LABOUR MARKET ECONOMICS

Eighth Edition

Dwayne Benjamin
University of Toronto

Morley Gunderson
University of Toronto

Thomas Lemieux
University of British Columbia

Craig Riddell
University of British Columbia

Mc
Graw
Hill
Education

Labour Market Economics
Eighth Edition

ISBN-13: 978-1-25-903083-3
ISBN-10: 1-25-903083-0

1 2 3 4 5 6 7 8 9 0 WEB 1 9 8 7

Printed and bound in Canada.

Portfolio and Program Manager: Karen Fozard

Product Manager: Kevin O'Hearn

Executive Marketing Manager: Joy Armitage Taylor

Product Developer: Melissa Hudson

Senior Product Team Associate: Stephanie Giles

Supervising Editor: Jessica Barnoski

Photo/Permissions Editor: Karen Hunter

Copy Editor: Julie van Tol

Plant Production Coordinator: Michelle Saddler

Manufacturing Production Coordinator: Emily Hickey

Cover Design: Michelle Losier

Cover Image: Ben Hung/Getty Images Royalty Free

Interior Design: Lightbox Visual Communications Inc.

Composition: Aptara, Inc.

Printer: Webcom, Ltd.

Dedication

To our parents, Janet Wilson and Harry Benjamin, Ann and Magnus Gunderson, Lise and Vincent Lemieux, and Ethel and William Riddell, and to Craig Riddell's wife Rosemarie Riddell who died in 2013.

about the **AUTHORS**

DWAYNE BENJAMIN

Dwayne Benjamin is Professor of Economics and Chair of the Department of Economics, University of Toronto. He joined the University of Toronto in 1989 after receiving his PhD from Princeton University.

Professor Benjamin is an empirical microeconomist with research interests that focus on the interactions between households and markets, especially labour markets, and the resulting distribution of economic well-being. His research is grounded in the use of household survey data and has focused on two main arenas: rural areas of developing countries and contemporary Canadian labour markets. In the development sphere, his work includes studies of labour and land market performance in Indonesia, China, and Vietnam. In the Canadian context, he studied labour market outcomes of immigrants, the impact of minimum wages, and the impact of public pensions on retirement decisions. For his early work, he was awarded the Polanyi prize in 1992. More recently, his development-related research has concentrated on trends and determinants of inequality in China and Vietnam, while his current Canadian-oriented work focuses on household savings, in particular the role of savings and government programs (such as RESPs) in financing post-secondary education. He has published widely in top economics journals, and has also been awarded multiple Social Sciences and Humanities Research Council grants as well as others. From 2005–2008, he was managing editor of the *Canadian Journal of Economics* and also served from 2003–2014 as associate editor for the journal, *Economic Development and Cultural Change*.

MORLEY GUNDERSON

Morley Gunderson holds the Canadian Imperial Bank of Commerce Chair in Youth Employment at the University of Toronto, where he is a Professor at the Centre for Industrial Relations (Director from 1985 to 1997) and in the Department of Economics. He is also a Research Associate of the Centre for International Studies and the Institute for Human Development, Life Course and Aging, both at the University of Toronto. He has been a Visiting Scholar at various institutions, including the International Institute for Labour Research in Geneva, Switzerland (1977–1978), and Stanford University (1984–1985, 1991–1993, 1994–1996, and 1998–1999).

Professor Gunderson has published on various topics, including gender discrimination and pay and employment equity; the aging work force, pensions, and mandatory retirement; youth employment; the evaluation of labour market programs; minimum wage impacts; public sector wage determination; the determinants and impact of immigration; the causes and consequences of strikes; child care arrangements and labour market behaviour; workers' compensation, reasonable accommodation, and disability issues; labour market adjustment and training; volunteer labour supply; information technology labour market; labour markets in China; Aboriginal labour market issues; and the impact of trade liberalization and globalization on labour markets, labour policy, labour standards, industrial relations, human resource management, and workplace practices.

Professor Gunderson is on the editorial board of the *Journal of Labor Research* and the *International Journal of Manpower*. In 2002, he was awarded the Industrial Relations Research Association Excellence in Education Award in Labour Economics and the Gérard Dion Award in 2003 for Outstanding Contributions to the Field of Industrial Relations. In 2008, he was made a Fellow of the Royal Society of Canada, and in 2015 he received the Carolyn Tuohy Impact on Public Policy Award.

THOMAS LEMIEUX

Thomas Lemieux is Professor of Economics and Director of the Vancouver School of Economics, University of British Columbia. He received his PhD from Princeton University and has held positions at MIT and the Université de Montréal prior to joining the faculty at UBC in 1999. Lemieux was a Visiting Professor at Princeton and Berkeley, and a National Fellow at the Hoover Institution. He is a Research Associate at the National Bureau of Economic Research, and has received awards for his research, including the Canadian Economic Association's Rae Prize, UBC's Killam Senior Research Prize, and the Minnesota Award. He currently holds a Bank of Canada Fellowship Award, is a fellow of both the Society of Labor Economists and of the Royal Society of Canada, and a Past-President of the Canadian Economics Association. Lemieux was also a founding co-editor of the *American Economic Journal: Applied Economics*.

Professor Lemieux has published on a variety of topics in labour economics, including the underground economy, the impact of collective bargaining on wages and employment, the determination of wage differentials between ethnic groups and men and women, and the estimation sectoral choice models. He has also published work on applied econometrics topics, such as decomposition methods and regression discontinuity designs. Most of his recent research has focused on the determinants of earnings inequality in industrialized economies.

W. CRAIG RIDDELL

W. Craig Riddell is Royal Bank Faculty Research Professor in the Vancouver School of Economics at the University of British Columbia and former Academic Director of the Canadian Labour Market and Skills Research Network. He is also a Research Fellow of the Institute for the Study of Labor (Bonn, Germany), the Centre for Research and Analysis of Migration (University College, London), and the Institute for Research on Public Policy (Montreal). He received his PhD from Queen's University in 1977, and taught at the University of Alberta before joining UBC in 1979. He has been a Visiting Scholar at the Center for Labor Economics, University of California, Berkeley; Department of Economics, University of New South Wales, Sydney; the Research School of Social Sciences, Australian National University, Canberra; and the University of California, Santa Barbara. He has published numerous papers in leading academic journals as well as in outlets that reach a broader audience. His current research is focused on inequality, skill formation, unemployment, immigration, income assistance, unionization and collective bargaining, and unemployment insurance.

Professor Riddell is former Head of the Department of Economics at UBC, former Academic Co-Chair of the Canadian Employment Research Forum, and Past-President of the Canadian Economics Association. He is currently a member of Statistics Canada's Advisory Committee on Labour and Income Statistics and of the Board of Directors of the Centre for the Study of Living Standards. In addition to his scholarly activity, he has been active in policy advisory work, including serving as Research Coordinator for the Macdonald Royal Commission and Advisor to the B.C. Task Force on Employment and Training. In 2007–2008 he was a member of the Expert Panel on Older Workers established by the Government of Canada. He has received numerous awards, most recently the Mike McCracken Award for Economic Statistics for contributions to the development and use of labour market data.

BRIEF CONTENTS

CONTENTS

CHAPTER 3

LABOUR SUPPLY AND PUBLIC POLICY: WORK INCENTIVE EFFECTS OF ALTERNATIVE INCOME MAINTENANCE SCHEMES   71

CHAPTER 4

LABOUR SUPPLY OVER THE LIFE CYCLE   103

CHAPTER 6
LABOUR DEMAND, NON-WAGE BENEFITS, AND QUASI-FIXED COSTS 166

PART 3 LABOUR SUPPLY AND DEMAND TOGETHER

CHAPTER 7
WAGES AND EMPLOYMENT IN A SINGLE LABOUR MARKET 185

CHAPTER 10
WAGE STRUCTURES ACROSS MARKETS   272

CHAPTER 11
THE ECONOMICS OF IMMIGRATION   300

PART 5 UNIONS

CHAPTER 14
UNIONS AND COLLECTIVE BARGAINING 401

CHAPTER 15
UNION IMPACT ON WAGE AND NON-WAGE OUTCOMES 440

PART 6 UNEMPLOYMENT

CHAPTER 16
UNEMPLOYMENT: MEANING, MEASUREMENT, AND CANADA'S EXPERIENCE   478

CHAPTER 17
UNEMPLOYMENT: CAUSES AND CONSEQUENCES   495

PREFACE

Labour economists study the decisions of everyday life, especially how people earn a living. We even offer the analytic tools to help you decide whether to take labour economics, English, quantum mechanics, or nothing at all (see Chapter 9). In Canada, most people earn a living at their jobs; that is, from the earnings they receive from selling their labour services through the labour market. Not surprisingly, many of the most important issues of public policy hinge on our understanding of how the labour market works. What causes unemployment? Why are some people's earnings so low that they need social assistance? Why are women often paid less than men? Should governments pay subsidies for post-secondary education?

The discipline of labour economics provides a framework for critical thinking about these sorts of questions. At the core of the discipline is the neoclassical supply and demand model. This model allows the construction of logical, internally consistent arguments concerning economic variables, such as employment and earnings. But models have to be used carefully and evaluated for their applicability in the real world. Labour economists, therefore, combine theoretical reasoning with empirical evidence. The interplay between economic theory and evidence is complex. On the one hand, empirical evidence is used as a way to evaluate the theory and to calibrate the ingredients of theoretical models (e.g., how much taking an additional year of schooling raises a person's earnings). But, on the other hand, economic theory also serves a vital role in "purely" empirical exercises. Without theory, labour economics would appear as "just one damn fact after another"[1] (which is not to diminish the value of establishing a "fact" in the first place).

In this book, we provide students with the tools for critical thinking about labour market problems. As the subtitle indicates, we aim to develop student facility at both theoretical and empirical critical thinking. Another important organizing principle is the focus on public policy. The book is meant to provide a consistent theoretical framework that can be applied not only to current policy issues but also to new policy issues as they emerge over time. Policies that are relevant today may not be relevant tomorrow, but a good theoretical foundation will always be relevant. Just as importantly, what constitutes evidence? We are constantly bombarded with claims that a particular viewpoint has "the facts" on its side. How can we recognize plausible empirical arguments?

We also believe that economic institutions matter, especially in labour markets. While economic theory and sound empirical methodology are portable to studying labour markets in most countries, we have chosen the balance of topics in this book to reflect Canadian interests. For example, unions are a more important feature of the Canadian landscape than that of the United States. Unemployment has also been a more prominent feature of the Canadian labour market for many years, though things have changed recently. Our book reflects these differences. We also provide a corresponding emphasis on the evaluation of Canadian labour market policies, drawing heavily on Canadian evidence. Given the explosion of empirical research in Canada since the 1990s, it has been quite easy to maintain an emphasis on Canadian data, examples, institutions, problems, and policies—though harder to keep up with the pace of research. However, given the increased internationalization of the Canadian economy, Canadian issues are discussed within the context of a more general theoretical and empirical framework, applicable to the labour problems of most developed countries.

Key Changes

We undertook this revision with two main objectives. First, to improve the readability of the text, making it more student friendly and accessible to a broader audience. Second, to update the content of the chapters to provide fresh material.

Enhanced and Updated Coverage of Topics

Labour economics is a dynamic area of research, especially in Canada. We have tried to ensure that the empirical evidence, for both first-order descriptive statistics and the results of applied research, is up-to-date. All of the tables and figures have been updated with the most recently available data. We gave our reviews of public policy an overhaul, and we have enhanced our discussion of the following topics, which feature prominently in the research agenda of labour economics in the 21st century:

- Added an appendix, Research Designs in Labour Economics, to Appendix 1A.

- Chapter 3 was updated to cover new developments relating to the social safety net in Canada and other countries, such as the increased use of refundable tax credits rather than traditional welfare, the consequences of the Quebec Family Policy that provided highly subsidized child care, and the Canada Child Benefit introduced in 2016.

- Added a new exhibit on the "China Syndrome" and the effect of Chinese imports on local labour markets in Chapter 5.

- Added a new exhibit on the rise of the "Gig Economy" in Chapter 6.

- A new exhibit on the $15 minimum wage movement was added to Chapter 7.

- A new exhibit on whether sex workers receive a compensating pay premium for their risk of providing unprotected sex was included in Chapter 8.

- Added a new exhibit, "Big Data" and Lifetime Returns to Schooling, in Chapter 9.

- A new section in Chapter 9 has been included to discuss changes in returns to education and inequality (originally included in the "Empirical Evidence" section).

- The Main Questions section in Chapter 10 has been updated to include a new material.

- A new exhibit in Chapter 10 discusses employer-employee data and firm wage effects.

- Chapter 11 was significantly updated given the changes in data, policy, and research since the last revision. There were major updates on the discussion of policy, as well as evidence on the impact of immigration and immigrant outcomes in Canada. All statistics, references, and pedagogy were updated.

- Significant content, reference, and statistical updates were made in Chapters 12–15.

- In Chapter 16, the data and research were updated to reflect the experience of the 2008–2009 financial crisis and the associated worldwide recession, called the "Great Recession" in the United States.

- Chapter 17 was substantially changed overall, with the sections on displaced workers and unemployment insurance expanded and updated. Material on the growing use of the Internet in job search and matching has also been updated and expanded.

Economics Preparation

The text was written for students who have had an introductory course in economics and preferably, but not necessarily, a course in microeconomics. Formal mathematical analysis is rarely utilized, though high school algebra and elementary regression analysis are used where appropriate. The text is also suitable as a basis for graduate labour courses in business schools and economics departments.

Learn without Limits

McGraw-Hill Connect® is an award-winning digital teaching and learning platform that gives students the means to better connect with their coursework, with their instructors, and with the important concepts that they will need to know for success now and in the future. With Connect, instructors can take advantage of McGraw-Hill's trusted content to seamlessly deliver assignments, quizzes, and tests online. McGraw-Hill Connect is a learning platform that continually adapts to each student, delivering precisely what they need, when they need it, so class time is more engaging and effective. Connect makes teaching and learning personal, easy, and proven.

Connect Key Features:

SmartBook®

As the first and only adaptive reading experience, SmartBook is changing the way students read and learn. SmartBook creates a personalized reading experience by highlighting the most important concepts a student needs to learn at that moment in time. As a student engages with SmartBook, the reading experience continuously adapts by highlighting content based on what each student knows and doesn't know. This ensures that he or she is focused on the content needed to close specific knowledge gaps, while it simultaneously promotes long-term learning.

Connect Insight®

Connect Insight is Connect's new one-of-a-kind visual analytics dashboard, now available for instructors, that provides at-a-glance information regarding student performance, which is immediately actionable. By presenting assignment, assessment, and topical performance results together with a time metric that is easily visible for aggregate or individual results, Connect Insight gives instructors the ability to take a just-in-time approach to teaching and learning, which was never before available. Connect Insight presents data that helps instructors improve class performance in a way that is efficient and effective.

Simple Assignment Management

With Connect, creating assignments is easier than ever, so instructors can spend more time teaching and less time managing.

- Assign SmartBook learning modules.
- Edit existing questions and create your own questions.
- Draw from a variety of text specific questions, resources, and test bank material to assign online.
- Streamline lesson planning, student progress reporting, and assignment grading to make classroom management more efficient than ever.

Smart Grading

When it comes to studying, time is precious. Connect helps students learn more efficiently by providing feedback and practice material when they need it, where they need it.

- Automatically score assignments, giving students immediate feedback on their work and comparisons with correct answers.
- Access and review each response; manually change grades or leave comments for students to review.
- Track individual student performance—by question, assignment or in relation to the class overall—with detailed grade reports.
- Reinforce classroom concepts with practice tests and instant quizzes.
- Integrate grade reports easily with Learning Management Systems including Blackboard, D2L, and Moodle.

Instructor Library

The Connect Instructor Library is a repository for additional resources to improve student engagement in and out of the class. It provides all the critical resources instructors need to build their course.

- Access Instructor resources.
- View assignments and resources created for past sections.
- Post your own resources for students to use.

Instructor Resources

- Instructor's Manual
- Instructor's Solutions Manual
- Computerized Test Bank
- Microsoft® PowerPoint® Lecture Slides

Superior Learning Solutions and Support

The McGraw-Hill Education team is ready to help instructors assess and integrate any of our products, technology, and services into your course for optimal teaching and learning performance. Whether it's helping your students improve their grades, or putting your entire course online, the McGraw-Hill Education team is here to help you do it. Contact your Learning Solutions Consultant today to learn how to maximize all of McGraw-Hill Education's resources.

For more information, please visit us online: http://www.mheducation.ca/he/solutions

ACKNOWLEDGMENTS

Various people have aided in the preparation of this book. Our colleagues and fellow labour economists within Canada are too numerous to mention. However, we are particularly indebted to our colleagues at the University of British Columbia and the University of Toronto, and to a number of anonymous referees who made comments and suggestions for improvements on this and the seventh edition. At McGraw-Hill Education, Kevin O'Hearn provided important initial impetus on the direction of the revision and ongoing support; Melissa Hudson and Tammy Mavroudi meticulously organized and coordinated the construction of the book, from first drafts to completion; and Jessica Barnoski, Supervising Editor, and Julie van Tol, Copy Editor, provided valued editorial assistance. We especially wish to thank our wives, Christine, Melanie, Nicole, and Rosemarie, for their patience, support, and encouragement.

The eighth edition has benefited from a number of perceptive reviews, which were a rich source of suggestions for this revision. Reviewers include the following:

Elizabeth Dhuey	University of Toronto
Bruno Fullone	George Brown College
Ana Ferrer	University of Calgary
Stéphanie Lluis	University of Waterloo
Joseph Marchand	University of Alberta
Amy Peng	Ryerson University
Miana Plesca	University of Guelph
Glen Stirling	University of Western Ontario

AEJ App	*American Economic Journal: Applied Economics*
AER	*American Economic Review*
BPEA	*Brookings Papers on Economic Activity*
CJE	*Canadian Journal of Economics*
CPP	*Canadian Public Policy*
Ecta	*Econometrica*
EI	*Economic Inquiry*
EJ	*Economic Journal*
IER	*International Economic Review*
ILRR	*Industrial and Labor Relations Review*
IR	*Industrial Relations*
IRRA	*Industrial Relations Research Association Proceedings*
IER	*International Economic Review*
JASA	*Journal of the American Statistical Association*
JEH	*Journal of Economic History*
JEL	*Journal of Economic Literature*
JEP	*Journal of Economic Perspectives*
JLR	*Journal of Labor Research*
JHR	*Journal of Human Resources*

JOLE	*Journal of Labor Economics*
JPE	*Journal of Political Economy*
JPubEc	*Journal of Public Economics*
LE	*Labour Economics*
MLR	*Monthly Labor Review*
PLI	*Perspectives on Labour and Income*
QJE	*Quarterly Journal of Economics*
RI/IR	*Relations Industrielles/Industrial Relations*
R.E. Studies	*Review of Economic Studies*
R.E. Stats	*Review of Economics and Statistics*
SEJ	*Southern Economic Journal*
WEJ	*Western Economic Journal*

Other journals have been included in the References section without an abbreviation for their title.

The references listed in this text tend to focus on more recent articles, especially those with a Canadian focus; earlier references can be found in previous editions.

CHAPTER 1

Introduction to Labour Market Economics

LEARNING OBJECTIVES

LO1 See that, as in other markets, supply and demand curves can be used to find the equilibrium values of wages and employment levels.

LO2 Understand that earnings, hours, and hourly wages are quite unevenly distributed in the Canadian labour market.

LO3 Understand that, in addition to market forces, legislative and institutional factors play an important role in labour market outcomes.

LO4 Learn about the different types of data sets, such as time-series data, cross-section microdata, and panel data, that are used in labour market research.

LO5 Learn how regression analysis contributes to our understanding of labour economics.

MAIN QUESTIONS

- Who are the main actors in the labour market, and what particular roles do they play?
- How can features of the labour market be divided into labour supply and labour demand factors?
- What types of policy questions does labour economics address?
- What characteristics of the labour market make it distinctive from other markets, justifying a special sub-discipline of economics?
- What is the neoclassical model of the labour market? Are there alternative approaches?

Labour economics is the study of the outcomes of decisions each of us can expect to make over our lifetime. As a subject of inquiry, it is relevant to both our everyday lives and to the broader issues of society. This makes labour economics interesting, practical, and socially relevant, as well as controversial.

Decisions by Individuals, Firms, and Governments

Labour market decisions that affect our everyday well-being are made by the three main actors, or participants, in the labour market: individuals, firms, and governments.

For individuals, the decisions include when to enter the labour force; how much education, training, and job search to undertake; what occupation and industry to enter; how many hours to work; whether to move to a different region; when to accept a job; when to quit or look for another job; what wage to demand; whether to join a union or employee association; and when to retire. There may also be decisions as to how to allocate time between market work and household responsibilities.

Many aspects of labour market behaviour are positive experiences, such as obtaining a job, getting a wage increase or promotion, or receiving a generous pension. Other experiences are negative, such as being unemployed or permanently displaced from one's job, or experiencing discrimination or poverty.

Employers have to make decisions also, such as how many workers to hire; what wages and benefits to offer; what hours of work to require; when to lay off workers or, perhaps ultimately, to close a plant; what to outsource; and how to design an effective pension and retirement policy. These decisions are increasingly being made under pressures from global competition, free trade, industrial restructuring, deregulation, and privatization. As well, the decisions of employers must be made in the context of a dramatically changing work force, with respect to such factors as age, gender, and ethnic diversity. The legislative environment within which employers operate is also constantly changing in a number of areas: human rights and anti-discrimination legislation; employment standards laws with respect to things such as minimum wages, maternity leave, and hours of work and overtime; legislation regarding workers' compensation and occupational health and safety; legislation regarding pensions and mandatory retirement; and labour relations laws that regulate the process of collective bargaining.

Governments, through their legislators and policymakers, establish the environment in which employees and employers interact. In part, this involves a balancing act between providing rights and protection to individuals while not jeopardizing the competitiveness of employers. It also involves decisions as to what to provide publicly in such areas as training, information, employment insurance, workers' compensation, vocational rehabilitation, income maintenance, pensions, and even public sector jobs.

Labour economics deals with these decisions by individuals, employers, and government—decisions that affect our everyday lives and that lead to consequences we can all expect to experience. While this makes labour economics interesting and relevant—and controversial—it also puts a premium on the existence of a solid framework from which to analyze these decisions and their consequences. The purpose of this book is to provide and apply such a framework.

Parts of the book may be more challenging and seem less interesting than the sections more obviously related to policy and other applications; however, they provide the basic tools and theoretical framework that are crucial to understanding labour market behaviour. In many cases, the immediate application of economic theory to labour market issues facilitates understanding of the basic tools of economics itself; that is, the application economic theory to interesting and important issues in the labour market facilitates a deeper understanding of economic theory itself.

In labour economics, however, the ultimate usefulness of economic theory is in building an understanding of labour market behaviour. "The proof of the pudding is in the eating"; that is, the usefulness of basic economic theory in the labour area must be demonstrated by its ability to help us understand labour market behaviour. This is one of the objectives of this book.

Subject Matter of Labour Market Economics

Labour market economics involves analyzing the determinants of the various dimensions of labour supply and demand, and their interaction in alternative market structures to determine wages, employment, and unemployment. Behind this simple description, however, lies a complex array of behaviours, decision making, and dimensions that often relate labour economics with other disciplines and areas of study.

Labour supply, for example, involves a variety of dimensions. It includes population growth, which involves decisions pertaining to fertility and family formation, as well as to immigration and emigration, all of which are amenable to economic analysis. Labour supply also involves the dimension of labour force participation; that is, determining what portion of the population will participate in labour market activities as opposed to other activities, such as household work, education, retirement, or pure leisure. For those who participate in the labour market there are consideration, such as of hours of work, including trends and cyclical patterns, and such phenomena as overtime, moonlighting, part-time work, work sharing, flexible work-time arrangements, and compressed workweeks. These things tie labour economics to such areas as demography and personnel and human resource planning.

In addition to these *quantity* dimensions of labour supply, there are also *quality* dimensions that are amenable to economic analysis. Quality dimensions include education, training, and health. These dimensions, along with labour mobility, are often analyzed as human capital investment decisions, emphasizing that they involve incurring costs today in exchange for benefits in the future. Quality dimensions of labour supply also include work effort and intensity—dimensions that are analyzed in the context of efficiency wage theory and optimal compensation systems. This connects labour economics to issues of personnel and human resource management as well as to the key policy issue of productivity, often involving education and training considerations.

Labour supply analysis also involves determining the work incentive effects of income maintenance and tax-transfer schemes. Such schemes include demogrants (e.g., the Old Age Security Pension), negative income taxes, wage subsidies, income taxes, unemployment insurance, welfare, disability payments, workers' compensation, and private and public pension plans. This ties labour economics to the interesting and controversial areas of poverty and income distribution, as well as to tax and social welfare policy.

The **labour demand** side of the picture focuses on how firms vary their demand for labour in response to changes in the wage rate and other elements of labour cost, including fringe benefits and legislatively imposed costs. The impact of quasi-fixed costs that may be involved in hiring, training, and even terminating workers are also important. Since the demand for labour is a derived demand—derived from the demand for the firm's output—this side of the picture is influenced by such issues as free trade, global competition and outsourcing, industrial restructuring, privatization, public sector retrenchment, mergers and acquisitions, and technological change. It is increasingly important to analyze the demand side in the context of changes that are occurring in the international global environment.

The various dimensions of labour supply and demand are interesting and informative not only in their own right but also because their interaction determines other key **labour market outcomes**: **wages**, **employment**, **unemployment**, and **labour shortages**. These outcomes are influenced by the interaction of labour supply and demand in alternative market structures, including the degree of competition in the product market as well as the labour market. They are also influenced by unions and collective bargaining, as well as by legislative interventions, including minimum wages and equal pay and equal opportunity laws. This highlights the interrelationship of labour economics with industrial relations and labour law.

The various wage structures that emerge include wage differentials by occupation (e.g., engineer versus waiter), by industry (e.g., public versus private sector), by region (e.g., Newfoundland and Labrador versus Ontario), and by personal characteristics (e.g., men versus women). Economic analysis outlines the determinants of these wage structures, how and why they change over time, and how they are influenced by such factors as demand changes, non-wage aspects of employment, and noncompetitive factors including unions, legislation, occupational licensing, and labour market imperfections. For some wage structures, like male–female wage differentials, the economic analysis of discrimination offers insight into why wage differentials arise and persist, and how they will be affected by legislation and other policy initiatives.

Wage differentials between union and non-union workers can be explained by basic economic analysis that incorporates bargaining theory. In order to fully understand how unions affect wages, it is also necessary to understand why unions arise in the first place and how they affect the non-wage aspects of employment. Labour economics is also applied to understanding why certain institutional arrangements exist in the labour market, including unions, seniority-based wage increases, and various personnel practices.

There is increasing recognition that wages can have strong impact on incentives, such as to acquire education and training, to move, to stay with a job or quit or retire early, and to work harder and more productively. The effects of these changes are analyzed in various areas of labour market economics: human capital theory, optimal compensation systems, efficiency wages, and private pension plan analysis. This, again, highlights the interrelationship of labour economics with industrial relations and personnel and human resource management.

Unemployment is analyzed at both the microeconomic and the macroeconomic levels. At the micro level, the emphasis is on theories of job search, implicit contracts and efficiency wages, and the impact of unemployment insurance. At the macro level, the relationships between wage changes, price inflation, productivity, and unemployment are emphasized.

LO1, 2   Preliminary Explorations of Labour Market Outcomes

The fundamental subject matter considered by labour economics is how individuals earn a living, and especially how they do so by selling their labour services in the labour market. Labour economists are interested in both the average level of earnings from the market and the distribution; that is, how unequal are labour market outcomes (and why)?

Table 1.1 shows selected descriptive statistics concerning these outcomes. The tabulations are based on a large sample of approximately 47,000 Canadians, referring to their incomes and labour activity in 2011. The sample is drawn from the Survey of Labour and Income Dynamics (SLID), Statistics Canada's survey that tracked incomes and labour market activities between 1993 and 2011. In this table, we restrict attention to individuals in their main working years, between the ages of 20 and 65. It shows the average levels of various types of income, and the percentage of people with each particular source of income. The averages are also broken down separately for men and women.

Looking first at the full sample, we see that earnings (from the labour market or self-employment) averaged $36,556 per person. Labour earnings are, by far, the largest source of income for Canadians; they constitute 90 percent of non-transfer income and 84 percent of total income. Income is earned by 83 percent of Canadians aged 20 to 65 at some point during the year, though they may not work for the entire year. Government transfers, such as employment insurance or social assistance, are another important source of income received by 69.2 percent of the sample. Transfer income is also closely related to labour market outcomes, because it is low labour income that usually qualifies someone to receive the transfer. Finally, note that income taxes reduce earned income by about 17 percent (on average).

Regarding labour market activities, 80 percent of Canadians in the sample worked at least one hour over the year, the average being 1487 hours worked. The average wage was $24.20 per hour. Finally, excluding people who worked in self-employment (i.e., worked for themselves), it remains the case that almost two-thirds (62.8 percent) of individuals had the labour market as a source of earned income.

The next four columns compare these outcomes for men and women. Most striking is the gap between men's and women's earnings; the ratio of men's to women's earnings is 1.66. Some of this can be explained by differences in hours worked. Men were slightly more likely to work (80.4 percent versus 76.0 percent), and they work longer hours, an average of 1487 hours per year versus 1279. The male–female ratio of hours worked is, thus, only 1.16, which falls short of explaining the earnings difference. We can also see that the hours explanation is not the whole story, because the ratio of men's to women's wages is $26.46/$22.03 = 1.20. Later in this book, we spend considerable time trying to explain the earnings and wage differentials between men and women, in particular assessing the extent to which this differential is driven by discrimination, as opposed to "legitimate" (or explainable) differences in productivity. Finally, note that some of the earnings differential is offset by the higher taxes paid, and lower government transfers received, by men.

TABLE 1.1	Sources of Income for Individual Canadians, 2011					
	Full Sample		**Men**		**Women**	
	Mean	**% positive**	**Mean**	**% positive**	**Mean**	**% positive**
Earnings	36,556	82.5	45,645	86.2	27,475	78.8
Investment income	1571	27.6	1909	27.8	1234	27.4
Pension income	1504	5.6	1834	5.9	1175	5.3
Other income	809	15.5	770	14.7	849	16.4
Government transfers	3232	69.2	2505	65.6	3958	72.7
Subtotal	43,673	98.2	52,662	98.7	34,691	97.7
Income taxes	7395	68.3	9972	74.2	4821	62.3
After-tax total	36,277	98.3	42,689	98.7	29,870	97.9
Annual hours worked	1487	80.4	1696	84.9	1279	76.0
Average hourly wage	24.20	69.5	26.46	71.4	22.03	67.6
Worked, but not self-employed	62.8		64.1		61.5	

NOTES:

1. Income figures are average values for all individuals aged 20 to 65, in 2011 dollars. The "% positive" column reports the percentage of individuals with positive (or negative) income for that source. The income averages are calculated over the whole sample, including individuals with zero income.

2. The "average hourly wage" is the implicit average hourly wage (SLID variable, "cmphrw28," calculated on the basis of earnings and hours across all jobs. Note that the product of hours and wages will not equal earnings, and the average wage is calculated only over those who worked.

SOURCE: Adapted from Statistics Canada's Survey of Labour and Income Dynamics public use microdata, 2011. All computations on these microdata were prepared by the authors. The responsibility for the use and interpretation of these data is entirely that of the authors.

While the averages shown in Table 1.1 are informative, they hide considerable variation, or dispersion, of outcomes across individuals. In Figure 1.1 we plot a histogram of the distribution of labour earnings. In this figure, we restrict our sample to those who have positive earnings and whose earnings come exclusively from wages and salaries (i.e., we exclude the self-employed). Each bar on the histogram shows the fraction of individuals with a particular level of earnings. To aid in interpretation, we also show three reference lines: the 10th, 50th, and 90th percentiles. While earnings may range from a low of $1250 per year to a high of $190,000 per year, most people had earnings between $9000 and $92,500.[1] The 10th percentile (or first decile) is $9000. This means that 10 percent of individuals had earnings below $9000 per year. The median (or 50th percentile) is $39,000. This means that half of the sample had earnings below, and half above, $39,000. Finally, the 90th percentile is $92,500, indicating that 90 percent of people had incomes below this level, or, conversely, that 10 percent had earnings higher than this. One common measure of income dispersion is the ratio of incomes at the 90th to the 10th percentiles. In this case, a "high income" earner (at the 90th percentile) earned about 10 times more ($92,500/$9000) than a "low income" person (at the 10th decile).

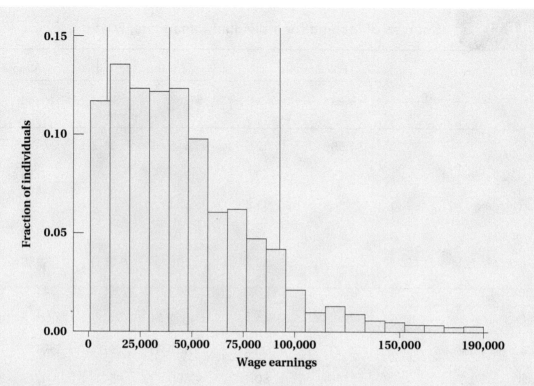

Figure 1.1 The Distribution of Individual Labour Earnings, 2011

This is a histogram showing the distribution of labour earnings for a large sample of Canadians in 2011. Each bar shows the proportion of the sample with earnings in the range indicated on the horizontal axis. For reference purposes, we also show vertical lines corresponding to the 10th percentile, median, and 90th percentile.

NOTES:

1. In this figure, we show the distribution of average annual wage earnings. For clarity, we show only the middle 98 percent of the distribution; that is, that part of it with labour earnings above the first percentile ($1250) and below the 99th percentile ($190,000).

2. Reference lines corresponding to the 10th percentile ($9000), median ($39,000), and 90th percentile ($92,500) are also shown.

SOURCE: Adapted from Statistics Canada: see Table 1.1.

How much of this difference is due to differences in wage rates, which depend on individual productivity, education, and luck, and how much depends on differences in hours worked, which may depend on a variety of factors, ranging from preferences to the inability to find work (unemployment)? To take a quick look at this, we can break total earnings, WH, into its constituent parts: wages, W, and hours, H. The separate distributions for hours and wages are shown in Figures 1.2 and 1.3.

Looking first at hours, there is considerable variation, with hours ranging from as low as 98 per year to as high as 3585 per year. Recall also that 20 percent of individuals do not work at all (i.e., have zero hours), and they are not represented in this figure. Someone may have high earnings because she works a lot (3500 hours corresponds to 67 hours per week, 52 weeks per year!), or has low earnings because she works very little, if at all. Despite the dispersion in hours worked, most people work around 2000 hours per year, which corresponds to the typical 40 hours per week for 50 weeks per year. One of the primary objectives of labour economics is to explain the variation in hours across individuals, and, in particular, why some people work fewer than 100 hours per year (if at all) while others work more than 2500 hours per year. Are low hours voluntarily chosen, or are they the result of unemployment?

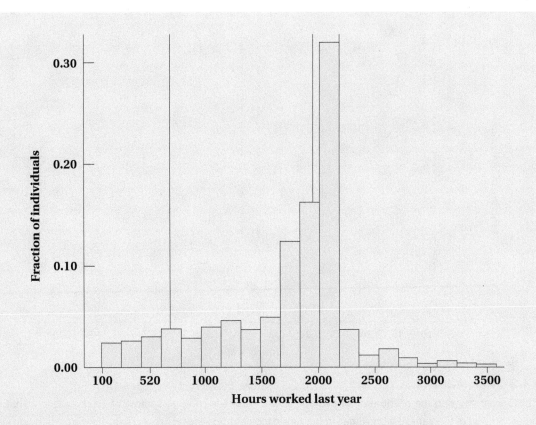

Figure 1.2 The Distribution of Individual Annual Hours Worked, 2011

This is a histogram showing the distribution of hours worked for a large sample of Canadians in 2011. Each bar shows the proportion of the sample with hours worked in the range indicated on the horizontal axis. There are 20 bars, so each bar corresponds to (approximately) a range of 170 hours. For reference purposes, we also show vertical lines corresponding to the 10th percentile, median, and 90th percentile.

NOTES:

1. This figure shows distribution of annual hours worked in 2011. For clarity, we only show the middle 98 percent of the distribution; that is, that part of it with hours above the first percentile (98) and below the 99th percentile (3585).

2. Reference lines corresponding to the 10th percentile (696), median (1955), and 90th percentile (2190) are also shown.

SOURCE: Adapted from Statistics Canada: see Table 1.1.

The wage distribution is depicted in Figure 1.3. Wages in this sample ranged from $9.00 to $69.82 per hour. (Again, the graphs have been trimmed of the top and bottom 1 percent.) Most people had wages between $11.00 and $40.36 per hour, corresponding to the 10th and 90th percentiles. Notice that the ratio of wages at the 90th to the 10th percentiles is 3.67, which is much less than the case for earnings; that is, wages are considerably more equally distributed than earnings. The higher inequality of earnings results from the combined inequality of hours and wages. Still, if everyone is created equal, why is there such dispersion in wages? Labour economists attempt to answer this question, exploring the factors discussed in the previous section and relying heavily on the neoclassical supply and demand model.

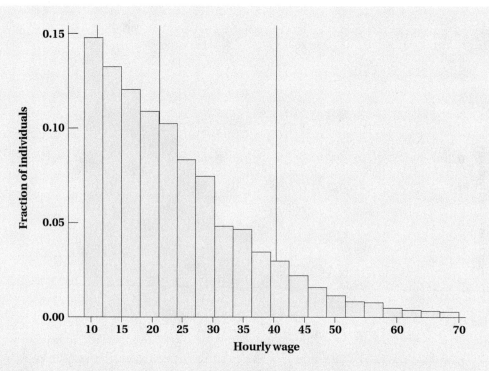

Figure 1.3 The Distribution of Individual Average Hourly Wages, 2011

This is a histogram showing the distribution of average hourly wages for a large sample of Canadians in 2011. Each bar shows the proportion of the sample with wages in the range indicated on the horizontal axis. For reference purposes, we also show vertical lines corresponding to the 10th percentile, median, and 90th percentile.

NOTES:

1. In this particular figure we show the distribution of average hourly wages. For clarity, we only show the middle 98 percent of the distribution; that is, that part of it with wages above the first percentile ($9.00), and below the 99th percentile ($69.82).

2. Reference lines corresponding to the 10th percentile ($11.00), median ($21.26), and 90th percentile ($40.36) are also shown.

SOURCE: Adapted from Statistics Canada: see Table 1.1.

The Supply and Demand Model: Workhorse of Labour Economics

The wide-ranging set of topics discussed in the first few pages hints at the breadth of subject matter in labour economics, while the previous empirical explorations show how this broad range of labour market outcomes can be distilled into two variables: employment and wages. Explaining employment and wage outcomes will go a considerable way toward explaining many diverse labour market outcomes. It just so happens that economists have a powerful set of tools with which to explain quantities and prices—in this case, employment and wages. The foundation of that set of tools is the standard supply and demand model, which forms the core of this textbook.

There are two key ingredients in the **neoclassical supply and demand model**:

1. Behavioural assumptions about how buyers and sellers respond to prices and other factors.
2. Assumptions about how buyers and sellers interact, and how the market determines the level and terms of exchange.

Throughout this text we will develop, build upon, and critically evaluate both ingredients. For now, we provide a quick overview of the supply and demand framework, with special emphasis on the nature and interpretation of the competitive equilibrium.

The familiar supply and demand model as applied to the labour market is depicted in Figure 1.4. The objective of this model is to yield a prediction concerning the level of employment and wages likely to prevail in a market. With a well-developed behavioural model, we can also conduct "thought experiments," whereby we change assumptions concerning the supply or demand side of the market, and explore the logical consequences for employment and wages.

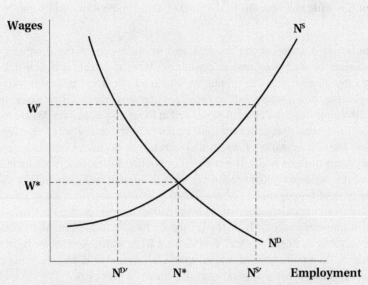

Figure 1.4 Wages and Employment in a Competitive Labour Market

The labour supply curve, N^S, depicts the desired amount of labour that individuals would like to sell at each wage rate, holding all other factors constant. Similarly, the demand curve, N^D, shows how much labour firms would like to hire at each wage rate (holding all other factors constant). The equilibrium combination of employment and wages (W^*, N^*) is given by the intersection of supply and demand. Only at W^* is it the case that the quantity supplied equals the quantity demanded.

The supply curve, N^S, represents the behaviour of the sellers' side of the market. We usually imagine that the labour supply decision is made by individuals, and that it depends on many variables. However, in this exercise we hold all factors constant except the wage, and then plot the amount of labour that would be offered for sale at each wage rate. Similarly, the demand function N^D shows the amount of labour that firms would be willing to hire at each wage rate. Obviously, labour demand will also depend on many variables besides the wage, but these variables are held constant. The question is, then, if individuals and firms simultaneously act in their own best interests, selling and buying labour according to their supply and demand curves, what wage and employment combination will prevail in the market? The assumption of competitive behaviour permits strong predictions concerning the labour market outcomes.

Wages and Employment in a Competitive Labour Market

In the simplest model, buyers and sellers of labour interact competitively in the labour market—that is, they take the market wage as given and supply or demand the relevant quantity of labour according to their supply or demand functions.

No single agent has the power to affect the market wage by its actions. How then is the market wage determined? We might imagine a mythic auctioneer using trial and error to establish a market clearing price; however, such an auctioneer does not actually exist. Before discussing how the market wage is determined, economists try to characterize the **equilibrium**; that is, the properties the market wage should satisfy. Of the continuum of possible wages that could prevail in the market, economists focus on the wage that clears the market—the wage that sets supply equal to demand. This equilibrium is depicted in Figure 1.4.

Why is this intersection so appealing to economists? First, at W^*, supply equals demand at N^*; that is, at (W^*, N^*) is the optimal labour supplied by workers (it lies on N^S) and the optimal labour demanded by firms (it lies on N^D). The easiest way to see why this is, at least, a reasonable candidate combination of W^* and N^* to prevail in the market is by considering any other combination. We maintain the assumption that the agents in the labour market are optimizing; that is, they will choose to supply or demand N according to their supply and demand functions. Let us also assume that exchange is voluntary; that is, individuals cannot be forced to buy or sell unless they choose to do so. Consider a wage W above W^*. At this wage, N^D

will be exchanged since firms cannot be forced to hire any more labour. At this wage, supply exceeds demand. There is, in principle, no reason why this wage will not prevail in the market, but it would be difficult to characterize this as a market equilibrium. At this wage there would be workers willing to work for slightly less and firms willing to hire at a slightly lower wage. Thus, there would be competitive pressures for the wage to fall. In the absence of rigidities, we might expect wages to fall toward W*. A similar argument (in reverse) would apply to a situation where the market wage was below W*. Thus, if we believe that there are equilibrating mechanisms in the market, the combination of W* and N* is a reasonable candidate to prevail in the labour market.

It is worth exploring in more detail some of the features and implications of the competitive equilibrium, since this **market-clearing model** underlies most of **neoclassical economics**. One implication is that in markets with homogeneous workers (individuals who are the same in terms of productive characteristics) and homogeneous jobs (jobs that are equally desirable from the workers' point of view), wages will be equalized across workers. Firms would not pay more than the going market wage, because they can employ as much labour as desired at the going wage rate. Workers would not accept less than the market wage because there are equally satisfactory jobs available at the going wage rate. We can, thus, use the supply and demand model to explore the determinants of wages across markets, an important first step in trying to explain wage differentials across different groups of individuals. But our first prediction is that otherwise identical workers should be paid the same. This implication of the basic competitive equilibrium is illustrated in Figure 1.5 for the case of two industries or regions employing the same type of homogeneous labour. Panel (a) shows the situation in which the labour market is not in equilibrium (even though demand equals supply in each individual labour market) because employees in sector A are receiving a lower wage than employees in sector B. In the presence of full information, and in the absence of mobility costs (costs of changing from one sector to another), workers would move from sector A to sector B, thus increasing labour supply in B and reducing it in sector A. As a consequence, wages would fall in sector B and rise in sector A. This process would continue until wages are equalized across the two sectors, as illustrated in panel (b).

Mobility costs could account for some persistence of earnings differences across sectors, at least in the short run, especially if the sectors are geographically separated. However, these differences are unlikely to persist in the longer run. As older workers retire and young workers enter the labour market, new entrants will tend to choose the higher-paying sector over the lower-paying sector, thus bringing about wage equality across the homogeneous work force.

Another implication of the basic competitive equilibrium is the absence of **involuntary unemployment**. This is also illustrated in panel (b) of Figure 1.5. In labour market equilibrium, there are no individuals who would like to work at the going market wage, W_e, unable to find work at that wage. There are some individuals who are "voluntarily unemployed" in the sense that they would be willing to work at a higher wage (e.g., at wage W_0), but at the wage W_e the value of their time spent in leisure or household production exceeds the value of their time spent in market work. (This aspect is evident from the rising labour supply curves in these two labour markets.) This labour supply decision *may* explain our finding in Figure 1.2 that many individuals choose low hours of work.

The absence of involuntary unemployment implies that there are also no unexploited "gains from trade" that would mutually benefit employers and unemployed workers. For example, if there existed an unemployed worker who would be willing to work at a wage below the existing market wage, both the worker and the hiring firm would benefit from a job match.

A related implication of the basic competitive labour market equilibrium is that there will be no queues for or rationing of jobs. The predicted absence of queues follows from the assumed homogeneity of jobs (thus, making all jobs equally satisfactory in terms of working conditions, job security, and so on) and the property of equalized wages across jobs and sectors. As a consequence, there are no jobs worth waiting for or lining up for. Similarly, in the absence of queues, there is no need for firms to ration jobs.

Whether these predictions of the basic competitive model accord with observed labour market behaviour is another question. Wages may not adjust quickly to "clear" the labour market (i.e., to equate labour demand and supply). Involuntary unemployment of workers appears to be a frequent, if not persistent, feature of many labour markets. Large and persistent differentials in the wages paid to apparently homogeneous workers also appear to prevail. In addition, there is evidence that the jobs that pay the highest wages are also more desirable on other grounds, such as working conditions, job security, career prospects, and non-wage benefits.

These simple observations suggest that this neoclassical model is not strictly true. So why build an entire discipline, let alone a textbook, around such a model? First, it may be that there is no better alternative; that other models of the labour market are even worse. More importantly, the model may still serve as a useful approximation and be useful for looking at policies, especially those that affect prices in the labour market. In essence, the "proof of the pudding is in the eating," so that whether this model is useful or not will depend in part on the extent to which it is useful in predicting the consequences of policy changes that affect the labour market.

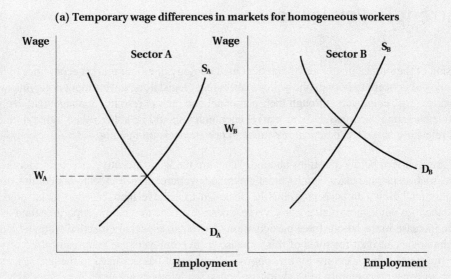

(a) Temporary wage differences in markets for homogeneous workers

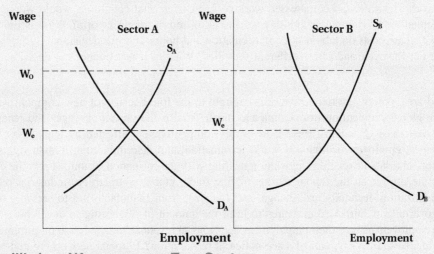

(b) Labour market equilibrium in markets for homogeneous workers

Figure 1.5 Equilibrium Wages across Two Sectors

The supply and demand model can be applied across labour markets. Consider the relative wages of identical (homogeneous) workers in two separate markets (e.g., regions or occupations). In panel (a), the equilibrium wage, W_A, is lower in sector A than that, W_B, in sector B. This cannot be a permanent equilibrium, unless there is a barrier preventing workers in sector A from moving to sector B. These barriers could be imperfect information about the higher wage opportunities or other costs associated with switching regions or occupations. Absent these barriers, we would expect individuals to move to sector B, shifting out the supply curve in sector B, until the wage is equal in the two sectors and there are no longer incentives for individuals to switch sectors. This cross-sector equilibrium is illustrated in panel (b), where the equilibrium wage is W_e.

Nevertheless, it is still unsatisfying that a model, even if useful for some purposes, is at odds with reality. The apparent inconsistencies between the predictions of the basic competitive model and observed behaviour have motivated considerable recent theoretical and empirical research. A central theme of this research is that much of the behaviour we observe in labour markets can be explained in terms of the responses of employers and employees to imperfect information, incentives, and risk and uncertainty; all features of economic life that are ignored in simple supply and demand models. A common feature of these theories, which we will address in this and future chapters, is that the wage performs functions in addition to clearing the labour market—the wage may also act as an incentive device, a risk-sharing mechanism, a part of a matching process, or a signal of the productivity of the worker on the job. Because the wage rate serves more than one function, it need not—indeed, generally will not—perform its market-clearing function fully.

Current Policy Issues

The previous discussion of the subject matter and theoretical methodology of labour market economics highlighted a number of areas of current policy of concern to both public policymakers (e.g., legislators, government policymakers, and the courts) and private policymakers (e.g., employers, through their personnel and human resource management decisions, and unions, through their collective bargaining actions). Labour market economics should be able to shed light on many of these issues, illustrating its social relevance as well as practical relevance in private decision making.

In the labour supply area, current policy questions abound. What are the work incentive effects of income maintenance and tax transfer programs, such as income taxes, employment insurance, welfare, earned income tax credits, disability payments, and workers' compensation? How can such programs be designed to achieve their broader social objectives of reducing poverty and other inequalities while minimizing any adverse incentive effects that could jeopardize their existence? Why has there been a dramatic increase in the labour force participation of women, especially married women? Do improvements in home production technologies account for some of this increase? Can employers use features of their private pension plans to encourage early retirement? What accounts for the long-run decline that has occurred in the average workweek? Why do some workers require an overtime premium to work longer hours, while others are willing to moonlight at a second job at a rate that is less than the rate in their primary job? Why has there been an increase in alternative work-time arrangements, including part-time work, flextime, and compressed workweeks? Under what conditions would workers voluntarily accept work sharing arrangements; for example, a four-day workweek in return for no layoffs? What is the impact of increased commuting time and daycare costs on labour force participation and hours-of-work decisions? What factors influence how we allocate time over our life cycle and across different activities? What factors influence our decision to have children, and when to have them?

In the labour demand area, policy questions have been brought to the fore because of new competitive pressures, many of these emanating from global competition from China and India. What is the impact of wages and other elements of labour cost on the competitiveness of Canadian firms? How is this competitiveness affected by legislated policies, with respect to such factors as wages, employment, hours of work, termination, anti-discrimination, human rights, health and safety, workers' compensation, and labour relations legislation dealing with the formation of unions and the conduct of collective bargaining? What is the impact on the labour market of free trade, global competition, industrial restructuring, mergers and acquisitions, privatization, technological change, and the shift from manufacturing to services and high-technology industries? Should governments introduce measures to limit the amount of offshoring to developing countries like China and India? How will employers change their employment decisions in response to legislation on minimum wages, equal pay for work of equal value, severance pay, and advance notice of termination? Is social networking and technological change reshaping the way workplaces are organized? Can new jobs be created by policies to reduce the use of overtime through higher overtime premiums or regulations on maximum hours of work?

With respect to wage determination and wage structures, policy issues also abound. Why has wage inequality been increasing in Canada and other developed countries over the past several decades? To what extent are changes in the income distribution due to technological change and globalization of production versus changes in labour market policies and institutions, such as minimum wages and unionization? Is the middle class declining, and if so what accounts for increased wage polarization? Do public sector workers receive higher pay than comparable private sector workers? How important are fringe benefits in the total compensation picture, and why do fringe benefits prevail in the first place? How quickly do immigrants assimilate into the Canadian labour market? Does increased immigration lower the wages of native-born Canadians? Are workers in risky occupations compensated for that risk through wage premiums? Do workers "pay" for pension benefits by receiving lower wages than they would receive in the absence of such pensions? Why do male–female wage differentials prevail, and have they been changing over time, especially in response to legislative initiatives? How can employers design optimal compensation systems to induce productivity from their work force, including executives? Why does mandatory retirement exist, and what will happen to wage structures if it is banned? Why do wages seem to rise with seniority even if there is no productivity increase with seniority? Why do some employers seem to pay wages that are excessively high to meet their recruitment and retention needs?

With respect to unemployment, many old questions prevail, and new ones are added. Is unemployment different now than it was in earlier periods? Has job stability declined in recent years? What has happened to the unemployment of young people as the baby boomers age through the labour force? Are immigrants more likely to experience unemployment than the Canadian born? Does our aggregate unemployment rate reflect a large number of people experiencing short bouts of unemployment or a small number of people experiencing long bouts of unemployment? Did this change in the Great Recession of 2008? Why do workers and unions not take wage cuts to ameliorate unemployment? How have we managed to achieve relatively low rates of inflation and unemployment in recent years? What impact has unemployment insurance had on our unemployment rate?

These are merely illustrative of the myriad current policy questions that are relevant for public policy as well as for private personnel and human resource practices, and for collective bargaining. They indicate the social and practical relevance of labour economics, and the controversy that surrounds the field. The tools of labour market economics developed in this text will provide answers to many of these questions and shed light on others.

Similarities and Differences Between the Labour Market and Other Markets

A key issue in labour market economics is whether or not the labour market is so different from other markets that the basic tools of economics, especially the supply and demand model described earlier, do not apply. The following discussion illustrates some of these peculiarities and their implications for labour markets.

Various Actors with a Variety of Goals

As discussed previously, the labour market has three main actors, or stakeholders—labour, management, and government—each with different subgroups and objectives, or agendas. For example, within labour there is union labour and non-union labour, and within organized labour there are different types of unions (e.g., craft or industrial and professional associations) as well as possible differences between the leadership and the rank-and-file membership. Within management, the goals of stockholders may differ from the goals of chief executive officers, which, in turn, may differ from the goals of middle management. With increased emphasis on employee participation, the distinction between middle management and workers may be blurred. Within the catch-all of government, there are federal, provincial, and local levels. As well, there are often differences in the units that make the laws (e.g., legislators and regulators), that enforce the laws (e.g., courts, administrative agencies, and tribunals), and that design the laws and operate particular programs (e.g., policy units and bureaucrats). As well, the distinction between making, designing, and administering the law and policies often becomes blurred in practice. For example, the jurisprudence and case law of the courts and administrative tribunals can shape the interpretation of the law to such an extent that it can be more important than establishing new laws.

Sociological, Institutional, and Legislative Constraints

More so than most markets, the labour market is riddled with sociological, institutional, and legislative constraints, among others. In the sociological area, for example, family and community ties and roles can affect labour mobility, the role of women in the labour market and the household, and the career and educational choices of women. Social norms may also influence what are considered appropriate wage structures and who should do certain jobs.

Institutions are also important in labour markets. This is most obvious with respect to unions, especially in Canada where about a third of the work force is unionized. An increasingly large fraction of the workforce is also covered by various forms of licensing requirements. As is well known, workers in traditional professions like medicine, law, or accounting need to obtain a professional license before they are allowed to practice in a given jurisdiction. Over the years, these requirements have covered a growing number of occupations, such as servers in licensed establishments, cosmetologists, cooks, and so on. Note that earlier perspectives on labour economics were characterized as "institutional," emphasizing the importance of institutions and institutional arrangements in understanding labour market behaviour.

Legislative constraints are also crucial in labour markets. Employment standards laws set minimal or "community" standards with respect to such things as minimum wages, hours of work and overtime, statutory holidays, parental leave, and severance pay and advance notice requirements. Human rights and anti-discrimination legislation are important, as are laws on health and safety and workers' compensation. Labour relations laws also establish the framework for the formation of unions and the conduct of collective bargaining. Separate statutes often exist for workers in the public sector, sometimes circumscribing the right to strike and providing alternative dispute resolution procedures, including binding wage arbitration. The labour market may also be affected by other laws and regulations, such as those affecting immigration, free trade, unemployment insurance, pensions, training and education, and even environmental protection.

Market Imperfections

The labour market, more so than most other markets, is subject to market imperfections and other constraints. For example, imperfect information may make it difficult to decide which type of education to undertake, or whether to make a geographic or occupational move. Asymmetric information (e.g., the employer has information not available to workers) may make it difficult to demand compensating wage premiums for workplace hazards, or to agree to wage concessions in return for employment security. Transaction costs may make it difficult to finance human capital investments in areas like education, training, or mobility. Uncertainty and risk may make it difficult to make occupational-choice decisions that are affected by uncertain future demand and supply conditions.

Complex Price, Serving a Variety of Functions

The essential price that is determined in the labour market—the price of labour services, or the wage rate—is a complex price that is called upon to serve a variety of functions. It reflects a variety of factors: the returns to investments in education, training, or mobility; compensation for risk or undesirable working conditions; a "rent," or surplus, for being a member of a union or professional association or perhaps being employed in a particular industry; discrimination; and supply and demand decisions on the part of other participants in the labour market. As well, the wage rate is only one component of total compensation, with fringe benefits making up an increasingly larger share.

The **wage rate** is also called upon to perform a variety of functions. It allocates labour to its efficient uses; that is, to particular occupations, industries, and regions. It encourages optimal investments in human capital, such as education, training, labour market information, job search, and mobility. It is used to enhance performance, work effort, and productivity. It is also called upon to provide an adequate standard of living and family income, and to alleviate poverty and the manifestations of discrimination. In the labour market, issues of efficiency, equity, and fairness are intricately connected.

In part for these reasons, there are often strong moral overtones to labour market issues and the resultant wage that emerges. This is compounded by the fact that even though the wage is the price of labour services, the labour services and the labourer are inseparable. Dignity, perceptions of self-worth, and social attitudes are tied to the wage. Hence, phrases like *a decent wage, a living wage, the social wage, a just wage*, and *equal pay for work of equal value* are common expressions in labour economics.

Clearly, the labour market has a number of characteristics that differentiate it from many other markets. This raises the issue of whether the basic tools of economics apply in a market with such a complex array of participants and goals; sociological, legal, and institutional constraints; market imperfections; and pricing that are called upon to serve a variety of functions.

Our perception is that these are differences in degree and not in kind; other markets have some of these peculiarities, as well as others of their own. Moreover, these differences make the basic tools of economics more relevant, not less so, to understanding labour market behaviour and the impact of these peculiarities of the labour market. Economic analysis deals with decision making and trade-offs under risk, uncertainty, transaction costs, information problems, and market imperfections. It deals with the interplay among various market participants, those often with conflicting objectives. It deals with the impact of legal, institutional, and even sociological constraints—after all, the methodology of economics is a matter of optimizing subject to the constraints.

Economics has even proven useful in understanding why many of these constraints and institutional arrangements arise in the first place. As illustrated later in the text, economic efficiency rationales can be given to explain the existence of a variety of phenomena that may appear to be "irrational" or inefficient: purely seniority-based wage increases, the simultaneous existence of moonlighting and overtime, wages that appear "excessive" relative to what is necessary to recruit and retain workers, strikes that appear "irrational," an unwillingness to accept wage concessions in spite of high unemployment, the provision of job security in the public sector, payment through fringe benefits rather than cash compensation, and the existence of personnel practices such as mandatory retirement. In some cases, these phenomena may be the result of mistakes or bargaining power, but in other cases they may be the efficient institutional arrangement to deal with other problems in labour markets. Economics can shed light on why these arrangements arise in the first place as well as indicate their impact on the labour market. This often requires an interdisciplinary understanding that blends labour economics with other areas, such as industrial relations, personnel and human resource management, labour law, sociology, psychology, and history.

Summary Observations and Format of This Book

The previous discussion highlighted how labour economics is both practically relevant to our everyday lives and also relevant to broader social issues. The discussion also emphasized that the peculiarities of labour economics make economics more relevant, not less so, to understanding not only the impact of these peculiarities and institutional features, but also to why they arise in the first place. These issues make the study of labour markets relevant, controversial, and interesting.

In covering these issues, the text is divided into 17 chapters, which, in turn, can be divided into three groups. The first group, Chapters 2 through 7, constitutes the main core of theoretical work in labour economics: the neoclassical supply and demand model. The focus of these chapters is on the determination of employment and wages in a single labour market.

Chapters 2, 3, and 4 examine the supply side of the labour market. The underlying theory of labour supply is first outlined, emphasizing the income-leisure choice framework as a way to analyze the decision of whether and how much to work. While the ostensible objective of this theory is to provide the theoretical underpinnings of the labour supply function in the neoclassical model, it is more fundamentally a theory of individual rationality in the face of economic constraints. This basic theory underlies all of the remaining chapters in the book. While it can be daunting at first, Chapter 2 on labour supply is a chapter that forms a foundation for topics that are not even directly related to labour supply. The income-leisure framework is then applied to analyzing the work incentive effects of income maintenance programs in Chapter 3. This chapter emphasizes the means by which various features of government policy can be incorporated into the budget constraint, or opportunity set, and how they, ultimately, may affect work choices made by individuals. Chapter 4 explores features of labour supply over time, and over an individual life cycle. Home production is introduced as an additional consideration for understanding differences between the labour supply of men and women. The retirement decision is also analyzed, emphasizing the role of private and public pensions.

Chapters 5 and 6 address the demand side of the market. Attention turns from the decisions of individual worker-consumers to firms, emphasizing how employers change their demand for labour in response to changes in the wage rate and other determinants of labour demand. Factors affecting the magnitude of the possibly adverse employment effects of wage increases are investigated. Also analyzed are the effects on labour demand, and the employment of recent trends, such as global competition, free trade, industrial restructuring, privatization, offshoring, and deregulation. Canada's labour cost position in the competitive international environment is outlined, and the usefulness of such information in evaluating the impact of trade on labour markets is discussed. The impact on labour demand and employment of quasi-fixed costs, such as hiring and training costs and the cost of certain fringe benefits, are also analyzed, especially in the context of the willingness of employers to engage in worksharing or restrictions on overtime to create new jobs.

Chapter 7 deals with the interaction of labour demand and supply in a single market. Wage and employment determination under a variety of assumptions about the degree of competition is presented. First, the competitive model is explored and used to analyze the impact of payroll taxes on employment and wages. Second, we consider the case of imperfect competition, whereby employers have an extreme form of market power: monopsony. The discussion of employment and wage determination under these alternative market structures is then used as background to empirical debate regarding the impact of minimum wages.

The second group of chapters (Chapters 8 through 15) extends the neoclassical theory of wage and employment determination in a single market to wage structures *across* markets. Chapter 8 develops the theory of compensating wage differentials that underlies most of the subsequent discussion of earnings structures. Chapter 9 discusses human capital theory and investigates the role of education and training in the labour market. Considerable attention is paid to the empirical analysis of the connection between education and individual earnings. A unifying framework for the study of wage structures, the human capital earnings function, is also developed. This framework is exploited in Chapter 10 in an analysis of wages by various categories: occupation, industry, region, and firm size. Particular attention is also paid to private–public sector wage differentials.

Chapter 11 looks at the earnings of immigrants, and the degree to which their earnings grow after arrival in Canada. This aspect of the economics of immigration is cast into the wider context of immigration policy and the impact of immigration on the Canadian labour market. Chapter 12 focuses on earnings differentials by sex and investigates the degree to which these differentials may be attributed to discrimination. The chapter also reviews the various policy initiatives in this area, including pay and employment equity. Optimal compensation systems are analyzed in Chapter 13 and applied to explain, for example, the existence of institutional rules and personnel practices, such as mandatory retirement.

Chapters 14 and 15 analyze the impact of unions and collective bargaining in the labour market. Union growth and the varying incidence of unions across industries and regions are discussed, as is a comparison of unionization between Canada and the United States. Union preferences are analyzed and used in the context of contract theory and bargaining theory. Chapter 15 focuses on the impact of unions on wages, employment, non-wage aspects of employment, and productivity.

The third group of chapters (16 and 17) departs from the purely neoclassical model of employment and wage determination to consider the possibility that the labour market does not clear instantly (i.e., supply and demand do not get equated instantly), a fact resulting in unemployment. The meaning and measurement of unemployment is analyzed in Chapter 16. A great deal can be learned about the nature of unemployment by examining its structure and dynamic properties. Chapter 17 documents many of the suggested leading explanations for the existence of unemployment, ranging from imperfect information and search in a largely neoclassical context to alternative theories that have been offered to explain why wages may not adjust to clear the labour market. The macroeconomic relationship between aggregate wage changes, inflation, and unemployment is also examined.

The emphasis in the text is on a balance of theory, evidence, and application to important issues of social policy and private employment practices. By its very nature, however, labour economics has a more empirical tilt than most other fields within economics. While economic theory is a helpful guide when thinking about important policy issues, almost invariably the impact of a policy depends on *how much* a given policy is likely to affect economic outcomes. In the absence of controlled laboratory experiments, researchers have to infer the impact that economic variables have on each other by observing existing or past empirical relationships. Some of these inferences are more plausible than others.

Throughout the book, then, the challenges of conducting empirical research are featured. By its very nature, this research is specific and temporal. While the theory of labour supply and demand is "true," given the assumptions, empirical results that hold at one time may cease to be relevant at another. For this reason, a discussion of evidence is a review of current and past evidence, conducted by specific researchers with specific data. These particular bits of evidence, however, usually contribute to a wider, more consistent mosaic of economic relationships that can serve as a guide to policymakers.

One of the more useful trends in empirical labour economics has been to conduct careful comparative studies of economic outcomes across countries. To some extent, this merely reflects the increased internationalization of our economy and the need for external benchmarks when assessing magnitudes of variables in Canada. More importantly, however, by comparing economic outcomes between economies as similar as those of Canada and the United States, differences that exist between these outcomes can be associated with differences in the underlying economic structure or policy environment. While evidence of this nature is only suggestive, it represents some of the more important advances in labour economics over the past few years, and it is highlighted where ever possible in the text.

LO4, 5 Appendix 1A: Regression Analysis and Research Designs[2]

Throughout this book, we emphasize empirical evidence that pertains either to the theoretical model being discussed or the policy question being analyzed. Empirical labour economists address a variety of such questions, a small sample of which is listed below:

- Do labour supply curves slope upward? (Chapter 2)
- Does unemployment insurance reduce incentives to work, increasing the duration that someone is unemployed? (Chapter 3 and Chapter 17)
- Do minimum wages "kill" jobs? (Chapter 7)
- How much does education increase earnings? (Chapter 9)
- How much of the difference between men's and women's earnings can be attributed to labour market discrimination? (Chapter 12)
- Does increased immigration adversely affect the employment outcomes of the native born? (Chapter 11)

- Do higher wages adequately compensate individuals for working in unpleasant conditions? (Chapter 8)
- How much do unions affect the wage structure of the economy; that is, what is the premium that workers receive for being organized within unions? (Chapter 15)

Sometimes, the evidence is a simple graph, chart, or table of means. More often in labour economics, because it is relationships between variables that are of direct interest, empirical evidence refers to results from **regression analysis**. Our objective here is not to dwell on the mathematical aspects of regression analysis; several helpful sources that do are listed in the text references. Rather, our objective is to review some of the terminology and issues that will allow a more informed reading of the empirical evidence as it is described in the book. With modern computing capabilities, even the most basic spreadsheet can estimate regressions, so we shall not discuss computational aspects of estimating regressions. Besides, the difficult part of regression analysis or empirical work is not, usually, implementing the estimation procedure, but rather obtaining informative data and choosing a reasonable regression to run in the first place. Our discussion in this brief appendix will, therefore, focus on how regression results can be interpreted.

The foundation of all empirical work is data; that is, recorded measurements of the variables we are trying to summarize or explain. Increasingly, access to data is becoming quite easy as data libraries and statistics bureaus cooperate in providing computer-readable files. These data sets can be downloaded over the Internet or accessed on CD for use on personal computers. Labour economists employ a wide variety of data sets, but there are some sources that we will encounter more frequently in this book. A useful way to catalogue these data sets is by the nature of the unit of observation:

1. **Aggregate** or **time-series data** report economy-wide measures like the unemployment rate, inflation, GDP, or CPI. The variables are usually reported for several years (i.e., over time) and often for several economies (countries or provinces). A common database of such series is Statistics Canada's CANSIM, which has information on literally thousands of variables at national, provincial, and city levels.

2. **Cross-section microdata** report measures of variables (such as earnings, hours of work, and level of education) for individuals at a point in time. Common data sets of this type (there is considerable use of these throughout the text) are from the censuses of Canada conducted every five years; the monthly Labour Force Survey (LFS); and, in the United States, the monthly Current Population Survey (CPS).

3. **Panel data (longitudinal data)** combine the features of cross-section and time-series data by following sample individuals for several years. This selection allows economists to study the dynamics of individual behaviour, such as transitions into and out of the labour market. In Canada, the Survey of Labour and Income Dynamics (SLID) was conducted between 1993 and 2011 and followed individuals for a few years, focusing on labour market outcomes. The National Longitudinal Survey of Children and Youth (NLSCY) follows a sample of young Canadians over a longer period of time. In the United States, the Panel Study of Income Dynamics (PSID) and various National Longitudinal Surveys (NLS) have followed individuals over a longer time, and many panel data–based studies are based on these sources.

In order to illustrate the main ideas of regression analysis, we employ a very simple example that should also provide rudimentary insights into the discussion of earnings determination in later chapters. We explore the relationship between hockey player performance and player compensation. Specifically, we estimate the relationship between goals scored and player salaries. While the policy relevance of this topic is limited, at least that particular labour market should be familiar to many readers. To keep matters "simple" we also focus only on those players playing forward positions (centre, left wing, and right wing), since salaries of goal tenders and defencemen will probably be determined by different criteria than those used to evaluate players whose principal function is to score goals.

The underlying theory of player compensation is straightforward. As will be discussed in more detail in the text, individual pay depends primarily on the economic value of the contribution of one's labour. In this context, we would expect player pay to depend on the amount of additional revenue he generates (or is expected to generate) for the team. While it involves some additional assumptions, it is not unreasonable to imagine that the main contribution a forward player makes to a team is scoring goals, helping the team win games, and, ultimately, generating more revenue for the team. What we seek to estimate here is the additional pay a player can expect to make by scoring another goal.

We do this by comparing the salaries of hockey players who score different numbers of goals. We expect the forces of supply and demand to generate higher salaries for the higher-scoring players. For example, imagine that there are only two types of players: stars who score lots of goals, and "grinders" who serve a primarily defensive or limited offensive role. Presumably, the teams will place a greater value on those scoring more goals, for reasons described above. If we assume that there are two distinct markets for these types of players, then salary determination may be depicted by supply and demand graphs, such as those in Figure 1.A1. Here we can see that the better players earn more because of higher demand and scarcer supply. What we are trying to estimate is the extra earnings a player could expect if he could acquire the skills necessary to move from the grinder to the star market. Of course, in the real world there is a continuous distribution of hockey talent (goal-scoring availability), so we are estimating the returns to marginal improvements in performance.

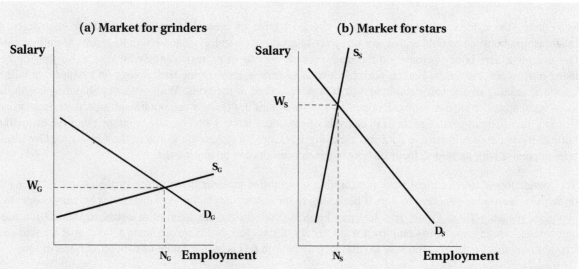

Figure 1.A1 Supply and Demand and the Relative Earnings of Star versus Grinder Hockey Players

Consider the separate markets for two types of players: grinders (low skill) and stars (high skill). The equilibrium wage for each type of player is determined within each submarket. Because they generate less revenue, the demand for grinders is lower than for stars. Since it requires less skill to be a grinder, we can also assume that the supply is greater at each wage than for high-skilled players. The combination of lower demand and higher supply results in a lower wage for grinders, W_G, than for stars, W_S.

As suggested earlier, the first step in such an inquiry is to obtain data on the key variables we believe help explain player salaries. In this case, data on player performance statistics and salary are readily available. We use data on player performance in 2014–2015 and their salaries in 2015–2016. Data on lifetime performance would probably be better, but these more limited data will be sufficient to illustrate the main ideas of regression analysis.

Figure 1.A2 shows a scatter plot of player salaries against the number of goals scored in the previous year. Each point in this scatter plot indicates the combination of goals scored and salary for an individual player. For example, Alex Ovechkin scored the highest number of goals in 2014–2015 (53) and he was paid $10,000,000 in 2015–2016. Most of the observations lie below $3,000,000 in annual salary and 30 goals scored. There are a few observations corresponding to high salaries and higher goal scoring. An "eyeball" summary of this graph suggests that players who score more goals also make more money. Regression analysis is little more than a formalization of this data summary exercise.

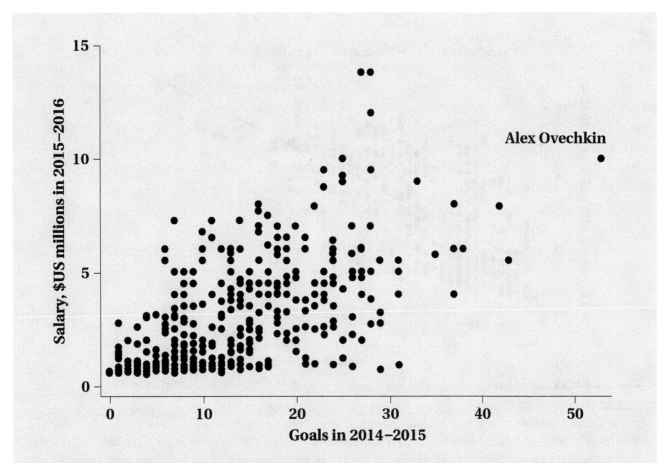

Figure 1.A2 NHL Player Salaries by Goals Scored in the Previous Year, 2014–2015

This is a scatter plot of player salaries in 2015–2016 against their goals scored the previous year (the 2014–2015 season). Each point corresponds to a specific player, relating the number of goals he scored to his salary. Alex Ovechkin, for example, scored 53 goals, and was paid $10,000,000.

NOTE: Sample includes only players (forwards) who played at least 20 games in the 2014–2015 season. Sample size is 410.

SOURCE: Based on data http://stats.nhlnumbers.com, accessed November 2015.

In Figure 1.A3, we show a plot of the same data, except that we transform the salaries into "ln(Salary)." Why? It is common practice in labour economics to use logarithms; some of the reasons for this are outlined in Exhibit 1A.1 and later in Chapter 9. For our purposes here, the primary reason is that it is easier to summarize the relationship between log salaries and goals with a straight line than it is with the raw levels of salaries. This is especially true given the range of salaries paid to players (from $500,000 to $10,000,000).

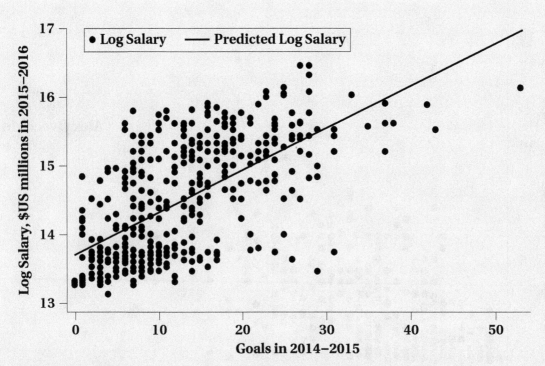

Figure 1.A3 Logarithm of NHL Player Salaries by Goals Scored in the Previous Year, and Fitted Regression Line

This is a scatter plot of the logarithm of player salaries in 2015–2016 against their goals scored the previous year (the 2014–2015 season). Each point corresponds to a specific player, relating the logarithm of his 2015–2016 salary to his goals scored. In addition, the estimated regression line, based on a regression of log salary on goals scored, is also presented on this graph.

NOTES:

1. Sample includes only players (forwards) who played at least 20 games in the 2014–2015 season. Sample size is 410.

2. The predicted log salary is based on the regression results reported in Table 1.A2, where log salary = 13.718 + 0.061 × Goals.

SOURCE: Based on data http://stats.nhlnumbers.com, accessed November 2015.

EXHIBIT 1A.1

Natural Logging

In labour economics, especially in the presentation of empirical results, it is common to encounter logarithms. Many students find logarithms (or logs) quite intimidating, but, in fact, the use of logs often simplifies economic theory and empirical work. There are at least two (related) contexts in which you will encounter logs in labour economics.

1. First, logs are helpful in expressing elasticities. The elasticity of labour supply with respect to the wage expresses the effect of a change in the wage on hours of labour supply in proportional, or percentage, terms. This is usually more convenient than expressing the relationship in the original units of measurement. For example, we could state that a $1 per hour rise in the wage increases annual labour supply by 50 hours. In order to facilitate comparison across studies, however, it is usually preferable to report that a 10 percent increase in the wage leads to a 2.5 percent increase in labour supply; that is, the elasticity is 0.25. The elasticity is unit free and gives the proportional (or percentage) change in hours associated with a proportional (or percentage) change in the wage. What does this have to do with logs? The conventional formula for an elasticity is

$$E = \frac{\Delta Y}{\Delta X} \times \frac{X}{Y} = \frac{\Delta Y}{Y} \div \frac{\Delta X}{X}$$

where "Δ" refers to the change in a variable. As it turns out, changes in the logarithms of variables directly yield the proportional changes, so that the elasticity can be expressed as

$$E = \Delta \ln Y / \Delta \ln X$$

This is especially convenient in estimating elasticities, because the estimated slope of a regression of ln Y on ln X gives a direct estimate of the elasticity.

2. Second, for many economic phenomena, changes in key variables lead to multiplicative, or proportional, changes in others. For example, economic growth is usually expressed in percentage terms, rather than in so many billions of dollars. We usually hear that GDP grew by 2 percent, or some comparable figure. An economy with a constant growth rate will grow exponentially, as each year's growth is added to the base of the next year, much as interest is added to the principal in a savings account with compound interest. An approximation of this growth process, or any similar relationship between a variable y and a variable x, is

$$y = Ae^{rX}$$

This equation is a simple representation of a variable y that grows continuously at rate r with X.

In labour economics, many productive characteristics are best described as having a multiplicative effect on wages. For example, an additional year of education might raise wages by 10 percent. Each additional year of education would then raise wages by 10 percent as much. In that case, wages can be expressed as a function of years of schooling, as in the equation above. The figure illustrates the relationship between the level of wages and years of schooling, for a simple example, where the base wage is $6 per hour and the returns to a year of schooling is 10 percent. Also shown in this graph is a plot of the log wage against the years of schooling. Notice that, unlike the relationship in levels, the logarithmic relationship yields an exact straight line. Again, for the purposes of estimating regressions, this is the preferred linear specification of the relationship between wages and education. Transforming such variables into (natural) logs is, thus, a common exercise.

Useful Properties of Logs

$\ln e = 1$	$\ln (a/b) = \ln a - \ln b$	$\ln (Ae^{rx}) = \ln A + rx$
$\ln ab = \ln a + \ln b$	$\ln a^x = x \ln a$	$\ln (1 + r) \approx r$

A Comparison of W and ln(W) as Functions of Schooling

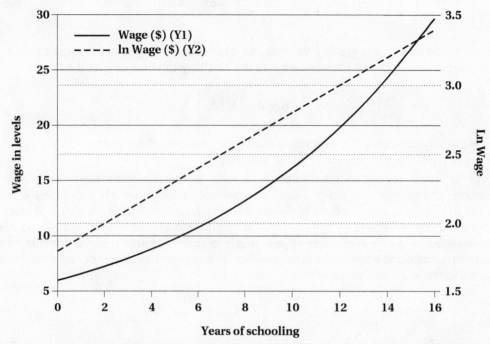

This line shows a hypothetical relationship between wages and the number of years of schooling. In this example, we assume that the logarithm of wages is a linear function of schooling. The dashed line corresponds to the log wage, and the second (right-hand) axis provides the relevant scale. While the log wage is linearly related to the level of schooling, the wage (in levels) is nonlinear, as can be seen by the solid line and the relevant first (left-hand) vertical axis.

One simple way to more formally summarize the data in Figures 1.A2 and 1.A3 is to array the average salaries by the number of goals scored. Table 1.A1 illustrates the results of this exercise. Here we can see that average player salaries rise from $1.49 million to $3.12 million when "Goals Scored" moves from 0–9 goals per year to 10–19 goals per year, an increase of approximately $1,630,000 for the extra 10 goals. This implies a return of about $1,630,000/10 = $163,000 per goal. The return for scoring goals can also be estimated as players move to the other categories; average salaries rise by $1.65 million for moving from the 10–19 to the 20–29 goals per year category, by almost $1 million for moving from the 20–29 to the 30–39 category, and also by almost $1 million for moving up to the 40–49 goals per year category. There is a huge payoff ($3.3 million) for moving from the 40–49 category to the 50-plus category. This is probably an understatement, as some of the highest earning players in 2015–2016 (i.e, Sidney Crosby, Patrick Kane, and Jonathan Toews) scored fewer than their normal output of goals in 2014–2015. In terms of logarithms, we see that the log salary rises by about 0.70 for moving between the lowest and second-lowest categories, and then less than 0.50 per 10 goals thereafter.

TABLE 1.A1	Tabulation of NHL Player Salaries by Goals Scored, 2015–16		
Goals Scored, 2014–15	Sample Size	Salary ($US millions)	ln (Salary)
0–9	173	1.49	13.99
10–19	148	3.12	14.71
20–29	74	4.77	15.19

30–39	12	5.76	15.45
40–49	2	6.70	15.70
50 +	1	10.00	16.12

NOTES:

1. Each column indicates the sample size or sample average for the corresponding goal-scoring category.

2. Sample includes only players (forwards) who played at least 20 games in 2014–2015. Sample size is 410.

SOURCE: Based on data http://stats.nhlnumbers.com, accessed November 2015.

A regression function calibrates, more formally, the relationship that was apparent in the table. Rather than letting our eyes fit a line through the data plotted in Figure 1.A2 and Figure 1.A3, or approximating the relationship between two variables from a table, regressions are calculated to provide an estimate of the function that "best fits" the data. Imagine that we want to estimate the following relationship between salary and goals:

$$\text{Salary} = a + b \times \text{Goals}$$

This is the equation for a straight line. In this example, salary is the dependent variable, while goals is the independent, or explanatory, variable. If we believed this were an exactly true and complete model of player salaries, all of the data would lie on the line implied by this equation, and estimation would be very simple. Of course, we know that this is only an approximation, and there are many other factors (leadership ability, "marketability," past performance, long-term contracting issues, and luck) that affect player salaries. We can lump all of these factors together into an error term, e, so that our augmented model is

$$\text{Salary} = a + b \times \text{Goals} + e$$

For any given line that we can draw through the points in the scatter plots, this "model" will fit perfectly. Individual player salaries will equal the "predicted" salary that is on the line, plus the difference between the actual salary and the predicted salary. However, we are interested in explaining as much of the salary as we can with goals and would like as little as possible left to the residual, e. While there are many ways to formalize this idea, in practice, most researchers choose the line that minimizes the sum of the (squared) residuals, or distance between the line and the actual observation. This **ordinary least squares**, or OLS, estimator yields a line that best predicts salary with goals scored, at least according to this criterion. The output of regression analysis will be estimates for the parameters of this line: a) the intercept, and b) the slope.

The estimated regression line for these data is shown in Figure 1.A3 with log salary as the dependent variable. It is upward sloping, though the precise slope is hard to read directly from the graph. The slope of the line will tell us (on average) how much player salaries rise with goals scored. Specifically, the estimated slope will allow us to conduct the "thought experiment" of how much extra a player would earn if he scored one more goal. The numerical estimates of the regression are reported in Table 1.A2. We show the estimated results for both levels (dollars) and logarithms. In column (1) for levels, we see that each additional goal is associated with $169,907 of additional earnings. In logarithms, column (4) suggests that each goal is associated with an additional 0.061 log dollars, which can be interpreted as an additional 6.1 percent in salary.

In addition to the **coefficient**, or **parameter** estimates, regression analysis and the associated statistical theory yield estimates of the stability, or reliability, of the estimates, at least within the sample. The **standard errors** of each coefficient provide a measure of the precision with which we are likely to have estimated the true parameter. If the estimation procedure were repeated on other samples of similar hockey players, the coefficients would likely vary across samples even if the underlying salary determination were the same, since no two samples are identical (because of e). The standard error is an estimate of the variability (due to **sampling error**, e) that we would expect for estimates of the coefficient across these samples. Coefficients and standard errors are used together to conduct tests of statistical hypotheses. The most common hypothesis we will encounter is whether a given coefficient is, statistically, significantly different from zero. Even if one variable has no effect on another, given sampling error, it is unlikely that the estimated coefficient would equal zero exactly. For this reason, we generally pay attention only to coefficients that are at least twice as large as their standard errors. This is related to the common disclaimer in the reporting of poll results—that the polling procedure yields estimated percentages which are within a given range of the true percentage 19 times out of 20, so that we should take the specific reported value with a well-defined grain of salt. While this is an approximation of the basic, formal statistics underlying hypothesis testing, it should be sufficient for most empirical research discussed in the book.

TABLE 1.A2	Estimated Effects of Performance on Player Salary in 2015–16 (standard errors in parentheses)					
		Salary ($US) mean = 2,844,749			In (Salary) mean = 14.52		
	Means	(1)	(2)	(3)	(4)	(5)	(6)
Intercept		615,243	197,067	62,994	13.718	13.576	13.521
		(165,213)	(160,787)	(167,676)	(0.057)	(0.056)	(0.058)
Goals	13.12	169,907	88,349	94,695	0.061	0.034	0.036
		(10,482)	(13,753)	(13,869)	(0.004)	(0.005)	(0.005)
Assists	18.49		80,495	82,944		0.027	0.028
			(9626)	(9604)		(0.003)	(0.003)
Plus/minus	−0.27			−20,422			−0.008
				(7809)			(0.003)
R-squared		0.39	0.48	0.49	0.41	0.49	0.50

NOTE: Sample includes only players (forwards) who played at least 20 games in 2014–2015. Sample size is 410.
SOURCE: Based on data http://stats.nhlnumbers.com, accessed November 2015.

The ratio of the coefficient to its standard error is called the **t-ratio**, and the test for **statistical significance** is basically a determination of whether this ratio exceeds 2 in absolute value. In the example reported in Table 1.A2, the t-value for goals scored is much greater than 2 (e.g., $169,907/10,482 = 16.21$), so we can reject the possibility that the estimated relationship between goals and salaries is due to pure chance or sampling error.

Another statistic commonly reported in regression analysis is the **R-squared**. We do not focus much on R-squareds in this text, but the R-squared is a measure of the goodness of fit of the regression. It indicates the proportion of the variance of the dependent variable that is accounted for, or explained, by the explanatory variables. In column (1) of Table 1.A2, the R-squared is 0.39, which indicates that goals scored in the previous year account for 39 percent of the variation of player salaries. Sadly, this is probably as good a fit of regression as we will encounter in labour economics!

Of course, we do not believe that this simple one-variable regression could possibly explain all of the variation in player salaries. There are other aspects of hockey performance that we also expect to contribute to team victories and revenue. For example, defensive play or setting up goals for other players (assists) may also be rewarded. These other factors can easily be accommodated in **multiple regression** analysis, which is nothing more than adding more variables to the regression equation. At one level, the effect of additional variables, like assists, is of independent interest, and for this reason the expanded set of regressors may be desirable. However, there is a more important reason to add additional variables.

Our objective is to estimate the additional earnings a player can expect by scoring another goal. We accomplish this by comparing earnings across players who have scored different numbers of goals. We, thus, attribute the additional earnings a 30-goal scorer earns compared to a 10-goal scorer entirely to the extra 20 goals scored. What if the 30- and 10-goal scorers differ in other ways? What if the 30-goal scorer is also a better player overall (in other dimensions)? We may then over-attribute the salary difference to the goal scoring alone. What we really want to do is compare otherwise identical players who differ only in the number of goals scored. We cannot perfectly do this, but by including additional explanatory variables, we can control for, or hold constant, these other factors. Of course, we can hold constant only observable, measured factors, and there will always exist the possibility that any estimated relationship between two variables is purely spurious, with one variable merely reflecting the effects of unobserved variables with which it is correlated. We will encounter many such problems as we evaluate empirical research in labour economics. For example, do highly educated individuals earn more because they have the extra schooling, or is schooling merely an indirect indicator of their inherent ability and earnings capacity? Do union members earn higher wages because of the efforts of the union or because unionized firms are more selective in hiring more productive workers? We must always be careful in noting that regression coefficients indicate correlation between variables. As tempting as it may be, it may be very misleading to apply a causal interpretation to this association.

In columns (2) and (5) we add the variable "Assists" to the regression to see whether goals scored alone was capturing some of the effects of omitted player quality. Apparently this was the case. The estimated return to scoring a goal drops by half when we control for the number of assists. Players who score more goals also tend to perform well in other dimensions, like assisting other players to score goals. In fact, assists are rewarded similarly to goals.[3] In column (2), the economic return to scoring a goal for a player with a given level of assists is $88,349. In this way, the multiple regression framework holds constant player ability in one dimension to see how variation in another is associated with player salary. Similarly, for players scoring the same number of goals, an extra assist is associated with $80,495 in additional salary.

Finally, in order to see whether forwards are compensated for their defensive abilities, we include a measure of the players' "plus-minus" (the difference between team goals scored for and against while a player is on the ice—a large "minus" for a player indicates that even though he may score goals, the opposing team often scores when he is playing). In columns (3) and (6) we see that the estimated coefficients on plus-minus are small and *negative,* although including this variable has little effect on the other coefficients. In both the levels and logarithmic specification, the plus-minus coefficient is also statistically significant. It appears that forwards are not rewarded, and may even be penalized, for their defensive skills—they are primarily paid to set up or score goals.

Appendix 1B: Research Designs in Labour Economics

Throughout this text, we place considerable emphasis on theory and evidence, and much of the available evidence comes from research projects carried out by labour economists. In this section, we briefly summarize some of the principal research strategies, or "research designs," used by labour (and other) economists. Examples of these research designs will appear throughout the text.

Sometimes, the research question of interest is purely descriptive in nature; for example, "What is the difference in average earnings in Canada between men and women?" or "Is wage inequality rising and if so by how much?" The data in Table 1.1 provide an answer to the first question using information from the Survey of Labour and Income Dynamics for 2011. For the second question, we would first choose suitable measures of wage inequality (such as the ratio of the earnings of the person at the 90th percentile of the wage distribution to that of the person at the 10th percentile of the distribution, as discussed in the context of Figure 1.1) and then calculate these measures at various points in time.

Although informative, answers to such descriptive questions often raise further questions relating to causal linkages and mechanisms. For example, "Why are the average earnings of women lower than those of men?" or "What were the underlying forces driving the rise in wage inequality in Canada over the past several decades?" Furthermore, in many cases the research question of interest involves identifying cause and effect; for example, estimating the causal impact of a labour market intervention or policy change (or, to use terminology from medical science, a treatment). Answering such questions requires suitable data and an appropriate research design. As we just discussed, multiple regression may be part of the research strategy, but this statistical method alone may not be sufficient to provide credible answers.

Identifying and estimating causal impacts is often challenging. The nature of the challenge is easily explained. We can observe the outcomes experienced by individuals (or families, firms, cities, regions, etc.) who received the treatment, but we cannot observe what would have occurred in the absence of the intervention. What would have happened to these individuals if they had not received the intervention is referred to as the "counterfactual outcome." To estimate the causal impact of the treatment we would want to compare the observed outcomes (or outcomes) to the counterfactual outcome(s), but the latter is inherently unobservable.

For example, suppose that you injure your ankle playing sports. Your doctor prescribes physiotherapy, and you begin treatment. Six weeks later your ankle is healed. Did the physiotherapy cause (i.e., lead to the result) the ankle to heal, or would your ankle have healed on its own? You cannot answer this question because you can't observe the counterfactual outcome, the healing that would have taken place if you hadn't had the physiotherapy treatment.

Research designs are empirical strategies for estimating the counterfactual outcomes. One key distinction is that between experimental and nonexperimental methods. Among nonexperimental methods there are a variety of research strategies that may be employed, depending on the nature of the research question and data availability (e.g., using regression analysis to estimate the effect of scoring more goals on a player's salary).

Experimental methods involve random assignment to "treatment" and "control" groups. This research design represents the gold standard for credible evidence of causal impacts, and for this reason it is widely used when feasible, ethical, and cost-effective. Those in the treatment group receive the intervention, such as a drug in the case of a pharmaceutical trial designed to test the effectiveness of a newly developed medicine. Those randomly assigned to the control group do not receive the intervention, although in the case of a pharmaceutical trial they receive a placebo (a pill that looks identical to that received by those in the treatment group but contains no medical ingredients).

Random assignment ensures that the treatment and control groups are statistically indistinguishable prior to the beginning of the treatment. By statistically indistinguishable, we mean that the two groups are not, statistically, significantly different on any dimension that might be relevant to the effectiveness of the treatment, whether it be by age, gender, intelligence, health, physical fitness, motivation, ambition, strength, dexterity, and so on. As a consequence, the behaviour of the control group provides an unbiased estimate of the counterfactual outcomes; that is, what would have happened to the treatment group in the absence of the intervention.

Experimental research designs have two additional advantages. First, the statistical techniques needed are very simple and do not require additional assumptions. In many cases, the researcher can obtain unbiased estimates of the impact of the intervention by comparing the mean (average) outcome(s) of the treatment group to those of the control group. Second, these methods are easy to explain to, and be understood by, policymakers and the general public, unlike some econometric methods.

Examples of social experiments that you will read about in this text include the negative income tax (guaranteed annual income) experiments carried out in the 1960s and 1970s in Canada and the United States and welfare-to-work experiments, such as Canada's Self-Sufficiency Project carried out in the 1990s (both covered in Chapter 3) and experimental evaluations of job training and job search assistance programs discussed in Chapter 9.

A variety of nonexperimental research designs can be employed. These are sometimes referred to as studies that use observational data to distinguish them from studies that employ experimental data. Relative to random assignment designs, all nonexperimental methods have potential limitations. Typically, better data allows researchers to minimize the limitations. In addition, multiple regression is also often needed to control for potentially confounding factors.

1. Before–after comparison of those treated

This method compares the outcomes experienced by those who received the intervention before and after the treatment. It, therefore, requires longitudinal data (in order to follow the same individuals over time). The method is often unconvincing, as it assumes that the outcomes experienced before the treatment provide a good estimate of the counterfactual. This could be the case in some situations, but often there may be other reasons why the post-treatment outcomes differ from the pre-treatment outcomes. For example, consider a program that offers job search assistance to workers who recently lost their job. Comparing post-intervention employment rates to pre-intervention employment rates is unlikely to provide a good estimate of the impact of the job search assistance program, because some of the unemployed workers would have found jobs even without the program. In these circumstances, a more convincing research design would incorporate a comparison group of recently unemployed workers who did not participate in the job search assistance program. If the comparison group is otherwise very similar to those who did participate in the program, their outcomes could provide a good estimate of the counterfactual.

An important concern when using this research design is that factors other than the intervention may influence post-treatment outcomes. For example, in the case of the job search assistance program, economic conditions may have changed between the pre-treatment and post-treatment periods. For these reasons, multiple regression is often used to control for observable factors that may influence the outcomes.

2. Post-treatment comparison of treated and comparison groups

This method compares the outcomes experienced by those who received the intervention to those of a similar group of individuals (or regions, countries, firms, families, etc.) that did not receive the intervention. It requires only cross-section data on the two groups. The key assumption is that the outcomes experienced by the comparison group provide a suitable estimate of the counterfactual outcome that would have been experienced by the treatment group in the absence of the intervention. Thus, the choice of a suitable comparison group, one that is as similar as possible to the treatment group, is crucial to the credibility of this method. In the absence of random assignment, the treatment and comparison groups are likely to differ on some dimensions. Multiple regression is, therefore, used to control for observable differences in the two groups.

The main limitation of this method is the absence of data on the treatment and comparison groups prior to the intervention. For example, consider an educational intervention, such as smaller class sizes or the addition of teacher's aides designed to improve student performance on achievement tests. Use of this research design would involve comparing classes of students in the treated group, such as those taught in smaller classes, to similar classes with regular class size. However, it is possible that the achievement levels of the comparison group of classes differed from those of the treated group prior to the intervention. Not being able to take these pre-treatment differences into account is likely to result in biased estimates.

3. Before–after comparison with a comparison group

This method removes important limitations of the first two research designs discussed above. It requires data on both the treatment group and a suitable comparison group prior to and after the intervention. The outcomes experienced by the comparison group are used to estimate the counterfactual. Multiple regression is typically also used, both to control for observable differences between the treatment and comparison groups and to control for changes over time in other influences.

The main threat to the validity of this research design is that there may be unobserved factors that influence whether individuals are in the treatment or comparison group, and that are also correlated with the outcomes of interest. This will generally result in biased estimates, even if multiple regression is used to control for observed differences between the treatment and comparison groups. An important case in which this occurs is referred to as "self selection," or selection bias. Consider, for example, a training program designed to improve the skills and employability of individuals facing labour market challenges. The before–after comparison with another group's research design would employ pre-program and post-program data on trainees and a comparison group of non-trainees. Multiple regression would be used to control for any observed differences between the trainees and non-trainees. However, typically the program participants would have chosen to apply for training, whereas those who didn't receive training would have chosen to not apply. The program participants are a self-selected sample, and they may have chosen to receive training on the basis of factors that are unobserved by the researcher, such as motivation, a desire to improve their earnings, and so on. If those unobserved factors are also correlated with the outcome of training (skill enhancement, employability, and earnings) the comparison of trainees and non-trainees will typically suffer from selection bias. Examples of potential selection bias, and methods to deal with it, will arise several times in this book.

4. Natural experiments (or quasi-experiments)

Natural experiments or quasi-experiments are a frequently used research design in labour economics. In structure, they are very similar to the before–after comparison with a comparison group's design discussed previously. They arise when some event occurs that results in some individuals (or regions, cities, firms, etc.) receive a treatment or intervention while others do not. Those who receive the intervention constitute the treatment group, and those who did not receive it constitute the comparison group. The event could be a policy change, a natural disaster, or any change in social or economic circumstances that affects some individuals and not others. Ideally, the event occurs for exogenous reasons; that is, for reasons that are unrelated to the treatment of interest. If so, selection bias will not be a problem as those who are affected by the intervention (and those not affected) did not choose to be affected. In these circumstances, there may be unobserved differences between the treatment and comparison groups but these are unrelated to the outcomes of interest. Multiple regression can be used to control for observed differences between the treatment and comparison groups.

Summary

- There are three main groups of actors in the labour market: individuals, firms, and government. Individuals make decisions concerning how they will earn a living, whether and how much to work, what type of work they will do, and what kinds of skills they will acquire in order to work. Firms make decisions about how much and what type of labour they will hire. Governments set various policies, many of which have direct implications for the decisions of individuals and firms, and also affect the operation of the labour market itself.

- While there are many dimensions to the decisions made by these actors, we can distill the outcomes of the decisions to individual outcomes, especially concerning earnings, employment (or hours), and wages. Preliminary explorations with individual-level data show considerable dispersion in these outcomes for Canadians and systematic differences between men and women. These empirical features, or "labour market facts," merit further investigation in this book.

- The neoclassical supply and demand model is a powerful tool that can be used to analyze these outcomes, especially employment and wages. The model comprises behavioural assumptions concerning buyers and sellers, summarized by the supply and demand curves for labour. In addition, the neoclassical model assumes that the labour market is in equilibrium; that is, that the labour market clears where supply equals demand. This is a very powerful assumption that allows the model to predict a unique employment and wage outcome in a market.

- Most of this book is organized around the supply and demand framework. It begins with a thorough development of the behavioural models underlying labour supply and demand. Next, employment and wage determination in a competitive labour market is summarized and the assumption of perfect competition is relaxed. The neoclassical framework is then applied to explaining wages across labour markets, especially with respect to the role of education in generating wage differentials. The remainder of the book focuses on markets and outcomes that are not as well characterized by the simple neoclassical model; it includes topics such as discrimination, internal labour markets, unions, and unemployment.

- The appendix to this chapter reviews regression analysis, a statistical tool used to summarize the relationships between variables.

Keywords

aggregate	panel data
coefficient	parameter
cross-section microdata	R-squared
employment	regression analysis
equilibrium	sampling error
involuntary or voluntary unemployment	standard errors
labour demand	statistical significance
labour market outcomes	t-ratio
labour shortages	time-series data
labour supply	unemployment
market-clearing model	wage rate
multiple regression	wages
neoclassical economics	
neoclassical supply and demand model	
ordinary least squares	

Endnotes

1. For clarity of the graphics, we have trimmed the sample of the lowest and highest earners, dropping the top and bottom 1 percent from the sample. However, the percentiles are calculated over the entire sample.

2. More thorough discussions of regression analysis, statistics, and issues of research design can be found in any good econometrics book (e.g., Wooldridge 2016). Angrist and Pischke (2014) provide an accessible introduction to research design.

3. As it turns out, we cannot reject the hypothesis that the coefficients on goals and assists are the same; that is, given the sampling error, it is possible that the estimated coefficients on goals and assists were generated by a model where goals and assists have the same returns.

CHAPTER 2

Labour Supply: Individual Attachment to the Labour Market

LEARNING OBJECTIVES

LO1 Define the key elements of labour force measurement—employment, unemployment, labour force participation, and hours worked—and explain how they are measured and reported by Statistics Canada.

LO2 Illustrate graphically how the income-leisure model reflects the trade-offs that consumers face in deciding whether and how much to work.

LO3 Distinguish theoretically between the work choices made by individuals and the economic opportunities that they choose from.

LO4 Explain, using diagrams, how an increase in the wage rate leads to offsetting income and substitution effects, and how this yields an ambiguous effect of wage changes on labour supply.

LO5 Interpret the economic and other factors affecting a married woman's decision to work, and show how this decision can be captured within the income-leisure (labour supply) model.

MAIN QUESTIONS

- How do we measure labour market attachment? How did labour market attachment evolve over the twentieth century?
- What is the labour force participation decision, and how does it fit into the general theory of labour supply?
- How can we incorporate the possibly different factors that determine men's and women's labour supply decisions?
- Is there any theoretical reason to believe that labour supply increases with the market wage?
- What is the evidence regarding the responsiveness of individual labour supply to changes in the wage?
- Why are workers paid an overtime premium, rather than just a higher wage, in order to induce them to work overtime?

At its core, the subject matter of the study of labour supply is how individuals earn a living by selling labour services through the labour market. While there are important quality dimensions to labour supply, such as the levels of skill that someone brings to the market, the focus of the next three chapters is on the quantity of homogenous labour offered. The guiding theoretical question is whether or not labour supply is an upward-sloping function of the wage rate.

Why might market labour supply curves increase with the wage rate? In introductory courses, supply curves are commonly drawn as upward-sloping functions of the market price. Why not borrow from this, and merely assert that labour supply, as a special case of "supply," is also upward sloping in its price? Of course, such reasoning is circular and provides no insight as to why more labour would be offered at a higher wage. The classical economists provide one possible explanation. They argued that labour supply was upward sloping, at least in the long run, because higher wages would spur population growth, thereby increasing the number of labourers. Modern labour economists do not pursue that line of reasoning. Instead, we take the population as fixed at a point in time, and focus on individual decisions of how much to work. These decisions can be broken down into participation (whether to work) and hours (how much to work). Why might these two dimensions of individual labour supply decisions be increasing in the wage rate? Intuition suggests that people will want to work more if the return for doing so increases. As we shall see, however, intuition alone can be misleading. Nevertheless, incentives to work lie at the heart of the study of labour supply.

In this chapter, we develop a model of individual labour supply. The basic theoretical framework is the labour-leisure (or income-leisure) choice model, and it can be applied to both the participation and the hours dimensions. Within this framework, we analyze the effect of changes in wage rates and other economic variables on preferred hours of work, and from this derive the individual's supply curve of labour. An important strength of this model is that it can easily be adapted to explore the impact of more general types of incentives, such as those provided by government tax and transfer programs. Accordingly, we exploit the labour-leisure model in the following chapters, especially Chapter 3, where we incorporate government programs, like social assistance (welfare), into the individual's decision to work. Before turning to the theoretical model, however, we define some important concepts and investigate several labour supply features of the Canadian labour market.

A Guide to This Chapter

This can be a daunting chapter, especially for newcomers to the topic; in addition to an avalanche of definitions, the discussion may occasionally seem abstract and theoretical. And, especially, when the primary conclusion is that labour supply *can either increase or decrease* with the wage rate, it also may seem that the ratio of insight to effort is low. However, appreciating the complexity of the decision in the model is a first step toward a better understanding of real-world labour supply behaviour, which is even more complicated. Furthermore, much of the material in labour economics—even topics not so obviously related to labour supply, like how long to attend school—require an understanding of this theory. It is worth remembering the basic idea underlying the model: workers are rational decision makers, making choices from among various opportunities presented by the labour market. We divide the chapter into two sections.

Section One: The Theory of Labour Supply

The objective of Section One is to begin with a model of individual behaviour and trace it through the implications for the market supply of labour. Ultimately, we derive a labour supply function that relates labour supply to the market wage. We begin with an explanation of how economists quantify labour market attachment, dividing this attachment into participation (whether to work) and hours (how much to work) components. After exploring participation and hours patterns in Canada, we develop the basic income-leisure model that underlies both dimensions of labour supply. Using this model, we investigate how participation and hours respond to changes in the economic environment (like the wage). Finally, we summarize the empirical evidence on the effect of wages on labour supply.

Section Two: Extensions and Applications

The objective of Section Two is to use the labour supply model to explore a number of features of the labour market, exclusive of government tax and transfer programs which we treat separately in the next chapter. In particular, we look at the impact of labour market constraints (like unemployment) on individual labour supply, and the means by which the model can account for multiple job holding (moonlighting) and the structure of overtime premiums.

Section One: **The Theory of Labour Supply**

LO1   # Quantifying Labour Market Attachment

Many students are, initially, surprised to see the relative attention paid to labour supply by economists. Perhaps based on their own experience, their caricature of a labour supply decision is that virtually everyone wishes to have a full-time job or career. However, is it really the case that most people participate in the labour market, working the standard workweek of around 40 hours? As we shall see, there is actually considerable variation in the degree of attachment of individuals to the labour market.

Labour Force Participation

The **labour force participation decision** is basically a decision to participate in paid labour market activities as opposed to other activities, such as unpaid work in the home, volunteer work, education, or retirement. As such, it influences the size and composition of our labour force and has an impact on household activities, education, and retirement programs.

The policy implications of these changes can be dramatic. Changes in the size and composition of our labour force affect our growth and unemployment rates, as well as the occupational and gender composition of the labour force. The latter, in turn, affect such factors as relative wages, demands for unionization, daycare, and equal pay and equal employment opportunity legislation. Changes in household activities can involve family formation and mobility. Retirement programs can be affected insofar as new labour force participants will add contributions to pension funds, while those who retire (i.e., do not participate in the measured labour force) will be a drain on the funds.

As illustrated in Figure 2.1, the **labour force** consists of those persons in the eligible population who participate in labour market activities, as either employed or unemployed. The eligible population is the portion of the population that is surveyed as potential labour force participants (i.e., civilian non-institutional population, 15 years old and over, excluding Yukon, Northwest Territories, Nunavut, and those living on Indian reserves). Persons from that potential population of labour force participants (POP) are categorized as either in the labour force (LF) or not in the labour force (NLF). Those in the labour force are either **employed** (E), or **unemployed** (U), with the latter being not employed but seeking work. People are classified as "employed" if they did any work at all in the survey period (even one hour). They are also considered as employed if they are normally employed but happen not to be at work at the time of the survey because, for example, they are ill or on strike. Note that the definition of "work" is somewhat vague, but is designed to capture those working for pay, either in the formal labour market or implicitly in self-employment. Students may work hard on their courses, but this is not considered being employed; only students working for pay are considered employed. Accordingly, people not in the labour force are usually students, retirees, persons in the household, those unable to work, and some discouraged workers who have simply given up looking for work. According to labour force definitions, the latter are not categorized as unemployed because they are not seeking work.

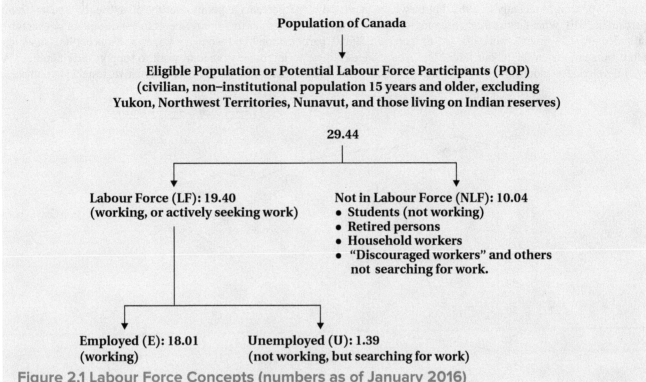

Population of Canada

↓

Eligible Population or Potential Labour Force Participants (POP)
(civilian, non–institutional population 15 years and older, excluding
Yukon, Northwest Territories, Nunavut, and those living on Indian reserves)

29.44

Labour Force (LF): 19.40
(working, or actively seeking work)

Not in Labour Force (NLF): 10.04
- **Students (not working)**
- **Retired persons**
- **Household workers**
- **"Discouraged workers" and others**
  not searching for work.

Employed (E): 18.01
(working)

Unemployed (U): 1.39
(not working, but searching for work)

Figure 2.1 Labour Force Concepts (numbers as of January 2016)

The labour force is the sum of those individuals either working (employed) or not working but searching for work (unemployed). The unemployment rate is the percentage of the labour force that is unemployed, while the labour force participation rate is the percentage of the eligible population in the labour force.

NOTES:

1. Population figures in millions.

2. Labour force participation rate: LFPR = LF/POP = 19.40/29.44 = 65.9%.

3. Unemployment rate: UR = U/LF = 1.39/19.40 = 7.2%.

SOURCE: Adapted from the Statistics Canada publication, "Labour Force Information," Catalogue 71-001-X, February 2016, http://www.statcan.gc.ca/pub/71-001-x/71-001-x2016001-eng.pdf, accessed February 17, 2016.

The **labour force participation rate (LFPR)** is the fraction of the eligible population that participates in the labour force (LFPR = LF/POP). The unemployment rate (UR) is the proportion of the labour force that is unemployed (UR = U/LF).

The Canadian Labour Force Survey (LFS) conducted by Statistics Canada is currently based on a monthly sample of approximately 56,000 households, yielding detailed labour force data on approximately 100,000 individuals. The results are published monthly in "Labour Force Information" (Statistics Canada, Catalogue No. 71-001-X). The survey is described in more detail in that publication.

While the LFS provides the most frequently used estimates for our labour force, employment, and unemployment figures, other sources are available. In particular, the Canadian census, which is conducted every five years and the most recent being in 2011, referred to activity in 2010 (implemented as the National Household Survey that year). The census is more comprehensive (not based on a sample from a larger population), and consequently includes richer details relating to such factors as employment and unemployment by industry and occupation. However, its use is limited because it is conducted only every five years, there is a considerable lag before the results are published, and its reliability on labour force issues may be questioned because, unlike the Labour Force Survey, it does not focus only on labour force activity.

Labour force participation rates have changed significantly over the twentieth century, especially for women. Figure 2.2 shows trends in participation based on a combination of census and Labour Force Survey data. As we can see, male participation has declined from just over 90 percent of the eligible population to 71 percent by 2010. Women's rates were below 30 percent as recently as 1961, but they have increased by 33 percentage points over the 50 subsequent years, to 62 percent in 2010. What factors might account for these changes? Was it primarily improvements in contraception or changing attitudes toward women's work that led to increased female participation? Did women's wages rise since 1960, inducing more women to enter the labour force? Did men's wages fall, requiring more women to work to support their families? A well-developed economic model would aid in analyzing these explanations and also provide alternative, testable hypotheses.

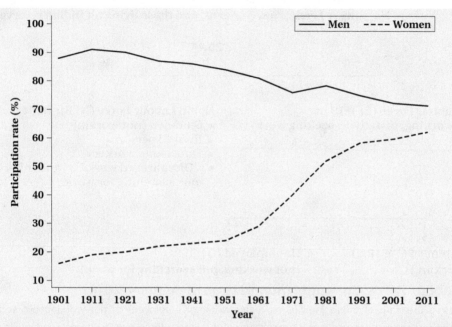

Figure 2.2 Labour Force Participation Rates by Sex, Canada, Census Years 1901–2011
Labour force participation rates for men and women are plotted by census years, beginning in 1901. The general trends suggest a gradual reduction of labour force attachment for men, in contrast to a sharp increase for women, beginning in the 1950s.
SOURCES: M. Gunderson, "Work patterns," in *Opportunity for Choice: A Goal for Women in Canada*, ed. G. Cook (Ottawa: Statistics Canada, 1976), p.97 for 1901–1971, reproduced by permission of the Minister of Supply and Services Canada. Participation rates for 1981–2011 are calculated from the Labour Force Survey, Statistics Canada, Table 282-0002.

Figure 2.2 hides as much variation in participation as it shows. For example, participation varies significantly by age and marital status. We focus on these demographic and lifecycle dimensions of labour supply in Chapter 4. Table 2.1 highlights another important aspect of cross-sectional variation in participation: differences across countries. For this particular (and incomplete) sample of countries, labour force participation ranges from a low of 52.9 percent in Egypt, to 78.2 percent in Denmark and Canada. A careful examination of the numbers in Table 2.1 yields at least two insights. First, most of the variation in overall participation is due to differences in the participation rate of women. Second, participation rates for women seem to be positively related to the level of economic development, with the richer countries having higher female participation rates, or at least smaller gaps between men and women.

TABLE 2.1	Labour Force Participation Rates by Sex, Selected Countries, 2014				
Country	Abbreviation	Overall	Male	Female	Difference
Denmark	DNK	78.2	80.6	75.7	4.9
Canada	CAN	78.2	81.8	74.7	7.1

Country	Abbreviation	Overall	Male	Female	Difference
Germany	GER	77.4	82.7	72.0	10.7
Australia	AUS	76.7	82.8	70.7	12.1
United Kingdom	GBR	76.4	82.2	70.5	11.7
Bangladesh	BGD	73.6	86.6	60.6	26.0
Russia	RUS	73.6	79.0	68.8	10.2
United States	USA	71.8	77.4	66.2	11.2
France	FRA	71.0	75.4	66.8	8.6
Hong Kong	HKG	68.9	78.9	60.4	18.5
Jamaica	JAM	67.8	74.3	61.5	12.8
Chile	CHL	67.8	80.0	55.6	24.4
Poland	POL	67.3	74.2	60.5	13.7
Philippines	PHL	67.1	81.3	52.8	28.5
South Korea	KOR	66.1	76.2	55.6	20.6
Mexico	MEX	65.0	83.3	48.3	35.0
Italy	ITA	64.2	74.4	54.0	20.4
South Africa	ZAF	56.6	64.3	49.2	15.1
Pakistan	PAK	56.6	85.9	25.9	60.0
Nigeria	NGA	56.3	63.8	48.6	15.2
Egypt	EGY	52.9	79.3	26.0	53.3

NOTES: Participation rates for the population 15–64 years old. "Difference" is the difference between the male and female participation rates. The list of countries is ranked in descending order, from the highest to the lowest overall participation rate.

SOURCE: All data from the World Bank Indicators; http://databank.worldbank.org/data, accessed May 24, 2016. The Labour Force Participation rates are based on International Labour Organization (ILO) estimates. The specific series are Overall (SL.TLF.ACTI.ZS); Male (SL.TLF.ACTI.MA.ZS); and Female (SL.TLF.ACTI.FE.ZS).

This second point is illustrated in Figure 2.3, where we plot the participation rates against one measure of economic development—the logarithm of per capita GDP (national income). One guiding question, which can be only suggestively addressed given the exploratory nature of this exercise, is whether the labour force participation patterns we observe represent different points along an upward-sloping labour supply function. While it is reasonable to assume that wages for both men and women are higher in richer countries, there are also many other factors that differ across countries. That said, what might we potentially learn about labour supply behaviour from these figures? The first panel shows that male participation is essentially flat, unrelated to per capita income, and possibly wages. Does this mean labour supply for men is also flat? Not necessarily. Perhaps as countries get richer, even though their wages rise, men do not have to work as hard, or for as long, in their lifetime, and perhaps they are better able to afford early retirement. This may even be easier if their wives are also able to work at higher-paying jobs.

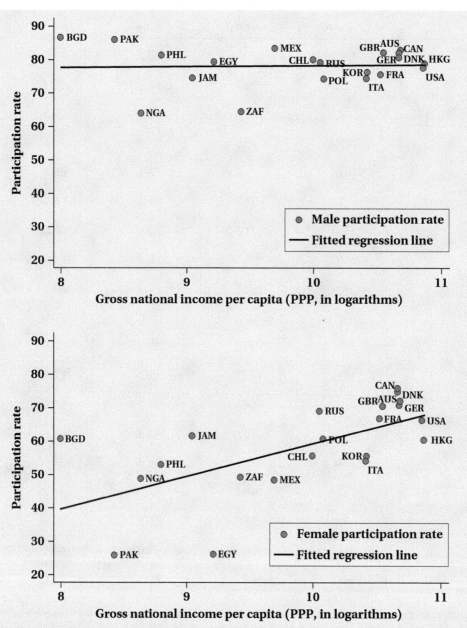

Figure 2.3 Male and Female Participation Rates by Level of Economic Development

This figure shows how male and female participation varies with the level of economic development as measured by per capita GDP. In addition to the data points indicated by the country abbreviations (explained in Table 2.1), we also show the estimated regression line relating the participation rate to log per capita income. The top panel shows that the male participation rate is generally flat, and unrelated to national income, while the second panel shows that women's participation rises with national income.

This figure plots the participation rates for men and women against the per capita national income of the country (in natural logarithms). The participation data and country abbreviations are detailed in Table 2.1. Per capita GNI is taken from the World Bank World Development Indicators (http://databank.worldbank.org/data), accessed May 24, 2016. This "PPP" (purchasing power parity) adjusted measure of per capita national income accounts for differences in the cost of living between countries. We also show the estimated OLS regression line for each series as a function of log per capita income.

In the second panel, we see a strong upward-sloping relationship between national income and female participation. Again, this is far from definitive evidence, but the data are consistent with richer countries having higher-paying opportunities for women (i.e., higher wages) and, thus, higher female participation rates. In richer countries the fertility rate of women is also lower, possibly further facilitating their movement into the labour force. Notice that there are other variables besides income that explain differences in participation rates. Countries above the regression line have relatively high rates of female participation for their level of development, while countries below the line have lower rates. Among lower income countries, Bangladesh, the Philippines, and Jamaica have higher female participation rates, especially when compared to Pakistan and Egypt. Perhaps differences in culture or attitudes to women's market work explain these differences. A good model of labour supply should be able to account for such differences. Taken together, these results point to a positive link between economic development and a reduced gap in the participation rates between men and women. As countries get richer and as women's education and labour market opportunities improve, a convergence occurs in the economic roles of men and women, at least as far as their participation rate is concerned.

Hours

The **hours-of-work aspect** of labour supply involves a variety of dimensions, including hours per day, days per week, and weeks per year. Changes in any or all of these dimensions can alter the hours-of-work aspect of the labour supply decision. Phenomena such as the eight-hour day, the shorter workweek, and increased vacation time are institutional embodiments of a reduction in hours of work. Similarly, moonlighting, overtime, flexible working time, and compressed workweeks are institutional arrangements that alter the typical pattern of hours of work.

The policy importance of the hours-of-work decision is illustrated in a variety of ways. Changes in hours of work can affect not only the quantity but also the quality of our overall labour supply (and hence national output), as well as absenteeism, turnover, employment opportunities, and the demand for related activities—notably, those involving leisure time and flexible working hours. Changes in hours of work, in turn, can be affected by changes in the age and sex structure of the labour force, the prominence of two-earner families, government policies and laws, and, of course, the wage rate.

In the short run, hours of work appear to be relatively fixed with little scope for individual variation. The eight-hour day, five-day workweek, and fixed vacation period are fairly common for many wage and salary earners. However, the increased importance of flexible working hours is altering these arrangements. In addition, occupational choice provides an element of flexibility as people choose jobs partly on the basis of the hours of work required. Individuals may also be able to combine jobs, perhaps two part-time jobs or a full- and a part-time job, in order to work the desired number of hours for a given wage rate.

Figure 2.4 illustrates the apparent degree of flexibility that Canadian workers have in the number of hours they work per week. The work patterns of women are quite varied, while men are more likely to work the typical 40-hour week. However, even for working men, less than half work 40 hours per week. The next largest proportion (22 percent) works between 30 and 39 hours per week, while about 13 percent work more than 50 hours. Women, on the other hand, are as likely to work part-time (less than 30 hours) as exactly 40 hours. However, they are less likely than men to work more than 40 hours per week. Might these patterns be explained by labour supply theory? Perhaps relatively higher wages for men lead to higher average hours worked, especially for the highest paid? Alternatively, women may prefer to work part-time so that they can better meet family commitments. Or maybe women are underpaid in the labour market, and so work fewer hours? As with participation, a good theory of labour supply should be able to accommodate these features, and the potential explanations, of labour market attachment.

As previously mentioned, the length of the workweek is also more flexible than one might think. At the beginning of the twentieth century, the average factory worker worked almost 60 hours per week, the equivalent of six 10-hour days. It wasn't until the 1960s that the average hours in manufacturing conformed to the more familiar 40-hour workweek (eight hours per day, for five days). More recently, average hours have dropped below 40 hours per week. And average hours worked are even lower, closer to the mid-30s, once we account for increased vacations and holidays.

Since real wages have risen over the century, this long-run decline in hours worked appears inconsistent with an upward-sloping labour supply function. Instead, it suggests an independent effect of increased wages: as societies become wealthier, they need not toil as hard and can afford to take more time off. It is hoped that the theoretical model will clarify the ways in which wages can affect labour supply.

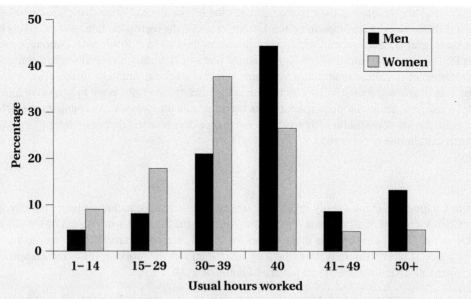

Figure 2.4 Distribution of Hours Worked Per Week by Sex, January 2011

This histogram shows the distribution of usual hours worked per week for men and women. Only 45 percent of men work exactly 40 hours per week, while 28 percent of women work exactly 40 hours. Women are more likely to work part-time (under 30 hours per week), while men are more likely than women to work overtime (in this case, 50 or more hours per week).

SOURCE: Adapted from Statistics Canada, "Labour force survey estimates (LFS), by usual hours worked, main or all jobs, sex and age group, unadjusted for seasonality, monthly," Table 282-0015, CANSIM Database, http://www5.statcan.gc.ca/cansim/a26?lang= eng&id=2820015, February, 2016.

LO2, 3   Basic Income-Leisure Model

The objective of the **labour supply model** is to represent an individual's choice of hours worked, given his or her market opportunities and the value he or she places on their nonmarket time. We wish to model this person as doing the best they can, subject to the constraints of the labour market and the limited availability of time. The model is an extension of standard microeconomic consumer theory, a brief review of which can be found in Appendix 2 on our OLC site. As such, we divide the individual's decision-making problem into two parts: what he or she would like to do (preferences) and the choices available (constraints). The assumption of rationality brings the two parts together, yielding a unique characterization of an individual's choice as a function of preferences and market constraints.

Preferences

We assume that individual preferences can be distilled into **preferences** over two "goods": consumption of goods and services, and leisure. **Leisure** embodies all nonlabour market activities, including household work and education, as well as pure leisure activities. The phrase "leisure" is somewhat of a misnomer since it includes activities that are not leisure activities. The term is used here, however, because it is the phraseology used by Robbins (1930) in his original work on the subject, and it has been retained in the literature as a summary term for "nonlabour market activities."

We can graphically represent consumer preferences with **indifference curves**. Indifference curves and budget constraints are used extensively in developing the theory of labour supply. Those unfamiliar with indifference curve analysis should review the online appendix to this chapter before proceeding further.

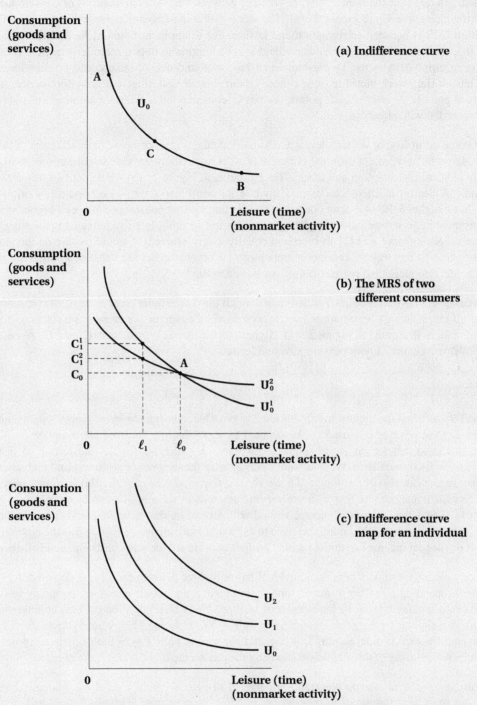

Figure 2.5 Consumer Preferences: Consumption-Leisure Indifference Curves

Indifference curves plot combinations of consumption and leisure that yield the consumer equal levels of utility. The absolute value of the slope of an indifference curve gives the marginal rate of substitution (MRS); that is, the amount of leisure the consumer is willing to accept in exchange for giving up some consumption. The indifference curve in panel (a) exhibits diminishing MRS, as the consumer requires more leisure to offset the decline in consumption as his or her level of consumption falls (from A to C, versus C to B). In panel (b), we compare the MRS's of two consumers. (Note: Indifference curves cannot cross for a single individual.) Beginning at A, consumer 2 has a lower valuation of leisure and, conversely, a higher value on consumption, requiring a smaller increase in consumption (C_1^2 versus C_1^1) to offset the decline in leisure from ℓ_0 to ℓ_1. Finally, panel (c) shows representative indifference curves for an individual. Utility is increasing as the consumer has more leisure and consumption (i.e., as combinations move further from the origin.

The individual is indifferent (has the same utility, or welfare) between various combinations of consumption and leisure as given by the indifference curve U_0 in Figure 2.5(a). The slope of the indifference curve exhibits a diminishing **marginal rate of substitution** (MRS) between consumption and leisure. For example, at point A, the individual has an abundance of consumption and, thus, is willing to give up considerable consumption to obtain more leisure; hence, the steeply sloped indifference curve at point A. At point B, the individual has an abundance of leisure and is, therefore, willing to give up considerable leisure (i.e., work more) to obtain more labour income and, thus, consumption; hence, the relatively flat indifference curve at point B. At intermediate points, such as C, consumption and leisure are more substitutable because the individual is not saturated with either.

While we cannot compare **utility**, or welfare, levels across individuals, we can compare marginal rates of substitution across consumers. This allows us to represent different preferences, at least partially, by indifference curves with different MRSs, at various combinations of consumption and leisure. For example, in Figure 2.5(b) we depict two different consumers. For consumer 1, bundle A lies on indifference curve U_0^1, while for consumer 2 the same bundle lies on indifference curve U_0^2. Consumer 1 has a higher MRS at A than consumer 2. This implies that consumer 1 places a higher value on leisure (at A) than does consumer 2. To induce consumer 1 to give up leisure from ℓ_0 to ℓ_1 requires compensating him or her with an increase in consumption from C_0 to C_1^1 to keep him equally happy, whereas it would require an increase to only C_1^2 to compensate consumer 2. In this way we can incorporate those factors that affect the value of **nonmarket time**, such as the value of work at home, into individual preferences as manifested in the MRS.

We assume that consumers have well-defined preferences over all the conceivable combinations of consumption and leisure. This implies that all combinations lie on some indifference curve. Consumer preferences can then be represented by an indifference curve map, as illustrated in Figure 2.5(c). Higher indifference curves such as U_1 and U_2 represent higher levels of utility since they involve more of both consumption and leisure.

Constraints

The individual will try to reach the highest indifference curve possible, constrained by economic opportunities provided by the labour market. Let the price of consumption be denoted by P, so that the value of consumption is PC. In this simple model we ignore saving so that we can set PC equal to income. This allows a simple transformation of our model from **consumption-leisure** to **income-leisure**. We now want to summarize the income (or consumption) and leisure combinations from which the consumer can choose. In Figure 2.6 we show a few examples of **potential income constraint**. These are "potential" income constraints because they indicate varying amounts of income that can be obtained by giving up leisure and working instead. The actual amount of income earned will depend on the chosen amount of work plus the amount of income received from other sources; the latter is referred to as "nonlabour" income and shown as the amount Y_N. Alternative phrases used for the potential income constraint include **budget constraint**, income constraint, and **full-income constraint**.

Consider first a very simple situation where the individual has only three discrete choices, as depicted in Figure 2.6(a). She can do no paid work, spending all of her available time, T, engaged in nonmarket activities, including leisure. In this case, the most that she can consume is given by her nonlabour income, Y_N (which might be 0). This combination is denoted by A. She could work part-time, increasing her income by I_P to $I_P + Y_N$, reducing her leisure by h_P to $\ell_P = T - h_P$ (point B). Alternatively, she could work full-time, earning $I_F + Y_N$, and consuming $\ell_F = T - h_F$ units of leisure (point C). In this case, she need only compare the utility of three bundles, choosing the one on the highest indifference curve.

The more conventional potential income constraint is depicted in Figure 2.6(b). This linear budget constraint allows the individual to choose from a continuum of income-leisure bundles, ranging from 0 hours of work to T hours of work. The slope of the constraint depends on the person's wage rate, W. For each hour worked, the individual gives up one hour of leisure but earns W of additional income. The constant slope reflects an assumed constant wage rate for each hour worked. Persons with a higher market wage, such as W_1 where $W_1 > W_0$, will be able to earn more income by giving up leisure and working more; hence, the slope of W_1 is steeper than the slope of W_0.

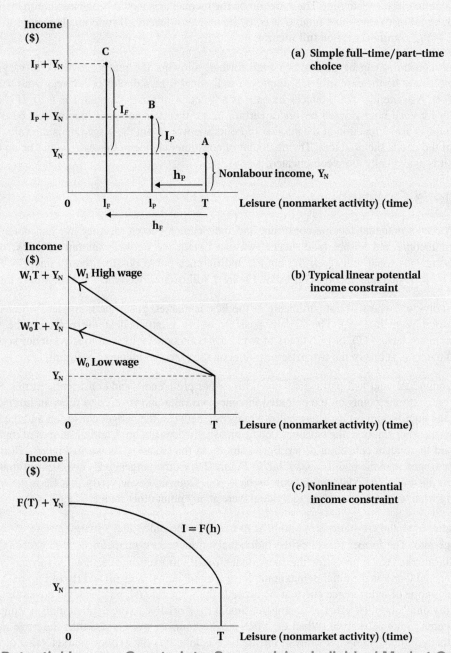

Figure 2.6 Potential Income Constraints: Summarizing Individual Market Opportunities

Budget sets, or potential income constraints, show the combinations of income (or consumption) and leisure available to an individual. In panel (a), the individual has only three choices: (1) not working (point A), obtaining T hours of leisure, no labour earnings, and nonlabour income of Y_N; (2) working part-time for h_P, obtaining l_P hours of leisure, and earnings l_P (plus nonlabour income Y_N); or (3) working full-time, obtaining l_F leisure, and l_F earnings (plus Y_N). Panel (b) shows the more conventional opportunity set, where the individual is free to choose any number of hours to work at the wage rate, W. Higher wages yield a steeper budget constraint and higher potential income. Panel (c) illustrates the possibility that the "wage rate" is not constant per hours worked, as would be the case for a self-employed person.

Perhaps the simplest way to understand how wage changes (as well as other factors, such as taxes and transfers, which will be examined later) affect the potential income constraint is to first mark the endpoint on the leisure axis. This endpoint is the maximum amount of leisure available (T). Depending on the units in which leisure is measured, it could be 24 hours per day, 7 days per week, 52 weeks per year, or some combination, such as 8736 hours per year. The potential income constraint is then derived by plotting the income people receive as they give up leisure and work additional hours; that is, they move leftward from the maximum leisure endpoint. The endpoint on the income axis would be the maximum income the individual could attain by working all of the available time; that is, by having zero leisure. If individuals choose to work T, the most they can earn is $WT + Y_N$, commonly called **full income**.

The potential income constraint can be generalized even further, allowing the returns to work to vary with the amount worked. One example would be the case of a self-employed individual (like a doctor or lawyer), who sells output that she produces to the market. Assume that she produces income as a function of hours worked, $I = F(h)$. If she has diminishing marginal productivity for each hour worked beyond a certain point, then her potential income can be depicted by Figure 2.6(c). Here, her income is also a function of the number of hours she works, but the wage rate is the value the market places on an hour's worth of the goods she produces. The treatment of consumer choice in this case would be no different than that in panel (b), though it is analytically more complicated.

The Consumer's Optimum

By putting the individual's potential income constraint and indifference curves together, we can obtain the **consumer's optimum** amount of income and leisure (and, hence, we can obtain the optimal amount of work, or labour supply). The **utility-maximizing** individual will reach the highest indifference curve possible, constrained by the labour market opportunities as given by the potential income constraint. Figure 2.7 illustrates two types of outcomes to this choice problem.

Panel (a) shows an individual who will not participate in the labour market, given the individual's preferences, nonlabour income Y_N, and market wage rate W_0. The highest possible utility is attained at the point on the budget constraint corresponding to maximum leisure (T), or zero hours of work. This outcome is referred to as a **corner solution** because the individual equilibrium occurs at one of the two extreme points on the potential income constraint.

Panel (b) shows an individual who will participate, given his or her preferences and constraints. In this case, the optimum occurs between the two extreme points on the potential income constraint and is referred to as an **interior solution**. With an interior solution, the equilibrium is characterized by a tangency between the budget constraint and the highest attainable indifference curve. At a corner solution, the tangency condition usually does not hold, and the slopes of the highest attainable indifference curve and the budget constraint differ. For example, in the situation shown in Figure 2.7(a), the indifference curve is more steeply sloped than the budget constraint. In Figure 2.7(b), the tangency E_0 involves optimal leisure of ℓ_0 and labour supply or work $h_0 = T - \ell_0$, yielding income $W_0h_0 + Y_N$. One can easily verify that E_0 is the utility-maximizing equilibrium by seeing what would happen if the individual were at any point other than E_0.

A useful way to characterize the consumer's optimum is to compare the individual's marginal rate of substitution (MRS) with the market wage rate. The former measures the individual's preferences, or *willingness* to exchange nonmarket time for income, while the market wage measures the individual's *ability* to exchange leisure for income. Consider first the participation decision, and focus on the point of maximum leisure, point A in panels (a) and (b) of Figure 2.7. When the MRS at zero hours of work (slope of indifference curve at A) exceeds the wage rate (slope of budget constraint), as at point A in Figure 2.7(a), the individual's implicit value of nonmarket time is high relative to the explicit market value of that time, and the individual will therefore not participate. When the MRS at zero hours of work is less than the wage rate, as at the point A in Figure 2.7(b), the individual's implicit value of leisure time is less than the explicit market value of that time, and the individual will participate in the labour market. In this case, the individual increases hours of work until the MRS between income and leisure equals the wage rate, thereby exhausting all "gains from trade" associated with exchanging nonmarket for market time.

In analyzing labour force participation behaviour, economists often use the concept of a **reservation wage**, which is defined as the wage rate at which an individual would be indifferent between participating and not participating in the labour force; that is, the wage at which an individual would be indifferent between work in the labour market as opposed to engaging in nonlabour market activities, such as household work, retirement, or leisure activities, all of which require time. If the market wage rate were equal to the reservation wage W_R, the individual's potential income constraint would be given by the line RR' in Figure 2.7(a) and 2.7(b). That is, the reservation wage is the slope of the individual's indifference curve at zero hours of work. If the market wage is less than the reservation wage, as in Figure 2.7(a), the individual will not participate in the labour force. If the market wage exceeds the reservation wage, as in Figure 2.7(b), the individual will participate in the labour force, since the return from engaging in labour market activity exceeds that individual's valuation of time in nonlabour market activities.

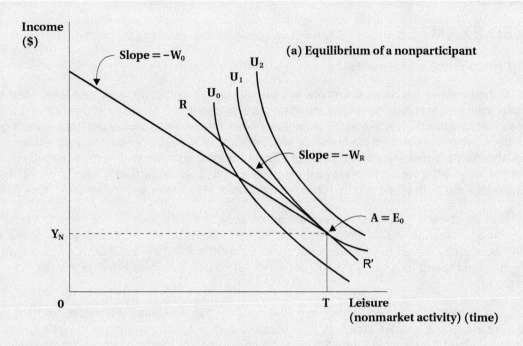

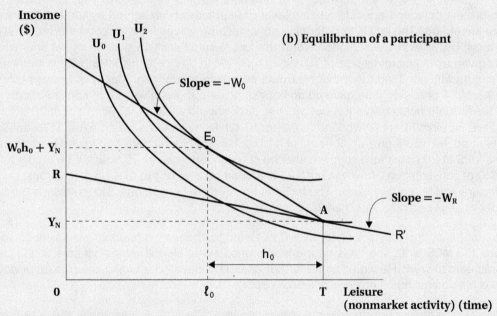

Figure 2.7 The Consumer's Labour Supply Decision

The utility-maximizing choice of hours worked is illustrated. In panel (a), the consumer's optimum occurs at A, with leisure equal to T and consumption Y_N yielding the highest utility. This person does not work. The reservation wage is given by the slope of RR' and is the MRS at this point. If the wage were higher than RR', the individual would participate. In panel (b), E_0 is an interior solution, where the indifference curve U_2 is tangent to the budget constraint. This consumer chooses ℓ_0 units of leisure and consumption (income) of $Y_N + W_0 h_0$.

WORKED EXAMPLE

Working Part-Time at University

Jack and Jill both attend the same university and are deciding whether to work part-time while they are in school. Both have identical financial situations: their parents give them a weekly allowance of $100, and they can work as much as they would like at the local Mega-Mart, at a wage of $10.00 per hour. Over a given week, they each have sleep and personal maintenance requirements of 10 hours per day, leaving a total of 7 × 14 = 98 hours available for discretionary activities. Out of this 98 hours, they have to decide how much time to spend working at the Mega-Mart versus time with their studies, partying, socializing with friends, or watching TV. Our simplified analysis distills this time into two choices: working at Mega-Mart and "nonmarket" time (leisure).

Panels (a) and (b) show a graphical representation of Jack and Jill's identical opportunity sets, or budget constraints. At one extreme, if Jack does not work, he can subsist on his $100 allowance. At the other, if he worked 14 hours a day, seven days a week, he could earn 98 × $10.00 = $980.00. Combined with his $100 allowance, he could spend (or save) $1080.00 per week. Of course, he would have no downtime and would be unable to study.

While Jack and Jill have identical opportunity sets, they do not have the same preferences, and, therefore, might make different choices. Consider Jack first. One possible choice for him would be to work one day, or eight hours per week (Point A). He would earn $80 that he could use, for example, to pay for nicer clothes or buy better-tasting protein powder. He would attain a level of happiness represented by the indifference curve U_0. Is this what he should do? The key is to determine how much he values his time compared to what he is being paid to give it up; is the extra consumption worth the lost leisure? Jack's valuation of his time when working eight hours is given by his marginal rate of substitution (MRS). In this case, his MRS is 2; he does not value his time very much. An MRS of 2 indicates that he would be willing to work an additional hour as long as he was paid at least $2. More precisely, if he gave up an hour's leisure but was given $2 of consumption, he would be indifferent. Clearly, eight hours of work is not optimal. Jack should work more. What about 20 hours (Point B)? This would leave him indifferent to working eight hours. While he would earn an extra $120 dollars to spend however he wanted, he would give up 12 hours of leisure, leaving him no better off (given his preferences) than at Point A. His MRS at 20 hours also suggests that he should work less. At 20 hours, if he works one hour less he gives up $10 of consumption. However, his MRS is $16, so he is willing to give up $16 of consumption to gain one hour of leisure and be equally happy. The fact that he needs to give up only $10 makes it a "no brainer" that he should work at least one hour less than 20.

The only point on his opportunity set where he will not want to change his hours of work is at 15 hours of work (Point C). Here, the MRS is 10, and he is on the indifference curve U_1. He values his time at $10 per hour, the same as he can earn at work. He would be no further ahead by altering his work schedule up or down an hour. Fifteen hours is his optimal hours of work, or labour supply.

Jill, by contrast, has the same opportunities but values her time differently. For example, she may place a greater priority on studying or spending time with friends, as compared to personal consumption. She is considering working one half-day per week, for four hours (Point A). However, her MRS at 4 hours is $20, which is much higher than the wage. In other words, she values her time at $20 per hour at this point. Since she would be paid only $10 for an hour's work, it would make sense for her to reduce her labour supply. In fact, even if she reduces her labour supply to zero, she finds her time is more valuable than Mega-Mart is willing to pay. At zero hours of work, her MRS is $15. Unfortunately for Jill, there are no more hours of leisure available at any price. The best she can do is choose not to work at all (Point B) and not participate in the labour market, thus attaining utility represented by U_1. She will still be able to consume $100 at this point. Only if the Mega-Mart was willing to pay her more than $15 per hour would she want to work, as $15 is her reservation wage, given by RR'.

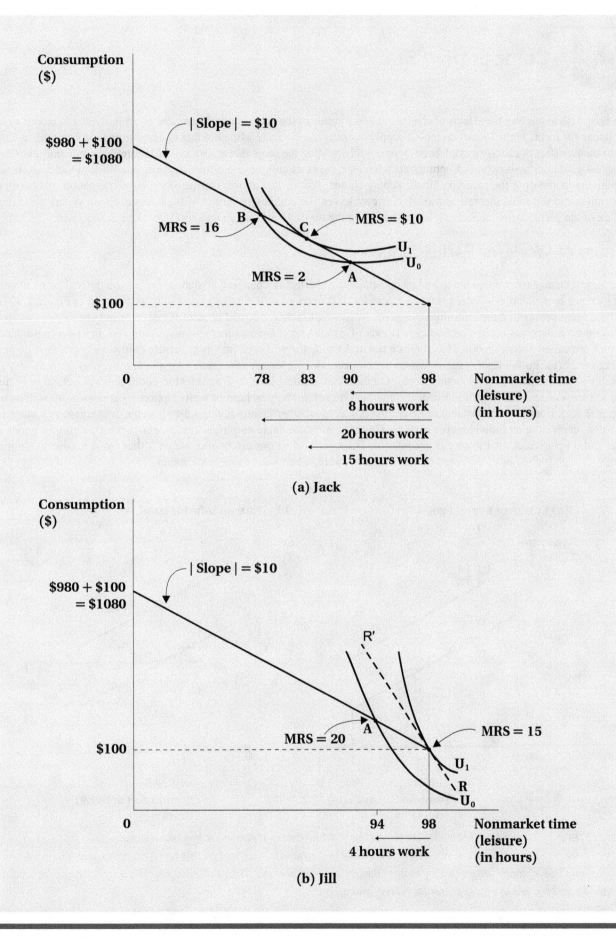

(a) Jack

(b) Jill

LO4   Comparative Statics

We now wish to analyze the effects of changes in key features of the economic environment on an individual's labour supply decision. We focus on the impact on labour supply of changing the wage while holding nonlabour income constant, and then focus on the effect of changing nonlabour income while holding the wage rate constant. The theoretical methodology is quite simple—given our assumption of optimizing behaviour, we need only compare the consumer equilibrium under alternative conditions, comparing the resulting labour supply choice. As we saw above, the decisions on participation and hours are integrated into the same theoretical model. However, given the continuous nature of the hours decision versus the discrete nature of the participation decision, it is worth treating the two sides of the labour supply problem in sequence.

Hours of Work for Participants

The easiest change to examine in the budget constraint is the effect of changing nonlabour income on desired hours of work. An increase in nonlabour income results in a parallel shift outward of the budget constraint, as depicted in Figure 2.8. This shift outward means that the consumer can purchase more of both goods and leisure. Whether or not she decides to spend more on both depends on her preferences. Goods of which she consumes more in response to an increase in nonlabour income are called normal goods. If leisure is a **normal good**, she will consume more leisure (and work less), as is depicted in Figure 2.8(a). In this figure, she increases her consumption of leisure (thus decreasing labour supply) from ℓ_0 to ℓ_1 as a result of the increase in nonlabour income. On the other hand, if leisure is an **inferior good**, she will actually consume less leisure, concentrating the additional income (and more) on the purchase of consumption. This possibility is shown in Figure 2.8(b). Economic theory makes no predictions as to whether leisure is normal or inferior. It is an entirely empirical question, depending on individual preferences. However, most available empirical evidence suggests that inferior goods are rare, and, in particular, that leisure is not inferior. Through most of our discussion, we will, thus, treat leisure as a normal good—though it must be emphasized this is a matter of pure, albeit reasonable, assumption.

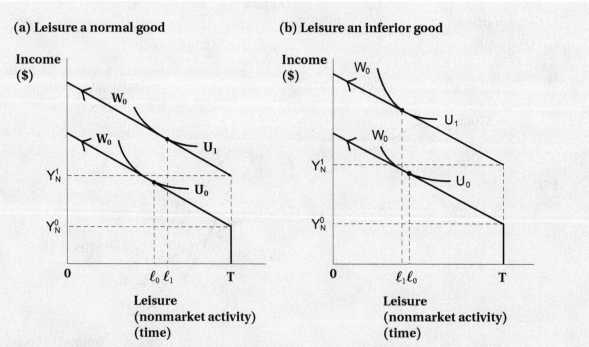

Figure 2.8 The Effect of an Increase in Nonlabour Income on Labour Supply

Panels (a) and (b) compare the impact of an increase in nonlabour income (from Y_0 to Y_1) on hours worked. In (a), the consumer "buys" more leisure (works less), as leisure is a normal good. In (b), the consumer buys more consumption but less leisure (and works more), as leisure is an inferior good.

What will happen to the equilibrium amount of effort if wages are increased? Among the classical economists, Adam Smith discussed the "short-run" response of labour to an increase in the wage rate:

The wages of labour are the encouragement of industry, which, like every other human quality, improves in proportion to the encouragement it receives. . . . Some workmen, indeed, when they can earn in four days what will maintain them through the week, will be idle the other three. This, however, is by no means the case with the greater part. Workmen, on the contrary, when they are liberally paid by the piece, are very apt to over-work themselves, and to ruin their health and constitution in a few years.[1]

As this quote suggests, a change in the wage rate has two effects. On the one hand, the higher wage rate means that for each quantity of work, the worker now has more income from which to buy more of all goods, including leisure. This is termed the **income effect**, and in the case of a wage increase, it leads to reduced work, assuming that leisure is a normal good. On the other hand, the individual may work more because the returns for work are greater; that is, the opportunity cost of leisure, or the income foregone by not working, is higher and, hence, the person may substitute away from leisure. This is termed the **substitution effect**, and in the case of a wage increase, it leads to increased work. In the case of a wage change, therefore, the income and substitution effects work in opposite directions; hence, it is ultimately an empirical proposition as to whether a wage increase would increase or decrease the supply of work effort.

EXHIBIT 2.1

Importance of Paying Attention to Both Income and Substitution Effects

Income and substitution effects are relevant for other types of consumption decisions besides labour supply. Quite often, when prices change there will be offsetting (or reinforcing) responses to (1) the expanded budget caused by the price change (income effect) and (2) the shift in relative prices (the substitution effect). Failure to account for these potentially offsetting effects can lead to unexpected responses to incentives. As an example, consider the use of higher salaries to attract workers to a remote location.

The capital of Brazil, Brasilia, was constructed as a planned new city. It was built in the undeveloped heartland of Brazil, in the Amazon jungle area. This movement of the capital from the popular coastal area was done, in part, to encourage development in the otherwise isolated area.

Because of that isolation, it was difficult to recruit civil servants to work in the new capital, and wages were raised in order to encourage recruitment. This worked; in essence, it induced a substitution effect whereby the higher wages elicited a voluntary increase in labour supply to this region.

Unfortunately, the higher wages also induced an income effect that worked at cross purposes to the objective of encouraging the civil service to permanently move to the new capital and become part of a new, integrated community; that is, with their new, higher income, many of the civil servants could afford to maintain another residence in Rio de Janiero on the coast. They could also afford to fly regularly out of Brasilia, leaving it to spend their greater wealth.

Over time, a more permanent, committed community developed. Nevertheless, this example highlights the importance of paying attention to both the income and substitution effects of wage changes. The emphasis on incentive effects in many similar policy discussions often ignores the possibility that an income effect can undo a perfectly reasonable substitution effect.

The income and substitution effects of a wage change are illustrated in Figure 2.9. After the wage increases from W_0 to W_1, the new equilibrium is E_1. This is the net, or bottom-line, effect of the wage change. What we wish to know is, does economic theory allow us to state whether this new equilibrium entails more or less labour supply? Like all price changes, this increase in the price of leisure can be broken down into an income effect and a substitution effect. This is critical in understanding how wage changes affect labour supply.

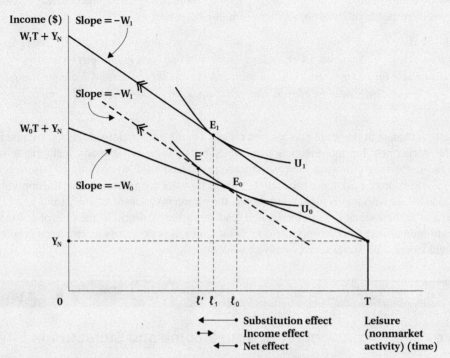

Figure 2.9 Income and Substitution Effects of a Wage Increase

A wage increase from W_0 to W_1 has an ambiguous impact on hours worked. On the one hand, leisure is more expensive, and the substitution effect leads the consumer to switch away from leisure toward consumption (E_0 to E'). On the other, the increase in full income makes the consumer "richer." With leisure a normal good, the income effect leads the consumer to purchase more leisure (E' to E_1). The net result depends on the relative magnitudes of the income and substitution effects. In this example, the substitution effect dominates, and the consumer works more.

The substitution effect represents the effect of a pure increase in the relative price of leisure. That is, the substitution effect is that part of the consumer's adjustment that would occur if she were forced (or allowed) to remain on the original indifference curve U_0, but maintain a tangency with a budget line with slope given by the new wage, W_1. In consumer theory, the substitution effect is sometimes called the compensated price effect, since it refers to the effect of a price change whereby the individual is kept as well off (i.e., compensated) as she was before the price change. Given our assumption of diminishing MRS, economic theory unambiguously predicts that leisure demand should fall with an increase in its price, holding utility constant. This is depicted in Figure 2.9 with the movement from E_0 to E and the resulting change in leisure demand, ℓ_0 to ℓ'. In fact, this is the only empirically testable prediction of labour supply theory: the substitution effect for leisure demand is negative or, equivalently, the substitution effect for labour supply is positive. The theory predicts that compensated labour supply curves must slope upward.

The income effect is given by the movement from E to E_1 The wage rate is held constant at the new wage rate, W_1, but potential income increases to reflect the higher wage rate. The implicit shift in the budget constraint is given by the parallel shift of the constraint from the dashed line to the actual final budget constraint.

If leisure is a normal good, the income effect offsets the substitution effect, since it leads to an increase in the demand for leisure. In Figure 2.9, the substitution effect dominates the income effect; hence, in this illustration, the wage increase resulted in a net increase in the amount of work. However, the income effect can dominate the substitution effect, in which case a wage increase will result in a decrease in the amount of work supplied.

The overall income effect can itself be broken down into two parts. First, the increase in the price of leisure *decreases* purchasing power, as it would for any other good. With a price increase, all else equal, our command over resources falls. This conventional income effect is offset, however, by the fact that full income also increases with the wage increase. Maximum potential earnings rise by $(W_1 - W_0)T$, the consumer's available time, as valued by the increase in the wage rate. This increase in full income leads to a net increase in income available for the purchase of goods and leisure.

Participation

The effects of changes in the wage rate and nonlabour income on labour force participation are illustrated in Figure 2.10. For a participant, an increase in the wage rate has both income and substitution effects; because these are opposite in sign, hours of work may either increase or decrease. However, even if the income effect dominates the substitution effect so that hours of work decline, an increase in the wage rate can never cause a participant to withdraw from the labour force. This prediction of income-leisure choice theory is illustrated in Figure 2.10(a). As the wage increases, the household can achieve higher levels of utility and would never choose to not participate in the labour force that yields the utility level U_0.

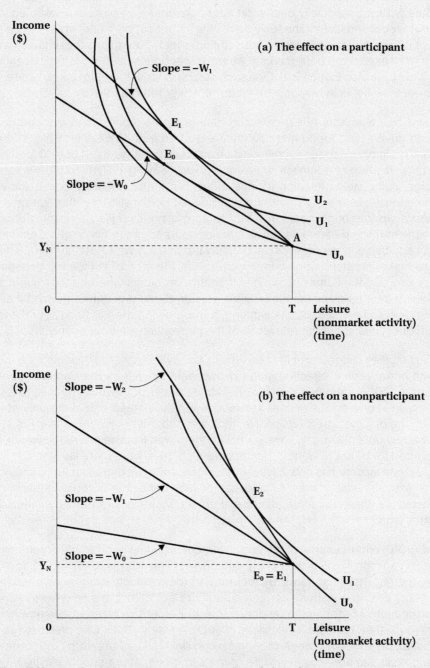

Figure 2.10 The Effect of a Wage Increase on Participation

As a wage increase may lead to a reduction in hours worked, it will never induce a participant, panel (a), to stop working: the wage is still higher than the reservation wage. A nonparticipant, however, may be induced to work if the wage rises above the reservation wage. In panel (b), the consumer chooses to work at W_2, but not at the lower wages W_0 and W_1.

EXHIBIT 2.2

Do Taxi Drivers Work Longer on Rainy Days?

It's a cold, rainy day in New York City, and even walking a block is a test of endurance. What a great day to be a taxi driver. While fares are regulated, finding passengers is relatively effortless, and the hourly income from driving (the wage) is as good as it gets. It's a great day to quit *early*.

What can we learn about labour supply from cab drivers? How much discretion do individuals really have in their hours worked, especially over short time horizons? Can someone wake up in the morning, anticipate a higher wage, and instantaneously adjust his labour supply? And what are the prospects that the income effect offsets the effort-inducing substitution effect? To explore these questions, economists increasingly turn to specialized labour markets where the economic setting more closely resembles the labour-leisure model (See also Exhibit 2.4). One such setting is for self-employment, where individuals are relatively free to set their hours in response to higher or lower returns to work.

Colin Camerer and his co-authors (1997) collected data on hours worked and average daily incomes of New York City cab drivers, and found that cab drivers worked *less* on days with higher wages (average returns to work). The implied labour supply elasticities were as large as −1.0: a 10 percent increase in wages leading to a 10 percent decrease in hours worked, leaving daily income the same. This could reflect a very large, completely offsetting income effect, but it also could be consistent with behaviour outside the conventional labour supply model. It may instead be consistent with a "target income" model, whereby individuals work enough hours in a day to earn a pre-specified amount of income. A higher wage simply means that the person has to work fewer hours to reach his target. Camerer et al. review the psychological and behavioural reasons people may behave this way. Possibly, people maintain simple rules of thumb to make decisions of how much to work in the face of fluctuating economic conditions. Or, perhaps, they use target incomes to avoid self-control problems whereby they might be tempted to quit too early. Setting a target gives them a tangible objective, and a guilt-free threshold after which they can stop working. The authors, and others working in the growing area of behavioural economics, raise several important questions about the relevance of the conventional labour supply model.

Three more-recent studies suggest that the taxi drivers' behaviour may still be explained by labour supply theory, albeit with large income effects. Using his own data as well as the Camerer et al. data on taxi drivers, Henry Farber (2005) identified similar work-income patterns; however, he tries to test between the two competing explanations: target income and labour supply. Instead of looking only at hours worked, Farber focuses on the quitting-time decision. He finds that cab drivers are more likely to stop working as they earn more money on a given day, consistent with the target income model. However, he shows that this can be accounted for by hours worked, *not* income. Cab drivers are more likely to quit the more hours they work. Daily earned income has no statistically significant effect, controlling for hours. A target income does not seem to explain quitting times. Instead, cab drivers' behaviour is consistent with a conventional labour supply model: as they work more, they get tired and value leisure more (i.e., their MRS of leisure rises the more they work).

Ashenfelter et al. (2010) address some of the potentially confounding econometric problems by exploiting quasi-experimental variation in the wages of the cab drivers. The returns to driving a cab in New York are driven largely by the regulated cab fares. By focusing on the relatively exogenous changes in cab fares caused by regulatory changes, Ashenfelter and co-authors estimate that cab drivers reduce their hours worked by approximately 2.5 percent in response to a 10 percent increase in average hourly returns to driving. In other words, they estimate an elasticity of approximately −0.25. Like previous researchers, they find that the substitution effect of a wage change for cab drivers is swamped by the income effect. Their evidence also suggests that previous estimates of the cab driver labour supply elasticity were too large, probably because of econometric problems.

Farber (2015) uses the richest data set so far, based on complete records of taxi rides in New York City between 2009 and 2013. He is able to use the methodology of each preceding study in order to determine whether it is methods or data that drive the results. He obtains similar estimates to Ashenfelter et al. (i.e., small, negative supply elasticities), but once he corrects for the way that the "wage" is constructed (earnings divided by hours), he estimates positive labor supply elasticities. Farber concludes that taxi-driver behaviour is inconsistent with a target-income model, and that, consistent with labor supply theory, when the returns to working are higher, cab drivers work longer hours.

All of these studies are based on the "pre-Uber" taxi market. With Uber, and the evolving practice of surge pricing, the returns from working in high-demand times (like rainy days) are even higher, and will provide fruitful research grounds for studying labour supply. Indeed, the entire premise of surge pricing is to encourage drivers to accept more passengers and to draw drivers into the market at peak times, better equating supply and demand. This requires the substitution effect to dominate the income effect. It remains to be seen whether surge pricing increases taxi driver labour supply (and taxi availability in the rain) enough to offset the grumbling of passengers.

For a nonparticipant, an increase in the wage rate may result in the individual entering the labour force or it may leave labour force participation unchanged, depending on whether the now-higher market wage exceeds or is less than the individual's reservation wage. As illustrated in Figure 2.10(b), the increase in the wage from W_0 to W_1 leaves the individual's preferred outcome at E_0; that is, out of the labour force. However, the further wage increase to W_2 results in the individual's entering the labour force (point E_2). This prediction can be explained in terms of income and substitution effects. An increase in the wage rate raises the opportunity cost of leisure time and tends to cause the individual to substitute market work for nonmarket activities. However, because the individual works zero hours initially, the income effect of an increase in the wage rate is zero. Thus, for nonparticipants, a wage increase has only a substitution effect that tends to increase hours of work.

These predictions can also be expressed in terms of the reservation wage. An increase in the market wage will not alter the labour force status of participants because the market wage already exceeds their reservation wage. However, an increase in the market wage may cause some nonparticipants to enter the labour force, if the increase in the wage is sufficiently large that the now-higher market wage exceeds the reservation wage.

Together, these two predictions of the income-leisure choice model imply that an increase in the wage rate can never reduce and may increase labour force participation. The effects of an increase in nonlabour income on labour force participation are opposite to those of an increase in the wage rate. If leisure is a normal good, an increase in nonlabour income will never cause a nonparticipant to enter the labour force and may cause some participants to withdraw from the labour force. These predictions follow from the fact that an increase in nonlabour income has a pure income effect. Thus, if leisure is a normal good, the amount of time devoted to nonmarket activities must either rise (if the individual was a labour force participant in the initial equilibrium) or not decline (if the individual was already at the maximum leisure point initially).

These predictions of the income-leisure choice model can, alternatively, be stated using the concept of a reservation wage. If leisure is a normal good, an increase in nonlabour income will increase the individual's reservation wage. (Proof of this statement is left as an exercise; see Review Question 6 at the end of this chapter.) Thus, some participants will withdraw from the labour force, their reservation wage having risen above the market wage, while nonparticipants will remain out of the labour force, their reservation wage having been above the market wage even prior to the increase in nonlabour income.

The determinants of an individual's labour force participation decision can be conveniently categorized as to whether the variable affects the individual's reservation wage, market wage, or both. Other things being equal, a variable that raises the individual's reservation wage would decrease the probability of participation in labour market activities. Such variables could be observable in the sense that data are often available on characteristics such as the presence of children, the availability of nonlabour market income, and the added importance of household work as on a farm. Or the variables could be unobservable in the sense that data are not directly available on the characteristic, such as a preference for household work.

While some such variables may affect, primarily, an individual's reservation wage and, hence, have an unambiguous effect on his or her labour force participation decision, others may affect both the market wage and the reservation wage and, hence, have an indeterminate effect on the labour force participation decision. An increase in a person's age, for example, may be associated with a higher market wage that makes participation in labour market activities more likely. However, it may also raise the individual's reservation wage if the disutility associated with work increases relative to leisure time, and this may induce the person to retire from the labour force.

Deriving the Individual Supply Curve of Labour

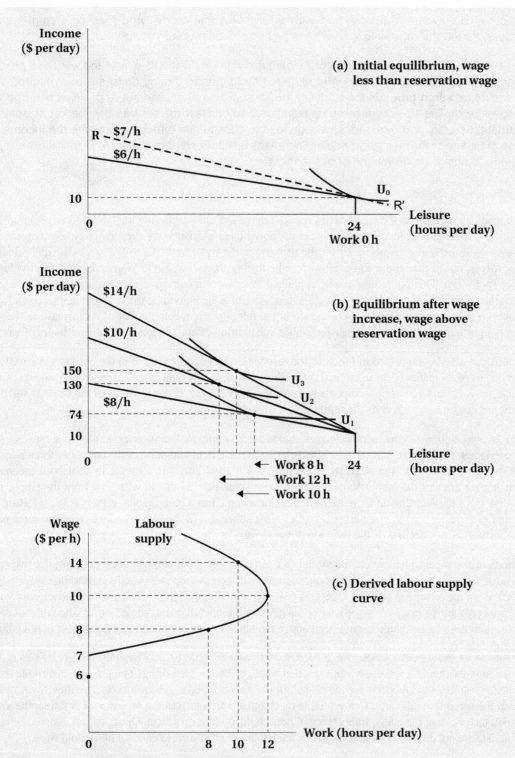

Figure 2.11 Deriving the Individual Supply Curve of Labour

The individual labour supply curve, relating desired hours of work to the wage rate, can be derived by tracing out the labour supply choices (tangencies) in response to different wages, reflected in the slope of the budget constraint. Labour supply is zero until the wage equals the reservation wage. For higher wages, the slope of the labour supply function depends on the relative magnitudes of the income and substitution effects.

We have now met the principal theoretical objectives of this chapter—establishing the avenues through which wage changes affect labour supply, and investigating the slope of the **labour supply schedule**. As the early writings of Robbins (1930) indicate, the income-leisure choice framework can be used to derive the individual's labour supply schedule, which indicates the amount of labour that will be offered at various wage rates. By varying the wage rate, we can obtain a schedule of corresponding desired amounts of work, and, hence, trace out the individual's labour supply curve.

Derivation of an individual's labour supply schedule is further illustrated by the specific example of Figure 2.11, where leisure and work are measured in units of hours per day and wages in units of wages per hour. Income is the hourly wage rate multiplied by the hours of work. Figure 2.11(a) illustrates the desired hours of work for a wage rate of $6 per hour. In this case, the market wage is below the individual's reservation wage of $7, so the individual does not participate and desired hours of work is zero. The corresponding income is just the value of nonlabour income, $10 per day. This gives us one point on the individual's labour supply schedule of Figure 2.11(c); at $6 per hour, the labour supply would be zero hours. Indeed, this would be the labour supply until the market wage reaches $7 per hour. In Figure 2.11(b) we see how hours evolve as wages are raised above the reservation wage. At $8 per hour, the equilibrium hours of work is eight hours per day, and the corresponding daily income is $64 of earnings, plus nonlabour income, for a total of $74. This gives us the second point on the labour supply schedule: at $8 per hour, labour supply would be eight hours. As the wage rises to $10 per hour, hours increase to 12 hours per day. In this particular case, the substitution effect of the wage increase outweighs the income effect so that hours of work increase. This yields a third point on the supply schedule. Finally, in Figure 2.11(b), wages are raised to $14 per hour and the individual is observed to decrease work effort to 10 hours per day. This yields a fourth point on the supply curve in Figure 2.11(c). At the higher wage rate, the income effect of the wage increase begins to dominate the substitution effect and the labour supply schedule becomes backward bending. In fact, this may be a reasonable approximation for many individuals—at low wage rates they have an abundance of unmet needs such that higher wages will induce them to work more in order to fulfill these needs. At higher wages, many of their needs are fulfilled so that additional wage increases will be used to purchase leisure.

LO5 Empirical Evidence

One of the first areas of empirical research in labour economics was the estimation and testing of models of labour supply. The research focused on two sets of questions. First, does labour supply behaviour conform to the predictions of economic theory, and second, how responsive is labour supply to changes in the wage?

Participation, Married Women

The basic theory of labour force participation is often tested with data on married women since they may have more flexibility to respond to the determinants of labour force participation. In addition, their participation has increased dramatically over the past few decades, and this has policy implications for such things as sex discrimination, family formation, and the demand for child care facilities.

Empirical evidence in both Canada and the United States tends to confirm the predictions based on the economic theory of participation. For Canada, some illustrative figures are given in Table 2.2. Here we report participation rates for women with different characteristics that are likely to affect participation. We expect those variables that increase the market wage will be positively associated with participation, while those factors that increase the reservation wage will be negatively related to participation. In the table we show four columns. The first gives the percentage of women in each category (e.g., age group). The second gives the average participation rate by the various categories. The third shows the difference in participation between a given category and the base category (always the lowest category). The final column presents estimates of the same differentials as in the third column, but it shows regression-adjusted estimates that control for the other factors (age, education, number of children, and husband's income).

| TABLE 2.2 | Labour Force Participation Rates of Married Women, Canada 2011 |

	Percentage of Married Women	Participation Rate[a]	Raw Difference from Base Group[b]	Adjusted Difference from Base Group[c]
All Women, Total		**76.0**		
Age				
20–24	1.8	86.1	N/A	N/A
25–34	19.4	88.0	1.9	0.6
35–44	23.5	86.2	0.1	1.2
45–54	26.8	84.9	−1.3	−2.0
55–64	21.2	60.2	−25.9	−26.7
65–74	7.3	22.8	−63.3	−61.8
Children, under 18 years old, at home				
No children	55.7	69.2	N/A	N/A
One child	16.7	87.6	18.3	−1.3
Two children	19.9	86.1	16.9	−4.5
Three children	5.8	77.3	8.0	−13.1
Four or more children	2.0	64.7	−4.6	−24.5
Education				
Less than grade 9	3.6	34.4	N/A	N/A
Some high school	7.0	58.7	24.3	12.0
High school graduate	15.4	65.7	31.2	15.5
Some post secondary	9.8	75.9	41.5	19.7
Non-university, post-secondary certificate	37.8	81.6	47.2	26.7
Bachelor's degree	18.7	83.2	48.8	26.4
Higher than bachelor's degree	7.8	86.9	52.5	30.3
Husband's income				
Under $10,000	7.8	70.1	N/A	N/A
$10,000–$19,999	9.0	68.4	−1.7	8.9
$20,000–$29,999	9.7	67.3	−2.8	4.6
$30,000–$49,999	23.8	75.0	4.9	7.3

$50,000–$74,999	21.0	80.2	10.1	7.4
$75,000–$99,999	14.4	81.5	11.4	5.7
$100,000–$149,999	9.1	81.2	11.2	6.0
Over $150,000	5.0	78.2	8.1	3.0

NOTES: Sample based on all married women between the ages of 20 and 75, with husband present.

a. Participation is defined as having been in the labour force for at least one week in the previous year (2011).

b. Difference in participation rate from the base group (the lowest category).

c. Difference in participation rates from the base group, controlling for the other factors (age, education, fertility rate, or husband's income), estimated by ordinary least squares. The base group for the adjusted differences is, women aged 20–24 with no children, less than grade 9 education, with husbands earning less than $10,000.

SOURCE: This analysis is based on the Statistics Canada, "Survey of Labour and Income Dynamics (SLID)," 2011. All computations, use, and interpretation of these data are entirely that of the authors.

Participation for married women appears to peak in the 25–34 age group, with the steepest decline for those over 64 years of age. Whether this can be interpreted as a pure aging or retirement effect will be addressed in more detail in Chapter 4. The effect of children on women's participation is puzzling at first blush; women with no children work less than those with more children. However, this raw correlation confounds the fertility effect with other factors, notably age (married 20 to 24-year-olds may still be in school). In the last column, adjusted differences, we see in fact that labour force participation strictly declines with the number of children at home.

EXHIBIT 2.3

The Economics of Sleep

Sleep occupies more of our time than any other activity, with approximately one-third of our adult life devoted to sleeping. Casual observation suggests that many of our students undertake that same time allocation during class!

Presumably, we derive satisfaction from sleeping, and it is an important component of leisure and an input into our production of other activities. Hence, it should be amenable to economic analysis.

Biddle and Hamermesh (1990), in fact, provide empirical evidence from a variety of sources indicating that the demand for sleep is negatively related to the price, or opportunity cost, of sleeping. That is, other things equal, people of higher potential earnings sleep less because it costs them more (in terms of foregone income) to sleep longer.

Education has a pronounced positive effect on participation. In principle, higher education should be associated with higher market wages, and an increased likelihood of working. Alternatively, education may be correlated with preferences for working, or reduce fertility, so that the reservation wages of more-educated women may also be lower. The education coefficients alone are not enough to disentangle these competing explanations, though both are consistent with the model of participation. Finally, the results for husband's income illustrate some of the difficulties in identifying pure income effects. We would expect that the reservation wages of women with high-income husbands would be higher, at least if the wife's nonmarket time is a normal good. However, the results in column 4 do not show this; women with high-income husbands are *more* likely to work, though the effect is less pronounced for women whose husbands have high incomes that are over $150,000. Part of the problem in isolating a possibly larger income effect is the fact that more-educated, higher-income working women tend to marry more-educated, higher-income husbands. Unobserved preferences for work are correlated with husband's income, a classic case of omitted variables bias. This "assortative mating" confounds the income effect.

Evidence of the Elasticity of Labour Supply

A large number of econometric studies have estimated the "shape" of the labour supply schedule; that is, the responsiveness of labour supply to changes in the wage rate. As discussed previously, there are a number of components to that responsiveness. The total, or gross, or **uncompensated elasticity** of labour supply is the percentage change in labour supply that results from a 1 percent increase in the wage rate. Its sign is theoretically indeterminate because it reflects both the expected negative income effect of the wage change and the expected positive substitution effect. The **income elasticity** of labour supply is the percentage change in wages that results from a 1 percent increase in nonlabour income. It is expected to be negative, reflecting the leisure-inducing effect of the wage increase. The **compensated elasticity** of labour supply is the percentage increase in labour supply that results from a 1 percent increase in the wage rate, after compensating the individual for the increase in income associated with the wage increase (i.e., after subtracting the income effect of the wage increase). The compensated wage elasticity of labour supply is expected to be positive, since it reflects the pure substitution effect (movement along an indifference curve) as the wage rate increases the price of leisure, inducing a substitution away from more expensive leisure and into labour market activities. For this reason, the income-compensated wage elasticity is also often called the pure substitution elasticity.

Knowledge of the separate components of the labour supply elasticity may be important for policy purposes. For example, the uncompensated wage elasticity would be used to predict the labour supply response to a wage subsidy (since it has both income and substitution effects), but the compensated wage elasticity would be used if it was assumed that the higher income would be taxed back. The income elasticity would be relevant to predicting the labour supply response to a lump-sum government transfer.

As indicated, a large number of econometric studies have estimated these various elasticities that constitute the labour supply response to a wage change. The results differ substantially, depending upon such factors as the econometric technique and data. Especially for women, the results can differ depending upon whether the labour supply response refers to the participation decision, the hours-of-work decision conditional upon participation, or a combination of both. For women, this can be important because there tends to be more flexibility in their participation decision and, hence, it is important to take account of potential econometric problems. In particular, the subsample of labour force participants may be a select sample in terms of unobservable characteristics (like attitudes toward career or work) that can influence wages. These characteristics may, in turn, confound the estimated wage elasticity if conventional regression analysis is used. As well, their labour supply decision may be more affected by discontinuities associated, for example, with fixed costs of entering the labour market, such as daycare costs. The differences in female labour supply responses often reflect differences in the extent to which these factors are taken into account in the estimation procedure.

EXHIBIT 2.4

Take Me Out to the Ball Game . . .

What lessons can economists draw by studying the labour supply of baseball stadium vendors? There is a long history in labour economics of trying to estimate "the" elasticity of labour supply, since it is such an important parameter for public policy. However, the labour supply elasticity almost certainly varies across groups in the population, and also over time. Increasingly, researchers focus their efforts on estimating the impact of specific changes in labour market opportunities on employment decisions, instead of estimating the more general "labour supply elasticity." For example, they may focus on identifying the impact of a tax change or income support scheme on the hours or participation decision. The economic theory of income and substitution effects is still a useful tool in interpreting the results from such exercises.*

But there still remains an important role for trying to estimate the elasticity of labour supply, especially in evaluating the one truly testable implication of labour supply theory—that the substitution effect is positive. This is not an easy task for a number of reasons, but especially because of the difficulty of isolating the substitution effect from the income effect. Consider the apparently simple exercise of regressing the number of hours worked on an individual's wage and nonlabour income. Ideally, we would like to use the estimated wage coefficient in order to construct the substitution elasticity, under the assumption that we can estimate the income effect from the nonlabour income elasticity. A number of statistical problems make this difficult.

First, it is difficult to measure nonlabour income. Almost all forms of income are somehow related to labour earnings; government transfer income depends on having low labour earnings (because of either low wages or low hours), and investment income is generally higher for those with higher wages and hours. This could lead to either an over or understatement of the true income effect. Second, individual preferences may be correlated with wages. For example, ambitious people may have both higher wages and higher hours. We would, thus, exaggerate the impact of wages on the labour supply decision such people. Third, an increase in someone's wage may have a long-run impact on his lifetime earnings potential, leading to a potentially large income effect. Thus, without a clean estimate of either the wage or the income elasticities, it is difficult to test whether the wage response reflects a positive substitution effect. An ideal "experimental design" would involve comparing an individual's labour supply decisions on a day-by-day basis, when the individual has complete knowledge of his or her "long-run" income and the patterns of wage rates across different days. In this way, a researcher could attribute higher effort on high-wage days to a pure (positive) substitution effect.

That's where the baseball vendors come in. In a clever study that follows this ideal procedure, Gerald Oettinger (1999) examines the labour supply of vendors in a professional baseball stadium (in Arlington, Texas). He finds that vendors are more likely to work on days where the expected returns (sales, and thus wages) are higher. Apparently, vendors respond to the size of the anticipated crowd, the opposing teams, the Texas Rangers's performance, the weather, and promotional events (such as Free Hat Day). Even taking into account the fact that the labour supply response also leads more vendors to show up (and thus soak up some of the additional sales), Oettinger estimates that a 1.00 percent increase in the expected daily wage leads to a 0.60 percent increase in the number of vendors working. Because he can identify each vendor's daily choices, he can hold constant individual preferences, nonlabour income, and the value of the time endowment over the entire baseball season, and this response can reliably be interpreted as a pure substitution effect. While the estimated labour supply elasticities may not generalize to other types of workers, Oettinger's paper shows how the careful study of even a very specific group of workers can, more generally, shed light on the possible validity of labour supply theory.

*See Blundell and MaCurdy (1999).

In spite of the substantial variation that exists in the results of the different studies, a number of generalizations can be made. Table 2.3 provides an illustrative representation of those results based on a number of reviews that have been done in the literature (as cited in the source to the table). The numbers used in the first row of Table 2.3 for both sexes are simply based on a "rounded approximation" of those elasticities from the 50 studies and the 13 newer ones. For that reason, they are meant to be illustrative and representative rather than strict averages of the results of the different studies. The separate figures for males and females are also meant to be only illustrative.

TABLE 2.3	**Estimated Elasticities of Labour Supply**		
Sex	**Uncompensated (Gross, Total) Wage Elasticity of Supply**	**Compensated (Substitution) Wage Elasticity of Supply**	**Income Elasticity of Supply**
Both sexes	0.25	0.40	−0.15
Men	−0.10	0.10	−0.20
Women	0.80	0.90	−0.10

SOURCES: As discussed in the text, these are "representative illustrative" numbers based on different reviews of over 50 econometric studies of labour supply. These reviews include Hansson and Stuart (1985), Killingsworth (1983), Killingsworth and Heckman (1986), and Pencavel (1986).

The following generalizations are illustrated in Table 2.3:

1. The overall labour supply schedule for both sexes is likely to be slightly upward sloping; that is, a wage increase does lead to a slight increase in the amount of labour supplied to the labour market. The representative elasticity of 0.25 indicates that a 1 percent increase in real wages would lead to a one-quarter of 1 percent increase in labour supply. This small uncompensated total elasticity is a result of the positive pure compensated (substitution) elasticity slightly outweighing the negative income elasticity.

2. For males, however, the labour supply schedule is likely to be slightly backward bending; that is, real wage increases are associated with a reduction in the amount of labour supplied to the labour market. This overall effect is very small and could well be zero (i.e., vertical or perfectly inelastic labour supply) or even slightly forward sloping. The small overall negative elasticity is a result of a weak positive substitution elasticity being outweighed by a weak but slightly larger negative income elasticity.

3. For women, the labour supply schedule is more strongly forward sloping; that is, an increase in real wages is associated with a more substantial increase in the amount of labour supplied to the labour market. This is the result of a strong positive substitution elasticity outweighing the weak negative income elasticity.

4. The strong positive total elasticity for females is sufficiently strong to outweigh the weak negative total elasticity for males, so that the aggregate supply schedule for both sexes is likely to be forward sloping, as discussed.

5. The substantial variation in the magnitudes of these effects across studies suggests that these representative numbers be used with caution. As well, there is increasing evidence that the female labour supply response is closer to the male response than portrayed in these early studies—a result that should not be surprising if female labour market behaviour is becoming more like male behaviour over time. Pencavel (1998) uses data through the mid-1990s, and estimates overall female labour supply elasticities around 0.20 for annual hours worked. The corresponding elasticity for the subsample of married women was over 0.40; significantly higher than the consensus estimate for men, but lower than the 0.80 reported in Table 2.3.

Section Two: Extensions and Applications

One of the most important assumptions of the labour supply model is that individuals can freely choose any package of consumption and leisure along the linear potential income constraint. Unfortunately, this assumption may not be valid for those individuals facing constraints in the labour market. There may be no work available at the going wage rate, resulting in unemployment for the individual. Alternatively, the individual may have only limited choice over the number of hours worked. As we suggested previously, however, the model is quite flexible, and some of these issues can be incorporated into the existing framework.

Added and Discouraged Worker Effects

Recall that the definition of the labour force includes both the employed (those who wish to work and have jobs) and the unemployed (those who wish to work but do not have jobs). One interesting question pertains to how labour force participation responds to changes in the unemployment rate. Specifically, in periods of high unemployment, people may become discouraged from looking for work and drop out of the labour force, returning to household activities or to school, or perhaps even entering early retirement. This is termed the **discouraged worker** effect. On the other hand, in periods of high unemployment, some may enter the labour force to supplement family income that may have deteriorated with the unemployment of other family members. This is termed the **added worker** effect.

Changes in unemployment are a proxy for transitory changes in expected wages and other income, and, thus, the discouraged and added worker effects can be interpreted as short-run substitution and income effects, respectively. That is, if unemployment is high, then opportunities in the labour market are lowered temporarily; thus, the price of leisure (opportunity cost of foregone income from not working) is reduced temporarily. The wage might fall below an individual's reservation wage, leading him to drop out of the labour force. On the other hand, the high unemployment means that it is more likely that family income is lowered temporarily, lowering other household members' reservation wages and inducing them to participate in labour market activities so as to restore that income.

Since the added and discouraged worker effects operate in opposite directions, one lowering the reservation wage and the other lowering the returns to working, it is necessary to appeal to the empirical evidence to see which dominates. Again, most of the empirical tests have been based on data of married women, since they are more likely to respond to changes in unemployment. In the United States, the empirical evidence clearly indicates the dominance of the discouraged worker effect for most married women. That is, in periods of high unemployment, women become discouraged from entering the labour force to look for work, and this dominates any tendency to add themselves to the labour force to maintain their family income. In Canada, however, the empirical evidence is mixed.

Hidden Unemployment

The discouraged worker effect also gives rise to the problem of **hidden unemployment**, a topic that we will return to in a later chapter on unemployment. During a recession, when the unemployment rate is high, there may also be a large number of discouraged workers who do not look for work because they believe that no work is available. They are considered to be outside the labour force because they are not working or actively looking for work. However, because they would look for work were it not for the high unemployment rate, they are often considered the hidden unemployed—people whom the unemployment figures tend to miss because they are considered outside the labour force rather than unemployed persons in it.

The notion of the discouraged worker is especially important as groups like married women and teenagers become a larger portion of our potential labour force. Such persons often have a loose attachment to the labour force, moving in and out in response to changing economic conditions. They often, but not always, have other family income upon which to rely. For these reasons they are often labelled "secondary" or "marginal" workers—unfortunate misnomers if they are used to belittle the employment problems or the contribution to the family income of such workers. This is especially the case if they are contrasted with "primary" workers or "breadwinners," terms often used to describe the employment position of males.

However, because of their flexibility with respect to labour market activities, married women and teenagers do constitute a large portion of discouraged workers who would enter the labour force and look for work if employment prospects increased. Hence, there is the recent emphasis in labour force surveys to find out exactly what these people are doing, and why they are not looking for work.

Clearly, the decision to include such persons either in the category of unemployed or as outside of the labour force is a difficult one. Research by Jones and Riddell (1999) suggests that while the marginally attached are closer in behaviour to the unemployed than the remainder of the nonemployed, it is not strictly appropriate to pool them with either group.

Moonlighting, Overtime, and Flexible Working Hours

Any analysis of the hours-of-work decision must confront the following basic question: why is it that some people moonlight at a second job at a wage less than their market wage on their first job, while others require an overtime premium to work more? This apparent anomaly occurs because people who moonlight are underemployed at the going wage on their main job, while people who require an overtime premium are already overemployed at the going wage on their main job. Underemployment and overemployment, in turn, occur because different workers have different preferences, and they tend to be confronted with an institutionally fixed work schedule. The fixed hours of work, in turn, can arise because of such factors as legislation, union pressure, or company personnel policy. The need for interaction among employees (or between employees and the firm's physical capital) may cause the employer to set standardized hours of work rather than allow each employee to work his or her preferred number of hours. Again, economic theory will enable us to analyze the labour market impact of these important institutional constraints.

The fixed-hours-of-work phenomenon is illustrated in Figure 2.12(a). In this case, the worker is faced with two constraints. The first is the usual budget constraint TY_1 as determined by the person's hourly wage. This restricts the worker's maximum choice set to the triangular area TY_1O, where O denotes the origin. The second constraint, the fixed workday of TL_c hours (recall that work is measured from right to left), restricts the worker's maximum choice set to the area L_cCY_cO: the worker can take no more leisure than OL_c (work no more than TL_c), and earn no more income than OY_c, even if he worked more than TL_c. In effect, this reduces the worker's realistic choice set to only point C, since C will always be preferred to other points within L_cCY_cO.

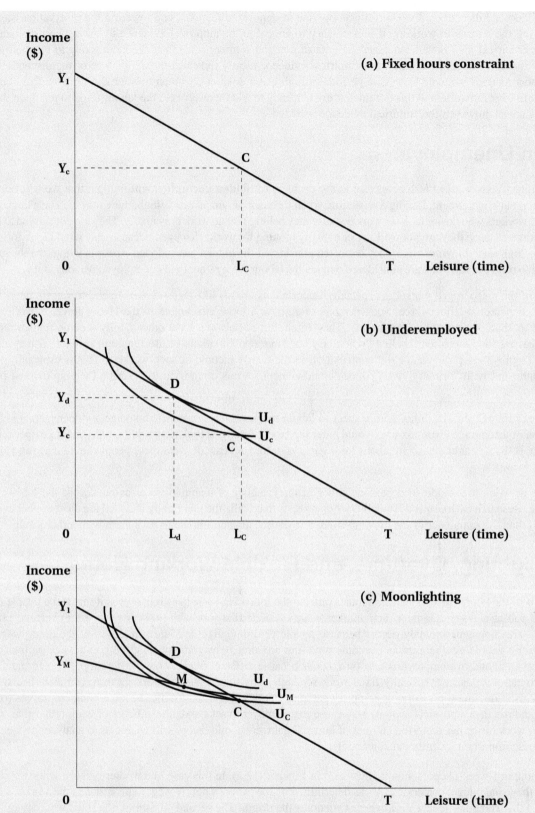

Figure 2.12 Fixed Hours Constraint, Underemployment, and Moonlighting

Consumers may be constrained in their choice of hours worked and confronted with the point C, a fixed hours and income "package." As shown in panel (b), given the wage, the consumer would rather choose D, working T − L_D hours. As this exceeds the available hours of work, the consumer is underemployed. As shown in panel (c), if a second job is available, even one paying a lower wage, the consumer may choose M, working T − L_C on the main job, and moonlighting on the second.

EXHIBIT 2.5

Are Women Working to Pay the Mortgage?

In the labour supply model, individuals are assumed free to choose whether to work. As we saw with the added worker effect, someone's labour supply may increase in response to unexpected declines in family income caused by the unemployment of a breadwinner. In such circumstances, increased female participation need not be associated with improvements in family well-being.

Mortgage precommitments and borrowing constraints provide another reason a woman's labour market participation may reflect household constraints as much as enhanced opportunities for women. Nicole Fortin (1995) examines the labour force attachment of a sample of Canadian women according to the mortgage-holding status of the household. She finds that as a family's mortgage commitments approach the fraction of family income permitted by the bank, the wife's participation rate increases sharply. One (extremely simplified) way to model this is to treat the mortgage payment as a predetermined financial commitment, outside the household's current choice set. In that case, larger mortgage payments have a similar effect on participation as a reduction in family income. More generally, higher mortgage commitments, especially those close to the maximum that banks will permit, reduce the wife's reservation wage. Of course, this ignores the fact that house purchases are a choice that households make, distinguishing the interpretation from the added worker effect. The joint aspect of the housing and labour supply decision is treated more thoroughly in Fortin's paper. Furthermore, interest rate or housing price swings may lead to genuine changes in the budget constraint that look like typical income effects.

Fortin estimates that the effect of mortgage commitments can be quite large. For example, the effect on a woman's participation of moving into a category where the ratio of mortgage payments to husband's income is close to the maximum of what banks will tolerate has as large an effect as the presence of two preschool children (though in the opposite direction). Del Boca and Lusardi (2003) explore the same question in an Italian context. They exploit changes in the financial sector in Italy in the early 1990s to see whether improved access to mortgages induced more women into the labour market. Even accounting for the possibility that causality runs in both directions—that is, households with women are more likely to qualify for mortgages at the same time that having a mortgage may lead more women to work—they find similar results to Fortin. Married women's work decisions are strongly linked to the need for families to meet mortgage commitments.

Moonlighting and Underemployment

Some individuals, however, may prefer to work more hours at the going wage rate. Figure 2.12(b) illustrates the case for an individual whose preferences (indifference curve U_d) are such that he would prefer to be at D, working TL_d hours at the going wage and taking home an income of Y_d. However, because of the hours-of-work constraint, the worker must be at C, obviously being less well off since $U_c < U_d$. In fact, the difference between U_d and U_c is a measure of how much the worker would be willing to give up in order to have the fixed-hours constraint relaxed.

A variety of implications follow from this analysis. The worker is **underemployed** because he would like to work more at the going wage rate. Because of the additional constraint of the fixed working hours, the worker is also less well off ($U_c < U_d$) and may be seeking a different job that would enable him to achieve his desired equilibrium at D. In addition, the worker may be willing to engage in **moonlighting** and do additional work at a wage rate that is lower than the wage rate of the first job.

This moonlighting equilibrium is illustrated in Figure 2.12(c) by the budget constraint CY_m. (To simplify the diagram, the details of Figure 2.12(b) have been omitted.) This new budget constraint rotates downward from CY_1 because the moonlighting wage, which is less than the regular wage as given by the slope of CY_1, applies only to hours of work beyond TL_c. In spite of the lower moonlighting wage, the worker is willing to work more hours (move from C to M) because of the greater utility associated with the move ($U_m > U_c$). That is, workers who are underemployed at the going wage rate would be willing to moonlight at a lower wage rate on their secondary job.

Overtime and Overemployment

Other individuals, however, may prefer to work fewer hours at the going wage rate. Figure 2.13(a) illustrates the situation where the worker would prefer (maximize utility) to be at D, working TL_D hours for an income of Y_d. However, because of the institutionally fixed workweek, she is compelled to be at C, being less well off ($U_C < U_d$) even though she takes home more income ($Y_c > Y_d$).

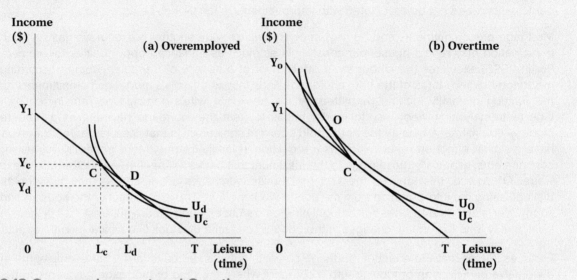

Figure 2.13 Overemployment and Overtime

A consumer may be constrained to work more hours than desired. In this case, he or she would prefer to work at D, at fewer hours than C, though C is still preferred to not working at all. However, this consumer could be induced to work more hours, corresponding to point O, if offered a higher wage rate for hours worked after C.

Such a worker is **overemployed** at the going wage rate and consequently would support policies to reduce the institutionally fixed workweek. In addition, she also may be seeking a different job that would enable her to work fewer hours at the going wage rate, and she may even exhibit absenteeism and tardiness as ways of moving toward her desired workweek. Because such a worker is already overemployed at the going wage rate, she would not willingly work more hours at the wage rate; however, she may be induced to do so by an **overtime premium**.

This overtime premium is illustrated in Figure 2.13(b) by the budget constraint CY_0 that rotates upward from CY_t because the overtime premium, which is greater than the normal wage that determines the slope of TY_1, applies only to overtime hours of work beyond TL_c. If, for example, the overtime premium is time and a half, then the overtime budget constraint has a 50 percent greater slope than the regular straight-time budget constraint. As long as the worker is willing to give up some leisure for additional income, then there is an overtime premium that will induce her to work more; for example, to move to point O on Figure 2.13(b) (on the indifference curve U_0). Because the worker is overemployed at the going wage rate, the overtime premium is necessary to get her to work more hours.

The person works longer hours even though he is overemployed at the going wage rate because the overtime premium results in a large substitution effect by making the price (opportunity cost, income forgone) of leisure higher only for the overtime hours. The overtime premium has a small income effect, because the budget constraint rotates upward *only* for the overtime hours; consequently, it does not have an income effect for the normal straight-time hours. Recall that the substitution effect was illustrated by a changed *slope* in the budget constraint, while the income effect was illustrated by a *parallel shift* of the constraint. Since the overtime premium changes the slope for the overtime hours, it is primarily a work-inducing substitution effect, with little leisure-inducing income effect.

Overtime Premium versus Straight-Time Equivalent

The importance of the relative absence of the income effect in the overtime premium can be illustrated by a comparison of the overtime premium with the straight-time equivalent. One might logically ask the question, if workers are constantly working overtime, why not institutionalize that into a longer workday and pay them the straight-time equivalent of their normal wage plus their overtime wage?

This alternative is illustrated in Figure 2.14. The overtime situation is illustrated by the budget constraint TCY_0, with TC being the normal wage paid during the regular work period and CY_0 being the overtime premium paid for overtime hours. The normal wage is assumed not to change as a result of the overtime premium. The regular work period would be TL_c hours and overtime hours would be L_cL_0. (To simplify the diagram, these points are not shown; however, as in Figure 2.13(a), they are simply the points on the horizontal leisure axis, vertically below their corresponding equilibrium points.) The straight-time hourly equivalent for TL_0 hours of work is given by the budget constraint, TO, the slope of which is a weighted average of the slopes of the regular wage, TC, and the overtime premium, CO. The straight-time hourly equivalent is derived by simply taking the earnings associated with the overtime plus regular time hours of work, TL_0, and determining the straight-time wage, TO, that would yield the same earnings.

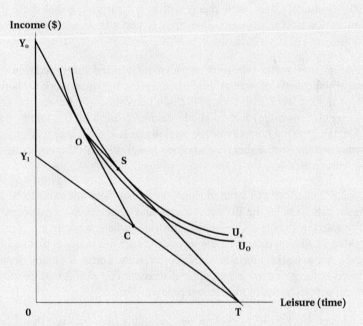

Figure 2.14 Overtime Premium versus Straight-Time Equivalent

An overtime premium can be used to induce a worker to choose hours corresponding to the point O, after paying the straight-time wage to point C. Why not simply offer the consumer a straight-time equivalent, equal to the average wage associated with the earnings and hours at O? The income effect associated with the higher wage received from the first hour worked will lead the consumer to choose fewer hours worked (at S) than when the higher (overtime premium) is paid only on hours in excess of those at C.

A worker who is paid the straight-time equivalent, however, would not voluntarily remain at O, but would rather move to the point S, which involves less work. This is so because the wage line, TSO, has a larger leisure-inducing income effect, whereas the overtime premium, COY_0, is dominated by the work-inducing substitution effect (rotation of the budget constraint). In essence, since the overtime premium is paid only for hours *beyond* the regular workday, the person has to work more to get the additional income.

Overtime premiums, therefore, may be a rational way for employers to get their existing work force to voluntarily work more hours, even if they are overemployed at their regular workday. Employers, in turn, may want to work their existing work force longer hours rather than hire additional workers, in order to spread their fixed hiring costs over longer hours. The importance of these fixed hiring costs will be analyzed in more detail when labour demand is discussed.

Workers need not be overemployed at their going wage rate for the overtime premium to work. One can easily portray the situation for a worker in equilibrium at the regular wage rate who would unambiguously work more when offered an overtime wage premium, but who may work less if offered a straight-time hourly wage increase. Firms that want to work their existing work force longer hours may prefer a wage package that involves a low regular wage and a high overtime premium to a package that costs them the same but that involves a straight-time wage increase.

Again, what at first glance appear to be costly and irrational actions on the part of firms—in this case, the coexistence of overtime and moonlighting rates and a preference for overtime premiums over straight-time equivalent earnings—may well be rational actions when viewed in the larger picture where the parties are optimizing with respect to legal institutional constraints and when the varying preferences of individual workers are considered. Rather than rendering economic theory irrelevant in the force of such constraints, they highlight the usefulness of economics in analyzing the impact of the constraints and in explaining why, in fact, they may arise as an endogenous institutional response to the peculiarities of the labour market.

Allowing Choice in Working Hours

As illustrated previously, the composition of the work force has been changing dramatically in recent years. This is evidenced by such phenomena as the increased labour force participation of women, the dominance of the two-earner family, and the aging of the workforce. Given such changes, it is not surprising that these different groups would have different tastes and preferences for alternative work-time arrangements in the labour market. As well, they will face different household constraints.

For example, two-earner families may prefer part-time employment for one party, reduced hours of work for the other party, and flexible work-time arrangements, as well as the right to refuse overtime work for both parties. This would enable them to better combine labour market work with their household activities. In contrast, the one-earner family may prefer a long workweek (e.g., with regular overtime) for the single earner so as to earn a family income similar to that of the dual-earner family. In essence, the growing diversity of the work force has given rise to a growing diversity of preferences for alternative work-time arrangements. Preferences for such arrangements are no longer dictated by the former stereotypical male breadwinner in a single-earner family.

The basic income-leisure choice framework can be used to illustrate that there are gains to be had by employers providing alternative work-time arrangements to meet the divergent tastes and preferences of an increasingly heterogeneous work force. These benefits are illustrated in Figure 2.15. Point C illustrates where workers are constrained to operate given the all-or-nothing choice of working TL_c hours (points on the leisure axis are not marked, to simplify the diagram) at the going wage (slope of TY_t). However, many workers have different preferences. Some, for example, may prefer to be at point D. Because they are overemployed at the going wage rate, their discontent ($U_c < U_d$) may be exhibited in the form of costly absenteeism, high turnover, and perhaps reduced morale and productivity.

Obviously, firms that allowed such workers to work their desired hours of work could save on these costs. Alternatively, such firms could lower their wage rates and still retain their work force. This is illustrated by the wage line TY_f, which could be lowered until the point of tangency, F, with the original utility curve, U_c. Workers are equally well off at C and F (same level of utility U_c) even though F implies a lower wage rate, simply because they are at an equilibrium with respect to their hours of work. In essence, they are willing to give up wages in return for a work schedule that meets their preferences.

Competition for such jobs would ensure that firms could offer lower wages in return for more flexible work schedules. In this sense, the gains from flexible work schedules could be recouped by the firm to cover the other costs that may be associated with such schedules. Firms that offer more flexible hours need not lower wages but may take the benefits in the form of reduced absenteeism, lower turnover, and improved worker morale. Various combinations of reduced wages (downward-rotated wage line) and improved worker morale (higher indifference curve), of course, are possible.

While there are benefits from allowing workers to choose their preferred hours of work, there are also costs, especially if such flexibility is given to different workers in the same establishment. Individual differences in hours worked can give rise to problems of monitoring, supervision, communication, scheduling, and coordination. One compromise is flextime, whereby the workers are required to work a fixed number of hours (e.g., eight per day), and certain core hours (e.g., 10:00 a.m. to 3:00 p.m.), but the beginning and ending times are flexible. This helps meet the divergent preferences of different workers (e.g., late risers versus early risers), enables some with child-raising responsibilities to be home when children return from school, and facilitates avoiding rush hour commuting problems.

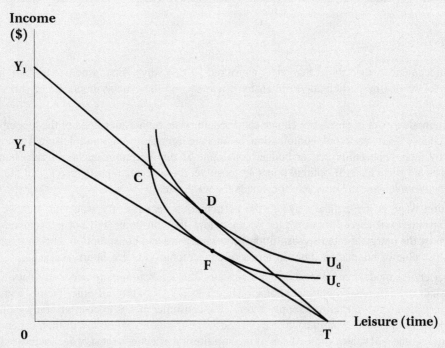

Figure 2.15 Gains from Alternative Work Schedules
Consumers may be willing to pay for flexibility in choosing their hours worked. A consumer constrained to working at C would be indifferent to any lower wage and hours package lying on the indifference curve U$_C$. The wage could fall as low as that represented by TY$_F$, where the consumer would choose hours associated with point F.

Compressed workweeks are another alternative work-time arrangement. Common compressed schedules include four 10-hour days or even three 12-hour days. These are often attractive to employees because of the longer weekends that are involved. They also enable the amortizing, or spreading, of fixed daily commute costs over a longer workday. For example, a two-hour commute over three 12-hour days is six hours of commute time per week, as against ten hours based on a five-day week. As well, the 12-hour day may avoid rush-hour commutes. Such compressed workweeks have been used in some areas (e.g., nursing) as a recruiting device to help attract and retain personnel.

Clearly, there may be costs associated with such alternative work-time arrangements and these have to be weighed against the potential benefits. The point made here, and illustrated in the income-leisure framework, is that there are potential benefits to meeting the divergent tastes and preferences of workers. As well, these benefits are likely to be growing as a result of the increasing diversity of the work force.

Summary

- Individual attachment to the labour market is measured in two ways: first, whether an individual is working or searching for work (the participation dimension); and second, how many hours he or she works (the hours dimension).

- The microeconomic model of consumer choice can accommodate both dimensions of the labour supply decision. Consumers choose their preferred combination of income (consumption) and leisure (nonmarket time), as represented by their opportunity set, or budget constraint. If this optimum occurs at zero hours of work, the individual does not participate. If optimal hours are positive, the individual participates, and the marginal rate of substitution between leisure and consumption equals the wage rate.

- The reservation wage is the critical wage to the participation decision: for wage rates above the reservation wage, the consumer will choose to work; for wages below, the consumer will not participate. The reservation wage is given by the marginal rate of substitution between leisure and consumption, at zero hours of work—that is, the person's value of nonmarket time (in terms of consumption) at zero hours worked.

- The consumer choice model can be used to build an individual's labour supply curve. By varying the wage rate, we can trace out the consumer's optimal choice of hours worked, holding all other factors constant. For wages below the reservation wage rate, labour supply is zero. The consumer moves to positive hours supplied as the wage exceeds the reservation wage. The impact of increased wages on hours worked will then depend on the relative magnitudes of income and substitution effects. If the substitution effect is largest, wage increases lead to increases in labour supply; if the income effect dominates, wage increases lead to decreases in labour supply.

- The labour-leisure choice model can be used to investigate a variety of labour market phenomena, such as the "added worker effect," the structure of overtime wage premiums, and the willingness of individuals to accept flexibility in work hours in exchange for lower wages.

Keywords

added worker	labour force
budget constraint	labour force participation decision
compensated elasticity	labour force participation rate (LFPR)
consumer's optimum	labour supply model
consumption-leisure	labour supply schedule
corner solution	leisure
discouraged worker	marginal rate of substitution
employed	moonlighting
full income	nonmarket time
hidden unemployment	normal good
hours-of-work aspect	overemployed
income effect	overtime premium
income elasticity	potential income constraint
income-leisure	preferences
indifference curves	reservation wage
inferior good	substitution effect
interior solution	uncompensated elasticity

underemployed	utility
unemployed	utility maximizing

Review Questions

1. What would happen to an individual's labour supply schedule if leisure were an inferior good? Use an income-leisure diagram to illustrate your argument.

2. A labour force survey yields the following estimates:

Population 15 and older	30m
Employed	22m
Not working, but actively seeking work	1m
Full-time students	2m
Retired	3m
Not working, discouraged because of lack of jobs	0.5m
Not working, household workers	1.5m

   Calculate the labour force participation rate and the unemployment rate.

3. Draw your own budget constraint. To simplify the problem, treat your savings and any allowances from family as predetermined nonlabour income that can be evenly spread over a year (or so).

   a. First take the time horizon of a week. How much consumption can you support if you don't work for pay? How many hours over the week are you available for work, excluding sleep and personal maintenance? What is your wage rate? What is the maximum you can earn, including allowance for holding multiple jobs, if necessary?

   b. Repeat the same exercise with the time horizon of a year, where "weeks of work" (including the summer) is the unit of analysis.

4. Use the basic income-leisure choice framework to analyze the possible labour supply response of various groups to changes in their wage rate. The different groups could include the following:

   a. The poor who are at a minimum subsistence and who aspire to middle-class consumption patterns.

   b. The wealthy who have acquired an abundance of material goods and who now aspire to be members of the idle rich.

   c. Workers who have a fairly strong attachment to the labour force and who are reluctant to change their hours of work.

   d. Workers who have a weak attachment to the labour force and who have viable alternatives to market work.

   e. "Workaholics" who have strong preferences for labour market work.

5. Illustrate the case where an individual responds differently to a wage increase and a wage decrease of the same magnitude. Specifically, have the person become "locked in" to a certain consumption pattern associated with the higher wage.

6. Use the income-leisure choice model to show that an increase in nonlabour income will increase the individual's reservation wage if leisure is a normal good.

7. On the basis of the diagrams of Figure 2.12, illustrate how an underemployed worker would respond to

   a. An offer to work as many more hours as the worker would like at the going wage.

   b. Payment of an overtime premium for hours of work beyond C.

   c. An offer to work an additional fixed number of hours, as determined by the employee at the going wage.

8. On the basis of the diagrams of Figure 2.13, illustrate how an overemployed worker would respond to

   a. An offer to work as many hours as the worker would like at the going wage.

   b. Payment of the moonlighting rate for hours of work beyond C.

9. On the basis of Figure 2.13(b), precisely illustrate the following overtime rates for hours worked beyond TL_C:

   a. Time and a half

   b. Double time

   c. Time and a half for the first two hours of overtime and double time thereafter

Problems

1. Consider an individual with $5000 of annual nonlabour income. She has total available time of 80 hours per week, for $52 \times 80 = 4160$ hours per year. Her current wage rate is $15.00 per hour, and she currently chooses to work 2000 hours in a year.

   a. Draw a labour-leisure diagram, carefully illustrating her current labour supply decision.

   b. The wage rate rises to $18.00 per hour, and she decides to work 2040 hours. At $18.00 per hour, if she worked 2200 hours per year, she would have been indifferent to her original work decision (in (**a**). Show her new choice on a diagram, and calculate the income and substitution effects associated with the wage change. Calculate the compensated and uncompensated elasticities of labour supply implied by her response to the wage increase.

2. Assume that the following regression equation has been estimated, where P_W is the labour force participation rate of married women (measured as a percentage with average $\overline{P} = 35.0$), Y_H is the husband's wage income (measured in thousands of dollars, with average $\overline{Y}_H = 10$), Y_W is the wife's expected "wage" (expected income from working a fixed number of hours, measured in thousands of dollars, with average $\overline{Y}_W = 6$), and u_H is the male unemployment rate (measured as a percentage, with average $\overline{U}_H = 6.0$):

$$P_W = -7Y_H + 18Y_W - 0.5u_H$$

   a. What is the expected effect of an increase of $1000 in the income of the husbands on the participation rate of their wives?

   b. What is the expected effect of an increase of $1000 in the wage of the wives themselves?

   c. Break the latter down into its separate income and substitution effects.

   d. Given the magnitude of the latter two effects, what would be the impact on female participation of an equal pay policy that increased the expected wages of females by $1000 while at the same time decreasing the expected earnings of their husbands by $1000?

   e. Calculate the pure income and the gross or uncompensated wage elasticities of participation, evaluated at the means.

   f. Does this equation shed any light on why the labour force participation of married women has increased over time, even though their nonlabour wage has also increased?

3. Consider two individuals with endowments of $T = 60$ hours (per week) of leisure, nonlabour income of Y, and a wage of $7.50 per hour. At this wage, assume that workers are constrained by their employers to work 40 hours per week, or not at all.

   a. On a carefully labelled diagram, show the equilibrium for a worker for whom 40 hours is the optimum labour supply and a worker who would like to work 20 hours, but still prefers the 40-hour week to not working. Compare the marginal rates of substitution for these individuals at 40 hours per week.

   b. The average part-time wage is $7 per hour, in contrast to $7.50 wage for full-time workers. Using the above model, provide an explanation for this difference in wage rates.

4. Assume that women's marginal rate of substitution of leisure for consumption is given by the following function:

$$\text{MRS} = A(x)\frac{C}{\ell}$$

where C is consumption (with price = 1) and ℓ is leisure. A(x) is a taste-shifting function of the following form:

$$A(x) = \exp\left(\beta_1 x_1 + \beta_2 x_2 + \ \dots\ + \beta_k x_k + \varepsilon\right)$$

where the x_j are k different observable factors that affect her preferences, and ε represent unobservable factors that affect the MRS. ε has the property that it can be described by a probability density function, such as the normal or uniform density.

   a. Show that this functional form for the MRS represents preferences that exhibit a diminishing marginal rate of substitution. Give specific examples of x_j that may affect the MRS, and explain how they will affect the MRS. Give a graphical example.

   b. Assume that an individual woman has nonlabour income, y, (including her husband's income) and a time endowment of T. Derive an expression for this woman's reservation wage, w*. Show that if the market wage is w, this expression implies that a woman will participate if

$$\ln w > \ln y - \ln\ T + \beta_1 x_1 + \beta_2 x_2 + \ \dots\ + \beta_k x_k + \varepsilon$$

Rewrite this as an expression of the form, participate if $\varepsilon < Z$, where Z depends on the market wage, nonlabour income, and preferences. *Hint:* Remember $\ln(ab) = \ln a + \ln b$; $\ln(a/b) = \ln a - \ln b$, etc.

   c. Assume that Z has a standard normal distribution. Using your results from (**b**), graphically show and explain how nonlabour income, the market wage, and the various taste shifters affect the probability of a woman participating in the labour market.

5. Using carefully labelled diagrams, indicate the expected impact on the labour force participation of married women by changes in each of the following factors, other things held constant:

   a. An increase in the education of women.

   b. A more equal sharing of household responsibilities between husband and wife.

   c. A reduction in the average number of children.

   d. An increased tendency to have children spaced more closely together.

   e. An increase in the earnings of husbands.

   f. Daycare paid out of general tax revenues.

   g. Allowing daycare expenses to be tax deductible.

   h. Paying homemakers a fixed sum out of general tax revenues for household work.

6. Using the income-leisure framework, formally analyze the added worker effect; that is, the impact on the wife's labour supply of an adverse shock to her husband's job. For concreteness, assume that the wife has a wage rate of $10 per hour, and that her husband's employer has forced him to take a pay cut of $5, from $20 per hour to $15 per hour, but allowed him to continue working at 40 hours per week (if he wishes). Consider two approaches:

   a. In the first, take the husband's hours as given, and analyze the household choice over consumption and wife's leisure.

   b. In the second, focus on the choice of husband versus wife's labour supply, allowing both to adjust their hours, and putting the consumption decision in the background.

   c. Compare the pros and cons of the two approaches. In particular, use the two approaches to compare the impact on the wife's labour supply of unemployment compensation for the husband equal to $200 per week.

7. Susan claims labour supply theory is nonsense. She determines how much income she needs to support her "addiction" to maintaining and insuring her 1967 Mustang convertible. She then works as many hours as necessary. "No crazy income and substitution effects for me," she asserts. Is she right?

Depict her labour supply choice in an income-leisure diagram and break a wage increase down into its constituent income and substitution effects.

8. Curious George must decide how much to work. He has 60 hours per week available that he can spend either working or engaging in leisure (which for him is creating various kinds of mischief). He can work at a wage rate of $5 per hour. The Man with the Yellow Hat (who looks after George) also gives him an allowance of $100 per week, no matter how much George works. George's only source of income that he can use for consumption (mostly bananas) is this allowance plus his wage earnings.

   a. In a carefully labelled diagram, draw George's consumption-leisure budget constraint. Show an equilibrium where George chooses to work 40 hours per week.

   b. In an effort to have George pay for other household expenses, the Man with the Yellow Hat decides to tax George 50 percent of his *wage income*. Using the same diagram you drew in (**a**), where George works 40 hours, show what happens to his labour supply. To do this, show one possible outcome, and break the change down into income and substitution effects.

   c. Instead of the wage tax, the Man with the Yellow Hat could impose a "poll tax," a lump-sum tax independent of George's wage earnings. This tax must raise the same revenue as the wage tax in (**b**), and could be accomplished by reducing George's allowance. Draw the budget constraint with the new tax *and* the wage tax, and compare the work incentive effects of the poll tax to the wage tax in (**b**). As in (**b**), assume that George was working 40 hours before any taxes were imposed.

Endnotes

1. Adam Smith, *The Wealth of Nations* (ed. E. Cannan), Book I (London: Methuen and Company, Ltd., 1930), p. 83.

PORTRAIT IMAGES ASIA/Shutterstock.com

CHAPTER 3

Labour Supply and Public Policy: Work Incentive Effects of Alternative Income Maintenance Schemes

LEARNING OBJECTIVES

LO1 Differentiate between different types of income maintenance programs, including demogrants, social assistance, unemployment insurance, earned income tax credits, worker's compensation, and child care benefits.

LO2 Graphically illustrate how key aspects and program parameters of income maintenance programs can be captured by budget constraints.

LO3 Using the labour supply (income-leisure) model, analyze and compare the work incentive effects of different income maintenance programs. Also, be able to show how individual well-being can be compared across programs within this framework.

LO4 Discuss the key challenges to estimating the "real world" effects of income maintenance programs on work incentives.

LO5 Evaluate the potential validity or shortcomings of empirically based arguments concerning the merits of one income maintenance program versus another, and be able to cite representative studies from the empirical economics literature.

MAIN QUESTIONS

- Can the myriad government transfer programs in Canada be analyzed in a common framework? If so, is there a way to determine the "best" type of income transfer program, at least in terms of its effects on work incentives?

- Does unemployment insurance unambiguously reduce incentives to work, thereby reducing overall employment?

- Can welfare programs be designed in a way that minimizes adverse work incentives, directing benefits to those who most need it?

- How can we incorporate disabilities into the labour supply model? Can workers' compensation reduce the incentive of injured workers to return to work?

- How do child care subsidies encourage the labour force participation of women? How can child care costs be incorporated into the labour supply model?

As a response to the problems of income loss and poverty, governments in Canada spend over 10 percent of GDP on various **income maintenance schemes** aimed at raising the income of certain groups and to supplement low wages. Table 3.1 shows that Old Age Security and payments under the Canada/Quebec Pension Plan are, by far, the largest transfer programs, followed by Employment Insurance, social assistance, child tax benefits, and workers' compensation. Because of the social and economic hardships due to poverty and low income, discussion of income maintenance programs is often controversial and emotive. Many considerations go into the design of these programs, and no single program can address the multiple reasons income may be low. However, as we shall see, most of these programs have adverse **work incentives**, and these possible incentive problems can be analyzed within the labour supply framework. But before doing that, it is important to understand the motivation for the various types of income maintenance programs. Given that it is desirable that we should transfer income to those with low income, why would governments design a program that discourages work?

TABLE 3.1	Spending of the Federal and Provincial Governments on Income Maintenance Programs in 2009 ($ billions)
Canada/Quebec Pension Plan	39.3
Old Age Security	35.0
Employment Insurance	18.8
Social Assistance	13.2
Federal Child Tax Benefits	9.7
Workers' Compensation	6.0
Others	54.7
Total	176.6

SOURCE: Adapted from Statistics Canada http://www.statcan.gc.ca/tables-tableaux/sum-som/l01/cst01/govt05a-eng.htm, accessed June 22, 2016, CANSIM Database, Table 384-0009 and Catalogue no 13-213-XDB. The series was discontinued in 2011; 2009 is the last available year.

In designing a transfer program, consider first the issue of "universality" versus "targeting" of a social program.[1] For simplicity, imagine that there is a well-defined poverty line, z. If person i's income, y_i, falls below z, we define him or her as poor, and one objective of an income maintenance program may be to eliminate poverty; that is, raise income (at least) to z. An administratively simple program would be to give everyone in the economy the same transfer, $t_i = z$, no matter what their income, y_i. Under this universal scheme, or demogrant, poverty would be completely eliminated. However, it is also the most expensive way to eliminate poverty, and many benefits would go to the nonpoor, an example of "leakage." People who are not poor would receive the same benefits as those who really needed help. An alternative program would entail perfect targeting; that is, give everyone exactly enough transfer to reach the poverty line: $t_i = z - y_i$. Only those people with incomes below the poverty line would receive transfers, and they would all attain income level z. As long as individual income is unresponsive to the transfer rule, and ignoring the higher administrative costs associated with determining individual incomes (means testing), this perfectly targeted program would be cheaper than the universal program. In fact, in the absence of adverse incentive effects, the perfectly targeted program is the least expensive possible way of eliminating poverty. However, notice that the perfectly targeted transfer program guarantees that individuals with incomes below z are topped up to z. For every extra dollar of income earned, the transfer is reduced by one dollar. If earning income is a costly activity, individuals may reduce work effort (and, thus, their income) so that the transfer program becomes more expensive. By their very nature, targeted programs build in disincentives to earn income, because low income is a condition for receiving the benefit. Perhaps surprisingly, those programs whose main selling feature is that they are directed only at the poor have the worst disincentives for work.

There are several reasons why it is very important to design income support that minimizes work disincentives. For instance, traditional economic analyses focus on the economic inefficiencies due to the fact that income support programs reduce the supply of labour below its optimal level. In addition, as Atkinson (1998) points out, even when they are effective at reducing poverty, programs with adverse work incentives may result in the social exclusion of unemployed workers who benefit from the programs but then, eventually, become disconnected from the main society by being absent from the labour market.

Another issue in program design concerns whether low income is regarded to be of a permanent or a transitory nature. The appropriate response to low income would, thus, depend on whether we believe that an individual is having a bad year, or whether she is likely to be poor every year. Take, for example, the case of a worker who gets laid off from a job. Since many people manage to find a new job in a matter of weeks or months, the income of the worker will be reduced only during a relatively brief period of time, at least relative to the length of a career. In these circumstances, workers will generally be eligible for unemployment insurance, which is designed to provide temporary income support in the event of job loss. Similarly, workers' compensation programs provide temporary income support to workers unable to work because of a workplace injury.

In the case of permanent injuries or disabilities, however, people become eligible for a different set of income maintenance programs (such as disability benefits under the Canada/Quebec Pension Plans and provincial welfare programs). Similarly, individuals permanently out of the labour force can receive welfare payments once they have exhausted their unemployment insurance benefits. Yet another set of programs can help the reintegration into the labour market of individuals who have been out of work for a long period of time. For example, providing child care subsidies to mothers of young children may help them go back to work. Similarly, training programs managed as part of welfare or unemployment insurance systems can help individuals improve their earnings potential and return to work.

In the real world, the distinctions between permanent and transitory income are much harder to make. Yet we can see that the various income maintenance programs are designed to address problems arising from different sources of low income. We will also see that hours worked are not immutable to the transfer program, and may depend on work incentives. The income-leisure framework from Chapter 2 is a useful way to analyze these issues, because it can accommodate many of the key elements of our discussion: wages and nonlabour (transfer) income, the choice of hours worked, final income, and consumer welfare (well-being).

We now turn to an analysis of a variety of "programs": demogrants, welfare, negative income taxes, wage subsidies and earned income tax credits (or refundable tax credits), employment insurance, disability payments and workers' compensation, and child care subsidies. Throughout this chapter, we discuss only "passive" income support, focusing on static work incentives. The possible "dynamic" (or long-run) incentives for investing in human capital (skills) are ignored as are programs designed to enhance skills, until Chapter 9.

LO1, 2, 3   Static Partial Equilibrium Effects in Theory

The basic income-leisure choice framework provides a convenient starting point to analyze the work incentive effects of alternative income maintenance schemes. The analysis is restricted to the static, **partial equilibrium effects** of alternative income maintenance programs. That is, it does not consider dynamic changes that can occur over time, or **general equilibrium effects** that can occur as the impact of the program works its way through the whole economic system. For example, the withdrawal of a large enough number of workers from the work force to take advantage of an income maintenance program may result in higher wages as employers try to compete for a more-limited number of workers. Higher wages make work more attractive, which draws back some individuals into the work force and reduces the adverse impact of income maintenance programs on labour supply.

Income support programs affect behaviour by altering the individual's opportunities (their potential income constraint). To analyze the effect of specific programs on the income constraint, ask first what is the effect on nonlabour income, and second, what is the effect on the slope of the constraint—that is, what happens as the individual gives up leisure and works more? Throughout this analysis, Y is defined as income after taxes and transfer payments and E as labour market earnings, equal to wages times hours worked.

Demogrant

Perhaps the simplest income maintenance program to analyze is a lump-sum transfer, or **demogrant**. As the name implies, a demogrant means an income grant to a specific demographic group, such as lone-parent families with children, all persons aged 60 and over, or all family units irrespective of their wealth. There are only a few examples of pure demogrants. The best recent example in Canada is the former Universal Child Care Benefit (UCCB) program, which provided monthly benefits to all families with children under the age of 18. This program, subsequently replaced by the Canada Child Benefit, paid $160 per month for each child under the age of 6 and $60 per month for each child between 6 and 18 years of age. Demogrants are characterized by their complete universality: the benefit received does not depend on income or earnings. The Canada Child Benefit, introduced in 2016 to replace the UCCB and other federal child benefit programs, is not a pure demogrant, since the level of benefit depends on family income. That is, benefits are "clawed back" (gradually reduced as income increases) and families with incomes above a ceiling level receive no benefits. In this way, benefits target families with relatively low incomes. Another example of a targeted demogrant is the Old Age Security (OAS) program, which provides monthly benefits to individuals over the age of 65. Although pure demogrants are uncommon, they are worth analyzing in their abstract form because many income maintenance programs share the features of demogrants.

As illustrated by the dashed line in Figure 3.1, a demogrant shifts the potential income constraint vertically upward by the amount of the grant. The slope of the new income constraint is the same as the original constraint since the relative price of leisure has not changed; a demogrant generates no substitution effect. The new equilibrium, E_d, is above and to the right of the original equilibrium; that is, work incentives are unambiguously reduced. This occurs because the demogrant involves only a leisure-inducing pure income effect. The increase in actual take-home income is less than the amount of the demogrant because some of the demogrant is used to "purchase" leisure, hence reducing earned income. This can readily be seen in Figure 3.1; if the individual did not alter working time, the outcome would be at the point E_1 (yielding income Y_1) vertically above the original equilibrium E_0, whereas income with the demogrant is given by Y_d.

Recent evidence suggests that demogrants have exactly this simple income effect on labour supply. Schirle (2015) studies the effect of the Universal Child Care Benefit (UCCB) on the labour supply of married women. Using a difference-in-difference strategy, she compared the labour market behaviour of married couples with children and with differing eligibility for the UCCB both before and after the introduction of the UCCB in 2006. The first group had children under five years old and received the benefit while the second had children older than five and did not receive the benefit). She found that the introduction of the UCCB had strong negative effects on labour supply, consistent with Figure 3.1. Women who were eligible for the benefit reduced their participation and their hours worked when compared to the behaviour of those who were not eligible for the benefit.

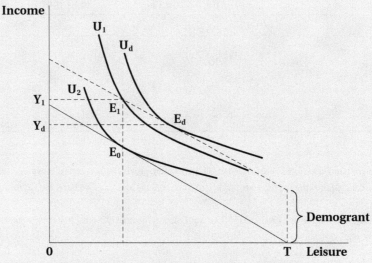

Figure 3.1 Work Incentive Effects of a Lump-Sum Demogrant

The demogrant generates a parallel shift of the budget constraint. If leisure is a normal good, the new equilibrium will occur at a point like E_d, with lower labour supply than the original E_0. Income will not rise by the full value of the demogrant. This would occur only if E_1 were the optimal choice, with hours of work unchanged. But this will not happen if leisure is normal.

Welfare

In Canada, **welfare**, or **social assistance (or income assistance)**, programs are administered by the provinces but financed partly by the federal government under the Canada Social Transfer program. This block funding arrangement provides federal contributions to health, education, and social programs operated by the provinces, but allows provinces to allocate these funds to these programs according to their priorities (e.g., a province may choose to spend less on welfare and more on post-secondary education). Income assistance levels vary by province and benefit amounts vary according to factors such as family type (single parent, couple) and employability. Benefits also depend on the needs of the family and the family's assets and other sources of income. As illustrated in Table 3.2, the total income (including welfare payments) of single parents with one child tends to be about 81 percent of the poverty-line level of income, with considerable variation by province.

TABLE 3.2	Income[a] of Welfare Recipients by Province, 2014 (lone parent, one child)	
Province	**Annual Income ($)**	**Income as % of Poverty Line[b]**
Newfoundland	21,254	102
Prince Edward Island	18,562	91
Nova Scotia	16,384	79
New Brunswick	17,684	85
Quebec	19,600	80
Ontario	19,040	78
Manitoba	15,480	63

Province	Annual Income ($)	Income as % of Poverty Line[b]
Saskatchewan	19,351	93
Alberta	16,626	68
British Columbia	17,277	70
Average (unweighted)	18,126	81

NOTES:

a. Includes basic social assistance (welfare), additional benefits, federal child benefits, provincial tax credits, provincial child benefits, and GST credit.

b. The Caledon Institute of Social Policy, following the previous practice of the National Council of Welfare, uses Statistics Canada's low income cut-offs (LICO) as their measure of the poverty line.

SOURCE: Tweddle, Battle, and Torjman, *Welfare in Canada, 2014* (Ottawa: Caledon Institute of Social Policy, November 2015). Available online, accessed at http://www.caledoninst.org/Publications/PDF/1086ENG%2Epdf

Consider a simplified welfare program. For those who are eligible for welfare, their potential income constraint is given by the dashed line in Figure 3.2. If they do not work, they receive the full welfare payment. Hence, at the point of maximum leisure (zero work), their income constraint shifts, vertically, upward by the amount of the welfare payment. Under traditional welfare programs, if individuals work and receive labour market earnings, they are required to forgo welfare payments by the exact amount of their labour market earnings. In effect, there is a 100 percent tax on earnings. In fact, the implicit tax may even be greater than 100 percent if, for example, they also lose medical or housing subsidies. With the 100 percent tax, the potential income constraint is horizontal at the amount of the welfare payment; that is, as they work and earn income, they forgo a comparable amount in welfare and, hence, their total income remains the same. Every dollar earned results in a dollar reduction in welfare. Of course, once they reach their original labour market wage constraint, their take-home pay will be indicated by their original wage constraint. At this point their welfare payments have been reduced to zero so they cannot be "taxed" any further by being required to give up welfare.

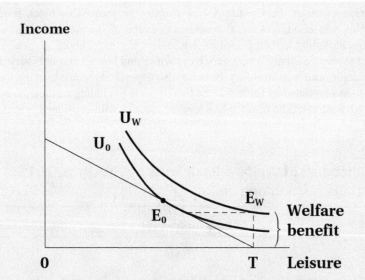

Figure 3.2 Work Incentive Effects of a Welfare Benefit with 100 Percent "Clawback"

Without a welfare program, E_0 is the optimal choice, and the person works. With welfare, the person receives a fixed level of income, irrespective of hours worked. From zero hours worked, wage earnings net of reduced welfare benefits are zero, and there are no returns to working (until benefits are exhausted). The optimal choice would thus be E_W, and nonparticipation.

If the welfare payment is sufficiently high, the individual will have a strong incentive to move to the corner solution at E_W where he will not work at all. There is no incentive to work more (move to the left of E_W) due to the 100 percent implicit tax on income. Even though the person's take-home pay, Y, is lower at E_w than E_0, he chooses E_w because it involves considerably more leisure. Clearly, this type of welfare program has extreme potential adverse effects on work incentives. Of course, for many people on welfare, work is not a viable alternative; for example, if they are disabled or unemployable. Yet for others, work would be a viable alternative if there were not a 100 percent implicit tax on earned income.

This analysis suggests a variety of ways of reducing the number of people on welfare. Traditionally, we think of making eligibility requirements more stringent or reducing the magnitude of welfare for those who are eligible. These changes would, of course, be successful. In Figure 3.3(a), for example, if the welfare payment were lowered to an amount lower than the height of U_0 at the point of maximum leisure, there would be no incentive to go on welfare since the individual would be maximizing utility at E_0. Although successful in reducing the number of people on welfare, these changes may have undesirable side effects, not the least of which are denying welfare to those in need and providing inadequate income support to those who are unemployable.

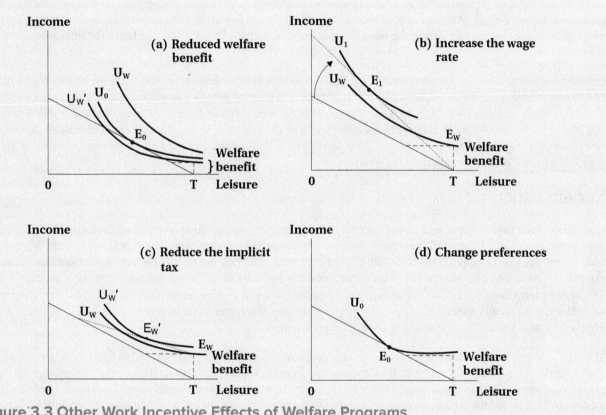

Figure 3.3 Other Work Incentive Effects of Welfare Programs
Changes can be made to the welfare program depicted in Figure 3.2 to improve work incentives. In (a), the benefit is reduced so that nonparticipation yields U_w, and the person prefers working E_0. In (b), a higher wage rate can make working more attractive, as E_1 yields utility U_1 versus U_w. In (c), the implicit tax is reduced so that the welfare recipient can keep some of her earnings. This increase in the returns to work can lead to participation at E'_w In (d), we see the case where sufficient stigma (for example) is attached to being on welfare, so that E_0 is the preferred choice.

One alternative to these policies would be to increase the market wage rate of those on welfare and thereby encourage them to voluntarily leave welfare and earn income. In Figure 3.3(b), an increase in the market wage rate would pivot the wage constraint upward from T. At some higher wage rate, the individual clearly would be induced to move to a higher indifference curve that would involve more work effort than that when under welfare (i.e., a new equilibrium to the left of E_w, E_1). The increased market wage could come about through training, job information, mobility, a government wage subsidy, or institutional pressures, such as minimum wages or unionization. Obviously, these policies may be costly or, in the case of minimum wages and unionization, may involve a loss of jobs. However, they could have the benefit of voluntarily reducing the number of people on welfare and, hence, increasing work incentives.

Another way of improving work incentives would be to reduce the 100 percent implicit tax on welfare. In most welfare programs, this is accomplished by requiring welfare recipients to give up only a portion of their welfare if they earn income by working. For example, if recipients are required to give up 50 cents in welfare for every dollar earned in the labour market, they would have some incentive to work because the implicit tax rate would be 50 percent. In Figure 3.3(c), this could be shown by a wage constraint starting at E_w, with a negative slope of 50 percent of the slope of the labour market wage constraint reflecting the fact that the recipient takes home 50 percent of every dollar earned by working. The negative income tax, discussed below, is a general scheme designed to ensure that individuals receiving income support face an implicit tax on income from work that is significantly less than 100 percent.

An alternative solution to reducing the number of welfare recipients would be to alter the preferences of welfare recipients away from being on welfare and toward labour market activity. In Figure 3.3(d), this would imply changing the shape of the indifference curves. If, for example, at all points to the right of E_0, the indifference curve U_0 were flat, then the individual would not have opted for the welfare equilibrium E_w. The flat indifference curve would indicate a reluctance to accept any cut in income even to get substantial increases in leisure. Traditionally, preferences have been altered by attaching a social stigma to being on welfare. Alternatively, preferences could be altered toward income-earning activities, perhaps by making potential recipients feel more a part of the nonwelfare society, or perhaps by attempting to break the intergenerational cycle of welfare.

Recently, welfare reform has also emphasized the distinction between "employables" and "nonemployables" and has often set a requirement that the employables work or be registered in a training program as a condition of eligibility for the receipt of welfare. Such programs—termed *workfare*—have often been directed at families who are believed able to engage in paid employment. In the case of single-parent families, one of the problems is that this can entail expensive daycare needs. Nevertheless, it may encourage participation in the workforce as well as enhance the longer-run employability of recipients by providing them with work experience or training.

Negative Income Tax

Negative income tax or guaranteed annual income plans involve an income guarantee and an implicit tax rate of less than 100 percent applied to labour market earnings. Income after taxes and transfers would be $Y = G + (1 - t)E$, where G is the basic guarantee, t is the implicit tax rate, and Y and E, as defined earlier, are take-home pay and labour market earnings, respectively. Most negative income tax plans differ insofar as they involve different values of the basic guarantee and the tax rate. The term *negative* income tax is used because recipients will receive more from the guarantee than they will pay out in taxes, even though they do face a positive implicit tax rate. Guaranteed annual income schemes have frequently been proposed by policy analysts from a variety of political perspectives.[2]

Although a comprehensive guaranteed annual income program has never been implemented in Canada, some programs that apply to particular groups—for example, the Canada Child Benefit, which supplements the income of families with children, and the Guaranteed Income Supplement, which supplements the income of individuals over 65—have the negative income tax design. That is, there is a basic guarantee received by those with income below a certain level; those with higher income receive less income supplementation according to the program's implicit tax rate, and those whose income exceeds the program's breakeven point receive no benefits.

A negative income tax plan with a constant rate is illustrated by the dashed line in Figure 3.4. As with the demogrant and welfare, at the point of maximum leisure, the basic income guarantee shifts the potential income constraint upward by the amount of the guarantee. Thus, even if the individual does not work, she has positive income equal to the amount of the guarantee. Unlike welfare, as the individual works, income assistance is not reduced by the full amount of labour market earnings. However, income support does decline as income from work increases; thus, labour market earnings are subject to a positive implicit tax rate. Take-home pay does not rise as fast as labour market earnings; hence, the income constraint under the negative income tax plan is less steeply sloped than the original labour market income constraint. At the point B, often referred to as the breakeven point, income received from the negative income tax program has declined to zero. Thus, to the left of this point the original income constraint applies.

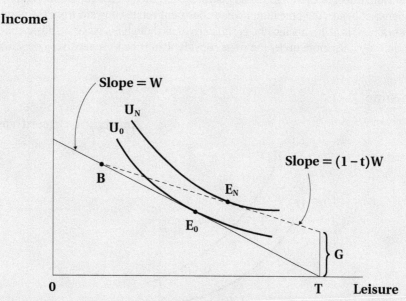

Figure 3.4 Work Incentive Effects of a Negative Income Tax

A negative income tax is a welfare program with a less than 100 percent tax-back rate. Such a program will reduce work incentives (compared to no program). The guarantee level, G, shifts out the budget constraint, producing a work-reducing income effect. Leisure is also cheaper, (1 − t)W as against W, so the substitution effect will lead to fewer hours worked. No benefit is received when income is higher than the breakeven level, B.

Assuming leisure is a normal good, the new equilibrium for recipients of the negative income tax plan will clearly lie to the right of the original equilibrium E_0: work incentives are unambiguously reduced relative to a situation in which there is no other form of income support. This occurs because the income and substitution effects both work in the same direction to reduce work effort. The tax increase on earned income reduces the relative price of leisure, inducing a substitution into leisure and, hence, a reduction in work effort. The tax increase also has an income effect (working in the opposite direction); however, for *recipients* this is outweighed by the guarantee so that, on net, their new potential income constraint is always above the original constraint—that is why they are defined as recipients. Because the potential income of recipients is increased, they will buy more of all normal goods, including leisure. Thus, the income effect works in the same direction as the substitution effect, reducing work effort.

The income-leisure choice framework predicts that work incentives will be unambiguously reduced as a result of a negative income tax plan. But this does not negate the viability of such a program. The adverse work incentive effects may be small, or the increased "leisure" may be used productively, such as in job search, mobility, education, or increased household activities. In addition, the reduction in labour supply may have other desirable side effects, such as raising the wages of low-wage labour since it is now a relatively scarcer factor of production. Perhaps most importantly, the adverse incentive effects were predicted when a negative income tax was imposed in a world without other taxes and transfers. In most circumstances, a negative income tax scheme is intended to replace some welfare programs that have even larger adverse incentive effects. In this sense, work incentives may increase relative to incentives under welfare (as will be discussed in more detail in subsequent sections). While the basic conclusions from the work-leisure model should not be ignored, they must be kept in proper perspective. Empirical information is needed on the magnitude of any adverse work incentive effects and on the form in which leisure is taken. In addition, the effects on work incentives will depend on the programs that the negative income tax scheme is intended to replace.

Wage Subsidies and Refundable Tax Credits

Since one of the problems with the negative income tax and welfare is that the tax on earnings may discourage work effort, some have suggested that, rather than tax additional earnings, the government should subsidize wages in an attempt to encourage work. Although there are a variety of forms of a **wage subsidy**, the simplest wage subsidy schemes have the common result that the recipient's per-hour wage rate is supplemented by a government subsidy.

The static, partial equilibrium effect of the wage subsidy is illustrated by the dashed line in Figure 3.5. For the recipients, it is exactly like a wage increase; hence, the potential income constraint rotates upward from the point of maximum leisure T. If the person does not work (i.e., is at T), his income is still zero even though his wage is subsidized. However, as the person works more, his take-home pay rises more under the wage subsidy than if he were receiving only his market wage.

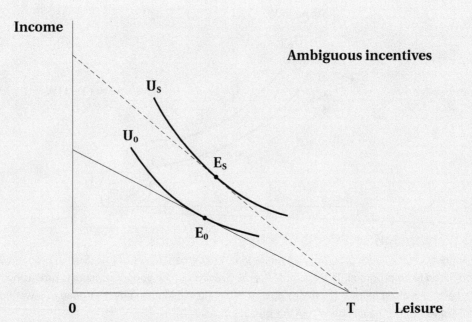

Figure 3.5 Work Incentive Effects of a Wage Subsidy

The work incentives of a wage subsidy are the same as for a wage increase; the work-inducing substitution effect may be offset by the income effect (as it is here, in the movement from E_0 to E_S).

Just as an increase in wages has both an income and a substitution effect, which work in opposite directions insofar as they affect work incentives, so will the wage subsidy have an ambiguous effect on work incentives. The higher wage means higher potential income from which the individual will buy more of all normal goods, including leisure; hence, work incentives are reduced via the income effect. This income effect will function even though the individual has to work to receive the income; the increased leisure could come in the form of reduced hours or longer vacations or periodic withdrawals from the labour force or reduced work from another family member. The higher wage also means that the price (opportunity cost) of leisure has now increased; hence, work incentives are increased via this substitution effect. On net, theory does not indicate which effect dominates; hence, the work incentive effects of a wage subsidy are ultimately an empirical proposition.

Although the work incentive effects of a wage subsidy are theoretically indeterminant, other things being equal (the recipient's welfare, their post-transfer income, or the size of the subsidy), the adverse work incentive effects of the wage subsidy are not as great as those of the negative income tax. Remember that under a negative income tax plan, both the income and substitution effects go in the direction of reducing hours of work. Work incentives are better under the wage subsidy because it increases the wage by the amount of the subsidy while negative income tax reduced the wage by the amount of the implicit tax.

Although the work incentive effects are greater under a wage subsidy than under a negative income tax, this does not necessarily make the wage subsidy a better plan. The key disadvantage of the wage subsidy is that it is poorly targeted to the population in need. Although it may help the working poor, it does nothing to help those who legitimately cannot work. For the latter group, a negative income tax plan would at least provide a guaranteed minimum income. Furthermore, high-income individuals would also be eligible for support under a pure wage subsidy program. Like a demogrant, a wage subsidy is an extremely expensive way of helping the people in need.

Because of these obvious cost issues, pure wage subsidies, like demogrants, are rarely used in practice. For a wage subsidy to be viable, it needs to be targeted to low-income individuals. The most natural way of targeting a wage subsidy program is to condition the subsidy on "low earnings," and possibly other demographic characteristics associated with need, such as being a single parents with children. Interestingly, this type of "income-tested" wage subsidy has become very popular in both the United States and the United Kingdom, and is also used in Canada and several European countries. In the United States, the program is known as **Earned Income Tax Credits**, or EITCs. Introduced in 1975, and with major expansions in the program since the 1990s, the EITC has grown to be one of the largest components of the U.S. welfare state, one that has supplanted traditional welfare as the income support program for working-age individuals (see Nichols and Rothstein 2015, for a useful review of the U.S. EITC program and its evolution). In 2013, for example, 26.7 million families received $63 billion in federal EITC benefits. In addition, the federal EITC is supplemented by the Child Tax Credit, which is similar in size, and by state and local EITCs. The UK program, referred to as the Working Families Tax Benefit (WFTB), provides even higher benefit levels to recipients and, like the EITC, has become a core part of the UK social safety net (Blundell 2006). A similar Canadian program, the federal Working Income Tax Benefit, or WITB, started in 2007. However, expenditure on WITB was only about $1 billion annually as of 2015, so Canada's program is dwarfed by those in the United States and UK on a per-capita basis. Provincial welfare programs, despite their flaws due to high implicit tax rates, remain the primary source of support for those in need in Canada.

In the United States and United Kingdom, these tax credit programs for working families with low incomes are supported across the political spectrum because of the unique combination of targeting and relatively strong work incentives. Labour earnings are required to receive benefits, and, thus, there is broad political support for this program targeted to the "working poor." In addition, these programs are relatively inexpensive to administer. They operate through the tax system, and unlike traditional income assistance programs they do not require case workers and an associated government bureaucracy.

The EITC, WFTB, and WITB are refundable tax credits, or subsidies, that are paid irrespective of other income taxes paid. Application and receipt is a normal by-product of completing a tax form. An EITC-type program is typically divided into three parts. In the first, or "phase-in," part of the program, workers receive a wage subsidy that is proportional to their earnings (thus, the marginal tax rate, equal to 1 minus the slope of the schedule, is negative). As base example, for a single individual under the WITB, the subsidy begins after the first $3000 of earnings, which in 2012 equalled 25 percent of earnings. The subsidy increases to a maximum level of $970. Once the subsidy reaches the prescribed maximum value, it remains constant (plateaus) for a "flat range" of earnings. The subsidy is gradually phased out, disappearing once earnings reach a high enough level. For the WITB, phase-out begins after earnings exceed $11,000, at which point benefits are reduced by 15 percent for excess earnings. The WITB disappears when earnings reach $18,000. Work effort is thus implicitly taxed in the phase-out part of the program. As a result, the effect of the EITC or WITB on hours of work depends on whether an individual is in the phase-in (where work is subsidized), flat range (where benefits are constant), or phase-out (where work is taxed) part of the program.

Canada's WITB is a much smaller program than its U.S. and UK counterparts for two principal reasons. First, the WITB affects a very narrow and low income range, with phase-outs starting around $11,000 in annual income for singles and $16,000 for families. WITB earnings supplements are fully phased out beyond $18,000 for individuals and $28,000 for families. Second, the maximum benefit under WITB is very small relative to that in the United States and UK—less than $1000 for singles and less than $2000 for families (in 2012 dollars).

Figure 3.6(a) shows in more detail the work incentives of a simplified refundable tax credit program like the EITC or WITB. Between A and B, the phase-in part of the program consists of a standard wage subsidy. The maximum value of the total subsidy is reached at point B, when the worker has earnings of Y_L. Between earnings of Y_L and Y_H we are in the flat range (between B and C). After point C is reached, the subsidy is gradually phased out between C and D. Interestingly, the refundable tax credit combines the features of both a negative income tax program (between C and D) and a wage subsidy program (between A and B). In both cases, as in the flat range, the income effect tends to reduce work effort. The substitution effect may increase or decrease work effort, depending on what the work effort of the individual would be in the absence of the EITC or WITB. Figure 3.6(a) shows how three different types of individuals might respond to the introduction of a refundable tax credit. Individuals at point a move to point b in the phase-in section; individuals at point c move to point d in the flat range; while individuals at point e move to point f in the phase-out section. The phase-in section is similar to a standard wage subsidy. For individuals starting at point a, the substitution effect increases work effort while the income effect reduces work effort. As in the case of the work subsidy, the overall impact on work effort is ambiguous. Indeed, Figure 3.6(a) depicts a situation in which hours worked are slightly lower at point b, where the income effect dominates the substitution effect. In both cases, however, the refundable tax credit increases the welfare of low-income workers who are better off with than without the earnings supplement.

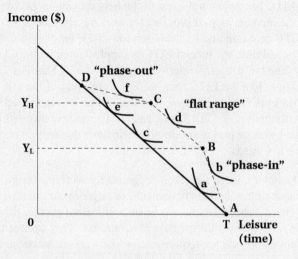

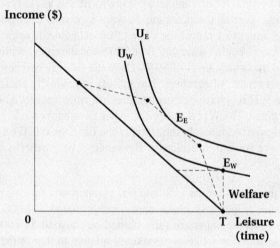

Figure 3.6 Work Incentives of a Refundable Tax Credit

A refundable tax credit, such as EITC or WITB, has an ambiguous effect on hours-of-work incentives, but it nonetheless provides better incentives than a traditional welfare program, and also encourages participation. The impact of the tax credit on work incentives is illustrated in (a). Between A and B, the phase-in part of the program consists of a standard wage subsidy. The maximum value of the subsidy is reached at point B, when the worker earns Y_L. Between B and C, the subsidy is unchanged (the "flat range"). Beginning at point C, when the worker has earned Y_H, the subsidy is gradually phased out until zero subsidy at point D. The phase-out section is like a negative income tax. Individuals in the phase-in section move between points and hours of work can either increase or decrease, depending on the magnitude of income and substitution effects. In the flat range, individuals move from points c to d, where there are only income effects (so hours of work are reduced). In the phase-out section, income and substitution effects reinforce each other, and hours of work are reduced (as in e versus f). Incentives for participation are unambiguously higher with the refundable tax credit. In option (b), the EITC or WITB results in increased hours of work (and participation) to E_E, compared to a traditional welfare program (E_W).

In the flat range, the program exerts only an income effect and labour supply is reduced, assuming leisure is a normal good (individuals move, for example, from points c to d). Finally, the phase-out section of the EITC or WITB is like a negative income tax. For individuals starting at point e, both the substitution and income effect reduce work effort to point f, just as they do for a negative income tax. While the net effects on hours worked (the "intensive margin") may be ambiguous, the effect on participation (the "extensive margin") is clearer. For most individuals who would have chosen not to participate, those for whom the market wage was less than their reservation wage, the wage subsidy improves the returns to work, and this increases the probability of participation.

The work incentives of refundable tax credits look even better when compared to a traditional welfare program. Figure 3.6(b) shows that in absence of an EITC or WITB, the individual would choose to not work (at E_W), collect welfare, and get utility U_W. With the tax credit, the individual will be induced to work at E_E and attain a higher utility level, U_E. For individuals who would otherwise be on welfare, the EITC or WITB provides a strong incentive to join the work force, as long as the benefit is high enough. This helps explains why EITC-type programs are increasingly popular in both the United States and United Kingdom and, to a lesser extent, in Canada.

Employment Insurance

Employment insurance (EI) is the largest income security program for non-elderly individuals in the country, covering approximately 92 percent of the labour force.[3] EI also accounts for about 15 percent of non-old-age-related income security expenditure. The replacement rate is 55 percent of lost earnings (subject to a maximum), with the benefit duration ranging from 14 to 45 weeks, depending upon the rate of unemployment in the region. In order to qualify for the benefits, individuals must have worked between 420 to 700 hours, the equivalent of 12 to 20 weeks at 35 hours per week, again depending on the unemployment rate of the region.

Like other income maintenance programs, unemployment insurance (UI) primarily affects work incentives by changing the budget constraint faced by individuals. The chapter's Worked Example shows that the incentive effects of UI are complex because they are very different, depending on how strongly attached individuals are to the labour market. As a result, UI may provide more work incentives for certain individuals, but fewer incentives to work for others. As in the case of other income maintenance programs, however, it is assumed that if individuals want to increase their labour supply, the jobs are available for them to do so. However, in regions or periods of high unemployment this may be an unrealistic assumption. Individuals may be constrained by the lack of jobs on the demand side. Phipps (1990, 1991) shows that, both theoretically and empirically, this can have an important effect in altering the work incentive effects of income maintenance programs, like unemployment insurance. Specifically, reforms to UI to cause increased work incentives may be thwarted, in part at least, by the fact that increasing the *incentive* to work (a supply-side phenomenon) does not guarantee that more people will work if the jobs are not available (a demand-side phenomenon).

WORKED EXAMPLE

Unemployment Insurance and Work Incentives

The effect of UI on work incentives can be analyzed using the income-leisure choice framework. To simplify the analysis, consider a stylized example of an unemployment insurance scheme that gives recipients 60 percent of their weekly pay for a maximum period of 20 weeks and requires a minimum of 14 weeks of employment in order to qualify for benefits.

This hypothetical scheme is illustrated in the figure below using a one-year time horizon. The solid line AF is the potential income constraint in the absence of a UI program, and the line ABCDF, including the dashed segment ABCD, is the constraint with unemployment insurance. If the individual works fewer than 14 weeks during the year, he does not qualify for UI benefits and his income constraint is the segment DF. If the individual works 14 weeks, he is eligible for benefits for an additional 20 weeks; thus, his income at 14 weeks of work equals his labour market earnings for the 14 weeks plus 20 times 60 percent of his normal weekly wage earnings. His annual income would be $Y = 14W + (0.60)20W$, where W is weekly wage earnings. This results in point C in the figure, the vertical distance between C and D equalling $(0.60)20W$.

As the person works additional weeks (moves from right to left, from the point C) he can earn his weekly earnings as well as his unemployment insurance, at least for some period of time. Because he cannot legally work and collect unemployment insurance at the same time, he will reach a point where a week's work "costs" him a week of collecting UI. For example, if he works 50 weeks, he can collect UI only for the two remaining weeks of the year. Any week worked that reduces his 20 weeks of eligible UI collection thus has an additional opportunity cost. So, as long as he does not reduce his entitlement to collect UI benefits, the slope of the income constraint from point C is parallel to the original wage constraint. He can collect his full UI benefits as well as earn W per week worked. His UI entitlement is reduced as soon as weeks of leisure fall below 20. This parallel component of the budget constraint is, thus, the segment from C to B, at 20 weeks of leisure.

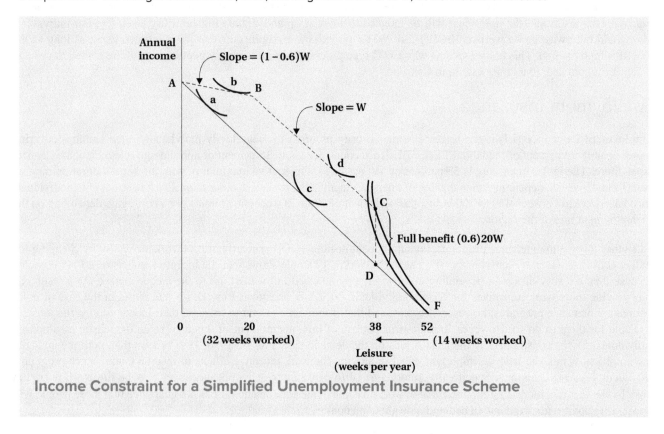

Income Constraint for a Simplified Unemployment Insurance Scheme

After working 32 weeks, available leisure, or time for collecting UI, is reduced. Thus, the returns to working are less than the wage. Between 32 and 52 weeks worked, the return to working is the labour market earnings minus the foregone UI benefits. Since one week's benefits are equal to 0.6W, the returns to working an additional week over this portion of the budget constraint is W – 0.6W, or 0.4W. This segment is labelled AB in the figure.

The nature of the work incentive effects of unemployment insurance depend on where the individual would be located in the absence of the UI system. Three different possibilities are shown in the figure. For individuals working more than 32 weeks (e.g., at point a on AF), the income and substitution effects work in the same direction to potentially decrease weeks worked (moving to point b on AB). For individuals such as those originally at point c on AF, the unemployment insurance system constitutes a pure income effect, again potentially decreasing work incentives (moving to point d on BC). These adverse work incentive effects are potential because the vast majority of people will not collect UI. Many employees would not leave their job because they may not be able to return once they have exhausted UI. However, for those with a guaranteed or reasonably certain job—be it seasonal, with family friends, in household activity, or perhaps one of many low-paid, dead-end jobs that cannot attract other workers—there may be an incentive to collect UI. In addition, the incentive would certainly be there for those who have lost their job, perhaps because of a recessionary phase in the business cycle, and hence have no labour market alternatives.

The third possibility illustrated in the figure applies to individuals who would be outside the labour force in the absence of a UI program. These individuals are originally located at point F, reflecting the high value of their time devoted to nonmarket activities. Many such individuals would choose to remain outside the labour force and neither work nor collect UI. Others, however, would enter the labour force and work a sufficient number of weeks in order to qualify for UI benefits, locating at point C in the figure. In this case, the UI program has increased work incentives by making it attractive for these individuals to devote less time to nonmarket activities and to enter the labour force for relatively brief periods. Similar conclusions apply to those who would work fewer than 14 weeks in the absence of a UI system (i.e., those who would be located in the segment DF).

In summary, the basic income-leisure choice model predicts that work incentives may be either increased or decreased by UI. Some of the individuals who would, in the absence of a UI system, either be outside the labour force or work fewer weeks than are required to qualify for UI benefits, will increase their weeks worked per year in order to receive UI. In contrast, some of those individuals who would, in the absence of a UI system, work more than the minimum number of weeks required to qualify for UI will reduce their weeks worked per year and increase the number of weeks during which UI benefits are received. These impacts are likely to be more pronounced in regions where seasonal and other forms of part year work are available. Both of these consequences of UI are likely to increase the unemployment rate—the former because it draws into the labour force individuals with marginal employment attachments who devote much of their time to nonmarket activities, and the latter because it reduces employment and increases unemployment of those with strong labour force attachment.

EXHIBIT 3.1

The Senate Inadvertently Helps Social Science Research

One useful way to determine whether policy details affect behaviour is to exploit differences in program parameters across regions. For unemployment insurance, the model described in the figure in the Worked Example predicts a possible bunching of workers at the minimum weeks worked required in order to qualify for UI; that is, 14 weeks. In the Canadian EI system, the qualification period, or entrance requirement (ER), varies across regions according to the local labour market conditions. These variable entrance requirements (VERs) are set higher where the unemployment rate is higher.

To see whether the ER indeed generated a bunching of workers with jobs lasting exactly the minimum number of weeks, Christofides and McKenna (1996) compare the distribution of job durations across regions with different ERs. They find evidence that, indeed, there is a correlation between the VERs and the bunching of the job durations at the minimum required weeks.

One potential problem, however, is that the VER is set on the basis of the local unemployment rate, so that, implicitly, the VER may depend on the underlying distribution of job durations. If that is the case, then the causality runs from behaviour to policy, rather than vice versa. To get a clean estimate of whether the ER affects job duration, one would like the VER to be set independently of local economic conditions.

That is precisely what happened in 1990. Unless ratified by the Senate in January 1990, the VERs were to revert to a common ER of 14 weeks in all regions. However, because of a dispute between the House of Commons and the Senate over the introduction of the GST, the necessary legislation was delayed. Thus, for most of 1990, all regions had an ER of 14 weeks, which represented an increase in the ER for those areas with the highest unemployment rates. This "natural experiment" provided an opportunity for economists to study the effect of a change in the ER on the distribution of job durations. Two separate studies, Green and Riddell (1997) and Baker and Rea (1998), exploit this episode, and find that the job duration distribution was indeed sensitive to the ER. Their results suggest, in part, that individual labour supply reacts to parameters of the UI system.

Evidence supporting these predicted labour supply and unemployment consequences is provided in several empirical studies. A noteworthy example is Kuhn and Riddell (2010) who use the natural experiment provided by the experience of Maine and New Brunswick over the period 1940 to 1991. The economies, labour forces, and industrial structures of Maine and New Brunswick are very similar. Prior to 1950, the U.S. state of Maine and the Canadian province of New Brunswick had very similar UI programs, and the incidence of part-year work (working less than the full year) and the overall unemployment rates were very similar. However, subsequently the generosity of the UI program in New Brunswick was increased substantially, first in the 1950s and later in the 1970s, while the Maine UI program remained relatively unchanged. Kuhn and Riddell (2010) use the Maine experience as a counterfactual estimate; that is, used it to predict what would have occurred in New Brunswick in the absence of two major expansions of the UI program there. They find that the increased generosity of UI in New Brunswick resulted in increased labour force participation and more part-year work among those with limited labour force attachment (e.g., movements from point F to point C in the Worked Example above), and reduced work activity and increased part-year work among those with strong labour force attachment (e.g., movements from point a to point b and from point c to point d in the Worked Example). By the end of their sample period (1990), 13 percent of working age men in Maine's northern counties (those most similar to New Brunswick) worked part-year, versus 26 percent in New Brunswick. Kuhn and Riddell's estimates imply that more than 75 percent of this differential can be attributed to the more generous UI program north of the border. These labour supply responses also increased the New Brunswick unemployment rate substantially. The impact of the UI system on unemployment is discussed further in Chapter 18.

Disability Payments and Workers' Compensation

Income maintenance programs for the disabled also exist in a variety of forms, such as workers' compensation, disability pension entitlements from public and private pensions, long-term disability insurance (with premiums usually paid from joint contributions from employers and employees), and court awards for personal injury. As indicated in Table 3.1, expenditures on workers' compensation programs are large, at almost $6 billion a year. Long-term disability programs account for more than $4 billion of the $39 billion a year spent under the Canada/Quebec Pension Plan. In most cases, of course, the work incentive effects of such income maintenance programs are not of interest, as payment is made precisely because the disability legitimately prevents a person from working, and the person may have little discretion over how much to work. In some cases, however, there may be more discretion over whether to work and, if so, how much to work or when to return to work. In such cases, the work incentive effects of disability income maintenance programs become a legitimate policy concern.

Prior to examining the impact of disability compensation, it is informative to examine the effect of the disability or injury itself.

Effect of Disability on Budget Constraint

Depending upon its nature, the injury may have a number of different effects on the individual's budget constraint (i.e., ability to earn income). A partially disabling injury could reduce the amount of time the individual can spend at the job, but not affect the person's performance and, hence, wage at the job. This is illustrated in Figure 3.7(a). Without any disabling injury, the worker's choice set is YH_f, given the market wage rate as illustrated by the slope of the budget constraint. In this particular case, the worker chooses E_0 with corresponding utility of U_0 and hours of work (measured right to left) of H_0. The partially disabling injury, for example, could reduce the amount of time the worker is able to work, from H_0 to H_p. The worker's choice set is now limited to E_pH_f, with a corresponding drop in utility to U_p. If the injury were completely disabling so that the person could not work at all, then the person would be constrained to H_f, with no labour market income and utility reduced to U_f. This again highlights the misnomer associated with the phrase "leisure"—it is a catch-all for all activities outside the labour market, ranging from pure leisure to being unable to work because of disability.

In addition to affecting one's ability to earn income, a disabling injury may also entail medical expenses. This affects the budget constraint, reducing income by the amount of medical expenses at each level of hours of work, analogous to a reduction in nonlabour income. Because costs associated with medical expenses shift the budget constraint inward without altering its slope, they will have a pure income effect, unambiguously reducing leisure and increasing hours of work, assuming leisure to be a normal commodity.

A disability that reduced one's ability to earn wages in the labour market would give rise to conventional income and substitution effects, and hence have an indeterminate effect on hours of work. That is, the returns to work are reduced and, thus, one would work less (substitution effect). But one's wealth is also decreased, thereby reducing one's ability to purchase commodities, including leisure, thus inducing more work (income effect).

A disability may also have a differential effect on the disutility associated with work, or the ability to enjoy non–labour market activities. For example, if the disability gave rise to more pain and suffering associated with labour market activities than with household work, it would rotate the household indifference curve as in Figure 3.7(b) so that the indifference curves U_d' and U_d'' are steeper in the disabled state, U_d', than in the non-disabled state, U_0. That is, to remain at the same level of utility, the disabled individual would require more income in return for a given increase in hours of work. For a given market wage rate (as given by the slope of the budget constraint), this would induce a substitution from labour market to nonlabour market activities, reducing work time from H_0 to H_d (work being measured from right to left on the diagram).

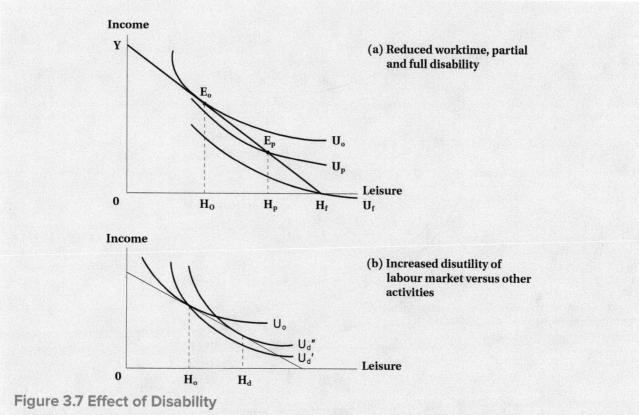

Figure 3.7 Effect of Disability

The effect of a disability can be incorporated into the work decision in a variety of ways. In panel (a), the individual's potential working time is reduced to a maximum of H_P or H_F, under either partial or full disability. In (b), the worker's opportunity set remains unchanged, but the disutility of work increases. Indifference curves become steeper at H_0 (from U_0 to U'_d) and desired work falls to H_d.

Obviously, a disability may result in a variety of the above effects. They were treated separately here only for expositional purposes. It is a relatively straightforward matter to portray them in various realistic combinations. For example, the disability may reduce the time one is able to work, reduce the wage, impose medical costs, and increase the disutility associated with labour market work as opposed to other activities. In such circumstances, the budget constraint and utility isoquants will change to reflect each of these effects, and the incentive to work will be affected accordingly.

Effect of Compensation

To offset the impact the previously discussed type of disability, various forms of compensation exist, including workers' compensation, disability pension entitlements from public and private pensions, long-term disability insurance, and court awards. The effect of such compensations upon well-being or utility and work incentives depends on the form of compensation.

Workers' compensation, for instance, is designed to support the recipient's income so it is not reduced by as much as it would be in the absence of the compensation. For example, it may compensate for two-thirds of the loss in one's former income, in which case the worker's compensation budget constraint appears as the dashed line $E_0Y_dH_f$ in Figure 3.8(a). That is, as the worker is compelled to reduce work activity (move to the right of E_0), income does not fall by the full drop in take-home pay (as it would along E_0H_f) but rather falls by the proportion that it is not supported by workers' compensation. If workers' compensation were two-thirds of one's income loss, then the fall in income would be one-third.

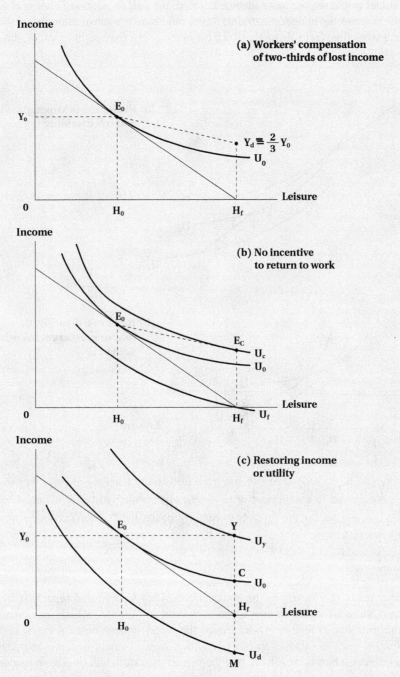

Figure 3.8 Effect of Compensation

What is the appropriate level of compensation for a worker who has suffered an injury? Workers' compensation conventionally compensates someone (for example) by assuming a full disability (H_F) and providing disability benefits of two-thirds of the pre-injury income: $Y_d = 2/3Y_0$ in panel (a). Assuming that benefits are reduced by 1/3W for each hour worked, the new budget set is indicated by the dashed line. This may lead the individual to stop working, at E_C in panel (b) and obtaining utility U_C, which is higher than before the injury (U_0). Panel (c) considers the case of an individual who cannot work and who also has medical expenses, M. The "ideal" compensation would be enough to bring him to U_0, which is unobservable. More conventionally, a court may award him $Y_0 + M$, which yields U_y. Thus, ignoring pain and suffering, he would be overcompensated.

The policy challenge is to design a compensation scheme that compensates those who are legitimately disabled and, hence, in need of compensation but yet provides an incentive for them to return to work where feasible. The potential for an adverse work incentive effect for those who could legitimately return to work is exhibited by the fact that the workers' compensation budget constraint is like the previously discussed budget constraint under a negative income tax; that is, the additional income enables one to afford to work less (income effect). Further, the reduced opportunity cost of leisure time that comes about because one forgoes disability payments as one increases hours of work (substitution effect) also discourages work activity. Obviously, for those who have no discretion over their ability to engage in more work activity, the incentive effects are not at issue. For some, however, these may discourage a return to work activity that they are capable of doing.

The availability of the full budget constraint $E_0 Y_d H_f$ presupposes that such compensation is available for any combination of partial disabilities that would reduce the person's work between H_0 and H_f. That is, depending upon preferences, workers could locate anywhere along the segment $E_0 Y_d$. If the compensation is available only if one could prove full disability, H_f, then the worker's options would be only the points Y_d and E_0. Assuming Y_d was above the indifference curve U_0 as shown in Figure 3.8(a), then the worker would choose the point Y_d.

Figure 3.8(b) illustrates a situation where the worker receives workers' compensation for the full disability and has no incentive to return to work, assuming of course that such an option were feasible. The compensation ($E_c H_f$) is such that the worker is better off not working and receiving the compensation (point E_c) than he would be by returning to work (point E_0); that is, utility under compensation (U_c) is greater than utility under work (U_0). Even though income by working would be greater than income under compensation, it is insufficient to offset the disutility associated with the additional work.

No provision of compensation, however, risks the effect that individuals who legitimately cannot return to work have their utility level reduced to U_f. Clearly, lowering the compensation level so that U_c is below U_0 would induce a return to work from those who can legitimately engage in work; however, it creates a risk of penalizing those who legitimately cannot return to work. Also, when one considers the considerable medical costs and pain and suffering that are often associated with disability, it becomes less likely that compensating someone for a portion of their lost earnings would make them better off.

Different amounts of compensation are also involved, depending upon the position to which the recipient is to be returned. Figure 3.8(c) illustrates the situation where a permanently disabling injury prevents the individual from working at all (i.e., forces the individual to locate at H_f) and gives rise to medical costs of $H_f M$. These events reduce the individual's well-being from U_0 to U_d. A court award to compensate for the individual's loss of earnings, YH_f, plus medical costs, $H_f M$, would lead to a total award of YM. This would clearly leave the individual better off than before ($U_y > U_0$) because the individual is not experiencing the disutility associated with working. If, however, the disability results in pain and suffering, then the individual's ability to enjoy goods and leisure consumption may be reduced and the individual could be worse off than before, even with the compensation award of YM (and possibly even with some additional compensation for pain and suffering).

If the court wanted to restore an individual to his former level of well-being or utility, U_0, then an award of CM would be appropriate. The problem is in assessing the value the individual may attach to not having to work. This is given in the diagram by YC, which is the income reduction the individual would have willingly accepted to reduce work activity from H_0 to H_f (equal to $E_0 Y$) and to remain indifferent to being at E_0 with utility U_0. The problem is that YC is not observed; all that is observed is the person's income, YH_f.

This clearly illustrates the dilemma any court or administrative tribunal would have in arriving at compensation to "restore the person in whole." Amounts will vary, depending on whether this is interpreted to refer to the previous level of income or to welfare or well-being.

Child Care Subsidy

One of the most hotly debated social programs in recent years has been the provision of daycare or **child care subsidies** to facilitate the employment of those with children. Analysis of the daycare subsidy requires first an investigation of how child care costs might affect a parent's labour supply decision.

Daycare costs can be modelled as a special case of **fixed costs** associated with working. The assumption in this case is that the cost of child care is incurred only if the person works, and that the cost is independent of hours worked. It is a straightforward exercise to extend the analysis to the case where the cost depends on the actual hours worked.

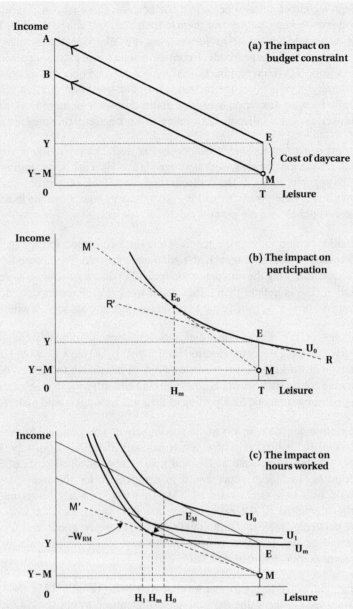

Figure 3.9 The Effect of Child Care Costs on Labour Supply

Daycare costs can be incorporated into the budget constraint as a fixed cost, M. If a parent does not work, the consumption opportunity is E, but as soon as the parent works, the budget constraint falls to MB. Effectively, therefore, the hours-income budget line is given by EMB. As seen in panel (b), this results in an increase in the reservation wage from RR' to MM'. For a parent who works, the adverse income effect will lead to an increase in labour supply, from H_0 to H_1 in panel (c).

The effect of the daycare cost on the potential income constraint is illustrated in Figure 3.9(a). The fixed cost of daycare is analogous to a vertical drop in the individual's budget constraint immediately upon entering the labour market. That is, immediately upon engaging in labour market activities, the individual incurs the fixed costs $M = EM$, which are analogous to a drop in income of EM. (The point M is slightly to the left of the vertical line ET to indicate that the costs are incurred only if one engages in labour market activity; that is, moves to the left of T.) These fixed costs are avoided if one does not work in the labour market but remains at E. In summary, in the absence of child care costs, the person faces income constraint AE, whereas with fixed child care costs, the person faces BME.

We can separately examine the effect of these costs on the individual's participation and hours decisions. We first look at participation. In the presence of such fixed costs, the individual's reservation wage is depicted by the slope of the line MM in Figure 3.9(b). This is the minimum wage above which one would enter the labour market. It is the wage at which one would be indifferent between engaging in labour market activities at E_0 and remaining at home with the children at E. Market wages below the reservation wage would not induce labour market participation because the individual would be better off by engaging in nonlabour market activities, like taking care of the children at home, at E, and attaining utility level U_0. Market wages above the reservation wage would induce labour force participation and the amount of work would be determined by the tangency of the new, higher indifference curve and the higher budget constraint (not shown in this diagram).

Clearly, the individual's reservation wage in the presence of fixed daycare costs is greater than the person's reservation wage in the absence of these costs. This is illustrated in Figure 3.9(b) by the fact that the slope of the line MM is greater than the slope of the individual's indifference curve at the point E, the latter slope being the person's reservation wage RR in the absence of fixed costs. (This can be formally proved by the fact that the line MM is tangent to U_0 at the point E_0 that is to the left of E of the same indifference curve, and the indifference curve becomes steeper as one moves to the left of E because of the hypothesis of diminishing marginal rate of substitution.) Simply stated, child care costs associated with entering the labour market increase the reservation wage by making labour market work less attractive than caring for the children at home.

Fixed costs can also have an impact on the hours-of-work dimension of labour supply. This impact is more complicated than the labour force participation decision.

First, consider a person for whom the market wage exceeds the reservation wage MM in the presence of daycare costs. Figure 3.9(c) shows the initial equilibrium at E_0 with hours of work H_0 when there are no child care costs. The existence of daycare costs M associated with entering the labour market is akin to a reduction in non-labour income to $Y - M$. This shifts the budget constraint down in a parallel fashion since market wages have not changed. If leisure is a normal good, this pure income effect from the reduced income increases hours of work from H_0 to H_1. Essentially, when there are fixed costs, one has to work more hours to make up for the income loss associated with the cost of daycare.

In addition to increasing hours of work for those who are participating in labour market activity, fixed child care costs also create a discontinuity, or "gap," in the implied labour supply schedule. This can be seen in Figure 3.9(c). The distance TH_M indicates the number of hours below which it would not be worthwhile to enter the labour market, given the reservation wage W_{RM} created by the daycare costs EM. It is not possible to amortize the fixed costs of entering the labour force over so few hours; hence, there is a discrete jump in labour supply from zero to TH_M hours. Geometrically, it is not possible for there to be a tangency between the budget constraint MM and the indifference curve U_M in the region $E_M E$. This is so because the slope of MM is always greater than the slope of the indifference curve to the right of E_M. In this way, daycare costs discourage part-time work.

In summary, fixed child care costs increase reservation wages and this, in turn, decreases labour force participation. However, for those who do participate, hours of work will be increased. The fixed child care costs also create a discontinuity in labour supply, making part-time work less likely. Intuitively, daycare expenses make entering the labour force less attractive, especially for a few hours. However, once in the labour force, the individual will work more hours to compensate for the loss of income associated with the child care costs. Clearly, fixed costs like daycare have a complicated effect on the various dimensions of labour supply.

To simplify the discussion of the impact of a daycare subsidy, consider a simple program that eliminates the entire cost of child care; for example, the provision of free public daycare. Also, as with the other programs, we ignore the impact of taxes needed to finance the daycare subsidies.

By removing the fixed costs associated with daycare, the reservation wages would be reduced. This, in turn, would induce labour force participation among those who otherwise found the fixed daycare costs too inhibiting a barrier to labour force participation. Even part-time work might be attractive since there would no longer be a need to amortize the fixed daycare costs over longer working hours.

For those who are already participating in the labour force, the daycare subsidy would not affect their participation decision; that is, it would never cause them to leave the labour force. This is so because, if they were already participating, their reservation wage was already below their market wage; hence, lowering their reservation wage would only strengthen their decision to participate in the labour market.

The daycare subsidy would, however, induce those who already were participating in the labour force to work fewer hours. This is so because the subsidy is like a demogrant given to those who have children in daycare, causing them to buy more of all normal commodities, including leisure, and hence, the results in a reduction in hours worked. Alternatively stated, by eliminating the fixed cost of daycare, the subsidy reverses the effect of the fixed cost of working, as illustrated in Figure 3.9(c).

In the end, subsidies to daycare can have a complicated effect on the various dimensions of labour supply, encouraging labour force participation and part-time work but reducing the hours of work for those already participating (assuming the subsidies are not on a per-hour basis). The net effect on total hours of work is, therefore, ambiguous. Obviously, making the subsidy available only to those who are not already participating in the labour force would ensure that total hours of work would increase. However, this can create inequities (and some interesting politics!) because similar groups who are already participating in the labour force would not receive the subsidy.

EXHIBIT 3.2

Daycare at $5 a Day and Female Labour Supply

In the late 1990s, the Quebec government introduced a new program to make daycare more affordable to all families. The idea was to reduce the cost of daycare to $5 a day by directly subsidizing daycare centres. At the time, most daycare centres charged over $20 a day per child. The "$5 a day" program thus made daycare much cheaper for most families. From a theoretical point of view, the $5 a day program can be considered a daycare subsidy.

Baker, Gruber, and Milligan (2008) use Quebec's $5 a day program as a natural experiment in order to estimate the effect of daycare subsidies on labour supply. Their basic idea is to compare the labour supply of Quebec women with young children before and after the introduction of the program. To control for other possible sources of change in labour supply over time, they further compare the change in labour supply of mothers in Quebec to the change in labour supply in other provinces where the $5 a day program was not introduced. After controlling for these various factors, Baker, Gruber, and Milligan find that the $5 a day program increased the participation rate of mothers with young children by 7.7 percentage points. Stalker and Ornstein (2013) use census data through 2006 to further explore this question, and confirm that women's labour supply, especially for married women, increased in response to the subsidy. This provides strong support to the view that daycare expenses are an important barrier to work for women with young children.

But think of the children. The more controversial strand of this literature examines the impact of the Quebec daycare subsidy on child outcomes: does daycare hurt children? The results are striking. Baker, Gruber, and Milligan (2008) and Kottelenberg and Lehrer (2013) show that many health outcomes, especially those pertaining to mental health and non-cognitive skills (behaviour) are adversely affected by switching children from maternal to institutional daycare. Using recent data that tracks children through their mid-teens, Baker, Gruber, and Milligan (2015) show that the Quebec daycare policy drew more children into daycare (away from their mothers), significantly worsening an array of mental health outcomes, and even increasing criminal behaviour. While the subsidy program may have encouraged more women to work rather than care for children, it seems to have had adverse, unintended consequences for the children. As a footnote, the program is also expensive, and in response, the program has been scaled back. By 2015, the minimum price of daycare had risen to $7.55 per day, and furthermore, the price now depends on family income, reaching $20.70 for households with income of $158,000.

LO4, 5   Illustrative Evidence of Incentive Effects

The previous theoretical analysis suggests that income maintenance program parameters can be important determinants of the work incentives of potential recipients; however, the model also emphasizes that a person's overall budget constraint matters. Economic opportunities, whether in terms of job availability or the wage rate, are an equally important part of an individual's decision to work in the presence of an income maintenance program. Knowing how large a role is played by the structure of the support program is of obvious importance in the design of policy.

These issues can be illustrated with the example of welfare participation. Consider Figure 3.10, which shows per capita welfare use and a base-case benefit level for Ontario during the past 34 years. While there are differences in the magnitudes and timing, the broad patterns in Ontario are similar to those in other provinces, and also in jurisdictions in the United States. The proportion of per capita welfare beneficiaries increased steadily over the 1980s, with sharp increases in the early 1990s. This was followed by an equally sharp decline over the last half of the 1990s, and a modest increase since 2008. The real value of the maximum benefit level for single employables is given by the vertical bars. They track the welfare recipiency rate very closely. There were steady increases in generosity over the 1980s, with significant improvements in benefit levels in the early 1990s. However, the historically high caseloads, combined with fiscal pressures associated with the 1991 recession and the change in federal funding formulas (the replacement of the CAP with the CHST) made the benefit levels politically unsustainable. Welfare benefit levels for employables were significantly cut, and other restrictions on welfare receipt (including workfare provisions) were introduced in 1995.

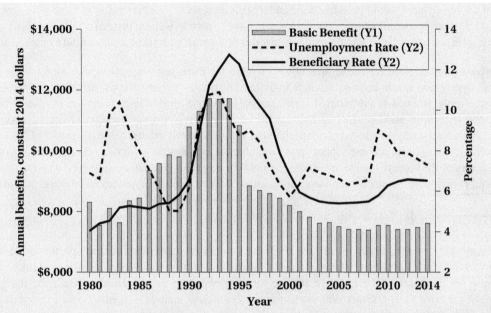

Figure 3.10 Welfare Benefits, Labour Market Conditions, and the Welfare Beneficiaries, Ontario

The average number of welfare beneficiaries per capita (including children) per year is plotted for the years 1980 through 2014 (units on the right-hand axis, Y2). Alongside this series, we show the value of the annual maximum benefits available for a single employable person, expressed in constant year 2014 dollars (units on the left-hand axis, Y1), and the Ontario unemployment rate (units on axis Y2).

NOTES:

1. The Basic Benefit is the maximum welfare benefit for a single employable person, deflated by the CPI (using a 2014 base year).

2. The Unemployment Rate is the average annual unemployment rate for Ontario.

3. The Beneficiary Rate is the percentage of the population receiving welfare (including dependents) during a given year.

Looking at these two series alone, there is an obvious correlation between welfare benefits and the number of people collecting benefits. The much harder question to answer is whether the relationship is purely causal, with causality running from benefits to welfare program participation. Moreover, are welfare program parameters the whole story in explaining the pattern of welfare use? It would certainly be premature to draw that conclusion.

First, it is possible that at least some of the correlation is driven by causality, running from the level of welfare use to the level of benefits. How are welfare benefits set? This is a political decision, reflecting the preferences and motivations of governments. At least during the late 1980s and early 1990s, Ontario governments viewed themselves as more sensitive to the needs of welfare recipients, who formed an important part of their political constituency. As this became an increasingly sizeable group, benefits were increased to meet their needs. Thus, a larger number of welfare beneficiaries could lead to increased levels of benefits ("responding to need"). The story does not carry easily past 1995 when welfare benefits were cut, though it is also the case that declining welfare caseloads would remove some of the political pressure to maintain welfare benefit levels. This "story" of welfare benefits potentially depending on the number of welfare beneficiaries extends to using differences in welfare rates to explain differences in welfare use across jurisdictions. A positive correlation may simply reflect the fact that, in some provinces or states, there is a more generous attitude toward welfare recipients, which is reflected in both higher levels of benefits and higher numbers of beneficiaries.

A much bigger problem is the possible confounding of welfare benefit changes with other factors. For example, the model of welfare participation underlines the importance of labour market opportunities in the participation decision. Low wages, or high unemployment, will make welfare "more attractive" than work. The unemployment rate is a useful proxy for labour market conditions; it is plotted alongside the other series in Figure 3.10. Especially starting in 1988, there is a very strong correlation between the unemployment rate and the number of welfare beneficiaries. At least some of the decline in welfare use in Ontario must be attributed to the strong labour market conditions of the latter 1990s. Note also that in the early 1990s, the high level of unemployment would have had an even larger impact on the welfare rolls, as there were new restrictions on the collection of UI benefits, meaning larger numbers would have to turn to welfare instead of UI. The onset of the recession in 2008, with the attendant increase in unemployment, saw the first notable increase in the welfare beneficiary rate.

Given these considerations, it is still striking how closely related the three series are. How can we formally disentangle the relative impacts? One option would be to extrapolate individual responses to incentives from the nonexperimental literature on general labour supply. But this is a dubious strategy, not only because of their wide variation in results, but also because they generally apply to middle- and high-income families. More reliable evidence on incentive effects of income maintenance programs comes from both nonexperimental and experimental sources directly related to the behaviour of low-income workers in response to changes in specific income support programs. **Nonexperimental evidence** relates measures of labour supply to various parameters of the income maintenance scheme, notably wages and nonlabour income. In addition, there have been large-scale "social experiments" in the United States and Canada concerning prototype income support schemes.

Nonexperimental Evidence

An ideal empirical study of the impact of welfare programs on labour supply and welfare participation would link this joint decision to an individual's wage, nonlabour income, household demographic characteristics, and the welfare program parameters. Using the language of the negative income tax programs, the key parameters would be the guarantee level, G, and the benefit tax-back rate, t. Other real-world parameters would include earned-income exemptions and workfare requirements. A researcher could then evaluate whether individuals facing higher guarantee levels were more likely to be on welfare and work less (if they worked), and whether lower tax rates encouraged welfare recipients to work more hours.

An important caveat must be applied, however, even when interpreting results from an ideal study. As noted by Ashenfelter (1983), welfare participation may be sensitive to program parameters for purely mechanical reasons that have nothing to do with the income and substitution effects described in the labour supply model. For example, when the income on welfare, G, exceeds what an individual would earn in absence of welfare ($Y = Wh$), the individual will always choose welfare over work, irrespective of the precise magnitude of substitution and income effects. As a result, most of the studies we discuss should be viewed more as addressing whether "welfare programs matter" rather than testing the labour supply models outlined in this chapter.

Setting aside this interpretation issue, data limitations make the "ideal" empirical study difficult in a nonexperimental setting. The primary difficulty is in obtaining a data set that contains detailed information on both welfare recipients and nonrecipients and on their personal characteristics, where individuals face observably different welfare program parameters. Only in few isolated cases, such as the one described in Exhibit 3.2, is it possible to conduct an "almost ideal" empirical study using nonexperimental data. Excellent summaries of the existing nonexperimental studies for Canada and the United States are provided by Lacroix (2000) and Moffitt (2002).

One line of research uses administrative data from provincial governments.[4] These data offer detailed income and benefit information for welfare recipients, and especially beneficial information tracking the welfare recipient over a relatively long period of time. Unfortunately, administrative data have limited information on individual socioeconomic characteristics, and, more seriously, there is no information on nonrecipients, meaning these data cannot be used to study the welfare participation decision. Also, since the data are collected at the provincial level, they are not suitable for estimating the impact of program parameters: For a given province and time period, everyone in the sample faces the same program. While there may be some variation over time, such studies are vulnerable to the problems discussed in connection with Figure 3.10.

That said, these studies yield several important findings, particularly concerning welfare dynamics. First, most beneficiaries use welfare for less than a year before leaving the program. As Lacroix (2000) reports, in Quebec, just over one-half of single men and slightly fewer single parents who initiate benefits leave welfare during the first year. For British Columbia, over 85 percent of single men leave within the first year; indeed, three-quarters within the first six months. Similar numbers apply to single parents, with almost 75 percent of welfare spells over in less than a year. This highlights the fact that for most people welfare serves as temporary income assistance.

However, a less rosy picture emerges when we look at welfare recipients at a single point in time. For any given month, the vast majority of welfare cases are "long term." Almost 85 percent of single men on welfare in Quebec have been on welfare for longer than one year, and more than 40 percent for over six years. For single parents, 95 percent of recipients have been on welfare for more than a year, and almost two-thirds for six years or more. The British Columbia numbers are less grim, but the distribution of beneficiaries is still heavily skewed toward long-term, "permanently" low-income users.

EXHIBIT 3.3

Age Discrimination: Bad for Young People, Good for Research

Welfare programs are often designed for single mothers with dependent children. Young, employable males are not traditionally targeted for benefits. Following this principle, until August 1989, Quebec welfare benefits for singles or couples without children and under the age of 30 were much lower than for those age 30 and older. For example, a single employable individual age 29 was eligible only for a monthly benefit of $185, compared to $507 for someone 30 or older. Setting aside the merits of targeting, this seems like a blatant example of discrimination against young adults. Indeed, some of the young welfare claimants who were denied the higher welfare benefits sued the Quebec government on the basis of the Charter of Rights and Freedoms that prohibits discrimination because of age. Their case went all the way up to the Supreme Court of Canada where it was only narrowly defeated in a split decision (*Gosselin v. Quebec* 2002).

This policy undeniably hurt many young people who had to survive on a grossly inadequate amount of money. But what is bad for some may be good for others, especially those doing social science research. Indeed, the policy created a very sharp difference ("discontinuity") between the work incentives for people just below age 30 and those just above age 30. There are no reasons to believe that people a few months short of their 30th birthday are much different than those who just had their 30th birthday, in terms of their work opportunities and taste for work, among other things. Comparing groups of people just above and just below age 30 thus provides a unique opportunity to see how welfare benefits affect work effort for two otherwise comparable groups. The research methodology that exploits the discontinuity of policy (in this case, the big jump in welfare benefits at age 30) is known as regression discontinuity design.

Using administrative data on welfare claimants, Fortin, Lacroix, and Drolet (2004) find that the higher benefits lead to much longer welfare spells. In other words, people who started receiving much higher benefits after turning 30 ended up spending much more time on welfare. These findings are echoed by Lemieux and Milligan (2008), who find that employment rates of male high school dropouts in Quebec in 1986 sharply dropped by 4 percentage points for those above the age of 30. Turning 30 was therefore associated with sharply higher benefits and a propensity to stop working in favor of collecting welfare. These two nonexperimental studies provide compelling evidence that welfare benefits do, indeed, reduce incentives to work.

One further point is worth highlighting. Most evidence in Canada and the United States suggests that welfare beneficiaries exhibit "negative duration dependence"; that is, even controlling for other determinants of being on welfare, the longer one is on welfare, the less likely one is to leave welfare. This may arise because skills deteriorate, employers regard welfare as a negative signal, or those who stay on welfare have conventionally unobserved characteristics (termed unobserved heterogeneity) that are not controlled for in the statistical analysis, and that make them less likely to leave welfare.

Studies of the determinants of welfare participation rely on cross-province differences in the generosity of welfare programs. Allen (1993) uses the 1986 Canadian Census, while Charette and Meng (1994) and Christofides, Stengos, and Swidinsky (1997) use the Labour Market Activity Survey (LMAS) from 1988–1989. Each of these studies finds a strong association between labour market earnings potential and welfare use; those with low predicted earnings, a relatively permanent characteristic, are more likely to use welfare. The evidence on the welfare program parameters is more mixed. However, this arises to some extent because of the limited variation in programs and the difficulty in distinguishing program effects from other, unobserved differences between provinces. Dooley (1999) addresses this limitation by pooling several cross-sectional, individual-level data sets (Surveys of Consumer Finances) over a period covering the 1980s into the early 1990s. This allows him to exploit greater within-province variation in program generosity. Dooley's study focuses on single mothers, and he finds very strong evidence linking both the welfare guarantee levels and the individual earnings characteristics to welfare use. He shows that a significant part of the increase in welfare use during the 1980s can be explained by the relative increase in generosity of welfare benefits, combined with stagnant or declining labour market opportunities for low-skilled women.

Milligan and Stabile (2007) also use a cross-provincial approach in order to study how the benefit tax-back rate, or claw-back rate, of welfare programs affect work incentives. As mentioned earlier, most welfare programs had, traditionally, very high tax-back rates. This changed in Canada in 1998, when most provinces agreed to integrate the new National Child Benefit into their welfare programs. For welfare claimants with dependent children, a significant part of the welfare benefit was replaced by the National Child Benefit. Unlike welfare benefits that are taxed back very quickly as work income increases, welfare claimants are allowed to keep the full amount of the National Child Benefit until they reach a fairly high level of earnings. As a result, the tax-back rate of this new, integrated welfare program was substantially reduced. Milligan and Stabile find that this change greatly improved work incentives and that it can account for about one-quarter of the decline in welfare caseloads in Canada between 1997 and 2000.

A third type of study uses aggregate data like that shown in Figure 3.10, pooling data over time periods and across provinces in order to estimate the impact of provincial welfare programs on welfare caseloads.[5] The consensus from this research is that a variety of factors, including the generosity of welfare benefits, the unemployment rate, and restrictions on the collection of unemployment insurance, all played a role in the increase in welfare caseloads between 1985 and 1994. Berg and Gabel (2015) use provincial-level data to study the effect of all dimensions of provincial welfare programs on caseloads between 1986 and 2009. They show that the most important explanation for the drop in welfare caseloads was the introduction of work requirements (workfare). Such changes in program structure were often introduced alongside benefit cuts (e.g., as in Figure 3.10), and it was these work requirements, more than the benefit cuts themselves, that reduced the attractiveness of welfare relative to working.

The weight of the nonexperimental evidence thus suggests that welfare participation does indeed depend on the generosity and structure of welfare programs. But it also underlines the other important part of the welfare participation equation: individual labour market and income earning opportunities. While our model is helpful in understanding welfare participation, the evidence presented here, however, cannot be taken as evidence that the model is correct in the sense of predicting marginal adjustments in hours in response to welfare program incentives.

Experimental Evidence

Negative Income Taxes

The available **experimental evidence** from the experimental negative income tax literature comes from one Canadian and four U.S. negative income tax experiments: New Jersey and Pennsylvania (1968–1972); rural areas of North Carolina and Iowa (1970–1972); Seattle and Denver (1970–1978); and Gary, Indiana (1971–1974). The Canadian experiment was carried out in Manitoba during the period 1975–1979. Different families were given different amounts of basic guaranteed income and their labour market earnings were subjected to various tax rates. Their work behaviour was then compared to that of a control group of similar families that were not under a negative income tax plan.

Moffitt and Kehrer (1981, p. 24) summarize the effect on work incentives of the four U.S. experiments on the basis of an average tax rate of 0.50 and a guarantee level about equal to the poverty line. The conclusions are that (1) overall hours of work are unequivocally reduced by the presence of the negative income tax; (2) the disincentive effects vary considerably by demographic group, with the reduction in hours of work ranging from 1 to 8 percent for husbands, 0 to 55 percent for wives, and 12 to 28 percent for female heads of families; (3) the work reduction for men occurred more in the form of reduced employment to zero hours of work for a small number of men than it did in marginal reductions in the hours of work of those who remained employed; (4) some marginal reductions in hours of work did occur through reduced overtime; (5) the reduced employment often occurred in the form of a lengthening of time spent between jobs for men and increased school attendance for youth, but these responses did not appear to lead to subsequent wage gains; (6) for most groups, disincentive effects generally occurred in response to both the guarantee and the implicit tax rate, although the groups seemed more responsive to changes in the guarantee than the tax rate; (7) the longer the program, the greater the disincentive effects, suggesting that the disincentive effects may be larger for a permanent as opposed to a transitory program. Hum and Simpson (1991) found somewhat smaller impacts of hours worked in the Canadian negative income tax experiment. Hours worked declined between 0.8 and 1.6 percent for men, between 2.4 and 3 percent for married women, and between 3.8 and 5.3 percent among single women.

The Self-Sufficiency Project

The **Self-Sufficiency Project** (SSP) was a large-scale social experiment carried out in Canada and designed to provide a rigorous test of the impacts of financial incentives on leaving welfare; a policy to "make work pay."[6] Thus, it differed substantially in structure from the negative income tax experiments. This pilot program yielded significant insights into the general question of the role of incentives in the work decision of welfare recipients. The experiments were conducted in New Brunswick and British Columbia with a sample of approximately 5600 single parents (mostly women) with dependent children who had been on welfare for at least a year, over the period 1992–1999. The original sample was randomly divided into treatment and control groups, with the treatment group offered a generous earnings supplement, and the control group offered nothing.

The earnings supplement offer worked as follows. Those in the treatment group were given one year from the beginning of the project to leave welfare for a full-time job, where "full-time" meant at least 30 hours per week. If they took such a job, their welfare benefits were eliminated, but they would receive an earnings supplement equal to half the difference between their earnings and an earnings benchmark initially set at $30,000 in New Brunswick and $37,000 in British Columbia. The supplement approximately doubled their welfare income. Participants could collect this supplement for a maximum of three years providing that they maintained full-time employment. They were also free to return to social assistance at any time. The key idea with this type of program was to make work much more financially attractive than welfare, contingent on working full-time. So how many took up the offer?

At the outset of the program, the proportion of welfare recipients working full time was 6 percent. By the deadline for supplement eligibility (after one year), about 30 percent of the program group was working full time. One estimate of the impact of the program would, therefore, be 24 percent (30 minus 6); that is, the earnings supplement induced a 24 percentage point increase in the number of single parents leaving welfare for full-time work. But this estimate would be wrong, since some of these individuals would have left welfare anyway. In order to gauge how many would have left welfare without the offer of the earnings supplement, we can use the control group. The control group also had 6 percent of women working full time at the outset of the program but 15 percent after one year. Thus, the true (experimental) estimate of the "treatment effect" is 15 percent (30 minus 15); that is, the earnings supplement encouraged (caused) an additional 15 percent of welfare recipients to leave social assistance. This is a large impact, especially given that single parents with dependent children have the lowest exit rates from income assistance of any group. However, after the initial eligibility period, the gap between the treatment and control groups gradually declined. For example, by 36 months after random assignment (i.e., two years after the end of the eligibility period), 27 percent of the treatment group versus 18 percent of the control group were working full time, yielding a 9 percent "treatment effect."

EXHIBIT 3.4

Welfare Reform in the United States

The early and mid-1990s witnessed several important changes to welfare programs in both Canada and the United States. In the United States, the impetus for change was similar to that in Canada: the fiscal pressures of high caseloads in the early 1990s and accumulated concerns with the incentive effects of existing welfare programs. The centerpiece of U.S. welfare reform was the passage in August 1996 of the Personal Responsibility and Work Opportunity and Reconciliation Act, or PRWORA. This act eliminated the traditional welfare program, AFDC (Aid to Families with Dependent Children), and replaced it with TANF (Temporary Assistance to Needy Families).

Rebecca Blank (2002) provides a comprehensive review of the program changes brought by PRWORA, as well as the early evidence on the impact of welfare reform. Her paper also highlights the practical challenges of evaluating the impact of a sweeping change in policy. The names of the legislation (PRWORA), and the resulting new program (TANF), reflect the nature of the policy changes. First, as a condition of federal funding, states administering welfare programs needed to implement work requirements for welfare beneficiaries. Second, a time limit of five years was imposed on lifetime eligibility for welfare benefits. This codified the objective that welfare be insurance for temporary adverse income shocks. The block structure of TANF funding also freed states to experiment with the details of implementing of their programs, generating significant cross-state variation in actual program design.

So what happened? Identifying the specific impact of welfare reform turns out to be quite difficult. First, while states may have varied in the details of implementing welfare reform, the changes mostly occurred at the same time. The mid-1990s also saw major changes to the returns to work. First, the United States was in the midst of a boom, with rising wages and declining unemployment. Second, two key federal policies increased the returns to work for everyone: the federal minimum wage increased and the benefits associated with the Earned Income Tax Credit (EITC) rose significantly. The combined effect of these changes was to increase real, full-time potential earnings for a single mother with children by 20 percent between 1989 and 2000. The stricter rules for welfare and the major increase in returns to work should combine to increase both participation and hours of work. Indeed, outcomes for the welfare-eligible population suggest that the reforms were a huge success. Welfare caseloads (the number of beneficiaries) declined by more than 50 percent over the last half of the 1990s. The labour force participation rate of single mothers with children increased by 10 percentage points: from 67 to 77 percent. And poverty rates for families headed by single mothers declined from 35.4 to 24.7 percent. But how much credit for these improvements could be apportioned among welfare reform, increased returns to work for low-wage workers, and a booming economy? Rebecca Blank outlines a long list of empirical challenges associated with disentangling the impact of these factors, as well as the various strategies used by researchers. While the evidence is still young, it appears that all three sets of factors were important, including the details of the structure of the new welfare programs. In other words, "welfare matters" for work incentives. Further research is necessary to more precisely identify the relative contribution of the factors. It remains to be seen how effective the new programs were in responding the recession of 2007–2009.

The Self-Sufficiency Project generated encouraging results in a number of other dimensions. In year 3, only 61 percent of the treatment group were collecting welfare, as against 70 percent in the control group. Of course, some of the program group were collecting the earnings supplement. Taken over the whole sample, in year 3 the program participants collected an extra $1000 in annual benefits (welfare plus earnings supplement). This, combined with the additional average annual earnings of $800, means that their overall living standards improved by almost $2000 per year. So, while the earnings supplement was more expensive than welfare, it had the twin benefits of leveraging $1 of transfer income into $2 of total income and of getting significantly more single parents into the labour force, which could potentially have important long-run benefits for the women and their children.

What happened in the long run, after the program was over and SSP benefits were no longer available? Did program participants gain a long-run advantage because of their additional labour market attachment? A follow-up survey 54 months (four and one-half years) after random assignment indicates not. The difference in full-time employment rates between treatment and control groups vanished, with approximately 28 percent of both groups working full-time. Average annual earnings were also the same. Similarly, based on administrative data from the British Columia and New Brunswick's social assistance programs, treatment-control differences in welfare receipt had faded to zero by month 69 after random assignment (Card and Hyslop, 2005).

The combination of a large short-term response to the financial incentive, and little or no long-run impact, has received considerable policy and research interest. In their comprehensive assessment of the SSP, Card and Hyslop (2005) show that the two SSP time limits generated an "establishment incentive" to find a full-time job and exit welfare within 12 months and an "entitlement incentive" to choose work over welfare once eligibility was established.

Subsequent research by Riddell and Riddell (2014) points to another factor contributing to the absence of a long-term impact of the SSP earnings supplement on employment and welfare receipt. They find that members of the SSP treatment group were substantially less likely than those in the control group to upgrade their education during the demonstration project. This was the case in all dimensions: high school completion, enrolment in a community college or trade school, and enrolment in university. This suggests that "work first" policies emphasizing full-time employment may reduce educational activity, which in turn could have adverse consequences for the long-run earnings capacity of welfare recipients. In other words, during the SSP demonstration, both the treatment and control groups improved their human capital and earnings capacity, but by different means; the treatment group acquired relatively more work experience whereas the control group acquired relatively more formal education. Because the financial incentive had the unintended side effect of reducing educational upgrading by the treatment group, the differences in earnings capacity between the two groups at the end of the project was reduced, contributing to smaller impacts on employment and welfare receipt.

The story, however, is not of a demonstration project that "did not matter." The SSP affected work incentives while the financial incentive was in place, and sped the process by which welfare beneficiaries moved back into the labour market. The behaviour of the control group, the gradual but substantial exit from income assistance over time, was also revealing and itself an interesting finding. Furthermore, the finding that the control group made substantial investments in formal education, especially in the form of high school completion, provides additional insights into a key mechanism contributing to exit from social assistance.

Summary

- Income maintenance schemes are designed to top-up low incomes, which can arise for any of a variety of reasons, be permanent or transitory, and may be due either to low wages or hours. By their very nature, means-tested programs can have strong disincentives to earning income.

- The income-leisure (labour supply) framework is a useful way to analyze work incentive effects. While programs vary in details, most will generate income effects (by shifting the opportunity set outward) or substitution effects (by changing the returns to work).

- Demogrants are pure lump-sum transfers, based only on immutable individual characteristics like age or sex. While these transfers are independent of income, they will still have adverse work incentive effects as long as leisure is a normal good.

- Welfare programs are designed to increase the income of individuals with low income. The degree to which they have adverse work incentive effects depends on how strictly benefits are reduced in response to higher earnings. The more severely benefits are reduced with higher earnings, the stronger the disincentives will be for welfare recipients to work.

- Negative income taxes, or guaranteed annual income programs, are generalizations of welfare programs. They were proposed as an alternative to welfare programs with steep earnings tax-back rates.

- Wage subsidies make work more attractive but are very expensive unless they are targeted to the working poor. One increasingly popular form of targeted work subsidy is called a refundable or earned income tax credit.

- Unemployment insurance is designed as an insurance scheme responding to short-run reductions in available hours of work, especially due to cyclical changes in labour market conditions. However, such schemes can also have work incentive effects. For those with strong labour force attachment, the incentives will be to reduce work activity, but for nonparticipants and those with limited work attachment, the returns to qualifying for UI will actually encourage them to increase work activity.

- Workers' compensation is designed to address income losses arising from workplace injuries. There are a variety of ways to incorporate injuries or disabilities into the labour supply model.

- Child care expenses can be modelled as fixed costs associated with working. As such, child care subsidies can be viewed as a reduction of these fixed costs. Generally speaking, these subsidies will encourage labour market participation by parents.

- Estimating the actual (as opposed to the theoretical) impact of income maintenance programs on labour supply is difficult. Many of the empirical issues can be illustrated through the important case of welfare programs. The weight of evidence from research on the impact of these programs shows that both the generosity of welfare benefits and individual labour market opportunities predict participation in welfare programs.

Keywords

child care subsidies	partial equilibrium effects
demogrant	Self-Sufficiency Project
Earned Income Tax Credits	social assistance or (income assistance)
employment insurance	wage subsidy
experimental evidence	welfare
fixed costs	work incentives
general equilibrium effects	workers' compensation
income maintenance schemes	
negative income tax	
nonexperimental evidence	

Review Questions

1. Use the work-leisure choice diagram to illustrate that, under normal circumstances, if an individual is given a demogrant, take-home pay will not increase by as much as the demogrant. Why is this so?

2. Illustrate the work incentive effects of a demogrant on a disabled person who is unable to work.

3. Use the work-leisure choice diagram to illustrate the following cases where an individual is

   a. Unwilling to go on welfare because the welfare payment is too low

   b. Indifferent between welfare and work

   c. Induced to move off welfare because of an increase in her wage

   d. Induced to move off welfare because of a change in preferences between income and leisure

   e. Induced to move off welfare by a reduction of the 100 percent implicit tax on earnings

4. In a diagram like the figure in the Worked Example, depict the case in which the individual must work eight weeks before becoming eligible to collect. Depict the case of a two-thirds rather than a 60 percent replacement rate.

5. In a diagram like Figure 3.8, depict the worker's compensation system involving a 90 percent replacement of the pre-injury wage earnings.

6. Use Figure 3.10 as the basis of a "debate" on the statement, "welfare reforms in Ontario worked." Construct arguments both for and against this proposition.

7. One important feature of the 1996 Welfare Reform in the United States was the introduction of time limits. In most states, this lifetime limit is now 60 months. This means that individuals who have received welfare payments during 60 months over their lifetime are no longer eligible for welfare. Discuss the relative merits of this measure in the case where low income is due to transitory factors (like job loss) or permanent factors (like low wage or partial work disabilities).

Problems

1. "The negative income tax involves a positive guarantee that has a pure income effect of reducing work effort. It also involves a tax increase on the earned income of recipients, and this has both an income and a substitution effect working in the opposite direction in their effect on work incentives. Consequently, we are unable to predict unambiguously the static, partial-equilibrium effects a negative income tax plan would have on work incentives." Is the last statement true or false?

2. Most jurisdictions allow welfare recipients to earn a small amount of labour market earnings before the tax back of welfare benefits begins. Using the work-leisure diagram, show how this more realistic welfare program compares to the one described in Figures 3.2 and 3.3. In the late 1990s, the Ontario government increased the amount of labour income disregarded (i.e., allowed before welfare benefits are taxed back), at the same time reducing the overall level of benefits. Analyze the expected impact on labour supply of a prospective welfare recipient of this change in the welfare program.

3. Use the work-leisure framework to illustrate that if we hold the post-subsidy income of the recipients constant, or the size of the subsidy constant, a negative income tax will involve more adverse work incentives than a wage subsidy would.

4. Consider an individual who must drive to his place of work. Assume that there are 16 available hours in the day, that his wage rate is $20 per hour, and that he has nonlabour income of $100 per day. The commute takes one hour each way, and it costs $40 in expenses for the round trip. Using a work-leisure diagram, depict his labour supply choice, including his reservation wage. Analyze the impact of an increase in commuting costs on his participation and hours decision. Analyze the impact, first, of an increase in commuting time from two to four hours per day, and, second, of an increase in driving expenses from $40 to $60 per round trip, keeping commuting time at two hours.

5. The U.S. Earned Income Tax Credit (EITC) has been described as one of the most successful elements of U.S. antipoverty public policy, especially as it directs benefits toward the working poor. For the 2010 tax year, the EITC worked (approximately) as follows. Low-wage workers received additional income from the federal government, depending on how much they earned and how many children they had. Consider an individual with one child:

   i. There was no credit if nothing was earned.

   ii. The credit equalled $0.34 per dollar earned, and peaked at around $3050, when the worker earned $8950.

   iii. It remained at $3050 until the worker earned around $16,450.

   iv. It was phased out gradually, by $0.16 per dollar earned, until eliminated completely if the worker earned $35,535 or more per year.

   a. Assuming the worker faced no other taxes, graph the budget constraint associated with the EITC for a typical worker earning W per hour.

   b. Analyze how the imposition of the EITC affects hours of labour supplied. Assuming that substitution effects are larger than income effects for the typical low-wage worker, does the credit necessarily increase hours of work for all those who are eligible? Why or why not?

   c. Analyze the impact of the EITC on an individual's labour force participation decision, assuming that the individual was not working in the absence of the EITC.

   d. The Canadian EITC-type program, the Working Income Tax Benefit (WITB), provides no credit until labour earnings reach a minimum of $3000. The benefit is then calculated on the basis of "earnings minus $3000." What would happen to the work incentive effects of the EITC if a similar $3000 threshold was added to the EITC (holding everything else constant)?

6. Consider the following earnings supplement program, modelled after the Self-Sufficiency Project. An individual can work a maximum of 60 hours per week, at a wage rate of $5 per hour. Welfare benefits are fixed at $200 per week, with a 100 percent tax back on labour earnings. Finally, the earnings supplement equals half the difference between an individual's labour earnings and the benchmark earnings of $450 per week. This supplement can be collected only if the individual forgoes welfare benefits and works a minimum of 30 hours per week.

Draw the individual's budget constraint, and analyze the work decision.

7. The different programs discussed in this chapter often have ambiguous effects on work effort. It is, nonetheless, possible to compare the work incentives of two programs by looking at what happens when the individual is indifferent between two programs. Use this approach to compare the work incentives of the following two pairs of programs:

   a. Earned income tax credit compared to welfare

   b. Wages subsidy compared to a negative income tax

   In both cases, use graphs to show the hours of work chosen under the two programs by an individual who is indifferent between the two programs.

Endnotes

1. See Besley and Kanbur (1993) for more detailed discussion of these general issues.

2. In one of the most comprehensive studies of its kind, the 1985 Report of the Royal Commission on the Economic Union and Development Prospects for Canada (the Macdonald Commission) recommended fundamental reform of existing income maintenance programs. The centrepiece of its proposal was the Universal Income Security Program (UISP), a negative income tax program that would supplement the income of families with low incomes.

3. Throughout this book, we refer to a generic program as "UI," and the specific Canadian program as "EI." Most of the workers who are not covered are self-employed.

4. See Lacroix (2000) for an excellent summary of this research. Important examples of welfare research using administrative data are Duclos, Fortin, Lacroix, and Roberge (1998) for Quebec; Barrett and Cragg (1998) for British Columbia; and Dooley and Stewart (1999) for Ontario.

5. See, for example, Fortin (1995), Fortin and Cremieux (1998), Brown (1995), and Dooley and Stewart (1998).

6. See Social Research and Demonstration Corporation (2002) for a complete report on the SSP. All figures reported in our discussion are based on this final report.

PORTRAIT IMAGES ASIA/Shutterstock.com

CHAPTER 4

Labour Supply over the Life Cycle

LEARNING OBJECTIVES

LO1 Explain why it is misleading to compare behaviours and outcomes of different-aged individuals, concluding that the observed differences can be attributed to the pure effects of "age."

LO2 Distinguish between the theoretical effects a temporary increase in wage and a permanent increase in wage might have on an individual's labour supply decision.

LO3 Paraphrase, for non-specialists, factors highlighted by economists when considering the question, where do babies come from?

LO4 Describe Canada's three-tier public and private pension system.

LO5 Explain, using diagrams, how changes to Canada's public pension program can affect the age at which individuals choose to retire, and how this can affect retirement incomes.

MAIN QUESTIONS

- Do men's and women's labour supply patterns evolve similarly as they age?

- Is there a difference in the way individuals respond to wage changes if the possibility that people make labour supply decisions with planning horizons as long as their entire life is taken into account?

- What complexities are added to the labour supply framework once we try to model labour supply in each period of a lifetime?

- How might we incorporate the development of labour-saving household appliances into a model of female labour supply?

- How can economic analysis help in our understanding of fertility behaviour and the relationship between fertility and women's labour supply?

- What factors determine the retirement age? In particular, what roles do public and private pension plans play in this decision?

The previous two chapters have emphasized the purely "economic" determinants of labour supply—market wages, nonlabour income, and government programs. One of the more interesting other correlates of labour supply is age, and labour economists have spent considerable effort trying to explain why labour supply appears to vary systematically over an individual's life cycle.

As a first step in exploring **life-cycle labour supply**, Figure 4.1 illustrates the labour force participation rates by age groups for men and women. These age-participation profiles are shown for each of five census years: 1971, 1981, 1991, 2001, and 2011. The men's profiles demonstrate the conventional inverted-U-shaped characteristic of life cycle labour force patterns in most countries; participation increases sharply as men move into their twenties, peaks for ages 30 to 50, then declines as conventional retirement ages approach. While the profiles are very similar in each census year, notice that the participation rates of older men declined significantly between 1971 and 2001, suggesting that men were retiring earlier. This trend was slightly reversed in 2011, with the participation higher than in 2001 (but still below that of 1971).

The women's profiles are more complicated and provide an important example of the perils of inferring dynamic (i.e., life cycle) behaviour from cross-section data. Focus first on the 1971 profile. If interpreted as a stable representation of the pure effects of age on labour force participation, then we can use this profile to predict how many women will work as they age. One can imagine telling the following story. A typical woman increases her labour supply after high school into her early-20s, reduces it sharply to raise a family, then gradually returns to work after age 35, until retirement.

However, as can be seen in Figure 4.1, predictions based on this story would be wrong. Consider 20-year-old women in 1971; that is, those born in 1951. They have a participation rate around 60 percent. If they followed the 1971 cross-section profile, we would predict a participation rate of about 40 percent for these women when they reached 30 years old (10 years later). By looking at the 1981 profile, however, we see that their participation rate was much higher, at around 63 percent. Their participation rate is almost 20 percentage points higher than that for 30-year-olds in 1971. As can plainly be seen from this figure, more generally, the age-participation profile has not been stable for women. In 1971, 20-year-old women differ from 30-year-old women in more ways than their age. Being 10 years younger, they were also born into a society with different economic and social conditions surrounding women's work. Based on a single cross-section, it is difficult to disentangle the "pure" effect of age from a birth **cohort effect**.

The only way to reliably isolate the true effect of age is to track a specific cohort over time, across censuses. With the combined censuses, we observe the true age trajectory at 10-year intervals. For women born in 1951, we observe them five times: at age 20 (in 1971), age 30 (in 1981), age 40 (in 1991), age 50 (in 2001), and age 60 (in 2011). Figure 4.1 shows the implied participation-age path for two different birth cohorts estimated in this manner. For each cohort, the labour force participation rate generally increases with age (until retirement). Women's profiles are, thus, shaped similarly to men's, though with a slower entry into the labour force at younger ages. The figure also clearly shows that the participation rate of 30-year-old women increased dramatically between 1971 and 1991. There was less change between 1991 and 2011. To the extent that the cross-section profiles stabilize, we can also see that the smaller cohort effects lead to a closer correspondence between the cross-section and actual age profiles, as demonstrated by a more recent birth cohort (e.g., born in 1961).

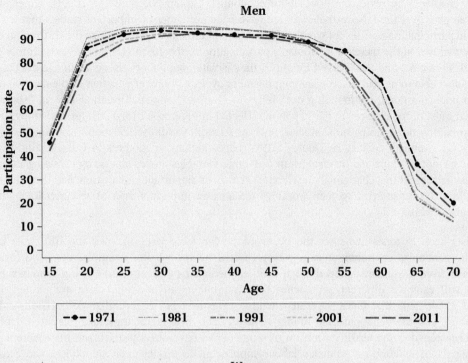

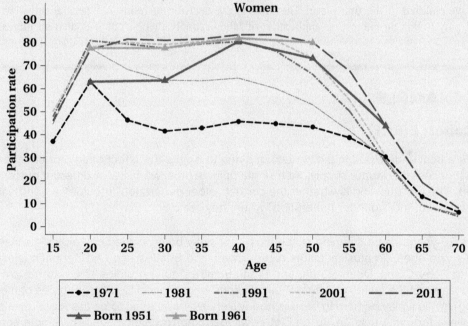

Figure 4.1 Age–Labour Force Participation Profiles

Each panel shows the participation rates of men or women by age, for five years: 1971, 1981, 1991, 2001, and 2011. The men's panel shows a strong inverted-U-shaped relationship between age and participation, following the traditional life-cycle pattern. The women's panel is more complicated because of the shift of the profiles over time, especially from 1971. The cross-section profiles from the earlier censuses (dashed lines) do a poor job of predicting behaviour because of the confounding of age and cohort effects. The "actual" age effects are indicated by the thicker lines for two selected cohorts (born in 1951 and born in 1961).

SOURCE: Based on data from Statistics Canada: 1971, 1981, 1991, and 2001 Census of Population, and the 2011 National Household Survey. While we report these as single-age and birth-year groups, they are based on 5-year bins (15-19, 20-24, …, 65-69, 70-74).

The focus of this chapter is on reviewing how labour economists explain the pure age effects, rather than on why these effects may be changing over time. Nevertheless, there have been a number of important studies that try to document and explain this shift in participation profiles for women. Beaudry and Lemieux (1999) analyze the shifting profiles for Canadian women and the slowdown in the increase in women's participation in the 1990s. Using methods similar to those sketched in connection with Figure 4.1 and the Worked Example, they isolate pure cohort effects from age effects. While it is more difficult, they are also able to net out macroeconomic business cycle, or time, effects that also cause the observations from different years to bounce around, confounding our ability to observe "long-run" relationships in "short-run" data. Their results suggest that most of the changes in participation reflected in Figures 4.1 (and 2.2) are driven by (permanent) cohort effects. As for explaining these shifts, most studies, such as Claudia Goldin's 1990 book examining changes in women's participation over the twentieth century or Dooley's 1994 paper looking at mothers in Canada, find that the increase in participation rates cannot be explained by changes in economic variables alone; that is, by changing incentives for women to work. These results suggest that changing "preferences" remain an important explanation, and the nature of these changes (e.g., in the attitudes toward married women working) remains an important area of research for both economists and sociologists (see also, Exhibit 4.1).

Labour economists seek to assess whether the observed labour force patterns over the life cycle can be explained by changes in the economic environment in a way predicted by theory. For example, does the inverted-U shape of participation derive from a similarly shaped wage profile, mediated by an upward-sloping labour supply function? In this chapter, we will examine different approaches to this problem. In addition, there are (at least) three important life cycle–related phenomena that merit separate attention. The first is the school-work decision—when and whether to acquire education, and the commensurate timing of work. This is a major topic and the subject of the chapters on human capital. The second is the fertility decision of women. We have already discussed the theoretical apparatus used to analyze the impact of children on women's labour supply, but in this chapter we explore the economic aspects of the decision to have children in the first place. The third is the decision to retire, or "permanently" withdraw from the labour force. Not only is this an interesting application of labour supply theory, but it is also an increasingly important public policy issue.

WORKED EXAMPLE

What Is a Cohort Effect?

Cohort effects are best understood in the context of trying to isolate the effect of age, or time, for the evolution of a variable (not necessarily labour supply). At a single point in time, we observe different outcomes for people of different ages. The key question is whether the current "older generation" provides a good estimate of what the outcomes will be for the "younger generation" when they are older.

- Will today's 20-year-olds be listening to the music currently being played on "oldies" or classic rock radio stations? As one ages, do musical tastes move toward the Beatles and Led Zeppelin (classic rock), and, ultimately, to Perry Como, Dean Martin, and Frank Sinatra ("golden oldies")? Or do the playlists of these radio stations reflect the tastes of different generations who listened to different types of music when they were young? While it may be hard to believe, today's oldies music used to be the "cool" music of the young. Hard to believe though it may be, Justin Bieber will be tomorrow's oldies music. Simple comparisons at a single point in time by age can result in misleading conclusions regarding the aging process.

- Fifty-year-olds (usually) live in bigger houses than do 30-year-olds. Should today's 30-year-olds expect to live in as big houses when they are 50? Perhaps obviously, it depends on whether today's 30-year-olds will be as rich when they are 50 as the current crop of 50-year-olds. If current 50-year-olds come from a richer generation, then maybe today's 50-year-olds are not a good basis for predicting the kind of house a 30-year-old can expect to own in 20 years.

Roughly speaking, differences in the lifetime trajectories of different generations—birth cohorts—are what we define as cohort effects.

Consider the hypothetical data in the table showing the labour force participation rates for women as they age through their 20s. The true behaviour reflected in this table is that participation increases by one percentage point per year between the ages 25 and 30 (for a total of 5 percentage points). This is true for both cohorts. The older cohort of the two had a participation rate of 75 percent at age 25 (in the year 2000) and 80 percent at age 30 (in the year 2005). The younger cohort has a participation rate of 80 percent at age 25 (in the year 2005) and 85 percent at age 30 (in the year 2010). Now imagine a researcher with only one data set, from 2005, trying to estimate how labour supply changes between ages 25 and 30. In 2005, both cohorts have participation rates of 80 percent, implying there is *no* increase in labour supply between ages 25 and 30. This is the wrong answer! The shifting profiles of participation make it impossible to be sure that differences in participation at a point in time reflect true differences in age. In this example, the younger cohort has a permanently higher participation rate than the older cohort, *for a given age*, and the implied cohort effect is 5 percent. It is only with repeated observations of the same cohort that we can disentangle the pure effect of age from other factors correlated with age (i.e., cohort of birth). Note that cohort effects do not have to be constant over the age profile; it is entirely possible that two cohorts differ in behaviour at age 30 but are the same at age 50.

In this example, we also simplified matters by neglecting a third possible confounding factor: time effects. Time (or year) effects would further cloud the picture. What if participation rates in 2005 were unusually high, possibly because of a booming economy? This would make it difficult to isolate the true age effects, even with two cross-sections and repeated observations on the same cohort. Other methods would have to be employed in order to filter out the year-to-year fluctuations from the normal effect of aging.

Observed in	2000	2005	2010
Older Cohort, born in 1975:			
Age	25	**30**	35
Participation Rate	75%	**80%**	85%
Younger Cohort, born 1980:			
Age	20	**25**	30
Participation Rate	75%	**80%**	85%

EXHIBIT 4.1

Where Do Cohort Effects Come From?

In Figure 4.1, 60 percent of women born in 1951 worked when they were 20 (in 1971). Women born just ten years later, in 1961, had a participation rate 15 points higher! Why did their age profile shift so dramatically? More generally, why did the participation rate of women rise over the twentieth century?

According to the labour supply model described in Chapter 2, we would expect at least some of the reason to be changes in economic circumstances, especially higher wages for women. Maybe husbands (or potential husbands) had lower incomes, and the adverse income effect led more women to work? Claudia Goldin (1990) argues that, in fact, economic variables in the labour supply model explain very little of the evolution of female labour supply. More important is the evolution of *men's* preferences, and broader social attitudes toward women's work. Goldin (1995) outlines one such channel that possibly helps explain women's increased participation over time, as well as differences in participation between countries (as shown in Table 2.1). As an economy develops, the labour market opportunities improve for both men and women. However, most of these new jobs are in low-status industrial positions. Social stigma against men with working wives imposes a psychic cost on families with women working; men are viewed as poor providers if their wives must work in factories. Improved incomes for men, thus, permit more women to withdraw from agriculture, but the stigma associated with factory work keeps them at home. It is only when white-collar, "respectable" jobs emerge that married women's participation becomes acceptable. Less stigma is attached to husbands whose wives are pursuing a career, especially if the job requires at least secondary-level education. It, therefore, wasn't enough for women's opportunities (and wages) to improve, but the nature of work and the social acceptability of their working did also.

More-direct evidence of the importance of preferences (or social attitudes) is provided by research on the effect of World War II on the economic role of women. During the war, large numbers of women entered the labour force, replacing the men in factories who had enlisted to serve in the armed forces. For most women, this increase in participation, however, was temporary; by the time these women were in their 50s, their labour force behaviour was the same as that of previous generations (Acemoglu, Autor, and Lyle 2004). But it had a lasting, *indirect* effect. Fernandez, Fogli, and Olivetti (2004) extend the work of Acemoglu, Autor, and Lyle (2004), exploiting cross-state variation in the enlistment rate of men in the United States and the resulting variation of the work patterns of women during the war. They find that the impact of women working during the war was the changed attitudes of their daughters and, especially, of their sons toward women working outside the home. Fernandez, Fogli, and Olivetti (2004) focus on the cohort of women born between 1930 and 1935 who were too young to be directly affected by the war. This is the first cohort to have a permanent increase in lifetime labour supply; that is, to be working more at age 50 than previous generations did. The increase in participation was largest for women born in states where enlistment rates for men during the war were highest. Furthermore, men whose mothers worked during the war were significantly more likely to be married to a working wife, controlling for other economic factors. It, thus, seems that the war altered the attitudes of families toward the economic role of women; being a working mom made it more acceptable for her son to marry a working woman.

More recently, Goldin and Olivetti (2013) show that an important subset of women did have their labour supply permanently and directly altered by Word War II; that is, higher-educated women who worked at white-collar jobs during the war were more likely to continue working after the war was over.

This is just one example of the process by which preferences evolve, and it is one piece of the puzzle of why the role of women changed so dramatically at the end of the twentieth century, or why women's roles vary so much across otherwise similar countries.

LO1, 2   Dynamic Life-Cycle Models

There are two distinct approaches we could take in devising a theory of life cycle labour supply. The objective of the exercise is similar to that in Chapter 2: a model relating labour supply at various points in time to the economic environment over time; specifically, wages (and prices) and other income. From such a model, we could compare theoretical labour supply for individuals facing different wages, either at a point in time, or over their entire lives.

The first approach would treat an individual's life cycle labour supply as a sequence of static labour supply problems. Each period, the individual would respond to the economic environment that exists in that period. Such an approach would allow us to use our existing models to make predictions; for example, as long as the substitution effect dominated, individuals would work most when their wages were highest. If income effects were large, this prediction would be modified accordingly. While this approach is satisfactory for a number of problems, it ignores the possibility that individuals may be forward looking. If individuals look to the future, they may react today to changes in their anticipated wage path, or to other changes to their future economic environment. Similarly, they may react differently to wage changes that are temporary versus those expected to be permanent.

For these reasons, economists have devised a theoretically more appealing dynamic framework. It turns out that this framework is little more than an extension of the static model we have already described. The basic idea is that individuals plan out their lifetime labour supply, given their expected lifetime environment. Given this long-run perspective, their labour supply decision in any one time period is connected to their decisions in all time periods; today's labour supply depends on today's wage and income, but also on the wage rates and income in the future. One important implication is that substitution effects from unexpected, temporary wage changes may be larger than static labour supply responses—small changes in the current wage affect the price of leisure but have only small effects on lifetime income.

For the simplest version of the model, we assume that an individual lives and potentially works for N periods, and that there is no uncertainty regarding the values of economic variables in the future. As it turns out, very little is changed by incorporating uncertainty into this framework. The person is assumed to have preferences, not just regarding "consumption" and "leisure" today, but over consumption and leisure in each of her N periods of life. We can represent these preferences by the utility function

$$u = U\left(C_1, C_2, \ \ldots, \ C_N, \ \ell_1, \ell_2, \ \ldots, \ \ell_N\right)$$

The individual is then assumed to maximize this utility function, choosing her optimal consumption and leisure in each period, subject to her expected lifetime budget constraint. For simplicity, let us assume that there is no nonlabour income, that the price of consumption is constant, and that the individual knows that she will face wages of $W_1, W_2, \ldots W_N$ over her lifetime. What does her budget constraint look like?

For ease of exposition, consider the case where there are only two periods (today and tomorrow, or this year and next year). Lifetime labour supply will be summarized by H_1 and H_2, hours worked in each period. It seems reasonable to imagine that lifetime consumption should equal lifetime earnings, or

$$C_1 + C_2 = W_1 H_1 + W_2 H_2$$

This implies that if the consumer chose to do so, she could consume everything in the first period; that is, $C_1 = W_1 H_1 + W_2 H_2$. This assumes that the person can, without cost, transfer resources from the future to the present, essentially borrowing her future income to finance current consumption. Try doing this at a bank! A bank will almost certainly charge interest on such loans. Similarly, it is unlikely that our consumer-worker would postpone consumption (or save) unless offered interest on her savings.

Assume that the individual can borrow and lend freely at the interest rate r. The correct relationship between income and consumption is actually given by

$$C_1 + \frac{C_2}{(1+r)} = W_1 H_1 + \frac{W_2 H_2}{(1+r)}$$

so that the **present value** of consumption equals the present value of income.[1] That this is the correct representation can be seen by considering what consumption in period 2 would be if the individual saved or borrowed. First, consider an individual who saved some of her period 1 earnings to consume in period 2. Her consumption in period 2 would then be her income in period 2, plus the principal and interest from her savings ($W_1 H_1 - C_1$) from period 1:

$$C_2 = W_2 H_2 + (1 + r)(W_1 H_1 - C_1)$$

This is a simple rearrangement of the present value representation. If she borrowed on the basis of future income to finance consumption in period 1, her period 2 consumption would be equal to her period 2 income, less the principal and interest on the loan ($C_1 - W_1 H_1$):

$$C_2 = W_2 H_2 + (1 + r)(C_1 - W_1 H_1)$$

This is also a simple rearrangement of the present value formula.

We can rewrite the budget constraint in more conventional terms of consumption and leisure:

$$C_1 + \frac{C_2}{(1+r)} + W_1\ell_1 + \frac{W_2\ell_2}{(1+r)} = W_1T + \frac{W_2T}{(1+r)}$$

In terms of N periods, we merely extend the formula to N periods so that the discounted present value of consumption and leisure is equal to the discounted present value of the lifetime labour endowment.

The resulting labour supply functions give labour supply in any period as a function of wages in each of the time periods, as well as interest rates and the present value of lifetime resources. The income and substitution effects that form the basis of comparative statics exercises with these **dynamic labour supply** functions are more complicated than the simple static model. MaCurdy (1981) deals with many of these complications, and some of the simpler ones can be illustrated with a diagram based on that source.

Figure 4.2 illustrates two hypothetical age-wage profiles indicating how wages may at first increase over the life cycle, and then decline later. The higher profile depicts the situation where an individual gets a greater wage at each and every age. The small "blip" in the higher profile illustrates the situation where an individual receives a temporary, one-time only, **unanticipated wage increase** at age t. There are three possible sources of wage changes occurring in this diagram, and each has different income and substitution effects, thus leading to different labour supply responses. For illustrative purposes, the three wage changes—from A to B, B to C, and C to D—are assumed to be of the same magnitude, as illustrated by the same vertical distance.

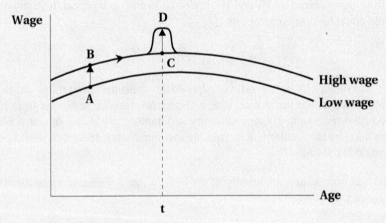

Figure 4.2 Dynamic Life Cycle Wage Changes

The labour supply response depends on how much the income effect of higher lifetime earnings offsets the substitution effect of the higher value of time. A permanent increase in the wage profile (A → B) generates the largest income effect, while a fully anticipated rise in wages (B → C) yields no change in lifetime income, and no income effect. A transitory (temporary) increase in wages (C → D) generates a small (intermediate-level) income effect.

NOTES:

A → B, permanent unanticipated wage increase (smallest labour supply response)

B → C, evolutionary anticipated wage increase (largest labour supply response)

C → D, transitory unanticipated wage increase (medium labour supply response)

Points A and B and the difference between them reflect two people whose wages differ by a permanent amount at each and every age in their life cycle. That difference would be associated with conventional income and substitution effects working in opposite directions. That is, the high-wage individual at B would have a higher opportunity cost of leisure and, hence, work more (substitution effect). However, that individual would also have a higher expected lifetime income (a higher present value of the lifetime labour endowment) and, thus, be able to afford more leisure and less work (income effect). Since the income and substitution effects work in the opposite directions, the labour supply of the high-wage individual may be greater or less than the labour supply of the lower-wage individual over their lifetimes.

The wage increase from B to C along an individual's given wage profile is an **evolutionary wage change** associated with aging over the life cycle. To the extent that such wage changes are fully anticipated and known with certainty, they will not create a leisure-inducing income effect as they occur. Rather, the income effect is spread over the life cycle, independent of when the wage change occurs. Basically, because it is already accounted for in the consumer's optimization problem (in the present value of the lifetime labour endowment), a fully anticipated wage increase is "no news" to the consumer-worker, so there is no adjustment to a change in resources. The evolutionary wage change, however, does have a substitution effect, making leisure more expensive (hence, inducing work) in the years of peak earnings in one's career. The substitution effect essentially reflects that a forward-thinking consumer will buy leisure when it is cheapest, or work more when the returns to doing so are highest. Because there is no leisure-inducing income effect, the labour supply response to anticipated evolutionary, life cycle wage changes (termed the **intertemporal substitution** response) will be larger than the labour supply response at a given age (i.e., not adding up over the life cycle) to permanent, unanticipated differences, like the wage profile shift from A to B, the latter labour supply response being muted by the leisure-inducing income effect.

WORKED EXAMPLE

Comparing Lifetime Wage Profiles and Labour Supply

In the intertemporal labour supply model, we imagine an individual making a lifetime plan of how much to work each year. Labour supply in a given year will depend on individual attitudes toward work, total lifetime income, and the wage in one year versus another. For concreteness, consider an individual planning her labour supply between ages 25 and 65. To keep the numbers simpler, let's also ignore the distinction between a salary and a wage. Think of the "wage" as the annual earnings (or salary) that would arise if the person worked full time (2000 hours) for a year. Assume her starting wage is $60,000 per year from age 25, and is expected to grow at 2.5 percent per year until her last year of potential work, age 65. At any given age (say, 40) her wage will, thus, be 2.5 percent higher than in the previous year; in this specific case, her wage would be $89,070 at age 40, versus $86,898 at age 39. If her intertemporal wage elasticity was 0.1, then we would expect her to work 0.1 × 2.5 percent = 0.25 percent more hours at age 40 compared to 39. This would be her plan, unless something changed. (This corresponds to the movement from B to C in Figure 4.2.)

Now, confront her with an alternative wage profile: starting at $70,000 at age 25 and growing (as before) at 2.5 percent until retirement. In this case, at age 40 she would be paid a wage of $101,381. How much more would she work with this wage at age 40 than she would under the previous scenario, where she was paid only $89,070? Will she work more at all? The answer depends on offsetting income and substitution effects. In the first case, with an interest rate of 5 percent, the present value of lifetime earnings is calculated as $1,506,430.24 (use a spreadsheet!). In the second scenario, with the same 5 percent interest rate, the present value of lifetime (potential) earnings is $1,757,501.95. This is $251,071.71, or 16.7 percent, higher than with a starting salary of only $60,000. The second wage profile, thus, makes her a lot richer. So, on the one hand, the substitution effect of the higher wage should lead her to work more. On the other hand, she might choose to use some of her higher earnings to buy leisure, and actually work less over her life cycle (and at age 40). A permanent wage increase, thus, has a significant income effect that offsets the substitution effect. (This corresponds to the movement from A to B in Figure 4.2.)

Finally, imagine she is confronted with a third profile. This is the same as the first one, except there is a transitory wage increase at age 40, to $90,000. After that, the profile reverts back to its previous trajectory. The substitution effect is pretty clear; she should work even more at age 40 than before. Offsetting this, however, is a small income effect; the present value of her lifetime wages is $1421.11 higher than under the first scenario. This is a pretty small change in lifetime wealth (compared to a base of $1.5 million). But if leisure is a normal good, she will still work slightly less than if there was no income effect, and this income effect will dampen the substitution effect induced by the transitory (temporary) wage increase. (This corresponds to the movement from C to D in Figure 4.2.)

The wage difference between C and D represents a transitory, unanticipated, one-time wage difference, except at age t, between two individuals whose wage profiles are otherwise similar (both high-wage profiles). The difference may be associated, for example, with a period of overtime pay that is not expected to be repeated. This wage difference will have the usual work-inducing substitution effect at year t, since the income forgone by not working is very high. There will also be a small leisure-inducing income effect spread over the life cycle, associated with the fact that the individual with the higher wage at D will have a slightly higher lifetime wealth because of the transitory wage difference. The present value of the lifetime labour endowment is only slightly affected by the one-time-only wage change. Because the wage difference is transitory and not permanent, however, the labour supply response to the transitory wage difference at age t will be larger than the labour supply response to a permanent wage difference, as between A and B, at age t, because the latter has a stronger, more permanent leisure-inducing income effect. Basically, individuals with the higher **transitory wage** at D will be able to afford to work slightly less over their life cycle; however, they will likely work more at the particular age t to take advantage of the high, temporary wage.

Clearly, the three sources of wage differences outlined above have different effects associated with whether the wage differences are permanent or temporary and anticipated or unanticipated. The different income effects, in turn, imply different labour supply responses to the wage differences. The anticipated evolutionary change from B to C has a pure substitution effect and is not offset by any leisure-inducing income effect. Hence, it will have the largest positive labour supply response to a wage change. The transitory wage difference between C and D has mainly a work-inducing substitution effect. However, there is a mild offsetting leisure-inducing income effect spread over the life cycle. In contrast, the permanent wage difference between A and B, at a given age, has a larger offsetting leisure-inducing income effect, and hence, it will have the smallest labour supply response to a wage increase (in fact, the response may be negative). The labour supply responsiveness to a wage change, therefore, may be ordered as the largest response stemming from an evolutionary change (pure substitution effect), a medium response emanating from a transitory wage change (mainly substitution but slight offsetting income effect), and the smallest (possibly negative) response emanating from a permanent wage change (reflecting offsetting substitution and income effects).

Clearly, in a dynamic life-cycle context, the substitution and income effects emanating from a wage change can vary, depending on whether the wage change is permanent or temporary and anticipated or unanticipated. This, in turn, means that the labour supply response will differ, depending upon the source of the wage increase in a dynamic life-cycle setting. While theoretically important, the life-cycle model has been called upon to explain a variety of labour market phenomena, ranging from the pure age-related topics that we are about to discuss, to year-to-year variations in employment at the macro level. Overall, the empirical performance of the model remains disappointing (see Card, 1994, for a review of the evidence), but the theoretical issues raised, and the insights the model offers over the simple static model, make the life-cycle model hard to set aside.

Household Production and the Evolution of Preferences

In the previous discussion, we noted that labour supply and consumption over one's life depend on preferences over the timing of work and consumption over the life cycle, as well as the trajectory of wages and prices. These preferences may vary systematically with age, helping to explain why people work more in their "prime" than when young or old. Changes in preferences, as opposed to wages, may also explain, for example, why women's labour supply increases from age 25 to 40. And we have also seen the potential role played by preferences in explaining the shifts in the profiles over time (e.g., generating cohort effects as described in Exhibit 4.1).

However, it is somewhat unsatisfying to explain so much as changing preferences, which are inherently unobservable. For this reason, economists have developed more detailed models of labour supply that incorporate a richer set of economic factors possibly explaining what we otherwise relegate to preferences in the simple labour supply model. Consider again the key condition for utility maximization in the labour-leisure choice model:

$$MRS = W$$

The MRS is the marginal rate of substitution between consumption and leisure, and W is the wage rate. As we explained in Chapter 2, the MRS is a person's subjective valuation of an hour of leisure in terms of consumption, and it is defined by how much consumption she would give up for another hour of leisure. We also discussed some of the factors that might lead to a higher or lower MRS—notably, shifts in preferences. For women, we highlighted the factors that affect the value of their time at home, and that leisure encompassed all nonmarket time, including time spent doing housework.

Perhaps the simplest modification of the basic utility maximization framework is that offered by exponents of the **household production model** introduced by Gary Becker (1965, 1976) and Kelvin Lancaster (1966). This perspective emphasizes that households are producers as well as consumers, and that the time of household members is an important ingredient in the production of household goods and services, and, ultimately, in the economic well-being of the household. The household production view underscores the misnomer "leisure" as it has historically been used in the income-leisure choice framework. Rather, household time consists of pure leisure, household work, and other activities that facilitate consumption (through household production). The household's allocation of its scarce time resource, then, is the focus of the household production function approach. This approach focuses on the technological considerations of production of household-consumed goods and services, instead of relying so heavily on the "black box" of differences in tastes to explain certain elements of behaviour. It extends the explanatory power of consumer demand analysis, primarily by expanding the concept of the space "price" of a good to include the time costs of obtaining utility from the good (or its processing).

Basic Framework

As with the conventional utility maximization model, households obtain utility from the consumption of goods and services, $Z = Z_1, Z_2, Z_3, \ldots, Z_n$:

$$u = f\left(Z_1, Z_2, \ldots, Z_n\right)$$

The main innovation is to recognize that these "fully processed" goods and services, or commodities, in turn depend on a more fundamental set of market-purchased goods, $X = X_1, X_2, \ldots, X_k$, which are combined with household time, h, to produce Z. A household production function summarizes how household time is combined with market-purchased inputs to produce the utility-generating final goods:

$$Z_i = g_i\left(X_1, X_2, \ldots, X_k, h_i\right)$$

The X_i are market-purchased goods (or services) and h_i is the time spent producing Z_i with X. The main point is that leisure is not a purely separate good, and that nonmarket time (time spent not working outside the home) is divided into a number of household production tasks and is an input in producing utility from consumption.

This framework underscores the technological requirement that time is an input into production of household consumption. Some goods, like a store-bought chocolate cake, will require very little processing by the household, and the distinction between X_i and Z_i is minor. Others will require more effort. A well-maintained lawn (a Z_i) requires various purchased inputs, X, such as seed, perhaps chemicals, water, a lawn mower, gasoline, among others, as well as considerable labour input from the homeowner. We denote such goods as relatively **time-intensive commodities** as opposed to those, like store-bought chocolate cake, which are **goods-intensive commodities**.[2] In this model, we account for the fact that there is economic activity associated with turning the X into Z, and, moreover, that the nature of this activity may affect labour market behaviour.

The potential value of the household production model can be seen through a simple example. Assume that a woman has preferences over food and leisure, so that the components of Z are nutrition and rest.

$$u = f\left(\text{nutrition, rest}\right)$$

Nutrition can be attained either through purchasing precooked food or raw food, so that the market goods (Xs) are the two different types of food. Assume that raw food needs to be prepared at home, and that it takes time to cook food so that it is edible. For simplicity, assume it takes d units of preparation time, h, to produce one unit of edible nutrition, Z.

The consumer, thus, has to decide how much precooked and raw food to buy, as well as how much time to spend in one of three activities: work outside the home (at wage W), leisure (rest), and food preparation (h). This **tripartite choice** is essentially the same as the one in Chapter 2, except that we now subdivide nonmarket time into pure leisure (or rest) and housework. We can use this basic model to explore the impact of changes in the woman's economic environment on how she divides time between the three activities, as well as on the combination of market goods.

Again, for simplicity, we can approximate the various prices that the woman faces for the three goods:

Price of Leisure (W)

This is the same as the standard model—an hour of rest comes at the opportunity cost of an hour of potential labour earnings, at a wage rate of W, which could be used to purchase goods and services (in this case cooked or raw food).

Price of a Unit of Nutrition from Raw Food ($P_R + W_d$)

More generally, the price of nutrition (Z) from raw food could be a more complicated function of the amount of raw food being prepared, the amount of precooked food being used, the stock of kitchen appliances, and potential help from family members. For expositional purposes, we can imagine (on the margin) the price of a unit of nutrition is some value of raw food (P_R) plus the value of the time it takes to prepare the food, W × d. The cost of obtaining nutrition from raw food, thus, depends on the technology of cooking (captured by the time input, d) as well as the opportunity cost of time, W.

Price of a Unit of Nutrition from Precooked Food (P_C)

The ready-to-eat food arrives at the table for a purchase price of P_C. The main innovation in this model is that we explicitly recognize that part of the "price" of nutrition derived from raw food is the time cost for preparation. The opportunity cost of an hour of preparation is, like leisure, an hour's wage.

Comparative Statics

Each price change will generate income and substitution effects, which may offset or reinforce each other. In this discussion, we will ignore for simplicity that all the variables are determined simultaneously and that the total effects of changes may be more complicated. Our main objective is to provide a sketch of the theoretical "flavour" of the model. For each price change, we could evaluate the impact on the overall consumption of nutrition, the composition of nutrition (prepared versus raw food), time spent cooking, leisure (rest), and labour supply. Again, for simplicity, we highlight only the more interesting results.

A Decrease in the Price of Precooked Food (P_C)

This entails a reduction in the relative price of the goods-intensive good, or an increase in the relative price of the labour-intensive good. The substitution effect should, thus, induce the person to substitute away from raw toward precooked food. The composition of nutrition would, thus, change. The income effect of the lower price would lead to an increase in the consumption of all normal goods. Therefore, the income and substitution effects both point to higher consumption of prepared food. The effect is ambiguous for raw food, but if the substitution effect dominates, less raw food would be purchased, and less time would be spent cooking. If leisure is also a normal good, we might also expect this change to lead to an increase in leisure, as less time is spent in food preparation.

A Decrease in the Price of Raw Food (P_R)

A decrease in the price of the labour-intensive good would have the opposite effect. The income and substitution effects would both lead to a tilt toward more home-cooked food. The extra time needed to prepare this would have to come from leisure or work.

An Increase in the Wage Rate (W)

This is where the home production model is most helpful, as it explicitly recognizes that the opportunity cost of time affects the composition of demand for time-intensive or goods-intensive consumption. If the wage rises, then the opportunity cost of time spent cooking rises, and the relative price of raw food–based nutrition rises. The income and substitution effects both suggest an increase in the demand for precooked food; the higher wage makes the woman wealthier, permitting her to buy more of everything, and the higher wage makes home cooking relatively more expensive. Clearly, a richer version of this model can help explain the evolution of the demand for a variety of home services, traditionally carried out by stay-at-home women, in terms of rising labour market opportunities for women (i.e., increases in W). Rising wages will tilt demand away from time-intensive goods.

A Decrease in Preparation Time (d)

What happens if there is a labour-saving device (dishwasher, microwave oven, or other home appliance) that makes home cooking a snap, reducing the time required to generate a given amount of nutrition? Or, what if the husband is more willing to pitch in, reducing the wife's required time input? A reduction of d will reduce the relative price of home-cooked food (versus store-bought). The substitution effect of this price change will have the wife producing more home-cooked meals, but at a lower time cost. The income effect may allow her to "cash in" some of the time savings in terms of greater leisure. But the largest effect may be to increase the real wage for the woman—she can more easily turn her market income into nutrition for her family. This increase in the returns to work (relative to cooking at home) may lead to higher female labour supply, depending on the income and substitution effects, and higher family preferences for leisure versus nutrition. Indeed, Greenwood, Seshadri, and Yorukoglu (2005) argue that improvements in household production technology (i.e., reduction in the time cost of home production usually performed by women) help explain the joint evolution of the demand for household durables and women's labour force participation.

Discussion and Some Implications

The commodities that provide the ultimate source of satisfaction, generally, require both time and goods in order to yield utility. This observation has significant implications. If real wages increase, the demand for goods-intensive commodities will increase at a relatively rapid rate due to the fact that the income and substitution effects reinforce each other. The consequences of this tendency are evident in many aspects of life: the growth of fast-food outlets and prepared foods; attempts to combine activities, sometimes with additional goods input (e.g., jogging with iPods instead of sitting down while listening to music); and even the choice of forms of exercise (the popularity of jogging compared to walking). If real wages rise in the future, households will be driven to more goods-intensive as opposed to time-intensive forms of consumption.

The household production function perspective has other implications that may not have been obvious from the conventional exposition of household commodity demand and labour supply behaviour. It reminds us, for example, that the consumption decisions of households depend not only upon their income and relative commodity prices, but also upon factor prices (especially the opportunity cost of their time) and factor productivity. Also, households with an efficient household production function have a larger opportunity, or choice, set than those with less efficient production functions. Such households are potentially better off.

Emphasis on the household as a producer as well as a consumer also reminds us of the importance in household consumptions and time allocation decisions of various laws of production. The principle of comparative advantage emphasizes that it may be economically efficient for different members of the household to specialize in their respective areas of comparative advantage. This may mean, for example, that it is economically efficient for one party to specialize in labour-market tasks and the other to specialize in household tasks, depending upon their relative earning power in the labour market and productivity in household tasks. Such specialization may be artificially induced, however, if female market wages are reduced because of discrimination. This can lead to a vicious circle whereby females specialize in household tasks because their market wages are lower due to discrimination, and this household specialization prevents them from acquiring the labour market experience that would give them a potential comparative advantage to specialize in labour market tasks.

Economies of scale may also be an important law of production that has relevance to the concept of the household production function. For example, the average *per person* cost of preparing a meal may be high for a single person but not for a family of six; hence, inducing the single person to enter co-operative arrangements or to eat more often in restaurants. Similarly, the extra cost of watching an additional child may be small once the fixed costs are incurred for watching one child; hence, the emergence of co-operative daycare arrangements. Also, within the same family, the extra cost of raising a third child may be less than that of the second child, which in turn is less than that of the first child; hence, the rationale for per capita poverty measures that do not simply divide family income by the number of family members.

The household production function approach also emphasizes the importance of the family as a decision-making unit and, thus, the importance of joint decision making amongst family members with respect to various elements of behaviour. For example, the decisions to get married, participate in labour-market activities, and have children are all intricately related for all family members. This also means, for example, that a change in the wage rate or price of time for one family member may affect not only his own allocation decisions, but also the decisions of other family members. Formally stated, cross-price effects can be important across family members.

The importance of allocating time over the life cycle is also highlighted in the household production function approach. For example, it may be economically rational to engage in time-intensive activities when the opportunity cost of time is low, perhaps because productivity is lower at certain stages in the life cycle. Thus, it may be efficient to work intensively and for long hours during the peak-earnings years of one's career and to engage in more leisure time when one's earnings are lower. For example, it may be efficient for students to take time off for time-intensive travel before they have established a career in the labour market, or for older workers to partake in early or partial retirement programs once they have passed the peak earnings years of their careers.

Lastly, from a methodological point of view, the household production function perspective de-emphasizes the importance of tastes and preferences in determining behaviour. Rather, the emphasis is on more objective constraints faced by households in their consumption and production decisions.

Fertility and Childbearing

As we saw in Figure 4.1, women's participation is lowest during their childbearing years, suggesting that issues of **fertility** and family formation are important in understanding women's labour supply over the life cycle. In our discussion of labour force participation, we addressed the impact of children and child care costs on the value of women's nonmarket time and their reservation wages. However, children are not randomly brought to doorsteps by storks but usually are the result of some degree of family planning. It is reasonable to imagine that economic considerations may affect the decision of whether and how many children to have. Certainly, in planning life cycle labour supply, women must consider the interrelationships between education, work, and having children.

Largely on the basis of the pioneering work of Becker (1960) and Mincer (1963), economists have applied the principles of consumer demand theory to the decision to have children.[3] The more sophisticated analyses of fertility behaviour are cast in a dynamic setting, much like the one outlined above. A fully dynamic setting allows one to account for the intertemporal nature of the fertility decision, including the possible consequences on future wages of withdrawal from the labour force. A dynamic setting also allows one to look at questions regarding the timing and spacing of births, rather than just the number of children a woman may choose to have. We will restrict ourselves to an overview of the simpler aspects of the economics of fertility, illustrating the potential importance of economic variables in affecting women's labour supply during the childbearing part of their life cycle.

EXHIBIT 4.2

The Pill and Women's Careers

While Figure 4.1 shows the shifting age profiles and associated cohort effects for women's labour force participation, it hides dramatic changes in the nature of women's work. Women have moved steadily into professional careers like law, medicine, and dentistry. Several factors are behind these shifts, but what credit can be given to the birth control pill (The Pill)? *The Economist* (December 1999, p. 102) suggests that oral contraceptives may be considered the technological development "that defines the 20th century," because of their liberating power for women's choices. But why would The Pill make such a difference to women's career paths?

Claudia Goldin and Lawrence Katz (2002) argue that the primary influence was in university dormitories. They explore the role of The Pill in U.S. women's college and marriage decisions from a variety of angles. It was approved for use by the U.S. FDA in 1960 and quickly adopted by most young, married women. Throughout the 1960s, married women used it and reduced their fertility. But the expectations of reduced fertility did not immediately induce young, single women to enrol in education-intensive occupations. Goldin and Katz argue, instead, that it was not until single women could obtain The Pill that they began making these educational investments. For most of the 1960s, it was difficult for single women to get The Pill; there were restrictions on the ability of doctors to prescribe birth control pills to single women below the age of majority, 21 years old at the time. But in 1971, the age of majority was lowered to 18 by constitutional amendment, with the primary motivation of extending the vote to Vietnam draft-age men. The adoption of this amendment was staggered across states, and there is a striking correlation between the time a state lowered its age of majority and the time single women in that state started using The Pill. Furthermore, there is a correlation between these dates and increases in the enrolment of women in professional programs, as well as the delay in marriage by young women, facilitating the pursuit of professional careers.

So why would birth control for single women affect their schooling decisions? Goldin and Katz highlight two channels. First, it reduced the possibility of unwanted pregnancies and allowed women and men to have premarital sex without jeopardizing the woman's educational plans. Second, eliminating the stark choice between sex (and early marriage) versus a career, it allowed women to postpone marriage. This had a ripple effect through the "marriage market." Prior to The Pill, a delay of marriage meant that a woman would face a smaller pool of potential husbands, as many men had already partnered with women not pursuing professional careers. But the ability to have sex and delay marriage meant that fewer women were married right out of university, leaving a deeper pool of potential husbands a few years later. Thus, Goldin and Katz argue, the primary liberating effect of The Pill on women's careers was to facilitate the combination of premarital sex with a university education.

More recently, Martha Bailey (2006) has extended Goldin and Katz's line of research, exploring whether The Pill affected women's labour force behaviour more generally, not just for those women in college or university. She confirms that The Pill had a significant impact on the labour supply of younger women in the broader population by delaying their fertility and increasing their labour supply. This increase in labour supply appears to have been permanent, persisting through the life cycle. Her results go some way in explaining cohort effects, like those observed in Figure 4.1, for cohorts of women reaching their 20s in the late 1960s and early 1970s.

Although many find it obnoxious to think of children, even analogously, as if they are "consumer durables," few would deny that at least some families delay or alter their child-bearing decisions because they cannot yet afford to have children (perhaps until they have at least saved for the down payment on a house or finished paying for their education) or because it is too costly to have another child (perhaps because it would mean an interruption in a wife's career in the labour market). As long as these and other economic factors affect the decision to have children for some families, economic factors will have some predictive power in explaining variations in birth rates.

As suggested by consumer demand theory, the basic variables affecting the fertility decision are income, the price or cost of a child, the price of related goods, and tastes and preferences. Labour supply theory reminds us of the importance of time, the trade-off between consumption and nonmarket time, and the competing returns to working for pay versus staying at home.

Variables Affecting Fertility

Income

Economic theory predicts that, *other things being equal*, there will be a positive relationship between income and the desired number of children, assuming children are analogous to normal goods. The problem is that in the real world other things are not equal. Specifically, factors such as contraceptive knowledge and the cost of having children tend to be related to the income variable so that it becomes difficult to separate the pure effect of income alone. (See Exhibit 4.3.)

EXHIBIT 4.3

Are Children Normal Goods?

In economics, normal goods are the things that we spend more on as our income increases; that is, they have a positive income elasticity of demand. At first glance, it appears that children are not like normal goods, in that higher-income families and wealthier countries tend to be associated with small family sizes. Children, like potatoes, seem more like an inferior good that we purchase less of as our income rises!

The problem with the empirical evidence is that the gross-negative relationship between income and family size is the result of two opposing forces. On the one hand, high-income families and countries have more wealth, which should lead to larger family sizes, if children are like normal goods (i.e., a pure income effect). On the other hand, women in high-income families and wealthy countries tend to have high potential earnings power and this makes the (opportunity) cost of children higher; that is, women of high earnings power forgo more income if they take time out of the labour market to bear and raise children.

As indicated subsequently, the negative effect of the higher "price" of having a child tends to outweigh the positive income effect whereby higher earnings are used to "buy" more children. When the potential earnings of women are controlled for (e.g., through econometric analysis), a positive relationship between income and family size prevails. Children are like normal goods!

EXHIBIT 4.4

Fertility and Labour Supply

How much do children reduce the labour supply of women? If parents decide to have an additional child, how much less likely is a woman to work for pay? One way to address this question would be to compare the labour supply decisions of women with different numbers of children. For example, the difference in number of weeks worked of women with one child from that of those with two children could be interpreted as the causal effect of an additional child on labour supply.

However, as this section emphasizes, fertility and labour supply are outcomes of a more complicated, probably joint, decision-making process. It is unlikely that fertility decisions are made independent of labour supply, and vice versa. For example, women who choose to have larger families might be less inclined to work in the first place, and this difference in preferences is confounded with the possibly independent effect of fertility on labour supply.

Absent the co-operation of a scientifically inspired stork, economists have attempted to identify natural experiments whereby the number of children can be treated as exogenous to (or independent of) the labour supply decision. Angrist and Evans (1998) provide a very clever example of this methodology. They point out that among families with two children, parents with "matched sets" (one boy and one girl) are less likely to have a third child than those with two children of the same sex. Presumably, parents like having a mixture of sexes of children. It seems reasonable to treat the sex composition of the first two children as independent of labour supply preferences of parents with two children. It also turns out that women with two children of the same sex are less likely to work than those with one boy and one girl. It is difficult to explain this except by the fact that they are also more likely to have a third child.

Thus, while Angrist and Evans estimate that women with three or more children are 16 percent less likely to work than women with only two children, only 10 percentage points of this is due to the causal effect of children on labour supply, and the remaining 6 percent is due to the underlying preference for women with three children to stay at home anyway.

Price, or Cost, of Children

Economic theory also predicts that the demand for children is negatively related to the price, or cost, of having children. Phipps (1998) calculates the implicit cost of children in Canada by estimating the amount of income it would take to restore a family with one child to the same level of material well-being as a similar childless couple. A typical Canadian couple with a family income of $60,000 would require about $9300 per year to compensate it for the extra costs associated with having a first child. Additional children are slightly cheaper.

Although direct costs, such as the additional food, clothing, and housework, associated with raising a child are an important aspect of the cost of children, the main element in the cost of having a child is the income foregone by the spouse (in our society this tends to be the wife) who takes time away from labour market activity to bear and raise the child.

An increase in the potential earnings of wives can have both income and substitution effects on the decision to have children. The consumption substitution effect says that wives with high potential earnings will have fewer children because the higher opportunity cost (forgone income) of having a child induces them to substitute away from the expensive alternative of having children and to engage in less-expensive activities that do not impinge as much on their earning capacity. The income effect, on the other hand, says that wives with a high earning capacity can contribute more to family income, and this will enable the family to spend more on all commodities, implying greater expenditures on children if children are normal goods. Thus, the income and substitution effects of a change in the wife's earning capacity have opposing effects on desired family size.

Price of Related Goods

A rise in the price of complementary goods (e.g., medical expenses, daycare, education) would tend to reduce our desired number of children. Conversely, a fall in their price, perhaps from public subsidies, could encourage larger family sizes. In most cases, the cost of any one of these related commodities is probably not large enough to have any appreciable effect on family size. However, dramatic changes in the private cost of some of these items, such as free university tuition or universally free daycare, could have an impact, as could any trend in the overall extent of government support for medical care, family allowances, maternity leave, education, or daycare.

Tastes and Preferences

Economists tend to regard tastes and preferences as exogenously given from outside the economic system. In the area of family formation, our tastes and preferences have dramatically changed, related to our ideas on religion, family planning, and the women's liberation movement in general. These factors have all changed over time in a fashion that would encourage smaller family sizes.

Some would argue that these changes were not really exogenous to the economic system, but rather were a result of some of the more fundamental economic changes. For example, such factors as improved job opportunities for females may have made women's liberation more necessary to ensure more equal employment opportunities. The dramatic increase in the number of women working outside the home may have changed attitudes toward women, their role in society, and the nature of the family. Cause and effect works both ways; tastes and preferences both shape and are shaped by the economic system.

Education also has an important bearing on tastes and preferences. Not only does it raise the income forgone by raising children, but increased education may also widen our horizon for other goods (travel, entertainment outside the home), enable family planning, and encourage self-fulfillment through means other than having children.

Technology

The term technology is often used by economists as a general rubric to describe the general technological and environmental factors that influence our economic decisions. In the area of fertility and family formation, birth control knowledge and contraceptive devices have had an important impact on the number of children, primarily by equilibrating the actual with the desired number of children. Medical advances with vasectomies and tubal ligation can have a similar impact. The reduction in infant mortality over time should also reduce the number of births, since in times of high infant mortality it was often necessary to have large families simply to have a few children survive to adult age.

Most of the technological advances discussed so far are ones that would encourage or enable smaller families. Some, such as reduced danger and discomforts during pregnancy and advances in fertility drugs and operations, work in the opposite direction, to encourage or enable more childbearing. These have been especially important for women who have postponed childbearing to later in their life. Other advances, such as processed food and disposable diapers, have made care for children easier.

Empirical Results

The empirical evidence on fertility behaviour is confusing to interpret because of the difficulty of holding other factors constant when observing actual behaviour. For example, it is difficult to isolate the effect of family income independent of the effect of the wife's education, because highly educated wives tend to marry husbands with high incomes. If we observe fewer children in high-income families, is this because of their high income, or is it because wives in such families tend to be highly educated and, hence, their foregone income or cost of having children is high?

EXHIBIT 4.5

China's One-Child Policy

Out of concern for excessive population growth, in 1979 China adopted a one-child policy designed to reduce fertility, ideally, to one child per family. The policy was enforced by a variety of mechanisms, including both rewards for families that complied and fines for families having too many children. It was applied most strictly in cities and more unevenly in the countryside. By the early 1990s, the total fertility rate (the number of children ever born to a woman) had declined from three to fewer than two children per woman, and the sex ratio had tilted decidedly in favour of boys.

How much credit or blame should be given to this "central planning" of fertility? As usual, it is difficult to tell. China's pattern of demographic transition—that is, the reduction in births combined with an increase in life expectancy—looks very much like that of other East Asian countries as they have gone through the process of economic development. As economies develop, and the returns to women's work and education improve, the increase in women's opportunity cost of time naturally leads to a reduction in fertility. Furthermore, as incomes rise, parents substitute toward the quality of their children's investments (like education) and away from quantity. Several researchers, such as Shultz and Zeng (1999), highlight the importance of women's labour market opportunities in their fertility decisions, helping to explain why fertility would have declined for purely economic reasons. However, this does not mean that the policy had no independent effect. Shultz and Zeng (1995), and McElroy and Yang (2000) show that the economic incentives associated with the one-child policy also appear to have influenced the decision of how many children a couple has. In providing an overall assessment, Whyte, Fang, and Cai (2015) argue that the policy's coercive restrictions unambiguously reduced fertility, but that its impact has largely been exaggerated (especially by the government that justified the policy). Economic factors, especially rapid economic growth, explain most of the decline in fertility. Recognizing its limitations, effective as of January 1, 2016, the one-child policy was abolished in favour of a two-child policy. It remains a matter of future research to determine to what extent such restrictions, as opposed to economic factors, explain differences in fertility.

The results of most empirical studies generally confirm the economic predictions. Specifically, there tends to be a negative relationship between the number of children and the cost of having children as measured, for example, by the wife's potential labour market earnings. As well, there tends to be a weak positive relationship between income and family size after holding constant the impact of other variables, notably the earnings potential of the wife.[4] This positive relationship is especially likely to prevail between income and *expenditures* on children, since higher income is used to purchase more quality (as measured by expenditures per child) as well as quantity (number of children).

When the earning potential of the wife is *not* held constant there tends to be a negative relationship between fertility and income; that is, poor countries and poor families tend to have larger family sizes. This is due, however, to the low earnings potential of women in such situations, with this negative effect of their potential earnings dominating the positive effect of income. This highlights the probability that a viable population control policy, for less-developed countries especially, will improve the job opportunities for women (see Exhibit 4.5). This will raise the (opportunity) cost of having children, and if the empirical estimates are applicable, this should outweigh any tendency to have more children because of the additional income generated by their employment.

EXHIBIT 4.6

The Benefits of a Distinct Society (I)

Can governments use cash to encourage Canadian parents to have another child? Given the high costs of raising children, how high would such a subsidy have to be? The government of Quebec offered such a subsidy during the 1990s. The program, Allowance for Newborn Children (ANC), in place from 1988 to 1997, paid nontaxable benefits to families in Quebec that had children. When it was first introduced, the program offered $500 for a first child, $500 for a second, and $3000 for a third. By 1997, the subsidy for a third child had risen to $8000! So, while the government of China was attempting to reduce fertility, the government of Quebec was trying to increase the number of Quebecers. Were there any takers?

Part of the problem in answering this question stems from the difficulty in knowing what would have happened to fertility in Quebec in the absence of a program. However, given the similarities in fertility behaviour in the rest of Canada, the rest of Canada can serve as a control group for the "treatment group" in Quebec. Furthermore, we would expect that the effect of the program would be strongest for parents moving from two to three children, taking advantage of the largest subsidy. Kevin Milligan (2005) exploits this strategy to estimate the impact of the ANC on fertility in Quebec. Some of his results are reproduced in the table below.

	Total Fertility Rates by Region			
	Quebec	Change (from 1987)	Rest of Canada	Change (from 1987)
1987	1.37		1.66	
1992	1.67	+0.30	1.74	+0.12
1997	1.52	+0.15	1.57	−0.09
DD 1992		+0.18		
DD 1997		+0.23		

NOTE: DD is the "difference in differences" between Quebec and the rest of Canada, comparing the change in TFR from 1987 in the two regions.
SOURCE: Based on numbers reported in Milligan (2005) Figure 1, which is, in turn, based on provincial vital statistics.

In 1987, the TFR (number of children ever born to a woman) was significantly lower in Quebec than the rest of Canada. This reflected a steep decline in fertility in Quebec, in absolute terms and relative to the rest of Canada, beginning in 1960. By 1992, after the program had been in place for five years, the TFR in Quebec had increased by 0.30 children per woman. However, part of this was apparently due to factors unrelated to the ANC, as women in the rest of Canada also had their TFR rise by 0.12. The difference in these changes, the "difference in differences," is 0.18, which may be interpreted as the effect of the "treatment" of the ANC. By 1997, fertility in both regions declined, but the gap between Quebec and the rest of Canada had declined to 0.05, implying an impact of the program of 0.23.

Milligan further shows that the increases in fertility were greatest for those families who had two or more children already, and were thus eligible for the large subsidy. His more detailed econometric analysis employing a variety of data sources also confirms that, for a price, Quebecers could be encouraged to have more children.

EXHIBIT 4.7

Did the "Family Allowance" of the Poor Laws Increase Birth Rates?

The Poor Laws of early nineteenth-century England essentially provided a system of child allowances whereby workers often received additional income from their parish if they had more children. Malthus argued against such laws on the grounds that they simply encouraged larger family sizes, which in the long run would simply increase poverty.

There has been, and continues to be, considerable debate on the impact of the Poor Laws. Recent econometric evidence, however, indicates that after controlling for the effect of other variables on birth rates (Boyer 1989), the Poor Law system of family allowances did lead to higher birth rates. Malthus appears to have been correct at least in his argument that family allowances leads to higher birth rates.

Most recent empirical work addresses the impact of government policy, as opposed to economic variables more generally. This empirical evidence also indicates that government policies can affect fertility by altering the economic determinants that influence family size. For example, Milligan (2005) investigates the impact of Quebec's tax incentive scheme to increase fertility, and finds that the policy succeeded in encouraging families to have more children (see Exhibit 4.6). Even in nineteenth-century England, the family allowance of the Poor Laws apparently led to increased birth rates (see Exhibit 4.7).

LO4, 5   Retirement Decision and Pensions

The **retirement decision** is essentially a decision by older persons not to participate in the labour force. It is amenable to analysis utilizing labour force participation theory. The retirement decision is treated separately simply because it is an area of increasing policy concern and, as the references indicate, it has developed its own empirical literature. Here, we apply the basic income-leisure framework to the retirement decision. Subsequently, Chapter 13 deals with the reasons for the existence of mandatory retirement rules that lead to a "bunching" of retirement dates, often around age 65.

The notion of retirement has many meanings, ranging from outright leaving the labour force, to reducing hours worked, to simply moving into a less onerous job. The process itself may also be gradual, beginning with a reduction in time worked (perhaps associated with a job change) and ending in full retirement. Throughout this section, we will generally talk of retirement as leaving the labour force; however, the importance of various forms of quasi-retirement and the often gradual nature of the retirement process should be kept in mind.

The policy importance of the retirement decision stems from the fact that it can have an impact on so many elements of social policy. For the individuals themselves and their families, the retirement decision has implications on things from their financial status to their psychological state. For the economy as a whole, the retirement decision also has macroeconomic implications with respect to such factors as private savings, unemployment, and the size of the labour force, all of which have implications for the level of national income.

In addition, there is concern over the solvency of public pension funds if large numbers retire and few are in the labour force to pay into the fund. This problem may be especially acute over the next 10 to 20 years, as the post–World War II baby-boom generation reaches retirement age and, with smaller cohorts of younger workers, there are fewer people paying into the funds.[5]

The policy importance of the retirement decision is further heightened by the fact that it is an area where policy changes can affect the retirement decision. This is especially the case with respect to such factors as the mandatory retirement age and the nature and availability of pension funds. However, to know the expected impact of changes in these factors, we must know the theoretical determinants of the retirement decision and the empirical evidence on the retirement response.

Theoretical Determinants of Retirement

Mandatory Retirement Age

The term **mandatory retirement provisions** refers to both compulsory retirement provisions and automatic retirement provisions. Under automatic retirement, people *have* to retire at a specific age and cannot be retained by the company. Under compulsory retirement provisions, however, the company can compel the worker to retire at a specific age, but it can also retain the services of a worker, usually on a year-to-year basis.

The term is somewhat of a misnomer, since there is no magic age embodied in *legislation* that says a person *must* retire by a specific age. The mandatory retirement age may be part of an employer's personnel policy, or it may be negotiated in a collective agreement. In addition, there is an age at which public pensions become available, although they do not *prevent* people from continuing to work. As well, aspects of labour legislation may not apply to workers beyond a specific age. Thus, the so-called mandatory retirement age, age 65, previously the magic number in North America, is really a result of personnel policy and is influenced, but not determined, by government programs. It is neither fixed nor immutable.

By December 2012, with some exceptions, mandatory retirement was eliminated for employers in federal jurisdictions. This completed a trend of the gradual elimination of mandatory retirement across Canada's provinces in response to human rights decisions and growing concern about discrimination on the basis of age. Still, some Canadian workers are employed in jobs subject to a mandatory retirement provision, where there are "bona fide occupational requirements (BFOR)"; for example jobs where physical dexterity is important (see Gomez and Gunderson 2011). Others, like partners in big law firms, may legally be allowed to sign contracts that mandate their retirement at a fixed age (like 65). The Supreme Court has ruled that such contracts are enforceable, and do not constitute age discrimination. Why might employers and employees agree to such contracts, and why was mandatory retirement so important historically? These questions are discussed in more detail in the later chapter (Chapter 13) on optimal compensation systems.

Wealth and Earnings

Economic theory, in particular the income-leisure choice theory discussed earlier, indicates that the demand for leisure—as indicated, for example, by the decision to retire early—is positively related to one's wealth and is related to expected earnings in an indeterminate fashion. The wealth effect is positive, reflecting a pure income effect; with more wealth we buy more of all normal goods, including leisure in the form of retirement. The impact of expected earnings is indeterminate, reflecting the opposing influences of income and substitution effects. An increase in expected earnings increases the income forgone if one retires and, therefore, raises the (opportunity) cost of retirement; this has a pure substitution effect, reducing the demand for retirement leisure. On the other hand, an increase in expected earnings also means an increase in expected wealth and, just like wealth from nonlabour sources, this would increase the demand for retirement leisure. Since the income and substitution effects work in opposite directions, the impact on retirement of an increase in expected earnings is ultimately an empirical proposition. Thus, the increase in our earnings that has gone on over time, and that presumably will continue, should have an indeterminate effect on the retirement decision.

Health and the Nature of Work and the Family

As people age and approach retirement, their health and the health of their spouses can obviously influence the retirement decision. This can be the case especially if their accumulated wealth or pension income enables them to afford to retire because of health problems.

The changing nature of work may also influence the retirement decision. For example, the trend toward white collar and professional jobs and away from more physically demanding blue-collar jobs may make it easier and more appealing for people to work longer. Emerging labour shortages may provide an incentive for employers to encourage older workers to return to the labour force. On the other hand, the permanent job loss of older workers due to plant closings and mass layoffs may make earlier retirement more attractive for these workers, especially if their industry-specific skills make it difficult for them to find alternative employment.

The changing nature of the family can also affect the retirement decision, albeit in complicated ways. The decline of the extended family may make retirement less attractive. The dominance of the two-income family may lead to one spouse not retiring from the labour market until the other also retires, given the joint nature of the retirement decision. However, the increased family income associated with both parties working may enable them both to be able to afford to retire early. The "deinstitutionalization" of health care with its emphasis on home care as opposed to institutional care may force the retirement of one spouse in order to care for the other.

In the income-leisure choice framework, many of these factors affect the shape of the individual's indifference curve (preferences for labour market work versus preferences for leisure or household work in the form of retirement). Others can affect the budget constraint or wage line, which depicts the market returns to labour market work. For example, health problems that make labour market work more difficult will increase the slope of the indifference curve (requiring more income per unit of work to maintain the same level of utility). This, in turn, will induce a shift toward retirement leisure. Alternatively stated, it increases the individual's reservation wage and, therefore, makes retirement more likely if the reservation wage exceeds the market wage.

A permanent job loss will lead to a reduction in the market wage if alternative jobs are lower paid. This downward rotation of the wage line has opposing income and substitution effects, as previously discussed. The returns to work are reduced (substitution effect) and this may induce retirement as the market wage now may fall below the reservation wage. In contrast, income or wealth has fallen (income effect), and this may compel the individual to postpone retirement.

Universal Old Age Security Pension

In addition to being affected by the mandatory retirement age, wealth and earnings, health, and the changing nature of work and the family, retirement decisions can be affected by various features of public and private pension plans. In fact, a growing area of research in labour economics has involved indicating how these various features of pension plans can have intended and unintended effects on retirement decisions. This highlights the fact that pensions are not simply forms of saving for retirement but active policy and human resource management instruments that can be used to influence the retirement decision.

As indicated in Exhibit 4.8, there are several sources of pension income in Canada. The universal "old age" pension is given to all persons over the age of 65. In addition, persons who have worked in the labour market likely will have built up eligibility for the Canada/Quebec Pension Plan (CPP/QPP). As well, many will have an employer-sponsored occupational pension plan. In fact, many receive pension income from all three sources.

All three tiers of the pension income support system also have features that affect the retirement decision. In fact, increased attention is being paid to utilizing these features of pension plans to influence the retirement decision, for purposes of public policy and human resource management.

For most people, the universal **Old Age Security** (OAS) pension is basically a demogrant, an unconditional grant given to all persons over the age of 65. In the income-leisure choice framework, the budget constraint is shifted outward in a parallel fashion, by the amount of the pension. The shift is parallel to the original budget constraint because the pension is given irrespective of the recipient's work behaviour. There is no change in the returns to work—recipients receive their full market wage as well as pension. (This ignores, of course, the income taxes, or "clawback," that applies to high earners.)

As a demogrant, the old age pension has the work incentive effects of a demogrant (discussed previously in Chapter 3 and illustrated in Figure 3.1). That is, there is a pure income effect, enabling the recipient to buy more of all normal commodities, including more leisure in the form of earlier retirement. Alternatively stated, the pension enables people to be able to afford to retire earlier.

The **Guaranteed Income Supplement** (GIS) may also be paid to persons over 65 and in need as determined by a means test. There is a 50 percent implicit "tax back" feature to the GIS in that the payments are reduced by $0.50 for every dollar earned by persons who continue to work and earn income. So the GIS shifts the budget constraint upward by the amount of the supplement, and then reduces its slope by 50 percent (i.e., rotates it downward and to the left) because of the implicit tax-back feature. On net, the budget constraint has both shifted outward and reduced its slope. The outward shift, or income effect, implies more income, or wealth, which in turn implies earlier retirement. The reduction in the slope, or substitution effect, implies that the returns to labour market work are reduced (i.e., the opportunity cost of retirement is lower), which also increases the likelihood of retirement. That is, both the income and substitution effects of the GIS increase the probability of retiring from the labour force.

EXHIBIT 4.8

Canada's Three-Tier Public and Private Pension System

1. **Universal Old Age Security Pension**

   - Financed by general tax revenue.

   - Demogrant, or flat amount, paid to all persons over age 65, irrespective of need or past contributions or work history.

   - The maximum monthly benefit for a single person in June 2016 was $570.52. Benefits are reduced for high earners. The reduction in benefits equals 15 percent of earnings higher than $72,809.

   - May be supplemented by a means-tested Guaranteed Income Supplement (GIS), based on need. The maximum monthly benefit for a single beneficiary in 2016 was $773.60.

2. **Social Insurance Pension: Canada/Quebec Pension Plan**

   - Financed by compulsory employer and employee contributions through a payroll tax for all workers, whether paid or self-employed.

   - Benefits related to contributions based on payroll tax applied to past earnings, but not necessarily self-financing, since funds for current pensioners come from payments from current work force. The maximum monthly benefit in 2016 was $1093.

   - Virtually universal participation, with average CPP contributions in 2012 of approximately $2950 per contributor.

3. **Employer-Sponsored Occupational Pension Plans**

   - Financed by employer, sometimes with employee contributions.

   - Benefits depend on type of plan: flat benefit plans pay a flat benefit per year of service, earnings-based plans pay a percentage of earnings per year of service, and defined contribution plans pay on the basis of returns earned by contributions to the fund.

   - Covered 32 percent of the labour force and 38 percent of paid workers in 2013.

Also, private savings, privately arranged pensions, and savings through such mechanisms as Registered Retirement Savings Plans (RRSPs). In 2014, approximately 23 percent of tax filers contributed to RRSPs, with a median contribution of $3,000.

NOTES: 1) OAS, GIS, and CPP benefit levels are reported, and updated regularly, on the Employment and Social Development Canada website, www.esdc.gc.ca; 2) Statistics for employer-sponsored pension plans, and RRSP contributions, are based on the authors calculations from series in CANSIM (Statistics Canada).

Social Insurance Pensions: Canada/Quebec Pension Plan (CPP/QPP)

Social insurance pensions refer to public pension schemes that are financed by compulsory employer and employee contributions through a payroll tax, and pay pensions based on past earnings to those who qualify by virtue of their age and work experience. Some social insurance pensions (e.g., Social Security in the United States, but not the **Canada/Quebec Pension Plan** in Canada) also have a **retirement test** or work-income test whereby the pension gets reduced if the recipient works and continues to earn income. This is an implicit tax on earnings because it involves foregoing pension payments as one earns additional income. In addition, there is usually an explicit payroll tax on earnings used to finance the social insurance fund.

The retirement test tends to be prevalent in the vast majority of countries with social insurance. Developing economies usually require that persons' complete withdrawal from the labour force in order to receive the pension (i.e., implicit 100 percent tax on earnings), mainly because such countries cannot afford to pay pensions to people who also work. In contrast, some countries with the longest history of social insurance schemes have no retirement test, allowing the person to retain full earnings and pension. The motivations for this may vary. In France it appears to be because pension benefits are low and earnings are needed to supplement income, while in Germany it seems to be because of a desire to encourage the work ethic.

In the Canada Pension Plan, the retirement test was eliminated in 1975, while the United States eliminated the retirement test for most Social Security recipients in 2000. In the United States, the retirement test now applies only to individuals who choose to retire before their normal retirement age.[6] If someone chooses to initiate Social Security benefits between age 62 and the normal retirement age, benefits are reduced by $0.50 for every dollar of earned income above a specific threshold. In 2016, this threshold was $15,720.

These features of the Canadian and American social insurance pension schemes can have a substantial impact on the retirement decision. The pension itself, like all fixed benefit payments, has a pure income effect inducing retirement. In addition, for those who work, the implicit tax of the pension reduction associated with the retirement test and the explicit payroll tax used to finance the scheme both lower the returns to work, thus making retirement more financially attractive. That is, both taxes involve a substitution effect toward retirement because the opportunity cost of leisure in the form of retirement is lowered by the amount of tax on forgone earnings. To be sure, the tax on earnings also involves an income effect working in the opposite direction; that is, our reduced after-tax income means we can buy less of everything, including leisure in the form of retirement. However, this income effect is outweighed by the income effect of the pension itself, since for all potential recipients their income is *at least* as high when social insurance is available. Thus, as with the negative income tax plans analyzed in Chapter 3, both the substitution effect and the (net) income effect of the features of social insurance serve to unambiguously induce retirement.

These features of social insurance and their impact on retirement can be modelled somewhat more formally, along the lines of the income-leisure framework developed in Chapter 2. With Y defined as income after taxes and transfers, W the wage rate, T the maximum amount of leisure (l) available, B the pension received upon retiring, p the explicit payroll tax used to finance social insurance, and t the implicit tax involved in the pension reduction through the retirement test, the budget constraint with a social insurance pension is,

$$Y_p = B + \left(1 - p - t\right) W\left(T - \ell\right)$$

This can be compared to the constraint without social insurance, which is,

$$Y_o = W\left(T - \ell\right)$$

The new budget constraint is illustrated in Figure 4.3 for various possible social insurance schemes. Figure 4.3(a) illustrates the case when there is no retirement test (e.g., Canada/Quebec Pension Plans); that is, the recipient is given a pension and is allowed to work without forgoing retirement. (For simplicity, the payroll tax for financing the pension has been ignored. With the payroll tax as a fixed percentage of earnings, the budget constraint would have rotated downward from the point B.) The new budget constraint is $Y = B + W(T - \ell)$, when p = 0 and t = 0. Such a pension scheme simply has a pure income effect, encouraging potential recipients to retire. Although it is not shown in the diagram, the new indifference curve may be tangent to the new budget constraint at a point such as E_p above and to the right of the original point E_0. The new equilibrium may also involve a corner solution at B, in which case the recipient retired completely, or it may be at a point like E_p, signifying partial retirement. Or, if leisure is not a normal good, it may be at a point vertically above E_0, in which case the recipient continued to work the same as before and received the full pension.

Figure 4.3(b) illustrates the new budget constraint under a full retirement test whereby the pension recipient is required to give up $1 of pension for every $1 earned. This implicit 100 percent tax rate makes the budget constraint similar to the one for welfare discussed in Chapter 3, and the adverse work incentive effects are similar. In particular, there will be a strong incentive to retire completely (move to point B).

The typical case with a partial retirement test is illustrated in Figure 4.3(c). The first arm of the budget constraint, TB, indicates the pension benefits payable upon complete retirement. (Income is $Y_b = TB$ when leisure is OT.) The second arm, BC, illustrates that up to a specific threshold amount of labour market earnings, $Y_c - Y_b$, for working $T - \ell$, the recipient may keep the full pension benefits of $Y_b (= TB)$, so that her total income with pension and labour market earnings could be up to Y_c. As indicated previously, this threshold amount of earnings, $Y_c - Y_b$, was $14,160 in the United States in 2011. The new arm of the budget constraint is parallel to the original constraint of TY_m because the implicit tax is zero; that is, recipients who work keep their full labour market earnings.

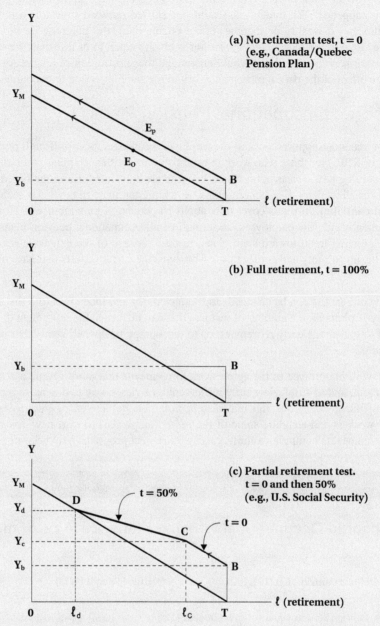

Figure 4.3 Budget Constraints under Social Insurance Pensions (assuming payroll tax p = 0)

This figure illustrates the work incentives associated with public pension plans under varying assumptions regarding retirement tests, or the clawing back of benefits. In panel (a), beneficiaries receive benefits Y_b, and there is no penalty for working. In panel (b), the individual faces a 100 percent retirement test, so that earnings are fully clawed back until the benefit is exhausted. In panel (c), the retirement test applies to earnings over $(Y_c - Y_b)$, only when the person works $T - \ell_C$, after which benefits are reduced by \$0.50 for every dollar earned.

The third arm, CD, illustrates the implicit tax that is involved when the recipient is required to give back a portion of the pension for the additional labour market earnings of $Y_d - Y_c$ that result from the additional work of $\ell_c - \ell_d$. An implicit tax of 50 percent results in the slope of CD being one-half of the slope of the original constraint TY_m; that is, for every dollar earned, the recipient forgoes \$0.50 in pension. When the recipient's labour earnings exceed $Y_d - Y_b$, at point D, then the person would no longer receive any pension and any additional work activity of $\ell_d - 0$ would result in additional income as shown by the fourth arm of the budget constraint DY_m.

The work incentive effects of the new budget constraint, $TBCDY_m$, are such as to unambiguously induce retirement. Basically, two things have happened. The budget constraint has shifted outward (upward to the right) from the original constraint of TY_m, and this has a wealth, or income, effect encouraging the purchase of more leisure in the form of retirement. In addition, the slope of the new budget constraint is always equal to or less than the original constraint; that is, the opportunity cost of leisure is reduced and this would encourage the substitution of leisure for other commodities. Both the income and substitution effect of the partial retirement work in the same direction to encourage early retirement.

Employer-Sponsored Occupational Pension Plans

The third tier of pension income support consists of **employer-sponsored/occupational pension plans**, (also called Registered Pension Plans, or RPPs) for those who work in establishments with such plans. As indicated in Exhibit 4.9, such plans can be classified according to the basis upon which benefits are calculated. Earnings-based plans are most common, covering almost two-thirds of all workers. Flat-benefit plans, which predominate in the union sector, cover about 13 percent of plan members. **Defined contribution plans** cover only about 16 percent of plan members. However, because these tend to exist in small establishments with few employees, about half of all occupational pension plans are defined contribution plans. As well, there is a growing trend toward such plans, in part because of the extensive regulations being put on the defined benefit plans and the uncertainty and conflict over who owns the surplus assets that have often been generated in the defined benefit plans.

Because the level and pace of benefits can be changed, and inducements and incentives to retire sooner versus later can be manipulated, **defined benefit plans** have a number of features that can influence the retirement decision of workers. In fact, such features can be used to encourage early retirement, or to discourage postponed retirement past the normal retirement age established by the plan.

This aspect is likely to grow in importance as the aging work force means that more people are in the age groups likely to be affected by early retirement, and as firms view early retirement as a viable way to downsize their work force. If the early retirement payments are sufficiently generous, this may also be in the mutual interest of employees, opening new promotion opportunities for younger workers and enabling some of the retired employees to start new careers. As well, if mandatory retirement is banned or becomes less common, voluntary early retirement programs may become more prominent.

EXHIBIT 4.9

Employer-Sponsored Occupational Pension Plans, 2014 (% of members in parentheses)

Defined Contribution (17%)	Defined Benefit (71%)	
	Flat Benefit (12%)	Earnings–based (59%)
• Pension benefits equal the accumulated value of the contributions made by, or on behalf of, employees. • Usually in smaller establishments • 37% of plans covering 17% of members.	• Fixed benefit for each year of service; e.g. $50 per month per year of service, with a maximum of 35 years of service (i.e., $1,750 per month). • Predominantly in the union sector • 3% of plans covering 12% of members.	• Pension based upon years of service and percent of earnings in final years, best years, or career average • Typically, 2% of earnings for each year of service, up to a maximum of 35 years of service • 56% of plans covering 59% of members.

NOTES : Numbers do not add up to 100 percent because we do not report hybrid and other plans that combine features of both defined benefit and defined contribution plans.

SOURCE: This analysis is based on Statistics Canada CANSIM database, http://www5.statcan.gc.ca/cansim/, Tables 280-0012 and 280-0017, accessed June 13, 2016. All computations, use, and interpretation of these data are entirely that of the authors.

Empirical Evidence

The general empirical evidence on the determinants of retirement is reviewed in Lazear (1986), Lumsdaine and Mitchell (1999), and Gruber and Wise (1999), while Baker and Benjamin (2000) provide an overview of the Canadian evidence. Researchers use a variety of data sources, including those we have discussed already (labour force surveys and censuses). They also exploit cross-country and cross-jurisdictional data in order to identify the impact of particular features of national public pension schemes (see Exhibit 4.10, for example).

In addition to these more conventional sources, labour economists use two U.S. surveys specifically designed for studying the elderly: the Retirement History Survey (RHS) and the more recent Health and Retirement Survey (HRS). These are longitudinal surveys that follow a sample of older workers for several years. This allows researchers to track the labour force status and relevant economic variables (such as pensions, wealth, and wages) from one year to the next, as the workers age. These sorts of data permit a more detailed investigation of the labour force dynamics associated with retirement. In a similar vein, economists occasionally gain access to company personnel records, which allows a careful analysis of the impact of private pensions on the retirement decision. The most credible studies of this type have been able to exploit "surprises" in the features of private pensions (such as temporary buyouts or offers of early retirement) to explore the sensitivity of the retirement decision to these program parameters.

EXHIBIT 4.10

The Benefits of a Distinct Society (II)

One of the features of Canada's public pension program is that it is split into two separate jurisdictions: Quebec administers the QPP while the federal government (with the provinces) administers the CPP in the rest of Canada. This differentiates Canada from most other countries, which have single, country-wide pension plans. The CPP and the QPP are virtually identical in terms of policy parameters, such as contribution rates, levels of benefits, and rules governing eligibility. Occasionally, however, the two jurisdictions have been out of step in important ways. This has had real advantages for empirical research on the impact of pension plans on retirement behaviour, since differences across the plans can be exploited to identify possible effects of program parameters on retirement.

In most countries, for example, retirement rates have been trending upward, as more individuals opt for early retirement (retirement before age 65). At the same time, most retirement plans have become increasingly generous, especially with respect to early retirement. It is tempting to causally link these two trends, but one can never be sure whether the correlation is merely spurious and retirement trends are independent of the changes in pension plans. In 1984, Quebec began to allow early retirement for individuals aged 60 to 64; that is, individuals in this age group could now retire and collect a reduced QPP pension. The CPP did not permit early retirement until 1987. Thus, for three years, early retirement was permitted in Quebec but not in the rest of Canada. This provided an opportunity to examine the impact of early retirement provisions on retirement behaviour. Did early retirement take off in Quebec relative to the rest of Canada during this interval of different policies? Baker and Benjamin (1999) explore this question, and find that in fact there is little evidence of differential retirement patterns in Quebec over this time period, suggesting that the public pension plans did little to affect behaviour. Most of the individuals who opted for early retirement would have done so anyway. Some may have had poor labour market opportunities, while others may have had generous private pensions. Thus, while Canada's constitutional bickering can be quite annoying, it can pay dividends for social science research.

Most studies find that characteristics of public and private pension plans affect retirement decisions in ways we would expect, given the theory outlined above. However, the estimated responses have generally been small—certainly not large enough to explain the dramatic changes in retirement behaviour that have occurred over the past 30 years. This is an active area of empirical research, and more recent studies attempt to incorporate information on health, and also recognize that retirement decisions are jointly made by husbands and wives, complicating the simple models outlined here.

Summary

- As individuals age, there are several systematic patterns in their labour supply—withdrawing to have children, and eventually retiring from the labour force—that require modifications of the static labour supply model developed in Chapter 2.

- Interpretation of the cross-section correlation between age and labour force status as representing the pure effect of age is problematic, especially for women. This arises because of cohort effects, or the difficulty of separating out age from vintage (or year of birth) at a single point in time. Specifically for women, the age-participation profiles have been shifting upward over time, as each subsequent cohort of women is more attached to the labour market than previous ones.

- Incorporating individual decisions to work in one time period versus another involves a straightforward extension of the static labour supply model. Principally, this entails allowing for preferences to work at various points in one's life, and more importantly, the specification of the lifetime budget constraint: the present value of lifetime consumption equals the present value of lifetime income.

- The inter-temporal labour supply model can be used to conduct a variety of thought experiments concerning the impact of wage changes at different points in the life cycle on the evolution of work patterns.

- The household production model helps explain how preferences evolve; specifically, why household valuation of nonmarket time may change with the introduction of technologies that improve the production of goods and services within the household. This model emphasizes that many goods entail significant time input in order to be consumed. Especially to the extent that household production was performed by women, the model can be used to better understand the factors that contribute to the changing economic role of women, inside the family, and in the labour market.

- Children can have an important impact on the labour supply of parents, especially mothers; however, children are themselves the outcome of parents' choices. Economic models of fertility explore the connections between economic variables like income and wife's wages on the decision regarding whether and how many children to have, as well as interactions between fertility and labour supply.

- Retirement is another important life -cycle labour supply decision that is affected by a myriad public and private pension plans. The static labour supply model can easily be augmented along the lines shown in Chapter 3, in order to incorporate some of the main features of public pension plans.

Keywords

Canada/Quebec Pension Plan	intertemporal substitution
cohort effect	life-cycle labour supply
defined benefit plans	mandatory retirement provisions
defined contribution plans	Old Age Security
dynamic labour supply	present value
employer-sponsored/occupational pension plans	retirement decision
	retirement test
evolutionary wage change	time-intensive commodities
fertility	transitory wage
goods-intensive commodities	tripartite choice
Guaranteed Income Supplement	unanticipated wage increase
household production model	

Review Questions

1. Why has there been a long-run decline in fertility over time, even though income has risen?

2. Briefly outline the Becker-Lancaster approach to consumer demand theory (household production) and its applicability to labour market economics. Specifically, indicate some of the labour market implications of this theory that we would not have been able to derive from conventional consumer demand theory.

3. What does the economics of fertility suggest to us about differences in family size between urban and rural areas of less-developed countries?

4. Discuss the extent to which the mandatory retirement age is both an exogenous determinant of the retirement decision and an endogenous result of the retirement decision.

5. On the basis of Figure 4.3(a), draw the indifference curves, before and after the pension, for persons who

    a. retire completely,

    b. retire partially, or

    c. work the same as before.

   Compare their income in each case.

6. On the basis of Figure 4.3(b), draw the indifference curve for a person who is indifferent between retiring completely and continuing to work. Why would a person ever be indifferent between these two alternatives assuming that retirement is regarded positively? On the basis of the various factors given in the diagram, indicate how people may be induced to stay in the labour force rather than retire.

7. On the basis of Figure 4.3(c), draw the indifference curve for a person who

    a. retires completely,

    b. works part time and earns income only up to the maximum amount before it becomes retirement tested; that is, benefits are reduced if the individual works too much,

    c. works and earns income up to the maximum amount before it becomes retirement tested at a 100 percent implicit tax, or

    d. works and earns so much income that no pension is forthcoming.

   Compare the pension cost under each alternative.

Problems

1. The evaluation of the labour supply response to a tax cut can be quite different in a dynamic setting from what it is in a static setting. Discuss the relative impact of a permanent versus a transitory tax cut on labour supply, and compare the analysis to the static model.

2. Consider the two-period dynamic labour supply model discussed in this chapter. What, if any thing, happens to current labour supply if the interest rate rises from 2 to 10 percent?

3. Use a simple supply and demand diagram to illustrate how either supply-side or demand-side factors may underlie the cohort effects implicit in Figure 4.1. What factors could be assigned to the supply side or the demand side in explaining how the curves would shift? How could an empirical researcher disentangle the relative magnitudes of the supply and demand factors in explaining the increase in the number of women working now, as against 1950?

4. Utilize your knowledge of household production theory to indicate the following:

   a. The expected effect of a wage increase on the wife's labour supply.

   b. The expected effect, on the demand for children, of an increase in the wage of a wife.

   c. Why the substitution effect for labour supply may be larger for women than men.

   d. The effect on one spouse's labour supply, of his or her spouse's disability, where the spouse requires home (not institutional) care.

   e. The effect on this same spouse's labour supply, as in (d), if the government (or private insurance) provided financial compensation to the family.

5. The importance of cohort effects in female labour supply seems to have diminished over time, as seen in Figure 4.1. What factors may account for this? Does this mean cohort effects are probably unimportant to predicting future female labour supply? Discuss possible factors that may arise in the future to shift women's age-participation profiles, in any direction.

6. Using the economic theory of fertility, analyze the expected impact on the TFR (total fertility rate) and women's labour supply of the following:

   a. An increase in women's wages.

   b. Elimination of the family allowance for high-income women.

   c. An increase in the deduction for child care expenses.

   d. Increasing educational levels for women.

7. Financial advisers say it's never too early to think about retirement. Analyze the impact on the current labour supply of a 25-year-old of the following news: "The Canada Pension Plan will be insolvent in 40 years, and in addition to a reduction of pension and old age security benefits, the government will have to increase the CPP payroll tax for all workers."

8. Consider an individual aged 64 who is eligible to collect full social security (public pension) benefits of $6000 for a year. She has no other income, but can work at a weekly wage rate of $600 for a maximum of 52 weeks. Receipt of benefits from the social security program is retirement tested. Specifically, the individual can earn up to $9000 in annual wage income without a reduction in benefits; however, after $9000 of earnings, benefits are reduced by 50 percent for every dollar earned, until the benefits are exhausted.

   a. Carefully draw and label the budget constraint for this individual.

   b. Consider an individual whose labour supply decision is such that she receives YA in social security benefits, so that $0 < YA < \$6000$ (i.e., she receives positive but reduced benefits). On the carefully labelled diagram from part (a), show her labour supply decision.

   c. "Elimination of the retirement test (i.e., allowing the individual to keep all benefits, irrespective of his or her labour earnings) will unambiguously increase the labour supply of the individual described in part (b)." True or false? Explain, using a carefully labelled diagram.

9. You have been asked to estimate the impact on retirement of a policy raising the replacement rate from 40 to 60 percent of final earnings, and of lowering the implicit tax of the retirement test from 50 to 30 percent. You have access to comprehensive microeconomic data where the individual is the unit of observation. Specify an appropriate regression equation for estimating the retirement response, and indicate how you would simulate the impact of the change in the two policy parameters.

10. On the basis of a social insurance pension scheme where income, Y_P, is,
$$Y_P = B + (1 - t)E$$

   and B is the pension, t is the tax-back rate of the retirement test, and E is earnings, solve for the following:

   a. The breakeven level of earnings, E_b, where the recipient no longer receives any pension income (*Hint:* Income without the pension scheme is $Y_0 = E$, and therefore the breakeven level of earnings, E_b, occurs when $Y_0 = Y_P$ or the pension benefit, $B - tE$, equals zero)

    b. The breakeven level when there is also a threshold level of income, Y_t, before the taxback rate of the retirement test is applied, so that,

$$Y_P = B + Y_t + (1 - t)E$$

    c. The dollar value of the breakeven level of earnings in parts (a) and (b) when B = $6000, Y_t =$10,000, and t = 0.5.

11. In an income-retirement choice diagram, indicate the effect on an individual's indifference curves and/or budget constraint and subsequent retirement decision of each of the following:

    a. Retirement of one's spouse.

    b. Illness of one's spouse.

    c. Improvements in health of the elderly.

    d. Permanent displacement from a high-wage job in the steel industry to a low-wage job in the restaurant sector.

    e. Improvements in the retirement leisure industry (e.g., condominiums, recreation, travel) such that retirement is now relatively more attractive.

Endnotes

1. The discounted present value, or present value, gives the current value equivalent of a stream of money received (or paid) at different time periods. The present value provides the current "financial equivalent" of a flow of money, assuming that one can borrow all the future money (and pay it back, principle and interest) at an interest rate of r. For a flow of money $y_1, y_2, \ldots, y_T$ across T time periods, with a constant interest rate, r, the present value is given by the formula:

$$y_1 + \frac{y_2}{(1+r)} + \frac{y_3}{(1+r)^2} + \ldots + \frac{y_T}{(1+r)^{T-1}} = \sum_{t=1}^{T} \frac{y_t}{(1+r)^{t-1}}$$

   If an individual so chose, he could consume the entire present value of lifetime income in the first period, paying all his future income back (in principle and interest) for the remainder of his life.

2. Even the store-bought chocolate cake requires more time input than you might think; it requires shopping and serving time, which may not be trivial. It also requires time to eat, unless you are willing to combine eating a piece of cake with leisure activities, or driving, etc.

3. Excellent reviews are found in Hotz, Klerman, and Willis (1997); Montgomery and Trussell (1986); and Schultz (1997).

4. On the basis of Canadian data over the period 1948 to 1975, Hyatt and Milne (1991b) estimate the elasticity of demand for children to be 1.38 with respect to male income, and −1.55 with respect to female wages.

5. See Baker and Benjamin (2000) for further discussion of these issues.

6. The normal retirement age is defined as the age at which one can retire and receive full pension benefits. Early retirement in the United States can be initiated at age 62 (60 in Canada). The normal retirement age in Canada is 65, while in the United States it is gradually being raised from 65 to 67 (it will be 67 for everyone born after 1960).

PORTRAIT IMAGES ASIA/Shutterstock.com

CHAPTER 5

Demand for Labour in Competitive Labour Markets

LEARNING OBJECTIVES

LO1 Understand how firms decide how much labour they need to employ to produce a certain amount of goods or services. The theory of labour demand provides the tools required to understand how firms make these decisions.

LO2 Labour demand decisions are made both simultaneously with other input decisions, and after factories and machines have been built. Learn how labour demand decisions differ in these two circumstances; that is, in the short run versus the long run.

LO3 Understand why labour demand functions are downward sloping (i.e., decreasing functions of the market wage), and learn that this law of demand holds regardless of the time horizon used by the firm in its decisions or the structure of product market completion.

LO4 Learn about the factors that affect the elasticity of demand for labour. For example, does it matter whether a firm operates as a monopolist or a perfect competitor in the product market?

LO5 Understand the impact of free trade, and of international competition more generally, on the Canadian labour market.

MAIN QUESTIONS

- Is there any empirical support for the convention that labour demand functions are downward sloping?

- How can we characterize the competitiveness of Canadian labour in an increasingly globalized world economy? How have the productivities and wages of Canadian workers evolved over time compared to the rest of the world? Does this bode well for future employment prospects of Canadian workers?

- What is the impact of the Internet and technological change on the demand for labour?

- How can we use labour demand functions to assess the impact of offshoring and globalization on the wages and employment of Canadian workers?

The general principles that determine the demand for any **factor of production** apply also to the demand for labour. In contrast to goods and services, factors of production are demanded not for final use or consumption but as inputs into the production of final goods and services. Thus, the demand for a factor is necessarily linked to the demand for the goods and services that the factor is used to produce. For instance, the demand for land suitable for growing wheat is linked to the demand for bread and cereal, just as the demand for construction workers is related to the demand for new buildings, roads, and bridges. For this reason, the demand for factors is called a **derived demand**.

In discussing firms' decisions regarding the employment of factors of production, economists usually distinguish between short-run and long-run decisions. The **short run** is defined as a period during which one or more factors of production, referred to as *fixed factors*, cannot be varied, while the **long run** is defined as a period during which the firm can adjust all of its inputs. During both the short and the long run, the state of technical knowledge is assumed to be fixed; the *very long run* refers to the period during which changes in technical knowledge can occur. The amount of calendar time corresponding to each of these periods will differ from one industry to another and according to other factors. These periods are useful as a conceptual device for analyzing a firm's decision making rather than for predicting the amount of time taken to adjust to change.

By demand for labour we mean the quantity of labour services the firm would choose to employ at each wage. This desired quantity will depend on both the firm's objectives and its constraints. Usually, we will assume that the firm's objective is to maximize profits. Also examined is the determination of labour demand under the weaker assumption of cost minimization. The firm is constrained by the demand conditions in its product markets, the supply conditions in its factor markets, and its production function, which shows the maximum output attainable for various combinations of inputs, given the existing state of technical knowledge. In the short run, the firm is further constrained by having one or more factors of production whose quantities are fixed.

The theory of labour demand examines the quantity of labour services the firm desires to employ given the market-determined wage rate, or given the labour supply function that the firm faces. As was the case with labour supply, our guiding objective is in deriving the theoretical relationship between labour demand and the market wage, holding other factors constant. In this chapter, we will assume that the firm is a perfect competitor in the labour market. In Chapter 7, we relax this assumption and explore the case where the firm faces the entire market supply curve and operates as a monopsonist. In that case, it is not sensible to think of the firm as reacting to a given market wage. However, as we shall see, the basic ingredients of the theory of input demand can easily be adjusted to this problem.

In some circumstances, however, thinking of either the firm or the labour it hires as operating in a competitive environment fails to capture the way markets actually work. The employer and employees may negotiate explicit, or reach implicit, contracts involving both wages and employment. When this is the case, the wage-employment outcomes may not be on the labour demand curve because the contracts will reflect the preferences of both the employer and the employees with respect to both wages and employment. Explicit wage-employment contracts are discussed in Chapter 15 on unions, and implicit wage-employment contracts are discussed in Chapter 17 on unemployment (because of the theoretical links between implicit contracts and unemployment). Even under these circumstances, however, we shall see that the theory of firm behaviour described in this chapter is the foundation for employment determination outside the perfectly competitive framework.

The chapter ends with an extended discussion on the impact of the global economy on the demand for Canadian labour. The relative cost and productivity of Canadian labour is examined, as are the possible channels by which offshoring and changes in international trade patterns may impact the employment of Canadian workers. In particular, we present evidence on the impact of trade agreements, like NAFTA, on the Canadian labour market.

Categorizing the Structure of Product and Labour Markets

Because the demand for labour is derived from the output produced by the firm, the way in which the firm behaves in the product market can have an impact on the demand for labour, and hence, ultimately, on wage and employment decisions. In general, the firm's product market behaviour depends on the structure of the industry to which the firm belongs. In order of the decreasing degree of competition, the four main market structures are (1) perfect competition, (2) monopolistic competition, (3) oligopoly, and (4) monopoly.

Whereas the structure of the product market affects the firm's derived demand for labour, the structure of the labour market affects the labour supply curve that the firm faces. The supply curve of labour to an individual firm shows the amount of a specific type of labour (e.g., a particular occupational category) that the firm could employ at various wage rates. Analogous to the four product market structures are four labour market structures. In order of the decreasing degree of competition faced by the firm in hiring labour, these factor market structures are (1) perfect competition, (2) monopsonistic competition, (3) oligopsony, and (4) monopsony. (The "-opsony" ending is traditionally used to denote departures from perfect competition in factor markets.)

The product and labour market categorizations are independent in that there is no necessary relationship between the structure of the product market in which the firm sells its output and the labour market in which it buys labour services. The extent to which the firm is competitive in the product market (and, hence, the nature of its derived demand for labour curve) need not be related to the extent to which the firm is a competitive buyer of labour (and, hence, the nature of the supply curve of labour that it faces). The two *may* be related, for example, if it is a large firm and thus dominates both the labour and product markets, but they need not be related. Hence, for *each* product market structure, the firm can behave in at least four different ways as a purchaser of labour. There are, therefore, at least 16 different combinations of product and labour market structure that can bear on the wage and employment decision at the level of the firm.

In general, however, the essence of the wage and employment decision by the firm can be captured by an examination of the polar cases of perfect competition (in product and/or factor markets), monopoly in the product market, and monopsony in the labour market. We will begin by examining the demand for labour in the short run under conditions of perfect competition in the labour market.

LO1, 2   Demand for Labour in the Short Run

The general principles determining labour demand can be explained for the case of a firm that produces a single output, Q, using two inputs: capital, K, and labour, N. The technological possibilities relating output to any combination of inputs are represented by the **production function**:

$$Q = F(K, N) \tag{5.1}$$

In the short run, the amount of capital is fixed at $K = K_0$, so the production function is simply a function of N (with K fixed). The quantity of labour services can be varied by changing either the number of employees or the hours worked by each employee, or both. For the moment, we do not distinguish between variations in the number of employees and hours worked; however, this aspect of labour demand is discussed in Chapter 6. Also discussed later is the possibility that labour may be a quasi-fixed factor in the short run.

The demand for labour in the short run can be derived by examining the firm's short-run output and employment decisions. Two decision rules follow from the assumption of **profit maximization**. First, because the costs associated with the fixed factor must be paid whether or not the firm produces (and whatever amount the firm produces), the firm will operate as long as it can cover its **variable costs** (i.e., if total revenue exceeds total variable costs). **Fixed costs** are sunk costs, and their magnitude should not affect whatever is currently the most profitable thing to do.

The second decision rule implied by profit maximization is that, if the firm produces at all (i.e., is able to cover its variable costs), it should produce the quantity Q^* at which **marginal revenue** (MR) equals **marginal cost** (MC). That is, the firm should increase output until the additional cost associated with the last unit produced equals the additional revenue associated with that unit.

If the firm is a price-taker, the marginal revenue of another unit sold is the prevailing market price. If the firm is a **monopolist**, or operates in a less than perfectly competitive product market, marginal revenue will be a decreasing function of output (the price must fall in order for additional units to be sold). With capital fixed, the marginal cost of producing another unit of output is the wage times the amount of labour required to produce that output. Expanding output beyond the point at which MR = MC will lower profits, because the addition to total revenue will be less than the increase in total cost. Producing a lower output would also reduce profits, because at output levels below Q^* marginal revenue exceeds marginal cost. Increasing output would add more to total revenue than to total cost, thereby raising profits.

The profit-maximizing decision rules can be stated in terms of the employment of inputs rather than in terms of the quantity of output to produce. Because concepts such as total revenue and marginal revenue are defined in terms of units of output, the terminology is modified for inputs. The total revenue associated with the amount of an input employed is called the **total revenue product** (TRP) of that input; similarly, the change in total revenue associated with a change in the amount of the input employed is called the **marginal revenue product** (MRP). Both the total and marginal revenue products of labour will depend on the physical productivity of labour as given by the production function, and on the marginal revenue received from selling the output of the labour in the product market.

Thus, the profit-maximizing decision rules for the employment of the variable input can be stated as follows:

- The firm should produce, providing the total revenue product of the variable input exceeds the total costs associated with that input; otherwise, the firm should shut down operations.
- If the firm produces at all, it should expand employment of the variable input to the point at which its marginal revenue product equals its marginal cost.

The short-run employment decision of a firm operating in a perfectly competitive labour market is shown in Figure 5.1. In a competitive factor market, the firm is a price-taker; that is, the firm can hire more or less of the factor without affecting the market price. Thus, in a competitive labour market, the marginal (and average) cost of labour is the market wage rate. The firm will, therefore, employ labour until its marginal revenue product equals the wage rate, which implies that the firm's short-run labour demand curve is its marginal revenue product of labour curve. For example, if the wage rate is W_0, the firm would employ N_0^* labour services. However, the firm will shut down operations in the short run if the total variable cost exceeds the total revenue product of labour, which will be the case if the average cost of labour (the wage rate) exceeds the average revenue product of labour (ARP). Thus, at wage rates higher than W_1 in Figure 5.1 (the point at which the wage rate equals the average product of labour), the firm would choose to shut down operations. It follows that the firm's short-run labour demand curve is its marginal revenue product of labour curve below the point at which the average and marginal product curves intersect (i.e., below the point at which the ARP_N reaches a maximum).

The short-run labour demand curve is downward sloping because of **diminishing marginal returns** to labour. Although the average and marginal products may initially rise as more labour is employed, both eventually decline as more units of the variable factor are combined with a given amount of the fixed factor. Because the firm employs labour in the range in which its marginal revenue product is declining, a reduction in the wage rate is needed to entice the firm to employ more labour. Similarly, an increase in the wage rate will cause the firm to employ less labour, thus raising its marginal revenue product and restoring equality between the marginal revenue product and marginal cost.

At this point, it may be worth highlighting a common misconception concerning the reason for the downward-sloping demand for labour. The demand is for a given, homogeneous type of labour; consequently, it does *not* slope downward, because as the firm uses more labour it uses poorer-quality labour and, thus, pays a lower wage. It may well be true that when firms expand their work force they often have to use poorer-quality labour. Nevertheless, for analytical purposes, it is useful to assume a given, homogeneous type of labour so that the impact on labour demand of changes in the wage rate for that type of labour can be analyzed. The change in the productivity of labour that occurs does so because of changes in the amount of the variable factor combined with a given amount of the fixed factor, not because the firm is utilizing inferior labour.

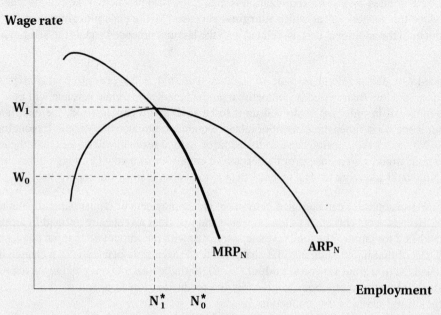

Figure 5.1 The Firm's Short-Run Demand for Labour

Profit maximization requires labour to be employed until its marginal cost (the wage) equals its marginal benefit (marginal revenue product). For the wage, W_0, the profit-maximizing employment level is N_0^*. At wages higher than W_1, labour costs exceed the value of output, so the firm will hire no labour. The labour demand schedule is, thus, MRP_N, below where ARP_N reaches its maximum (the thicker part of the curve on the figure).

Wages, the Marginal Productivity of Labour, and Competition in the Product Market

The demand schedule of a profit-maximizing firm that is a wage-taker in the labour market is the locus of points for which the marginal revenue product of labour equals the wage rate. The marginal revenue product of labour (MRP_N) equals the marginal revenue of output (MR_Q) times the **marginal physical product** of labour (MPP_N). Thus, there is a relationship between wages and the marginal productivity of labour.

The marginal revenue of output depends on the market structure in the product market. The two polar cases of perfect competition and monopoly are discussed here. A perfectly competitive firm is a price-taker in the product market. Because the firm can sell additional (or fewer) units of output without affecting the market price, the marginal revenue of output equals the product price; that is, for a competitive firm,

$$MRP_N = MR_Q \times MPP_N = p \times MPP_N \tag{5.2}$$

Because it is the product of the market price and the marginal product of labour, this MPP_N term is also sometimes called the **value of the marginal product** of labour. A firm that is competitive in both the product and the labour markets will, thus, employ labour services until the value of the marginal product of labour just equals the wage; that is, the demand for labour obeys equation 5.3:

$$p \times MPP_N = MRP_N = w \tag{5.3}$$

Equation 5.3 follows from the MR = MC rule for profit maximization: the MRP_N is the increase in total revenue associated with a unit increase in labour input, while the wage, w, is the accompanying increase in total cost. Alternatively stated, the labour demand curve of a firm that is competitive in both the product and the labour market is the locus of points for which the real wage, w/p, equals the marginal physical product of labour.

The polar case of noncompetitive behaviour in the product market is that of monopoly. In this situation, the firm is so large relative to the size of the product market that it can influence the price at which it sells its product. It is a price-setter, not a price-taker. In the extreme case of monopoly, the monopolist makes up the whole industry; there are no other firms in the industry. Thus, the industry demand for the product is the demand schedule for the product of the monopolist.

As is well-known from standard microeconomic theory, the relevant decision-making schedule for the profit-maximizing monopolist is not the demand schedule for its product, but rather its marginal revenue schedule. In order to sell an additional unit of output, the monopolist has to lower the price of its product. Consequently, its marginal revenue, the additional revenue generated by selling an additional unit of output, will be lower than its price. As shown in Figure 5.4(b), the marginal revenue schedule for the monopolist will, therefore, lie below and to the left of its demand schedule. By equating marginal revenue with marginal cost so as to maximize profits, the monopolist will produce less output and charge a higher price (as given by the demand schedule, since this is the price that consumers will pay) than if it were a competitive firm on the product market.

This aspect of the product market has implications for the derived demand for labour. The monopolist's demand for labour curve is the locus of points for which,

$$MR_Q \times MPP_N = MRP_N = w \qquad (5.4)$$

The differences between equation 5.3 and 5.4 highlight the fact that when the monopolist hires more labour to produce more output, not only does the marginal physical product of labour fall (as is the case with the competitive firm), but the marginal revenue from an additional unit of output, MR_Q, also falls. The monopolist produces less output than a competitive firm and will, therefore, demand less labour. Furthermore, because both MPP_N and MR_Q fall when N increases in equation 5.4, then the monopolist's demand for labour falls faster than it would if it behaved as a competitive firm in the product market, in which case only MPP_N would fall, as given in equation 5.3.

LO1, 2 Demand for Labour in the Long Run

In the long run, the firm can vary all of its inputs. For expositional purposes, we will continue to assume two inputs, labour, N, and capital, K, and one output, Q. However, the general principles apply to firms that employ many inputs and produce multiple outputs. As in the previous section, the demand for labour is derived by varying the wage rate that the firm faces for a given homogeneous type of labour and tracing out the profit-maximizing (or cost-minimizing) quantity of labour that will be employed by the firm.

For conceptual purposes, the firm's production and employment decisions are usually examined in two stages. First, the minimum-cost method of producing any level of output is examined. Second, given that each output will be produced at minimum cost, the profit-maximizing level of output is chosen.

Isoquants, Isocosts, and Cost Minimization

As before, output is assumed to be produced according to the technology represented by the firm's production function, $Q = F(K, N)$. In this case, capital and labour are chosen together to maximize profits. The first stage of profit maximization (**cost minimization**) is depicted geometrically in Figure 5.2. The top part of the diagram, Figure 5.2(a), gives the firm's **isoquant**, Q_0, which shows the various combinations of labour, N, and capital, K, that can produce a given level of output, Q_0. This isoquant reflects the technological constraints implied by the production function. For any level of desired output, there will be a corresponding isoquant offering the menu of combinations of capital and labour that could be employed to produce the level of output. Higher levels of output will require higher levels of inputs, and isoquants corresponding to higher output levels (like Q_1) lie to the "northeast" of the Q_0 isoquant.

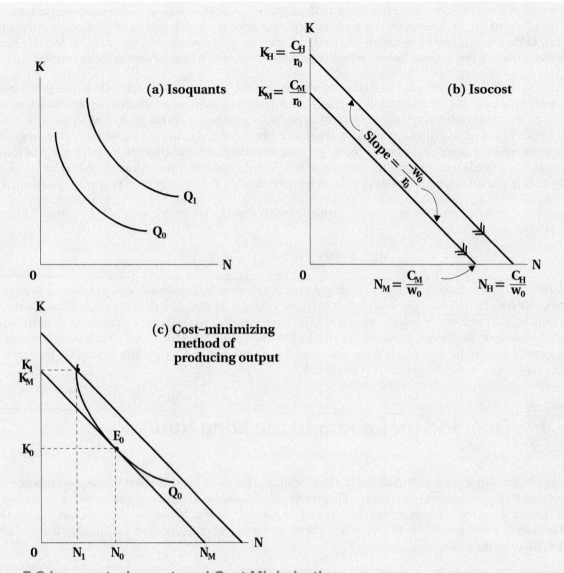

Figure 5.2 Isoquants, Isocost, and Cost Minimization

Cost minimization entails producing a given output, Q_0, using the cheapest possible combination of capital, K, and labour, N, and it depends on both technology and the relevant input prices. The technology is represented by isoquants (panel (a)), which show the different ways Q_0 can be produced with K and N. Panel (b) summarizes the costs associated with using any combination of K and N. For example, all points along the line $K_M N_M$ cost the same, C_M. Panel (c) shows the cost-minimizing choice, E_0. Here, Q_0 is produced in the least expensive way: no other point on the isoquant for Q_0 lies closer to the origin (i.e., on a lower isocost line). At the point E_0, the firm uses (K_0, N_0) to produce Q_0, and, furthermore, the tangency between the isocost line and isoquant implies that the marginal rate of technical substitution equals the ratio of input prices (w_0/r_0).

The slope of the isoquant represents the **marginal rate of technical substitution** (MRTS) between the inputs. The MRTS reflects the ease with which capital and labour can be substituted to produce a given level of output. Isoquants exhibit diminishing MRTS, as it becomes harder to substitute away from a factor when there is less of it. For example, in the upper left segment, when an abundance of capital is used, a considerable increase in the use of capital is required to offset a small reduction in the use of labour if output is to be maintained. In the lower right segment, when an abundance of labour is used, labour is a poor substitute for capital, and considerable labour savings are possible for small increases in the use of capital. In the middle segment of the isoquant, labour and capital are both good substitutes. Successively higher isoquants, or levels of output, such as Q_1, can be produced by successively larger amounts of both inputs.

Clearly, under differing technologies, we expect the difficulty of substitution to vary. If hoeing requires one hoe per worker, purchasing additional hoes without the workers, or hiring extra workers without hoes, will not allow much of an increase in output. In that case, production would be characterized by a low level of substitutability between the inputs. On the other hand, it might be easier to substitute weeding labour for herbicides. One could imagine using a lot of labour and doing all the weeding by hand, or hiring only one worker to apply large quantities of chemicals. Intermediate combinations would also be feasible. In that case, the level of substitutability will be high. The substitutability of one factor for another will clearly have an effect on the responsiveness of producers to small changes in the relative prices of the two factors.

The firm's objective will be to choose the least expensive combination of capital and labour along the isoquant Q_0. The costs of purchasing various combinations of capital and labour will depend on the prices of the inputs. Figure 5.2(b) illustrates the firm's **isocost line**, $K_M N_M$, depicting the various combinations of capital and labour the firm can employ, given their market price and a total cost of C_M. Algebraically, the isocost line is $C_M = rK + wN$, where r is the price of capital and w the price of labour, or wage rate.[1] The position and shape of the isocost line can be determined by solving for the two intercepts, or endpoints, and the slope of the line between them. From the isocost equation, for fixed prices r_0 and w_0, these endpoints are $N_M = C_M/w_0$ when $K = 0$, and $K_M = C_M/r_0$ when $N = 0$. The slope is simply minus the rise divided by the run, or $-[C_M/r_0 \div C_M/w_0] = -w_0/r_0$; that is, the price of labour relative to the price of capital. This is a straight line as long as w and r are constant for these given types of labour and capital, which is the case when the firm is a price-taker in both input markets. Isocost lines will pass through each possible combination of capital and labour that the firm could hire. For example, a higher isocost line, $K_H N_H$, is also depicted in Figure 5.2(b). Costs are increasing as the isocost lines move to the northeast (away from the origin).

A profit-maximizing firm will choose the cheapest capital–labour combination that yields the output Q_0. In other words, it will choose the combination of K and N on the isoquant Q_0 that lies on the isocost line nearest the origin. Figure 5.2(c) combines the isoquants and isocost lines to illustrate the minimum-cost input choice that can be used to produce Q_0. This is clearly E_0, where the isocost is tangent to the isoquant. That this should be the minimum-cost combination is most easily seen by considering an alternative combination, K_1 and N_1. The isocost line corresponding to this combination is associated with a higher total cost of production. In this case, costs could be reduced by using more labour and less capital, and by moving toward the combination at E_0.

As with the consumer optimum described in Chapter 2, the tangency between the isoquant and isocost lines has an economic interpretation. At the optimum for the firm, the internal rate of input substitution, given by the marginal rate of technical substitution (the slope of the isoquant), equals the market rate of substitution, given by the relative price of labour and capital (the slope of the isocost line). This tangency can also be expressed in terms of the relative marginal products of capital and labour:

$$MRTS = \frac{MPP_N}{MPP_K} = \frac{w}{r} \tag{5.5}$$

In the short run, we saw that the value of the marginal product of labour was equal to the wage. In the long run, the relative value of the marginal product of labour is equal to the relative price of labour.

The second stage of profit maximization entails choosing the optimal level of output. The determination of the profit-maximizing level of output (the output at which marginal revenue equals marginal cost) cannot be seen in the isoquant-isocost diagram. What is shown is how to produce any output, including the profit-maximizing output, at minimum cost.

At E_0, the cost-minimizing amounts of labour and capital used to produce Q_0 units of output are N_0 and K_0, respectively. If Q_0 is the profit-maximizing output, this gives us one point on the demand curve for labour, as depicted later in Figure 5.3; that is, at the wage rate w_0, the firm employs N_0 units of labour.

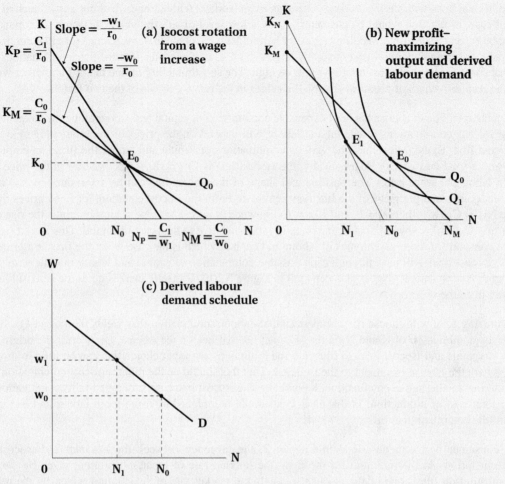

Figure 5.3 Deriving the Labour Demand Schedule

This figure shows how an increase in the wage is associated with a change in the quantity of labour demanded, and, ultimately, how a labour demand curve can be traced out. In panel (a), an increase in the wage from W_0 to W_1 rotates the isocost curves, and E_0 (the profit-maximizing employment level at W_0) is no longer optimal. The new optimal input combination is depicted in panel (b), where the firm is also producing a lower level of output. The new tangency between the isoquant (for Q_1) and isocost curve yields labour demand of N_1, which is lower than N_0. The relationship between wages (W_0 and W_1) and the optimal quantity of labour demanded (N_0 and N_1) is summarized by the labour demand schedule in panel (c).

LO3   Deriving the Firm's Labour Demand Schedule

The complete labour demand schedule for the long run, when the firm can vary both capital and labour, can be obtained simply by varying the wage rate and tracing out the new, equilibrium, and profit-maximizing amounts of labour that would be employed. This is illustrated in Figure 5.3. An increase in the wage from w_0 to w_1 causes all of the isocost curves to become steeper. For example, at the initial input combination, K_0 and N_0, the isocost line rotates from $K_M N_M$ to $K_P N_P$. Clearly, the total cost of continuing to produce Q_0 using K_0 and N_0 will rise. If the firm chose to rent only capital at the new cost level, C_1, it would be able to rent more capital services than before—up to $K_P = C_1/r_0$. On the other hand, even though costs have risen, if the firm spent C_1 entirely on labour, it could hire only up to $N_P = C_1/w_1$. Finally, panel (a) shows that the cost-minimizing (and profit-maximizing) condition no longer holds at E_0, because the isoquant is not tangent to the new isocost line.

As depicted in Figure 5.3(b), given the higher wage rate w_1, the firm will maximize profits by moving to a lower level of output Q_1, operating at E_1, and employing N_1 units of labour. This yields a second point on the firm's demand curve for labour depicted in Figure 5.3(c); that is, a lower level of employment, N_1, corresponds to the higher wage rate, w_1, compared to the original employment of N_0 at wage w_0.

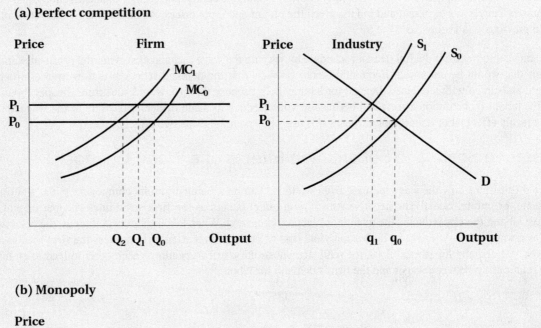

(a) Perfect competition

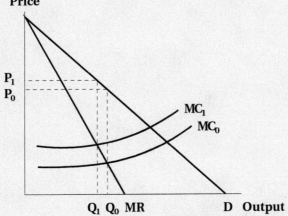

(b) Monopoly

Figure 5.4 The Effect of a Cost Increase on Output

The profit-maximizing level of output falls when the wage increases. Profit maximization requires that $MC(Q) = MR(Q)$. A wage increase raises marginal costs, from MC_0 to MC_1, as shown in panel (a). For a competitive firm, marginal revenue equals the price, and at the original output price, P_0, output would decline to Q_2. However, the shift of the MC schedule for all firms leads the industry supply curve to shift from S_0 to S_1, and market price to rise from P_0 to P_1. Each firm produces Q_1 (where $MC_1 = P_1$), while the industry produces q_1. Similar logic applies to a monopolist, panel (b). The MR function is unchanged by the wage increase, but marginal costs rise from MC_0 to MC_1. This leads to lower output Q_1, where $MR = MC_1$.

To complete the explanation of the firm's response to a wage increase, Figure 5.4 shows how the profit-maximizing output levels (Q_0 and Q_1 in Figure 5.3b) are determined. The wage increase shifts up the firm's marginal and average cost curves. In a perfectly competitive industry, each firm reduces output, which raises the market price of the product. In the new equilibrium, the output of each firm and total output are lower than in the original equilibrium. The monopolist responds to the increase in costs by raising the product price and reducing output. The analysis of the intermediate market structures (monopolistic competition and oligopoly) is similar; in general, an increase in costs, all things being equal, leads to an increase in the product price and a reduction in output. Note, however, that although the firm moves to the lower isoquant (Q_0

to Q_1 in Figure 5.3b), its total costs may increase (as shown in Figure 5.3b where $K_N > K_M$) or decrease. Producing a lower output tends to reduce total costs, but the higher wage tends to raise total costs. The net effect, therefore, depends on the magnitude of these offsetting forces. In this respect, the analysis of the response of the firm to an increase in an input price is not exactly analogous to the response of the consumer to a commodity price increase. In consumer theory, income (or total expenditure on goods) is assumed to be exogenously determined. But firms *do not* have predetermined budget constraints. In the theory of the firm, total cost (or total expenditure on inputs) is endogenous rather than exogenous, and depends on the profit-maximizing levels of output and inputs, given the output and input prices. As these change, total costs may change, as depicted previously in Figure 5.3(b).

Clearly, one could trace out the full demand schedule by varying the wage rate and observing the profit-maximizing amounts of labour that would be employed. Economic theory predicts that the demand schedule is downward sloping (i.e., higher wages are associated with a reduced demand for labour) both because the firm would substitute cheaper inputs for the more expensive labour (substitution effect) and because it would reduce its scale of operations due to the wage and, hence, cost increase (**scale effect**). For conceptual purposes it is useful to examine these two effects.

Separating Scale and Substitution Effects of a Wage Change

Figure 5.5 illustrates how the wage increase from w_0 to w_1 can be separated into its component parts: a substitution effect and a scale, or output, effect. The negative substitution effect occurs as the firm substitutes cheaper capital for the more expensive labour, thereby reducing the quantity of labour demanded. When labour is a normal input, the negative scale effect occurs as a wage increase leads to a higher marginal cost of production that, in turn, reduces the firm's optimal output and, hence, derived demand for labour. Thus, the scale and substitution effects reinforce each other to lead to an unambiguously inverse relationship between wages and the firm's demand for labour.[2]

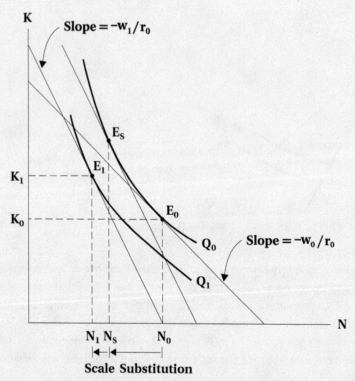

Figure 5.5 Substitution and Scale Effects of a Wage Change

A wage increase from w_0 to w_1 leads to a rotation of the isocost curves. If a firm continued to produce Q_0, the cost-minimizing input combination would move from E_0 to E_S. The associated decline in labour demand from N_0 to N_S is called the *substitution effect*. But the wage increase also leads to a reduction in output, from Q_0 to Q_1. The implied reduction in labour employed from E_S to E_1 is a direct consequence of the output reduction, and the associated reduction in employment from N_S to N_1 is called the *scale effect*.

The scale effect can be isolated by hypothetically forcing the firm to continue producing Q_0. This is illustrated by the hypothetical isocost line that is parallel to the new isocost w_1/r_0, but tangent to the original isoquant Q_0 at E_s. The only difference between E_s and E_1 is the scale of operation of the firm (Q_0 as opposed to Q_1), since the relative price of labour and capital are the same; that is, both are w_1/r_0. Therefore, N_s to N_1 can be thought of as the scale effect—the reduction in employment that comes about to the extent that the firm reduces its output in response to the wage increase. Except in the unusual circumstance in which labour is an inferior input, the scale effect works through the following scenario. Wage increases imply cost increases, which lead to a reduced optimal scale of output, which, in turn, leads to a reduced demand for labour.

The difference between E_0 and E_s, on the other hand, is simply due to the different slopes of the isocost lines. They both represent the same output, Q_0. Consequently, the difference between E_0 and E_s reflects the pure substitution of capital for labour to produce the same output, Q_0. Therefore, N_0 to N_s can be thought of as a pure or output-constant substitution effect, representing the substitution of relatively cheaper inputs for the inputs whose relative price has risen. Both scale and substitution effects work in the same direction to yield an unambiguously downward-sloping demand schedule for labour. The fact that labour demand slopes downward in both the short run and the long run is often referred to as a law of demand, since this is a case where economic theory makes unambiguous predictions about the connection between these two important labour market variables.

For capital, the substitution and scale effects of an increase in the wage rate work in opposite directions. The substitution effect (E_0 to E_s) increases the demand for capital as the firm uses more capital and less labour to produce a given level of output. However, the reduction in output from Q_0 to Q_1 causes a reduction in demand for all normal inputs; thus, the scale effect (E_s to E_1) reduces the demand for capital. The overall, or net, effect on capital thus depends on which of the two effects is larger. In general, an increase in the wage may cause the firm to employ more or less capital.

WORKED EXAMPLE

The Effect of Offshoring on Employment

While it is standard to use capital and labour as the two basic production factors, labour demand theory works just as well when other production factors are considered. One prominent example discussed later in the chapter is the case where the two production factors are Canadian and foreign labour. Understanding the respective roles of Canadian and foreign labour in production is at the core of the debate about the consequences of offshoring.

Consider the case of two firms. Toy Inc. (Toy) is a toy maker that can either hire workers in Canada or abroad to assemble toys. Since workers assembling toys in Canada and abroad perform very similar tasks, they are very close substitutes in production. As a result, the isoquants for Toy do not have much curvature and have a slope of about –1, the marginal product of a foreign worker being about the same as the marginal product of a Canadian worker (remember that the slope of the isoquant, the MRTS, is the ratio of marginal products). Another way to see this is that Toy produces exactly the same number of toys, Q_0, with 100 Canadian workers and 20 foreign workers (point A on the figure) than with 20 Canadian workers and 100 foreign workers (point B). So firing 80 Canadian workers to replace them with 80 foreign workers has no impact on output.

Why would Toy replace Canadian workers with foreign workers? The figure for Toy shows that point A is the point Toy would choose when Canadian wages are $10 while foreign wages are $12.50. The slope of the isocost curve, –12.5/10, is equal to the slope of the isoquant at this point. This would be the case, for example, when Toy can hire only U.S. workers at $12.50 an hour because of geographical proximity. But once it becomes possible to hire Mexican workers at $8 an hour (after taking into account higher transportation costs), the new isocost curve has a slope of –8/10, and it is now optimal for Toy to move to point B. The move from point A to B is a *pure substitution effect* since output is maintained at the same level, Q_0, on the same isoquant. In addition, the decrease in the wage of foreign workers reduces the overall marginal cost. The resulting scale effect enables Toy to hire 40 additional foreign workers and 30 additional Canadian workers to expand production to Q_1 at point C. Combining both substitution and scale effects, Toy reduces its Canadian employment from 100 to 50 workers when the foreign wage declines from $12.5 to $8. This is clearly a case where outsourcing work abroad does reduce Canadian employment.

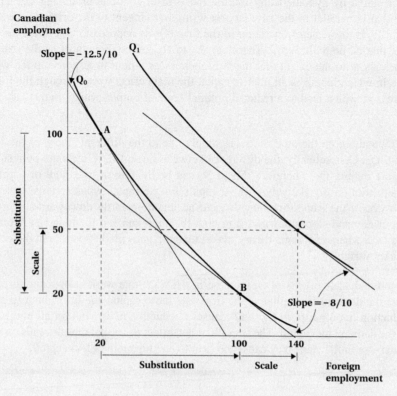

Toy Inc.

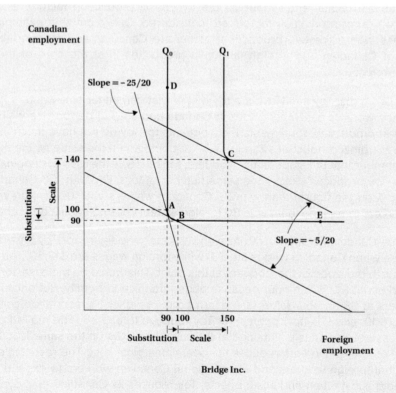

Bridge Inc.

The situation is quite different, however, for Bridge Inc. (Bridge), a Canadian engineering firm specialized in building bridges at home and abroad. Unlike Toy, Bridge employs very different workers in Canada and abroad. All the engineers, designers, and managers work in Canada, while construction workers are hired in the country where bridges are being built. Far from being substitutes, Canadian and foreign workers are now close complements in production. As a result, the isoquants in the figure for Bridge are L-shaped. The shape of the isoquants shows that output remains the same when more and more Canadian engineers are hired (from point A to D) if no additional foreign construction workers are hired to execute the final work. In other words, hiring more engineers but no more construction workers leaves Bridge on the same isoquant, and output remains at Q_0. Similarly, hiring more construction workers from B to E also leaves output unchanged if no additional engineers are hired to plan how to construct the bridge.

Point A represents the choice of output of Bridge when it pays $20 an hour to Canadian workers and $25 an hour to construction workers for projects in the United States. With globalization, however, the market in China becomes accessible and Bridge can now hire construction workers at $5 an hour to do similar work there. As before, the effect of the lower foreign wage can be decomposed into a substitution effect and a scale effect. Moving along the initial isoquant, Bridge slightly reduces Canadian employment, from 100 to 90 workers (point B), and increases foreign employment from 90 to 100 when the foreign wage falls from $25 an hour to $5 an hour. But the lower foreign wage reduces marginal costs, which leads to an expansion of output to point C. Bridge hires 50 additional Canadian workers and 50 additional foreign workers as a result of this scale effect. In the end, the adverse impact of the substitution effect on Canadian employment (10 jobs) is more than offset by the scale effect (50 jobs). The fact that Bridge employs more foreign workers than before (150 instead of 90) does not result in a decline of Canadian employment. Globalization and offshoring may, thus, be good or bad for Canadian employment. Everything depends on whether Canadian and foreign workers are substitutes or complements in production.

The Relationship Between Short- and Long-Run Labour Demand

The division of the firm's response to a wage change into the substitution and scale effects is also useful in understanding the difference between the short-run and long-run labour demands. In the short run, the amount of capital is fixed; thus, there is no substitution effect. The downward-sloping nature of the short-run labour demand curve is a consequence of a scale effect and diminishing marginal productivity of labour. In the long run, the firm has the additional flexibility associated with varying its capital stock. Thus, the response to a wage change will be larger in the long run than in the short run, all things being equal. This relationship is illustrated in Figure 5.6. The initial long-run equilibrium is at E_0. The short-run response to the wage increase, from w_0 to w_1, involves moving to a new equilibrium at E_0^1. Here, the firm is employing less labour (N_0^1 versus N_0) but the same amount of capital, K_0. In the long run, the firm also adjusts its capital stock from K_0 to K_1, shifting the short-run labour demand curve to the left. The new long-run equilibrium is at E_1. The long-run labour demand curve consists of the locus of points, such as E_0 and E_1, at which the firm has optimally adjusted employment of both labour and capital, given the wage rate and other exogenous variables.

Labour Demand under Cost Minimization

Economic analysis generally assumes that firms in the private sector seek to maximize profits. However, organizations in the public and quasi-public sectors—such as federal, provincial, and municipal public administration; Crown corporations; and educational and health institutions—generally have other goals. These goals will determine the quantity of output, or services provided, and the amount of labour and other productive inputs employed. Although the factors that determine the output of these organizations may vary, such organizations may seek to produce that output efficiently; that is, at minimum cost.

The distinction between the scale and substitution effects is useful in analyzing the demand for labour in these circumstances. An organization whose output of goods and/or services is exogenously determined, but that seeks to produce that output at minimum cost, will respond to changes in wages by substituting between labour and other inputs. That is, with output fixed (determined by other factors) there will be a pure substitution effect in response to changes in the wage rate. Labour demand will, therefore, be unambiguously downward sloping but more inelastic than that of a profit-maximizing firm because of the absence of an output effect.

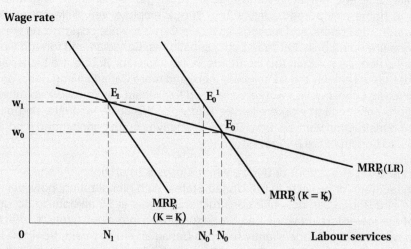

Figure 5.6 The Demand for Labour in the Short and the Long Run

For a given w_0, consider a firm in long- and short-run equilibrium; it has no desire to change its level of labour or capital. The wage rises to W_1. In the short run, K_0 is fixed and employment falls to N_0^1. In the long run, the firm adjusts to capital, K_1, and long-run employment of N_1. Long-run labour demand is thus flatter than the "family" of short-run labour demand schedules associated with any fixed level of capital, since the potential for substitution is greater.

Although a cost-minimizing organization will respond to a wage increase by substituting capital for labour, its total expenditure on inputs (total costs) will, nonetheless, rise. This aspect is illustrated in Figure 5.5. The equilibrium E_s involves greater total costs than the original equilibrium, E_0. The increase in total costs is, however, less than would be the case if the organization did not substitute capital for labour in response to the wage increase (i.e., if the firm remained at the point E_0 in Figure 5.5).

LO4   Elasticity of Demand for Labour

The previous analysis indicated that the demand for labour is a negative function of the wage rate. Consequently, in this static, partial-equilibrium framework, an exogenous increase in wages, other things held constant, would lead to a reduction in the quantity of labour demanded. The exogenous increase in wages, for example, could emanate from a union wage demand, a wage parity scheme, or wage-fixing legislation, such as minimum wages, equal pay, fair-wage legislation, or extension legislation. Although there may be offsetting factors (to be discussed later), it is important to realize that economic theory predicts there will be an adverse employment effect from these wage increases. The magnitude of the adverse employment effect depends on the elasticity of the derived demand for labour. As illustrated in Figure 5.7, if the demand for labour is inelastic, as in Figure 5.7(a), then the adverse employment effect is small; if the demand is elastic, as in Figure 5.7(b), then the adverse employment effect is large.

From a policy perspective, it is important to know the expected magnitude of these adverse employment effects, because they may offset other possible benefits of the exogenous wage increase. Consequently, it is important to know the determinants of the **elasticity of demand for labour**. As originally outlined by Marshall and formalized by Hicks (1963, pp. 241–6 and 374–84), the basic determinants of the elasticity of demand for labour are the availability of substitute inputs, the elasticity of supply of substitute inputs, the elasticity of demand for output, and the ratio of labour cost to total cost. These factors are related to the magnitude of the substitution and scale effects discussed previously. Each of these factors will be discussed in turn, in the context of an inelastic demand for labour in Figure 5.7(a), which implies a wage increase being associated with a small adverse employment effect.

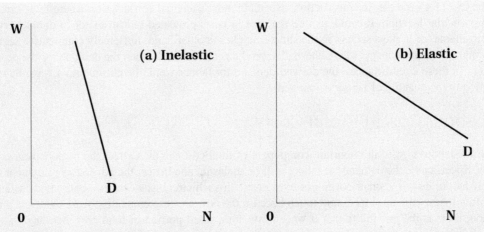

Figure 5.7 Inelastic and Elastic Demand for Labour
Steeper labour demand functions, as in panel (a), are usually more inelastic than flatter ones, as in panel (b). For a given percentage increase in the wage (from a common starting point), the reduction in employment is lower for the more-inelastic demand curve.

Availability of Substitute Inputs

The derived demand for labour will be inelastic, and hence, the adverse employment effect of an exogenous wage increase will be small, if alternative inputs cannot be substituted easily for the higher-price labour. This would be depicted by an isoquant that is more an L-shaped as opposed to a negatively sloped straight line; that is, the marginal rate of technical substitution between other inputs and labour is small. This factor relates to the magnitudes of the substitution effect.

The inability to substitute alternative inputs could be technologically determined (e.g., if the particular type of labour is essential to the production process) or it could be institutionally determined (e.g., if the union prevents such substitution as outsourcing or the use of non-union labour or the introduction of new technology). Time also is a factor, since in the long run the possibility of substituting cheaper inputs is more feasible.

Examples of workers for whom substitute inputs may not *readily* be available are construction tradespeople, teachers, and professionals with specialized skills. Even in these cases, however, substitutions are technically possible in the long run, especially when one considers alternative production processes and delivery systems (e.g., prefabricated construction, larger class size with clickers and other computer-enabled devices, and the use of paraprofessionals).

Elasticity of Supply of Substitute Inputs

The substitution of alternative inputs can also be affected by changes in the price of these inputs. If the substitutes are relatively *inelastic* in supply, so that an increase in the demand for the inputs will lead to an increase in their price, then this price increase may choke off some of the increased usage of these substitutes. In general, this is probably not an important factor, however, because it is unlikely that the firm or industry where the wage increase occurs is such a large purchaser of alternative inputs that it affects their price. Certainly, in the long run, the supply of substitute inputs is likely to be more elastic.

Elasticity of Demand for Output

Since the demand for labour is derived from the output produced by the firm, then the elasticity of the demand for labour will depend on the price-elasticity of the demand for the output, or services produced, by the firm. The elasticity of product demand determines the magnitude of the scale effect. If the demand for the output produced by the firm is inelastic, so that a price increase (engendered by a wage increase) will not lead to a large reduction in the quantity demanded, then the derived demand for labour will also be inelastic. In such circumstances, the wage increase can be passed on to consumers in the form of higher product prices without there being much of a reduction in the demand for those products and, hence, in the derived demand for labour.

This could be the case, for example, in construction, especially nonresidential construction where there are few alternatives to building in a particular location. It could also be the case in tariff-protected industries, or in public services where few alternatives are available, or in most sectors in the short run. On the other hand, in fiercely competitive sectors, such as the clothing or personal computer industry where alternative products are available, then the demand for the product is probably quite price elastic. In these circumstances, the derived demand for labour would be elastic and a wage increase would lead to a large reduction in the quantity of labour demanded.

Share of Labour Costs in Total Costs

The extent to which labour cost is an important component of total cost can also affect the responsiveness of employment to wage changes. Specifically, the demand for labour will be inelastic, and hence, the adverse employment effect of a wage increase small, if labour cost is a small portion of total cost.[3] In such circumstances, the scale effect would be small; that is, the firm would not have to reduce its output much because the cost increase emanating from the wage increase would be small. In addition, there is the possibility that if wage costs are a small portion of total cost then any wage increase more easily could be absorbed by the firm or passed on to consumers.

For obvious reasons, this factor is often referred to as the "importance of being unimportant." Examples of the wage cost for a particular group of workers being a small portion of total cost could include construction craftworkers, airline pilots, and employed professionals (e.g., engineers and architects). In such circumstances, their wage increases simply may not matter much to the employer, and consequently, their wage demands may not be tempered much by the threat of reduced employment. On the other hand, the wages of government workers and miners may constitute a large portion of the total cost in their respective trades. The resultant elastic demand for labour may therefore temper their wage demands.

Empirical Evidence

Clearly, knowledge of the elasticity of demand for particular types of labour is important for policymakers, enabling them to predict the adverse employment effects that may emanate from such factors as minimum wage and equal pay laws or from wage increases associated with unionization, occupational licensing, or arbitrated wage settlements. Estimates of the elasticity of the demand for the particular type of labour being affected would be useful in predicting the employment effect of an exogenous wage increase. However, even without precise numerical estimates, judicious statements still can be made on the basis of the importance of the various factors that determine the elasticity of the demand for labour.

Hamermesh (1986, 1993) reviews the extensive empirical literature that can be used to calculate estimates of the elasticity of demand for labour. He concludes, largely on the basis of private-sector data from the United States, that the elasticity ranges between −0.15 and −0.75, with −0.30 being a reasonable "best guess."[4] That is, a 1 percent increase in wages would lead to approximately a one-third of 1 percent reduction in employment. This adverse employment effect is, roughly, equally divided between the substitution and scale effects; that is, the substitution and scale effects are approximately equal. In a recent **meta-analysis** of 151 labour demand studies, Lichter, Peichl, and Siegloch (2015) find a median estimated elasticity of -0.551, with 87 percent of estimates lying between 0 and -1. Lichter, Peichl, and Siegloch show that elasticities appear to have increased (in absolute terms) over time, which explains the difference relative to the earlier surveys by Hamermesh. They also show that most of the other propositions regarding labour demand elasticities seem to be reflected in the empirical evidence. For example, the labour demand elasticity decreases as the skill level of the labour increases, and the long-run elasticity is larger than the short-run elasticity.

Canadian studies have obtained broadly similar estimates. For example, Gordon (1996) found that the elasticity of demand for the whole Canadian manufacturing sector was in the –0.1 to –0.3 range for the 1961–1986 period. There are also a number of other Canadian studies based on microeconomic industry- or firm-level data. These studies also yield elasticity estimates in the middle of the range suggested by Hamermesh. Card (1990) analyzes manufacturing employment in unionized firms, using contract-level data, and finds an implied labour demand elasticity of −0.62. In a study of public sector employment, teachers in school boards in Ontario, Currie (1991) also estimates an elasticity in the neighbourhood of −0.55. Since the technology and market conditions vary across these diverse settings, it is remarkable that the empirical studies paint such a consistent picture of the price elasticity of the demand for labour.[5]

Changing Demand Conditions, Globalization, and Offshoring

LO4, 5

Traditionally, labour demand theory has been used to understand how factors like payroll taxes, union wage settlement, and minimum wages affect the employment decision of firms by raising the cost of labour. For example, in a perfectly competitive labour market, payroll taxes increase the wage (including taxes) paid by the firm, which reduces its demand for labour. As we just saw, the elasticity of employment with respect to the wage also depends on the availability of other inputs that can be substituted for labour.

Labour demand theory can also be used, however, to shed light on how employment decisions of Canadian firms are being reshaped in an increasingly globalized world. Examples of the impact of globalization on domestic employment abound in the popular media. Governments and workers are regularly asked to provide tax advantages and wage concessions to keep (or create) manufacturing plants in Canada. The fear is that multinational firms would otherwise open new plants in other parts of the world where labour is cheaper. The threat on employment posed by offshore **outsourcing**, or **offshoring**, has also attracted a lot of attention in media and political circles. For instance, there has been widespread opposition to the **Trans-Pacific Partnership (TPP)** that was signed in February 2016 by the governments of Canada, the United States, Japan, and nine other countries. For instance, presidential candidate Donald Trump strongly opposes the TPP, and free trade agreements more generally, on the grounds that they kill jobs in the United States. There are also mounting concerns that information and communication technologies, or **ICTs** have made it much easier for firms to offshore some of their business in other parts of the world.

Offshoring is not a new phenomenon in the manufacturing sector. Back in the 1980s, a number of U.S. firms started building assembly plants in the **Maquiladora** region of Mexico right next to the U.S. border to exploit much cheaper labour costs. The idea was to outsource the less-skilled assembly work to Mexico while still manufacturing the parts to be assembled (a more skilled task) in the United States. The number of Maquiladora plants further expanded with the enacting of the North American Free Trade Agreement (NAFTA) between Canada, the United States, and Mexico.

What has changed more recently is that ICTs make it possible to outsource services, not simply manufacturing activities, to other countries. Call centres, accounting departments, software development, and even medical diagnosing are being moved to India. For example, some U.S. hospitals now send X-rays by email to India where radiologists earning a fraction of the salary of their U.S. counterparts make the diagnosis and email it back to the United States. So, while the first wave of offshoring in the manufacturing sector predominantly affected less-skilled assembly line workers, there is now a fear that even highly trained professionals may see their jobs "offshored" to developing countries.

Of course, discussing the impact of globalization on labour markets would not be complete without mentioning the staggering economic growth of China. The way things are going, some may wonder whether any manufacturing jobs will be left in Canada and other industrialized countries in a decade or two. Not to forget, of course, the never-ending trade disputes between Canada and the United States about softwood lumber, beef, or other goods and services, or the concern that a high Canadian dollar would force firms to reduce their work forces. The point is that international trade, globalization, and offshoring are dominating the jobs debate in Canada, the United States, and many other countries. Labour demand theory helps clarify the role of these factors and to separate the rhetoric from the hard facts.

The Impact of Trade on a Single Labour Market

The simplest way to look at the impact of globalization is to start with the case where Canadian firms compete with foreign firms for the same product. Since the demand for labour is derived from the output of firms, the demand for labour of Canadian firms will be affected by changes in the product market conditions. With increased trade liberalization, increased competition from cheaper, foreign-produced goods effectively lowers the price that comparable Canadian-produced goods can sell for. In a competitive market, this leads to a decline in the value of the marginal product of domestic (Canadian) labour, since the $MRP_N = p \times MPP_N$. This results in a shift inward of the demand curve for Canadian labour. If the wage of Canadian labour remains constant, then this *must* result in a decline in demand for Canadian labour (all else constant). In order to maintain the profit-maximization condition, however, there are two other possible margins of adjustment besides employment. First, the wage rate could decline enough to offset the decrease in the value of Canadian output. Alternatively, the marginal productivity of labour could increase, offsetting the price decrease.

In many sectors of the economy, however, there are no such things as "Canadian" and "foreign" firms. Modern corporations, rather, produce goods and services by combining capital and labour inputs from Canada and other countries. As we just discussed, ICTs now make it possible for small firms and not just large multinational corporations to outsource some of the work in other countries. The theory of labour demand in the long run is easily adapted to this setting where Canadian labour is one of several inputs available to firms. Just like firms can substitute capital for labour in the long run, global firms can also substitute foreign labour for Canadian labour. When both foreign (F) and Canadian labour (C) are available, profit maximization requires the maintenance of the condition,

$$\frac{MPP_{N,C}}{MPP_{N,F}} = \frac{W_C}{W_F} \tag{5.6}$$

If ICTs or the removal of trade barriers effectively reduces the price of foreign labour, W_F, then we would expect to see a substitution, or outsourcing, toward foreign labour. This simple intuition would seem to suggest that production (and, thus, jobs) will always move to the lower-wage country. Indeed, all else equal, this would be true if Canadian and foreign labour were perfect substitutes in production.

This simple intuition suggests fairly bleak prospects for the Canadian labour market in an era of increased globalization. Fortunately, the simple intuition misses some important points. First, it is not clear that Canadian and foreign labour are substitutes in production. This is important, since cheaper foreign labour results both in a substitution and a scale effect. Because cheap foreign labour reduces production costs, firms produce more and the scale effect increases the demand for both Canadian and foreign labour, provided that both are normal inputs in production. If foreign and Canadian labour are very close substitutes, however, the substitution effect may be large enough to offset the scale effect and result in a decrease in the demand for Canadian labour. Fear of the consequences of offshoring are typically based on this view, that foreign labour is a perfect substitute that merely "replaces" Canadian labour. At the other extreme, if Canadian and foreign labour are perfect **complements** in production, the scale effect will dominate and both Canadian and foreign labour will increase. This is illustrated in more detail in the chapter's Worked Example.

EXHIBIT 5.1

The China Syndrome: the Effect of Chinese Imports on Local Labour Markets

Back in 1970, about a quarter of all jobs in Canada and the United States were in the manufacturing sector. More than four decades later, this proportion has declined to only about 10 percent in both countries. While some of this change is undoubtedly linked to secular trends, such as technological change (e.g., robots replacing workers), a popular belief is that trade, and trade with China in particular, has played an important role in these dramatic changes.

In their influential work on the "China Syndrome," Autor, Dorn, and Hanson (2013) observe the share of total U.S. spending on Chinese goods increased from 0.6 percent in 1991 to 4.6 percent in 2007, with most of the change happening since China joined the World Trade Organization (WTO) in 2001. They study the impact of growing Chinese imports on local labour markets using a research design that compares what happened in regions that competed to different degrees with Chinese firms. For example, local areas where the toy industry is more prevalent should be more adversely affected by competition from China (that now dominated this particular industry worldwide) than local areas specializing in higher-end products, such as airplanes.

Autor, Dorn, and Hanson (2013) find that rising Chinese imports cause higher unemployment, lower labour force participation, and reduced wages in local labour markets more exposed to Chinese competition. They conclude that one-quarter of the decline in U.S. manufacturing employment can be linked to this factor. They also find that government transfers, such as unemployment insurance benefits and disability payments, increased sharply in more trade-exposed labour markets. These large effects may help explain why international trade remains a contentious political issue in the United States and other countries, including Canada.

The second important point to note is that the profit-maximization condition involves *both* sides to the equality; while relative labour costs matter, the relative marginal products (marginal rate of technical substitution) matter as much. If Canadian labour is twice as productive with the same level of employment, then a profit-maximizing global employer will choose to hire as much Canadian labour as possible, even at twice the price. This does not diminish the importance of labour costs in assessing the impact of trade on labour markets, but merely emphasizes the need to consider **productivity** at the same time. A focus on labour costs alone ignores the symmetric role that productivity plays. As long as Canadian workers are sufficiently more productive than Indian workers, firms will not move to India in response to wage differences.

The following tables provide some international comparisons of various aspects of labour costs and productivity. They highlight Canada's changing position in an increasingly integrated world economy. Since it is labour cost relative to productivity that influences competitiveness, the tables provide information on various dimensions: compensation costs (including some fringe benefits), productivity, and unit labour costs, which reflect both compensation costs and productivity (i.e., labour cost per unit of output).

Table 5.1 compares compensation costs in Canada to a variety of countries throughout the world. The costs are converted to Canadian dollars on the basis of the exchange rate, and hence, they reflect fluctuations in the exchange rate. They are specified on an hourly basis so they are adjusted for differences in hours worked. The costs for each year are indexed to the Canadian costs, which are set equal to 100, so that they are all expressed as percentages of the Canadian costs. For example, in 2015, compensation costs in the highest-cost country, Switzerland, were 213 percent of Canadian costs (i.e., 113 percent above Canadian costs), while the costs in the lowest-cost country of Mexico were 19 percent of those in Canada. The figures of Table 5.1 indicate that Canada is reasonably competitive on an international basis in terms of compensation costs. We are significantly below high-wage countries like Germany, Switzerland, Belgium, and the Scandinavian countries but significantly above low-wage countries like Mexico and the newly industrialized economies of Korea and Taiwan (though the gap is narrowing). Canadian costs are slightly lower than those of the United States, our major trading partner. An important point to bear in mind, however, is that one should not be entirely cheered by declining wages. From a welfare perspective, while low wages might make one more competitive, they do not necessarily make one better off. National standards of living depend, crucially, on high wages derived from high productivity. This further emphasizes the importance of considering productivity along with wage costs.

TABLE 5.1	Compensation Costs,[1] Various Countries,[2] 1997, 2005, 2015 (as % of Canadian compensation costs)		
Country	**1997**	**2005**	**2015**
Switzerland	165	153	213
Norway	140	160	161
Belgium	157	156	150
Denmark	128	141	144
Germany	156	144	137
Sweden	135	135	135
Austria	135	123	127
Australia	104	109	125
Finland	121	128	124
United States	125	115	122
France	134	124	121
Netherlands	123	126	118

Country	1997	2005	2015
Ireland	94	113	116
Italy	107	105	102
United Kingdom	104	113	102
Canada	**100**	**100**	**100**
Singapore	66	50	82
Spain	75	79	76
Japan	119	96	76
New Zealand	65	62	75
Korea	50	56	73
Israel	63	51	70
Greece	63	58	50
Portugal	35	36	36
Taiwan	38	30	31
Mexico	19	21	19
Trade-Weighted Measures [3]			
OECD	116	109	119
Europe	123	119	132
East Asia[4]	48	48	62

NOTES:

1. Defined as (1) all payments made directly to the worker, before payroll deductions of any kind, and (2) employer expenditures for legally required insurance programs and contractual and private benefit plans. In addition, for some countries, compensation is adjusted for other taxes on payrolls or employment (or reduced to reflect subsidies), even if they are not for the direct benefit of workers, because such taxes are regarded as labour costs. All figures are on an hours-worked basis and are exchange-rate-adjusted and therefore reflect exchange rates and wages and fringe benefits.

2. In descending order, from high to low, in terms of 2015 compensation costs.

3. Averages for groups of countries, weighted by the amount of trade (exports and imports) with the United States.

4. The "East Asia" category includes Hong Kong, Korea, Singapore, and Taiwan but not China and Japan.

SOURCE: The Conference Board, "International comparisons of hourly compensation costs in manufacturing." Available online, accessed May 2016, www.conference-board.org/ilcprogram/.

The continued success of higher-wage countries like Germany and Sweden shows the viability of being able to compete on the basis of productivity and quality, as opposed to low wages. The extremely low wages of many of the Asian countries and Mexico highlight that it is not possible for Canada to compete on the basis of labour costs alone. Rather, it is important to be able to develop "market niches" on the basis of high productivity and high-value-added production and quality service (i.e., on the basis of a high value of marginal productivity of labour).

Table 5.2 shows how Canadian costs and productivity have evolved since 1990, relative to other countries. Hourly productivity is an estimate of the value of output produced per hour of labour input, and corresponds to the average product of labour. From this table, we can see that Canada had a relatively slower productivity growth over this period compared to the other countries in the table. Korea had, by far, the highest productivity growth (446 percent!). However, from a labour allocation perspective, unit labour costs in Korea hardly changed at all (they increased by 4 percent). The explanation for this apparent puzzle is that hourly compensation moved in tandem with productivity growth in Korea. As a result, unit labour costs remained more or less constant over this period. By contrast, hourly compensation grew less in Canada than in most other countries. This means that the relatively average performance of Canada in terms of unit labour costs was achieved at the expense of poor growth in hourly compensation. Productivity growth was simply not large enough to allow Canadian firms to substantially raise wages without increasing unit labour costs. Productivity grew even less in countries like Norway and Australia. At the same time, hourly compensation increased faster in these countries than in Canada, which made these countries less competitive (higher labour costs). Countries like the United States and Sweden were in a more enviable position as they achieved significant reductions in their labour costs thanks to large improvements in productivity. This allowed them to increase hourly compensation substantially over the 1990–2014 period. The fact that productivity increased much faster in the United States than in Canada over recent years raises important concerns, since standards of living are, ultimately, linked to productivity.

TABLE 5.2	Change in Productivity,[1] Hourly Compensation,[2] and Unit Labour Costs[3] in Manufacturing, 1990–2014 (various countries)		
Country	**Hourly Productivity**	**Hourly Compensation**	**Unit Labour Cost**
Italy	37	92	32
Australia	53	188	96
Norway	53	178	87
Canada	66	108	31
Belgium	80	126	18
United Kingdom	84	116	35
France	93	134	12
Germany	94	139	27
Japan	97	88	-16
Netherlands	97	124	21
Denmark	102	136	28
United States	162	118	−14
Sweden	221	104	−35
Taiwan	270	90	−44
Korea	451	446	4

NOTES:

All figures represent the percentage increase, relative to 1990 base year.

1. Output per hour.

2. Compensation is defined as (1) all payments made directly to the worker, before payroll deductions of any kind and (2) employer expenditures for legally required insurance programs and contractual and private-benefit plans. In addition, for some countries, compensation is adjusted for other taxes on payrolls or employment (or reduced to reflect subsidies), even if they are not for the direct benefit of workers, because such taxes are regarded as labour costs. All figures are on an hours-worked basis and are exchange-rate-adjusted, and therefore reflect exchange rates and wages and fringe benefits.

3. Hourly compensation per unit of output (i.e., adjusted for productivity).

SOURCE: U.S. Department of Labor, Bureau of Labor Statistics, "International comparisons of manufacturing productivity and unit labor cost trends." and The Conference Board, "International Comparisons of Manufacturing Productivity & Unit Labor Costs Trends." Available online, accessed May 2016, www.conference-board.org/ilcprogram/.

Figure 5.8 provides a more detailed view on the competitive position of Canada relative to our largest trading partner, the United States. The graph summarizes the same information as in Table 5.2 for every year between 1989 and 2014, comparing trends in labour costs and productivity in the two countries. There are three important points to note. First, Canada's unit labour costs are much higher now than they were in the 1990s (relative to those of the United States). This has occurred because hourly compensation has fallen more slowly than productivity. The second point is that the relative costs fluctuate quite a bit. Most of this fluctuation turns out to be driven by the exchange rate. For example, unit labour costs decreased between 1989 and 2001 as the Canadian dollar fell from 85 cents (U.S.) to 64 cents. Labour cost then increased very sharply as the exchange rates appreciated by almost 50 percent since 2001, going from 64 cents in 2001 to around parity a few years ago, before declining again since 2013. The third point is that, since the late 1990s, productivity (output per hour) has steadily declined relative to the United States.

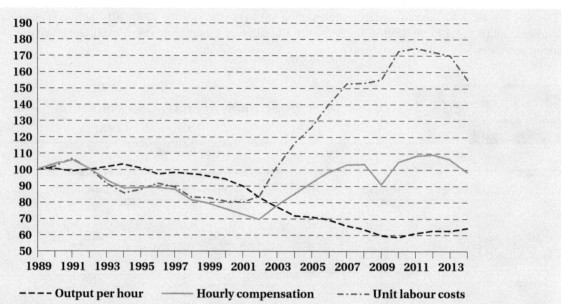

Figure 5.8 Relative Trends in Labour Costs and Productivity: Canada Relative to the United States (base year 1989)

This figure shows relative trends in productivity and labour costs in Canada and the United States. Each point shows the ratio of a cost (or productivity) index in Canada to that in the United States, with 1989 as the base year. For example, in 2007 unit labour costs were 60 percent higher in Canada than in 1989, compared to the United States. Note that these figures do not compare the levels of costs between Canada and the United States, only their trends (relative to 1989).

NOTES: Points represent the relative value of indices of Canadian to U.S. labour costs and productivity (as defined in the notes to Table 5.2). The base year is 1989 (index = 100 for both Canada and the United States).

SOURCE: Author's calculations based on U.S. Department of Labor, Bureau of Labor Statistics, "International comparisons of manufacturing productivity and unit labor cost trends." and The Conference Board, "International Comparisons of Manufacturing Productivity & Unit Labor Costs Trends." Available online, accessed May 2016, www.conference-board.org/ilcprogram/.

The recent and dramatic increase of labour costs in Canada relative to those in the United States is an increasing source of concern among policymakers and other observers of the Canadian economy. For instance, former Governor Mark Carney of the Bank of Canada remarked that the combination of an appreciating currency and poor productivity performance is threatening the prospects of an export based recovery (Bank of Canada 2011). This would, in turn, have adverse consequences on the employment performance of Canada in the years to come.

Cross-Sectoral Impact of Trade

The above discussion is illuminating on a number of issues related to trade and labour markets. In particular, it emphasizes the important role of the productivity of labour as a determinant, as much as the wage, on where employment is likely to grow in an increasingly global economy. Unfortunately, the single-market framework is too divorced from underlying trade theory to allow us to make more insightful statements about the impact of increased trade on employment and wages.

The following simple trade model illustrates a couple of additional points. It shows the underlying motivation for expanded trade—the possible gains to an economy from increased openness. It also emphasizes the importance of cross-sectoral adjustment in evaluating the labour market effects of trade. While the model is quite simplified, its assumptions provide a useful framework for evaluating the impact of recent trade agreements.[6]

Consider a small economy (relative to the world) that produces and consumes only two products: beer and wine. Assume that the economy is completely closed—that is, that it engages in no trade, so that consumers can consume exactly only what they produce. Such an economy is illustrated in Figure 5.9(a). The **production possibility frontier (PPF)** is given by PP . If labour were allocated entirely in the production of beer, then 100 units (cases) could be produced. Alternatively, if labour were moved entirely into wine production, 15 cases could be produced.

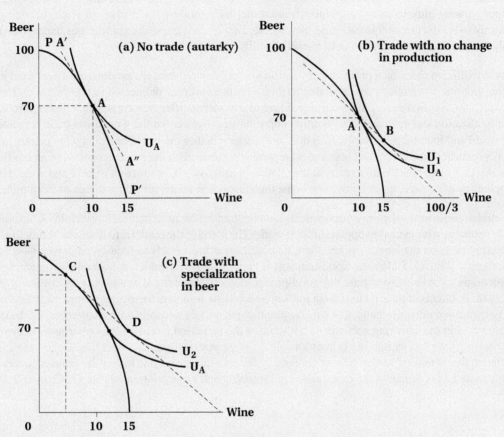

Figure 5.9 Trade, Consumption, and Production in a Simple Economy

Consumers can be made better off with trade. Panel (a) shows the no-trade outcome, where consumption is based on the domestic production possibility frontier, PP'. At the chosen point A, five cases of beer trade for one case of wine. In panel (b) consumption possibilities expand if wine can be purchased in the world market, at a price of three cases of beer for one case of wine. Even without changing production, consumers can attain utility level $U_1 > U_A$. Consumption expands further (in panel (c)) if the economy specializes in producing beer, moving to the point C. On the basis of this production, consumers can attain U_2, associated with consumption point D.

In this economy, consumption possibilities correspond exactly to production possibilities, so a representative or collective consumer must choose from the points on PP the combination of beer and wine that maximizes utility. This optimal consumption and production package is given by the tangency between the indifference curve UA and the PP at point A (for autarky). At this point, the implicit rate of trade (or price) of beer for wine is given by the dashed line, A A , and is equal to five. In other words, one case of wine "trades" for five cases of beer: the consumer's marginal rate of substitution between beer and wine is five (he would be willing to exchange five cases of beer for one case of wine and remain equally happy). And the marginal rate of transformation is also equal to five: in order to produce one more case of wine, labour would have to be reallocated so that output of beer fell by five cases.

Now consider an agent for the world market offering to trade wine and beer with this economy. Note that this agent will only trade wine for beer, or vice versa—she will not give either away. Importing (buying from the agent) necessarily entails exporting (selling to the agent). Similarly, the small economy will not engage in trade unless it yields an improvement in utility. Suppose that the agent offers to exchange one case of wine for five cases of beer. This represents no opportunity (on the margin) for the small economy to engage in trade. In order for the international agent to offer something to the small economy, there must be a difference between the world price and the autarkic price. Consider instead a world price of three cases of beer for one case of wine. On the margin, rather than giving up five cases of beer for the case of wine by shifting production on its own, the small economy *could* trade three cases of beer for the case of wine, at a savings of two cases. This represents an improvement in consumption opportunities, and the set of such opportunities is shown in Figure 5.9(b), under the assumption that production remains exactly as it did before trade. At the extreme, the country could sell its entire production of beer (70 cases) in exchange for 70/3 cases of wine. This would allow it to consume a total of 70/3 cases of imported wine plus 10 cases of (identical) domestic, for a total of 100/3 cases of wine. Consumption need not correspond exactly to production in this case, and the expanded set of consumption opportunities makes the small economy unambiguously better off, allowing it to achieve a level of utility indicated by U_1.

If the economy is willing to reorganize production by shifting more labour toward the production of beer (and implicitly away from wine), consumption possibilities are expanded further. This possibility is delineated in Figure 5.9(c). Here, production moves to C, while consumption moves to D, corresponding to a higher indifference curve, U_2. Openness to trade can result in increased specialization and enhanced consumption opportunities. Notice that the gains from trade depended only on the divergence of world and internal *relative* prices. It does not matter whether the world beer and wine market is dominated by a "super-mega" producer that can produce beer and wine with less labour than the small economy, or an inefficient producer of both goods. All that matters is the difference in the relative productivity in production of beer and wine. This is the basic notion of comparative advantage, the driving force in the theoretical arguments regarding the gains from trade.

This simple model illustrates why most economists favour free trade as a general principle. Consumers are made unambiguously better off with increased opportunities to trade. The value of the model also lies in its ability to assess the likely impact of increased trade on the labour market. First, it suggests that trade leads to sectoral adjustment—some sectors will expand while others will shrink. Unless the world economy is "giving away" its output, at least one sector must expand in order for the small economy to be able to purchase the world-produced goods. Looking at aggregate employment statistics may not tell the full story of the effects of trade on the labour market. Second, the argument for the gains from trade assumes that there is a representative consumer, or equivalently, that the consumption pie is shared equally with all members of the small economy. If the labour allocated in the shrinking sector does not share in the increased consumption opportunities, then the argument that trade is necessarily welfare-enhancing is questionable. In more practical terms, unless the "losers" are compensated, or costlessly shifted to the "winning" sector, it is not necessarily the case that freer trade makes the small economy better off. We will be pursuing these issues further in our examination of inequality and wage differentials later in Chapter 9.

Evidence

With these theoretical insights behind us, let us turn to the more-specific question of how freer trade has affected the Canadian labour market, especially since the Canada–U.S. Free Trade Agreement (CUFTA) and NAFTA were implemented in 1989 and 1994, respectively. The effects were expected to be positive; job gains exceeding job losses, increases in real wages, and reductions in unemployment. However, more than two decades later, controversy remains about the actual effects of these free trade agreements (FTAs), with opponents attributing mass layoffs and plant closings to the CUFTA and NAFTA. In particular, there has been a renewed controversy in the United States about NAFTA, with republican presidential nominee Donald Trump threatening to pull the United States out of NAFTA if elected. However, it has been difficult to isolate the independent impact of CUFTA and NAFTA, in part because they were phased in over a long time period, but more importantly, because it was only one of many interrelated forces affecting the labour market at the time (Betcherman and Gunderson 1990). The other forces include those discussed in this section: global competition, industrial structuring, technological change, privatization, and subcontracting. The CUFTA also coincided with a recession in both Canada and the United States, and a high Canadian dollar (recall Figure 5.8).

An increasing consensus is emerging about the overall impact of the CUFTA. First, there were definite short-run adjustment costs, especially in heavily protected industries; that is, those that had the largest tariff reductions. Gaston and Trefler (1997) estimate that of the 400,000 jobs lost in Canada between 1989 and 1993, between 9 and 14 percent (around 40,000 jobs) can be attributed to the FTA, netting out the variety of other contributing factors. To some extent, both Gaston and Trefler and another study by Beaulieu (2000) attribute the adjustment costs to inflexibility (wage rigidity) in the Canadian labour market. Implicit in our discussion of the gains from trade is a costless reallocation of labour from the shrinking sector to the expanding one. If this reallocation is impeded by labour market imperfections, the potentially adverse consequences of trade are magnified. Gaston and Trefler's results emphasize the importance of labour market structure in assessing the benefits of freer trade.

However, Trefler (2004) and Melitz and Trefler (2012) also show that while the short-run costs are evident, there have also been significant long-run benefits of the FTA, especially in terms of higher labour productivity. The reallocation of labour out of the less productive into the more productive plants has led to increases in labour productivity of 0.6 percent per year in all of manufacturing, and a "staggering" 2.1-percent-per-year increase in those manufacturing industries most affected by free trade. While painful in the short run, the specialization in more-productive activities (or modes of production) generates long-run benefits, largely in line with what we would expect using the simple trade models, such as those discussed in Figure 5.9.

Turning to the issue of service offshoring, the available evidence suggests that the impact of offshoring to China, India, and other developing countries has been modest. Trefler (2010) provides a useful review of the recent evidence where he points out that the lion's share of Canada's trade in services remains with other rich countries, such as the United States or Europe. So, while the offshoring of software development services and call centres to India (to take this example) has been growing rapidly, it remains too small to have a noticeable impact on the Canadian labour market. This is not to say that the growing trade with China and India has and will keep having a small impact on Canadian workers. If China starts selling cars to Canada, the recent job losses in the auto sector in Ontario would likely become even more severe. There is just no evidence yet that highly skilled workers in the service sector have experienced labour market difficulties as a result of the stellar economic performance of China, India, and other fast-growing developing nations.

Other Demand-Side Factors

As noted previously, there have been a number of other important changes occurring on the demand side of the Canadian labour market. Industrial restructuring has also been prominent, associated mainly with the decline of blue-collar, often unionized, well-paid jobs in heavy manufacturing. As outlined in more detail later in the chapter on wage structures, these middle-wage jobs have been displaced by jobs at polar ends of the occupational distribution. At the high end are professional, managerial, and administrative jobs; at the low end are the low-wage jobs in services and retailing. This phenomenon has been described as the "declining middle" and it has led to increased wage polarization.

The large factories of the heavy-manufacturing, "smokestack" industries have often given way to more-flexible, modular factories linked together by advanced communications and just-in-time delivery systems that require little inventory. Flexibility and adaptability are crucial, and the need for these elements has led to increases in subcontracting, permanent part-time work forces, and contingent work forces that are utilized as demand changes. The industrial restructuring has often been accompanied through mergers and acquisitions, often leading to workforce reductions (downsizing) and pressures for concession bargaining.

Technological change has continued its advance, especially in areas of information and communication technologies (ICTs). These technologies and the Internet have dramatically reshaped the internal organization of firms and business practices. Robotics has been introduced on the factory floor and the assembly line, and computer-assisted technology has been utilized in virtually every aspect of the production cycle.

These various changes emanating from the demand side of the labour market have significant implications for both labour markets and human resource practices, and for industrial relations policies in general. They imply greater demands for a flexible and adaptable work force, just like the flexibility that is required from the product market side from which the demand for labour is derived. The work force must be willing and able to do a broader array of job assignments and to integrate quality control as an integral part of the job. The product market changes place greater emphasis on a workforce that is trained in the general skills required for continuous upgrading and retraining and is also able to do a variety of tasks ("multi-skilling") associated with the broader job assignments and the emphasis on quality control. As part of the individual worker's responsibility for quality control, there is less emphasis on direct supervision and more emphasis on employee involvement in decision making.

EXHIBIT 5.2

Free Trade and Jobs

In 1990 and 1991, opponents of free trade linked the Canada–U.S. Free Trade Agreement (CUFTA) to the significant job loss experienced in Canada over this time period. Hardly a day went by without the media reporting of one factory or another closing down and moving to the United States. While employment has recovered significantly since that time, to what extent were CUFTA opponents correct in laying blame on free trade for these job losses? As it turns out, this is a difficult question to answer. The job losses at the time coincided with four other major adverse economic factors: (1) a severe recession that occurred in both Canada and the United States; (2) a high Canadian dollar, the increased value of which may have offset any favourable effects of U.S. tariff reductions (recall Figure 5.8); (3) high relative Canadian interest rates, which may have contributed to higher relative economic contraction; and (4) ongoing structural adjustment, and other manifestations of technological change and globalization.

Gaston and Trefler (1994, 1997) present a thorough and careful attempt to disentangle these factors. Given lags in data availability, their studies focus on changes up to 1993, corresponding to the depths of the last recession. They point out that any "conviction" of the FTA for job destruction depends on establishing a link between job loss and trade and, furthermore, to the tariff changes that could be associated with changed trade patterns. The aggregate employment conditions at the time cannot be blamed on the FTA, or at least FTA proponents can reasonably argue that other factors might have been responsible. Thus, the Gaston and Trefler studies look at cross-industry variation in employment growth, compared across the two countries.

They show that employment decline, especially in "sunset" or declining industries, was more severe in Canada. This could be associated with changed tariffs. However, some of the more severe employment declines occurred in industries that were less affected by the FTA (automobiles, steel, and lumber, for example). In the end, they attribute only about 9 to 14 percent of the overall job loss (around 400,000 jobs) to tariff changes resulting from the FTA. Furthermore, they point out that some of this loss would have been reduced if Canadian wages had adjusted more toward the U.S. levels. Townsend (2007) finds that workers in industries most impacted by FTA-induced tariff reductions did eventually experience a substantial decline in wages. This suggests that wages eventually adjusted, which may in turn explain why Canada had a strong employment performance in the late 1990s.

The demand-side changes are also pressuring for compensation that is more flexible and responsive to the changing economic conditions and to the particular economic circumstances of each individual enterprise. This, in turn, puts pressure toward the breakdown of historical pattern bargaining that often prevailed, whereby establishments frequently followed the wage settlements established by certain key pattern-setting firms. This may no longer be viable given the different demand conditions facing different firms. Lemieux, MacLeod, and Parent (2009), indeed, show that the growth in performance-pay schemes closely parallels the decline in collective bargaining coverage.

The changes emanating from the demand side of the labour market have also led to numerous changes in workplace practices. Jobs have often been redesigned to provide for both *job enlargement* (the horizontal addition of a variety of tasks of similar complexity) and *job enrichment* (the vertical addition of tasks of different levels of complexity).

Whether these changes are part of a fundamental transformation or a continuous evolution of the workplace and the labour market is a debatable issue. What is certain is that the demand-side forces are having a substantial impact. The impact is particularly pronounced because the forces tend to work in the same direction, thereby compounding their individual effects. When coupled with many of the supply-side pressures highlighted previously (aging workforce, continued labour force participation of women, dominance of the two-earner family), they emphasize the dynamism that will continue to characterize the Canadian labour market.

Summary

- Labour demand is derived demand; that is, labour is hired in order to produce goods that are sold in the product market. For this reason, labour demand is always connected to the product market, especially in terms of the degree of competition, whether from foreign or domestic producers.

- Labour is only one of several factors of production. In the short run, we imagine that all of these other factors are fixed, and labour is the only variable input. The profit-maximizing level of labour demand will be chosen so that the marginal benefit equals the marginal cost of hiring an additional unit of labour. The marginal cost is the wage rate, while the marginal benefit is the revenue associated with the extra production by that worker, its marginal revenue product (MRP_N). Therefore, the short-run labour demand function is given by the MRP_N schedule, where employment is determined by $W = MRP_N$.

- In the long run, labour can be substituted with other inputs like capital. An increase in the wage will have two effects on the quantity of labour demanded. First, even if output remains the same, the firm will substitute toward capital and away from labour (the substitution effect). Second, the increase in marginal cost will lead to a reduction in the optimal output, and a further reduction in labour demanded (the scale effect).

- Labour demand curves unambiguously slope downward, in both the long and short run. The long-run function is more elastic (at any given wage), because of the greater degree of flexibility in substituting other inputs for labour.

- The impact of globalization and offshoring on the Canadian labour market can be analyzed in the context of a simple labour demand model, where employment in Canada depends on labour productivity and labour costs in Canada versus the rest of the world. However, a richer model allowing for more than a single sector provides a better understanding of the cross-sectoral impacts of increased trade on employment, wages, and economic welfare, and also highlights the important role played by comparative advantage in determining trade and employment patterns.

Keywords

complements

cost minimization

derived demand

diminishing marginal returns

elasticity of demand for labour

factor of production

fixed costs

ICTs

isocost line

isoquant

long run

Maquiladora

marginal cost

marginal physical product

marginal rate of technical substitution

marginal revenue

marginal revenue product

meta-analysis

monopolist

offshoring

outsourcing

production function

production possibility frontier (PPF)

productivity

profit maximization

scale effect

short run

total revenue product

Trans-Pacific Partnership (TPP)

value of marginal product

variable costs

Review Questions

1. Why is the point E_0 in Figure 5.2(c) a stable equilibrium? Show the firm's expansion path. That is, show how the firm's input mix evolves as output is increased.

2. What is meant by an inferior factor of production? How would the firm's demand for labour be altered if labour were an inferior factor of production?

3. "The firm's demand schedule for labour is a negative function of the wage because as the firm uses more labour it has to utilize poorer-quality labour, and, hence, pays a lower wage." True or false? Explain.

4. Derive the firm's demand schedule for labour if it were a monopolist that could influence the price at which it sells its output. That is, relax the assumption that product prices are fixed and trace the implications.

5. With reference to Tables 5.1 and 5.2 and Figure 5.8, discuss Canada's changing international competitive position as regards unit labour cost. Discuss the relative importance of the various dimensions of unit labour cost.

6. "Given our wage costs relative to those in the Asian newly industrialized economies, in China, and in Mexico, it does not make sense to try and compete on the basis of restraining labour costs. Rather, we should concentrate on other ways of competing, including the development of market niches that involve a high-wage, high-value-added strategy." Discuss.

7. "Our real concern on an international basis is that our unit labour costs have increased relative to those of the United States, and this has occurred just at the time when we need to be most competitive, given NAFTA. A prudent policy would be to maintain a low exchange rate." Discuss.

8. During the 2004 U.S. presidential campaign, Senator John Kerry proposed to introduce a special tax on profits of firms attributable to their offshore activities. Discuss under which conditions such a tax would achieve its intended goal of increasing domestic employment.

Problems

1. Output of lawn-care services, measured in number of lawns, depends on the hours of lawn-maintenance labour, given a fixed capital stock, according to the production function:

$$Q = 2\sqrt{L}$$

The marginal product of labour is therefore given by $\dfrac{1}{\sqrt{L}}$. Assume that the price of lawn services is $10 per lawn.

   a. Solve for the labour demand function.

   b. Calculate the labour demand, output, and profits for wages equal to the following (i.e., fill in the remainder of the table):

Wage	Labour	Output	Profits
$1	_____	_____	_____
$2	_____	_____	_____
$5	_____	_____	_____
$10	_____	_____	_____

How do profits vary along the demand curve?

2. Bicycle Helmet Testing Services requires capital (a hammer) and labour to be used in fixed proportions (one labourer per hammer per day of testing). Assume also that it takes one day of steady bashing to fully test one helmet. Show the isoquant for a helmet-testing firm corresponding to 100 helmets tested. Show the cost-minimizing input combination if a day's labour costs $50, a hammer costs $10 to rent for one day, and the firm wishes to test 100 helmets. Depict the scale and substitution effects if the wage decreases to $25 per day. What does the short-run labour demand function look like? What does the long-run labour demand function look like?

3. "The provision of health services requires the labour of doctors and nurses. If the wage rate of nurses increases, while doctor's wages are unchanged, the demand for doctors will increase." True or false? Explain.

4. Assume that fruit-picking can be done by children or adults, but that adults are twice as efficient as children (they pick twice as fast). The production function for fruit-picking is thus

$$Q = 10 \times \left(2L_A + L_C\right)$$

where output is measured in bushels of apples, labour is measured in days, L_A is the number of days of adult labour, and L_C is the number of days of child labour.

   a. Depict the isoquants for a typical orchard (in terms of fruit-picking).

   b. Assume the wage rate of adults is $100 per day, and the wage for children is $60 per day. Show the isocost lines.

   c. Show the profit-maximizing input choice where the profit-maximizing output is 1000 bushels of apples. Depict the scale and substitution effects if the wage of child labour falls to $25 per day.

   What does the demand curve for child labour look like?

5. For each of the following examples, choose the case with the lower (more inelastic) wage elasticity, evaluated at a common point where the wage is $15 per hour:

   a. A farm's demand for farm labour for weeding, in a jurisdiction where chemical herbicides are banned for environmental reasons, versus a jurisdiction where they are not.

   b. A coal mine's demand for labour, where the mine has a local monopoly in the sale of coal, versus a mine that sells coal in a competitive market.

   c. The demand for workers in a cigarette factory versus the demand for workers in a fast-food restaurant.

   d. The demand for computer programmers versus secretaries for factories in Silicon Valley.

   e. The demand for "beer tasters" (quality-control engineers) versus beer production line workers in a brewery.

6. Consider a very simple representation of the before-trade Canadian and U.S. economies. Both countries produce only automobiles and food, according to the technology represented in the following production possibility frontiers:

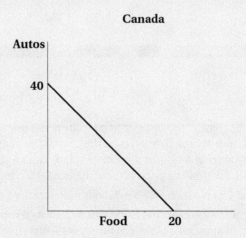

Canada

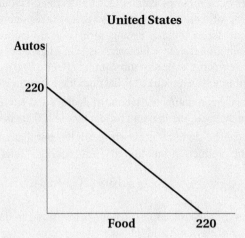

Assume that the working populations of Canada and the United States are 25 and 250, respectively.

a. Using well-labelled diagrams, show that Canada can gain from trade with the United States. Carefully describe what will happen to Canadian production, employment, and wages after free trade with the United States. Be careful to state your assumptions.

b. Recognizing that the above model is a simplification of the real world, analyze the likely short- and long-run employment consequences of free trade with the United States on Canadian employment and wages.

c. "Within four years of the implementation of the Canada–U.S. Free Trade Agreement (FTA) in 1989, employment in Canadian manufacturing dropped by 400,000. This shows that the FTA killed jobs." True or false? Explain.

7. When capital and labour are complements in production, increasing capital results in a *higher* marginal product of labour, and vice versa. By contrast, when capital and labour are substitutes, increasing capital results in a *lower* marginal product of labour, and vice versa.

a. In light of this observation, explain why it is that an increase in the wage reduces the demand for labour but increases the demand for capital when labour and capital are substitutes, while the demand for capital also declines when they are complements.

b. Redraw Figure 5.6 in the two cases where labour and capital are substitutes and complements. Carefully explain whether K_1 is larger or smaller than in each case, and why the $K_0 \text{MRP}_N$ curve shifts the way it does in the long run.

Endnotes

1. If the firm rents its capital equipment, the cost of capital is the rental price. If the firm owns its capital equipment, the implicit or opportunity cost of capital depends on the cost of the machinery and equipment, the interest rate at which funds can be borrowed or lent, and the rate at which the machinery depreciates. In the analysis that follows, we will assume that the firm is a price-taker in the market for capital.

2. Nagatani (1978) proves that this is true even when labour is an inferior factor of production.

3. Hicks (1963, pp. 245–46) proves formally that this is true as long as the elasticity of demand for the final product is greater than the elasticity of substitution between the inputs—that is, as long as consumers can substitute away from the higher-priced product more easily than producers can substitute away from higher-priced labour. This factor thus depends on the magnitude of both the substitution and the scale effects.

4. Hamermesh (1993, p. 135).

5. See Hamermesh (1993), especially Chapter 3, for a more detailed, comprehensive summary of these and other studies.

6. See Johnson and Stafford (1999) for a theoretically more rigorous treatment of the links between trade and labour markets, and a summary of evidence pertaining to these links.

CHAPTER 6

Labour Demand, Non-wage Benefits, and Quasi-fixed Costs

LEARNING OBJECTIVES

LO1 Outline the concept of quasi-fixed costs of labour, explaining how, unlike wages and salaries, these are costs a firm has to pay regardless of the number of hours worked by each employee.

LO2 Discuss the distinction between workers and hours as components of the labour input, and outline the potential insights gained from this perspective.

LO3 Discuss the importance of non-wage benefits as a share of total compensation, and how these non-wage benefits affect the way we model labour demand.

LO4 Describe how quasi-fixed costs create a wedge between the value of the marginal product and the wage rate, and the implications of this for labour hoarding and other dynamic decisions of the firm.

MAIN QUESTIONS

- Many payroll taxes (such as employer contributions to unemployment insurance) have ceilings, or maximum payments per worker. How can this feature of payroll taxes actually reduce employment?

- Why is less-expensive, unskilled labour more likely to be laid off during a downturn than more-expensive, skilled labour?

- Can restrictions on the length of the workweek or the amount of overtime permitted lead to the creation of more jobs for others?

- Did short-time work schemes and other worksharing programs helped save jobs during the Great Recession of 2008–2009?

The previous chapter analyzed the demand for labour when labour is a variable input into the production process. In these circumstances, a change in the amount of labour used in production (the number of employee hours) leads to a proportionate change in labour costs. Furthermore, the change in labour costs depends only on the overall magnitude of the change in the labour input and not on the composition of the change in terms of the number of employees versus hours worked per employee. However, some labour costs may be *quasi fixed* in the sense that they are independent of the number of hours worked by the firm's workforce. These quasi-fixed costs may arise because of the costs of hiring and training new workers, the costs of dismissing employees, and from non-wage benefits, such as holiday pay, contributions to pension plans, and unemployment insurance.

Quasi-fixed costs have important implications for a variety of labour market phenomena, such as work schedules, part-time work, overtime work, hiring and layoff behaviour, and unemployment.[1] This chapter examines firms' employment decisions when labour is a quasi-fixed factor of production.

Non-wage Benefits and Total Compensation

The analysis of labour income and labour demand is complicated by the fact that wages and salaries are only one aspect of total compensation, and, therefore, only one aspect of the cost of labour to the employer. Figure 6.1 illustrates the main components of total compensation and the most commonly used terminology for these components. Pay for time not worked (holiday and vacation pay, parental leave) is generally included in wage and salary income as reported by Statistics Canada. However, for some analytical purposes, it may be desirable to treat this as a separate compensation category. In particular, for some employees, payment for time not worked is a quasi-fixed cost in the sense that the magnitude of holiday and vacation pay to which the employee is entitled is independent of hours worked.

As is illustrated in Table 6.1, **non-wage benefits** (indirect labour costs) are a large and increasing component of total compensation. Between 1957 and 1984, non-wage employee benefits as a percentage of direct labour costs (gross payroll) increased from 15.1 to 32.4 percent, but have been fairly stable since then. Among benefits, pay for time not worked has remained an important category and bonuses a small component. The two fastest-growing components of benefits have been a) pension and welfare plans and b) legally required payments for workers' compensation, unemployment insurance, and CPP/QPP.

The existence and growth of non-wage benefits are interesting phenomena to explain, especially given the basic economic proposition that unconditional cash transfers (e.g., wages) are generally more efficient than **transfers-in-kind** (e.g., non-wage benefits). This proposition follows from the fact that recipients who receive cash could always buy the transfers-in-kind if they wanted them, but they are better off because they could buy other things if they wanted those more. Applied to employee benefits, why wouldn't employees and employers prefer wage compensation, since it would enable employees to buy whatever benefits they want rather give them something they may not value?

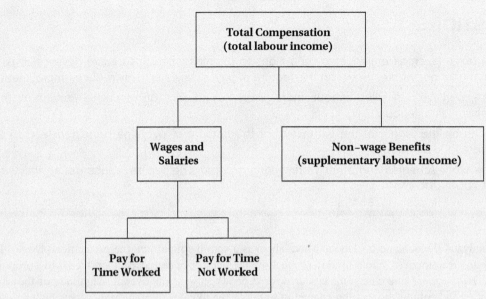

Figure 6.1 Components of Total Compensation

Total compensation includes wages plus non-wage benefits. The wage and salary component can be further divided into the part directly corresponding to time worked and that which does not depend on time worked (such as vacation pay).

TABLE 6.1	Non-wage Benefits in Large Firms:[1] Components and Changes Over Time				
Non-wage Benefit Categories	**Percentage of Gross Payroll**				
	1957	**1984**	**1989**	**1998**	**2015**
Payments required by law[2]	2.0	4.4	5.3	9.3	10.0
Pay for time not worked	6.7	14.9	13.9	12.4	-
Pension and welfare plans	6.4	9.4	9.9	11.5	-
Bonuses, profit sharing, other	1.3	3.7	4.4	3.5	-
Total of benefits not required by law	14.4	28.0	28.2	27.4	25.0
Total non-wage benefits	16.4	32.4	33.5	36.7	35.0

NOTES:

1. Figures are for all industries. Separate figures for manufacturing and nonmanufacturing are not dramatically different.

2. Includes workers' compensation, unemployment insurance, and Canada/Quebec pension plans.

SOURCES: KPMG Peat, Marwick, Stevenson, and Kellogg, *Employee Benefit Costs in Canada* (Toronto), 1989, and 1998 (for the 1957–1998 data) and KPMG, *Competitive Alternatives* (Toronto), 2016 (for the 2015 data) .

There are, obviously, a variety of possible reasons for the existence and growth of non-wage benefits. They are sometimes not taxed and, as taxes have increased over time, this increasingly makes non-wage benefits a preferred form of compensation. There may be economies of scale and administrative economies for group purchases through the employer of such things as pension and insurance plans. While many of these economies still could be had through completely voluntary group plans, letting people choose their benefits can be a problem because of **adverse selection**. For instance, healthy individuals may not want to pay for expensive health or dental insurance benefits. As a result, those who want these insurance benefits will have to pay more for them, since the pool of insured workers will be more expensive to cover as these workers will use the health and dental benefits more extensively. This adverse selection can eventually lead to a situation where insurance benefits are not provided at all, despite the fact that they would be valuable to workers.

There is also the possibility that workers think they are receiving non-wage benefits free, in the sense that if they did not have these benefits their wages would not rise by a corresponding amount. More likely, workers may simply prefer non-wage benefits because it is an easy way of purchasing benefits that they value. In some cases, like increased vacations and holidays with pay, it is a way of institutionalizing the increased purchase of more leisure that accompanies their growing wealth.

Employers may have accepted the increased role of employee non-wage benefits for reasons that are beneficial to them. Paid vacations and holidays, for example, enable more-effective planning of the production process than would be the case if the workers' desire for increased leisure came in the form of lateness, absenteeism, work slowdowns, or turnover. Similarly, workers' compensation, unemployment insurance, and health insurance can reduce the need for employers to have contingency plans for workers involved in industrial accidents or subject to layoffs or health problems. In addition, some employee benefits may alter the behaviour of workers in a fashion that is preferred by the employer; for example, subsidized cafeterias can reduce the need for long lunch breaks by keeping employees in the plant, the provision of transportation can ensure that workers get to work on time, company health services can reduce absenteeism and provide a check on a worker's health, and pensions and other seniority-related benefits may reduce unwanted turnover. Employers may also prefer non-wage benefits because they provide work incentives. Some employee benefits, such as company pension plans and seniority-based vacation pay, represent **deferred compensation** in that these benefits are received later in the employee's career. Workers who leave the firm early in their careers do not receive these benefits. With some of their compensation in the form of deferred benefits, existing employees will be less likely to quit in order to seek or accept employment elsewhere. In addition, deferred compensation raises the cost to the employee of being fired for poor work, absenteeism, and so on, thus strengthening work incentives. These effects of deferred compensation on turnover and work incentives are discussed further in Chapter 13.

Deferred compensation can also act as a sorting or screening device, enabling the employer to hire those workers who are most likely to remain with the firm. Employers for whom turnover is very costly, perhaps because of the costs of hiring and training new workers, can screen out potential employees who do not expect to remain with the firm for an extended period by making deferred compensation a significant proportion of total compensation, a compensation package that is most attractive to potential employees who expect to remain with the firm for a long period of time. Such screening mechanisms are especially valuable when the employer is unable to predict which job applicants are likely to leave the firm after a brief period and which are likely to remain with the firm.

Governments may also prefer non-wage benefits (and, hence, grant favourable tax treatment) because they may reduce pressures for government expenditures elsewhere. Employer-sponsored pensions may reduce the need for public pensions; contributions to the Canada (or Quebec) Pension Plan may reduce the need for public care for the aged, at least for the aged who have worked; and increased contributions for unemployment insurance directly reduce the amount the government has to pay to this fund. In addition, many non-wage benefits are part and parcel of the whole package of increased social security, and, hence, the reasons for their growth are caught up with the reasons for the growth of the whole welfare state.

LO1, 2   Quasi-fixed Labour Costs

General Definition

Employers can change their labour input by changing the number of employees, the hours per employee, or both. The way in which they adjust will depend upon the relative costs of the different options.

Variable costs of labour are affected by the *total* hours of labour employed, regardless of whether the increase in total hours comes from an increase in the number of employees or from an increase in the hours per employee. For example, if the only cost of labour is the hourly wage rate, then costs will increase by the same percentage whether the labour input is expanded by increasing employment or hours per employee. In such circumstances, the firm's costs would increase by the same amount regardless of whether the labour input was expanded by increased employees or by hours per employee.

Wage costs are, therefore, a variable labour cost, as are non-wage benefits that are proportional to wages. Other labour costs, however, are **quasi-fixed costs** in the sense that they are incurred per employee and are independent, or largely independent, of the hours of work per employee. They may be *pure* quasi-fixed costs in the sense that they are fixed per employee and are completely independent of the hours of work of each employee. Or they may be *mixed* variable and quasi-fixed costs in that they increase more rapidly for a given proportionate increase in the number of employees as opposed to hours per employee. In either circumstance, the firm would no longer be indifferent between whether the labour input (employees times hours per employee) expanded through increasing the number of employees or increasing the hours per employee. Increasing the number of employees would be more costly as a result of the quasi-fixed costs.

A distinction should also be made between *recurring* and *nonrecurring*, or "one time," quasi-fixed costs. **Payroll taxes** to finance public pensions and unemployment insurance are examples of recurring non-wage labour costs; these taxes are remitted regularly (e.g., monthly) to the relevant government agencies. Examples of nonrecurring costs include hiring and orienting new employees and dismissing employees whose services are no longer required.

Examples of Quasi-fixed Costs

At the hiring stage, firms incur quasi-fixed costs associated with the recruiting, hiring, and training of new workers. These costs are independent of the hours the employees subsequently work. Under such circumstances, there is an obvious incentive to try to amortize these fixed costs over longer hours and a longer worklife for these employees rather than to hire new employees and incur their additional fixed costs.

Expected termination costs also have a fixed-cost component as, at the *hiring stage*, the firm may anticipate incurring these costs should it subsequently lay off or dismiss the worker. Such costs become expected quasi-fixed costs at the hiring stage, even though they may not be incurred until a subsequent period. Although expectations of such costs are incurred when a new employee is hired, they do not increase, or at least not by the same proportion as wage costs, when an existing employee works additional hours.

Employers' contributions (payroll taxes) to certain income maintenance programs may also have an element of fixed cost, when those contributions have a ceiling. Employer contributions to workers' compensation and public pensions, for example, have an annual income ceiling. Unemployment insurance has a weekly earnings ceiling below which contributions are a certain percentage of earnings, and beyond which contributions are zero. Thus, once this ceiling is reached, it pays employers have these people work additional hours since no further payroll taxes are incurred, rather than hire new employees and incur the payroll taxes. These payroll taxes are variable costs until the ceiling is reached, and thereafter they become fixed costs, creating the incentive to work existing employees more hours rather than incurring the costs associated with hiring new workers.

Similarly, **employment standards legislation** often requires employees to have been employed for a certain minimum period before they are eligible for some benefits, such as paid holidays and advance notice of termination. When the employee reaches this minimum period, these benefits become fixed costs for the employer; they are independent of the additional hours worked by the employee. As with other fixed costs, they encourage the employer to work existing employees longer hours and they discourage the hiring of new employees for whom such costs will be incurred.

Employers' contributions to life insurance, medical, and dental plans can also have a quasi-fixed-cost component to the extent that they are fixed per employee. In such circumstances, costs are increased by hiring a new employee but not when an existing employee works more hours.

Not all non-wage benefits have a quasi-fixed component. For some, like employer-sponsored occupational pension plans, employer contributions are based on a percentage of earnings. In this case, the employers' contributions are proportional to earnings, and are the same whether the labour input increases through an increased number of employees or increased hours per employee. The same situation prevails for vacation pay, which is a percentage of earnings.

General Effect of Quasi-fixed Costs

As indicated, one general effect of such quasi-fixed costs is to increase the marginal cost of hiring an additional worker (sometimes termed the extensive margin of adjustment) relative to the marginal cost of working an existing worker longer hours (sometimes termed the intensive margin of adjustment). The quasi-fixed costs distort the labour expansion decision of the firm away from employment and toward more hours, as a way to minimize the quasi-fixed costs. Alternatively stated, the firm will want to amortize its fixed costs over the existing workforce as much as possible rather than hire new workers and incur additional quasi-fixed costs. This is especially so for skilled workers, where such quasi-fixed costs may be especially large, mainly because of training costs.

On the supply side of the market (recall the discussion in Chapter 3), fixed money costs of work reduce the probability that an individual will enter the labour market, but increase the hours of work once having entered. In the same way, quasi-fixed costs of employment have a differential effect on the demand side; employers would be reluctant to hire more workers (and incur the fixed costs), but once the workers are hired, the employers would like them to work longer hours in order to amortize the fixed costs.

Nonrecurring fixed costs of employment alter the firm's hiring and layoff decisions, making them longer term in nature. If the firm must incur some hiring and training costs when hiring a new employee, the firm will not hire that employee unless the addition to revenue is at least as great as the addition to costs, including the hiring and training costs. However, as long as the employee is expected to remain with the firm for several periods, it is not essential that the additional revenue equal or exceed the additional costs *each period*. Rather, the firm will continue hiring additional workers until the present value of additional future revenues equals the present value of additional costs. Thus, rather than hiring until the current wage equals the current value of marginal product (the employment rule discussed previously, summarized in equation 5.1), in the presence of nonrecurring fixed costs of employment the profit-maximizing employment rule becomes

$$H + T + \sum_{t=0}^{N} \frac{W_t}{(1+r)^t} = \sum_{t=0}^{N} \frac{VMP_t}{(1+r)^t} \tag{6.1}$$

H + T   are hiring and training costs (assumed to be incurred in the first period, for simplicity)

W_t is the wage rate in period t

VMP_t is the expected value of the marginal product in period t

r   is the firm's discount or interest rate

N   is the expected length of employment

The left-hand side of equation 6.1 is the present value of the costs of hiring an additional worker (i.e., the present value of the marginal costs) and the right-hand side is the present value of the marginal revenue.

Several implications of equation 6.1 are worth noting. The hiring decision depends on the firm's expectations about the future, in particular the expected duration of employment, expected wage rates, and expected product market conditions (which determine the value of the marginal product of labour in future periods). Another implication is that, because of the hiring and training costs on the left-hand side of equation 6.1,

$$\sum_{t=0}^{N} \frac{VMP_t}{(1+r)^t} > \sum_{t=0}^{N} \frac{W_t}{(1+r)^t} \tag{6.2}$$

Thus, when hiring an additional worker, the firm must anticipate that the value of the marginal product will exceed the wage in most, if not all, future periods. As will be seen below, this prediction of the theory has implications for the firm's layoff behaviour in response to unanticipated changes in demand.

The small but growing empirical literature on dynamic labour demand confirms some of the theoretical discussion on quasi-fixed costs. Hamermesh (1993) reviews the literature in detail, while Hamermesh and Pfann (1996) provide a more recent review of the general literature on **dynamic factor demand**. Most studies find that firms behave as if costs associated with adjusting their level of employment are important. The intuition that the employment level (number of workers) is more costly to adjust than are employee hours is is also borne out in the data, so that the worker-hours distinction merits further attention. Another important distinction is that between the net and gross costs of adjustment. Hamermesh (1995), for example, uses firm-level microdata and finds that the costs associated with changing the employees (direct hiring and firing costs, or gross costs of adjustment) are as important as costs associated with changing the number of employees (or net costs of adjustment). While there have been fewer direct studies on the relative adjustment speeds of different types of labour, it is generally found that skilled labour is adjusted more slowly than unskilled labour. This has important implications for the incidence of unemployment over the business cycle, a phenomenon we address in the next section.

WORKED EXAMPLE

Quasi-fixed Costs and Training

According to the Government of Canada's *Innovation Strategy*, "To succeed in the global, knowledge-based economy, where highly skilled people are more mobile than ever before, a country must produce, attract, and retain a critical mass of well-educated and well-trained people" (Government of Canada 2002). While this ambitious goal is laudable, it also represents a major challenge from a labour market point of view. The problem is that there is little incentive for firms to invest time and money in a new worker unless the worker stays long enough for the firm to reap some of the benefits from this investment. Note that training is an important aspect of human capital, which we will discuss in more detail in Chapter 9.

Equation 6.1 can be used to illustrate this dilemma in the context of a simple example. Consider a high-tech firm that needs to hire and train a young worker; a cost of $15,000. The worker is paid $25,000 a year but produces, once fully trained, $30,000 worth of output every year. In terms of equation 6.1, this means that $H + T = \$15,000$, $W_t = \$25,000$, and $VMP_t = \$30,000$. To simplify the calculations, we assume that the interest rate, r, is equal to zero (therefore, future value = present value). The table below illustrates how costs compare with benefits over different employment durations.

During the first year, the firm spends more on the worker ($40,000) than the worker produces ($30,000). If the worker was to leave the firm at the end of the year, the firm would, thus, lose $10,000. It is only in the third year that the firm breaks even. The firm starts making profit only if the worker stays on for more than three years. The decision of the firm to hire more workers is, thus, closely linked to the duration of employment. If the firm expects that workers will stay for three years or more, it should hire more workers to increase profits. Otherwise, it should reduce employment to cut its losses. By doing so, the VMP of remaining workers should be higher than $30,000 a year.

Employment Duration (N)	Costs			Benefits (ΣVMP_t)	Total Profit	Yearly Profit
	Fixed (H + T)	Variable (ΣW_t)	Total			
1 year	$15,000	$25,000	$40,000	$30,000	-$10,000	-$10,000
2 years	15,000	50,000	65,000	60,000	-5000	-2500
3 years	15,000	75,000	90,000	90,000	0	0
4 years	15,000	100,000	115,000	120,000	5000	1250
5 years	15,000	125,000	140,000	150,000	10,000	2000

LO3, 4   Some Phenomena Explained by Fixed Costs

The existence and growth of such fixed costs may help to explain, in part at least, the existence and growth of a number of labour market phenomena. The desire of employers to work their existing workforce overtime, in spite of overtime premium wage rates and possible fatigue effects, may be explained in part by the fact that fixed costs make it relatively cheaper to work the existing workforce longer hours than it is to hire new workers.

Quasi-fixed costs of employment may also explain, in part, the popularity of temporary-help agencies, outsourcing, and the rise of the "gig economy." Employers avoid the quasi-fixed costs of hiring new employees when they outsource or engage the services of temporary-help agencies. Likewise, the success of Uber is in part based on the fact its drivers are independent contractors who use the Uber app software but have to provide for themselves the capital (their car) used to perform their jobs.

The layoff behaviour of firms will also be affected by quasi-fixed costs of employment. Once an employee has been hired and trained, the associated nonrecurring costs become sunk costs. Because these costs cannot be recovered, they will not influence the firm's decision making with respect to its existing workforce (for whom the hiring and training expenses have been incurred), but the costs will influence decisions regarding potential employees (for whom the expenses have not yet been incurred).

EXHIBIT 6.1

Quasi-fixed Costs and Temporary-Help Agencies

In both Canada and the United States, a growing fraction of workers are employed under non-standard employment arrangements, such as temporary-help agencies. In 2015, 190,000 Canadians and 3.5 million Americans were employed by firms in the employment services industry (most of which consist of temporary-help firms). While this sector remains smaller in Canada (1.2 percent of the workforce) than in the United States (2.5 percent of the workforce), it is growing rapidly. Between 1991 and 2015, the number of jobs in employment services firms grew at an annual rate of 9.3 percent, compared to 1.7 percent for the whole Canadian labour market.

What explains the growing popularity of temporary-help jobs? Houseman (2001) suggests several motivations to use temporary-help agencies. Not surprisingly, firms tend to use the services of these agencies when they need an employee only for a short period. The three main reasons mentioned by firms for using temporary-help agencies are, indeed, filling vacancies until a regular employee is hired, filling in for an absent regular employee, and providing needed assistance at times of unexpected increases in business. Another important reason mentioned by firms is that they like using temporary-help agencies to "save on wage and/or benefit costs."

All of these reasons for using temporary-help agencies can be linked to quasi-fixed costs. When a firm requires a worker on a short-term basis, equation 6.1 shows that it is not profitable to pay the full hiring and training costs. Temporary-help agencies reduce firms' costs since they are responsible for hiring and providing appropriate training. In this sense, the existence of temporary-help agencies is a market response to the problem of quasi-fixed costs. Firms also reduce other non-wage benefit costs, such as health insurance or pensions, by hiring temporary workers who do not have access to these benefits since they are not regular workers. Substituting too many regular employees with workers from temporary-help agencies to save on benefit costs is probably not a wise strategy, however, for firms that still need to develop a stable, loyal, and productive workforce.

At the time an employee is hired, the firm anticipates that the present value of future marginal products will exceed the present value of future wage costs, as shown in equation 6.2. This excess of the value of the worker's contribution to the firm over the cost of that worker creates a "buffer" which reduces the risk that the worker will be laid off. In particular, even if there is an unanticipated decline in product demand, thereby reducing the value of the marginal product of labour, the firm may nonetheless choose not to lay off any employees, because the present value of the revenue associated with an employee, although lower than anticipated, remains higher than the present value of the costs. Because of the unanticipated decline in demand, the firm's return on its investment in hiring and training costs will be lower than expected; however, the return may still be positive, indicating that it is worthwhile to retain the employee. This will be the case especially if the decline in demand is believed to be temporary in nature, or if workers who are temporarily laid off may not be available for recall when demand returns to normal levels. In such circumstances, the company may rationally engage in **labour hoarding** of workers in a cyclical downturn, and may pay deferred compensation or seniority-related wages or benefits to discourage its experienced workers from leaving.

EXHIBIT 6.2

The Rise of the "Gig Economy"

As noted in Exhibit 6.1, a growing fraction of jobs are based on non-standard work arrangements, such as those provided by temporary-help agencies. More recently, there has been a lot of talk about the growth of the "sharing" or "gig" economy, the most prominent example being the famous transportation network company, Uber, that now operates in most large cities in North America.

While smartphones, apps, and the Internet have played a central role in the growth of companies like Uber, quasi-fixed costs can also help explain the growth of these new types of work arrangements. Unlike traditional jobs where employers have to provide training and capital to workers, in the gig economy it is typically workers themselves who pay the quasi-fixed costs of labour (e.g., use their own car when working for Uber).

But, for all the talk about the gig economy, it still appears to account for only a small fraction of all jobs. For example, a recent survey conducted by Katz and Krueger (2016) indicates that about 0.5 percent of workers provided services through online intermediaries, such as Uber. However, Katz and Krueger show that the fraction of workers in any type of alternative work arrangement has grown from 10.1 percent in 2005 to 15.8 percent in 2015. This means that alternative work arrangements account for all the (net) new jobs created in the United States in the last 10 years!

While these changes have not been as dramatic in Canada, data from the Labour Force Survey indicates that the fraction of workers with fixed term, contract, or casual jobs has increased from 8.1 percent in 1997 to 10.5 percent in 2015. So, while the gig economy still accounts for a small fraction of jobs, there is no doubt that non-standard work arrangements are on the rise in both Canada and the United States.

This implication of nonrecurring fixed employment costs is illustrated in Figure 6.2. Panel (a) shows the case in which there are no fixed costs of employment. At the wage W_0, employment will be N_0^*. A decline in labour demand from VMP to VMP^1 will result in a drop in employment from N_0^* to N_0^1. Panel (b) shows the case in which the employer incurs nonrecurring hiring and training costs, $H + T$. At the wage W_0, employment will be N_0 rather than N_0^*, as would occur in the absence of the hiring and training costs. For the N_0 employees hired, the value of their marginal product is VMP_0; because of the fixed costs, the employer does not expand employment to the point at which the VMP equals the wage. The "buffer," $VMP_0 - W_0$, implies that employment will not necessarily fall in response to a decline in labour demand. For example, at the wage W_0, employment would remain at N_0 even if the employees' value of the marginal product fell to VMP^1.

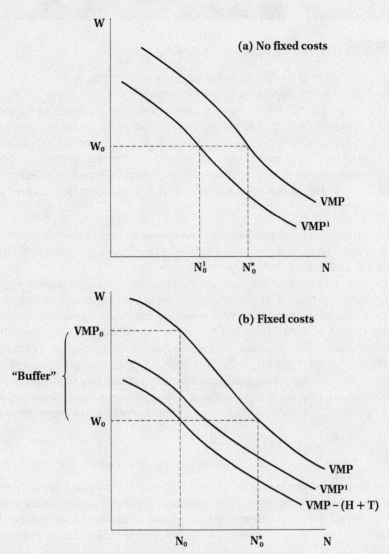

Figure 6.2 Nonrecurring Fixed Employment Costs and Changes in Labour Demand

In panel (a), a decline in market conditions leads to an inward shift of the VMP schedule, from VMP to VMP^1. The profit-maximizing level of employment falls from N_0^* to N_0^1 at the prevailing wage of W_0. By contrast, if there are fixed costs of hiring workers, employment may not fall as much. First, the original level of employment will be at N_0, not N_0^*, as employers choose employment so that the wage equals the VMP net of hiring and training costs, VMP – (H + T). At N_0, the VMP (VMP$_0$) exceeds W_0 by a "buffer," H + T. As long as the new VMP^1 > VMP – (H + T) = W_0, it will not be optimal for the firm to change its employment level from N_0.

Fixed costs of employment can also explain the observation that layoff rates are much higher among low-skilled workers than they are among those who are highly skilled. Considerable evidence exists that hiring and training costs are significantly larger for high-skilled workers. Thus, they have a larger buffer (excess of value of marginal product over wage rate) protecting them from unanticipated declines in demand compared to unskilled and semi-skilled workers. This prediction is illustrated by comparing panels (a) and (b) of Figure 6.2, the former showing the situation facing unskilled workers and the latter that of skilled workers.

EXHIBIT 6.3

Labour Hoarding in the Automobile Industry

Most of the evidence suggesting the importance of quasi-fixed costs and labour hoarding is indirect. First, surveys of the labour force confirm that skilled workers are less likely to be unemployed than unskilled workers. This may have nothing to do with labour hoarding, however, as it may simply reflect that skilled workers are employed in firms that are relatively unaffected by business cycle conditions. Second, average labour productivity usually falls during recessions. This is puzzling, because we would expect labour productivity to increase as less labour is employed (by the assumption of diminishing marginal productivity of labour). Labour hoarding would provide one possible explanation—productivity falls during recessions because firms retain workers who have nothing to do; that is, those whose productivity is worth less than their wage.

Ana Aizcorbe (1992) provides direct evidence on labour hoarding in the automobile industry. Using plant-level data from car assembly plants in the United States over the period 1978–1985, she shows that firms employed up to 5 percent more workers than necessary, given the level of production in each plant. Aizcorbe also investigates another explanation for apparent labour hoarding besides the quasi-fixed-cost explanation provided in the text. Increasing returns to specialization (or scale) would imply that layoffs, or a reduction in the size of the workforce, could lower the average productivity of the remaining workers. One possible rationale for these increasing returns arises from the nature of production in assembly plants. The main way to reduce output is to slow down the assembly line. One cannot, for example, just lay off the part of the line that attaches fenders. The resulting slowdown of line speed can reduce the intensity and productivity of the remaining workers, especially if they are asked to perform additional tasks. Aizcorbe finds that both of these explanations (increasing returns and conventional labour hoarding) are significant features of employment adjustment in car plants in response to downturns.

Quasi-fixed costs may also foster the segmentation of labour markets into a protected sector (where employment stability is relatively guaranteed so as to amortize the quasi-fixed costs) and a sector that cannot compete for these jobs because firms would have to incur additional fixed costs upon hiring such workers. In essence, once an employee has been hired and trained, the firm is not indifferent between an existing employee and an otherwise identical potential employee.

To the extent that fixed costs inhibit the hiring of new workers (at the extensive margin), employers may try to meet their labour demand needs by expanding not only at the intensive margin of more hours, but also at the intensive margin of a greater *intensity* of work effort. That is, employers may try to work their existing workforce not only longer hours but also harder, rather than hire new workers. Just as labour supply had quality and quantity dimensions, so does labour demand, and these various dimensions may be affected by relative prices, including fixed costs.

Quasi-fixed costs may also explain some of the employers' resistance to engage in worksharing practices. For example, having all of the company's employees work a four-day as opposed to five-day workweek and hiring 20 percent more employees at the same wage would increase labour costs if there were quasi-fixed costs associated with hiring the new employees. Similarly, having two workers engage in job sharing (e.g., by each working half of the week) would increase the quasi-fixed costs because of the additional employee. Such costs may also make it more expensive to engage part-time employees, unless there are compensating offsets in the wage component or in some of the quasi-fixed costs, such as non-wage benefits.

Worksharing and Job Creation

The recession that started in the summer of 2008 pushed the unemployment rate to levels that had not been seen in generations in the United States and Europe. While Canada fared relatively better in this regard, the high levels of unemployment generated some renewed interest in **worksharing** as a way to "create jobs" or, at least, to share the scarce number of jobs that seem to be available. This interest has been supported by workers' preferences for flexible work-time arrangements, the result, in part, of the growth of the two-earner family and the changing age and sex composition of the workforce.

Reduced work-time arrangements could take a variety of forms, including delayed entry into the labour force, early retirement, a shorter workweek, reduced overtime, or increased vacation time. The key question is, would any of these reductions in the work-time of some individuals lead to new jobs for other individuals?

Overtime Restrictions and Job Creation

In recent years, the question of the effect of work-time reductions has become extremely important with respect to reductions in the workweek, especially through restricting the use of overtime. The paradox of some workers working overtime, seemingly on a regular basis, while other workers in the same community and often in the same plant are on layoff, has led to increasing pressure to restrict the use of overtime. This restriction could come in a variety of forms: reducing the standard workweek beyond which an overtime premium must be paid, increasing the overtime premium, establishing or reducing the statutory maximum hours that are allowed, making it more difficult to get special permission to exceed the statutory limit when exemptions are allowed, or granting workers the right to refuse overtime. Changes in any or all of these features of overtime legislation could be used to restrict the use of overtime.

There is considerable empirical evidence that legislation aiming to curb the use of overtime by increasing the overtime premium or reducing the standard workweek beyond which an overtime premium must be paid do reduce weekly hours of affected workers. For instance, Friesen (2001) exploits interesting differences in overtime legislation across Canadian provinces to estimate the impact of this legislation on a variety of labour market outcomes. She finds modest effects for use of both the overtime premium and the standard workweek beyond which overtime must be paid on total hours of work.

A more difficult question to answer is whether these kinds of policy changes would translate into new jobs. On this issue there is also considerable controversy. In a simple accounting sense, if firms have to reduce the number of overtime hours by some workers, one may think that they will need to hire other workers in order to maintain the same level production. While many proponents of hours restrictions as a way of creating jobs tend to believe in this accounting logic, economics tells us that these types of policies can have a number of unintended effects preventing them from achieving their stated job-creation goals.

For example, firms may not comply fully with the legislation and, thus, some workers whose overtime hours were restricted may moonlight. Friesen (2001), indeed, finds that stricter overtime rules tend to result in more hours of moonlighting. Furthermore, although firms may substitute new employees for the more expensive overtime hours, they would also reduce their *overall* demand for labour, because it is now more expensive and because the demand for the firm's output will be reduced as it passes some of the cost increase on to consumers in the form of higher product prices. These are, respectively, the familiar substitution and scale effects that occur in response to an increase in the price of a factor of production.

As well, there may be productivity changes that affect the number of new jobs created if hours of work are reduced. On the one hand, if fatigue effects make overtime hours less productive than the hours of work of new workers or rehires, then the number of new jobs created will be diminished because the overtime hours can be replaced by fewer regular hours. On the other hand, workers who work the overtime may already be the most productive of all workers; that is, in fact, why they are asked to work overtime. If that is the case, then reducing the overtime hours of the most productive workers may have the potential for creating a larger number of jobs for less-productive workers, albeit at an obvious cost—one that could reduce the job-creating potential because of the substitution and scale effects discussed previously.

The job-creating potential of either cutting overtime hours or reducing the standard workweek also may be offset by the fact that persons who are unemployed or on layoff (who are less likely to be skilled) may not be good substitutes for full-time workers (who are likely to be more skilled). The problem may be particularly acute in the case of highly skilled workers who simply cannot be replaced by most unemployed persons. The job-creating potential of reduced hours of work is further complicated by the fact that, in the long run, there are not really a fixed number of jobs in the economy. In fact, the notion that there is a fixed number of jobs is known as the lump-of-labour fallacy. It is a fallacy because it ignores the fact that people who hold jobs have other effects on the economy (known as general equilibrium effects). For example, they may increase aggregate demand through their increased disposable income, and they may reduce aggregate wages by augmenting the supply of labour. Both of these effects would increase the number of jobs available in the economy.

EXHIBIT 6.4

Non-wage Benefits and Part-Time Work

Part-time employment, defined as working fewer than 30 hours per week, has grown rapidly in Canada during the past several decades, both in absolute terms and relative to full-time employment. For example, part-time employment constituted less than 4 percent of total employment in 1953 but has grown steadily over time to reach 19 percent in 2016.

What factors lie behind the growth of part-time and other forms of flexible or non-standard employment, such as short-term and contract work, within the temporary-help industry and certain types of self-employment? Most part-time employees are women or young workers. Thus, supply-side factors associated with the changing composition of the labour force, particularly the increased participation of women and youth, may also have played a role. However, evidence suggests that demand-side factors have also contributed to the rise in part-time employment, since wages of part-time workers are considerably lower than those of comparable full-time workers. Doiron and Barrett (2001) show that the wage gap between full-time and part-time workers is especially large (close to 15 percent) for involuntary part-time workers who would prefer to work full-time but cannot find a full-time job. Perhaps more importantly, hourly non-wage labour costs are, generally, substantially lower for part-time workers due to their lower likelihood of being covered by unemployment insurance, workers' compensation, the Canada and Quebec Pension Plans; much lower levels of employer sponsored benefits; and exclusion from some labour standards legislation (e.g., regulations requiring payment for statutory holidays). Because such non-wage labour costs have been growing rapidly, we would expect an increased tendency for employers to substitute part-time for full-time workers.

Evidence that such substitution has occurred in the United Kingdom is provided in an econometric study by Patricia Rice (1990). Changes in the structure of National Insurance payroll taxes resulted in a significant increase the average hourly cost of full-time young adult workers, while reducing that of part-time adult workers. In most industries, part-time adults and full-time youth were found to be substitutes in production. The consequence of these tax changes was a rise in part-time adult employment and a sharp decline in youth employment.

Buchmueller (1999) reaches a similar conclusion for the United States. Using detailed establishment data, he finds that employers who offer more-generous fringe benefits are also more likely to hire low-wage, part-time workers.

Thus, while an individual who takes a job or works long hours at a particular establishment may be taking a job from someone else who could work at that establishment, this need not be the case for the economy as a whole; what is true for a given establishment may be a fallacy for the economy as a whole. Perhaps this is best illustrated by the example of the increased labour force participation of females. Few analysts today would say that every job taken by a female means one fewer job for a male. Even though that may be true for a particular job in a particular establishment (just as a job taken by a male means that particular job is not occupied by a female) it is not true for the economy as a whole. Females working in the labour market also create demands for other goods and services, especially those formerly produced in the household. This in turn creates jobs elsewhere.

In essence, a job held by one person does not mean that another person does not have a job. This applies to jobs held by females or immigrants, by older workers who do not retire, or by persons who work long hours or overtime. Conversely, restricting their work in particular establishments (e.g., by mandatory retirement or restricting overtime) may open up some new jobs in that establishment, but this may not lead to more jobs in the economy as a whole when one considers the general equilibrium effects as previously discussed.

For all of these reasons, the job-creating potential of policies aimed at reducing the number of hours worked by full-time workers is regarded with some skepticism. There is increasing evidence that these types of measures, indeed, fail to create new jobs. Skuterud (2007) looks at the decision of the province of Quebec to reduce its standard workweek from 44 to 40 hours between 1997 and 2000. He finds that while this change did reduce by 20 percent the fraction of workers working more than 40 hours a week, the policy failed to raise employment in the province or in industries that were most affected by this policy change.

Studies for other countries reach similar conclusions. For instance, Crépon and Kramarz (2002) find that the decision of the French government to reduce the standard workweek from 40 to 39 hours did not help create jobs. Despite this, the French government went ahead with a further reduction in the workweek from 39 to only 35 hours, a move that also failed to create jobs (Chemin and Wasmer 2009). This more-recent evidence suggest that policies aimed at creating jobs by reducing the statutory workweek of full-time workers should be regarded with a fair dose of skepticism.

While these measures likely fail to promote employment creation in the long run, we discuss in Exhibit 6.5 how other forms of worksharing may be viable, temporary methods to share scarce jobs in times of high cyclical unemployment until the economy returns to full employment. It may also be important to remove any impediments that may prevent the parties from entering into otherwise mutually beneficial voluntary worksharing arrangements. As indicated previously, the ceilings on payroll taxes for workers' compensation, public pensions, or unemployment insurance make it more attractive for employers to work their existing employees longer hours once the ceiling on the payroll tax has been reached, since no further taxes then have to be paid. Having the premiums based on hourly earnings with a ceiling based on hourly earnings would remove the bias against hiring new workers. Similarly, prorating employer contributions to medical, dental, and life insurance plans according to hours worked, rather than having fixed contributions per employee, would reduce their existing bias against employment sharing.

EXHIBIT 6.5

Short-Time Work and the Great Recession of 2008–2009

In the wake of the financial crisis of the summer of 2008, most industrialized countries have experienced some of the most dramatic increases in unemployment since the Great Depression of the 1930s. One of the most hard-hit countries was Spain where the unemployment rate increased from 7.9 percent in May 2007 to a staggering 20.6 percent in September 2010. Over the same period, the U.S. unemployment rate more than doubled, from 4.6 to 9.6 percent. Canada fared much better with a relatively modest increase in the unemployment rate, from 6 to 8 percent. Most remarkably, the unemployment rate in Germany declined from 8.5 percent to 6.6 percent during the same period despite the fact that the large export-oriented German manufacturing sector experienced a steep, though temporary, decline in output during this time period.

What can explain such a dramatic difference in the employment performance of these different countries during this period? Cahuc and Carcillo (2010) and Hijzen and Venn (2011) argue that the presence of large and effective short-time work scheme programs in countries like Germany played an important role in keeping unemployment low during the recession. Short-time work (STW) programs are public schemes aimed at keeping unemployment low during recessions by providing income support to workers in firms that agreed to implement worksharing programs to protect employment. For example, the government provides some income support to workers who agree to reduce their weekly hours of work in response to an adverse demand shock.

Hijzen and Venn (2011) show that out of the 19 OECD countries they studied, 11 countries (including Canada) had some kind of STW schemes prior to the recession, while five other countries introduced such programs in response to the crisis. However, the fraction of workers receiving an income compensation for reduced work at the peak of the crisis in 2009 varied considerably among countries with existing STW: from less than 1 percent in Canada, the United States, or Spain to more than 3 percent in Germany. Based on these findings, both Cahuc and Carcillo (2010) and Hijzen and Venn (2011) conclude that STW schemes have played in important role keeping unemployment low in Germany as well as in Japan.

However, these authors also warn against possible long-term consequences of these programs, since governments could end up subsidizing, on a long-term basis, firms in declining sectors, thereby preventing them from making more-efficient adjustments in their use of labour. Cahuc and Carcillo suggest addressing this issue by introducing a experience rating system, whereby firms using STW schemes the most intensively would eventually have to pay for a large share of the compensation provided to workers on reduced workweeks.

Subsidizing Employment Sharing

One potentially viable method of encouraging worksharing is to offer financial incentives for firms and workers to choose worksharing instead of layoffs. Unfortunately, standard EI programs discussed in Chapter 3 instead provide an incentive to choose layoffs instead of worksharing. Under a standard EI program, workers are eligible for EI only once they are out of work because of temporary layoffs, plant closings, or other forms of job loss. There is, thus, an incentive for firms to use layoffs, subsidizing employment reduction with EI.

As a response to these unintended consequences of regular EI programs, in 1982 Canada modified its unemployment insurance program to allow firms to apply for unemployment insurance for workers who willingly participate in worksharing. The scheme, basically, provides EI benefits for anyone giving up an average of one day of work per week so that other workers in the firms would not be laid off. Although EI provides only a partial replacement for lost income (55 percent under the current program), workers may voluntarily choose to take a day off since they get an extra day of leisure by giving up less than half of a day's pay. Implicitly, the EI-funded subsidy to shorter workweeks is also a subsidy to firms. Gray (2000) provides a comprehensive review of the Canadian and international experience with "subsidized short-time compensation," the more general term used for government-subsidized worksharing.

As Gray points out, Canadian experience suggests that the program "works," in the sense that when offered the subsidy many firms chose to participate. In fact, the program has been oversubscribed, with more firms applying to participate than the budget allows. Program evaluation also suggests that the participating firms reduced layoffs, at least as measured by the number of employees enrolled in the program and the implicit reduction in hours worked. Unfortunately, it is less clear that the subsidy yielded long-run employment protection. Frequently, workers were laid off after the subsidy ran out. Did the firms and workers "take the money and run"? Gray notes, "it would be an exaggeration to characterize the Work Sharing program as prone to widespread misuse by beleaguered, subsidy-hungry firms (and their employees) attempting to avoid restructuring" (Gray, 2000, p. 14). While worksharing subsidies were intended to help firms through short-term downturns, firms and workers may in good faith have believed that demand conditions would soon improve.

Declining firms present problems of their own for policymakers, but long-term subsidization of employment is increasingly recognized as the inappropriate response (the Atlantic fishery represents an important example). Gray offers a number of suggestions for fine-tuning worksharing subsidies that try to target the program more effectively to firms genuinely experiencing short-run reductions in demand. For example, subsidies could be restricted to times of aggregate downturn (like recessions) to reduce the possibility that worksharing subsidies are not simply delaying economic restructuring.

Workers and the Demand for Worksharing

In addition to the costs to the firms and to the government, the feasibility of worksharing depends on the willingness of workers to go along with the scheme. Most union seniority rules are biased in favour of layoffs versus worksharing; the youngest workers bear the cost of the downturn, while the others are fully cushioned from the adverse (short-term) shock. David Gray (1998) uses rich industry-level data from France to explore the determinants of the propensity of firms to choose worksharing over layoffs, or vice versa.

He finds that three particular theoretical predictions are confirmed by the data. First, worksharing is more likely to be chosen in industries where workers have more seniority, because stringent job protection laws make it expensive to lay off workers with more seniority. Second, industries where workers have higher salaries are less likely to opt for worksharing because high-wage workers have to take a relatively larger wage cut under typical worksharing schemes. Third, industries already characterized by high rates of turnover and quitting, where adjustment costs are presumably lower, are less likely to use worksharing.

Closer to home, Huberman and Lacroix (1996) compare the relatively unsuccessful experience of worksharing at Bell Quebec (Quebec branch of Bell Canada) in 1994 to the much more successful experience of a similar program implemented by Volkswagen in Germany during the same period. These case studies identify two key factors that made the Volkswagen program much more successful than the one introduced by Bell. First, there is a long tradition of temporarily reducing hours to preserve jobs in Germany, while the North American tradition is to simply lay off workers during downturns. Second, the worksharing program at Volkswagen was implemented in tandem with other agreed-upon changes in the whole organization of work in the firm. By contrast, worksharing was introduced at Bell without adjusting other aspects of the collective agreement between workers and the firm. In particular, in layoffs, seniority provisions were preserved. This meant that more-senior workers were at no risk of losing their jobs at any time, with or without worksharing. Not surprisingly, very few of these senior workers agreed to participate to the worksharing program that was always voluntary in nature (unlike the program at Volkswagen). As a result, too few workers at Bell agreed to reduce their hours for worksharing to be a viable alternative to the layoffs that eventually occurred.

Summary

- Non-wage benefits, such as paid vacations, pensions, and other social insurance contributions, account for almost 40 percent of labour compensation. While this is more complicated than the simple "wage" that we use as the price of a unit of labour, the complexity of compensation may not affect the validity of the labour demand model. For example, if non-wage benefits are strictly proportional to the wage, the distinction is not important. However, non-wage benefits are often complex functions of the number of employees and hours worked.

- Many of these compensation costs are quasi fixed in that they are incurred once a worker is hired (possibly recurring annually), but do not change with the number of hours worked. Other labour costs, such as hiring, training, and firing costs, are also quasi fixed.

- The fact that some costs do not increase proportionately with hours worked drives a wedge between the marginal cost of hiring an additional worker (the extensive margin) and having an existing employee work more hours (the intensive margin). This generates an important distinction between the number of workers and hours worked per worker in yielding a given labour input. Some of these quasi-fixed costs will bias firms toward working their existing employees more intensively instead of hiring additional employees.

- The fixed costs associated with adjusting the number of employees (hiring, training, and firing costs) also generate a wedge between the value of the marginal product (VMP) of labour and the wage rate, since these costs must be paid by the surplus of VMP over wages. This wedge can operate in favour of a worker when demand for a firm's output declines. As long as the lower VMP is still higher than the wage, firms will have an incentive to retain workers instead of laying them off. This labour hoarding is more likely to apply to skilled workers for whom the quasi-fixed costs are higher.

- Because the labour cost structure may favour layoffs as the way to reduce labour input, governments around the world have introduced various regulations and programs, such as *short-time work schemes* (worksharing), which are aimed at encouraging firms to reduce hours per worker instead of the number of workers.

Keywords

adverse selection

deferred compensation

dynamic factor demand

employment standards legislation

labour hoarding

non-wage benefits

payroll taxes

quasi-fixed costs

transfers-in-kind

worksharing

Review Questions

1. Explain the factors that affect the firm's choice between the number of employees and hours per employee.

2. Firms often respond to decreases in demand by laying off some of their workforce. However, some groups of workers are more likely to be laid off than others. Provide an explanation for this phenomenon.

3. Would it ever be rational for a firm to retain an employee whose current marginal revenue product is less than his current wage? Explain.

4. "In the absence of hiring, training, and other fixed costs of employment, the firm does not need to forecast the future when making employment decisions. However, in the presence of these fixed costs the firm's employment decision necessarily involves planning for and forecasting the future." Discuss.

5. Discuss how regulations concerning the overtime premium (e.g., mandating it be two times rather than 1.5 times the wage rate) and subsidies for worksharing may increase the level of employment. Who benefits from such schemes? Who loses?

6. Firms regularly hire outside consultants to do specialized work instead of relying on in-house expertise. Discuss why this may be a profitable strategy for the firm.

Problems

1. Consider a firm that pays a salary of $10,000 and offers employees a compulsory benefit of three units of term life insurance (i.e., term life insurance that pays out three times salary if a person dies). Assume that term life insurance can be purchased for $2000 per year per unit in the insurance market. Unattached Jane is considering working for this company, and is evaluating her salary and benefits package. She imagines (incorrectly) that she can take the cash equivalent of the life insurance if she chooses.

   a. Draw her budget constraint, with consumption of non-insurance on the Y-axis and units of insurance on the X-axis, assuming that she can convert the three units of life insurance into cash.

   b. Depict her constrained choice, C, of $10,000 income and three units of insurance, and compare this to a situation where she would prefer only one unit of life insurance. With these assumptions, is there any way that she is better off with the firm's offer than with the cash equivalent?

   c. What if the implicit price of insurance is cheaper if offered by the firm? Draw the new budget constraint, assuming that she can convert her three units of consumption into cash at this cheaper rate. Is it possible that the compulsory three units might actually be optimal for Jane? Why might life insurance be cheaper for the firm to offer than Jane could purchase on the open market?

2. Assume that firms have a two-period planning horizon. For any workers hired, the value of the marginal product of labour in each period is given by VMP_1 and VMP_2, and the wages are W_1, W_2.

   a. Assume that there are no hiring costs. What is the relationship between the VMP and wage rate in each period?

   b. What happens to employment if VMP_2 is lower than expected in the second period?

   c. In order to reduce layoffs in the situation where VMP falls in the second period, the government introduces a "layoff tax." Show how this affects the employment decision in period 2, assuming that the tax was unexpected in period 1.

   d. How would your answer change if the firm was aware of the tax in period 1?

   e. Many European countries have legislation regarding severance pay that makes termination of employees costly to employers. What impact would introducing such legislation have on employer behaviour related to dismissals and new hires? What groups in society are likely to benefit, and what groups are likely to lose, from this type of legislation?

3. Currently, the payroll tax for Employment Insurance and the CPP/QPP are structured (approximately) as follows:

$$\text{Tax} = \begin{cases} t\text{Wh if Wh} \leq \overline{E} \\ t\overline{E} \text{ if Wh} > \overline{E} \end{cases}$$

   a. Why might the government put such a cap on the payroll tax?

   b. Assume that output depends on labour input as the simple sum of the number of hours worked by employees (i.e., an hour worked by an existing or new employee is equally productive). Derive the marginal cost of hiring an additional hour of labour services, depending on the number of hours worked by the employee (incorporating the payroll tax).

   c. Show how the structure of these taxes may affect the firm's choice between workers and hours.

   d. Would it be a good idea to eliminate the cap on the payroll taxes?

4. "The level of benefits offered to part-time workers is often below that offered to full-time workers doing the same job. A priority for labour standards legislation should be to end this discriminatory practice, especially since many part-time workers are women. Part-time workers would be better off if firms were forced to pay them the same benefits." True, false, or uncertain? Explain.

5. Consider a firm that exists for one period. The value of labour's (L) marginal product is given by $\text{VMP}_L = P \times \text{MP}_L$, where P is the price of output, and $\text{MPL} = 10 - 0.5L$. The wage rate is $10.

   a. Assume that there are no hiring or training costs. If the firm expects the price of output to be $10, what is the optimal level of employment, L_0? If the firm hires these workers, but then finds out that the price of output is $5, what will the firm do?

   b. Assume now that there are hiring and training costs of $20 per worker. If the firm expects the price of output to be $10, what is the optimal level of employment? How does this compare to your answer in part (a)? If the firm hires these workers but then finds out that the price of output is $5, what will the firm do? What if the price is $2? Explain.

   c. Explain (qualitatively) how your answer to part (b) would change if the hiring and training costs were higher or lower. How can these results be used to predict patterns of layoffs across occupations and industries during economic downturns?

6. Medical doctors are a good example of a profession in which it is very expensive to train workers. Medical students have to go through a long and expensive education program before they can start practicing as professional doctors. For the purpose of this exercise, assume that the marginal product is fixed so that the value of the marginal product, VMP, can be written as the product of hours of work, h, and the value of the hourly marginal product, VHMP. Total wages paid are the product of the hourly wage rate, w, and hours. In terms of the notation used in equation 6.1, it follows that $\text{VMP} = \text{VHMP} \times \text{h}$ and $W = w \times h$.

   a. Use equation 6.1 to show that for given values of VHMP and w, higher hiring and training costs result in higher hours of work. Would this model predict that specialists should work longer hours than general practitioners? Discuss.

   b. A growing fraction of doctors are women who, because of family and other responsibilities, may choose to not work as long hours as many male doctors used to. As a result, average hours worked by doctors will likely decline in the future. Assuming that hiring and training costs remain unchanged, discuss in the context of equation 6.1 what adjustments need to be made to either w, VHMP, or N to maintain the profit-maximizing employment rule in the face of lower hours of work. Keep in mind that since doctors are self-employed, they have quite a bit of latitude in choosing their hours of work.

Endnotes

1. Seminal contributions in this area were made by Oi (1962) and Rosen (1968). Other contributions include Hart (1984, 1987) and Hamermesh (1989, 1995).

PORTRAIT IMAGES ASIA/Shutterstock.com

CHAPTER 7

Wages and Employment in a Single Labour Market

LEARNING OBJECTIVES

LO1 Starting with individuals' labour supply decisions and firms' labour demand choices, construct market supply and demand curves, and compute the equilibrium wage and employment levels.

LO2 Contrast the equilibrium level of wage and employment under perfect competition to the case where in the market for goods there is imperfect competition, a monopoly, an oligopoly, or monopolistic competition.

LO3 Explain why, compared to the case of perfect competition, employment and wages are lower when the firm is a monopsony in the labour market.

LO4 Describe how the minimum wage has a negative effect on employment under perfect competition, but that the effect can turn positive when a firm is a monopsony.

LO5 Discuss how estimating the effect of the minimum wage on employment has been the source of some controversy.

MAIN QUESTIONS

- How is the equilibrium wage and employment level determined in a single labour market?

- How does imperfect competition affect the way in which we use the supply and demand model to analyze wages and employment determination?

- Are payroll taxes "job killers"? Is employment lower in Europe than in North America because of higher taxes?

- What is monopsony? How do wage and employment outcomes differ in labour markets where firms have market power in the hiring of labour? How much worse off might workers be if they have few alternative places of employment?

- Do minimum wages do more harm than good?

In this chapter, we complete the neoclassical model by analyzing the interaction of labour supply and demand in a single market. The firm may be operating in a **competitive** product market or a **noncompetitive market** (monopoly, oligopoly, monopolistic competition). Alternatively, the firm may be competitive or not competitive (i.e., possess some market power or monopsony) in the labour market. Throughout the analysis, we assume that workers are selling their labour on an individual basis. In later chapters, we analyze the situation of collective bargaining via unionization.

In dealing with the interaction of supply and demand in various market structures, it is important to be specific about the level of aggregation that is being analyzed. In this section, we begin at the level of aggregation of the individual firm, and, consequently, focus on the firm as the decision-making unit. Subsequently, we move to the "market," dealing with higher levels of aggregation, such as the occupation, industry, region, and economy as a whole—the levels at which the market wage is determined in competitive labour markets. We then relax the assumption of perfect competition in the product market. As will be seen, this does not substantially alter the supply and demand analysis. We describe the use of the supply and demand framework in policy analysis, with an extended investigation into payroll taxes.

Relaxing the assumption of perfect competition in the labour market has a greater impact on the analysis of wage and employment determination. We move from this discussion of monopsony to an in-depth examination of the impact of minimum wages on the labour market, where the monopsony and perfectly competitive models of the labour market have been brought to bear in the interpretation of the existing empirical evidence.

A Guide to Chapter 7

Chapter 7 pulls together the components of the supply and demand framework developed in Chapters 1 to 6, exploring how firms and workers interact in the market in determining the level of employment and wages. The key model is the competitive, neoclassical, and market-clearing "supply and demand" model. This model underlies the topics in the remainder of the text. The main objective of this chapter, then, is to see how the model works, and to consider some of the ways in which it may be wrong, while exploring how firms and workers interact in the market in determining the level of employment and wages.

One obvious set of ways in which the model may be wrong is in the assumption of perfect competition; that is, the assumption that no one firm or individual can affect the prevailing wage. They may do so in a number of ways:

- One possible route that imperfect competition may take is via the product market, where employers may have some degree of monopoly power. We saw in Chapter 5, and will see it confirmed here again, that while the slope of the labour demand function may be affected, the basic labour supply and demand framework is unaffected by imperfect competition in the product market.

- Alternatively, there may be imperfect competition within the labour market itself. For example, there may be only a few (or one) employers, in which case workers have few options of where to work. The case of a single employer is called monopsony, and it significantly affects the way in which employment and wages are determined in a labour market. Imperfect competition could run the other way as well. Labour may be sold to firms on a monopolistic basis by labour unions. Because unions play such an important role in the labour market, we defer their study to separate chapters (Chapters 14–16).

THE OUTLINE OF CHAPTER 7 IS AS FOLLOWS:

1. Imperfect competition in the product market, and its impact on the labour demand function.
2. The competitive supply and demand model; solving for and interpreting the equilibrium, and applying the model to an evaluation of payroll taxes.
3. Monopsony in the labour market, or employment determination when firms (but not workers) can affect the wage.
4. Measuring the impact of the minimum wage on employment. Traditionally, this topic would be discussed in a labour demand chapter. However, recent empirical evidence requires an understanding of the impact of minimum wages on monopsonistic markets before it can be presented.

LO1   The Competitive Firm's Interaction with the Market

We first examine the case in which the firm is a competitive seller of its output in the product market and a competitive buyer of labour in the labour market. In essence, the firm is so small relative to both markets that it can sell all of the output it wants at the going price of the product, and it can buy all of the labour it wants at the going wage rate. The firm is both a price-taker and wage-taker: it cannot influence either the product price or the wage rate.

This situation is depicted in Figure 7.1(a) and (b) for two competitive firms. In both cases, their supply schedules for a given homogeneous type of labour are perfectly elastic (horizontal) at the market wage rate, W_c. The firms are wage-takers, not wage-setters, and, consequently, can employ all of the labour they want at this market wage rate.

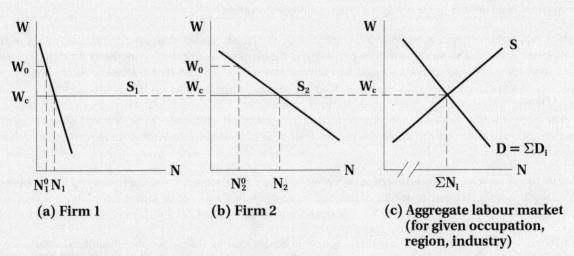

(a) Firm 1   (b) Firm 2   (c) Aggregate labour market (for given occupation, region, industry)

Figure 7.1 Competitive Product and Labour Markets

Market demand for labour is the sum of the demand for labour by each firm at each wage. At wage W_0, market demand is $N_1^0 + N_2^0$, plus remaining firms' demand at W_0. In a competitive market, each firm faces perfectly elastic labour supply at the prevailing wage. For the whole market, the market supply of labour is relevant, and, as shown in panel (c), W_c is the equilibrium wage.

The market wage rate for this specific, homogeneous type of labour is determined by the interaction of supply and demand in the aggregate labour market, as depicted in Figure 7.1(c). This aggregate labour market could be a regional labour market for a particular occupational category of labour; for example, the Halifax labour market for junior accounting clerks. By assuming that the firms are in the same region and are hiring the same homogeneous occupational type of labour, we are able to minimize the intervening influence of these factors on the wage determination process and, thereby, focus on the issue of wage and employment determination at the disaggregate, or microeconomic, level of the firm. In the subsequent chapters on wage structures, these assumptions are relaxed sequentially and the resultant wage structures analyzed.

The demand schedules for labour in the two firms are the schedules of the value of the marginal products of labour, defined as the marginal physical product of labour times the price at which the firms can sell their products. (These were derived formally in Chapter 5.) Since the firms are assumed to be competitive sellers of their products, their product prices are fixed at p_1^* and p_2^*. Only if the firms are selling the same output would their product prices have to be the same; otherwise, p_1^* need not equal p_2^*. The magnitude and the elasticity of the demand for labour also are depicted as being different, simply to emphasize that the market wage is the same, irrespective of these factors. The demand schedules determine the level of employment in each firm; in this case, N_1 and N_2 units of labour, respectively, in firms 1 and 2.

The **market demand curve**, as depicted in Figure 7.1(c), is the summation of the demand curves of the individual firms, such as those shown in Figures 7.1(a) and (b). Conceptually, the market demand curve can be obtained as follows. For any specific wage rate, such as W_0 in Figure 7.1, determine the quantity of labour that each firm in the market would wish to employ. For the two firms depicted in Figures 7.1(a) and (b), these quantities are N_1^0 and N_2^0, respectively. Adding these quantities gives the total market demand at that wage rate. Repeating this process for all wage rates traces out the market labour demand curve.

In summary, when the firm is a **competitive buyer of labour**, it faces a perfectly elastic supply of labour at the market wage. When the firm is a competitive seller of its output on the product market, it regards the price at which it sells its output on the product market as fixed, and its derived demand for labour schedule is the value of the marginal product of labour, defined as the marginal physical product of labour times the fixed price at which the firm sells its output. Because the labour supply schedule to the firm is perfectly elastic at the market wage rate, the intersection of the firm's labour supply and demand schedules determines the employment level of the firm for that particular type of labour—wages are determined elsewhere; specifically, in the aggregate labour market for that particular type of labour.

The previous analysis was based on the long-run assumption that the firm could get all of the labour it needed at the market-determined wage rate. That is, in order to expand its workforce, it need hire additional workers only at the going wage rate—there is no need to increase wages to attract additional workers.

In the short run, however, even a firm that is competitive in the labour market may have to raise its wages in order to attract additional workers. This situation is often referred to in the literature as **dynamic monopsony**. In such circumstances, the firm's short-run labour supply schedule could be upward sloping, as depicted by the schedule S_s in Figure 7.2. In the short run, in order to expand its workforce so as to meet an increase in the demand for labour from D to D , the firm may have to pay higher wages, perhaps by paying an overtime premium to its existing workforce, or by paying higher wages to attract local workers within the community. The resultant expansion of the workforce can be depicted as a movement up the short-run supply curve in response to the new, higher wage of W_s, occasioned by the increase in the demand for labour from D to D .

In the longer run, however, a supply influx of other workers will be forthcoming because the firm is paying an above-market wage (i.e., $W_s > W_c$) for that particular type of labour. The supply influx may not be instantaneous, but could occur in the long run because it may come from other firms or perhaps from outside of the labour force, and such adjustments take time.

The new supply influx in response to the higher wage could be depicted by the S_s supply schedule of labour. The supply influx would depress the temporarily high, short-run wage of W_s back to its long-run level of W_c. Thus, the long-run supply of labour schedule to the firm, S_1, can be thought of as a locus of long-run equilibrium points, traced out by various shifting short-run supply schedules of the firm, as the firm tries to expand its workforce.

In essence, temporary wage increases above the competitive norm are consistent with the firm being a competitive buyer of labour in the long run. In fact, short-run wage increases can be a market signal for the supply response that ensures that market forces operate in the longer run.

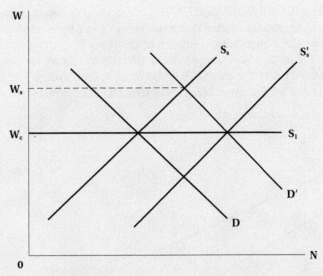

Figure 7.2 Short-Run and Long-Run Labour Supply Schedules to the Firm

Long-run labour supply to the firm, S_1, is perfectly elastic at W_c. In the short run, mobility restrictions may yield upward-sloping labour supply, such as S_s. At higher wages, more workers will want to work at the firm, and at lower wages the firm will lose some (but not all) of its workers. If demand shifts from D to D', the firm can hire more workers at W_s. In the long run, workers will be attracted to this firm, shifting labour supply to S_s', until the firm is paying W_c.

Imperfect Competition in the Product Market

Monopoly

When an industry is competitive in the product market, the industry demand for labour is obtained by aggregating the labour demand of each of the firms in the industry, as illustrated in Figure 7.1. In the case of monopoly in the product market, the firm *is* the industry, and, therefore, there is no need to distinguish between the firm's labour demand and that of the industry as a whole.

As discussed in Chapter 5, the labour demand schedule for the competitive firm on the product market is given by

$$w^* = MPP_N \times p_Q^* = VMP_N \text{ [competitor]}$$

(7.1)

where the value of the marginal product of labour (VMP_N) is used to distinguish

$$w^* = MPP_N \times MR_Q = MRP_N \text{ [monopolist]}$$

(7.2)

which applies to the monopolist, since its output price is not fixed. Rather, for the monopolist, marginal revenue is the relevant factor.

The difference between equations 7.1 and 7.2 highlights the fact that when the monopolist hires more labour to produce more output, not only does the marginal physical product of labour fall (as is the case with the competitor), but also the marginal revenue from an additional unit of output, MR_Q, falls. This latter effect occurs because the monopolist, unlike the competitive firm, can sell more output only by lowering the product price and this, in turn, lowers marginal revenue. Because both MPP_N and MR_Q fall when N increases in equation 7.1, then the monopolist's demand for labour falls faster than it would if it behaved as a competitive firm in the product market, in which case only MPP_N would fall, as given in equation 7.2.

The difference between the labour demand schedule for a monopolist and the schedule that would prevail if the industry were competitive in the product market is illustrated in Figure 7.3. This comparison is most meaningful if it involves two situations that are identical except for the difference in market structure. To carry out the comparison, begin with a large number of price-taking firms. Aggregating the labour demand of each of the firms in this competitive industry gives the industry demand curve $D_C = \Sigma VMP_N$ in Figure 7.3. Now, suppose these firms form a cartel and set the product price to maximize total industry profit, as would a monopolist that owned all of the firms in the industry. The labour demand schedule for the monopolist is $D_M = MPP_N \times MR_Q = MRP_N$. Since $MR_Q < P_Q$, then D_M lies below D_c.

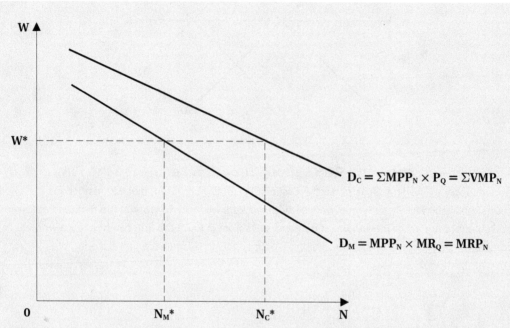

Figure 7.3 Monopolist versus Competitive Demand for Labour

In a competitive product market, demand for labour is given by $D_C = \Sigma MPP_N \times P_Q = \Sigma VMP_N$. If a monopolist purchased these firms, demand for labour would be $D_M = MPP_N \times MR_Q = MRP_N$. At W^*, the demand for labour is lower for the monopolist; that is, $N^*_M < N^*_C$, because the monopolist produces lower output. Furthermore, the demand curve is steeper for the monopolist, since MR_Q falls as employment and output increase, whereas P_Q remains the same.

The monopolist (or a cartel of firms acting like a single monopolist) raises the industry price relative to the competitive equilibrium level, which reduces output and employment. Thus, at any particular wage (e.g., W^* in Figure 7.3), employment will be lower if the industry is monopolized than in an otherwise identical competitive industry.

As long as the number of workers employed by the monopolist is small relative to the size of the relevant labour market, the fact that the monopolist has market power in the product market does not translate into market power in the labour market. A standard monopolist that simply tries to maximize profits should just pay the going competitive wage. As we will see below, however, there are other reasons a monopolist may end up paying more than the equilibrium market wage.

Monopolistic Competition and Oligopoly

Between the polar cases of competition and monopoly in the product market are a variety of intermediate cases. Firms can be monopolistically competitive, a situation characterized by many firms that are small relative to the total market, but with products that are differentiated in some way, giving the firm some discretion in its price-setting. In such circumstances, the demand for the firm's product is not perfectly elastic, as in the competitive case, but it rather has some degree of inelasticity, reflecting the fact that if the firm raises its price it will not lose all of its market, and if it lowers its price it will not gain all of the market. Under monopolistic competition, as is the case in perfect competition, there are no barriers to entry by new firms. This "free entry" property implies that firms cannot earn above-normal or monopoly profits in the long run.

Oligopoly industries are characterized by few firms that produce sufficiently similar products so that the actions of one firm will affect the other firms. Consequently, the firms will react to the actions of the other firms, and will take into account the possible reactions of their rivals in making their own decisions. There are many ways in which the firms can react, and, consequently, there is a large number of possible ways to categorize oligopoly situations. Oligopoly industries are, generally, characterized by some barriers to entry by new firms so that above-normal profits may be earned by oligopolists in the long run.

The general conclusions reached in the previous analysis of perfect competition and monopoly continue to apply to the intermediate cases of monopolistic competition and oligopoly. In particular, market power in the product market is consistent with the firm being competitive in the labour market (or labour markets) in which it operates. Thus, firms that exercise some discretion or even exert considerable control over the product price may be wage-takers in the labour market. In these circumstances, they would pay the market wage for the types of labour they employ, and could increase or decrease their employment without affecting the prevailing market wage.

Product Market Structure and Departures from Market Wages

The previous analysis highlights that, as long as market power in the product market does not translate into market power in the labour market, there is no particular reason to expect a profit-maximizing firm not to simply pay the going market wage. It is important to realize, however, that when a monopolist pays the going market wage, all of the monopoly profit or "rent" goes to the owners of the firm. Workers employed by the monopolist earn the same wage as they would if they worked for a competitive firm making zero profits. As we will see in Chapter 14, however, this scenario is unlikely to hold when workers employed by the monopolist are members of a union that collectively bargains with the employer. In such a setting, there is clear empirical evidence that unions are able to negotiate a wage above the going market wage, thereby redistributing some of the monopoly profits to workers in terms of higher wages. Existing empirical evidence suggests that even when workers are not unionized, they still tend to earn higher wages in industries where firms earn higher profits because of market power in the product market or other considerations.[1]

Similarly, organized workers employed by oligopolistic firms will also, likely, be able to negotiate a wage above the going market wage. A leading example of this phenomenon is the North American automobile sector that was traditionally dominated by the "Big Three" automakers (General Motors, Ford, and Chrysler). While the sector has been under intense foreign competition since at least the 1980s, it was widely believed to be a typical case of an oligopoly making excess profits during the decades following World War II. Unions were also, traditionally, very strong in this sector and managed to turn part of the oligopolistic profits into better-than-average wages and work conditions.

This situation is quite different for firms that operate under monopolistic competition. Under monopolistic competition, free entry implies that firms should not earn above-normal profits in the long run (though they may in the short run, as would occur if there was an unexpected increase in demand for the product). Such firms are also, generally, small in size, such as retail outlets that are differentiated by location and possibly also by the merchandise carried. For these reasons, we would expect firms that are monopolistically competitive in the product market but perfectly competitive in the labour market to pay the prevailing market wage, over which changes in their employment levels will exert no influence.

Working with Supply and Demand

One of the most common types of applied policy analysis is to simulate the effects of a policy change on the equilibrium level of employment and wages. In order to do this, it is necessary to be able to solve explicitly for the market equilibrium. Consider the most general form of the model, with labour supply and demand functions given by

$$N^S = f(W; X)$$

$$N^D = g(W; Z)$$

W, N^S, and N^D are **endogenous variables** in this system, while Z and X are **exogenous variables**. Economic theory guides us in sorting out what are the various shifters, Z and X, that will affect labour supply and demand.

To solve the system, we invoke market clearing and set $N^S = N^D$. Then we solve for W* and N* (two equations with two unknowns). The results, which express N and W as functions of the parameters and the exogenous variables, are called the **reduced form**. Once we have solved for the reduced form, we can easily simulate the effect on the equilibrium of changing X and Z .

Linear Supply and Demand Functions

A useful example is to consider the simplest functional form for the supply and demand functions: straight lines. Equations for these functions are

$$N^D = a + bW; \quad b < 0$$

$$N^S = c + fW; \quad f > 0$$

Setting $N^S = N^D$, we can solve for the equilibrium, or reduced form:

$$W^* = \frac{a - c}{f - b}$$

Substituting W* into either the supply or demand equation yields the equilibrium employment:

$$N^* = \frac{af - bc}{f - b}$$

It is easy to add other variables (shifters), like the X or Z, to our models to make them more realistic:

$$a + bW + \delta X = c + fW + \phi Z$$

yielding,

$$W^* = \frac{a - c}{f - b} - \frac{\phi Z}{f - b} + \frac{\delta X}{f - b}$$

where Z and X represent other supply and demand factors that shift the position of the supply and demand functions.

If we know how policy changes affect the position of the demand or supply function (i.e., how they affect a or c), then, given estimates of the other parameters, we can simulate the effect of the policy change on the equilibrium.

The equilibrium wage and employment can also be illustrated graphically using a standard supply and demand graph illustrated in Figure 7.4. In order to match the form of the above supply and demand equations with the economists' unconventional reverse representation of functions, it is worth re-expressing these equations in terms of W as

$$W = -\frac{a}{b} + \frac{1}{b}N$$

$$W = -\frac{c}{f} + \frac{1}{f}N$$

These are equations for straight lines. For example, the slope of the demand curve is given by 1/b, while the intercept is −a/b. Many "thought experiments" take the form of changing the "intercept"; that is, shifting the position of the supply or demand function, keeping the slopes constant. Note that for these linear demand and supply functions, the absolute change or the slope is constant, so the elasticity varies. Since the elasticity is given by $\frac{\Delta N}{\Delta W} \times \frac{W}{N}$, if the slope is constant, the elasticity will vary with $\frac{W}{N}$.

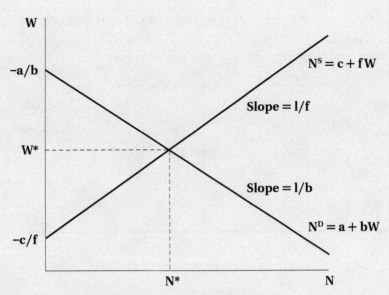

Figure 7.4 Linear Supply and Demand Functions

The supply function is given by N^S = c + fW, transformed so that the vertical axis is the wage, the horizontal axis is employment, the slope is 1/f, and the intercept is −c/f. The demand function is given by N^D = a + bW, but after its axes are switched, the slope is 1/b and the intercept is −a/b. The equilibrium (N*, W*) is given by the intersection of the functions.

The equilibrium values of W* and N* in Figure 7.4 correspond to the analytical expressions derived above. It is sometimes useful to work with log-linear instead of simple linear functions. In this case, the functional form for the supply and demand functions is given by

$$\log N^D = \alpha + \beta \log W, \quad \beta < 0$$

$$\log N^S = \lambda + \eta \log W, \quad \eta > 0$$

The convenience of the log-linear functional form comes from the fact that the slope parameters β and η are the demand and supply elasticities. The slopes of the log-linear functions are constant, and so too are the elasticities. Because economists often have estimates of these elasticities, the reduced form turns out to be easier to use for simulating the impact of changes in policy.

The solution for the reduced form proceeds identically to the linear case. For simplicity, denote $n^S = \log N^S$, $n^D = \log N^D$, and $w = \log W$. An equilibrium, $n^* w^*$, will occur as before, where $n^S = n^D$, and, implicitly, $N^S = N^D$.

Application: Incidence of a Unit Payroll Tax

A common use of these equilibrium models is in the evaluation of tax policy. After income taxes, the most contentious tax studied by labour economists is the payroll tax. A payroll tax is a tax levied on employers, based on the level of employment, usually proportional to the firm's payroll. Common examples of payroll taxes in Canada include CPP/QPP premiums, workers' compensation, unemployment insurance, and health insurance levies in some provinces. Table 7.1 illustrates these payroll taxes for 1971 and 1997, drawing on Lin (2000). Generally, payroll tax rates have grown in importance, especially for unemployment insurance and the CPP/QPP. In fact, the combined tax rate for employer and employee contributions to the CPP/QPP grew steadily over time to reach 9.9 percent in 2003. It has remained at that level since then. These taxes are often viewed as taxes on employers, rather than on workers. As such, they are often attacked as taxes on jobs, or "job killers." By investigating the possible impact of such taxes on wages and employment, we can evaluate the truth to these claims. To keep the notation simple, we will consider a simple per-unit tax, T, applied on a per-employee basis to firms. We will use the linear system of equations developed earlier to further simplify the analysis.

TABLE 7.1	Payroll Taxes as a Percentage of Labour Income by Type of Payroll Tax, Canada, 1971 and 1997	
Type of Payroll Tax	**1971**	**1997**
Workers' compensation	0.73	1.61
Unemployment insurance	1.06	4.98
Canada/Quebec pension	2.12	3.92
Health and/or education	0.21	1.71
Total	**4.12**	**12.23**

SOURCE: Authors' calculations based on data provided by Lin (2000). Payroll Taxes in Canada Revisited: Structure, statutory parameters, and recent trends. *Canadian Tax Journal*, 48:577–625.

Workers are paid the wage W for a unit of work, while firms pay W + T per unit hired—W to the employee, and T to the government. On the face of it, it appears that the common sense debate has substance; the employers pay the tax to the government (the workers do not), and this is likely to reduce employment because it raises the cost of hiring labour. Unfortunately, this "common sense" ignores the impact of the tax on the labour market and the adjustments that might occur.

The effect of the tax on labour demand is depicted in Figure 7.5. The initial equilibrium is labelled A, with equilibrium employment N_0 and wage W_0. The imposition of the tax shifts the demand schedule N^D down by T units for every employment level. The initial demand curve gives the optimal labour demanded at a cost of W per unit, whereas the shifted curve accounts for the fact that the price of labour is now W (to the workers) plus T (to the government), for a total of W + T. If there were no other changes in the labour market (i.e., the wage stayed the same) demand would fall from N_0 to N . As we can see, however, as long as the supply curve is not horizontal, the equilibrium wage drops to W_1, and employment falls only to N_1. The lower wage effectively means that the workers pay some portion of the tax. In fact, at the new level of employment, N_1, we can account for who pays the tax. Workers' wages are lowered by $W_0 - W_1$ (given by BC in Figure 7.5), and this represents their share. The remainder of T, CD, is paid by the firm. Therefore, the **incidence of the tax** does not necessarily fall only on the party that physically pays the tax or fills in the forms.

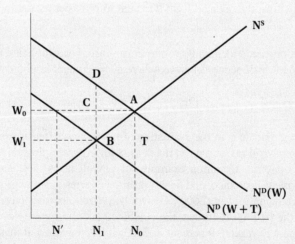

Figure 7.5 The Effect of a Payroll Tax on Employment and Wages
The initial equilibrium is A, at a wage of W_0. The payroll tax, T per worker, raises the price of labour to W + T. This shifts labour demand down by T units at each employment level. The new equilibrium is denoted by B, at the lower wage W_1. Some of the tax is paid by workers through lower wages. The workers' share of the tax is given by the vertical distance BC, while the incidence of the tax on employers is the remainder of T, which is given by CD.

Algebraically, we can see this by substituting the appropriate post-tax prices into the demand and supply equations:

$$N^D = a+b(W + T) = a+bW + bT$$

$$N^S = c+fW$$

So that

$$a+bW + bT = c + fW, \text{ and } W_1 = \left(\frac{a-c}{f-b}\right) - \frac{b}{b-f} \times T < W_0$$

where W_0 is the equilibrium wage in the absence of the tax.

EXHIBIT 7.1

Why Do Americans Work So Much More than Europeans?

There is an emerging puzzle about the effect of payroll and other taxes on employment. On the one hand, studies like Beach and Abbott (1997) that look at the effect of payroll taxes within countries generally fail to find evidence that payroll taxes are the job killers they are made out to be. On the other hand, a growing number of studies point out that there is a strong negative relationship between taxes and employment across countries. For example, Prescott (2004) argues that differences in taxes are the primary reason more-heavily taxed Europeans now work much less than Americans. Davis and Henrekson (2005) reach a similar conclusion looking at a richer set of cross-country data.

As we saw in Figure 7.5, an increase in taxes shifts down the labour demand curve along the labour supply curve. The impact of taxes on employment, thus, critically, depends on the elasticity of labour supply. When labour supply is very elastic, a small increase in taxes can result in a large negative employment effect. By contrast, taxes have little effect on employment when the labour supply curve is inelastic.

For the entire working-age population, Americans adults now work, on average, 25.1 hours a week compared to 18.0 hours a week in France and 18.6 in Germany. In other words, Americans now work 35–40 percent more hours per week than do people in France or Germany. Prescott argues that taxes can explain this large and growing gap, provided that the labour supply elasticity is large enough. To see how large the elasticity needs to be, note that tax rates are 15 to 20 percentage points higher in France and Germany than in the United States (depending on how taxes are measured). The elasticity of hours of work with respect to tax rates must, therefore, be around 2 for a 15–20 percentage point gap in taxes to translate into a 35–40 percentage point gap in hours of work. This is a much larger elasticity than what is typically found in the empirical studies of labour supply discussed in Chapter 3. Indeed, Alesina, Glaeser, and Sacerdote (2005) argue that taxes cannot explain differences in hours of work between the United States and Europe because the elasticities required are implausibly large.

Alesina, Glaeser, and Sacerdote instead argue that European labour market regulations explain the bulk of the difference in employment and hours of work between the United States and Europe. They also conjecture that a "social multiplier" in leisure may be playing a role in the U.S.–Europe difference. The idea is that leisure is more valuable when other people also take time off, as they do in Europe, than when other people take little time off, as they do in the United States. If this reasoning is correct, it implies that the marginal utility of leisure is higher in Europe than in the United States, and that Europeans rationally choose to consume more leisure than do Americans. This social multiplier is closely linked to the concept of social capital popularized by Putnam (2000) in his aptly titled book, *Bowling Alone*. The fact that it is not much fun to go bowling when nobody else does nicely illustrates how the marginal utility of leisure depends on how much leisure other people also consume.

This example highlights how social interactions can have important implications for economic behaviour. Indeed, developing new economic models and empirical tests of social interactions is an active area of research in economics.

Thus, of the T tax dollars, the worker's wage is reduced from the original level by $\frac{b}{b-f}$T. This is the worker's share of the taxes. Clearly, the worker's share will depend on the relative slopes of the supply and demand functions. For example, if b = −3 and f = 1, the workers' share is $\frac{-3}{-3-1}$ = 0.75, so that most of the tax is shifted to workers in terms of lower wages.

Note that the effect of a payroll tax may differ in the short and long run. For example, if labour supply is perfectly inelastic in the long run (f = 0), workers will end up paying the entire tax and the employment level will be unaffected. In the short run, with more elastic labour supply, firms will pay part of the tax, and employment will be lower than before the tax (but again, not as much as would be the case if the market wage did not adjust). It is an empirical question what the ultimate incidence of the payroll tax is.

Kesselman (1996) provides a useful summary of the state of empirical knowledge on payroll taxes, as well as a critical review of some of the theoretical and practical issues related to the simple model we have just outlined. One important point he raises is that since the government needs to raise a given amount of revenue, it must use some form of tax, and all taxes have distortionary effects on markets. The question is then, which tax distorts least. Kesselman concludes that payroll taxes may actually be useful and relatively efficient tax instruments, especially if the tax is collected for a particular purpose, such as CPP/QPP. For example, compared to income taxes, payroll taxes are generally easier to administer, compliance is easier, and evasion is lower. The growing body of empirical evidence also seems to support the conclusion that, in the long run (as suggested by the model above), the incidence of payroll taxes falls largely on workers, and that the disemployment effect is small. There may be some disemployment effects in the short run, but it does not appear that payroll taxes are the job killers they are made out to be.[2]

LO3   Monopsony in the Labour Market

To this point, we have examined the wage and employment decision when the firm is both a competitive seller of its output in the product market and a competitive buyer of labour in the labour market. We also relaxed one of those assumptions, that of a competitive seller of its output, and examined the labour market implications when the firm is a noncompetitive seller of its output, but still a competitive buyer of labour in the labour market. In this section, the assumption of being a competitive buyer of labour is relaxed. So as to trace out the implications of this single change, termed **monopsony**, the firm is still assumed to be a competitive seller of its product.[3] The results of relaxing both assumptions simultaneously, those of competition in the labour market and in the product market, follow in a straightforward fashion from the results of each separate case.

Simple Monopsony

The situation in which a firm is sufficiently large relative to the size of the local labour market, so that it influences the wage at which it hires labour, is referred to as monopsony. The monopsonist is a wage-setter, not a wage-taker. In order to attract additional units of labour, the monopsonist has to raise wages. Conversely, if it lowers the wage rate it will not lose its entire workforce.

Consequently, the monopsonist faces an upward-sloping labour supply schedule rather than a perfectly elastic labour supply schedule at the going wage, as was the case when the firm was a competitive buyer of labour. This labour supply schedule shows the average cost of labour for the monopsonist, because it indicates the wage that must be paid for each different size of the firm's workforce. Since this same wage must be paid for each homogeneous unit of labour, then the wage paid at the margin becomes the actual wage paid to all of the workers, and this same average wage is paid to all.

The firm's labour supply, or average cost-of-labour schedule, is not its relevant decision-making schedule. Rather, the relevant schedule is its *marginal* cost of labour, which lies above its average cost. This is so because when the firm has to raise wages to attract additional units of labour, in the interest of maintaining internal equity in the wage structure, it also has to pay that higher wage to its existing workforce (intramarginal workers). Thus, the marginal cost of adding an additional worker equals the new wage plus the addition to wage costs imposed by the fact that this new, higher wage must be paid to the existing workforce. Consequently, the marginal cost of adding an additional worker is greater than the average cost, which is simply the wage.

This situation can be depicted by a simple hypothetical example. Suppose the monopsonist employed only one worker at a wage of one dollar per hour. Its average cost of labour would be the wage rate of one dollar. This would also be its marginal cost; that is, the extra cost of hiring this worker. If the monopsonist wanted to expand its workforce, however, it would have to pay a higher wage of, for example, $1.20 to attract an additional worker. Its average cost of labour is the new wage of $1.20 (i.e., (1.20 + 1.20)/2). However, the marginal cost of adding the new worker is the new wage of $1.20 *plus* the additional $0.20 per hour it has to pay the first worker in order to maintain internal equity in the wage structure. Thus, the marginal cost of the second worker is $1.40 per hour, which is greater than the average cost, or wage, of $1.20. If a third worker costs $1.40, then the average cost, or wage, of the three workers would be $1.40, while the marginal cost of adding the third worker would be $1.80, composed of $1.40 for the third worker plus the additional $0.20 for each of the other two workers. (This example is further extended in the first three columns of the table in the Worked Example, "Minimum Wage and Employment under Monopsony" presented later in this chapter.)

The monopsony situation is illustrated diagrammatically in Figure 7.6. The essence of monopsony is that the firm faces an upward-sloping supply schedule for labour and, hence, has a marginal cost-of-labour schedule that lies above the supply, or average cost, schedule. The firm maximizes profits by hiring labour until the marginal cost of an additional unit of labour just equals the marginal revenue generated by the additional unit of labour. Marginal revenue is given by the value of marginal product (VMP) schedule in this assumed case of the firm being a competitive seller of its product. This equality of marginal cost and VMP occurs at the employment level N_M.

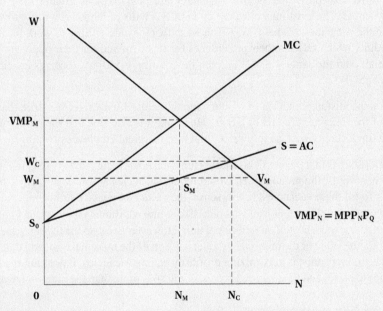

Figure 7.6 Monopsony

The marginal benefit of hiring an additional worker is $VMP_N = MPP_N \times P_Q$. The supply curve, S, indicates the wage needed to induce a given number of workers to work for the firm. That wage is also the average cost of labour, so S = AC. The marginal cost of labour, MC, is higher than the average cost, because the firm must raise the wage for all of its existing employees, not just the marginal employee hired. The profit-maximizing employment level, N_M, occurs at $MC = VMP_N$. In order to attract N_M workers, the firm must pay W_M.

The VMP curve for the monopsonist is not its demand curve for labour in the sense of showing the various quantities of labour that will be demanded at various wage rates. This is so because the monopsonist does not pay a wage equal to the VMP of labour. For example, in Figure 7.6, at the wage W_M, the quantity of labour demanded is N_M, not $W_M V_M$, as would be the case if VMP were a demand schedule equating W with VMP. In essence, the demand for labour is determined by the interaction of the MC and VMP schedules, and this depends on the shape of the supply schedule (and, hence, the MC schedule) as well as the VMP schedule. This line of reasoning is analogous to that underlying the fact that a product market monopolist has no supply curve for its product.

Implications of Monopsony

The level of employment, N_M, associated with monopsony is lower than the level, N_c, that would prevail if the monopsonist behaved as a competitive buyer of labour, equating the supply of labour with the demand. The monopsonist restricts its employment somewhat because hiring additional labour is costly, since the higher wages have to be paid to the intramarginal units of labour.

For N_M units of labour, the monopsonist pays a wage of W_M, as given by the supply schedule of labour. The supply schedule shows the amount of labour that will be forthcoming at each wage, and for a wage of W_M, then N_M units of labour will be forthcoming. This wage is less than the wage W_c that the monopsonist would pay if it employed the competitive amount of labour N_c. The monopsonist wage is also less than the value of the marginal product of N_M units of labour. That is, the monopsonist pays a wage rate that is less than the value of the output produced by the additional unit of labour (although the value of that output does equal the marginal cost of producing it). This monopsony profit, or difference between wages and the value of marginal product of labour, has been termed a measure of the monopsonistic exploitation of labour, equal to $VMP_M - W_M$ per worker or $(VMP_M - W_M) N_M$ for the monopsonist's workforce. This monopsony profit accrues to the firm because its wage bill, $W_M N_M$, is less than the market value of the marginal output contributed by the firm's labour force, $VMP_M N_M$.

Although monopsony leads to a wage less than the value of the marginal product of labour, it is also true that intramarginal workers are receiving a seller's surplus; that is, the wage they are paid, W_M, is greater than their reservation wage as indicated by the supply schedule. The existing workforce up until N_M units of labour is willing to work for the monopsonist for a wage that is less than the wage they are paid, W_M. The wage that they are willing to work for is illustrated by the height of the labour supply schedule, which reflects their preferences for this firm and for their opportunities elsewhere. However, to the extent that they are all paid the same wage, W_M, then the existing workforce receives a seller's surplus, or economic rent, equal to the triangle $S_0 S_M W_M$.

This is why the term "monopsonist exploitation of labour" should be used with care. It is true that the monopsonist pays a wage less than the value of the marginal product of labour. However, it is also true that the monopsonist pays a wage greater than the reservation wage (opportunity cost, supply price) that intramarginal employees could get elsewhere for their labour.

A final implication of monopsony is that there will be equilibrium vacancies (equal to $V_M - S_M$ in Figure 7.6) at the wage paid by the monopsonist. In other words, the monopsonist would report vacancies at the wage it pays, but it will not raise wages to attract additional labour to fill these vacancies. In this sense, the vacancies are an equilibrium, since there are no automatic forces that will reduce the vacancies. The monopsonist would like to hire additional labour *at the going wage* since the value of the marginal product exceeds the wage cost of an additional unit. However, because the higher wage would have to be paid to intramarginal units of labour, the value of the marginal product just equals the marginal cost, and that is why there are no forces to reduce the vacancies. The monopsonist is maximizing profits by having vacancies. It does not reduce the vacancies because it would have to raise wages to do so, and the marginal cost of doing so is more than the marginal revenue.

Characteristics of Monopsonists

As long as there is some inelasticity to the supply schedule of labour faced by a firm, then that firm has elements of monopsony power. To a certain extent, most firms may have an element of monopsony power in the short run, in the sense that they could lower their wages somewhat without losing all of their workforce. However, it is unlikely that they would exercise this power in the long run, because it would lead to costly problems of recruitment, turnover, and morale. Facing an irreversible decline in labour demand, however, firms may well allow their wages to deteriorate as a way of reducing their workforce.

In the long run, monopsony clearly will be less prevalent. It would occur when the firm is so large, relative to the size of the local labour market, that it influences wages. This could be the case, for example, in the classic one-industry towns in isolated regions. Such firms need not be large in an absolute sense; they are simply large relative to the size of the small local labour market, and this makes them the dominant employer. Monopsony may also be associated with workers who have particular preferences to remain employed with the monopsonist. In such circumstances, wages could be lowered and they would stay with the monopsonist because their skills or preferences are not transferable.

Thus, a mining company could be a monopsonist, even if it were reasonably small, if it were located in an isolated region with no other firms competing for the types of labour it employed. The same company could even be a monopsonist for one type of labour—for example, miners—while having to compete for other types of labour—for example, clerical workers. Conversely, an even larger mining company might be a competitive employer of miners if it were situated in a less isolated labour market and had to compete with other firms. It is size relative to the local labour market that matters, not absolute size.

Monopsony may also be associated with workers who have specialized skills (specific human capital) that are useful mainly in a specific firm, or with workers who have particular preferences to remain employed with a specific firm. Because their skills or preferences are not completely transferable, such workers are tied to a single employer which, therefore, possesses a degree of monopsony power. Contractual arrangements in professional sports, for example, often effectively tie the professional athlete to a specific employer (team), giving the employer a degree of monopsony power. At a minimum, the employer need pay a salary only slightly higher than the player's next-best alternative salary (e.g., in minor leagues or in another line of work), which would be considerably less than the value of his skills in a competitive market. In practice, a much higher salary is usually paid in order to extract maximum performance. When players are free agents—for example, when different leagues compete—the resultant salary explosions attest to the fact that the competitive salary is much higher than the monopsonist salary.

The professional sports example illustrates the important fact that although monopsonists pay less than they would if they had to compete for labour, they need not pay low wages. In fact, unique, specialized skills are often associated with high salaries, albeit they might even be higher if there were more competition for their rare services. Monopsony does not imply low wages; it implies only wages that are lower than they would be if there was competition for the particular skills.

Perfect Monopsonistic Wage Differentiation

The previous discussion focused on what could be labelled simple monopsony—a situation where the monopsonist did not differentiate its workforce but rather paid the same wages to all workers of the same skill, both marginal and intramarginal workers. In terms of Figure 7.6, all workers were paid the same wage, W_M, even though intramarginal workers would have been willing to work for a lower wage, as depicted by their supply price. The resultant seller's surplus, or economic rent (wage greater than the next-best-alternative), is appropriated by the intramarginal workers.

This highlights another implication of monopsony. The monopsonist may try to appropriate this seller's surplus by differentiating its otherwise homogeneous workforce so as to pay each worker only his or her reservation wage. If the monopsonist were able to do this for each and every worker, the result could be labelled **perfect monopsonistic wage differentiation**. In this case, the supply schedule would be its average cost of labour *and* its marginal cost, because it would not have to pay the higher wage to the intramarginal workers. In such circumstances, the discriminating monopsonist would hire up to the point N_c in Figure 7.6.

In fact, there is an incentive for the monopsonist to try to expand its workforce by means that would make the cost of expansion peculiar only to the additional workers. In this fashion, the monopsonist could avoid the rising marginal cost associated with having to pay higher wages to intramarginal workers. Thus, monopsonists may try to conceal the higher wages paid to attract additional labour so as not to have to pay their existing workforce the higher wage. Or they may try to use non-wage mechanisms, the costs of which are specific to only the new workers. Moving allowances, advertising, or other more expensive job search procedures, and paying workers for paper qualifications that are largely irrelevant for the job are all ways in which monopsonists may try to expand their workforce without raising wages for all workers.

Evidence of Monopsony

Boal and Ransom (1997) provide an excellent overview of theory and evidence pertaining to monopsony in the labour market. Although the empirical evidence is by no means conclusive, there does appear to be evidence of monopsony in at least some particular labour markets. Scully (1995) discusses evidence of monopsony in professional baseball, especially among the star players. The dramatic increase in player salaries following the introduction in 1977 of the free agent system (which significantly increased competition among teams for players, who were no longer tied to teams) also indicates that monopsony power was important in this labour market. However, in their study of salary determination in the National Hockey League, Jones and Walsh (1988) find only modest evidence of monopsony effects on player salaries. Thus, the evidence relating to the importance of monopsony in markets for professional athletes is not entirely conclusive. The professional sports example is also interesting in that it highlights the point that monopsony power need not be associated with low salaries—just salaries that are lower than they would be in the presence of competition in the labour market.

Empirical studies carried out in the United States, the United Kingdom, and Canada have also found evidence of monopsony in the labour markets for teachers (e.g., Currie 1991; Merrifield 1999; Ransom and Sims 2010), professors (e.g., Ransom 1993), and nurses (see Exhibit 7.3) In Canada, these labour markets are now highly unionized; thus, the employer–union bargaining models developed later in this book may be more appropriate than the simple monopsony model of this chapter. In her study of the labour market for Ontario school teachers, Currie (1991) noted that both a bargaining model and a demand-supply framework are consistent with the data. The estimates associated with the demand-supply framework indicate that labour demand is very inelastic and labour supply is slightly upward sloping; that is, school boards possess a small amount of monopsony power in wage-setting. The extent to which these results can be generalized, even within the occupations where some monopsony was found, remains an open question. In addition, the extent to which it is monopsony power rather than other factors that is associated with lower wages could be open to debate.

It is unlikely that monopsony can be an extremely important factor in the long run. Improved communications, labour market information, and labour mobility make the isolated labour market syndrome, a necessity for monopsony, unlikely at least for large numbers of workers. As these factors improve over time, monopsony should diminish.

By contrast, monopsony may be quite common in the short run. Most firms can lower their offered wage and still recruit new employees, albeit at a slower pace than at a higher offered wage. Similarly, firms that offer a higher wage are likely to experience both more applicants and a higher acceptance rate of job offers. In these circumstances, firms face an upward-sloping labour supply curve in the short run, even though they may face a perfectly elastic labour supply curve over a longer horizon. This situation of "dynamic monopsony" is especially likely to occur in an environment of imperfect information in which workers are searching for jobs and employers are searching for employees. These and other implications of imperfect information are examined further in Chapter 17.

Manning (2003) goes one step further and argues that monopsony is, in fact, a much more natural way of understanding how labour markets work than is the traditional competitive model. Manning's view is based on two key observations. First, there are frictions in the labour market. Second, employers set wages. The first observation is clearly not controversial. Changing one's job or leaving the labour force is a costly decision that people do not undertake unless the benefits of doing so are large enough. And, as we just said, it is clear that firm can set wages, at least in the short run. The difficult question is not whether these imperfections exist, but how significant they are, and whether even small frictions can lead to very different policy prescriptions.

Manning argues that monopsony provides a better explanation than the competitive model for a whole range of labour market phenomena, such as unemployment, employers' wage policies, and employment effects of the minimum wage, to mention a few examples. As we will shortly see in the case of the minimum wage, there is still much debate about whether monopsony or the competitive model best describe the way the labour market actually works. These debates aside, Manning makes an important point by showing how even small frictions can result in monopsony power, and how this can lead to very different conclusions about the desirability of different labour market policies.

LO4, 5   Minimum-Wage Legislation

Minimum-wage laws provide a useful illustration of the practical relevance of our theoretical knowledge of neoclassical labour markets. The estimation of the impact of minimum wages has also been an important area of research and considerable disagreement in recent years. In Canada, labour matters are usually under provincial jurisdiction; hence, each province has its own minimum-wage law. Federal labour laws cover approximately 10 percent of Canadian workers. Industries of an interprovincial or international nature—for example, interprovincial transportation and telephone communication, air transport, broadcasting, shipping, and banks—are under federal jurisdiction. The influence of federal laws may be larger to the extent that they serve as a model for comparable provincial legislation.

The recent evolution of minimum wages in Canada and the United States is presented in Figure 7.7. For the Canadian wage, we show a population-weighted average of the provincial minima, while for the U.S. we show the federal minimum. The minimum wage is shown relative to the average manufacturing wage, an important benchmark for the relative price of low-skilled labour. The graph shows that, until recently, the Canadian and U.S. minimum wages have been tracking each other quite closely. After declining sharply between 1975 and 1985, the relative value of the minimum wage remained around 35 percent of manufacturing wages in the United States after 1985, with some large swings linked to increases in the minimum wage in 1990–1991, 1995–1996, and 2007–2009. The relative value of the minimum wage was also stable in Canada over most of this period, but increased substantially after 2005 to reach its highest level in decades (about 45 percent of manufacturing wages).

EXHIBIT 7.2

Estimating the Incidence of Payroll Taxes

It is less than ideal to use theoretical formulae in order to estimate the incidence of a payroll tax; an important distinction must always be made between even well-informed simulation and estimation. In order to estimate the impact of a payroll tax, a researcher would need to provide direct evidence of a link between a change in a payroll tax and a change in employment and wages. This exercise can be difficult for a number of reasons:

- The tax changes may be very small; for example, moving from 4 percent to 5 percent. Given the noise and underlying variation in employment and wages, it may be difficult to detect the impact of such a small change.

- Causality may run in both directions. The tax changes may themselves depend on the state of the labour market being increased when wages and employment are relatively high. In this case, we might find a positive relationship between payroll taxes and employment and wages, yet it would be inappropriate to conclude that the taxes *raised* employment and wages.

- Especially when combined with the previous two problems, it may be difficult to hold constant the many other factors that affect employment and wages.

Jonathan Gruber (1997) explores the impact of a dramatic change in payroll taxes in Chile that avoids these problems. In 1981, Chile privatized its social security (public pension) system, moving from a payroll tax–based, pay-as-you-go system (like the CPP/QPP) to an individual, savings-based system. In 1980, the payroll tax to support the old pension system was 30 percent for employers and 12 percent for employees. In May 1981, the new system was implemented, and payroll taxes were slashed so that they were down to 8.5 percent (for employers) by 1982. The new social security system was financed by contributions from employees.

The obvious question concerning payroll taxes is whether the reduction in payroll taxes led to higher wages, higher employment, or both. To some extent, the tax reduction had to lead to higher wages, because the government legislated firms to increase nominal wages by 18 percent as a consequence of the drop in payroll taxes. However, inflation was running at 25 percent at the time, so it is not obvious that workers enjoyed any real wage increase corresponding to the payroll tax reduction.

Using detailed firm-level data on employment and wages, Gruber explores the impact of the shift in tax regimes. He exploits differences in wages and employment over time (before and after 1981) and differences in the likely impact of the tax change across firms. His results show that virtually all of the tax reduction led to higher wages, with little effect on employment. His results are, thus, consistent with the "back of the envelope" calculations which imply that workers bear most of the incidence of payroll taxes and that these taxes have negligible effects on employment.

The rationale behind minimum-wage laws has not always been explicit. Curbing poverty among the working poor, preventing "exploitation" of the unorganized non-union sector, preventing "unfair" low-wage competition, and even discouraging the development of low-wage sectors have all been suggested as possible rationales. In the early days of union organizing, it is alleged, minimum-wage laws were also instituted to curb unionization—that is, if the wage of unorganized labour could be raised through government legislation, there would be less need for unions. As is so often the case with legislation, its actual impact may be different from its intended impact, or at least it may have unintended side effects. Economic theory may be of some help in shedding light on this issue.

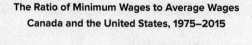

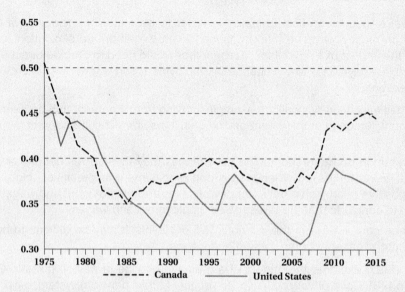

Figure 7.7 The Ratio of Minimum Wages to Average Wages, Canada and the United States, 1975–2015

This figure shows the relative value of the minimum wage to the average wage, from 1975 to 2015, for both Canada and the United States. For Canada (dashed line), the graph shows the ratio of a weighted average of provincial minimum wages to the average manufacturing wage in each year. For the United States (solid line), the graph shows the ratio of the federal minimum wage to the average manufacturing wage.

NOTES: For Canada, minimum wage is a population-weighted average of provincial minimum wages. The minimum-wage data are reported in Labour Canada, *Labour Standards in Canada*, 1976–1987; and Labour Canada, *Employment Standards Legislation in Canada*, 1989–2015. The average wage is the average manufacturing wage, retrieved from CANSIM, adapted in part from CANSIM database, http://cansim2.statcan.gc.ca/. For the U.S., minimum wage is the mandated federal amount, while the average manufacturing wage was retrieved from the website of the Bureau of Labor Statistics on June 22, 2016 (http://www.bls.gov/data/#wages).

Expected Impact: Competitive Labour Market

The primary model for evaluating the impact of minimum wages is the neoclassical supply and demand model. Indeed, it is the evaluation of minimum wages that provides one of the most common illustrations of the insights provided by this simple model. Economic theory predicts that a minimum wage in a competitive labour market will have an adverse employment effect; that is, employment will be reduced relative to what it would have been in the absence of the minimum wage. This is illustrated in Figure 7.8, where W_c and N_c are the equilibrium wage and level of employment, respectively, in a particular competitive labour market. After the imposition of the minimum wage, W_m, employers will reduce their demand for labour to N_m. Thus, $N_c - N_m$ is the adverse employment effect associated with the minimum wage. In addition to the $N_c - N_m$ workers who would not be employed because of the minimum wage, an additional $N_s - N_c$ workers would be willing to work in this sector because the minimum wage is higher than the previous prevailing wage. Thus, the queue of applicants for the reduced number of jobs is $N_s - N_m$, with $N_c - N_m$ representing workers laid off because of the minimum wage and $N_s - N_c$ representing new, potential recruits who are attracted to the minimum-wage jobs.

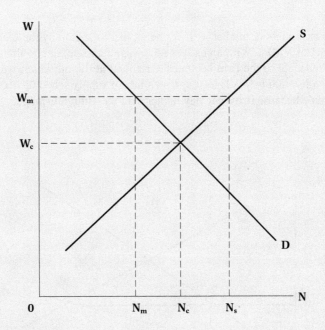

Figure 7.8 Minimum Wage

In this figure, the equilibrium wage and employment level are given by W_c, N_c. If a binding minimum wage, W_m, is set above the equilibrium wage, labour demanded will equal N_m, while labour supply is N_s. Since exchange is voluntary, employment will be determined by the demand side (employers do not have to hire workers if they do not want to). In this case, employment will be N_m, which is below the competitive level, and there will be an excess supply of labour equal to $N_s - N_m$.

The adverse employment effect $N_c - N_m$ occurs as firms substitute other, relatively cheaper, inputs for the higher-priced labour, and as they reduce output in response to the higher costs. These are the familiar substitution and scale effects, respectively, that give rise to the downward-sloping demand schedule for labour. (In the short run, there would also be a disemployment effect, but the reduction in employment would be less than the long-run effect incorporating the scale and substitution effects.) The adverse employment effect need not mean an increase in measured unemployment; some who lose jobs in the sectors covered by the minimum-wage law may go to the uncovered sectors or drop out of the labour force.

The magnitude of this adverse employment effect depends on the elasticity of the demand for labour. If the demand for labour were relatively inelastic, then the adverse employment effect would be small. Unfortunately, in those sectors most affected by minimum-wage legislation—low-wage industries like the restaurant sector, accommodation, and retail—the demand for labour is possibly quite elastic, especially in the long run, reflecting the availability of substitute inputs and products as well as the fact that labour costs are often a substantial proportion of the total cost. In addition, since many of these sectors are often thought of as "fiercely competitive," it is unlikely that the minimum-wage cost increases could be absorbed by the industry through a reduction in monopoly profits.

Expected Impact: Monopsony in the Labour Market

The existence of monopsony has interesting implications for the employment impact of an increase in the minimum wage (Stigler 1946). This discussion also applies to other exogenous wage increases; for example, unionization, equal pay laws, or other forms of wage fixing. Specifically, over a specified range, an exogenous minimum-wage increase may actually *increase* employment in a monopsonistic firm. This seemingly paradoxical proposition first will be demonstrated rigorously, and then explained heuristically and by way of an example.

Formal Exposition

Figure 7.9 illustrates a monopsonistic labour market with W_0 being the wage paid by the monopsonist for N_0 units of labour with a value of marginal product of VMP_0. With an exogeneous wage increase, due to the imposition of a minimum wage to W_1, the new labour supply schedule to the firm becomes horizontal at the minimum wage. This is so because the firm cannot hire at wages below the minimum wage. Thus, the firm's labour supply schedule becomes W_1S_1S; to the right of S_1 it becomes the old supply schedule because firms can pay higher than the minimum wage.

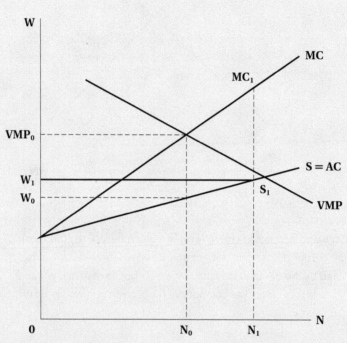

Figure 7.9 Monopsony and a Minimum Wage

A minimum wage can increase employment under monopsony. The original monopsony wage is W_0, and employment is N_0. If the minimum wage is above W_0, but still below the competitive wage, the resulting marginal cost schedule is given by the minimum wage (W_1) until the firm must pay a higher wage in order to attract workers (at N_1), after which the marginal cost schedule reverts to the original MC schedule (at MC_1). The profit-maximizing level of employment occurs when marginal cost equals marginal benefit of hiring labour, at N_1 in this case. The resulting employment is higher than N_0 but lower than the competitive level.

The relevant marginal cost schedule, therefore, becomes $W_1S_1MC_1MC$. It is the same as the labour supply schedule for the horizontal portion W_1S_1, because both marginal and intramarginal workers receive the minimum wage and, consequently, marginal cost equals average cost equals the minimum wage. Similarly, to the right of S_1, the marginal cost schedule becomes the old marginal cost schedule MC_1MC, reflecting the relevance of the portion of the old supply schedule S_1S. The jump in marginal cost between S_1 and MC_1 occurs because when the firm expands its workforce beyond N_1 units of labour it has to raise wages to do so, and the wage increase applies to all intramarginal workers who previously were receiving the minimum wage.

After the imposition of the new minimum wage, the monopsonist would equate MC with MR (i.e., VMP) and, hence, employ N_1 units of labour at the minimum wage W_1. Wages have increased from W_0 to W_1 and, paradoxically, employment has increased from N_0 to N_1. In fact, for wage increases up to VMP_0, employment would increase, reaching a maximum increase for wages at the intersection of the supply and VMP schedules.

Heuristic Explanation

Why would wage increases ever lead to employment increases on the part of the firm? The answer to this seeming paradox lies in the fact that the minimum wage negates or makes redundant a certain portion of the firm's supply and marginal cost of labour schedule. Faced with the new constraint of the minimum wage, the firm no longer need concern itself, at least up to a point, with the fact that if it wants more labour it will have to raise wages and pay these higher wages to all workers. In other words, it is no longer inhibited in its employment expansion by the rising marginal cost of such expansion. Consequently, it will expand employment because, although the wage it pays is higher, the marginal cost of expansion is lower, since it already pays the minimum wage to its intramarginal workers.

This does not mean that the monopsonist would welcome a minimum-wage increase because then it would not have to worry about the rising marginal cost of labour. The minimum wage obviously reduces profits to the monopsonist; otherwise, it would have self-imposed a minimum wage without the need for legislation. The monopsonist is basically responding to a different set of constraints. The minimum-wage constraint simply leads to more employment, at least over a limited range of wage rates.

Practical Importance

While, in theory, minimum wage increases can lead to employment increases in situations of monopsony, in practice the importance of this factor depends on the extent to which monopsony is associated with workers who are paid below minimum wages. Low-wage labour markets that would be affected by minimum wages tend to be concentrated in the service sector (e.g., hotels, restaurants, and theatres). Employers in these sectors tend to be small businesses, and the pool of low-wage labour from which they draw is large. On the surface, the conditions giving rise to monopsony do not seem prevalent. Recall, however, our earlier discussion of dynamic monopsony. Even at a fast-food restaurant like McDonald's, it is unlikely that the firm faces a perfectly elastic supply curve, at least in the short run. Perhaps, because of imperfect information about job opportunities, small decreases in the wage paid may not lead to a complete abandonment of the firm by its workers. In other words, the firm faces an upward-sloping supply schedule, akin to that of a pure monopsonist.

Expected Impact: Other Possible Offsetting Factors

In a dynamic context, other things are changing at the same time as the minimum wage, and these changes may offset, in part at least, the adverse employment effect. For example, the demand for labour could increase, perhaps because of an exogenous increase in the demand for output or because of an increase in the price of substitute inputs. While this may mitigate some, or perhaps even all, of the unemployment associated with the minimum wage, it is still true that employment would be even higher were it not for the minimum wage. Hence, there is still an adverse employment effect relative to the situation with no minimum wage. This can easily be illustrated in Figure 7.9 by shifting the demand schedule upward and to the right, and tracing out the new level of employment with and without the minimum wage.

EXHIBIT 7.3

Monopsony in the Labour Market for Nurses

The labour market for nurses is often cited as being characterized by monopsony, in part because of a belief that hospitals, the main employer of nurses, possess considerable market power in wage-setting. In addition, the labour market for nurses has frequently displayed persistent shortages, an outcome that is consistent with monopsony. (Recall that a monopsonist will wish to employ more labour at the monopsony wage, and therefore, will report unfilled job vacancies. However, the monopsonist will not wish to raise the wage in order to attract more applicants.)

However, skeptics point out that the market for nurses is often national or international in nature and that nurses are geographically very mobile. Thus, even though a particular hospital may have considerable market power in its own town or city, it must compete in a larger labour market for nurses and may be somewhat of a wage-taker in that larger market.

Thus, on a priori grounds, there are arguments both for and against the hypothesis that the labour market for nurses is characterized by monopsony. As is frequently the case in labour economics, the debate can be resolved only by empirical analysis. Indeed, whatever beliefs are held on the basis of deductive reasoning, empirical analysis is needed to determine whether the extent of monopsony is quantitatively significant, or whether the amount of monopsony power is sufficiently small that the market is essentially competitive in nature.

Sullivan (1989) provides direct information on the quantitative importance of monopsony using techniques similar to those used in industrial organizations to measure the extent of monopoly power in product markets. His analysis suggests that U.S. hospitals have significant monopsony power in the short run, and even over a longer time horizon may exercise considerable market power. In particular, the (inverse) elasticity of labour supply to hospitals is estimated to be 0.79 over a one-year horizon and 0.26 over a three-year horizon. Staiger, Spetz, and Phibbs (2010) find even stronger evidence of monopsony by looking at a natural experiment in Veterans Affairs (VA) hospitals in the United States. They show that, consistent with an inelastic labour supply curve, nurse employment did not change much in response to an exogenous change in nurse wages induced by a reform in the wage-setting system of VA hospitals in 1991. By contrast, Matsudaira (2014) looks at a natural experiment where some nursing homes had to increase their staffing levels in response to new state regulations (in California). In does not appear that these nursing homes had to increase wages to attract more nurses, which is more consistent with a competitive model than with monopsony. One possible explanation for these different findings is that hospitals are larger employers than nursing homes and may find it easier to exert some monopsony power in the market for nurses.

WORKED EXAMPLE

Minimum Wage and Employment under Monopsony

The response of a monopsonist to a minimum wage increase is illustrated in the hypothetical example in the table below. The symbols refer to those in Figure 7.9. The firm's labour supply schedule is given in column 2, with hypothetical increments of $0.20 per hour necessary to attract an additional worker. The resultant marginal cost schedule is given in column 3, and rises faster than the average wage cost because of the necessity to pay intramarginal workers the extra wage. In the absence of the minimum wage, the monopsonist would equate MC with VMP and, hence, employ four workers.

With the imposition of a minimum wage equal to $2 per hour, the firm's labour supply schedule becomes as in column 4. For the seventh worker, the minimum wage is redundant, since that worker would not work for less than $2.20 per hour, as indicated earlier in column 1. With the minimum wage, the firm's new marginal-cost-of-labour schedule becomes as in column 5. It is constant at the minimum wage for up to six workers, because the firm simply pays the minimum wage to all workers. There is a large jump in MC associated with the seventh worker, however, because to acquire the seventh worker the firm has to pay not only the $2.20 for that worker but also an additional $0.20 for each of the previous six workers, for a total of $3.40 (i.e., 2.20 + 6(0.20)).

Given the new marginal cost schedule associated with the minimum wage, the firm will equate MC with VMP by employing five workers. The minimum wage increase results in an increase in employment, from four to five workers.

Monopsony profits before the minimum wage were (VMP − w)N = (2.20 − 1.60)4 = 2.40 dollars per hour. After the minimum wage, they are reduced to zero in this particular case, because the minimum wage was set exactly equal to the VMP of the fifth unit of labour. (In Figure 7.9, for example, there would still be some monopsony profits even after the minimum wage.)

TABLE 7.2	Hypothetical Example of Monopsonist Responding to Minimum Wage				
	No Minimum Wage		**Minimum Wage**		
Units of Labour N (1)	**Wages** $S = AC$ (2)	**Marg. Cost** MC (3)	**Wages** $W_1 S_1 S = AC$ (4)	**Marg. Cost** $W_1 S_1 MC_1 MC$ (5)	**Value of Marg. Prod.** VMP (6)
1	1.00	1.00	2.00	2.00	3.00
2	1.20	1.40	2.00	2.00	2.50
3	1.40	1.80	2.00	2.00	2.30
4	1.60	2.20	2.00	2.00	2.20
5	1.80	2.60	2.00	2.00	2.00
6	2.00	3.00	2.00	2.00	1.80
7	2.20	3.40	2.20	3.40	1.60

It is possible that some of the adverse employment effect may be offset by what could be labelled a "shock effect." Because of the cost pressure associated with the higher minimum wage, employers may be induced into utilizing other cost-saving devices that they should have introduced even without the minimum wage. The minimum wage simply serves as the catalyst for the introduction of cost-saving efficiencies. Similarly, labour itself may be induced into becoming more productive, perhaps because of the higher wage or the queue of applicants vying for their jobs. The existence of these shock effects, however, requires that there be some slack in the system; that is, that firms were not maximizing profits or minimizing costs in the first place, because otherwise they would have instituted these possibilities even without the minimum wage.

There are possible situations when employers may be able to absorb the wage cost increases without reducing employment. If the firm were an oligopolist and would lose a substantial share of the market by raising its product price, it might try to absorb the wage cost increase. However, it is likely that the low-wage industries which are most affected by the minimum wage are competitive rather than oligopolistic.

Thus, while there is the theoretical possibility of these factors offsetting, in part at least, the adverse employment effect of minimum-wage laws, their practical relevance is in question. It does not seem likely that they could be of great importance in the long run, especially in those low-wage sectors most affected by minimum wages. Subject to some qualifications, then, economic theory points to the conclusion that, in all probability, minimum-wage laws reduce employment opportunities. In addition, the impact will fall disproportionately on unskilled workers who are often most in need of work experience. This is the case, for example, with respect to younger workers and women who could utilize employment, even at low wages, as a means of acquiring the on-the-job training and labour market experience necessary to move on to higher-paying jobs. For this reason, some would argue that minimum-wage laws actually harm the very people they are allegedly designed to help.

This disemployment effect does not necessarily mean that minimum-wage laws are undesirable, although that is likely to be the conclusion of many economists. The benefits of the wage increases to some have to be weighed against the costs of reduced employment opportunities to others.

Empirical Evidence on Actual Impact

As may be expected, it is difficult to ascertain the actual impact of minimum-wage legislation, largely because so many other factors are also changing over time, and it may take a long time for all of the adjustments to occur. In addition, the adjustment processes may be subtle and difficult to document empirically. For example, a clothing manufacturer, when faced with a minimum-wage increase, may outsource to households specific tasks, such as sewing on buttons or collars, or a restaurant may increase its usage of prepackaged foods. How does one accurately compare the employment reduction in the clothing establishment or the restaurant with the employment creation in the household or the food processing sector to arrive at a net employment effect of the minimum wage?

In spite of the obvious difficulties, there have been numerous attempts to measure the employment impact of minimum-wage laws, mainly in the United States. Most of the early research was conducted using aggregate U.S. time-series data. A typical study entailed the estimation of a regression of a measure of teen employment as a function of the federal minimum wage, with controls for aggregate labour market conditions. This early research is thoroughly summarized in Brown, Gilroy, and Kohen (1982). Minimum wages were, generally, found to reduce employment, with the employment elasticity between -0.1 and -0.3. In other words, a 10 percent increase in the minimum wage was associated with a 1 to 3 percent decline in teen employment (all else being equal).

The Canadian evidence to that point reinforced the conclusions from the U.S. research. Both Swidinsky (1980) and Schaafsma and Walsh (1983), for example, found significant disemployment effects. The methodology employed in these studies was somewhat different than those from the United States, in part because the Canadian researchers had the benefit of cross-province in addition to time-series variation in the minimum wage. The Canadian minimum-wage effects also tended to be at the higher end of the range from the United States.

As depicted in Figure 7.7, the minimum wage in real terms declined significantly over the 1980s. The decline was sufficiently large to motivate researchers to investigate whether there was a corresponding increase in teen employment, as would be predicted based on the pre-1980s empirical evidence. However, these studies failed to find an increase in teen employment. In fact, Wellington (1991) and Grenier and Seguin (1991) found that the disemployment effect of minimum wages virtually disappeared in the United States and Canadian data, respectively. Their results cast doubt on the foundation of the previous consensus among economists.

In part because they had fallen so low, minimum wages were increased in the early 1990s. Several labour economists took advantage of the opportunity to exploit this discrete policy change.[4] Indeed, several states had already increased their minimum wages, providing the opportunity for cross-jurisdictional measurement of the impact of minimum wages. The most influential of these new studies was that of Card and Krueger (1994) (see Exhibit 7.4). In this and a few other associated studies, they did not find evidence of a disemployment effect, and even found evidence suggesting that increases in minimum wages were associated with increases in employment, which is more in line with the monopsony model.[5] Not surprisingly, their results have not gone unchallenged, and a number of studies, such as Neumark and Wascher (2000), question the results of Card and Krueger, and provide some evidence consistent with the traditional evidence of a disemployment effect.[6] However, recent studies by Dube, Lester, and Reich (2010) and Allegretto, Dube, and Reich (2011) that use up-to-date and geographically detailed data, generally, support the earlier conclusion of Card and Krueger that minimum wages do not have adverse employment effects.

Baker, Benjamin, and Stanger (1999) incorporate the increases in minimum wages that occurred in most provinces of Canada in the early 1990s. Their research, which benefits from the additional cross-jurisdictional variation in minimum wages across labour markets over what is available in the United States, focuses on the dynamics of minimum-wage responses. The general conclusion of Baker, Benjamin, and Stanger (1999) is that minimum wages tend to reduce youth employment in Canada. This result has been confirmed in recent work by Baker (2005); Campolieti, Fang, and Gunderson (2005); and Campolieti, Gunderson, and Riddell (2006). Brochu and Green (2013) also find modest employment effects on teenagers, but no effect for older workers. Interestingly, they show that, contrary to the predictions of a simple competitive model, firms don't tend to layoff workers (including teenagers) following an increase in the minimum wage. In fact, firms are less likely to both hire and lay off workers following an increase of the minimum wage, a finding that Brochu and Green (2013) rationalize using a search model (see Chapter 17 for more discussion of search theory).

where lowercase letters represent natural logs; that is, $\ell^D = \ln L^D$, $\ell^S =$ ...
$A' = \ln A$ and $B' = \ln B$.

Graph these functions with l and w on the axes.

Algebraically, solve for the equilibrium wage and employment levels. Notice that a ...
and supply elasticities, respectively.

c. The government is considering a *proportional* payroll tax, so that taxes are collect ...
wage, where the tax rate is denoted t. With a payroll tax, the effective cost of labo ...
+ t) W. Use the approximation that $(1 + t) = t$, and solve for the new market wag ...
workers, and employment.

Explain how the share of the taxes paid for by the workers depends on the rela ...
elasticities. Using reasonable estimates of these elasticities, calculate the probable ...
tax. How might your answer differ between the short and the long run?

d. An alternative tax would have the workers pay an income tax of t percent on their ...
reducing their wage to $(1 - t)$ W. Use the same approximation and logic as in pa ...
level of employment and worker take-home pay will be the same as with a payro ...
rate.

4. "Monopsonists are at a disadvantage relative to competitive buyers of labour, because ...
wants to expand its workforce it has to raise wages, while the competitive buyer can get ...
the going wage." True or false? Explain.

5. a. Consider a firm that sells its output in a perfectly competitive product market, and hi ...
competitive labour market. The value of the marginal product of labour (in dollars) ...

$$VMP_L = 30 - 2L$$

Assuming that the firm is a profit maximizer and can hire labour at $W per unit, de ...
function.

b. Given that there are 10 identical firms (like the firm described in part (a)) in the i ...
market labour demand is given by,

$$L^D = 150 - 5W$$

The supply function of labour to this market is given by,

$$L^S = 10W$$

Solve for the equilibrium wage and level of employment in this market.

c. In an effort to stimulate employment in this industry, the government offers firms a ...
of labour hired. Analyze the effects of the subsidy on the level of employment and the ...

d. The government's opposition parties accuse the government of catering to "corporat ...
the wage subsidy/handout. They suggest that the money would be better spent by p ...
the hands of the workers. They propose that the government should directly give wor ...
for each unit of labour worked. Evaluate the argument put forward by the opposition ...
workers' employment and incomes (wages plus government bonus) to the scheme in p ...

6. "Suppose it was found that university professors' salaries depended on the occupation ...
example, suppose that professors whose husbands were doctors had higher salaries tha ...
businesses. This is clear evidence of monopsony." True or false? Explain.

7. "It is not possible to say on theoretical grounds whether monopolists will pay higher ...
perfectly competitive firms." True or false? Explain.

8. The other side of payroll taxes are the benefits associated with the taxes. For example, ...
and the CPP/QPP are funded out of payroll taxes. Future benefits from these programs ar ...

Given the simplicity of the minimum-wage policy lever, it is somewhat distressing that measuring its effect has been so difficult. Nevertheless, the minimum-wage debate provides an interesting example of the difficulty of conducting empirical research in economics. The emerging consensus (subject, obviously, to more evidence) seems to be that minimum wages have small disemployment effects, at least in the long run. Whatever the ultimate resolution, the lessons from the debate extend beyond the effects of minimum wages. Most importantly, they indicate that labour markets are more complicated than the models described in textbooks.

EXHIBIT 7.4

Minimum Wages and Fast-Food Jobs

The best way to measure the effect of a policy change on behaviour is through a controlled experiment. In the context of minimum wages, the ideal experiment might involve imposing a particular minimum wage in one labour market and a different minimum wage in an otherwise identical labour market. The researcher could then compare the different employment outcomes across labour markets. Because the only difference between the two is the level of the minimum wage, any difference in employment could be attributed to the difference in minimum wages. Of course, such experiments cannot be conducted, and labour economists have to seek policy changes in labour markets that, as closely as possible, approximate the experimental ideal.

Card and Krueger (1994) analyze a change in minimum wages that very closely approximated such an experiment. In April 1992, the minimum wage in New Jersey increased from $4.25 to $5.05 per hour but remained at $4.25 in neighbouring Pennsylvania. Anticipating an opportunity to measure firm adjustments to the new minimum wages, Card and Krueger surveyed a sample of fast-food restaurants in both states a few months before and eight months after the increase in the New Jersey minimum wage. Based on expected results, it is difficult to imagine that an increase of the minimum wage by almost 20 percent would not affect employment. In fact, they found no evidence of a disemployment effect, and, if anything, found evidence of relative increases in employment in New Jersey. The employment evidence was, thus, more in line with the monopsony model, although auxiliary findings on fast-food prices were not consistent with the monopsony story. The Card and Krueger study presented a serious challenge to the conventional view of minimum wages, and not surprisingly, generated an increased interest in minimum-wage research.

Neumark and Wascher (2000) and Card and Krueger (2000) re-evaluated this "experiment" with a variety of corroborating data sets. They, generally, found small (positive in the case of Card and Krueger, negative in the case of Neumark and Wascher) and insignificant effects. More recently, Dube, Lester, and Reich (2010) re-examine the evidence using all pairs of contiguous counties in the United States where the minimum wage takes on different values on the two sides of state borders. They failed to find a significant effect of minimum wages on employment. Taking all this evidence together, it does not appear that minimum wages have much of an effect (positive or negative) on employment in the restaurant industry.

Note, finally, that whether minimum wages have modest (as Canadian studies suggest) or no employment effect (as U.S. studies suggest) is perhaps not the most important question from a policy point of view. A broader and arguably more important question is whether the minimum wage is an effective tool for fighting poverty and redistributing income. Although minimum wages have been shown to decrease the wage gap between low wage and high-wage workers (e.g., Fortin and Lemieux 2015), there is a clear consensus in the U.S. and Canadian literature that minimum wages have not been an effective tool for reaching these goals. The main reason is that the link between poverty (low incomes) and low wages is quite weak because (a) many of the poor do not work, so raising wages cannot possibly help them, and (b) many low-wage workers are youth living in high-income families.

4. Is it possible for a multi-million–dollar professional sports player to be subject to monopson labour? Is it possible for workers who are subject to monopsony to be receiving an economi their labour services? Could workers who are receiving an economic rent for their services disadvantaged workers?

5. Explain why a minimum-wage increase, over a certain range, would lead to a monopsonist employment. Given this possibility, could the monopsony argument be relied on to ne minimum-wage legislation who argue that minimum wages will have an adverse employmen harm some of the very people they were designed to help? Could minimum wages ever be ap monopsony situations? Could wage-fixing via unionization be applied more selectively?

6. On the basis of Figure 7.9, discuss the favourable impact on resource allocation of setting a the intersection of the S and VMP schedules. Heuristically, in what sense are resources alloca at that point than at the monopsonist's equilibrium? If the monopsonist followed a polic differentiation in the absence of the minimum wage, what would be the implications for r Compare the income distribution consequences of the two alternatives, minimum wages differentiation.

7. Consider the following statement about a government that provides a wage subsidy: "It does the subsidy is paid to the worker or to the firm since employment and total pay received by and subsidy) will be the same in both cases." Graph labour supply and demand curves to statement is right or wrong.

Problems

1. "The imposition of a minimum wage above the prevailing market wage will unam employment." True or false? Explain.

2. There are two types of hockey players: (1) goal-scoring "stars" and (2) "grinders," or "non-s short supply so that there are not enough star players to fully stock the teams in the NHL. O the supply of non-stars is unlimited. Using carefully labelled diagrams, describe the relative non-stars for each of the following situations:

   a. Each hockey team in the NHL keeps all of the revenue it generates. Players are drafted b no ability to change teams on their own accord; that is, they must play for the team that their whole career, unless they are traded.

   b. Players become free agents after a few years. That is, players are free to change teams (go bidder) after a few years with the team that drafted them.

   c. There is free agency for players, but teams agree to share all their gate and TV revenues them into a pool and divide it equally among the team owners).

3. Consider a labour market with labour demand and supply functions given by the following equa

$$L^D = AW^a$$

$$L^S = BW^b$$

   a. What would you expect the signs of a and b to be? Plot each of these curves, and grapl equilibrium wage and employment level.

   b. Often, it is easier to work with logarithms. Show that the following is an alternative way above labour supply and demand equations:

$$\ell^D = A' + aw$$

$$\ell^S = B' + bw$$

contributions, just like retirement benefits from private pension plans are linked to previous contributions. In this sense, payroll taxes do not represent a pure income loss from the point of view of individuals, since they also entitle workers to some future benefits. The fact that workers value the benefits provided by payroll taxes can be captured in the supply and demand model of Figure 7.5 by considering the amount workers are willing to pay for these benefits. If workers are willing to pay an amount G for the benefits, they will be willing to work the same number of hours at a salary W without benefits or at a salary W − G with the benefits.

   a. Illustrate the difference between the standard labour supply curve without benefits and the labour supply curve when workers do get benefits for which they are willing to pay G.

   b. Re-analyze the effect of payroll taxes on employment (Figure 7.5) when workers are willing to pay G for the benefits that come with the payroll taxes. Contrast the case where G = T with the case where G < T.

Endnotes

1. See, for example, Blanchflower, Oswald, and Sanfey (1996).

2. See Hamermesh (1993) for an overview of the empirical evidence on payroll taxes. Dahlby (1993); Beach, Lin, and Picot (1996); Beach and Abbott (1997); and Lin (2000) provide Canadian evidence. Also see Exhibit 7.2 for interesting evidence from Chile.

3. See Thornton (2004) for an interesting discussion of how Cambridge economist Joan Robinson coined the term "monopsony" over tea with Cambridge classical scholar B.L. Hallward. Robinson had asked Hallward to make up a word parallel to monopoly but with the emphasis on buying rather than selling. Even though the greek word "opsonein" refers specifically to purchases of "dried fish," Hallward thought that the word "monopsony" sounded better than other alternatives he thought of.

4. Brown (1999) provides a comprehensive overview of the empirical research on minimum wages. See also Goldberg and Green (1999) for a general discussion of the social and economic benefits of minimum wages in Canada.

5. See Card and Krueger (1995) for a comprehensive review and critique of the empirical research on minimum wages. In this book they also summarize much of the new research that exploits cross-jurisdictional variation in the relative minimum wage, often finding zero or positive employment effects of the minimum wage.

6. See the collection of book reviews of Card and Krueger's "Myth and Measurement" in *Industrial and Labour Relations Review* (1995) for a critical evaluation of their methodology and conclusions. Neumark and Wascher (2000) and Card and Krueger (2000) provide a thorough reconsideration and evaluation of the impact of the 1992 New Jersey minimum-wage change.

CHAPTER 8

Compensating Wage Differentials

LEARNING OBJECTIVES

LO1 Explain how labour market transactions between employers and employees are able to attach a "price" (compensating wage) to various attributes of a job, including working conditions, shift work, pension and health benefits, and risk.

LO2 Describe the conditions under which the market can yield an optimal amount of risk at the workplace, and the conditions under which that amount is not likely to be optimal.

LO3 Explain the conditions under which government health and safety regulations can affect the level of safety in the workplace in a way that either increases social welfare or decreases it.

LO4 Discuss how there is "no such thing as a free lunch" in that workers generally "pay" for desirable workplace characteristics by accepting a lower wage in return for such characteristics.

LO5 Explain how estimates of the compensating wage premium that is paid for workplace risks can be used to provide estimates of the value of a (statistical) life.

MAIN QUESTIONS

- What factors determine the relative pay rates across different jobs?
- Can workers with identical skills be paid different wages in the neoclassical model?
- Does increased safety regulation make workers better off or worse off?
- Are workers adequately compensated for performing unpleasant tasks or facing the risk of death on the job? Under what conditions might firefighters and police officers be paid the same, assuming their skills were equally valuable to society?

In previous chapters, we discussed labour demand and various aspects of labour supply, and how they interact to determine the wages and employment of a homogeneous group of workers. This chapter focuses on the **wage differentials** that arise when workers and jobs are not homogeneous but differ because of positive characteristics, such as non-wage benefits, and negative characteristics, such as risk.

Purposes of Wages and Wage Structures

The discussion of wage determination is complicated by the fact that wages and wage structures are called upon to serve a variety of purposes in our economy. **Wage structures** are the relative prices of labour that are utilized to allocate labour to its most productive and efficient use, and to encourage human capital development—education, training, mobility, job search—into areas yielding the highest return. Wages are also the prices that compensate workers for undesirable job characteristics, and, hence, they can ensure that the supply of and demand for such characteristics are in balance. In addition, wages are an important component of family income and may play an important role in the achievement of an equitable distribution of income, as we saw in Chapter 1. Our macroeconomic objectives of full employment, price stability, and a viable balance of payments can also be affected by wage developments, just as wage determination is affected by the macroeconomic environment.

There is a complex nexus between wages and productivity. Usually, we think of high wages as being the result of high productivity that can come about, for example, through various forms of human capital formation, or through technological change. (With respect to the latter factor, wage increases are one way of distributing the gains of general productivity improvements; price reductions are another.) However, there is the possibility of cause and effect working the other way as well; that is, high wages may induce productivity improvements through improved morale, health, and intensity of work effort, as well as reductions in absenteeism and turnover. In addition, wage increases may induce efficient changes elsewhere in the system—changes that should have occurred earlier but that would not occur without the shock induced by a wage change.

The matter is further complicated by the fact that wages and wage structures serve a social role, in that prestige is associated with wages; hence, the importance of *relative* positions in the wage hierarchy and the importance of key comparison groups. The social role of wages is further heightened by the fact that labour services are inseparable from the person who provides the services—hence, the importance of the human element in labour market analysis.

Clearly, wages and wage structures are called upon to serve a variety of, often conflicting, roles in our economic system in particular and in our social system in general. Perhaps this is why there is so much emotive conflict over various policies, such as minimum wages or wage controls or equal pay legislation, that affect wages.

LO1 ## Theory of Compensating Wages

The idea behind **compensating wage differentials** cannot be stated any more succinctly than originally posed by Adam Smith:

> *The five following are the principal circumstances which, so far as I have been able to observe, make up for a small pecuniary gain in some employments, and counter-balance a great one in others: first, the agreeableness or disagreeableness of the employments themselves; secondly, the easiness and cheapness, or the difficulty and expense of learning them; thirdly the constancy or inconstancy of employment in them; fourthly, the small or great trust which must be reposed in those who exercise them; and fifthly, the probability or improbability of success in them. (Adam Smith, The Wealth of Nations, Chapter X, page 100.)*

Smith then goes on to provide numerous examples in which compensating wage differentials are at work. For example, he cites public executioners as well-paid but in a particularly unpleasant line of work. While individuals now pursue very different careers than they did in Smith's days, the five sources of compensating wage differentials he identified more than two centuries ago remain very important in a modern economy. For instance, people put their lives in the hands of airline pilots and neurosurgeons. Not surprisingly, these "high trust" occupations (Smith's fourth principle) that also require very expensive training (second principle) are very well paid. Another modern example are high-technology entrepreneurs. Some entrepreneurs "make it big" and become very wealthy, but scores of others lead ventures that eventually fail. There were no such entrepreneurs back in Smith's days, but this high-risk occupation is a prime example of Smith's fifth principle.

Wages, thus, serve the purpose of compensating employees for undesirable working conditions or for negative or costly attributes associated with a particular job. Such conditions include an unsafe or unhealthy work environment, long commute time, undesirable and inflexible working hours, lengthy training or other human capital requirements, and even the need for workers with discriminatory preferences to work in an integrated work environment. Wages also compensate—by being lower than they would otherwise be—for desirable working conditions, such as flexible hours, stimulating tasks, and a pleasant working environment, including workplace practices that facilitate work-family balance. As illustrated subsequently, many of these characteristics are associated with particular occupations, industries, regions, or firms and, hence, form part of the rationale for wage structures associated with these factors.

As a result, compensating wage differentials can account for some of the wage differences across occupations and other job characteristics discussed in more detail in Chapter 10. For instance, compensating wage differentials may explain why high-risk occupations, such as construction, pay more than low-risk occupations, such as clerks. Compensating wage differentials may also account for some of the gender wage gap (Chapter 12) if men work on more-risky jobs than women.

In this chapter, the theory of compensating wages (Rosen 1986) is illustrated with respect to compensating wages associated with the risk of injury or illness that can result from an unsafe or unhealthy work environment—an area where the theory has seen considerable development and empirical application. The analysis, naturally, extends to other job amenities or disamenities, and these are outlined. The compensating wage associated with any job attribute is also termed the hedonic price of that attribute.

Single Firm's Isoprofit Schedule

Figure 8.1(a) illustrates a single firm's **isoprofit schedule**, I, defined as the various combinations of wages and safety that the firm can provide while maintaining the same level of profits. For the firm, both wages and a safe work environment are costly to provide, resulting in a negative trade-off between the two; that is, the firm can provide more safety and maintain profits only if it can pay a lower wage. The isoprofit schedule exhibits a diminishing marginal rate of transformation between wages and safety. That is, in the upper left portion, such as at point A, where the firm is providing little safety, it can provide additional safety in a relatively inexpensive fashion with minor basic changes in its safety technology (e.g., better lighting, signs, guard rails). Here, it is in a stage of increasing returns with respect to the provision of safety. In such circumstances, the firm can provide these inexpensive safety features without requiring much of a wage reduction in order to maintain a constant profit level; that is, the isoprofit schedule is relatively flat.

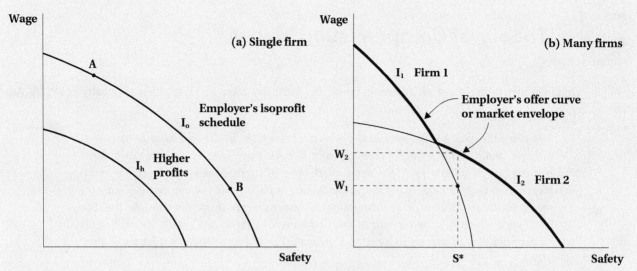

Figure 8.1 Employer's Isoprofit Schedules and Offer Curve

Panel (a) depicts isoprofit schedules, such as I_0, that show combinations of wages and safety yielding the same level of profits. The high-safety/low-wage package at B yields the same profits as the lower-safety/higher-wage package at A. Profits increase as the combinations move closer to the origin, and I_h represents higher profits than I_0. Panel (b) shows the isoprofit schedules of firms with different safety technologies. Firm 2 is inherently safer, and its flatter isoprofit curve (I_2) reflects the fact that it can offer a higher level of safety without reducing wages as much as firm 1 (I_1). The bold line represents the "market envelope" available to workers in equilibrium. At S*, firm 1 can offer W_1, but workers will not accept this, since they could have the same level of safety but the higher wage W_2 as well at firm 2. Firm 2 is more attractive at higher levels of safety, but firm 1 will dominate firm 2 at lower levels of safety because it can pay higher wages.

Conversely, in the bottom right segment, as at point B, where the firm is providing considerable safety, it can provide additional safety only through the introduction of more-sophisticated and costly safety procedures. It is in a stage of diminishing returns in the provision of safety, having already exhausted the cheapest forms of safety provision. That is, as the firm moves from left to right on the horizontal axis and provides additional safety, it will start with the cheapest forms of safety provision and then move to the more expensive. In such circumstances, it will require an even larger wage reduction to compensate for its additional safety costs in order to maintain the same level of profits; that is, the isoprofit schedule will become steeper as more safety is provided and the firm moves from point A toward B.

Lower isoprofit schedules, like I_h in Figure 8.1(a), imply higher levels of profits. That is, profits are the same at all points along I_h just as they are the same at all points along I_0. However, profits are higher along I_h than I_0. This is so because, to the firm, both wages and safety are costly to provide. Hence, providing both lower wages and lower safety means higher profits.

Different Firms with Different Safety Technologies

Different firms can have different abilities to provide safety at a given cost. Hence, different firms may have differently shaped isoprofit schedules even for the same level of profit (e.g., even if they all operate at the competitive level of zero excess profits).

Figure 8.1(b) illustrates the isoprofit schedules for two firms (or industries, or occupations). Firm 1 exhibits rapidly diminishing returns to providing a safe work environment. Additional safety can be provided only if wages drop quite rapidly to compensate for the safety costs, if profits are to be maintained. This could be the case, for example, for firms in sectors that are inherently dangerous, such as mining or logging. In contrast, firm 2 may be in an inherently safer industry and, hence, be able to provide high levels of safety without having to substantially lower wages to maintain profits. Competitive equilibrium requires that excess profits of firms 1 and 2 are reduced to zero (i.e., $I_1 = I_2 = 0$).

The outer limits of the two isoprofit schedules (bold line), called the employers' *offer* curve, or **market envelope curve**, show the maximum compensating wages that will be offered in the market for various levels of safety. Points within the envelope will not prevail in the market because they will always be dominated by points on the envelope. For example, for a given level of safety, S^*, firm 2 is able to offer the wage W_2 and maintain its given level of profit, I_2. Firm 1, in contrast, can offer only the wage W_1 and continue to meet the zero profit condition. Hence, firm 2's offer will dominate firm 1's offer for levels of safety, like S^*, to the right of the intersection of the isoprofit schedules; firm 1's offer will dominate to the left of the intersection. In other words, workers would always go to employers that offer the highest compensating wage for every level of safety; hence, only points on the outer segments of the isoprofit schedules will prevail in a competitive market.

Single Individual's Preferences

As with any other items they value, individuals will have preferences for wages and safety. These preferences can be illustrated by a typical indifference, or isoutility, curve showing various combinations of wages and safety that yield the same level of utility, as depicted in Figure 8.2(a). The curvature of the indifference curve illustrates a diminishing marginal rate of substitution between wages and safety. That is, at points in the upper left segment, such as A, where the individual does not have a very safe work environment, that individual would likely be willing to give up considerable wages to get a slightly safer work environment. Hence, the indifference curve is steep. Conversely, at points such as B where the individual has a safer work environment, the individual may not be willing to give up much in the form of wages to obtain additional safety, and hence, the indifference curve is relatively flat. Higher indifference curves, like U_h, indicate higher levels of utility since the individual has more of both wages and safety, both of which yield utility.

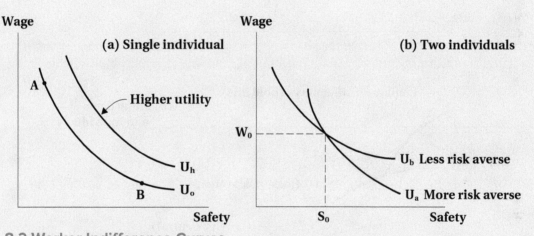

Figure 8.2 Worker Indifference Curves

Indifference curves, such as U_0, plot combinations of wages and safety that yield the same utility. Not everyone has the same preferences for safety. At the combination S_0, W_0 in panel (b), the indifference curve for person U_a is steeper than for person U_b, reflecting a greater willingness to give up wages in return for more safety.

Different Individuals with Different Risk Preferences

Different individuals may have different risk preferences and, hence, may show a different willingness to give up safety in return for a **compensating risk premium** in the form of higher wages. Figure 8.2(b) illustrates a more risk-averse and a less risk-averse individual. As indicated at the point of intersection of the two schedules, the more risk-averse individual requires a larger compensating wage in return for giving up some safety and accepting a riskier work environment.

Equilibrium with Single Firm, Single Individual

Figure 8.3(a) illustrates the market equilibrium for a single firm and single individual as the point of tangency, E_c, between the firm's isoprofit schedule, I_c, and the individual's indifference curve, U_c. This outcome occurs because a perfectly competitive market yields the maximum worker utility, subject to the firm's earning zero economic profits. The compensating wage, W_c, given the level of safety, S_c, is the highest the firm is able to offer for that level of safety, given the zero profit constraint. For movements to the left of S_c, the additional wage that the individual requires for accepting more risk (i.e., slope of the indifference curve) is greater than what the firm is willing to give (i.e., slope of the isoprofit schedule) in order to maintain the same competitive profit level. Conversely, for movements to the right, what the worker is willing to give up for additional safety is insufficient to compensate the employer so as to maintain the same competitive profit level. Thus, given the constraint I_c (due to the zero profit condition), worker utility is highest at E_c.

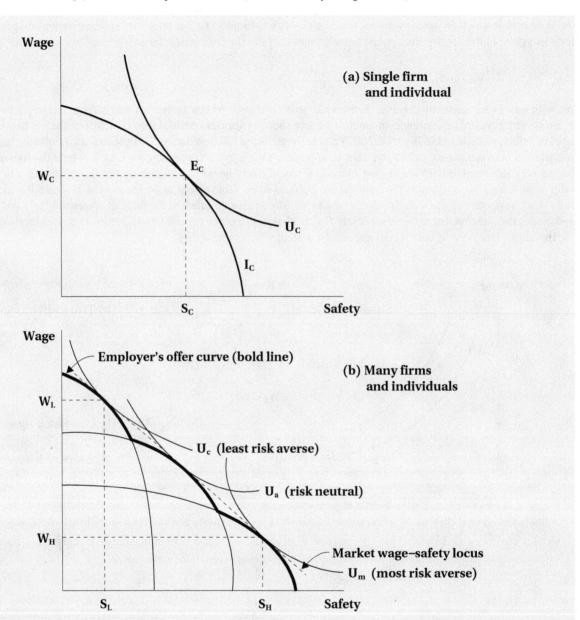

Figure 8.3 Market Equilibrium

With a single firm and individual, the equilibrium is given by W_C and S_C. Perfect competition restricts the possible combinations to those on I_C, the firm's zero-profit isoprofit schedule. Workers will choose jobs that yield the highest utility, which is given by the tangency at E_C. Panel (b) shows the case of many firms and individuals. The market envelope is shown in bold, and represents the wage-safety opportunities available to workers (employers' offer curve). Some people will choose to work at less-safe jobs (such as S_L) in exchange for higher wages (such as W_L), while the more risk-averse will opt for greater safety (such as S_H) in exchange for lower wages (such as W_H). The set of equilibrium compensation packages is given by the market wage-safety locus, which shows the rate at which the market compensates individuals for working in less-safe conditions.

Higher indifference curves are not attainable for the worker because they would lie outside of the feasible choice set as dictated by the employer's isoprofit schedule, I_c, which gives the competitive level of profits. Higher isoprofit schedules would imply profits that are below the competitive level. Conversely, under competitive conditions, individuals would not have to accept combinations of lower wages and safety that would put them on indifference curves below U_c (and employers on isoprofit schedules that are closer to the origin, implying profits above the competitive norm) because workers could move to firms that would offer higher compensating wages and still maintain competitive profits. Of course, if firms could offer lower combinations of wages and safety (e.g., if worker mobility were restricted or they did not know the risk to which they were exposed), then workers would be on lower indifference curves and firms would have higher profits.

Equilibrium with Many Firms and Individuals

Figure 8.3(b) illustrates the market equilibrium that will prevail when there are many firms and individuals. Assuming perfect competition, individuals will sort themselves into firms (occupations, industries) of different levels of risk (i.e., along the market envelope schedule) and receive differing compensating wages for the different levels of risk. The least risk-averse individual, for example, will enter a high-risk firm in order to get the higher wage, W_L, associated with the low level of safety, S_L. Conversely, the most risk-averse individual will enter the low-risk work environment and accept the lower wage, W_H, in order to have the safe work environment, S_H.

The set of tangencies between the various isoprofit and indifference schedules gives the various equilibrium combinations of wages and safety that will prevail in the market. This is termed the **wage-safety locus** (dashed line in Figure 8.3(b)). The *slope* of that locus of wage-safety combinations gives the change in the wage premium that the market yields for *differences* in the risk of the job. The slope of that line can change for different levels of safety. It is determined by the interaction of workers' preferences and the firms' technology for safety, and these basic underlying determinants may change with the level of safety. The only restriction on the slope of the line is that it be negative, reflecting the fact that compensating wages are required for reductions in safety, given worker aversion to risk and the fact that safety is costly to firms.

The fact that the slope of the wage-safety locus can change magnitude but not direction means, for example, that the compensating wage premium required for *additional* risk may be very high in an already risky environment. Whether that is true, however, is an empirical proposition since it depends upon whether there are sufficient workers willing to take that risk in return for the higher wage, and whether firms could reduce the risk in ways that are less costly than paying a wage premium for workers to accept the risk.

In such circumstances of perfect information and competition (assumptions that will be relaxed later), the market will pay a compensating wage premium for undesirable working conditions, such as risk. This will induce workers to sort themselves into jobs depending upon their aversion to risk. It will also induce employers to adopt the most cost-effective safety standards (not necessarily the safest) since they can save on compensating wages by increasing their safety. In this fashion, the need of employers to carry on production in a manner that may involve some risk is required to confront the equally compelling need of workers for desirable working conditions, and vice versa. The price that mediates these competing objectives is the compensating wage paid for the undesirable working conditions. Such prices are often termed **shadow, or implicit, prices** because they are embedded in the market wage rather than attached explicitly to a job characteristic.

Obviously, the markets for each and every characteristic are likely to be "thin" (i.e., involve few buyers and sellers). For example, a worker who wants (and is willing to pay for) a job that is reasonably safe, close to home, and that allows flexible working hours, may not have a large set of jobs to choose from. Of course, if enough workers want those characteristics, then employers will find it is in their interest to provide them, because of the lower wages they can pay in return for providing the desired work characteristics. Nevertheless, it is easy to see that there may not be a large number of buyers and sellers for each and every characteristic, and, hence, the shadow price yielded by the market for each characteristic may not be the same as the competitive price that would prevail if there were many buyers and sellers for *each* characteristic.

Effect of Safety Regulation

Perfectly Competitive Markets

The effect of safety regulation depends, critically, upon whether markets are operating properly or not to compensate workers for occupational risk. In markets that are operating perfectly, the effect of regulation may be perverse. This is illustrated in Figure 8.4(a). For a single representative firm and individual, the competitive equilibrium is given at E_c, with the wage W_c being paid for the level of safety S_c. In the absence of any external effects on third parties for which the market does not extract appropriate compensation, the level of safety, S_c, can be considered socially optimal in the sense that the price mechanism, through compensating wages, ensures that neither employers nor employees want to move from the level of safety S_c. By moving from S_c, neither party can be made sufficiently better off to compensate the other party so that they are no worse off.

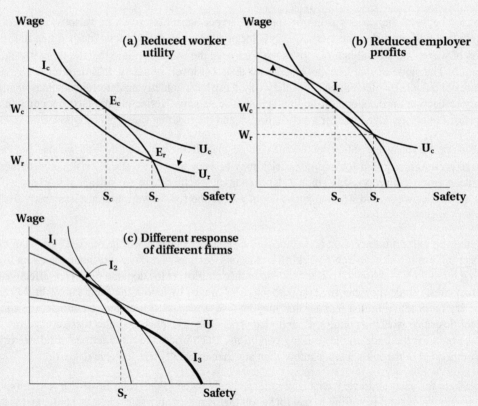

Figure 8.4 Responses to Safety Standard

In a competitive market, a legislated increase in safety will make people worse off. In panel (a) the optimal safety level is S_C. At a regulated level of S_r, the zero-profit constraint means that the firm can provide this only at the lower wage W_r. The worker is worse off, as the regulated combination, E_r, lies on a lower indifference curve, U_r. In panel (b), the worker's utility is maintained at U_C, but the firm's profits are reduced to I_r. If profits are negative, the firm will go out of business. Panel (c) extends the argument to several firms. The impact of the regulation will depend on the firm's technology, and some firms (such as firm 1) will go out of business.

A regulatory agency that required the parties to increase the level of safety to S_r would actually make one or both parties worse off, in this particular situation of perfectly competitive markets. This is illustrated in Figure 8.4(a), where the firm remains on its isoprofit schedule (it has to if this is the competitive level of zero excess profits) and the individual worker is on a lower level of utility U_r, with compensating wage W_r. The worker's level of utility under regulation is lower (i.e., $U_r <$

U_c), because the worker is not voluntarily willing to accept the wage reduction from W_c to W_r in return for the safety increase from S_c to S_r; if given the choice, the worker would return to E_c. In this particular example, the firm was no worse off after the regulation (i.e., on the same isoprofit schedule) but the worker was worse off (i.e., on a lower indifference curve). If the firm originally had excess profits, it could absorb the cost increase associated with the safety regulation and not go out of business. In such circumstances, the worker need not be worse off after the regulation. This is depicted in Figure 8.4(b), where the firm moves to a higher isoprofit schedule, I_r, (with lower profits, because it is experiencing both higher wage and safety costs) and the worker stays on the same indifference curve. The worker still receives a reduction in the compensating wage, from W_c to W_r, but this is exactly offset by the increase in safety, so that utility remains constant at U_c. In this case, the firm bears the cost of the safety regulation by taking lower profits.

WORKED EXAMPLE

Attracting Doctors to Rural Communities

A perennial problem of smaller communities in Canada is to attract doctors. Stories about small towns about to lose their last remaining doctor often make it in the national news. Even movies have been inspired by this problem (see, for example, *Seducing Doctor Lewis* by Canadian filmmaker Jean-François Pouliot). This phenomenon happens despite the fact that doctors can earn very substantial salary premia (provided by the government) by establishing their practices outside Canada's main population centres.

The theory of compensating wages provides a simple way of understanding this phenomenon. The problem is that most doctors, for professional and personal reasons, prefer to live and work in urban areas even if they earn, as a result, a lower salary. This is illustrated in the figure, which shows the preferences of Dr. Lewis and Dr. Brown. Both doctors can earn $100,000 a year (net of taxes, administrative costs, etc.) when they set up their practice in an urban area. The indifference curves also show that Dr. Brown is willing to pay more than Dr. Lewis to live in a large city. He is indifferent between earning $190,000 in a rural area and $100,000 in a city, whereas Dr. Lewis is indifferent between earning $140,000 in a rural area and $100,000 in a city. These indifference curves are depicted by U^O_{Brown} and U^O_{Lewis}, respectively. In other words, Dr. Brown needs a compensating wage of at least $90,000 to move to a rural area, while Dr. Lewis needs a compensating wage of $40,000.

Consider three salary premia relative to $100,000, aimed at attracting doctors to rural areas: point A, 25 percent; point B, 50 percent; and point C, 100 percent. Both Dr. Brown and Dr. Lewis would be on a lower indifference curve, U^A_{Brown} and U^A_{Lewis}, by accepting the rural job with the 25 percent premium than by choosing the urban job paying $100,000. As a result, neither of them will be willing to move to the rural area. Once the premium is increased to 50 percent, however, Dr. Lewis is now on a higher indifference curve in the rural area (U^B_{Lewis}) than in a city (U^O_{Lewis}). He will thus decide, unlike Dr. Brown, to move to the rural area. Recruiting a second doctor is very costly, since the government must now pay a full 100 percent premium to finally convince Dr. Brown to move to the rural area ($U^C_{Brown} > U^O_{Brown}$).

This example illustrates the difficult trade-off involved in recruiting doctors to rural areas. Some doctors may be willing to move provided a premium is being offered. But the premium may have to be very large to fully staff the hospitals and clinics in rural areas (e.g., recruiting both Dr. Lewis and Dr. Brown in the above example). Given the tight budget constraints in the health care sector, one can easily see why governments may prefer to pay a lower salary premium even if this means understaffing and lower quality services in rural areas.

Location Decision of Dr. Lewis and Dr. Brown

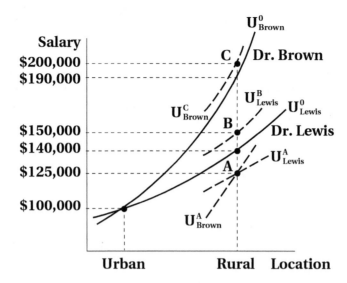

Realistically, the cost of the safety regulation will likely be borne by workers in the form of compensating wage reductions and by firms in the form of lower profits, their respective shares depending upon their relative bargaining powers.

Not all firms will be affected in the same fashion. For some, the safety regulation may be redundant since they are already meeting the standard. Others may be put out of business, unless their workforce accepts wage concessions. This is illustrated in Figure 8.4(c) for three firms that are assumed to be operating under a competitive profit constraint so that excess profits are zero (i.e., $I_1 = I_2 = I_3 = 0$). For firm 3, a uniform safety standard of S_r would be redundant since it is already providing a safer work environment than required by the standard; that is, the relevant portion of its isoprofit curve making up part of the market wage envelope always lies to the right of S_r. Firm 2 could meet the standard and stay in business only if its workforce were willing to provide wage concessions (and, hence, receive a lower level of utility) for the firm to stay on its zero-profit isoprofit schedule. (For simplicity, only the indifference curve for a representative worker of firm 2 is shown.) Firm 1 would go out of business because its isoprofit schedule is below that of firm 2 in the relevant region of the safety standard S_r; that is, for the minimal level of safety, S_r, firm 2 could offer a higher compensating wage than firm 1 and still stay in business. Workers in firm 1 would go to firm 2 if the standard were improved, even though they would prefer to be in firm 1 with no standard. This competitive analysis, of course, assumes that firm 2 can absorb the workers with no adverse general equilibrium effects.

While this analysis suggests that the application of a uniform safety standard has the desirable effect of weeding out firms whose safety technology is such that they cannot meet the standard, it must be remembered that they were able to pay a sufficiently high wage to attract certain workers who were willing to accept the inherent risk. By imposing a uniform standard, the regulators are saying that firms which cannot meet the standard will not be able to operate no matter how much they are able to pay to have workers willingly accept the risk.

Imperfect Information

The previous analysis assumed perfect information about the level of safety involved. Such an assumption, however, may be unrealistic in situations where employers may have a vested interest in not disclosing information about health hazards, and where the latency period before an occupational disease shows up can be very long. In such circumstances, workers may think that they have a higher level of safety, and hence, utility, for the compensating wage they receive.

This situation of **imperfect information** is depicted in Figure 8.5. For a given compensating wage, W_a, associated with an actual level of safety, S_a, workers may perceive their level of safety to be greater at S_p. Their (mis)perceived level of utility would be U_p, while their actual level would be U_a. In such circumstances, any imposed safety standard between S_a and S_r could improve workers' utility without making employers worse off since they would be on the same or a lower isoprofit schedule (lower schedules representing higher profits). The optimal standard would be at the point of tangency E_0, between the employer's isoprofit schedule and the employee's highest attainable indifference curve.

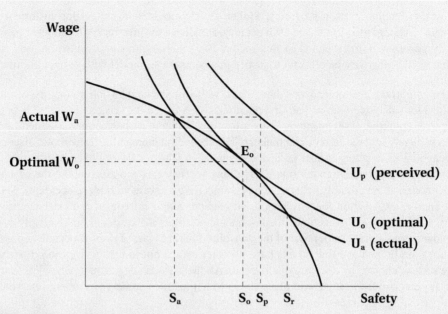

Figure 8.5 Effect of Imperfect Information

Suppose that workers are paid W_a, believing they are getting safety level S_p, yielding utility U_p. However, the actual level of safety is S_a, yielding actual utility of U_a. A regulator could force the firm to offer a higher level of safety while allowing it to pay lower wages. Any wage-safety combination along the isoprofit schedule, with a safety level higher than S_a but lower than S_r, would make the worker better off. The optimum would occur at E_0, with a safety level S_0 and wage W_0.

Providing the parties with the correct information would also lead to the optimal amount of safety, because workers would increase their utility by moving to offers in the range of the offer curve between S_a and S_r. Ultimately, they would arrive at E_0, accepting the wage reduction from W_a to W_0 in return for the increase in safety from S_a to S_0. With full information, market forces can also lead to the optimal amount of safety.

LO3   Rationale for Regulation

If a perfectly competitive market with proper information can lead to the socially optimal amount of safety at the workplace, why does regulation persist, especially since it runs the risk of making both employers and employees worse off? While no easy answer to this question exists, a number of plausible explanations can be given, in addition to the possibility that it may simply be a well-meant mistake. First, information is not perfect and may be hidden by employers or improperly discounted by workers. Second, competition may not prevail for the buying and selling of each and every job characteristic, including safety in the work environment. Workers simply may not have much choice in the risk of their work. Third, workers who opt for risk in return for a high wage may not pay the full cost of their decisions to the extent that the state bears some of the medical or workers' compensation costs if the risk comes to fruition. Fourth, society may feel that workers ought not to have to sell their health and safety to make a living, even if they are willing to do so. If regulating safety means a lower compensating wage, then it may be best to try to take care of that problem through other income-maintenance schemes. Fifth, the willingness of workers to accept some risk in return for a compensating wage premium may be dictated by the existing amount of risk to which they are currently exposed. If that risk is reduced by law for everyone, they may actually prefer the new level of risk even though earlier they were unwilling to accept the wage reduction to achieve the reduced risk. Although economists tend to regard preferences as given, preferences in fact may be influenced by our existing state. Lastly, there may be the feeling that the market simply may not yield the compensating wages necessary to ensure the socially optimal amount of safety.

Safety Regulation: The Behavioural Economics View

The emerging field of behavioural economics also suggests a number of reasons government should regulate workplace safety and provide workers' compensation programs. Shiller (2005) provides an interesting historical perspective on the introduction of workers' compensation in the late 19th century, and discusses how recent findings in behavioural economics can be used to justify government intervention in this sector. The same arguments can also be used to justify workplace safety regulations that would otherwise be difficult to justify in a competitive model with perfect information.

Shiller mentions four important phenomena that have been well documented in laboratory experiments and that have interesting implications for safety regulation. The first phenomenon is called the "risk as feelings" hypothesis: the idea that emotions often take over cognitive assessments in risky situations. Patterns of behaviour suggested by rational choice are postponed, or even completely ignored in decision making. The second phenomenon, "hyperbolic discounting" (as opposed to the standard exponential discounting model used, for example, in Chapter 9), is linked to the idea that people put too much importance on the present, relative to the future. By doing so, they care too much about the paycheque they get right now, and do not care enough about possibly negative future events (like a severe workplace accident). The "theory of mental departments" is yet another explanation for why people may ignore major infrequent risks despite the fact that they also protect themselves against minor, and sometimes inconsequential, risks. Finally, people may simply refuse to believe that risks are involved in dangerous situations because of the "wishful thinking bias." This is especially a possibility in situations where job opportunities are limited and individuals have no other choice but to take a risky job. For their mental stability they may rationalize such a "choice" by downplaying the risk. All these cases suggest that, when left to themselves, workers may not take sufficient precautions against workplace risks, which justifies some government intervention in the form of safety regulations.

Of course, just saying that people don't make the right choices for themselves and that governments know better is at odds with the usual economic approach for analyzing the effect of government policies. The danger with these types of arguments is that they can be used to justify any government intervention on the grounds that people don't know what they are doing. What is different with the behavioural economics approach is that it relies on a mix of laboratory experiments, formal theoretical modelling, and empirical evidence to propose alternatives to the simplest maximizing behaviour under perfect (or imperfect) information used in the standard economic approach. This provides useful guidance on how people actually do behave in settings where they are confronted with serious but unlikely risks, as is often the case with workplace or other accidents.

Empirical Evidence on Compensating Wages

Methodological Problems

Obtaining empirical evidence on the existence of compensating wages for desirable or undesirable working conditions is difficult because of the problem of controlling for the myriad positive and negative job characteristics in order to isolate the separate effect of one characteristic. This is compounded by the fact that situations of strong employee bargaining power often have high wages, good fringe benefits, and good working conditions. While there could still be a trade-off between wages and a better work environment, there is often insufficient variation in the data to identify the trade-off with any degree of precision. In some cases, it may be direct and explicit. For example, collective agreements or company pay policies may specify a premium for underground as opposed to above-ground mining, or for the night shift as opposed to the day shift. Premiums for an isolation allowance or even hazard pay may be explicitly mentioned with the explicit price stated.

In other circumstances, however, the compensating pay premium is not explicitly given but rather is embedded as part of an individual's wage rate and, hence, is a shadow price associated with the job characteristic. It can be estimated only by comparing wages in jobs that are similar except for the one characteristic. Given that jobs involve a multiplicity of characteristics, this is not an easy task and usually requires fairly sophisticated statistical procedures.

The most extensive literature in this area pertains to compensating wages for the risk of injury or death on the job, although Sandy and Elliott (2005) have also applied it to the risk of acquiring an occupationally related, long-term illness while on the job. These studies have been plagued by a number of econometric problems that are typical of statistical work in economics and illustrate the general problems involved with estimating compensating differentials.

For example, in addition to higher wages being paid to compensate for undesirable working conditions, cause and effect may work the other way, as undesirable working conditions may result from lower wages—that is, low-wage individuals cannot afford to buy a safe work environment and the forgone income from an accident is less to them. These income and substitution effects, respectively, cause them to buy less occupational health and safety. Failure to account for such reverse causality can lead to a **simultaneous equation bias** in the estimates of compensating wages for workplace hazards. Simultaneous equation techniques to account for the two-way causality have been employed in a few studies.

Errors-in-variables problems may also exist, especially in those studies that relate an *individual's* wage to an *aggregate* measure of risk, such as the injury rate in the person's industry or occupation. Such aggregate measures of risk are likely to be subject to considerable random error as a proxy for the risk that an individual will face in that occupation. Econometrically, it can be shown that this will lead to an underestimation of the compensating wage paid for risk. Some recent studies have been able to deal with this issue by using more accurate and detailed data on risks that individuals face (Aldy and Viscusi 2008; Kneisner et al. 2010).

Omitted variable bias may also exist to the extent that crucial variables affecting wages and also correlated with risk are not controlled for in the measurement of the wage-risk trade-off. For example, bargaining power of workers (as possibly represented by unionization) may lead to high wages and low risk. Failure to control for this factor may mean that there appears to be little or no wage premium paid for the risk. In reality, the low wages in risky jobs may reflect the fact that workers with little bargaining power end up in jobs of low wages and high risk. The low wages in risky jobs may reflect the disproportionate absence of bargaining power of workers in those jobs, not the absence of a wage premium for risk. One method to control for such difficult-to-measure variables as preferences or an individual's bargaining power is to use longitudinal or panel data that follows the same individual over time so that such factors can be assumed to be relatively constant or fixed over time. (e.g., Brown 1980; Duncan and Holmlund 1983; Hwang, Reed, and Hubbard 1992; Hinterman et al. 2010; Keisner and Leeth 2010; and Kneisner et al. 2010).

Sample selection bias problems may also prevail to the extent that wage-risk premiums are estimated on a subsample of risky jobs, perhaps because actuarial data is available only on risky occupations (e.g., Thaler and Rosen 1975). In such circumstances, the risk premiums obtained from the subsample of risk-taking individuals may not give an accurate estimate of the compensating wage paid for a random worker. See Ashenfelter and Greenstone (2004b) for a discussion of this issue as well as of how natural experiments can be used to get more credible estimates of the wage-risk trade-off.

More generally, account needs to be taken of the process via which individuals choose jobs, occupations, and careers. Specifically, those individuals who have the least aversion to an undesirable job characteristic or are better equipped to deal with it are, other things equal, the most likely to choose jobs with that characteristic. Thus, the compensating wage needed to attract *additional* workers into an occupation may be higher than was needed to attract those already in the occupation. Recent research has tried to take into account this simultaneous determination of job risk and occupational choices (Garen 1998; Goddeeris 1988) and the fact that risk may be **endogenous**, with risky jobs being chosen by those most able to deal with it, or for risk takers for whom it matters least (Garen 1998; Gunderson and Hyatt 2001; Sandy and Elliott 2005; Shogren and Stamland 2002; Kneisner et al. 2010; and Hintermann et al. 2010). Viscusi and Hersch (2001), for example, use smokers to identify risk takers and find that such risk takers are willing to work in hazardous jobs for a smaller compensating wage premium.

Discussions of many of the difficulties of estimating wage-risk trade-off along with evidence of such trade-offs are given in Bonhomme and Jolivet (2008), Baughman et al. (2003), DeLeire and Levy (2004), Felfe (2012), and Gronberg and Reed (1994).

LO5

EXHIBIT 8.1

What Is a Life Worth . . . Statistically Speaking?

Since the evidence on compensating wages for the risk of fatal injury indicates what individuals are willing to pay in the form of accepting lower wages for reductions in such risks, it has been used to obtain estimates of the *statistical* value of a life. Such estimates, in turn have been widely used in situations as diverse as court awards for accidents causing death and cost-benefit assessments of the amount of money to devote to public safety or to environmental policies that would reduce fatal risks.

For example, based on administrative data from the Ontario Workers' Compensation Board, Gunderson and Hyatt (2001) estimate that, on average, a typical worker must be paid $2816 (in 1988 dollars) more per year to assume an additional 0.001 probability of a fatality on the job. In other words, a firm with 1000 workers would save $2816 in annual wage costs if it were able to reduce the risk of an occupation-related fatality by a probability of 1 in 1000. Alternatively, a group of 1000 workers would be willing to pay $2,816,000 to statistically reduce the risk of death by one person (among them) per year. This willingness to pay can be taken as a measure of the **value of a (statistical) life**. They indicate that this is in the mid-range of typical estimates, based on Canadian data. Updating this 1988 value-of-life estimate of $2.8 million to adjust for inflation would imply a value of approximately $4.78 million in 2011 dollars. Those estimates in Gunderson and Hyatt (2001) are based on the conventional methodology for estimating compensating wage premiums for fatal risk. When they allow for the endogenity of job choice and self-selection of risk-averse workers into safe jobs, they obtain much higher estimates, suggesting that the conventional methods may underestimate the amount workers are willing to pay for safer workplaces and, hence, the value they attach to a "statistical" life.

Cropper, Hammitt, and Robinson (2011) summarize the existing reviews of the U.S. estimates of the statistical valuation of a life based on the literature on compensating wages for workplace risk, highlighting that the estimates range from $2.0 million to $11.1 million in 2009 dollars. Clearly, individuals have revealed a preference or willingness to pay to reduce fatal risks, although the precise magnitude of that estimate is subject to considerable uncertainty. Interestingly, Viscusi and Aldy (2007) provide evidence of a "senior discount" in the statistical valuation of a life, in that older workers appear willing to accept a lower compensating wage to reduce risk, perhaps reflecting the fact that they have fewer expected remaining years to live.

Coucher and Horrace (2012) estimate the wage premium that climbers in the Himalaya are willing to pay for guides with a better safety record, controlling for a wide range of other factors that can affect the risks of mountain climbing. From this, they estimate the value of a statistical life of about $5 million, which is in the mid range of typical estimates.

Based on Chinese data, Guo and Hammitt (2009) also find a compensating wage premium for fatal risk. Interestingly, they find that the compensating wage premium is lower when unemployment is high, suggesting that workers are willing to take on more risk for the same pay when fewer jobs are available. Their estimates imply a statistical value of life in China of only US$45,000. They cite other Chinese studies that find similar magnitudes, as well as studies from numerous other developing countries that show magnitudes vastly below U.S. estimates. Clearly, people in poorer countries are willing (more realistically, constrained) to take on more risk in return for smaller wage increases than are people in richer countries. Conversely, safety and a lower risk of fatalities are luxuries that come with wealth.

Wage-Risk Trade-offs and Value of Life

Such econometric problems are typical of the applied econometrics literature; hence, the econometric evidence on compensating wages for occupational risk is likely to be neither more nor less reliable than typical econometric estimates. Reviews of such evidence are contained in Rosen (1986), Jones-Lee (1989), Moore and Viscusi (1990), Viscusi (1993), and Gunderson and Hyatt (2001). The general consensus appears to be that compensating wage premiums are paid for work hazards, and they increase with the seriousness of the risk; that is, they are larger for risks of death than for risks of injury, and, for risks of injury, they are larger for permanent than for temporary injuries. In fact, for less-serious injuries, compensating wage premiums are often found not to exist. A limited amount of evidence also suggests that the compensating wage premiums are reduced when the risk is partly covered by workers' compensation systems, and that compensating wage premiums are larger in union than in non-union environments. Powel (2012) finds that the before-tax compensating pay premium for risk increases when income taxes are high because more of the premium is taxed away. Canadian empirical evidence tends to confirm the U.S. findings (Meng 1989; Meng and Smith 1990; Cousineau, Lacroix, and Girard 1992; Martinello and Meng 1992; Gunderson and Hyatt 2001).

EXHIBIT 8.2

Do Sex Workers Receive a Risk Premium for Providing Unprotected Sex?

A novel application of occupational risk premiums is with respect to whether sex workers receive a pay premium for providing unprotected sex that can put them at risk of acquiring a sexually transmitted disease but is often preferred by customers. Gertler, Shah, and Bertozzi (2005) provide evidence that sex workers in Mexico receive a risk premium of about 15 percent per transaction for engaging in sex without a condom. Arunachalam and Shah (2013) review the literature and provide their own evidence of a risk premium in this area. Canadian evidence of the offer and acceptance of pay for unprotected sex is provided in Johnston et al. (2010).

Desirable and Undesirable Job Characteristics

A number of other studies have investigated the presence of compensating differentials associated with other elements of Smith's first factor affecting relative wages ("the agreeableness or disagreeableness of the employments themselves"). Such studies have estimated compensating wages for desirable and undesirable job characteristics, such as poor working conditions (Fernandez and Nordman 2009), the uncertainty or amount of pension benefits (Gunderson, Hyatt, and Pesando 1992; Montgomery, Shaw, and Benedict 1992; Smith 1981; Schiller and Weiss 1980), the mandatory requirement to work overtime (Ehrenberg and Schumann 1984), commuting time (Leigh 1986; Mulalic et al. 2014), amenities across cities (Albouy, Leibovici, and Warman 2013), shift work (Kostiuk 1990), retirement characteristics (Ehrenberg 1980), fringe benefits in general (Eriksson and Kristensen 2014), and the willingness of employers to accommodate the return of injured workers (Gunderson and Hyatt 1996). To date, no one has challenged Smith's conjecture that "the most detestable of all employments, that of public executioner, is, in proportion to the quantity of work done, better paid than any common trade whatever" (Smith, p. 100).

Given the growing importance of issues surrounding the provisions of health care benefits by employers in the United States, increased attention has been paid to any trade-off between health care benefits and wages. Evidence of a trade-off is found, for example, in Adams (2007) and Olson (2002). Lluis and Abraham (2013) discuss the literature in that area, highlighting that many, but not all, studies find evidence of such a trade-off. In their own empirical work, which deals with many of the methodological issues discussed previously, they find evidence of a trade-off for workers who are provided health insurance as the only fringe benefit, but they are unable to disentangle a trade-off when employees are offered health care as part of a comprehensive package of benefits, as is often the case in high-wage firms.

EXHIBIT 8.3

Inequality of Workplace Amenities

One of the most important, and most studied, features of the U.S. labour market is the dramatic increase in wage and earnings inequality beginning in the 1970s and extending into the early 2000s. As we saw in Chapter 6, wages are only one component of compensation. Once due account is taken of non-wage (financial or pecuniary) benefits, total financial compensation inequality increased even more than wage inequality (Farber and Levy 2000; Pierce 2001). But what about other aspects of job quality? Was there a potentially offsetting reduction in the inequality of workplace amenities? For example, if there was an across-the-board improvement in workplace safety that workers implicitly value financially, the increase in wage inequality would overstate the increase in total compensation (financial and nonfinancial) with due allowance for nonpecuniary benefits.

Hamermesh (1999) investigates this question by exploring changes in the distribution of workplace injuries across industries. Were relative decreases in wages in low-wage industries offset by relative improvements in worker safety? Apparently not. If commonly accepted dollar values are attached to workplace safety, overall compensation inequality increased even more than wage inequality! Hamermesh shows that this pattern also happened in the 1960s, when wage inequality was falling. In that time period, relative wage improvements in lower-paying jobs were accompanied by relative improvements in workplace safety. Furthermore, his results extend beyond workplace safety to other amenities. During the 1980s and 1990s, high-wage workers saw relative improvements in their discretion over work hours; evening and shift work was increasingly concentrated among low-wage workers. It appears that when "the rich get richer," they implicitly spend a disproportionate share of their higher wages on improvements in working conditions.

Employment Security

Several papers have also addressed Smith's conjectured third factor, "the constancy or inconstancy of employment." Smith suggested that individuals would have to be compensated for bearing the risk of unemployment. Describing the seasonal nature of work for a mason or bricklayer, Smith notes that "his employment at all other times depends upon the occasional calls of his customers. He is liable, in consequence, to be without any [employment]. What he earns, therefore, while he is employed, must not only maintain him while he is idle, but make him some compensation for those anxious and desponding moments which the thought of so precarious a situation must sometimes occasion" (Smith, p. 103).

Most empirical researchers find evidence of compensating differentials for the risk of unemployment. This is usually accomplished by investigating the statistical significance of a measure of predicted or anticipated unemployment in a wage regression. Important work in this area is outlined in Ashenfelter and Abowd (1981), Murphy and Topel (1987), Adams (1985), Hatton and Williamson (1991), Li (1986), Moretti (2000), and Averett et al. (2005).

One complication addressed by these researchers and Topel (1984), is that we do not observe a pure "market" outcome for the determination of wages and unemployment risk because of the public provision of unemployment insurance. The existence of alternative forms of insurance reduces the need for wages to accomplish this on their own, and perhaps explains the small differentials found by some researchers. Topel (1984), for example, finds that the compensating differential is reduced considerably when the negative consequences are somewhat offset by unemployment insurance. Leonardi and Pica (2013) find that the compensating wage premium was reduced slightly when additional protection against unjust dismissal was provided by legislative reforms in Italy, but this only applied to workers who changed jobs and not to incumbent workers.

Family-Friendly Work Practices

Although it was not a workplace characteristic that was likely prominent in Smith's time, the value that individuals attach to **family-friendly workplace practices** that facilitate *work-family* balance is increasingly important today given the growth in two-earner families that are trying to balance work and family pressures. The admonition that many young families now give when referring to their parents' generation is, "you lived to work; we work to live." Such families should be willing to pay for the availability of family-friendly practices in the workplace, which are generally costly to employers, by accepting lower wages in return. Conversely, employers should be able to shift at least part of the cost of such practices back to workers in the form of lower compensating wages. The literature in this area is more limited and just beginning to emerge, and it faces the usual difficulties of separating out the effect of family-friendly work practices from the myriad other factors that affect pay, as well as controlling for the endogeneity of family-friendly practices in that those with high earnings may "purchase" more of such policies.

Heywood, Siebert, and Wei (2007) account for this endogeneity and estimate a substantial trade-off between pay and family-friendly work practices in general, with the trade-off being prominent for such practices as the availability of parental leave, flexible working hours, job sharing, and ability to take time off work and make it up later. They found no trade-off for support for child care or for allowing working at home. They suggest that this could reflect the possibility that these are the practices that may "pay for themselves," by allowing workers to pay more attention to their work as opposed to their family. Interestingly, they found that if they did not control for the endogeneity of workplace practices they did not find a trade-off, highlighting that the gross relationship often observed regarding the tendency of high-paying jobs to have desirable workplace practices does not negate the fact that there is an underlying trade-off.

Further support for the hypothesis that there is a trade-off between wages and family-friendly work practices is found in Bonhomme and Jolivet (2008), Baughman et al. (2003), DeLeire and Levy (2004), and Felfe (2012). It is also evidenced by the fact that mandated maternity leave has led to a drop in the wages of married women of childbearing age in both the United States (Gruber 1994) and in Europe (Ruhm 1999).

Policy Implications

A number of policy implications associated with compensating wage differences for undesirable job characteristics have already been discussed. In particular, competitive markets can yield the optimal amount of these characteristics, with compensating wages being the price that equilibrates markets. This ensures that the need of employers to carry on production in a manner that may involve undesirable working conditions confronts the need of workers for desirable conditions, and vice versa. This also implies, for example, that the optimal amount of safety is not zero; people are seldom willing to pay the price of attaining that otherwise desirable state.

In such competitive markets, regulations setting a uniform standard, such as a health and safety standard, run the risk of making the parties worse off, largely because compensating wages will adjust in a fashion that workers themselves would not have accepted for the improved working conditions. If there is imperfect information, or markets fail for other reasons, then regulation can make workers better off.

To the extent that wage premiums fully compensate workers for the expected risk of a job, then compensating them if the risk comes to fruition can involve double compensation. Of course, once this is anticipated by the parties, then the compensating wage premium itself will fall, and will be paid only for the uncompensated risk. Thus, the compensating wage paid for the risk of injury or being unemployed will be smaller, respectively, in situations with workers' compensation and unemployment insurance.

The notion that a job involves a set of positive and negative characteristics, each with its own implicit price, also has important implications for the analysis of wage differentials by such factors as occupation, industry, or region. As is shown subsequently, the wage associated with each of these factors can have a component that reflects the compensating wage premiums paid for certain undesirable characteristics associated with each occupation, industry, or region. This will be important for understanding the existence and persistence of interoccupation, interindustry, and interregional wage structures.

Summary

- While the discussion of Chapters 1 to 7 emphasized that equally productive people in the labour market are paid the same wage, wages clearly vary across individuals. This chapter develops the tools to show why wages can be expected to differ across individuals, even if all are equally productive, when the labour market is made up of submarkets that are integrated into a single, more broadly defined but integrated "labour market."

- Wages will be higher for some individuals in order to compensate them for doing unpleasant jobs (or incurring additional costs of employment), while others will willingly accept lower pay for jobs with more amenities.

- The model of compensating wage differentials can be applied to any job characteristic, but the most common application is workplace safety. Firms can choose their production technology to offer workers greater safety, or they can economize on safety and offer the savings to workers in the form of higher wages. For any firm, there will generally be a trade-off in offering more safety or higher wages, holding constant the level of profits. In the broader labour market, however, the competition between firms for workers will imply that, for any level of safety, the technologically highest-possible wage will be offered, while firms earn zero economic profits. The resulting "menu" of wage-safety combinations is called the employers' offer curve.

- Workers have preferences among combinations of wages and workplace safety. Obviously, they would like more of both, but at any level of utility, workers are willing to accept some additional risk in exchange for higher wages. Not all workers have the same attitudes toward workplace risk and will put differing values on workplace safety. Workers will sort across firms according to their relative tastes for wages or safety. Those who are least tolerant of risk will choose to work for those firms offering more safety, at the price of lower wages, while those who are less concerned about safety will work at the riskier but higher-paying jobs.

- In comparing wages across jobs with different levels of safety, the resulting equilibrium choices of workers and firms will yield a "market wage-safety locus." Given that most workers value safety (i.e., on the margin they are willing to buy some additional safety in the form of lower wages at *some* price), and that safety is costly for firms to supply, we expect that the wage-safety locus will show a negative relationship between wages and safety; that is, wages will be lower for safer jobs, *all else equal.*

- Empirical analysis of compensating wage differentials attempts to estimate the extent to which wage differentials across individuals reflect differences in workplace amenities, such as job safety. However, it is difficult to hold everything, such as productivity, constant when doing this analysis, and, typically, we observe higher-paid individuals also having more job amenities. Nevertheless, most carefully executed studies find that wages are indeed higher (on average) for individuals with more dangerous or unpleasant jobs, after holding other determinants of wages constant.

- Primarily as a byproduct of the underlying assumptions of perfect competition and perfect information (workers choose the optimal amount of safety given technological constraints), the theory of compensating differentials can be used to show that government regulation of workplace safety can make workers worse off. However, if the government is more informed about workplace risks than workers are, it is possible that government regulation of safety can improve the welfare of workers. Recent research in behavioural economics also suggests a number of reasons governments may want to intervene given that people do not behave as rationally as they are usually assumed to when confronted with risky situations.

- Estimates of the wage-risk trade-offs can also be used to calculate the value of a (statistical) life and to illustrate that workers generally "pay" for workplace amenities, such as a safer work environment or a family-friendly workplace, by accepting lower wages in return for such amenities.

Keywords

compensating risk premium

compensating wage differentials

endogenous

errors-in-variables problems

family-friendly workplace practices

imperfect information

isoprofit schedule

market envelope curve

omitted variable bias

sample selection bias

shadow or implicit prices

simultaneous equation bias

value of a (statistical) life

wage differentials

wage-safety locus

wage structures

Review Questions

1. Assume that a firm has predetermined sales revenue of $100, which it produces with one unit of labour. It can produce its output with varying degrees of safety, at a cost of $10 per unit of safety. Its total costs are given by $TC = W + 10S$, where W is the wage it pays its worker and S is the amount of safety provided.

   a. Graph the isoprofit schedule for this firm, for level of profits = 0, and profits = 50.

   b. Assume that there is another firm, with a predetermined level of sales revenue equal to 75. Its total costs are given by $TC = W + 5S$. Assume that both firms earn zero profits. On a carefully labelled graph, show the "employer's offer curve" for these two firms, analogous to Figure 8.1.

2. A downtown law firm has offered you a summer job sorting and filing papers for 40 hours per week (8:30 a.m. to 5 p.m., with a half-hour for lunch), at a wage rate of $15 per hour. Assume that this is your only job. What is the lowest wage rate that you would be willing to accept in order to switch to the following job?

   a. The same job, but with a "free lunch" at the cafeteria.

   b. The same job, but with extra two paid breaks of a half-hour each per day.

   c. The same job, but with the freedom to work your 40 hours any time of day or night over the course of the week.

   d. A job with the same 8:30–5:00 schedule (with a half-hour for lunch), but working outside for 40 hours a week, picking garbage off the streets.

   e. A job with the same schedule, but as a taste tester at the local brewery.

   f. A job with the same schedule, but as a fashion photographer's assistant for a national men's or women's magazine (take your pick!).

   g. A job with the same schedule, but working "on the front lines" at a chicken processing plant.

3. Referring to Figure 8.3 panel (a), explain why a wage-safety combination with higher safety than S_C but a lower wage than W_C will not exist in equilibrium.

4. Is it possible for each individual to have a distaste for working with a particular disamenity (i.e., be willing to accept a lower wage in order to have less of the disamenity), but for there to be no market compensation for working with the disamenity?

5. Explain how safety monitoring improvements in firms will change the benefits or cost of safety regulation in Figure 8.5.

6. Discuss how and why the compensating differential for the risk of death on the job can be used as the basis for an estimate of the value of human life? Does this seem like a reasonable basis upon which to make such a calculation?

7. Under imperfect information, workers make the "wrong choices" about workplace safety because they just don't know what the real risks are. Under the "wishful thinking bias," they know what the real risks are but just refuse to believe it and manage to convince themselves that their job is not that risky after all. From the point of view of the government, does it matter whether the problem is imperfect information or wishful thinking? More specifically, discuss (under the two different scenarios of imperfect information versus wishful thinking) the effect of the following two policies aimed at reducing workplace injuries: (1) providing better information about risks to workers, and (2) legislating specific safety measures to be implemented in workplaces.

8. With the growth of two-earner families, workers often attach a substantial value to family-friendly workplace practices and are willing and able to pay for them. They are generally costly, however, for employers to provide. Discuss how compensating wage mechanisms can solve this problem.

Problems

1. Suppose there exists a simple economy with two kinds of workers: J (for "jocks") workers who like physical labour, and L (for "lazy") workers who dislike physical labour. Further, suppose that in this economy there are two kinds of jobs: O (for "office") jobs, which involve little or no physical labour; and F (for "forestry") jobs, which involve substantial physical labour. The J workers will work for $6 per hour in the F jobs, and for $8 per hour or more in the O jobs, while the L workers will work for $6 per hour in the O jobs and $10 per hour or more in the F jobs. Neither group will work for less than $6 per hour. The L workers are indifferent between an F job at $10 per hour and an O job at $6 per hour, while the J workers are indifferent between an F job at $6 per hour and an O job at $8 per hour.

   a. Draw the supply curve of labour to the two sectors (O and F), assuming that there are 100 of each type of worker.

   b. Suppose the demand for labour curves (which are derived from the demand for the products of the two sectors) intersect the labour supply curves at L = 150 and L = 50 in the F and O sectors, respectively.

      i. What is the equilibrium differential?

      ii. Which workers are earning an economic rent, and what is the amount of the rent earned?

      iii. Which workers are earning no economic rent?

2. A simple economy has two sectors, A and B, both of which use labour as an input in production. Both A and B jobs are equally desirable from the point of view of workers. Also, all workers have the potential to do either job. However, a training period must precede employment in either job. For simplicity, we will assume that the training is financed by the worker. Each period, some workers retire in each sector, and new workers enter the labour force.

   a. If the training periods for the two jobs are equal in length and cost, what is the equilibrium differential in earnings between the two jobs?

   b. Assume the conditions given in part (a), and assume further that the labour markets are initially in equilibrium. Then, suppose there is an increase in demand for the products of sector A. What will happen in the two labour markets, both immediately and in the long run?

   c. Suppose job B requires a longer and more expensive training period than job A. Will there be an equilibrium earnings differential between the two jobs?

3. Workers care about only two aspects of their compensation: wages and paid vacations.

   a. Using carefully labelled diagrams, describe the relationship between wages paid by firms offering longer paid vacations and those offering shorter vacations.

   b. If you found, in fact, using data from "the real world," that higher-paying jobs also offered longer vacations, would this be evidence against the argument you sketched in part (a)?

c. What would happen to the wage structure if the government forced all firms to offer at least four weeks of paid vacation?

4. After a rash of injuries in the Big Choke Coal Mine, members of the Parliamentary Committee in Search of Things to Regulate drafted legislation to increase the level of safety in the mine. Economists hired by the mine countered in the committee hearings, arguing that wages at the mine were higher than any other mine, and that by legislating a higher level of safety, the workers would be made worse off.

Outline and evaluate the argument of the economist, describing the conditions under which either the company's economist, or the parliamentary committee, has the correct policy recommendation.

5. The current unemployment insurance program, Employment Insurance, offers special benefits to fishers. Because it is seasonal in nature, and fishing regions often have few alternative employment opportunities, fishers usually find themselves unemployed outside fishing season. They can claim EI benefits for the off-season. Some policymakers have mused openly about eliminating EI benefits for seasonal workers, like fishers.

"Given the returns to fishing, if EI benefits were eliminated, no one would be able to remain in fishing, and a culturally important way of life would be destroyed." Critically evaluate this statement.

6. A labour economist estimates the following regression relating annual earnings to the risk of on-the-job death in the worker's industry:

$$\text{EARNINGS}_i = \alpha + \beta \, \text{RISK}_i + \varepsilon_i$$

where RISK_i is the annual death rate per 10,000 workers. She obtains a statistically significant estimate of $\hat{\beta} = -30.03$.

a. Interpret this coefficient. Is this estimate consistent with the economic theory of compensating differentials? If not, does this mean that the theory is wrong?

b. In a second attempt, the labour economist adds other control variables to the regression, X_i, such as the worker's age, education, union status, and occupation, and estimates,

$$\text{EARNINGS}_i = \alpha + \sum_{j=1}^{K} \gamma_j X_{ji} + \beta \, \text{RISK}_i + u_i$$

and she obtains an estimate of $\hat{\beta} = 43.10$. Why might she obtain a different result than in part (a)? Interpret the new coefficient, and calculate the implied value of a human life. Explain your answer.

7. Mercer Human Resource Consulting company, www.mercerhr.com, provides annual estimates of city rankings based on an index of their "quality of life," an index considering a variety of city characteristics, including cultural and recreational amenities, crime, political stability, and traffic congestion. In 2000, Vancouver was the highest-ranked city in the world (tied with Zurich). Montreal and Toronto also scored well, tied at 19th place. If an economist estimated an earnings regression across the 215 cities as follows,

$$W_i = \alpha + \beta \text{QOLI}_i + \varepsilon_i$$

where W_i is the average earnings in city i, and QOLI_i is the quality-of-life index, she would invariably find that $\hat{\beta} > 0$. Does this mean that the theory of compensating differentials, when applied to city amenities, is wrong? Explain how an economist might be able to test the theory with this type of data.

8. Using the labour-leisure choice model developed in Chapter 2, consider the case of the following two workers. Worker A, who would choose to work exactly 40 hours a week at the going wage rate of $10 an hour, and worker B, who would prefer to work 30 hours at the same going wage. Both workers, however, have to work 40 hours at $10 an hour for their employer because of rigid work shifts.

a. Using budget constraints and indifference curves, first illustrate the choices of workers when they are free to choose their hours of work. Then show what happens when both worker A and B are forced to work 40 hours a week. How does the slope of their indifference curves compare at the same point (40 hours of work) on the budget constraint?

b. The firm now wants to induce workers to supply an extra 10 hours of overtime work, in addition to the regular 40 hours work week. Illustrate the overtime premium that worker A and worker B require in order to accept to work these extra 10 hours. Is the premium higher for worker A or worker B?

c. Discuss how overtime premia are linked to the theory of compensating wages.

CHAPTER 9

Human Capital Theory: Applications to Education and Training

LEARNING OBJECTIVES

LO1 Discuss how the decision to invest in human capital (schooling or on-the-job training) can be analyzed as a standard investment decision based on a comparison between the costs and benefits of the investment.

LO2 Explain how the most expensive part of an investment in human capital is the opportunity cost of one's time.

LO3 Explain why trying to estimate the monetary return to education by simply comparing the earnings of more- and less-educated workers can be misleading due to the ability bias or because education is used as a "signal" in the labour market.

LO4 Describe how the return to education is quite large and has been changing over time in Canada.

LO5 Discuss the circumstances under which either workers or employers are the ones who should pay for training programs.

MAIN QUESTIONS

- Why are more-educated workers generally paid more than less-educated workers? What factors determine the market rate of returns to education?

- If education is such a worthwhile investment, why doesn't everyone have a Ph.D.?

- Are more-educated people paid more because of the learning they acquired, or do higher levels of education merely indicate these individuals' inherently greater productivity?

- What is labour market signalling and screening? How might education serve a role as a signal? If education is used primarily as a screening device, why might the private and social rates of return to education diverge?

- Should the government subsidize early childhood learning programs?

- Are government-funded training programs worth the money?

In the chapters on labour supply, we emphasized the *quantity* aspects of labour supply, ranging from family formation to labour force participation to hours of work. Labour supply also has a *quality* dimension encompassing human capital elements, such as education, training, labour market information, mobility, and health. In addition, in the previous chapter on compensating wages, we indicated that compensating wages may have to be paid to compensate workers for the costly process of acquiring human capital, like education or training. The approach developed in that chapter can be applied to costly attributes necessary to do a job, just as it can be applied to negative job attributes like risk.

While the economics of education and health are often the subject matter of separate courses and texts, they—along with training, job search, and mobility—have a common theoretical thread: human capital theory. This chapter presents the basic elements of human capital theory and applies it mainly to the areas of education and training.

 Human Capital Theory

The essence of **human capital theory** is that investments are made in human resources so as to improve their productivity and, therefore, their earnings. Costs are incurred in the expectation of future benefits; hence, the term "investment in human resources." Like all investments, the key question becomes, is it economically worthwhile? The answer to this question depends on whether or not benefits exceed costs by a sufficient amount. Before dealing with the investment criteria whereby this is established, it is worthwhile to expand on the concepts of costs and benefits as utilized in human capital theory. In this chapter, only the basics are touched upon. A wealth of refinements and precise methodological techniques is contained in the extensive literature on human capital theory and its application.

In calculating the costs of human capital, it is important to recognize not only direct costs, such as books or tuition fees in acquiring a university education, but also the **opportunity cost** or income forgone while people acquire the human capital. For students in university or workers in lengthy training programs, such costs can be the largest component of the total cost. The evaluation of these opportunity costs can prove difficult, because it requires an estimation of what the people would have earned had they not engaged in human capital formation.

In addition, it is important to try to distinguish between the consumption and the investment components of human capital formation, since it is only the investment benefits and costs that are relevant for the investment decision. In reality, this separation may be difficult or impossible—how does one separate the consumption from the investment benefits of acquiring a university degree? For example, a consumption benefit of studying English literature is that it helps one appreciate and enjoy reading old novels. Studying literature also helps improve one's writing, which is an investment benefit that is highly valued in a modern economy. Nevertheless, the distinction between consumption and investment benefits must be made qualitatively, if not quantitatively, especially in comparing programs where the consumption and investment components may differ considerably.

A distinction must also be made between private and social costs and benefits. **Private costs and benefits** are those that accrue to the parties making the investment and, as such, will be considered in their own calculations. **Social costs and benefits** are all those that are accrued by society, including not only private costs and benefits but also any third-party effects, or externalities, that accrue to parties who are not directly involved in the investment decision. Training disadvantaged workers, for example, may yield an external benefit in the form of reduced crime, and this benefit should be considered by society at large even though it may not enter the calculations of individuals doing the investment.

A further distinction can be made between real costs and benefits as opposed to pecuniary, or distributional or transfer, costs and benefits. **Real costs** involve the use of real resources, and should be considered whether those resources have a monetary value or not. Pecuniary or **transfer costs** and benefits do not involve the use of real resources, but rather involve a transfer from one group to another; some gain while others lose. While it may be important to note the existence of such transfers for specific groups, it is inappropriate to include them in the calculation of social costs and benefits since, by definition, gains by one party involve losses by another. For example, the savings in unemployment insurance or social assistance payments that may result from a retraining program are worth noting, and for the unemployment insurance fund they may be a private saving, yet from the point of view of society they represent a reduction in a transfer payment, not a newly created real benefit.[1] Similarly, the installation of a retraining facility in a community may raise local prices for construction facilities, and this may be an additional cost for local residents. Yet, it is a pecuniary cost, since it involves a transfer from local residents to those who raised the prices. While such a transfer may involve a loss to local residents, it is not a real resource cost to society as a whole, since it represents a gain for other parties.

From the point of view of the efficient allocation of resources, only real resource costs and benefits matter. Transfers represent offsetting gains and losses. However, from the point of view of distributive equity, or fairness, society may choose to value those gains and losses differently. In addition, costs and benefits to different groups may be valued differently in the economic calculus.

Thus, in the calculation of the benefits from a training program, it is conceivable to weigh the benefits more for a poor, disadvantaged worker than for an advantaged worker. The appropriate weighting scheme obviously poses a problem, but it could be based on the implicit weights involved in other government programs, or in the progressive income tax structure, or simply on explicit weights that reflect a pure value judgment.

LO1, 2   Private Investment in Education

The main elements of human capital theory can be outlined by considering decisions relating to investment in education. As noted previously, the basic ideas are more than 200 years old:

> When any expensive machine is erected, the extraordinary work to be performed by it before it is worn out, it must be expected, will replace the capital laid out upon it, with at least the ordinary profits. A man educated at the expense of much labour and time to any of those employments which require extraordinary dexterity and skill, may be compared to one of those expensive machines. The work which he learns to perform, it must be expected, over and above the usual wages of common labour, will replace to him the whole expense of his education, with at least the ordinary profits of an equally valuable capital. (Smith, *The Wealth of Nations*, p. 101)

This passage emphasizes a few key points regarding the investment in and returns to education: (1) the increase in wages associated with the acquired skill is a "pure" compensating differential—that is, not a payment for innate ability, but merely compensation to the individual for making the investment; (2) the costs of education, particularly, include the opportunity costs of other pursuits in terms of both time (the wages of common labour) and other investments; and (3) the analytic framework for the individual decision is analogous to the investment in physical capital.

This decision is illustrated in Figure 9.1, which shows alternative income streams associated with different levels of education: incomplete high school (10 years of education at age 16), high school completion (age 18), and university or college degree (age 22). These three outcomes are used for illustration only. In general, we may regard "years of education" as a continuous variable, each year being associated with a lifetime income stream. The earnings in each year are measured in present value terms to make them comparable across different time periods.

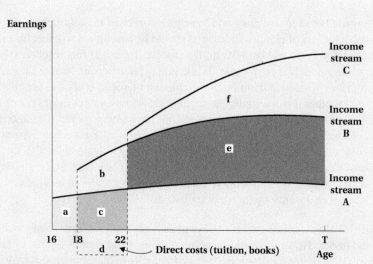

Figure 9.1 Education and Alternative Income Streams

A 16-year-old faces three earnings trajectories. He can drop out of high school at age 16, becoming part of income stream A for the remainder of his working life. If he completes high school, he earns nothing between ages 16 and 18, but has income stream B after graduation. The opportunity cost of staying in school is the forgone earnings (area a), while the benefits are increased earnings, (area b + e). If he attends university, he incurs direct costs in addition to forgoing income stream B while attending university. The total cost of attending university equals the area b + c + d, while the benefit is the higher earnings stream (from B to C), corresponding to area f.

The shapes of the earnings streams, or of an **age-earnings profile**, reflect two key factors. First, for each profile, earnings increase with age but at a decreasing rate. This concave shape reflects the fact that individuals, generally, continue to make human capital investments in the form of on-the-job training and work experience once they have entered the labour force. This job experience adds more to their productivity and earnings early in their careers due to diminishing returns to experience. Second, the earnings of individuals with more years of education, generally, lie above those with fewer years of education. This feature is based on the assumption that education provides skills that increase the individual's productivity and, thus, earning power in the labour market. Because of the productivity-enhancing effect of work experience, individuals with more education may not begin at a salary higher than those in their age cohort with less education (and, therefore, more experience). Nonetheless, to the extent that education increases productivity, individuals with the same amount of work experience but more education will earn more, perhaps substantially more.

Which lifetime income stream should the individual choose? To address this question we will initially make several simplifying assumptions:

1. The individual does not receive any direct utility or disutility from the educational process.

2. Hours of work (including work in acquiring education) are fixed.

3. The income streams associated with different amounts of education are known with certainty.

4. Individuals can borrow and lend at the real interest rate r.

These assumptions are made to enable us to focus on the salient aspects of the **human capital investment decision**. The first assumption implies that we are examining education purely as an investment, not as a consumption decision. The second assumption implies that the quantity of leisure is the same for each income stream so that they can be compared in terms of income alone. Assumption three allows us to ignore complications due to risk and uncertainty. The fourth assumption, often referred to as **perfect capital markets**, implies that the individual can base the investment decision on total lifetime income, without being concerned with the timing of income and expenditures. The consequences of relaxing these simplifying assumptions are discussed below.

In these circumstances, the individual will choose the quantity of education that maximizes the net present value of lifetime earnings. Once this choice is made, total net lifetime earnings (or human capital wealth) can be distributed across different periods as desired by borrowing and lending.

As illustrated in Figure 9.1, human capital investment involves both costs and benefits. The costs include both direct expenditures, such as tuition and books and opportunity costs in the form of forgone earnings. For example, in completing high school, the individual forgoes earnings equal to the area a associated with income stream A between the ages of 16 and 18. The benefits of completing high school consist of the difference between earnings streams A and B for the remainder of his working life, equal to the areas b + e in Figure 9.1. For a high school graduate contemplating a university education, the additional costs include the direct costs (area d) and forgone earnings equal to area b + c, while additional benefits equal the earnings associated with income stream C rather than B (area f). As Figure 9.1 is drawn, a university education yields the largest net present value of lifetime income. However, for another individual with different opportunities and abilities, and therefore different income streams, one of the other outcomes might be best.

The costs and benefits can be more formally represented in terms of the present value formula introduced in Chapter 4. Consider the case of an 18-year-old high school graduate faced with the decision to work after completing high school or to enrol in a post-secondary education (community college or university). To keep things simple, assume that if the student starts working right after high school, she will earn a fixed annual salary Y from age 18 until she retires at age T. At age 18, the net present value of this sequence of earnings over the T − 18 remaining years of work, PV, is

$$PV = \frac{Y}{(1+r)^0} + \frac{Y}{(1+r)^1} + \dots + \frac{Y}{(1+r)^{T-18}}$$

$$= Y + \sum_{t=1}^{T-18} \frac{Y}{(1+r)^t} \approx Y + \frac{Y}{r}$$

The last part of the equation shows that the present value is equal to the sum of earnings in the first year of work, Y, plus the discounted sum of earnings in future years, which is approximately equal to annual earnings Y divided by the interest rate r.[2] To obtain this simple formula for the present value, we have assumed that earnings were constant as a function of age, while from the discussion of Figure 9.1 we, generally, expect earnings to grow as a function of age. Allowing for earnings growth would make the formula more complicated without, however, adding much to the analysis.

Now consider the marginal cost and benefit of investing in further (post secondary) education. As illustrated in Figure 9.1, the cost consists both of the direct cost of schooling, D, plus the forgone earnings while attending school, Y. The marginal cost, MC, of investing in a further year of schooling is MC = Y + D.

On the benefits side, assume that a further year of schooling permanently increases the salary of the student by ΔY. We can use the same approach as above to compute the present value of this alternative stream of earnings. Since annual earnings are now $Y + \Delta Y$ instead of Y, the present value of net income with one further year of education, PV^*, is

$$PV^* \approx \frac{Y + \Delta Y}{r} - D$$

The net gain from an additional year of schooling is given by the difference in the two present values:

$$PV^* - PV \approx \frac{\Delta Y}{r} - (Y + D)$$

The first term on the right-hand side of the equation, $\Delta Y/r$, is the marginal benefit (MB) of the investment in education. The second term, $Y + D$, is the marginal cost (MC). As long as marginal benefits exceed marginal costs, it is optimal to keep investing in human capital. In fact, it is optimal to invest up to the point where marginal benefits are equal to marginal costs. The decision is illustrated graphically in panel (a) of Figure 9.2. The optimal investment in schooling, E^*, is at the intersection between the marginal cost and marginal benefit curves. Marginal costs rise with years of schooling because forgone earnings, Y, rise with schooling. Direct costs, D, also tend to rise with years of schooling. For example, access to public elementary and secondary schools is free, while post-secondary institutions charge substantial tuition fees. By contrast, marginal benefits, generally, decline with years of education due to diminishing returns to education (ΔY declines as schooling increases) and the shorter period over which higher income accrues.

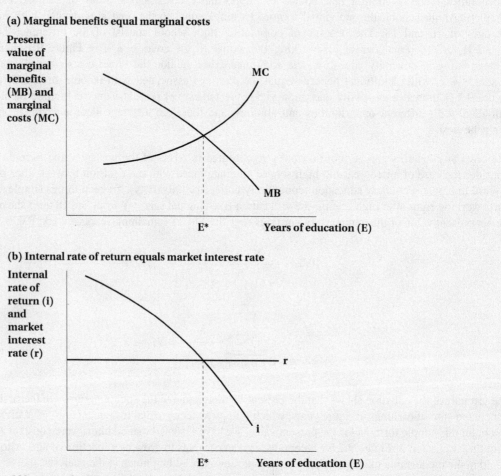

Figure 9.2 Two Ways of Stating the Decision Rule for Optimal Human Capital Investment

Individuals choose the human capital investment that maximizes the net present value of lifetime earnings. One way to show this is illustrated in panel (a). The net benefit of obtaining education level E equals the difference between benefits and costs, and is maximized by setting marginal benefit (MB) equal to marginal cost (MC). The MB of another year of school is the extra earnings generated by the human capital. With diminishing returns, MB will decline with years of education. The MC of another year of school includes direct costs, such as tuition fees, plus the opportunity cost of forgone earnings, which generally increase with years of education. The optimal level of education occurs at E*, where MB = MC. Alternatively, the individual could calculate the implicit (or internal) rate of return, i, for each level of education, corresponding to the discount rate that yields a net present value of zero for the investment. The internal rate of return as a function of years of schooling is given by the schedule i in panel (b). The individual should invest until the internal rate of return equals the opportunity cost of the investment, given by the interest rate r. This condition yields the same educational choice, E*, as in panel (a).

Human capital decisions, like those involving financial and physical capital, are also often expressed in terms of the rate of return on the investment. For any specific amount of education, the **internal rate of return** (i) can be defined as the implicit rate of return earned by an individual acquiring that amount of education. The optimal strategy is to continue investing as long as the internal rate of return exceeds the market rate of interest r, the opportunity cost of financing the investment. That is, if at a specific level of education i > r, the individual can then increase the net present value of lifetime earnings by acquiring more education, which may involve borrowing at the market interest rate, r. Similarly, if i < r, the individual would increase lifetime earnings by acquiring less education. Because the present value of marginal benefits and marginal costs are generally declining and increasing functions, respectively, of years of education, the internal rate of return falls as educational attainment rises. As illustrated in panel (b) of Figure 9.2, the point at which i = r yields the optimal quantity of human capital.

It is easy to see that the level of education at which MB = MC is the same as the level of education at which i = r. Using the above formula, MB = MC can be written as

$$\frac{\Delta Y}{r} = Y + D$$

A simple manipulation of the formula yields

$$i = \frac{\Delta Y}{Y+D} = r$$

The expression on the left-hand side of the equation turns out to be the internal rate of return, i. It represents how large are the pecuniary gains from investing in education, Y, relative to the cost of the investment (Y + D). The internal rate of return declines with years of education for the same reasons mentioned while discussing marginal costs and benefits above. First, the numerator Y decreases with years of education because of diminishing returns. Second, the denominator Y + D increases with years of education because of rising opportunity and direct costs.

Perhaps the most obvious implication of the theory is that human capital investments should be made early in one's lifetime. Educational investments made at later stages earn a lower financial return because forgone earnings increase with work experience and because of the shorter period over which higher income is earned. A related implication is that individuals expecting to be in and out of the labour force, perhaps in order to raise children, have less financial incentive to invest in education and will (other factors being equal) earn a lower return on any given amount of human capital investment.

This framework can be used not only to explain human capital investment decisions but also to predict the impact of changes in the economic and social environment and in public policy on levels of education. For example, changes in the degree of progressivity of the income tax system are predicted to alter levels of educational attainment. Because optimal human capital investment decisions are based on real, after-tax income, an increase in the progressivity of the income tax system would shift down high-income streams (such as C in Figure 9.1) relatively more than low-income streams (such as A), thus reducing the demand for education. Similarly, policies such as student loans programs alter the total and marginal costs of education and, thus, levels of educational attainment.

Not all individuals have or obtain sufficient information to make the detailed calculations needed to determine the optimal quantity of education. Nonetheless, people do take into account costs and benefits when making decisions, including those with respect to human capital investments. Consequently, as is frequently the case in economic analysis, models that assume rational decision making may predict the behaviour of individuals quite well, especially the average behaviour of large groups of individuals. Optimization errors that result in a specific individual's choice of education deviating from the optimum level tend to offset each other and, thus, may have little effect on the average behaviour of large groups of individuals.

Decisions relating to investment in education are also complicated by the fact that the simplifying assumptions used in the above analysis may not hold in practice. The process of acquiring education may directly yield utility or disutility. The existence of this consumption component does not imply that the investment aspect is irrelevant; however, it does indicate that human capital decisions may not be based on investment criteria alone. Individuals who enjoy learning will acquire more education than would be predicted on the basis of financial costs and benefits, while the opposite is true for those who dislike the process of acquiring knowledge. The decision continues to be based on costs and benefits, but these concepts need to be broadened to include nonfinancial benefits and costs.

EXHIBIT 9.1

Innovative Ways of Financing Higher Education?

In the simplest human capital investment model, the decision to go to college or university depends on a simple comparison between the internal rate of return to this human capital investment and the prevailing interest rate at which students could, in principle, borrow to finance their education. In reality, however, a number of other factors may also influence this decision. For instance, high tuition fees may deter students from going to college or university if they have problems borrowing money from financial institutions. Recent evidence for Canada shows that higher tuition fees reduce post-secondary enrolment (Fortin 2005), especially among youth from lower-income backgrounds (Coelli 2009). Many students may also understate the benefits (and internal rate of return) of higher education. For instance, a recent poll shows that low-income Canadians overstate university tuition by $2000 and understate the annual earnings of university graduates by more than $20,000 (Canada Millenium Scholarship Foundation 2004).

Guaranteeing access to a high-quality post-secondary education is a major topic of policy interest in Canada and many other countries. A major challenge is to provide a good quality education without raising tuition fees to a point that would discourage many from getting a post-secondary education. In response to these concerns, several countries have introduced a tuition repayment scheme called an income-contingent loan. The idea is that students take on a loan to finance their studies, but then repay only according to their income in the future. When income falls short of a certain threshold, they don't have to pay anything. The repayment rate then increases the higher the income of graduates is. Riddell (2003) reviews the experience of several countries, and particularly of Australia, with income-contingent loans. He concludes that Australia succeeded at improving the funding of universities, without reducing access, by raising tuition fees and introducing income-contingent loans in parallel. Repayments simply come as deductions from pay cheques (just like income tax), which greatly simplifies the repayment process from the students' point of view. While Canada does not offer a full income-contingent loan program, the Repayment Assistance Plan helps student reduce student loan repayments when their income fall below a certain threshold.

One reason why income-contingent loans may be more effective than traditional students loans is that, for psychological reasons, students appear to have a strong aversion to debt. Using a randomized experiment conducted at NYU Law School, Fields (2009) shows that seemingly comparable aid packages can have a surprisingly large impact on enrolment decisions. Students offered a tuition subsidy program (to be repaid if the student found a high-paying job) were more likely to enrol in law school than those offered a loan (to be waived if the student went for a lower-paid public interest job). Since the programs were similar in terms of present value, the results indicate that one needs to go beyond the simple human capital investment model to understand how financial aid programs can enhance the access to post-secondary education.

WORKED EXAMPLE

Computing the Returns to Education

To help understand the various formulas used to compute present values and the internal rate of returns to education, consider the following example. Mary is an 18-year-old high school graduate who can take a job paying $30,000 without further education. The prevailing interest rate is 5 percent. Mary plans to work from age 18 until retirement at age 65. If she decides to start working right away, the present value (at age 18) of the stream of income will be equal to her earnings at age 18 ($30,000) plus the discounted value of future earnings. For instance, her earnings at 19 are still $30,000, but we have discounted them to reflect the fact that a dollar earned sometime in the future is not worth as much as a dollar earned today. In particular, if Mary can put the dollar earned today in a savings account with a 5 percent interest rate, she will get back $1.05 next year. A dollar earned next year is, thus, worth less by a factor of 1.05 relative to a dollar earned today. By the same token, if the $1.05 was left in the bank for one more year, it would then grow to 1.05 × 1.05 = 1.1025 dollars two years from now. This means that $30,000 earned next year is worth only $30,000/1.05 in dollars of today, and that $30,000 earned two years from now is worth only $30,000/1.1025 in dollars of today. The same procedure can be used to compute the discounted value at any period in the future. For instance, Mary will eventually retire 47 years (65 minus 18) after having started working. A dollar put in the bank today will be worth 1.05 multiplied by itself 47 times by age 65. This can be written down as 1.05 raised to the 47th power (1.05^{47}), and is equal to 9.91. This means that a dollar earned at age 18 is worth 9.91 times more than a dollar earned at age 65.

We obtain the present value of earning $30,000 a year from age 18 to 65 by adding up current and future discounted earnings:

$$PV_{HS} = 30,000 + \frac{30,000}{1.05} + \frac{30,000}{1.05^2} + \ldots + \frac{30,000}{1.05^{47}}$$

$$= 30,000 + 28,571 + 27,211 + \ldots + 3028$$

$$= 569,430$$

Earning $30,000 a year from age 18 to 65 is, thus, worth more than half a million dollars in present value terms. Note also that since $30,000 at age 65 is worth only about a tenth ($3028) of $30,000 at age 18, it does not matter so much in terms of present value whether Mary retires a couple of years before or after age 65. This is the reason we can approximate a stream of future income Y using the formula Y/r, which is based on the idea that Mary would never retire and work forever. Using the approximation formula for the present value we get

$$PV_{HS} = 30,000 + \frac{30,000}{.05} = 30,000 + 600,000$$

$$= 630,000$$

which is only about 10 percent larger than the exact figure of $569,430.

Now, assume that after completing a one-year post-secondary program, Mary would earn $33,000, or 10 percent more than if she had stopped her education right after high school. The present value would now be given by

$$PV_{PS} = 0 + \frac{33,000}{1.05} + \frac{33,000}{1.05^2} \ldots + \frac{33,000}{1.05^{47}}$$

$$= 0 + 31,429 + 29,932 + \ldots + 3331$$

$$= 593,373$$

The extra year of schooling, thus, increases the present value of future income by $23,943 ($593,373 − $569,430). This largely exceeds realistic estimates of the direct costs of schooling (tuition fees, books, etc.). Mary should, thus, go ahead and acquire an extra year of education. We reach the same conclusion using the approximation formula. Remember that the benefit of education is given by $\Delta Y/r$. This is equal to $3000/.05 = $60,000 in Mary's case. Subtracting the opportunity cost of $30,000, Mary still gains $60,000 − $30,000 = $30,000 in present-value terms, which is close to the $23,943 figure obtained using the exact formula.

Finally, we can compute the internal rate of return using the formula $i = \Delta Y/(Y + D)$. When there are no direct costs (D = 0), we get i = 3000/30,000 = 10 percent. Since this exceeds the interest rate of 5 percent, Mary should go ahead and invest in one more year of schooling. With tuition fees of $3000, the internal rate of return is about 9 percent (3000/(30,000 + 3000)), which still largely exceeds the interest rate. Direct costs indeed have to go up to $30,000 for Mary not to undertake the investment, since we would now have i = 3000/(30,000 + 30,000) = 5 percent, which no longer exceeds the interest rate of 5 percent.

In addition to increasing one's future earnings, education may open up a more varied and interesting set of career opportunities, in which case job satisfaction would be higher among those with more education. The consequences may be even more profound. For example, the acquisition of knowledge may alter peoples' preferences and, therefore, future consumption patterns, possibly enhancing their enjoyment of life for a given level of income. In principle, these aspects, to the extent that they exist, can be incorporated into the theory, but they clearly present challenges for measurement and empirical testing. Similarly, the returns to education are unlikely to be known with certainty so that investment decisions must be based on individuals' expectations about the future. Because some alternatives may be less certain than others, attitudes toward risk will also play a role. Risk-neutral individuals will choose the amount of education that maximizes the expected net present value of lifetime earnings, while risk-averse individuals will place more weight on expected benefits and costs that are certain than on those that are uncertain.

Financing is, generally, an important aspect of any investment decision. In the case of human capital investments, financing is particularly problematic, because one cannot use the value of the human capital (i.e., the anticipated future earnings) as collateral for the loan. In contrast, machinery and equipment, land, and other physical assets can be pledged as loan collateral. There is, therefore, a fundamental difference between physical and human capital in terms of the degree to which "perfect capital markets" prevail. In the absence of subsidized tuition, student loan programs, and similar policies, the problems associated with financing human capital investments could prevent many individuals from choosing the amount of education that would maximize their net present value of lifetime earnings. Even in the presence of these policies, borrowing constraints may exert a significant influence on decisions regarding education.

This discussion of human capital theory has focused on the private costs and benefits of education, because these are the relevant factors affecting choices made by individuals. However, the acquisition of knowledge may also affect third parties, in which case the social costs and benefits may differ from their private counterparts. These issues are discussed further, below, in the context of public policy toward education.

LO3   Education as a Filter

The previous model emphasizes the role of education as enhancing the productive capabilities of individuals. A contrasting view of education, where it has no effect on productivity, is provided by the following simple model based on the seminal work of Spence (1974).

Imperfect information is a common feature of many labour markets, and it gives rise to phenomena that cannot be accounted for by the simple neoclassical model. Some important variables that enter into economic decision making are not observable (or are observable only at great cost) until after (perhaps a considerable amount of time after) a decision or transaction has taken place. In these circumstances, employers and employees may look for variables believed to be correlated with or related to the variables of interest. Such variables, which are observable prior to a decision or transaction being made, perform the role of being market signals. In this model, worker productivity is unknown when hiring decisions are made, and education plays a role as a signal of the productivity of employees. This model is important in its own right because education may act, at least in part, as a **signalling** or sorting device, and because it illustrates the more general phenomenon of signalling in labour and product markets.

In the model described here, education acts only as a signal; that is, we assume for simplicity and purposes of illustration that education has no effect on worker productivity. This assumption is made in part to keep the analysis as simple as possible, and in part to illustrate the proposition that job market signalling provides an alternative explanation of the positive correlation between education and earnings.

Employers in the model are assumed to not know the productivity of individual workers prior to hiring those workers. Even after hiring, employers may be able to observe the productivity only of groups of employees rather than that of each individual employee. However, employers do observe certain characteristics of prospective employees. In particular, they observe the amount of education obtained by the job applicant. Because employers are in the job market on a regular basis, they may form beliefs about the relationship between worker attributes, such as amount of education and productivity. These beliefs may be based on the employer's past experience. In order for the employer's beliefs to persist, they must be fulfilled by actual subsequent experience. Thus, an important condition for market equilibrium is that employers' beliefs about the relationship between education and productivity are, in fact, realized.

If employers believe that more-educated workers are more productive, they will (as long as these beliefs continue to be confirmed by actual experience) offer higher wages to workers with more education. Workers, thus, observe an offered wage schedule that depends on the amount of education obtained. In the model, we assume that workers choose the amount of education that provides the highest rate of return. Any consumption value of education is incorporated in the costs of acquiring education.

To keep the analysis as simple as possible, we assume that there are two types of workers in the economy. Low-ability workers (type L) have a marginal product of 1 (MP = 1), and acquire s units of education at a cost of $s. High-productivity workers (type H) have a marginal product of 2, and acquire s units of education at a cost of $s/2. Note, as explained above, that the productivity or ability of workers is given, and is independent of the amount of education obtained. Note also that the more-able workers are assumed to be able to acquire education at a lower cost per unit of education obtained. This situation could arise because the more-able workers acquire a specific amount of education more quickly, or because they place a higher consumption value on (or have a lower psychic dislike for) the educational process.

The assumption that more-able workers have a lower cost of acquiring education is important. As will be seen, this is a necessary condition for education to act as an informative signal in the job market. If this condition does not hold, low- and high-ability workers will acquire the same amount of education, and education will not be able to act as a signal of worker productivity.

To see what the market equilibrium might look like, suppose that employers' beliefs are as follows:

$$\text{If } s < s^* \text{ then MP} = 1$$

$$\text{If } s \geq s^* \text{ then MP} = 2$$

That is, there is some critical value of education (e.g., high school completion, university degree) and applicants with education less than this critical value are believed to be less productive, while applicants with education equal to or greater than this value are believed to be more productive.

In these circumstances, the offered wage schedule (assuming for the purposes of illustration that the labour market is competitive so that firms will offer a wage equal to the expected marginal product) will be as shown in Figure 9.3. That is, applicants with education equal to or greater than s^* will be offered the wage w = $2, and applicants with education less than s^* will be offered the wage w = $1. In Figure 9.3 it is assumed that s^* lies between 1 and 2.

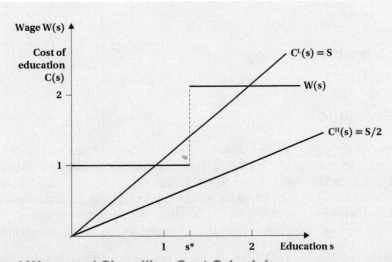

Figure 9.3 Offered Wage and Signalling Cost Schedules

Employers offer the wage schedule W(s) with an educational requirement of s^*, where employees are paid 2 if they have education $s \geq s^*$ and 1 if they have education level $s < s^*$. Low-ability workers' cost of acquiring education is given by $C^L(s)$. Their return acquiring s^* is given by $2 - C^L(s^*) < 1$, so they are better off not going to school, and accepting the lower wage. The net benefit of education to the high-abilitied is given by $2 - C^H(s^*) > 1$, so they are better off acquiring the education level s^* rather than being pooled with the low-abilitied (at wage 1). In this equilibrium, only the high-abilitied acquire education, and all workers are paid their marginal products.

Also shown in Figure 9.3 are, for each type of worker, the cost functions C(s) associated with acquiring education. Note that low-ability workers are better off by acquiring 0 units of education. This choice gives a net wage of $1; because the cost of acquiring zero units of education is zero, the gross wage and net wage are equal in this case. In contrast, low-ability workers would receive a net wage of w = $2 − s* < $1 if they were to acquire sufficient education to receive the higher-wage offer given to those with education equal to or greater than s*.

However, the high-ability workers are better off by acquiring education level s = s*. This choice yields a net wage of w = $2 − s*/2 > $1, whereas choosing s = 0 yields, for these individuals, a net wage of w = $1.

Thus, given the offered wage schedule, if s* lies in the range 1 < s* < 2, the low-ability workers will choose s = 0 and the high-ability workers will choose s = s*. Thus, employers' beliefs about the relationship between education and worker productivity will be confirmed. Those applicants with low education will in fact be the less productive, and those with higher education will be the more productive. Employers will, therefore, not have any reason to alter their beliefs or the offered wage schedule. Given the offered wage schedule, workers will continue to choose to acquire the educational "signal," such that the level of education is a good predictor (in this simple model it is a perfect predictor) of productivity. This outcome is a market equilibrium even though, by assumption, education does not increase the productivity of any individual worker; that is, education acts strictly as a signalling or sorting device in this case. Looked at from the outside, it might appear that education raises productivity, because those with more education are more productive and receive higher earnings. However, this is not the case; education simply sorts the otherwise heterogeneous population into two distinct groups.

This simple model illustrates the central result of the theory of market signalling. This theory has been used to explain numerous other phenomena, such as the use of a high product price to signal the quality of the product, the use of product warranties to signal product quality, and the use by employers of an applicant's employment experience (e.g., number of jobs, amount of time spent unemployed) to signal worker quality.

Of course, we do not expect that education acts strictly as a filtering or signalling mechanism, as is the case in the simple model just outlined. Most educational programs probably provide some skills and knowledge that raise the productivity of workers. However, it is possible that some forms of education or training act primarily as a signal, while other forms involve, primarily, human capital acquisition, which raises productivity and earnings. The extent to which education serves as a signalling device versus a form of human capital acquisition is an interesting and important question. The policy implications of the models, for example, are quite different. For the signalling model, educational subsidies represent a pure transfer to high-ability individuals, and are indefensible on equity grounds.

Empirical Evidence

Education and Earnings

Because of the importance of the topic, but also because of an abundance of data sets with information on earnings and education, labour economists have spent considerable effort measuring the **returns to schooling**, and attempting to evaluate the neoclassical human capital model. Figure 9.4 shows age-earnings profiles for four educational categories of Canadian males: (a) some elementary and high school but no high school diploma, (b) high school diploma (11 to 13 years of elementary and secondary schooling, depending on the province) but no further schooling, (c) some post-secondary education but no university degree, and (d) a university degree. (The profiles for females are qualitatively similar.)

As these data indicate, there is a strong relationship between education and lifetime earnings, on average. The income streams of those with more education lie above the streams of those with less education. Two additional patterns are evident. First, earnings increase with age and, thus (presumably), labour market experience until around age 50, and then decline slightly. As noted previously, this concave relationship between age and earnings is generally attributed to the accumulation of human capital in the form of on-the-job training and experience, a process that displays diminishing returns. Second, earnings increase most rapidly up to age 45 to 49 for those individuals with the most education. Thus, the salary differential between groups with different amounts of education is much wider at age 50 than at ages 20 or 30.

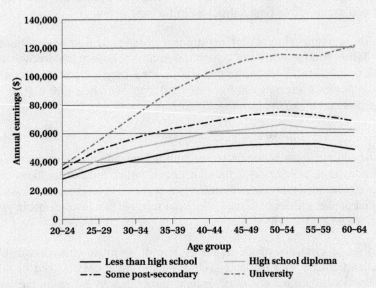

Earnings by Age and Education, Canadian Males, 2010

Legend:
— Less than high school
—·— Some post-secondary
—— High school diploma
—·· University

Figure 9.4 Earnings by Age and Education, Canadian Males, 2010

This graph shows the average earnings by age group for different levels of education. For example, the lowest line shows the relationship between age and earnings for those men who have not completed their high school education. Their earnings generally increase with age, as they accumulate on-the-job experience. The age-earnings profiles are higher on average for those men with more education, being highest for university graduates.

NOTES:

1. Earnings are average wage and salary income of full-year (49-plus weeks), mostly full-time (30 hours per week or more) workers.

2. Education categories are defined as (1) *less than high school*–elementary school or high school, but no high school diploma; (2) *high school diploma*–holds a high school diploma (11 to 13 years of high school, depending on the province) but no further schooling; (3) *some post secondary*–some post-secondary education, but not a university degree; (4) *university*–at least a bachelor's degree.

SOURCE: Data from Statistics Canada, Individual Public Use Microdata Files, 2011 National Household Survey.

EXHIBIT 9.2

"Big Data" and Lifetime Returns to Schooling

Most studies that estimate the returns to schooling rely on cross-sectional data, such as the Canadian census (or the 2011 National Household Survey used in Table 9.2), to compare the earnings of individuals with different levels of schooling at a given point in their lifetime. By contrast, the theory of human capital investment is based on the comparison of earnings streams over one's whole lifetime (see Figure 9.1). This disconnect between theory and empirics has to do with the fact that, until recently, there were no data available to track down earnings of individuals over their whole lifetime.

This has changed recently, thanks to the availability of new matched data sets and "Big Data," more generally. For instance, Frenette (2014) combines data from the 1991 Census (that provides information on schooling) with income tax information for the years 1991 to 2010. This allows him to compute cumulative earnings over 20 years for a sample of Canadians born in 1955 to 1957 who were just starting their careers in 1991. Frenette finds that men with a bachelor's degree earned, on average, a total of $1,707,340 (expressed in constant 2010 dollars) over 20 years, compared to $975,323 for high school graduates. The gap between lifetime earnings of university and high school graduates remains very large at about $440,000 when expressed in present value using a 5 percent discount rate ($1,071,624 and $628,364 for university and high school graduates, respectively).

Although lifetime earnings are lower for women than for men, women with a bachelor's degree earn much more over a 20 years period ($972,869) than those with a high school diploma ($524,627). Even in present value terms, the gap in lifetime earnings is about $280,000 ($610,516 and $331,373 for those with a bachelor's degree and those with a high school diploma, respectively).

These differences in the present value of earning streams of several hundreds of thousands of dollars are orders of magnitude larger than the costs of education (tuition fees, etc.). Moreover, the lifetime benefits of education are still understated in Frenette's study as they only include earnings over one's first 20 years of career. These findings strongly reinforce the existing evidence that higher education is one of the best investments one can make in his or her lifetime.

Data on earnings by age and education can be used together with information on direct costs to calculate the internal rate of return on investments in education, analogously to those described earlier. Such calculations can be useful to individuals wishing to know, for example, whether a university education is a worthwhile investment. They can also be useful input for public policy decisions. In particular, efficient resource allocation requires that investments in physical and human capital be made in those areas with the greatest return.

Table 9.1 shows one such set of estimates of the monetary rate of return to education in Canada as of 2000 (from Moussaly-Sergieh and Vaillancourt, 2009). Like most such estimates, these are obtained by comparing the earnings of individuals with different levels of education at a point in time, rather than by following the same individuals over time. Other factors that might also account for earnings differences across individuals are taken into account using multivariate regression analysis. The estimates shown are the private after-tax rates of return to the individual, taking into account such costs as tuition fees and forgone earnings.

TABLE 9.1	Estimates of the Private Returns[1] to Schooling in Canada, 2000	
Level of Schooling	**Males**	**Females**
Bachelor's degree[2]	12	14
Master's degree	3	5
Ph.D.	nc[2]	4
Medicine	21	22
Bachelor's Degree by Field of Study	**Males**	**Females**
Education	9	14
Humanities and fine arts	nc	10
Social sciences[3]	11	14
Commerce	9	19
Natural sciences	9	8
Engineering and applied science	9	14
Health sciences	18	18

NOTES:

1. Rates of return by level of schooling are calculated relative to the next-lowest level. For example, the return to a bachelor's degree is relative to completed secondary school, and the return to a master's degree is relative to a bachelor's degree.

2. "nc" indicates "not calculated" because that estimated returns were not significantly different from zero, statistically.

3. Social sciences includes law degrees.

SOURCE: Adapted from *Extra Earning Power: The Financial Returns to University Education in Canada*, p. 3. C. D. Howe Institute. Used with permission.

Note that the rates of return are highest for the bachelor's level, as would be expected if there is diminishing returns to the level of human capital (e.g., as shown in Figure 9.2). Females benefit more from additional education than males, a result consistent with the general finding that the gap between male and female earnings is largest at low levels of education and least at high levels of education. Burbidge, Collins, Davies, and Magee 2012 show fairly similar results, except for master's degrees, for which the rate of return (for a median worker) is closer to 10 percent for both men and women.

Although rates of return to undergraduate education are generally high, there are also large differences in these rates of return by the type of education obtained. The bottom part of Table 9.1 illustrates these differences for fields of study of a holder of a bachelor's degree. Those obtaining degrees in health sciences (such as medicine, dentistry, and related fields) earn particular the highest return, while those graduating in humanities and fine arts earn much lower returns.

The Human Capital Earnings Function

Estimates of the rate of return to education are generally obtained by comparing different individuals at a point in time. After controlling for other observed factors that influence earnings, the differences in individuals' earnings are attributed to differences in educational attainment. This is primarily accomplished through the estimation of a **human capital earnings function**. In its simplest form, this function is nothing more than a least-squares regression of earnings on education, with controls for other factors believed to affect earnings. Because of its importance to labour economics, however, it is worth reviewing some of the details involved in the specification and estimation of the returns to schooling in this regression context.

The human capital earnings function is easily derived in the case where the direct costs of education are either zero or negligible relative to opportunity costs. In this case, the formula used above to obtain the internal rate of return can be written as

$$i = \frac{\Delta Y}{Y} \approx \Delta \ln Y = r$$

We use the fact that proportional change in a variable is approximately equal to the change in the logarithm. This means that at the margin, increasing schooling by an extra year increases log earnings by r. In other words, the slope of the relationship between log earnings, ln Y, and schooling, S, is equal to r. In general, we can write the implied relationship between these two variables as

$$\ln Y = \alpha + rS$$

where α represents what an individual without any schooling would earn. The equation shows how human capital theory predicts that the log of earnings, as opposed to the level of earnings, should be linearly linked to the number of years of schooling. In this equation, r is, thus, interpreted as the rate of return to schooling. This reflects the fact that the interest rate, r, should indeed be equal to the internal rate of return, i, when people make optimal investments in human capital. The human capital investment model also provides an additional reason for working with logarithms instead of levels. Remember from Exhibit 1A.1 that using logs is also popular in economics because they are simpler to interpret.

Since schooling is clearly not the sole determinant of earnings, empirical studies typically add a number of additional variables to the earnings function. For instance, Figure 9.4 shows that earnings rise with age (or experience). Furthermore, unobservable components, such as ability or motivation, are also important determinants of earnings. A more general earnings equation is, thus,

$$\ln Y = \alpha + rS + \beta\, AGE + \varepsilon$$

where ε is the unobservable component, or error term.

The functional form could be generalized further by permitting the returns to age, or schooling, to vary with the level of schooling or age, for example, by including quadratic terms in schooling or age.

The human capital earnings function then yields a straightforward regression equation. By regressing log wages on years of schooling, and possibly other factors, we obtain an estimate of the returns to schooling. In this particular equation, the return to schooling is simply the coefficient on years of education. The coefficients on the other variables (like age, or potential labour market experience) also have the interpretation as rates of return to the given characteristics.

The easiest way to illustrate the empirical methodology of estimating these earnings functions is to examine some actual earnings-schooling data. We have drawn a random sample of women from 35 to 39 year of age who held full-time jobs in 2010 from the 2011 National Household Survey. By comparing the earnings of these women by education level, we can estimate the return to education, holding age constant. This is illustrated in Figure 9.5. The individual observations are plotted, as well as the estimated regression of log earnings on years of schooling from this sample. While the regression function fits quite well, yielding a rate of return to schooling of 10 percent per year, there is still considerable dispersion around this function. On average, earnings rise with education, but there are plenty of examples of low-educated women earning more than the higher-educated ones. These women may be the "anecdotes" used by high school dropouts to justify their decisions, but it is clear that such women are the minority.

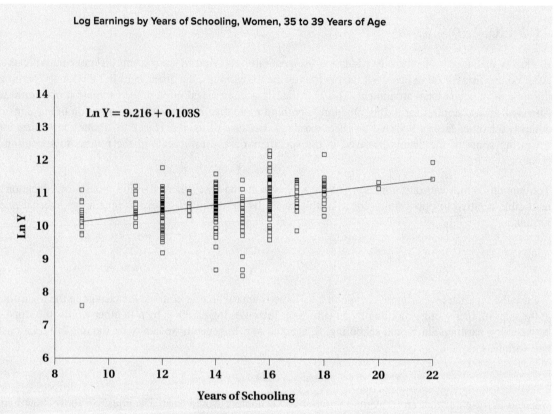

Figure 9.5 Log Earnings by Years of Schooling, Women 35 to 39 Years of Age, 2010

This scatter plot shows the relationship between education and earnings for a sample of 35- to 39-year-old women in 2010. Each point represents a particular woman, with her level of education and annual earnings. Also shown is the estimated regression line, which shows the level of predicted earnings for women with a given number of years of schooling. While most observations lie close to the regression line, there are obviously some women whose earnings are higher than predicted, and some whose earnings are lower than predicted.

NOTES: This figure shows the log annual earnings-schooling pairs and the predicted log earnings from a regression of log earnings on the years of schooling.

SOURCE: Data from Statistics Canada, Individual Public Use Microdata Files, 2011 National Household Survey.

In summary, the most conventional approach to estimating the returns to schooling is to estimate the human capital earnings function. The simplest, most common specification replaces age with a quadratic function of **potential experience**:

$$\ln Y = \alpha + rS + \beta_1 EXP + \beta_2 EXP^2 + \varepsilon$$

This function is linear in schooling and quadratic in potential labour market experience. Since actual work experience is rarely included in data sets, it is usually approximated by potential experience, equal to

$$Age - Schooling - 5$$

which is an estimate of the number of years an individual was working but not at school.[3] We have estimated this equation on the full sample of full-year, full-time men and women from the 2011 National Household Survey. The results are reported in Table 9.2. The rate of return to schooling for men is estimated as 8.3 percent, while that for women is 11.2 percent. Consistent with Table 9.1, the returns to education are higher for women than men. The returns to experience, however, are significantly lower for women than men. This is perhaps due to the fact that "potential experience" is an especially poor proxy for actual work experience for women, who generally have more intermittent attachment to the work force. We will return to this in our chapter on discrimination.

TABLE 9.2	Estimated Returns to Schooling and Experience, 2010 (dependent variable: log annual earnings)	
	Men	**Women**
Intercept	9.114 (742.25)	8.537 (631.62)
Years of schooling	0.083 (116.57)	0.112 (140.33)
Experience	0.053 (77.02)	0.042 (64.32)
Experience squared	− 0.0008 (59.03)	− 0.0006 (44.95)
R-squared	0.151	0.198
Sample size	125,680	101,985

NOTES: The regressions are estimated over the full samples of full-year (49 or more weeks worked in 2005), mostly full-time men and women, respectively. Absolute t-values are indicated in parentheses, with t-values greater than 2 generally regarded as indicating that the relationship is statistically significant, and unlikely due to chance.

SOURCE: Data from Statistics Canada, Individual Public Use Microdata Files, 2011 National Household Survey.

LO3   Signalling, Screening, and Ability

The earnings function provides a convenient framework for summarizing the relationship between education and earnings in the labour market. The estimated rate of return yields the average difference in earnings between groups of individuals with different levels of education. The difficult question, however, is whether this correlation represents a "pure" causal relationship between education and earnings. If the return to education is estimated as 10 percent, then providing an additional year of schooling to a lower-educated group of workers should raise their earnings by 10 percent. If there are systematic differences between the less educated and the more educated that affect both earnings and schooling, then the correlation between earnings and education may reflect these other factors as well. In that case, our estimate of the rate of return to schooling would be biased. One of the advantages of the multiple regression framework is that it allows a researcher to control for these other factors, data permitting.

One potential determinant that is difficult to control for is ability, by which we mean ability in the workplace, not learning ability (though these may be correlated). If more-able individuals are also more likely to invest in education, some of the estimated return to education may in fact be a return to innate ability. In other words, there are those who are more able would earn more even in the absence of education. We may be incorrectly attributing their higher earnings to education rather than to their innate ability.

One theoretical rationale for the potential importance of "omitted ability bias" is the hypothesis that higher education may act as a filter, screening out the more-able workers rather than enhancing productivity directly. According to the extreme form of signalling/screening hypothesis discussed above, workers may use education to signal unobserved ability while firms use education to screen. In the equilibrium of this model, workers who obtain more education are more productive and receive higher earnings. Yet, by assumption, education does not affect worker productivity.

Early empirical tests of the signalling/screening hypothesis were not always conclusive (Riley1979; Lang and Kropp 1986), though more-recent work is more supportive. For instance, Ferrer and Riddell (2002) document important "credential effects" in the Canadian labour market that are hard to reconcile with a simple human capital investment model. Bedard (2001) shows that, as predicted by the standard signalling model of Figure 9.3, low-ability workers have fewer incentives to pretend they are high-ability workers when the quality of the pool of high-ability workers goes down. Most would agree that the pure signalling model in which education has no impact on productivity does not appear capable of explaining observed behaviour (Rosen 1977; Weiss 1995). If knowing about their workers' ability is so important, employers should invest more in learning about these abilities instead of exclusively relying on the education system to do so. Indeed, Lang and Siniver (2011) show that although individuals with a degree from an elite institution initially earn more than others in the labour market, the earnings gap for individuals with similar abilities eventually dissipates over time. This suggests that, consistent with Altonji and Pierret (2001) and Arcidiacono, Bayer, and Hizmo (2010), employers gradually learn about the productive ability of their workers. So, while signalling effects may be important early in one's career, there are unlikely to last once employers know who are their good and not so good workers, regardless of their level of education.

EXHIBIT 9.3

The Rate of Return to Taking "Serious" High School Courses

Most of the empirical evidence on estimated returns to schooling focuses on the average rate of return to a "year" of education, without any regard for the actual courses taken over that year. Altonji (1995) provides some of the first estimates of the effect of high school course selection on future labour market outcomes. Using the NLS, he observes the wages in 1985 of a large sample of high school graduates from the class of 1972.

Controlling for a variety of family background variables, as well as characteristics of the high schools (or classmates), Altonji finds almost no economic payoff for students who took more-academically oriented high school courses. For example, switching from less-academically oriented courses (like industrial arts, physical education, or commercial studies) to the same number of science, math, or English courses would increase future earnings by less than 0.3 percent. Thus, the academic "package" of a year's worth of these courses has no higher rate of return than a generic year of high school.

As noted by Altonji and discussed further in Weiss (1995), this evidence is more consistent with the screening/signalling view of education than with the pure human capital model. The premise of human capital theory is that it is the purely productivity-enhancing features of education that employers are paying for. If that is the case, course content should matter more than just the number of years of education. On the other hand, the signalling model suggests that employers infer other characteristics from the level of education, such as individual perseverance and work habits. In that case, employers will care more about whether the person finished high school than whether they took this course or that one. Furthermore, employers may not know about the particular course choices of students, in which case, they will be basing their hiring and compensation decisions on the level of education. It is gaps like the ones detected by Altonji—gaps between measured human capital investments and the labels attached to them—that provide the most convincing evidence of the role of signalling and screening in the labour market.

Even in the absence of education acting as a signal, there may be a correlation between unobserved ability and the level of education. As we emphasized in the human capital model, education is a private investment decision. People acquire additional education if it increases their earnings enough to offset the costs of doing so. For example, two individuals may be comparing the earnings associated with becoming a lawyer versus a plumber. The model outlined earlier assumed that the two individuals were equally able, in terms of both their work ability and their ability to complete law school. Assuming that the jobs are otherwise equally desirable, in equilibrium, the return to schooling would be such that these individuals were indifferent between the two career paths, and the higher lawyer's salary would be a pure compensating differential for the cost of attending law school. If the one choosing to be a plumber instead went to law school, her earnings would be the same as the person who chose the legal career.

Imagine now that one of the individuals was of higher overall ability. For her, law school would be a relative breeze, so she would choose the legal path. Similarly, because of her higher ability, she would make higher-than-average earnings as a lawyer. Comparing her earnings to the plumber would then overstate the returns to education that the plumber would receive if she had chosen law school. Alternatively stated, the actual difference in earnings would be smaller than predicted if the plumber and lawyer switched career paths. Of course, the bias could work the other way. Ability may be multidimensional. Perhaps the lawyer would make a lousy plumber. In that case, the observed difference in earnings between the plumber and lawyer would understate the difference that would exist if the plumber and lawyer switched occupational paths.

Addressing Ability Bias[4]

The best way to determine how much education improves productivity, and thus increases earnings, would be to conduct an experiment. Separate groups of individuals would be randomly assigned different levels (and possibly types) of education, independent of their ability, family background, and other environmental factors. At a later date, the incomes of these groups would be compared. Because of the random assignment to groups, on average, differences in earnings between the groups would only be due to the different levels (or types) of education. But in the absence of such experiments, economists seeking more reliable evidence concerning the relationship between education and earnings have tried to find a **natural experiment** that isolates the influence of education from the possible effects of unobserved ability factors.

The basic methodology can be illustrated using a stripped-down earnings function. We specify a simple relationship between earnings and schooling:

$$\ln Y = \alpha + \beta S + \varepsilon,$$

so that log wages depend only on the level of schooling, S, and unobserved talent, ε. As we explain in the online appendix to the chapter, the ordinary least squares (OLS) estimate of the return to schooling β is biased, termed the **ability bias**, because unobserved talent, ε, is correlated with schooling. In simple intuitive terms, the solution to this problem is to find a setting in which schooling for an individual, or average schooling for a group of individuals, is not related to unobserved talent or ability.

A first such setting is the case of twins who should have the same level of ability or talent since they share the same genetic and family environment. Despite this, twins often end up with different levels of education. Looking at whether differences in schooling between twins have an effect on differences in earnings should, therefore, yield estimates of the returns to education that are not afflicted by the ability bias. Behrman, Hrubec, Taubman, and Wales (1980) provide one of the first examples of this approach. They use a sample of male identical twins who were veterans of World War II. In their data, the simple relationship between education and income indicates that every additional year of schooling adds approximately 8 percent to annual earnings. However, when attention is focused on twins alone (i.e., the relationship between differences in education and differences in earnings for pairs of twins as described above), the estimated return to an additional year of education falls to between 2 and 2.5 percent. These estimates suggest that differences in unobserved ability may account for much of the estimated return to education. However, in this type of analysis, measurement error in the amount of education obtained will bias the estimated returns toward zero. Even small errors in reported education are magnified when looking at differences instead of levels of education. Thus, considerable uncertainty about the true impact of education remained following the Behrman et al. study.

In a later study, a team of Princeton University labour economists collected data on a large sample of identical twins attending the annual "Twins Festival" in Twinsburg, Ohio.[5] In addition to the usual measures of earnings and education, they obtained an independent source of information on education level in order to minimize the possible influence of measurement error. They asked each twin about his or her sibling's level of education, giving them a second estimate of the level of schooling for each person. This second estimate could be used to "corroborate" or provide a more accurate estimate of the effects of schooling differences on the earnings differences of the twins.

Using the conventional approach, Ashenfelter and Rouse (1998) estimated an OLS return to education of about 11 percent, slightly higher than most other datasets. Exploiting the twins feature of the data to control for innate ability, the return to education fell to 7 percent, suggesting considerable ability bias. However, once they accounted for the possibility of measurement error, the estimated returns rose to 9 percent, which was still lower than the conventional OLS results. Their results confirm that omitted-variables bias is a problem, but not a large one.

Another approach is to try to mimic an experiment by finding a mechanism that affects ("assigns") education levels to groups of individuals in some way independent of the individual's expected returns to schooling. In that setting, the average level of schooling of each group should be unrelated to the average level of unobserved talent or ability of the group.

There are a number of studies based on this natural experiment methodology, whereby the main innovation is arguing that the division by groups satisfies the condition that schooling is unrelated to unobserved talent or ability. One such study uses the natural experiment associated with compulsory school attendance laws (Angrist and Krueger 1991). Such laws, generally, require students to remain in school until their 16th or 17th birthday. However, because children born in different months start school at different ages, compulsory attendance laws imply that some children are required to remain in school longer than others. Of course, for those who remain in school longer than the minimum required period, such as those who obtain some post-secondary education, these laws will not influence the amount of education obtained. However, for those who wish to leave school as soon as possible, compulsory attendance laws require students born in certain months to remain in school longer than those born in other months. Because month of birth is unlikely to be correlated with ability or family background, any variation in educational attainment associated with compulsory school attendance laws is likely to be randomly distributed in terms of ability and environmental background. Angrist and Krueger find that season of birth is, indeed, related to educational attainment in the United States; in particular, those born early in the year (and who therefore attain the legal dropout age earlier in their education careers) have a slightly lower average level of education than those born later in the year. Furthermore, those who attend school longer because of compulsory schooling laws receive higher earnings. Angrist and Krueger estimate the impact of an additional year of school (due to compulsory attendance requirements) on the earnings of males to be an increase in earnings of 7.5 percent. Because ability is unlikely to be related to month of birth, this estimate should be free of any bias associated with unobserved ability.

Oreopoulos (2006a, 2006b) uses changes in compulsory schooling laws in Canada and the United Kingdom to estimate returns to education that are not contaminated by ability biases. He finds that the returns to education remain quite large (10 percent or more) even after controlling for ability biases, though Devereux and Hart (2010) obtain a smaller returns to education using a similar approach for the United Kingdom. Of course, these studies provide evidence regarding the relationship between schooling and earnings for levels of education around that of high school completion. Other natural experiments would be needed to obtain similar evidence for post-secondary education (see Exhibit 9.4).

Card (1995) uses proximity to a college as another way to identify the "experimental" effects of acquiring post-secondary education. Individuals born in areas with nearby colleges or universities effectively face a lower cost of schooling. As long as account is taken of other possible differences in family background that may be related to both geographical location and earnings potential, this difference in the cost of education can be used to isolate the returns to education. Card found that the standard estimates of the return to schooling were typical, around 7.5 percent. Once proximity was used to "control" for possible individual ability bias, the estimated returns rose to around 14 percent. Again, there was no evidence of ability bias.

In concluding this discussion of the empirical evidence relating to education and earnings, several observations should be made. First, looking across these recent studies, it seems our initial intuition that the returns to education were overstated because of ability bias, was exaggerated. Second, the returns to education discussed here are restricted to the private monetary benefits. Additional benefits to the individual—such as any enjoyment derived directly from acquiring knowledge, a more varied and interesting career, or even an enhanced ability to enjoy life—would increase the private returns to education. Third, the social returns to education may differ from the private returns for a variety of reasons. It is also important to note that estimates usually provide the *average* rate of return for all those making a certain educational investment. Policies, such as those relating to the allocation of resources, should be based on *marginal*, not average, calculations; that is, for social efficiency, funds should be allocated among various physical and human capital investments such that the social rate of return on the last dollar invested in each project is equal.

Finally, with a few exceptions (e.g., Frenette 2014), note that the calculated returns to education are based on cross-sectional data (different individuals at a point in time). This procedure will be accurate only if the age-earnings profiles for each educational category are approximately constant over time, apart from overall earnings growth affecting all groups. To the extent that earnings differentials by education narrow or widen over time, the actual realized return to educational investments will be smaller or larger than that estimated on the basis of cross-sectional data.

EXHIBIT 9.4

Investing in Early Childhood Education

One of the important principles in human capital theory is that it pays off to make investments in learning and training early in life, since one can then benefit from the return on these investments for a longer time period. Over the last decade, economists and other social scientists have paid increasing attention to "very early" investments in human capital among preschool children. Part of this increased focus is due to the fact that children from disadvantaged backgrounds are already behind other children in terms of test scores and health outcomes at the time they enter kindergarten or Grade 1 (Almond and Currie 2011). More generally, given the critical importance of the very early years in one's long-term development, it seems natural to broaden the focus of educational policies beyond what happens when children start formal schooling at age 5 or 6.

In both Canada and other countries, these concerns for early childhood development have lead to some policy debates about the appropriate role of preschool child care as an additional instrument in educational policies. For instance, the $5-a-day child care policy introduced in Quebec in the late 1990s is one example of a policy measure aimed at providing affordable child care for all preschool children. But, since subsidizing child care is an expensive proposition, economists have been studying whether such early childhood interventions yield enough benefits to justify this particular form of government intervention.

One of the most extensively studied programs was a small venture known as the Perry Preschool project conducted in the United States in the 1960s. Children from disadvantaged family environments were randomly assigned into an expensive and high-quality child care program. Despite the substantial costs of the program, benefits measured much later in life were even larger thanks to improvements in education, income, and a reduced propensity to commit crimes (Anderson 2008). It is difficult to draw firm conclusions from this small program, however, since its costs were prohibitive and it only involved a small group of very disadvantaged children. Indeed, evaluations of the more broadly based U.S. program Head Start yield more mixed results. Currie and Thomas (1995) and Deming (2009) find that many of the benefits of the program fade out as children, and in particular African American children, get older.

Closer to home, Baker, Gruber, and Milligan (2008) conclude that Quebec's $5-a-day child care program did not have a positive impact on affected children. In a follow-up paper (Baker, Gruber, and Milligan 2015), they fail to find any positive impacts on outcomes, such as health and criminal behaviour later in life. This is an important finding, since the Quebec program is universal and, therefore, affects a broader cross-section of the population than the aforementioned U.S. programs. So while high-quality daycare programs have been shown to be beneficial for children from disadvantaged backgrounds, the available evidence suggests that such programs have more modest benefits for the rest of the population of preschoolers.

EXHIBIT 9.5

The Benefits of a Distinct Society (III)

"Conscription if necessary, but not necessarily conscription."

These famous words of Prime Minister William Lyon Mackenzie King spoken during World War II reflected his strong desire to avoid controversy over the issue of conscription (the draft). Canada was deeply divided over whether conscription should be implemented, with the fault line at the Quebec border. In a 1942 referendum on whether the federal government should have the power to draft men into military service, over 70 percent of Quebecers were opposed, while an equally large majority in the rest of Canada were in favour. For many reasons, there were sharp differences between Quebec and the rest of Canada with respect to the war effort in Europe. While there was eventually limited conscription at the end of the war, almost all of Canada's soldiers were volunteers, and regional enlistment patterns reflected the "Quebec–the rest of Canada" attitudes toward the war. Of the male population between the ages of 18 and 45 in 1945, 46 percent of men in Ontario had voluntarily served in the war, as against only 23 percent in Quebec. Basically, men outside Quebec were twice as likely to have served in the Canadian Army, Air Force, or Navy.

What does this have to do with estimating the returns to education? In order to ease the return of war veterans into the labour market, the federal government provided strong financial incentives for veterans to attend university or other sorts of training programs. The Veterans Rehabilitation Act (VRA) offered returning soldiers living allowances and covered tuition expenses if they chose to attend university. Because so many more young men from Ontario than Quebec had served as soldiers, they were significantly more likely to be eligible for these benefits. In essence, the combination of the VRA and the differential probability of military service between Ontario and Quebec generates a natural experiment for estimating the impact of university attainment.

In terms of the notation in the text, the population can be divided into two groups; for example, 18- to 21-year-olds (in 1945) from Ontario, and the same age group from Quebec. Because the Ontario men were more likely to be veterans, we would expect they would be more likely to attend university, and thus have higher education than the same-aged men from Quebec. As long as there were no other reasons for differences in labour market outcomes between men in Ontario and Quebec, we could attribute higher lifetime earnings for the Ontario men to their higher education. For example, we would have to assume that the Quebec and Ontario labour markets were otherwise similar, and that veteran status had no independent impact on earnings. David Card and Thomas Lemieux (2001) implement this procedure, including a careful evaluation of the necessary assumptions, to estimate the returns to education. They find that Ontario men born in the mid-1920s (who were 18 to 21 in 1945) were indeed more likely to attend university than comparable men in Quebec, and, moreover, that they were more likely to attend university than those Ontario men born before or immediately after them (who would not have been eligible for VRA benefits). Card and Lemieux estimate that the VRA increased the education of the veteran cohort of Ontario men by 0.2 to 0.4 years. Furthermore, they estimate an OLS rate of return to schooling of 7 percent, but a much higher (14 to 16 percent) rate of return when they exploit the natural experiment. As with the growing body of related research, they find that the conventional OLS estimate of the returns to schooling is, if anything, biased downward (possibly by measurement error), as opposed to inflated by ability bias.

Social Returns to Education

All the empirical studies mentioned up to now look only at the private returns to education. As mentioned at the beginning of the chapter, increased education may also have social benefits or spillover effects on individuals other than the ones undertaking the investment in education. Estimating the magnitude of these social benefits has been an active area of research in recent years. As in the case of the private benefits of education, it is often difficult to separate the causal effect of education from mitigating factors that are difficult to control for (like ability in the case of private returns). The potential problem here is that cities or regions of Canada with a productive advantage may also be attracting more-educated migrants from other parts of the country. For example, if a number of highly productive high-tech firms open plants in a particular area, this may attract highly educated workers. This type of phenomenon may mislead researchers into thinking that a more educated population increases productivity above and beyond what we expect based on private returns only, while causality is in fact running the other way around (high productivity attracts more-educated workers).

To confront these problems, recent studies have exploited natural experiments and other underlying sources of regional differences in educational achievement to estimate the social returns to education. For example, Acemoglu and Angrist (2001) use variation in educational attainment associated with compulsory schooling laws and child labour laws in the United States to examine whether there is evidence of external returns to higher average schooling at the state level. They find small (about 1 percent) social returns in excess of private returns, but these are imprecisely estimated and not significantly different from zero (see also Ciccone and Peri 2006). Because compulsory schooling laws principally influence the amount of secondary schooling received, these results suggest that there are not significant knowledge spillovers associated with additional high school education. Subsequent studies by Moretti (2004a, 2004b) and Iranzo and Peri (2009) find stronger evidence of externalities associated with post-secondary education (graduates of four-year colleges in the United States). Sand (2013) shows, however, that these findings only hold using older data from the 1980s, and that there is no evidence of human capital externalities in more recent data.

A number of studies have also used a variety of natural experiments to show that education has a favourable impact on a variety of outcomes other than earnings. For example, research shows that more-educated people tend to live longer (Lleras-Muney 2005), commit fewer crimes (Lochner and Moretti 2004), and participate more in civic activities, like voting (Milligan, Moretti, and Oreopoulos 2004), than less-educated people, although recent studies show these findings are not as robust as those on the causal effect of education on earnings (Clark and Royer 2013; Stephens and Yang 2014). Comprehensive surveys of empirical work on social returns to education are available in Riddell (2003), Moretti (2004c), and Oreopoulos and Salvanes (2011).

Increased Returns to Education and Inequality

Education and Inequality

In the previous section, we reviewed the econometric quest for an estimate of "the" return to schooling. Increasingly, researchers have recognized that the return to education is not an immutable parameter but varies across individuals (Card 1999) and over time. Labour economists have been particularly interested in the variation of the returns to schooling over time.

Part of the interest derives from a pronounced increase in the returns to schooling during the 1980s and 1990s, especially in the United States. These **increased returns to education** have coincided with more-general increases in income inequality in society: the growth of the "top 1 percent" and the "decline of the middle class," widely discussed in the press. Before examining the evidence, it is worth pausing to clarify the potential linkages between the schooling literature and the wider literature on income inequality. To begin, this entails emphasizing the distinction between wages, earnings, and income.

Most studies of income inequality, starting with Blackburn and Bloom's 1993 comparative study of the United States and Canada, focus on the distribution of family income. This measure includes both the income of all family members (i.e., husbands and wives) and both labour earnings and nonlabour income, such as government transfers and investment income. Increases in individual earnings inequality need not translate into increases in inequality of family income, particularly if husbands' and wives' income changes are offsetting, or if government transfers smooth changes in the earnings distribution. Beach and Slotsve (1996), for example, show that overall income inequality did not increase significantly in Canada during the 1980s, even though men's earnings inequality has increased sharply. By contrast, more-recent evidence from Frenette, Green, and Milligan (2009) and from Heisz and Murphy (2016) shows that family income inequality increased sharply over the 1990s, before stabilizing again since 2000. As Gottschalk (1997) emphasizes, labour economists do not have much understanding, to this point, of how family income (as distinct from individual earnings) evolves in response to changing economic conditions. The determinants of family income are much more complicated. As Picot and Heisz (2000) suggest, the increase in Canadian family income inequality is associated with an increase in the number of lone-parent families, an increasing tendency for high-earning men and women to marry each other (assortative mating), and a decline in income transfers to low-income households during the early and mid-1990s. Of more interest to us in this section, then, is the distribution of labour market earnings, particularly for men.

The link between earnings inequality and returns to schooling is not quite complete. First, earnings are the product of wages and hours, and the changes in hours worked, perhaps due to changes in the incidence of unemployment, may be as important as changes in wages. Some evidence of the importance of this distinction is provided by Beach and Slotsve (1996) and Freeman and Needles (1993).

Second, wages themselves may be becoming more unequal in ways that do not correlate with returns to schooling. In fact, most studies of wage inequality focus on the overall distribution, not the relative wages of high and low educated. For the United States, the distinction is not important. Katz and Autor (1999); Gottschalk (1997); Juhn, Murphy, and Pierce (1993); and Lemieux (2006) show that the trend toward greater wage inequality is the result of both increased returns to schooling and increased inequality within education groups (wage inequality has increased among university graduates, not just between university graduates and high school dropouts).

As it turns out, however, the distinction is much more important in Canada, where there has been a significant rise in wage inequality with a more modest increase in the returns to schooling. Richardson (1997), Picot (1998), and Picot and Heisz (2000) document the sharp increase in wage and earnings inequality in Canada, and the relatively flat time profile for returns to education. More recent evidence by Boudarbat, Lemieux, and Riddell (2006, 2010) indicate that, although returns to schooling have been increasing steadily in Canada, the lion share of the growth in inequality has been happening within education groups.

Picot (1998) and Picot and Heisz (2000) emphasize that earnings differences associated with age, with older workers faring much better than younger, play a more important role than those linked to education in the 1980s and 1990s. These changes have been partly reversed, however, in more recent years (Boudarbat, Lemieux, and Riddell 2010). Nonetheless, there appears to be an increase in the returns to age, possibly reflecting increased returns to labour market experience, itself a form of human capital. However, as is carefully illustrated by Beaudry and Green (2000), this is not the case. Instead, the returns to labour market experience have been largely constant, but the entry position of younger workers has been steadily deteriorating, whatever their education level. Thus, earnings differences between young and old reflect possibly permanent "cohort effects" instead of increased returns to aging. Today's young workers have no reason to expect that their earnings will rise to the level of those of current older workers.

In addition to documenting the trends and patterns in the returns to skill (or wage inequality), many studies attempt to provide an explanation. Excellent summaries of these explanations are provided in Johnson (1997), Topel (1997), Katz and Autor (1999), Goldin and Katz (2008), and Autor (2014) for the United States, and Fortin et al. (2012) for Canada. The explanations can most easily be cast in the context of a two-sector supply and demand framework, with markets for skilled and unskilled labour. First, increases in the relative supply of unskilled labour might depress the wages of the unskilled. Second, increases in the relative demand for skilled workers would raise their wages. Two hypotheses have been offered for an increase in the demand for skilled workers. Skill-biased technological change in favour of skilled workers would increase their relative demand. This would occur if new technologies (such as computers) and educated labour were complements in production. Alternatively, increased globalization and competition from low-skilled labour in developing countries might reduce the demand for less-skilled labour domestically. A third distinct possibility lies outside the supply and demand framework; labour market institutions, like minimum wages or the influence of trade unions, may have changed in a way that hurts the unskilled more than the skilled. For example, declines in the real minimum wage (documented in Chapter 7) and in the degree of unionization (documented in Chapter 14) may have adversely affected the wages of the less skilled.

Increasing Returns to Education Since 1980

In the first few decades of the post–WW II period, the monetary return to education remained relatively stable in both Canada and the United States. The most important development during this period was a modest decline in the rate of return to education during the 1970s. One explanation of this phenomenon was the substantial increase in the proportion of the population going to university, particularly the entry into the labour force of the baby boom generation during the 1970s. Freeman (1976) argued that the demand for educated workers also declined, so that not all of the change in relative earnings could be attributed to temporary developments on the supply side. Dooley (1986) examined these competing explanations in the Canadian setting using data for the period 1971–1981. He concluded that the entry of the large baby boom cohort during this period did lower earnings growth for this group, but that this demographic effect could not account for the observed narrowing of earnings differentials by level of education. Dooley's results, thus, suggest that demand-side forces may also have played a role.

This declining trend was abruptly reversed in the 1980s. This reversal was especially sharp in the United States. For instance, Katz and Murphy (1992) show the increasing skill premium for both observable and unobservable skill (university education), though Lemieux (2006) points out that unobservable skills have played a minor role since about 1990. For Canada, Freeman and Needles (1993); Bar-Or et al. (1995); and Murphy, Riddell, and Romer (1998) conclude there was little change in returns to schooling in the 1980s and early 1990s. More-recent evidence shows, however, that the return to education has increased substantially since the mid-1990s. In particular, Boudarbat, Lemieux, and Riddell (2010) show that the gap between university and high school educated men increased by about 5 percentage points during the period 1980 to 2005. The most recent evidence indicates, however, that returns to schooling have been declining since 2005 (Frenette and Morissette 2014; Fortin and Lemieux 2015). The Canadian-specific development (no such decline happened in the United States) appears to be linked to the extractive resources (mostly oil and gas) boom that increased the demand for "middle-skill" jobs and, thus, favoured high school graduates over university graduates.

Most empirical research has concentrated on explaining the increased returns to education in the United States. Empirical studies, generally, attempt to sort out the relative contribution of demand and supply factors. On the demand side, the shift in employment out of heavy manufacturing industries and toward financial and business services has brought about a decline in demand for labour in semi-skilled and unskilled blue-collar jobs and an increase in demand for skilled, educated workers in the service sector. The underlying source of this change in demand remains a subject of debate. On the supply side, there were fewer educated baby boomers graduating and entering the United States labour force during the 1980s.

While there is no consensus on the relative contribution of the different supply- and demand-side factors, there is reasonable agreement that demand-side factors were most important, especially in the 1980s (Bound and Johnson 1992; Katz and Murphy 1992; Murphy and Welch 1992; Katz and Autor 1999). That is, the technological change and industrial restructuring that occurred was biased in favour of more-skilled and more-educated workers. As well, the increased international competition and imports tended to adversely affect low-wage workers, while increased exports positively affect higher-wage workers. On the supply side, there was a slower growth in the influx of educated college graduates so that higher wages were not constrained by that factor in the 1980s.

While there is some agreement as to the overall importance of demand factors (i.e., there is agreement that supply factors cannot explain most of the increase in inequality), there remains disagreement as to which demand factors were most important. A first set of studies published in the 1990s proceeded by attempting to relate changes in the skill premium across occupational or industry groups. Because technology is inherently unobservable, it tends to be a "residual" explanation, while trade-based explanations can be more directly evaluated with trade data. Bound and Johnson (1992) and Johnson (1997) emphasize the inability of trade to explain changes in the wage structure, and argue that skill-biased technological change is the most likely explanation. Goldin and Katz (1996) look at the broader patterns of technological change in the 20th century. They note, first of all, that technological change need not be biased in favour of high-skilled labour. The technological innovations of the industrial revolution tended to hurt skilled artisans in favour of unskilled labour working in factories. However, the 20th century saw most technological change complementary with skill; that is, the technological innovations in production resulted in relative increases in the demand for skilled labour.

Krueger (1993) was the first to look more explicitly at the role of computer technologies in the growth in the return to schooling. He finds that employees who work with computers, all else equal, have higher wages. As it turns out, however, the observed linkage between use of computers and wages may have been spurious, reflecting other unobserved job characteristics. Using different data from Krueger, a study by DiNardo and Pischke (1997) shows that similar finding exist for using pencils or telephones on the job, suggesting that Krueger's "computer use" may have been proxying for the type of job, rather than the impact of technology on wages. Another challenge to the technological change explanation is that inequality grew much less in the 1990s than in the 1980s (Card and DiNardo 2002; Beaudry and Green 2005). This is puzzling since most indicators suggest that technological change was more pronounced in the 1990s than in the 1980s.

In response to these shortcomings, more-recent studies have refined the technological change explanation by pointing out that one needs to go beyond the narrow concept of skills to really understand how new information and communication technologies have reshaped the labour market. Autor, Levy, and Murnane (2003) introduce the concept of routine-biased technological change. The idea is that jobs where workers perform routine tasks which can be done by a computer or robotic machinery instead are the ones that are the most affected (negatively) by technological change. Interestingly, these jobs are concentrated in the middle of the wage distribution, which helps explain the **polarization of wages** phenomena that has been documented in the United States during the 1990s. Autor and Acemoglu (2011) argue that better understanding the connection between wages, skills, and the task content of jobs (routine dimension, etc.) is essential for understanding how these technologies have resulted in increasing earnings inequality. Looking across local labour markets, Autor and Dorn (2013) find that the "routinization" hypothesis helps explain polarization in both wages and employment observed since the early 1990s. Green and Sand (2015) also find a substantial increase in employment polarization in Canada, but show that this did not translate into wage polarization as in the United States. Manning, Goos, and Salomons (2014) show pervasive evidence of employment polarization across 16 Western European countries, though, as in Canada, there is little evidence of wage polarization in these countries.

Despite these differences, one common development in Canada and the United States is the large growth of the earnings of the "top 1 percent" relative to rest of the workforce. Saez and Veall (2005) and Veall (2012) show that income and earnings are increasingly concentrated at the top of the distribution, though the changes have not been as dramatic in Canada as in the United States. Lemieux and Riddell (2016) show that education has been playing an important role in these changes, as workers in the top 1 percent are substantially more educated then the rest of the population. For instance, they show that 67 percent of workers in the top 1 percent have at least a bachelor's degree, compared to only 21 percent for the entire population.

It remains unclear, however, why earnings at the very top have increased so much more than in the rest of the labour market. The puzzle gets deeper when looking at broad set of countries. For example, Atkinson, Piketty, and Saez (2011) show that, while income concentration at the top has increased substantially in Canada, the United States, and the United Kingdom, it has hardly changed at all in countries such as France, Germany, and Japan. This suggests that simple explanations based on technological change or the routinization hypothesis cannot account for surprisingly diverse patterns of inequality change across countries. Other explanations need to be considered as well.

One set of alternative explanations has to do with the role of labour market institutions. In particular, DiNardo, Fortin, and Lemieux (1996) and Fortin and Lemieux (1997) show that the decline in unionization in the United States contributed considerably to the relative decline in the fortunes of less-skilled workers. DiNardo and Lemieux (1997) and Donald, Green, and Paarsch (2000) compare earnings distributions in Canada and the United States, and show that the lower-wage inequality in Canada derives from the greater degree of unionization. DiNardo and Lemieux argue that most of the greater increase in wage inequality during the 1980s (*not* returns to schooling) can be explained by the relative decline in unions in the United States. A follow-up study by Card, Lemieux, and Riddell (2004) shows, however, that unionization has been declining as fast in Canada as in the United States during the 1990s and early 2000s. This suggests that other factors beside unionization must, thus, be invoked to explain why inequality increased more in the United States than in Canada over the last 10 to 15 years.

Going even further down the skill distribution, DiNardo, Fortin, and Lemieux also show that the real decline in the legislated minimum wage was associated with the widening of the wage distribution. Fortin and Lemieux (2015) show that increases in the real value of the minimum wage in Canada since about 2005 have helped increase wages at the bottom of the wage distribution and reduce wage inequality. More generally, Lemieux (2008, 2011) argues that institutions help explain important cross-country differences in the growth in inequality over the last few decades.

Taken together, these findings raise many questions for policymakers. On the one hand, increased returns to schooling make it even more imperative to encourage individuals to acquire education. The penalty for dropping out of high school is becoming increasingly large. In light of these findings, Goldin and Katz (2008) suggest that the single easiest way to improve the income distribution may be to reduce inequality in schooling attainment by encouraging more people to obtain post-secondary education. On the other hand, returns to schooling have been increasing, even with dramatic increases in university enrolment. Given that schooling is one of the most important factors leading to income inequality, and that the private returns to schooling have increased significantly, subsidies to education may (if poorly directed) actually contribute to a widening of the income distribution. Foley and Green (2016) argue that targeting expenditures on early childhood development and secondary school toward low-income households has greater potential to reduce inequality both in the long term and across generations.

LO5 Training

Like education, training is a form of investment in human capital in which costs are incurred in the present in the anticipation of benefits in the future. The benefits accrue because training imparts skills that raise the worker's productivity and, thus, value in the labour market.

In this section, we focus on some *economic* aspects of training rather than on an institutional description of training in Canada. The main focus of our analysis is to shed light on the following questions: Who pays for training? Is a government subsidy warranted? How should training be evaluated?

Who Pays?

In his classic work on the subject, Becker (1964, pp. 11–28) distinguishes between **general training** and **specific training**. General training is training that can be used in various firms, not just in those that provide the training. Consequently, in a competitive market, firms will bid for this training by offering a higher wage equal to the value of the training. Since competition ensures that the trainee reaps the benefits of general training in the form of higher earnings, then the trainee would be willing to bear the cost of training as long as benefits exceed costs. If a company were to bear the cost of such training, it would still have to bid against other companies for the services of the trainee.

This argument is illustrated in Figure 9.6(a). In the absence of training, the individual can earn the alternative wage W_a equal to the value of marginal product without training (VMP_a). During the training period, the value of the worker's output is VMP_t, which could be zero. After training, the worker's value to *any* firm in this labour market rises to VMP*. The costs and benefits are as shown. If the investment is worthwhile, the employee can finance the training and earn the benefits by being paid a wage equal to the VMP at each point in time; that is, the worker receives W_t = VMP during training and W* = VMP* after the training period. The firm could incur the costs and hope to reap the benefits by paying the worker W_a before and after training. However, because the employee can earn W* elsewhere, the firm's strategy won't work. Thus, in the absence of bonding arrangements (as are used for limited periods in the armed forces for certain types of general training, such as pilot training), general training will be financed by employees.

With specific training, however, the training is useful only in the company that provides the training. Consequently, other companies have no incentive to pay higher earnings for such training and the trainee would not bear the cost because of an inability to reap the benefits in the form of higher earnings. The sponsoring company, however, would bear the costs, providing these exceed the benefits. In addition, the sponsoring company would not have to pay a higher wage for those persons with specific training, since other firms are not competing for such trainees.

This case is also illustrated in Figure 9.6(a). The firm pays the alternative wage, W_a, during and after training, incurring costs of $W_a - VMP_t$ during the training period and receiving benefits of VMP* $- W_a$ after the completion of training.

Specific human capital may also be a shared investment. This arrangement is particularly likely when there is some uncertainty about the continuation of the employment relationship due to shifts in labour demand affecting the worker's VMP, and shifts in supply affecting the alternative wage, W_a. If the sponsoring company pays for the specific training, as shown in Figure 9.6(a), it faces the risk that the employee may quit at some point after the training period, thus reducing the employer's anticipated return on the investment. Because the worker is receiving no more than the alternative wage, the cost of quitting is low. Even a small increase in W_a could cause the worker to go elsewhere. However, the cost to the company is high, because the trained employee is worth more to the firm than he or she is being paid. In these circumstances, the sponsoring company may pay trainees a wage premium to reduce their turnover and, hence, to increase the probability that the company will recoup its investment costs. To compensate for the wage premium, the firm may lower the wage paid during the training period, in which case the two parties share the costs and benefits of training.

This situation is shown in Figure 9.6(b). The firm pays $W_t < W_a$ during the training period and W* $> W_a$ after training. Both parties incur costs and reap benefits as shown. The shared investment minimizes the risk that either party will wish to terminate the employment relation, because both the employer and employee are earning rents after the completion of training. The employer's rents of VMP* $-$ W* each period reduce the risk that the employee will be laid off due to a decline in demand. Only when the worker's value to the firm falls below W* will the firm consider layoffs. The employee's rents of W* $- W_a$ each period reduce the risk that the employee will quit in response to an improvement in labour market opportunities. Only when the alternative wage rises above W* will the employee consider quitting.

This analysis indicates that specific human capital investments provide an incentive for firms and workers to maintain their employment relationship in the face of external shocks to demand and supply. The return on the shared investment acts like glue keeping the two parties together. These incentives for long-term employment relationships and their consequences are discussed further in Chapter 17 in the context of implicit contracts, in Chapter 13 in the context of deferred compensation, and in Chapter 6 in the context of layoffs.

In competitive markets, then, trainees will pay for general training, whereas specific training investments may be paid by the sponsoring company or shared by the two parties. The form of payment may be subtle, as, for example, when trainees in an apprenticeship program forgo earnings by accepting a lower wage rate during the training period, or when companies forgo some output from workers when they provide them with on-the-job training.

The sharp distinction made in panels (a) and (b) of Figure 9.6 between the training and post-training periods may not hold in practice. Much on-the-job training is informal and takes place gradually as employees learn different facets of their job and its place in the overall organization. In these circumstances, earnings can be expected to rise gradually, as shown in Figure 9.6(c), rather than abruptly. The concave shape of the earnings profile reflects the assumption that there are diminishing returns to on-the-job training and work experience. As noted previously, this shape is typical of age-earnings profiles (see Figure 9.4).

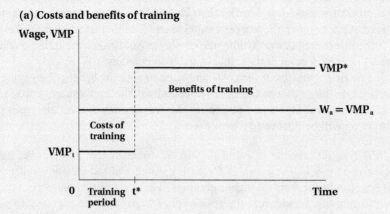

(a) Costs and benefits of training

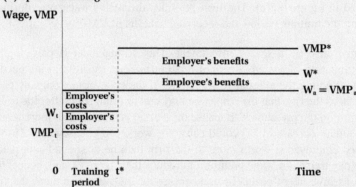

(b) Specific training as a shared investment

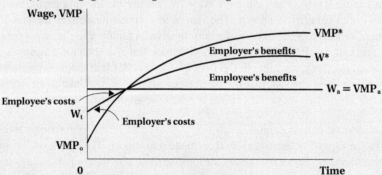

(c) Earnings growth with gradual training

Figure 9.6 Costs, Benefits, and Financing of Training

Panel (a) illustrates the costs and benefits of training. In the absence of training, a worker has productivity VMP_a and can earn W_a elsewhere. After period t^* of training with reduced productivity, VMP_t, the worker's productivity increases to VMP^*. With general training, the firm has no incentive to pay for training, since, post-training, the worker can be poached by other firms for a wage up to VMP^*. As a result, the worker implicitly pays for all training costs by accepting a wage, VMPt, below her alternative without training, W_a.

When the human capital is firm specific, the firm can finance some of the training without concern that the employee will be poached, since her additional training is of no value to other firms. Panel (b) shows the case where the employer and employee share the costs and benefits of the investment in specific training. Post-training, the employee is paid W^*, which is higher than her alternative wage, so she is less likely to quit. In return, the employee helps pay for the training by accepting a lower wage, W_t, during the training period. In panel (c), earnings rise and training is offered more gradually. The configuration of wages and marginal product is such that employees accept lower wages early in their career in return for higher productivity and wages later on.

In practice, the distinction between general and specific training can be difficult to make. Training often contains elements of both. Indeed, Parent (1999) shows that training is often specific to the industry in which a worker in employed. That type of training will remain valuable when the worker gets another job in the same industry, but not if she moves to a different industrial sector. Likewise, Kambourov and Manovskii (2009) argue that a fair amount of training is specific to the occupation of the worker, while Robinson and Poletaev (2008) and Gathmann and Schoenberg (2010) show that human capital specificity is linked to the type of tasks performed on the job, which vary a fair amount across occupations. These cases illustrate that, in practice, training cannot be strictly divided into a component that is completely general and one which is specific to the firm where the training is undertaken. Nonetheless, the distinction between general and specific training is useful for conceptual purposes.

Appropriate Role of Government

If trainees will pay for and benefit from general training, and sponsoring companies and employees will share the costs and benefits of specific training, why should governments be involved in the training process? In other words, are there situations when the private, unregulated market does not provide a socially optimal amount of training?

This possibility may exist for trainees who cannot afford to purchase training (perhaps by accepting a lower wage during the training period) and who cannot borrow because of an inability to use their human capital (future earnings) as collateral for a loan. Imperfect information, regulatory restrictions, or contract enforceability problems may prevent private institutional arrangements like apprenticeships from fully developing to provide the optimal amount of training (see Gillian Hamilton 1995, 1996, and 2000 for a discussion of these issues in the context of apprenticeship contracts in early 19th-century Montreal, and Gunderson and Krashinsky 2015, for recent estimates of the returns to apprenticeship training in Canada).

These labour market imperfections likely explain why firms often appear to be paying for some general training. For instance, Acemoglu and Pischke (1998) analyze the case of the successful German apprenticeship system where training is quite general but firms, nonetheless, pay for most of it. They argue that it is profitable for firms to train their workers as others firm are unlikely to "poach" trained workers because of imperfect information in the labour market. Dustmann and Schoenberg (2012) argue that training may be too complex to be specified in a legally enforceable contract, and that firm-based training is more common in countries like Germany where commitment to training provision is more widespread. In a related contribution, Acemoglu and Pischke (1999) show that when wages are compressed because of institutions, such as unions or minimum wages, wages don't fully reflect the increase in productivity that comes with general training. As a result, workers don't have a strong incentive to invest in general training, and governments (or firms) can play a useful role by subsidizing investments in general training.

A suboptimal amount of general training may also be provided by companies where on-the-job training is a natural by-product of their production process. Workers simply acquire training in their everyday work tasks. However, because it is difficult to know how much training they are acquiring and at what cost, they may be reluctant to pay for such training. In these circumstances, training may have public-good characteristics in that it is available to all workers, and yet it is difficult to exclude those who don't pay for the training. To be sure, only those who are willing to work for lower wages could be hired (and in this way nonpayers are excluded). However, the indirect nature of the training makes it difficult for the purchasers to know how much training they are acquiring.

Evaluation of Government Training Programs

Our discussion to this point makes clear the importance of education and training in determining individual earnings. It is not surprising that policymakers view training as an important tool, whether or not some of the theoretical arguments in favour of government intervention hold. Given the popularity of proposed training programs, one would imagine that there was evidence that these programs were cost effective, even if they only displaced the private provision of training. Perhaps surprisingly, the evidence in support of government training programs is quite mixed.

The evaluation of government training programs provides a classic example of the difficulties of performing reliable **program evaluation**. Training is evaluated by the extent to which it improves an individual's earnings, either by increasing his wage rate or by improving his chances of obtaining a job in the first place. The difficulty, which we have encountered before, is that we never observe what the trained individual's earnings would have been in the absence of training. We observe the **treatment group** but we may not have a plausible **control group**. Consider first (perhaps cynically) a politician's measure of the effectiveness of training; that is, a comparison of an individual's earnings before and after training:

$$Y_{After} - Y_{Before}$$

There are several reasons this is a poor measure of the impact of training. Each problem suggests a different solution.

First, the individual's earnings may have been especially low before training. Individuals may be enrolled in programs when they have experienced bad luck in the labour market. On average, even if training had no effect, we would expect these individuals' earnings to revert to their long-run value. Thus, we may attribute an increase in earnings to a "mean reverting" rebound in earnings that would have occurred anyway. The obvious remedy for this problem is to use an appropriate comparison group, where the group comprises individuals who also had extraordinarily low earnings, but did not obtain training. This is a special case of the more general problem plaguing such estimates of the impact of training; that is, the trainees may have experienced wage growth in the absence of training. Whether it is because low earnings are individually transitory or because there are economy-wide trends upon which trainees can ride, for some individuals we might observe increases in earnings that have nothing to do with training. This problem, again, has a straightforward solution; that is, earnings growth of the trainees must be compared to a carefully selected comparison group of individuals who did not receive training. An estimate of the effect of training on earnings would then be the "difference-in-differences":

$$\left(Y_{After} - Y_{Before} \right)_{Trained} - \left(Y_{After} - Y_{Before} \right)_{Not\ Trained}$$

To address the problems just described, a data set with detailed information on individuals who did not receive training, but who are otherwise comparable to those who did, would be sufficient to construct a control group.

Unfortunately, there are difficulties in implementing such a procedure, because one can never obtain data on the "same types" of individuals without an experiment. There are good reasons to believe that individuals who receive training and those who do not will differ in unobservable ways that lead to an overstatement of the impact of training. First, if enrolment in training programs requires initiative on the part of the trainee, then this self-selection will yield a pool of trainees more likely to have these positive, unobservable characteristics than the pool of nontrained individuals. Individuals may choose to enrol in training programs if they have private information suggesting they would particularly benefit. The same sort of selection may operate on the part of the training providers. Given resource limitations, administrators of training programs will naturally choose to offer training to those individuals most likely to succeed. It would then be inappropriate to assign the difference in earnings between trained and untrained individuals entirely to training. Part of the difference may be the result of innate differences in the earnings capacities of the individuals.

The best solution to this evaluation problem is to conduct an experiment, randomly assigning individuals into training programs or control groups, then following up their labour market outcomes. Such experiments have been conducted in both Canada and the United States, and, increasingly, in European countries. LaLonde (1986) demonstrates some of the advantages of employing these experiments instead of artificially constructing control groups, though Heckman and Smith (1995) point out that these experiments are no panacea, and in fact have their own shortcomings. In fact, as Heckman, Lalonde, and Smith (1999) emphasize, whatever procedure is used, the most important determinant of the reliability of the evaluation is the careful construction of a control or comparison group. If chosen properly, a nonexperimental comparison group can serve almost as well as an experimental one.

LaLonde (1995) and Heckman, LaLonde, and Smith (1999) review the empirical results from evaluating a variety of training programs in the United States, employing experimental and nonexperimental (econometric) procedures. The results (in terms of cost effectiveness) vary by program. Training is directed to two distinct groups: disadvantaged workers and dislocated, or displaced, workers. Disadvantaged workers tend to be young, and come from poor backgrounds. The U.S. evidence suggests that there are modest returns to training for disadvantaged women, but little positive evidence for men. Displaced workers tend to be older, blue-collar men displaced from relatively high-paying jobs. This is the group often discussed when governments propose adjustment programs in response to the impact of globalization or other substantial changes in market structure. LaLonde (1995) and Heckman, LaLonde, and Smith (1999) find only limited evidence that training programs help these individuals.

More recently, Card, Kluve, and Weber (2010, 2015) take a broader look at these issues by conducting a meta-analysis study of approximately 200 recent econometric evaluations of **active labour market programs** (including training programs) from around the world. They find that programs emphasizing human capital accumulation (e.g., training programs) have a larger impact than other active labour market programs. Although impacts are close to zero in the short run, they become more positive two to three years after completion of the program. They also find, like Heckman, LaLonde, and Smith, that training programs tend to have a larger impact for women than for men. An interesting new finding is that training programs appear to be quite effective for the long-term unemployed, and to be more effective in recessionary environments. Reassuringly, Card, Kluve, and Weber show that experimental and nonexperimental studies yield similar estimates of the impact of training programs. On balance, Card, Kluve, and Weber find that training programs appear to be more effective than is suggested by earlier U.S. evidence. Nonetheless, it is unlikely that training programs lasting a few months will provide the same benefits as much longer full-time university programs and will vault large numbers of individuals out of poverty or restore skilled workers' years of lost industry-specific human capital.

Summary

- The individual decision to acquire education can be treated like any investment. The human capital investment decision is based on a comparison of the present value of the net benefits of obtaining varying levels of education. The optimal choice will maximize the present value of net benefits, accounting for the direct costs of schooling as well as the opportunity cost of the time spent in school.

- Because it is costly for people to acquire education, workers will need to be compensated in the labour market by higher wages in order to justify the investment in additional human capital. As long as firms are willing to pay these higher wages (because higher-educated workers are more productive), there will be a positive return to education.

- It is also possible for wages to be positively related to education even if education does not improve individual productivity. This can occur when education serves as a signal for underlying ability, and firms cannot otherwise distinguish between high- and low-quality workers. As long as education is correlated with underlying ability, firms will be willing to pay for more highly educated workers.

- The empirical evidence strongly shows that, on average, earnings increase with education. One convenient way to summarize the relationship between earnings and education is through the human capital earnings function. The human capital earnings function relates the log of earnings to the level of education, and other covariates like potential labour market experience. The coefficient on years of schooling in this equation is called the "return to schooling."

- An important interpretation problem arises in determining whether the estimated returns to schooling represent the "causal" effect of schooling on earnings. The estimated coefficient may overstate the true causal effect, if (for example) more-highly educated individuals would have earned more than less-educated individuals even with the same amount of schooling as the less educated. This problem of "ability bias" has been addressed by a number of studies that exploit natural experiments, where it is believed that differences in schooling are not driven by differences in labour market ability.

- A significant amount of human capital investment occurs through on-the-job training. However, whether the worker or the firm pays for this human capital depends on whether the training yields general or firm-specific human capital. The firm will not pay for general human capital, since workers can be poached away by other firms. The poaching problem does not exist for firm-specific training. However, even with firm-specific human capital, the firm and worker may share the investment, so that the worker will have an incentive to remain with the firm after training.

- Economists and policymakers often want to know whether government training programs improve the incomes of program participants. However, evaluation of these programs requires a carefully constructed "control group," ideally the product of a formal experiment, since a comparison of trainees earnings before and after the training program may overstate the benefits of the training.

Keywords

ability bias	perfect capital markets
active labour market programs	polarization of wages
age-earnings profile	potential experience
control group	private costs and benefits
general training	program evaluation
human capital earnings function	real costs
human capital investment decision	returns to schooling
human capital theory	signalling
increased returns to education	social costs and benefits
internal rate of return	specific training
natural experiment	transfer costs
opportunity cost	treatment group

Review Questions

1. Discuss the parallels between physical capital and human capital.

2. How would you evaluate the extent to which acquiring a university education is a sound investment, economically? Be precise in the information you would require and exactly what you would do with it.

3. You have been asked to evaluate an on-the-job training program in a particular company. Specify exactly what sort of information you require, and what you would do with it.

4. The federal government supports a variety of human resource programs, including education, training, mobility, labour market information, and health. Could you propose any techniques that may be useful to suggesting how resources should be allocated to the various functions?

5. Should governments subsidize human resource programs? If so, why? Be precise in your answer by indicating where, if anywhere, the private market may fail to yield a socially optimal amount of human resource development.

6. Give an example of each of the following as errors in a cost-benefit calculation: ignoring opportunity cost, failing to discount benefits, double counting, considering sunk cost with no alternative value, ignoring a real externality, considering a pecuniary externality, and ignoring consumption benefits.

7. Compare the virtues of on-the-job versus institutional training.

8. Should the government subsidize higher education in the case where schooling is a valuable signal of ability but private returns are zero? How would your answer change if there were also large social returns to schooling?

Problems

1. Assume that you are deciding whether to acquire a four-year university degree. Your only consideration at this moment is the degree as an investment for yourself. Costs per year are tuition fees of $600 and books at $100. The government also pays to the university an equivalent amount to your tuition fees to cover the real cost. If you didn't go to university, you could earn $6000 per year as an acrobat. With a university degree, however, you know that you can earn $10,000 per year as an acrobat. Because of the nature of your chosen occupation, your time horizon for the investment decision is exactly 10 years after university; that is, if the investment is to be worthwhile, it must be so within a 10-year period after graduation. The market rate of interest is 5 percent. Would you make the investment in a degree?

2. "You can't teach an old dog new tricks—in fact, you shouldn't." Discuss.

3. Madeleine is a high school graduate deciding whether to go to university. She (like everyone else) lives for two periods after high school. In the first period, she can work (without university) for a salary of Y_H, or she can attend university. If she attends university, she must pay $5000 in fees (tuition, books), but she will also earn $5000 from a summer job. In the second period, she will continue to earn Y_H if she did not attend university, or she will earn Y_U if she went to university. The interest rate at which money can be borrowed or invested is r.

   Show that she will attend university if

   $$Y_U > (2 + r)Y_H$$

   Explain how an increase in the interest rate would affect her decision to attend university.

4. This question continues the analysis of Madeleine's decision to attend university (from Probem 3).

   In order to decide whether to attend university, she needs to know whether the condition (in Problem 3) is true, and, more generally, how much a university education would increase her earnings.

   She has a well-designed labour force survey with information on earnings, education, and other sociodemographic characteristics. If she divides her sample into two groups, 1 and 2, she can estimate the returns to schooling (per year) with the following estimator:

   $$\hat{\beta} = \frac{\overline{Y}_1 - \overline{Y}_2}{\overline{S}_1 - \overline{S}_2}$$

   where $\overline{Y}_j$ is average individual earnings from group j, and $\overline{S}_j$ is the average level of schooling for individuals in group j. Suppose that the true model of earnings for groups 1 and 2 is given by

   $$Y_i + \alpha + \beta S_i + \varepsilon_i$$

   a. Her first instinct is to divide the sample into two groups: those with a four-year university degree (S_U), and those with only high school (S_H). Derive the conditions under which her estimator will yield an unbiased (i.e., correct, on average) estimate of β, and interpret.

   b. Assume that she has information on each individual's parent's income. Assume also that individuals from poorer families face higher borrowing costs than those from richer ones. How might this affect individual university attainment decisions? Use the condition in Problem 3. How might she exploit this information in order to obtain an unbiased estimate of β? Be sure to discuss the necessary assumptions for this strategy to work.

5. Yun has just finished high school. He has three periods of time left in his working life, and is considering three career options:

   • Obtain a job in a hotel, earning $20,000 per year for each of the remaining three periods of his working life.

   • Attend community college, earning a diploma in human resources. The diploma takes one period to complete, with tuition fees equal to $5000. After graduation, he will earn $50,000 per year for the remaining two periods of his life.

   • Attend university to obtain his Ph.D. in art history. The degree takes two periods to complete, with tuition fees of $10,000 per period. After graduation, he will earn $90,000 per year for the one remaining period of his working life.

   Assume that the interest rate is 10 percent per period.

   a. Which career path should he follow?

   b. Yun has always wanted to be an art historian. If he chooses to be an art historian, what is the implicit consumption value he places on being an art historian?

   c. Who among the population is likely to choose this career path—the children of rich or of poor parents? Why?

   d. Should the government subsidize tuition fees for art history? Why or why not?

6. Assume that there are two types of workers in equal proportion (i.e., 50 percent of each type). High-ability workers have productivity of $50,000, while low-ability workers have productivity of $30,000. Firms will pay workers their marginal product, but they cannot distinguish between the two types of workers. If firms cannot distinguish between workers, they must pay all workers the same wage, equal to the average marginal product. In equilibrium, firms must earn zero profits.

   However, workers can buy S units of education. The cost to high-ability workers of acquiring S units of education is $S/2, and for low-ability workers, it is $S. Education has no impact on workers' marginal products.

   a. What is the equilibrium wage rate for the high- and low-ability workers in the absence of education; that is, assuming that education is unaffordable to either the high- or the low-ability workers?

   b. Now assume that education is available as described. Assume that firms use the following rules to pay workers:

   If S < 31,000, then pay the worker $30,000

   If S ≥ 31,000, then pay the worker $50,000

   How much education will the high- and low-ability workers obtain, and what will be their wages? Provide a careful explanation and diagram.

   c. Returning to the theoretical model, in an effort to encourage low-ability workers to obtain schooling, the government subsidizes and reforms education so that the cost of schooling is reduced. The cost to high-ability workers is now $S/3, and to low ability, $S/2.

   Show that the pay scheme adopted by firms in part (a) does not yield an equilibrium. What is the equilibrium level of schooling and education?

7. A researcher wishes to evaluate the effectiveness of a one-year job skills training program for disadvantaged women. She has surveyed the women as they entered the training program in January 2005, and then one year after the end of the program, in January 2007, obtaining estimates of their average earnings in each year. The women's average earnings in January 2005 were $10,000, and they were $15,000 in January 2007.

   a. "A reasonable estimate of the impact of the training program is that it raised trainee earnings by $5000." Critically evaluate this statement.

   b. The researcher consults her annual reports from Statistics Canada, and reads that the average full-year, full-time female worker in Canada had earnings of $35,000 in January 2005, and $38,000 in January 2007. Can she use this information to construct a better estimate of the impact of training? Can you suggest a better comparison group? Explain.

8. In the simplest human capital investment model, people know exactly what the rate of return to their investment is. In reality, however, there is considerable uncertainty surrounding the actual rate of return. Consider the case of Janelle who needs to borrow $25,000 to go to university and get a degree. Janelle thinks that there is a 50 percent chance that the degree will enable her to get a "good job" paying $10,000 more a year once she has graduated. She also thinks, however, that there is a 50 percent chance that her investment won't pay out at all. Now consider two ways in which she can borrow the $25,000 she needs to go to university

    a. Take on a standard student loan that needs to be repaid at a rate of $2500 per year after she has graduated.

    b. Take on an income-contingent loan (ICL) where she has to pay back $5000 per year if she gets the good job, but where she has nothing to pay back if she does not get that job.

        i. Show that both the expected cost (repayments of loan or ICL) and benefits (increased earnings) are the same under the standard loan and the ICL. Discuss why Janelle will be indifferent between the two choices provided that she is "risk neutral." (Risk-neutral agents care only about expected values. For example, they are indifferent between receiving $1 for sure and receiving a ticket from a lottery with a 1 percent probability of winning a $100 prize.)

        ii. Like most people, however, Janelle would like to protect herself against risk. This is the reason people buy insurance against all types of adverse events. How do the net benefits (earnings gain minus repayment costs) compare under the standard loan and the ICL if Janelle was to get the good job after graduation? How do they compare if she doesn't get the good job? Using these figures, explain why Janelle may decide to go to university when an ICL is available, but may decide not to go to university when only a standard loan is available.

Endnotes

1. This discussion ignores the possible real resource costs involved in operating and financing unemployment insurance or social assistance programs. If savings in unemployment insurance or social assistance payments reduce the real resources required to operate and finance these programs, then a real externality is involved in addition to the transfer externality.

2. This formula is similar to one used to compute the present value of a very long-term bond that pays forever a stream of interest income I. In that case, the present value of the bond is known to be I/r. By analogy, we can think here that human capital (high school education in this case) produces a stream of income Y over time. Note that the formula exactly holds when the retirement age goes to infinity. In practice, the approximation is very good with normal retirement ages (e.g., T = 60 or 65) and realistic interest rates of around 5 percent.

3. Age alone might be a poor proxy for labour market experience, since individuals who do not attend school can obtain additional human capital through work experience (as long as they are working). Comparing earnings by education level as in Figure 9.5 (controlling for age alone) would then involve comparing individuals who differed not only by education, but also systematically by work experience. The difference in earnings due to difference in education would be understated, since higher-education individuals also had lower work experience (on average).

4. See Card (1999) for a thorough discussion of these issues and a review of the empirical literature on the estimation of returns to schooling.

5. See Ashenfelter and Krueger (1994) and Ashenfelter and Rouse (1998) for descriptions of the Princeton Twins Survey and a presentation of the empirical evidence.

6. David Card (1995b) and (1999) provides some preliminary exploration of alternative hypotheses.

PORTRAIT IMAGES ASIA/Shutterstock.com

CHAPTER 10

Wage Structures across Markets

LEARNING OBJECTIVES

LO1 Discuss the large differences in wages paid to different workers depending on the kind of job they hold (industry and occupation) and where they work (region and size of the firm).

LO2 Explain the several factors that account for the wage differences across labour markets, including supply and demand factors and other explanations, such as compensating wages differences, institutional rigidities, and short-run disequilibrium.

LO3 Discuss how the Roy model provides a more general approach to wage setting when different workers have different levels of skills and productive abilities.

LO4 Explain how interindustry wage differentials may be generated by "efficiency wages," whereby firms pay higher wages because worker productivity depends on the wage rate.

LO5 Learn that the public sector is one particularly large industry (over one-fifth of employment in Canada) that pays higher wages and other forms of compensation than do other industries.

MAIN QUESTIONS

- Why might wages vary across labour markets, even among apparently identical workers?

- Are public sector workers overpaid?

- Why are wages higher in Alberta than in Ontario?

- What are the main determinants of the decision to migrate from one province to another?

- Large firms pay higher wages to workers than do small firms. Can this be taken as evidence against the neoclassical supply and demand model of the labour market?

- Which industries and occupations provide the highest wages for their workers? Can these higher wages be accounted for by differences in the skills of the workers?

There are as many wage structures as there are ways of classifying workers. In Chapter 9, for example, we investigated how wages varied systematically across individuals with different levels of education or skill. Casual observation suggests that there are a number of other interesting dimensions worth exploring, including occupation, industry, region, large versus small firms, men versus women, race or ethnicity, immigrant status, union status, and public versus private sector.

Some of these categories represent special challenges to the neoclassical model of the labour market we have developed to this point. Others have important policy implications. We cover some of these in separate chapters on immigration, discrimination, and unions. In this chapter, we focus on wage variation across occupations, industries, regions, firm sizes, and public versus private sectors.

Explorations with the 2011 National Household Survey

The easiest way to summarize wage structures across various categories is in the context of the **earnings function** we developed in Chapter 9. Recall that, in its simplest form, it is a function relating an individual's earnings to his or her characteristics that are believed to determine productivity. The most common specification in labour economics is

$$\ln Y_i = \alpha + rS + \beta_1 \, EXP + \beta_2 \, EXP^2 + \varepsilon_i \tag{10.1}$$

which states that individual (log) earnings depend on formal schooling, labour market work experience, plus unobserved ability or luck. When estimated by ordinary least squares, the coefficients on years of schooling, S, and experience, EXP, can approximately be interpreted as rates of return; that is, the percentage increase in wages associated with a unit change in the productive characteristic.

We can easily augment this equation to allow earnings to depend on other characteristics. Consider adding K other measures of individual characteristics X_j:

$$\ln W_i = \alpha + rS + \beta_1 \, EXP + \beta_2 \, EXP^2 + \gamma_1 X_1$$
$$+ \gamma_2 X_2 + \ldots + \gamma_K X_K + \varepsilon_i \tag{10.2}$$

In this equation, the γ_j also has the interpretation as (approximate) rates of return to the characteristics X_j, controlling for the other factors, such as human capital.

To be more concrete, we estimate the earnings function from Chapter 9, augmented with indicators for the individual's occupation, industry, and region. The results are reported in Table 10.1 for men who worked full-year, full-time in 2010, using data from the 2011 National Household Survey. Consider first the results for region or province. Table 10.1 shows the percentage difference in annual earnings (wages) across provinces, holding constant the individual's level of schooling, experience, industry, and occupation. Ideally, this represents a pure **regional wage differential** that cannot be attributed to the possibility, for example, that wages vary across regions because of differing industrial mixes. We will discuss the challenges of interpreting these differentials later in the chapter. For now, we wish to summarize only the broad patterns.

TABLE 10.1	Earnings Differentials by Province, Occupation, and Industry, Canada, 2010

Province

	% Jobs	Premium
Newfoundland and Labrador	1.4	−4.6
Prince Edward Island	0.4	−14.7
Nova Scotia	2.7	−10.1
New Brunswick	2.3	−9.5
Quebec	23.4	−11.9
Ontario	40.0	—
Manitoba	3.5	−7.1
Saskatchewan	2.8	4.1
Alberta	12.5	15.7
British Columbia	12.0	1.5

Occupation			Industry		
	% Jobs	Premium		% Jobs	Premium
Senior management	2.0	52.8	Agriculture, forestry, and fishing	1.5	−32.6
Middle management	5.0	34.7	Other primary	2.3	42.9
Other management	9.0	14.8	Utilities	1.7	32.9
Professionals (business and finance)	3.1	19.4	Construction	9.0	−5.2
Finance and administration	6.1	−11.9	Manufacturing	16.2	—
Clerical	1.2	−20.1	Wholesale trade	7.1	−0.4
Professionals (science)	7.4	19.0	Retail trade	9.4	−24.0
Other science occupations	6.1	1.8	Transportation and warehousing	7.1	−0.6
Professionals (health)	0.9	51.7	Information and culture	2.9	4.6
Other health occupations	1.1	1.4	Finance and insurance	4.0	9.6
Professionals (education and social services)	5.0	14.5	Real estate and leasing	1.6	−10.2
Other education and social occupations	3.2	16.1	Professional services	7.5	−1.9
Professionals (arts, culture, and recreation)	1.5	−19.3	Administrative and support, and waste management	3.3	−26.0
Sales and service supervisors	4.4	−5.7			
Sales representatives	6.3	−16.8	Educational services	4.8	−12.8
Sales and services support	4.0	−32.4	Health and social assistance	3.5	−21.6

Occupation			Industry		
	% Jobs	Premium		% Jobs	Premium
Trade workers	15.0	—	Accommodation and food	3.4	–53.7
Transportation and trade helpers	10.0	–21.4	Other services (except public administration)	5.1	–23.8
Supervisors and technicians (primary and secondary sectors)	5.9	–9.6	Public administration	9.6	4.8
Labourers	3.0	–27.5			

NOTES: This table reports the earnings differentials in percentage terms, implied by the coefficients on indicator variables for each province, industry, and occupation. The premiums are expressed relative to the base group (Ontario, construction trades, and manufacturing, respectively). The "% Jobs" indicates the distribution of observations across categories. The earnings function is estimated on a sample of full-year, full-time males with only wage and salary income. The regression includes years of schooling, a quadratic in potential experience, and the indicators for region, industry, and occupation. Observations from the territories are excluded.

SOURCE: Data from Statistics Canada, Individual Public Use Microdata Files: 2011 National Household Survey.

The reported premiums are the percentage differences in earnings of having a given characteristic that is different from a base category. For the provincial indicators, the base category is Ontario, Canada's largest province. The premium is the percentage difference in wages between the province reported in the table and Ontario. Thanks to the oil and gas boom that was still going strong in 2010 (Fortin and Lemieux 2015), the highest-wage province is Alberta, where wages exceed those paid in Ontario by 15.7 percent. Saskatchewan and British Columbia follow with wages 4.1 percent and 1.5 percent above those paid in Ontario, respectively. The other provinces have wages significantly below those in these richest provinces. Note that these differentials are adjusted (by estimating a multiple regression) for the fact that the industrial composition is different across provinces.

The **occupational premiums** are reported relative to construction trades, traditionally male jobs. The highest-paid occupational groups are "senior management" and "health professionals" (mostly physicians) with wages 52.8 and 51.7 percent higher, respectively, than those paid in construction trades. These occupational differentials already account for the fact that education levels vary across these education groups, so the differentials *do not* reflect differences in the level of schooling required for these jobs. For a given level of education, therefore, it appears worth avoiding most service occupations if you are interested only in money. If one cannot be a manager, careers in sciences or health seem like relatively lucrative choices. Finally, the **industry premiums** are reported relative to manufacturing. The largest premium is for "other primary" industries, which includes oil and gas extraction and mining. The lowest paid workers are in accommodation and food industries (and note, again, this is not because they have less schooling, on average). Having documented the existence of these systematic differences in wages across submarkets, the question then arises as to how these differentials can emerge and be sustained in a competitive, integrated labour market.

Theoretical Issues

While each type of differential has its own explanation, or raises its own theoretical problems, there are several common conceptual issues. Consider a single labour market comprising identical workers who can freely choose to work in one of two submarkets. Why might wages vary across these markets? First, there may be different educational requirements for different jobs. In this case, the differences in earnings should simply reflect the returns to schooling. What if the differential remains even after accounting for this difference in human capital? There are a number of possibilities:

- *Compensating differentials.* Earnings may vary because of differences in **nonpecuniary benefits** across sectors. Wages would be higher in the market where jobs were less pleasant (see Chapter 8).
- **Immobility** *across sectors.* Contrary to our assumption, individuals may not be able to freely choose sectors. This may be because one sector requires a special skill that cannot be acquired through schooling; that is, our assumption that individuals are identical is invalid. Alternatively, there may be barriers to mobility across sectors caused by government regulation or noncompetitive features in the labour market. In this case, it is not reasonable to treat the two submarkets

as parts of a common, integrated labour market. More troubling, the differential may indicate that at least one of the submarkets cannot be characterized by the neoclassical, market-clearing supply and demand model.

- *Short run versus long run.* Perhaps less troubling, the unexplained differentials may reflect only a short-run, transitory **disequilibrium** across the markets. This may be due to adjustment costs of mobility across markets.

- **Unobserved heterogeneity**. Finally, the differentials may have no theoretical implications but simply reflect the fact that our data are coarse and imperfectly measured. Differences across the submarkets may be the consequence of differing skills or human capital that are not captured by "years of schooling" or other crude measures of human capital. In this case, we may have a fully integrated labour market, and wage variation across submarkets merely reflects differences in average productivity of the individuals in each market.

While labour economists may find the following wage structures intrinsically interesting, they are more generally interested in whether the earnings differentials indicate that the labour market is not fully integrated, and in the fact that there is a significant departure from the neoclassical supply and demand framework.

Occupational Wage Structures

In the National Occupational Classification (NOC) an **occupation** is defined as a collection of jobs, sufficiently similar in work performed to be grouped under a common title for classification purposes. The two key factors used to classify occupations are the skill level (education and training) required to perform the duties of an occupation, and the skill type, referring to the type of work performed. Workers who perform the same kind of work in different establishments or industries are classified in the same occupation.

The occupation wage structure refers to the wage structure between various occupations or occupational groups. The occupational groups can be broadly defined as, for example, one of the 40 NOC two-digit major groups, such as senior management or clerical, or industrial, electrical, and construction trades. (The 20 occupational classifications in Table 10.1 are a slightly aggregated version of these groups.) Or they can be one of the 500 four-digit codes (in the 2011 NOC) for which census data are often available. Examples of four-digit occupations are data entry clerks (occupation 1422) or bricklayers (occupation 7281).

Figure 10.1 illustrates the occupational wage differential (skill differential) that exists between two hypothetical occupations; for example, skilled welders and unskilled labourers. The demand schedules for each occupation are simply the aggregation of the demand schedules of the various firms that utilize each type of labour. The schedules could be large or small, elastic or inelastic, depending on the circumstances.

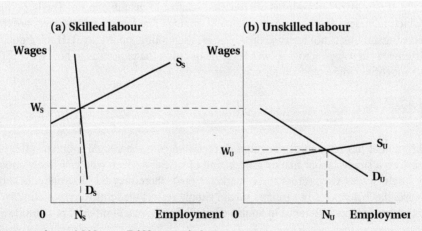

Figure 10.1 Occupational Wage Differentials

The demand curves for skilled and unskilled labour are given by D_S and D_U. The supply curve represents the number of people willing to work in a given occupation at a given wage rate, all else equal. To the extent that skilled labourers incur training costs, we expect the skilled labour supply curve, S_S, to be higher than the unskilled labour supply schedule, S_U. We also expect the supply curves to be upward sloping, as higher wages will attract more workers to that type of job. The equilibrium wages for the skilled and unskilled occupations are given by W_S and W_U.

The supply schedules for each of the occupations are upward sloping, reflecting the fact that higher wages are required to attract additional workers into the occupations, away from other occupations or nonlabour market activities. The higher wages are often necessary to attract additional workers because of different worker preferences for the various occupations, or because of increasing costs associated with acquiring the skills necessary to do the work. Those who prefer the occupation or who have a natural talent for doing the work would enter at the lower wages. Higher wages would be necessary to attract those who did not have a preference for the occupation or who could do the work only by a more-costly acquisition of the skills.

The supply schedule, therefore, can be thought of as reflecting a ranking of actual and potential workers in the occupation, where those who most prefer the occupation or who have an innate talent for it are ranked at the beginning (and, hence, require a lower wage to enter), and those who least prefer the occupation or for whom the acquisition of the skills would be more costly are ranked at the end (and, hence, require the higher wage to enter). If all preferences were identical and there were no increasing costs associated with entering the occupation, then the supply schedule would be perfectly elastic at the going wage for the occupation.

The degree of elasticity of the supply schedule to each occupation also depends on the responsiveness of alternative sources of labour supply that, in turn, depend upon such factors as labour market information and mobility, training requirements, immigration, and the general state of the economy. For example, in the short run, the labour supply schedule to an occupation may be inelastic (and, hence, a demand increase would lead to more of a wage increase than an employment increase) for a variety of reasons: potential recruits to the occupation are not yet aware of the high wages, recruits have to be trained to enter the occupation, fulfilling some of the occupational demand through immigration takes time, and the labour market is currently tight so there is no ready surplus of labour from which to draw.

In the long run, however, most of these factors would adjust to the new demands, and the labour supply schedule to the occupation would be more elastic. It may not be perfectly elastic if the new sources of supply are more costly than the original sources. However, in the long run, if all of the supply responses had sufficient time to adjust, and if the new sources of supply were not more costly than the original sources, then any inelasticity to the labour supply in an occupation would reflect the different preferences of workers, which would result in a need to raise wages to attract workers who do not have a strong preference for the occupation.

Reasons for Interoccupational Wage Differentials

Given the basic determinants of occupational supply and demand, standard economic theory predicts that the forces of competition will ensure an equal present value of net advantage at the margin in the long run across all occupations. If this does not prevail, then competition ensures that workers at the margin of decision will move from jobs of low net advantage to ones of high net advantage. This does allow for considerable variation in the occupational wage structure to reflect the main determinants of wage structures: the nonpecuniary aspects of the job (including human capital requirements), short-run adjustments, and noncompetitive forces.

For example, with respect to compensating differences for nonpecuniary aspects, occupations differ in their nonpecuniary characteristics, such as pleasantness, safety, responsibility, fringe benefits, seasonal or cyclical stability, and the certainty of their return (see Exhibit 10.1). As discussed in Chapter 8 on compensating wage differentials, **interoccupational wage differentials** may exist, therefore, to compensate for these nonpecuniary differences.

Part of the wage paid in a particular occupation may reflect a wage premium to compensate workers for the costly acquisition of human capital necessary to do a particular job. A competitive wage premium would be one that just yields a competitive rate of return on the investment in human capital.

Short-run adjustment factors may also affect the occupational wage structure. For example, an increase in the demand for skilled workers, perhaps because of technological change, would lead to an outward shift in the demand schedule for skilled labour, as in Figure 10.1(a). Cortes (2016) shows, for instance, that wages in "non-routine" occupations where workers cannot be replaced by computers or robots did increase in recent years. In the short run, the supply schedule to the skilled occupation may be fairly inelastic because of a long training period required to do the skilled work. Thus, wages would rise in this occupation, and this would be a short-run signal for workers in other occupations to acquire the skills necessary to work in the skilled occupation.

In response to the short-run wage premium in the skilled occupation, new workers will enter this occupation, and this increased supply will reduce the wage premium until it is just large enough to restore an equality of net advantage at the margin; that is, until no further gains in net advantage are possible. The new equality of net advantage may or may not be associated with the old occupational wage differential. This depends on the preferences of workers in the occupations (i.e., on the slopes of the supply schedules to each occupation). If the skilled occupation had an upward sloping supply schedule and, therefore, higher wages were necessary to attract the additional workers, the new skill differential may be greater than before. The skilled workers who were already in the occupation (intramarginal workers) would receive an additional rent because they were willing to work in the occupation at the old wage but now receive the new, higher wage that was necessary to expand the number of workers in the occupation.

EXHIBIT 10.1

Starving Artists and Superstars—Myth or Reality?

Is there any truth to the stereotype of the starving artist—the person who gives up material gain in return for the creative rewards of an artist? In theory, this is a distinct possibility, since low monetary rewards are consistent with compensating nonpecuniary aspects of a job, such as fame and creative recognition. As well, artists may bequeath a legacy of art or fame to their heirs. Also, it simply may be an occupation that attracts risk-taking individuals who are willing to gamble for the "big break" that will lead to fame and fortune.

Contrary to the stereotypical view, empirical evidence reported in Filer (1986) indicates that artists tend to have similar earnings to otherwise comparable individuals in other occupations. The results reported in Table 10.1 suggest that artists do earn less than workers in most other, though not all, occupations, given their experience and education. Artists in Canada suffer a 4 percent penalty, which may be a small price to pay, especially for someone who enjoys being an artist.

This being said, it is true that there are a disproportionate number of artists at the low end of the earnings spectrum within the artistic profession. This confirms the stereotype that some may have very low incomes while others have very high incomes. Furthermore, the evidence shows that, if anything, earnings inequality among artistic performers has increased substantially over time. For instance, Krueger (2005) shows that "superstars" have done much better than other performers over the last 25 years. In particular, the share of total ticket revenue accruing to the top 1 percent of rock concert performers in the United States increased from 26 to 56 percent between 1981 and 2003! This far exceeds the growth in earnings inequality for all workers discussed in Chapter 9.

Noncompetitive factors can also affect the occupational wage structure. For example, occupational licensing on the part of professional associations, by regulating entry into the profession, can effectively lead to a reduction in the supply of labour to the occupation and, hence, artificially high salaries. Kleiner (2006) and Kleiner and Krueger (2013) show that a growing fraction of the workforce is covered by some form of occupational licensing. Unions, especially craft unions through the hiring hall (a union controlled employment centre) and apprenticeship requirements, can also exclude people from some occupations and crowd them into others, raising wages in the former and depressing them in the latter. The importance of unions has been declining over time, however. In fact, Kleiner and Krueger (2013) point out that that substantially more workers are now covered by occupational licensing requirements rather than by union collective bargaining agreements. Other policies may also work directly on wages rather than indirectly through the supply of labour. Minimum wage legislation would affect low-wage occupations and equal pay for equal work laws would affect wages in female-dominated occupations.

 LO3   Heterogeneous Workers and the Roy Model

In the above discussion, we have looked at the simplest possible case where all workers are equally productive and should, therefore, earn the same wage when working in the same occupation. The reality is much more complex since workers differ both in terms of their observed (e.g., education and experience) and unobserved (e.g., motivation, talent, etc.) attributes. Furthermore, casual observation suggests that people who choose different lines of work tend to have different abilities and talents. For instance, being successful in theoretical physics and in professional hockey require very different sets of talents. The most prominent physicists in leading universities would likely do extremely poorly in professional hockey, and vice versa.

Finding a competitive equilibrium when different workers earn different wages in different occupations is much more challenging than in the simple case with homogeneous workers. In general, there will be some occupational rents in the competitive equilibrium even if the market clears in the sense that no worker would prefer to choose another occupation. For instance, people who become professional hockey players likely earn much more playing hockey than they would earn in any other occupation. But even if the "law of one price" does not hold in this case, the labour market still clears in the sense that other workers do not want to try to get a job in the NHL instead of being, for instance, theoretical physicists. Following the famous expression coined in international trade theory, what happens here is that different workers have a **comparative advantage** in different occupations, and each chooses the occupation in which they earn the most money.

This more general model of occupational choice with heterogeneous workers is known as the **Roy model**. The approach was first introduced by Roy (1951) where he used, as an example, the choice between becoming a hunter or a fisherman (see Exhibit 10.2). The Roy model has been used extensively for estimating the magnitude of occupational wage differences when workers are heterogeneous. Generally speaking, individuals are believed to be *endowed* with skills that are valued in the marketplace, in which case the wage premium that is paid to them reflects their natural embodiment of these skills. The individual may be endowed with a skill that is useful in a variety of occupations (e.g., strength, dexterity, or intelligence) or one that is unique to one or a few (e.g., ability to sing or put the puck in the net). Using an empirical version of the Roy model with panel data, Gibbons et al. (2005) conclude that most of the interoccupational wage differentials can be linked to these skill differences across occupations.

EXHIBIT 10.2

The Roy Model of Earnings Determination

In a simple competitive labour market where all workers have the same skills and abilities, wages should become equalized across jobs and occupations. The reason this law of one price holds is that if one job pays more than another, many workers will try to get this higher-paying job, and this induced increase in supply will depress wages until they become equalized across all jobs. While wages may differ across jobs because of compensating wages differences, institutional rigidities, or short-run disequilibrium, the consensus in the empirical literature is that these factors cannot account for most of the differences in wages across occupations (Gibbons et al. 2005), firm size (Brown and Medoff 1989), or industries (Krueger and Summers 1988).

Does this mean that the competitive model of the labour market has to be tossed away because the law of one price fails to hold in practice? As it turns out, the law of one price should only hold in the special case where all workers are identical in terms of their skills and productive abilities. Since this is obviously an oversimplification, it follows that we can have a competitive equilibrium in the labour market in which the law of one price does not hold.

This important point was first illustrated in a famous contribution by Roy (1951) who considered a simple labour market with two occupations: fishing and hunting. Fishermen have to catch trout, which is a fairly skilled job, while hunters face the much simpler task of catching rabbits. To quote Roy (1951), ". . . the rabbits are plentiful and stupid and even the less-skilled man can ensnare a fair number in a year's hunting while the exercise of a quite appreciable degree of skill does not enable the better hunters to catch many more." Roy then goes on and points out that ". . . the trout, on the other hand, are particularly wily and fight hard, so that many men would undoubtedly starve if they had to eat only what they themselves caught; but nevertheless the real fisherman can obtain very big catches in a year's fishing, although such catches are pretty rare occurrences."

It is easy to see that, in this context, "less skilled" workers will choose hunting over fishing since the value of the rabbits they catch far exceeds what they would earn from fishing. By contrast, highly skilled workers will choose fishing over hunting. Importantly, the labour market will clear since none of the fisherman would rather go into hunting, and vice versa. Interestingly, some "middle skilled" workers will be indifferent between hunting and fishing. For this group of workers, the law of one price will hold, since they will be indifferent (in terms of earnings) between working in fishing or hunting.

This simple example illustrates several important features of the Roy model. First, people choose their occupation (or type of job or employer) on the basis of comparative advantage. In the above example, highly skilled workers have a comparative advantage in fishing and tend to sort themselves into this particular line of work. Second, comparative advantage results in a selection bias, since workers with different sets of observed and unobserved skills tend to sort themselves into different jobs or occupations. Third, most workers earn rents in equilibrium in the sense that the wage in the job they choose is higher than what they would get in other jobs. Fourth, we still have a market clearing equilibrium, because no worker would prefer to switch to a different kind of job in equilibrium.

These remarkable properties of the Roy model provide a much richer description of the actual labour market than does the standard competitive model with identical workers. This explains why this model is widely used in empirical studies of wage differences across occupations, industries, and firm size, where it is important to have a model that is realistic enough to capture the observed features of the labour market. The simple competitive model remains useful, however, for understanding how the forces of demand and supply help shape the wage structure across these different dimensions, since it is harder to work analytically and solve for the equilibrium in the Roy model (see, however, Acemoglu and Autor 2011, who propose a simpler but more tractable version of the Roy model)

Regional Wage Structures and Geographic Mobility

The existence of pronounced regional wage differentials is a well-documented fact in Canada as in most economies (see Table 10.1, for example). As with most wage structures, however, what is less well known are the reasons for the differentials and the extent to which a pure geographic wage differential would persist in the very long run.

 ## Reasons for Regional Wage Differentials

Economic theory predicts that the forces of competition would ensure an equality of net advantage at the margin associated with identical jobs in each region. That is, if the non-wage aspects of employment (including the probability of obtaining employment) were the same, competition would ensure that wages for the same job would be the same across all regions. Competitive forces could operate in the form of workers moving from the low-wage regions to the high-wage regions, or in the form of firms moving from high-wage regions to low-wage regions to minimize labour cost. As workers leave the low-wage region, the reduced supply would raise wages, and as firms enter the low-wage region, the increased demand would also increase wages. The converse would happen in the high-wage region, and the process of the mobility of labour and/or capital would continue until an equality of net advantage was restored in the long run.

To the extent that different people have different geographic preferences, the supply of labour for a given occupation in a particular region may not be perfectly elastic. That is, for a region to expand its workforce, higher wages may have to be paid to attract workers from other regions. This could obviously be the case in the short run, but it may also be the case in the long run to the extent that geographic preferences exist. In such circumstances, some workers may be receiving location rents in the sense that they would prefer to remain in a particular region even if wages were lower.

The equality of net advantage at the margin predicted by economic theory does allow for considerable variation in the interregional wage structure; however, as with interoccupational wage differentials, that variation would have to reflect compensating differences, short-run adjustments, or noncompetitive factors.

The compensating differences are most obvious, and they include wage compensation for such factors as cost of living, remoteness, and climate. For instance, Albouy, Leibovici, and Warman (2013) compare wages and cost of living differences across Canadian cities and conclude that they largely reflect a compensation for differences in amenities, such as climate, cultural factors, etc. Another potential source of regional wage differences comes from compensation for nonprice externalities, such as pollution and congestion. Short-run interregional wage differentials could also be present, and, in fact, serve as the signals that are necessary to induce the mobility that will lead to a long-run equilibrium.

Noncompetitive factors may also affect the regional wage structure. Not only is geographic mobility hindered by the barriers that arise because of the high direct and psychic costs of moving, but also it can be hindered by artificial barriers and public policies that have an indirect, and perhaps unintentional, impact on mobility.

Occupational licensing, for example, can hinder geographic mobility. Some provinces may not recognize training done in other jurisdictions, others may have residency requirements, and others may even require citizenship. In addition, trade unions that control hiring (i.e., have the "hiring hall") can require that people who have worked in the zone be hired first, hence discouraging others from entering the zone. While these policies do achieve other objectives, they also reduce the effectiveness of interregional mobility as a force to reduce interregional wage differentials.

Social transfer programs that try to reduce income disparities will obviously have different regional impacts and this could reduce regional mobility. Albouy (2012) argues, for instance, that the equalization payments in Canada substantially reduce mobility across provinces. In such circumstances, governments are faced with a basic dilemma; as they use transfer programs to reduce income inequality, they reduce part of the incentive for people to engage in regional mobility, unless the transfer programs are conditional upon geographic mobility. Regional expansion policies can encourage capital to move into low-income areas, but this also reduces the mobility of labour from that region and, hence, reduces some of the market forces that would reduce inequalities. Obviously, these policies can achieve other important objectives—noticeably, perhaps, a more equitable distribution of regional income—but they do have the effect of reducing the effectiveness of geographic mobility as a force to reduce geographic wage differences.

Migration Decision

As the previous section indicates, economic theory predicts that the forces of competition would serve to reduce pure regional wage differentials so that they reflect compensating differences, short-run adjustments, or noncompetitive factors. Those forces of competition were the movement of capital from high- to low-wage areas, and the movement of labour from low- to high-wage areas.

This latter movement—geographic mobility, or **migration**—can be treated as a human capital decision, the determinants of which are discussed in Chapter 9. That is, geographic mobility will occur as long as the marginal benefits exceed the marginal costs to the individuals making the decision. Benefits can include such factors as expected income (which, in turn, can be a function of earnings and job opportunities as well as transfer payments), climate, and the availability of social services. Costs can include the usual costs of information seeking and moving, as well as the psychic costs associated with geographic moves. In addition, the migration decision may depend on one's ability to finance the move—a problem that is particularly acute in human capital theory, because one cannot legally use human capital (e.g., the larger expected earnings) as collateral to finance any necessary loan.

The human capital framework provides a variety of empirically testable propositions concerning the mobility decision. Other things being equal, relative to older workers, younger workers would tend to engage in more job mobility because they have a longer benefit period from which to recoup the costs, their opportunity cost (forgone income) of moving is lower as are their direct costs if they do not have a home to sell or family to move, and their psychic costs are probably lower because they have not established deep ties in their community. In addition, they may not be locked in by seniority provisions or pensions that are not portable. Mobility should be from areas of high unemployment toward areas of low unemployment. It should also increase at the peak of a business cycle when job opportunities are more abundant, and decrease in a recession when jobs are scarce. Mobility in and out of Quebec is likely to be lower than in other regions of Canada because of language and cultural differences. In addition, distance is an inhibiting factor because it increases moving costs and uncertainty as well as the psychic costs associated with being uprooted from one's familiar environment.

WORKED EXAMPLE

Oil Shocks and Regional Wage Differences

After reaching a low of less than US$20 a barrel in the late 1990s, the price of oil stabilized to around US$100 in the 2011 to 2014 period before declining to less than US$50 since then. The value of the Canadian dollar relative to Canada's main trading partner, the United States, closely followed the evolution of oil prices over this period.

The Canadian dollar went from about 65 cents (0.65 US$) in the late 1990s to parity when oil prices reached US$100 before falling again in the most recent years. These price shocks had very different impacts on different parts of the country. Until 2014, the higher exchange rate made it harder for manufacturing firms based in Ontario and Quebec to compete internationally, while oil-rich Alberta experienced a long economic boom. As a result, despite the recent setbacks, wages in Alberta remain much higher than in the rest of the country (see Table 10.1).

The figure below illustrates how this emerging regional wage gap is easily understood in a simple demand and supply model of regional labour markets. To simplify the story, we assume that (real) wages increased by 5 percent in Alberta but remained constant in Ontario. Panel (a) in the figure shows the demand and supply curves for Ontario. As long as the two curves remain stable over time in Ontario, the wage remains stable at its equilibrium level of $20. By contrast, panel (b) in the figure shows what happens in Alberta when increasing oil prices shift up the demand curve from D_0 to D_1. In the short run, the labour supply curve remains constant at S_0 and the labour market equilibrium moves from point A to point B. As a result, the equilibrium wage increases from $20 to $21, a 5 percent increase.

If workers were perfectly mobile across provinces, the higher wage in Alberta would attract workers from other parts of the country up to the point where wages would be equalized across regions. Panel (b) in the figure shows that this happens once migration to Alberta is large enough to shift the labour supply curve from S_0 to S_1. The equilibrium then moves to point C and the wage in Alberta return to its level of $20. With wages equalized again across provinces, there is no longer an economic incentive for people to move from Ontario to Alberta.

What this simple model does not tell us, however, is how long it takes for the market to adjust and regional wage differences to disappear. If historical evidence is any guide, the answer is that, despite recent setbacks in Alberta, it will take at least several years for these wage differentials to disappear. The reason is that interprovincial migration flows are not generally large enough to quickly equalize interprovincial wage differences. For instance, according to Statistics Canada data for 2000 to 2015, Alberta's net gain from migration has been about 25,000 people per year. Let's compare this figure to the number of migrant workers required to shift the supply curve from S_0 to S_1. Since the movement from B to C is along the demand curve, the elasticity of demand tells us by how much the number of workers has to increase to reduce wages by 5 percent. If the elasticity was equal to one, employment would also have to increase by 5 percent from B to C. Since there are about 2 million workers in Alberta, this means that we need 100,000 people (.05 × 2 million) to move to Alberta. This is four times the normal number of people who move to Alberta every year, suggesting it would take many years for the labour market to fully adjust.

Effect of an Oil Shock on Regional Wages

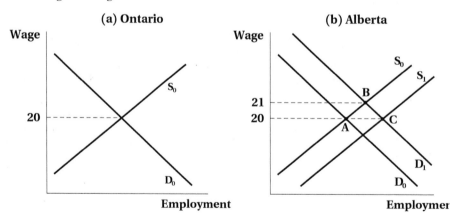

Empirical evidence tends to verify the implications of migration as a human capital decision. Osberg, Gordon, and Lin (1994) explore the determinants of interregional and interindustry mobility of individuals in the Maritimes. Using the 1986–1987 Labour Market Activity Survey (LMAS), they find that younger individuals and those with higher expected wage gains are more likely to migrate. Finnie (2004) uses a database of longitudinal tax records that allows him to accurately follow individuals over a 13-year period (1982–1995). More recently, Bernard, Finnie, and St-Jean (2008) have expanded this analysis up to 2004. These analyses of the determinants of interprovincial migration are in accordance with what we would expect from the human capital model. Younger workers are more likely to move, as they have a longer period over which to reap the benefits of moving. It is more costly for people who are married with children to move, and, not surprisingly, they have lower mobility. Francophones are also less likely to leave Quebec, as their language skills do not transfer easily to other provinces. Finally, these studies find that individuals who are down on their economic luck are more likely to move, especially if they live in a high-unemployment province. Similar results concerning migration decisions and the human capital model have been found by Cousineau and Vaillancourt (2000) and Coulombe (2006), using the Canadian census. The economic incentives of government programs can also affect the migration decision. Day (1992) shows that interprovincial migration flows reflect the fact that people tend to move to provinces with more-generous social programs, lower taxes, and higher expenditures on health and education. Day and Winer (2012) provide a comprehensive empirical analysis of the link between internal migration and public policy in Canada.

But why do regional wage disparities persist? Migration should tend to reduce wage differentials, at least to the point where there is no incentive (on the margin) for people to move. Low-wage regions would simply be nicer places to live, as workers accept lower wages in return for local amenities. Similarly, investment flows should reduce earnings differentials, as firms build factories in low-wage areas. In fact, evidence from the United States and Canada suggests that regional earnings differences are eroding over time. For example, empirical evidence from the United States indicates that the wage differential between North and South had disappeared by the 1970s, after controlling for the differences in cost of living and the human capital endowments of the workforce (Bishop, Formby, and Thistle 1992; Farber and Newman 1987). This wage convergence occurred as firms located to the low-wage South (thereby reducing the demand for labour in the North and increasing it in the South) and as workers left the South for jobs in the high-wage North (thereby increasing the supply of labour in the North and reducing it in the South). More-recent evidence suggests that regional wages have stopped converging in the 1990s (Barro and Sala-i-Martin 1999). Berry and Glaeser (2005) even find that wages across metropolitan areas had started diverging again in the 1990s, though the effect disappears after controlling for changes in human capital. Economic convergence of incomes also appears to be happening in Canada. Coulombe and Day (1999) and Cousineau and Vaillancourt (2000) show that interprovincial differences in per capita income levels are generally diminishing over time. Differences remain substantial, however, and vary over time as different regions of Canada are hit with difference shocks. For instance, incomes went up in Alberta relative to the rest of the country during the oil and gas boom that ended around 2014. While Chan and Morissette (2016) show that young workers reacted to these changes by increasingly moving to Alberta, the induced migration flows were clearly not large enough to reduce the income differentials.

Finally, there is also anecdotal and formal evidence that the nature of regional mobility has been changing over time. There has been a long-term decline in the real cost of air transportation, which makes it increasingly possible for people to work in a region of Canada without having to permanently live there. Using detailed tax data, Laporte, Lu, and Schellenberg (2013) show that, in 2008, 6 percent of workers in Alberta were interprovincial employees working in that province but living somewhere else. Morissette and Qiu (2015) show a comparable fraction of interprovincial employees in Saskatchewan, and a much higher fraction in Yukon, Nunavut, and the Northwest Territories. New technologies also make it increasingly possible to work away from home, which means that the traditional notion of regional mobility is less relevant than it used to be.

Interindustry Wage Differentials

As the Canadian *Standard Industrial Classification* manual indicates, industrial designations refer to the principal kind, or branch, of economic activity of establishments in which individuals work. The industries may be broadly defined sectors; for example, agriculture, mining, manufacturing, construction, transportation, trade, and public administration. Or they may be more narrowly defined. For example, within the nondurable manufacturing sector there are food and beverage, tobacco, rubber, textile, and paper industries. The interindustry wage structure indicates the wage differential between industries, however broadly or narrowly defined.

Theoretical Determinants of Interindustry Wage Differentials

The average wage in an industry will reflect a variety of factors, including the occupational composition and personal characteristics of the workforce, and the regional domination of some industries. Consequently, pure **interindustry wage differentials** are difficult to calculate because they reflect other wage structures; notably, those by occupation, region, and personal characteristics of the workforce.

If we could net out the effect of these other wage structures, however, so that we were comparing wages across industries for the same occupation, the same type of worker, and the same region, then the pure interindustry wage differential would reflect only the different characteristics of the industry. This is what we attempt to do with the exercise reported in Table 10.1. Many of these different wage-determining characteristics are similar to the ones analyzed as determinants of the interoccupational wage structure—nonpecuniary aspects of the jobs in each industry, short-run adjustments, and noncompetitive forces. If there are no differences in any of these aspects, competitive forces should ensure that all industries pay the same wage for the same type of labour. The basic determinants of interindustry wage differentials, therefore, can be categorized according to the basic determinants of any wage structure—nonpecuniary characteristics of the industry, short-run demand changes, and noncompetitive factors.

Interindustry wage differences, for example, may exist to compensate for differences in the nonpecuniary aspects of the work in different industries. Such factors could include unpleasant or unsafe work conditions, or seasonal or cyclical employment. Workers in the construction industry, for example, may receive a wage premium in part to compensate for risk as well as the seasonal and cyclical nature of much of the work.

Interindustry wage differences may also reflect short-run demand changes. The wage differences are the price signal necessary to encourage reallocation from declining sectors to expanding ones. Different industries are affected in different fashions by various demand changes emanating from such factors as technological change or free trade and global competition. For example, freer trade will lead to an expansion of export-oriented industries and to a contraction of industries most affected by imports. This should lead to a wage premium in the expanding export sector, which, in turn, is the price signal to encourage the reallocation of labour from the declining import sector to the expanding export sector.

There may also be a variety of noncompetitive factors that could affect the interindustry wage structure. Monopoly rents may differ by industry, and these may be captured, in part, by workers, especially if they are unionized. Even in declining industries, or industries subject to severe import competition, the rents going to workers could increase if they were able to appropriate a larger *share* of the declining rents. This could occur, for example, if the declining nature of the industry meant that there was no threat of entry, and the firm had no alternative use for its plant and equipment, and, therefore, no viable threat to relocate if labour appropriates a larger share of the rents. In essence, labour is still able to "milk a dead cow," at least for a time.

Other noncompetitive factors can also affect the interindustry wage differential. Minimum wage laws obviously affect low-wage industries, such as personal services (laundries, hotels, restaurants, and taverns), retail trade, and parts of nondurable manufacturing, especially clothing. Equal-pay laws will affect industries with a high proportion of females (which often are also low-wage industries); for example, nondurable manufacturing retail trade, services and finance, insurance, and real estate. Fair-wage laws and wage-extension laws tend to be most important in the construction sector. Occupational licensing and unionization tend to be most prominent in high-wage industries—in part, of course, because they may have raised wages in those industries. In summary, basic economic theory suggests that, in the long run, competitive forces should eliminate pure interindustry wage differences. To the extent that they exist, interindustry wage differences should reflect only such factors as compensating wages for the nonpecuniary characteristics of the industry, short-run demand changes, or noncompetitive factors.

LO4

Efficiency Wages, "Good Jobs," and Interindustry Wage Differences

As will be discussed in more detail in Chapter 17 (Unemployment: Causes and Consequences), firms may rationally pay wages above the market-clearing level so as to improve morale, reduce turnover and absenteeism, elicit effort, reduce shirking, reduce the threat of unionization, and lead to a queue of applicants so as to reduce recruiting and hiring costs. It may be efficient for the firm to pay wages above the market-clearing wage because of its positive effects on labour productivity or on reducing costs in these other areas. These productivity-enhancing wages are called **efficiency wages**. Such higher wages are rents to the workers who receive them, in the sense of being payments in excess of the market-clearing wage and in excess of their next-best-alternative job, assuming it is at the market-clearing wage. In fact, it is the receipt of this rent, or excessive wage payment, that elicits the desirable behaviour on the part of workers. Although they are payments above the market-clearing wage, these are competitive wage differentials in the sense that they are consistent with the profit-maximizing behaviour of firms and will not be eliminated by the forces of competition.

The desirability of paying efficiency wages may well differ by industry, thereby giving rise to persistent interindustry wage differentials.[1] For example, industries that utilize expensive capital equipment or for which the training costs make turnover costly may find it profitable to pay such efficiency wages to have a trustworthy workforce and low turnover. Such interindustry wage differentials may also persist over time if the efficiency rationales for paying a pure wage premium also persist over time.

Such high-wage jobs also correspond to the notion of "good jobs" as opposed to "bad jobs." The good jobs are those in industries that pay wages in excess of the market-clearing wage. Workers in those jobs are fortunate in the sense that the efficiency wage premium is a pure rent, not a compensating wage premium paid for undesirable working conditions or costly human capital. It is a rent or wage premium designed explicitly to make it a good job so that workers will not want to lose the job. As such, they are likely to exhibit good work characteristics with respect to such factors as absenteeism, turnover, and honesty. Obviously, to the extent that there is disutility associated with having to deliver such good work characteristics, then the higher wage would simply be a compensating wage premium associated with such characteristics. The essence of efficiency wages, however, is that they are rents, or pure wage premiums, and not compensating wages.

Efficiency wage premiums are different from conventional rents in that they are not extracted from the firm through, for example, the monopoly power of a union. Rather, they are voluntarily paid by the firm to serve a positive human resource management function, such as eliciting loyalty or honesty or reducing turnover. Workers are paid the marginal product of their labour; that marginal product is simply enhanced by the productivity-inducing aspects of the higher wage. For workers, however, it is like a conventional rent in that the wage premium is greater than any disutility they experience from the actions (increased loyalty and honesty, reduced turnover, absenteeism, or shirking) that they undertake as a result of the efficiency wage premium.

Workers who are displaced from those "good" jobs (perhaps because of industrial restructuring or import competition) would lose those rents if they are displaced to jobs that may simply pay the market-clearing wage. The loss of such efficiency wages may be one of the reasons for the large wage losses that are often experienced by workers who are displaced because of a plant closing or permanent job loss. Furthermore, Beaudry, Green, and Sand (2012) show that cities which lose good jobs because of industrial restructuring tend to also see wage declines in other sectors that are not directly affected by these changes. Because of these "spillover" effects on other jobs, they conclude that loss of good jobs has negative effects on a local economy that go substantially beyond the direct impact on workers who used to hold these good jobs. Likewise, Marchand (2015) and Fortin and Lemieux (2015) find that, in Canada, so-called good jobs in the oil and gas industry also have large spillover effects on other sectors. See also Green (2015) who provides a thorough discussion of the recent research on the good jobs in Canada and abroad.

The existence of efficiency wages or other sources of rents may also provide a theoretical rationale for industrial policies designed to protect the so-called good-wage jobs (Dickens and Lang 1988; Katz and Summers 1989a). Policies could include subsidies to high tech or other industries where such jobs may prevail, or even minimum wage laws that reduce employment in low-wage jobs that are unlikely to embody any efficiency wage. Tariffs could also protect good jobs in industries that pay efficiency wages. However, in developed countries, high-wage industries tend to be export oriented, and low-wage industries tend to be subject to import competition. Therefore, freer trade to enhance both exports and imports should increase the number of good jobs related to low-wage jobs; that is, free trade and not protectionism would be the best policy to enhance the number of jobs that pay efficiency wage premiums, especially if workers can be reallocated from the lower-wage, import-competing jobs to the higher-wage, export-oriented jobs.

In summary, countries may want to protect or encourage jobs that pay efficiency wages, because they are good jobs in the sense that firms want to pay the high wages (i.e., it is in their profit-maximizing interest to do so) and workers obviously want to receive such high wages because they are rents in excess of their next-best alternative wage. Countries that happen to have such jobs are fortunate, just like countries that happen to have endowments of natural resources.

While efficiency wages can provide a *theoretical* rationale for industrial policy to protect certain good jobs, this should not be taken as a justification for all such policies. This is especially the case because the encouragement and protection of efficiency wages is subject to a degree of policy control. Sensible policy application, however, requires answers to a number of questions: Can efficiency wage premiums be precisely identified so as to target policies to encourage such jobs? What will be the ultimate outcome if all jurisdictions (countries, provinces, states, regions, etc.) compete for such jobs? Are there ways of dealing with the distributional consequences if the already high-wage jobs effectively become protected or subsidized? If industrial policies are used to protect or encourage efficiency wages, what will happen when employers and employees try to have other jobs protected and encouraged in the same fashion? Answers to these and other questions would be useful to shed light on this important policy issue.

Empirical Evidence on Interindustry Wage Differences, Efficiency Wages, and the Impact of Deregulation

Systematic evidence on the existence of pure interindustry wage differences is difficult to compile because of the problem of controlling for other factors that affect the wage difference across industries. Different industries, for example, utilize different skill mixes, and they are concentrated in different regions and are composed of firms of different sizes. Hence, interindustry wage differences often confound wage differences by other factors, such as occupation, region, or plant size.

In microeconomic data sets where the individual worker is the unit of observation, it is possible to use econometric techniques to control for the influences of some of these different factors, and to thereby isolate a pure interindustry wage differential. The econometric results indicate that interindustry wage differences do reflect the conventional determinants of wage structures: nonpecuniary differences in the jobs, short-run demand changes, and noncompetitive factors. However, the studies also indicate that even after controlling for these factors, a pure interindustry wage differential, or efficiency wage, seems to prevail.[2] Some industries simply pay higher wages than appear necessary to compensate for the nonpecuniary aspects of the job or to meet short-run demand changes or because of noncompetitive factors. As well, this interindustry wage pattern appears quite stable over time; high-wage industries tend to remain high-wage industries.

That these are rents or payments above the market-clearing wage is supported by other indirect evidence. Workers who change industries are likely to gain or lose the full amount of the rent premium associated with that industry, suggesting it is the industry and not their own individual characteristics that gave rise to the wage premium. As well, the wage premium goes to workers throughout the occupational spectrum in an industry (e.g., secretaries, blue-collar workers, and managers) suggesting that it is something in the industry itself that generates the premium. The higher wages also tend to be associated with lower quit rates and large queues of applicants, and this would not prevail if the premium were simply a compensating premium for skills or nonpecuniary aspects of the job. While these observations suggest that the wage premiums are rents, it is more difficult to determine whether they reflect efficiency wages or the results of noncompetitive factors associated with each industry.

The interindustry wage structure tends to be quite stable over time and across different countries (Katz and Summers 1989b; Krueger and Summers 1988). That is, high-wage industries tend to be high-wage industries for considerable periods of time, and they tend to be high-wage industries in countries with very different labour market structures and institutional features. Industries that pay efficiency wages tend to be capital intensive, and, typically, are composed of large firms with considerable market power and ability to pay. These industries are also, usually, highly unionized and have a workforce of above-average education and low quit rates.

Table 10.2, based on Canadian data, illustrates the magnitude of the pure interindustry wage differential that prevails after controlling for the effect of a wide range of other factors that can influence wages across industries. Clearly, the differences are substantial. High-wage industries like tobacco products and mineral fuels, respectively, pay wage premiums of 33.4 percent and 25.5 percent above the competitive norm (i.e., above the average wage paid to workers of comparable wage-determining characteristics in other industries). Conversely, the service industries tend to pay wages considerably below the competitive norm: 31.8 percent below in religious organizations, and 20.3 percent below in accommodation and food services.

TABLE 10.2	Pure Interindustry Wage Differentials, Canada, 1986*

Industry	Wage Premium
Primary Industries	
Mineral fuels	25.5
Mining services	22.7
Forestry	18.9
Metal mines	18.9
Nonmetal mines	13.7
Quarries and pits	0.1
Fishing and trapping	−9.5
Manufacturing	
Tobacco products	33.4
Petroleum and coal	20.8
Chemicals	14.4
Paper	12.0
Primary metals	11.5
Wood products	8.7
Transport equipment	7.2
Rubber and plastics	7.1
Printing and publishing	6.4
Nonmetallic minerals	4.8
Metal fabricating	3.7
Electrical products	2.6
Machinery	0.8
Miscellaneous manufacturing	−3.4
Food and beverages	−3.5
Clothing	−8.1
Leather	−10.0
Furniture and fixtures	−14.4
Textiles	−19.0
Construction	
Special trade	17.0
General contractors	11.4
Related services	−2.4
Utilities, Communication, Transportation	
Utilities	14.4
Communications	10.5
Transportation	8.7
Storage	6.3

Industry	Wage Premium
Trade	
Wholesale trade	3.8
Retail trade	−11.1
Finance, Insurance, Real Estate	
Insurance carriers	13.7
Finance	9.3
Insurance and real estate agencies	−4.1
Other Services	
Business management	4.8
Education	−1.0
Miscellaneous	−2.8
Health and welfare	−3.1
Amusement/recreation	−11.4
Personal services	−16.7
Accommodation/food	−20.3
Religious organizations	−31.8

*Percentage wage differential between the wage in each particular industry and the average two-digit industry wage, after controlling for the effect of other wage-determining factors. Data is from Statistics Canada's 1986 Labour Market Activity Survey. The industries are listed in descending order of the magnitude of the industry wage premium within each major industry group.
SOURCE: S. Gera and G Grenier, "Interindustry wage differenatials and efficiency wages: Some Canadian evidence," *Canadian Journal of Economics* 27 (February), 1994, pp. 86−87. Reproduced with permission of Blackwell Publishing Ltd.

These extreme examples of the largest differences above and below the competitive norm also highlight the potential difficulty of fully controlling for the other factors that could affect interindustry wage differences. For example, some of the wage premium in tobacco products could reflect a compensating premium for the uncertainties associated with the restructuring of that industry. Some of the wage disadvantage in accommodation and food services may reflect the fact that some of the compensation may occur in the form of "tips." Some of the wage disadvantage in religious organizations may reflect perceived compensation in nonmonetary forms. Some of the wage gaps may also be the consequence of demand shocks that take some time to become dissipated by labour market adjustments (Gray and Qiu 2010).

Whether these interindustry wage premiums reflect noncompetitive factors or efficiency wages, there is empirical evidence to suggest that industry wage premiums will be dissipated by international competition. This has been documented in studies that tend to find a negative correlation between average industry wage levels and the extent of import penetration into the industry.[3] It has also been documented in a number of recent studies that relate individual wages to measures of import penetration into the industry in which the individuals work.[4]

There is also empirical evidence indicating that industries which are concentrated, in the sense that they are dominated by a small number of firms in the product market, tend to pay higher wages, presumably because of their monopoly profits. In his study of Canadian interindustry wage differentials, Grey (1993) finds that more-concentrated industries, as well as those with more export orientation, have higher unexplained wage differentials. Industries that are regulated also pay higher wages, presumably because the higher wage costs can be passed on to consumers in the form of rate increases without there being much of a reduction in the demand for the regulated service and, hence, in the derived demand for labour. Conversely, the deregulation that has occurred in the 1980s and 1990s has led to substantial reductions in wages in those industries. Rose (1987), for example, found that the union wage premium was cut almost in half after deregulation of the trucking industry in the United States. The wages of unionized truck drivers fell by almost $4000, or 14 percent, as a result of deregulation.

In the case of the airline industry, Card (1986) also found that wage reductions occurred after deregulation, albeit the magnitudes were smaller than in trucking. This finding is consistent with Hendricks (1994) who concludes after looking at the evolution, over time, of various wage differentials for airlines, trucking, railroads, busing, and telephones that the strongest impact of deregulation occurred in trucking. Card's finding was attributed in part to the fact that the large airline carriers were still able to maintain a monopoly position because of their control over key airline terminals as a result of the "hub and spoke" system.

While the deregulation movement has slowed down in recent years, the outsourcing of labour by large firms has contributed to a decline in wages for some particular types of jobs. For example, Goldschmidt and Schmieder (2015) show that many firms have outsourced their food, cleaning, security, and logistics services in response to competitive and cost pressures over the years. Wages on these jobs have declined by 10 to 15 percent, on average, in response to these changes.

In summary, the empirical evidence strongly suggests that industries which are subject to greater competitive pressures on the product market (e.g., import competition, deregulation, more competing firms) tend to pay lower wages. The evidence also suggests the existence and persistence of pure interindustry wage differentials or rents that are consistent with the payment of efficiency wages. More empirical work is necessary, however, to document the precise magnitude of these wage differences and their basic determinants.

Interfirm Wage Differences and Firm Size

Wage differences may also exist across firms within the same industry and region and for the same occupational group. As with other wage structures, economic theory suggests that such wage differences should reflect the basic determinants of wage structures: nonpecuniary differences in the nature of the jobs, short-run demand changes, and noncompetitive factors. Firms that pay high wages, for example, may have poor working conditions or short-run demand increases or noncompetitive conditions, such as a monopoly position in the product market or a union in the labour market, or they may find it in their interest to pay efficiency wages above the competitive norm.

Until recently, studies on interfirm wage differences focused on the positive, and puzzling, empirical relationship between wages and firm size, with larger firms tending to pay higher wages (see Brown and Medoff, 1989, and Oi and Idson, 1999, for a comprehensive review of the evidence, and Lluis, 2009, for more-recent evidence for Canada and the United States). This relationship has been somewhat of a puzzle to economists, because there is little theoretical reason to expect such a relationship once one has controlled for the effect of other factors that influence wages.

Certainly, other factors that influence wages may be correlated with firm size, giving the appearance that it is the size of the firm that affects wages. For example, large firms tend to be unionized and, hence, may pay a union wage premium. Even if they are not unionized, they may pay that premium to minimize the threat of being organized. Large firms may be more likely to have monopoly profits that may be shared with labour. They may also be more likely to be capital intensive and, hence, employ more skilled workers, thereby confounding the occupational wage differential with a firm-size wage differential. Some of the wage advantage in large firms may be a compensating wage premium for their more structured and formalized work requirements.

In such circumstances, the wage premium in large firms arises because large firms are more likely to have these wage-enhancing characteristics: unionization, skilled workers, rents, and undesirable working conditions. It is not firm size, per se, that matters, but rather the correlation of firm size with these other wage-determining factors. These factors may be conventionally observable factors, as were the previously mentioned ones, or they could be conventionally unobservable factors that are difficult to control for in statistical procedures that isolate the pure effect of firm size on wages. For example, such unobservable factors could include motivation or skills that are not measured by years of education or training. Large firms may attach a premium to these characteristics because of their importance in the capital intensity and interrelated production of such firms.

Large firms may also be more likely to pay efficiency wages. As discussed previously, these are wage premiums above the market-clearing wage. They are voluntarily paid by firms in order to encourage loyalty and reduce costs associated with turnover, shirking, monitoring, and supervision. These may be more important for large firms, given their capital intensity and possibly higher costs of monitoring and supervision. In essence, a high-wage policy may pay more for large firms than smaller firms. In such circumstances, the wage premium need not be a premium for workers who have better observable or even unobservable characteristics. It can be a pure rent or "prize" that elicits the positive behaviour on the part of workers so as not to risk losing the prize.

Morissette (1993) uses 1986 LMAS data from Canada to try to disentangle the relative importance of each of the factors contributing to the positive relationship between firm size and wages. He controls for a number of worker and firm characteristics, but still finds a large firm-size premium. A worker moving from a firm with fewer than 20 employees to one with over 500 employees would expect a wage increase of almost 19 percent. Morissette also eliminates the simple compensating wage differential explanation by showing that large firms tend to have better working conditions, for example, as reflected in the provision of pension plans. This evidence seems to suggest that efficiency wage or noncompetitive explanations underlie the firm-size effect.

The Roy model (see Exhibit 10.2) can also be used to understand the source of wage differences across firm size. To the extent that more skilled workers have a comparative advantage in larger firms, unobserved workers differences could account for a large share of the firm-size premium. Using panel data from the Survey of Labour and Income Dynamics (SLID) to estimate a Roy model for firm size, Ferrer and Lluis (2008), indeed, conclude that worker heterogeneity explains a large share of the firm-size effect. Interestingly, an earlier study by Reilly (1995) had also concluded that unobserved differences across workers (as captured by differences in the use of computer technologies) accounted for most of the firm-size wage premium.

One key reason many studies have focused on the role of firm size in wage determination is that this variable is often available in standard data sets, such as the Labour Force Survey. Thanks to advances in computing power and the availability of large **employer-employee data** sets, it is now possible, however, to go beyond firm size and estimate firm wage premia for each and every firm in the economy (Exhibit 10.3). This approach was pioneered by with Abowd, Kramarz, and Margolis (1999) who find, using French data, that firm wage premia account for a substantial share of the wage dispersion in the labour market. Understanding the source of these large and persistent wage differences is an area of active research.

EXHIBIT 10.3

Employer-Employee Data and Firm Wage Effects

Imagine a data set where we know the earnings and the employer of each and every worker in a country, and observe these workers across 10 years or more as they change employer, experience earnings growth, or lose their job. Not so long ago, it would have been inconceivable to have access to such a wealth of information. But with advances in computing power and data storage, it is now possible to conduct very sophisticated econometric analyses on these very large employer-employee data sets.

Abowd, Kramarz, and Margolis (1999) were the first to use these employer-employee data to understand how much of the dispersion of wages in the economy was due to firm effects (some firms pay better than others) or worker effects (some workers earn more regardless of who they work for). While Abowd, Kramarz, and Margolis used French data, recent studies for other countries, such as Germany (Card, Heining, and Kline 2013) and Portugal (Card, Cardoso, and Kline 2016) have reached similar findings; namely, that both worker and firm effects play an important role in wage determination. For instance, Card, Heining, and Kline find that more than half of total wage dispersion is due to worker effects, while firm effects account for about 20 percent of wage dispersion.

The fact that some workers earn more than others regardless of the firm they work for can be explained by differences in human capital (experience and education) or underlying differences in ability or effort. It is more challenging for standard economic theory to explain why different firms appear to be paying different wage to otherwise comparable workers. Under perfect labour market competition, we should instead observe different firms paying the same market wage for workers of a given level of human capital and ability.

There is mounting evidence, however, that the perfectly competitive model is an overly simplistic approach. For instance, Syverson (2011) documents very large differences in productivity across firms, even in narrowly defined industries. In light of this, it is perhaps not surprising to see that more-productive firms pay more than less-productive firms. Source of labour market imperfections have then to be introduced to explain how these differences can persist over time. For instance, Postel-Vinay and Robin (2002) argue that search and matching fictions can account for some of these differences, while Card, Cardoso, Heining, and Kline (2016) propose an explanation based on monopsony power.

While much remains to be learned about the sources of wage differences across firms, this example illustrates how the much richer employer-employee data now available to economists help provide a much better understanding of which model (perfect competition, monopsony, etc.) best describes how the labour market really works.

Public–Private Sector Wage Differentials

The issue of **public–private sector wage differentials** is a topic of interindustry wage determination since the public sector is simply one of many industries. However, the public sector is singled out for special attention for various reasons; it is a large sector, it is the subject of policy concern mainly because of strikes and wage settlements, its impact may spill over into the private sector, and it has peculiarities that make wage determination somewhat unusual.

As our earlier discussion indicated, the theoretical determinants of interindustry wage differentials include compensating adjustments for nonpecuniary differences, short-run adjustments, and noncompetitive factors. Just as these broad categories provided a convenient framework for analyzing the determinants of interindustry wage differentials, they also are convenient for categorizing the theoretical determinants of the particular interindustry wage differential examined in this chapter, the public–private sector wage differential.

The public sector can be broadly defined to include education, health, and government enterprises, and the more-narrowly defined government employment at the federal, provincial, and municipal levels. This definition is based on whether the employer is either funded or owned by the government. Figure 10.2 shows the breakdown of public sector employment in Canada from 1981 to 2012. Total public sector employment grew through the 1980s, peaking in 1992 when there were over three million employees, approximately one-quarter of the employed labour force, working for the government or government-funded employers. Public sector employment dropped sharply in the mid-1990s and started increasing again to reach an all-time high of almost three and a half million workers by 2012. Note, however, that the public sector accounts for a smaller share of the overall workforce (22 percent) than it did back in the 1980s.

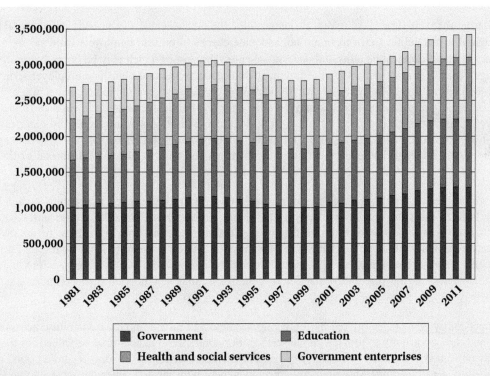

Figure 10.2 Public Sector Employment, Canada, 1981–2012

This graph shows the level of employment in the broadly defined public sector in Canada from 1981 to 2012.

NOTES: Each bar represents annual average employment in four public employment sectors: government (federal, provincial, and municipal), education (local school boards, colleges, and universities), health and social services, and government-owned businesses.

SOURCE: Authors' calculations based on Statistics Canada, CANSIM series D466212, D466028, D466358, D466371, D466384, D466240, D466266, and D466490.

The total employment figures hide different trends in the sub-components. The main declines occurred through downsizing of all three levels of public administration (government), and the privatization of government enterprises, such as Air Canada, Canadian National, and Petro-Canada. The health and education sectors also shrank slightly over the 1990s but are now a larger share of the public sector than in 1981, so that the education sector now accounts for 28 percent of public sector workers (as against 24 percent in 1981) and the health sector accounts for 26 percent (as against 22 percent in 1981). Clearly, even after the downsizing of the 1990s, the public sector remains a large and important employer.

Theoretical Determinants of Public–Private Wage Differentials

Compensating Adjustments for Nonpecuniary Differences

Interindustry wage differentials may reflect compensating adjustments for differences in the nonpecuniary aspects of employment across industries. With respect to the private and public sectors, nonpecuniary advantages may exist with respect to such factors as job security, fringe benefits, and political visibility. To the extent that these advantages prevail in the public sector, we would expect a correspondingly lower wage to compensate for the advantages. However, to the extent that these advantages are dissipating over time, we may also expect public sector wages to rise relative to those in the private sector to compensate for the loss of these nonpecuniary advantages.

Job security often is discussed as being more prevalent in the public than in the private sector. Theoretically, this may be the case because job security could be necessary to prevent the abuses of political patronage. That is, without a modicum of job security, civil servants could be replaced each time a new political party came into power, or whenever a politician wanted to gain favour by granting patronage in the form of civil service jobs. To avoid this potential abuse, and to ensure a degree of continuity in the public sector workforce, a degree of job security may be granted. Larger elements of the public sector also may be able to easily provide such job security because their size gives them a portfolio of jobs within which to reallocate their workforce.

As with job security, there are theoretical reasons to suggest that the public sector may provide more-liberal fringe benefits. This occurs because in the public sector there are not adequate checks to prevent employers from saving on *current* wage costs by granting liberal retirement benefits and pension schemes, the cost of which may be borne by *future* generations of taxpayers. Fringe benefits that are payable in the future, such as early retirement plans and employer-sponsored pensions, can be viewed as deferred wages in the sense that workers would willingly give up some current wages for these future benefits. Such deferred compensation systems may be a way for the public sector to shift costs to future generations of taxpayers; however (as discussed in the later chapter on optimal compensation systems), deferred compensation also may exist as part of an optimal compensation system to ensure honesty and work effort. Such a system may be especially important in the public sector, to the extent that other mechanisms, such as the threat of dismissal or the monitoring of output, are not available.

In the private sector, there is a built-in check to ensure that employers are constrained in granting such deferred benefits; eventually they have to meet the obligation of paying for them. However, in the public sector, unless such benefits are fully funded, their costs will be borne by future taxpayers. To the extent that they have little or no say in the current political process, there is no automatic mechanism to prevent public sector employers from saving on current wage costs by granting liberal deferred cost items, such as early retirement or substantial pensions or pensions indexed for future inflation. The only check is the possibility that future generations may not honour such commitments made by their predecessors.

Additional nonpecuniary advantages offered by the public sector could include political visibility, access to control over political rules, and the opportunity to provide public service. For some, these factors may be valued for their own end; for others, they may be valued as a means to other objectives. For example, some workers may regard a period of public sector employment as a low-wage apprenticeship period that provides them with inside knowledge, access to power sources, and contacts in the political arena. These factors may be of immense value (and, hence, lead to higher remuneration) in future private sector jobs as consultants, lobbyists, or simply partners in firms that do business with the government or that would benefit from inside political information.

For others, public sector employment may provide "the nonpecuniary satisfaction of doing good"—to use a phrase utilized by Reder (1955). This could be a reason, for example, for people to do volunteer work for churches or charities, or for some to accept lower salaries in such nonprofit institutions. It may be a more prevalent phenomenon throughout the public sector, especially in teaching or health care. The term "public service" means just that to many people.

The nonpecuniary factors that we have discussed—job security, fringe benefits, and political visibility—generally, are ones for which there are theoretical reasons to believe that they would be greater in the public than in the private sector. Certainly, conventional wisdom and casual empiricism seem to suggest this to be the case. To the extent that it is true, the public sector would be expected to have lower wages to compensate for these factors.

Noncompetitive Factors

Interindustry wage differentials may also reflect noncompetitive factors, and it is in this area that the differences between public and private sector labour markets become most pronounced. Specific features that have important implications for public-private wage differentials and their changes over time revolve around the fact that the public sector can be characterized as subject to various peculiarities, including a political constraint rather than a profit constraint, possible monopsony, an inelastic demand for labour, and a high degree of new unionization. Each of these factors will be discussed in turn, with an emphasis on their implications for public-private wage differentials and their changes over time.

Political Rather Than Profit Constraint

The public sector usually is not subject to a profit constraint as traditionally exists in the private sector. Rather, the profit constraint is replaced by an ultimate political constraint, and there is the belief that the political constraint is less binding. This occurs because taxpayers are diffuse, often ill informed, and can exert pressure only infrequently and with respect to a package of issues. Public sector managers also are diffuse in the sense that lines of responsibility are not always well defined and "buck-passing" can prevail. Workers in the public sector, on the other hand, are often portrayed as a unified, distinct-interest group providing direct pressure for wage increases. A more serious imperfection of the political process arises from the fact, discussed earlier, that *future* taxpayers have little or no representation in *today's* political process.

While these features of the political constraint suggest the possibility that it is less binding than the profit constraint, there still are constraining influences on wage settlements in the public sector. Taxpayer scrutiny is now extremely strong and, in fact, politicians may gain from appearing to be cost-conscious guardians of the public purse by reducing wage costs. Even the alleged diffuse nature of management in the public sector may work against employees; it can be difficult to win wage gains if one doesn't know with whom one is bargaining.

Perhaps the most important feature of the political constraint that works against public sector workers is that, during a strike, tax revenues keep coming in to the public sector even though wage expenditures are reduced and public services are not provided. This is in contrast to the private sector, where employers are under considerable pressure to settle because they are losing customers and sales revenues during a strike. To be sure, there can be pressure from taxpayers to have the wage savings go into general tax revenues or into tax reductions because services are not provided. Nevertheless, the fact remains that this political pressure is less stringent than the profit constraint when firms lose customers and revenues during a strike.

Monopsony

To the extent that the government sector is often the dominant employer in particular labour markets, governments may utilize their monopsony power to pay lower wage rates than if they behaved competitively. Political forces may pressure them to act as model employers and not utilize their monopsony power; nevertheless, there is also pressure to be cost conscious, which may lead them to exercise their monopsony power.

In fact, the empirical evidence cited earlier in the chapter on monopsony suggested that for at least two elements of the public sector, teaching and nursing, there was some evidence of monopsony. The extent to which these results can be generalized for other elements of the public sector, or for the teaching and nursing professions as a whole, remains an unanswered empirical question.

To the extent that monopsony power exists and is exercised in the public sector, public sector wages would be lower than they would be in the absence of monopsony. However, the pressure of monopsony also means that, for a range of wage increases, unions would not have to be concerned about employment reductions. In fact, as illustrated in the chapter on monopsony, wage increases may actually lead to employment increases, suggesting the possibility of a substantial union wage impact in monopsonistic labour markets.

Inelastic Demand for Public Sector Labour

The possibility of a substantial union impact on wages in the public sector is furthered by the possibility that the demand for labour in the public sector may be wage inelastic. In such circumstances, unions could bargain for substantial wage increases without worrying about large reductions in the employment of their members. The inelasticity of the demand for labour may occur because noncompetitive forces restrict the utilization of substitute inputs as well as substitute services.

Many of the services produced in the public sector are so-called essential services that are not provided in the private sector, and when they are so provided, they are often under governmental regulation. Since consumers (taxpayers) are unable to substitute other services for those provided by the public sector, their demand for these services may be relatively price (tax) inelastic. In essence, wage increases can be passed on to taxpayers in the form of tax increases for the essential services without taxpayers reducing their demand for these services and, hence, the derived demand for labour.

This is strengthened by the fact that there are often few good inputs to substitute for public sector labour as it becomes expensive. This may reflect the nature of the public sector production function, but it may also reflect the fact that the public sector is heavily professionalized, and professional labour tends to have a degree of control over the utilization of other inputs, including nonprofessional labour.

While these factors suggest that the demand for public sector labour would be wage inelastic, other factors are at work in the opposite direction. Specifically, the high ratio of labour cost to total cost in many public services suggests that the demand would be elastic. In addition, substitute inputs and services certainly could be utilized, especially in the long run. Even the essentiality of the service may work against public sector employees by restricting their right to strike and reducing public sympathy during a strike. In addition, the employers may stall in the bargaining process, knowing that the essential elements of the service will be maintained and, as indicated earlier, tax revenues are still forthcoming.

Since theory does not indicate unambiguously whether the demand for public sector labour would be elastic or inelastic, we must appeal to the empirical evidence. The evidence from various U.S. studies indicates that the demand for labour in the public sector is inelastic, and that, the more essential the service, the greater the inelasticity (Gunderson and Riddell 1991, p. 167).

Unionization

A final noncompetitive factor, unionization, may also affect the wages of public sector workers relative to their private sector counterparts. This is especially the case when the unionization is coupled with the other factors discussed in this chapter—the inelastic demand for public sector labour, the possible monopsony in some public sector markets, and the absence of a profit constraint.

In Canada, the growth and high degree of unionization in the public sector is documented, for example, in Ponak and Thompson (2005). Some sectors, like the federal civil service, are organized almost to their full potential. Others, like teaching and health, are also predominantly unionized. Interestingly, in Canada, the United States, and the United Kingdom, a majority of unionized jobs is now found in the public sector because of the ongoing decline in unionization in the private sector (Card, Lemieux, and Riddell 2004).

Competitive Floor but Not Ceiling

The previously discussed factors—absence of a profit constraint, monopsony, inelastic demand, and the high degree of recent unionization—all suggested that wage determination may be different between the public and private sectors, and that noncompetitive factors may give rise to an interindustry wage differential between the public and private sectors. Most of the factors, with the exception of monopsony, would appear to favour a noncompetitive wage advantage in the public sector, although a variety of subtle constraining influences are present.

However, there is a stronger reason to expect the wage advantage to be in favour of public sector workers. This is so because the forces of competition would ensure that wages in the public sector would not fall much below wages in the private sector for comparable workers. If they did, the public sector would not be in a competitive position to recruit labour, and would experience problems of recruitment, turnover, and morale. That is, competition would ensure a competitive *floor* on wages in the public sector.

These same competitive forces, however, need not provide an effective *ceiling* on wages in the public sector. To be sure, if public sector wages exceeded wages of comparable workers in the private sector, there would be queues of applicants and excessive competition for public sector jobs. Nevertheless, employers in the public sector are not under a profit constraint to respond to these disequilibrium signals; they need not lower their relative wage. They *may* not pay an excessive wage if the political constraint is a binding cost constraint; nevertheless, there is no guarantee that this will be the case. In essence, the forces of competition ensure a floor, but they need not provide an effective ceiling on wages in the public sector. Hence the potential bias, in theory, for wages in the public sector to be in excess of wages in the private sector for comparable workers.

Empirical Evidence

Empirical studies of wage differentials between the public and private sectors try to isolate the "pure" public sector premium; that is, the impact of working in the public sector, controlling for human capital, age, sex, industry (type of service), occupation, and possibly union status. The simplest way to do this is within a regression framework, such as that in equation 10.2. The researcher includes an indicator variable (or "dummy" variable) of whether a worker works in the public sector, along with the other control variables (X). The coefficient on the public sector indicator is interpreted as the public sector pay premium. An alternative approach generalizes the regression approach, and takes into account the possibility that the pay structure may differ in the two sectors. For example, the impact of gender may be different in the public sector because of more stringent pay equity provisions, or the experience profiles may be flatter. This decomposition procedure, which is more fully developed in Chapter 12 on discrimination, divides the public–private differential into two parts: (1) the part due to differences in skills or endowments of the worker and (2) surplus returns or economic rent (the "pure" public sector premium).

EXHIBIT 10.4

Are There Queues for Government Jobs?

One of the best measures of whether a job is "overpaid," and whether incumbent workers, therefore, receive economic rents, is whether there are queues of qualified applicants for such jobs. This is so because queues provide a good bottom-line measure of the total compensation of the job (wages and fringe benefits) relative to the requirements and working conditions of the job. That is, as an alternative to trying to estimate, for example, pure public-private wage differentials after controlling for the effect of other legitimate wage-determining characteristics, it may be desirable to estimate queues of qualified applicants.

Krueger (1988a, 1988b) does so on the basis of a number of different U.S. data sets. He finds that there are substantial queues for federal government jobs. As well, as the ratio of federal earnings to private sector earnings increases, the application rate for federal government jobs increases, as does the quality of such applicants.

The two approaches yield similar conclusions. Evidence for Canada is provided in Gunderson, Hyatt, and Riddell (2000).[5] Using Labour Force Survey data from 1997, they estimate that public sector workers earn a premium of about 9 percent. Generally, the premium is higher for women, reflecting the impact of pay equity policies, and lower for higher-skilled employees, reflecting wage compression in the public sector. Similarly, Hou and Coulombe (2010) show that the premium is higher for visible minorities, suggesting there is less discrimination against this group of workers in the public than in the private sector, while Mueller (1998) shows that the premium is higher for people a the low-end of the wage distribution. One of the more striking findings of Gunderson, Hyatt, and Riddell, using census data from 1971, 1991, and 1991, is that the public sector pay premium has actually been rising over the past 30 years, from about 5 percent in 1971 to 9 percent in the 1990s. The Canadian evidence agrees with results from the United States, where the estimated public sector premium is also in the 5 to 10 percent range.[6]

These empirical results, which suggest only modest premiums, indicate that severe policies are not necessary, at least at this stage, to restrain public sector wage settlements. Nevertheless, constant vigilance is required, especially to prevent current taxpayers from passing public sector costs on to future taxpayers in the form of deferred compensation.

Summary

- The wage (or earnings) structure can be cut along many dimensions besides workplace amenities and education, as explored in the previous chapters. In particular, we are often interested in how earnings vary by occupation, region, industry, and public versus private sector. The human capital earnings function is especially helpful in summarizing how earnings vary in these dimensions, because it allows us to isolate the "pure" impact of working in a specific region or job, controlling for all of the other factors, especially age and education (skill).

- Simple supply and demand diagrams can be used to explain why wages differ across sectors. In equilibrium, we expect wage differentials to exist because of differing demand conditions, combined with differences in the supply of workers. That said, wage differentials may be exacerbated by impediments to mobility of workers between sectors, and nonequilibrium wage differences may persist, even in the long run, if workers cannot move from the low- to the high-wage sector.

- Wage setting across sectors gets more complicated when different workers have different levels of skills and productive abilities. The Roy model provides a more general approach to wage setting in these circumstances. Wages are no longer perfectly equalized across sectors, as workers with different skills choose the sector in which they earn more than in any other job. Interestingly, the market still clears, in the sense that all workers are satisfied with the job they have and would not want to choose a different sector of employment.

- While barriers to mobility can often explain persistent wage gaps across sectors (like regions in Canada), these gaps may be generated by more complicated economic behaviour. For example, interindustry wage differentials may be generated by "efficiency wages," whereby firms pay higher wages because worker productivity depends on the wage rate. In this case, some industries will be high-wage industries, even in the long run, despite queues of workers who would like to switch from lower-wage industries. Because it would reduce worker productivity, firms in high-wage industries are unwilling to cut wages to increase employment and, thus, clear the cross-industry labour market.

- The public sector accounts for about one-fifth of the employed labour force in Canada, including workers in government (public administration), as well as government-owned or funded firms and agencies (hospitals, schools, colleges, universities, and Crown corporations). An important policy question asks how much public employees should be paid, and in particular, whether through their unions and political pressure they are able to extract excessive wages. Most evidence suggests that there is a small premium (5 to 10 percent) for working in the public sector, controlling for observable human capital determinants of earnings.

Keywords

comparative advantage

disequilibrium

earnings function

efficiency wages

employer-employee data

immobility

industry premiums

interindustry wage differentials

interoccupational wage differentials

migration

nonpecuniary benefits

occupation

occupational premiums

public–private sector wage differentials

regional wage differential

Roy model

unobserved heterogeneity

Review Questions

1. Discuss the various factors that determine the shape of the labour supply schedule for an occupation. Give an example of an occupation that may have an elastic supply schedule and one that may have an inelastic one, and indicate why this is so. If the two occupations received an equal increase in the demand for their labour, what would happen to the skill differential between them?

2. Discuss the expected impact on the occupational wage structure of each of the following policies:

    a. An increase in unionization

    b. An increase in public subsidies to education, training, job search, and mobility

    c. Wage-price controls

    d. Child labour laws

    e. Laws governing the minimum age one can leave school

    f. A reduction in rural-urban migration

    g. An increase in immigration

    h. An exogenous influx into the labour force of younger workers and married women

    i. Stricter control of entry into the medical profession

3. It could be argued that market forces will not prevent cities from growing beyond a socially optimal size, because pollution or congestion externalities associated with city growth are not accounted for through the market mechanism. Discuss the extent to which wage adjustments may reflect these externalities. Will the wage adjustments ensure a socially optimal city size?

4. Discuss the ways in which government social transfer programs may decrease or increase geographic mobility. To the extent that they decrease mobility, should they be removed? Are there ways of mitigating their adverse effects on geographic mobility?

5. Why might large firms pay higher wages than small firms? Why might this relationship prevail even after controlling for the effect of other wage-determining factors, such as the differences in the skill distribution and in working conditions?

6. On the basis of your knowledge of the determinants of the elasticity of demand for labour (for a review, see Chapter 5), would you expect the demand for public sector labour to be inelastic or elastic? Why? Why might one expect the elasticity to differ across different elements of the public sector?

7. Criticisms of public sector wages as being too high often implicitly assume that private sector wages are the correct norm. What is so virtuous about private sector wages, given that they can reflect market imperfections, unequal bargaining power, and a variety of non-economic constraints? Discuss.

8. Most studies show that wages are higher in the public than in the private sector. Table 10.1 shows, however, that most industries in which public sector workers are concentrated (government services, educational services, health and social services) exhibit a negative wage premium. Is this inconsistent with the other studies? Discuss.

Problems

1. "In a competitive economy, there can be no such thing as a pure interindustry wage differential in the long run." True or false? Explain.

2. "Efficiency wages cannot prevail in the long run, because there would always be a queue of qualified applicants for the jobs that paid the efficiency wage premiums. In such circumstances, the employer could increase the hiring standards or the job requirements and the wage premium would, therefore, reflect a compensating wage for the greater skill requirements or more-difficult requirements of the job." True or false? Explain.

3. Consider an economy of only two industries, one high wage and the other low wage. Each employs the same number of workers, equally divided between two groups: skilled and unskilled. Skilled workers are identical with each other in the two industries, and so are the unskilled. The low-wage industry pays its skilled labour $10 an hour and its unskilled labour $5, during both a recession and an expansion; that is, it has a rigid wage structure. The high-wage industry pays its skilled labour $20 per hour in both a recession and an expansion, but it pays its unskilled workers $5 during recession and $15 during expansion; that is, only its skilled wages are rigid over the business cycle.

   For the whole economy, calculate the interoccupational wage differential (ratio of skilled to unskilled wages) in both the recession and the expansion. Calculate the interindustry wage differential (ratio of high- to low-wage industries) for both skilled and unskilled workers in both the recession and the expansion. Why does the interoccupational wage differential contract in the expansion and widen in the interindustry?

4. A researcher has access to the 2000 Labour Force Survey, and estimates the following regression:

$$\ln W_i = 10.46 + 0.336 PUBLIC_i$$

   where W_i is individual annual earnings, and $PUBLIC_i$ is an indicator of whether the individual works in the public sector. Calculate the implied ratio of public to private sector earnings. The researcher concludes that this is evidence that public sector workers earn economic rents; that is, that they are overpaid. Critically evaluate the researcher's conclusions, and explain how the researcher could refine her estimate.

5. Differences in the elasticity of demand for labour between the public and private sectors, by themselves, are not sufficient conditions for a wage differential between the two sectors. True or false? Explain.

6. Grant, a young Newfoundlander, has just graduated from high school and is deciding what to do with the rest of his life, which lasts two periods (like everyone else's). His main decision is whether to stay in Newfoundland or migrate to Toronto. If he stays in Newfoundland, he will earn Y_0 in period 1 and Y_1 in period 2. If he moves to Toronto, he will incur a moving cost of M (in the first period), and he will be unemployed (with zero earnings) for the first period. In his second period in Toronto, he will earn Y_T. The interest rate at which money can be borrowed or invested is r.

   a. On a carefully labelled diagram, illustrate Grant's migration decision; that is, show his earnings paths as a function of time, depending on whether he lives in Newfoundland or Toronto.

   b. Show that he will move to Toronto if

$$\left(Y_T - Y_1\right) > \left(1 + r\right)\left(Y_0 + M\right)$$

   What is the economic intuition underlying this result? How does an increase in the interest rate affect the migration decision? Why?

   c. As a potential labour economist, Grant realizes that he needs to have estimates of Y_T and Y_1 in order to make a wise migration decision. He reads in the newspaper that average earnings of Newfoundlanders in Toronto are $\overline{Y}_T$, while Newfoundlanders earn an average of $\overline{Y}_1$ if they stay in Newfoundland. (Both magnitudes refer to second-period earnings) With specific reference to the result in part (b), discuss the potential error that Grant may make by using $\overline{Y}_T$ and $\overline{Y}_1$ as the basis of his estimate of the return to migration.

7. Debbie is deciding which career to pursue. She cannot decide between becoming a veterinarian or a pharmacist. Assume that both careers require the equivalent of six years of post-secondary education. A recent increase in the demand for pharmacists has led to shortage, and incomes of pharmacists are about $20,000 higher than those of veterinarians. All else equal, Debbie would rather be a veterinarian, but for a $20,000 higher salary, she is tempted to study pharmacy. As a rare, economically literate guidance counsellor, use a figure like Figure 10.1 to advise Debbie on her career choice. Be sure to distinguish between the short- and the long-run supply of labour to an occupation.

8. Assume that, on average, an applicant waits 12 months before being hired into a government job (as a mail clerk). George could work as a mail clerk in the private sector immediately for a salary of $2500 per month, but he chooses instead to remain unemployed and wait for the government job. In the meantime, he collects $500 per month in unemployment insurance benefits (for 12 months). Assume that the government job lasts two years,

that his private sector job will last just as long (plus the year he can wait for the government job), that salaries are constant, that the interest rate is 10 percent per year, and that leisure has no value to George. Determine the minimum public sector premium that must exist for George's decision to be rational.

What are the pros and cons of using queues as a measure of rents or excess payments paid to workers in the public sector?

9. Several studies, such as Krueger and Summers (1988), show that interindustry wage differentials tend to be stable over time, and countries. Because of data limitations, however, many such cross-country comparisons look at only raw wage differentials that are not corrected for differences in skills or human capital of workers employed in these industries. In a detailed comparison of the United States and Sweden, however, Edin and Zetterberg (1992) show that interindustry wage differentials are much smaller in Sweden than in the United States, once differences in workers' skills (observed and unobserved) are controlled for. An important difference between the two countries is that, unlike the United States or Canada, Sweden has a highly centralized wage-setting system. With this in mind, discuss what the case of Sweden and the United States teaches us about the underlying sources of interindustry wage differentials.

Endnotes

1. In theory, efficiency wages could vary by any of the factors that give rise to wage structures, such as occupation or region as well as industry. In practice, however, the theoretical rationales for efficiency wages suggest that they will differ by industry and by firm size and not so much by occupation and region. Hence, the efficiency wage literature tends to be associated with the literature on wage differences by industry and firm size, and not by the other factors that give rise to wage structures.

2. See Dickens and Katz (1987); Gibbons, Katz, Lemieux, and Parent (2005); Katz and Summers (1989b); Krueger and Summers (1987, 1988); and Murphy and Topel (1987) for U.S. data, and Gera and Grenier (1994) for Canadian data. These studies also review the earlier studies that documented a substantial interindustry wage differential based on aggregate industry data.

3. See, for example, Grossman (1986, 1987), Lawrence and Lawrence (1985), Revenga (1992), and Grey (1993).

4. See, for example, Dickens and Lang (1988), Freeman and Katz (1991), Katz and Summers (1989a), and Gaston and Trefler (1994, 1995).

5. Gunderson, Hyatt, and Riddell (2000) employ the simpler, "dummy variable" approach. For evidence employing the alternative (decomposition) approach, see Gunderson and Riddell (1995). For other surveys of evidence on the public sector premium in Canada, see Gunderson (1998).

6. Borland and Gregory (1999) provide a detailed summary of the methodological issues entailed in estimating the public sector wage premium, as well as extensive international evidence.

CHAPTER 11

The Economics of Immigration

LEARNING OBJECTIVES

LO1 Provide a descriptive profile of immigrants to Canada, including the following information: how many immigrants arrive each year, where do they come from, and where do they settle?

LO2 Describe Canada's immigrant point system, and the role it plays in determining the admission of immigrants to Canada.

LO3 Use the supply and demand framework to evaluate the theoretical impact of immigration on the labour market, and use this model to discuss the empirical evidence of the impact of immigration.

LO4 Define the concept of "immigrant earnings assimilation," and explain the pitfalls of using a single cross-section data set to estimate the rate of assimilation.

LO5 Sketch a simple economic model of migration, including an answer to the question, when should someone move countries?

MAIN QUESTIONS

- How have patterns of immigration to Canada changed over the past 60 years? From which countries do immigrants come, and where do they settle upon arrival in Canada?

- What is the "point system," and what impact does it have on immigration to Canada?

- Overall, does immigration have a positive or negative impact on the labour market outcomes of the native born? In particular, are higher levels of immigration associated with downward pressure on wages or increases in unemployment?

- In what respects do immigrants assimilate? How long does it take for an immigrant's earnings to catch up to those of a native-born Canadian?

- Are immigrants a net drain on the public treasury, especially through higher dependence on social assistance?

From the narrow perspective of the human capital earnings function, immigrant status may be viewed as just another determinant of individual wages. In fact, documenting and interpreting the correlation between immigrant status and earnings is the subject of intense research in labour economics. However, this focus arises from a much wider interest in the economics of immigration.

While immigration has always been an important feature of Canadian labour market policy, several factors have conspired to move it to the forefront of economic policy discussion. First, there is some concern that immigration contributes to a deterioration in labour market conditions, especially in the form of higher unemployment and wage polarization. Second, government fiscal pressures keep social programs lean, and there is some perception (perhaps unwarranted) that immigrants pose a special burden to these programs. Third, immigrants come from a diverse set of countries, substantially changing the ethnic composition of the Canadian population. Some view these changes as a challenge to Canadian multiculturalism policy. Others note that immigrants from non-European countries may face greater difficulties in assimilation than was the case with earlier immigrants. To the extent that the new immigrants come from developing countries, their skills (vocational or language) may indeed be less of a match for the Canadian labour market. Finally, whatever the particular policy motivation, immigrants are a numerically important group in the labour market. This is true, not just in the traditional immigrant-receiving countries like Canada, the United States, and Australia, but also in the United Kingdom, France, Germany, and other parts of Europe. Immigration, as much as trade, is an important manifestation of globalization in the Canadian labour market.

Even confined to its economic aspects, immigration is too large a topic to cover in one chapter. There are a number of potential subtopics that would be worth describing.

Among them are the following:

1. *Economic models of migration.* How might we model the individual decision to migrate to a particular country? To what extent can we explain immigrant flows across countries by the economic variables implied by these models?

2. *Economic performance of immigrants.* Once they arrive in Canada, how quickly do immigrants adjust to their new labour market? What factors seem to explain success (or failure) in the Canadian labour market?

3. *The impact of immigrants on native-born outcomes.* Do immigrants adversely affect the labour market outcomes of the native-born population? Are some groups hurt more than others? Are immigrants net contributors to the public treasury?

4. *Policy evaluation.* What policy mechanisms are at the government's disposal to minimize the adverse effects of immigration (or maximize the benefits)? Should immigration levels be increased or decreased? Should family reunification be the dominant criteria for admission to Canada? Does it really matter who is admitted to Canada?

Our discussion is largely confined to the last three topics. The economic model of migration is a straightforward extension of human capital theory briefly outlined in Chapter 10. (See also our discussion of "the brain drain" in this chapter.)

A Profile of Immigration to Canada

Any description of the main features of immigration to Canada is principally a confirmation of the prominence of immigrants in the Canadian labour market. As such, the following provides a backdrop for the discussion of public policy toward immigration, and the potential impact of immigration on the labour market.

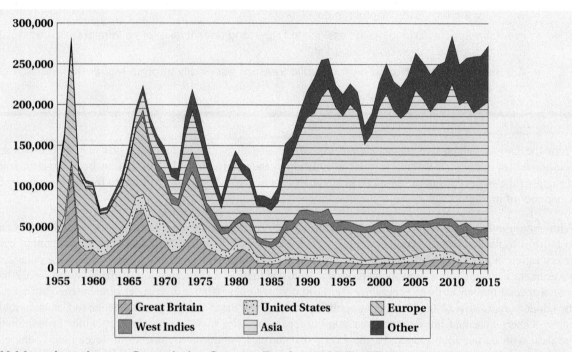

Figure 11.1 Immigration to Canada by Source Region, 1955–2015

This figure plots the number of immigrants to Canada from six major immigrant source regions for each year from 1955 to 2015. The distance between each line and the one below it represents the number of immigrants from that region, so that the areas (bands) between lines show the relative size of immigration from a region. Total immigration is given by the sum of immigration from the six regions. The figure, thus, illustrates patterns in the total flow of immigration, fluctuating, with peaks at around 200,000–250,000, as well as a declining share of immigrants from Great Britain and the United States, and an increasing share from Asia.

NOTES: "Europe" is total Europe minus Great Britain. "Other" is the total of other regions/countries not otherwise listed; notably, Africa, Australasia, and Central and South America.

SOURCE: Authors tabulations based on data retrieved from CANSIM, Statistics Canada (1955–2013), and for 2013–15, CIC Admissions of Permanent Residents by Country of Citizenship, see "Permanent Resident Admissions by Source Country," http://open.canada.ca/data/en/dataset/ad975a26-df23-456a-8ada-756191a23695.

Figure 11.1 shows the level and patterns of immigration by source region since 1955. Green (1976, 1995) provides more detailed documentation of the early features of these patterns, especially including an important historical perspective on immigration over the 20th century. This figure illustrates a number of important points. First, until the mid-1980s, overall immigration levels fluctuated considerably. Subsequently, Canada steadily admitted over 200,000 immigrants per year, with the exceptions of 1998 and 1999. From 2000 onward, immigration levels have increased, to over 270,000 in 2015. However, even these high numbers are not unprecedented. The annual flow is only slightly higher than was experienced in the peak years of the late 1950s, mid-1960s, and mid-1970s. On a per capita basis, immigration levels are actually slightly lower. In the past, however, immigration levels varied more, year-to-year, and they were more cyclical, with levels significantly curtailed during recessions. The recessionary years of the early 1990s and 2008–2009 did not see such a decline in immigration. The steady flow of immigration irrespective of economic conditions is unprecedented. Second, this figure shows that the source regions have changed dramatically. In the mid-1960s, the main source regions were Great Britain, the United States, and Western Europe. By the early 1990s, the largest region was "Asia" (a decidedly broad grouping). Other countries, principally those in South and Central America, have also gained in relative importance. Table 11.1 provides a more detailed breakdown of the source countries for 2005 and 2015, showing the top 10 source countries for those two years. There is general stability in the composition of immigrants over this time period; one-half of the top 10 source countries are in Asia. But some changes are worth noting. First, the composition of immigrants from Asia has changed. In 2005, China was the largest source country, accounting for 16 percent of all immigrants to Canada. By 2015, the Philippines overtook China, providing almost 19 percent of immigrants to Canada. India was the second most important source, comprising about 15 percent of Canada's immigrants in both years. Second, in any given year there will be idiosyncratic reasons why one country is in the top 10. In 2015, for example, almost 10,000 immigrants came from Syria, mostly as refugees. Variations in the sources of global conflict or economic crises generate temporary churning in the distribution of immigrants. While this changing mix of source countries may not have any bearing on the economic consequences of immigration, it certainly affects public perceptions of immigration, and, more objectively, has a clear impact on the ethnic composition of the population.

TABLE 11.1	Top Ten Immigrant Source Countries, 2005 and 2015			
Rank	2005		2015	
1	China (PRC)	42,568	Philippines	50,831
2	India	36,179	India	39,525
3	Philippines	18,137	China (PRC)	19,531
4	Pakistan	14,314	Iran	11,669
5	United States	8392	Pakistan	11,329
6	United Kingdom	7253	Syria	9853
7	Colombia	6424	United States	7523
8	Iran	5837	France	5807
9	Korea, Republic of	5826	United Kingdom	5451
10	Romania	5048	Nigeria	4133
Top 10 source countries	149,978			165,652
Percentage accounted for by top 10	57			61
Percentage accounted for by top four	42			45
Others	112,268			106,168
Total	262,246			271,820

SOURCE: Citizenship and Immigration Canada, "Permanent Resident Admissions by Source Country," http://open.canada.ca/data/en/dataset/ad975a26-df23-456a-8ada-756191a23695.

Figure 11.2 demonstrates another important feature of immigration to Canada. Based on the 2001 and 2011 censuses of population, this figure shows the regional variation of immigrant concentrations across major metropolitan areas. Immigrants are defined to be those individuals born outside Canada who have attained landed immigrant status (i.e., legal permanent immigrants to Canada). In 2011, 20.7 percent of all Canadian residents were born outside of Canada, compared to 18.3 percent 10 years earlier—an increase of 2.4 percentage points. This percentage is also significantly higher than the United States, where a still-large 13 percent are foreign born. However, aggregated national figures mask the potential impact of immigration. Immigrant concentrations vary considerably, from over 46 percent in Toronto and 40 percent in Vancouver, to under 5 percent in Quebec cities outside Montreal. Figure 11.2 also shows that the relative importance of immigration is changing differently across cities. Immigrant shares are growing most obviously in Toronto and Vancouver, but also Calgary, Montreal, and Winnipeg. While economists often speak of the impact of immigration on the national labour market, it is likely that the impact varies across cities. Indeed, the variation of immigrant concentrations across cities represents a possible way to identify the impact of immigration on the labour market.

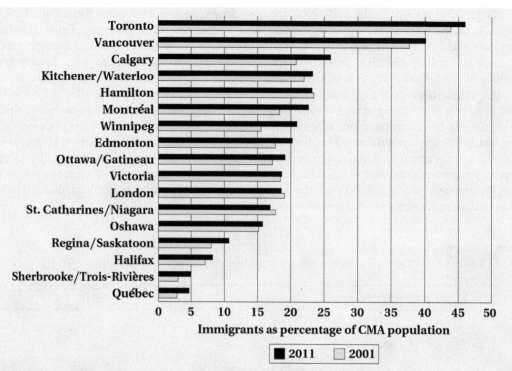

Figure 11.2 Immigrant Concentration by Census Metropolitan Area, 2001 and 2011

This bar chart shows the fraction of the population of Canada's largest cities (Census Metropolitan Areas, or CMAs) that are immigrants (i.e., permanent immigrants to Canada, born outside of Canada). For each city we show two bars: the percentage of each city that are immigrants in 2011, and the corresponding percentage for 2001. The cities are sorted in descending order of the percentage of the population that were immigrants in 2011.

NOTES: Reported figures are the percentage of the population of each CMA that are permanent immigrants to Canada.

SOURCE: Authors tabulations based on the 2001 Individual Public Use Microdata Files, Census of Canada, 2001, and National Household Survey, 2011, Statistics Canada.

LO2   The Policy Environment

Immigration policymakers essentially have two "levers" that they can manipulate: (1) the number of immigrants to be admitted and (2) who among the set of potential immigrants is admitted. The history of Canadian immigration policy illustrates the extremes in the application of these tools. At the beginning of the 20th century, immigration to Canada was essentially open to anyone, with the notable exception of immigrants from China. While there was a strong preference to recruit immigrants from northern Europe, only the very sick, destitute, and criminals were actively screened (Green 1995). By the mid-1960s, both the quantity and type of immigrants were significantly restricted, though there ceased to be active discrimination on the basis of country of origin. Before outlining how these immigrant admission tools are used, it is worth discussing the fundamental, though largely unresearched, question regarding the objectives of immigration policy. It is difficult to assess the failure or success of immigration policy without some idea of what policymakers are trying to achieve.[1]

We begin by ignoring the important political dimension of immigration policy, and assume that policymakers are attempting to maximize "national welfare." The question is then, whose welfare enters into this objective function? What are the relative weights attached to the existing stock of Canadian residents versus potential immigrants? Most likely, the greater weight is placed on maximizing the benefit of immigration to the existing population. Immigrants, for example, may be admitted for the skills they bring to the Canadian labour market, alleviating specific skills shortages or, more generally, contributing to economic growth. The problem with the delineation between current residents and immigrants, however, is that the "existing population" evolves as new immigrants join the club. The welfare of the existing population and potential immigrants cannot be neatly separated, because today's immigrants are tomorrow's residents. For example, today's immigrants will ultimately wish to be reunited with family members. Family reunification then becomes another motivation for immigration that is addressed to maximize the welfare of the "ultimately" current residents of Canada.

Humanitarian concerns for potential immigrants will provide another motivation for admitting individuals to Canada. Such concerns may be purely political (provide individuals sanctuary from political persecution) or they may be economic (provide individuals with sanctuary from poverty). In practice, it is difficult to disentangle these factors, and it may be easier to summarize them as merely providing immigrants with an opportunity to better their lives.

Canadian immigration policy has been driven by both the self-interested and the altruistic (humanitarian) concerns described above. This is reflected in the historical development of the immigration policy levers. Green (1976, 1995) and Green and Green (1995, 1999) provide a comprehensive summary of the history and details of Canadian immigration policy.

As will become apparent, the two policy dimensions, or the number and nature of immigrants, are not independent. Nevertheless, it is worth discussing them separately. Every year, the federal government announces the planned number of immigrants to be admitted the following year. These levels are chosen in consultation with the provinces and with an eye to minimizing any adverse impact of immigration. Accordingly, planned admissions would be reduced in recessionary times. Of course, fewer immigrants would find Canada an attractive destination during a recession. The ultimate level of immigration would then be the result of a mixture of immigrant supply and demand factors.

Immigrants enter Canada by a number of different avenues, each reflecting the competing motivations for immigration described above. Broadly speaking, immigrants can be divided into **assessed and non-assessed classes**. The assessed classes are those immigrants who are evaluated on the basis of their likely contribution and success in the Canadian labour market. These include the traditional **independent immigrants**, now called the "skilled worker class," most commonly described in economic models of migration. These are individuals who apply for admission to Canada on the basis of their skills and are evaluated on a relatively objective **point system**. This system, introduced in 1967, currently applies to the majority of immigrants. Points are awarded for the specific skills that the immigrant has, with extra points awarded for skills perceived to be in shortage in Canada, and especially for already having a job offer in Canada. The details of the point allocation are described in Exhibit 11.1. The point system provides the government with the most direct method of controlling the types of immigrants admitted to Canada. In principle, with enough information, the point system could be used to limit immigration only to those individuals virtually certain to succeed in Canada, with no possible displacement of Canadian workers. There are other, smaller, economically assessed classes, like live-in caregivers, and the business classes, which include investors, entrepreneurs, and self-employed who are not evaluated under the same point system as skilled workers but must meet certain economic objectives.

EXHIBIT 11.1

Canada's Immigration Point System, 2016

Immigrants can be considered for immigration to Canada in the skilled worker class. To qualify, potential immigrants must satisfy all of the following criteria:

1. **Work experience:** Individuals must have at least one year of recent full-time work experience in a broadly defined skilled occupation.
2. **Language:** Individuals must meet a minimum score on a sanctioned language test, establishing their fluency in either English or French.
3. **Minimum funds:** Individuals must demonstrate sufficient "start-up" funds to support themselves on arrival in Canada. For a single person this is approximately $12,000, while a family of four would need to prove they had almost $23,000.
4. **Minimum score:** Individuals need to obtain a minimum score according to six selection criteria. In 2016, the minimum score was 67 points out of a maximum 100. The following table illustrates the current scale and the scores for various skills and attributes that are predictors of likely economic success in Canada:

Factor	Maximum Score
Education	**25**

- Higher points are awarded for more education, sharply increasing with completed university or equivalent.
- A mere 5 points are awarded for someone who has only completed high school.
- Points increase sharply for completing at least one year of post-secondary education (leading to a diploma or degree). A two-year equivalent diploma or degree earns 19 points.
- An Ph.D. earns the maximum 25 points, while an MA earns 23. A bachelor's degree is worth 21 points.

Official Languages	**28**

- A maximum of 24 points is given for proficiency in one official language (English or French).
- Candidates must meet minimum thresholds in four language tests (speaking, listening, reading, and writing) for either English or French.
- An additional 4 points are awarded for demonstrated proficiency in the other official language.

Work Experience	**15**

- Points are awarded for full-time work experience, ranging from 9 points for one year, to 15 points for six or more years.

Age	**10**

- The maximum of 10 points is awarded to applicants aged 18 to 35. No points are awarded to those younger than 18, or older than 47.

Arranged Employment in Canada	**10**

- Ten points are added if the applicant has already arranged a job in Canada.

Adaptability	**10**

- Points are awarded (to a maximum of 10) for:
  - Spouse's education, language, and Canadian work experience
  - Previous legal work experience in Canada
  - Past studies in Canada
  - Family relationship in Canada
  - Arranged employment (bonus points)

If they meet the minimum standard, immigrants are then added to the pool for "Express Entry," a refinement to the point system adopted in 2015. Under Express Entry, once added to the pool, potential immigrants are ranked by several criteria, notably their (and/or their spouse's) education and experience, but also job offers from employers who can also select immigrants from the pool. Successful immigrants are, thus, "twice filtered": first by the point system described above, and second by the "Comprehensive Ranking System" applied to the pool of eligible potential immigrants.

SOURCE: *Six Selection Factors--Federal Skilled Workers*, http://www.cic.gc.ca/english/immigrate/skilled/apply-factors.asp, Government of Canada, Immigration, Refugees and Citizenship Canada.

The non-assessed classes (**family class immigrants** and **refugee class**) currently make up 37 percent of all immigrants, a lower proportion than in the early 1990s when it was as high as 63 percent. Reunification of family members with Canadian residents is a high priority of government policy. The definition of "family" has varied over the years, with the changes made to the closeness of relatives admissible under these criteria. Unlike skilled workers who undergo skills evaluation, family class immigrants are not selected with any consideration of the likelihood of their success in Canada. The same is true of refugees. In fact, likelihood of economic success is of no consideration for refugees, since they are admitted on the basis of humanitarian grounds, usually to facilitate escape from political persecution or violence.

Figure 11.3 plots the time series of immigration to Canada, by broad class of immigrant, since 1966. A few patterns are worth noting. First, the economically assessed classes are the largest group, comprising well over half of immigrants (63 percent) in 2015. However, the relative importance of this group has fluctuated over time, with changes in immigration policy. When the point system was first introduced in 1967, most immigrants were assessed. Over the mid-1970s, the family class grew steadily in importance and, until the mid-1990s, formed the "base" of the immigration numbers in any given year. The size of the family class was not very sensitive to economic conditions or the total number of immigrants admitted to Canada. In fact, it was the assessed classes in this time period that essentially formed the margin of adjustment, being substantially reduced when immigration totals were cut. This changed in the mid-1990s when concerns of the economic performance of immigrants led to an increased emphasis on skills, and the assessed classes became more prominent. The refugee class fluctuates with global political conditions, peaking, for example, in the late 1970s with Vietnamese refugees, and more recently with refugees from Syria. The share of refugees has been relatively constant since the early 1990s.

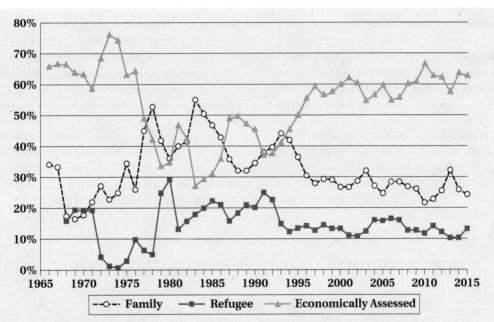

Figure 11.3 Immigration to Canada by Class of Immigrant, 1966 to 2015

This figure plots the number of immigrants to Canada each year from 1966 to 2015 by admission category. "Economically assessed" immigrants are primarily the skilled worker (or independent) class, assessed under the point system, and the small business or entrepreneur class. The "family" class are those immigrants sponsored by Canadian residents (as family members).

NOTES: Reported figures are the percentage of annual total of immigration to Canada by class of entry (admission class). The economically assessed class is an aggregate of skilled workers, entrepreneurs, and other classes admitted under the point system.

SOURCES: Data from 1980 through 2015 comes from Citizenship and Immigration Canada, "Permanent Resident Admissions by Category," http://open.canada.ca/data/en/dataset/ad975a26-df23-456a-8ada-756191a23695. Data prior to 1980: authors' tabulations based on statistics reported in Employment and Immigration Canada, *Immigration Statistics*, various issues; Supply and Services Canada; and Citizenship and Immigration Canada.

A number of policy questions immediately arise. How much of a problem for the Canadian economy is created by the fact that the family class is unassessed? Do family class immigrants perform more poorly than the skilled worker class? Even within the assessed classes, how well does the point system pick those most likely to succeed? How sensitive is immigrant performance to the overall level of immigration?

To address these particular issues, as well as more general ones, policymakers need to know the answers to a few important empirical questions:

1. *What is the impact of immigrants on the Canadian market?* If immigrants have no adverse effects (or possibly even positive ones), then this permits humanitarian concerns to dominate. It also reduces the need for governments to intensively assess potential immigrants. On the other hand, if there are adverse consequences, then it will matter more how many and who is let in.

2. *How do immigrants fare in Canada?* Answering this informs the policymaker of the factors important for success in Canada, and yields possible evidence on the failure or success of previous admissions policy. It also provides indirect evidence regarding the first concern. If immigrants have difficulty adjusting to the Canadian labour market, it seriously questions the ability of the labour market to absorb the level and type of immigrants being admitted. Furthermore, if immigrants perform poorly, they may have more direct adverse effects on the Canadian economy, potentially becoming a burden on transfer programs. Of course, the evidence could just as easily show that immigrants are on average quite successful and net contributors to the public treasury.

LO3   The Impact of Immigrants on the Labour Market

Of most direct interest to policymakers in setting immigration levels is the **impact of immigrants** on the labour market. A simple supply and demand model can be used to outline the principal theoretical issues.[2] Most directly, the addition of new immigrants to a labour market increases the population of potential workers and increases the supply of labour. This first-order effect on the labour market is illustrated in panel (a) of Figure 11.4. One can easily see why the native born might oppose immigration. Wages are unambiguously depressed, unless the demand curve is perfectly elastic (horizontal). Employment increases, but if for some reason the wage does not fully adjust to clear the market, unemployment might also ensue.

This simplistic representation ignores many other effects of immigration on the labour market that could offset these adverse consequences. First, as described above, immigrants are often selected on the basis of their occupational skills. If these skills are in short supply so that the market is in temporary disequilibrium, then immigrants may relieve the shortage without any adverse effect on wages or unemployment. Of course, only a small minority of immigrants are likely to fill this role, so skills shortages alone are unlikely to offset the negative impact of immigration on wages, assuming Figure 11.4(a) is the otherwise correct representation of the labour market.

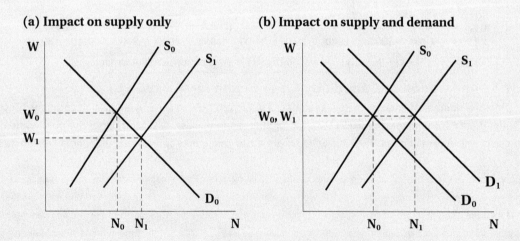

Figure 11.4 The Impact of Immigration on Employment and Wages

An increase in the number of immigrants will shift out the supply curve of labour, from S_0 to S_1. If this is the only change in market conditions, the new equilibrium will have lower wages, W_1 as against W_0, and higher employment, N_1 as against N_0. Panel (b) allows for the possibility that immigration also shifts out the demand curve. In this example, the increase in demand is exactly enough to offset the change in supply, so that the new wage, W_1, equals the original wage, W_0, and all the new immigrants are employed.

More likely, immigrants may cause the demand curve to shift outward, as illustrated in Figure 11.4(b). Immigrants purchase goods and services in Canada, and this will increase the derived demand for labour. Immigrants may also alter trade patterns in ways that could affect the demand for labour.[3] This could arise because of improved information flows between new immigrants and their source countries. Alternatively, "importing" labour may be a substitute for importing the goods produced by that labour in the originating country. Immigrants may also disproportionately invest in Canadian firms, creating additional employment. Clearly, this is the motivation for the admission of business class immigrants. Even if immigrants themselves do not invest, others may invest in production facilities that take advantage of the new immigrant labour. In Figure 11.4(b), the increase in demand is drawn in such a way that there is no adverse effect on wages. Whether this is the relevant outcome depends on the relative shifts of the supply and demand curves, as well as the slopes (elasticities) of the functions. Economic theory can take us only so far in this policy exercise.

Another important consideration is the relevant labour market upon which we expect immigration to have an impact. Is it the national labour market, or the Vancouver, Toronto, Montreal, or Regina labour markets? Is it the high-skill or low-skill labour markets? Can we view these markets in isolation, or are there important linkages across them? For example, the admission of high-skilled immigrants might lower the price of high-skilled labour, but if this labour is complementary with low-skilled labour, then demand for low-skilled labour would be positively affected. A similar argument would hold if immigrants were low skilled but the beneficiaries of the immigration are the high skilled. The overall impact on the market would then depend on the skill composition of immigrants, as well as on the complementarity of high- and low-skilled labour.

As it turns out, estimating the impact of immigration on the labour market is quite difficult. Part of the problem stems from the factors outlined above: the impact may be complicated, vary across markets, and be diffuse at the national level. This makes it more difficult to know where to begin to look for the effect of immigration. Unfortunately, even where there is some confidence that one can isolate a market in which immigration should have an effect (positive or negative), economists encounter the same problem as in most other empirical exercises; we never observe what labour market conditions would prevail in the absence of immigration—that is, the **counterfactual** case. The problem of the absence of a reasonable comparison market is compounded by the fact that, with few exceptions, immigrants do not arrive randomly in a particular market. Immigrants are, generally, attracted by good economic prospects, whether in terms of higher wages or employment probabilities. This simultaneous determination of immigration and labour market outcomes confounds the evaluation of the impact of immigration. The most credible empirical investigations of the impact of immigration focus on this issue, and have adopted different strategies for constructing counterfactual evidence.

One promising approach is to exploit cross-city variation in immigration. Consider again Figure 11.2. If the economies were otherwise identical, one could imagine comparing labour market outcomes in Toronto, with an immigrant concentration in 2011 of 46 percent, to Montreal, with an immigrant concentration of 23 percent. Given Toronto's 23 percent higher concentration of immigrants, if immigrants had a depressing effect on the labour market one would expect that city to have lower wages and possibly higher unemployment than Montreal. The problems with this procedure are manifest in this prediction. There may be other features of the cities that differ and have nothing to do with the fraction of immigrants. One way to address this problem is to relate *changes* in labour market outcomes to *changes* in immigrant shares; for example, within cities between 2001 and 2011. This allows us to control for long-run differences between the economies of Toronto and Montreal. From Figure 11.2, we would then base our inference on the differences in *changes* in wages and unemployment between Montreal and Toronto, compared to *changes* in the share of immigrants (an increase in Toronto of 2.2 percentage points, versus an increase in Montreal of 4.3 percentage points). We would then determine whether wages declined more, or grew less slowly, in Montreal where the immigration share increased more than in Toronto. Again, we can see the limitations of this approach. Presumably, immigrants move to the city where economic conditions are most promising; that is, where labour market outcomes are likely to be improving. We never really see what the economy of Toronto would have looked like without immigration, and looking at changes in the Montreal economy may not be informative. Nevertheless, by finding variables that help predict immigration but are relatively independent of economic factors (e.g., the pre-existing ethnic composition of a city), progress can be made in addressing this problem.

Because of the larger sample sizes and larger number of cities (markets), this approach has been used in the United States, where Altonji and Card (1991) use cross-city variation in immigration patterns between 1970 and 1980 to identify the impact of immigration on a variety of labour market outcomes. Because most immigrants to the United States are low skilled, Altonji and Card also focus their attention on the labour market outcomes of the comparably low-skilled native born. As mentioned, the positive correlation between immigration and positive labour market outcomes is likely to lead to an understatement of adverse labour market consequences, if such consequences exist. For this reason, Altonji and Card also try to account for this simultaneity by using previous immigration patterns to help predict cross-city flows of immigration. They find virtually no evidence of a link between immigration and labour market outcomes.

But previous immigration patterns themselves may be related to long-run economic opportunities in a city. An "ideal" solution to this problem is to exploit natural experiments, whereby immigration levels to a particular labour market are at least arguably exogenous to local economic conditions. There have been a few such studies that exploit historical episodes where immigration was determined by political factors and a relatively convincing case can be made for the exogeneity of the immigration. The empirical method is otherwise similar to the cross-city approach. Comparisons are made between the economic outcomes in the market receiving the "immigration shock" and those markets that did not receive the shock. Not surprisingly, the method is not without its own flaws, and the results can be sensitive to the choice of comparison market. Even if we believe that the immigration shock is exogenous, we observe only the "treatment" market, and may not have a perfect counterfactual, or control, market.

The first paper to use this approach is Card (1990) (See Exhibit 11.2). He examines the impact of the Mariel boatlift on the Miami labour market, and finds very little evidence of an adverse effect of this historically large influx of immigrants. More recently, Borjas (forthcoming) has challenged Card's conclusion, though not the quasi-experimental methodology, noting that one subset of the Miami labour market (native-born high school dropouts) were adversely affected. Several papers followed Card's, exploiting similar episodes of major, politically motivated migration to estimate the impact of immigration on labour markets. Two papers, for example, look at the impact of the repatriation of European "colonials" on their home country labour markets. Hunt (1992) examines the impact of the return of Europeans to France after Algerian independence in the 1960s, while Carrington and de Lima (1996) explore the impact of the return of Portuguese citizens following Marxist revolutions in former Portuguese colonies in Africa. While the evidence is mixed, neither of these studies conclude that these significant shocks to the labour markets were associated with adverse outcomes for natives. As another example, Friedberg (2001) evaluates the impact of large-scale Russian immigration to Israel from 1989 to 1995. Over this period, the arrival of over 600,000 Russian immigrants increased the Israeli labour force by almost 14 percent. By exploiting the uneven occupational distribution of the Russian Jews (both before and after their arrival in Israel), and the subsequent changes in the Israeli occupational wage structure, she shows that this increase in immigration had no adverse effect on the wages of native-born Israelis.

EXHIBIT 11.2

Fidel Castro and Immigration Research

Because immigrants are likely to settle in labour markets that provide the best economic opportunities, comparing the economic outcomes of high- and low-immigrant cities may not provide a clean estimate of the impact of immigration. Even if immigrants depressed wages in the high-immigration city, this effect might be masked by the otherwise better economic performance of that city. One way around this problem is to find examples where political, rather than economic, motivations were the principal determinants of immigrant settlement.

David Card (1990) exploits one such episode. Emigration from Cuba is tightly restricted, but between May and September 1980, Fidel Castro permitted approximately 125,000 Cubans to leave Mariel for the United States. About half of these immigrants settled permanently in Miami, leading to a 7 percent increase in the labour force, especially of low-skilled workers. Associated with this immigration was an immediate downturn in the Miami economy. The unemployment rate rose from 5 percent in April 1980 to 7.1 percent in July. The homicide rate rose by 50 percent, and there were serious riots in the poorer sections of Miami, with 13 deaths.

So, does this suggest that the Mariel boatlift hurt the Miami labour market? Card's answer is no; even cities that did not receive these immigrants suffered similar deterioration in their labour markets. We can think of Miami as the "treatment" group in a natural experiment, and the measured impact on Miami cannot be interpreted without a reference, or control, group. Card constructs a control group with a composite of cities with characteristics similar to those of Miami (Atlanta, Houston, Los Angeles, and Tampa). The difference-in-differences methodology then estimates changes in the Miami labour market from before to after the arrival of the Mariel immigrants versus the changes in the comparison group. For example, to estimate the effect on the labour market, Y, two years after the Mariel boatlift, one only needs to calculate

$$\left(Y_{1982} - Y_{1979}\right)_{\text{Miami}} - \left(Y_{1982} - Y_{1979}\right)_{\text{Comparison}}$$

Statistically significant differences could be interpreted as evidence of the effect of immigration on the Miami labour market.

Card finds no detectable effect of the Mariel boatlift on the Miami labour market. There is no evidence that the unemployment rates or wages of even the low-skilled workers were adversely affected by this major labour market shock.

More recently, George Borjas (forthcoming) offers a reappraisal of Card's research design. In particular, he disaggregates the "low skill" group that Card created, and focuses instead on the subset of native-born workers most similar to the Mariel immigrants: high school drop outs. Borjas also constructs different sets of "control group" cities to explore the robustness of Card's conclusions. He finds much larger adverse impacts of the Mariel immigrants on this especially vulnerable part of the skill distribution, an effect that is masked by Card's aggregation of low skill. Clearly, even when pursuing a straightforward, transparent research design, there are many choices that can affect the bottom-line conclusions.

While Borjas, Freeman, and Katz (1992, 1996) acknowledge that natural experiments may help address the concern that immigration to any particular city depends on exogenous economic opportunity, they offer an explanation as to why no effect is typically found: other economic adjustments. There are two main candidate forms of adjustment. First, the native born may move out of cities experiencing major influxes of immigration. This means that immigrants shift the supply curve of labour out less than we expect in a narrowly defined city market, so the effect in that market is smaller. Immigrants still shift the overall national supply curve of labour, but the impact is more diffuse, spread over several labour markets, and harder to find. The second form of adjustment is through trade and investment. For example, firms may set up shop in cities with large stocks of low-priced immigrant labour. This corresponds to an outward shift of the labour demand curve (as in panel (b) of Figure 11.4). Even an otherwise exogenous increase in immigration can thus lead to a shift in both the supply and demand curves. Shifts in relative labour demand across cities will therefore complicate and hide the otherwise adverse impact of immigration on the overall labour market. Given these difficulties, Borjas, Freeman, and Katz (1992, 1996) propose a more indirect approach to calibrate the impact of immigration on wages. First, they estimate the impact of immigration on the supply of various skill groups, and they then simulate the effect on wages and employment, analogous to the discussion surrounding Figure 11.4. Using this approach, they argue that, while the overall impact of immigration on wages and employment is limited, U.S. immigration patterns have had a negative impact on the employment and wages of low-skilled natives. In fact, they point to immigration as one of the more important factors leading to increased wage polarization.

More-recent papers have tried to combine insights from both approaches, though they come to slightly different conclusions. These papers spend more time discussing and defining the relevant labour market being affected by immigration, as well as taking account of economic adjustment that may mitigate the impact of immigration on a particular market. Card (2001) extends the cross-city approach using the 1990 U.S. census while, most importantly, exploiting within-city differences in the skill mix of immigrants and potential impacts on the local occupational wage structure. He also directly estimates the impact of immigration on total labour supply to any particular market, measuring the extent to which native out-migration offsets the increase in supply of a within-city skill group. On this question, he finds no evidence of offsetting native migration; adding one immigrant to a labour market increases "supply pressure" by one person. His main results on wages are consistent with previous studies (i.e., small overall effects), except, he finds that, where increases in immigration led to disproportionate increases in the share of unskilled workers, the wages of low-skilled workers were slightly adversely affected. He estimates that high levels of low-skilled immigration, such as experienced over the 1980s, adversely affected the wages of other low-skilled workers in the most affected cities (like Miami and Los Angeles) by between 1 and 3 percent.

Borjas (2003) also divides the labour market by skill level. However, he argues that the adjustments across cities are inherently difficult to control for, and instead focuses on the national U.S. labour market. His study, thus, divides the U.S. labour market into skill submarkets across time periods instead of cities. Using data from 1960–2001, he finds an overall negative adverse impact of immigration on low-skill wages. A 10 percent increase in the immigration-induced supply of workers reduces wages by 3 to 4 percent. Given the concentration of immigrants in low-skill labour markets, he concludes that immigration to the United States between 1980 and 2000 lowered the wages of native-born high school dropouts by

9 percent. Borjas also shows that results are sensitive to the spatial definition of the market. When he focuses on state-level rather than national-level outcomes, the estimated impact of immigration is only one-third as large. This is consistent with offsetting economic adjustment at the local level, as suggested by Borjas, Freeman, and Katz.

Card (2009) provides some reconciliation of the cross-city and national time series approaches, but raises further questions about the appropriate definition of the labour market. The issues he raises illustrate the gap that exists between a simple conceptual framework, like that used in Figure 11.4, and "real world" implementation. At the same time, Card's presentation highlights the value of such a framework for organizing a discussion of this complex question. In Borjas's (2003) study, the labour market is subdivided into four skill groups: 1) high school dropouts, 2) high school graduates, 3) those with some post secondary, and 4) university (college) graduates. Each skill group is in its own isolated labour market, independently affected by immigrants as depicted in Figure 11.4. Card (2009) argues that this configuration is inappropriate. He proposes, instead, that high school dropouts and high school graduates work at essentially the same jobs and, as perfect substitutes, can be grouped into the same labour market (low skilled).[4] Similarly, those with some high schooling and those with completed post-secondary education can be combined into a single high-skill labour market. This means that the effect of low-skilled immigrants should be measured incorporating all low-skill native born, not just the relatively small group of high school dropouts. With this apparently small change in the definition of "market," Card estimates that immigration has no significant effect on the wages of native-born workers. In addition, Card shows that immigrants and natives with the same observed skill levels are not perfect substitutes, and, as a result, the addition of more immigrants of a given skill does not shift the supply for native-born workers of that skill as much as would be the case if they were perfect substitutes. Instead, Card argues, the impact of increased immigration is borne primarily by other immigrants: an increase of low-skill immigrants lowers the wages of other low-skill immigrants.[5]

Aydemir and Borjas (2011) raise a further unsettling point about the difficulty of estimating the impact of immigration. Virtually all research is conducted using the largest possible samples from the U.S. census. However, once the data are partitioned into submarkets along skill and location dimensions, sample sizes become dangerously small for precisely estimating the impact of immigration. The resulting measurement (or sampling) error biases researchers away from finding effects, even if they are there. They illustrate this point using Canadian census data, and also provide the primary evidence on the impact of immigration on native-born wages in Canada. Using the complete samples of the Canadian census available at Statistics Canada, and partitioning the national labour market into five skill groups, they show that there is a well-determined negative effect of immigration on native-born wages in Canada. They also show that the effect is almost undetectable in the commonly used, publicly available Canadian census data, because the small sample sizes are too small. Turning to the cross-city approach, they show that the small sample problem is significantly worsened. Furthermore, using Canadian data yields only 27 "cities" that can be compared over time, as opposed to almost 200 such markets in the United States; therefore, a distinct "small sample" problem. Using the complete censuses, they estimate only small and statistically insignificant effects of immigration on Canadian native-born wages at the city level. Aydemir and Borjas conclude that many of the small estimated effects of immigration are driven by data problems that especially affect the local labour market approach. For this, and the conceptual reasons previously discussed, they conclude that the national market, time-series approach is better. Using this approach yields negative effects of immigration on native outcomes in Canada as well as the United States.

More-recent papers build on this earlier literature, incorporating the concerns regarding the exogeneity of immigrants to the labour market, the definition of skill group, and the adjustment of native-born workers that can offset the impact of immigration. Using Danish administrative data covering the entire population of Denmark, Foged and Peri (2016) exploit the exogenous placement of refugees across Danish municipalities to track outcomes for native-born residents of the municipalities. They find that the low-skilled refugees, indeed, had an impact on the low-skilled native labour market, but that, in response, the native-born invested in their own skills to mitigate these effects. In other words, rather than just move geographic markets to avoid competition with immigrant labour, low-skilled Danes moved "up market" in the skill distribution. Another paper highlighting the adaptability of labour markets to immigrant supply shocks is Cadena and Kovak (2016). Instead of the native born moving in response to increased competition from immigrants (e.g., Borjas, Freeman, and Katz 1996), they show that previous immigrants themselves are highly sensitive to changing local economic conditions. Cadena and Kovak show that low-skilled Mexican migrants to the United States are more mobile than low-skilled native-born workers, and in response to the financial crisis of 2008 it was the migration of these Mexican immigrants from hard-hit cities to more prosperous ones that helped cushion the blow on low-skilled domestic workers.

What conclusions can be drawn, especially as an input into policy formation? First, policymakers need to be aware that there is no simple answer to the question of whether immigration has an adverse impact on the labour market. To the extent that an effect exists, it is hard to find; immigrants likely choose to live in places that can accommodate them, and other forces of economic adjustment mitigate the potentially adverse labour supply effect. Second, there is a strong skill dimension to the impact of immigration. Immigrants to the United States tend to be lower skilled than those to Canada, and it is not clear that even the mixed results from the U.S. literature will apply to Canada. Even with the caveats raised by Aydemir and Borjas concerning sample sizes, investigating the impact of immigration on labour market outcomes in Canada remains an important area begging for future research.

LO4   Economic Assimilation

Primarily because of the relative abundance of data, most research on immigration has focused on the immigrants themselves. By charting immigrant economic performance, especially over time, economists obtain, at least, indirect evidence on the absorptive capacity of the labour market. By correlating economic success with observable characteristics, results from this exercise can, in principle, aid in the design of admission criteria. Finally, since one of the general public concerns is that immigrants do not succeed and subsequently become burdens of the state, evidence on immigrant performance can directly support or allay these concerns.

Economic assimilation can occur in a number of possible dimensions. Immediately after arriving in Canada, immigrants may face a period of unemployment as they search for a job. Thus, we might expect immigrants to assimilate in terms of their hours worked, perhaps starting out at a lower level than similar native-born individuals, but catching up after spending time in Canada. We may expect their wages to follow a similar pattern. Upon arrival in Canada, immigrants may lack some of the less observable skills that the native born have—language, knowledge of the local labour market, and more specific (but unobservable) skills particular to firms in Canada. Their educational credentials may not be fully recognized. With time, however, we would expect their wages to grow to the level of native born. In fact, if immigrants are **positively selected**—that is, that immigrants are among the most motivated and able (in terms of unobservables)—their wages may eventually exceed those of the native born. Earnings growth may also reflect the dissipation of discrimination, at least to the extent that immigrants who have been in the country for a longer period are likely to be less discriminated against than recent arrivals.

Most studies of assimilation focus on earnings as a summary of economic performance. Earnings will summarize both hours worked and wages, though, by focusing on full-year, full-time workers, these studies effectively concentrate on wages. The objective of most of this research is the immigrant assimilation profile. Figure 11.5 shows the key features of this profile. Consider two otherwise identical individuals, one native born entering the labour market at age 20 and the other a 20-year-old immigrant entering the labour market immediately upon arrival in Canada. The native-born Canadian will experience wage growth as he ages (the returns to experience). Initially, the immigrant may suffer an earnings penalty, called the **entry effect**. As the immigrant ages, his earnings should also rise. Assimilation will refer to the difference in the returns to age experienced by the immigrant and the comparable native, and is usually measured as a function of **years since migration** (YSM). If immigrants experience assimilation (i.e., enjoy additional returns to age), it is possible that their earnings will catch up to the native born. This catch-up or time to equality is marked by T in Figure 11.5. After T years of YSM, immigrant earnings exceed that of the native born. If assimilation is slow, or the entry effect is sufficiently large, then the implied time to catch up may exceed the individual's working life. In that case, immigrants effectively never catch up to the native born.

Early studies of immigrant assimilation, such as Chiswick's 1978 investigation for the United States, found large entry disadvantages offset by rapid earnings growth. The methodology employed in these studies was quite straightforward. Most census data include information on individual human capital characteristics, earnings, and immigration status. One can then estimate a conventional earnings function, augmented by the indicators of immigrant status. By comparing recently arrived immigrants to comparable natives, one can readily estimate the entry effect. By then comparing earnings of recent immigrants to those who have been in the host country longer, one can impute the rate of earnings assimilation. As pointed out by George Borjas (1985), however, such a procedure can lead to misleading results regarding assimilation, and also miss important changes in the entry effects of immigrants. This would be the case if immigrant performance is deteriorating (or improving) over time. Because it illustrates some of the general empirical problems involved in estimating assimilation, and also outlines some of the important areas of debate in the recent literature, we describe this problem in some detail.

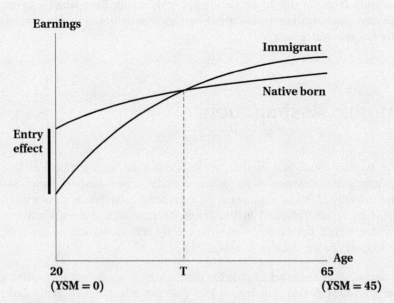

Figure 11.5 Hypothetical Assimilation Profile, 20-Year-Old Immigrant

We, typically, measure assimilation by the extent to which immigrant earnings catch up to those of the native born. Consider two otherwise identical people at age 20, one native born and the other a new immigrant. At age 20, the immigrant's years since migration (YSM) equals zero, and his earnings are initially below those of the native born, due to what is called the *entry effect*. Over time, the native-born wages will rise with age for conventional reasons, as would the immigrant's. However, with years in Canada, the immigrant's earnings may grow even faster, as he accumulates Canada-specific human capital. These excess returns to age, or returns to YSM, are due to what is called *assimilation*. If the rate of assimilation is high enough, immigrant earnings may catch up, for example, by age T.

The problems that arise when using a single cross-section of data to estimate assimilation profiles are similar in spirit to those outlined in Chapter 4 in the context of disentangling age from birth-year effects. The problem of cohort effects, as applied to assimilation profiles, is illustrated in Figure 11.6. Panel (a) illustrates the ideal scenario, for which the single cross-section would be appropriate. Consider the earnings of the cohort of immigrants who arrived between 1986 and 1990, labelled IM8690. Their initial earnings are at the level labelled A, and they grow by the indicated amount to point B in 1995. Now, assume that we have data in 1995 that allows us to compare the earnings of the most recent cohort, IM9195, to IM8690. Because IM8690 immigrants have been in Canada on average for five years longer, we might attribute the difference in earnings between the two groups (point B versus point D) to assimilation (ignoring, for the moment any other sources of earnings growth in the economy). If entry and assimilation rates are the same across cohorts, this will be an accurate estimate.

Now consider the situation in panel (b), where the assimilation rate is constant across cohorts, but their entry positions differ. IM8690 begins at point A, and has their earnings rise to point B in 1995. However, we would seriously overstate immigrant assimilation by attributing the entire difference in earnings between IM9195 and IM8690 in 1995 (point B minus point D) to the latter's five years in Canada. Their earnings are also higher because they started out at a better position; IM9195 starts off at point D rather than the earnings associated with point A. By looking at 1995 data alone, there is no way to disentangle the changing entry, or cohort, effect (the distance from D to F) from genuine assimilation (the distance from F to B). For this reason, the only credible way to obtain estimates of assimilation is to follow cohorts of immigrants over time; for example, by combining data from 1995 and 2000. For IM9195, this would entail a comparison of point E with point D. Even with this method, there may be pitfalls. One possibility is that out-migration of immigrants leads to systematic changes in the composition of the underlying immigrant cohorts (see Lam 1994). The immigrants comprising IM9195 in 2000 may have a different composition than they did when they first arrived in 1991. On one hand, some of the unsuccessful immigrants may have returned home (see Lubotsky 2007); on the other, some of the more successful may have migrated to the United States. Average incomes of the IM9195 cohort might then be different in 2000 than they were in 1995 for reasons that have nothing to do with earnings growth of the average immigrant arriving in 1991.

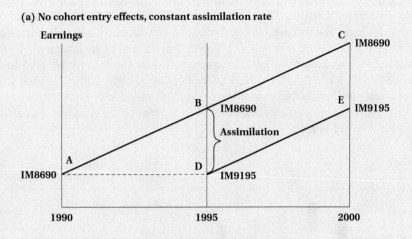

(a) No cohort entry effects, constant assimilation rate

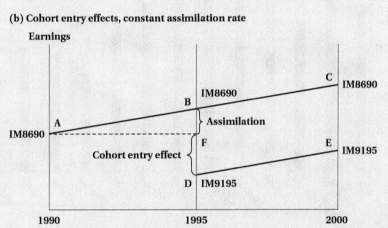

(b) Cohort entry effects, constant assimilation rate

Figure 11.6 Measuring Earnings Assimilation: Disentangling Cohort and Assimilation Effects

This figure shows the potential pitfalls of using cross-sectional data to compare rates of assimilation. Panel (a) shows the ideal case. Each cohort of immigrants has the same starting point (entry effect) and same rate of assimilation. A cross-section estimate of assimilation is based on comparing the earnings of IM8690 to IM9195 in 1995, where the immigrants who arrived between 1986 and 1990 (IM8690) have been in Canada five years longer than the newer immigrants (IM9195). This difference is given by BD, which corresponds to the actual earnings growth of IM8690 who started out at A, the same level as IM9195 (at D). Panel (b) shows what happens if the entry position of immigrant cohorts is shifting. Here, genuine earnings growth of IM8690 is given by BF, but the difference in earnings between IM8690 and IM9195 is BD. Part of the difference is due to the lower starting point, or cohort entry effect of IM9195 (D versus A). The cross-section estimate of earnings growth for IM9195 (BD) would overstate assimilation, confounding actual growth and the change in initial earnings. Only with data from 1990, and following IM8690 from A to B (in 1995), would the genuine assimilation of BF be identified.

Cohort effects represent more than just a nuisance for labour economists measuring assimilation. The changing entry position of immigrants is of considerable interest in its own right. If immigrant performance is deteriorating, it becomes important to document and explain. Is it because the immigrants themselves are not as capable as previous cohorts? If so, can this be linked to changes in immigration policy? Alternatively, is it the economy that is changing, whereby the labour market is less able to provide employment for immigrants with particular skills?

Figure 11.7 illustrates the issues described above by arraying immigrant earnings by cohort for the 2006 Census and 2011 National Household Survey. Here, average annual earnings (expressed in year 2010 dollars) are shown for a sample of full-year, full-time employed men so that the patterns primarily reflect differences in wages. Focus first on the 2005 means (the black bars). By looking from right to left, we can see that average earnings, generally, rise as we compare immigrants who have been in Canada longer. To some extent, these differences reflect the fact that those immigrants are also older, but they may also reflect genuine assimilation. The entry effect can be estimated by comparing the most recent immigrants (2000 to 2004) with the native born. In this case, the entry effect is approximately $14,880, a quarter less than natives (the raw numbers used in these calculations are reported in Problem 3 at the end of the chapter). A cross-section estimate of assimilation can be obtained for this cohort, IM0004, by comparing their earnings to the 1995 to 1999, IM9599, cohort. In 2005, IM9599 earned $57,430 while IM0004 earned an average of $49,898. The difference is $7532 and this can be interpreted as the effect of being in Canada five years since entry. If assimilation profiles are the same for both cohorts, and they both started out with the same earnings, we expect IM0004 to experience the same earnings growth, and end up with as high earnings in 2010 as IM9599 had in 2005.

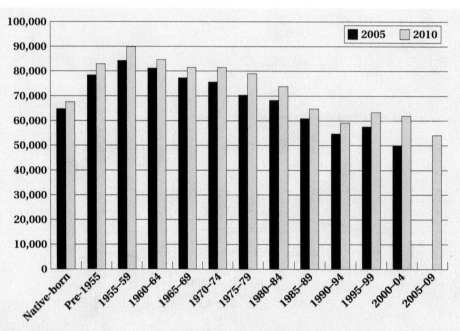

Figure 11.7 Annual Earnings by Immigrant Cohort, 2005 and 2010

A cross-section estimate of assimilation compares the earnings of immigrant cohorts within a given year. Looking right to left, immigrants who have lived in Canada longer have, generally, higher earnings. A quasi-panel estimate of assimilation follows actual cohorts' earnings over time (e.g., between 2005 and 2010). This entails a comparison of the height of the black and grey bars for each cohort. Between 2005 and 2010, all cohorts' earnings increased, suggesting positive assimilation. However, a better estimate of assimilation nets out changes to aggregate economic conditions, using native-born earnings growth as a benchmark. In this case, most immigrant cohorts, especially recent ones, experienced economic assimilation, as their earnings grew more than those of the native born.

NOTE: Reported figures are average annual earnings of men by immigrant cohort. "Native" refers to Canadian born, while each immigrant cohort is grouped by year of entry. Averages are computed for full-year, full-time employed men between 20 and 64 years of age who had only wage and salary income. Incomes of 2005 are adjusted by the CPI to year 2010 dollars.

SOURCE: Authors' tabulations from the Public Use Microdata files, Census of Canada, 2006, and National Household Survey, 2011, Statistics Canada.

The "quasi-panel" genuine cohort assimilation rate is estimated by comparing the earnings of each cohort across censuses; that is, by comparing the heights of the black and grey bars for each cohort. All of the immigrant cohorts saw earnings growth between 2005 and 2010. IM0004, for example, experienced earnings growth to $61,699, an increase of $11,801, which is substantially higher than what we predicted based on IM9599's earnings in 2005. The actual growth in earnings of this cohort is not quite an estimate of assimilation, since some of this growth might be due to general wage growth for everyone in the economy. For this reason, we want to net out aggregate wage growth, using the native born as a benchmark. Native-born earnings rose by $2469, so the estimated earnings assimilation for IM0004 is $9332, or almost 19 percent of their initial earnings. This is actually a slightly higher estimate of assimilation than is traditionally found in the literature. In this example, the cross-section underestimates the actual earnings growth of the IM0004 cohort, though the difference is not large. This is not always the case. When it exists, the gap in earnings between the cross-section and the quasi-panel provides an estimate of the change in immigrant fortunes. If the cross-section exaggerates potential assimilation, then immigrant performance is declining. The reverse is true of the cross-section underestimates assimilation. Another way to describe cohort effects is to compare the position of two cohorts at the same point on their assimilation profile (i.e., with the same years in Canada). For example, we could compare IM0004 after "five" years in Canada (i.e., in 2010) with IM9599 with the same years in Canada (i.e., in 2005). We can also compare entry effects. Perhaps as a source for optimism, recent immigrants arrived between 2005 and 2009, (IM0509) had real earnings in 2010 almost $4000 higher than did recent immigrants (IM0004) in 2005. Why this is the case is the subject of future research. Perhaps immigrants from 2005 to 2009 had higher skills, or maybe labour market conditions were more favourable.

WORKED EXAMPLE

Comparing Cross-Section and Quasi-Panel Estimates of Assimilation

A key input in evaluating immigration policy is knowing how quickly immigrants integrate into the Canadian economy. One benchmark for this integration is how quickly immigrant earnings catch up to comparable native-born Canadians' earnings. How can we estimate this speed of economic "assimilation"? One obvious way is to follow immigrants over time, asking, how much higher are their average earnings after living in Canada five years longer? This is the quasi-panel approach. Is it possible to take a short cut and simply compare a group of immigrants at a point in time to another group who have been in Canada, say, five years longer? That is the cross-section method. Whether the shortcut works depends on whether there are immigrant "cohort effects."

The results discussed in the main text using the 2006 and 2011 censuses show one example. In this Worked Example, we use data from the 1996 and 2001 censuses to explore similar questions. The following table displays mean earnings for full-year, full-time employed men, in constant 2000 dollars, analogous to those reflected in Figure 11.7.

Entry effect: This is the difference in income between new immigrants and the native born. In this case, the only new immigrants we observe are IM9195 in 1995. The entry effect for IM9195 is given by the difference between average earnings of IM9195 and the native born; that is, $46,999 − $31,423 = $15,576, or about $15,576/$46,999 ≅ 33 percent less in income than native born. This is a substantial difference.

Cross-section microdata: For cohort IM9195, a five-year cross-section estimate of their assimilation over the next five years can be obtained by comparing the earnings of IM9195 and those of IM8690 in 1995, as IM8690 immigrants have been in Canada an average of five years longer. The cross-section estimate is, thus, given by $36,580 − $31,423 = $5157, or about $5157/$31,423 ≅ 16.4 percent over five years. This would be a reasonable estimate of earnings growth (assimilation) for IM9195 if they have the identical immigration experience to IM8690. It will be a poor estimate if the experience is different; for example, if IM8690 started out with higher earnings than IM9195, or if economic conditions were vastly different over the next five years.

Quasi-panel: The quasi-panel approach tracks the actual cohorts over time (or their statistical representatives, thus, the "quasi" qualifier). In this approach, we also net out economy-wide changes in earnings. For IM9195, we see that their 2000 earnings are $38,652, or $38,652 − $31,423 = $7229 higher than they were in 1995. We cannot attribute the entire increase to immigrant assimilation, however, as earnings may have changed for everyone. Indeed, we see that native-born earnings increased by $48,641 − 46,999 = $1642. IM9195 earnings did grow faster than the native born, by $7229 − $1642 = $5587. In this case, the quasi-panel estimate is almost identical to what the 1995 cross-section predicted. To see that this is not always the case, we can conduct the same exercise for IM8690, observed in 1995. To predict their earnings five years later, we compare their earnings to the earlier cohort (IM8185), yielding $42,294 − $36,580 = $5714. Tracking them to 2000, however, we see that their earnings only grew by $5008, and given that native-born earnings grew by $1642, their quasi-panel estimate of earnings growth from assimilation is $5008 − $1642 = $3366. For this cohort, the five-year earlier cohort was a poor predictor for subsequent earnings growth.

By comparing the entry effects and subsequent assimilation for different cohorts, we can further learn what conditions contribute to varying levels of immigrant success in the labour market.

Cohort	Observed in 1995	Observed in 2000	Change between 1995 and 2000
Native born	$46,999	$48,641	$1642
IM8185	42,294	45,962	3669
IM8690	36,580	41,588	5008
IM9195	31,423	38,652	7229

Not surprisingly, given its prominence in Canadian public policy, the economic performance of immigrants and, data permitting, incorporating the quasi-panel methodology just described have been given considerable attention by researchers and undergone much study. Canadian research has also been aided by the relatively high frequency of the Canadian census: every five years. As each census is released, researchers evaluate the predictions of immigrant assimilation based on the previous censuses and incorporate new patterns into our broader understanding of the degree to which immigrant earnings catch up to those of the Canadian born, as well as the factors that are correlated with immigrant economic assimilation. Improvements in data have also contributed to an acceleration of research on this topic, especially the development of longitudinal, administrative databases. In particular, the *Longitudinal Immigrant Database* (IMDB) and *Longitudinal Administrative Database* (LAD) allow detailed tracking of earnings outcomes of immigrants and native born (the LAD), combined with complete information on immigration records (IMDB).

Whatever the data source, all Canadian studies confirm that immigrants are doing poorly in the labour market (especially in terms of entry effects), and moreover, that their performance is steadily worsening.[6] How does this line up with the apparent success of immigrants and improving entry effects we see in Figure 11.7? For one thing, the numbers in this figure are unadjusted for immigrant characteristics. Immigrants have increasing levels of observed skills (like education), so those that arrived after the year 2000 should do better based on this; given their level of skills, they actually do worse than comparable immigrants in earlier cohorts. Second, it is not sufficient to use average outcomes for all native-born men to control for the differing economic conditions in the survey years and across entry cohorts. This affects estimation of the entry, as well as the assimilation effects. As emphasized by Green and Worswick (2012), macroeconomic conditions, especially those affecting all new labour market entrants (e.g., immigrants as well as recent graduates) affect both the level and growth rates of labour market earnings.[7]

When adjustments are made for these factors, a relatively disappointing picture emerges concerning immigrant assimilation in Canada. First, as just mentioned, the entry effect is worsening over time; immigrants are starting out further behind the native born. This decline is partly attributed to changes in the source countries of immigrants, where more-recent immigrants may have skills (e.g., language) that are a poorer match for the Canadian economy. Second, most evidence strongly points to a "skills" explanation for the gap between immigrant and native-born earnings. Warman and Worswick (2015) document a significant mismatch between the skills immigrants have before arriving in Canada, and the occupations they end up working in. Immigrant skills do not transfer well. Stated differently, the return to a year of education is much lower for immigrants educated outside Canada. Ferrer and Riddell (2008) note, however, that immigrants benefit disproportionately from having formal certifications of completed degrees. This suggests Canadian employers have difficulty evaluating the education of immigrants. Using data that more precisely measure skills, such as literacy, Ferrer, Green, and Riddell (2006) confirm that low immigrant English literacy skills explain a significant portion of the immigrant earnings deficit. In addition to education, the evidence also highlights significantly lower returns to "experience," which means that older immigrants to Canada suffer a particularly large penalty. Whatever work experience they had in their home country receives a low return in Canada. The low return to "foreign human capital" also begs the question of what exactly we mean by "immigrant." Foreign birth is probably not the only relevant determinant, as it makes a difference where the individual acquired formal education and work experience. As Schaafsma and Sweetman (2001) note, "age at immigration matters"; someone who immigrates to Canada as a baby and receives all of her schooling in Canada is not the same kind of immigrant as someone who arrives at age forty. The third pattern is that, while assimilation rates vary across cohorts and with different durations in Canada, they are uniformly too low for the average earnings of any cohort of immigrants to be able to catch up to comparable native born. There is nothing in the data, and certainly no reasonable extrapolation that can be made, which suggests immigrants who arrived in Canada after 1980 will catch up to the native born. A fourth pattern is the, generally, similar outcomes for men and women. There may, occasionally, emerge modest differences in assimilation—women tend to suffer a slightly smaller earnings entry effect, for example—but the similarities far outweigh the differences.

To what extent should policymakers be concerned? If immigrants are better off in Canada than in the country they left, what difference does it make how they compare to other Canadians? Certainly, if poor economic performance is the result of discrimination, there ought to be a policy response (see Exhibit 11.3, for example). But what if that is not the reason, and weaker performance is the result of "legitimate" economic factors, such as the returns to skills? One possible concern, however, is that immigrants not able to obtain employment or with low earnings capacity may turn to social welfare programs, and this may have adverse effects on the public treasury. Baker and Benjamin (1995a, 1995b); Crossley, McDonald, and Worswick (2001); and Ostrovsky (2012) directly examine this question (see Exhibit 11.4), and show that, despite poor economic outcomes, immigrants actually make less use of unemployment insurance and social assistance. At least, using the native born as a benchmark, there is no evidence that immigrants represent an extra burden to taxpayers in these dimensions. In fact, Jadvani and Pendakur (2014) use the 2006 Census to estimate a balance sheet of immigrant net contributions to the Canadian treasury and find that taxes paid by immigrants almost completely offset the value of transfers received from the government. There is an, approximately, $500 annual transfer from Canadian native-born taxpayers to each immigrant, an estimate which varies across censuses (e.g., Akbari 1995), involves considerable extrapolation of future earnings (and taxes), and ignores the contribution of immigrants' children. Nevertheless, fiscal concerns about the cost of immigration seem second order, though point to the value of selecting immigrants more likely to succeed in Canada.

EXHIBIT 11.3

How Important Is "Canadian Experience" in Getting a Job?

Why do immigrants struggle so much in the labour market when they arrive in Canada, especially given that over half of new immigrants have been selected through the point system? Poor knowledge of Canadian labour market institutions; a lack of skills specific to Canada; and, possibly, weak English-language facility might contribute to these adjustment problems. Compounding this, immigrants may also have difficulty signalling their level of qualifications; very few have attended Harvard or Princeton. Indeed, a great deal of policy discussion addresses the general problem of "credentials recognition." Perhaps a third-party agency could provide reliable and widely accepted validation of foreign credentials, making immigrants more attractive to Canadian employers? Is this likely to make a difference? Are employers likely to respond to such stamps of approval?

To address this question, Phil Oreopoulos (2011) implemented a compelling experiment (audit study) to evaluate employer responses to immigrant applicants with varying educational backgrounds and sources of work experience. He submitted approximately 13,000 "fake" applications with resumes to 4000 job postings, mostly in the Greater Toronto Area (GTA). The type of applicant was randomly assigned, with four different applications submitted per job posting. Key sources of variation were (1) whether the applicant had an English or "foreign" name, (2) whether the applicant attended an equally prestigious Canadian or home-country university, and (3) whether the applicant's otherwise identical work experience was from Canada or their home country (all working for major international firms). The types of applicants (resumes), and the resulting call-back rates from the employers are listed in the following table:

	Comparison 1: English-named immigrants from Britain	Comparison 2: Immigrants from India/Pakistan/China
Base Group: **English names** **Canadian university (Cdn univ)** **Canadian experience (Cdn exp)**	0.158	0.157
Type I **Foreign name, Cdn univ, Cdn exp**	N/A	−0.044* (0.009)
Type 2 **Foreign name, Foreign univ, Cdn exp**	−0.029 (0.019)	−0.047* (0.011)

	Comparison 1: English-named immigrants from Britain	Comparison 2: Immigrants from India/Pakistan/ China
Type 3 Foreign name, Foreign univ, Mixed exp	−0.001 (0.023)	−0.072* (0.010)
Type 4 Foreign name, Foreign univ, Foreign exp	−0.017 (0.021)	−0.098* (0.009)

NOTES: (1) Results based on Table 4 of Oreopoulos (2011); (2) Each column reports the following: first, the base callback rate for Canadian-born applicants with English names, education, and experience; then, second, the difference in callback rates between the base group and immigrants from Britain; then, third, the difference between the base group and an immigrant from India, Pakistan, or China. (3) Each row represents an applicant with different combinations of Canadian or foreign university and/or work experience. (4) Standard errors for the differences are shown in parentheses, with "*" indicating statistical significance at the 5 percent level.

SOURCE: Philip Oreopoulos, "Why do Skilled Immigrants Struggle in the Labour Market? A Field Experiment with Thirteen Thousand Resumes," *American Economic Journal – Economic Policy,* Vol 3. No. 4, November 2011, pp. 148-171. Used with permission.

The "base" applicant was a Canadian-born male or female with one of four English last names, a Canadian university degree, and Canadian work experience. As can be seen in the first row, approximately 16 percent of this group received a callback from an employer. A second type of "applicant" had one of the same English names, but was an immigrant from Britain. While British immigrants had slightly lower callback rates than otherwise identical Canadian-born and educated applicants, the difference was small and statistically insignificant. Neither education nor work experience in Britain were discounted. By contrast, even a Canadian-educated immigrant with a Chinese, Indian, or Pakistani last name was 4.4 percentage points less likely to receive a call back. Having a Canadian university degree, as opposed to a well-regarded foreign university degree, made little difference. This suggests that recognition of foreign academic credentials was not a major concern for employers. Instead, it seems that work experience in Canada matters a great deal, even though the resumes reported foreign work experience only from big name, internationally recognized companies. Applicants with only foreign work experience were a further 5.1 percentage points less likely to get a callback than similar immigrants with Canadian work experience.

The results of this study suggest that immigrants with non-English names are at a disadvantage in the Canadian labour market, at least partially for reasons that have nothing to do with observable qualifications—possibly discrimination. A large part of the problem is also the recognition of foreign work experience, and the information that employers can infer about potential employee quality from such information. It is difficult to imagine how these factors would be mitigated by improved recognition of foreign credentials.

EXHIBIT 11.4

Immigrants and Government Transfers

A common concern expressed about the impact of immigration is that immigrants are prone to using Canada's social transfer system, be it the collection of welfare, employment insurance, or residence in public housing. Baker and Benjamin (1995a, 1995b) directly examine this question, asking whether immigrants make more use of social insurance than the native born. Using the Survey of Consumer

Finances (SCF) for 1985 and 1990, they compare use of social services by various immigrant cohorts, and track their use over time. The following table illustrates some of the patterns of program use in 1990.

	Men Collecting EI	Families Receiving Social Assistance	Households Receiving a Rent Subsidy
Native born	16.8%	9.4%	3.9%
Immigrants 1966–70	13.4	5.1	2.5
Immigrants 1976–80	16.7	8.8	3.7
Immigrants 1986–90	13.4	10.4	5.9

SOURCE: SCF, 1991, reported in Baker and Benjamin (1995a).

As a group, immigrants are less likely to use each of these programs than are the native born. The differences are even more pronounced once one controls for differences in economic characteristics, including the fact that recent immigrants have poor labour market economic outcomes. A much harder question concerns trends in welfare and transfer program use. Are new immigrants becoming more reliant on these programs over time? Do immigrants tend to use transfer programs the longer they are in Canada? Baker and Benjamin find evidence of an increasing trend toward welfare use, mirroring the deteriorating labour market outcomes. To some extent, this can be explained by the disproportionately high fraction of refugees (who were not allowed to work) in the late 1980s. Baker and Benjamin also find evidence that immigrants assimilated *into* (not out of) transfer programs.

However, Crossley, McDonald, and Worswick (2001) show that identifying the dynamics of transfer program use is problematic when using only two surveys. In fact, they find no evidence of deteriorating immigrant outcomes, and certainly not of assimilation into transfer programs. Instead, they emphasize the importance of business-cycle conditions in determining the propensity for immigrants to use transfer programs, such as EI or welfare. More recently, Ostrovsky (2012) uses the LAD and IMDB (1993 to 2007) to explore the dynamics of EI and social assistance (SA) participation. He finds no evidence of rising EI use across cohorts, nor evidence that immigrant use of EI increases with years in Canada (beyond what one would expect given increased eligibility). Similarly, he finds no evidence of rising reliance on SA for more recent cohorts. As with native-born Canadians, SA is becoming a less important source of support than universal child tax benefits (like the CCB).

One final cautionary note: while less reliance of immigrants on either EI or SA may be attractive to the treasury, there are important questions as to whether this reflects greater self-reliance or difficulty in accessing these programs (Konig and Banting 2013).

LO1, 2, 4   Immigrant Outcomes and Public Policy

One of the more important questions considers possible links between immigration policy and the patterns of immigrant assimilation just described. For example, how effective have the policy levers outlined at the beginning of the chapter been in selecting immigrants most likely to succeed in Canada? Researchers have adopted two approaches to addressing this question. First, in the absence of data directly linking policy variables to immigrant outcomes, researchers exploited comparative, cross-country differences in immigrant outcomes to draw inferences concerning the impact of the policy environment. Second, with new administrative data sets, researchers have been more able to directly link individual immigrant policy characteristics (e.g., class of immigrant) to their economic performance in Canada.

On the comparative side, one of the most fruitful approaches has been to compare immigrant performance in Canada and the United States. Since Canada introduced the point system in 1967, immigration policy has differed significantly, at least in principle, between the two countries. In the 1960s, both countries adopted policies designed to eliminate the pro-European orientation that dominated immigration policy to that point. Canada instituted the point system to more objectively evaluate the suitability of immigrants to Canada, while the United States instead moved to a family reunification–based immigration system.[8]

Despite the different systems, however, the two countries have seen similar patterns in immigrant assimilation over the past 25 years; namely, a marked decline in the entry position of recent immigrants. While assimilation rates are higher in the United States, the entry position of immigrants is generally lower. Borjas (1993) examines observable skills, such as schooling, as well as the earnings of immigrants to the two countries in order to assess the possible effects of Canada's point system. He argues that the main effect of the point system has been to tilt immigration to Canada away from source countries that provide, on average, low-skill workers. For example, he suggests that immigrants to Canada have a higher education level than those to the United States, not because the point system favours the most-skilled from a given country, but because it reduces admissions from less-developed countries where workers are less skilled, on average.[9] He shows that the resulting differences in immigrant source countries account for most of the difference in immigrant performance (in terms of entry position) between the two countries. In another interesting exercise, he compares the performance of U.S. immigrants in Canada to Canadian immigrants in the United States. If the point system was effective in picking winners, especially compared to the more open U.S. policy, we might expect American immigrants to do better in Canada than Canadian immigrants in the United States. He shows that the opposite holds; that is, that Canadians do better in the United States than vice versa.

Other studies have challenged the sharpness of the Borjas conclusion, arguing that the point system, indeed, had some impact on "picking winners" from particular source countries, though these studies also reinforce his conclusion that the changing source-country mix is correlated with changing immigrant fortunes. Green and Green (1995) provide a detailed investigation on the linkages between immigration policy changes (like the point system) and the occupational mix of immigrants.[10] They show that, overall, it is difficult to find an impact of the point system on the occupational mix of immigrants, especially accounting for source country characteristics. This, and their finding of the importance of source country composition, is in accordance with Borjas's interpretation. However, they further show that the absence of a "post-1967" effect on immigrant skills is not due to ineffectiveness of the point system, but rather that the point system is dominated by immigration non-assessed classes (family and refugee). Thus, they argue that the point system actually has a significant impact on tilting immigrant selection toward more-skilled groups, once full account is taken of the limited nature in which it is applied.

Kaushal et al. (2016) use longitudinal data from both countries (the Survey of Labour and Income Dynamics (SLID) in Canada, and the Survey of Income and Program Participation (SIPP) for the United States) covering the period 1996 to 2008. They find that immigrant assimilation rates are significantly lower in Canada than in the United States. However, this is mostly driven by lower-skilled immigrants in the United States, who have higher earnings growth than higher-educated immigrants to either country. Immigrants to Canada are more highly educated, on average, than immigrants to the United States, and this is reflected in a lower overall earnings assimilation rate.

Instead of comparing immigrant outcomes with the United States, Clarke and Skuterud (2013) make the comparison between Australia and Canada, as both countries have similar point systems and similar levels of immigration per capita. They find that immigrants to Canada fare relatively poorly (as they did compared to the United States), both in terms of lower entry effects and slower assimilation. Some of this they attribute to weaker labour market conditions in Canada, but the greater part seems related to immigrant selection. Once they hold constant the source country (that is, compare immigrant outcomes for the same source country to Australia and Canada; e.g., India), the differences largely vanish. Since neither country discriminates on the basis of source country, the difference arises from the screening criteria that tilt the balance of immigrants to those from more-successful source countries. In the late 1990s, Australia tightened its rules pertaining to language and skills, which seems to have paid off in yielding immigrants more likely to succeed.

Research on the importance of class of admission has been significantly advanced by the assembly of the Longitudinal Immigration Database (IMDB) and the Longitudinal Survey of Immigrants to Canada (LSIC). These databases link immigrant characteristics from landing (admission) records—notably, immigrant class, education, and other skills—to income-related information from income tax records (IMDB) or household survey data (LSIC). These data sets are also longitudinal, so they permit following an (anonymous!) individual immigrant's earnings over time. Based on the IMDB, a series of reports (Abbott and Beach 2009; Citizenship and Immigration Canada 1998; Citizenship and Immigration Canada 1999) show unambiguous evidence that economically assessed immigrants have more skills (language and education) than other immigrants, and that, in turn, they fare much better in Canada—they earn more, their earnings grow faster, and they are less likely to require employment insurance or social assistance. Differences in earnings across immigrant classes tend to fade, however, with the passage of time. Untangling the reasons behind these differences across classes—that is, whether they are due to differences in source country, education and other skills, or unobservable talent—remains an important topic for future research. Using early waves of the LSIC, Aydemir (2011) explores differences in the short-run employment outcomes of immigrants from assessed and non-assessed classes. He also confirms that the main consequence of the point system is the selection of immigrants with favourable labour market traits (like education), which facilitate immigrant adjustment. However, selection based on observable skills is no guarantee of success; as noted elsewhere, human capital acquired abroad does not transfer well to Canada. Sweetman and Warman (2013) use later waves of the LSIC and are able to more precisely estimate the longer term links between class of immigrant and subsequent earnings. They find strong evidence that economically assessed immigrants do better than both family-class and refugee immigrants. The notable exception is privately sponsored refugees. Possibly because of the much stronger support they receive form their sponsors (e.g., community and church groups), they perform almost as well as economically assessed immigrants (conditional on their skill level). In summary, Canadian immigration policy strongly affects the types of immigrants who are admitted to Canada, and this, in turn, is related to their economic performance.

Hou and Picot (2014) use the LAD/IMDB (covering the years 1982 through 2010) to explore the other "lever" of immigration policy: the number of immigrants admitted. They find that cohort size matters; the larger the immigrant cohort, the poorer they do in Canada. This is consistent with a simple supply and demand model, where new immigrants compete in the same labour market. For a given state of demand, the more immigrants there are, the lower the wages will be for those immigrants. Hou and Picot also confirm the basic findings on the admission class of immigrant, and, thus, their paper nicely encapsulates the links between policy and outcomes that we discussed at the outset of the chapter.

LO5   The Impact of Immigration on Source Countries

While it does not enter significantly into Canadian immigration policy determination, one of the most interesting and controversial aspects of international migration is the issue of the so-called **brain drain**. The problem arises because countries, especially less-developed ones, may lose their most-skilled labour to the more developed countries. It is the skilled workers who tend to leave because they can afford to do so, they have the knowledge of foreign opportunities (perhaps acquired while studying abroad), and they can usually amass sufficient points to enter the host country.

The problem is especially acute with countries that heavily subsidize the education and training of their workers. In such circumstances, the home countries bear the cost of the education, and the skilled emigrant reaps all of the benefits in the form of higher earnings in the host country. In many circumstances, these skilled workers are the very persons that the developing economy can least afford to lose.

The brain drain often occurs when students from less-developed economies go to more-developed economies for advanced education and training. The psychic costs associated with the cultural and environmental change have already been incurred, and the direct cost of education or training is often borne by the home country. By definition, the income opportunities are greater in the more developed host country; hence, the temptation to stay.

For countries that are net losers of highly skilled labour, there are some possible remedies, but they all involve other problems. Having the individuals themselves pay for their own education and training would at least ensure that they were paying the costs for the benefits they could receive if they emigrate. However, especially in developing economies, this may hinder large numbers of otherwise poor people from acquiring the education or training. Placing an "exit tax" equal to the amount of the human capital cost borne by the state is theoretically possible, but difficult to enforce, and it may be politically unpopular as it becomes compounded with issues of human rights. Recruiting your own students abroad and encouraging their return is a policy that is utilized, but it does have costs and it may be vacuous if viable job opportunities cannot be provided. Providing job opportunities at high wages, of course, is easier said than done, especially in countries that have followed a conscious policy of minimizing wage differentials, possibly for equity reasons. Finally, some countries actually benefit significantly from the brain drain, in that their workers abroad send home remittances that may be an important part of household income for those staying home. As in so many elements of public policy, a variety of delicate trade-offs are involved.

The Brain Drain and Canada

While the immigration to Canada by skilled individuals from developing countries does not cause loss of sleep for most Canadians—we're happy to poach the best and brightest from anywhere in the world—the brain drain is relevant to Canada to the extent that it, too, is a source country, especially of immigrants to the United States. Indeed, the emigration of highly skilled Canadians to the United States periodically receives considerable media attention, and it is often used as one argument in favour of income tax cuts. Despite the hyperbole, and for a variety of reasons (especially data limitations), research on the brain drain remains thin. However, economists have addressed a number of relevant questions in this area.

The first pertains to the size of the brain drain, and whether it is in fact getting worse. It turns out that answering this question is difficult.[11] To start with, the Canadian government does not collect data on people leaving Canada. This leaves only indirect Canadian sources. One is the "Reverse Record Check," a double check performed by Statistics Canada to evaluate the coverage of the census. This survey is helpful for establishing the residence of those sampled, and whether they have moved to the United States. It is, therefore, helpful in counting exits in census years, but it yields no other information on the migrants. A second source is tax records. By tracking tax filers, it is possible to identify the year they switch from Canadian to U.S. addresses. Again, this is useful for counting people who leave Canada, with the added bonus of revealing the taxpayer's income before leaving Canada. On the negative side, tax data contain very little in the way of demographic information, and there are no observations for people who do not file income taxes. The other sources are from the U.S. perspective. The decennial U.S. censuses, and the annual American Community Surveys collect information on country of birth and country of residence last year, so Canadian-born residents of the United States can be identified, along with information on their income and demographic characteristics. Administrative data from the Department of Homeland Security can be used to tally the number of Canadians obtaining visas to the United States. However, it can be difficult to sort out permanent from temporary migration using these data.

Once the pros and cons of the various data sources are taken into account, it is possible to get reasonable estimates of the flow of Canadians into the United States. Each year, between 60,000 and 75,000 individuals move from Canada to the United States. About half of these people are Canadian born, with the remainder split evenly between Americans returning to the United States, and immigrants born outside Canada moving to the United States.[12] As a stock, the 2012 American Community Survey indicates that there are approximately 800,000 Canadian-born residents of the United States.[13] While levels fluctuate, there has been an increase in migration to the United States since the early 1990's, facilitated to some extent by labour mobility provisions in NAFTA. However, as noted by Helliwell (1999) and others, the current level of migration to the United States is low by historical standards. More alarming is the composition of the migrants; they are disproportionately highly educated and high earners. There is an especially high flow of doctors, nurses, natural scientists, and university professors. While the annual flow represents less than 1 percent of the current stock of these occupations in Canada, it can be a large fraction of new graduates. For example, one-quarter of the new classes of nurses and doctors in the mid-1990s moved to the United States. Similarly, movers were disproportionately drawn from Canadians who earned over $100,000 before they left. Card (2003) uses large samples of micro data (U.S. and Canadian censuses, and pooled Current Population Surveys from 1995 to 2002) to document the performance and characteristics of Canadians living in the United States, with a comparison to their potential earnings in Canada. His results confirm that Canadians in the United States tend to be higher educated than average Americans, but, of more concern to Canada, they are also drawn from the highest education groups in Canada. This migration raises the skill level in the United States at the expense of Canada. Furthermore, the high education level of Canadian emigrants probably understates the skill loss to Canada, as Canadians in the United States appear to be "positively selected"; that is, they earn more in the United States than we can predict on the basis of observed skills alone. To a large extent, these migrants are probably attracted by the relative high returns to skill in the United States as compared to Canada.

The second line of questioning pursues these basic facts to evaluate the potential impact of the brain drain. To some extent, the analysis could proceed along the lines of Figure 11.4, only in reverse. However, at least in aggregate, it is unlikely that an annual outflow of 35,000 people would have much impact on the Canadian labour market, given that it is difficult to detect the impact of adding 250,000 immigrants. But in more narrowly defined markets, emigration may matter; it could be the case that doctors and nursing shortages are exacerbated by the brain drain, which increases the wages of those who remain. In this sense, the brain drain may increase health care costs by increasing the price of health care professionals. Another way to measure the impact of the brain drain is to calculate the loss of goods and services produced by Canadians in the United States. Assume, for example, that a NAFTA visa holder earns the equivalent of C$150,000 in the United States. If she would have earned the same amount in Canada, this represents a loss of $150,000 worth of GDP, and about $50,000 of tax revenue. With 50,000 such visa holders, the loss of GDP and tax revenue is in the billions. So, to the extent that the migrants are disproportionately high-income earners, and these individuals pay a disproportionate share of income taxes, the brain drain has an undeniable effect on the Canadian treasury. However, as our "back of the envelope" calculations show, it is easy to "cook up" estimates of the cost of the brain drain. More problematic is the task of constructing the counterfactual case; that is, estimating how much income these emigrants would have made had they stayed in Canada. Presumably, they moved to the United States because they could make more money; that is, they are more productive in the United States than in Canada. As the income differential for an individual between the two countries reflects their higher productivity in the United States, it is unreasonable to assume that their incomes could be replicated in Canada.

The final question concerns what, if anything, to do about the brain drain. The policy implications have received increasing attention.[14] A common proposal is to cut income taxes, making it more attractive to remain in Canada. There are a number of potential problems with this suggestion (at least in this context). First, potential emigrants remain a small fraction of the population, and it does not make sense to let the "tail wag the dog" in setting tax policy. Obviously, the responsiveness of Canadians to taxes is an important ingredient in setting tax rates, but it would be an overstatement to assume that most high-income Canadians are on the verge of moving to the United States. Second, an important key input in evaluating the benefits of a tax cut to stem the brain drain is knowledge of the sensitivity of migration to the tax rate. When asked about the importance of various factors in their decisions to move, a sample of recent graduates living in the United States ranked higher Canadian taxes low on their list of reasons for leaving Canada (Frank and Belair 1999). The most important reason for moving was a better job, and the corresponding higher income. Assume, for example, that a new graduate can earn $50,000 staying in Canada or $65,000 moving to the United States. This doesn't seem like a big difference. However, if we take an estimated age-experience profile (e.g., from Table 9.2), and simulate a person's earnings growth over a 40-year career, assuming a 5 percent discount rate yields a present value of over $400,000 for taking the U.S. job instead of the Canadian. The most striking mystery (to economists) is why anyone faced with this decision would stay in Canada at all![15] It is also clear that small changes in the income tax rate will do little to change this calculation. As Card (2003) notes, Canadian migration to the United States is drawn to the relatively high returns to skill in United States, and there are no simple policy levers to dramatically raise the returns to skill in Canada.

WORKED EXAMPLE

To Move or Not to Move?

Under what conditions would it be optimal to move to the United States? The economic model of migration assumes that individuals calculate the expected utility of moving compared to the expected utility of staying. A key input in this decision will be the expected present value of earnings in the United States compared to Canada.

To illustrate the ingredients that go into this decision, consider an individual facing the following hypothetical income streams in Canada and the United States. The person is 25 years old, and can earn $100,000 per year for 40 years in Canada (starting at age 26), versus $110,000 per year in the United States for the same 40 years (all figures are assumed to be fully adjusted for differences in income taxes, the exchange rate, and the cost of living). The respective present values of income streams, assuming an interest rate of 5 percent, are as follows:

$$PV(Canada) = \sum_{t=0}^{39} \frac{\$100,000}{(1.05)^t}$$

$$= \$100,000 \times 18.0170407$$

$$= \$1,801,704.07$$

$$PV(United\ States) = \sum_{t=0}^{39} \frac{\$110,000}{(1.05)^t}$$

$$= \$110,000 \times 18.0170407$$

$$= \$1,981,874.47$$

The difference in the present value of income streams is $180,170.41.

On purely a purely financial basis, the person should move if the associated "moving costs" are less than $180,170.41. For simplicity, we can define moving costs as any one-time costs associated with changing locations. While there will be several components of moving costs, one of the largest possible components will be the difference in the price of housing. Obviously, this cost will depend on the specific cities one is comparing. But if the house in the United States was $200,000 more expensive than a comparable house in Canada, then, for this person, there would not be an economic case for moving. If the financial costs of moving were zero, the decision may still not be obvious, depending on how much the person "values" living in Canada. For this person to stay in Canada, assuming the moving costs are zero, he or she must value living in Canada by at least $180,170.41.

As in the human capital model described in Chapter 9, this model of migration underscores the optimality of moving when young, in order to capture the maximum benefits of the investment in moving.

For someone from a poorer country than Canada, the calculation is similar, but possibly more stark. Using the same interest rate and time horizon, but earnings of $10,000 in Mexico and $35,000 in the United States (again, entirely hypothetical numbers) the returns to moving are,

$$\left(\$35,000 - \$10,000\right) \times 18.0170407 = \$25,000 \times 18.0170407 = \$450,426.$$

When the returns to migration are so high, it is not surprising that people should go to such great lengths to move to the United States. Even allowing individuals a preference for staying in their home country, modest differences in earnings levels can lead to big incentives to move.

It should be noted that this example describes the simplest case, where earnings are certain and constant. A richer example, using the same model, could incorporate real-world earnings dynamics, especially the fact that migrant earnings may be initially lower in the new country, and that it may take several years for the investment to pay off. In such a case, the role of discounting in the present value calculation would be more prominent, as migrants would need to trade off future benefits against higher immediate costs. Migrants would clearly need some idea of what the "assimilation profile" looked like for new immigrants. An even richer model would incorporate risk—not every migrant succeeds in his destination country. The calculations, however, would follow similar lines to the above example.

A second policy prescription is to ensure that emigrants are replaced by immigrants from outside Canada. In fact, Zhao, Drew, and Murray (2000) report that for every university-educated emigrant, Canada receives four university-educated immigrants, including one at the master's degree or Ph.D. level. Clearly, immigration can at least partially offset the loss of human capital to the United States. Furthermore, labour mobility (such as that under NAFTA) is a two-way street, allowing Canadian and American professionals to move between countries to jobs for which they are a good match. However, no matter how many qualified immigrants come to Canada, it would presumably be better to have both the new immigrants and those people who moved. In the long run, there will continue to be a brain drain as long as the United States provides better opportunities than Canada. Defining the set of policies that would create this happy situation certainly lies outside the scope of this textbook, and is an obvious topic for future research.

Summary

- Canada currently receives approximately 250,000 immigrants per year. This number has fluctuated over time; for example, sometimes being lower during economic downturns. Compared to 60 years ago, immigrants are significantly more likely to come from Asia than Western Europe. Most immigrants settle in large cities, especially Toronto and Vancouver.
- The Canadian government has two main policy instruments for controlling immigration. First, it can set a target number of total immigrants. Whether the target binds will depend to some extent on the supply side, the number of people who want to immigrate to Canada. Second, the government can affect the mix by determining how many

immigrants will be admitted in the assessed and non-assessed classes. Since the 1990s, the government tilted the mix toward more-skilled immigrants by increasing the number of immigrants assessed by the points system and decreasing the size of the family reunification class.

- Policymakers and economists can use the simple supply and demand framework in order to simulate the potential impact of immigration on the labour market (i.e., on the employment and wages of the native born). If the only effect of immigration is to shift out the supply curve, we would predict that immigration would depress wages. However, the impact of immigration may be offset by shifts of the labour demand curve, in which case the impact of immigration is indeterminate.

- Empirically evaluating the impact of immigration on the labour market is difficult, because it is impossible to know what would have happened in the absence of immigration. A common approach, for example, is to compare native-born wages across cities with different levels of immigration. This can be a difficult empirical strategy if immigrants choose to go to cities with more-prosperous labour markets or if native-born workers move in response to immigration or if firms invest in factories to take advantage of the pool of immigrant labour. All of these factors will make it difficult to detect an adverse effect, even if one exists. Researchers have employed a variety of strategies to circumvent these problems, including exploiting natural experiments, whereby there were large sudden inflows of immigrants to particular labour markets. The "consensus" estimates of the impact of immigration suggest that the impact is modest, though possibly, increases in unskilled immigrants reduces low-skilled wages.

- Another important empirical question is how immigrants perform in their new labour markets. Economists are particularly interested in how much lower the earnings of immigrants are than those of the native born when they first arrive (the entry effect), how quickly immigrant earnings grow after arrival (assimilation), and ultimately, whether their earnings catch up to those of the native born. It can be difficult to estimate these assimilation profiles, unless one uses data sets that permit following cohorts (or samples of cohorts) of immigrants over time. The assimilation rate in Canada has generally been low over the past 40 years, with the exceptions of the economic expansions in the late 1980s and late 1990s.

- Emigration is the opposite of immigration, and the flow of emigrants from Canada to the United States has received considerable attention in the context of the brain drain. The data suggest that the number of migrants to the United States is small on an annual basis, but many of these migrants come from high-skilled occupations in short supply in Canada.

Keywords

assessed and non-assessed classes

brain drain

counterfactual

economic assimilation

entry effect

family class immigrants

impact of immigrants

independent immigrants

point system

positively selected

quasi-panel

refugee class

years since migration

Review Questions

1. Visit the Citizen and Immigration website, www.cic.gc.ca, and review the information for applicants to Canada. In this section there is a detailed discussion of the point system described in Exhibit 11.1. Evaluate yourself, and determine whether you qualify as an immigrant to Canada.

2. Describe the point system and its role in Canadian immigration policy. Discuss the policy objectives it is designed to meet, and review the empirical evidence that reflects upon its effectiveness.

3. Carefully define economic assimilation in the context of a human capital earnings function. Outline some of the empirical difficulties encountered in estimating earnings assimilation. How can evidence on assimilation patterns of immigrants in Canada and the United States be used to evaluate the impact of Canadian immigration policy?

4. "An increase in the immigration of low-skilled workers has an unambiguously adverse impact on the wages of low-skilled native-born workers." Discuss the theoretical and empirical validity of this statement using a framework similar to Figure 11.4.

5. Explain how the data summarized in Figure 11.2, on cross-city variation in the concentration of immigrants, could form the basis of an empirical investigation of the impact of immigration on the Canadian labour market. Critically review the evidence from the United States that employs such a procedure.

6. Most studies of economic assimilation show a steady decline in the entry earnings of immigrants, combined with slow rates of assimilation. Discuss the possible factors that may explain this deterioration: why might immigrant performance vary over time?

7. Discuss what is meant by the brain drain, why it arises, and possible solutions to the problem.

8. Most evidence shows that highly educated individuals can earn significantly higher salaries in the United States than in Canada. The economic model of migration emphasizes the importance of the difference in present values of lifetime incomes between locations in the migration decision. But not every highly educated Canadian moves to the United States. Does this cast doubt on the usefulness of the economic model of migration? Explain.

Problems

1. Consider the following tabulation of (fictitious) average earnings for native-born Canadians and two cohorts of immigrants.

Group	Year of Observation	
	2000	2005
Native born	$40,000	$41,000
Immigrants, 1996–2000	32,000	36,000
Immigrants, 1991–1995	38,000	39,000

Use these data to provide a description of the immigrant assimilation profile (entry effect and assimilation rates).

2. A researcher wishes to investigate the impact of immigration on the Canadian labour market. She uses time-series data on the number of immigrants and the national unemployment rate from 1961 to 2015 to estimate the following relationship:

$$\text{dur}_t = \alpha + \gamma \text{d} \ln \text{imm}_t + \varepsilon_t$$

where dur$_t$ is the change (from one year to the next) in the unemployment rate, and d ln imm$_t$ is the change in the logarithm of the number of immigrants arriving in Canada.

   a. Explain what economic theory suggests should be the sign of γ.

   b. She obtains the following regression estimates (with standard errors in parentheses):

Intercept   0.015 (0.147)

d ln imm$_t$ −1.56 (0.75)

She interprets her results as showing that, far from adversely affecting the Canadian labour market (and increasing the unemployment rate), increases in immigration actually reduce unemployment. Critically evaluate her interpretation. In your answer, you should discuss the following:

    i. Under what conditions her interpretation may be correct

    ii. The reasons her interpretation may be flawed

    iii. Any evidence that you know sheds light on these issues

3. The following table shows the average earnings of various immigrant cohorts and the native born for 2005 and 2010 (all values expressed in year 2010 dollars), corresponding to Figure 11.7.

   a. Calculate the cross-sectional entry effect (in levels) for the 2000–04 (IM0004) cohort. Interpret.

   b. Use the 2005 cross-section to estimate the effect on earnings of being in Canada an additional five years for the IM9094 cohort; that is, the effect of being in Canada 17.5 instead of 12.5 years. Use this to predict IM9094's earnings in 2010.

   c. Compare your estimate from part (b) to IM9094's actual earnings in 2010. Provide a better estimate of the earnings assimilation of the IM9094 cohort. Explain and interpret. Compare this to the cross-sectional estimate from part (b) and suggest an explanation as to why they are different.

4. Assume that the labour market can be described by the following supply and demand equations:

$$S{:}e = a + bP + cW$$

$$D{:}e = \alpha + \beta P + \eta W$$

where e is the log of employment, W is the log wage, and P is a log of the "population."

   a. Interpret b and β. Explain how immigration may shift the population. Define γ as the elasticity of population, P, with respect to immigration, I. Why might γ vary across markets?

   b. Solve for the equilibrium wage and employment level as a function of the population.

Average Earnings by Immigrant Cohort

Cohort	Label	2005 YSM	2005 Earnings ($)	2010 YSM	2010 Earnings ($)
Native-born	Native	N/A	64,778	N/A	67,247
Pre-1955	IM55P	52.5	78,179	57.5	82,584
1955–59	IM5559	47.5	84,124	52.5	89,472
1960–64	IM6064	42.5	81,041	47.5	84,469
1965–69	IM6569	37.5	76,992	42.5	81,410

		2005		2010	
Cohort	Label	YSM	Earnings ($)	YSM	Earnings ($)
1970–74	IM7074	32.5	75,444	37.5	81,139
1975–79	IM7579	27.5	70,287	32.5	78,927
1980–84	IM8084	22.5	68,018	27.5	73,671
1985–89	IM8589	17.5	60,881	22.5	64,565
1990–94	IM9094	12.5	54,478	17.5	59,185
1995–99	IM9599	7.5	57,430	12.5	63,253
2000–04	IM0004	2.5	49,898	7.5	61,699
2005–09	IM0509			2.5	53,888

NOTE: "YSM" refers to the average years since migration.

c. Assume the following parameters: $c = 0.1$ and $\eta = -0.3$, which are in accordance with the empirical literature. Using the answer to part (b), evaluate the impact of an increase in immigration on equilibrium employment and wages under two scenarios:

   i. $\beta = 0$; $b = 1$
   ii. $\beta = 1$; $b = 1$

   Assume that the elasticity of population with respect to immigration is 1. Interpret your results, using a figure like Figure 11.4.

5. A common representation of the assimilation profile of an immigrant cohort is to express log earnings as a function of years in Canada (or YSM, years since migration). We begin with a model for the gap between an individual's, i's, earnings (from cohort j at time t, $\ln y_{ijt}$) and comparable native-born Canadians $\left(\ln \tilde{y}_{Nit}\right)$. The gap for an individual is given by

$$\ln \tilde{y}_{ijt} \equiv \ln y_{ijt} - \ln \tilde{y}_{nit} = \alpha_j + \beta YSM_{ijt} + u_{ijt}$$

Taking averages over individuals in a cohort, we have,

$$\ln \tilde{y}_{jt} = \alpha_j + \beta YSM_{jt}$$

This expression represents the difference in average log earnings in year t between comparable native born and immigrants from cohort j as a function of YSM.

   a. Graph a profile for $\ln y_{jt}$, where $\alpha_j = 0.25$ and $\beta = 0.01$. Interpret α_j and β. How many years does it take for an immigrant from cohort j to catch up to the comparable native born level of earnings?

   b. What would it mean for β to have a subscript j: β_j? Based on an assimilation profile with β_j, derive a general expression for the time it takes cohort j to catch up to comparable natives.

6. Assume that the starting salary for a computer programmer in the United States is C$75,000 as against C$50,000 in Canada, that the starting age is 25, and that the person expects to be continuously employed until age 65. Assume, further, that earnings can be expected to grow at 6 percent per year in both jobs.

a. Calculate the present value of earnings under the two alternatives, assuming a discount rate of 5 percent. How much would a potential migrant have to value living in Canada in order to stay?

b. What factors can you identify (and possibly value) that might offset the benefits of moving?

c. Calculate the present value of moving at each age. When would you expect a person to move, if he or she were going to move?

It is recommended that you use a spreadsheet in order to make these calculations. (In Excel, the relevant function for calculating present values is "NPV.")

Endnotes

1. Borjas (1996) provides a non-technical discussion of these issues, while Borjas (1995) offers a slightly more technical presentation of the economic benefits of immigration. Green and Green (1995) document the variety of goals, economic and non-economic, that have played important roles in the evolution of Canadian immigration policy.

2. For a detailed discussion of the potential impact of immigrants on the labour market, Borjas (1994, 1995) and Friedberg and Hunt (1995) provide quite readable and comprehensive surveys of the issues and evidence through the mid-1990s. Borjas (1999, 2014) provide more technical, and also more general, overviews of the immigration literature.

3. See, for example, Kuhn and Wooton, 1991; Globerman, 1995; Baker and Benjamin, 1997a; and Head and Ries, 1998.

4. Note that the difference in skill-group definition is also at the heart of differences between Card's 1990 Mariel Boat Lift results, and those from Borjas (forthcoming).

5. The debate concerning the appropriate degree of substitutability between (1) Equally-skilled native-born and immigrant labour; and (2) High-school drop outs and high school graduates continues in Ottaviano and Peri (2012), and the comment by Borjas, Grogger, and Hanson (2012).

6. See Warman and Wosrwick (2015) and Clarke and Skuterud (2013) for immigrant assimilation results based on the 2006 Census. Green and Worswick (2012) document the same deterioration of outcomes using the IMDB/LAD, while Kaushal et al. (2016) use the SLID. For earlier research with previous censuses, see Picot and and Sweetman (2005), Aydemir and Skuterud (2005), Grant (1999), Bloom, Grenier, and Gunderson (1995), and Baker and Benjamin (1994).

7. See also Aydemir and Skuterud (2005), Green and Worswick (2004), and McDonald and Worswick (1998) for a discussion of the importance of macroeconomic conditions to the estimation of immigrant assimilation profiles.

8. See Alan Green (1995) for a detailed historical comparison of immigration policy between the two countries.

9. Educational differences between immigrants and the native born are also documented in Duleep and Regets (1992) and Baker and Benjamin (1994). Green (1999) explores skill differences along occupational dimensions, and shows that immigrants are more highly represented in skilled occupations.

10. David Green (1995) evaluates the correlation between the intended and actual occupation of immigrants. Intended occupation is the basis of admission through the point system. He finds that the correlation is quite high, though primarily because of observable skills on the part of immigrants, rather than any additional predictive power of their stated intended occupation.

11. See see Zhao, Drew, and Murray (2000) and Dion and Vézina (2010) for a discussion of measurement issues pertaining to Canadian migration to the United States.

12. Dion and Vézina (2010).

13. Zong, Rkasnuam, and Batalova (2010).

14. See Finnie (2001), Kesselman (2001), and an IRPP Symposium (1999) for discussion of the policy issues. Policy discussions are as cyclical as the brain drain: when Canadian emigration levels are low, the topic receives little attention.

15. DeVoretz and Iturralde (2001) address this very question, and explore a broad variety of determinants of mobility from Canada to the United States.

CHAPTER 12

Discrimination and Male–Female Earnings Differentials

LEARNING OBJECTIVES

LO1 Describe the factors that give rise to the male–female pay gap (or any pay gap for minority groups) and, especially, the importance of discrimination in explaining that gap.

LO2 Outline the methodologies that have been used to estimate discriminatory pay gaps and the challenges associated with those methods so as to have an appreciation of the difficulties of determining the extent of discrimination.

LO3 Explain how discriminatory pay gaps may be sustained in markets even though they can entail inefficient practices by not hiring the best people given their wages.

LO4 Discuss the pros and cons of different policy initiatives for combating discrimination.

LO5 Explain the factors giving rise to changes in the male–female pay gap over time, and how those factors may change in the future.

LO6 Describe the mechanics and complexities of pay equity policy initiatives.

MAIN QUESTIONS

- How can otherwise equally productive men and women be paid different wages in a competitive labour market? Will competitive market forces dissipate discrimination?
- What methods are used to measure the extent of discrimination in the labour market?
- How much discrimination against women exists in the Canadian labour market? Is there evidence of discrimination against other groups?
- What policies have been adopted to address the effects of discrimination? Which policies have been effective?
- How has the gender pay gap changed over time and why? What is the expectation for the future?

The economic analysis of discrimination provides a good application for many of the basic principles of labour market economics. In addition, it indicates the limitations of some of these tools in an area where non-economic factors may play a crucial role. In fact, many would argue that discrimination is not really an economic phenomenon, but rather is sociological or psychological in nature. While recognizing the importance of these factors in any analysis of discrimination, the basic position taken here is that economics does have a great deal to say about discrimination. Specifically, it can indicate the labour market impact of the sociological or psychological constraints and preferences. More importantly, economics can indicate why the gender pay gap has changed over time, and what this may portend for the future. It may also shed light on the expected impact of alternative policies designed to combat discrimination in the labour market.

Sex discrimination appears to have existed for a long time, at least as evidenced by the fact that the Bible recommended paying females 60 percent of the pay of males—a ratio that is fairly close to that which prevails today (see Exhibit 12.1). The terms *sex discrimination* and *gender discrimination* are used interchangeably in this chapter, although the former is often used to denote biological differences and the latter to denote cultural and socially determined differences.

EXHIBIT 12.1

It's Been 0.60 Since Biblical Times

"The Lord spoke to Moses and said, 'Speak to the Israelites in these words. When a man makes a special vow to the Lord which requires your valuation of living persons, a male between twenty and fifty years old shall be valued at fifty silver shekels, that is shekels by the sacred standard. If it is a female, she shall be valued at thirty shekels'" (Leviticus 27:1–4).

Clearly, a female/male earnings ratio of 30/50 = 0.6 is not a new phenomenon. It has existed—or at least been endorsed—at least since biblical times!

Although the focus of this analysis is on gender discrimination in the labour market, it is important to realize that discrimination can occur against various groups and in different markets. Discrimination can occur in the housing market, product market, capital market, and human capital market (e.g., education and training), as well as in the labour market. It can be based on a variety of factors, including race, age, language, national origin, sexual orientation, or political affiliation, as well as on sex.

Labour market discrimination can come from a variety of sources. *Employers* may discriminate in their hiring and promotion policies as well as their wage policies. To a certain extent, the forces of competition would deter employers from discriminating, since they forgo profits by not hiring and promoting females who are as productive as their male counterparts. However, profit-maximizing firms must respond to pressure from their customers and male employees. For this reason, they may be reluctant to hire and promote females, or they may pay females a lower wage than equally productive males. In addition, firms in the large not-for-profit sector (e.g., government, education, hospitals) may be able to discriminate without having to worry about losing profits by not hiring and promoting females.

In addition to discrimination on the part of employers, *male co-workers* may also discriminate for reasons of prejudice, misinformation, or job security. Akerlof and Kranton (2000), for instance, provide examples of how males in typical "male" jobs may find their masculinity threatened, and thus refuse to co-operate with or informally train female co-workers. Representing the wishes of a male majority, craft unions may discriminate through the hiring hall or apprenticeship system, and industrial unions may discriminate by bargaining for male wages that exceed female wages for the same work. Another potential source of discrimination is some *customers* who may be reluctant to purchase the services of females or who may not patronize establishments that employ females, especially in positions of responsibility (see Exhibit 12.2).

EXHIBIT 12.2

Discrimination or Productivity Differences? Evidence from Baseball Cards

Conventionally, the extent of discrimination is measured by estimating the earnings differential between, for example, males and females or blacks and whites, after controlling for productivity differentials that could be regarded as legitimate determinants of wages. It is extremely difficult, however, to control for productivity differentials. Even if the extent of discrimination can be estimated, it is difficult to determine the extent to which it emanates from customers, co-workers, or employers.

Nardinelli and Simon (1990) examine the market for baseball cards to get around many of these problems. It is a highly competitive market with competitive prices for the cards, and it is possible to link price to objective measures of productivity (i.e., performance of the players). Evidence indicates that the price of cards is 10 to 13 percent lower for nonwhite players than for white players of the same productivity (i.e., performance). This can be taken as evidence of pure *customer* discrimination since neither employers nor co-workers systematically influence the price. Based on a survey of the literature, Guiliano, Levine, and Leonard (2010) find evidence of customer discrimination in most (but not all) studies, and their own evidence from retail stores finds only weak evidence of customer discrimination, although they indicate that many employers hire on the basis of believing that their customers have discriminatory preferences.

The focus of the chapter is on labour market discrimination that occurs when groups who have the same productivity or productivity-related characteristics, such as education, experience, and training, are treated differently purely because of their demographic group or personal characteristics, such as sex, race, age, national origin, or sexual orientation. The different treatment could occur in such forms as wages or the occupation into which they are placed, and it can occur at various phases of the employment relationship through recruiting, hiring, promoting, training, and terminating.

In order to better understand the economics of gender discrimination, various theories of discrimination are first presented. This is followed by a discussion of the methodologies used to measure the discriminatory portion of that differential and the empirical evidence on the extent of sex discrimination in the labour market, as well as discrimination against other groups. The chapter concludes with a discussion of alternative policies to combat discrimination in the labour market.

Theories of Labour Market Discrimination and Some Evidence

Alternative theories of sex discrimination in the labour market can be classified according to whether they focus on the demand or supply side of the labour market, or on noncompetitive aspects of labour markets.

Demand Theories of Discrimination

Demand theories of discrimination have the common result that the demand for female labour is reduced relative to the demand for equally productive male labour. This can occur because employers have a prejudice against hiring female labour, customers have an aversion to buying from female labour, or co-workers have an aversion to working with female workers. The resultant decreased demand for female labour would reduce the employment of females, and, unless the supply of female labour is perfectly elastic, reduce the wages of females relative to the wages of equally productive males. How does discrimination lead to a reduction in the demand for female labour?

According to Becker (1957, p. 14), employers act as if $W_f (1 + d_f)$ were the net wage paid to females, male co-workers act as if $W_M(1 - d_m)$ were the net wage they receive when working with females, and consumers act as if $P_c(1 + d_c)$ were the price paid for a product sold by a female. In all cases, the discrimination coefficient, d, represents the cost, in percentage, associated with hiring, working with, or buying from females. For example, a firm that has a discrimination coefficient of 0.10 , and which can hire all the female labour it wants at $6 per hour, would act as if it paid $6 (1 + 0.10) = $6.60 each time it hired a female. Clearly, such discrimination reduces the demand for females relative to equally productive males.

Charles and Guryan (2008) emphasize that such wages are determined by the market transactions of the prejudices of the marginal employer with which such minorities interact, and not by the prejudices of the average employer. Minorities will obviously seek out those employers who discriminate the least. Their evidence indicates that one-quarter of the black–white wage gap in the United States is due to such prejudice.

Arrow (1973) gives a neoclassical theory of discrimination based on the firm's desired demand for labour when the firm maximizes utility (rather than simply profits), and the firm's utility is increased by employing fewer workers from minority groups. Again, this results in a reduced demand for female labour and lower female wages.

The demand for female labour relative to male labour also depends on information concerning their relative productivity. If employers consistently underestimate the productivity of females, they would correspondingly reduce their demand for female labour. This misinformation on the part of employers may be due to their own ingrained prejudices, as well as to erroneous information fostered by male customers and co-workers.

Because information on individual workers is extremely costly to acquire, employers may judge individual females on the basis of the average performance of all females. **Statistical and signalling theories of discrimination** are discussed and evidence provided in Bjerk (2008), Coate and Loury (1993a, 1993b), Lundberg (1991), Lundberg and Startz (1983), Oettinger (1996), and Frederiksen (2008). If efficiency wage premiums are paid to reduce costly turnover, individual females who expect to stay in the labour market may find it difficult to credibly signal their intent. In such circumstances, employers may judge them as having the average turnover of all women (which employers perceive to be higher than that of males) and, hence, may not place them in the jobs that pay the efficiency wage premiums. Although, from the employers' viewpoint, such statistical judgment may be efficient, it could be inequitable for many individual females.

Supply Theories of Discrimination

Supply theories of discrimination have the common result that the supply of female labour is increased by discrimination because of crowding, or, conversely, that the female asking wage is reduced by discrimination.

The **crowding hypothesis** was first outlined by Edgeworth (1922, p. 439) when he referred to "that crowding of women into a comparatively few occupations, which is universally recognized as a main factor in the depression of their wages." As formalized by Sorensen (1990), it implies that females tend to be segregated into "female type" jobs. The resulting abundance of supply lowers their marginal productivity and, hence, their wage. Thus, even if females are paid a wage equal to their marginal productivity, their wage will be less than male wages that are not depressed by an excess supply.

In a similar vein, dual labour market theory posits two separate and distinct labour markets. The primary, or core, labour market (unionized, monopolistic, expanding) provides secure employment at high wages. The secondary, or peripheral, labour market (non-unionized, highly competitive, declining) is characterized by unstable employment at low wages. Men tend to be employed in the primary labour market, women in the secondary labour market. Prejudice on the part of the dominant group and its desire to exclude female competition will prevent the entry of women into the primary labour market. Unions, occupational licensing, discriminatory employment tests, and barriers to education and training can all work against the entry of females into the core labour market. Female immobility may also result because of women's stronger ties to the household and their tendency to move to the places where their husbands are employed. For these various reasons, females tend to be crowded into jobs in the secondary labour market with its concomitant unstable employment and low wages. Their low wages and undesirable working conditions may, in turn, create high absenteeism and turnover, which further depress wages in the secondary labour market.

In a related vein, Zeytinoglu and Cooke (2008) use Canadian data from the 1999 Workplace and Employee Survey to indicate that females dominate non-standard employment, defined as regular part-time, temporary full-time, and temporary part-time employment. Within the female labour force, workers in all three types of non-standard employment are less likely to be promoted than workers in regular full-time employment, but the same is not true for the male labour force. As a result, barriers to promotion appear to be more structural for women than for men, which may adversely contribute to the gender wage gap.

Females' asking (reservation) wages may be reduced it they engaged in less job search because it is more costly having to search for nondiscriminating job offers, and their job search and mobility are more limited because they tend to be more tied to their household and, perhaps, to the employment location of their husband or partner (Benson 2015; Black 1995; Blackaby, Booth, and Frank 2005; Bowlus 1997; Eriksson and Lagerstrom 2012; Flabbi 2010; and Webber 2015, 2016). As well, their ability to negotiate higher pay may be reduced if their threat of leaving their employer is made less credible by their ties to their household. It is noteworthy that women tend to quit and leave the labour force for non-monetary reasons, such as household responsibilities and illness in the family, while men tend to quit for better job opportunities (Sicherman 1996).

Recent studies in behavioural economics that combine economics and psychology have documented that females tend to be more risk averse and less competitive and aggressive in their bargaining, as well as less confident in their ability compared to males (even when their abilities are equal and they have feedback information to that effect). Evidence on this is provided, for example, in Asmat and Petrongolo (2014); Booth (2009); Booth and Nolen (2013); Buser, Niederle, and Oosterkerk (2014); Dietrich, Knabe, and Leipold (2014); Dohmen and Falk (2011); Flory, Leibbrandt, and List (2015); Fisman and O'Neill (2009); Frick (2011); Garratt, Weinberger, and Johnson (2013); Gerdes and Gransmark (2010); Gneezy, Leonard, and List (2009); Gupta, Poulsen, and Villeval (2013); Kuhn and Villeval (2014); Lavy (2013); Le et al. (2010); Niederle and Vesterlund (2007); Ors, Palomino, and Peyrache (2013); and Santos-Pinto (2012). Those studies also referred to hundreds of experimental studies in psychology as well as economics. These factors, in turn, can inhibit females from competing for higher paying jobs, especially in managerial and executive ranks. Fortin (2008) provides evidence indicating that some of the male–female pay gap arises because females tend to value jobs that emphasize people and family over money. Mueller and Plug (2006) also provide evidence indicating that it pays to be antagonistic if you are a man, but not if you are a woman (Exhibit 12.3).

EXHIBIT 12.3

It Pays to Be Antagonistic and Disagreeable . . . If You Are a Man but Not a Woman!

Based on personality tests applied to a sample of high school graduates in the United States, Mueller and Plug (2006) provide evidence that men have considerably more of the personality trait of being antagonistic and disagreeable, and they were rewarded for that trait, while women have less of the trait and were not rewarded for it. It seems that it pays to be antagonistic and disagreeable if you are a man, but the opposite if you are a woman!

Supply theories of discrimination also emphasize the importance of preferences in determining various decisions with respect to education, training, hours of work, working conditions, and occupational choice—all of which can influence the jobs that women take and the pay they receive. The importance of these preferences is emphasized, for example, in Butler (1982), Daymont and Andrisani (1984), and Filer (1983, 1986). Eschriche (2007) and Eschriche et al. (2004) indicate how such preferences can be shaped by a socialization process and transmitted intergenerationally in a self-perpetuating fashion. Of course, the extent to which these "choices" reflect preferences as opposed to discriminatory constraints, those perhaps arising from outside the labour market, is an interesting and important question.

In the area of education, for example, women disproportionately "choose" or are streamed into fields of study such as humanities, history, and social sciences where the male–female pay gap is large (perhaps because of the large number of females) rather than professional fields or graduate degrees where the gap is small or nonexistent (Morgon 2008). Furthermore, there is some persistence in the choice of many fields of study on the part of females (Andres and Adamuti-Trache, 2007 for Canada). The importance of field of study in contributing to the male–female pay gap is emphasized in Black et al. (2008), Brown and Corcoran (1997), Paglin and Rufolo (1990), and Zafar (2013) and in references cited therein. Given the small number of female faculty members at universities, females are often taught by males and there is evidence based on the random assignment of students to faculty that female students perform better when assigned to female faculty (Carrell, Page, and West 2010). Florian and Oreopoulos (2009) also find positive effects in college performance from same-sex role models. See Exhibit 12.4 for evidence on mathematics as a field. Warman, Woolley, and Worswick (2010) document that the male–female gap in academic salaries at Canadian universities has narrowed between 1970 and 2001, but a substantial gap remains, largely reflecting differences in rank and also field of study. Based on Canadian data from a large research-oriented university, Doucet, Smith, and Durant (2012) find that the male–female pay gap is largely explained by differences in rank and seniority as females are less likely to be promoted to higher ranks and acquire seniority. They find that female faculty are also less likely to receive market based pay increases or pay increases associated with being appointed to Canada Research Chairs, which they interpret as subject to discretionary decisions. Based on U.S. data, Manchester and Barbezat (2013) find that females in economics departments allocate their time away from academic publishing, in part because of constraints imposed by child care responsibilities.

EXHIBIT 12.4

Gender and Mathematics

Differences in educational attainment and choice of field of study across genders may be the result of a labour market discriminatory "feedback" effect. For example, if women anticipate receiving lower wages than their male counterparts then, *ceteris paribus*, their incentive to invest early into human capital is commensurately reduced. Fryer and Levitt (2010) show that differences in the educational attainment in mathematics between boys and girls start at very early ages. Using data from the Early Childhood Longitudinal Study Kindergarten Cohort (ECLS-K) from the United States, the authors find that there are no average differences in mathematics scores between genders upon entry to school, but girls lose more than two-tenths of a standard deviation relative to boys over the first six years of elementary school. Since the ability gap is realized at an early age, it is unlikely to result from direct feedback effects from labour market discrimination, although such feedback effects could still influence parents' willingness to invest in their children's education. Fryer and Levitt's evidence may suggest that other socio-cultural factors are affecting the educational attainments of men and women at early ages.

Noncompetitive Theories of Discrimination

In theory, male–female wage differentials for equally productive workers are inconsistent with competitive equilibrium. As long as females could be paid a wage lower than that of equally productive males, firms that do not have an aversion to hiring females would increase their profits by hiring females. The resultant increased demand for females would bid up their wages, and the process would continue until the male–female wage differential is eliminated for individuals of the same productivity. Firms that do not have an aversion to hiring females would be maximizing profits by employing large numbers of females; firms that have an aversion to hiring females would be forgoing profits by employing only males. According to competitive theory, discrimination leads to a segregation of males and females, not wage differentials. It also implies that discrimination should be reduced over time, since firms that discriminate will go out of business as they forgo profits to discriminate. Evidence of this is provided subsequently.

Nevertheless, some would argue that these predictions of competitive economic theory are at variance with the facts. Male–female wage differentials seem to persist. **Noncompetitive theories of discrimination** seek to explain why discriminatory wage differentials seem to persist.

Arrow (1973) attributes the persistence of male–female wage differentials to costs of adjustment and imperfect information. Even if they do acquire the information that profits can be increased by hiring low-wage females to do certain jobs performed by higher-wage males, firms cannot immediately replace their male workers with an all-female workforce. There are fixed costs associated with recruiting and hiring; consequently, firms want to spread these fixed costs as much as possible by retaining their existing workforce. Firms may replace male turnover by new female recruits, but they would be reluctant to immediately replace their male workforce. In essence, Arrow implies that the long run may be a very long time.

Queuing theories based on efficiency wages may also explain the persistence of male–female wage differentials for equally productive workers. Arrow argues that some firms pay efficiency wages that are wages greater than competitive market wages in order to reduce turnover, improve morale, or secure the advantages of always having a queue from which to hire workers. Other firms pay greater than competitive wages because of union or minimum wage pressure, or because of a necessity to share monopoly or oligopoly profits with their workers. The resultant higher-than-competitive wage enables these high-wage firms to hire from a queue of available workers. Rationing of the scarce jobs may be carried out on the basis of discrimination or nepotism, where nepotism is a form of discrimination in that it involves favouring a particular group, which disadvantages the group not receiving the favouritism. Thus, discriminatory wage differentials may exist in a long-run competitive equilibrium when profit-maximizing firms minimize labour costs by paying high wages in order to reduce turnover or improve morale, or because they face institutional constraints, such as unions or minimum wage legislation.

The persistence of discrimination can also be fostered by noncompetitive mechanisms, when political pressures can replace market pressures. Reflecting male wishes, governments can discriminate both in their own hiring practices and in the provision of education and training. In the case of sex discrimination, this would reduce the skill endowment of minorities and reduce the number of professional-managerial females who would hire fellow females. Also reflecting the preferences of some males, unions could discriminate against females, especially in apprenticeship and training programs. Interest groups may use the power inherent in governments, unions, and business monopolies to further their own ends through discrimination and segregation.

A more radical perspective regards discrimination as deliberately fostered by employers as part of a conscious policy of "divide and conquer" (Reich, 1978; Roemer, 1979). Employers will deliberately pit workers against each other and utilize a reserve of unemployed workers as a means of disciplining the workforce and reducing working-class solidarity and power. In this perspective, group power is more important than the economic forces of supply and demand in determining wages.

Monopsony is another noncompetitive factor that can affect female wages relative to male wages, mainly in two ways (Madden 1972; Manning 2003; Webber 2014, 2015; Ransom and Oaxaca 2010). First, if females tend to be employed by monopsonists, their wages will be reduced correspondingly. Because of their immobility (tied to household and to husbands' places of employment), females may not have the effective threat of mobility necessary to receive a competitive wage, as discussed previously in the job search models. Their labour supply elasticity to the firm may be small to the extent that their ties to the household make them relatively insensitive to wage changes. Second, monopsonists may try to differentiate their workforce so as to pay the higher wage rate only to some employees. One obvious way of differentiating workers is by sex. Thus, the company may pay higher wages to male employees and yet not have to pay these higher wages to its female employees who do the same work, simply because the female employees do not consider themselves direct competitors with male employees doing the same job. Employers find it in their interest to foster this attitude, since it enables them to maintain the wage differentials based on sex. Evidence that monopsony may explain part of the male–female wage gap is provided in Barth and Dale-Olsen (2009) for Norway; Hirsch, Schank, and Schabel (2010) for Germany; and Ranson and Oaxaca (2010) and Webber (2015, 2016) for the United States.

The concept of **systemic discrimination** (not to be confused with *systematic discrimination*) has been advanced to explain discrimination that may be the unintended by-product of historically determined practices. It may result, for example, from informal word-of-mouth recruiting networks (the "old-boy system") that perpetuate the existing sex composition of the workforce. Or it may result from certain job requirements pertaining to height or strength that may no longer serve a legitimate purpose. In situations where wages are institutionally set above the competitive norm, such job requirements may simply cause rationing of the scarce jobs and serve little or no function related to productivity.

Productivity Differences: Choice or Discrimination?

Female wages may differ from male wages because of productivity differences that arise from differences in the human capital endowments and in the absenteeism and turnover of males and females. The human capital endowments could include *acquired* attributes, such as education, training, labour market information, mobility and labour market experience, as well as more *innate* characteristics, such as intelligence, strength, perseverance, or dexterity. In an increasingly mechanized society, the innate characteristic for which there may be the greatest difference—physical strength—takes on reduced importance. Baker and Cornelson (2016), however, provide evidence of gender difference in sensory, motor, and spacial attitudes, and argue that these differences can explain much of the occupational differences that continue to prevail between men and women.

Because of their dual role in the household and in the labour market, women traditionally have a shorter expected length of stay in the labour market. For example, Drolet (2002a) shows that men and women differ considerably in the continuity of the work they experience and that women are more likely to combine periods of paid work with periods of labour force withdrawals for family reasons. Baker and Drolet (2010) show, using Canadian data from a variety of sources, that usual weekly hours for full-time women aged 25 to 54 are about three to four hours less than those of men. Consequently, women have a reduced benefit period from which to recoup the costs of human capital formation. In addition, their time in the labour market can be intermittent and subject to a considerable degree of uncertainty. Depending upon the nature of the household tasks they perform, this can lead to a depreciation of their human capital that is valued in the labour market and inhibit them from acquiring continuous labour market experience. For this reason, it may be economically rational for females (or firms) to be reluctant to invest in female human capital that is labour market oriented. Of course, if the skills they develop in household activities are valuable in the labour market (e.g., time management and multitasking, or doing a wide range of different tasks) their human capital need not deteriorate from spells of household work.

The human capital decision, therefore, may reflect rational choice; however, it is important to consider that these choices may also be subject to discriminatory constraints. Females may be discriminated against through the returns they receive for acquiring human capital as well as in borrowing to finance the cost of human capital formation. In addition, family and peer group pressures may close off certain avenues of human capital formation. Young girls, for example, may be conditioned to become nurses instead of doctors, or secretaries instead of lawyers.

Most importantly, female responsibility for household tasks (see Exhibit 12.5) may reflect discrimination more than choice. Whatever the reason, females tend to acquire less labour market oriented human capital than males, and, consequently, their wages and employment opportunities are reduced in the labour market. This occurs even if in the labour market there is no discrimination on the part of firms, co-workers, or customers. Differences in wage and employment opportunities may reflect productivity differences, which, in turn, may come about because of rational economic choice as well as discrimination prior to entering the labour market.

EXHIBIT 12.5

Do Differences in Family Commitments Affect the Pay Gap between Male and Female Managers?

On the basis of survey data of middle managers in a large Canadian organization, Cannings (1991) determined that female managers spend about four times as much time on household work than male managers. Only 15 percent of the females, but 69 percent of the males, thought that their own careers were more important to their families than the careers of their spouses. Ten percent of the females had professional or managerial husbands who would be willing to move for the sake of the career of their wife; in contrast, 28 percent of the males had professional or managerial wives who would be willing to move for the sake of the career of their husband.

Clearly, family commitments and constraints are more important to female managers than they are to male managers. Statistical analysis of the determinants of the earnings of male and female managers indicates that these differences in family commitment accounted for about 20 percent of the earnings gap that prevailed between otherwise similar male and female managers. Families are not "equal opportunity employers!"

This is further illustrated by the fact that hours devoted to household work has a negative effect on women's wages (Hersch and Stratton 1997). In contrast, men's labour market productivity and, hence, their wages, increase after becoming married, which is at least partially attributable to their increased specialization in labour market work following marriage (Rodgers and Stratton, 2010).

Productivity and, hence, wage differences may also occur because of differences in the absenteeism and turnover of females. This is especially the case if female turnover occurs primarily as a result of leaving the labour force (which would reduce earnings, as explained earlier), and male turnover occurs primarily as a result of moving to a higher-paying job. Sicherman (1996) finds that women tend to quit for reasons not related to money, like household responsibilities and caring for a family member who is ill, while men tend to quit to go to a better job. The empirical evidence on differences in quit rates and turnover rates by sex tends to be mixed. Some studies find quit and turnover rates to be higher for women than men so that women accumulate less tenure, seniority, and training at a particular job (Becker and Lindsay 1994; Light and Ureta 1995; Sicherman 1996; Ureta 1992). However, other studies find that after controlling for the effect of other variables that affect turnover (e.g., wages, education, occupation, age) there is no significant difference in the turnover rates of men and women (Blau and Kahn 1981; Meitzen 1986). In other words, to the extent that women have higher turnover rates then men, it tends to be because women are employed in occupations and low-wage jobs that have high turnover. For example, Frederiksen (2008) shows that, while women have higher unconditional turnover rates than men, the differences are eliminated by comparing job separation probabilities for employees in similar workplaces and job characteristics. As well, most studies find that any differences in turnover rates tend to be declining over time, and that the wage gap is smaller when comparisons are made between males and females with the same continuity in the labour forces (Light and Ureta 1992).

Differences in household responsibilities can lead to a situation where women develop a comparative advantage in household tasks and men develop a comparative advantage in labour market tasks. This leads to each specializing in their area of comparative advantage, reinforcing discriminatory behaviour against women performing labour market tasks. The specialization, in turn, leads to cumulative effects whereby women become less prone to accumulate the continuous labour market experience that leads to higher earnings. This leads them to be especially vulnerable in case of divorce or if they return to the labour market after a prolonged absence due to child raising.

The fact that the household responsibility of females is so important in these aspects of productivity makes it more understandable that there will be increased pressure for a more equitable division of labour in the household, as well as more daycare facilities for children and "family friendly" parental leaves. Based on U.S. data, Lowen and Sicilian (2009) indicate that women are more likely to receive family friendly fringe benefits, such as paid parental leave, flexible work schedules, child care, and sick leave. In addition, in empirical work that attempts to control for productivity differences between males and females, we should be careful in interpreting the productivity-adjusted wage and employment patterns as ones that are free of discrimination. The discrimination may simply be occurring outside the labour market, affecting productivity and, hence, wages in the labour market. Lundberg and Startz (1998) analyze the cumulative effect of post- and pre-labour–market discrimination, and review the earlier literature on that topic.

LO2   Measuring Discrimination

Defining discrimination is much easier than measuring it. It is rare, though not unheard of, to find cases of discriminating firms engaging in overtly and directly observable discriminatory practices. Instead, economists and others look for indirect evidence of discrimination as reflected in unequal outcomes between groups. Of course, for any two groups there may be legitimate differences in earnings that have nothing to do with discrimination. Economists, therefore, look for evidence of unequal outcomes (like pay or promotion rates) *net* of differences in productivity. Unfortunately, productivity is rarely measured.

Where equally qualified men and women perform the same job in the same firm, but are paid differently, this is generally taken as prima facie evidence of discrimination (economically and legally). But such situations represent only a tiny fraction of the potential discrimination in the economy, and publicly available, firm-level data sets are rarely available to the public (though see Exhibits 12.7 and 12.9).

Much economic research focuses on the economy-wide earnings ratio. It is in this wider arena where the unobservability of productivity becomes an empirical problem. Viewed differently, it is another manifestation of the more general empirical problem in economics. Because we cannot perform controlled experiments to address every empirical question, we have to artificially construct counterfactual evidence. In this case, we have to construct counterfactual evidence for women's earnings: what would women earn if they were men? We wish to hold all productive characteristics constant, and imagine changing the workers' sex to see how their pay would be adjusted. (In this case, the difficulty of conducting the experiment is evident, though individual cases exist.) Thus, any difference in pay that cannot be accounted for by productive characteristics might be deemed discrimination, although it can also reflect unobserved characteristics that cannot be controlled for in the analysis.

The framework most commonly employed by economists is a straightforward application of the human capital earnings function previously developed. The procedure is attributed to Blinder (1973) and Oaxaca (1973), though it is usually referred to as a **Oaxaca decomposition**. The objective is to decompose the difference in earnings between men and women (or any two groups) into that part due to productivity and that due to discrimination.

To begin, we wish to explain,

$$\frac{Y^F}{Y^M}$$

That is, the ratio of women's to men's wages. Our earnings functions provide models for the levels of pay for men and women. Suppose that we have our standard human capital models of earnings,

$$\ln Y^M = \beta_M X_M$$

and

$$\ln Y^F = \beta_F X_F$$

where X_M and X_F are men's and women's productive characteristics, and β_M and β_F are the market rewards (rates of return), or pay schedules, for these characteristics. Then, taking logs of the male–female wage ratio, we have the simple expression,

$$\ln\left(\frac{Y^M}{Y^F}\right) = \ln Y^M - \ln Y^F = \beta_M X_M - \beta_F X_F$$

By adding and subtracting the term $\beta m X_F$, we obtain,

$$\ln Y^M - \ln Y^F = \beta_M X_M - \beta_F X_F - \beta_M X_F + {}_M X_F$$

Rearranging, we get,

$$\ln Y^M - \ln Y^F = \beta_M\left(X_M - X_F\right) + \left(\beta_M - \beta_F\right)X_F$$

which yields the decomposition.

In the absence of discrimination, pay differences should arise only from differences in the X's (productive characteristics), not differences in the β's (the pay scales). The first part of this expression, $\beta_M(X_M - X_F)$, gives the predicted difference in earnings that would arise if men and women were paid on the same basis, but had different characteristics. The second component, $(\beta_M - \beta_F)X_F$, yields the part of the differential due to differences in pay structure. The first component is often referred to as a measure of the differential due to **pre-market characteristics**, while the second, unexplained component, is often labelled as that due to labour market discrimination, although it can also reflect unobserved factors that cannot be controlled for in the analysis.

The basic framework is illustrated in Figure 12.1. This figure shows two pay scales, one for men and one for women, as well as the wage corresponding to two individuals, a woman with productive characteristic X_F, and a man with X_M. The woman is paid $\ln Y_F$ according to her pay schedule (measured by the vertical distance to point A), while the man is paid $\ln Y_M$ according to his pay schedule (measured by the vertical distance to point D). The overall differential is, thus, the vertical distance between points A and D. The point B represents what the woman would have been paid if she had been paid according to the man's pay schedule. In this way, the "counterfactual" is constructed. The difference between A and B is, thus, labour market discrimination, or the difference in earnings due entirely to differences in pay schedules. The vertical distance CD is the additional pay that the man earns because of his higher level of X (according to the male pay schedule), and is, thus, that part of the earnings difference that can be explained by pre-market characteristics.

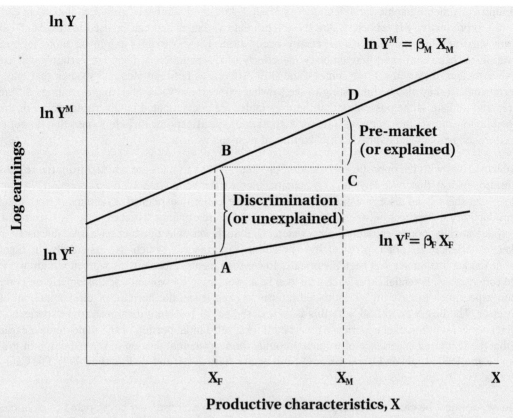

Figure 12.1 Graphical Illustration of the Oaxaca Decomposition

The lines indicate the relationship between pay (vertical axis) and productive characteristics (horizontal axis) separately for males (top line) and females (bottom line). The positive slope of both lines indicates that both males and females receive higher pay for more productive characteristics. The fact that the male line is steeper than the female line indicates that males also receive a higher return (i.e., greater pay) for additional productive characteristics. The fact that the intercept is higher for males than for females indicates that males also receive greater "base" pay than females. Since the base pay (i.e., intercept) of males and the monetary returns to productive characteristics (i.e., slopes) are greater for males than for females, the male line is always above the female line—that is, male pay is always higher than female pay for any given level of productive characteristics.

With data on the X's and Y's, the earnings functions, or pay scales, can be estimated. The decomposition can then be based on the regression coefficients and average measured male and female characteristics.

$$\ln Y^M = \hat{\beta}_{0M} + \hat{\beta}_{1M}\overline{X}_{1M} + \dots + \hat{\beta}_{KM}\overline{X}_{KM}$$

$$\ln Y^F = \hat{\beta}_{0F} + \hat{\beta}_{1F}\overline{X}_{1F} + \dots + \hat{\beta}_{KF}\overline{X}_{KF}$$

Thus, we can decompose the differences in mean log earnings (and, thus, the raw earnings ratio) into that part due to differences in observable X's and that part due to differences in β's: **explained and unexplained differentials**, respectively. A hypothetical example is illustrated subsequently in the Worked Example, "Analyzing the Determinants of Male and Female Earnings."

While the procedure is relatively simple to employ, there are a number of important caveats for interpretation, and difficulties in implementation. First, there is the question of what are the admissible X's (productive, "pre-market" characteristics). Most researchers would agree that the standard human capital variables, such as experience and education, are legitimate predictors of productivity and earnings. However, schooling decisions of women and men may be affected by discrimination in the labour market. A neat separation of pay differences due to pre- and post-labour–market discrimination may, therefore, be difficult. Empirically, demographic variables, such as marital status and number of children, also affect earnings, though their relationship to productivity is less clear. Are these legitimate variables that can be used to "explain" earnings? More problematic are variables like industry and especially occupation. These variables might be more legitimately viewed as outcome variables themselves, and may embody the effects of discrimination. They are certainly difficult to label as pre-market. Nevertheless, they will capture some of the skill differences between men and women that may be legitimate earnings determinants. It may also be interesting to see to what extent these variables explain earnings differences, even if we are not prepared to dismiss the possibility that these variables are contaminated by discrimination. For this reason, it is usually worthwhile to estimate the decomposition for a number of specifications, including ones that do not control for the differences in the occupational and industrial distributions of men and women.

A second problem arises with the opposite specification problem; what variables are omitted from the regressions (termed unobserved heterogeneity) that may lead to a systematic bias in the estimation of discrimination? At one extreme, a diehard believer that there is no discrimination could attribute the entire unexplained difference in earnings to legitimate, unobserved productivity differences between men and women. More reasonably, there are specific variables that we might imagine are systematically poorly measured for women. One such variable is experience. As discussed in Chapter 9, labour market experience is often proxied by "potential experience," which is essentially a function of age. Women's labour market attachment has been historically lower than men's, especially as women withdraw from the labour force for child care reasons. Potential experience may then be a poor proxy for women's actual experience compared to men. We might then expect men to have higher estimated returns to experience, not because of discrimination, but because of measurement error. The best way to deal with this is, obviously, to try to obtain data on actual experience. Such studies find that differences in labour market experience do account for a substantial portion of the male–female earnings gap, and, importantly, that the increased experience of women accounts for a substantial portion of the reduction of the gap in recent years (Blau and Kahn 1997; Light and Ureta 1995; O'Neill and O'Neill 2005; and Wellington 1997). For Canadian evidence see Drolet (2002a, 2002b) and Kidd and Shannon (1994).

At the very least, we must be careful in interpreting the results of this exercise, and be prepared to examine the numbers underlying the "bottom line" reported differentials. There is also a high return to finding data sets that permit one to address some of these econometric problems.

WORKED EXAMPLE

Analyzing the Determinants of Male and Female Earnings

Assume that the following wage equations were estimated separately for males (subscript m) and females (subscript f). ED denotes years of education (averaging 14 for males and 15 for females), EXP denotes years of labour market experience (averaging 10 for males and 7 for females), MAR being married (average of .50, or 50 percent, being married for both males and females) and CHILDREN the presence of children in the household (average of .60, or 60 percent, having children present for both males and females). When the dependent variable is in logarithmic form, the estimated coefficients give the percentage change in wages associated with a one-unit change in the explanatory variable.

$$\ln W_m = .40 + .07ED_m + .06EXP_m + .05MAR_m + .01CHILDREN_m$$

$$\ln W_f = .01 + .10ED_f + .04EXP_f - .02MAR_f - .05CHILDREN_f$$

a. What do these coefficients imply about the differential effect of education, experience, marital status, and the presence of children on the wages of males and females? The returns to acquiring additional education are higher for females compared to males, but the effect of experience is lower for females compared to males. Males who are married tend to earn more than males who are not married, after controlling for the other included variables that affect earnings, while the married state has a negative effect on the earnings of females. The same is the case for the presence of children in the household.

b. Based on these coefficients and the mean values of the explanatory variables, calculate the expected ln wages for both males and females. "Plug in" the mean values for the explanatory variables, and calculate the expected, E, ln wage as

$$E(Ln\ W_m) = .40 + .07(14) + .06(10) + .05(.5) + .01(.6) = 2.01$$

$$E(Ln\ W_f) = .01 + .10(15) + .04(7) - .02(.5) - .05(.6) = 1.75$$

Since one property of regression analysis is that the regression coefficients are such that when multiplied by the average value of the explanatory variables they yield the mean of the dependent variable, then E(LnW) = WA where WA is the average ln wage.

c. What is the average total or "raw" ratio of female to male ln wages? The raw ratio of female to male ln wages, as indicated in part (b), is E (Ln W_f)/E(Ln W_m) = WA_f/WA_m = 1.75/2.01 = .87.

d. Calculate the expected ln wages for an average female, assuming she was paid according to the same pay structure as the average male. Plug in the average value of the female characteristics into the male wage equation to get the hypothetical ln wages W^*_f, which females would get if paid according to the male pay structure.

$$ln\ W^*_f = .40 + .07(15) + .06(7) + .05(.5) + .01(.6) = 1.90$$

e. Calculate the expected ln wage for an average male, assuming he was paid according to the same pay structure as the average female. Plug the average value of the male characteristics into the female wage equation to get the hypothetical ln wages, W^*_m, which males would get if paid according to the female pay structure.

$$ln\ W^*_m = .01 + .10(14) + .04(10) - .02(.5) - .05(.6) = 1.77$$

f. What is the hypothetical difference in ln wages if females were paid according to the male pay structure, as in (c) above? The equation below gives the calculation, indicating that there still would be a gap in favour of males of 11 log points. This implies a ratio of female/male pay of exp(-.11) = 0.897 if females were paid according to the male pay structure, as opposed to the 0.87 ratio of their actual wage as given in part (c) above. The remaining gap is attributable to differences in their pay-determining characteristics.

$$ln\ W^*_f\ -\ E(Ln\ W_m) = 1.90\ - 2.01 = -.11$$

g. What is the hypothetical difference in ln wages if males were paid according to the female pay structure, as in (d) above? The equation below gives the calculation, indicating that there still would be a gap in favour of males of 2 log points. This implies a ratio of female/male pay of exp(-.02) = 0.98 if males were paid according to the female pay structure, as opposed to the 0.87 ratio of their actual wage as given in part (c) above. The remaining gap is attributable to differences in their pay-determining characteristics.

$$E(Ln\ W_f)\ -\ Ln\ W^*_m = 1.75\ -1.77 = -0.02$$

h. Why do these two ratios differ? The two ratios differ because in one case the male regression coefficients are used to weight, or evaluate, the female endowments of characteristics, and in the other case the female regression coefficients are used to weight, or evaluate, the male endowment of characteristics. This is akin to an index number issue where different prices are used to weight, or evaluate, different bundles.

i. Is one more appropriate than the other? There is no single correct procedure, although it seems more logical to use the male weights or returns to evaluate the female characteristics, because the male coefficients are generally regarded as the nondiscriminatory norm. Other procedures, however, have been used in the literature, such as a weighted average of the two coefficients.

j. How do these adjusted ratios compare to the unadjusted ratio, as calculated in (c) above, and what does that imply? The adjusted ratios are both higher than the unadjusted ratio of female to male earnings. This implies that if either females were paid according to the male pay structure or males were paid according to the female pay structure, the ratio of female to male wages would rise. That is, a part of the male–female wage gap reflects differences in pay that males and females receive for the same characteristics. This is often labelled a measure of "discrimination," although it can also reflect other unobservable pay-determining factors that are not controlled for in the regression.

While most of the empirical studies of the effect of discrimination use some variant of the Oaxaca decomposition technique, other methodologies are also used, including procedures that involve direct estimates of productivity (Exhibit 9), or audit studies involving interviews or auditions where the characteristics of the applicants are "blinded" (Exhibit 10), or correspondence studies where resumes of equally productive workers who differ only in terms of their signalling of gender or minority status or sexual orientation are sent out and call-backs or job offers recorded.

LO3   Additional Evidence on Male–Female Pay Differentials

Evidence on the factors influencing male–female pay differentials was provided previously when the alternative theories of labour market discrimination were outlined. Further evidence, with particular reference to Canadian studies, is provided here.

Numerous studies have reviewed the empirical procedures and the evidence on male–female wage differentials and the determinants of those differentials. Reviews of earlier Canadian and U.S. studies are contained in Gunderson (1989, 2006), Drolet (2001), Baker and Drolet (2010), and Vincent (2013). Reviews of U.S. studies are given in Altonji and Blank (1999); Bertrand (2011); Blau, Ferber, and Winkler (2002); Blau (1998); Blau and Kahn (2000, 2003, 2008); Holzer and Neumark (2000); and Jarrell and Stanley (2004). The extensive literature in this area is exhibited by the fact that Weichselbaumer and Winter-Ebmer (2005) provide a meta-analysis of 263 international studies on the male–female pay gap. The following generalizations emerge from those various reviews:

- Before adjusting for the effect of different factors that can influence the male–female pay gap, females in Canada tend to earn about 60 percent, or slightly more, of what males earn. This is often referred to as the gross earnings ratio. The ratio tends to increase to around 70 percent based on full-time, full-year workers, and to around 80 percent based on hourly wages that control for hours of work differences that can occur within full-time, full-year workers. The ratio increases to around 85–90 percent, and sometimes higher, after controlling for such factors as actual work experience, type of education, occupation, and other workplace characteristics.

- In essence, the ratio tends to increase (i.e., the male–female pay gap decreases) as adjustments are made for various factors, such as women working fewer hours, having less continuous work experience, having fields of study in education that tend to be less labour market oriented, working in lower-paying occupations and smaller firms, and having a disproportionate burden of household responsibilities that can affect their job search, mobility, and labour market performance. Some of these factors themselves, however, may reflect discrimination, although much it may occur outside of the labour market.

- The male–female pay gap is smaller in the public sector and in unionized environments, likely reflecting such factors as egalitarian pay practices, compressed wage structures, and sensitivity to their public image.

- The pay gap is dissipating substantially over time, although that convergence has slowed in recent years. The declining gap likely reflects a variety of factors: more accumulation of experience and continuity of experience on the part of women; increases in the education of females as well as more labour-market-oriented education; the greater importance of market forces that dissipate discrimination associated with factors such as global competition, deregulation, and privatization; the greater emphasis on "brain over brawn" facilitated by technological change and especially the IT revolution; the dissipation of stereotypes as more women enter the labour market; more-equitable divisions of labour within the household; a growth in demand for female-dominated occupations, such as health and education, and a decline in demand in male-dominated jobs, such as blue-collar manufacturing; the decline of male unionization and a relative increase of female unionization; and, possibly, increased anti-discrimination legislation.

- The gap is smaller in countries with centralized bargaining structures, where wage structures tend to be compressed and equal pay issues are incorporated into centralized bargaining.

- The discriminatory gap is smaller the greater the degree of competition in product markets and labour markets, suggesting that competitive forces can help dissipate discrimination (see Exhibit 12.6).

EXHIBIT 12.6

Are Markets a Minority's Best Friend?

As discussed previously, competitive market forces should dissipate discrimination since it is a costly practice to not hire the best people for the job or to bypass the opportunity to hire female workers who are paid less than equally productive male workers. Empirical evidence tends to bear this out in that discrimination is less when private-sector employers are subject to more competition in their product and service markets. Such evidence is found in Ashenfelter and Hannan (1996); Black and Brainerd (2004); Black and Strahan (2001); Hellerstein, Neumark, and Troske (2002); Jones and Walsh (1991); and Meng (2004). This suggests that "markets may be a minority's best friend," and that fostering competitive market forces through such means as trade liberalization, deregulation, and privatization can be "part of the solution."

Similar positive effects of greater competition in the labour market are found based on a correspondence study in which resumes were sent to employers in Belgium. Applicants with foreign-sounding names were equally likely as natives to be invited to a job interview when labour markets were tight and vacancies were difficult to fill, but they were half as likely to be invited when markets were not tight (Baert et al. 2015). Similarly, in Sweden the share of females in employment increased substantially after the takeover of an inefficient firm. The takeover firm applied more-efficient practices after the takeover, including the increased employment of females (Heyman, Svaleryd, and Vlachos 2013).

The "flavour" of the discrimination literature can be illustrated by a more detailed discussion of a number of studies, with particular emphasis on Canadian ones. For example, based on the 1991 Survey of Consumer Finances, Baker et al. (1995) estimate a raw earnings differential of 0.402 in Canada. Depending on the specification, they find that most of this gap is not explained by differences in pay-determining characteristics, with the unexplained gap reflecting discrimination or unobserved factors that cannot be controlled for by conventional measures of pay-determining factors.

Using the Labour Market Activity Survey (LMAS) data for 1989, and looking at wages instead of earnings, Kidd and Shannon (1994) estimate a raw differential of 0.295. Using traditional measures of labour market experience, they find that 0.22 of this differential is unexplained. However, when they used a measure of predicted labour force attachment, which is primarily a function of household responsibilities, to correct the measure of labour market experience, they find that the unexplained component of the earnings differential drops by one-half. Similarly, Drolet (2002a, 2002b) finds the gap to be substantially smaller after controlling for differences in actual labour market experience. This highlights that discrimination and inequality of responsibilities and opportunities originating from outside the labour market may be as important, or even more important, a source of male–female wage inequality as discrimination from within the labour market itself. This is especially the case with respect to the unequal division of labour related to household responsibilities (especially child raising), which can manifest itself in different labour market behaviour pertaining to such factors as hours worked, absenteeism, turnover, mobility, career interruption, training, and occupational choice.

Drolet (2002b) uses data from the 1999 Workplace and Employee Survey (WES), a survey that matched workers with their workplace, enabling an analysis of the effect of differences in workplace characteristics. She found that female hourly wages were about 80 percent of male wages *before* adjusting for different productivity-related factors that can affect wages. Female wages increased to about 92 percent of male wages *after* adjusting for differences in worker characteristics that can affect pay, such as education, general work experience, company-specific tenure, marital status, dependent children, part-time status, union status, region, occupation, as well as workplace characteristics, such as firm size, non-profit organization, foreign-held organization, self-directed work groups, performance pay, overtime pay, training, workplace part-time rate, and industry. Workplace characteristics were more important than worker characteristics in explaining the pay gap. The ratio of female to male wages of 0.92, after adjusting for differences in other factors that affect pay, implies a small wage gap of about

8 percent, some of which reflects discrimination and some reflecting other unmeasured factors. In a more recent study, Drolet and Mumford (2012) also find that the gender wage gap in Canada was about 10 percent, after controlling for workplace and other factors that affect pay.

Also based on Canadian data, Phipps, Burton, and Lethbridge (2001) find that child-related interruptions negatively affect female earnings both because human capital depreciates and because time spent on household activities likely has a negative effect on labour market productivity.

A number of Canadian studies find, perhaps surprisingly, that the occupational segregation of women into lower-paying jobs does not explain a large portion of the male–female wage gap in Canada (Baker et al. 1995; Baker and Fortin 1999, 2001, 2004; Kidd and Shannon 1994; with similar evidence for the United States given in Macpherson and Hirsch 1995). This captures the fact that a large part of the gap reflects the segregation of females in low-wage establishments and industries. Also, there is not a strong negative relationship between female pay and the proportion of females in the particular occupation, in Canada. Baker and Fortin (2001, 2004) attribute this to the high degree of unionization in Canada, especially in public sector jobs, such as education and health and welfare, where women are relatively well paid. However, as pointed out by Kidd and Shannon (1996b), to some extent this reflects the poor measures of occupation. Occupation has greater explanatory power with more-narrowly defined occupations (e.g., separating out doctors and nurses from "health occupations"). Again, beyond an accounting exercise, it is doubtful that we want to treat occupation as a pre-market characteristic. Nevertheless, these findings highlight the potential importance of policies to reduce occupational segregation and to encourage the occupational advancement of women. Such initiatives include equal employment opportunity policies, as well as the provision of education and training that is labour-market oriented. They also highlight the limitations of conventional equal pay legislation involving comparisons between men and women within both the same job and the same establishment, since pay differences are likely to be small in those circumstances.

Based on German data, Ludsteck (2014) finds that jobs with high proportions of females have a larger male–female wage gap. However, he finds that much of this is due to the fact that females who are employed in male-dominated jobs tend to have a wage premium based on their above-average unobserved ability. Also based on German data, Janssen and Backes-Gellner (2016) find that women employed in stereotypical male jobs tend to be less satisfied with their job but more satisfied with their income. Apparently, they receive a pay premium to compensate for the possible harassment and other negative aspects of being employed in stereotypically male jobs that leave them less satisfied with their job.

In addition to being disproportionately employed in low-wage occupations, women tend to be employed in low-wage establishments (Drolet 2002a, 2002b; Reilly and Wirjanto 1999) and industries. This further emphasizes the limitations of equal pay policies, since comparisons are allowed only within the same establishment and, therefore, also the same industry. Kidd and Shannon (1996a) emphasize this point in their comparison of earnings differentials in Australia and Canada. In Australia, comparisons could be made across firms and across industries since wages for approximately 80 percent of employees were determined by centrally administered tribunals at the state and federal levels. As a result of being able to make such comparisons across firms and industries, the gap in Australia was only 0.14 (most of which is still unexplained), which is about half the level in Canada where such wage-setting procedures will likely never occur.

Evidence also exists that suggests **glass ceilings** whereby large male–female pay gaps exist at the high end of the pay distribution, as females are less likely to be promoted to the very high-paying jobs. Such evidence is discussed in Baker et al. (1995), Javdani (2015), and Yap and Konrad (2009) for Canada; Arulampalam, Booth, and Bryson (2007) and Christofides et al. (2013) for Europe; and Johnstron and Lee for Australia (2012). Gunderson and Xiu (2014) review the international studies and provide evidence of a glass ceiling for China.

In a survey of large Canadian corporations, Kathy Cannings (1988a) found that female managers earned, on average, 87 percent of the pay of male managers. They were also only 80 percent as likely to be promoted in any given year of their career with the organization. Some of this difference in promotion opportunities can be explained by differences in such factors as formal education and productivity-related characteristics. However, even after controlling for differences in these factors, female managers were significantly less likely to be promoted than male managers.

Based on U.S. data, Bertrand and Hallock (2001) find that female executives earned about 45 percent less than male executives, mainly because they were less likely to be in the top positions or in large corporations. Their position in these areas, however, is improving dramatically. Blau and Devaro (2007) use a cross-sectional survey of employers in four metropolitan areas in the United States in the mid-1990s to show that women have lower probabilities of promotion than men, but that there are essentially no differences in wage growth across genders with or without promotions.

Based on U.S. data, Gayle, Golan, and Miller (2012) find that the overall pay and promotion gap between male and female executives occurs mainly because females exit their jobs more often than males. For the smaller number of females who do continue, they actually have higher pay and promotion probabilities then males. Much of this may reflect the fact that the "survivors" are a select group in terms of their ability as executives.

Based on Danish data, Smith, Smith, and Verner (2013) find that the probability of promotion into VP and CEO positions is considerably lower for females than males, even after controlling for various factors that influence promotions. Much of the difference reflects the fact that female VPs tend to cluster in areas such as HR, R&D, and IT where promotion rates into CEO positions are lower compared to areas such as sales or production that are dominated by males. The extent to which this clustering itself reflects discrimination is an open question.

Gregor-Smith, Main, and O'Reilly (2014) find evidence of gender bias in the appointment and pay of women to boards of directors in the United Kingdom. They find no evidence, however, that gender diversity on boards of directors improves corporate performance. Negative effects on firm profits as a result of quotas of females on boards of directors in Norway are found in Matsa and Miller (2013), a finding likely reflecting the fact that organizations with increased representation of females on the board engaged in fewer workforce reductions so that relative labour costs increased.

Doiron and Riddell (1994) document that for Canada the impact of unions on wages tends to be greater for females than males. However, as females are slightly less likely to be unionized, these opposing effects imply that unions do not substantially affect the male–female wage gap.

Evidence on the effect of legislated job-protected maternity leave tends to be conflicting. On the one hand, such job-protected leave could increase female wages to the extent that it allows them to return to their original or similar job and to retain their seniority and their wage. On the other hand, it could decrease female wages to the extent that it makes employers reluctant to hire females since expected leaves are costly to employers; or they may hire women only if they can pay a compensating lower wage. Based on U.S. data, Waldfogel (1996) finds no effect on women's wages, while Gruber (1994) finds that mandated maternity leave in U.S. health plans has a negative effect on women's wages. Based on international data, Ruhm (1999) also finds a negative effect on women's wages. In Canada, Baker and Milligan (2008) exploit variations in statutory job-protected leave entitlements across time and provinces to show that the introduction of modest entitlements increases the proportion of mothers employed and on leave but has little effect on the length of time that they are home with their children. Moreover, the authors show that maternity leave entitlements increase job continuity with pre-birth employers, for reasons that some women come back to the workforce rather than permanently quitting. To the extent that reduced job separation probabilities increase investments into human capital and increase wages (as suggested in Drolet 2002a), these programs may have a positive effect on women's wages, although more research on this subject is still warranted.

Baker and Drolet (2010) construct a new time series on hourly wages in Canada from a number of different data sets. They emphasize that hourly wages is a preferred measure since it reflects the "price" of labour, rather than earnings, which confounds that price with time worked. As well, wages are the target measure for policies such as pay equity. They find that the hourly wage ratio is considerably higher than the earnings ratio. Specifically, the wage ratio for full-time, full-year workers aged 25–54 had reached 0.85 in 2006, compared to 0.72 for the earnings-based ratio. The wage ratio is also much higher for younger workers, single persons, and university graduates. Importantly, the wage ratio has improved over the last 15 years, while the earnings ratio has remained stagnant. Drolet (2011) also discusses the rise in the wage ratio across the wage distribution, and the fact that it increased more at the bottom of the wage distribution than at the top. Boudarbat and Connelly (2013) provide similar evidence for post-secondary graduates in Canada, although the wage gap actually increased slightly in the upper half of the wage distribution. Schirle (2015) provides evidence that the wage gap has declined across all provinces, although more in some than in others.

Evidence that the gap is small or nonexistent when females first enter the labour market but that it increases with time spent in the labour market prevails in other countries as well (Simpson 1990). Based on UK data, for example, Manning and Swaffield (2008) document this phenomenon and attribute it to a number of inter-related characteristics of females: less acquisition of subsequent training and continuous labour market experience; less risk taking, competitive behaviour, and emphasis on money as opposed to family and altruism; and less job shopping. They emphasize, however, that the majority of the pay differences remain unexplained even by this wide array of considerations.

Evidence that the male–female pay gap is declining over time, albeit more slowly in recent years, is also documented in U.S. studies (Beaudry and Lewis 2014; Blau and Kahn 1997, 2006; Kassenboehmer and Sinning 2014; and Weinberger and Kuhn 2010). Much of that decline in the gap reflects improvements in the productivity-related characteristics of females, including their increased labour market experience and the continuity of that experience, as well as education and, especially, education that is labour market oriented. Other contributing factors include a possible decline in stereotyping and discrimination, an increased importance in the "knowledge economy" of skills that females often possess (Bacolod and Bloom 2010; Beaudry and Lewis 2014) with a decline in the importance of manual-labour skills often possessed by males (i.e., an increased premium on brains over brawn), and the fact that unionization rates fell more slowly for females compared to males. Other factors include the greater importance of market forces associated with the dissipation of discrimination, such as global competition, deregulation and privatization; a more equitable sharing of household tasks; a growth in demand for female dominated occupations, such as health and education, along with a decline in demand in male-dominated jobs, such as blue-collar manufacturing; and, possibly, increased anti-discrimination legislation.

There is also some evidence of a positive selection bias in that women with conventionally unobserved traits that yield a wage premium were increasingly drawn into the higher end of the labour market, perhaps in response to the growing wage inequality and rising returns to skills and education that females possessed (Blau and Kahn 2006; Mulligan and Rubinstein 2008; Weinberger and Kuhn 2010; Black and Spitz-Oener 2010). While the evidence indicates that the male–female pay gap has declined over time, a gap still remains, and discrimination appears "alive and well" for explaining part (albeit likely a declining part) of that gap (but see Exhibit 12.7).

In her presidential address to the American Economics Association, Claudia Goldin (2014) outlined what she surmised would be the "last chapter" leading to gender equality in the labour market. She outlined that there has been a "grand convergence" in gender roles in various dimensions: labour force participation, labour market experience, paid hours of work, unpaid hours of work at home, occupations, fields of study in education, and education where female education now exceeds that of males. And these determinants of earnings have led to a convergence (not necessarily equality) in earnings. She argues that the gender gap in pay would be reduced further and perhaps eliminated "if firms did not have an incentive to disproportionately reward individuals who labored long hours and worked particular hours." (p. 1091). She refers particularly to the corporate, financial, and legal occupations where long hours of work and willingness to be available are rewarded with huge premiums. These are essentially compensating pay differences in return for giving up flexibility and control over one's hours. This, in part, reflects the lack of good substitutes for scarce talent. With respect to the gender pay gap, it reflects the difficulty that women have in working extremely long hours, and in giving up control over their hours in light of child care and household responsibilities. Some firms have provided more flexibility given the high cost of requiring long and inflexible hours, but the adaptation has been slow. She argues that the last chapter toward greater gender equality will require more of such flexibility in hours worked. Whether market forces will foster this flexibility, given the high cost to firms of paying for such long hours and to individuals in giving up control over the hours, is an open question. Policy initiatives to foster that grand convergence are also not obvious.

EXHIBIT 12.7

Perhaps There Is No Discrimination!

In a study that is likely to generate considerable controversy (if not ire!) June O'Neill and Dave O'Neill (2005) conclude, "labour market discrimination [against women] is unlikely to account for a differential of more than 8 percent and may not be present at all" (p. 26). Their study is based on the U.S. National Longitudinal Survey of Youth (NLSY) cohort that had reached age 35–43 in 2000. Their study is different from most in that they are able to control for a variety of conventionally unmeasured factors, such as the extent and continuity of experience, as well as job-related characteristics and workplace amenities that are "family friendly." They find, for example, that labour force withdrawal for child care or family responsibilities is associated with a similar 8 percent reduction in wages for both men and women; however, 55 percent of women and only 13 percent of men withdraw for those reasons.

Based on Canadian data, Marie Drolet (2002b) estimates the adjusted ratio of female to male wages to be about 0.92 after controlling for a wide array of workplace characteristics, such as firm size, flexible hours, performance pay, and non-profit and part-time employment. Her study is different from most in that she uses a data set (the 1999 Canadian Workplace and Employee Survey [WES]) that has measures of workplace characteristics that are not available in most conventional data sets that analyze discrimination. Drolet emphasizes, however, that women may disproportionately be placed or segregated into jobs with characteristics that are associated with low pay, such as being in small firms and in the non-profit sector, as well as in part-time employment and without performance pay.

Both studies cite others that find the gap to be much smaller after controlling for such conventionally unobserved factors that are not present in most data sets.

Differences in fringe benefits can also account for a portion of the male–female gap when measured on the bases of total compensation. For example, Solberg and Laughlin (1995) find the ratio of female to male wages to be 0.96 within occupations, when based on a total compensation including fringe benefits, as compared to 0.87 when based only on wages. Although arguments have been made that the male–female pay gap reflects a compensating wage paid to males because they receive lower pension fringe benefits than do females, since females live longer, Pesando, Gunderson, and McLaren (1991) provide evidence that this is more than offset by the fact that females are less likely to have pension plans and, when they do, they are less likely to accumulate seniority-based service credits or wage increases. As such, the male–female pay gap may be understated by the exclusion of pension fringe benefits. However, Lowen and Sicilian (2009) show, using longitudinal data from the United States, that there are no gender differences in family neutral fringe benefits, such as medical, life, and dental insurance; retirement benefits; profit sharing; and job training, after controlling for other personal and job characteristics. Moreover, while women are shown to receive more family friendly fringe benefits than men, these differences have negligible effects on explaining gender wage gaps. Overall, the effect of fringe benefits on wage differentials is unresolved in the empirical literature.

Clearly, debate will continue as to the actual magnitude of the male–female wage gap that can be attributed to discrimination, especially after controlling for the effect of such factors as experience and the continuity of that experience, workplace characteristics, and fringe benefits. These factors are often not available in conventional data sets. As such, more and better data in these areas will be helpful to narrow the range of the debate. There is still the issue, however, of the appropriateness of controlling for these factors if differences in their prevalence between males and females reflect discrimination, perhaps outside the labour market.

While the debate will continue over the extent of discrimination, the reviews of the literature on sex discrimination invariably conclude that some portion of the male–female wage gap reflects discrimination, although much of it may emanate from forces outside the labour market. The following are examples of those conclusions. "We believe that the evidence suggests there is ongoing discrimination in the labor market, both against blacks as well as women" (Altonji and Blank 1999, p. 3191). "[M]ost studies do find some residual wage gap that they attribute to discrimination. When the gap is close to zero that usually results from the inclusion of control variables whose values themselves may reflect discrimination" (Gunderson 1989, p. 51). "[E]mployer discrimination continues to play a role in generating different labour market outcomes by race and sex" (Holzer and Neumark 2000, p. 499). "Clearly, women experience significant discrimination in pay. Almost all studies confirm this" (Jarrell and Stanley (2004, p. 828, based on their meta-analysis of 104 estimates of the gender pay gap).

The study by Jarrell and Stanley (2004) also found the interesting result that those studies done by male researchers tended to find *larger* discriminatory gaps than did the studies by female researchers, even after controlling for other methodological factors that can influence their estimates. They suggest that this could reflect male researchers "bending over backwards" so as to be perceived as objective in the way they conduct their research!

EXHIBIT 12.8

What Do the Womb, the Plow, and the Pill Have in Common?

A number of recent studies have provided insight into the importance of different factors in explaining the decline of the male–female wage gap, but also of many of its origins that have a legacy effect in sustaining the gap. Bhardwaj and Lakdawala (2013) highlight how in India discrimination begins in the womb in that investments in prenatal care are higher for boys than for girls, especially in regions known to have preferences for boys and for women whose previous children are female. Alesina, Giuliano, and Nunn (2013) provide evidence that societies in which agriculture originally depended on the plow disproportionately depended on strength and, hence, favoured males. These societies still tend to have less-equal gender norms, as measured by such factors as reported gender-role attitudes and female participation in such areas as the workplace, politics, and entrepreneurial activity. Janssen et al. (2016) highlight the importance of gender norms, given that pay gender gaps are largest in regions within Switzerland that vote against equal rights for women and men. Similar effects of gender norms across 25 OECD countries are found in Fortin (1995) and for the United States in Kosteas (2013) and references cited therein. Bailey, Hershbein, and Miller (2012) provide evidence that the availability of birth control pills in the 1960s and 1970s enabled women to delay their marriage, increase their education, and time their births in manners that enhanced their careers and, hence, earnings. They cite other studies with similar findings. In essence, while the womb and the plow may have long-lasting effects on female labour market outcomes, these effects can be altered by innovations such as the pill.

Most of the empirical studies from which the empirical evidence on discrimination was derived use variants of the Oaxaca decomposition or similar procedures to indirectly estimate the extent of discrimination. More-direct procedures (see Exhibits 12.9 and 12.10) also provide evidence of discrimination.

EXHIBIT 12.9

Studies with Direct Estimates of Productivity

Very few empirical studies of discrimination have direct estimates of productivity to detect discrimination defined as wages that are not commensurate with productivity (e.g., a ratio of female–male wages that is less than the ratio of their productivity). Productivity is generally inferred from indirect measures, such as experience and education.

A small number of studies, however, do use more-direct measures of productivity, although the results are not always in agreement. For example, based on U.S. data, Hellerstein, Neumark, and Troske (1999) estimate production functions to obtain the marginal productivity of females relative to males. They find that female productivity is somewhat less than male productivity, but the ratio of their wages is much less than the ratio of their productivity, suggesting a discriminatory pay gap. Smith (2002) finds that the productivity of female veterinarians is equal to that of male veterinarians, but that their pay is about 9 percent lower. Using firm-level data from Israel, however, Hellerstein and Neumark (1999) find that the ratio of female to male wages is about equal to the ratio of their productivity.

Blackaby, Booth, and Frank (2005) infer the productivity of male and female economists in the UK based on measures such as actual experience and career breaks, as well as publications, research grants, and teaching performance. (The fact that the latter is used as a measure of productivity may come as a surprise to you as students!) They find that female academic economists do receive lower pay after controlling for such measures of productivity. They indicate that this occurs largely because females receive fewer outside offers than do men, and outside offers or "raiding" is the primary mechanism whereby academic economists can get their pay increased either directly (if they accept the offers and move) or indirectly (if their own institution matches such offers). Blackaby, Booth, and Frank suggest that the reduced number of outside offers reflects the fact that other universities do not make offers for females as often as for males, since they feel the women are less likely to accept them and disrupt family life by moving. As well, their own institution may feel less pressure to respond and match such outside offers, because they feel that women have a less-credible threat of leaving, being more tied to their family commitments.

EXHIBIT 12.10

Direct Evidence of Discrimination from Audit and Correspondence Studies

The vast majority of empirical evidence on discrimination is indirect, based on estimating wage equations and conducting Oaxaca-type decompositions of the male–female wage gap. More-direct evidence is obtained with audit studies done with otherwise similar individuals and correspondence studies done with otherwise similar resumes.

In an audit study, Neumark, Bank, and Van Nort (1996) had two otherwise equally qualified male and female college students apply for jobs in a variety of restaurants. They found that the males were more likely to get interviews and, ultimately, job offers (at a higher wage) in the higher-priced restaurants, while females got jobs in the lower-priced restaurants, and at a lower wage. They interpret this as reflecting customer discrimination; apparently customers, for whatever reason, were prepared to pay more to be waited on by a male waiter in the more-expensive restaurants.

Goldin and Rouse (2000) analyze the effect of "blind" auditions adapted by a number of orchestras in the United States in the 1970s and 1980s. In such auditions, the performer was separated from the judging panel by a screen so that the panel would not know the personal characteristics of the performer. They found that the blind auditions had a large and positive effect on the hiring of female musicians, after controlling for other characteristics that could influence such hiring. They argue that this accounted for a large amount of the increased proportion of female musicians that were hired in recent years.

In a correspondence study, Bertrand and Mullainathan (2004) sent fictitious resumes with similar characteristics except for the ethnic "soundingness" of the applicants' names to job vacancies posted in newspaper advertisements in various cities in the United States. The results suggested that, on average, black applicants must apply to 15 jobs for every 10 jobs that whites must apply to in order to obtain a call-back for an interview.

Neumark (2012) cites various audit and correspondence studies as well as criticisms of those methodologies, and provides responses to those criticisms. Guryan and Charles (2013) and Heckman (2008) provide critiques of the audit and correspondence studies. Bartos et al. (2016) provide evidence from correspondence studies that employers engage in "attention discrimination" in that they more quickly dismiss job applications with minority sounding names.

 # Empirical Evidence for Other Groups

Most empirical research on discrimination in Canada has focused on male–female earnings disparities. Very little attention has been paid to other potentially disadvantaged groups (but see Exhibit 12.11 and 12.12). This has not been the case in the United States, where a high percentage, including most of the pioneering theoretical and applied work, of discrimination research has focused on racial discrimination, especially black-white differentials (for a review see Altonji and Blank 1999, and Fryer 2011). Partially due to data limitations, evidence and research on earnings differentials by ethnic groups in Canada is somewhat scanty, but what little there is has raised a number of important questions for future research.

EXHIBIT 12.11

Discrimination against the Homely: Beauty Pays

Are better-looking people paid more? If so, does this represent employer discrimination against the less attractive? In an innovative article, Hamermesh and Biddle (1994) explore the role of physical beauty in the labour market. They use survey data from Canada and the United States that contain subjective measures of looks. Interviewers were asked to rate photographs of the respondents on a 1 to 5 scale (strikingly handsome through homely). Most people were judged as average looking. Very few were rated at the extremes, and Hamermesh and Biddle focus on the average, the above average, and the below average.

Controlling for human capital characteristics, they find that the penalty for being unattractive (rather than average) is around 5 to 10 percent. The penalty is slightly higher for men than women. The premium for beauty was estimated to be slightly smaller, at about 4 to 5 percent; again, similar for men and women. An obvious question is whether or not this reflects employer discrimination. Because of consumer discrimination, better-looking employees may increase profits for their employers. This is obviously true for modelling agencies and movie studios, and may also be important in occupations where interpersonal contact is important. Hamermesh and Biddle use the fraction of an occupation that hires better-looking workers as a proxy for the importance of good looks. They find that there is some evidence that this measure affects earnings, but that individual looks still matter, even for those employed in occupations where beauty is less likely to be important. Their results suggest that the attitudes of employers toward nonproductivity-related characteristics of their employees may affect individual pay.

Sorting out cause and effect in such studies is difficult, since beauty can be correlated with other, unobservable factors, such as health and self-confidence, that are difficult to control for in conventional econometric procedures. There may even be reverse causality in that successful persons in the labour market may be able to invest more in products and services that enhance their looks. Many of the studies subsequent to the original Hamermesh and Biddle (1994) article have dealt with those methodological issues, invariably finding a robust beauty premium. Such evidence is found in Belot, Bhaskar, and van de Ven (2012); Dechter (2015); Hamermesh (2011); and Scholz and Sicinski (2015), and in studies they reviewed.

Kuhn and Shen (2013) provide evidence from China where job advertisements are allowed to state preferences for gender, age, and height and where employer preferences for women are related to their beauty, age and height. Such preferences become less important for higher levels of skills, where the value of education and qualifications are more important.

A number of recent studies have examined the effect of skin tone on wages and employment, generally finding that lighter-skinned individuals (i.e., closest to white) within each racial group have better outcomes, with this effect diminishing over time. Akee and Yursel (2012) and Kreisman and Rangel (2015) provide such evidence and cite earlier studies in that area.

EXHIBIT 12.12

Discrimination against Gays and Lesbians

The human rights codes of all jurisdictions in Canada provide protection against discrimination on the basis of sexual orientation. With increased attention being given to such human rights issues, and the increase in the number of same-sex marriages, a number of recent studies have examined labour market discrimination against gays and lesbians. In a meta-analysis that summarized the results of 31 previous studies, beginning with Badgett (1995) and including Carpenter (2008) for Canada, Klawitter (2015) concluded that gay men earn less than heterosexual men, and that much of the difference can be attributed to discrimination. Specifically, after controlling for other determinants of wages, gay men earned an average of 11 percent less than heterosexual men, with estimates ranging from zero to 30 percent less. Lesbian women on average earned 9 percent *more* than otherwise comparable heterosexual women, although the variation in the estimates is much greater, ranging from 25 percent less to 43 percent more. One possible rationale for the finding of a lesbian wage premium is that lesbian women do not generally expect to raise a family and hence invest more in labour market skills when compared to heterosexual women who may invest more in skills related to raising a family (Black et al. 2003). This is substantiated by the finding in Daneshvary et al. (2009) that lesbians who were previously married do not receive a lesbian wage premium.

Plug, Webbink, and Martin (2014) utilize data that indicates the extent to which prejudice against gays and lesbians varies by occupation. They find that gays and lesbians, understandably, shy away from occupations where prejudice against them is greatest. Such restrictions on occupational choice can obviously lower their earnings. Because of their lower earnings and restrictions on occupational choice, gays and lesbians tend to be less satisfied with their jobs compared to heterosexual men and women. (Canadian evidence in Leppel 2014).

A small number of studies have examined the effect of legislation that prohibits discrimination against lesbian, gay, bisexual, and transgender (LGBT) persons. For gays, based on 22 states that have such legislation in the United States, Martel (2012) finds that gay men face a wage penalty of roughly 20 percent, after controlling for the effect of other factors that affect wages, and that the legislation has reduced this penalty by about one-fifth. He cites three other studies that find similar positive effects of the legislation.

George and Kuhn (1994) examine white–**Aboriginal earnings differentials** using the 1986 census. Focusing on natives (Aboriginals) living off reserves, they find a raw gap of 0.14 for men with any Aboriginal origins, and 0.087 for women with any Aboriginal origins. Depending on the breadth of controls included in the earnings function, they find that anywhere from one-quarter to one-half of this differential can be explained by observable characteristics. They find that education plays an important role in diminishing the earnings difference between whites and native people, which holds promise. Less promisingly, they find that Aboriginal outcomes look much worse once those living on reserves are included in the sample. Additional Canadian evidence on the earnings gap between Aboriginal and non-Aboriginal persons, much of which is attributable to discrimination, is provided in Baker and Benjamin (1997), Hum and Simpson (1999), Lamb (2013), and Pendakur and Pendakur (1998, 2002, 2011). Pendakur and Pendakur (2011) found that the large pay gaps eroded somewhat between 1995 and 2005. The gaps were largest for registered or Status Indians, followed by those who self-reported Aboriginal identity, with the gap smallest for those with Aboriginal ancestry (but not identity or registry).

Exploration of **ethnic–white earnings differentials** for other groups inevitably confronts the reality that most nonwhites in Canada are also immigrants (Skuterud 2010). This makes research difficult for two reasons. First, it requires a separation of earnings differences that are to be attributed to immigrant status as distinct from ethnicity. This is best accomplished by comparing immigrants of different ethnicity separately from native born of different ethnicity (e.g., comparing immigrant whites to immigrant blacks, and native-born whites and native-born blacks as separate exercises). This is where data constraints become a problem, since there are often very few native-born members of ethnic minorities in publicly available data sets. For example, Baker and Benjamin (1994) report that there are only 60 native-born blacks in the public use samples of the 1981 census who had the earnings characteristics usually required for estimation of wage regressions.

Similar results were found for economics departments in the United States in Kolpin and Singell (1996). Interestingly, they also found that the departments that disproportionately hired females improved the most in citation rankings (a measure of productivity).

Studies on gender or race discrimination in the United States, which use the National Longitudinal Survey of Youth (NLSY79) data set, control for direct measures of productivity by including respondents' scores on the Armed Forces Qualification Test (AFQT). Briefly, the AFQT is a test conducted on United States military applicants was given to all survey respondents in the NLSY79 and designed to measure aptitudes in a variety of subject areas: science and mathematics, language and writing, mechanical comprehension, and electronics information. For example, Munasinghe, Reif, and Henriques (2008) find that the wage return to job tenure is substantially lower for women than men, and that the wage return to experience is higher for women than men, after controlling for productivity, or "ability," scores on the AFQT. Neal and Johnson (1996) and Arcidiacono, Bayer, and Hizmo (2010) find that wage gaps of black workers with high school education in the United States are substantially reduced after controlling for differences in ability scores, suggesting that discrimination in the labour market partly derives from pre-market factors affecting racial differences in investments into human capital and ability formation.

Nevertheless, there have been a few studies that provide evidence on ethnic wage differentials in Canada. Stelcner and Kyriazis (1995) conduct Oaxaca decompositions for several ethnic groups (mostly European) from the 1981 census. They find that most ethnic groups have earnings that are similar to Canadians of "British" ethnicity. For visible minorities, they find that African-Canadian men earned 18 percent less than British Canadians, with most of this differential unexplained. On the other hand, Chinese Canadians also earned 18 percent less than British Canadians, but this was actually more than would be predicted on the basis of their observable characteristics, such as education. Christofides and Swidinsky (1994) use the 1989 LMAS to compute decompositions based on a coarse "visible minority" indicator. They find that men from visible minorities earned about 15 percent less than whites, and that most of this differential could not be explained by observable characteristics. The differential was much smaller for women, at about 3 percent.

Reitz et al. (1999, p. 421) also find that the earnings disadvantage for immigrants varies considerably according to the country of origin of the migrant. For example, relative to other male European immigrants, earnings were lower by 6 percent for Italians, 15 percent for West and South Asians and Chinese, and up to 25 percent for Greek, black, and other Asian groups. Reitz and Breton (1994) also provide survey evidence for Canada indicating that negative attitudes toward immigrants vary substantially by ethnicity.

Baker and Benjamin (1997) provide decompositions by ethnic group and immigrant status based on the 1991 census. Following the lead of Reitz and Breton (1994), they also provide a comparison of the Canadian findings with those from the United States, in order to assess the question of whether Canadian multicultural policy provides a more hospitable environment for minorities in Canada than the "melting pot" of the United States. Their results are summarized in Table 12.1, with the results for Canada in the top panel and for the United States in the bottom panel. In Canada, there is generally a substantial overall gap between the unadjusted, or gross, earnings of whites and those of the various ethnic groups who are born in Canada. The gap is largest for South Asians (e.g., Bangladesh, India, Pakistan) and smallest (actually negative) for Southeast Asians (e.g., Philippines, Korea, Vietnam). After controlling for differences in various wage-determining characteristics, the "unexplained gap" or "discrimination" appears to account for roughly half of the overall gap. The pure ethnic earnings disadvantage relative to whites is 22 percent for South Asians, 17 percent for blacks, 9 percent for Aboriginals, 6 percent for Chinese, and 2 percent for Southeast Asians. It is labelled a pure ethnic earnings gap, or "ethnic discrimination," because it reflects ethnic status after controlling for the effect of various observable wage-determining characteristics, including immigrant status.

TABLE 12.1	Ethnic Wage Differentials, Various Groups Born in Canada or United States				
Black	South Asian[a]	Southeast Asian[b]	Chinese	Aboriginal	
Canada					
Total gap 0.293	0.536	−0.022	0.193	0.179	
"Discrimination" 0.171	0.222	0.023	0.058	0.091	
United States					
Total gap 0.328	0.176	−0.079	−0.205	0.304	
"Discrimination" 0.123	0.055	−0.007	−0.047	0.136	

NOTES: The total gap is the percentage by which the earnings of whites exceed those of the ethnic group, reflecting both the differences in their wage-determining characteristics and the differences in pay for the same characteristics. The latter is the differences in the regression coefficients from an Oaxaca-type decomposition as discussed in the text, and is labelled here as "Discrimination."

[a] E.g., Bangladesh, India, Pakistan

[b] E.g., Philippines, Korea, Vietnam

SOURCE: Baker and Benjamin (1997, Tables 5 and 11, specification 3 including industry and occupation controls).

Reasons for the variation in this pure ethic earnings gap across the different ethnic groups are not obvious, and, in fact, the variation highlights that it likely does not all reflect discrimination, since there is no obvious reason pure discrimination should vary so much across the different groups. Some of the variation likely reflects differences in factors such as the quality of schooling or credential recognition, or perhaps in ethnic social capital and networks of the different groups. Thus, more research is necessary to uncover these underlying factors.

Interestingly, the pure ethnic earnings gap attributable to discrimination is smaller in the United States compared to Canada for every ethnic group except Aboriginal persons. In fact, two of the five ethnic groups (Southeast Asians and Chinese) receive higher returns (i.e., the gap is negative) for their wage-determining characteristics than white Americans with the same observable characteristics. Furthermore, the ranking of the different ethnic groups with respect to the magnitude of the gap is not the same in the United States as in Canada, raising further questions about why this should be.

Clearly, this analysis raises numerous interesting questions in need of further research. Why do the pure ethnic earnings differentials vary across the different ethnic groups in both countries? Why do they differ between Canada and the United States? And why does the ranking of the different groups in terms of the magnitude of the gap differ across the two countries?

Pendakur and Pendakur (1998, p. 530) do a similar analysis for persons who designate themselves as visible minorities—another way of designating ethnic status. They also find that after controlling for various wage-determining characteristics, visible minorities have an earnings disadvantage relative to otherwise comparable "whites" in Canada. For males, the earnings disadvantage was 8.2 percent for visible minorities who were born in Canada, and it doubled to 16.2 percent for visible minorities who were new immigrants. The 8.2 percent estimate is taken as a pure estimate of the effect of visible minority status independently of immigrant status since it exists for visible minorities who were born in Canada and, hence, who are not immigrants. It is interesting that for females they found no earnings disadvantage for visible minorities who were born in Canada, and a smaller disadvantage of 7.8 percent for visible-minority women who were new immigrants.

Hum and Simpson (1999) do a similar analysis to isolate the pure wage effect associated with visible minority status, after controlling for the impact of various wage-determining characteristics. They also attempt to control for the possible selection bias that could occur, because persons in the labour market may have different wage offers than persons who do not enter the labour market, although such effects are extremely difficult to identify. Hum and Simpson find that most visible minority groups experience a significant wage disadvantage relative to otherwise comparable Canadian-born persons. However, when they do the analysis separately for foreign-born and Canadian-born visible minorities, they find that the earnings disadvantage of being a visible minority arises mainly among the foreign-born immigrants. Visible minorities who are born in Canada do not generally experience any significant wage disadvantage, except for black males. This leads them to conclude (p. 392) that "there is no significant wage gap between visible minority and non-visible minority group membership for native-born workers. It is only amongst immigrants that the question of wage differentials for visible minorities arises." Clearly, this points up the fact that more research would be desirable to reconcile these results with those of Baker and Benjamin (1997) and Pendakur and Pendakur (1998).

Pendakur and Pendakur (2007) analyze ethnic wage gaps across the earnings distribution. They find that the pattern of the wage gap differs across groups. The pay gap is largest at the top of the pay distribution for persons of Chinese origin, while those from Southeast Asia have the largest gap at the bottom of the distribution, and black workers face great disparity throughout the distribution.

Hou and Coulombe (2010) focus on differences in the ethnic pay gaps for observationally equivalent persons in the private and public sector using the 2006 Canadian Census data. They find little pay gap in the public sector except for black women. In the private sector, pay gaps prevail for all ethnic groups and it is especially large for black men and women.

One area where there is a dearth of evidence on discrimination in Canada is with respect to persons with disabilities. This is surprising, since they are one of the four employment equity groups in Canada, and there have been a number of studies on the topic in the United States which find evidence of such discrimination (reviewed in Baldwin and Johnson 2006, with more recent evidence in Baldwin and Choe 2014). The methodological issues are difficult because disability, by definition, implies functional limitation and this can affect productivity. Nevertheless, these methodological problems have been dealt with in the U.S. literature in various ways, such as by incorporating measures of prejudice and by focusing on those who say their disability is not a limitation at work. A recent study for the UK, in fact, finds that the discriminatory portion of the wage gap between persons with and those without a disability largely disappears after fully controlling for productivity differences (Longhi, Nicoletti, and Platt 2012). Based on Canadian data, however, Gunderson and Lee (2016) find that persons with a disability that does not affect their performance at work are still paid about 10 percent less than a comparison group with no disability but with the same pay-determining characteristics. Clearly, this is an area that merits more attention in Canada.

Policies to Combat Sex Discrimination

Because of the variety of sources and forms of discrimination, policies to combat it have also tended to take a variety of forms. Public policy initiatives in this have been in three areas: equal pay legislation, including pay equity or equal pay for work of equal value; equal employment opportunity legislation, including employment equity or affirmative action; and policies designed to facilitate female employment and to alter attitudes and preferences. Each of these will be discussed in turn.

Conventional Equal Pay Legislation

All Canadian jurisdictions have **conventional equal pay legislation**, which requires equal pay for equal work within the same job and within the same establishment. The courts and enforcement agencies have generally interpreted equal work as work that is *substantially similar*, with minor differences being allowed, especially if offset by differences in other aspects of the work performed. For example, the work could be considered the same even if males do occasional heavy lifting, especially if females do other occasional tasks not done by males.

The scope of conventional equal pay legislation is limited by the fact that it deals with only one aspect of discrimination—wage discrimination within the same job within an establishment—and, as our earlier discussion of the empirical evidence indicated, this is probably a quantitatively small aspect of discrimination. In addition, enforcement of the law can be difficult because this usually relies upon individuals to complain, and because there are problems with interpreting what is meant by equal work, although the courts have interpreted this rather broadly.

Equal Value, Pay Equity, or Comparable Worth Legislation

In part because of the limited potential for conventional equal pay policies to narrow the overall male–female earnings gap, further legislative initiatives have been advocated on the pay side in the form of equal pay for work of equal value. The phrases equal value, **pay equity**, and **comparable worth** are usually used interchangeably, although "equal value" is often used internationally, "pay equity" is usually used in Canada, and "comparable worth" is used most often in the United States.

Existence of Equal Value Legislation

Pay equity or equal value legislation or voluntary arrangements with governments are common across jurisdictions in Canada, generally requiring a proactive plan as discussed subsequently. As indicated in McDonald and Thornton (2015), in most Canadian jurisdictions pay equity is restricted to the public sector either by law (Manitoba, New Brunswick, Nova Scotia, PEI) or by voluntary practice (British Columbia, Saskatchewan, Newfoundland and Labrador). Alberta does not have a legislative requirement or a voluntary arrangement applied in practice. Only Quebec, since 1996, and Ontario, since 1987, have pay equity legislation that also applies to elements of the private sector. The federal jurisdiction, Northwest Territories, Nunavut, and the Yukon have complaints-based rather than proactive legislation that applies to both the public and private sectors. In the United States, comparable worth legislation is largely confined to the public sector and in a small number of states.

In Europe, the principle of equal pay for work of equal value is incorporated into the European Community law. Its practical application, however, is severely limited by the fact that it is largely complaints-based, enforcement tends not to be prominent, and job evaluation procedures that are used to determine the "value" of a job are not common.

In Australia, a form of comparable worth was adopted in 1972 when the country's national wage awards made by wage tribunals (which set wages for the majority of workers) eliminated wage differentials across occupations designated as predominantly male and predominantly female. However, this decision, which substantially raised the wages of females, was based on legislative fiat, not on the results of job evaluation procedures. Hence, this method of eliminating wage differentials is not a comparable-worth procedure in the conventional sense. The centralized process whereby wages tend to be set by arbitration through tribunals is particularly conducive to making equal value awards, although they tend not to be based on formal job evaluation procedures as in North America.

Equal Value Procedures

Equal value policies generally require an equality of pay between jobs of equal value, where value is determined by a job evaluation scheme that is free of gender bias (Gunderson 1994, 2010). Such schemes generally involve comparisons between jobs that are designated as predominantly male and predominantly female—where gender predominance (meaning, involving 70 percent or more of either sex) is designated. The next step involves determining the *factors,* such as skill, effort, responsibility, and working conditions, that are believed to be the important determinants of the value, or worth, of a job. For the various jobs, job evaluators, then, usually assign point scores for each of these factors. The points are summed to get a total point score for each job (which implies equal weights for a point score for each of the factors), or different weights or ranges of scores could be assigned to the scores of each factor on an a priori basis. Predominantly female jobs are then compared to predominantly male jobs of the same total point score, and the wages adjusted to those of the predominantly male jobs. In situations where this equal value approach has been applied, wages in female-dominated jobs typically have been only 80 to 90 percent of wages in male-dominated jobs of the same job evaluation point scores. The jobs can be in different occupations as long as they have the same job evaluation point scores. One case within the federal jurisdiction, for example, involved a comparison of predominantly female librarians with predominantly male historical researchers.

Economic versus Administrative Concepts of Value

This procedure highlights the fact that equal pay for work of equal value involves an **administrative concept of value**, where value is determined by the *average* value of the *inputs*, such as skill, effort, responsibility, and working conditions that are involved in a job. This is in contrast to the *economic* concept of the value of the marginal product of labour, whereby value is determined by the value of the *output* produced by an *additional* unit of labour. The administrative concept of value is akin to the notion of value-in-use (i.e., the average value of inputs), while the economic concept involves value-in-exchange (i.e., marginal contribution to the value of output). According to the economic concept, inputs that are in abundance of supply may have little value-in-exchange (and, hence, command a low market wage) even though they may have a high value-in-use because they involve substantial average inputs of skill, effort, responsibility, and working conditions. This is analogous to the diamond-water paradox, whereby diamonds have a high value-in-exchange (because of their scarcity) but water has a low value-in-exchange (because of its abundance) in spite of its high value-in-use.

The equal value concept, in fact, explicitly rejects the notion that market forces should be the prime determinant of the value and, hence, pay for jobs. This rejection is based on the belief that market forces reflect discrimination. Even if market forces enable employers to hire workers in predominantly female jobs at rates of pay that are lower than those paid to workers in predominantly male jobs, proponents of comparable worth would argue that such an outcome is socially unacceptable, because it reflects discriminatory segregation and the systematic undervaluation of female-dominated jobs. The belief is that females should not have to leave female-dominated jobs to get the same pay as those in male-dominated jobs that require the same inputs of skill, effort, responsibility, and working conditions.

In essence, the primacy of market forces of supply and demand is rejected in that the value and, hence, remuneration of a job is not deemed to be low simply because there is an abundance of labour willing to do the work, or because there is little demand for that type of labour. This is in contrast to the economic emphasis on the market forces of supply and demand to determine the value and, hence, remuneration of a job.

While there is a sharp contrast between the economic and comparable worth concepts of value, the two concepts do not have to be diametrically opposed. Skill, effort, and responsibility are scarce resources and, hence, will receive a market premium, just as they are assigned point scores by job evaluators. Similarly, compensating wage premiums are paid in the market for undesirable working conditions, just as they can be assigned point scores by job evaluators. In fact, it is possible to apply the premiums that the market yields for the various factors of skill, effort, responsibility, and working conditions based only on the male-dominated jobs, and then to apply those premiums to weigh the scores of the female-dominated jobs. This yields the value of those female-dominated jobs had they been paid the same market premium as the male-dominated jobs. This procedure is termed a **policy capturing approach** in that it is a policy that simply captures the pricing mechanism used for the male-dominated jobs and extends it to the female-dominated jobs. Comparable worth approaches can also pay attention to market forces by allowing exceptions for occupations that are in scarce supply.

Clearly, market forces do not have to be ignored by the principle of comparable worth, but it is equally clear that the comparable worth concept of value is different from the economic concept of value. The former is an administrative concept of value based upon job evaluation procedures; the latter is based upon market forces of supply and demand.

Rationale for Equal Value Initiatives

Equal value initiatives have been rationalized on the basis of being able to deal with *both* wage discrimination and occupational segregation—the latter on the grounds that comparisons can be made across different occupations as long as they are of the same value, as determined by job evaluation procedures. This is important because occupational segregation generally is believed to be a more important contributor to the overall earnings gap than wage discrimination, and conventional equal pay can deal with only the latter. Equal value policies have also been rationalized on the grounds of securing redress for those women who do not want to leave predominantly female jobs to get the same pay as those in predominantly male jobs of the same value, as determined by job evaluation procedures.

Scope of Equal Value Initiatives

The scope of equal value policies is potentially large because it enables comparisons across occupations, unlike conventional equal pay policies, which uses comparisons only within the same occupations. However, the scope of equal value policies will be limited in a complaints-based system by the fact that it is difficult for individuals or even groups to lodge a complaint under such a complicated procedure. For individuals, the fear of reprisals may also be a deterrent. For this reason, supporters of comparable worth have advocated a **proactive system-wide** procedure whereby employers would be required to have a bona fide job evaluation system in place to help achieve pay equity. Even if such a system were in place, the scope of comparable worth would be limited by the fact that comparisons are restricted to only jobs within the same establishment and, hence, also industry.

Design Features of Comparable Worth

If comparable worth becomes more prominent as a policy initiative, a large number of program design features will have to be worked out to facilitate the practical implementation of the policy (Gunderson 1994, 2010). Such design features include the definition of gender predominance for comparing male-dominated with female-dominated jobs; the job evaluation procedure for establishing the value of a job; the procedure for relating the job evaluation point scores to the pay of jobs; the procedure for adjusting pay in undervalued jobs and in overvalued jobs; the definition of establishment and of pay itself; the appropriate exemptions, if any; and the optimal enforcement procedure, including whether a complaints-based or more proactive system-wide procedure should be followed. These and other design features can have a substantial impact on the scope of equal value initiatives and, hence, on their positive and negative consequences, thereby illustrating the maxim "the devil is in the details."

Pay Equity Example

A hypothetical example can illustrate many of the issues associated with the application of pay equity. In Figure 12.2 the evaluation points for each job are plotted on the horizontal axis, and the pay for each job is plotted on the vertical axis. The upper line is the **payline** for the male-dominated jobs (e.g., 70 percent or more males) and the bottom line is the payline for the female-dominated jobs (e.g., 70 percent or more females). The points around each line are the particular male or female jobs in the establishment. They illustrate the combination of pay and points associated with each job. The paylines could have been simply drawn or "eyeballed" to fit the scatter of points, or they could be estimated by statistical techniques, such as regression analysis. They could be straight lines, as in this example, or nonlinear if the relationship between pay and points is nonlinear. The slopes could be the same, in which case the same absolute pay difference would be associated with different job values, and, therefore, the percentage difference would be smaller in the jobs of high pay and points. Or the slopes could be different, as in this example where the higher-paying jobs are associated with higher absolute wage differences, albeit a possible constant percentage differential.

A number of observations are worth noting. The male payline is above the female payline, indicating that male-dominated jobs tend to receive higher pay than female-dominated jobs of the same value, where value is measured by job evaluation points. Typically, the female payline is 80 to 90 percent of the height of the male payline, indicating that female-dominated jobs tend to be paid 80 to 90 percent of the pay in male-dominated jobs of the same job evaluation score. (They are drawn further apart here simply to avoid clutter in the diagram.)

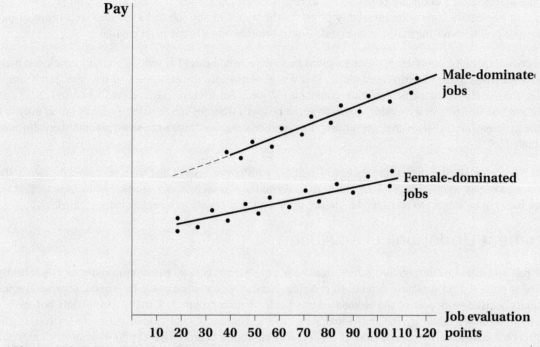

Figure 12.2 Pay Equity Case

The vertical axis is the pay in jobs and the horizontal axis is the "value" of the job as given by evaluation points. The positive slope of both lines indicates that persons in both male-dominated and female-dominated jobs receive higher pay for higher job evaluation points. The fact that the male line is steeper than the female line indicates that males also receive a higher return (i.e., greater pay) for additional job evaluation points in this particular illustration. The fact that the intercept is positive for both males and females indicates that both males and females receive some base level of pay that is independent of their job evaluation points. The fact that the intercept is higher for males than for females indicates that males also seem to receive greater "base" pay than females.

Some of the female-dominated jobs at the lower end of the job evaluation scores do not have direct male **comparator jobs** of the same value. This raises the issue of whether projection of the male payline (the dashed line segment) would be allowed to offer hypothetical male comparators (sometimes termed **phantom jobs**) indicating what such male jobs would have been paid, based the relationship between pay and points in the other male jobs. In fact, it may even be an issue whether extrapolation of the male payline is allowed within the sample points of the male-dominated jobs, or whether a male comparator job of comparable job evaluation points is required before a comparison can be made.

Although not shown in this particular diagram, it is possible that some female "dots" (pay for points) could lie above the male payline, or above a male dot of the same value. This would simply indicate that some female jobs could pay more than male jobs (hypothetical or actual) of the same job evaluation score. Similarly, it is possible that a male dot could lie below the female line; however, such outlying dots are not likely to occur, though they are possible. It is also possible to have multiple male or female dots at the same point score. This would simply indicate that unequal pay for work of the same value can exist within female-dominated jobs or within male-dominated jobs.

The diagram also illustrates alternative wage adjustment procedures that are possible. The **line-to-line** procedure would raise the female payline to the male payline, thereby eliminating the systematic differences in pay between male-dominated and female-dominated jobs. The random deviations in pay that previously prevailed around the female payline would remain, just as they remain for male-dominated jobs around the male payline. Some female jobs would be "overvalued" (i.e., above the male payline), and others would be "undervalued" (i.e., below the male payline) just as they were overvalued and undervalued relative to the previous female payline, and just as some male-dominated jobs are overvalued and others undervalued relative to the male payline.

The **point-to-line** procedure, in contrast, would raise all the points around the female payline to the male payline. This would remove both the systematic differences, as evidenced by differences in the heights of the paylines, as well as the random deviations that previously prevailed around the female payline. Random deviations for male jobs around the male payline would still prevail, unless it became a company policy to try to remove such random deviations. This would be hampered, however, by the fact that pay equity legislation invariably prohibits the wages in any job to be reduced as a result of pay equity, in which case male points above the male payline could not be brought down to the male payline.

Other adjustment procedures are also possible. A **point-to-point** procedure would raise the female point to the closest male comparator point (as is specified in the Ontario legislation). This would not require the estimation of paylines, but it would require decision rules for the choice of particular male comparators' jobs. An average payline could be used that is an amalgam of the male and female lines, or a corridor approach could be used, whereby the female payline is raised only to a lower boundary of the male payline. A single average adjustment could be calculated, with the same amount then allocated to each female-dominated job.

These are meant to be simply illustrative of the technical and administrative issues that can be associated with the implementation and design of pay equity. These issues can have a substantial impact on the magnitude of the awards that are made, and, hence, are likely to be subject to considerable debate if the policy becomes more extensively applied.

Equal Employment Opportunity Legislation

In contrast to equal pay and equal value policies, which deal with pay discrimination, **equal employment opportunity legislation** is designed to prevent discrimination in recruiting, hiring, promotion, and dismissals. In general, provincial equal employment opportunity legislation is part of the Human Rights Code of each province. Usually, complaints concerning discrimination in employment are made by the individual party to the Human Rights Commission. An officer of the commission tries to reach a settlement by conciliation. If this is unsuccessful, a board of inquiry investigates and makes a final decision. Most provinces have appeal procedures to regular courts, although courts are generally loath to interfere with the decisions of administrative tribunals, unless it has made severe procedural errors, that is. Although the commissions generally act only on complaints, on a more informal basis they can and do persuade employers to increase their quotas of female employees.

In spite of the fact that this procedure is time-consuming and cumbersome, equal employment opportunity legislation does have the virtue of increasing the demand for female labour at the recruiting, hiring, and promotion stages. This, in turn, should increase female wages *and* employment. Unlike equal pay laws, which increase female wages at the expense of their employment, equal employment opportunity legislation would work through the market to increase both the wages and employment of females. However, equal employment opportunity legislation is likely to be more beneficial to new recruits or women seeking to change their jobs; it may do little to help incumbent females in their existing jobs.

Some have argued that equal pay and equal employment legislation are complementary, in that one is useless without the other. The argument is that without equal employment opportunity legislation, equal pay would result in employers refusing to recruit, hire, and promote females. Similarly, without equal pay, equal employment opportunity legislation would result in employers hiring females but paying them lower wages than equally productive males. However, this ignores the economic argument that the increased demand for females resulting from equal employment opportunity legislation would work through the market to increase female wages. Equal pay may be a natural by-product of equal employment opportunities.

Affirmative Action or Employment Equity

While equal employment opportunity legislation is designed to remove discriminatory barriers so as to ensure an equality of *opportunity*, affirmative action is a more intrusive form of intervention, focusing on *results* and not just on opportunities. The rationale is that an equality of opportunity is insufficient to compensate for the legacy of a cumulative history of discrimination as well as of systemic discrimination that may be the unintended by-product of certain personnel policies. True equality may require some preferential treatment for women, at least on a temporary basis, to ensure an equality of starting points. The hope is that temporary affirmative action programs may break the circle of entrapment whereby women are relegated to low-wage, dead-end jobs, which, in turn, foster labour market behaviour that keeps them in such jobs.

Affirmative action legislation tends to be called **employment equity** legislation in Canada—a phrase coined by the 1984 Abella Commission—in part to differentiate it from the earlier U.S. initiatives, which tended to be criticized on the grounds of requiring rigid quantitative quotas for the hiring of the target groups. In Canada, legislated employment equity currently exists only in the federal jurisdiction, which covers about 10 percent of the Canadian workforce. It is embodied in the Employment Equity Act of 1986, amended in 1995 to include the federal civil service. A separate employment equity program was also adopted in 1986 for federal contractors as part of a federal contract compliance program. Employment equity programs have also been adopted in particular cities or municipalities and can be utilized on a voluntary basis without being considered a form of reverse discrimination by the courts.

The federal programs were to apply to four designated groups identified by the Abella Commission as particularly susceptible to systemic discrimination. The four designated groups are women, visible minorities, disabled persons, and Aboriginal people.

Employment equity essentially involves four steps.

- First, an internal audit is conducted within the firm, usually based on a survey, to determine the internal representation of the designated groups and their position within the firm.
- Second, this internal representation is compared to the external availability of these groups in the relevant external labour market, as given for example by census data.
- Third, targets or goals are established to achieve an internal representation of the designated groups that is similar to their availability in the relevant external labour market.
- Fourth, a plan and timetable for achieving these targets are established.

In the United States, affirmative action has a longer history. It is part of the federal contract compliance program under Executive Order 11246 of 1965, and subsequent orders. It can also be imposed by the courts as a form of redress under the general anti-discrimination legislation: Title VII, the Equal Employment Opportunity Provision of the Civil Rights Act of 1964. When first instituted, affirmative action was targeted toward blacks, but in the 1970s it was also targeted toward women.

Policies to Facilitate Female Employment

In addition to the various direct policies, such as equal pay and equal employment opportunities legislation and affirmative action, there are a variety of policies that can indirectly affect the employment opportunities and wages of women. These could be labelled **facilitating policies**, in that they are generally designed to expand the range of choices open to women, thereby facilitating their participation in labour market activities in a nondiscriminatory fashion.

Currently, women tend to have the primary responsibility for household tasks, especially the raising of children (Zhang 2009). This may reflect historical tradition, comparative advantage (which itself may be historically determined), or discrimination within the household. Whatever the origin, this responsibility can create tensions over the equitable division of labour within the household when both parties engage in labour market work.

To minimize some of this tension and to expand the employment opportunities available to women, facilitating policies have been suggested. Improved availability of daycare, and family-friendly workplace practices, such as flexible working hours, part-time jobs, and childbirth leaves, are examples of such facilitating policies. In the interests of equality, they would apply to males as well as to females, so as to maximize the opportunities for households to allocate their labour among various market and nonmarket alternatives.

Certainly, such policies are not without costs, which could be substantial in some aspects, such as subsidized daycare. Consequently, there is legitimate debate over the efficiency of such policies. What is less contentious, from the perspective of economics at least, is that at a minimum of such facilitating policies be allowed to emerge in response to market demands. This may require, for example, that daycare expenses be tax deductible or that quality regulations do not excessively restrict the availability of daycare. Or it may require that government policies not discourage flexible working arrangements by increasing quasi-fixed costs of employment, which may encourage employers to utilize only a core of male workers.

To a large extent, these institutional features—flexible hours, part-time jobs, child care leaves, and daycare arrangements—are emerging like endogenous responses to the increased labour market role of women. Their emergence, however, may be subject to impediments reflecting discrimination, government policies designed to achieve other objectives, or simply the slow operation of market forces subject to inertia and fixed costs.

Considerable debate emerges over the appropriate role of public policy in this area. Some would argue that such facilitating policies should be discouraged in order to preserve the traditional sex division of labour. Others argue that public policies should be neutral by simply removing impediments to the emergence of these facilitating policies.

Others argue for a more active role—subsidized daycare, extended child care leave—to compensate for discrimination elsewhere in the system, including past discrimination.

The role of **protectionist labour standards** policies takes on an interesting light in the context of policies designed to facilitate the labour market work of women. Such protectionist policies could include special provisions requiring employers to provide free transportation for women on night shifts, prohibiting the employment of women in some specific occupations, or placing restrictions on the hours of work for females. The earliest labour standards laws in Canada had their origins in the Factory Acts of the 1890s. Some may argue that such protective devices would enable women to take on some jobs they would otherwise be reluctant to do. Most would argue that such protective devices simply protect male jobs by reducing the employment opportunities of females and by perpetuating the stereotype of women as in need of outside protection. If such protection is desirable, it should be provided to all workers, male and female, through labour standards laws or collective agreements.

This suggests another institutional arrangement for facilitating the labour market work of females—unionization. The rationale for increasing the role of women in unions is twofold. The first is to have women share in the wage and job security gains that unions obtain for their members. In order to obtain these gains, it is necessary for women not only to unionize but also to aspire to powerful positions within the union or at least ensure that their minority rights are guaranteed. The second rationale for increasing the role of women in unions is to ensure effective monitoring of equal pay, equal employment opportunities, and affirmative action.

Females may be more willing and able to press for equal pay and employment opportunities through the union both because the apparatus is available (shop steward, grievance procedure) and because reprisal by the company is less likely when the worker is protected by a union.

Banning pay secrecy laws or practices can enable women to be informed that they may be underpaid. This, in turn, can facilitate their bargaining for higher pay. Kim (2015) provides evidence from the United States that such legislative bans on pay secrecy have increased the pay of women, especially higher educated ones, narrowing the male–female wage gap.

LO5   Alter Preferences and Attitudes

Economics traditionally regards tastes and preferences as exogenously given, and then inquires into what happens to the demand for something when such factors as relative prices and income change. In the area of sex discrimination, this is a legitimate inquiry. Equal pay and equal employment opportunity legislation can be viewed as policies designed to raise the "price" of discrimination to those who discriminate. The price in this case is the legal cost, which includes court costs and the expected fine, as well as possible adverse publicity. The contention is that raising the price of discrimination will reduce the quantity demanded.

In the area of discrimination, however, some have suggested the utilization of public policies designed to alter the basic tastes and preferences giving rise to discrimination, since tastes and preferences of employers, co-workers, and customers are an important source of discrimination. The dominant group, for example, may find it important to foster uniform preferences for discrimination and to punish nondiscriminators. Preferences are also shaped by the media, the education system, and the socioeconomic system in general. Preferences are neither immutable over time, nor are they likely to be the same for all firms, employees, or customers. For this reason, many anti-discrimination policies are designed to alter basic tastes, preferences, and attitudes. Recent work in economics, for example, has emphasized **endogenous preferences** (i.e., understanding why and how preferences are formed) rather than simply taken them as exogenously given.

In practice, of course, changing basic tastes and attitudes is a difficult task. Specific policies have been instituted and include removal of sex stereotyping in schoolbooks, guidance programs, and television; provision of information on the labour market performance and attachment of females; and politicization of women to raise their own group awareness. The process will be slow, but many argue that the results, at least, will be long lasting.

Impact of Policy Initiatives

While there is considerable empirical evidence on the magnitude of the male–female wage differential and its determinants, there is much less evidence on the impact of various policy initiatives, and most of the studies were done earlier, shortly after the initiatives were introduced (Altonji and Blank 1999; Gunderson 1989, 1995).

Conventional Equal Pay Policies

Econometric studies in the area of equal pay for equal work have found those equal pay policies not to have had any impact on closing the male–female earnings gap. This lack of impact likely reflects the limited scope for such policies, since they could deal only with male–female wage differences within the same occupation and establishment, and such differences are unlikely to be very large compared to differences across occupations and establishments. As well, reliance on a complaints procedure may deter enforcement since individuals may be reluctant to complain.

In the United States, conventional equal pay policies are combined with equal employment opportunity initiatives under Title VII of the Civil Rights Act; therefore, the separate impact of equal pay is difficult to disentangle, especially because both should serve to raise the wages of women. The econometric studies of that legislation tend to find somewhat inconclusive results. Some studies find positive effects on the earnings of women, some find no effect, and when the effects are positive they tend to be small.

In contrast, more-positive effects of equal pay policies are found in Britain (Zablaza and Tzannatos 1985a, 1985b) where the policy was incorporated into the process of centralized collective bargaining that occurs in that country. This suggests that a conventional equal pay policy may be more effective in reducing the earnings gap when it is incorporated by the private parties into more-formal systems of centralized collective bargaining, rather than having legislative systems rely on complaints, as is done in the more market-oriented decentralized systems of wage determination and collective bargaining that prevail in North America.

Affirmative Action

A number of econometric studies have evaluated the impact of affirmative action under the federal contract compliance of Executive Order 11246 in the United States. This legislation did benefit the minority groups to which it was targeted—mainly black males in the earlier years of the program. Much of that benefit, however, came at the expense of losses to other minority groups—mainly white females—to which the program was not targeted in the earlier years. However, when the affirmative action programs began to be more targeted toward females, they too benefited from them. The legislative initiatives also tended to be more effective in an expanding economy than during a recession, and when it was aggressively enforced. Court-mandated affirmative action requirements were also found to improve the economic status of female employees in Ransom and Oaxaca (2005). Kurtulus (2012) provides evidence that affirmative action programs in the United States improved the employment and occupational advance of women and minorities, and she cites earlier studies with similar findings.

Comparable Worth and Pay Equity

The impact of comparable worth (pay equity) programs has also been analyzed in a number of studies, usually based on the application of the policy in a number of public sector jurisdictions in Canada and the United States (Altonji and Blank 1999; Gunderson 1995). Average wage adjustments of $3000 to $4000 per recipient were common at that time, although there is considerable variation in the adjustments. However, such adjustments occur only in particular organizations, and they go to the portion of the workforce that is in female-dominated and whose jobs are undervalued. (See Exhibit 12.13 for a discussion of the now-famous federal pay equity case in Canada.) When the costs are amortized over the whole workforce of the particular public sector, they are in the neighbourhood of 4 to 8 percent of payroll costs. Typically, in the same public sector workforces, the ratio of female earnings to male earnings (in all public sector jobs, not just those that receive the adjustment) is around 0.78 before the comparable worth adjustment and 0.84 after the adjustment (but see Exhibit 12.15). This increase of 0.06 in the earnings ratio implies that comparable worth closes about one-third (i.e., 0.06/0.22) of the earnings gap of 0.22 (i.e., 1.00–0.78).

EXHIBIT 12.13

So It Took a Little While (15 Years!): The Federal Pay Equity Award

On December 19, 1984, the Public Service Alliance of Canada (the largest union of federal government employees) filed a pay equity complaint to the Canadian Human Rights Commission (responsible for handling federal human rights issues) against the Treasury Board of Canada (the employer of federal government employees). PSAC alleged that the predominantly female clerical and regulatory group was paid lower wages than the predominantly male program administration group even though their work was of equal value. This subsequently mushroomed into complaints filed on behalf of other female-dominated occupation groups. On July 29, 1998, the federal Human Rights Tribunal, in a 203-page decision based on 262 days of hearings, ruled in favour of PSAC, giving the parties one year to voluntarily agree to the specifics of the implementation procedure or they would be imposed by the tribunal. The Treasury Board appealed to the Federal Court of Canada, but the appeal was rejected. The parties then came to an agreement on October 29, 1999—almost 15 years after the original complaint. Clearly, the mills of the gods grind slowly.

The settlement was for approximately $3.6 billion (most of which was back pay) affecting approximately 230,000 current and former federal employees, of which only about 54,000 were still working for the government at that time; many of the others were deceased. The awards occurred in such female-dominated jobs as clerks, secretaries, librarians, data processors, hospital workers, and education support staff. The settlement averaged over $15,000 per employee, by far the largest and most significant pay equity award in history.

The process involved 15 job evaluation committees evaluating 1700 jobs from nine female-dominated groups and 1407 jobs from 53 male-dominated groups. There was endless wrangling over issues, such as gender bias in job evaluation as well as the appropriate wage adjustment procedure with phrases like "level to segment" comparisons and "female points to the weighted quadratic male composite line" being part of the debate.

For details of what has been appropriately named "A Pay Equity Saga," see Sulzner (2000).

These estimates of the impact of comparable worth are based on particular public sector cases where the policy has been applied. They are also based on estimates of the gap within a particular public sector employer, and this gap of around 0.22 is only a little over one-half of the earnings gap that prevails in the economy as a whole. Simulations of the potential economy-wide impact of comparable worth in the United States have estimated that the policy would close, at most, 8 to 20 percent of the overall gap of 0.41 (Johnson and Solon 1986), or 15 to 20 percent of the gap (Aldrich and Buchelle 1986). The policy can close only a portion of the overall gap because much of the gap reflects the segregation of females into low-wage firms and industries, and comparable worth does not involve comparisons across different firms or industries.

The potentially limited impact of comparable worth in the wider labour market is confirmed with preliminary evidence from Ontario. Gunderson (1995) examines early evidence from surveys of firms, and finds that the pay adjustments were smaller, on average, in the private sector. These smaller settlements were reflected in much smaller changes in wage costs for private firms: 0.6 percent of payroll for large firms versus 2.2 percent in the public sector. McDonald and Thornton (1998) also report that few females received pay equity adjustments in the private-sector firms they surveyed in Ontario.

These studies suggest that comparable worth would likely close about one-third of the pay gap within particular elements of the public sector. For the economy as a whole, it would likely close a smaller portion, perhaps 8 to 20 percent of the gap. This highlights the fact that the policy can close a substantial portion of the earnings gap, but most would remain even after a comprehensive application of the program.

EXHIBIT 12.14

It Pays to Lobby

In 1985, the state of Iowa announced a pay equity award to its state employees that would have raised the ratio of female-to-male wages from 0.78 to 0.88, closing 44 percent of the male–female pay gap (Orazem and Mattilla 1990). However, male-dominated union and professional groups lobbied for modifications to the award to enhance their own pay. Because of their pressure, the award was subsequently amended so that the ratio of female-to-male wages was only 0.83, with the award thereby closing only 22 percent of the pay gap as opposed to 44 percent. Clearly, in a public sector environment, where political factors can be important in setting pay in the first place, those same factors can influence any changes in pay. What the state gives, the state can take away.

An even more pessimistic view of the potential for pay equity legislation emerges from Baker and Fortin (2004) in their comprehensive analysis of Ontario pay equity legislation (Exhibit 12.15). The good news is that they found only small adverse employment effects; the bad news is that this occurred because of small wage effects. In a more recent study, McDonald and Thornton (2015) also find Ontario's pay equity legislation to have had little or no effect on the male–female wage gap.

EXHIBIT 12.15

A Comprehensive Evaluation of Ontario's Pay Equity

Baker and Fortin (2004) provide a comprehensive and systematic econometric analysis of the effect of Ontario's pay equity legislation as it applies to the private sector. Their study is particularly important because it is the first to comprehensively examine the impact of proactive (as opposed to complaints-based) pay equity in a decentralized, private-sector labour market. The results are quite startling, and will likely generate considerable controversy. Their findings indicate that the legislation had the following effects on wages and employment (actually wage and employment growth) and the wage gap:

- No substantial impact on women's wages in female-dominated jobs, in part because such jobs tend to be in the smaller firms where implementation and compliance is difficult.
- A reduction in male wages in the female-dominated jobs.
- A slight reduction in the male–female wage gap in female-dominated jobs, mainly because of the fall in male wages.
- A reduction of female wages in the male-dominated jobs, which tended to be in the larger firms where compliance was more prominent.
- An increase in male wages in the male-dominated jobs.
- An increase in the male–female wage gap in those male-dominated jobs as a result of the decreased female wages and increased male wages.
- Overall, across all occupations, no substantial change in the male–female wage gap, because the reduction in the gap in the female-dominated jobs was largely offset by the increase in the gap in the male-dominated jobs.
- A small decrease in female employment in the larger firms where compliance is more likely.
- A small increase in female employment in the smaller firms where compliance is less likely.
- No substantial change in female employment as a result of these offsetting forces.

The lack of any substantial impact of the legislation is attributed largely to the fact that compliance and enforcement is extremely difficult in the small firms that employ the majority of women. This, in turn, reflects a variety of factors:

- The high cost of implementing the legislation in small firms, given the difficulty of amortizing the costs of job evaluation and consultants over a small number of employees.
- The difficulty of finding male comparator jobs (or estimating male paylines) when there are few male employees.
- The fact that female pay tends not to be substantially lower in female-dominated jobs.

Orazem and Matilla (1998) indicate that, paradoxically, pay equity could increase the proportion of women in both female-dominated and male-dominated jobs. This occurs because the elasticity of labour supply is greater for females than for males in female-dominated jobs, and the opposite in male-dominated jobs. So when real wages increase in female-dominated jobs, females enter those jobs in proportionately larger numbers than males, making them even more female-dominated. When real wages decrease in male-dominated jobs, males disproportionately leave, making them less male-dominated.

Summary

Although it is hazardous to draw a conclusion about the impact of the various policy initiatives from such a limited number of studies, some tentative generalizations can be made. The effects of equal pay and equal employment opportunity policies tend to be inconclusive, although there is some evidence that affirmative action policies in the United States have been effective for the target groups to which they have been applied. Comparable worth policies have reduced the earnings gap and resulted in considerable awards in the few situations where they have been applied; albeit, on a comprehensive basis, their scope will be limited by an inability to deal with the considerable portion of the wage gap that reflects the segregation of females into low-wage establishments and industries. The evidence on the adverse employment effects from comparable worth adjustments tends to be inconclusive.

It should be kept in mind, however, that estimating the impact of such policy initiatives is extremely difficult, especially given the other dramatic changes that are occurring simultaneously in the female labour market. This is especially the case since the policy initiatives themselves may be a function of the policy problem they are designed to eliminate, and the initiatives may be related to other unobservable factors that are the true cause of the changes in labour market behaviour. Such problems are not unique to these policy initiatives; they apply to estimating the impact of almost any social program.

Keywords

Aboriginal earnings differentials

administrative concept of value

affirmative action

comparable worth

comparator jobs

conventional equal pay legislation

crowding hypothesis

demand theories of discrimination

employment equity

endogenous preferences

equal employment opportunity legislation

ethnic–white earnings differentials

explained and unexplained differentials	point-to-point
facilitating policies	policy capturing approach
glass ceilings	pre-market characteristics
labour market discrimination	proactive system-wide
line-to-line	protectionist labour standards
noncompetitive theories of discrimination	queuing theories
Oaxaca decomposition	statistical and signalling theories of discrimination
pay equity	
payline	supply theories of discrimination
phantom jobs	systemic discrimination
point-to-line	

Review Questions

1. "If females are paid a wage equal to their marginal productivity, then sex discrimination in the labour market does not exist." Discuss.

2. "Male–female wage differentials for equally productive workers will not persist in the long run because the forces of competition would remove these differentials." In essence, market forces are "a woman's best friend." Discuss.

3. If we adjusted the gross male–female wage differential for all of the productivity-related factors that influence wages (e.g., education, experience, absenteeism, turnover, etc.) and found that the wage gap would be zero if males and females had the same productivity-related characteristics, would this indicate the absence of gender discrimination?

4. What impact would equal pay laws have on the wages and employment of female workers? What impact would equal employment opportunity laws (fair employment laws) have on the wages and employment of female workers?

5. For policy purposes, does it matter if the reason for discrimination is prejudice, erroneous information, or job security? Does it matter if the main source of discrimination is employers, co-workers, or customers?

6. Why might the wage gap be negligible for single, never-married males and females? If it is negligible, would this reflect the absence of discrimination?

7. Discuss reasons for the limited potential scope of pay equity legislation.

8. Would you expect the overall, unadjusted male–female pay gap to be increasing or decreasing over time, and why?

9. Comparable worth is akin to the elusive notion of a "just price," where the price is determined independently of the basic forces of demand (reflecting what people are willing to pay for a service) and supply (reflecting what people are willing to accept to provide the service). Discuss.

10. Discuss the pros and cons of the following design or implementation features of comparable worth:

    a. defining gender dominance as 60 percent as opposed to 70 percent of either sex

    b. constraining the male and female paylines to have the same slope as opposed to different slopes

    c. allowing projection of the male payline outside the sample range of the data in cases where the female-dominated jobs otherwise have no male comparator groups

    d. following a point-to-line versus a line-to-line versus a point-to-point wage adjustment procedure

11. Would you expect discrimination to be greater in the public sector or in the private sector, and why? Would you expect it to be greater in union or non-union sectors, and why?

12. From your knowledge of the various components of the overall male–female wage, discuss the potential scope of the various possible policy initiatives.

13. In designing a viable equal value policy, what steps might you take to minimize any inherent conflict between administrative concepts of value (as implied by job evaluation procedures) and economic concepts of value (as implied by market-determined wages)?

14. Assume that you have used a job evaluation procedure to establish the point scores for a number of male-dominated jobs and a number of female-dominated jobs in your organization. Indicate how you would estimate a payline between point scores and pay for each of the predominantly male and predominantly female jobs. What is the appropriate functional form for such paylines? Should they each have an intercept? If the pay in the undervalued female-dominated jobs is to be adjusted, should the female payline be raised to the male payline (line-to-line adjustment) or should the pay in each female job be raised to the male payline (point-to-line adjustment), or to some other value such as an average line or the pay of the closest male job? Should interpolation of the paylines be allowed, within the sample range of the data? Should extrapolation of the paylines be allowed outside of the sample range of the data?

15. If employers were to provide more family-friendly workplace practices, what would that do to the male–female wage gap and why?

16. What factors have led to a decline in the male–female pay gap over time? Are those trends likely to continue?

Problems

1. Suppose that a pay equity plan has just been put in place in your organization. The pay equity consulting firm did a job evaluation and assigned points to each of the male-dominated and female-dominated jobs. It then estimated the following male and female pay lines by ordinary least squares regression, where Y denotes annual earnings, P denotes job evaluation points, and the subscripts m and f denote male and female respectively:

$$Y_m = 5000 + 100P_m$$

$$Y_f = 4000 + 80P_f$$

Assume that you were an employee in a female-dominated job and that your job evaluation score was 200.

   a. What would your pay be before pay equity?

   b. What would it be after pay equity? What is the magnitude of your pay equity award?

2. In the above example, assume that the average job evaluation score was 300 points in male-dominated jobs and 200 points in female-dominated jobs.

   a. What is the average pay in male-dominated jobs and in female-dominated jobs?

   b. Use a Oaxaca decomposition to determine the average pay differential between male- and female-dominated jobs into two components: a portion attributable to the differences in job evaluation points (valued according to the male pay for such points) and a portion attributable to differences in pay for the same job evaluation points.

   c. Use that same decomposition, but this time evaluate the differences in job evaluation points according to the female pay for such points.

3. Assume the type of discrimination analyzed by Becker, in which firms act as if they pay $W_f (1 + d_f)$ when they hire females and $W_m(1 - d_m)$ when they hire males, where d_f and d_m, respectively, are discrimination and nepotism coefficients.

   a. Embed these in place of wages in the firms profit function and derive the firm's profit-maximizing demand for labour.

b. In the case where the value of the marginal products of male and female labour are the same, solve for the ratio of female to male wages when the discrimination and nepotism coefficients are both 0.10.

c. What is meant by a discrimination and nepotism coefficient that is 0.10?

4. Assume that a firm maximizes utility, which is a positive function of profits and a negative function of the number of females it employs. Assume further that males and females are equally productive and, hence, perfectly substitutable for each other in the firm's production function.

a. Show that female wages will be less than the value of their marginal product.

b. Show that female wages will be less than male wages if males are paid the value of their marginal product.

PORTRAIT IMAGES ASIA/Shutterstock.com

CHAPTER 13

Optimal Compensation Systems, Deferred Compensation, and Mandatory Retirement

LEARNING OBJECTIVES

LO1 Discuss why certain compensation arrangements that at first glance seem inefficient may be optimal mechanisms to align the incentives of employers and employees or stockholders and management.

LO2 Explain why these optimal compensation arrangements may change over time or differ across countries or workplaces.

LO3 Outline the "new economics of personnel" and evaluate whether it offers insights into the workplace and human resource practices of organizations.

LO4 Engage in the debate as to whether CEOs "are worth" their often astronomical pay or are essentially "milking their organization and its stockholders."

LO5 Discuss why mandatory retirement may exist and the implications of legislatively banning mandatory retirement.

MAIN QUESTIONS

- In what ways might labour markets within firms differ from labour markets outside of firms? What are the implications for neoclassical supply and demand models?

- Why do wages rise with seniority? Does worker productivity rise continually over the life cycle?

- Why are superstars paid so much more than "average" performers when the difference in their performance levels may be relatively small?

- What is mandatory retirement? Does it represent age discrimination or might it be an important feature of a well-functioning labour market?

- Why are the salaries of some CEOs and executives very high, and why has their pay, relative to the pay of an average worker, increased in recent years?

- Why does academic tenure exist? Should it?

- Under what circumstances would organizations match the outside offers of raiding firms?

Many features of our compensation system in particular, and of our personnel policies in general, seem peculiar and inefficient. For example, promotion and pay are often based on seniority and not necessarily on merit. Workers are often required to retire from specific jobs even though they could carry on many of the necessary functions. Some individuals receive astronomical pay, certainly relative to what they would receive in their next-best alternative activity, even though they appear to be only slightly better performers than others. In many circumstances, pay seems to resemble a tournament prize rather than payment equal to the marginal revenue product of the employee to the firm. In many circumstances, wages appear to be in excess of the amount necessary to recruit and retain a viable workforce to the firm.

To some, these examples of peculiar compensation practices are simply taken as illustrations of the fact that **internal labour markets** within the firm do not operate in the textbook fashion predicted by neoclassical supply and demand theory. They are regarded as inefficient pay practices, or the results of constraints imposed by unions. In recent years, however, basic economic principles have been applied to help explain, in part at least, the existence of various institutional features of labour markets, including compensation systems. An efficiency rationale was sought to explain their survival value. This is part of the trend away from simply regarding these institutional features as exogenously given and then analyzing their impact, and a movement toward explaining these institutional features (i.e., regarding them as endogenous) using basic principles of economics.

Explaining the variation in the use of such workplace and human resource management practices over time and across different work environments is an important new area of research in labour economics. The "new economics of personnel" is the phrase often used to describe this area. Lazear (1995, 1998, and 1999) is generally considered its modern founder, placing that literature in the mainstream of neoclassical labour economics. The literature of new economics of personnel also highlights the interrelationship of labour economics and practical issues of human resource management, including compensation practices and executive compensation. Discussions, summaries, and reviews of some of that rapidly emerging literature are given in Baker and Holmstrom (1995), Bebchuk and Fried (2003), Blakemore (1987), Gibbons (1998), Gibbons and Waldman (1998), Gunderson (2001), Holmstrom and Milgrom (1994), Lazear and Shaw (2007), Malcolmsom (1998), Mitchell and Zaidi (1990), Oyer and Schaefer (2011), Parsons (1986), Prendergast (1999), and Shaw (2009).

As is illustrated in these summaries of the literature and in many of the subsequent examples, this is a literature that often relies on game theory—dealing with "mechanism design issues" (in this case, personnel practices) in a world of uncertainty—as well as on monitoring cost and information asymmetries. This forms a significant "barrier to entry" for specialists in the field of personnel and human resource management in any interaction between them and economists working in the same area. It is hoped that such interaction will expand in the future—and, in fact, students who read this chapter may be motivated to "arbitrage that gap." As stated by Gibbons (1998, p. 30), "Much of the best economics on this subject [economics of personnel] is still to come, and it will exhibit stronger connections both to broader literature on organizational economics and to other disciplines that study organizations." Examples of such efforts include Aggarwal and Samwick (1999); Asch and Warmer (2001); Bandiera et al. (2007, 2010); Barron and Gjerde (1997); Boning, Ichniowski, and Shaw (2007); Drago and Garvey (1998); Ichniowski et al. (1997); Jones et al. (2010); Jones and Kato (2011); Kandel and Lazear (1992); Lazear (1991, 2004, 2007); Lazear and Oyer (2004a, 2004b); Lazear and Shaw (2007); McLeod and Parent (2009); Lindbeck (1997); Mengistae and Xu (2004); Main, O'Reilly, Pekkarinen, and Riddell (2009); Macdonald and Weisbach (2004); Murphy and Zabojnik (2004); Ortin-Angel and Salas-Fumas (2002); and Wade (1993), many of which deal with group norms and teamwork. While compensation is a key outcome in much of this analysis, other motivating factors might also include non-monetary "rewards," such as altruism, respect, attention, fairness, and even jealousy (Ellingsen and Johannesson 2007).

The new economics of personnel also suffers from a lack of data. This reflects, in part, the fact that conventional data sets focus, understandably, on easy-to-quantify measures, such as labour force participation, hours of work, and wages. The measures that are more the focus of personnel economics—such as effort, motivation, bonuses, and individual performance—are often more difficult to quantify and, hence, not collected in conventional data sets. They are occasionally obtained from confidential, proprietary personnel records of firms, but this makes them more difficult to verify and replicate, and it focuses attention on large firms. Consequently, the literature in this area has often been theoretical—too many theories and too few facts (see Exhibit 13.1).

EXHIBIT 13.1

Too Many Theories, Too Few Facts

The problem of lack of data to test the theoretical predictions of personnel economics has been recognized by many who work in the field. Here are some examples:

- "Most of the early work in personnel was theoretical. Primarily because of data shortcomings, research focussed on dreaming up theories that might explain the empirical regularities of human resource management" (Lazear, 1999, p. 200).
- "There are simply no easily accessible data bases with personnel data" (Prendergast 1999, p. 56).
- As indicated by the title of one review article: "Internal Labor Markets: Too Many Theories, Too Few Facts" (Baker and Holmstrom 1995).

There are, however, a growing number of studies (cited subsequently) that have utilized firm-level data sets linking individual measures of performance to the personnel practices of firms. Their methodology has even been given labels; for example, "insider econometrics" (Shaw 2009), signifying that they are internal to the firm, or "econometric case studies" (Jones and Kato 2011), signifying that they generally involve a single organization.

 Agency Theory and Efficiency Wage Theory

In many instances, the theoretical framework that has been applied is part of what is termed **principal-agent theory**. That perspective deals with the problem of designing an **efficient contract** between the principal (employer) and the agent (employee) when there are incentives to cheat. The problems are particularly acute when **monitoring costs** are an issue, or there is **asymmetric information** (i.e., one party has better information than the other and there is no incentive to reveal that information). In such circumstances, the parties may try to design contracts that elicit "truth telling" and ensure incentive compatibility so that no party has an incentive to cheat on the contract.

In such circumstances, the pay of workers need not equal their marginal revenue product to the firm at each and every point in time (a condition economists label the "spot" or "auction market"). Rather, their *expected* pay would equal their expected productivity over their expected lifetime with the firm. Such circumstances are often characterized by explicit contracts, like collective agreements which provide a degree of guarantee of the receipt of payment. Or they are often characterized by **implicit contracts** that rely largely upon reputation. Where reputation is weak, a compensating wage may be paid for the risk that the contract may be broken. Economists term such markets "contract" markets to highlight the long-term contract nature of the arrangements (Carmichael 1989; Lazear 1991).

The growing literature on efficient compensation systems is also related to the literature on efficiency wages (discussed previously, and in Chapter 17; also, Chen and Eden 2002; Fuess and Millea 2002), which argues that wages may both affect productivity and be paid according to the value of the marginal product of labour in the firm; that is, causality can run both ways. This efficiency wage literature has had a number of applications. The economic development literature has often emphasized the subsistence wage necessary for basic levels of nutrition. The Marxist literature has emphasized the subsistence wage necessary for the reproduction of the labour force. As will be discussed in the chapter on the impact of unions, much of the new literature on the impact of unions has emphasized that unions may arise in response to high wages (in addition to the conventional view that unions *cause* higher wages) and that such unions can have a positive influence on productivity. As discussed previously, one possible response to minimum wage legislation (or any other form of wage fixing) is for employers to be "shocked" into more-efficient practices; again, higher wages induce higher productivity. High pay also enables employers to hire from a queue of applicants and this may serve as a worker discipline device, making the cost of layoff high to the worker, especially if there is a pool of unemployed. The personnel literature, and many private personnel practices, has long recognized the potential efficiency gains of paying high wages (see Exhibit 13.2). Pay (and especially perceptions about the fairness of pay), in turn, has been recognized in the personnel literature as potentially being able to affect productivity. In all of these examples, the causality runs in the direction of pay affecting productivity. This supplements the conventional economic emphasis that pay is given in return for the value of the marginal product of labour to the firm. This two-way causality must be recognized in the design of any **optimal compensation system**.

EXHIBIT 13.2

Do High Wages Pay for Themselves?

Raff and Summers (1987) ask whether Henry Ford paid efficiency wages. On January 14, 1914, Henry Ford, overnight, doubled the going wage rate to $5 per day. As a result, there were huge queues of applicants, so much so that rioting developed and the lines of job applicants had to be controlled with fire hoses. Worker performance and productivity improved dramatically. Within a year, turnover fell to one-eighth, absenteeism to one-quarter, and dismissals to one-tenth of their previous level.

Henry Ford touted the high-wage policy—it was termed profit sharing—as good business rather than altruism. It certainly did have the effect of improving work effort and productivity, and it reduced the need for costly supervision. This raises the possibility that high wages may "pay for themselves," at least to a degree.

It is interesting to note that women and girls were excluded from eligibility for the $5 a day, largely on the grounds that they were not supporting a family. As well, a Sociological Department, with 150 inspectors, was established with the power to exclude workers from eligibility if they engaged in excessive drinking, gambling, untidiness, and consumption of unwholesome food!

Taylor (2003) disputes whether Ford meant to pay efficiency wages, arguing that the real intent was to spur consumption and, hence, increase aggregate demand, especially for his own cars. A meta-analysis summarizing 14 studies with 75 estimates of the efficiency wage effect finds strong empirical support for the existence of efficiency wages (Peach and Stanley 2009).

LO1   Economics of Superstars

Optimal compensation systems must also consider the fact that the value of the marginal product of labour may reflect the size of the market (scale) as well as the contribution of an employee to the productivity of others. As emphasized by Rosen (1981), small differences in the skill input of certain individuals may get magnified incredibly in the value of the marginal product of the service consumed by the public or co-workers in certain circumstances. This could be the case, for example, in a collectively consumed consumption good, like a concert or TV performance, where the size of the audience does not usually detract from the ability of others to watch. In such circumstances of a common demand, people are willing to pay to hear the best person because the additional price they have to pay to hear the best is shared among a large group of collective recipients. The additional *per person* cost of hearing the best person is small, because it is shared among the large audience. Hence, "the best" person may command a **superstar** salary that is astronomical relative to the next-best person, even though the superstar's ability or skill may be only marginally better than that of the next-best person. Small differences in skill get magnified into large differences in the value of the marginal product of the service when that service can be consumed by a large audience that can share the cost. This is obvious in the area of professional sports, especially when television creates a global marketplace (Rosen and Sanderson 2001). It can also occur in the area of "rockonomics" (Exhibit 13.3).

EXHIBIT 13.3

"Rockonomics" and the Economics of Real Superstars

Kruger (2005) documents that from 1996 to 2003 the average concert ticket price increased by 82 percent while the consumer price index (CPI) increased by only 17 percent. He examines a number of possible hypotheses and concludes that the economics of superstars can explain the longer-term trend but not this sharp recent rise in concert prices. He attributes the sharp rise in prices to the fact that the ability to download music led to a decline of the complementarity between live concerts and sales of records and discs. Concerts no longer lead to an increase in sales of records and discs. As such, live concerts had to generate their own revenues as unique events. He labels this the Bowie theory, after David Bowie, who is attributed as saying (p. 26) that "music itself is going to be like running water and electricity" so that performers had "better be prepared to do a lot of touring because that's really the only unique situation that's going to be left." Also see Hamlen (1991).

Similarly, if an individual can have a positive effect on the productivity of other workers in the job hierarchy, then the value of the marginal product of that individual's labour to the organization may be high, even if that positive effect is small for each worker. A small positive effect on each worker can accumulate to a large total effect when the number of affected workers in the organization is large. Hence, we may expect certain executives or talented individuals to receive a much larger salary than the next most talented individual, even though there may not be much difference in the skills of the two individuals. Small differences in skill get magnified into large differences in the value of an individual to an organization when those skills can improve the productivity of a large number of workers. The same can apply to effects on suppliers and customers. The expansion of world markets through globalization and trade liberalization that has occurred in recent years may account for some of the astronomical increase in the pay of CEOs of large multinationals; their talent may now be spread over a world market of customers, employees, and suppliers. Even if the CEOs are only slightly more talented than the next-best person, that small additional talent is worth a huge amount to an organization if it affects thousands of employees, millions of customers, and thousands of suppliers. We would also expect such talented individuals to be drawn to large organizations where the benefits of their talents could be spread over larger numbers (Baker and Hall 2004).

As pointed out by Rosen (1982), superstar salaries may also be necessary to ensure that the best people get sorted into their best match or highest-valued use, especially if they have unique talents peculiar to an organization and others are not good substitutes. A huge salary may not be necessary to motivate such people to work hard, but it may be necessary to ensure that their specific talents are matched with the right organization. This is especially the case when the effect of their talent gets spread over a large base of customers, employees, and suppliers, as discussed previously.

Salaries as Tournament Prizes

As pointed out in Lazear and Rosen (1981) and Rosen (1986), executive salaries often seem to resemble prizes for the winners of contests rather than compensation in return for the value of the marginal product of one's services. **Salaries as tournament prizes** are starkly illustrated in the situation of a company that has a number of vice-presidents, all of whom are of roughly comparable ability. However, the one who gets promoted, presumably on the basis of being the best, gets a huge increase in salary. The salary difference between the president and the vice-president seems to reflect a prize for winning a contest more than it does differences in ability or the value of the person to the organization. That is, the president is probably slightly more capable than the vice-president, yet the salary difference seems much more than the ability difference.

Such a compensation system may be efficient, however, if the organization is able to *rank* its executives only according to the *relative* value of their contribution to the organization. That is, the organization may be able to say that individual A is better than B who is better than C, and so forth. However, the organization is not able to assess the precise contribution of each individual or by how much the contribution of one individual exceeds that of another. If the organization is able to assess the productivity of the group, then it could pay individual wages equal to the *average* productivity of each person. However, this compensation system may not create much incentive to perform, since the individual's pay would be based on the productivity of the group, not the individual (i.e., the 1/N problem discussed subsequently). In fact, it may create perverse incentives for some individuals, who themselves know that they have below-average productivity, to enter the group and get the average pay. This adverse selection procedure (a common problem in markets with asymmetric information) could lead to a situation where the bad workers drive out the good workers.

In order to create performance incentives in such markets, organizations may pay a top salary that resembles a prize to the winner in the group. Even if most are paid a wage equal to the average productivity of the group, there will be an incentive to perform in order to be promoted to win the prize. The organization can judge the winner in order to award the prize because, by assumption, the organization can rank individuals on the basis of their performance, even though it cannot gauge their individual productivity.

Such compensation in the form of prizes may be particularly important for senior workers who otherwise have few promotional opportunities left in their career. There may still be an incentive to perform if one of those promotions means the prize of a large salary increase.

Such compensation systems in the form of prizes can also create perverse incentive structures. For example, they may discourage co-operative behaviour, since that could lead to one's competitor receiving the prize, unless, of course, the organization is able to identify and reward such team players. Contest prizes can create positive incentive effects to "win" the prize, but contests also create losers who may become disgruntled employees. They can also foster corruption and create incentives to lose (Exhibit 13.4). Prizes can also create incentives to work just hard enough to win the prize but not to work harder if it is not attainable (as is the case with some grading practices; see Exhibit 13.5). Such compensation systems may even encourage individuals to disrupt the performance of their competitors for the prize so as to enhance their own probability of winning. One can win a tournament by performing well or by making one's opponents play poorly! Drago and Garvey (1998), for example, found that compensation schemes based on relative performance can discourage workers from sharing their tools with fellow workers. The firm is also limited in the extent to which it can use prizes, since risk-averse individuals would not enter a contest for which the runners-up (e.g., vice-presidents) would receive nothing. Hence, it must balance the needs to provide an incentive to win a large prize against the needs to guarantee some payment to get people to enter the contest. Empirical evidence generally confirming predictions of tournament theory include Altmann, Falk, and Wibral (2012); Bognanno (2001); DeVaro and Kauhanen (2016); DeVaro and Waldman (2012); Ehrenberg and Bognanno (1990); Eriksson (1999); Garvey (1998); Harbring and Irlenbusch (2003); Hutchens (1987, 1989); Leonard (1990); Main, O'Reilly, and Wade (1993); and Moldovanu and Sela (2001).

DeVaro and Waldman (2012) highlight the signalling role of promotions in that when an individual is promoted within the organization, other competing employers regard this as a sign of quality and, therefore, increase their wage offers. This induces the promoting employer to increase the individual's wage to prevent them from being bid away. This discourages firms from promoting individuals, especially for those who do not have a high education credential that already signals high ability. They provide empirical evidence confirming their theoretical predictions.

Prizes in the form of awards that carry little or no direct monetary compensation can also create positive incentives to perform, especially if peer recognition is involved. Neckermann, Cueni, and Frey (2014) review the literature on the incentive effect of such awards and highlight that almost all studies find positive incentive effects. Their own study of the effects of recognition awards for call centre workers also finds positive effects on performance, although the effect is short-lived. Gerhards and Seimer (2016) also review the literature, further indicating that almost all studies find positive incentive effects of non-monetary awards. Their own study finds positive affects on performance through provision of either private feedback on being the best performer in the group, or public feedback by revealing this performance information to peers.

In the academic realm, they find positive incentive effects in the such things as enhanced publications and citations for economists winning the John Bates Clark Award for economists under the age of 40, or for being elected to the prestigious Econometric Society. Whether the incentive effect is due to enhanced productivity or to the fact that journal editors are more likely to accept a publication from someone with such enhanced prestige and certified qualifications and that other academics are more likely to cite such individuals is an open question. In contrast, Borjas and Doran (2014) find a *decline* in the productivity of mathematicians after winning the prestigious Fields Medal. They find that about half of the decline can be attributed to the fact that the winners tend to reallocate much of their time to "trying out" other fields, often outside of pure mathematics.

EXHIBIT 13.4

Sometimes It Pays to Lose!

We tend to think of compensation structures as designed to create incentives to win or work hard or to be co-operative or engage in other aspects of positive behaviour. In some circumstances, however, incentives can encourage participants to lose a tournament or contest.

Taylor and Trogdon (2002), for example, provide evidence that teams in the National Basketball Association (NBA) that were very unlikely to make the playoffs lost more than would be expected based on their quality and schedule in order to obtain a higher draft pick. This occurred when the draft was designed with the highest draft pick going to the team with the poorest record. When the draft procedure was changed to a lottery so that any team that missed the playoffs had the same chance at the top draft picks, this pattern of systematically losing disappeared. In the opposite direction, Stiroh (2007) provides evidence that individual performance in the NBA improves markedly in the year before players sign a multi-year contract but declines after the contract is signed.

Duggan and Levitt (2002) also provide evidence of sumo wrestlers in Japan likely rigging matches when it matters more to win, and "throwing" or intentionally losing matches when it does not matter much to lose. Such an incentive structure is created by a sharp nonlinearity in the payoff function for winning or losing. In most cases, each win of a match moves the person up the ranks. But there is a nonlinearity of much higher rewards for winning the eighth match in a season, since that yields a "winning record" of winning more than half of one's matches in the season (i.e., 8 out of 15). The rewards involve money and prestige as well as perks—the lowest-ranked wrestlers have to get up early in the morning and clean and prepare food for the others, while the top ones have servants! Duggan and Levitt find that wrestlers on the margin of winning their eighth match win far more often than would be expected, based on their record and on that of their opponent. They provide evidence that this is not due to additional effort the wrestlers would expend to win the match. Rather, they suggest that it reflects rigging matches where those for whom it pays more to win bribe those for whom the cost of losing is not high. In such circumstances, the parties respond to incentives both to win and to lose. For some, it "pays to lose."

EXHIBIT 13.5

Exert Just Enough Effort to Get the Grade—Students' Response to Grade Incentives

Grading practices are often nonlinear in that linear grades (e.g., 1 to 100) are converted to nonlinear categorical grades like A, B, C, D, F. These practices are similar to employment practices where pay is not based on a linear system (e.g., an extra dollar of pay for every unit of productivity or widget produced) but rather is based on job categories that are ranked. In such circumstances there may be an incentive to exert just enough effort to achieve the attainable target but little incentive to exert effort after the quota is reached or after it becomes unattainable. In the employment area, the effect of such distortionary incentives has been documented, for example, in Asch (1990), Larkin (2014), and Oyer (1998).

Oettinger (2002) finds that such strategic behaviours also exist for students in an Economics 101 course. He documents that there is unusual bunching of grades at just above or at the minimum levels required to achieve certain grade categories. As well, students who are on a grade borderline when going into a final exam score higher on the final exam, after controlling for pre-final performance. Some students exert just enough effort to get their target or achievable grade, but don't "waste" their effort to improve their performance if it is unlikely to move them into a higher grade category.

Such bunching of grades is consistent with strategic behaviour on the part of students making a rational calculation between partying and exerting just enough effort to get their target or achievable grade. But it is also consistent with strategic behaviour on the part of faculty who want to minimize hassles from students who missed a grade category by, say, one mark. Students aren't the only group who strategically respond to incentives in the grading area!

Efficient Pay Equality, Teams, Employee Co-operation, and Performance Pay

In establishing the pay structure within an organization, trade-offs are involved in determining the **optimal degree of inequality** of pay, as well as in achieving a balance of competitive and co-operative behaviour amongst employers (Che and Yoo 2001; Georg et al. 2010; Lazear 1989; Lazear and Shaw 2007). Some dispersion or inequality of pay is necessary as an incentive to perform well in order to to advance in the hierarchy, and perhaps, ultimately, to reach the top. However, too much inequality or dispersion may be inefficient in that it can discourage co-operative behaviour and **teamwork** in instances where only a few can rise to the top. It may even encourage sabotage of fellow employees' efforts to be promoted, if that will enhance your own chance of promotion. As well, a large degree of salary inequity may not be attractive to persons with a degree of risk aversion, or to those who are motivated by concepts of fairness. Pay inequality can also be counterproductive if it fosters jealousy among workers who feel they are not paid appropriately relative to their higher-paid peers, or feel their fellow workers are unfairly underpaid (Charness and Kuhn 2007, although they do not find evidence that workers' own effort is sensitive to the pay of co-workers). Sebastian et al. (2010) also found pay inequality that emanated from unequal rewards to result in enhanced productivity.

The challenge for compensation specialists and human resource managers is to establish the optimal degree of pay equality or salary compression that will provide performance incentives and yet encourage teamwork and co-operative behaviour, if that is important. The optimal degree of pay equality likely varies across different situations. A greater degree of pay equality or salary compression will be efficient if workers affect each other's output; it is difficult to measure each individual's contribution to the team, and co-operative effort is important for team production. In such circumstances, co-operative behaviour and teamwork have a greater potential to enhance group productivity, while sabotage has a greater potential to do the opposite. In the extreme, a completely egalitarian pay structure may prevail, although this suffers from the **1/N problem** (see Exhibit 13.6).

EXHIBIT 13.6

The 1/N Problem: What Do Team-Based Compensation and Restaurant Bills Have in Common?

In workplace teams (a growing phenomenon in the workplace), paying people on the basis of the average performance of team members is often advocated. This can make sense if it is difficult to measure individual performance, if team production is highly interrelated, and if co-operative team effort is to be encouraged. However, such an egalitarian compensation structure suffers from the 1/N, or "free rider," problem. Individuals receive only 1/N (i.e., the same share as everyone else, where N is the size of the team) of the total results of the team effort. This can be a very small amount if the workplace team is large, therefore, providing little incentive to work hard and contribute to the team, since hard workers would get the same as shirkers (Holmstrom 1982; Prendergast 1999). In small teams and partnerships, on the other hand, peer pressure can be brought to bear to deter shirking (Barron and Gjerde 1997; Goodman and Turner 2013; Kandel and Lazear 1992).

Abramitzky and Lavy (2012) highlight the 1/N problem in Israeli kibbutzim in instances when the output of the kibbutzim was shared equally. Some kibbutzim moved to a system of wages based on productivity and performance, which induced the youth to invest more in education that would enhance their productivity and wages.

At a more pragmatic level, the 1/N problem can be applied to sharing restaurant bills as well. If the bill is shared, each individual has an incentive to eat or drink too much and order the more-expensive food and drinks, since she pays only 1/N of the cost of what they all eat and drink. (Of course, she may be constrained by the fact that she pays the individual cost of indigestion and a hangover!) As the group size increases, this problem becomes more severe, since individual actions become less transparent. In contrast, in a small group that repeatedly eats together, such transgressors may not be asked out too often.

Different pay incentive schemes also may be appropriate for different levels within an organization, as well as for different organizational structures. For example, at higher levels within an organization, the potential for either co-operative or sabotaging behaviour may be greater than at lower levels. As well, the types of individuals who achieve those higher levels may be disproportionately "hawkish" and willing to engage in aggressive, competitive behaviour. In such circumstances, it may be sensible to pay higher-level managers bonuses on the basis of individual or group output rather than paying them on the basis of their relative performance. The latter could encourage non-co-operative behaviour or even sabotage on their part as well as on the part of their peers with whom they compete.

Firms may also try to discourage non-co-operative behaviour or sabotage by keeping such opposing contestants at arm's length; for example, by having them each head relatively autonomous business units. Selecting a president from within a company (i.e., **internal promotion**) also may be more feasible if that person is chosen from a group of vice-presidents heading autonomous units whose relative performance can be evaluated easily, and who cannot affect the relative performance of the other, competing vice-presidents through non-co-operative behaviour or sabotage. If such opportunistic behaviour is possible, then it may be necessary to choose a president from outside of the company (i.e., **external promotion**), though this may dilute the incentive of inside vice-presidents because of the reduced probability for internal promotion.

External promotion may also be necessary to prevent the internal contestants from colluding. That is, if the internal contestants know that one of them will be promoted based on their relative performance, they may have an incentive to collude and not work hard (i.e., to avoid the "rat race"), since one of them will still be promoted. The individual incentive to "defect" or cheat is obvious, so the group will have to be able to discipline such "rate busters" who work hard! In such circumstances, the firm may promote (occasionally at least) from the outside so that it has a credible threat of promoting from the outside in order to discipline the internal contestants. The pros and cons of external versus internal promotion are discussed, for example, in Baker, Gibbs, and Holmstrom (1994a, 1994b), Bognanno (2001), Chen (2005), and Chan (1996), as well as in references cited therein.

An interesting perspective on promotions is found in the Peter Principle. The Peter Principle argues that individuals are promoted on the basis of their competence in the job, and when they are no longer competent in their job they will no longer be promoted. This implies that individuals are promoted until they reach their level of *incompetence*, with the result that many individuals are languishing in jobs in which they are incompetent and they are not being promoted out of. Barmby, Eberth, and Ma (2012) provide some evidence to that effect. Lazear (2004) provides an alternative explanation based on the decline in productivity after a promotion being a statistical fact. Specifically, many individuals are promoted on the basis of having had a "good year" (i.e., a positive shock to their productivity). Such shocks, however, tend to be transitory. When the individual returns to their normal level of productivity (reversion to the mean) after their promotion, their productivity declines. It is not that they have been promoted to their level of incompetence. Rather, their promotion was a result of an unusual positive shock, and they have simply returned to their normal level of performance. Lazear provides other examples, including the "*Sports Illustrated* effect" whereby it is viewed as a curse for an athlete to be on the the cover of *Sports Illustrated* because his or her performance falls thereafter. Again, this reflects regression to the mean in that the athlete was put on the cover of *Sports Illustrated* as a result of experiencing an unusual positive shock to their performance. Afterwards, they simply reverted to their normal level of performance.

The optimal degree of competition and co-operation among employees is also likely to differ across firms and individuals. Some firms may get higher output, more innovation, and better quality by fostering competition. Others may do better by fostering co-operation amongst employees. Some workers may thrive on competition; others may be devoured by it and do their best work in a co-operative environment. In such circumstances, it is incumbent upon human resource managers to appropriately "mix and match" such workers. Workers themselves cannot always be relied upon to sort themselves into their appropriate environment, since there may be an incentive for the more hawkishly competitive employees to disguise that trait, enter the more "dovish," co-operative work environment, and then dominate that environment by their non-co-operative behaviour. In such circumstances, it may be rational for human resource managers to use personality traits as a hiring criterion so as to appropriately mix and match employees on the basis of the importance of competitive versus co-operative behaviour.

These examples highlight the fact that human resource policies which at first glance may appear to be inefficient (e.g., an egalitarian wage policy, paying attention to personality in the hiring decision) may be efficient practices encouraging co-operative behaviour among employees. In essence, basic economic principles may be able to explain the existence of a variety of human resource practices and compensation policies, including egalitarian wage structures within a firm, personality as a criterion in hiring, the establishment of semi-autonomous business units, and promotion from within the firm as opposed to from the outside. Explaining the variation in the use of such practices across time and different work environments is an important new area of research in labour economics. It also highlights the interrelationship of labour economics and practical issues of human resource management and compensation practices.

Up-or-Out Rules

Up-or-out rules are an example of a set of personnel practices that, at first glance, seem inefficient but that very well may have an efficiency rationale given imperfect and, especially, asymmetric information. Under such rules, employees are evaluated, usually at a specified point in their career, and are either promoted (i.e., "up") or terminated (i.e., "out"). These rules are common in universities, where assistant professors come up for promotion and either make the cut or are effectively terminated, and in law firms where junior personnel either become a partner or leave. This appears to be an inefficient practice, since it would seem more efficient to simply pay a lower wage to those with lower performance rather than lose them altogether. In other words, the rule seems to preclude normal market transactions or trades—lower wages for lower performance. Up-or-out rules are discussed in Kahn and Huberman (1988), O'Flaherty and Siow (1992, 1995), and Waldman (1990).

In a world of asymmetric information, however, when employers have better information on the value of the employee to them, and on their true ability to pay, then they have an incentive to not reveal that information and not promote the person to the higher-paying position. Up-or-out rules can encourage such information revelation, since employers are not given the low-cost option of not promoting good employees to the higher-paying job. If they bluff and argue that the employee is not a good performer or that they cannot "afford" the employee, they are compelled to terminate that person, which imposes a cost on them if the employee is, in fact, a good performer. As is common in models of asymmetric information, the institutional rules are an information revelation mechanism designed to get the parties with the private information to reveal that information by making the bluffing strategy costly to them.

Up-or-out rules can also serve a purpose when there are a relatively fixed number of junior, nonpromoted slots in an organization. In such circumstances, the organization may want to use some of these slots to evaluate a potential new candidate. If a nonpromoted employee continues to occupy a slot, he precludes an opportunity to bring in a new potential candidate. As stated by O'Flaherty and Siow (1992, p. 347), "If screening can be done only on the job, then the junior position has two roles. First, it is a direct factor of current production. Secondly, it allows the firm to observe the suitability of the junior employee for promotion to senior rank, thereby increasing future production. Even if a junior is capable in his current position, the firm may fire him in order to use his slot to observe another candidate with more promise for the senior rank."

Up-or-out rules can also exist in tournament-type compensation systems to deal with one of the disadvantages of tournament systems; that is, the creation of losers as well as winners, and the reality that losers may be disgruntled employees if they remain. They may, in fact, try to sabotage the winner in order to indicate that a mistake was made. In contrast, if they leave they may have a strong incentive to perform well in their new job in order to indicate that a mistake was made. Revenge can be a strong motivator! In circumstances where the employee may be a counterproductive performer if she remains but a very productive employee if she leaves, up-or-out rules may well be efficient contracts.

Up-or-out rules can also compel managers to make hard decisions and not to simply "coast," taking the easy way out by retaining mediocre performers rather than terminating them. Prendergast (1999 p. 30), for example, cites evidence from the personnel literature of the tendency to compress evaluation ratings because of a reluctance to give poor grades to poor performers. This is also one of the reasons for requiring relative evaluations. Up-or-out rules compel the manager to make a more extreme decision—retain the person and promote her to a higher position, or terminate her. The middle option of retaining her without a promotion is not possible.

While **tenure** at universities is an up-or-out rule that may exist for the reasons discussed above, it may also exist to provide job security, so that senior employees have an incentive to hire new persons who are better than themselves (see Exhibit 13.7).

EXHIBIT 13.7

Why Is There Academic Tenure?

Historically, academic tenure was perceived to be necessary to ensure freedom of expression in the university environment. Other rationales have been offered, including the possibility that it encourages researchers to undertake potentially risky but innovative research projects, since unsuccessful projects will not lead to job loss.

Carmichael (1988) offers an alternative explanation in that job security offered by tenure is necessary as an incentive for more-senior professors to hire junior professors who are better than themselves. Without such job security, professors would be reluctant to hire their potential replacement.

Tenure attracts much attention in this area in that the search and hiring decisions are done usually by the employees (i.e., by professors). In a sense, the university can be thought of as a workers' co-operative, run by the workers themselves! In order to provide an incentive to hire the best young people, academics are granted the job security of tenure after meeting certain competency requirements, usually after about six years as an assistant professor.

Again, what appears to be an inefficient work rule may well be an efficient practice, given the policy of recruiting and hiring being done by professors themselves. On the other hand, this may also only be a convenient rationale for those of us with tenure!

Raiding, Offer-Matching, and the Winner's Curse

Asymmetric information issues can also give rise to the problem of the **winner's curse** when organizations engage in **raiding** other organizations for top talent (Lazear 1986; Tranaes 2001). Because the person being recruited is employed at the organization being raided, that organization presumably has better information on the person than the raiding organization does. In such circumstances, the organization being raided presumably would engage in **offer-matching** of the outside offer *if* the individual were truly worth that amount, and the organization would not match the offer if the person were not worth that amount. The raiding organization, therefore, is successful only for those who were *not* worth its offer—hence, it would be subject to the "winner's curse."

There are, of course, mitigating circumstances that would alter this scenario, otherwise we would not expect to observe such raiding. Some individuals may be a better fit or match in the organization doing the raiding; hence, it would not make sense for the institution being raided to try to pay that match-specific offer. In such circumstances, raiding would ensure that individuals are allocated to their most valued use.

The raided institution may also not want to match the outside offer out of concern that this would lead to disgruntlement among its existing personnel if they do not get a similar pay increase. In such circumstances, the disgruntled employees may devote their time and energy into obtaining outside offers (some of which may be productive activity, but some of which may be a diversion from their normal activity). Or they may reduce their effort margin or work intensity if they have no intention of leaving.

In many situations, the information on a person's productivity is generally well known; it is not private information possessed only by the institution being raided. Most university departments, for example, know their own superstars as well as those of other universities. Universities that raid other universities also, generally, know who are "good citizens," generating positive externalities within their departments. Most even know the disruptive citizens who generate negative externalities, though that information may not be so publicly known. In such circumstances, the raiding institution is not likely to be subject to the winner's curse.

Piece Rates and Performance Pay

As the name implies, performance pay is compensation that is designed to reward and enhance performance. The performance can be based on the output, or number of "pieces," produced by an individual, as in the case of piece rates (Gibbons 1987; Kraft 1991; Lazear 2000). Or it can be more general, in that it is based on performance assessments of the individual as done through merit pay, or the performance of the work team or of the whole company, often in the form of bonuses.

Piece rates and performance pay have positive work *incentive effects,* because workers are rewarded for working harder and smarter, and, hence, producing more output. They also have positive *sorting, or selection, effects* for firms, because such systems would attract good workers willing to work hard. Firms would not have to worry about supervising and monitoring worker inputs and, hence, save on the costs of such monitoring.

Piece-rate systems require that the *output* of the individual be readily monitored so that payment can be based on that output. This can be costly, and it can lead to disputes if the parties do not agree on the accuracy of the monitoring. As well, such systems are harder to sustain if the individual does not have a large degree of control over the output, perhaps because it is affected by the work of others or by actions of the firm or by technological and other changes. A technological or other change that enables workers to produce twice as much output as before with no additional effort will lead to a renegotiation of the piece rate (or price per unit of output), and this may be difficult to establish, depending upon whether the change emanates from actions of the firm or is truly an exogenous change. Individuals on piece-rate systems may also be reluctant to do other tasks that could benefit the organization but for which a piece rate is not paid (e.g., assist other employees unless reciprocal favours are possible). As well, under piece-rate systems, workers may not care about the quality of the product or service unless it is tied to other rewards or penalties.

Overall, piece-rate systems will be more effective and better utilized when it is simple to measure and monitor the quantity and quality of the *output* produced, while the more conventional time-rate systems will be more effective and utilized when it is easy to measure and monitor the quantity and quality of the *input* that is provided. As well, piece-rate systems will be more common in jobs where turnover is high and it is not possible to induce positive incentives through deferred compensation systems that require long-term employment relationships, as discussed subsequently. Lemieux, MacLeod, and Parent (2009), for example, provide evidence that the use of performance pay has increased in recent years because skill-biased technological change has increased the premium on performance-related skills, and this has contributed to the growing wage inequality that is occurring. Heywood and Parent (2012), however, indicate that this applies only to white workers, resulting in a larger black–white wage differential for those in performance pay jobs. Anderson et al. (2009) provide evidence that much of the growing pay inequality reflects the star salaries paid for talent in the growing software sector, where innovation is important. Shaw (2007) suggests that performance pay has increased because new information technologies have facilitated the measurement of individual performance. Brenčič and Norris (2010) provide evidence that performance pay is less likely to be used when the job entails multitasking, quality control, or teamwork—characteristics that make it difficult to measure the output of the individual. Gibbs et al. (2009) provide evidence that multiple performance measures are used when there are multiple objectives to pursue and complex behaviours to modify. Goldin (1986) provides evidence that piece rates were most common in female jobs in the early 1900s because of the high turnover in those jobs. For a discussion of gender differences in performance pay see Exhibit 13.8.

With respect to the evidence on the effects of piece-rate systems, surveys of the literature suggest that these have both positive incentive and sorting effects (Prendergast 1999; Lazear and Oyer 2007). For example, Paarsch and Shearer (1999) provide empirical evidence of the incentive effects of piece-rate systems for tree planters in British Columbia—an industry suited for utilizing and evaluating piece rates, because planter output is easily observable on a daily basis. Specifically, other things equal, paying one cent more per seedling planted (on the basis of the average payment of 25 cents per seedling) increased average daily output by 67 trees. Paarsch and Shearer emphasize the importance of controlling for the endogeneity of the piece rate in that higher piece rates have to be paid in situations of difficult planting conditions; otherwise, workers will not work under piece rates. Without controlling for these planting conditions, higher piece rates led to lower output (where the lower output resulted from the difficult planting conditions), which would give the appearance of negative incentive effects—the opposite of what is predicted by theory. After controlling for the fact that higher piece rates have to be paid to compensate for the lower output associated with the more difficult planting conditions, the positive relationship between piece rates and productivity held, as predicted by the theory. Also see Shearer (2004).

EXHIBIT 13.8

Gender Differences in Performance Pay

There are theoretical reasons why females are more likely to receive performance pay and also for the opposite to prevail. Females are more likely to opt for performance pay, to the extent that it involves objective assessments based on output and, hence, is less likely to be based on discrimination. As well, if they have shorter expected tenure with an organization, they may opt for performance pay that is more based on "spot market" returns rather than look for deferred compensation systems that involve more implicit long-term contracts (Geddes and Heywood 2003).

Working in the other direction, performance pay with incentive bonuses may be more subject to the discriminatory assessments of performance on the part of supervisors (Gomez-Mejia and Balkin 1992; Reskin 2000; Elvira and Graham 2002). Females also may be more risk averse and, hence, reluctant to take on the risk of performance pay (Gneezy et al. 2003, 2004; Manning and Saidi 2010; Munoz-Builon 2010, and articles discussed previously in Chapter 12 on discrimination).

The empirical literature provides somewhat conflicting evidence, perhaps reflecting the different effects of these competing forces, as well as difficulties in determining a pure "gender" effect when pay systems may differ by such factors as the occupation, industry, and firms in which females are employed.

Evidence that women are less likely to receive performance-based pay then men is found in Cowling (2000) for the Netherlands, but the opposite is found for Belgium in Booth, in Frank (1999) for Britain, in Barth et al. (2008) for Norway, in Bertrand and Hallock (2001) for executives in the United States, and in Chauvin and Ronald (1994) for business school graduates in the United States. Evidence from laboratory experiments indicates that women are less likely to opt for performance pay when given a choice (Dohmen and Falk 2006).

Evidence that women are more likely to be paid performance-based piece rates is found in Brown and Heywood (2003) for Australia, and in Geddes and Heywood (2003) for the United States (although they are less likely to be paid commissions and bonuses). For Germany, Heywood and Jirjahn (2002) find that women are more likely to receive pay based on individual productivity and profit sharing, and not on group profit sharing.

Haley (2003) also found positive incentive effects of piece rates in the logging industry. They were slightly smaller than than those of Paarsch and Shearer (1999)—a fact that Haley attributes to the greater risk associated with working faster in logging than in tree planting. Lazear (2000) also provides evidence on the effect of shifting from hourly wages to piece rates in a large U.S. company that installed car windshields. The shift to piece rates increased productivity (output per worker) by about 44 percent. About one-half of this was due to the incentive effect of employees working harder because their effort was directly rewarded. The other one-half was due to "sorting"; the least productive workers left the company, and more productive workers stayed or joined the company. Bandiera et al. (2007) also provide evidence that managers whose performance pay depends upon the output of the workforce they manage target their efforts towards increasing the productivity of the most-able workers and also towards hiring the most-able workers. In a subsequent study, Bandiera et al. (2009) also find that when paid on the basis of performance pay, managers move away from favouring workers with whom they are socially connected and towards favouring high-ability workers whose output will enhance their own managerial performance pay. In essence, "friendship comes at a price," and when the price gets too high they don't favour their friends. In another, later study, Bandiera et al. (2010) also provide evidence that workers' productivity and pay in piece-rate systems is enhanced by working alongside friends who are more productive than themselves, suggesting that firms could enhance productivity by exploiting such social incentives at the workplace. It also highlights a whole new meaning to the concept of "will you be my friend."

Further evidence on the positive effect of piece rates and performance pay in a variety of different contexts is provided in Atkinson et al. (2008); Battisti and Vallanti (2013); Boning, Ichniowski, and Shaw (2007); Burgess et al. (2009); Dohmen and Falk (2011); Fabling and Grimes (2014); Gittleman and Pierce (2015); Jones, Kalmi, and Kauhanen (2010); Kahn and Sherer (1990); Long and Fang (2012); Lucifora and Origo (2015); Muralidharan and Sundararaman (2011); Parent (1999); Pekkarinen and Riddell (2008); and Shearer (2004), as well as in references cited therein.

Dufflo, Hanna, and Ryan (2012) randomly assign teachers in India to different treatment groups where they receive bonuses for showing up to teach as a way to curb the high absenteeism of teachers in India. Such bonuses have strong incentive effects in reducing absenteeism and in improving student performance in the long run.

In the United States, Sojourner, Mykerezi, and West (2013) analyze the effect of changes in teachers' pay, formerly based on a grid (i.e., pay based on educational qualifications and seniority), to a merit-based system; that is, pay-for-performance. They find positive effects on ultimate student test scores. Goodman and Turner (2013) analyze the effect of a group-based bonus scheme for teachers and find little effect when the teacher groups are large and subject to the 1/N-problem with its incentive to free ride. But there are positive effects on student performance when the teacher groups are small so that peer pressure are able to discipline the free riders.

In Ontario universities, Sen, Ariizumi, and Desousa (2014) find that universities reward productivity as measured by publications in top academic journals, as well as by receipt of research grants. However, they find no rewards for better teaching, a finding that will not surprise many students! They cite other studies with similar results.

The increased productivity from piece-rate systems does come at the cost of increased effort on the part of workers, and this increased effort, presumably, has some disutility. Copeland and Monnet (2009) provide evidence that the disutility from the increased effort is slightly less than half of the utility from the higher performance, based pay. It makes sense that the disutility from the increased effort must be less than the utility from the increased pay; otherwise, workers would not opt for such performance-based pay schemes. Frick, Goetzen, and Simmons (2013) provide evidence that performance-based pay has some hidden costs in the form of an incentive to increase quantity at the expense of quality, and to run the equipment for long hours instead of spending time on maintenance. Larkin (2014) provides evidence that employees in software sales "game the system" by altering the timing of their deal closures. Specifically, they both grant discounts and price items lower than required to make a sale in order to earn their commission in a time period most favourable to the salesperson, with the discount being unfavourable to their employer. Similar "timing gaming" is found in Oyer (1998).

Perhaps somewhat surprisingly, piece rates also exist in the medical profession. Medical doctors are typically paid in one of three main ways, each of which creates a different incentive structure. *Fee for service* is essentially a piece-rate system in which the doctor is paid for each service unit performed. This can occur in market-based systems where patients or insurance carriers essentially pay for the services performed during a visit (e.g., in the United States). Or it can occur in regulated systems, such as in Canada where the government sets the fee for the different services but the number of services performed depends largely on the decisions of the patient and the doctor (though it is usually subject to some government monitoring with respect to the need for the services, and sometimes subject to regulations with respect to the maximum amount that can be earned from fees). This system encourages doctors to "work hard" since they are paid by the "piece" (i.e., the service they produce). But it involves the risk that they may cut quality since they are not paid directly for better-quality service, although patients may not return if they feel they are not getting quality service (to the extent that they can judge quality in this area). It also allows the risk that doctors may have an incentive to "churn" patients—have them come back for repeat visits, follow-ups, or, in the extreme, visits that are not necessary. If there are maximum limits on the amount doctors can earn from fees (or reductions on the fee paid after a certain limit is earned), it can create the incentive to rapidly move patients through the system until the maximum is earned, and then to go on to other activities. It is for these reason that the public provider often has to monitor the output—in this case, the need for the service—and often has an incentive to introduce co-payments (shared by the patient) so that the patient has some monetary incentive not to abuse the system. Queues or waiting lists are often used to ration scarce services when prices are not used. Governments are also not able to know their costs in advance, although that is mitigated somewhat if there are caps on payments.

An alternative payment system for doctors is one based on *capitation,* or the number of potential patients in the doctor's service area or roster (e.g., in Britain). In effect, the doctor is on a form of salary, although that salary is contingent on the number of patients he can be expected to serve, based on his roster. In such circumstances, the doctor does not have a monetary incentive to see more patients or to provide quality service (or any service) since his pay is based on potential patients and not actual patients or actual services performed. He does have an incentive to try to get a roster of healthy patients or at least patients who will not come in for services. In this system, governments are able to know their costs in advance since it is essentially a form of salary.

A third payment system for doctors is one based on straight *salary,* where their pay is independent of the number of potential or actual patients they see. Such systems exist in the health maintenance organizations (HMOs) in the United States, and they can exist for doctors employed by companies or other organizations. While such doctors do not have a direct monetary incentive to "work hard," neither do they have an incentive to rush patients through the system or cut quality. As with the capitation system, governments are able to determine their costs in advance since it is essentially a salary.

Clearly, difficult trade-offs exist in trying to design an optimal compensation system that provides the best incentives in this important and costly area. As is typically the case in designing optimal compensation systems, those trade-offs depend upon such things as effectively monitoring the output or the input, and on information asymmetries and the extent to which doctors and patients respond to monetary incentives in the system.

Executive Compensation

The issue of **executive compensation** has received increased attention and public scrutiny in recent years, and especially since the recent financial crises of 2008–2009 (reviews in Abowd and Kaplan 1999; Bebchuk and Fried 2003, 2004; and Murphy 1999). Executive pay has increased relative to the average pay of workers. It is much higher in the United States (where the attention has focused) relative to other countries, such as Japan, and it has increasingly been tied to the performance of the firm, often through stock options. Stories abound in the popular press of occurrences skyrocketing executive pay in spite of the poor performance of their companies, suggesting that executive pay is not tied to performance.

The previous discussion of tournaments and superstars suggests that high executive salaries may be motivated in part by the need to pay "prizes" to the top persons to act as an incentive among other executives to strive for the "tournament prize." Making sure that the top person gets the job is especially important for an executive who is responsible for an extremely large organization. Correct decisions in these circumstances, for example, can have huge ramifications for the performance of large numbers of workers as well as for customers CEO and suppliers. In that vein, the incentive that is most important is not that which encourages the executive to work hard or to acquire managerial skills, but rather it is the incentive ensuring that the executive with the right talent gets *matched* with the organization that needs and values that talent the most (Rosen 1982). Paying a person a million dollars as opposed to one-half a million dollars per year is not likely to make her work any harder or be more productive. It may not even be necessary to have such a large "prize" as an incentive for potential candidates to strive for promotion to "win" it. However, it may be necessary in order to ensure that the appropriate person goes to the organization where her talent is valued most.

Popular impressions to the contrary, the empirical evidence tends to suggest that the compensation of top executives *is* positively related to the performance of their firm, but the pay-performance linkage is often weak and the direction of the causality is not well established (Bell and Van Reenen 2013; Conyon 2014; Doucouliagos, Haman, and Stanley 2012; Murphy 1985; Bertrand and Mullainathan 2001; Jensen and Murphy 1990; Kaplan and Rauh 2013; Zhou 2000; and references in those studies). Interestingly, Bryson, Forth, and Zhou (2013) find that CEO compensation in China follows similar patterns to those in Western countries, although in a slightly more muted fashion. The debate over the appropriateness of executive compensation tends to divide between those who feel that such superstar pay is necessary to create the right incentives in various areas—that is, to match appropriate CEOs with the right firm; to enable their talent to be spread over a large base of customers, suppliers, and workers; and to foster incentives below the CEO level to win the tournament prize. On the other side of the debate are those who feel that CEOs have "milked" their companies, in large part because of weak corporate governance structures.

On the efficient compensation side, Gabaix and Landier (2008) provide evidence that the increase in the size of firms that has occurred in recent years, often associated with multinationals and globalization, can explain much of the increase in CEO pay in the United States as well as the large variation in CEO pay across firms and between countries. Specifically, they indicate that the sixfold increase in CEO pay in the United States between 1980 and 2003 can be fully explained by the sixfold increase in size of firms (their market value) over that period. Updated evidence to include the period around the economic crisis of 2008–2009 confirms that relationship (Gabaix, Landier, and Sauvagnat 2014). Similar evidence of the importance of the increase in firm size in explaining the growth of executive compensation in the United States is provided in Conyon (2013, 2014), Gayle and Miller (2009), and Kaplan and Rauh (2013). Gayle, Golan, and Miller (2015) provide evidence for the United States indicating that executive pay increases along with firm size, and that most of this pay increase reflects a risk premium associated with the greater portion of risky incentive pay for executives in large firms. Abowd and Bognanno (1995) and Conyon and Murphy (2000) also provide evidence that much of the higher compensation of CEOs in the United States, as compared to those in Europe, can be attributed to larger firm sizes in the United States.

The link between executive compensation and firm performance is complicated by the institutional arrangements, or governance, whereby executive compensation is set. Executive compensation usually consists of a base salary and **stock options**—the latter providing an incentive for the CEO to improve the stock market value of the firm. Bullon (2010) provides evidence that most of the gender gap for high-level executives in the United States reflects the fact that females are much less likely to receive performance pay in the form of stock options. Typically, the compensation process involves the board of directors approving the executive pay recommendation made by a compensation committee. The boards of directors may have an incentive to award high executive salaries because they themselves are usually executives, and they are often appointed by the CEO whose salary they are determining. Shareholders may not be able to provide an effective check to this because of the complexities of evaluating the magnitude of the compensation package. As a result of these institutional arrangements for setting executive pay, some reforms have focused on making the process more open to the scrutiny of shareholders, to serve as an effective check.

Bertrand and Mullainathan (2001), for example, find that the relationship between CEO pay and firm performance is somewhat tenuous as CEOs are often rewarded for being "lucky" in that their whole industry happens to perform well for reasons that have nothing to do with their performance as a CEO. Bertrand and Mullainathan indicate that some of this could be optimal in that CEOs' outside offers may increase as the fortune of the industry improves or because firms may want their CEO to be able to forecast and respond to luck shocks. But they suggest that much of this likely reflects the fact that stockholders (principals) are not exerting sufficient control in governing the CEOs (agents). They find that when stockholders do exert sufficient control (e.g., there are large shareholders on the board of directors and the boards are independent of the CEO) then there tends to be a stronger link between pay and performance and a weaker link with luck. Malmendier and Tate (2009) provide evidence that superstar CEOs who win prestigious external awards for running their organization subsequently extract higher compensation but actually perform more poorly, in part because they spend more time on interests outside of running their company. This negative effect is stronger in organizations where there is weak corporate governance. Furthermore, Benmelech et al. (2010) find that stock options have induced managers to conceal bad news and to choose suboptimal investment policies in order to mask negative news to shareholders about future growth prospects.

The managerial power perspective is a more extreme position, viewing CEOs as, effectively, milking their corporation largely because of weak governance structures, as outlined above (Weisbach 2007). That perspective, which has gained some credence because of the recent financial crisis, is outlined in such titles as *In Search of Excess: The Overcompensation of American Executives* (Crystal 1991), *Pay Without Performance* (Babcock and Fried 2004) and "Endogenously Chosen Boards of Directors" (Hermalin and Weisbach 1998). Bivens and Mishel (2013) argue that because of weak governance, most of the high compensation of executives and CEOs reflects economic rents or excess payments above their next-best-alternative job, and hence, can be taxed without affecting the efficient allocation of their talents.

The discontent over executive pay has given rise to a "say on pay" response empowering shareholders to vote on the compensation arrangements of the executives of the firms in which they own shares. Gregory-Smith et al. (2014) find that in the UK, which pioneered the movement, such dissent was fostered by high executive compensation, but the impact of it was small. Furthermore, while the dissent itself did have a moderating effect on executive compensation, it was only for very high levels of compensation and when the dissent was strong. Based on UK data, Bell and Van Reenen (2013) find that when large institutional investors, such as pension fund managers, are significant shareholders they cause the pay-for-performance relationship to be much stronger, not only by rewarding executives when the firm performance is strong but also by penalizing them for negative performance. By contrast, firms with more dispersed ownership and less institutional investing only reward executives when firm performance is strong; they do not penalize them for negative performance. Overall, Bell and Van Reenen (2013) do find a strong positive relationship between pay and performance for executives and, especially, CEOs.

While the compensation of CEOs in private, for-profit firms has attracted the most scrutiny, increased attention is being placed on the compensation of executives in not-for profit organizations, including hospitals, charitable organizations, and even unions. Much of this reflects the fact that such organizations are increasingly paying attention to performance metrics, in part for funding reasons. Hallock (2002) and Hallock and Klein (2016) review much of that literature and conclude that although the level of compensation is often lower in non-profit organizations, executive pay is generally related to factors similar to those in the for-profit sector, such as the size and performance of the organization.

Although it does not directly relate to executive compensation, Lazear (2012) theorizes that successful leaders have the following attributes: extremely able and successful at tasks, communication skills that make their success visible, found in high variance industries where decision making has the greatest payoff, and tend to be generalists because of the wide range of decisions they have to make. Using data on Stanford alumni, he confirms those theoretical expectations. Also, as an important note for many students, those with better grades are less likely to obtain leadership positions! So, hang in there; it may be just a matter of time until your leadership ability is realized.

Deferred Wages

Evidence

Compensation often appears to be deferred in the sense that wages for the more senior employees are above the individual's productivity (Figure 13.1(a)). Alternatively stated, wages rise with seniority or experience, independently of the individual's productivity. Evidence on deferred compensation is reviewed in Lazear (1999) and Prendergast (1999), and more-recent evidence is provided in Dohmen (2004); Flabbi and Ichino (2001); Gersbach and Glaze (2009); Huck, Seltzer, and Wallace (2011); and Zwick (2012).

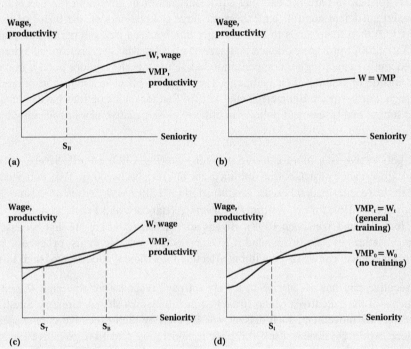

Figure 13.1 Wage Productivity Profiles

(a) Deferred wages contract market

Productivity, or the value of marginal productivity, is assumed to rise with seniority, though tapering off at higher levels. Wages start off below the individual's productivity profile (indicating underpayment relative to productivity) but they rise more rapidly than productivity, eventually reaching a breakeven point. They are above productivity at the higher levels of seniority (indicating overpayment relative to productivity).

(b) Spot market

Wages are equal to productivity at each and every level of seniority; that is, workers are always paid the value of their marginal product.

(c) Deferred wages with company-specific training

Wages are above the individual's productivity during the initial period up to S_t while they receive company-specific training. The sponsoring company benefits by that training (since it is usable only in that company), and hence, it "pays" for the training by accepting the fact that the worker will have lower productivity during that training period. Thereafter, a deferred wage profile prevails.

(d) General training

Wages are considerably below productivity in the initial period up to S_t, not only because of the deferred wage but also because the trainee is "paying" for the general training by accepting a lower wage during the training period. Trainees pay for the general training because they benefit by it; other firms will bid for their services since the training is generally usable in a wide range of organizations.

The deferred wage aspect would be even larger if one considers the fact that pension accruals become important in the years just prior to retirement; that is, for every additional year an individual works, that individual experiences not only a wage increase but also pension increments that are a cost to the employer but a compensation benefit to employees. Pension benefits themselves also can be considered part of the deferred compensation package (Lazear 1990; Pesando and Gunderson 1988; Pesando, Gunderson, and Shum 1992).

Associated Characteristics

Obviously, such deferred compensation systems will exist only in situations where there is some long-term commitment on the part of the firm to continue the contracted arrangements. Otherwise, the firm has an incentive to dismiss employees at the time the workers' pay begins to exceed their productivity (at the point of intersection, S_B, of the pay and productivity schedules of Figure 13.1(a)). Firms that engaged in such opportunistic behaviour, however, would develop a bad reputation and have to pay a higher regular compensating wage to employees in return for the risk that they may not receive their deferred wage.

Of course, firms that find themselves with an aging workforce with accumulated seniority and few younger workers (perhaps because of a decline in their hiring due to a decline in their product demand), may find it "profitable" to declare bankruptcy and hence sever their deferred wage obligations, especially if they can relocate elsewhere and hire younger workers at a wage less than their productivity. Obviously, if this were known by the new recruits, a compensating wage would be required for accepting employment in such a firm deliberately restructured to avoid its deferred compensation obligations. However, the true rationale for such bankruptcy can be difficult to detect, especially in situations of asymmetric information where the firm has more information than employees on the true profitability of the firm. As well, with "footloose capital" and the ability to relocate plants throughout the world, firms may have less need to worry about their reputation if they close plants in one country and reopen in another.

Given the fact that firms have a short-run incentive to renege on the deferred wage obligation when that obligation becomes due, such a compensation system will prevail only when there are certain checks and balances ensuring that the deferred compensation is paid. These checks and balances include the reputation of the firm, the payment of wages related to seniority, legal protection against unjust dismissal, and the fact that unions can provide a degree of "due process" to ensure that their members are not arbitrarily dismissed. Such checks and balances are characteristic of the longer-term contract market, where a longer-term employment relationship is expected, rather than the spot or auction market, where wages would equal the workers' productivity at each and every point in time (Figure 13.1(b)). As outlined by Hallock (2009), the job losses that more frequently occur for more-senior workers suggest that the implicit employment contract may be "fraying."

Rationales for Deferred Compensation

Such deferred compensation systems may serve a number of important functions and, hence, have an efficiency rationale. As emphasized by Lazear (1979, 1981), they may ensure honesty and work effort, because the worker wants to stay with the company to get the deferred wage. It is as if the worker posted a bond (equal to the excess of the worker's productivity over wages when young) that will be returned (in the form of wages in excess of productivity) when the worker has accumulated seniority with the firm. The returning of the bond (deferred compensation) will be done, conditional upon the worker having performed satisfactorily after a period over which past performance can be observed. Workers whose performance has not been satisfactory can be dismissed, subject to the checks and balances discussed previously. The greater honesty and work effort that results from such a system enhances productivity and, hence, provides the means for such workers to receive greater compensation over their expected work life.

This type of compensation system also reduces the need for constant, everyday monitoring of the productivity of workers. With deferred wages, monitoring can be made on a periodic, retrospective basis (i.e., examining past performance) with the worker being promoted and, hence, receiving the deferred wage conditional upon satisfactory performance (again subject to the previously discussed checks and balances). In contrast, under the spot market system (Figure 13.1(b)), where wages are equal to productivity at each and every point in time, productivity and performance must be assessed, or known, on a regular basis in order to compensate accordingly. The paradigm of the spot market is the piece-rate system, where payment is made directly according to output—a system that can exist only where output is easily measured (e.g., sales, logs cut, buttons sewn).

Deferred wages may also reduce unwanted turnover and, hence, enable firms to recoup their quasi-fixed hiring and training costs, which are usually incurred early in the employee's career with the company. Such costs to the firm are illustrated in Figure 13.1(c), by the area above the value-of-marginal product, VMP, line and below the wage line. In order to recoup these costs and amortize them over a longer work life of their employees, firms may want to defer compensation in order to provide employees with an incentive to stay with the firm.

WORKED EXAMPLE

Deferred Compensation

Assume a worker's productivity, or value of marginal product, VMP, is $10 per hour (i.e., VMP = 10) over her lifetime. Assume that she is paid according to a deferred compensation system whereby her starting wage of $5 per hour is increased by 0.2 for each year of tenure, T, she remains with the firm (i.e., W = 5 + 0.2T). Assume further that she starts working with the firm at age 20, and that there is no discounting.

a. Calculate at which age (or how many years tenure) the workers break even with this preferred compensation system; that is, the point at which wages are just equal to the workers' value of the marginal product. To solve for the breakeven tenure where wages are just equal to the worker's value of marginal product, set W = VMP; that is, 5 + 0.2T = 10, or T = 25. Thus, the worker's wage equals her productivity after 25 years at the firm. Since she starts at age 20 this occurs when she is T + 20, or 45 years old.

b. Solve for the mandatory retirement age at which the expected magnitude of the overpayment just equals the expected magnitude of the underpayment. To solve, use the information on the breakeven age and the symmetry of the magnitude of the "triangles" that would measure the underpayment (in the 25 years prior to the breakeven age of 45) and the overpayment that would occur over the next 25 years after the breakeven age—that is, at age 45 + 25 = 70.

c. Solve the annual amount of underpayment or overpayment at age 20, 30, 40, 50, 60, and 70. The *annual* amount of underpayment (−) or overpayment (+) is W − VMP, as calculated below at the various ages:

Age	Tenure, T	VMP	W = 5 + 0.2T	W − VMP
20	0	10	5	−5
30	10	10	7	−3
40	20	10	9	−1
50	30	10	11	+1
60	40	10	13	+3
70	50	10	15	+5

The training here is *company specific* in the sense that it is usable, mainly, in the company providing the training. As discussed in the previous chapter on human capital theory, if the training were *generally usable* in other firms the employee would have the incentive to pay for the training, often in the form of accepting a lower wage during the training program. In this case, the trainee's productivity and wage during training ($VMP_t = W_t$ in Figure 13.1(d)) would fall below what his productivity and wage would have been in the absence of training ($VMP_0 = W_0$). After the training period, the employee's productivity would increase and, since general training is usable anywhere, so would the trainee's wage (i.e., $VMP_t = W_t$ and both lie above $VMP_0 = W_0$ in the post-training period). In the case of general training, where the employee bore the cost of accepting a lower wage during the training period, the company would not have incurred any quasi-fixed costs, and hence, would have no incentive to pay a deferred wage, at least for that reason. In such circumstances, the wage profile would equal the productivity profile (i.e., $W_t = VMP_t$) as in a spot market. If deferred wages were desirable for other reasons, then these could be superimposed upon the general-training wage profile.

Deferred wages may also exist in order to provide workers with a financial interest in the solvency of the firm. Under the pure spot market of Figure 13.1(b), except for the transactions costs of finding a new job, the employee would be indifferent as to whether the firm went bankrupt or not, since employees would get a wage equal to their productivity elsewhere. With deferred wages, as in Figure 13.1(a), however, the employee stands to lose the deferred wage portion if the firm goes bankrupt. Thus, deferred wages, including pension obligations, provide employees with an interest in the financial solvency of the firm, and this, in turn, may encourage concession bargaining if the solvency of the firm is in jeopardy. The loss of deferred wages, for example, may be one reason for the larger income losses that are incurred by older workers when they lose their jobs and are displaced to their next-best alternative employment.

WORKED EXAMPLE

Piece Rates and Team Compensation

Assume that you and El Slacker are the only two employees at the company and that each of you are paid at a rate of $10 per unit of output, each unit of effort you provide yielding one unit of output. Assume further that your respective disutilities of effort are given by the schedule below in the third and fourth columns. The fifth and sixth columns are calculations of the respective pay each of you would receive based on multiplying your units of effort (and, hence, output) by the wage of $10 per unit of effort.

		Disutility of Effort		Pay (wage × effort)	
Unit of effort = output (1)	Wage per unit of effort (2)	You (3)	El Slacker (4)	You (5)	El Slacker (6)
1	10	5	7	10	10
2	10	6	8	20	20
3	10	7	9	30	30
4	10	8	10**	40	40
5	10	9	11	50	50
6	10	10**	12	60	60
7	10	11	13	70	70

a. Indicate how much effort each of you will provide. You would each adjust your effort margin so as to equate your disutility of effort to your wage. For you, this implies 6 units of effort, since at that point your disutility of effort just equals your wage. Prior to that, your disutility of effort is less than the pay you would receive for more effort, so it pays to exert more effort. After that point, your disutility of effort exceeds the pay you would receive for more effort, so it does not pay to exert more effort. For El Slacker, the optimal effort is 4 units, for the same reasons. The optimal efforts are denoted by ** in the table.

b. Indicate the pay that each of you will receive. Your pay under the piece-rate system would be $60, since you put forth 6 units of effort to produce 6 units of output for which you were paid $10 per unit of output. El Slacker's pay would be $40 since he put forth 4 units of effort to produce 4 units of output for which he was paid $10 per unit of output.

c. What is the total value of output produced? The total value of output produced is $100, based on $60 from you and $40 from El Slacker.

d. Assume your employer shifts from such a piece-rate system to a team-based compensation system where each of you share equally (i.e., 1/N, or 1/2) in the value of the output produced. What is the pay that each of you would receive? Each of you would receive 1/2 of the total output or $50.

e. Assume that if El Slacker reduces his effort under the team-based pay system he will be fired, as will you if you reduce your effort below what *he* provided. What is the level of effort that each of you will provide, and why? What is the total output? Since El Slacker will be fired if he reduces his effort, his effort will be the same, and he will still produce $40 of output. You, however, are out of equilibrium since you are exerting 6 units of effort to produce 6 units of output, but you are now receiving only $50, not $60 as before. This occurs because you have to share the value of your additional output with El Slacker. You now have an incentive to produce only as much as El Slacker (i.e., $40), because if you produce more you receive only one-half of the value of every additional unit of output you produce ($10). You cannot produce below his level of output or you will be fired. Output now drops to a total of $80.

Deferred wages may discourage "bad" workers ("lemons") from applying for such jobs, since information on their productivity will be revealed over time. This gets around the asymmetric information problem emanating from the fact that potential employees have better information than firms about some factors, such as their motivation, commitment, and willingness to work hard. To the extent that deferred wages have positive incentive effects, this can lead to higher productivity and, hence, higher expected lifetime wages.

Public sector employers may prefer deferred wages because this arrangement passes costs to future generations of taxpayers, the only check being the willingness of the future generations to honour these commitments. The deferred compensation may come in the form of more-liberal pension benefits or greater job security, so that one's *expected* wage (i.e., wage times the probability of receiving the wage) is higher. Deferred wages may also be legitimately needed more in the public than private sector to the extent that honesty is more important in the public sector and that monitoring and the measurement of current output is more difficult.

Deferred wages may also be preferred by employees, since these facilitate the synchronization of income and expenditures over the life cycle. That is, the shortfall of wages below productivity for junior workers can be regarded as a form of forced savings, paid out later in the form of wages in excess of productivity in later years. Whether this corresponds to their years of greatest expenditure needs, and whether saving in the form of deferred wages is better than private saving through capital markets, is an open question. Deferred wages may also correspond to a sense of equity and fairness to employees so that they receive wage increases commensurate with seniority, even if their productivity does not increase, or even declines. As well, if deferred wages have positive efficiency effects, employees may share in those gains by having higher wages over their life cycle. Employees may also regard deferred wages as a form of forced saving, or derive satisfaction from anticipating future consumption, evidence of which is found in Loewenstein and Sicherman (1991).

Clearly, there are a variety of possible rationales for deferred wages that confer benefits on both employers and employees. Even when the initial benefits would go largely to employers (e.g., increased work incentives, reduced monitoring costs, reduced unwanted turnover), such benefits would provide the means for them to compensate employees for any adverse effects of deferred wages. Employees could be compensated in the form of a higher lifetime wage profile and more job security. As mentioned previously, employees may also benefit from the lifetime employment aspects of the contract market, from the periodic rather than everyday monitoring, from the due process and seniority rules that provide security ensuring that deferred wages are paid, from the possible synchronizing of income and expenditures, and from the sense of equity and fairness that may be associated with wages based on seniority.

Rationale for Mandatory Retirement

To Enable Deferred Wages

While there clearly can be efficiency and equity reasons for deferred wages to exist, such a contractual arrangement requires a termination date in order to exist. Otherwise, employers run the risk of paying wages in excess of productivity for an indefinite period (as illustrated in Figure 13.1(a)). In such circumstances, a contractual arrangement involving deferred wages could not persist.

Lazear (1979) argues that **mandatory retirement** provides the termination date for contractual arrangements with deferred wages, and he provides empirical evidence indicating that mandatory retirement provisions are more prevalent in situations of deferred wages. The mandatory retirement date, MR in Figure 13.2, provides an equilibrium condition, enabling the expected present value of the wage stream to be equal to the expected present value of the productivity stream to the firm. Without that termination date to the existing contractual arrangement, it would be difficult or impossible for the deferred wage contract to exist, since the firm would be paying a wage in excess of productivity for an indefinite period. Mandatory retirement is the institutional rule that gives finality to the existing contractual arrangement. Viewed in this light, it is an endogenous institutional feature of labour markets that arises for efficiency reasons to allow deferred compensation systems to exist; it is not an exogenously imposed constraint, as is often perceived.

Figure 13.2 Mandatory Retirement Age

The mandatory retirement age (MR) is such that the present value of the underpayment (i.e., the area below the VMP line and the wage line) is equal to the present value of the overpayment (i.e., the area below the wage line and above the VPM line) in the latter period.

As discussed in the earlier chapter on retirement, the phrase "mandatory retirement" is somewhat of a misnomer, since it does not mean that the person is required to retire from the *labour force*. It means that the existing contractual arrangement is now terminated, and the employee must renegotiate an alternative arrangement with another employer or with the same employer (the latter being possible under compulsory but not automatic retirement). Presumably, any new arrangement would be for a wage commensurate with the worker's productivity, and this may involve a substantial wage drop, since deferred wages no longer would be paid. The wage drop need not reflect a decline of productivity with age; rather, it occurs because deferred wages are in excess of productivity for senior employees (in return for wages being below productivity in their early years with the company). In fact, this emphasizes that mandatory retirement need not exist because productivity (correctly or incorrectly) is perceived to decline with age. The appropriate response to such a phenomenon, if it existed, would be wage reductions rather than the requirement that the individual leave the job. Mandatory retirement could be an efficient compensation rule even if productivity continues to increase throughout a worker's working life (as it in fact does in the diagram).

Other Possible Rationales for Mandatory Retirement

In addition to enabling a deferred wage compensation system, other possible rationales may exist for mandatory retirement. It may facilitate work sharing by opening up promotion and employment opportunities for younger workers. While this may be true in particular firms and industries, as indicated in our previous discussion of work sharing, caution should be used in applying this argument to the economy as a whole so as to avoid the lump-of-labour fallacy. That is, there need not be a fixed number of jobs in the economy so that the job held by an older worker would mean that a younger worker would not have a job. The younger worker may not have that *particular job,* but by working longer, the older worker may be generating other jobs through increased consumption expenditures and by affecting wage levels.

Mandatory retirement may also create a greater degree of certainty about when an employee will retire from a particular job. For employers, this may facilitate planning for new staffing requirements, pension obligations, and medical and health expenditures, the last of which can be quite high for older workers. For workers, the advent of mandatory retirement may encourage pre-retirement planning and preparation of eventual retirement, preparation they may postpone indefinitely if the retirement date were not fixed. Retirement may also be facilitated by the fact that pensions, as a form of deferred compensation, are prominent in situations of mandatory retirement.

Mandatory retirement also reduces the need for monitoring and evaluating older workers, and it enables them to "retire with dignity," since they are retiring because of a common retirement rule and not because they are singled out for incompetence. Less productive workers can be "carried" to the retirement age by employers or co-workers, because that may be a short period and the departure is known with certainty. In contrast, without mandatory retirement, the performance of older workers will have to be monitored and evaluated, and dismissals may occur more frequently.

Arguments against Mandatory Retirement

The arguments against mandatory retirement tend to rest on human rights issues, with mandatory retirement being regarded as a form of age discrimination (see Exhibit 13.9). The appearance of age discrimination is further enhanced by the fact that employment standards or human rights legislation often has an age limit, not covering workers who are 65 years of age and older. The rationale for this age limit beyond which protection does not apply is to accommodate mandatory retirement, but by doing so it effectively precludes protection from age discrimination for persons beyond age 65. This apparent sanctioning of mandatory retirement provisions certainly makes the provisions look like a form of age discrimination. Stereotypes that give rise to discrimination are likely to be as prominent against older workers as against women, racial groups, or other visible minorities.

EXHIBIT 13.9

Do Age Discrimination Laws Facilitate Deferred Compensation Even Though They Ban Mandatory Retirement?

When mandatory retirement is banned, it is done through age discrimination legislation that prohibits mandatory retirement. If mandatory retirement exists in part to facilitate deferred compensation schemes (by providing a termination date to such arrangements, as those discussed in the text) this would suggest that age discrimination laws, by prohibiting mandatory retirement, would reduce the extent of deferred compensation schemes. This can be termed a "banning of mandatory retirement" effect, whereby banning mandatory retirement reduces the likelihood of deferred compensation.

Neumark and Stock (1999), however, indicate that age discrimination laws may provide a degree of employment security and protection to older workers who may be receiving deferred wages. They may protect older workers from employers who may behave opportunistically and lay off or fire workers when they begin to receive their deferred wage (whereby their wage begins to exceed their productivity). By providing this "protection effect," age discrimination laws may facilitate deferred wages even though they ban mandatory retirement. Neumark and Stock suggest that the age discrimination "protection" effect that would facilitate deferred wages is likely to dominate the "banning of mandatory retirement" effect that would discourage deferred wages, because firms could use subsidy and penalty features of their pension plans to substitute for mandatory retirement. That is, they could reduce pension benefits for those who carried on working if mandatory retirement were banned, and this would discourage continued employment with the firm.

Neumark and Stock exploit the cross-section variation in the extent of age discrimination legislation across different states in the United States to estimate the impact of age discrimination legislation on deferred compensation. They find that age discrimination legislation facilitated deferred compensation even though it banned mandatory retirement. In essence, the positive effect of age discrimination legislation in "protecting" deferred wages for older employees dominated the negative "banning of mandatory retirement" effect on deferred wages.

It is possible, however, to have age discrimination legislation and still allow mandatory retirement (e.g., to exempt it as not constituting age discrimination if, for example, there is the protection of a collective agreement and/or an employer pension plan). In such circumstances, deferred wages should be facilitated both by the protection of age discrimination and by the existence of mandatory retirement that terminates the deferred compensation arrangement.

Even if certain rules may be efficient, they may not be socially justifiable if they discriminate against individuals. Thus, even if mandatory retirement creates certainty for employers and employees, and facilitates retirement with dignity, if this occurs at the expense of some who want to continue working and are capable of working it still may be regarded as discriminatory against those individuals.

The abolition of mandatory retirement has also been supported on the grounds of improving the viability of public and private pensions, a growing concern as the aging population puts increasing pressure on pension obligations at the same time as a declining workforce provides fewer persons paying into pension funds. If workers continue to work beyond what was the former retirement age, they will be less of a drain on pensions. Of course, this argument assumes that those who continue to work will not draw full pension income, an assumption that is seldom explicitly stated. In fact, many unions tend to be concerned that banning mandatory retirement is simply a veiled excuse to reduce private and public pension obligations.

A Middle Ground

Given the pros and cons of mandatory retirement, it is not surprising that the debate over banning mandatory retirement is conducted at an emotive level. The real question, however, is, to what extent should legislation ban parties from entering into contractual arrangements (like mandatory retirement) that inhibit their freedom at some time in the future, presumably in return for other benefits, such as job and promotion opportunities when they are younger, pensions when they retire, and the benefits of a deferred compensation scheme? Clearly, legislation sanctions some contracts, like marriage contracts and loan contracts, that can inhibit freedom at certain points in time, presumably because of the other benefits they bring. Yet, the state does forbid other contracts, like indentured service and separate pay or promotion lines for females or racial groups, even if the individuals themselves are willing to enter into such contractual arrangements. Not all contractual arrangements are sanctioned by the state, especially if people can be misinformed or if they can be exploited because of a weak bargaining position.

One possible solution to prevent the worst abuses of mandatory retirement and yet preserve its benefits would be to remove the age ceiling on antidiscrimination legislation but to exempt bona fide collective agreements or employees covered by a bona fide pension plan. This would enable people to enter into arrangements involving mandatory retirement if they had the protection of a union. Presumably the union would be informed of the trade-offs involved, and it would represent the interests of its older workers, because all of its members could expect to become older and subject to any constraints such as mandatory retirement. Exempting employees covered by a bona fide pension plan would ensure that when workers become subject to the mandatory retirement constraint, they would retire with an adequate pension.

Such exemptions, however, would allow mandatory retirement to continue much in its present form, since most workers who are currently subject to mandatory retirement are also protected by a collective agreement and/or a pension plan. However, it would prevent potential abuse by the employer who engages in age discrimination or who requires mandatory retirement but does not provide a pension.

Impact of Banning Mandatory Retirement

In the United States, mandatory retirement was effectively banned through the 1986 amendments to the Age Discrimination in Employment Act, although there were some exemptions, including one for university professors (an exemption that expired in 1994). In Canada, the legal status of mandatory retirement is more complicated but it has, generally, been banned in most jurisdictions (Warman and Worswick 2010).

In the United States, earlier studies had suggested that the banning of mandatory retirement would not have a large effect on the continued employment of older workers, since most wanted to retire at or around the mandatory retirement age. This is, in large part, because penalties in the public and private pension system discourage older workers from continuing on in employment (Burkhauser and Quinn 1983). More-recent evidence from Neumark and Stock (1999, p. 1109) also indicates that banning mandatory retirement had little effect on postponing retirement, although they suggest that this may reflect limitations of their data. On the basis of better data (albeit data limited to only university professors) Ashenfelter and Card (2002) provide evidence suggesting that banning mandatory retirement has had a substantial effect on delaying the retirement of university faculty in the United States, the effect being largest at private research institutions where teaching loads are lowest. Similar effects are found in the University of North Carolina system (Clark and Ghent 2008). Warman and Worswick (2010) found that Canadian university professors were also more likely to continue working in situations where mandatory retirement was banned, with 23 percent likely to continue working until at least age 72. Based on Canadian data for all persons, both Reid (1988) and Shannon and Grierson (2004) found that labour force participation did not change substantially in the two provinces that have banned mandatory retirement—Manitoba and Quebec. Grant and Townsend (2013) find that immigrants are disproportionately likely to be adversely affected by mandatory retirement, because their late entry into the labour market means that they are less likely to accumulate pension benefits and retirement savings.

While research on the effect that banning mandatory retirement will have on the continued employment of older workers is scant (and not in agreement), there is virtually a complete absence of research on the impact that banning retirement will have on other aspects of the employment relationship. On the basis of the theoretical reasons for the existence of mandatory retirement in the first place, Gunderson (1983) outlined the *expected* impact a legislative ban on mandatory retirement would have on various aspects of the employment relationship.

To the extent that deferred compensation is no longer as feasible, the wages of younger workers will rise and the wages of older workers with more seniority will fall, as wage profiles will now have to more-closely approximate productivity profiles (i.e., the profiles will be more like Figure 13.1(b) than 13.1(a)). The wages of older workers may drop quite substantially to compensate for any increase in age-related fringe benefit costs, like medical and disability insurance. Those adjustments, in turn, may bring charges of age discrimination in pay practices. Until such wage adjustments occur, however, older workers may receive substantial "windfall gains" from the abolition of mandatory retirement, as their wages could now exceed their productivity for an indefinite period of time (i.e., beyond **MR** in Figure 13.2).

Not only will the wage profile "tilt" downward toward the productivity profile, but also, the whole productivity profile and wage profile will drop to the extent that productivity was enhanced by the deferred wage system; for example, because of enhanced work incentives and reduced monitoring. New efforts will also be made to restore the deferred wage system in a fashion that does not rely upon mandatory retirement for its existence. For example, periodic bonuses may be more prominent. If deferred wages are continued, employee voluntary buyouts or "golden handshakes" may become more prominent to encourage voluntary retirement. Actuarial reductions in pension benefits may also be used to encourage people to voluntarily retire. Pensions themselves may become less prominent to the extent that they were a part of the deferred compensation scheme.

Monitoring and evaluation of workers will likely increase to the extent that it is less feasible to use periodic evaluations based upon past performance. In addition, it will be more necessary to detect early signals of performance in younger workers and to provide documentation in the case of dismissals or wage reduction of older workers so as to avoid age discrimination charges.

The employment and promotion opportunities of younger workers may be reduced in particular jobs when older workers continue past the usual retirement age. The extent to which other job opportunities may open up because of the spending activities of those who remain in the workforce, or because of their effect on wage levels, is an empirical unknown. To the extent that deferred wages are not as prominent, promotion will take on a different meaning, since it will not mean promotion to receive the deferred wage. If wages are now equal to the worker's value of marginal product at each and every stage of the life cycle, then promotion by itself will be less important.

Training will decrease to the extent that deferred wages can no longer exist to discourage the unwanted turnover of those who receive company-specific training. However, training may increase to the extent that the expected benefit period, without mandatory retirement, is longer. Forecasting and planning will be more difficult, given the greater uncertainty about retirement ages.

Jobs may be redesigned to accommodate the older workers who stay, but they may also be designed to encourage them to leave. Some dismissals of older workers who otherwise may have been "carried" to the mandatory retirement age will be inevitable, and this will likely increase the amount of litigation over unjust dismissal cases. Layoffs of older workers may also be more prominent to the extent that seniority declines as a work rule that was coexistent with deferred compensation.

These are meant to be simple illustrations of the sorts of adjustments that may occur if one aspect of the intricate employment relationship is changed; in this case, if mandatory retirement is abolished. The adjustments may be minor if they are going on already in anticipation of mandatory retirement being banned, or if alternative procedures can arise to enable deferred wages, or if workers continue their trend toward earlier retirement. Nevertheless, we do not know if that trend will continue, especially as the proportion of the white-collar workforce grows, as retirement plans have more lead time to change, as larger numbers of co-workers postpone retirement, and if pensions dissipate. In addition, Canadian public pension plans do not have a tax-back feature as exists in the United States, so Canadian workers may be more prone to postpone retirement than are their American counterparts.

Clearly, the current debate over the pros and cons of banning mandatory retirement is not one that is likely to be resolved easily, and if it is resolved in favour of banning mandatory retirement, a number of repercussions are likely to follow. It is hoped that the application of some basic principles of economics can narrow the focus of the debate, though it may also make the issues more complicated than they appear at first glance. At the very least, these principles should provide us with information on the repercussions of a policy change and the alternative and complementary policies that may be desirable.

Summary

- Considerable new work is occurring in labour economics (often under the rubric of the "new economics of personnel") trying to explain the economic rationale that may lie behind the existence of various human resource and workplace practices within the internal labour markets of firms. Such practices at first glance often appear inefficient, but they may have a more complex efficiency rationale given uncertainty, monitoring costs, and information asymmetries.

- Examples of such practices discussed in the chapter include the following:
  - Efficiency wages or wage premiums that "pay for themselves"

  - Superstar salaries that are exorbitant

  - Egalitarian or compressed internal wage structures designed to encourage co-operation, especially among work teams

  - External compared to internal promotions from within the organization

  - The free-riding or 1/N problem that exists in partnerships, workgroups, and workplace teams

  - Up-or-out rules (including academic tenure at universities) under which employees are evaluated and then either promoted or terminated

  - Raiding and offer matching

  - Performance pay and piece rates (with an application to fee-for-service compensation schemes in medical practices)

  - Executive compensation systems that seem to resemble tournament prizes with large rewards for the winner

  - Deferred compensation systems where employees tend to be underpaid when younger and overpaid relative to their productivity when older

  - Mandatory retirement

- The theoretical framework underlying much of this work is agency theory, dealing with how to design efficient explicit or implicit contracts between the principal (employer) and the agent (employee or their representatives) when there are incentives to cheat (largely arising from uncertainty), monitoring costs, and information asymmetries. The contractual arrangements are often self-enforcing in the sense that they are designed to elicit the private information of the parties, providing them an incentive to engage in "truth telling" that improves market efficiency.

- Unfortunately, much of the work in this area has remained at the theoretical level, since there are few data sets linking individual employees to such practices, and when they exist they are often not publicly available (and, hence, not capable of being replicated) or they are from a single large organization, which raises the issue of generalizability and external validity. However, this is changing, and empirical research in this area, termed "insider econometrics," is a new frontier in labour economics.

Keywords

1/N problem	optimal degree of inequality
asymmetric information	principal-agent theory
efficient contract	raiding
executive compensation	salaries as tournament prizes
external promotion	stock options
implicit contracts	superstar
internal labour markets	teamwork
internal promotion	tenure
mandatory retirement	up-or-out rules
monitoring costs	winner's curse
offer-matching	
optimal compensation system	

Review Questions

1. Discuss the pros and cons of efficiency wages as opposed to deferred compensation as compensation systems to deter shirking and encourage work effort.

2. What should happen to the pay of superstars if there is technological change or increased globalization that enables the very best to reach a wider audience?

3. Under what circumstances would it be optimal for a firm to have a compressed versus a dispersed wage structure?

4. What is the 1/N or free-rider problem, and how can it be dealt with?

5. What are up-or-out rules, and what are their pros and cons?

6. What is the winner's curse in the case of organizations engaging in offer-matching of raiding organizations?

7. "If deferred compensation prevails and firms face an exogenous, unanticipated permanent reduction in their demand conditions, then they may have a strong incentive to engage in permanent layoffs or even bankruptcy." Discuss.

8. "While there may be advantages to deferred compensation, there are other ways besides mandatory retirement to enable deferred compensation." Discuss.

9. If mandatory retirement exists in part to enable deferred compensation, discuss the implication of banning mandatory retirement for different elements of the personnel function, including compensation policies.

10. "The relevant question is not, are you for or against mandatory retirement? Rather, it is, under what conditions should governments prohibit private parties from entering into arrangements like mandatory retirement?" Discuss.

11. "Any theory of executive compensation must be able to consistently explain two stylized facts—the increase in executive compensation that has occurred relative to average pay, and the higher executive compensation in the United States relative to that in other countries." Discuss.

12. In their analysis of labour markets in professional sports, Rosen and Sanderson (2001, p. F52) indicate, "When and if teachers use the Internet and other media to personally teach millions of students at one time, star teachers will earn at least as much as star athletes. Some writers of elementary textbooks are rumoured to approach star royalty status already." Discuss how this follows, based on the economics of superstars. As an aside, they were not referring to royalties from this textbook, which are closer to the minimum wage …

13. Should professors be paid piece rates on the basis of the number of articles or books they publish and the number of students they teach?

Problems

1. On the basis of the deferred wage profile of Figure 13.1, how would the analysis change if productivity began to decline after a certain age? Draw the new figures.

2. On the basis of the mandatory retirement portrayal of Figure 13.2, what would happen to the wage and productivity profiles if mandatory retirement were banned? Draw the new figures.

3. You are the human resource manager at a large organization. Each worker in your organization produces output valued at $10 per hour (i.e., VMP = $10). You want to deter shirking and turnover by paying a deferred wage profile where the hourly wage is $W = 2/3T$, where T is the tenure, or length of time that the person remains with the firm (i.e., after 10 years the person would earn $W = 2/3(10)$ or $6.67 per hour).

   a. Draw the diagram of the deferred wage profile.

   b. Could this profile persist?

   c. Solve for the breakeven point, or length of time the person would have to stay with the firm so that her wage would just equal their productivity.

   d. Determine the length of time she would have to stay with the firm for her expected wage over that period to just equal her expected productivity (assume no discounting so that a dollar today is the same as a dollar in the future).

   e. If the vast majority of the people start working with the firm at age 35, what mandatory retirement age would you pick to provide a termination date to that contractual arrangement?

   f. If a positive discount rate were assumed, what would that do to the mandatory retirement age?

   g. If you behaved in a short-run, opportunistic fashion and terminated all of your employees at the breakeven point, what would happen to that profile?

   h. If you had to downsize but wanted to maintain your reputation, you might want to offer an early retirement buyout package equal to the magnitude of the deferred compensation. What would that magnitude be for someone who has been at the firm for 15 years (assume 2000 working hours in a year or 50 weeks at 40 hours per week).

   i. Assume that you had unjustly dismissed an employee two years prior to his mandatory retirement age. An arbitrator deemed that you must compensate that employee for wage loss from the fact that if he had to obtain a job elsewhere it would be only at a wage equal to his value of marginal product at another firm (assumed equal to his VMP with your firm). Calculate the amount of that arbitration award.

   j. Assume that you have 10 workers, all of whom started at the same age, 35 years, and are now at the breakeven point in terms of how long they have been employed in your organization. You are a real hard-hearted person and you are trying to determine whether you should declare bankruptcy given your aging (and more expensive) workforce. You know that you can open up a new organization elsewhere and pay people the value of their marginal product. However, there are costs associated with going bankrupt and opening elsewhere. What is the magnitude of those costs that would make you indifferent between going bankrupt and continuing with your existing operation?

4. Outline the pros and cons of the different payment systems that exist for medical doctors, being sure to discuss the incentive effects they create. Who should like which scheme and why (among doctors, patients, and governments)? In your discussion, analyze the following schemes:

   • Fee-for-service with no annual maximum

   • Fee-for-service with an annual maximum

   • Capitation, or fixed salary, based on the number of patients in the doctors' roster

   • Fixed salary independent of the services rendered

5. One of the difficulties of a fee-for-service system is determining the (piece) rates that are to be paid for doctors for the different services performed. In Canada, these fee schedules are set by negotiations between the provincial governments and medical associations. One of the complications is that technological change can alter the amount of time or skill that it takes to perform a particular service. Discuss how this is a typical problem in piece-rate systems.

6. Ferrall, Gregory, and Tholl (1998) perform an econometric analysis of the determinants of the working time of Canadian physicians. They obtain the following results after controlling for the various other factors that determine working time:

   • Physicians who are in solo practice work many more hours than those who work in group practices where they share the returns.

   • Physicians in Quebec (which tends to have the most stringent caps on earnings) work significantly fewer hours than physicians in other provinces.

   • Physicians who work under fee-for-service see more patients but work fewer hours than physicians on salary.

   Are these facts consistent with the predictions of the theory of piece rates and of the 1/N problem presented in this chapter?

PORTRAIT IMAGES ASIA/Shutterstock.com

CHAPTER 14

Unions and Collective Bargaining

LEARNING OBJECTIVES

LO1   Explain the nature of unions and the role they play in the labour market.

LO2   Summarize key measures of union influence in Canada, such as the fraction of workers who are members of a union or covered by a collective agreement, and how these measures compare to those in other countries.

LO3   Describe the legal framework governing unions and collective bargaining, and how it has evolved.

LO4   Use economic models to explain why some workers are more likely to be unionized than others and why unions are more prevalent in some industries, occupations, regions, and countries than in others.

LO5   Describe the key factors that determine union objectives, and the constraints that unions face in trying to achieve their goals.

LO6   Explain and apply economic models that seek to explain how wages and employment are determined in unionized enterprises.

MAIN QUESTIONS

- What fraction of Canadian workers are members of unions? How has this evolved over time? How does this differ from other countries?

- Which types of workers are most likely to be covered by union contracts?

- What factors determine the level of unionization in the labour market?

- What motives underlie union behaviour? How, for example, do unions evaluate the trade-off between higher wages and improved job security?

- Can union behaviour be well represented by a purely economic model?

- How do firms and unions interact in the setting of employment and wages?

- Can economic theory account for apparently inefficient union practices like "featherbedding" and other restrictions placed on firm employment decisions?

- How can we incorporate "bargaining power" into a model of firm–union interaction?

Unions are collective organizations whose primary objective is to improve the well-being of their members. In Canada, this objective is met primarily through **collective bargaining** with the employer. The outcome of this process is a collective agreement specifying wages; non-wage benefits, such as those relating to pensions, vacation time, and health and medical expenses; and aspects of the employment relation, such as procedures relating to hiring, promotion, dismissal, layoffs, overtime work, and the handling of grievances.

There are two basic types of unions. **Craft unions** represent workers in a particular trade or occupation; examples are found in the construction, printing, and longshoring trades. **Industrial unions** represent all the workers in a particular industry regardless of occupation or skill; examples are found in the automobile, steel, and forest industries. Some unions combine elements of both types.

In addition to their collective bargaining activities, unions play a role in social and political affairs. Close ties between unions and social democratic political parties are common, especially in Western Europe. In Canada, the union movement provides financial and other support for the New Democratic Party. Unions also seek to influence the government in power, and accordingly have been involved in various forms of consultation and collaboration with governments and, in some cases, representatives of the business community. Although these and other political and social aspects of unions are important and deserve study, the major function of Canadian unions is to represent their members' interests in collective bargaining with employers, and it is this aspect of unions that is studied here.

This chapter begins with a discussion of the nature and significance of unions and collective bargaining in Canada. The extent of unionization in the labour force, how this has changed over time, how it compares with other countries, and the legal framework governing unionization and collective bargaining are described. Next, the determinants of the extent and incidence of unionization in the economy are examined; what factors result in some workers being represented by a union while other workers remain unorganized?

We then turn to the behavioural implications of unionization and collective bargaining. In order to understand the consequences of collective bargaining, we begin by examining union objectives and the constraints unions face in attempting to achieve those objectives. Then, we examine the firm's objectives and constraints and how the two parties interact to determine collective bargaining outcomes.

The following chapter is devoted to understanding the economic consequences of unions. Economists have paid particular attention to the impacts of unions on the wage structure, reflecting on the importance of wages for resource allocation, the living standards of working Canadians, and the impact of unions on wage inequality. However, as is emphasized in the next chapter, unions influence numerous labour market and economic outcomes in addition to their impacts on the wage structure.

LO1   Unions and Collective Bargaining in Canada

For a significant fraction of the Canadian labour force, wages and other conditions of employment are determined by collective bargaining. Table 14.1 provides several measures of the quantitative significance of unions in the labour market. Viewed over time, an upward trend is evident until the 1980s, with a modest decline since that time. **Union membership** as a proportion of the civilian labour force increased from about 9 percent in 1920 to about 24 percent in 2015. Union membership as a proportion of (civilian) nonagricultural paid workers—a measure that excludes from consideration the self-employed and those employed in agriculture—increased from 16 to 31 percent over the same period.

TABLE 14.1	Union Membership and Union Density in Canada, 1920–2015		
Year	Union Membership (000s)	Union Membership as a Percentage of Civilian Labour Force	Union Membership as a Percentage of Nonagricultural Paid Workers
1920	374	9.4	16.0
1925	271	7.6	14.4
1930	322	7.9	13.9
1935	281	6.4	14.5
1940	362	7.9	16.3
1945	711	15.7	24.2
1951*	1029	19.7	28.4
1955	1268	23.6	33.7
1960	1459	23.5	32.3
1965	1589	23.2	29.7
1970	2173	27.2	33.6
1975	2884	29.9	35.6
1980	3397	29.2	35.7
1985	3666	28.3	36.4
1990	4031	28.5	34.5
1995	4003	27.0	34.3
2000	4058	26.0	32.2
2005	4381	25.5	30.7
2010	4645	25.3	30.8
2015	4524	23.6	30.6

*The survey was not conducted in 1950.

SOURCE: Table 1: Union Membership in Canada, 2000–2010, published in *Labour Organizations in Canada 2015,* http://www.labour.gc.ca/eng/resources/info/publications/union_labour/union_coverage.shtml. Permission granted by the Ministry of Labour, 2015. Data for 2015 also taken from Statistics Canada, *Labour Force Survey,* January 2015.

The influence of unions may extend further than is suggested by these measures of the extent of union organization or **union density**. For example, in many private sector firms the extent of unionization is higher among non-office than among office employees. The wages and benefits negotiated for production workers may set a standard for non-union office employees in the same establishment. More generally, union agreements may influence the wages and working conditions of unorganized workers in the same industry, urban area, or region. As discussed below, in some countries the wages and working conditions in union agreements are extended to non-union workers in the same industry or sector.

LO3   The Legal Framework

Union representation and collective bargaining in Canada are regulated by an elaborate legal framework. The evolution of this framework reflects the changing social attitudes toward the role of unions and collective bargaining in Canadian society, and has contributed to the changes in the extent of union organization evident in Table 14.1. In general terms, the law with respect to collective bargaining in Canada has passed through three main phases. In the first phase, the period mostly prior to Confederation, the law discouraged collective bargaining. Judges interpreted the common law to hold that collective action by employees constituted a criminal conspiracy. There were also other criminal and civil constraints on both individual and group action by workers. In the second phase, which began in the 1870s, the law was "neutral" with respect to collective bargaining. In particular, the Trade Unions Act of 1872, amendments to criminal law, and other legislative actions removed many of the restrictions on union formation and the collective withdrawal of labour. However, the law did not encourage or facilitate unionization. This neutral stance lasted in Canada until the enactment in 1944 of the Wartime Labour Relations Regulations, Order-in-Council P.C. 1003, after which labour law facilitated union formation and, in turn, encouraged the spread of collective bargaining. P.C. 1003, which was partly modelled on the National Labor Relations Act (the Wagner Act) of 1935 in the United States, provided most private sector employees with the right to union representation and collective bargaining, established certification procedures, provided a code of unfair labour practices primarily intended to prevent employers from interfering with employees' right to union representation, and established a labour relations board to administer the law. Thus, in the post–World War II period, legislation facilitated collective bargaining.

These three phases in the history of collective bargaining applied primarily to the private sector. With the passage of the Public Service Staff Relations Act (PSSRA) in 1967 at the federal level and similar acts at provincial levels, governments encouraged collective bargaining and union formation in the public sector.

The Canadian labour relations policy that emerged in the 1940s had the following central features:

1. Workers who met the statutory definition of employee had the right to join and form unions.
2. Collective bargaining rights were protected under unfair labour practices legislation, which prohibited acts by both employers and unions to discourage or interfere with the employees' prerogative to bargain collectively.
3. A system of defining appropriate bargaining units and certifying bargaining representatives was established.
4. Once certified, the union became the exclusive bargaining representative of all employees in the bargaining unit.
5. Unions and employers were required to bargain in good faith.
6. These rights and obligations were administered and enforced usually by a labour relations board, but, in some cases, in court.

Another important aspect of the legal framework is the division of powers between the federal and provincial governments over labour legislation. The Constitution Act, 1867, has been interpreted by the courts as implying that jurisdiction over labour relations matters rests primarily with the provinces. Federal jurisdiction is limited to about 10 percent of the labour force—federal public servants; employees of federal Crown corporations; those employed in rail, air, shipping, and truck transportation; banks; broadcasting; uranium mines; and grain elevators.

LO2   Factors Influencing Union Growth and Incidence

Table 14.1 reveals that during the past nine decades, union growth in Canada has been substantial but erratic. In some periods, union membership declined in absolute terms (1920–1935, 1990–1995), in others it increased absolutely but declined relative to the labour force (1955–1965, 1975–2015), while in others union membership grew substantially more rapidly than the labour force (1965–1975, 1940–1950). The causes of union growth, both the upward trend and the variations around the trend, have long been a subject of scholarly research and debate. There are also significant cross-sectional differences in the extent of unionization—across countries, industries, regions, and occupations—which call for an explanation.

Table 14.2 shows two measures of the extent of union organization in the economy in 1980 and 2010, in several OECD countries. Union density—defined in this table as union membership as a percentage of paid (wage and salary) workers—in Canada is substantially higher than in France, Japan, or the United States, but much lower than in the Scandinavian countries (Denmark and Sweden). Also evident is the general tendency for union density to decline over the period in most advanced economies, although the magnitude of the decline differs substantially across countries. Canadian behaviour falls into a middle category, in terms of both the level of union density and the relative stability over the period. The divergent patterns displayed by Canada and the United States are particularly striking and are discussed in Exhibit 14.1.

TABLE 14.2	UNION DENSITY AND COLLECTIVE AGREEMENT COVERAGE IN SELECTED OECD COUNTRIES			
	Union Membership as a Percentage of Paid Workers		Collective Agreement Coverage as a Percentage of Paid Workers	
	1980	2010	1980	2010
Australia	50	18	84	58
Canada	34	27	37	29
Denmark	79	67	82	83
France	20	8	70	98
Germany	35	19	85	60
Italy	50	36	80	80
Japan	31	18	31	18
Netherlands	35	19	77	90
New Zealand	69	21	70	16
Sweden	78	69	88	88
United Kingdom	52	27	69	31
United States	22	12	25	13

SOURCE: J. Visser, ICTWSS Data base, version 5.0. Amsterdam: Amsterdam Institute for Advanced Labour Studies AIAS, October 2015. Open access database at www.uva-aias.net/208.

EXHIBIT 14.1

The Divergence of Unionization between Canada and the United States

As illustrated in Figure 14.1, Canada and the United States displayed similar patterns of union growth from the early 1900s until the mid-1950s. Since that time, trends in unionization have diverged sharply, with union density declining steadily in the United States, but growing in Canada until the mid-1980s and subsequently declining modestly. As a consequence, a huge intercountry differential has emerged in the extent of union coverage so that since the mid-1980s the fraction of the Canadian labour force represented by unions has been at least double that of the United States.

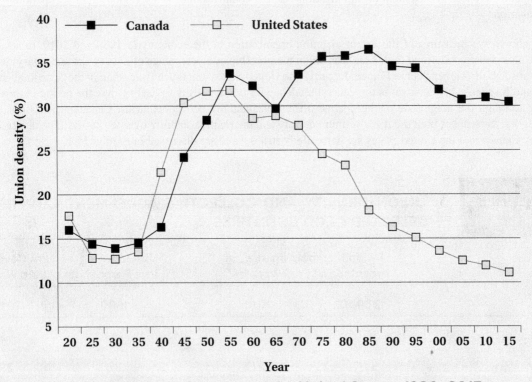

Figure 14.1 Union Density in Canada and the United States, 1920–2015

Union density is defined here as union membership as a percentage of nonagricultural paid workers. Union density rates for Canada and the United States are plotted at five-year intervals over the period since 1920. Union growth followed a similar pattern in the two countries from 1920 to the mid-1960s, after which time there has been a substantial divergence.

SOURCES: Human Resources and Social Development Canada, Directory of Labour Organizations in Canada, various issues; Union Membership and Coverage Database, www.unionstats.com.

A number of explanations have been advanced for the dramatic decline in union strength in the United States. Perhaps the most common explanation has to do with the changing structure of the economy and labour force. Specifically, most of the employment changes that have occurred in recent decades—away from manufacturing and toward services, away from blue-collar and toward white-collar, away from male and full-time and toward female and part-time, away from large firms and toward small firms—represent declines in the relative importance of sectors that traditionally have been highly unionized, and increases in the relative importance of sectors that traditionally had low union density. Thus, if union density remained constant in each sector, or for each type of worker, the economy-wide extent of unionization would decline due to these structural shifts.

Another explanation involves changes in the U.S. legal regime (the laws, their interpretation, and their administration and enforcement) relating to unions and collective bargaining during the post–World War II period. A related view is that the decline in U.S. unionization can largely be attributed to the rise in management opposition, both legal and illegal, to unions. Increased management opposition to unions may be due to changes in the legal regime, a more competitive economic environment, and a substantial union–non-union wage differential.

Another hypothesis is that there has been a reduction in the desire for collective representation because of the growth of substitute services. Governments have gradually provided more of the employment protection and non-wage benefits that were originally important factors underlying workers' desire for union coverage. In addition, employers have become increasingly sophisticated in their human resource practices and now provide services (e.g., grievance procedures) that workers previously received only in unionized firms.

A final hypothesis is that there has been, in the United States, a reduction in public sympathy toward unions and a reduction in workers' desire for collective representation.

Some evidence supporting each of these explanations has been put forward. However, beginning with Weiler (1983), the value of adopting a comparative Canada–U.S. perspective has increasingly been recognized. In particular, the many similarities between the economies of the two countries and their industrial relations systems results in a "natural experiment," thus, perhaps allowing some explanations of the decline in U.S. union strength to be rejected because they cannot account for the observed behaviour in Canada.

Many of the structural changes described above (rise in service sector, female, part-time, and white-collar employment) also occurred in Canada. Thus, it appears unlikely that the "structuralist" hypothesis can account for the behaviour of union density in both countries. Using comparable microdata on union incidence in the two countries at a point in time (December 1984), Riddell (1993) concludes that structural differences account for about 15 percent of the intercountry differential in union coverage; 85 percent is attributed to the fact that a Canadian worker with given characteristics is much more likely to be covered by a collective agreement than a U.S. worker with the same characteristics. The most important structural difference is the greater extent of public sector employment in Canada, which accounted in 1984 for about 7 percent of the unionization gap. (Public sector workers are much more likely to be unionized in both countries.) Similarly, analysis of changes over time by Riddell and Riddell (2004) concludes that structural changes in the economy account for little of the observed change in unionization during the 1980s and 1990s in either Canada or the United States (see Exhibit 14.2).

Differences in public support for unions also do not appear to be a contributing factor. Both Riddell (1993) and Lipset and Meltz (2004) show that social attitudes toward unions, as measured by public opinion polls, are not more favourable in Canada. In addition, the impact of unions on wages in the private sector is similar in the two countries. Thus, these hypotheses do not seem capable of explaining the observed behaviour in both societies. Equally unlikely is the "growth of union substitutes" view; Canadian governments have gone further than their U.S. counterparts in providing social and employment security.

These findings suggest that differences between Canada and the United States in the legal regime governing unions and collective bargaining may be able to explain the decline in the U.S. union movement and the divergent patterns of union growth in the two countries. Differences in such areas as certification and decertification procedures, bankruptcy and succession rights, first-contract negotiation, and union security arrangements have been argued to be factors contributing to the intercountry differential in union coverage.

A closely related factor is the greater extent of management opposition to unions in the United States in the form of legal and illegal practices to discourage union organization. U.S. laws allow employers more opportunities to oppose union formation, and stricter and more rapid enforcement of such laws in Canada result in lower incidence of illegal practices to discourage unionization.

Of course, laws regulating collective bargaining—and the administration and enforcement of such laws—do not operate in a vacuum. In a democracy the legal regime reflects the underlying social and political values of citizens. Scholars such as Lipset and Meltz (2004) have argued that Canadians' social and political values are relatively more collectivist and social democratic in nature than those of Americans, whose values are relatively more individualistic and free market oriented in nature. As a consequence, Canadians elect governments that are more supportive of unions than do Americans.

This observation fits with international experience (see Table 14.2). Countries with a strong social democratic tradition, such as the Scandinavian countries, are extensively unionized while countries with a strong individualistic tradition, such as the United States, have low unionization. Canada lies between the extremes of Scandinavia and the United States in terms of its social and political values, and in the importance of unions in the economy. The principal difficulty with this argument, which relies on deep-seated and long-lasting value differences between Canada and the United States, is that union density has not always been higher north of the 49th parallel (see Figure 14.1). Lipset and Meltz (2004) and Godard (2009) argue that the period during which U.S. unionization exceeded that in Canada, roughly from the mid-1930s to the mid-1950s, was an anomaly. According to this view, the extent of unionization in the U.S. economy subsequently returned to a level that reflects the underlying social and political values of Americans.

EXHIBIT 14.2

Round up the Usual Suspects: What Caused the Recent Decline in Unionization in Canada?

Although union density rates in Canada and the United States have diverged substantially since the 1960s (see Exhibit 14.1), the recent trend in the two countries has been similar—downward (see Figure 14.1 and Table 14.1). What are the principal causes of this recent decline in Canadian union strength?

Many of the "usual suspects" are summarized in Exhibit 14.1. Recent research provides some evidence about the relative importance of these various explanations.

Riddell and Riddell (2004) use data on individual workers in 1984 and 1998 to investigate the contributions of structural changes in the economy and labour force, such as the relative shift from manufacturing to services, the more rapid growth in part-time than full-time work, the rise in female labour force participation, and shifts in the industrial and occupational composition of employment. They find that very little of the recent decline in union coverage in Canada can be attributed to such structural changes. Instead, almost all the decline in union coverage can be attributed to a fall in the *likelihood that a worker with a given set of characteristics will be unionized.* See the Worked Example in this chapter for an illustration of such calculations. This evidence indicates that we need to look at other explanations for the recent drop in union strength.

One hypothesis involves the recent trend toward legislation believed to deter unionization. In particular, an increasing number of provincial governments have instituted mandatory voting as the union certification procedure. As has traditionally been the case in the United States, many unions in Canada must now win a secret ballot election to be certified as the exclusive bargaining agent of the proposed bargaining unit. This contrasts dramatically with the traditional "automatic certification" or "card check" procedure in Canada, in which unions simply had to obtain signatures of a sufficient proportion of the proposed bargaining unit to achieve certification. Before the 1980s, only one province, Nova Scotia, had mandatory voting for union certification. Since the late 1980s, however, an additional six provinces—Alberta, British Columbia, Manitoba, Newfoundland, Ontario and Saskatchewan—introduced such laws, although in two cases (Manitoba and Newfoundland) these changes were subsequently reversed. Since 2012, mandatory voting exists in five provinces, including the heavily populated provinces of Alberta, B.C., and Ontario.

What is the evidence on the impact of this legislation on unionization? Martinello (2000) conducts a study using data from Ontario over the period 1987–1998 and finds that, overall, union-organizing activity and union-organizing success rates were higher under the legislation introduced by the NDP regime of Bob Rae (which included automatic certification procedures) than under the legislation introduced by Mike Harris's Progressive Conservative regime (which required secret ballot elections for certification). Johnson (2002b) uses the variation over time and across provinces to identify the effect of mandatory voting and finds that a mandatory voting regime reduces union organizing success rates by 9 percentage points. Perhaps the most striking evidence comes from British Columbia, which altered legal regimes twice—replacing the card-signing system with mandatory voting in 1984 and then returning to automatic certification based on card signing in 1993. Riddell (2004) analyzes the consequences of these "before-after-before" changes in certification procedures and concludes that introduction of mandatory voting resulted in an approximately 20 percent decline in certification success rates.

Why should mandatory voting deter unionization? One reason could be the absence of peer pressure from union organizers and pro-union co-workers. Under a card-signing system, such pressure is likely to be considerably greater relative to a secret ballot election in which no one can observe the vote cast by any one individual. A second factor revolves around management opposition to the organizing drive. Mandatory elections provide employers with the opportunity to try to deter workers from voting in favour of union representation, an opportunity that is not or is less available in a card-check system. Evidence from the United States (see Flanagan, 2005, for a review) and Canada indicates that management opposition (both legal and illegal) influences the outcome of union organizing drives. In his analysis of the B.C. experience over the period 1978–1998 (which included two card-signing regimes and one mandatory voting regime), Riddell (2004) found that management opposition as measured by unfair labour practices was much more effective in the voting regime than in the card-signing regimes. Subsequent analysis of the experience in Ontario and B.C. by Campolieti, Riddell, and Slinn (2007) concludes that time delays between application and voting are correlated with management opposition, as well as being associated with substantial declines in the probability of union success.

Hence, empirical evidence indicates that legislative changes (in particular the introduction of mandatory voting in union certification procedures) and management opposition have contributed to the recent decline of unions in Canada.

The second measure of unionization is **collective agreement coverage**—the percentage of paid workers whose wages and working conditions are covered by a collective agreement. In countries such as Canada, Japan, the UK, and the United States, most bargaining takes place between an individual employer and union, and the collective agreements reached do not, generally, cover other workers. In contrast, centralized bargaining at the level of the industry, sector, or entire economy is common in many European countries and Australia. In addition, agreements reached between unions and employers are often extended to cover non-union workers in related firms and sectors. In these circumstances, there may be a substantial difference between union membership and collective agreement coverage. The extreme case is that of France, where union membership had fallen to 8 percent in 2010, yet 98 percent of wage and salary workers were covered by collective agreements! On the basis of a comparison of union density, one might have concluded that unions play a much smaller role in the French economy than in Canada (union density of 8 percent in France as against 27 percent in Canada) but the data on collective agreement coverage indicates that this is unlikely to be the case. More generally, collective agreement coverage in Canada is much lower than in most of these OECD countries, and exceeds only that of Japan, New Zealand, and the United States.

Canadian labour legislation provides that, once certified, the union is the exclusive bargaining representative for all employees in the bargaining unit, whether or not they are union members. Because some members of the bargaining unit choose not to join the union (although they are generally required to pay union dues), collective agreement coverage exceeds union membership. However, the gap between membership and coverage is small in Canada, Japan, New Zealand, the UK, and the United States compared to that in Australia and many European countries.

The extent of union organization in Canada varies considerably by province and various individual employee or employer characteristics. Table 14.3 shows some of these variations. Variations by industry and occupation (not shown) are also substantial. Public sector employees are much more likely to be unionized than workers in the private sector. Full-time workers are more likely to be unionized than part-time workers, but, in contrast to the historical pattern, males are no longer more unionized than females. There are also important differences by age; the likelihood of being unionized increases sharply with age to 45–54 years of age, and then declines. One of the strongest relationships is between unionization and workplace size, with workers in large establishments being much more likely to be represented by a union than those in small establishments.

TABLE 14.3	Union Membership and Collective Agreement Coverage as a Percentage of Paid Workers in Canada, 2015	
	Percentage of Paid Workers Who Are:	
	Union Members	**Covered by a Collective Agreement**
By Gender		
Both sexes	28.6	30.6
Females	30.4	32.4
Males	26.8	28.9
By Age		
15 to 24	13.2	15.0
25 to 34	27.7	29.9
35 to 44	32.1	34.3
45 to 54	34.4	36.4
55 and over	31.9	33.8
By Education		
Less than high school	18.1	19.6
High school graduate	22.1	23.8
Post-secondary diploma	32.7	34.9
University degree	32.6	35.0
By Province		
Newfoundland	35.1	37.3
Prince Edward Island	31.9	34.1
Nova Scotia	29.2	30.9
New Brunswick	28.4	29.3
Quebec	36.1	39.4
Ontario	25.2	26.8
Manitoba	33.6	35.9
Saskatchewan	31.7	33.2

	Percentage of Paid Workers Who Are:	
	Union Members	Covered by a Collective Agreement
Alberta	21.8	23.5
British Columbia	28.8	30.3
By Work Status		
Full-time	30.1	32.2
Part-time	21.9	23.5
By Sector		
Public sector	72.4	75.5
Private sector	15.0	16.7
By Workplace Size		
Under 20 employees	13.1	14.4
20 to 99 employees	28.8	30.9
100 to 500 employees	38.7	41.1
Over 500 employees	52.4	55.5
By Job Status		
Permanent job	28.9	30.9
Temporary job	26.4	28.9

SOURCE: Statistics Canada, Cansim Tables 282-0220, 282-0221 and 282-0224.

Explaining these differences in unionization—over time and by employee and employer characteristics at a point in time—is of considerable interest for its own sake. As discussed subsequently, this understanding is also important in interpreting research findings on the consequences of unions. Indeed, a central theme of recent research has been that union versus non-union status and the wage and non-wage effects of unions are jointly determined. That is, unionization may result in higher wages and improved working conditions, but also, higher wages and non-wage benefits may make unionization more likely to occur.

The growth and incidence of union organization can be analyzed using a demand and supply framework. The **demand for union representation** emanates from employees and depends on the expected benefits and costs of union representation. The **supply of union representation** emanates from the organizing and contract administration activities of union leaders and their staff. These demand and supply forces are discussed in turn.

On the demand side, the potential benefits of union representation may include higher wages and non-wage benefits, greater employment security (through protection from dismissal other than for cause), and protection from arbitrary treatment by management. Potential costs include direct costs such as union dues and time devoted to union activities, potential loss of income in the event of a work stoppage, and costs associated with the employer's actions should the employer be willing and/or able to attempt to discourage unionization. Several factors may be net benefits or costs depending on the individual employee's circumstances. Higher wages will benefit those who retain union jobs but may reduce employment opportunities of others. Unions typically alter procedures for determining promotions and layoffs—usually placing more emphasis on seniority—which will enhance some workers' opportunities and reduce those of others.

On the supply side, administering the contracts covering existing union members and organizing new (or previously non-union) workplaces are costly activities. Unions need to allocate their scarce resources to the activities that are expected to yield the greatest return, measured in terms of the union's objectives. Success in organizing new workplaces and in maintaining membership and union representation in existing organizations will depend on a variety of factors, including the resources devoted to contract administration and organizing drives, the activities of employers, and the economic and policy environment.

This demand and supply framework provides a useful conceptual model for analyzing the extent of union organization at a point in time and changes in unionization over time. The central concept is that the extent of unionization depends on the choices made by employees, the organizational and contract administration activities of union leaders, and the actions of employers. Those enterprises in which a majority of the employees perceive substantial net benefits from being represented by a union, and in which the actions of the employer will not significantly reduce these benefits, will have a high demand for unionization, and vice versa. The supply of union organizational and contract administration effort will be high to those enterprises in which the per-worker cost of organization and representation is low. The interaction of these demand and supply forces determines an equilibrium extent of union organization at a point of time. Some enterprises will be organized while others, because of either low demand or high organizational costs, will remain unorganized. Changes over time in the factors influencing demand and supply will result in changes in union density.

Under the Canadian legislative framework, there are several dimensions to the way the demand and supply factors interact and determine the **union status** of individual workers. First, a group of workers must become represented by a labour union, a process known as **certification**. Second, once certified, the union remains the exclusive bargaining representative of that group of employees (known as a **bargaining unit**) unless the union becomes decertified. Although the details of the mechanisms vary somewhat across provincial and federal jurisdictions and over time, certification and **decertification** are essentially majority decisions by the workers in the bargaining unit.

At any point in time, the stock of unionized and non-union enterprises and firms is, thus, a reflection of past certification and decertification decisions. The third influence on union status consists of the decisions of individual workers about whether to seek employment in unionized or non-union organizations. Fourth, the decisions of employers about which applicants to hire (and, in the case of workforce reductions, which workers to lay off) will also influence which individuals obtain (or retain) union jobs. Finally, because the economy and labour force are continually changing, the growth and decline of union and non-union firms over time will also impact on the union status of individual workers.

For these reasons, the determination of the union status of individual workers is the outcome of a complex set of forces, reflecting both past decisions and current developments. Because the stock of union and non-union employers at any point in time is, to an important extent, the outcome of past decisions, union density and collective agreement coverage display considerable inertia. Changes over time tend to be gradual, reflecting the extent to which growth in employment in unionized firms exceeds or falls short of growth in non-union employment, certifications of new or previously non-union organizations, and decertifications of previously union enterprises.

Empirical Evidence

This demand and supply framework was used in pioneering studies of union growth in the United States by Ashenfelter and Pencavel (1969) and in the United Kingdom by Pencavel (1971). Empirical studies by Swidinsky (1974) and Kumar and Dow (1986) have applied and extended this approach in the Canadian setting. These studies employed aggregate data.

More recently, the demand and supply framework has been used to analyze microdata in which the union status of each individual is observed. The supply and demand for unionization themselves are inherently unobservable. In a conventional market, we can appeal to an equilibrium assumption that supply equals demand, given by the observed quantity exchanged. With this assumption, the observed level of unionization would correspond to actual supply and demand. However, given the high degree of government regulation, and the imperfectly competitive nature of the "market" for unionization, this would be an untenable assumption. With mobility into the non-union sector, at least relative to the union sector, the most common characterization of the disequilibrium is one of excess (or unsatisfied) demand for unionization. That is, there are generally queues for union jobs, and those unable to obtain a job in a unionized organization either remain unemployed (waiting for a union job to open up) or take employment in the non-union sector.

The data requirements in this situation make precise measurement very difficult. Nevertheless, there exist a few data sets that ask individuals whether they desire to be unionized, and this permits estimation of demand, which, combined with actual union status, permits the estimation of unfulfilled demand. The probability of union coverage, given that an individual wishes to be covered, is taken as a measure of supply. Analogously, the proportion of uncovered individuals desiring coverage is taken as a measure of unfulfilled demand. Riddell (1993) uses this methodology, developed by Farber (1983), to explore whether the current difference in Canada and U.S. unionization rates is due primarily to demand or supply factors. If supply factors dominate, this would suggest that legislative or other cost of unionization factors are most important. Riddell finds that about two-thirds of the difference in rates can be attributed to differences in supply.

A subsequent study by Lipset and Meltz (2004) surveyed U.S. and Canadian employees about their desire for union representation. An advantage of their survey relative to earlier studies is that identical questions were asked of workers on both sides of the 49th parallel. Using the same methodology employed by Riddell (1993), Lipset and Meltz conclude that the demand for union representation is similar in the two countries—slightly more than one-half of all workers in Canada and the United States desire union representation. Because the extent of union coverage is much lower in the United States than in Canada (16 percent versus 36 percent in their study) their survey implies that there is much more unsatisfied demand in the United States than in Canada. Indeed, they estimate that about 90 percent of the Canada–U.S. unionization gap is due to supply-side factors—even greater than the two-thirds estimated previously by Riddell (1993)—leaving only a small amount attributable to demand-side differences. This evidence supports the view that Canada–U.S. differences in the legal regime and associated differences in management opposition to unions play a central role in the large intercountry unionization gap (see Exhibit 14.1). Recent studies by Johnson (2002a) and Riddell (2004) of the consequences of changes in laws regulating union certification provide further support for this conclusion (see Exhibit 14.2).

There have been a number of studies of the cross-sectional incidence of unionization according to observable factors, such as industry, enterprise and personal characteristics, region, and legislative jurisdiction. Although this literature will not be reviewed in detail here, the main findings and their consistency with the demand and supply framework will be discussed. Several factors suggested by the demand and supply framework have been investigated in empirical studies.

Social Attitudes toward Unions and Collective Bargaining

Both the receptiveness of employees to union representation and the resistance of employers may be affected by the prevailing attitudes regarding the role of unions and collective bargaining in society. In their pioneering U.S. study, Ashenfelter and Pencavel (1969) find that the percentage of Democrats in the House, a measure of pro-union sentiment, has a significant effect on U.S. union growth. Because society's attitudes toward unions tend to be reflected in labour legislation and its administration, measures of the legal regime (discussed below) capture social attitudes to some degree.

Subsequent studies of several countries have not found consistent evidence of an influence of indicators of the political and social climate, such as parliamentary representation. This mixed picture may reflect the difficulty of identifying such influences with aggregate time-series data. However, there is considerable evidence from studies using individual-level data that political and social attitudes of individual employees, and their perceptions of unions and their impact, are significant determinants of union membership (Schnabel 2003).

The Legislative Framework Governing Unionization and Collective Bargaining

Legislation governing the right of workers to act collectively and the machinery for administering and enforcing these rights are likely to exert an important influence on the demand for and supply of union representation. However, it must be recognized that labour relations legislation and its administration itself reflects certain underlying factors, such as society's attitudes toward unions; in the absence of good measures of social attitudes, it will be difficult to determine the independent impact of the legal regime. Further, union growth and a legislative environment that is conducive to union growth may be joint manifestations of underlying societal attitudes. Without favourable attitudes, the law may not have an independent influence.

The changes in the Canadian legislative framework described earlier have lowered the cost to employees of collective action and, until recently, increasingly restricted the employer's ability to attempt to discourage unionization. The former increases demand for unions by raising the net benefits to workers of union representation; the latter increases the supply by lowering the costs of organizing and representing workers. The legislative changes are, therefore, predicted to have encouraged union growth. Although this trend in labour legislation and its administration has occurred gradually over time, particularly important changes took place in the 1870s (e.g., the Trade Unions Act of 1872), the early 1900s (the Industrial Disputes Investigation Act of 1907 contained an implicit form of union recognition by banning strikes or lockouts over recognition issues), the 1940s (the enactment of P.C. 1003 gave workers the right to form and join unions and made illegal a number of practices by employers previously used to discourage collective bargaining; similar legislation was enacted in most provinces following World War II and the end of federal emergency powers), and in the 1960s (the extension to public sector employees of the right to collective bargaining).

Examination of Table 14.1 suggests that the changes in the legislative framework around 1944 and 1967 may have had a positive impact on union growth in Canada. Econometric studies such as Kumar and Dow (1986) support the view that labour legislation had a significant effect on the union growth process. In addition, the divergent patterns of union growth in Canada and the United States since the 1960s has been argued to be associated to a considerable extent with differences between the two countries in labour relations legislation and its enforcement (Exhibit 14.1).

Legislative changes introduced in several provinces in recent decades appear to have made new union organizing more difficult. Perhaps most significant has been the trend toward requiring secret-ballot elections for union certification (and decertification) decisions in Canadian jurisdictions. Exhibit 14.2 discusses the evidence on the impacts of these developments.

Other Economic and Social Legislation

The extent of union organization may also be affected by other economic and social legislation, although the direction of the effect is ambiguous. Employment standards such as those with respect to minimum wages, overtime premiums, statutory holidays, workplace health and safety, notice of layoff, and severance pay may narrow the gap in wages and working conditions between organized and unorganized workers, thus reducing the demand for unionization. On the other hand, such policies may have aided union growth by reducing competition from the lower labour costs that otherwise would have prevailed in the non-union sector in the absence of extending such benefits to unorganized workers. Social programs, such as public pensions, medical and health care, and unemployment insurance, may also have offsetting effects. Neumann and Rissman (1984) have suggested that the provision of certain welfare benefits by governments in the United States accounts for some of the decline in union strength there. In Canada, however, union density rose during the postwar period, an era of rapid expansion of the welfare state and significant improvements in employment standards.

Aggregate Economic Conditions

Early institutional economists emphasized the role of the business cycle in the growth of unions. Subsequent econometric studies have investigated the influence of such variables as the unemployment rate, the rate of growth of employment that is eligible for unionization, and the rate of price inflation. The general finding that the rate of union growth varies directly with the rate of growth of employment that is eligible for unionization is consistent with several hypotheses: (1) employer resistance to union formation is lowest when product demand is high and the labour market is tight and (2) the ability of unions to secure wage and benefit increases (and, thus, the perceived net benefit of being represented by a union) is highest when there is excess labour demand. However, even in the absence of these cyclical effects, a positive relationship between union growth and growth in employment eligible for unionization is expected. Employment growth in existing organized enterprises will result in an increase in the unionized labour force, unless the employees decide to decertify the union. In addition, some new enterprises and their employees will have characteristics (discussed below) that make them likely to become organized.

WORKED EXAMPLE

Decomposing Changes in Unionization into Structural and Propensity to Unionize Components

To help understand the methods used to determine how much of the observed change in unionization over time can be attributed to changes in the structure of the economy and the labour force (as discussed in Exhibit 14.1 and Exhibit 14.2), consider the following example. The data below show the composition of employment and union density by broad industrial groups over a particular time period (the example corresponds approximately to Canada over the 20-year period from the mid-1970s to the mid-1990s):

	Percentage of Employment of Paid Workers		Union Density	
	Base Period	Final Period	Base Period	Final Period
Goods-producing industries	32	24	43	38
Services-producing industries	68	76	26	32
All industries	100	100	31	33

First, note that overall union density in each year is a weighted average of union density in each sector, with the weights being the share of employment in each sector:

Union density in base period = .32 × 43% + .68 × 26% = 31.4%

Union density in final period= .24 × 38% + .76 × 32% = 33.4%

Between the base and final periods, union density changed by +2 percent.

Now, we ask the following counterfactual question. Suppose that union density in each sector remained at its base-period levels, but that the composition of employment changed between the base and final periods, as shown in the above table. Thus, we allow for structural change in the economy (the changing composition of employment) but we hold constant the propensity to unionize (the union coverage rate in each sector). Under this scenario, what would union density have been in the final period?

The answer to this question can be calculated as follows. If union density in each sector had remained at its base-period level, but the composition of employment had changed as was in fact observed, union density in the final period would have been,

Counterfactual union density = .24 × 43% + .76 × 26% = 30.1%

Thus, the change in union density due to structural change in the composition of employment is 30.1 − 31.4 = − 1.3 percent.

Using the results from the counterfactual union density calculation, we can now decompose the overall change of +2 percent into two components: (1) that due to changes in the sectoral composition of employment and (2) that due to changes in union density in each sector.

The total change in union density is 33.4 − 31.4 = 2.0 percent. The change in union density due to changing composition of employment is 30.1 − 31.4 = −1.3 percent. Because the two components sum to the total change, the change in overall union density due to changing union density in each sector is 33.4 − 30.1 = +3.3 percent.

The overall change of +2.0 percent can, thus, be decomposed into two terms: +3.3 percent due to changing union density in each sector (changes in the propensity to unionize) and −1.3 percent due to changing composition of employment (structural changes in the composition of employment).

Although the above reasons suggest that union growth will be pro-cyclical in nature, the experience of the Great Depression—during and subsequent to which the union movement displayed strong growth, especially in the United States—led Ashenfelter and Pencavel (1969) to hypothesize that severe business contractions will raise worker discontent, which, in turn, will spur unionization, perhaps with a lag. Although U.S. studies generally find that union growth is positively related to the severity of past recessions, Canadian evidence on this issue is mixed (Abbott 1982; Kumar and Dow 1986). It will be interesting to see if the "Great Recession" of 2008–2009 in the United States results in increased demand for union representation in that country. To date there is no sign of such a resurgence taking place.

Time-series studies also, generally, find that union growth varies directly with the rate of price inflation. This finding is consistent with the hypothesis that unions are viewed by workers as an effective vehicle for maintaining real wages.

Industry and Enterprise Characteristics

There are substantial differences across industries in the extent of union organization. Cross-sectional studies have found that union density tends to be higher in industries with larger firms or establishments, in more concentrated industries, in industries with more capital-intensive production processes, and in industries with more hazardous jobs. Martinello and Meng (1992) is a good example of this type of study with Canadian data.

These results can be interpreted using the demand-supply framework. The demand for union representation is likely to be higher in larger establishments because individual action becomes less effective the larger the group, and the need for formal work rules, communications, and grievance procedures is greater in larger organizations. In addition, the per-worker cost of union organizing is lower in larger establishments. Industries with hazardous jobs are also likely to be characterized by greater demand for a collective "voice" to represent workers' interests in the internal regulation of workplace health and safety.

Capital intensity may be associated with several effects. As with job hazards, capital intensive production processes may entail greater need for a collective voice relating to the organization and flow of work—aspects such as the speed of assembly lines, scheduling of shifts, and overtime regulations. In addition, high capital intensity implies that labour costs are a small fraction of total costs. This tends to make labour demand more inelastic and, thus, increases the potential wage gains from unionization.

The finding that more-concentrated industries tend to be more heavily unionized may reflect several factors. Concentrated industries, typically, have significant barriers to entry; there is, thus, less threat of non-union competition in the form of new entrants. In addition, unions may enable workers to share in the excess profits, or rents, earned by the established firms. Organizing costs may also be lower in more-concentrated industries.

Because of these differences across industries in the extent of union organization, changes over time in the economy's industrial structure will be accompanied by changes in union density, other things being equal. In Canada and most other industrialized countries, significant changes in industrial structure have occurred in the postwar period; employment has grown rapidly in services-producing industries and the share of service sector employment increased substantially, goods-producing industries (manufacturing and construction) have experienced slower employment growth and a decline in the share of total employment, employment in agriculture both declined absolutely and relative to the share of total employment, and other primary industries (mining, forestry, fishing, and trapping) have experienced positive employment growth but declining shares of total employment.

These trends in the industrial composition of employment have had offsetting effects on union growth. Several factors tend to increase union density: the decline in employment in agriculture, an industry with little unionization, and the growth in employment in public administration (employees of the federal, provincial, and municipal governments), a sector that has become extensively unionized since the mid-1960s. Robinson (1995) examines the incidence of unions in the public sector, in an attempt to isolate some of the underlying sources of this growth. Netting out differences in industry and personal characteristics, which turn out to have only a limited effect on unionization, he attributes most of the relative increase in public sector unionization to the lower per-member cost of organizing the large establishments that characterize the public sector.

However, other changes in industrial structure have tended to reduce the extent of union organization in the economy; that is, declining employment shares in manufacturing, mining, and forestry (sectors traditionally with above-average unionization), and increases in the share of employment in trade, finance, insurance, real estate, and other private-sector services (industries with low degrees of unionization).

Personal Characteristics

A number of personal characteristics affect the propensity to be a union member or to be represented by a union. Part-time workers and workers with intermittent labour force attachment are less likely to be organized. For these individuals, the net benefits of union representation—especially in the form of seniority provisions, pension benefits, and other forms of deferred compensation—are lower than is the case with full-time workers and employees with a permanent labour force attachment. The costs of organizing part-time workers and workers with intermittent labour force attachments may also be high. In part because they are more likely to work part-time and have tended to have less permanent attachment to the labour force, women were traditionally less likely to be represented by a union than men, although this is no longer the case.

As noted earlier, the extent of union organization is much higher among blue-collar than white-collar workers. Blue-collar workers are more likely to demand union representation because of less identification with management and, possibly, greater need for a collective voice in the determination of working conditions.

Age and experience have also been found in a number of studies to be related to the propensity to be organized. Although there are some conflicting results, this relationship appears to be concave; that is, the propensity to choose union representation at first increases, reaches a maximum, and subsequently decreases with age and/or experience.

An individual's position in the earnings distribution may also affect the net benefits of being represented by a union. As explained subsequently, unions tend to increase the wages of those at the lower end of the wage distribution by a relatively large amount and those in the upper tail of the wage distribution by a relatively small amount. Thus, individuals whose earnings would be above average in the absence of a union are less likely to favour union representation.

In summary, the growth of unions over time; the extent of union organization across industries, regions, occupations, and establishments; and employee characteristics are systematically related to a number of economic, social, and legal variables. These observed relationships are, generally, consistent with the demand-supply framework, which appears to provide a valuable conceptual device for understanding the growth and incidence of unions.

Theory of Union Behaviour

The economic analysis of firms and households begins from the assumption that the decision maker maximizes an objective function subject to the constraints imposed on the agent by the economic environment. Private-sector firms are usually assumed to maximize profits subject to the production function (which summarizes the technical possibilities available to the firm), the demand conditions in the product markets, and the supply conditions in the markets for inputs. This is the theory that underlies the demand for labour discussed in Chapter 5 of this text. It is a theory rich in testable implications, and one that has, generally, been found to accord with the available evidence. Similarly, the household is assumed to maximize utility—which depends on the quantities consumed of various goods, including leisure—subject to the budget constraint, which depends on the prices of goods and the wage rate. This is the theory that underlies the demand for goods and services in product markets and the theory of labour supply discussed in Chapter 2 of this text. This theory is also rich in testable implications, and has generally been found to be consistent with the evidence on household behaviour.

Economists have generally agreed that an understanding of union behaviour and its consequences must, likewise, begin with a theory of union objectives. The union can then be assumed to maximize its objective or utility function, subject to the constraints imposed on it and its members by the economic environment. However, our ability to characterize union preferences has long been controversial. The major aspects of this controversy were debated by Dunlop (1944) and Ross (1948) several decades ago. Dunlop advocated an "economic" approach in which the union is modelled as attempting to maximize a well-defined objective function subject to labour market constraints. (The specific objective function suggested by Dunlop is discussed below.) Ross criticized this approach and argued that union decision making can be understood only by treating the union as a political institution. The modern approach to union behaviour recognizes some merit in both positions in that the union is modelled as attempting to maximize a well-defined objective function, but attention is paid to the political nature of union decision making. Kaufman (2002) and Naylor (2003) provide surveys of the theoretical and empirical literature on union behaviour.

 LO5   ## Union Objectives

Unions are collective organizations whose leaders represent members of the bargaining unit, the rank and file, in collective bargaining with the firm. **Union objectives** refer to the goals of the organization. These need not be identical to the objectives of the individual members or to those of the union leaders. Three principal factors influence the relationship among the preferences of the members, the union leaders, and those of the union as a whole: (1) the information available to the rank and file about the available options, (2) the nature of the union's political decision-making process, and (3) the degree of homogeneity of the individual members' preferences. If the rank and file are well informed and the union's decision-making processes are highly democratic, the union leaders will make choices that have the support of a majority of the members. (Otherwise, they will be quickly replaced.) In these circumstances, the union's objectives are those that a majority of the rank and file would favour. However, asymmetric information (the members being less informed than the leaders) or imperfectly democratic decision-making processes may allow the union leaders to pursue their own objectives to some degree. In these circumstances, the objectives of the members and those pursued by the union may differ.

The degree of homogeneity of individual members' preferences is another important factor. If the rank-and-file have very similar preferences, it will be easy for the union leaders to determine the group's preferred choices. However, if preferences differ significantly across individuals or groups of individuals, the task of the union leaders is more difficult, and selecting an option that will be supported by a majority may require considerable skill and judgment.

Although various union objectives have been postulated, most involve two key aspects—the wages and employment of union members (abstracting from the various non-wage aspects of working conditions, for the moment). This suggests a union objective or utility function whereby utility is a positive function of both the wage rate and the employment of union members, and which may also depend on other variables as discussed below. Combinations of the wage rate and employment that are equally satisfactory to the union—the union's indifference or iso-utility curves—must be downward sloping because a higher wage is needed to compensate for lower employment, and vice versa. Furthermore, it is plausible to hypothesize that union preferences display a diminishing marginal rate of substitution between wages and employment; that is, holding utility constant, the union will be less willing to accept a wage reduction in return for a given increase in employment the higher the level of employment, and vice versa. This implies that the indifference curves have the convex shape displayed in Figure 14.2. (See Appendix to Chapter 2 for a review of indifference curves.) The shape of the indifference curve reflects the weights placed by the union on wages and employment. In particular, the smaller the weight given to employment the flatter is the indifference curve.

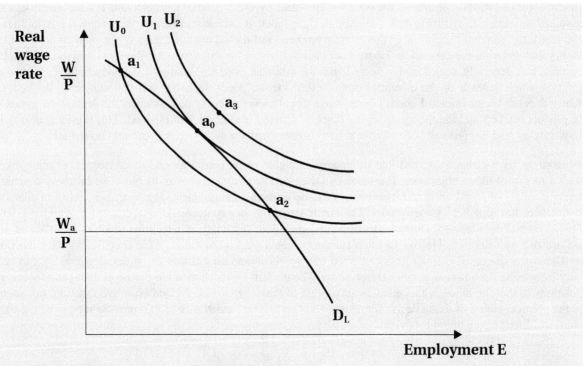

Figure 14.2 Union Objectives and Constraints

Union indifference curves plot combinations of wages and employment that yield equal utility. The indifference curves display diminishing marginal rate of substitution; as the union requires more employment to compensate for a one-unit reduction in the wage, the lower the wage. (See Appendix to Chapter 2 for discussion of the shape of indifference curves and the concept of diminishing marginal rate of substitution.) The indifference curves do not fall below the alternative wage because no level of employment would be sufficient to compensate for a wage below what union members could earn elsewhere. If the firm chooses employment, the union's constraint is the labour demand curve. The combination of wages and employment that yields maximum union utility is point a_0, where the indifference curve is tangent to the labour demand curve.

Union objectives are likely to depend on several additional variables. One is the overall price level, or the cost of living. Clearly, what matters to the workers is the real wage rate. A 10 percent increase (or decrease) in the nominal wage rate accompanied by a 10 percent increase (or decrease) in the price level leaves the workers' real income and, therefore, consumption and leisure possibilities unchanged. Union utility is also likely to depend on the **alternative wage** (i.e., the wage rate that union members could earn if employed elsewhere). Few workers will be willing to bear the costs of union representation (union dues and other costs discussed earlier) unless their compensation is equal to or greater than that available elsewhere for comparable work. For this reason, the alternative (real) wage is shown as a lower bound to the union's indifference curves in Figure 14.2.

In using the term "employment," we have not distinguished between hours worked and number of employees. Implicitly, hours worked are held constant, so that employment refers to the number of workers. This assumption is innocuous at this stage but needs to be relaxed when examining issues such as work sharing versus layoffs in response to temporary reductions in demand. Also, we have not discussed how the size of the union membership is determined. Membership size will matter to both the union leadership and the existing union members—the former because a larger membership implies more revenue from dues and possibly more power and prestige, and the latter because a larger membership may imply reduced employment opportunities, depending on how scarce jobs are rationed when employment demand is insufficient.

Some Special Cases

As noted earlier, various union objective functions have been suggested in the literature on union behaviour. Several of these are special cases of the utility function as illustrated in Figure 14.2, and examining these may increase our understanding of union objectives.

Maximize the Wage Rate, W

This would imply that the union places no weight on employment; that is, that the indifference curves are horizontal straight lines, as shown in Figure 14.3(a). Although this may seem implausible, the notion that in negotiating wages unions do not take into account the employment consequences of higher wages has a long tradition, including the influential work of Ross (1948), and is often stated by union leaders today.

Maximize Employment, E

This is the opposite extreme of the previous objective and implies indifference curves that are vertical straight lines, as shown in Figure 14.3(b).

Maximize the (Real) Wage Bill, WE

This objective, proposed by Dunlop (1944), implies that the indifference curves are rectangular hyperbolas as shown in Figure 14.3(c). (WE = a constant, is the equation of a rectangular hyperbola.) It has the advantage that the union attaches weight to both wages and employment. The wage bill is, of course, total labour income. It may appear plausible that union members would attempt to maximize their total income, especially if there is some mechanism for sharing the income between employed and unemployed members. The main defect of this objective function is that it disregards the alternative wage; indeed, it implies that the union may be willing to allow the wage to fall below W_a in exchange for higher employment.[1]

Maximize (Real) Economic Rent, (W – Wa)E

This objective is analogous to profit maximization for a monopolist; the alternative wage is the opportunity cost to each union member, so **economic rent** is analogous to total revenue (WE) minus total cost (W_aE). In this case, the indifference curves are rectangular hyperbolas with respect to the new origin (W_a,0), as shown in Figure 14.3(d).

This objective is the most plausible of the group, in that it hypothesizes that the union members seek to maximize their "total return," given what they could earn elsewhere. Again, the objective is most plausible when there is some mechanism for sharing the income between employed and unemployed union members.

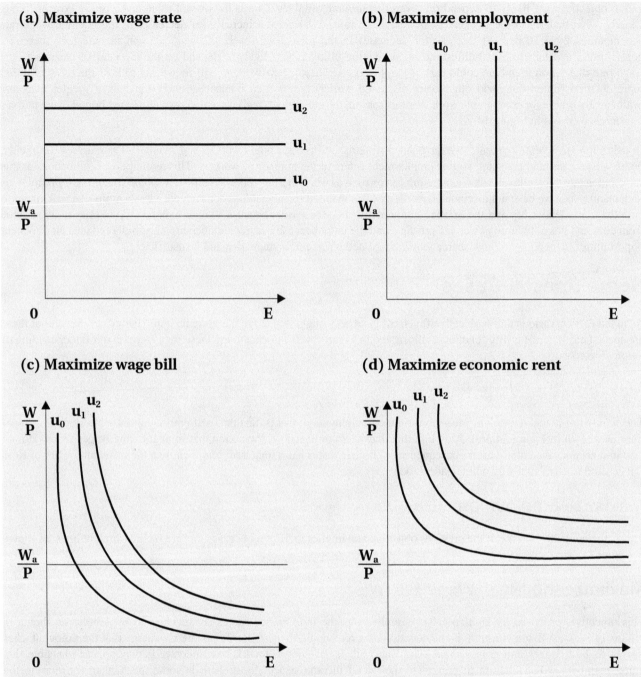

Figure 14.3 Union Objectives: Some Special Cases

The panels illustrate four special cases of the union utility function. In panel (a) the union maximizes the wage, placing no weight on employment. The indifference curves are horizontal straight lines in wage employment space. In panel (b) the union maximizes employment, placing no weight on the wage. The indifference curves are vertical straight lines. In panel (c) the union maximizes the wage bill; wages times employment. The indifference curves are rectangular hyperbolas and display a diminishing marginal rate of substitution between wages and employment. In panel (d), the union maximizes economic rent, the product of employment times the difference between the union wage and the alternative wage. The indifference curves are rectangular hyperbolas in wage-employment space above the alternative wage, and display a diminishing marginal rate of substitution between wages and employment.

Union Preferences: Some Additional Considerations

The task of deriving union objectives from the preferences of the constituent members is simplest when (1) members' preferences are homogeneous, (2) union leaders are constrained by democratic decision-making processes and the availability of information from pursuing their own objectives, and (3) union membership is exogenously determined. When these conditions do not hold, the economics of union behaviour is more complex.

Heterogeneous Preferences

The preferences of individual union members may differ for a variety of reasons. The union may represent several groups of employees with different occupations or skills. Industrial unions often contain highly skilled employees (usually a minority) in addition to semiskilled and unskilled workers. Alternatively, workers performing similar jobs may differ according to a number of personal characteristics, such as age, seniority, marital status, and alternative employment opportunities. Individual preferences may depend in a systematic way on these characteristics. For example, older workers may desire a greater emphasis on pensions and other forms of deferred compensation and less emphasis on current earnings in the total compensation package. Those with good alternative employment opportunities (high W_a's) may prefer a higher union wage than those with limited opportunities, for given levels of employment security. If layoffs take place in accordance with seniority, more-senior workers may wish to place more emphasis on wages and less emphasis on employment in union objectives. Clearly, these sources of heterogeneity may be important in particular settings, and the economic analysis of union behaviour should be able to account for their implications.

The conditions under which heterogeneous individual preferences can be aggregated into a group or social objective function is a central issue in the theory of public choice. One well-known result is the **median voter model**, which states that when choices over a single variable are made in a democratic fashion (i.e., by voting among alternatives) then, under certain conditions, the group's preferences will be identical to those of the median voter. The reason for this is that the outcome preferred by the median voter will defeat all others in a sequence of pairwise elections (votes between two alternatives). In the union context, this result implies that if, for example, the members' preferences with respect to the wage rate depend on the worker's seniority, the union's objective function will be that of the member with the median seniority (i.e., that individual for whom half the members are more senior and half the members are less senior).

The conditions under which the median voter model holds are fairly stringent. One key requirement is that the choice, or voting set, must be defined over a single variable (e.g., the wage in the union setting). Thus, with heterogeneous members, union preferences over multiple objectives (wages, employment, non-wage benefits, working conditions) cannot be derived from the assumption of pairwise voting among alternatives except under special conditions.

When the required conditions do not hold, a voting equilibrium will generally not exist; that is, no single set of outcomes will defeat all others in a sequence of pairwise elections. In these circumstances, the organization's choice may depend on factors such as the order in which alternatives are presented for voting.

Clearly, the assumptions of the median voter model do not apply precisely in the union setting. Unions typically do not choose among alternatives by conducting a sequence of pairwise votes. Most choices are made by union leaders, who are periodically elected by the membership. In addition, the union leaders often face trade-offs among several alternatives, such as wages, non-wage benefits, and employment. Nonetheless, when union members' preferences are heterogeneous, the median voter model may predict union behaviour reasonably well. Union leaders wishing to remain in office will adopt positions that are supported by a majority of the membership. When the members can be ordered by a preference-related factor, such as age or seniority, the choices of the median member, because of his or her central position in the distribution of preferences, may be more likely to receive majority support than any other set of choices.

Another approach to modelling heterogeneous preferences is the insider-outsider theory developed by Lindbeck and Snower (1988) and Solow (1985). The basic idea is that currently employed workers in a firm (the insiders) have greater influence over union bargaining strategies than do unemployed workers (the outsiders), even if some outsiders are union members. As a consequence, the weight placed on employment of outsiders may be considerably less than that placed on employment (and wages) of insiders. Thus, the union may be willing to trade off wages against employment of insiders, but may not be willing to accept lower wages of insiders in exchange for increased employment of outsiders. Insiders may be protected from competition from outsiders for a variety of reasons, including hiring and firing costs as well as negotiated provisions, such as seniority-based layoffs.

Union Leaders versus Union Members

Unions, like societies, generally do not conduct a referendum each time a decision must be made. Rather, union leaders are elected to implement policy, and their position of authority may allow them to pursue their own interests to some extent. Furthermore, because they specialize in contract administration and collective bargaining with the employer, union leaders generally have greater access than members do to information regarding the feasible options. In addition, the information that is received by the rank-and-file can be filtered to some degree by the leadership.

These observations suggest that union leaders may be able to pursue their own interests—such as maximizing dues revenue, expanding the union's membership and influence, and raising their own personal income. Nonetheless, the desire to remain in office (and perhaps other considerations) does constrain the leaders from deviating too far from the wishes of the membership. How binding these constraints are may well vary according to individual circumstances. A theory of union preferences based solely on the wishes of the members may not be able to account for all aspects of union behaviour. Nonetheless, it may provide a good approximation to observed behaviour.

Union Membership and Union Objectives

Changes in union membership may alter union preferences. For example, if employment in the industry or firm is expanding rapidly, not only will membership size increase but also the age and seniority of the median member will probably fall. The union's objectives, if the union represents members' preferences, will adjust to reflect the wishes of the younger, less senior workers. The opposite is likely to occur in declining sectors.

In formulating wage policy, the current union membership also influences the size of future membership and, thus, future union preferences. If the union pursues a high-wage policy, future membership will be reduced as employers substitute capital for labour and consumers substitute less-expensive products. Thus, union preferences may not be stable over time, but may depend on the wage policies adopted.

Union Constraints

The union cannot choose whatever wage and employment outcomes it desires, but must negotiate with the firm and must also take into account the consequences for its members of the outcomes of these negotiations. Initially, we will assume that the two parties negotiate over the wage rate, leaving the firm free to choose the level of employment at whatever wage rate is agreed upon by collective bargaining. (The possibility of negotiating over both wages and employment is discussed subsequently.) In these circumstances, the firm will choose the level of employment that maximizes profits given the negotiated wage; that is, it will choose employment according to the labour demand curve.[2] It follows that when the firm can unilaterally determine employment, the union is constrained by the firm's labour demand curve. That is, the firm's labour demand curve is analogous to a budget constraint for the utility-maximizing union.

In this situation, the union's preferred wage-employment outcome is the point a_0 in Figure 14.2, where the iso-utility curve u_1 is tangent to the labour demand curve. Wage-employment combinations, such as a_1 and a_2, are attainable but the union prefers a_0 to a_1 and a_2. Outcomes such as a_3 are not attainable if the firm can choose employment.

The firm will prefer wage-employment outcomes at which profits (Π) are higher to those at which profits are lower. The firm's **isoprofit curves**—combinations of wage rates and employment that yield equal profits—are shown in Figure 14.4. Note that lower curves imply higher profits; that is, $\Pi_3 > \Pi_2 > \Pi_1 > \Pi_0$. This is so because for any given level of employment, say E^*, profits are higher when wages are lower, other things equal.

Each curve attains a maximum at the point at which the isoprofit curve and the demand for labour curve intersect. This is so because if we fix the wage at, say, W^*, then profits must be highest at c because D_L shows the profit-maximizing quantity of E at each wage. Thus, as the firm increases employment from e to f to c, Π must increase (i.e., the firm must be moving to isoprofit curves with higher profit levels), reflecting the fact that each additional worker hired adds more to total revenue than to total cost (i.e., MRP > W where MRP is the marginal revenue product, the change in total revenue that results when one additional employee is hired). Similarly, as the firm increases employment from c to g to h, Π must fall, reflecting the fact that for $E > E^*$, MRP > W (i.e., each additional employee adds less to total revenue than to total costs).

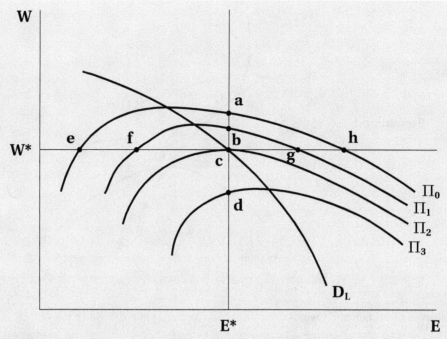

Figure 14.4 The Firm's Isoprofit Curves

Firm isoprofit curves plot combinations of the wage and employment that yield equal profits. Isoprofit curves are upward sloping to the left of the labour demand curve, are downward sloping to the right, and attain a maximum at the intersection with the labour demand curve.

It is important to recognize that, although the firm is maximizing profits at each point on the labour demand curve, the firm is not indifferent among these points, because each corresponds to a different level of profits. The higher the wage rate, the lower the maximum attainable level of profits.

Because profits rise as the firm moves down and to the right along D_L, the firm will prefer lower points on D_L to higher points. However, the firm is constrained by the fact that it cannot pay wages below the alternative wage that employees could get elsewhere. Thus, in Figure 14.5, I_f (I for "ideal") is the firm's preferred (W, E) combination while I_u is the union's preferred (W, E) combination. The **bargaining range** is the interval (W_a, W_u). The firm would not want the wage rate to fall below W_a, and the union would not want a wage higher than W_u, because a higher wage would not be worth the reduction in employment. Within the bargaining range, however, higher wages make the union better off and the firm worse off, and vice versa.

The bargaining range may be further limited by the need for the firm to earn a normal rate of return (zero economic profits) in order to remain in business, a constraint analogous to the requirement that employees receive a wage at least equal to that available elsewhere. The isoprofit curve corresponding to zero economic profits is shown as Π_0 in Figure 14.4; thus, if the wage were higher than W_0, the firm would go out of business. The wage at which profits are zero, W_0, may be above or below the union's preferred wage, W_u. (In a competitive equilibrium, W_0 and W_a coincide, and there is no scope for raising wages without forcing some firms to shut down operations.) When W_0 is below W_u, the upper limit to the bargaining range is W_0.

The theory outlined thus far does not predict a unique wage and employment outcome, but rather predicts that the wage rate will lie somewhere in the bargaining range (W_a, W_u), with the corresponding level of employment being determined according to the labour demand function. To complete the theory, we require an explanation of the determination of the bargaining outcome arrived at by the two parties. This requires a theory of bargaining, a subject taken up later. First, we examine two closely related possibilities: (1) that the union may attempt to alter the constraint and (2) that the firm and union may bargain over wages and employment, rather than leaving the latter to be unilaterally determined by the firm. In addition, the way unions can achieve their objectives by restricting supply is also discussed.

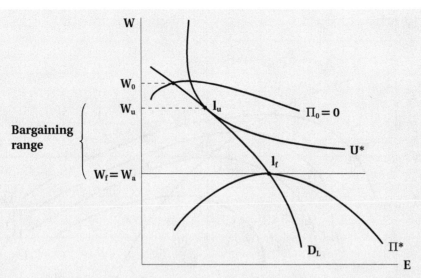

Figure 14.5 The Firm's and Union's Preferred Wage-Employment Outcomes and the Bargaining Range

The preferred outcomes of the firm and the union are illustrated for the situation in which the firm chooses employment given the wage. The union's preferred outcome, I_u, corresponds to the highest utility that can be attained, subject to being on the labour demand curve. The firm's preferred outcome, I_f, corresponds to the highest profits that can be attained, subject to the constraint that the wage must at least equal the alternative wage. The bargaining range is the set of wages between W_f and W_u.

Relaxing the Demand Constraint

Through collective bargaining with the employer, the union will attempt to reach a wage-employment outcome as close as possible to its preferred outcome I_u. However, unions can also enhance the set of available options by altering the constraint—either increasing labour demand or making the demand for labour more inelastic, so that increases in wages will have less-severe consequences for employment. Various union practices attempt to achieve these results. With respect to the goal of making labour demand more inelastic, recall from Chapter 5 that the elasticity of labour demand depends on (1) the elasticity of product demand, (2) the elasticity of substitution between labour and other inputs, (3) the share of labour in total costs, and (4) the elasticity of labour supply of other inputs. Union activity is, thus, often directed at restricting substitution possibilities by consumers in product markets and by employers in labour markets, the latter including the substitution of non-union for union labour in addition to the substitution of capital and other inputs for labour. Some restrictions come about through collective bargaining with the employer, while others are achieved by influencing public policy.

Because of the derived nature of labour demand, some attempts to alter the constraint focus on the product market. These include support for quotas, tariffs, and other restrictions on foreign competition in order to reduce the number of substitutes for union-produced goods and services (observed, for example, in the Canadian auto, textile, and shoe industries); opposition to deregulation, which generally enhances product market competition and may facilitate entry by non-union competitors (observed, for example, in the communications and transportation industries); advertising of the product (e.g., a union label on beer); and union attempts to organize all the firms in an industry in order to minimize substitution of non-union produced for union-produced goods and services.

Other union policies focus on the labour market. Unions are generally strong supporters of various forms of wage fixing for non-union labour, such as minimum wage laws and "fair wage" provisions in government contracts. Raising the wage of non-union workers reduces the potential for substitution of non-union for union labour—both directly through arrangements such as outsourcing of work by unionized employers and indirectly by the growth of non-union firms at the expense of union firms. Advocating fair wages for unorganized employees and higher minimum wages for both organized and unorganized workers may also be viewed by the union movement as an effective method of raising the living standards of the labour force and increasing labour's share of national income. Union support for full employment policies may reflect similar desires; such support can also be viewed as an attempt to increase labour demand generally, including the demand for union labour, as well as reducing the size of the pool of unemployed workers competing for jobs and, thus, weakening the position of employed union members.

Attempts to alter the constraint can have offsetting effects. In these circumstances, the union's optimal strategy will depend on the magnitude of the opposing effects. For example, raising the wages of unorganized workers limits the potential for substitution of non-union for union labour, but may also reduce the incentive for these workers to organize. The growth paths adopted by early craft unions also illustrate opposing effects. Some craft unions remained narrowly focused, representing a small group of highly skilled workers. An advantage of this arrangement is that the earnings of these workers often account for a small fraction of total cost. Other craft unions expanded to cover semiskilled and unskilled workers in the same enterprise and industry in order to minimize the substitution among different types of labour that would occur in response to an increase in the wage of the highly skilled group.

The potential for labour market substitution can also be reduced by restrictions on labour supply, such as limited immigration and control of entry through occupational licensing and apprenticeship arrangements. Restrictions on labour supply into the occupation or trade are most frequently employed by craft unions and professional associations, such as those representing doctors and lawyers. Unions also attempt to limit the employer's substitution possibilities by negotiating contract provisions, such as those relating to technological change, outsourcing, and work practices. This feature of collective bargaining involves the two parties in the negotiation of contracts relating to both wages and employment, a topic examined next.

LO4   Efficient Wage and Employment Contracts

Because unions generally care about the employment prospects of their members, we would expect the union to use its bargaining power to negotiate over employment as well as wages. Of course, the employer may resist this attempt because agreeing to certain levels of employment will have implications for the firm's profits. Nonetheless, if the union and its members care enough about employment, they may be willing to accept a lower wage in exchange for higher levels (or greater security) of employment. In these circumstances, the union and the firm may discover that an agreement with respect to both and employment is to their mutual advantage. Such **efficient wage and employment contracts** may be explicit (i.e., contained in the collective agreement) or implicit (i.e., an understanding that both parties respect).

In general, the firm and union can each benefit from negotiating a contract covering *both* wages and employment rather than having the firm choose employment subject to a fixed wage. That is, wage-employment outcomes on the labour demand curve imply unexploited "gains from trade" and, thus, are inefficient in the Pareto sense. (Recall that an outcome is said to be *Pareto-efficient* or *Pareto-optimal* if no individual or group of individuals can be made better off without making some individual or group of individuals worse off.)

This is illustrated in Figure 14.6. Starting at points on the labour demand curve, such as A and B, it is possible to make one or both parties better off by moving to outcomes in the respective shaded areas. At A′, both the union and firm are better off than at A, while at A″ the union is better off than, and the firm as well off as, at A. Note that at A″ it is not possible to move in any direction that does not make at least one party worse off. Thus A″ is a **Pareto-efficient wage-employment outcome**.[3] It is characterized by the union's indifference curve being tangent to the firm's isoprofit curve. This is a necessary condition for an efficient wage-employment arrangement.

The reasoning underlying this condition is as follows. The slope of the indifference curve measures the union's willingness to trade off wages against employment, holding utility constant. That is, it shows the largest wage reduction the union would accept in exchange for an increase in employment of one unit. Similarly, the slope of the isoprofit curve measures the firm's ability to substitute between wages and employment while holding profits constant. That is, it shows the minimum wage reduction the firm would require in exchange for an agreement to increase employment by one unit. When these slopes are not equal, unexploited gains from trade must exist. That is, by increasing employment by one unit and reducing the wage by more than the minimum the firm would require to maintain constant profits but less than the union would accept to maintain constant utility, both parties are made better off.

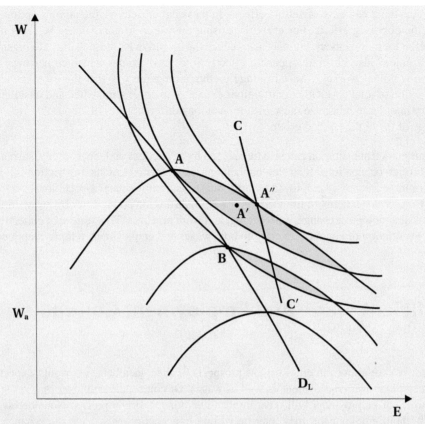

Figure 14.6 Efficient and Inefficient Wage-Employment Contracts

Wage-employment contracts on the labour demand curve are inefficient. For example, compared to the point A on the labour demand curve, both parties are better off at point A′, which yields higher union utility and higher firm profits. The set of Pareto-efficient wage-employment contracts, called the contract curve and shown as CC′, is the locus of points at which a union indifference curve is tangent to a firm isoprofit curve. Because the union indifference curves are downward sloping, this set of tangencies must occur to the right of the labour demand curve, where the firm isoprofit curves are also downward sloping.

The locus of the Pareto-efficient wage-employment outcomes is called the **contract curve** and is shown as CC′ in Figure 14.6. When the union cares about wages and employment (i.e., if the indifference curves are downward sloping), the contract curve must lie to the right of the labour demand curve. This follows from the fact that the isoprofit curves are upward sloping to the left of the labour demand curve, have a slope of zero where the two intersect, and are downward sloping to the right of the labour demand curve. Thus, the tangency conditions can be met only to the right of the labour demand function, where both the isoprofit and iso-utility curves slope downward.

In summary, both the firm and the union can benefit from negotiating a wage-employment outcome on the contract curve. Of course, the two parties will have differing views about which *particular outcome* on the contract curve should be chosen. Moving up CC′, the union becomes better off and the firm worse off, and vice versa. As before, there is a bargaining range and where the parties end up within that range depends on their relative bargaining strengths. The lower limit of the bargaining range is determined as before—the firm would not want the wage rate to be lower than would be required to attract workers. The upper limit is determined by a zero economic profit condition—in general, the union would not want wages and employment set at a level that caused the firm to cease operations.

Several implications follow from this analysis. Perhaps the most important implication is that the two parties have an incentive to negotiate wage-employment arrangements that may appear to be wasteful. Outcomes on the contract curve must involve the firm employing more labour than the firm would choose on its own, given the wage rate—that is, hiring redundant personnel, spreading a given number of tasks among more workers or paying workers for work not done. Such outcomes can be enforced by work rules of various kinds, arrangements that are often referred to as restrictive work practices or featherbedding. The above analysis shows why such practices may be to the mutual advantage of the employer and the union.

A second important implication is that, in the context of efficient contracts, the anticipated negative relationship (other influences being held constant) between wages and employment may not hold. The contract curve may be vertical or upward or downward sloping. Thus, it need not be the case in this setting that higher wages imply reduced employment, and vice versa. A more powerful union will generally be able to achieve higher wages *and* employment than a less powerful union, other things equal. (The meaning of the term *union power* is discussed further, later in this chapter.) Nonetheless, any particular union ultimately faces a trade-off between wages and employment, even when the contract curve is upward sloping, because the union is ultimately constrained by the need for the employer to earn a satisfactory level of profits in order to continue producing. Thus, the union is constrained by the locus of wage-employment combinations that yield this satisfactory level of profits, illustrated by the isoprofit curve Π_0 in Figure 14.5, a locus that is downward sloping to the right of the demand curve.

Obstacles to Reaching Efficient Contracts

While there is an incentive for firms and unions to bargain over both wages and employment and reach an outcome on the contract curve, there are also reasons for believing that outcomes on the labour demand curve may be more likely. One reason is that the information needed to recognize that there are unexploited gains from trade may not be available to both parties. For example, suppose the two parties are currently located at point A in Figure 14.6. As long as each has some information about the other side's preferences, then both will recognize that they are both better off at A than at A. What this requires is the firm knowing something about the union's willingness to trade off wages against employment, and similarly for the union. However, if neither party trusts the other, then each may be unwilling to reveal information about its preferences to the other, perhaps because of a fear that the other will later use this information to its own advantage. Indeed, there may even be an incentive to misrepresent one's preferences in bargaining situations—that is, not to "tell the truth, the whole truth, and nothing but the truth." In these circumstances, it may be difficult for the two bargainers to recognize a Pareto-improving change.

Also, while an agreement over wages is easily enforced, an agreement about employment may be difficult (i.e., costly) to enforce. Some enforcement mechanism is needed to prevent the firm from "cheating" on the agreement; this follows from the fact that at each wage rate the firm's profits are highest at the level of employment given by the labour demand curve. Thus, even though both sides are better off on the contract curve, given the negotiated wage rate, the firm always has an incentive to cut employment.

If the demand for labour is expected to remain constant during the contract period (the period during which the collective bargaining agreement is in effect), then an agreement about employment should not be difficult to enforce. Presumably, the union can keep track of its employed members, and if the firm is caught cheating (e.g., not replacing a worker who quits, retires, or is fired) the union will attempt to punish the firm (e.g., a strike, slowdown, etc.). However, many collective agreements cover a period of two or more years (almost all provide for a duration of at least one year) so that it is unlikely that labour demand will remain constant over the contract period. Thus, an agreement concerning employment would have to specify the level of employment for each of the many sets of circumstances that may prevail in the future.[4] This is the case for such factors as the future state of the product market and the costs of other inputs for the firm. From the workers' point of view, important variables would be the cost of living and wages in other firms and industries. Clearly, it may be very difficult and expensive to negotiate and enforce such a "contingent" agreement, depending on the different states of nature that may prevail.

The obstacles to negotiating efficient wage-employment contracts are often evident in concession bargaining. Unions have generally been reluctant to engage in concession bargaining unless job guarantees are part of the package, recognizing that without such guarantees the concessions may save few union jobs and may simply lead to higher firm profits. Firms are often reluctant to make explicit employment guarantees because of potential changes in product and labour market conditions.

Since an agreement covering all possible contingencies is unlikely to be workable, the two sides may try to approximate such an arrangement. This can be accomplished by tying employment to the output of the firm or to the use of other inputs. The most common such arrangement is to specify the minimum number of employees to be used for a given task; examples of such provisions are observed in railroads (size of freight train crews), airlines (number of pilots per aircraft), teaching (class size provisions), and musical performances (minimum size of orchestra). (Some of these provisions may also reflect other objectives, such as safety.) Such rules may not be difficult to enforce; further, they have the advantage that they allow the firm to adjust employment in response to fluctuations in the demand for the firm's product, yet oblige the firm to hire more employees in each state of demand than the firm would choose on its own.

The practice of negotiating work rules that restricts the firm's ability to control employment can, thus, be interpreted as a mechanism for approximating an efficient contract. In effect, the unconstrained demand curve D_L is replaced by a constrained demand curve, D_L^C, which shows the firm's profit-maximizing level of employment, given the work rules implicitly or explicitly agreed to by the two parties (see Figure 14.7). Although this constrained demand curve (or approximately efficient contract curve) is unlikely to coincide exactly with the contract curve, for each outcome on D_L there is a Pareto-superior outcome on D_L^C (i.e., a wage-employment outcome that makes both parties better off than on D_L).

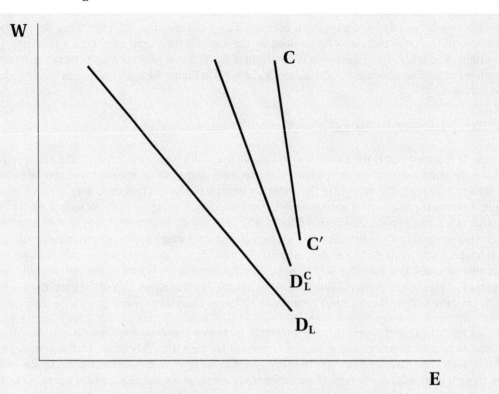

Figure 14.7 Inefficient, Approximately Efficient, and Efficient Contracts

The contract curve, or set of efficient wage-employment contracts, lies to the right of the labour demand curve D_L. However, the costs of writing, monitoring, and enforcing contingent contracts may prevent the two parties from reaching the contract curve in all situations. Rather, the firm and union may agree to the set of approximately efficient contracts, denoted by D_L^C, by negotiating work rules that restrict the firm's ability to control employment. For each point on the labour demand curve there is a wage-employment outcome on D_L^C that both the firm and the union prefer.

Previously, we noted that if the union is constrained by the labour demand curve, it is in the union's interest to shift the demand curve to the right or make it more inelastic. What wasn't clear was why the firm would accede to such requests. A primary insight of the analysis in this section is that featherbedding rules or restrictive work practices that force the firm to operate to the right of the unconstrained labour demand curve can be to the mutual advantage of both parties.

Efficient versus Inefficient Contracts: Summary

Two alternative models of the determination of wages and employment in unionized settings have been outlined. The first, which can be termed the "labour demand curve model," involves the two parties negotiating the wage rate and the firm unilaterally setting employment. Because the firm retains discretion over employment, this is also referred to as the "right to manage" model. The alternative model, the contract curve, or "efficient contracts" model, involves the two parties negotiating over both wages and employment. Which of these two models applies in any particular setting is an empirical question. The observation that both parties can improve their welfare by negotiating both wages and employment suggests strong incentives to reach an outcome on the contract curve, and provides an explanation of negotiated work rules as a rational response to these incentives. However, in many settings, employment is unilaterally determined by the firm and work rules appear to play a minimal role. This suggests that in many settings the costs of monitoring and enforcing an efficient contract are too high, given the variability in demand, to make this type of arrangement worthwhile.

Empirical Applications

Compared to the large number of empirical studies of the product demand and labour supply behaviour of households, and of the production and cost behaviour of firms, the number of studies of wage and employment determination in unionized labour markets is limited. Nonetheless, following pioneering research by Farber (1978) and Dertouzos and Pencavel (1981), a number of studies have been carried out.

Empirical applications of the theory of union wage and employment determination face several obstacles:

1. Choosing an appropriate specification of union preferences.
2. The presence of two alternative models of wage and employment determination, each of which is plausible on a priori grounds.
3. The need for a theory of firm–union bargaining to predict the specific wage-employment outcome chosen by the parties.

These are clearly major challenges. As noted previously, the issue of whether it is appropriate to characterize unions as attempting to maximize an objective function has long been a matter of scholarly debate. With respect to obstacles (2) and (3), the studies by Farber (1978), Dertouzos and Pencavel (1981), Pencavel (1984), and Carruth and Oswald (1985) assume that observed wage-employment outcomes lie on the labour demand curve and that the union is sufficiently powerful that it can achieve its preferred outcome, I_u, in Figure 14.5.

In contrast, studies such as those by Abowd (1989) are based on the assumption of efficient contracts; that is, that wage-employment outcomes are on the contract curve. Another group of studies—including Brown and Ashenfelter (1986), McCurdy and Pencavel (1986), and Martinello (1989)—have addressed the question of whether observed wage and employment outcomes are more consistent with the labour demand or contract curve models. The studies by Svenjar (1986) and Doiron (1992) have tackled the difficult task of incorporating bargaining into empirical models of wage and employment determination in unionized industries.

The Dertouzos and Pencavel study focuses on the International Typographical Union (ITU), a once-powerful closed-shop union representing printers. The employers are mostly newspaper firms. Recently, there have been important technological changes in the industry (computer typesetting, etc.) and employment has fallen drastically. The period studied, 1946–1965, is before these drastic changes to the collective bargaining setting.

Dertouzos and Pencavel argue that the union has a dominant power position, and that this justifies the assumption that the union can determine the wage. The union's power derives mainly from the vulnerability of local newspaper firms to a prolonged period of nonproduction. This vulnerability results from several factors: (1) the product cannot be stored, (2) both advertisers and subscribers have various alternative media they can turn to in the event of a strike, and (3) it is often costly and difficult to regain former subscribers and advertisers after a strike.

For the union local examined in the most detail, the *Cincinnati Post,* Dertouzos and Pencavel's estimates imply that the union cares about both wages and employment, but that relatively more weight is put on employment than would be the case if the union's objectives were maximization of economic rents. Pencavel (1984) finds that larger union locals have preferences that are approximately those of rent maximization, while smaller locals place more weight on employment.

Farber (1978) analyzes the wage and employment behaviour of the United Mine Workers in the U.S. bituminous coal industry over the period 1946–1973. The union was a dominant force in the industry due to the fragmented market structure (large number of essentially competitive firms), and is, thus, assumed to be able to dictate the wage. However, the union is constrained by the position and shape of the labour demand curve, which depend on substitution between (1) coal and other fuels in the product market, (2) labour and other inputs in coal production, and (3) union-produced and non-union-produced coal.

Farber's estimates imply that the union places a relatively high weight on employment relative to wages and benefits, higher than would be implied by wage bill or economic rent maximization. Other studies based on the labour demand model also find that unions place a relatively high weight on employment. For example, Martinello (1989) analyzes the behaviour of the International Woodworkers of America (IWA) in the British Columbia forest products industry. Although his primary objective is to compare the performance of the labour demand and contract curve models, his estimates for the labour demand model (assuming the union can set the wage) also imply that the union places a relatively high weight on employment.

On the basis of these studies, which are based on the labour demand curve model, there appears to be agreement on several issues: (1) both employment and wages are important to unions, (2) union preferences display a diminishing marginal rate of substitution between wages and employment, (3) union preferences are sensitive to the alternative wage, (4) unions generally place relatively more weight on employment than wages, (5) wage bill maximization is rejected as a union objective function, and (6) economic rent maximization is rejected in the majority of cases. In assessing these conclusions, it is important to keep in mind that only a small number of unions have been analyzed using modern econometric methods and that the conclusions are conditional on some key assumptions, in particular that the union can dictate the wage and the firm unilaterally sets employment.

The task of testing between the contract curve and labour demand models has been addressed in a number of papers. The basic methodology is to test whether, controlling for the contract wage, w, the alternative wage, w_a, helps predict employment. The alternative wage is an indicator that union preferences help predict employment off the demand curve, but on the contract curve. This would be the case, for example, if union preferences resembled those depicted in Figure 14.3(d) (maximize economic rent). In this case, the contract curve is vertical (see Problem 4 at the end of this chapter), so the level of employment is independent of the contract wage and varies only with changes in the alternative wage. In contrast, under the labour demand curve model, the contract wage should be the only wage relevant for employment determination.

Most studies employ contract-level data for specific unions and industries. For example, Brown and Ashenfelter (1986) and MaCurdy and Pencavel (1986) explore wage and employment outcomes in a sample of ITU contracts in the United States. Card (1986) focuses on airline mechanics in the United States. There are also a few studies that employ Canadian contract data. As mentioned above, Martinello (1989) tests the contracting and labour demand models for a sample of British Columbia forestry workers in the IWA. Christofides (1990) and Christofides and Oswald (1991) use an extensive contract-level data set covering many Canadian firms and unions to try to distinguish between the models.

At this point, there is not a consensus on the question of which model performs best. Most studies find that the contract curve model is more consistent with their data—alternative wages help predict employment levels, and contract wages are often only weakly related to employment (e.g., see Christofides and Oswald 1991). However, the evidence is far from conclusive; in particular, whether the efficient bargaining model is better than alternative frameworks that allow the outcome to be to the right of the demand curve remains to be seen. Furthermore, Manning (1994) questions whether the aforementioned empirical approaches can actually distinguish between the two models. As Card (1990) shows with Canadian contract data, the alternative wage may affect current employment because it helps predict future contract wages and need not have an efficient bargaining interpretation. As Currie (1991) notes, correlation of employment with alternative wages may actually be consistent with a perfectly competitive model of a unionized labour market (see Exhibit 14.3). Furthermore, Oswald (1993) shows that relatively few collective bargaining contracts contain language that explicitly sets employment levels. Thus, if efficient contracts are indeed achieved, this must be accomplished by indirect methods, such as negotiated work rules or by implicit rather than explicit contracts. The conditions under which outcomes are on the labour demand curve or the contract curve (or perhaps in between) is an important but unresolved question.

EXHIBIT 14.3

Are Ontario Teachers' Contracts Efficient?

Janet Currie (1991) attempts to distinguish between the monopoly union and efficient contracts models of union employment and wage determination for a sample of Ontario public school teachers over the period, 1975 to 1983. She finds that controlling for the contract wage, the alternative wage (the average wage in adjoining school districts) is negatively related to the level of employment, while the contract wage is insignificant. These findings are consistent with a vertical contract curve—that is, efficient employment determination in which employment is independent of the union wage.

However, as she notes, these results are also consistent with an entirely different model of the market for teachers: a simple supply and demand model. In that model, alternative wages shift the supply curve for teachers to a given school board. The supply of teachers would be lower to those boards paying wages below the neighbouring boards. Currie shows that, indeed, employment and wage determination in school boards is statistically consistent with a supply and demand model. Her results suggest that, despite the obvious violations of the assumptions governing firm-worker interaction in a unionized market, a competitive model may capture the essential features of employment and wage determination.

Perhaps the most important aspect of union wage and employment determination that is not addressed by the above studies is the incorporation of firm–union bargaining in the empirical analysis. In general, the labour demand and contract curve models predict a range of possible wage-employment outcomes rather than a unique outcome. In order to determine the particular settlement the parties will reach, we require a theory of bargaining, a subject that is examined in the online appendix to this chapter.

Union Bargaining Power

The term **bargaining power** arises frequently in discussions of firm–union bargaining. Like many terms that are widely used, the precise meaning is not always clear. In this section, we contrast two possible meanings of union bargaining power. For simplicity, we assume that the two parties negotiate over wages alone, leaving the firm to set employment. The extension of these ideas to the case of bargaining over wages and employment is straightforward.

One meaning of bargaining power is related to the elasticity of labour demand. A union facing an inelastic demand for labour can raise wages substantially with only minor adverse employment consequences. This notion of bargaining power is associated with the *willingness* to increase wages; other things equal, the more inelastic the demand for labour, the more willing is the union to raise the wage rate.

An alternative notion of bargaining power is associated with the *ability* to raise wages. According to this meaning of the term, a powerful union is one that can obtain a negotiated outcome close to its most preferred outcome. This aspect of union power depends not on the elasticity of labour demand but primarily on the relative costs of disagreement to each party.

Because these two aspects of bargaining power depend on different variables, it is possible for a union to be powerful according to one definition but weak according to another. This possibility is illustrated in Figure 14.8. Panel (a) shows a union that is willing to raise wages substantially but is unable to do so; the negotiated wage, W_c, is considerably below the union's preferred wage, W_u. Panel (b) shows a union that can obtain its preferred outcome but is not willing to raise wages substantially because of the employment consequences. Of course, in some circumstances a union may be powerful (or weak) according to both meanings. However, neither aspect of bargaining power alone ensures that the negotiated union wage will be substantially higher than the alternative wage.

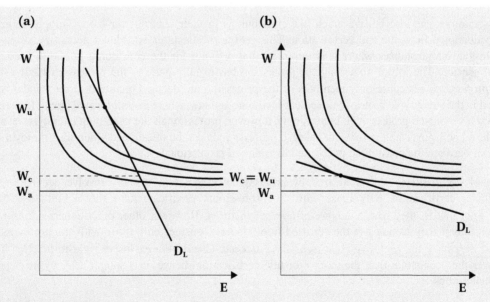

Figure 14.8 Alternative Aspects of Union Power

Two alternative aspects of union power, the "willingness" and "ability" to raise wages, are illustrated. Panel (a) shows a situation in which the union is willing to raise wages substantially because the demand for labour is relatively inelastic. Nonetheless, the union is limited in its ability to increase wages; it is able to achieve only the outcome W_c, which is substantially below its preferred wage. Panel (b) illustrates a union that is able to negotiate a contract wage W_c equal to its preferred wage W_u, but is not willing to raise the wage substantially due to the highly elastic demand for labour.

Union Power and Labour Supply

Most unions attempt to improve the wages and working conditions of their members directly by bargaining with the employer, and the strike threat is their primary source of bargaining power. However, craft unions and professional associations can raise the wages and working conditions of their members indirectly by controlling labour supply. For these organizations, restrictions on the supply of labour can constitute an important source of union power.

Restricting Supply: Craft Unions

By restricting the supply of labour, unions can raise wages artificially relative to the situation where competition prevailed in the supply of labour. Craft unions generally have sought to raise the wage of their members by controlling entry into their craft through the apprenticeship system, discrimination, nepotism, high union dues, and such devices as the closed shop (the worker has to be a member of the union *before* being hired; that is, the union controls the hiring hall). Because the supply of labour to the craft is reduced, wages will rise above the wage that would prevail in the absence of the craft restrictions.

Needless to say, the craft union will try to control the whole trade; otherwise, the benefits of the supply restriction would also go to non-union craft workers. Hence, the importance to the union of apprenticeship licensing, the closed shop, the union shop (the worker has to join the union after a probationary period of employment), or the agency shop (the worker must pay union dues but need not be a member of the union).

At the artificially high union wage rate, the quantity of labour supplied will exceed the quantity demanded. To the extent that the union controls entry, the scarce jobs can be rationed to the large number of workers who would like the jobs by such devices as discrimination, nepotism, or high union dues. To the extent that employers have a say in who is hired, they may ration jobs on the basis of discrimination or nepotism, but they may also ration on the basis of productivity-related factors, such as education, training, or experience. While these productivity-related factors obviously are useful requirements for employers, they may be set *artificially* high because the employer has an excess supply of applicants, given the higher unionized wage.

Restricting Supply: Professional Associations

Professional associations can also behave much like craft unions in their control over labour supply, largely through the processes of occupational licensing and certification. This setting of standards is deemed necessary, ostensibly to protect the public interest in circumstances where it is important but difficult for the consuming public to judge the quality of the professional service. The job of governing the profession has usually gone to the profession itself—hence, the term *self-governing professions*—because only members of the profession are deemed qualified to set standards. Traditionally, this has occurred in the stereotypic professions, such as medicine and law, where an uninformed clientele purchases complex services from a self-employed professional. Increasingly, however, professionals are becoming employed on a salaried basis, and the rationale for self-governing powers for salaried professionals can be questioned when the employer can provide an effective mediator between the consuming public and the salaried professional.

The techniques of occupational control utilized by professional associations usually involve occupational licensing or certification. Under certification, only those with the professional certificate have the right to use the professional designation, or title; that is, they have a *reserve-of-title certification*. However, other practitioners are allowed to practise in the profession, albeit they cannot use the certified title. Under licensing, only those with the professional licence can practise; that is, they have the *exclusive right-to-practise licence*. Clearly the exclusive right-to-practise licence involves more control over the occupation than the reserve-of-title certification; hence, it is sought after by most professional and quasi-professional groups.

Under licensing, the supply of labour to the occupation is restricted only to those with the licence. Under certification, the supply restrictions are less severe in the sense that others can practise in the profession, although competition is restricted because others cannot use the professionally designated certification. Whatever the impact on the quality of the service performed, the supply of labour to the occupation is restricted and wages rise accordingly. In this sense, professional associations like craft unions raise the wages of their members.

Although they receive higher wages, members of the profession may bear costs associated with the occupational licensing requirements. Such costs could include lengthy education periods as well as practical training periods, such as internship for doctors or articling for lawyers. There is a danger, however, in that the *incumbent* professionals may try to have the brunt of the licensing costs borne by *new* entrants into the profession. This could be accomplished by having increasingly stringent education or training requirements as a qualification for entry into the profession, with so-called "grandfather" clauses exempting those who are already practising. In this fashion, the new entrants bear more of the licensing costs (they will do so as long as the wage premium outweighs these costs), the existing practitioners who control the profession benefit from the restricted competition, and the consuming public gets increasingly qualified practitioners, albeit at a higher cost. Restricting grandfather clauses, or having licensing requirements set by persons other than existing practitioners, could go a long way to correcting this potential abuse of occupational licensing.

Summary

- Unions are collective organizations whose primary objective is to improve the well-being of their members. In Canada, this objective is met primarily through collective bargaining with the employer.

- There are two basic types of unions. Craft unions represent workers in a particular trade or occupation, while industrial unions represent the workers in a specific industry. Some unions combine elements of both types.

- A significant fraction of the Canadian labour force, about 24 percent in 2015, are union members. The importance of unions in Canada has increased over time. Union membership as a percentage of nonagricultural paid workers, a commonly used measure of union density, rose from 16 percent in 1920 to 31 percent in 2015.

- Union representation and collective bargaining in Canada are regulated by an elaborate legal framework that has changed substantially over time. The law provides workers with the right to form and join unions, and establishes procedures for administering and enforcing these rights. Canadian labour legislation has also traditionally regulated the use of work stoppages.

- Jurisdiction over labour legislation rests mainly with the provinces, with federal jurisdiction limited to about 10 percent of the labour force.

- The extent of union organization differs substantially across countries. On the basis of union density, Canada is in the middle of the pack among the OECD countries. However, collective agreement coverage in Canada is lower than in most OECD countries, and substantially below levels that prevail in many European countries.

- In Australia and many European countries, there is a large difference between union membership and collective agreement coverage. These differences arise because of centralized bargaining at the level of the industry, sector, or entire economy, and because union agreements are frequently extended to cover unorganized workers in the same industry or sector. In these circumstances, union membership may substantially understate the influence of unions in the economy. In Canada, the gap between union membership and collective agreement coverage is relatively small.

- The extent of union organization varies considerably by province and various individual employee and employer characteristics. Workers in the public and quasi-public sectors are the most heavily unionized, as are workers employed in large establishments.

- Economists use a demand-supply model to explain variations in unionization over time and across industries, regions, and types of workers at a point in time. The demand for union representation emanates from employees and depends on the expected benefits and costs of union representation. The supply of union representation emanates from the organizing and contract administration activities of union leaders and their staff. Employers' actions may influence either the demand or supply of union representation by altering the costs and benefits to employees and union leaders and organizers.

- The growth of unions over time; the extent of union organization across industries, regions, occupations, and establishment; and employee characteristics are systematically related to a number of economic, social, and legal/institutional variables. Both social attitudes toward unions and the legislative framework governing collective bargaining, which, in turn, may reflect society's views of unions, appear to influence union growth and decline. Aggregate economic conditions—in particular, employment growth, unemployment, and inflation—also affect union growth over time. Industry and enterprise characteristics, such as establishment size, industry concentration, capital intensity of production, and the extent of job hazards, contribute to explaining the large variations in union incidence across industries and establishments. Finally, worker characteristics, such as part-time employment, blue-collar employment, age, experience, and position in the wage distribution, also contribute to the determination of union status. These observed relationships are generally consistent with the demand-supply framework for understanding the growth and incidence of unions.

- The theory of union behaviour has long been a subject of debate. Some advocate an "economic" approach that assumes the union seeks to maximize an objective function subject to constraints. Others criticize this approach as not paying enough attention to the union as a political institution in which union leaders are elected to represent the wishes of the members and may perhaps also pursue their own objectives. The modern approach to union behaviour recognizes some merit in both positions in that the union is modelled as attempting to maximize a well-defined utility function, but attention is paid to the political nature of union decision making, especially the relationship between the preferences of individual members and those pursued by union leaders.

- Union objectives refer to the goals of the organization. The relationship between the preferences of the members, those of the union leaders, and the objectives of the organization as a whole depend on several factors, including (1) the information available to the rank-and-file about the available options, (2) the nature of the union's political decision-making process, and (3) the degree of homogeneity of the individual members' preferences.

- Union utility is postulated to be a function of the union wage and the employment of union members. Union indifference curves are downward sloping in wage-employment space, because a higher wage is needed to compensate for a reduction in employment, holding utility constant. Further, it is plausible to hypothesize that union preferences display a diminishing marginal rate of substitution between wages and employment, so that the indifference curves are convex in shape.

- Union objectives also depend on the price level and the alternative wage available to union members in their best alternative job. What matters to union members is their real wage; that is, the wage rate relative to the cost of living. The benefits to union members of belonging to the union also depend on the union or contract wage relative to their best alternative wage.

- The general union utility function depends on the real union wage, total employment of union members, and the real alternative wage. Some special cases of this utility function that have been proposed include (1) maximizing the (real) wage rate, which places no weight on employment in union preferences; (2) maximizing employment, which places no weight on the union wage; (3) maximizing the wage bill, the product of employment and the wage rate, which ignores the alternative wage; and (4) maximizing economic rent, the product of employment and the difference between the union wage and the alternative wage. The latter is the most plausible of these special cases, and is analogous to the union acting as a monopoly seller of labour to the firm, and maximizing the "total return," or profit.

- The task of deriving union objectives from the underlying preferences of individual members is easiest when individual members' preferences are relatively homogeneous. When this is not the case (e.g., older members wanting to place more weight in union decision making on pensions and less on current wages than younger members), the median voter model may be a good way to represent union preferences. According to this model, the preferences of the organization as a whole will be those of the median member (e.g., the member of median age in the case of preferences that differ according to the age of the member). The median voter model can be derived under certain conditions from a political model of union decision making.

- Union leaders may pursue their own objectives to some extent, but they are constrained by the desire to remain in office. A theory of union objectives that is based solely on the wishes of the members may not be able to account for all aspects of union behaviour but may provide a good approximation to observed behaviour in most circumstances.

- Union utility depends on the preferences of individual members; thus, changes over time in union membership may lead to changes in union objectives. For example, an increase in product demand will lead to an influx of new and possibly younger members, reducing the age and seniority of the median member.

- If the firm chooses employment subject to the negotiated wage rate, the union is constrained by the firm's labour demand curve. In this situation, the union's preferred wage-employment outcome occurs where the union indifference curve is tangent to the labour demand curve. The firm would prefer to pay the alternative wage—the minimum wage rate needed to attract labour to this sector. This leads to the "labour demand curve," or "right to manage" model, in which the two parties negotiate the wage rate and the firm chooses employment. The negotiated wage will lie somewhere in the bargaining range, between the alternative wage and the union's preferred wage rate.

- Unions may be able to enhance their available wage-employment outcomes by relaxing the demand constraint—either by increasing labour demand (shifting the demand curve to the right) or making labour demand more inelastic (making employment less responsive to increases in the wage). Such policies may include support for restrictions on competition in the product market, opposition to deregulation, and support for wage fixing legislation, such as minimum wage laws and "fair wage" provisions.

- In general, the firm and union can each benefit from negotiating a contract covering both wages and employment. Outcomes on the labour demand curve imply unexploited "gains from trade" that can be attained by exchanging a lower wage rate for increased employment such that both firm profits and union utility rise. The set of Pareto-efficient wage-employment contracts occurs where the union indifference curves are tangent to the firm's isoprofit curves, so that the rate at which the two parties are willing to exchange wages for employment is equalized at the margin. This set of Pareto efficient contracts, called the *contract curve*, lies to the right of the labour demand curve, thus implying that the higher wages that generally accompany unionization may not be associated with reduced employment.

- In principle, both the employer and union can benefit from negotiating over wages and employment, but in practice there are several obstacles to reaching efficient contracts. First, the parties must reveal to each other sufficient information to realize that there are unexploited gains from trade. Second, because demand may shift several times during the term of the agreement, thus altering the contract curve and the efficient levels of wages and employment, the contract must stipulate the employment level under a variety of contingencies. Third, there is a need for costly monitoring, because, for any given contract wage, the firm has an incentive to reduce employment to the labour demand curve, where profits are maximized at that wage rate. The costs of negotiating, monitoring, and enforcing such "contingent contracts" may be too high to make the effort worthwhile.

- Approximately efficient contracts may allow the firm and union to achieve most of the gains from trade associated with moving toward the contract curve without negotiating a fully contingent contract. These can be accomplished by tying employment to the output of the firm or to the use of other inputs. These arrangements allow employment to change in response to shifts in demand, but also constrain the firm to employ more workers than the profit-maximizing level at the contract wage. Examples of such contractual arrangements are observed in many sectors, including railroads (size of freight train crews), airlines (number of pilots per aircraft), and teaching (class-size provisions). The theory of efficient wage-employment contracts helps explain the existence and persistence of such "restrictive work practices"—practices that may appear to be socially wasteful.

- Empirical studies of union wage and employment determination face several challenges: (1) choosing an appropriate specification of union preferences, (2) the presence of two alternative models of wage and employment determination that are plausible on a priori grounds, and (3) the need for a theory of firm–union bargaining to predict the specific wage-employment outcome chosen by the parties.

- The earliest empirical studies assume that observed wage-employment outcomes lie on the labour demand curve and that the union is sufficiently powerful to achieve its preferred outcome. Another set of studies assumes that observed outcomes are efficient (i.e., on the contract curve). Recently, scholars have begun the difficult task of incorporating bargaining theory into the empirical analysis of union wage and employment determination.

- Studies of several unions and industries based on the labour demand curve model generally agree on a number of findings: (1) both employment and wages are important to unions, (2) union preferences display a diminishing marginal rate of substitution between wages and employment, (3) union preferences are sensitive to the alternative wage, and (4) unions generally place more weight on employment than wages.

- Several studies have attempted to test between the "labour demand curve" and "efficient contracts" models using contract-level data for specific unions and groups of firms. At this point there is not a consensus on which model performs best.

- Two possible meanings of the term "union bargaining power" are implied by the analysis in this chapter. One is related to the elasticity of labour demand. A union facing an inelastic demand for labour can raise wages substantially with only minor adverse employment consequences. This notion of bargaining power is associated with the *willingness* to raise wages. The second notion is associated with the *ability* to raise wages. According to this meaning of the term, a powerful union is one that can obtain a negotiated outcome close to its most preferred outcome. This aspect of union power depends not on the elasticity of labour demand but principally on the relative costs of disagreement to each party.

- Most unions attempt to improve the wages and working conditions of their members directly by bargaining with the employer. However, craft unions and professional associations can raise wages and improve working conditions indirectly by controlling labour supply. Mechanisms for restricting labour supply include limiting entry through the apprenticeship system, occupational licensing, and certification.

Keywords

alternative wage	**efficient wage and employment contracts**
bargaining power	**industrial unions**
bargaining range	**isoprofit curves**
bargaining unit	**median voter model**
certification	**Pareto-efficient wage-employment outcome**
collective agreement coverage	**supply of union representation**
collective bargaining	**unions**
contract curve	**union density**
craft unions	**union membership**
decertification	**union objectives**
demand for union representation	**union status**
economic rent	

Review Questions

1. Account for the differential growth of unionization between Canada and the United States in recent years.

2. "Differential legislative structures may account for some of the differential union growth between Canada and the United States; however, that raises the question of why the legislative structures are different. That is, legislation should be regarded as an endogenous variable and its existence explained." Discuss.

3. Discuss differences in the concepts of union density based on union membership and the proportion of the workforce that is covered by a collective agreement. What accounts for the differences in the magnitude in Canada? Which of the two measures is best for summarizing the significance of unions in the determination of wages and working conditions?

4. Outline the main legislative initiatives in Canada that have facilitated the development of unionization and collective bargaining.

5. The extent of unionization in Canada varies from one province to another. Discuss factors that could account for these differences.

6. Discuss the general factors that would explain the differences in union density across employee characteristics shown in Table 14.3.

7. Discuss why the objectives of union leadership may differ from the objectives of the rank-and-file. Discuss the implications of such differences.

8. Draw the union indifference curves (iso-utility curves) for the following situations:

   a. Wages and employment are perfect substitutes.

   b. There is a minimum wage below which union members will not reduce their wages in order to increase employment.

   c. At the current level of employment within the union, unions attach more disutility to a given employment reduction than the utility they attach to a corresponding employment increase.

   d. As their wealth increases, union members attach more weight to job security than to real income gains.

   e. The union objective is to maximize the wage bill.

   f. The union objective is to maximize total economic rent.

9. Discuss the effect of an increase in the alternative wage rate on the utility of the union.

10. Discuss the error in the following statement: "Because the firm is maximizing profits at each point on its demand curve, it is indifferent among these points."

11. Discuss the constraints that limit the "bargaining range" between unions and employers.

12. Discuss various ways in which unions may try to make the demand for labour more inelastic so as to minimize any adverse effect emanating from any wage increase.

13. Discuss why efficient wage and employment contracts are not on the firm's labour demand curve. That is, show how both labour and management potentially could be better off by agreeing to wage and employment combinations that are not on the firm's labour demand curve.

14. Discuss the obstacles that unions and management may face in arriving at efficient wage-employment contracts.

15. "Craft unions and professional associations will affect the wages of their members in a different manner than industrial unions." Discuss, and indicate why this may be the case.

16. "Self-government is an anachronism for salaried as opposed to self-employed professionals." Discuss.

17. Distinguish between occupational licensing and certification. Give examples of each.

Problems

1. "Any theory of union growth must be able to explain not only its long-run trend and short-run cyclical variation, but also why unionization varies across countries and across industries, regions, and occupations within a country." Discuss.

2. Given the determinants of unionization, discuss the future prospects for union growth in Canada.

3. Discuss why union members may differentiate in their preferences between hours of work and employment. What are the implications for union preferences?

4. Discuss the implications of unions being a democratic institution, reflecting the preferences of the median union voter. Why would the preferences of the median voter dominate in such a situation? What are the implications for minority rights within the union?

5. "If unions engage in concession bargaining to maintain job security, they should specifically bargain for a specific level of security to be associated with their wage concessions, rather than simply agreeing to the concessions and allowing the firm to choose the level of employment." Discuss.

6. Show that if the union's objective function is to maximize economic rent, the contract curve is vertical and employment corresponds to the level of employment that would prevail if the firm set employment subject to the constraint of paying the alternative wage.

7. What determines where the parties will settle on the contract curve? Could the indeterminacy of where the parties will be on the contract curve ever prevent them from arriving at an efficient contract?

8. Discuss how certain featherbedding rules may be efficient and sustain themselves in a competitive market environment. Does this mean that firms will never try to "buy out" such seemingly inefficient practices?

9. Some trade unionists have argued that wage concessions have not preserved jobs. Use the material developed in this chapter to illustrate the circumstances under which this concern may be legitimate, and the conditions under which the concern is not correct.

10. Show that if the union's objective is to maximize the wage paid, and if the firm and the union negotiate an efficient contract, then the contract curve will correspond to the labour demand schedule.

11. "The main foe of any union is various forms of substitution, not the firm."

    a. Explain the various forms of substitution that unions need to be aware of in formulating their bargaining objectives, and elaborate on the relationship between these forms of substitution and union bargaining power.

    b. The United Mine Workers studied by Farber (1978) had two instruments for affecting the monetary returns to and employment of their members—the hourly wage rate and the output tax (tax per ton of coal produced), the proceeds from which were distributed to members. Under what circumstances would the use of these two instruments allow the union to achieve outcomes that could not be achieved by affecting the wage rate alone?

12. "The argument that restrictive work practices and overstaffing provisions can be efficient doesn't make sense. Such practices imply that the marginal revenue product of the last worker hired is less than the wage rate paid to that worker, and this situation can't be efficient." Discuss.

13. Firms often complain about the restrictive work rules in their collective agreements. Why don't they "buy off" these rules by paying a higher union wage in exchange for removal of these restrictions? Explain and illustrate your explanation in a diagram.

14. Indicate conditions under which one may expect unions to have a substantial impact on the wages of their members.

15. If craft unions or professional associations can raise the wages in their trades above the competitive norm, excess supplies of applicants would result. Discuss how the scarce jobs may be rationed.

16. "If occupational licensing is necessary, the only group that could be entrusted not to abuse the powers of licensing would be the alumni of the profession, or at least members who were about to retire. Only they have knowledge about the profession, without having self-interest in abusing the power of licensing. Existing practitioners, while knowledgeable about the profession, have self-interest to restrict entry by putting unnecessarily costly entry requirements on new entrants into the profession. New entrants may not find it in their self-interest to put unnecessary restrictions on their entry into the profession, but they do not yet have sufficient knowledge about the profession and what is required for proper qualifications. The general public, while having an interest in ensuring quality performance without unnecessary restrictions, may not be able to judge what requirements are necessary for professional competence. Only alumni have knowledge of the profession without having a self-interest in excessive quality restrictions; consequently, they are the persons who should be entrusted with the powers of occupational licensing, if it is necessary." Discuss.

17. "Restrictions on the use of grandfather clauses would go a long way in reducing the abuses of occupational self-licensing." Discuss.

18. Indicate why incumbent practitioners in a profession may want to put excessive restrictions on entry into the profession.

Endnotes

1. To avoid this difficulty, Dunlop (1944) suggested that the union maximize the wage bill subject to a "membership function," which shows the wage rate needed to attract a given number of union members. The membership function is analogous to a labour supply function.

2. In the public and non-profit sectors the labour demand curve is derived under different assumptions about the organization's objective; for example, cost minimization. In these circumstances the demand curve shows the cost-minimizing level of employment for each wage rate.

3. Pareto efficiency is defined here in terms of the interests of the two parties. Whether such wage-employment outcomes are socially efficient (Pareto-efficient in terms of the interests of society as a whole) is unclear and will depend on a variety of other factors.

4. If D_L shifts, so does the set of Pareto-efficient (W, E) combinations. Even if an agreement for a specific level of employment could be enforced, there is no incentive for the two parties to reach such an agreement if the demand or supply of labour is expected to shift.

PORTRAIT IMAGES ASIA/Shutterstock.com

CHAPTER 15

Union Impact on Wage and Non-wage Outcomes

LEARNING OBJECTIVES

LO1   Discuss the difficulties in measuring the impact of unions on the wages of their members and the methodologies that are often used to overcome those difficulties. Illustrate some of the more recent econometric methods that are used to get causal estimates of the impact of unions on wages, including fixed-effects panel estimates, instrumental variables, regression discontinuities, and propensity score matching procedures.

LO2   Describe the mechanisms whereby unions may affect the wages of non-union workers.

LO3   Explain how unions affect pay wage inequality and the distribution of income.

LO4   Discuss how the impact of unions may differ across various characteristics, such as skill level, gender, the public and private sectors, and the degree of competition in the product market.

LO5   Describe how unions may affect productivity, investment, and the profitability of the firm, as well as overall efficiency in the economy as a whole.

MAIN QUESTIONS

- What are some of the difficulties of estimating the causal effect of unions on wages, and what are some of the newer procedures used to deal with those difficulties?

- By how much are unions able to raise the wages of their members? Which types of workers benefit most?

- What effects do unions have on the wages of non-union workers?

- Do unions increase or decrease the overall degree of income inequality?

- How much economic inefficiency can be blamed on the consequences of unionization?

- Are there positive effects of unionization on labour productivity?

- On balance, do unions reduce the profits of firms?

This chapter focuses on the impact of unions on various labour market outcomes. We begin by examining the impact of unions on the wages of their members and on the wages of other employees. The rest of the chapter discusses various non-wage consequences of unions—including their impact on fringe benefits, productivity, firm profitability, turnover (quits and layoffs), income distribution, investment, and the allocation of resources.

 LO1

Union Wage Impact

The impact of unions on wages has received more attention from economists than any other aspect of union behaviour. Most of the empirical research has been directed at measuring the **union–non-union wage differential**, the (percentage) difference in wages between union and otherwise comparable non-union workers. Our discussion of this research begins by outlining the relevant theoretical background and explaining some of the conceptual and measurement issues involved. We then proceed to a summary of the main empirical findings and a discussion of how these empirical results should best be interpreted.

The basic issues can be illustrated by imagining what evidence could be brought to bear on the question, what is the (average) effect of unionization on an individual worker's wage? The simplest way to tackle the question would be to compare the average wages of union (W_U) and non-union (W_N) workers. The percentage difference in wages would be given by

$$\hat{d} = \frac{\overline{W}_U - \overline{W}_N}{\overline{W}_N} \approx \ln \overline{W}_U - \ln \overline{W}_N$$

The first problem that one confronts is that the wages of non-union members may not be the same as the wages that would prevail in the complete absence of unions from the labour market (say, W_0). There are a number of theoretical reasons to believe that unions affect the wages of those employed in the non-union sector. We never really observe the counterfactual case to a union member's wages that would prevail if unions were removed entirely from the economy, and the wages of non-union employees may be a poor proxy.

The second problem is more practical, and concerns the more limited objective of measuring the impact of changing an individual's union status, given the level of unionization in the economy. The above measure, $\hat{d}$, measures only the "pure" effect of union status if union status is the sole difference between the union and non-union workers. For reasons discussed below, this may not be the case, and more-complicated statistical procedures have had to be employed in order for the estimator $\hat{d}$ to approximate a pure union effect.

Theoretical Background and Conceptual Problems

In many respects, the basic theory of the union wage impact is similar to that underlying the impact of other wage-fixing arrangements, such as minimum wage. However, there are some unique aspects of union wage determination, and these will emerge in what follows. We first examine the union wage impact in the simplest setting, and subsequently introduce additional complications.

In the analysis of union wage and employment determination in the previous chapter, the union workers' alternative wage—which in many situations may be taken to be the non-union wage—was taken as exogenously given. At this stage, however, it is important to recognize the impact of unions not only on the wages of union members but also on the wages of others. This requires a general equilibrium model. Most of the basic principles can be illustrated with a two-sector model, as shown in Figure 15.1(a). The two sectors, A and B, can be thought of as two different industries or regions employing the same type of labour, which is assumed to be homogeneous. There are a sufficiently large number of firms and workers that, in the absence of unions, the labour market is competitive. The equilibrium wage in the absence of collective bargaining is, therefore, W_0. (If there are differences in the desirability of jobs in the two sectors, a compensating wage differential would exist in equilibrium, as discussed in Chapter 8 of this text; allowing for this possibility would not affect the analysis other than to make it more complex.) Now, suppose a union organizes the workers in sector A and is able to raise the wage to W_U. Employment in sector A will, therefore, decline to E_1^A (We are assuming here that the firm can unilaterally set employment; the possibility of wage-employment outcomes to the right of the labour demand curve is discussed below.) The workers who are unable to obtain (or retain) employment in sector A will search for jobs in sector B, increasing labour supply to that sector by $a = E_0^A - E_1^A$. The additional labour supply depresses the wage in sector B, resulting in a new equilibrium wage of W_N. Employment expands to E_1^B, an increase (the amount b in Figure 15.1[a]) that is smaller than the reduction in employment in sector A. The difference $(a - b)$ in Figure 15.1(a) is due to the upward-sloping supply of labour to the economy; as the market wage falls in sector B, some individuals drop out of the labour force due to the market wage falling below their reservation wage.

In this economy, the union–non-union wage differential would be $\hat{d} = \dfrac{W_U - W_N}{W_N}$. Note that this is greater than the difference between the union wage W_U and the wage union members would receive in the absence of unionization (W_0). The difference arises because the higher wages associated with unionization force more workers to seek employment in the unorganized sector, with this spillover effect depressing wages there. In this respect, the impact of unions on wages in the two sectors is similar to that of firms in sector A paying efficiency wages, as discussed in Chapter 10.

According to this basic **two-sector model**, the magnitude of the union–non-union differential depends on (1) the elasticity of labour demand in each sector, (2) the ability of the union to raise wages in the organized sector, and (3) the elasticity of labour supply.

This basic model is consistent with the notion of a dual labour market. The primary sector (A) consists of firms or industries that have characteristics—such as establishment size, concentration in the product market, stability of employment, and the nature of production—that make unionization likely. The secondary sector (B) consists of firms or industries with the opposite characteristics. The reduction in employment in the primary sector (relative to what employment would be in the absence of wage increases associated with unionization) creates a widening of the wage gap between the two sectors, as those who cannot obtain employment in the unionized sector crowd into the non-union labour market, depressing wages even further in the secondary sector. These low wages may in turn be a source of many of the phenomena, such as high absenteeism and frequent turnover, that are characteristic of the secondary sector.

(a) Union wage impact in a two-sector model

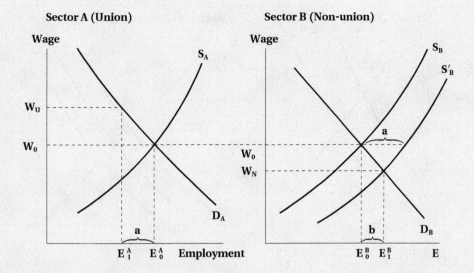

(b) Union wage impact with a threat effect

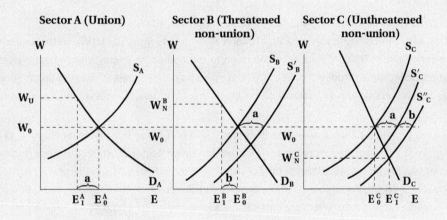

(c) Union wage impact with a vertical contract curve

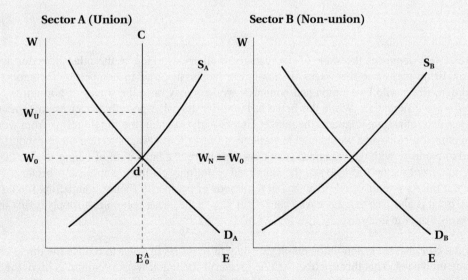

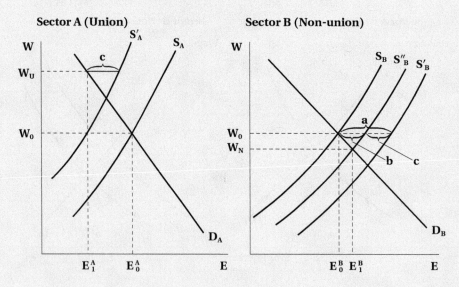

(d) Union wage impact with wait unemployment

Figure 15.1 Two-Sector Model of General Equilibrium

Both sectors start off with the competitive wage W_0. Unions raise wages from W_0 to W_U in the union sector, creating a reduction in employment of a. These displaced workers go to the non-union sector, shifting out the non-union supply schedule by a, and reducing wages from W_0 to W_N. This induces some individuals in the non-union sector to leave that sector (i.e., there is a movement down the supply curve given the lower wage), presumably to leave the labour force altogether.

The non-union sector is broken into two subsectors. In sector B, the non-union firm raises its wage to W_N^B to reduce the threat of being unionized. The displaced workers, b, go to the non-union sector C, which does not respond with a threat effect, further augmenting the increased labour supply of those who already came from the union sector, a.

With a vertical contract curve Cd, the union bargains for retaining the same level of employment, in spite of the higher wage. There is no adverse employment effect and, hence, no augmentation of labour supply in the non-union sector.

This is the same as panel (a) except that some of the displaced workers (the horizontal distance c) prefer to engage in "wait" unemployment, looking for jobs in the union sector. The net increase in employment in the non-union sector B, thereby, is only b = a – c.

While the spillover effect depresses the wage of unorganized workers, working in the other direction is the threat effect whereby non-union firms may raise the wages of non-union labour in order to compete with unionized firms for the workforce. In addition, firms with both union and nonunion workers may raise the wages of non-union labour in order to preserve traditional wage differentials. While this belief has intuitive appeal, especially because comparability appears to be so important in wage determination, it ignores the market factors—in particular, the supply influx from workers who cannot get jobs in the unionized sector—that would enable employers to pay lower wages to non-union labour. In essence, there may not be a need to compete with the unionized sector because there is a large pool of labour to hire that cannot get jobs in the high-wage, unionized sector. It is true that the unionized sector may get the top applicants because of the high wages, and it is the case that the reserve of labour may dry up in periods of prosperity (hence compelling the non-union sector to pay higher wages), but it is also true that those who cannot get jobs in the union sector are a supply influx into the non-union sector, and this lowers wages in that sector.

Nonetheless, it is the case that *some* non-union employers may raise wages in order to reduce the threat of their employees choosing to become unionized. This **threat effect** will be greater if the union wage premium is high, the non-union sector is easy to organize, the potential union is aggressive, or the employers have a strong aversion to unionization. In such circumstances, non-union employees may be paid close to the union wage (perhaps even higher, if the firm has a strong aversion to unionization) and provided with working conditions similar to those of union workers. Such employees could receive the benefits of unionization without bearing such costs as union dues or possible strike costs. However, such benefits may be precarious in that they hinge on the willingness of employers to provide them.

To illustrate the operation of the threat effect, we need to distinguish between those firms that choose to pay higher wages to avoid unionization, perhaps because of a strong aversion to unionization or because they are easy to organize, and those that will choose to pay the lowest wage needed to attract labour. This situation is shown in Figure 15.1(b). As before, the equilibrium in the absence of collective bargaining is the wage W_0 in each sector. The establishment of a higher union wage W_U causes some employers (sector B) to raise wages to W_N^B, despite the supply of individuals willing to work at lower wages. (W_N^B may be above or below the union wage, depending on the employer's aversion to unionization.) Employment declines in sectors A and B; thus, wages fall further in sector C than in the absence of the threat effect. In dual labour market analysis, sector C would be identified as the secondary labour market.

The impact of the threat effect on the union–non-union wage differential is ambiguous. The non-union wage is a weighted average of W_N^B and W_N^C, with weights being the employment in each sector. This average non-union wage may be higher or lower than the non-union wage that would prevail in the absence of a threat effect, W_N in Figure 15.1(a).

Two additional theoretical points should be noted; these can also be explained using the basic two-sector model. One is the possibility that the firm and union will negotiate wage-employment outcomes to the right of the labour demand curve, for reasons discussed previously in Chapter 14. Figure 15.1(c) illustrates the case in which the parties negotiate outcomes on a vertical contract curve. (Recall from Chapter 14 that the contract curve may be upward sloping, downward sloping, or vertical.) In these circumstances, the higher union wage is not associated with reduced employment in the union sector and, therefore, with depressed wages in the non-union sector. The union–non-union differential in this case is identical to the difference between the union wage and the wage union members would earn in the absence of collective bargaining. If the contract curve is downward sloping, the higher union wage will result in some displacement of labour to the non-union sector, and therefore, lower wages in that sector; however, these impacts will be smaller than will be the case if employment is on the demand curve.

The final complication to be discussed is that of **wait or queue unemployment**. The rationale behind this phenomenon can be understood by returning to the two-sector model illustrated in Figure 15.1(a). In that case, it was assumed that all of the workers unable to obtain jobs in the union sector would seek employment in the non-union sector. However, because union jobs pay relatively well, it may be rational to wait for a union job to turn up rather than to seek employment elsewhere. This strategy is most likely to be sensible when there is rapid turnover in the union sector (so that union jobs become available fairly frequently) and when it is difficult to queue for a union job while employed. When these conditions apply, some individuals may choose to remain attached to the union sector, albeit unemployed. As a consequence, the increase in supply to the non-union sector will be less than the reduction in employment in the union sector; compare Figures 15.1(a) and (d). The union–non-union wage differential will be smaller than in the case of no queuing unemployment, though higher union wages nonetheless have some depressing effect on the wages of non-union workers.

Higher union wages may also affect the demand for labour in the two sectors. This outcome is most likely to occur when the sectors constitute two groups of firms—possibly one group easy to organize and the other difficult to organize—in the same industry. Unless offset by higher labour productivity (a possibility discussed later) the union–non-union wage differential may enable non-union firms to expand their market share at the expense of union firms, thus shifting the demand for non-union (union) labour to the right (left). The final equilibrium in this case will generally involve a smaller union–non-union wage differential than that shown in Figure 15.1(a).

The above analysis of the union wage impact was based on several simplifying assumptions, including a homogeneous labour force and competitive labour markets (in the absence of collective bargaining). Several implications follow from relaxing these assumptions. With several different types of workers, changes in the wages of any one group will generally alter the wages of other groups. If union and non-union workers are employed in the same firm or industry, an increase in union wages will increase (reduce) the demand—and, therefore, the wages—for non-union labour, if the two groups are substitutes (complements) in production. In addition, the wages of non-union workers may be affected by various forms of wage-fixing, such as minimum wage rates and fair wage provisions, many of which are supported by unions to reduce competition based on lower non-union wages. In these circumstances, the wage in the unorganized sector may not decline sufficiently to absorb the workers displaced by higher wages in the union sector. Jobs will be rationed in both sectors and there will be a number of individuals willing to work at existing wage rates but unable to find employment.

In summary, collective action (in particular the strike threat) will generally enable unions to raise wages relative to a hypothetical labour market equilibrium without unions, thus creating a wage differential between union and comparable non-union workers. The magnitude of this differential depends not only on the ability and willingness of unions to raise wages but also on the impact on the wages of non-union workers. Clearly, the various factors discussed above can be at work simultaneously affecting the wages of non-union workers, and since they do not all work in the same direction, economic theory does not provide unambiguous predictions of the effect of unions on the wages of non-union workers. The wages of some non-union workers may increase for various reasons: the increased demand for substitute non-union labour, the threat effect, in response to legislative wage-fixing, or as part of the non-union sector adjusts to restore old wage relativities. In contrast, some non-union wages may decrease because of a decrease in the demand for complementary inputs, or because of the supply influx into the non-union sector created by the reduced employment opportunities in the unionized sector. Ultimately, the impact of unions on the wages of non-union workers is an empirical proposition.

Some Problems in Measuring the Union Wage Impact

Attempts to measure the union–non-union wage differential face a number of interrelated problems, the most important being those of controlling for other wage-determining factors, accounting for the joint determination of union status and the union wage impact, and separating cause and effect.

In estimating a *pure* union–non-union wage differential, it is important to control for other wage-determining factors so as to be able to attribute the differential purely to unionization. If, for example, unionized establishments tend to utilize more skilled labour than non-unionized establishments, it is crucial to control for these skill differences. Otherwise, the union–non-union wage differential may simply reflect the skill differential, not a pure union impact on wages. Controlling for differences in labour quality between the union and non-union sectors is especially important because, as indicated earlier, if unionized establishments pay a wage that is greater than the competitive wage, they may have a queue of applicants and may be able to hire the "cream of the crop" of applicants. Union firms faced with higher labour costs may also try to increase the job assignment, for example, by increasing the pace of work; however, such adjustments are likely to be resisted by the union.

In these circumstances, it is extremely important to control for differences in the characteristics of workers and job assignments. Otherwise, these omitted variables are likely to impart an upward bias because the union–non-union wage differential would reflect better-quality workers and perhaps more onerous job assignments in the union sector, in addition to the pure wage impact of unions.

Most contemporary studies use individual micro-level data to estimate the impact of union status on earnings. This permits the researcher to try to control for labour quality differences by including variables, such as education, training, and experience in a multiple regression framework. In fact, the most common procedure is to embed union status in the human capital earnings function described in previous chapters. In this way, the inclusion of the other regressors allows the investigator to control for observable factors believed to affect earnings in the absence of unions. The implicit model is then,

$$\ln W_i = \beta_0 + \beta_1 X_1 + \ldots \beta_K X_K + \beta_U \text{ IUNION} + \varepsilon_i$$

where the X's are the standard human capital variables and ε captures all the other, unobserved worker characteristics. An estimate of β_U would then be an estimate of the impact of union status (IUNION) on individual earnings, controlling for observed earnings characteristics.

Unfortunately, some of the factors believed to affect labour quality and earnings (e.g., motivation, work effort, and reliability) may not be observed by the economist. If these characteristics are correlated with union status, then some of the estimated effect that is attributed to union status may, in fact, merely reflect these unobserved differences between union and non-union workers. For example, information relating to the pace of work and job assignments is also often unavailable, although some studies (e.g., Duncan and Stafford 1980) have been able to control for these factors. Many studies are able to include only crude controls (such as occupation, industry, and region) for the characteristics of the job. Thus, it is not clear that the available data enables researchers to *fully* control for differences in productivity-related factors, although, as will be explained below, the quality of the available data has steadily improved.

These issues illustrate the problem of **selection bias** or the nonexperimental nature of union status, in the context of the union wage impact. As discussed in Chapter 14, union status is the outcome of decisions made by individual workers, employers, and union organizers. The omission from the estimated earnings equations of unobserved variables that are related to wages (such as motivation, work ethic, and reliability) will not bias the estimates of the union wage impact if these unobserved factors do not also influence the decisions relating to union status; that is, if the unobserved factors affecting wages do not also influence selection into the union sector. However, if factors unobserved by the researcher influence wages and selection decisions—for example, if ability is not observed by the researcher but is known by employers, perhaps because of screening procedures, and used to decide which applicants to hire—then the estimated union wage impact will be subject to selection bias. Addressing the selection bias problem is quite difficult, as it entails simultaneously explaining individual union status as well as the effect of unionization on wages.

The issue of the selection process determining which workers enter the union sector illustrates the more general problem of sorting out cause and effect in studies of the union impact. Usually, the argument is advanced that unions cause higher wages. However, there is the possibility that cause and effect also works in the opposite direction. That is, some firms may simply be high-wage firms, perhaps because of efficiency wage considerations relating to productivity and morale, perhaps because they are trying to reduce the turnover of workers with firm-specific human capital, they want to be known as a model employer, or they want a queue of applicants from which to hire. Unionization may be more likely to emerge in high-wage sectors because they are easier to organize or because the workers may be more likely to demand union representation. Workers in these firms will be reluctant to leave because wages are so high. Knowing that they want to stay in the high-wage establishment, and knowing that they will probably stay there for a considerable period of time because of the high wages, they may turn to devices to try to improve the everyday work conditions of the job. One such device may be unionization with its emphasis on due process, regulating the work environment, and administered rulings that provide a degree of certainty and security for the unionized workers.

In Hirschman's (1970) terminology, the restriction of **exit** increases the use of **voice**. In this case, voluntary quitting (exit) is reduced because of the high wages, and hence, workers seek to have more of a say (voice) in their job by collective bargaining.

This possibility of cause and effect working in both directions suggests that some of the wage advantage of union establishments may not be due to unions, but may be attributed to other factors; in fact, unionism itself emerges because of the wage advantage. This suggests that econometric studies of the impact of unions should be based on simultaneous equation models, which allow wages to be a function of unionism as well as unionism to be a function of wages.

Empirical Evidence on Union Wage Impact

In varying degrees, the numerous empirical studies of the wage impact of unions have attempted to deal with the measurement and modelling problems just discussed. Research has passed through several phases. Early studies based on aggregate data (e.g., industry or region) have given way to those using data based upon the individual worker as the unit of observation. Recent studies have attempted to account for the joint determination of union–non-union status and the union wage impact, and for unobserved quality differences between union and non-union workers. Much of the research has been carried out in the United States and our summary reflects this fact. However, during the 1980s, a number of data sets with information on the union status of individual employees became available in Canada. Accordingly, there is now a growing body of empirical literature on this important aspect of the Canadian labour market.

Early Studies

The classic work of H. Gregg Lewis (1963) both reviewed and reanalyzed the existing literature in the United States and provided new estimates up to 1958. While there was considerable variation in the estimated impact of the studies reviewed by Lewis, he attributed much of the variation to methodological differences. Lewis's estimate of the union–non-union differential, based on his own work and a reanalysis of earlier studies, was approximately 10–15 percent for the U.S. economy as a whole, being larger in recessions and smaller in the boom phase of the business cycle. This estimate of a 10–15 percent differential was associated with an increase in the average union wage of 7–11 percent and a decrease in the average non-union wage of approximately 3 or 4 percent.

Data availability imposed important limitations on these early studies. Because separate union and non-union wage series were not available, the union–non-union differential often had to be inferred from the average wage and the extent of unionization. This inference can be made only under certain restrictive assumptions; thus, the estimates should be treated with caution.

Since Lewis's work, there have been numerous additional studies, most utilizing new data sets where the unit of observation is the individual establishment or worker. Estimates of the union–non-union wage differential based on individual cross-sectional data have tended to produce a wider range of estimates compared to the 10–15 percent recorded by Lewis. However, this conclusion is subject to the qualification that some of the difference between union and non-union wages (after controlling for other wage-determining factors, such as education, age, and experience) may be a reflection of reverse causality and/or unmeasured (unobserved) quality differences between union and non-union workers. Recent research has focused on these issues.

Modelling Union Incidence and Impact

A number of studies have attempted to account for the joint determination of union status and the union wage impact. Ashenfelter and Johnson (1972), who were the first to formally deal with the **simultaneity** issue, used aggregate U.S. time-series data. They found that higher wages make unionization more likely, and that the estimated union wage impact is considerably smaller when the two-way causality is taken into account. Most subsequent studies have applied simultaneous equation methods with individual data. Generally, these studies model the wage determination process in the union and non-union sectors and the selection process determining which workers are employed in each sector. Thus, the researchers account for the possibility that the sample is not randomly generated with respect to union status; that is, union status is endogenously determined and some individuals have unobserved characteristics that make them more likely to be represented by a union than others. Such studies provide excellent illustration of the various methodologies that have been employed to estimate *causal* relationships (in this case the causal effect of unions on wages) rather than simply correlations or associations.

Longitudinal Studies

A recent development that has facilitated the estimation of such causal relationships has been the availability of longitudinal or panel data that provide observations on the same individuals over time. With longitudinal data, person-specific characteristics that are conventionally unobservable to the researcher (e.g., reliability, work effort, and motivation) can be taken into account if these characteristics are constant (i.e. fixed-effects) for each individual over time. In these circumstances, taking first-differences (differences from one period to the next) in the data provides a natural way of removing the effects of such characteristics. This cannot be done with conventional cross-section estimates, which compare different individuals at the same point in time.

The procedure can be illustrated with the earnings regression introduced previously. We assume that the unobservable component of individual i's earnings in year t, ε_{it}, has two components as follows:

$$\varepsilon_{it} = \lambda_i + v_{it}$$

In this case, λ_i captures all of the fixed characteristics of the individual that we believe may be correlated with his union status, while v_{it} represents a purely random error term that is uncorrelated with union status (or any other regressor). If we have two observations on each individual (e.g., in two different years), then we can take first differences:

$$\ln W_{it} - \ln W_{it-1} = \beta_1 \left(X_{1t} - X_{1t-1} \right) + \cdots \beta_K \left(X_{Kt} - X_{Kt-1} \right) + \beta_U \left(\text{IUNION}_t - \text{IUNION}_{t-1} \right) + \varepsilon_{it} - \varepsilon_{it-1}$$

By assumption,

$$\varepsilon_{it} - \varepsilon_{it-1} = \lambda_i + v_{it} - \lambda_i - v_{it-1} = v_{it} - v_{it-1}$$

That is, the λ_i term falls out, so that the error term in this regression is independent of these unobserved, fixed individual characteristics. If the unobserved variables are indeed constant over time, the use of longitudinal data allows the researcher to identify the union impact from the wage change for those individuals who *change* union status ($\text{IUNION}_t - \text{IUNION}_{t-1}$). Essentially, the estimated differential is an average of the earnings gain of those who moved from non-union to union jobs and the earnings loss of those who moved from union to non-union jobs, after controlling for other observable factors.

Longitudinal or panel data analyses in the United States (e.g., Mellow 1981; Mincer 1983; Moore and Raisian 1983; Jakubson 1991) generally find that the estimated union–non-union wage differential is about 10 percent, substantially smaller than suggested by cross-sectional estimates. In a recent study of college faculty in the United States, Hedrick et al. (2011) use panel data and estimate a union pay premium that is essentially zero. They argue that earlier estimates based on cross-section data, which tended to find that positive effects overstated the impact. Indeed, in general, when cross-sectional analyses are carried out on the same data sets, the estimated differentials are approximately double those obtained using data on those who change union status. This finding could be due to unobserved (by the researcher) differences in worker quality between union and non-union workers; if true, this conclusion has important implications for the interpretation of not only observed earnings differences between organized and unorganized workers but also observed differences in labour productivity between the two sectors. However, the assumptions underlying the longitudinal estimates could also be invalid.

In addition, longitudinal data have some deficiencies. There is evidence of error in the measurement of union status that may bias downward the estimated union–non-union wage impact (Freeman 1984). Thus the estimated average wage impact of 10 percent recorded in many of the longitudinal studies may be too low. Card (1996) presents direct evidence in this regard. Using 1987 and 1988 matched (longitudinal) CPS data, he estimates cross-section union wage effects on the order of 16 percent (typical of the literature). Estimation of a conventional **fixed-effects model** yields a much smaller union wage effect of about 6 percent. This suggests a significant amount of selectivity bias. However, external validation of the CPS union indicator suggests that approximately half of the individuals who appear to change union status are miscoded. The longitudinal approach depends on a reliable estimate of the earnings that individuals actually earn in their unionized and non-union state. If half of the individuals are actually miscoded, then the genuine wage differences associated with changing union status will be offset by the "noise" of the mismeasured observations. In the extreme case where union status is randomly reported, there should not be any systematic relationship between wages and "unknown" union status. This will generally lead to an understatement of the union effect. Card takes account of the misclassification problem, and finds that the resulting fixed-effect estimator leads to an estimated union effect of 16 percent, similar to the cross-section estimate.

A further problem is that the number of individuals changing status is typically only 3–5 percent of the total sample, resulting in small and possibly unrepresentative samples. Furthermore, the fact that those individuals who change status may not be typical individuals and that changes in union status may themselves be associated with other unobservable factors suggest that it would be hazardous to rely exclusively on the estimates from longitudinal studies.

Instrumental Variable Analysis

Instrumental variable (IV) analysis has also been used to control for the possibility that union status may not be exogenously determined, for example, if unions may be more likely to form in higher wage sectors in which case unions are a function of higher wages rather than a cause of higher wages. The same applies if union workers are different from non-union workers in unobserved characteristics (e.g., motivation) that can affect wages but that cannot be controlled for by simply including observable control variables in the analysis. IV analysis basically involves estimating a first-stage equation on the probability of being a union member and then using this probability in the second-stage wage equation. Similar procedures are involved in techniques such as the Heckman two-stage procedure to correct for selection bias. Proper identification in the first-stage union status equation generally relies on variables that affect union status but that do not affect wages. Such variables (termed identifying instruments) are extremely difficult to find. In part, for this reason such estimates are often unstable and outside of the range of what would be considered as reasonable estimates of the union impact (reviewed in Lewis 1985, 1986 and discussed in Renaud 1998).

Regression Discontinuity Studies

A number of recent studies have used a regression discontinuity (RD) procedure to estimate the causal impact of unions (DiNardo and Lee 2004; Frandsen 2014; Lee and Mas 2012). In the union impact literature, the RD procedure basically involves comparing those cases that barely won a certification election with those that barely lost the election. The rationale is that the difference between barely winning and barely losing can be considered random luck and, hence, can approximate the equivalent of exogenously randomly assigning people to union and non-union status in order to obtain causal estimates of the union impact. The intent is to make the treatment group (union workers) and the control group (non-union workers) as similar as possible. Those studies tend to find union wage effects that are small or zero.

DiNardo and Lee (2004), for example, use RD to analyse the effect of *new* unions that were formed over the period 1984 to 2001 in the United States. They find that such new unions had little or no impact on various outcomes, such as firm survival, employment, output, and productivity. This was so in large part because such newly formed unions also had no impact on wages. While these results are unusual in finding no wage impact, they are consistent with the possibility that unions may have moderated their wage demands in the face of barely winning the certification drive, as well as because of the constraints imposed by competitive market forces through deregulation, freer trade, and global competition.

The use of RD to approximate random assignment to union and non-union status also may have methodological issues. In closely contested elections, the parties may devote inordinate resources to winning knowing that this may tip the results in their favour rather than being a lost cause. If one side can devote more resources, then it no longer approximates random assignment. As well, the results of closely contested elections may not generalize to all elections. If the union barely wins a closely contested election, for example, it may not have the power to win large subsequent wage gains. As suggested by DiNardo and Mas (2012), larger gains may come from unions that win by a large margin.

Using the RD methodology, Frendsen (2014) also finds little or no union wage effects on workers who remain with the unionized firm after closely contested union elections. Importantly, however, he finds that the negligible *average* effect is a result of offsetting compositional changes in the union workforce; older, higher-wage workers tend to leave the firm while younger, lower-wage workers tend to enter or stay because of large redistributive effects from high-wage to low-wage workers. In essence, the negligible average union wage effect is, somewhat, a case of comparing apples and oranges. To the extent that those who remain with the firm after certification are are lower-wage workers, this would understate the true union wage effect.

Using the RD methodology on closely contested elections in nursing homes in the United States, Sojourner et al. (2015) find that unionization raised the wages of those who stayed by about 10 percent. The effects were higher at lower-paying levels and lower at higher-paying levels, so the composition of the workforce shifted towards lower-paid workers through both increased retention and reduced separation. Employment was reduced but there was no decline in care quality, suggesting that productivity increased. The union effects were larger in less-competitive product markets and where union density was lower, so threat effects were smaller. The growth or survival of nursing homes did not seem to be affected.

Clearly, the RD design is a potentially important methodology for estimating the causal effects of unionization. More work is merited in this area, however, to determine its ultimate usefulness.

Propensity Score Matching Procedures

Another empirical procedure that has been used to estimate the impact of unions is that of propensity score matching. The procedure, basically, involves matching unionized workers (the treatment group) with non-unionized workers (the comparison group) who have the same probability of being unionized but happen to be non-unionized. The intent is that this matching approximates random assignment (and, hence, controls for unobservable factors that can affect union outcomes) in that the two groups have the same probability of being unionized but because of random chance the union members happen to be unionized while the non-union members are not. The procedure involves estimating the counterfactual of what a union member would earn if they were non-union by matching them in a comparison group of non-union workers with the same probability of being unionized but who are not. Various matching procedures are still evolving and are commonly used to estimate the "treatment effect" of program interventions, such as training programs.

Eren (2007) utilises a propensity score matching procedure based on U.S. data for 1993 and estimates a union wage premium of 21.5 percent, which is at the high end of the union wage premiums.

Summary of Average Wage Impact in United States

Clearly, important advances have taken place in the measurement of the union wage impact, a reflection of improved data sources and more-sophisticated econometric methods. The accumulated U.S. evidence indicates that there is a statistically significant difference between the wages of union and otherwise comparable (to the researcher) non-union workers—probably on the order of 10 to 20 percent for the economy as a whole after controlling for observed worker characteristics other than union status. In a major extension of his earlier work, Lewis (1986) reviews almost 200 empirical studies of the impact of unions on wages in the United States. He concludes that the average union–non-union wage differential over the period 1967–1979 was approximately 15 percent, ranging from 9.6 to 16.4 percent. Based on their meta-analysis of 152 estimates from 114 studies for that same time period, Jarrell and Stanley (1990) find slightly lower estimates, ranging from about 8.9 to 12.4 percent.

However, there remains uncertainty about the magnitude of the union–non-union wage differential when the joint determination of unionization and its impact is taken into account. Unfortunately, the availability of better data and the application of more-sophisticated techniques have not yet resulted in greater consensus about the magnitude of the average union wage impact. Indeed, the range of estimates produced by these studies is sometimes wide, a reflection both of differences in data sets and differences in model specification. In a more recent study for the United States using matching procedures that essentially match union workers with otherwise equivalent non-union workers, Eren (2007) finds a substantial union wage premium of 21.5 percent. Given this wide variation in union impacts, research has attempted to determine which specification is most appropriate (Robinson 1989; Jakubson 1991; Green 1991; Card 1996). With the dramatic decline of unionization in the United States and internationally, however, interest in the topic of the union wage impact also appears to have declined, and there are fewer new studies in this area.

Canadian Evidence

Canadian studies of the average union wage impact are summarized in Table 15.1. Studies using aggregate industry data, plant-level data, and individual data have been carried out. The estimated union impact generally differs substantially across individual workers. The estimates reported in Table 15.1 are for the average individual in the sample. The estimates are broadly similar to those obtained in comparable U.S. studies. Average differentials (for the samples used) generally lie in the 10–25 percent range, with 15 percent being the estimate provided by Kuhn (1998) in his review. The estimated union wage impact is also sensitive to the econometric specification employed, and to the nature of the sample (e.g., manufacturing, hourly paid).

TABLE 15.1	Estimates of the Union–Non-union Wage Differential in Canada		
Author	**Time Period**	**Estimated Differential (%)**	**Characteristics of Sample; Other Comments**
1. Kumar (1972)	1966	17–23	Unskilled workers in manufacturing; aggregate data
2. Starr (1973)	1966	10–15	Unskilled male workers in Ontario manufacturing; disaggregate data (base wage at plant level)
3. Grant and Vanderkamp (1980)	1971	15	Individual data, annual earnings; "union member" includes membership in professional associations
4. Maki and Christensen (1980)	1974	51	Aggregate data, manufacturing
5. Christensen and Maki (1981)	1971–75	32	Aggregate data, manufacturing
6. MacDonald and Evans (1981)	1971–76	16	Aggregate industry data; 30 manufacturing industries
7. MacDonald (1983)	1971–79	20	Aggregate industry data; 30 manufacturing industries
8. Grant, Swidinsky, and Vanderkamp (1987)	1969–71	12–14 (1969) 13–16 (1970)	Individual longitudinal data, annual earnings; "union membership" includes professional associations
9. Robinson and Tomes (1984)	1979	24	Individual data on hourly paid workers
10. Simpson (1985)	1974	11	Microdata on wage rates for narrowly defined occupations

Author	Time Period	Estimated Differential (%)	Characteristics of Sample; Other Comments
11. Kumar and Stengos (1985)	1978	10	Union and non-union earnings data by industry
12. Kumar and Stengos (1986)	1981	12	Individual data; hourly earnings, representative sample
13. Robinson (1989)	1979–81	19–22	Individual data on hourly paid workers
14. Green (1991)	1986	15	Individual data on males; hourly earnings
15. Swidinsky and Kupfeschmidt (1991)	1986	15	Individual data on job changers
16. Lemieux (1993)	1986–87	20 (males, cross-section) 29 (females, cross-section) 16 (males, longitudinal) 17 (females, longitudinal)	Individual cross-section and longitudinal data; males and females
17. Doiron and Riddell (1994)	1984	15 (males) 24 (females)	Individual data; males and females
18. White (1994)	1989	18–20 (all workers) 9–10 (professionals)	Individual data; samples of all workers, professionals, and managers
19. Christofides and Swidinsky (1994)	1989	7 (white males 11 (white females) −14 (minority males) 21 (minority females)	Individual data
20. Kuhn and Sweetman (1998)	1983	9–14	Panel data of displaced workers who lost union job
21. Renaud (1998)	1989	10	Individual data
22. Gunderson, Hyatt, and Riddell (2000)	1997	8	Individual data
23. Fang and Verma (2002)	1999	8	Individual data linked to firm
24. Cleveland, Gunderson, and Hyatt (2003)	1991	15	Low-wage child care workers
25. Hosios and Siow (2004)	1973–90	2.4	University faculty
26. Martinello (2009)	1970–2004	Insignificant	Ontario university faculty

Variation in the Union Wage Impact

As would be expected on theoretical grounds, the estimated union–non-union wage differential varies considerably across firms, industries, workers, and over time. A number of generalizations about these variations emerge from the empirical literature, although for most generalizations there are exceptions in particular studies.

Variation by Union Density

The union–non-union wage differential tends to be larger when a high proportion of the relevant jurisdiction (industry, occupation, region) is organized. The relationship, however, is nonlinear; once a certain proportion of the jurisdiction is unionized, further increases have little additional effect on the differential. These findings can be interpreted in terms of two aspects of union power discussed previously: the elasticity of demand for unionized increases, the possibilities for the substitution of non-union for union labour decline, reducing the elasticity of demand for union labour. However, as more of the industry is organized, the remaining non-union firms may face a higher possibility that their workforce will organize, and thus, will tend to raise their wages. The gap between union and comparable non-union workers in the same jurisdiction will, thus, not continue to widen, and may even narrow.

Variation by Firm Size

Firm or establishment size has also been found to be positively related to both union and non-union wages in the majority of studies. The relationship is considerably stronger for non-union workers; thus, the wage differential between union and comparable non-union workers declines with firm or establishment size (Podgursky 1986, using U.S. data; Green, Machin, and Manning 1996, using UK data; Waddoups 2008, using Australian data). This outcome may reflect several forces. Unions usually attempt to standardize wage rates across firms and occupations—to "take wages out of competition"—which implies raising wages more in smaller firms, given the positive relationship between wages and firm size in the absence of unionization. Further, the threat of union organization is generally higher (due to reduced organizational costs per prospective member) in larger firms. Thus, larger non-union firms are more likely to match union wage scales than their smaller counterparts.

Variation by Occupation and Skill Level

Large differences in the estimated union–non-union differential are usually found to exist across occupations and skill levels. Skilled workers typically gain less from unionization than their semiskilled and unskilled counterparts (MacDonald 1983; Simpson 1985; Robinson and Tomes 1984; and Renaud 1998, for Canadian evidence), although there are specific examples of skilled trades, usually organized in craft unions, that exhibit large earnings differentials. As indicated in Table 15.2, the estimated union–non-union differentials decline almost monotonically with skill level; indeed, in the most-skilled categories, non-union wages exceed union wages. This outcome may largely reflect the fact that in many unions, especially industrial unions, skilled workers constitute a minority with little influence on the union's wage policy.

TABLE 15.2	Estimates of the Union–Non-union Percentage Wage Differential by Skill Level, Canada, 1974				
Skill Level	**All Industries**	**Manufacturing**	**Non-Manufacturing**	**Public Sector[a]**	**Private Sector**
1 (Low)	33.2	26.5	33.7	12.0	32.9
2	28.9	17.1	29.6	2.9	28.7
3	18.1	11.0	22.6	2.3	19.1
4	17.9	3.3	23.4	–1.0	19.0
5	12.4	–1.9	14.9	4.8	10.2
6	13.1	14.1	9.5	–24.3	15.0
7 (High)	–10.7	–11.1	–14.2	–33.4	–9.4
All Levels	18.6	11.5	20.9	–10.6	18.9

NOTE: [a] includes workers in health and education as well as public administration.

SOURCE: *Canadian Journal of Economics*, Simpson, W., 1985, 18, pp. 164–181: Table. Reproduced with permission of Blackwell Publishing Ltd.

An alternative perspective on the relationship between union and non-union wages and skill level is shown in Figure 15.2. (It should be understood that all other wage-determining factors are held constant.) Wages increase with skill level in both sectors. However, the increase is more gradual under collective bargaining, and at high-skill levels the union may even fall below the non-union wage. This type of relationship applies to a number of productivity-related characteristics (e.g., experience, education) in addition to skill. Simply stated, union wages are typically found to be less responsive to the personal characteristics of workers. The relationship between earnings and such factors as age, experience, education, and even marital status is weaker (i.e., age-earnings profiles are flatter, albeit higher) in the organized sector. When fringe benefits—which are typically of greater benefit to older, more-experienced workers—are included together with wages, this outcome is weaker, at least with respect to age and experience, but nonetheless remains.

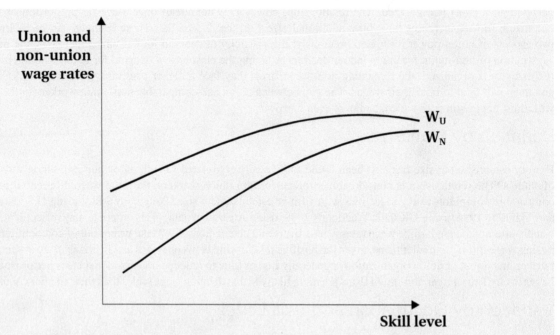

Figure 15.2 The Relationship between Union and Non-union Wages and Personal Characteristics

Wages increase with skill levels in both union and non-union sectors but more so in the non-union sector. The union wage premium is the vertical distance between the two lines—larger at low-skill levels and smaller at high-skill levels. In effect, unions obtain larger base increases (intercept) but they tend not to negotiate skill premiums (slope).

Direct evidence on the possible shapes of the earnings-skills relationships depicted in Figure 15.2 is provided in Lemieux (1993) for Canada, and Card (1996) for the United States. They provide longitudinal estimates of the union wage gap for workers with different skill levels, and find strong evidence that the wage gap is highest for low-skill workers, and is possibly zero for high-skill workers. For example, Lemieux estimates a wage gap of 21 percent for the lowest skill group, and less than 1 percent for the top skill group. Card estimates a wage gap of 28 percent for the bottom fifth of the skill distribution, but 0 and 11 percent for the top 2 quintiles of the skill distribution. Sojourner et al. (2015) find that unionization in nursing homes in the United States increases wages more for low-skilled than high-skilled workers so that, through retention and hiring, this induces a change in the composition of the nursing home workforce towards more lower-skilled and fewer higher-skilled staff. Blackburn (2008) also shows that the union wage premium is much lower for college graduates than for nongraduates in the United States.

Variation by Industry

The variation in the impact of unions across industries often reflects the extent to which excess profits or rents are prevalent for unions to extract. If product markets are protected from competitive forces, as through tariffs or regulations that restrict entry, then unions can extract some of the rents through higher wages. Conversely, if product markets are subject to more competition through deregulation, privatization, or freer trade or global competition, then unions are less able to extract rents.

The empirical evidence generally bears this out in that union wage premiums are lower when product markets are deregulated (Hirsch 1988, 1993) although there is considerable variation, depending upon the extent to which deregulation fosters additional competition (Bratsberg and Ragan 2002; and Hirsch and MacPherson 1998, 2000, and earlier references cited therein). Union wage premiums also tend to be lower when the sector is subject to greater foreign competition (Brown and Sessions 2004; Freeman and Katz 1991; Gaston and Trefler 1995; MacPherson and Stewart 1990; Shippen and Lynch 2002; although no effect is found in Bratsberg and Ragan 2002). The union can be exceptionally high in certain specific sectors, such as construction (Bilginsoy 2013; Blackburn 2008; Fang and Verma 2002), which are not subject to global competition. The decline of the union wage premium in recent years (documented subsequently) also bears out that union wage premiums dissipate under the forces of competition, since markets are increasingly deregulated, privatized, and subject to freer trade and global competition.

Variation by Public and Private Sector

With respect to the public sector, Lewis's (1990) survey of 75 U.S. studies concluded the the public sector union wage gap ranged from 8 to 12 percent, which was smaller than his estimate from about 15 percent from 200 studies in the private sector (Lewis 1985). Similar results are found in a more recent study by Bahrami, Bitzan, and Leitch (2009) although at a higher level (11.2 percent in the public sector compared to 22.7 percent in the private sector). Lewin, Keefe, and Kochan (2012) find that the impact of unions in the United States is lower in the public sector (3.7 percent) compared to the private sector (14.1 percent). Other recent evidence, however, suggests that the union wage premium is now similar in the public and private sectors, in part because it has fallen in the private due to competitive forces, but has risen in the public sector where competitive forces are mitigated (Belman, Haywood, and Lund 1997; Blanchflower and Bryson 2004).

In a recent study, Feiveson (2015) finds that cities in U.S. states with pro union collective bargaining laws spent more than one-half of federal transfer payments on public sector wage increases, while cities without such supportive laws spent more on increased government services.

In another recent study, Frandsen (2016) finds that laws which opened the door to public sector bargaining substantially increased unionism in the public sector. However, the effects varied by sector. For teachers, the effect on pay, benefits, and employment were minimal. Firefighters experienced a substantial increase in pay. For police, the effects on pay were modest, but the workweek was shortened substantially. Since the public sector is less subject to competitive market forces, this suggests that differing nonmarket forces can have different effects across various elements of the public sector.

This variation in the union impact is further illustrated for teachers in the United States. West (2015) reviews the literature and provides evidence of the union impact on teachers ranging from 0 to 28 percent. The extent to which this reflects differences in the bargaining power of teacher unions or other factors is an open and interesting question.

Canadian evidence generally supports the conclusion that the union wage impact is smaller in the public sector (Renaud 1998; Riddell 1993; Robinson and Tomes 1984; Simpson 1985). Robinson and Tomes (1984) find modestly lower differentials for hourly paid workers in the public sector (27 versus 34 percent in the private sector). However, only a minority of public sector workers are paid on that basis. As shown in Table 15.2, Simpson (1985) concludes that union–non-union wage differentials are significantly lower in the public than private sector for each skill group. Indeed, the differentials for higher-skill groups in the public sector are sufficiently negative that unionized public sector workers are estimated to earn *less* than comparable non-union public sector workers, while unionized private sector employees earn substantially more than their non-union counterparts. Lemieux (1993) confirms the higher union wage gap in the private sector in the cross-section specification, but finds the returns to union status are virtually identical in the first differenced (longitudinal) specification.

University Salaries

Porter (2013) reviews the literature on the effect of unions in universities. He indicates that the evidence is mixed, with most studies finding a small positive effect on average salaries, and some finding no effect. Canadian studies by Hosios and Siow (2004) and Martinello (2009), however, find that the small positive average effect. In their review of the literature, Henson et al. (2012) also document small or negligible effects of unions on faculty salaries. In their own study of community colleges, they find very small union wage effects of about 3 percent. Based on survey evidence from graduate student research and teaching assistants, Rogers, Eaton, and Voos (2013) find positive effects on pay and personal and professional support.

Variation by Gender

U.S. studies generally find that union wage premium is similar for males and females (48 U.S. studies surveyed in Lewis 1986). In Canada, there is evidence of a larger union–non-union differential for females (Christofides and Swidinsky 1994; Doiron and Riddell 1994; Kumar and Stengos 1986; Lemieux 1993; Renaud 1998). Unionization, thus, has two offsetting effects on the average earnings of Canadian males and females. Females benefit less from unionization because they are less likely to be covered by a collective agreement (see Exhibit 14.2 in Chapter 14). However, unions raise the wages of females more than those of males. Doiron and Riddell (1994) find that these two effects tend to offset each other.

Effect on Non-union Workers

In his earlier work, Lewis (1963) concluded that unionism has probably lowered the wages of non-union workers, this effect accounting for about 3 to 4 percentage points of the total estimated differential of 15 percent. Subsequent studies utilizing better data (Kahn 1978, 1980) also reach this conclusion. However, some more-recent studies find small positive effects of unions on the wages of non-union workers (Corneo and Lucifora 1997; Ichniowski, Freeman, and Lauer 1989; Neumark and Wachter 1995) at the city level, but negative effects at the industry level. As well, the overall average effect masks considerable variability, with some groups, such as non-union white males receiving a large wage increase from unionism. This outcome suggests the operation of both the threat and labour supply effects of union wage increases, as analyzed previously.

Effect on CEO Compensation

Given the increased interest in CEO compensation, it is informative to examine the impact of unions on CEO compensation. The expectation would be that CEO total compensation as well as any performance pay component (bonuses, stock options) would be lower in unionized establishments, given the union aversion to pay inequality and performance pay. As well, to the extent that unions appropriate any rent or surplus, there may simply be less left over for executives to appropriate. Also, boards of directors may be reluctant to pay high executive salaries and bonuses as that may complicate bargaining with the union, since it reveals a higher ability to pay. Working in the other direction, compensating pay premiums may have to be paid to attract and retain executives who have to deal with unions.

Based on U.S. data, DiNardo et al. (2000) find that higher levels of unionization within a firm are associated with lower levels of CEO cash pay (they did not have data on components like stock options). However, this effect generally becomes insignificant after controlling for industry and firm effects. Also, based on U.S. data, Banning and Chiles (2007) and Tzioumis and Gomez (2007) find that the unionization rate is associated with lower levels of *total* CEO compensation and a lower performance pay proportion of CEO compensation. Based on Canadian data, Singh and Agarwal (2002) find that unions were associated with higher executive compensation, but that effect disappeared after controlling for other variables, such as firm size.

Hallock and Klein (2016) provide evidence on the impact of unions on the compensation of union leaders in the United States. Their review of the literature highlights that the compensation of union leaders is positively related to factors that are similar to the compensation of executives in private organizations: size of the organization, its performance, and the complexity of the job. Their own results confirm a positive relationship between the size of the union and the wages of its members.

Variation Over the Business Cycle

With respect to the effect of business cycles on the union–non-union wage differential, Lewis concluded that it varies cyclically, widening in recessions and narrowing in booms; that is, union wages are less responsive to variations in economic and labour market conditions than non-union wages. This behaviour may partly result from the fact that collective agreements typically provide for fixed nominal wage rates, often for durations of two to three years, and these agreements overlap each other. At any point in time, only the fraction of union contracts being renegotiated is able to respond to changes in economic conditions. In the non-union sector, agreements are implicit rather than explicit, and wages can be adjusted in response to variations in economic conditions. However, even if union wage contracts were renegotiated frequently and did not provide for fixed durations (as is the case, for example, in the United Kingdom), union wages may well exhibit less cyclical variation than non-union wages. For reasons discussed subsequently, unions are likely to prefer employment reductions to wage reductions as a method of responding to temporary reductions in labour demand.

U.S. research (reviewed in Grant 2001) is generally divided as to whether union wages are more or less procyclical than are non-union wages. Canadian evidence on the cyclical behaviour of the union–non-union wage differential is extremely limited. As can be seen from Table 15.1, nine years (1971–1979) is the longest period for which estimates are available. MacDonald (1983) finds the differential rose almost continuously during this period, from 16.4 percent in 1971 to 22.8 percent in 1979. Because this was a period of generally rising unemployment and increasingly slack economic conditions, these results are broadly consistent with the hypothesis that the union wage impact varies counter-cyclically.

Variation Over Time

With respect to the trend, most studies find that the union wage premium has declined, at least since the 1980s (Addison and Belfield 2004; Bilginsoy 2013; Blackburn 2008; Blanchflower and Bryson 2004; Bratsberg and Ragan 2002; DiNardo and Lee 2004; Forth and Milword 2002; Hildreth 1999; Hirsch, Macpherson, and Schumacher 2004; Hirsch and Schumacher 2002; Stewart 1995). For Canada, Renaud (1997) finds that the union impact was approximately 15 percent at the beginning of the 1970s, rising to a peak of around 25 percent by the end of that decade, and falling to around 10 percent by the end of the 1980s. Gunderson, Hyatt, and Riddell (2000) also found that the union impact was approximately 8 percent by 1997, and Fang and Verma (2002) also document a decline to about 8 percent by 1999. Given the increased importance of competitive market forces, the union impact may be even smaller, based on more recent data.

WORKED EXAMPLE

Analyzing the Union–Non-union Earnings Differentials

Assume that the following annual earnings (Y) equations were estimated separately for union (subscript U) and non-union (subscript N) workers. ED denotes years of education (averaging 12 for union workers and 14 for non-union workers), SEN denotes years of seniority with the company (averaging 10 for union workers and 8 for non-union workers).

$$Y_U = 22{,}000 + 1000\ ED_U + 1000\ SEN_U$$

$$Y_N = 8000 + 2000\ ED_F + 500\ SEN_N$$

a. What do these coefficients imply about union wage-setting practices? The coefficients highlight that unions tend to bargain for a more egalitarian, or compressed, pay structure that gives a higher base pay (e.g., the intercept is higher in the union sector) but reduces the returns to skill-based characteristics, like education (e.g., the returns to education are lower in the union sector). Unions also bargain for seniority-based wage increases (i.e., the returns to seniority are higher in the union sector).

b. Calculate the expected earnings for the average union and non-union worker. The expected earnings for the average union and non-union worker can be calculated by substituting in the average value for their characteristics.

$$Y_U = 22{,}000 + 1000\ (12) + 1000(10) = 44{,}000$$

$$Y_N = 8000 + 2000\ (14) + 500\ (8) = 40{,}000$$

These values are also the average earnings of union and non-union workers, since a property of regression analysis is that the regression line passes through the means of the data; that is, the average union earnings is the sum of average values of the independent variables times the regression coefficients, plus the intercept.

c. What is the total or "raw" union–non-union earnings differential; that is, not adjusted for differences in their wage-determining characteristics of education and seniority? It is simply \$44,000 – \$40,000, or \$4000. In this example, the average union worker earns \$4000 more than the average non-union worker. This is \$4000/\$40,000, or 10 percent, more than the average non-union worker.

d. What are the expected earnings that a union worker would receive if paid according to the non-union pay structure? To calculate Y^*_U , simply substitute the average value of the union characteristics into the non-union earnings equation. That is,

$$Y_U^* = 8000 + 2000\,(12) + 500\,(10) = \$37{,}000.$$

e. What is the pure union earnings premium, adjusted for differences in their characteristics that influence earnings; that is, the percentage difference between what the average union worker is paid and what he would be paid, given his characteristics, if paid according to the pay structure of non-union workers? It is, $Y_U - Y_U^* = \$44{,}000 - \$37{,}000 = \$7000$ or expressed as a percentage of their hypothetical non-union pay, $\$7000/\$37{,}000 = 18.9$ percent.

f. Use the Blinder-Oaxaca decomposition technique (see Chapter 12) to decompose the average union–non-union earnings difference into its component parts; one component attributable to the average differences in their endowment of wage-determining characteristics, the other due to pay differences for the same characteristics.

The Blinder-Oaxaca decomposition is as follows, where $\overline{Y}$ is mean earnings, $\overline{X}$ is the mean values of the endowments of wage-determining characteristics, βs are the estimated coefficients including the intercepts, and the subscripts are as before.

$$\overline{Y}_U - \overline{Y}_N = \left(\overline{X}_U - \overline{X}_N\right)\beta_N + \left(\beta_U - \beta_N\right)\overline{X}_U$$

$$4000 = \left[(12 - 14)2000 + (10 - 8)500\right] + \left[(22{,}000 - 8000)1 + (1000 - 2000)12 + (1000 - 500)10\right]$$

$$= \left[-4000\right] + 1000 + \left[14{,}000 - 12{,}000 + 5000\right]$$

$$= \left[-3000\right] + \left[7000\right]$$

$$= \left[\text{endowment differences}\right] + \left[\text{pure pay differences}\right]$$

In percentage terms, $= [-75\%] + [175\%]$.

In this example, the pure pay difference of $7000 is more than the unadjusted earnings difference of $4000.

In a novel study that measures the "success" of unions by a combination of their wage premium and the proportion of the workforce they are able to organize to receive such a premium, Pencavel (2009) finds that union success increased from the early 1920s to the late 1940s, it peaked in the 1950s and 1960s, and then declined continuously since the early 1970s. He also found that they were more successful for black workers, and especially for black men. Relative to other countries with similar labour markets, the success ranking from low to high was the United States (lowest success), New Zealand, Canada, Australia, Japan, and Britain (highest success).

LO4   Union Wage Impact: Summary

Although exceptions can be found in particular studies, a number of generalizations emerge from the substantial body of empirical research on the wage impact of unions:

1. There is substantial evidence of a significant wage differential between union and non-union workers who are otherwise comparable in terms of observable characteristics. In Canadian studies, the average differential appears to be approximately 15 percent (in the range of 10 to 25 percent), similar in magnitude to estimates based on U.S. data. The earnings gap between union and comparable non-union workers varies across industries, firms, regions, occupations, and over time with aggregate economic conditions. Recent research suggests that the union wage premium has dissipated, likely in response to increased competitive market forces.

2. The overall impact of higher wages in the union sector on the average wage in the non-union sector is both theoretically and empirically inconclusive, with early studies tending to find small negative effects on non-union wages, but with some more-recent studies finding the opposite.

3. In unionized enterprises, wage differences among workers who differ according to various productivity-related personal characteristics, such as education, age, experience, skill, and marital status, are smaller than in non-union enterprises, and evidently, smaller than they would be in the absence of unionization. Thus, the financial "return" to additional amounts of these attributes—for example, years of education or experience—is generally lower with collective than individual bargaining.

4. The union–non-union wage differential is generally higher in the private than the public sector (in Canada, but not currently in the United States), higher in small firms and enterprises, higher for blue-collar than white-collar workers, higher when a large proportion of the relevant jurisdiction is organized, higher in recessions than booms, and higher in earlier periods when product markets were insulated from competitive market forces because of regulations or tariffs.

5. Unionization likely lowers the total compensation of CEOs as well as lowering the portion of their compensation that comes in the form of performance pay, like bonuses and stock options.

Canadian empirical evidence is consistent with these conclusions; however, only a limited number of studies have been carried out with Canadian data, and there is considerable scope for further research.

Clearly, a great deal has been learned about the effects of unions on wages. Nonetheless, several unresolved issues remain. These include the extent to which unionized firms respond to higher wages and the concomitant larger queue of applicants by hiring "higher-quality" workers; that unionized firms respond to higher wages by attempting to increase the job assignment, the pace of work, or the rigidity of work time; that earnings differences between union and comparable non-union workers are caused by unions raising their members' wages as opposed to unions being more likely to exist in firms that would choose to pay relatively high wages even in the absence of unions.

Unions, Wage Dispersion, and the Distribution of Income

There is significantly less **wage dispersion** among union workers than among comparable non-union workers. This generalization is found in the literature reviewed in Card, Lemieux, and Riddell (2004), and Rios-Avila and Hirsch (2014). Studies include Belman and Heywood (1990), Card (2001), Frandsen (2014), Freeman (1980a, 1982, 1993), Hirsch (1982), and Quan (1984) for the United States; DiNardo and Lemieux (1997), Meng (1990), and Lemieux (1993, 1998) for Canada; Hara and Kawaguchi (2008) for Japan; Dustmann and Schönberg (2009) for Germany; and Rios-Avila (2014) for Bolivia and Chile as well as the United States. This smaller variance is related to several aspects of union wage policy noted above. Unions tend to reduce wage differentials among workers who differ according to factors such as skill, age, experience, and seniority. Unions also attempt to standardize the wages of similar workers across establishments, especially those in the same industry or region. Further, unions have a larger impact on the wages of blue-collar workers than on white-collar workers. These policies imply that unions typically raise the wages of those at the lower end of the pay scale proportionally more than those at the upper end. As a result, the union wage distribution is both to the right (i.e., higher pay) and less dispersed (i.e., more compressed) than the non-union distribution, as is shown in Figure 15.3.

Although wage dispersion is substantially lower in the union than in the non-union sector, it does not necessarily follow that unionism is associated with reduced wage dispersion in the economy as a whole. By creating a wage differential between union and comparable non-union workers, unions also increase the variability of earnings relative to a hypothetical economy, without collective bargaining. Because of these offsetting factors—lower wage dispersion within the union sector but greater inequality between union and non-union workers—the direction of the overall impact of unionism on the wage distribution is indeterminate.

Studies by Hyclak (1979, 1980), Freeman (1980a), and Quan (1984) indicate that in the United States the net effect of unionism is to reduce wage dispersion. In a detailed analysis of the impact of labour market institutions on the distribution of wages, DiNardo, Fortin, and Lemieux (1996) confirm the significant equalizing effect of unions. In fact, they attribute an important role to the decline in unions for contributing to the increasing wage inequality in the United States (Chapter 14). They note that the decline in unions is associated especially with a drop in middle-level paying jobs, the better-paying blue-collar jobs traditionally being associated with the union sector. Lemieux (1993) uses a Canada–United States comparison to gauge the extent to which differences in unionization rates contribute to the different levels of wage inequality between the two countries. He estimates that the greater extent of unions in Canada explains 40 percent of the difference in wage inequality, suggesting that unions play an important role in reducing income inequality. DiNardo and Lemieux (1997) also find that the much greater decline in unionization that occurred in the United States compared to Canada over the period 1981 to 1988 accounted for two-thirds of the greater growth in wage inequality that occurred in the United States compared to Canada.

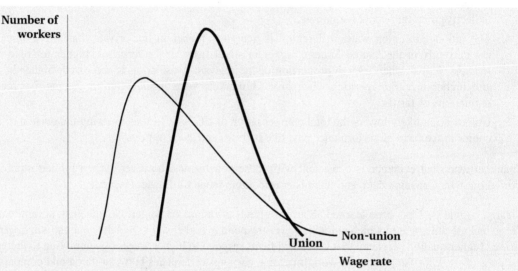

Figure 15.3 Wage Dispersion in the Union and Non-union Sectors

In the union sector, the wage distribution is more compressed (less dispersed) with fewer workers receiving low wages and few receiving very high wages. In effect, the tails of the distribution are compressed into the higher spike at the middle of the wage distribution in the union sector. The union distribution also tends to be to the right of the non-union distribution, reflecting the higher wages generally received in the union sector.

WORKED EXAMPLE

Union Wage Gains and Employment

Assume that the elasticity of demand for union labour is −0.3. Assume also that there is a 10 percent increase in employment growth due to a demand shock increase in the demand for the products produced by the bargaining unit and, hence, in the derived demand for union labour. Assume further that there are 100 unionized workers in the bargaining unit and that the union negotiates a 10 percent increase in union wages.

a. What is the potential new level of employment solely from the increase in the demand for the products of the union labour? It is simply 10 percent higher than the original 100, or 1.1(100) = 110.

b. What is the new level of employment solely associated with the union wage increase? Calculate from the elasticity formula.
Elasticity of employment associated with a wage increase is $E = \%\ \Delta N/\%\ \Delta W$, where E is elasticity, N is employment, W is wage, and % Δ is the percentage change. Substitute in $E = -0.3$ and $\%\ \Delta W = 10$, and solve for % ΔN. That is, $-0.3 = \%\Delta N/10$ or $\%\ \Delta N = -0.3(10) = -3\%$.

A 3 percent reduction in employment implies three fewer workers employed out of the original 100; that is, 97 employees after the wage increase.

c. What is the new level of employment after both forces are at work? It is 107, based on a gain of 10 from the demand shock increase and a loss of three from the union wage increase.

d. If employment has increased from its original level, does this imply no adverse employment effect from the union wage increase? No. There is still an adverse employment effect, since employment would have been 110 rather than

107 if there had been no union wage increase. The adverse employment effect is masked by the positive demand shock.

e. Assume that the government negotiates a free trade agreement that changes the demand for union labour from −0.3 to −0.5. What is the new level of employment after both forces in (a) and (b) above are at work? Use the new elasticity of −0.5 in part (b) above and solve for the adverse employment effect of 5 percent emanating from a 10 percent wage increase. This implies five fewer workers based on the base of 100. On net, the new level of employment is 105, based on a gain of 10 from the demand shock and a loss of five from the wage increase.

Assuming the new elasticity conditions and both the demand shock and the union wage gains are at work, what wage gains could "insiders" within the union win while maintaining the security of their employment at 100? To maintain the original level of employment at 100, the loss of employment due to a wage increase should be just equal to the gain in employment from the demand shock; that is, a decrease of 10 workers, or % ΔN = −10%, based on the original level of 100. Substitute this into the elasticity formula, set the elasticity equal to −0.05, and solve for the % ΔW.

$$E = \% \ \Delta N \ / \ \% \ \Delta W$$

$$-0.5 = -10\% \ / \ \% \ \Delta W$$

$$\% \ \Delta W = -10\% \ / -0.5 = 20\%.$$

That is, the insiders could get a 20 percent wage increase and still preserve their employment.

In their recent comprehensive study, Card, Lemieux, and Riddell (2004) find that unions have reduced wage inequality among men in Canada, the United States, and the United Kingdom but have had no effect on wage inequality among women. The decline of unionization in all three countries has also contributed substantially to the growing wage inequality in those countries.

LO4   Union Impact on Resource Allocation and Economic Welfare

Because they alter wages and employment, unions affect the allocation of labour and other resources in the economy. The nature and magnitude of this effect depends on several factors discussed previously in the context of the union wage impact. As was done earlier in this chapter, the consequences of unions are studied by comparing the situation with unions to a hypothetical economy without unions.

Figure 15.4 shows the allocative consequences of the union wage impact in a simple two-sector general equilibrium model in which outcomes are on the labour demand curve and the supply of labour to the economy is completely inelastic. With homogeneous workers and competitive labour markets, the equilibrium in the absence of unions implies a common wage (W_0) in both sectors. Because of the higher union wage W_U, the employment level declines to E_1^U in the union sector and increases to E_1^N in the non-union sector, reducing the wage there to W_N. With inelastic labour supply, the increase in employment in the non-union sector ($E_0^N E_1^U$) equals the reduction in employment in the union sector ($E_1^U E_0^U$).

These changes in wages and employment result in an **inefficient allocation** of society's resources and a reduction in the total output and income generated by the economy. The magnitude of this allocative inefficiency can be illustrated using the fact that, because the labour demand curve is the marginal revenue product curve, the area under the labour demand curve equals the total value of the output produced. Thus, the value of the output produced by the union sector declines by E_1^U a b E_0^U as a result of the union wage impact, while the value of output produced by the non-union sector increases by E_0^N d f E_1^N. Total income declines by E_1^U a E_0^U minus E_0^N d f E_1^N, an amount equal to the sum of the two shaded areas, **cab** and **edf**. (This follows from the fact that the area E_1^U c b E_0^U equals the area E_0^N d g E_1^N and the area **def** equals the area **dgf**, assuming a linear demand curve.)

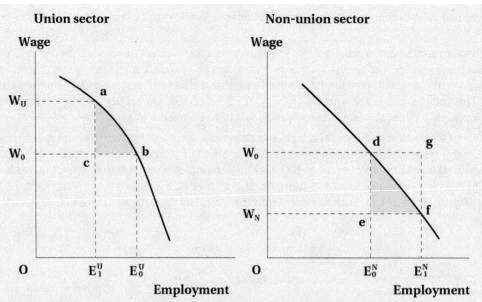

Figure 15.4 The Union Wage Impact and Allocative Inefficiency

With no unions, both sectors start with the competitive wage W_0 and employment E_0. Unions raise wages in the union sector to W_U, reducing employment by $(E_1 - E_0)$, all of whom go to the non-union sector. This creates deadweight losses—the triangles of **acb** in the union sector and **dgf** = **dfe** in the non-union sector. These losses are greater the larger the union–non-union wage differential (i.e., the height of the triangles), and the greater the elasticity of demand for labour, and hence, the resulting employment reallocation (i.e., the base of the triangles).

An alternative way of viewing the losses is to distinguish between deadweight or real resource losses and transfer losses, the latter representing a redistribution, not a loss, of output or income. For example, the loss of output E_1^U a b E_0^U in the union sector consists of two components: the loss of income E_1^U c b E_0^U to the displaced workers (which is a transfer loss since employers and ultimately customers are not paying that amount), and a real resource or deadweight loss **abc**, which represents what consumers are willing to pay for the output over and above what the workers were willing to accept to produce the output. When the displaced workers move to the union sector (E_1^U E_0^U = E_0^N E_1^N), their income is reduced from E_1^U c b E_0^U in the union sector to E_0^N e f E_1^N in the non-union sector. They, therefore, lose income of **edgf**. However, **edf** of that is a gain to the rest of society, reflecting their value of the output E_0^N d f E_1^N over and above what they have to pay for the additional output E_0^N e f E_1^N. Therefore, the only real resource loss is **dgf**, which equals **edf** given a linear demand curve. Thus, the total real output loss is **abc** plus **def**—the former represents what consumers are willing to pay for the loss of output in the unionized sector over and above what workers required to produce that output, and the latter represents the loss associated with the fact that the output increase is valued less in the non-union sector than the output loss in the union sector. The sum of these two components constitutes the welfare loss from union wage-fixing in an otherwise competitive market.

This reduction in the value of total output is referred to as a **deadweight loss**, because it is not offset by a benefit elsewhere. The misallocation of labour resources occurs because higher wages and reduced employment in the union sector push other workers into less-productive and more-poorly paying jobs in the non-union sector. As a result, there are too few workers employed in the union sector and too many in the non-union sector. The use of other resources is also affected. Relative to an efficient allocation of resources, firms will respond to the wage differential by utilizing excessively capital-intensive production techniques in the union sector and excessively labour-intensive techniques in the non-union sector.

The existence and magnitude of a deadweight loss associated with the union wage impact depend on several factors discussed earlier: the elasticity of labour supply, the amount of queuing unemployment, and the extent to which firms and unions negotiate wage-employment outcomes to the right of the demand curve. Depending on these various factors, the magnitude of the reduction in total output may be lower or higher than that shown in Figure 15.4. For example, in the situation depicted in Figure 15.1(c) in which union wages and employment lie on a vertical contract curve, employment in the two sectors is identical to that which would occur in a competitive labour market equilibrium, and no misallocation of labour resources results. In these circumstances, the higher union wage alters the distribution of income (increasing labour's share) but not total income. On the other hand, an additional output loss will occur if some individuals leave the labour force because the non-union wage falls below their reservation wage and/or some individuals choose to remain unemployed, hoping to receive a union job.

The potential allocative inefficiency associated with the union wage impact was illustrated using as a reference point an economy in a competitive equilibrium. From this starting point, any distortion, such as monopoly in the product market or wage-fixing in the labour market, will result in a misallocation of resources and a reduction in total income. However, if the starting point is an economy with existing distortions, then it is not necessarily the case that adding another distortion (e.g., union wage impact) will cause a reduction in society's economic welfare. This is the central proposition of the "theory of the second-best." The Canadian economy contains numerous distortions that would cause it to deviate from a first-best (Pareto-optimal) allocation of resources in the absence of unions; therefore, it is an empirical question as to whether the union wage impact improves or worsens allocative efficiency.

Early estimates of the deadweight loss were based on fairly crude methods and did not take into account other distortions in the economy. These studies estimated the loss for the United States to be about 0.15 percent of GNP (Rees 1963) and 0.33 percent of GNP (Johnson and Mieszkowski 1970) when the union–non-union wage differential was 15 percent. De Fina (1983), however, reports estimates based on a computable general equilibrium model of the U.S. economy incorporating several existing distortions. De Fina estimates the deadweight loss to be considerably less than that of earlier studies; when the union–non-union wage differential is 15 percent, the loss is less than 0.1 percent of GNP, while a differential of 25 percent produces an estimated loss of 0.2 percent of GNP. More-recent work by Fisher and Waschik (2000) for Canada, based on a general equilibrium model that incorporates other distortions and trade, finds a considerably smaller estimate of the deadweight loss of 0.04 percent (i.e., 0.0004) of GNP. They attribute these smaller effects in part to the fact that they did not simply impose an exogenous union wage increase, but also allowed unions to bargain for more-efficient contracts over both wages and employment (discussed previously in Chapter 14). Based on U.S. data, however, large deadweight losses as found in Vedder and Gallaway (2002), suggest that the issue is not settled.

Union Impact on Non-wage Outcomes

Unions bargain for a wide range of factors in addition to wages, and a more complete understanding of the economic and social consequences of unions will emerge from examining these other outcomes of collective bargaining. We begin by discussing the impact of unions on fringe benefits and proceed to working conditions, quit and layoff behaviour, and productivity and profitability.

Unions and Fringe Benefits

Non-wage, or fringe, benefits refer to employer payments such as those for pensions, medical and life insurance, vacations, holidays, and sick leave. Omitting these benefits understates both the cost of labour to the employer and the benefit received by the employee. Thus, total compensation is the relevant measure for both labour demand and supply decisions. (See Chapter 5 for a discussion of non-wage benefits and their effects on labour demand.) The omission of fringe benefits would not bias estimates of the impact of unions on the total compensation of union and non-union workers if non-wage benefits were the same proportion of total compensation in both sectors. However, evidence indicates that non-wage benefits account for a greater proportion of total compensation among union than non-union enterprises; that is, unions tend to have a greater impact on fringe benefits than on wages (Budd and Mumford 2004; Freeman 1981; Freeman and Medoff 1984; Freeman and Kleiner 1990; Renaud 1998; Long and Shields 2009). This implies that estimated union–non-union differentials understate the total compensation gap between organized and unorganized workers.

There are numerous reasons all parties—employees, employers, and governments—may prefer fringe benefits over wages as a form of compensation. (These are discussed in more detail in Chapter 5.) Workers may prefer fringe benefits because they are often not taxable or taxes are deferred. In addition, there may be economies of scale and administrative simplicity associated with group purchases. Employers may benefit from the fringe benefits provided to employees to the extent that they facilitate the planning and operation of the production process, provide appropriate work incentives, and reduce turnover. In periods of wage control, both parties may favour compensation via non-wage benefits. Governments may prefer fringe benefits (and, hence, grant favourable tax treatment) because private-sector expenditures on items, such as pensions, workers' compensation, and unemployment insurance, may reduce pressure for government expenditures in these areas.

While there are these reasons for the existence and growth of fringe benefits, the question remains as to why their magnitude is greater in the union than the non-union sector. There are several theoretical reasons why this is so.

To the extent that union workers are made better off by unionization, they can afford to buy more of everything, including fringe benefits. Thus, if the income elasticity of demand for non-wage benefits exceeds unity, union workers will devote a larger share of total income to fringe benefits than comparable non-union workers. Compounding this effect is the fact that the effective price, or cost, of nontaxable fringe benefits falls as income (and, therefore, the marginal tax rate) rises. However, Long and Shields (2009) suggest, using two waves of survey data from 250 Canadian firms in 2000 and 2004, that unions may extract employee benefits for their members at the cost (or from the "savings") of reduced base pay or individual performance pay. Thus, higher fringe benefits may simply reflect members' preferences rather than an ability of unions to extract rents in all areas of worker compensation.

The union's role in articulating its members' preferences regarding non-wage benefits may also affect the share of total compensation devoted to fringe benefits. As discussed previously, because of their political nature, unions can be expected to represent the wishes of the median union voter. In contrast, non-union employers will design their compensation packages to appeal to the marginal worker—the employee on the verge of joining or leaving the firm—who is likely to be younger and more mobile than the member of median age or seniority. Because the demand for such fringe benefits as pensions and life, accident, and health insurance increases with age, seniority, and family responsibilities, compensation packages in unionized enterprises are, thus, expected to devote a greater share to these non-wage benefits.

Fringe benefits in the form of deferred compensation are also expected to be more prevalent in unionized establishments. As discussed in Chapter 13, employers may prefer deferred compensation because of favourable work incentive effects (employees will work diligently in order to retain their jobs and, thus, receive the deferred payment later in their careers) and because it reduces turnover (employees who quit lose some or all of their deferred compensation; e.g., pensions and vacation rights). Deferred compensation will be attractive to employees if they are given a sufficiently high wage to compensate for some of it being deferred (and, hence, its receipt being uncertain), and/or if they are provided with sufficient guarantees that employers will, ultimately, pay the deferred wages. Such guarantees are more binding when they are provided in a collective agreement that, for example, protects against arbitrary dismissal. Thus, deferred compensation arrangements are expected to be more acceptable to union than non-union employees, other things equal.

Freeman's (1981) empirical analysis indicates that unionism increases fringe benefits both directly and indirectly (through higher levels of compensation for union workers). This suggests that the tendency of unions to represent the preferences of the median or inframarginal worker and the increased acceptability of deferred compensation to workers protected by a collective agreement help account for the increased significance of non-wage benefits in the union sector.

Unions may also become involved in the administration of their pension plans. Their involvement can have positive effects on the investment returns of their plan if they improve the monitoring of pension advisers or asset managers. They can have negative effects on those returns if they sacrifice returns to invest in projects that promote union goals, such as utilizing union labour or avoiding layoffs of union workers. Even and Macpherson (2014) provide evidence that the lowest performing pension plans in the United States were unionized plans, suggesting that unions were prepared to sacrifice returns for union goals. Interestingly, the effect did not prevail for defined contribution plans where individual union members directed their own plan investments. This suggested that individual union members were not prepared to sacrifice their pension returns to facilitate broader union goals.

Union Impact on Employment

In part because of the positive impact of unions on wages and fringe benefits, employers can be expected to respond by reducing employment of this more-costly factor of production—union labour. They may substitute away from higher-cost union labour and use more of the cheaper factors of production, such as capital and even non-union labour. The higher cost may cause them to raise their prices, in which case they may sell less output or even go out of business. These are, respectively, the familiar substitution and output effects of basic economic theory.

In the case of unions, however, the issue is complicated by the fact that unions bargain in terms of not only wages but also the level of employment. They may do so directly through such means as restrictions on layoffs, or indirectly through other mechanisms, such as restrictions on subcontracting, outsourcing, overtime, and plant closings, as well as bargaining over investment. Unions may also impose featherbedding rules that fix the ratio of labour to capital (e.g., the former rule of requiring a fireman on diesel locomotives when they switched from coal burning). Unions of professional workers may be able to restrict the use of cheaper nonprofessionals. In such circumstances, unions can affect the levels of both wages and employment—it is not simply a matter of bargaining over wages and letting the employer "move along the labour demand curve" to determine the level of employment.

The extent to which unions will opt for higher wages at the expense of employment (or slower employment growth) depends upon the preferences of unions and their members. If the median union voter is relatively safe from layoffs, unions may opt for higher wages. If union members' own jobs are at risk (as is increasingly the case with outsourcing, downsizing, and plant closings) they may bargain over both and may even accept wage concessions to preserve members' jobs. (See Chapter 14.)

Reviews of the empirical evidence suggest that employment growth is lower in union compared to non-union plants, although much of this reflects the fact that unions, traditionally, have been in declining industries and large plants where growth is slower. Separating cause and effect is extremely difficult in this area. Even after controlling for this, however, Freeman and Kleiner (1990) document slower employment growth in union firms in the United States, as does Long (1993) for Canada. Similarly, Krol and Svorny (2007) show that unionization negatively affects job creation during an economic recovery by examining state-level job growth following the November 1982 and March 1991 recessions in the United States.

Union Impact on Working Conditions and Job Satisfaction

In addition to their impact on wages and fringe benefits, unions affect a variety of working conditions. These changes may reflect both the collective bargaining objectives pursued by the union and the firm's response to the higher labour costs associated with unionism.

Union workplaces tend to be governed much more by various rules than comparable non-union settings. Collective agreements typically stipulate such factors as the way grievances are to be handled and the scheduling of worker hours. Non-union enterprises tend to be less rules oriented, and to exhibit more worker and management flexibility.

In addition to a more structured work setting and less-flexible hours, there is also evidence that unionized environments are characterized by a faster work pace. This may reflect the fact that unionism is more likely to occur in response to such working conditions or that employers are able to respond to the union wage effect by changing the conditions of work. Without being able to disentangle the true cause and effect, Duncan and Stafford (1980) estimate that about two-fifths of the union–non-union wage differential reflects a compensating wage for these more onerous working conditions. This conclusion is relevant to interpreting empirical evidence not only on union–non-union wage differences, but also on productivity differences between union and non-union workers, discussed subsequently. Hammer and Avgar (2005) review the literature and highlight that union workers consistently report less satisfaction, overall, with their jobs. They attribute much of this to unrealized expectations. Artz (2012) finds that unionized women report more dissatisfaction than unionized men. They attribute this to the lower influence of women within unions, especially in leadership positions. In a study of university faculty, Krieg et al. (2013) find no impact of unions on overall job satisfaction or on their authority to make decisions, but increased satisfaction with compensation and reduced satisfaction with faculty workload. For graduate student teaching and research assistants, Rogers, Eaton, and Voos (2013) find that unionization increases satisfaction with personal and professional support as well as with pay. Bryson et al. (2013) find that organizational changes leading to job-related anxiety and lower job satisfaction have their negative effects mitigated in unionized workplaces and when unions are involved in the process.

Brochu and Morin (2012) find that perceptions of job security are lower for union members than for non-union members, after controlling for other factors that can affect such perceptions. This could reflect any of a variety of factors: fear of losing their union wage premium, higher expectations, adversarial bargaining, or the possibility of an adverse employment effect from any union wage effect and resistance to wage concessions. This perceived job insecurity could also contribute to union workers' job dissatisfaction.

Berg et al. (2014) highlight that the effect of unions on work-life flexibility issues depends upon the bargaining priorities of the union, and not just the discretion of management. If unions emphasize workers' scheduling needs, then policies that lead to work-life balance are prominent; if unions emphasize wages, then work-life balance practices are given up in return for higher wages. In essence, unions can influence work-life balance depending upon their priorities, but they may have to give up wages in return for more of such balance.

In response to the economic realities of the new economic environment, unions may also be changing their bargaining strategy in order to survive. In particular, they may be de-emphasizing wage gains and emphasizing issues related to working conditions and work rules (see Exhibit 15.1).

EXHIBIT 15.1

Are New Unions Changing Their Stripes to Survive?

Freeman and Kleiner (1990) argue that newly formed unions in the United States in the 1980s may have been changing their bargaining strategy in order to survive. Specifically, they argue that newly formed unions at that time may have been moving away from their "monopoly" phase of trying to win large wage increases, and toward their "collective voice" phase of emphasizing practices that are important to unions, such as grievance procedures, seniority protection for layoffs and recalls, and posting and bidding for internal promotions. They argue that the collective-voice aspects may have been emphasized more in the 1980s for a variety of reasons:

- Unions may have been under more pressure to be cost conscious because of deunionization, deregulation, global competition, and high unemployment.
- New unions in the 1980s may have wanted to solidify their position by bargaining for items that give them a greater degree of security.
- New unions in the 1980s tended to disproportionately organize minorities and females, and since organizing was less frequent at that time (unions were declining), the plants they organized may have had particularly bad labour-management relations; hence, the emphasis on collective-voice aspects over money.

Freeman and Kleiner provide empirical evidence indicating that union wage gains in those newly formed unions in the 1980s were low (i.e., less than 5 percent) by historical standards, but that they did win improvements in grievance procedures, seniority protection for layoffs and recalls, and posting and bidding for internal promotions. They conclude that this represents a shift in union strategy in response to the realities of the new environment, with unions emphasizing their collective voice rather than their more costly monopoly union function.

Union Impact on Health and Safety

Unions can have an influence on health and safety at the workplace through a variety of mechanisms: enforcing health and safety and regulations, protecting workers who exercise a right to refuse work, and educating and informing workers of both their rights and responsibilities in this area. Donado (2015) reviews the literature based on 43 estimates from 25 studies across different countries, time periods, and industries. He finds that 22 of the estimates between unions and injuries were statistically insignificant, 16 were positive and significant, and only five were negative and significant, after controlling for the effect of other factors that affect injuries. In essence, unions either had no effect on injuries or were more likely to be associated with more rather than fewer injuries. This total effect masks an important difference, however, in that unions tend to be associated with fewer fatal injuries even though they are associated with more non-fatal injuries. His own evidence confirms this relationship.

Donado (2015) further investigates various possible explanations for the surprising positive relationship between unions and non-fatal injuries. These include the following:

- a reporting effect, as unions are more likely to ensure reporting non-fatal injuries while non-union firms may be less likely to report them (fatal injuries would have to be reported so this may explain why unionized firms have more non-fatal injuries but fewer fatal ones)
- a selection effect, as unions are more likely to organize more-hazardous workplace places (i.e., reverse causality)
- a compensating wage effect, as unions bargain for higher wages and management tries to offset some of the higher cost by investing less in health and safety

- workers themselves may respond to improved health and safety at the workplace by reducing their own safety enhancing measures and precautions

- union effectiveness in reducing fatal injuries may actually convert potentially fatal injuries into non-fatal ones (again accounting for their lower fatal injuries by higher non-fatal ones)

Donado (2015) investigates these possible explanations and concludes that none of them fully explain the positive association between unions and non-fatal injuries, but each may explain part of the association (with the exception of the compensating wage effect). He concludes (p. 179), "the impact of unions on reducing nonfatal injuries might be at best insignificant."

Morantz (2013) also reviews the literature and concludes that most studies find no statistically significant relationship between unions and health and safety outcomes at work after controlling for the effect of other factors that can affect such outcomes. Her own work, however, suggests the importance of a reporting bias. She finds that in the hazardous coal mining sector in the United States, unions do have a substantial effect on reducing *traumatic* injuries (14 to 32 percent reduction) as well as *fatalities* (29 to 83 percent reduction). These are injuries where both union and non-union firms invariably have to report the injury, so reporting bias is not prevalent and unions do seem to have an effect. However, she also finds that unions are associated with more *non-fatal* injuries, where reporting can be more discretionary and, therefore, subject to reporting bias, which leads to reporting of more *total* injuries. Non-union firms are more likely not to report such non-fatal injuries. In essence, unions have a *real* effect on reducing injuries but they also tend to have an effect on *reporting* more injuries, so this offsetting force gives the appearance that unions have no effect. This highlights the importance of drilling deeper into the data to distinguish real and perceived effects.

Union Impact on Turnover, Mobility, and Absenteeism

Unions also affect various aspects of **labour market turnover** and mobility—quits, layoffs, rehires, promotions, and terminations. Numerous U.S. studies (e.g., Freeman 1980b, 1980c; Blau and Kahn 1983; Rees 1994), a UK study (Addison and Belfield 2001), and a Canadian study (Swindinksy 1992) have found that the quit rate is significantly lower among union workers than comparable non-union workers. In part, this reflects the reluctance of workers to leave the higher-wage union environment. However, even after controlling for differences in wages, union workers quit less frequently than their non-union counterparts. Sojourner et al. (2015) also find that unions in nursing homes increase wages for lower-skilled staff and not for higher-skilled staff, so the composition of the workforce changes towards lower-skilled staff through their increased retention and hiring, while the opposite occurs for higher-skilled staff.

There may be several explanations for the lower quit rate of unionized workers in addition to the effect of any higher wages. As discussed previously, deferred compensation is more prevalent in union enterprises; such benefits provide an extra inducement to remain with the employer. Causality may also operate in the other direction. Deferred compensation, such as pensions and vacations tied to length of service, is more attractive to individuals who expect to remain with the firm for a long time. Thus, this type of compensation tends to act as a sorting or screening mechanism, attracting to union firms workers who are less likely to quit (and vice versa, in non-union firms).

The lower quit propensity among union workers can also be interpreted as reflecting their substitution of a "voice" mechanism for an "exit" mechanism (Freeman 1980b; Freeman and Medoff 1984). Union employees dissatisfied with their working conditions can attempt to bring about improvements through collective bargaining, while the main mechanism available to dissatisfied workers in non-union enterprises is the threat of seeking employment elsewhere.

Unions also affect the use of temporary layoffs, hours reductions, and wage reductions as mechanisms for responding to short-term fluctuations in demand. Collective agreements typically provide for a fixed nominal wage rate, possibly indexed to the cost of living, but rarely indexed to other variables, such as the state of the firm's product demand. With wages fixed, union firms rely more heavily on layoffs and recalls to respond to temporary fluctuations in demand than do otherwise comparable non-union firms, which make greater use of adjustments in wages and hours of work (Medoff 1979; Blau and Kahn 1983). In addition, seniority receives more weight in determining the order of layoffs and recalls in union firms. These differences in adjustment behaviour are consistent with the view that unions tend to represent the preferences of the median member. Having substantial seniority, such workers are unaffected by layoffs, except in the case of extremely large reductions in the workforce. In contrast, non-union employers respond to the preferences of the marginal worker. Being younger and less senior, such workers would prefer that all workers take a reduction in wages and/or hours rather than some workers being laid off in reverse order of seniority.

Internal mobility also differs between union and non-union employees and organizations. Promotion decisions depend much more on seniority in union than in non-union organizations, as do decisions about employee terminations (Blau and Kahn 1983). As with layoffs, the greater weight given to seniority in these organizational decisions can be seen as reflecting the preferences of the median union member.

Unions can also affect absenteeism due to sickness. Mastekaasa (2013) reviews the evidence and provides his own evidence indicating that unionized employees have much higher rates of absenteeism due to sickness than do non-union employees, after controlling for the effect of other factors affecting such absenteeism. Whether this is a result of unions legitimately protecting such workers from retribution on the part of management for such absenteeism or an abuse of such protection is an open question.

Union Impact on Privatization

Privatization of public services in areas ranging from garbage collection to crown corporations has increased in recent years in response to governments trying to inject competition and cut costs. As indicated in Jalette and Hebdon (2012), unions generally oppose privatization because of anticipated negative consequences on job losses, wages, and working conditions. They review the literature and provide their own evidence for Canada, indicating that government-provided services are frequently targeted for privatization because of their higher unionized labour costs, but that unions are frequently able to bolster support against privatization so that, on net, their is no relationship between unionization and actual privatization. The authors provide survey evidence indicating that the most successful strategy for unions in inhibiting privatization was to suggest alternatives to privatization, with strikes being the least successful strategy. Having an adjustment strategy for workers affected by privatization was found to reduce the resistance of unions. They highlight that the threat of privatization may be just as effective as privatization itself in reducing union-induced labour costs.

Union Impact on Productivity, Profitability, and Investment[1]

Union Impact on Productivity

Although the impact of unions on various aspects of productivity has been debated for a long time, the subject received little quantitative analysis until recently. This recent literature has confirmed that unions can have both positive and negative effects on productivity, so that the overall impact depends on the magnitude of various offsetting factors.

In discussing the impact on productivity, it is important to distinguish between the effects that occur directly as the outcome of collective bargaining and those that occur indirectly in the form of a behavioural response to higher wages. It is also important to recognize that unions may affect productivity not only in unionized firms but also elsewhere in the economy.

Economic theory predicts that firms will respond in several ways to the increase in labour costs associated with unionization. Relative to their non-union counterparts, union firms will utilize more capital and other inputs and less labour per unit of output. Union employers will also attempt to hire more-productive workers, and may try to increase job assignments and the pace of work.

Each of these responses to the union wage impact tends to raise labour productivity (output per worker) in the union sector and lower labour productivity in the non-union sector. Thus, a union versus non-union productivity comparison that does not control for differences in the amount of capital per worker, productivity-related worker characteristics, and the nature of the job assignment may well conclude that union workers are more productive than their non-union counterparts. Although this conclusion would be correct, it would not necessarily follow that unions benefit society as a whole by raising worker productivity. For example, as discussed previously, the union wage impact and its consequences for the allocation of labour and other resources results in a reduction in society's total output and income, even though output per worker in the union sector rises. Similarly, society as a whole will, in general, not benefit from distributing the labour force such that unionized firms employ the more productive workers and non-union firms the less productive. For these reasons, empirical analyses have attempted to determine whether unions and collective bargaining have direct effects on productivity in addition to those that arise as a consequence of the union wage impact. Such direct impacts, if positive, do imply a social benefit; if negative, they imply a social loss.

A common belief is that unions reduce productivity directly by inducing work stoppages and by negotiating restrictive work rules (featherbedding) that compel the employer to use excessive amounts of union labour and/or prevent the employer from introducing technological innovations. However, as emphasized by Freeman and Medoff (1979, 1984), unions may also have positive effects on productivity by reducing turnover, improving morale and co-operation among workers, improving communications between labour and management, and "shocking" management into more efficient practices.

Turnover is generally costly to firms because of expenses associated with hiring and training new workers to replace experienced personnel. While some turnover costs, such as expenditures on job advertising, may not affect measured productivity, others, such as having existing personnel devote less time to their own tasks and more to training new workers, do have this effect. In addition, lower turnover implies greater incentives for firms to engage in on-the-job training (Dustman and Schonberg 2009), which enhances productivity. For these reasons, the lower quit rate in union enterprises is expected to result in higher productivity than in otherwise comparable non-union enterprises. As discussed earlier, the differential in turnover can, in turn, be partly attributed to the union–non-union wage differential and partly to the direct impact of collective bargaining.

Unions may affect employee morale, the amount of co-operation among workers, and communications between labour and management in several, possibly offsetting, ways. Employee morale may be enhanced through various mechanisms: better wages, benefits, and working conditions; providing workers with a mechanism for expressing their collective preferences; and negotiating grievance, dismissal, and other procedures that protect workers from arbitrary treatment by management. Better morale may, in turn, raise productivity, although it is also possible that grievance procedures can be abused by workers, resulting in management and employee time being devoted to trivial matters. Also, making dismissal more difficult may reduce work effort and protect the incompetent. By making promotions much more dependent on seniority, unions may increase the amount of co-operation among workers because there will be less competition among employees for advancement. On the other hand, competition among workers for promotion may also enhance work effort and, thus, raise productivity. Unions also provide a formal mechanism for communication between workers and management, and these communications channels can be used to provide the firm with information about potential improvements in production techniques, product design, and the organization of the workplace. However, the union-management relationship can also become adversarial, with the consequence that there is less communication between the firm and its employees about potential improvements than in non-union organizations.

Some analysts have also suggested that unionization, and the accompanying increase in labour costs, may shock the firm into adopting more-efficient production and management techniques. This **shock effect** hypothesis assumes the existence of organizational slackness or inefficiency prior to unionization and is, therefore, consistent with "satisficing" behaviour on the firm's part, but not with optimizing behaviour (profit maximization and/or cost minimization). Although logically separate, the shock effect is difficult to distinguish empirically from the response of an optimizing firm to a change in relative factor prices—in this case, implementing a variety of changes in production techniques, hiring practices, and job assignments that result in the more efficient utilization of union labour.

In summary, economic theory suggests a variety of mechanisms through which unions may affect productivity. Because these mechanisms tend to both raise and lower productivity, the net impact is ambiguous. Empirical studies have found evidence of both positive and negative net impacts, suggesting that in some circumstances the productivity-enhancing mechanisms dominate, while in others the opposite occurs. To the extent possible, the studies have attempted to control for such factors as differences in capital per worker and in productivity-related worker characteristics, such as education and experience. The purpose, then, is to estimate the direct impact of unions on productivity; that is, to exclude those effects that are a consequence of the union–non-union wage differential.

Broadly based studies using aggregate data have generally produced inconclusive results. Using cross-sectional data for U.S. manufacturing industries, Brown and Medoff (1978) found a large, positive union impact on productivity when certain strong assumptions were made regarding the technology of production in union and non-union firms, but found no statistically significant impact under more general assumptions. With data for Canadian manufacturing industries, Maki (1983) obtains results that are even more sensitive to econometric specification, being positive when the Brown-Medoff assumptions are imposed but significantly negative under more-general conditions. Canadian evidence presented in Mitchell and Stone (1992) is also sensitive to the econometric specification. Adding to the conflicting results, Warren (1985) finds evidence of a negative union impact on productivity using aggregate U.S. time-series data.

Empirical studies based on more-disaggregated data generally appear to be much less sensitive to changes in specification. Using a large sample of individual U.S. firms, Clark (1984) estimates a small negative union impact on productivity. The growing number of econometric studies of individual industries provides evidence of both positive and negative impacts. In detailed studies of the U.S. cement industry, Clark (1980a, 1980b) finds that union labour was 6 to 8 percent more productive than non-union labour, an amount that approximately offsets the higher labour costs associated with the union wage impact. Large productivity effects have been estimated in residential and office construction (Mandelstamm 1965;

Allen 1984), a sector in which the union–non-union wage differential is also substantial. However, union and non-union labour are estimated to be equally productive in the construction of schools (Allen 1984). The difference may be due to the high degree of competition in residential and office construction relative to that for schools.

In a more recent study for Ireland, Liu, Guthrie, Flood, and MacCurtain (2009) find that an increase in union membership is associated with a significant decrease in the use of high-performance work systems. Such systems are widely believed to improve organizational performance, through such practices as rigorous staffing procedures, employee participation, job redesign, investments in training, and alternative approaches to compensation—all designed to improve employee competencies, discretionary authority, and motivation.

Recent reviews of the impact of unions on productivity generally conclude that the net effect is likely to be small, and as likely to be negative as positive (Addison and Belfield 2004; Hirsch 2004a, 2004b; Kahn 1998; Wilson 1995; Hirsch and Addison 1986). Hart and Sojourner (2015) find no impact of unions on productivity in charter schools where productivity is measured by student performance. In their meta-analysis of 73 studies, Doucouliagos and Laroche (2003b) conclude the union effect on productivity to be slightly positive in the United States, but slightly negative in the United Kingdom, although the estimates are sensitive to the type of data and empirical procedure.

Consistent with the hypothesis that product market competition plays an important role in the impact of unions on productivity is the general finding that there is no union–non-union productivity differential in the provision of public sector services, such as municipal libraries (Ehrenberg, Sherman, and Schwarz 1983), hospital services (Sloan and Adamache 1984), and building department services (Noam 1983), although Hoxby (1996) finds unions to have had a negative effect on the productivity of public school teachers. In general, the literature finds mixed effects of unions on productivity in the public sector (Gunderson 2005).

Labour-management relations also appear to be an important determinant of labour productivity. U.S. studies of unionized automobile plants (Katz, Kochan, and Gobeille 1983) and paper mills (Ichniowski 1986) find that productivity is negatively related to the number of grievances, a measure of labour-management relations.

Union co-operation and support can be an important ingredient for the success of quality improvement programs or profit-sharing programs introduced by employers. Based on U.S data, for example, Drago (1988) finds that union support facilitates the survival of quality circles where employees participate in problem solving. Kaufman (1992) finds profit-sharing plans to be more successful in union compared to non-union establishments. Cooke (1989, 1990, 1992, 1994) finds quality improvement and product quality to be higher in firms where unions are actively and co-operatively involved in quality improvement programs. Interestingly, Cooke (1994) finds profit sharing to enhance productivity more in union compared to non-union establishments, but because unions were able to appropriate more of the gains, such profit sharing contributed less to profits in union compared to non-union establishments. Block and Berg (2009) find that union co-operation in undertaking tasks traditionally performed by management in auto manufacturing had a substantial, positive effect on productivity and investment as well as sustaining employment security at relatively high wages. The importance of employment security in fostering union acceptance of high-performance work systems is also emphasized in Wenchuan et al. (2009).

Based on Canadian data on unionized establishments, Wager (1997, 1998) finds co-operative union management relations to be associated with various perceived positive organization outcomes, such as reduced conflict, turnover, absenteeism, job insecurity, and resistance to change as well as improved morale, innovation, productivity, product quality, and customer satisfaction. Based on Canadian and U.S. data, Kim and Voos (1997) find that managers' perception of the success of bonus or profit-sharing programs was similar for union and non-union establishments. However, in unionized establishments, union involvement was critical to success.

Of course, sorting out cause and effect is difficult in this area. Union co-operation and support can obviously foster such positive outcomes, but it is also possible that the positive outcomes facilitate union co-operation and support.

Management response to unionization may also play a significant role. In his study of cement plants that became unionized, Clark (1980a) found that existing managers were replaced with new managers who were less paternalistic or authoritarian, and who placed more emphasis on controlling costs, setting production standards, and improving communication and monitoring. This adjustment can be interpreted either as a "shock effect" or as an optimizing of firm's substitution of higher-quality managerial input in response to an increase in the relative price of production labour.

In summary, the impact of unions on productivity, long a controversial issue, has received considerable attention recently. Evidence on the average economy-wide impact is inconclusive. However, in specific industries, union labour has been found to be more productive, in some cases substantially so, than comparable non-union labour. This productivity differential persists after controlling for differences in capital per worker and observed productivity-related worker characteristics—differences that can be attributed to the union–non-union wage differential. However, the existence of a positive union impact on productivity is by no means assured. The direction and magnitude of the effect appears to depend on the management response to unionization, the quality of labour-management relations, and perhaps, the degree of product market competition.

The conclusion that in some industries union labour is significantly more productive than comparable non-union labour will no doubt surprise those who believe that by restricting management flexibility and negotiating various work rules unions reduce production efficiency. Skeptics are correct in claiming that several interpretations can be given to such evidence. Unions may organize the most-productive firms in the industry, perhaps because these are the most profitable and have the greatest potential for wage gains. Alternatively, as discussed previously in the context of the union wage impact, there may be unobserved differences in worker characteristics and/or job assignments that account for observed productivity differences. However, it also may be the case that, for the various reasons discussed above, union representation makes otherwise comparable workers more productive.

One interesting consequence of a positive union productivity effect is that it may explain the coexistence of both union and non-union firms in the same industry. In a perfectly competitive industry, unions must either organize all the firms in the industry (and credibly threaten to organize potential entrants) or the cost-increasing consequences of the higher union wages must be offset by higher productivity. When barriers to entry or other factors enable firms to earn above-normal profits, it is not essential that union wage gains be offset by the higher productivity of union labour. In these circumstances, unions may be able to capture some of the economic rents that would otherwise accrue to the firm's managers and/or owners.

Union Impact on Profits

Empirical evidence indicates that this in fact occurs. Despite differences in data sources, measurement of **profitability**, and methodology, numerous U.S. studies are unanimous in concluding that union firms are less profitable than comparable non-union firms. Such studies include Abowd (1989), Becker and Olson (1989, 1992), Belman (1992), Bronars and Deere (1990, 1994), Hirsch (1991a, 1991b, 2004), Magnani and Prentice (2010), Ruback and Zimmerman (1984), Voos and Mishel (1986), and Doucouliagos and Laroche (2009) in a meta-analysis involving 45 econometric studies with 532 estimates of the impact of unions on profits. The same is the case for UK studies (Addison and Belfield 2001; Machin 1991; Menezes-Filho 1997). While lowering profitability, unions do not appear to reduce profits by so much as to drive firms into bankruptcy, and thereby "kill the goose that lays the golden egg" (see Exhibit 15.2).

EXHIBIT 15.2

Do Unions Commit the Worst Crime against Working People?

Freeman and Kleiner (1999) cite Samuel Gompers, the first president of the American Federation of Labour in the late 1900s, when he said "the worst crime against working people is the company which fails to operate at a profit." Gompers clearly recognized the mutual interest that workers and employers had in the survival of the organization. As an aside, Gompers's facility with one-liners is also exhibited by his famous response to the question, "What does labour want?" His response was simple—"more"—but, as he obviously recognized, not so much more as to jeopardize the financial viability of the organization.

Recognizing that unions generally reduce profitability, Freeman and Kleiner (1999) analyze whether they do so by so much as to induce some firms into bankruptcy—to commit the "worst crime against labour." They find that unionized firms are no more likely to declare bankruptcy than are non-union firms. They, therefore, conclude that while unions reduce profits they do not "kill the goose that lays the golden egg."

The Canadian evidence is more equivocal. To some extent, this may reflect the differences in data sources (especially measures of profitability) and empirical methodology. Maki and Meredith (1986) investigate the relationship between unionization rates and industry-level profitability for a cross-section of Canadian industries over the period 1971–1981. They find that most measures of profits are negatively associated with unionization, consistent with the U.S. findings. Laporta and Jenkins (1996) find that unions reduced profits in monopolistic industries but increased them in competitive ones.

Canadian evidence is found in Martinello et al. (1995) who use a conventional **event study** methodology to isolate the effect of union certification on the stock market value of the firm. Basically, the event study methodology looks for unexplained changes in the share price around the timing of the event being analyzed (i,e., certification). If unions reduce profitability, then this should be anticipated by investors where unions are certified, leading to a drop in the stock market value of certified firms relative to the general change in the stock market value of firms. Martinello et al. examine a sample of 66 firms that experienced unionization drives (official applications for certification to the Ontario Labour Relations Board) over the period 1975–1991. They find very little relationship between changes in union status and firm share prices, suggesting that unions do not adversely affect profits. Another explanation, however, would be that union certification drives were correlated with periods of relatively good firm performance.

These results contrast with the previously discussed findings from the United States, as well as U.S. studies employing the event study methodology. Ruback and Zimmerman (1984), find that the effect of unionization on firm profits is anticipated by stock market participants. Equity values fell significantly when an application for a union representation election was announced. The decline was substantially higher in those cases in which the union subsequently achieved certification, suggesting that investors were also able to anticipate the outcome of the representation vote.

In a more recent U.S. event study, Lee and Mas (2012) find that a union election victory leads to about a 10 percent decline in the market value of firms after a period of 15 to 18 months. This is equivalent to about $40,500 per unionized worker, and implies an approximately 10 percent union wage premium.

Pearce, Groff, and Wingender (1995), however, found an asymmetry in that shareholder wealth did not increase when unions were decertified, perhaps reflecting the costs and uncertainty associated with implementing the new managerial strategies.

Union Impact on Investment

If unions reduce profitability one would expect to see less investment in unionized plants. This is especially the case if there is a risk of a **hold-up problem** whereby unions are able to appropriate the benefits of successful investments given that capital is fairly fixed and difficult to move once it is in place. Multinationals, especially, may allocate more of their investment in non-union organizations if their unionized ones are less profitable. This negative overall investment effect may be offset somewhat, however, by the possibility of substituting capital for labour if labour becomes more expensive because of a union wage premium or rigid work rules. As well, unions may actually bargain for additional investment to sustain employment.

The empirical evidence generally finds a negative effect of unions on investment (e.g., Odgers and Betts 1997 for Canada) as well as on research and development (Betts, Odgers, and Wilson 2001 for Canada). For the United States, see Allen (1988); Becker and Olson (1992); Bronars, Deere, and Tracy (1994); Cooke (1997); Connolly, Hirsch, and Hirschey (1986); Fallick and Hassett (1999); and Hirsch (1991a, 1991b, 1992). For the United Kingdom, see Addison and Wagner (1994) and Denny and Nickell (1991). For France, see Doucouliagos and Laroche (2003a), although they found the effect on investment to be negative only for militant unions.

In a meta-analysis of 208 estimates from 25 different studies across different countries, Doucouliagos and Laroche (2013) find that unions depress investment in innovations at the firm and industry level in all countries considered. This adverse effect is large, with unions associated with a 7 percent decline in innovation. It is declining over time, perhaps, because unions have less bargaining power to resist changes associated with innovation. The adverse effect of unions on innovation is larger in countries where labour markets are more flexible and less regulated, like in Canada and the United States, perhaps because workers have less protection against the adjustments associated with innovations and, hence, resist the innovations.

An interesting exception is Menezes-Filho, Ulph, and Van Reenen (1998), who find that in Britain the negative effect disappears if one excludes the high-tech industries that tend to invest considerably in research and development, and that tend to be non-union. In the other industries, unions do not appear to deter investment. They suggest that much of this may reflect the fact that British unions tend to emphasize jobs over wages and, hence, are reluctant to bargain in a way that may deter investment. In the United States, Karier (1995) is another exception, finding that firms in heavily unionized industries in the United States are no more likely to transfer their investments out of the country than are less unionized industries. However, Walsworth (2010) actually finds a small positive relation between the presence of a union and firms' abilities to innovate new products in Canada.

Summary of Union Impact on Productivity, Profitability and Investment

Overall, the evidence on the impact of unions on productivity, profitability, and investment suggests the following:

- Unions generally reduce quit rates as well as increase productivity, although there is conflicting evidence in the latter area.
- These positive effects tend not to offset the higher cost associated with unions, especially because of their higher wages and fringe benefits.
- As such, profitability is generally lower in unionized firms.
- However, unions are careful not to push firms into bankruptcy.

EXHIBIT 15.3

Is It Possible That New Unions Now Have No Effect on Outcomes?

In a recent study based on *new* unions that were formed over the period 1984 to 2001 in the United States, DiNardo and Lee (2004) find that such new unions had little or no impact on various outcomes, such as firm survival, employment, output, and productivity. This was so in large part because such newly formed unions also had no impact on wages. While such results are unusual in finding no impact, they are consistent with the possibility that the increased importance of competitive market forces through deregulation, freer trade, and global competition is restricting the extent to which unions can extract gains.

Their study is also unusual in that they utilize firm-level data and employ the methodology of a *regression discontinuity design* that is increasingly utilized to estimate the causal effect of a treatment or intervention—in this case, the formation of a union. Essentially, they compare outcomes in firms where unions *barely won* the certification vote and became unionized with those that *barely lost* the certification vote and became non-union. Such a procedure is designed to approximate the ideal experiment of random assignment to union and non-union status, since, for reasons they outline, barely winning or losing is largely random.

The procedure essentially gets around the selection biases that otherwise may occur, and work in opposite directions. On the one hand, unions could be more likely to organize in situations where firms are prosperous and likely to grow and survive. On the other hand, they may be more likely to be successful at organizing in firms that are poorly managed or face recent difficulties. In either case, union status can be *endogenous* and caused by the outcomes, rather than being exogenous and having a causal impact on the outcomes.

- In part because of this lower profitability, there tends to be less new investment and research and development put into unionized plants.
- For almost all of these results, however, there are exceptions—as is usually the case with empirical work.

Summary

- Unions affect the wages not only of their members but also of non-union workers, though in an indeterminate fashion. Some workers who are displaced from the union sector because of the adverse employment effect of the union wage premium go to the non-union sector, with that supply spillover depressing non-union wages. As well, the demand for non-union labour may change, but in opposing ways. On the one hand, the demand for non-union labour may decrease (and, hence, non-union wages fall) to the extent that it is a complement to union labour. On the other hand, the demand for non-union labour may increase (and, hence, non-union wages rise) to the extent to which it is a substitute for the now higher-priced union labour. The wages of non-union labour may also increase directly if employers raise their wages to reduce the threat of becoming unionized. Wages of non-union labour can also be affected by legislative initiatives that are often supported by unions (e.g., minimum wages) or if employers try to restore old wage relativities.

- Methodological problems associated with measuring the union impact include difficulties of controlling for other factors that influence wages, especially because employers have an incentive to alter items, such as qualifications and job requirements, in response to the higher union wage. Also, selection bias may occur if workers sort themselves (or are sorted by employers) into the union or non-union sector on the bases of unobserved factors; and reverse causality if high wages induce unionization.

- Although there are always exceptions, empirical studies on the impact of unions tend to find the following:
  - The union–non-union wage differential is likely around 15 percent, and within the range of 10–25 percent.
  - The union wage impact is falling in more recent years and now may be more in the neighbourhood of 10 percent.
  - The impact on non-union wages is likely small, although there is not a consensus as to whether it is positive or negative.
  - The union impact is larger at low-skill levels and smaller at high-skill levels, as unions tend to garner flat wage increases but reduce the returns to factors related to skill levels, such as education or training.
  - The union impact tends to be higher in the private sector compared to the public sector, in small firms compared to large firms, for blue-collar compared to white-collar workers, when a larger portion of the relevant jurisdiction is organized, and in recessions compared to booms.

- In the United States, the union wage impact is similar for females and males, but in Canada it is larger for females compared to males. However, because women tend to be less unionized, fewer women obtain the union wage premiums with these opposing effects cancelling out such that unions tend not to affect the overall male–female wage differential.

- Unions tend to compress wage structures within the union sector, but they also create a union–non-union wage differential that widens wage inequality, with most studies finding on net that unions reduce wage inequality in the economy.

- Because of the distortions created by their wage and employment effects, unions create welfare losses to society as a whole but those losses are small.

- The union impact on fringe benefits tends to be greater than the impact on wages.

- Unions reduce turnover and quits, and many studies (but by no means all) find that they have a positive impact on productivity. These positive effects tend not to offset the higher cost associated with unions, especially because of their higher wages and fringe benefits.

- As such, profitability is generally lower in unionized firms, although unions are careful not to push firms into bankruptcy and "kill the goose that lays the golden egg."

- In part because of this lower profitability, there tends to be less new investment put into unionized plants.

Keywords

deadweight loss	inefficient allocation
event study	labour market turnover
exit	profitability
fixed-effects model	selection bias
hold-up problem	shock effect

simultaneity

threat effect

two-sector model

union–non-union wage differential

voice

wage dispersion

wait or queue unemployment

Review Questions

1. Discuss the various wage structures and wage levels that unions can affect.
2. Discuss the various ways in which unions can affect the wages of non-union labour.
3. Why may one expect the skill level of union workers to be different from the skill level of non-union workers? What does this imply about union–non-union wage differentials? Why may one expect high wages to cause unionism, as well as vice versa, and what does this imply about union–non-union wage differentials?
4. If you expect the wage impact of unions to differ systematically with respect to certain conditions (e.g., extent of unionization in the industry or extent of concentration in the product market), how would you capture the interaction effect in a regression equation designed to measure the impact of unions?
5. Discuss why the union wage impact may vary according to such factors as industry, occupation, the stage of the business cycle, and the size of the firm.
6. Discuss the pros and cons of using longitudinal data to estimate the impact of unions.
7. Discuss the various ways in which unions can affect wage inequality in the economy.
8. Discuss the effect of unionization on the efficient allocation of resources. How would you measure these "welfare" effects?
9. Discuss the effect of unions on fringe benefits and working conditions.
10. Discuss the various ways in which unions may affect productivity.
11. How would you expect the union wage premium to be changing since the 1970s, and why?

Problems

1. Assume the following union impact equation:

$$W = 0.5CA + 0.004CA \times U + 0.003CA + CR - 0.01CA \times RLC + \text{other control variables}$$

where W is the wage rate in the establishment, CA represents the existence of a collective agreement in the establishment, U represents the percentage of the industry that is unionized, CR represents industry concentration, and RLC is the ratio of wage labour cost to value added.

   a. Theoretically justify the use of each of these explanatory variables.
   b. What sign would you expect for each regression coefficient?
   c. Why are the explanatory variables entered in the equation in that particular fashion—that is, multiplied by CA?
   d. What is the effect on wages of being covered by a collective agreement as opposed to not covered?
   e. Evaluate this effect at the following mean values of the explanatory variables: $\overline{U} = 40, \overline{CR} = 7, \overline{RLC} = 36$.

f. Compare this union impact in an establishment with the impact that would occur if the industry in which the firm operated was completely unionized, other things being equal.

g. Compare the union impact of (e) with the impact that would occur if the ratio of wage labour cost to value added were only 20 percent as opposed to 36 percent.

h. What does such an equation imply about the impact of the control variables on union and non-union workers?

i. How would you relax that implied assumption?

2. Assume you have estimated the following wage equations where W is the mean wage (or benefit), X is a vector of the mean values of the wage-determining characteristics, β is a vector of the estimated coefficients or returns to the characteristics, and the subscripts denote union and non-union status.

$W_U = X_U \beta_U$ for union workers

$W_N = X_N \beta_N$ for nonunion workers

a. Illustrate the hypothetical wage, W^*_U that union workers would receive if they had their own characteristics (i.e., X_U) but were paid according to the nonunion pay structure for those characteristics.

b. Show that the difference between this hypothetical wage and the actual wage of union workers is attributable to differences in the endowments of wage-determining characteristics between union and non-union workers, since both are paid according to the same pay structure, in this case the non-union returns, which are taken as the competitive norm.

c. Show that the difference between the actual wage of union workers and the hypothetical wage they would earn if they were paid according to the non-union pay structure is attributable to differences in their returns for the same wage-determining characteristics, in this case the union characteristics.

d. Add the differences calculated in (a) and (b) above to show that the average wage differential between union and non-union workers can be decomposed into two components: differences in the average value of the wage-determining characteristics, $(X_U - X_N)$, evaluated according to the non-union returns, β_N, and differences in the pay structure between union and non-union workers, $(\beta_U - \beta_N)$, evaluated with the union characteristics, X_U.

e. Give an interpretation to each of these two components in terms of union rents or wage premiums and endowments of wage-determining characteristics such as education or experience.

3. Assume you are head of the newly formed Airlines Pilots' Association and your brother is head of the newly formed Garment Workers' Association. Your union faces an elasticity of demand for labour of −0.2 and your brothers' union faces an elasticity of demand for labour of −0.6. You both can bargain only over wages.

a. If you both negotiated the average union wage premium of 10 percent that exists in the economy, what employment effects would result?

b. If you both were willing to accept a 2 percent reduction in the employment of your membership, what wage increase would you each bargain for?

c. If the airline that you bargained against just bought out another airline so there was very little competition, and this cut the elasticity of demand for labour that you faced by half, what wage would you now bargain for if you were willing to accept a 2 percent reduction in the employment of your membership?

d. If your brother's union now was bargaining with employers who were just exposed to increased international competition from countries with low-wage labour and this increased the elasticity of demand for labour that he faced from −0.6 to −1.0, what wage increase would he now bargain for if he were willing to accept a 2 percent reduction in employment?

e. Under these circumstances would you support or oppose the merger and your brother support or oppose free trade?

4. From Figure 15.4, the efficiency losses from the wage distortion imposed by unions is the triangle abc in the union sector plus the triangle dgf in the non-union sector. Assuming linear demand curves, this is equal to,

$$\frac{1}{2}\left(W_U - W_0\right)\left(E_1 - E_0\right) + \frac{1}{2}\left(W_0 - W_N\right)\left(E_0 - E_1\right),$$

or

$$\frac{1}{2}\left(W_U - W_N\right)\left(E_1 - E_0\right), \text{ since } \left(E_1 - E_0\right) = \left(E_1 - E_0\right)$$

It can be shown that this efficiency loss can be expressed as a percentage of national income in the economy (Rees 1963) as

$$\frac{1}{2}\Delta W_U \times \Delta E_U \times D_U \times L / Y, \text{ where}$$

ΔW_U = percentage union wage impact

ΔE_U = percentage reduction of employment in the union sector

D_U = union density or percent of labour force that is unionized

L/Y = labour's share of national income

Assuming that elasticity of demand for labour is -0.5 (so as to calculate the employment reduction), that 0.30 of the labour force is unionized (as is the case in Canada), and that labour's share of national income is 0.75, calculate this efficiency loss as a percentage of GNP on the basis of the following scenarios:

a. A union wage impact of 0.15, which is an approximate "best guess" for Canada.

b. A union wage impact of 0.10, which may be the case in more recent years given international competitive pressures and other forces.

c. A union wage impact of 0.15, but only 0.15 of the labour force being unionized as is approximately the case in the United States.

d. A union wage impact of 0.15 and a unionization rate of 0.30, but an increase in the elasticity of demand for labour from 0.5 to 1.0 given increased foreign competition.

e. A union wage impact of 0.10, but in return for the concession of such smaller wage gains unions getting guarantees of smaller employment adjustments that effectively reduce the elasticity of demand for labour from 0.5 to 0.25.

Endnotes

1. The discussion here does not deal with the impact of unions on macroeconomic indicators, such as inflation and unemployment under centralized or decentralized bargaining systems as reviewed in Flanagan (1999).

CHAPTER 16

Unemployment: Meaning, Measurement, and Canada's Experience

LEARNING OBJECTIVES

LO1 Explain how unemployment and the unemployment rate are defined and measured.

LO2 Explain why the measurement of unemployment is often controversial, and describe alternative measures that can be used.

LO3 Summarize the salient features of Canada's unemployment experience and how it compares to those of other developed countries.

LO4 Define the labour force participation rate and the employment rate, and explain why these measures are often used in addition to the unemployment rate to provide a complete picture of the state of the labour market.

LO5 Explain the meaning of the incidence and the duration of unemployment, and describe how each contributes to the extent of unemployment.

LO6 Describe the dynamic nature of the Canadian labour market and explain the implications of this feature for understanding movements in unemployment.

MAIN QUESTIONS

- How is the unemployment rate measured? Who is considered to be unemployed?
- How does Canada's unemployment experience compare to that of other countries?
- How do the incidence and duration of unemployment separately contribute to the overall unemployment rate?
- How long is a typical Canadian unemployed? Does this vary across groups in the population?
- Does the unemployment rate accurately reflect the amount of hardship felt by the jobless?

With the possible exception of the consumer price index (CPI), no single economic statistic receives as much attention as the unemployment rate. To a considerable extent, this attention reflects concern about the hardship that unemployment may impose on affected individuals and their families, and the waste of human resources that may be associated with unemployment. In addition, the unemployment rate is used as a measure of the overall state of the economy and of the degree of tightness (excess demand) or slack (excess supply) in the labour market. However, in spite of this evident interest, there is often confusion about what is meant by our unemployment statistics. This chapter examines the meaning and measurement of unemployment. The causes and consequences of unemployment and the role of public policy in this area are discussed in the following chapter.

Measuring Unemployment

The unemployed are generally defined as those who are not currently employed and who indicate by their behaviour that they want to work at prevailing wages and working conditions. The "prevailing wages" condition is important. Simply asking those who are not currently employed whether they want to work may not be very meaningful without stipulating the wage. Many individuals would be interested in working if they were handsomely paid.

In Canada, measurement of unemployment is based on Statistics Canada's Labour Force Survey. Additional information on the unemployed is available from administrative data on claimants of the Employment Insurance program and from other surveys carried out by Statistics Canada.

The **Labour Force Survey** (LFS) is conducted monthly by Statistics Canada. According to the LFS, people are categorized as **unemployed** if they did not have work in the reference period but were available for and searching for work. There are two exceptions to this general principle. The unemployed also includes individuals who were available for work but who were not seeking work because they were on temporary layoff from a job to which they expect to be recalled, or they had a new job to start within four weeks.

Apart from these exceptions, the general principle is that to be counted as unemployed, one has to be available for and searching for work. That is, it is necessary to engage in some form of job search, such as contacting employers or checking job ads, to be classified as unemployed. Job search is defined in the LFS as having looked for work sometime during the previous four weeks. Individuals who are not employed and who are not seeking work (such as students, individuals engaged in household work, those permanently unable to work, and retirees) are classified as being out of the labour force.

People are categorized as employed if they did any work for pay or profit, including unpaid work on a family farm or business, or if they normally had a job but were not at work because of such factors as bad weather, illness, industrial dispute, or vacation. The employed plus the unemployed make up the labour force, and the unemployment rate is defined as the number of unemployed divided by the labour force. Thus, the unemployment rate provides a measure of the proportion of the labour force that is not currently employed.

Canadian Experience

As Figure 16.1 illustrates, Canada's unemployment rate fluctuated widely during the period 1921–2015, to a considerable extent because of cyclical fluctuations in business activity. Several distinct episodes are evident:

- With the onset of the Great Depression in 1929, the unemployment rate soared from about 3 percent to almost 20 percent.
- A lengthy period of declining unemployment followed, and during World War II unemployment fell to very low levels.
- Following the war, unemployment remained low until the recession of 1957–1958. As the economy recovered from this recession, the unemployment rate gradually declined, reaching 3.4 percent in 1966.
- After the mid-1960s, the overall trend in unemployment was generally upward until the 1980s, although fluctuations around the trend also occurred.
- During the past three decades, unemployment rates have been gradually trending downwards, but noteworthy cyclical fluctuations around the trend continued to occur. The most-significant increases were experienced in the recession of 1974–1975 that followed the first OPEC oil shock; in the severe recession of 1981–1982, which resulted in the unemployment rate reaching 11.8 percent, the highest level since the Great Depression; in the recession of 1990–1992; and in the recent downturn in 2008–2009. During the economic expansion that followed the 1981–1982 recession, the unemployment rate gradually declined to a low of 7.5 percent in 1989. By 1992 the unemployment rate was back above 11 percent.
- After a brief economic slowdown in 2001, the Canadian economy experienced strong growth in the first part of the 21st century. By 2006, the unemployment rate had fallen to 6.0 percent, its lowest level since the early 1970s.
- The global financial crisis that began in 2008 resulted in a deep recession in many countries. Canada's economic downturn was less severe than that experienced in most other developed countries (and was especially mild relative to the U.S. Great Recession, the worst downturn in the United States since the Great Depression). Although Canada's unemployment rate rose to 8.3 percent in 2009, this level was substantially below that reached in the recessions of the early 1980s and early 1990s.
- Since 2009, Canada's unemployment rate has gradually declined, but in 2015 it remained below the level that prevailed prior to the 2008–2009 financial crisis.

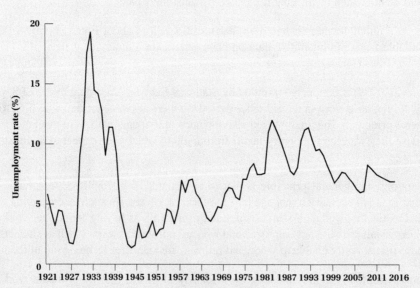

Figure 16.1 Unemployment in Canada, 1921–2015

The national unemployment rate is plotted by year over the period 1921–2015. Unemployment increased dramatically during the Great Depression, and fell to very low levels during World War II. During the postwar period, unemployment has fluctuated cyclically, initially around a generally rising trend. In the past three decades, this upward trend has been reversed.

SOURCE: *Historical Statistics of Canada (1921–1945)*, Statistics Canada CANSIM database.

LO2, 3, 4   Alternative Measures of Labour Force Activity

The **unemployment rate** is the most commonly used measure of aggregate labour market activity and the degree of labour force utilization. Two alternative measures are the *labour force participation rate* (the ratio of the labour force to the population of working age, or source population) and the **employment rate** (the ratio of employment to the source population). These statistics are shown for selected years in Table 16.1. With the exception of the most recent year (2015), the years are chosen so that they correspond to similar points in the business cycle. (The years 1956, 1966, 1973, 1981, 1989, 2000, and 2008 were the peak years of the business cycle in the postwar period.)

TABLE 16.1	Labour Force Participation, Employment, and Unemployment, Canada, 1946–2015[a]			
Year	Labour Force Participation Rate	Employment Rate	Unemployment Rate	Rate of Growth of Employment[b]
1946	55.0	53.1	3.4	
1956	53.5	51.7	3.4	1.8
1966	55.1	53.1	3.6	2.5
1973	59.7	56.4	5.6	3.0
1981	65.0	60.0	7.6	3.2
1989	67.2	62.1	7.5	1.8
2000	65.9	61.4	6.8	1.3
2008	67.6	63.4	6.1	1.8
2015	65.8	61.3	6.9	0.8

NOTES: [a]All statistics are based on authors' calculations from data on the civilian labour force (annual averages) derived from the CANSIM database.

[b]Civilian employment; growth rates are averages of compound annual increases from the level in the year in the row one line above to the level in the year one line below.

SOURCE: Authors' calculations based on data from the Statistics Canada CANSIM database.

Because they focus on somewhat different aspects of labour market activity, these three measures need not always move together. For example, after 1966, the unemployment rate rose sharply, yet at the same time both the employment rate and the fraction of the population participating in the labour force increased rather than decreased. Additional perspective on these divergent patterns is provided by the fourth column of Table 16.1; the rate of growth of employment between 1966 and 1981 was the most rapid of the postwar period. The combination of rapid employment growth and rising unemployment rates reflected several phenomena, including the substantial number of youth and women who entered the labour force, particularly after the mid-1960s. Although employment grew rapidly between 1966 and 1981, the growth in labour supply was even more substantial; thus, the unemployment rate rose. Since the early 1980s, the rate of growth in employment has fallen substantially. The growth rate of 1.3 percent per year in the 1990s represents the slowest rate of employment growth between cyclical peaks in the postwar period.

Of the three measures shown in the table, the one actually used for analyzing aggregate labour market activity will depend on the purpose of the analysis. The employment and labour force participation rates focus on the fraction of the working-age population that is employed and in the labour force, respectively, while the unemployment rate measures the fraction of the labour force that is out of work and searching for work. Because this chapter deals with unemployment, the main aggregate statistic referred to is the unemployment rate. However, the employment and labour force participation rates often provide useful additional information on labour market developments.

Hidden Unemployment or Marginal Labour Force Attachment

The measurement of unemployment raises some difficult and controversial issues. Hidden unemployment, or **marginal labour force attachment** , refers to situations in which individuals may be without work yet they desire work but are not classified as unemployed according to the official statistics. Such individuals are attached to the labour force to some degree, but are not sufficiently strongly attached that they are seeking work. One important example, especially during recessions and in regions where few jobs are available, is the phenomenon of the discouraged worker. This refers to individuals who are not employed, who may wish to work at prevailing wages, but who are not seeking work because they believe that no work is available. Other examples include individuals still awaiting recall after more than six months on layoff; forms of underemployment, such as individuals working fewer hours than they desire to work or normally work; and those temporarily employed in jobs that do not utilize their skills or training. Each of these examples illustrates the difficulties involved in making a satisfactory distinction between "employment," "unemployment," and "out of the labour force."

EXHIBIT 16.1

International Differences in Unemployment

Canada and the United States measure employment, unemployment, and labour force participation in very similar ways, using monthly surveys (Labour Force Survey and Current Population Survey, respectively) that share many features. Measures used in other countries differ in a variety of ways; however, the unemployment rate statistics shown in Figure 16.2 have been adjusted so that they are comparable to U.S. concepts.

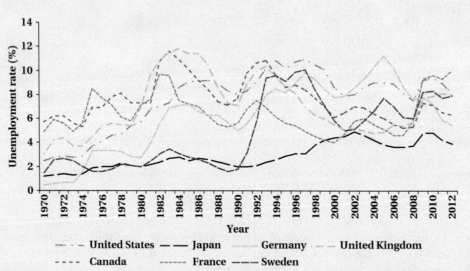

Figure 16.2 Civilian Unemployment Rates, 1970–2012 (approximating U.S. concepts)

SOURCE: U.S. Bureau of Labor Statistics (series discontinued in 2013).

As Figure 16.2 indicates, the unemployment rate has varied substantially over time within most countries, and also varies considerably across countries. During the 1950s and 1960s, unemployment rates in

North America were substantially higher than those in Japan, the United Kingdom, and most continental European countries. However, after the first OPEC oil price shock in 1973, unemployment rose sharply in several European countries (e.g., France, Germany, and the UK) and then escalated further during the 1980s. The 1990s saw further increases in unemployment in France and Germany, but lower unemployment in the UK. Japan, as well as a few European countries (e.g., Sweden), did not experience this dramatic rise in unemployment during the 1970s and 1980s, but both Japan and Sweden experienced much higher unemployment in the 1990s. By 2000, unemployment rates fell to historically low levels in the English-speaking countries (Canada, the United States, and the UK). However, many European countries, including France and Germany, continued to experience relatively high levels of unemployment. Similarly, Japan, which had unemployment rates of 1 to 2 percent in the 1970s and 1980s, faced dramatically higher rates in the following two decades.

Thus, Canadian and American unemployment rates, which were unusually high by international standards during the first two decades of the postwar period, were no longer so after the early 1980s. Indeed, unemployment rates in North America declined substantially during the long periods of economic expansion following the recessions of the early 1980s and early 1990s, whereas rates in many European countries remained stubbornly high. Japan and Sweden stand out as countries that were somehow able to adjust to the economic shocks of the 1970s and 1980s without experiencing dramatic increases in unemployment. However, both experienced large increases in unemployment during the 1990s, and by 2000 the unemployment rate in the United States was lower than that in Japan and Sweden, two countries with a tradition of low unemployment.

The worldwide financial crisis and the associated 2008–2009 recession resulted in dramatically higher unemployment in many advanced economies. The rise in unemployment was particularly acute in the United States, where the financial crisis began. After being regarded as a "low unemployment country" for about 30 years, during and after the Great Recession the United States could no longer claim that status. But the United States was not alone—following the 2008–2009 recession, unemployment rates were unacceptably high in most of the industrialized world.

Explaining these large differences in international experience is an important challenge for social scientists.

As discussed in Exhibit 16.2, some evidence on the quantitative significance of hidden unemployment in Canada is available. Since 1997, the Labour Force Survey identifies those who want work, are available for work, but are not seeking work for "personal" or "economic" reasons.[1] These "persons on the margin of the labour force" typically number between one-quarter and one-third of the officially unemployed. Exhibit 16.2 shows the consequences of including two types of "marginally attached" workers. In 2015, including discouraged workers increased the unemployment rate by 0.1 percentage points, and including a "waiting" group—those who state that they desire work but are not searching because they are waiting for recall, replies from employers, or a new job to start—added 0.7 percentage points. Including these two groups with the officially unemployed raises the unemployment rate from 6.9 to 7.7 percent, an increase of 0.8 percentage points, or almost 12 percent.

EXHIBIT 16.2

Supplementary Measures of Unemployment

The question of how best to measure unemployment has long been controversial. We frequently hear claims that the "true" level of unemployment is much greater than the official measure because of underemployment or "disguised" unemployment, such as discouraged workers who have stopped searching but still desire work. On the other hand, others claim that the official measure may overstate the amount of underutilization of labour because much unemployment is very short term in nature, representing mainly normal turnover in the labour market, and some searchers may not be serious about finding work.

Recognizing that there is no single best measure of unemployment suitable for all purposes, Statistics Canada produces a number of "supplementary measures of unemployment" (Statistics Canada 1999). As shown below, in 2015 these ranged in magnitude from R1 = 0.8 percent to R8 = 9.9 percent, when the official rate (R4) equalled 6.9 percent.

R1	Counting only those unemployed one year or more	0.8%
R2	Counting only those unemployed three months or more	2.5
R3	Made comparable to the U.S. official rate	5.9
R4	Official rate	6.9
R5	Official rate plus discouraged workers	7.0
R6	Official rate plus those waiting for recall, waiting for replies, and long-term future starts	7.6
R7	A measure of both unemployment and underemployment (involuntary part-time employment) expressed in full-time equivalents	9.1
R8	Official rate plus discouraged workers, those waiting for recall, those waiting for replies, and long-term future starts, and the underutilized portion of involuntary part-time workers	9.9

Measures R1 and R2 focus on groups for whom unemployment may represent particular economic hardship. Measures based on duration of unemployment may also be informative about the extent of mismatch between the skills and/or location of unemployed workers and available jobs, as discussed under the topic of "structural unemployment" in the next chapter.

R3 measures the Canadian unemployment rate on a comparable basis to the methods used in the United States. Differences in the Canadian and American definitions of unemployment are discussed by Riddell (2005). In recent years, these differences resulted in the U.S. unemployment rate being 0.6 to 1.0 percentage points lower than its Canadian counterpart for purely measurement reasons.

R5 adds to the officially unemployed those individuals who state that they desire work but are not searching because they believe no work is available in their area or suitable to their skills.

R6 includes the officially unemployed and three "waiting" groups who are conventionally classified as "out of the labour force": (1) waiting for recall to a former job, (2) waiting for replies from employers, and (3) have a job to start more than four weeks from the reference week of the survey. Note that the "waiting for recall" group does not include temporary layoffs, who are included among the officially unemployed even if not searching. Similarly, "long-term future starts" group does not include "future starts" who are included among the officially unemployed if they report that they have a job to start within four weeks.

R7 adds to the officially unemployed a measure of underemployment—those working part-time who state that they desire full-time work. Because this notion of underemployment is based on the gap between actual and desired hours of work, it is converted to full-time equivalents to make it comparable to measures of unemployment based on number of individuals rather than hours.

R8 adds to the officially unemployed all of the groups in R5, R6, and R7.

Whether individuals who desire work but are not seeking work should be classified as unemployed is a controversial issue. The observation that they are without work and state that they want work may argue for including them among the unemployed. According to this view, the fact that they are not searching for work may simply be a rational decision on how to spend their time; for example, if they believe that no jobs are available or if job search is costly. Similarly, waiting more than six months for recall may be sensible behaviour rather than wishful thinking, especially if the chances of recall are good and the job to which the individual expects to return is attractive relative to potential alternatives. In contrast, the absence of job search may indicate a low degree of labour force attachment, justifying the classification "out of the labour force."

These phenomena respond to changes in aggregate economic conditions. The number of discouraged workers increases during recessions and subsequently declines as the economy recovers. The number of individuals awaiting recall after more than six months displays a similar pattern. As a consequence, the increase in the unemployment rate in recessions is smaller than would be the case if those desiring but not seeking work were classified as unemployed. Similarly, the decline in the unemployment rate during the recovery is smaller than would be the case if these individuals were included in the unemployed.

Some evidence on the significance of underemployment is also available from the Labour Force Survey, which provides information on those working part-time who state that they desire full-time work. Adding these individuals raises the measured unemployment rate substantially (see R7). Once again, the measured unemployment rate may understate the extent of unutilized labour services, especially in recessionary periods.

Jones and Riddell (1999, 2006) provide empirical evidence on how "persons on the margin of the labour force" may distort measures of unemployment. They formally test whether these individuals behave more like the unemployed or those out of the labour force (where they are currently classified). Jones and Riddell show that the marginally attached behave as a distinct group, different from both the unemployed and the remainder of the "not in the labour force" category. Interestingly, "discouraged workers" are not the subgroup that most resembles the unemployed (rather than out of the labour force, where they are currently classified), but instead it is the group of individuals waiting for promised or potential jobs who most behave like the unemployed.[2] Similarly, Brandolini, Cipollone, and Viviano (2006) show that those who searched for work recently—for example, within the past six months—but who did not search during the past month (and are, thus, classified as not in the labour force) exhibit behaviour similar to that of the officially unemployed and distinct from that of those who did not recently search for work.

The major lesson to be learned from this discussion is *not* that the official unemployment rate is a poor measure of unemployment, but rather that the concept of unemployment is not sufficiently well defined that any single measure will suit all purposes. For many purposes, the official unemployment measure will be appropriate; however, in other situations, this should be supplemented by measures of hidden unemployment and underemployment. Because no single measure is likely to be suitable for all purposes, Statistics Canada publishes several supplementary measures of unemployment as described in Exhibit 16.2.

LO6   Labour Force Dynamics

Much recent research by economists has emphasized the dynamic nature of the labour force. Cross-sectional surveys like the Labour Force Survey provide a snapshot at a point in time, an estimate of the stock of persons in each labour force state. However, even if the magnitudes of these stocks remain approximately constant from one period to another, it would be a mistake to conclude that little change had taken place in the labour force. In fact, as Figure 16.3 illustrates, the flows between the three labour force states (employment, unemployment, out of the labour force) are large in comparison to the stocks, and the **gross flows** are huge in comparison to **net flows**. For example, on average over the period 1976–1991, between any pair of months, the number of unemployed declined only slightly (by 12,000). However, 235,000 individuals, 22 percent of those unemployed in an average month, became employed by the following month. This large gross flow from unemployment to employment was offset by a movement of 190,000 individuals in the opposite direction; the average net flow from unemployment to employment was thus 45,000 (235,000 minus 190,000). Similarly, 183,000 individuals, 17 percent of those unemployed, left the labour force between the average pair of months. However, this change was more than offset by the 216,000 individuals who entered the labour force and sought work. The net addition to unemployment of 33,000 due to the movements between unemployment and not in the labour force, thus, partially offset the net decline of 45,000 associated with the flows between unemployment and employment.

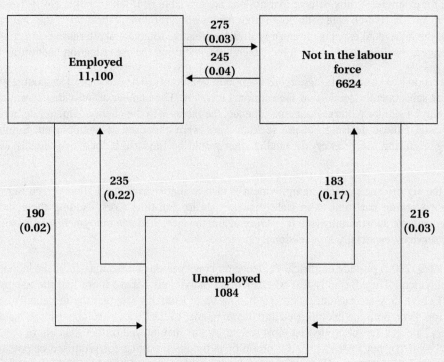

Figure 16.3 Labour Market Stocks and Flows, 1976–1991

This figure illustrates the large flows that occur each month between the labour force states of employment, E, unemploymen,t U, and not in the labour force, O. On average, every month 235,000 unemployed workers obtained jobs (i.e., moved from U to E), and 190,000 workers lost or left jobs and joined the pool of job searchers (i.e., moved from E to U). The average net monthly flow was, thus, 235,000 – 190,000 = 45,000 from U to E. The probability of an unemployed worker becoming employed the following month equals 0.22, and the probability that an employed worker becomes unemployed equals 0.02.

NOTES: All numbers are in thousands.

All stocks and flows are averages of monthly values from 1976 to 1991.

SOURCE: Stephen R.G. Jones, "Cyclical and seasonal properties of Canadian gross flows of labour." This article first appeared in Vol. XIX:I March 1993 of *Canadian Public Policy—Analyse de Politiques*. By permission.

Below each flow (in parentheses) in the figure is the average probability of moving from the origin state to the destination state. For example, on average over the period 1976–1991, the probability of an unemployed individual being employed in the following month was 0.22; the probability of moving from employment to unemployment was 0.02.

In summary, even though the number of unemployed changed only marginally from one month to the next over this extended period of time, many of the individuals unemployed in one month were no longer unemployed in the next month, with about 22 percent having obtained work and about 17 percent no longer seeking work. The picture that emerges from these data is that of a highly dynamic labour force in which there is a great deal of movement among employment, unemployment, and outside of the labour force each month.[3]

Table 16.2 provides data on the significance of the various flows into unemployment over the period 2005–2015. The picture of unemployment consisting almost entirely of individuals who lost their job (either temporarily or permanently) is clearly misleading; such job losers typically account for less than 40 percent of all unemployment. In recessions, such as during 2008–2009, the absolute and relative importance of job losers increases and the relative importance of job leavers declines. New entrants and re-entrants (those moving from out of the labour force to unemployed) constitute a substantial proportion (often 40 to 45 percent) of the unemployed.

TABLE 16.2	Decomposition of Unemployment by Reason, 2005–2015				
		Reason for Separation			
		Job Losers (%)			**New Entrants and Re-entrants (%)**
	National Unemployment Rate (%)	**Permanent**	**Temporary Layoffs**	**Job Leavers (%)**	
2005	6.8	28	7	10	42
2006	6.3	26	8	11	42
2007	6.0	27	7	11	43
2008	6.1	29	7	11	44
2009	8.3	33	8	8	40
2010	8.1	30	6	6	42
2011	7.5	27	5	9	43
2012	7.3	26	5	8	45
2013	7.1	28	5	8	44
2014	6.9	28	5	9	44
2015	6.9	29	5	8	44

NOTES: All statistics are based on authors' calculations from data on the civilian labour force (annual averages).

Components do not sum to the total because reasons for separation "Reason unknown" and "Future starts" are omitted.

SOURCE: Statistics Canada, CANSIM, Table 282-0216, 2016.

Incidence and Duration of Unemployment

Because of the dynamic nature of labour force movements, an understanding of unemployment requires information on the flows between various labour force states in addition to the stocks in each state at any point in time. Useful measures for this purpose are the **incidence of unemployment**—the proportion of individuals who become unemployed in any period—and the duration of unemployment—the length of time spent in the unemployed state before obtaining employment or leaving the labour force.[4] For any particular group of workers, incidence measures the probability of a member of the group becoming unemployed, while duration measures the length of time the individual remains unemployed, on average. Using the data in Figure 16.3, the incidence of unemployment for those employed in the average month was 1.7 percent (190,000 out of 11,100,000) while the incidence of unemployment among those out of the labour force in the average month was 3.3 percent (216,000 out of 6,624,000). The overall incidence among those either employed or not in the labour force was 2.3 percent. More commonly, incidence of unemployment is measured as a fraction of the labour force, so that it measures the percentage of the labour force that is newly unemployed. With this measure, the incidence of unemployment would be 3.3 percent over the time period covered in Figure 16.3.

The amount of unemployment at any point in time is affected by both the incidence and duration. Indeed, the unemployment rate (UR) can be expressed as the product of the incidence (I) and duration (D).[5]

$$UR = I \times D \tag{16.1}$$

Table 16.3 shows the unemployment rate and the incidence and duration of unemployment for various age-sex groups in Canada in 2015. The most striking feature of the data in Table 16.3 is that the groups with the highest unemployment rates (males and females 15–24 years of age) have the lowest duration (2.3 and 2.1 months, respectively) and the lowest incidence of long-term unemployment. The very high youth unemployment rate is associated with a high probability of becoming unemployed rather than requiring an unusually long time to find a job, or exiting from the labour force. Older workers, on the other hand, have the lowest unemployment rates within each sex group but the longest duration of unemployment. This reflects the fact that older workers are less likely to become unemployed; those that do require a longer than average period of time to find employment, or leave the labour force. The incidence and duration of female unemployment is generally less than that of men, as was the case in 2015.

TABLE 16.3	Incidence and Duration of Unemployment by Age and Sex, Canada, 2015				
Sex	**Age Group**	**Unemployment Rate**	**Incidence Rate**	**Duration (Months)**	**Unemployed > 6 Months (%)**
Men	15–24	15.0	6.4	2.3	11.0
	25–44	6.4	2.0	3.2	18.2
	45 +	6.0	1.5	4.0	27.6
	All	7.5	2.4	3.1	19.4
Women	15–24	11.3	5.4	2.1	8.2
	25–44	5.7	2.0	2.9	18.5
	45 +	5.1	1.4	3.6	25.9
	All	6.3	2.3	2.7	18.2

NOTES: The incidence rate is calculated as the percentage of the labour force that has been unemployed between 1 and 4 weeks. The average duration is calculated from the formula UR = I × D, given the incidence and unemployment rates in the first two columns.
SOURCE: This analysis is based on the Statistics Canada CANSIM database, Tables 2820002 and 2820048, 2016. All computations, use and interpretation of these data are entirely that of the authors.

Changing Perspectives on Unemployment

Public policy toward unemployment has occupied a central role in Canada, certainly since the Great Depression. Economists have often been charged with the task of discovering a "cure" for unemployment. As with any economic problem, the first step in designing an effective policy is to understand the "pathology" of unemployment. A common portrayal (or caricature) of unemployment in the media is that a 10 percent unemployment rate corresponds to 10 percent of the population engaged in a long term and futile search for nonexistent jobs. This is also a common view among those who experienced the Great Depression. The data summarized to this point goes a long way in dispelling this simple image, at least in "normal times." Several conclusions can be drawn:

1. The labour force is highly dynamic, with large flows into and out of unemployment each period.
2. Less than half the flow into unemployment in an average year is due to individuals losing their job; the remainder is associated with job leavers, new entrants, and re-entrants.
3. In 2015 (a time in which the economy was neither booming nor in recession), the average duration of unemployment was approximately three months, with less than one-fifth of all unemployment spells lasting more than six months.
4. The age groups with the highest unemployment rates have the shortest average unemployment durations, but the highest incidence of unemployment.

These general findings have important implications for the role of policies to deal with unemployment. The large amount of turnover in the labour force, the fact that job losers account for less than half the flow into unemployment, and the relatively short average duration of unemployment (especially among the groups with the highest unemployment rates) suggest that much unemployment may be caused not by a general shortage of jobs but by employment instability—brief spells of employment followed by periods of job search and/or exit from the labour force. In particular, the observed short duration of unemployment was regarded as evidence that most people could find an acceptable job fairly quickly. Back in the early 1970s, Feldstein (1973) used the term "the new unemployment" to describe this view of unemployment being primarily associated with rapid turnover and employment instability. This contrasted with the "old view" in which the unemployed were regarded as a stock of individuals without work for a lengthy period while waiting for a business upturn (the caricature painted in the previous paragraph). The new view suggested that policies aimed at reducing turnover and employment instability may be more successful in achieving lower levels of unemployment than policies aimed at increasing the number of jobs.

Subsequent research, such as that of Clark and Summers (1979) and Akerlof and Main (1980) for the United States, and Hasan and de Broucker (1982) and Beach and Kaliski (1983) for Canada, indicated that the new view of unemployment contained important elements of truth but was an overly simplistic picture of unemployment. Three conclusions emerged from this research, and taking these into account resulted in a "modified new view." First, although the average duration of completed spells of unemployment is fairly short, much unemployment is accounted for by those suffering lengthy spells of unemployment. An example may help to illustrate this point. Suppose that five individuals become unemployed, four for spells of one month each and the fifth for eight months. The average duration of unemployment for this group is 2.4 months, but two-thirds of all the unemployment (8 out of 12 months) is associated with the one long spell.

A second important consideration is that not all periods of unemployment end in employment. As Figure 16.3 suggests, a significant number of individuals end their search for work by withdrawing from the labour force. Some may leave the labour force to return to school, raise children, or work in the home. However, as discussed previously, some may want paid work but have stopped searching for work because they believe no work is available or for other "economic reasons." By not classifying as "unemployment" the period during which these individuals wanted work but were not searching for work, the duration of unemployment may be considered to be understated. For example, consider an individual who becomes unemployed, searches for work for two months, gives up and stops searching for three months, and then resumes the job search, finding work after a further two months. According to the official statistics, this person would have experienced two spells of unemployment, each lasting a brief two months. However, it could be argued that the individual experienced a single bout of unemployment lasting seven months. Even if this argument is rejected (i.e., the job search requirement for being considered unemployed is retained), it is clear that, when many spells of unemployment end in withdrawal from the labour force, the fact that the average duration of unemployment is fairly short does not imply that most of the unemployed can find an acceptable job fairly quickly. A related observation is that spells of unemployment that end in employment are, on average, longer than those ending in withdrawal from the labour force. Thus, the average length of time required to successfully find a job is understated by the duration statistics such as those reported in Table 16.3.

The third modification is related to the distribution of unemployment across the population. The implications of a specific unemployment rate differ according to how widely the unemployment is distributed. For example, an unemployment rate of 8 percent could mean that 8 percent of the labour force is unemployed all year (i.e., the distribution of unemployment is highly concentrated) or that all of the labour force is unemployed for 8 percent of the year (i.e., the distribution of unemployment is widely dispersed). The high rate of labour force turnover and the short average duration of unemployment led some analysts to believe that unemployment must be widely distributed among the labour force. In fact, this conclusion turns out not to be correct; unemployment is highly concentrated among a minority of the labour force. The reason for these apparently contradictory findings is that, even though the average duration of unemployment is short, a minority of individuals suffer repeated spells of unemployment, sometimes interrupted by periods out of the labour force. For these individuals, the "chronically unemployed," obtaining employment, especially durable employment, appears to be a difficult task.

The behaviour of Canadian unemployment has been dominated by cyclical changes: the recession of 1981–1982, recovery and expansion from 1983 to 1989, recession of 1990–1992, and recovery and expansion from 1993 to 2000. After a mild slowdown in 2001, Canada's economy subsequently experienced another period of strong growth that ended with the worldwide financial crisis and the recession of 2008–2009. During 1983, the unemployment rate reached 12 percent, its highest level of the postwar period (Figure 16.1). Only by 1989, following a long period of economic growth, did the unemployment rate return to its pre-recession level (however briefly). During the recession of 1990–1992, unemployment again climbed above 11 percent, and it did not fall below 8 percent until 1999. The 1980s and 1990s were, thus, characterized by higher unemployment rates at each point in the business cycle than was experienced in the 1960s and 1970s.

In contrast, during the early part of the 21st century there was less concern about unemployment until the worldwide economic downturn that began in 2008. During the period of strong economic growth from 2001 to 2008, Canada's unemployment rate fell to 6 percent, the lowest in over 30 years. In this environment it is not surprising that policy attention shifted from concern about high levels of unemployment to the problems associated with labour shortages.

During the 1980s and 1990s, much research and policy attention focused on international differences in unemployment experience, especially the dramatic increases in European unemployment since the 1970s and the persistence of high unemployment in those countries. As noted in Exhibit 16.1, during the 1950s and 1960s European countries typically had much lower unemployment than their North American counterparts. However, beginning with the OPEC oil price shocks of the 1970s and continuing during the 1980s and 1990s, unemployment rates in Europe shot up during economic downturns and have shown much less of a tendency than their counterparts in North America to decline during the subsequent expansion. In contrast to Europe, unemployment rates in the United States during most of the 1990s and 2000s were very similar to those experienced in the 1960s and 1970s (see Exhibit 16.1). Relative to the United States, Europe had gone from being a low-unemployment region to being a high-unemployment region, with the Canadian experience lying in-between these two extremes. Of course, the dramatic rise in U.S. unemployment during the 2008–2009 Great Recession and its persistence changed this perception, at least temporarily, and lead to a resurgence of interest in unemployment, especially long-term unemployment, and related policies.

Accompanying the rise in European unemployment was a substantial increase in the extent of long-term unemployment. Table 16.4 summarizes recent experience for the same countries whose unemployment rates are shown in Figure 16.2. In France and Germany, about 44 percent of the unemployed had been unemployed for a year or more, according to the most recent (2015) data. These proportions are lower in Japan and the United Kingdom, but they are nonetheless much higher than in North America, where the fraction of long-term unemployment is about 12 percent in Canada and 19 percent in the United States.

TABLE 16.4	International Differences in Long-Term Unemployment		
	Long-Term Unemployment as a Percentage of Total Unemployment		
	2005		2015
	12 Months and Over		12 Months and Over
Canada	9.6		11.6
France	42.5		44.3
Germany	54.0		44.0
Japan	33.3		35.5
Sweden	18.9		17.6
United Kingdom	22.4		30.7
United States	11.8		18.7

SOURCES: OECD, *Employment Outlook 2006* and *Employment Outlook 2016* (Paris: OECD, 2006 and 2016). J. Visser, ICTWSS Data base. version 5.1. Amsterdam: Amsterdam Institute for Advanced Labour Studies (AIAS), University of Amsterdam. September 2016.

For these reasons, there has been a shift in emphasis away from concern about employment instability and high turnover in the labour force toward unemployment that remains persistently high and is longer term in nature. This shift was especially evident in Europe where the problem of long-term unemployment was particularly severe. It thus appears that the new view of unemployment put forward in the 1970s needs to be replaced, or at least significantly modified. The changing nature of unemployment over time and across countries makes it difficult to design single, universally applicable policies to address unemployment.

Unemployment Rate as a Summary Statistic

The unemployment rate is widely used as an economic and labour market indicator about such things as the aggregate state of the economy, the tightness or looseness of the labour market, or the extent of hardship in the population. However, much of the previous discussion suggests that is unwise to rely on the unemployment rate alone for these purposes. It is not that the unemployment rate is wrong; rather, it may be asking too much of a single measure to indicate all these things, especially when dramatic demographic changes have occurred in the labour force and institutional changes have occurred in programs, such as unemployment insurance, pensions, and social assistance.

The unemployment rate is arguably most suited as a measure of the amount of unutilized labour supply. This purpose accounts for the emphasis that statistical agencies place on being "available for work" and currently "searching for work" in the official unemployment statistics. The concept of unutilized labour supply is necessarily somewhat ambiguous, because, as discussed in Chapter 2, both theory and evidence on labour supply behaviour indicates that the amount people want to work depends on how well they will be remunerated for their time and effort. The fact that those classified as unemployed are currently searching for employment is taken as evidence that they are willing to work at prevailing wages and working conditions.

Nonetheless, the unemployment rate is imperfect, even as a measure of unutilized labour supply, and should be supplemented with additional measures such as those described in Exhibit 16.2. Groups on the margin of the labour force may desire employment at prevailing wages but may not be currently searching because of discouragement or various forms of "waiting" for jobs to become available. These groups may display a weaker attachment to the labour force than those officially classified as unemployed, but also a stronger attachment than the remainder of those not in the labour force for reasons such as schooling, household production, and retirement.

The need to supplement the unemployment rate with other indicators increases when we consider some other uses to which this widely cited statistic is applied. As we have seen in this chapter, the unemployment rate provides a useful measure of the state of the economy and aggregate labour market—increasing in periods of slow or negative economic growth and falling in expansionary times. However, as illustrated in Figure 16.1, the time-series behaviour of unemployment displays not only these cyclical ups and downs but also a clear upward trend beginning in the 1960s, followed by a modest downward trend beginning in the 1980s. Thus, an unemployment rate of 6 percent is not likely to indicate the same degree of labour market tightness or looseness today as it did in earlier decades. At the present time, we would regard an unemployment rate of 6 percent as "low" and probably associated with an economy at or near a cyclical peak. In contrast, this level would have been regarded in the 1960s as very high, and likely an indicator of a weak labour market and a slumping economy.

The labour force participation rate and the employment rate are measures of aggregate labour market activity that can be used to provide a more complete picture of the state of the labour market. Often the three measures will move together; for example, a downturn in the economy is usually accompanied by rising unemployment and declining participation and employment rates. But, as we have seen, Canada also experienced periods in which the employment rate, the participation rate, and the unemployment rate were increasing (recall Table 16.1). In these circumstances, focusing on movements in the unemployment rate alone is likely to be misleading.

The unemployment rate is also often used as an indicator of the extent of hardship in an economy, region, or time period. Here, the need for considering additional measures is especially strong. Today, many of the unemployed are in families in which one or more other members are working. The rise of multi-earner families with two working parents and one or more working teenagers or young adults has resulted in a weaker link between unemployment and low family income than was the case in the past when there was more likely to be a single "breadwinner" in the family. At the same time, the unemployment rate is uninformative about the earnings levels of the employed, and the degree to which they may have fallen to a poverty level. Increases in earnings inequality may be associated with greater hardship without accompanying movements in unemployment.

Summary

- The unemployed are generally defined as those who are not currently employed, are available for work, and indicate by their behaviour that they want to work at prevailing wages and working conditions. The primary source of data on unemployment in Canada is the Labour Force Survey (LFS), carried out monthly by Statistics Canada.

- According to the Labour Force Survey, individuals are categorized as unemployed if they did not have work in the reference period but were available for and searching for work. Two exceptions to this principle are those on temporary layoff from a job to which they expect to be recalled and those with a job to start within the next four weeks.

- Canada's unemployment experience has varied widely. The onset of the Great Depression saw the unemployment rate soar from about 3 percent to almost 20 percent. During World War II unemployment fell to very low levels. The post–World War II period has been characterized by cyclical variations around a general upward trend until the 1980s, followed by a modest downward trend, subsequently.

- The unemployment rate is the most commonly used measure of labour market activity. Two additional measures are the employment rate and the labour force participation rate, defined, respectively, as the fractions of the adult population employed and in the labour force. Because they focus on somewhat different aspects of labour market activity, these three measures need not always move together. For example, since the mid-1960s, the unemployment rate has risen substantially but the labour force participation rate and employment rate have risen, not fallen.

- The measurement of unemployment raises difficult and controversial issues. Hidden unemployment, or marginal labour force attachment, refers to situations in which individuals may be without work, desire work, yet they are not officially classified as unemployed because they are not searching for work. Examples include discouraged workers and those who are waiting for potential or promised jobs to become available. The major lesson is not that the official unemployment rate is a poor measure, but rather that no single measure of unemployment is likely to be suitable for all purposes. Accordingly, Statistics Canada publishes several supplementary measures of unemployment.

- Canada's labour market is highly dynamic. Gross flows between the three labour force states (employment, unemployment, and out of the labour force) are large in comparison to the stocks in each state at any point in time, and huge in comparison to the net flows.

- Unemployment does not consist almost exclusively of individuals who lost their job, either temporarily or permanently. Job losers account for about 35 to 45 percent of flows into unemployment, with the proportion being highest in recessions. The remainder is accounted for by job leavers (about 10 percent) and new entrants and re-entrants (40 to 45 percent).

- Useful concepts for understanding unemployment dynamics are the incidence and duration of unemployment. For any group of workers, incidence refers to the probability of a member of the group becoming unemployed, while duration measures the length of time the individual can expect to remain unemployed. In a steady state, the unemployment rate can be expressed as the product of incidence and duration.

- Young workers have much higher unemployment rates than adults, but lower average duration of unemployment. The high youth unemployment rates are due to the high probability of becoming unemployed in any period. Older workers become unemployed less frequently, but experience longer unemployment spells once they become unemployed.

- Perspectives on unemployment have evolved substantially. During the 1970s, the traditional view, in which the unemployed were regarded as a mainly unchanging stock of individuals without work for a lengthy period, was challenged by a "new view" that emphasized the importance of employment stability and turnover in the labour market. Subsequent research modified this "turnover" view by noting that although the average duration of unemployment is fairly short, much of total unemployment is, nonetheless, accounted for by those experiencing repeated and/or long spells of joblessness. Furthermore, many unemployment spells end in labour force withdrawal rather than in employment, suggesting that unavailability of suitable employment is a reality for some workers.

- The unemployment rate is widely used as an indicator of the amount of unutilized labour supply, the state of the labour market and economy, and the degree of hardship in the population. For each of these purposes, it is unwise to rely on the unemployment rate alone.

Keywords

employment rate	marginal labour force attachment
gross flows	net flows
incidence of unemployment	unemployed
Labour Force Survey	unemployment rate

Review Questions

1. **a.** Discuss how the number of unemployed is measured in Canada.

    b. Discuss the strengths and weaknesses of this measure.

2. **a.** Explain the meaning of the following measures of labour force utilization: (i) labour force participation rate, (ii) employment rate, and (iii) unemployment rate.

    b. For each of these measures, describe circumstances under which that measure would be preferred to the other two.

    c. Under what conditions will these three measures all move in the same direction? Under what conditions would they move in opposite directions?

3. Explain the concept of hidden unemployment, or marginal labour force attachment. Discuss the pros and cons of including the hidden unemployed in our unemployment statistics.

4. Explain the distinction between gross flows and net flows among various labour force states.

5. In discussing the nature of unemployment, some analysts stress a shortage of jobs while others emphasize labour force turnover and employment instability.

    a. Elaborate on these competing perspectives on unemployment.

    b. Describe research findings that attempt to distinguish between these competing perspectives. Which view is correct?

6. Why might we expect younger workers to have higher unemployment rates than older workers, and what does this imply about the changes in our aggregate unemployment rate over time?

7. Why is it that the groups with the highest unemployment rates also have the shortest average duration of unemployment?

8. **a.** Indicate some of the purposes for which our aggregate unemployment rates are often used.

    b. Why might this single measure increasingly be inadequate for these purposes?

    c. What are some of the alternatives, and what are their strengths and weaknesses?

Endnotes

1. Prior to 1997 this information was collected in the annual Survey of Job Opportunities.

2. The group waiting for promised or potential jobs is included in Statistics Canada's measure "R6" (see Exhibit 16.2).

3. Gross flows data are subject to some limitations due to errors in measuring labour force status; see Jones (1993).

4. This is sometimes referred to as the duration of a "completed spell of unemployment" to distinguish it from the duration of an "interrupted spell" (i.e., a spell in progress). For further discussion of these duration concepts see Corak and Heisz (1995).

5. When the labour force is in a **steady-state equilibrium**—the fraction of the labour force in each state and the proportions flowing between states are constant—this relationship is exact. Otherwise, the relationship is only approximately correct. Equation 16.1 is an example of the steady-state identity that the stock at any point in time equals the flow times average duration.

PORTRAIT IMAGES ASIA/Shutterstock.com

CHAPTER 17

Unemployment: Causes and Consequences

LEARNING OBJECTIVES

LO1   Explain how imperfect information can lead to a labour market equilibrium in which unemployed workers and unfilled job vacancies co-exist.

LO2   Discuss and assess evidence on how technological change, especially the growing use of the Internet, is affecting job search and the matching of unemployed workers and unfilled job vacancies.

LO3   Explain how shifts in the structure of product demand can be a source of unemployment in the labour market.

LO4   Summarize empirical findings on job displacement and its consequences.

LO5   Describe leading models of worker and employer behaviour that give rise to employers paying above-market wages, thus, resulting in a labour market equilibrium with unemployed workers.

LO6   Explain the rationale for publicly provided unemployment insurance, and the ways that unemployment insurance may influence labour supply and unemployment.

LO7   Summarize the empirical evidence on the relationship between unemployment insurance and labour supply and unemployment.

MAIN QUESTIONS

- What role does wage rigidity play in explaining unemployment? What alternative theories to the conventional neoclassical model can help explain why wages may not adjust, even in the face of considerable unemployment?

- How does imperfect information manifest itself in the labour market? In what ways might imperfect information be an important cause of unemployment? What are the appropriate (or inappropriate) government responses to this feature of the labour market?

- How are technological changes, such as the Internet, affecting the way that workers search for jobs and employers search and screen for qualified workers? Is online search and matching improving the efficiency of the labour market?

- What are the consequences of job loss for workers and their families? Do some displaced workers suffer more than others from involuntary job loss?

- What role does unemployment insurance play in affecting the structure of unemployment in Canada? Does it do more harm than good?

The previous chapter discussed the meaning and measurement of unemployment and described the salient aspects of the Canadian experience. In this chapter, we examine the causes and consequences of unemployment and the role of public policy in this area. Given the diverse nature of unemployment, both across different groups in the population as well as over time, it should hardly come as a surprise that there is no single explanation of why the unemployment rate should be at a particular level.

Before discussing the possible causes of unemployment, it is useful to take one step back and consider again the simplest supply and demand model of the labour market of Chapter 7. Under perfect competition, the equilibrium wage clears the market at the point where the supply and demand curves intersect. Since the equilibrium point is on the supply curve, all workers willing to work at the going wage do so. People who prefer not to work at the going wage choose to do so because their reservation wage exceeds the going wage. For all these individuals, the decision not to work is a voluntary decision, and none of them should be looking for jobs at the going wage. In this simple model, nobody without a job is available for and searching for work, the two conditions listed in Chapter 16 for being classified as unemployed.

Since there is no unemployment in the simplest competitive model of the labour market, the causes of unemployment have to be found elsewhere. Indeed, we already saw in earlier chapters a number of possible reasons why there may be unemployment. For example, when the minimum wage is larger than the equilibrium wage (Figure 7.8), demand exceeds supply at the going (minimum) wage. Some individuals who would like to work at the minimum wage are unable to do so. It is natural to expect these individuals to keep looking for work until they find a firm willing to hire them. This makes them unemployed according to the usual definition of unemployment discussed earlier.

In addition to the minimum wage, other "institutional" factors, such as unions or a large public sector, can also cause unemployment by increasing the wage rate above its competitive level. But while these institutional explanations can surely account for some of the observed unemployment, there are many reasons to believe that most of the observed unemployment is linked to other factors. First, the wages of most workers in countries with highly decentralized labour markets, like Canada and the United States, are unlikely to be affected by institutional factors like unions and minimum wages. For unemployment among those workers to be linked to high wages, it must be that factors other than institutions keep wages above their competitive levels. We will see below how efficiency wages, implicit contracts, and insider-outsider models may result in wages above competitive levels and involuntary unemployment.

But even these more sophisticated models of unemployment linked to high wages cannot account for important aspects of unemployment. In particular, the fact that unemployment varies substantially with the state of the economy (i.e., the business cycle) suggests that demand factors can be an important underlying source of unemployment. This simple observation provides the foundation for Keynesian-style macroeconomic explanations of unemployment due to insufficient aggregate demand. Understanding business cycles and this important dimension of overall unemployment is beyond the scope of this book and is dealt with in courses in macroeconomics. A related source of unemployment linked to demand variation is seasonal unemployment.

Finally, if unemployment was solely due to high wages and low aggregate demand, it should essentially disappear in "red hot" local economies where firms are so desperate to hire more workers that they are almost ready to pay whatever its takes to hire them. As it turns out, however, even in the midst of the dot-com boom in the Silicon Valley or resource booms in provinces such as Alberta, Saskatchewan, and Newfoundland the unemployment rate never managed to get below a base level of 2 or 3 percent. This suggests a substantial amount of frictional unemployment associated with normal turnover of the workforce. We will see how models of job search and of the matching process between workers and employers provide a natural framework for understanding this particular type of unemployment. A related type of unemployment arises when sectoral shifts require workers who lost their job in one sector to find a job in another sector or region of the economy. Because it takes time for workers to adjust and find a job in a different sector, sectoral shifts create frictions that result in unemployment.

Most of the chapter will discuss how these various explanations can help understand the determinants of unemployment. With this in mind, we will then discuss what can be done about unemployment. From a policy perspective, a particularly contentious aspect of government policy toward unemployment is the provision of unemployment insurance. From initially being viewed as an important, progressive part of the social safety net, unemployment insurance (UI)[1] was subsequently painted as a major villain in the increases in unemployment following substantial expansion of Canada's UI program in the 1970s. We trace the debate on the role of unemployment insurance and examine the still-accumulating evidence on its role in affecting the unemployment rate.

Frictional and Structural Unemployment

The economic theories of frictional and structural unemployment are topics of continuing interest in labour economics and macroeconomics. One motivation for this interest is that it is well known that a substantial amount of unemployment tends to persist even when the overall economy does relatively well. In addition, it is equally well known that at any point in time both unemployed workers and unfilled job vacancies co-exist. Unemployment associated with normal turnover in the labour market—referred to as **frictional unemployment**—helps to understand these observations. Search theory provides the most natural way of understanding this type of frictional unemployment.

A related observation is that the stubbornly high level of unemployment experienced by many European countries during the last several decades seems to defy many theories of unemployment based on deficient demand or cyclical factors. Similarly, within Canada, some regions experience persistently above-average unemployment, while others have persistently below-average unemployment. **Structural unemployment** refers to situations in which there is a mismatch between labour demand and labour supply, either on occupational, skills, or regional dimensions. The sectoral shifts hypothesis also provides a related reason why unemployment may be quite high during periods of structural adjustment even when aggregate demand conditions remain strong.

Search Unemployment

The **job search** and **matching** process is associated with imperfect information on both sides of the labour market. Unemployed workers are not aware of all available jobs, their rates of pay, location, and working conditions. Employers with job vacancies are not aware of all individual workers and their characteristics. If both sides were fully informed, the process of matching workers and jobs could take place in a few days, if not hours. However, because the acquisition of information about job opportunities and job applicants takes time, unemployment and unfilled vacancies co-exist.

Following the important early contributions of Stigler (1962), McCall (1970), and Phelps et al. (1970), the economics of job search has received considerable attention. Pioneering work by Diamond (1982), Mortensen (1982), and Pissarides (1985) for which the three received the Nobel Prize in Economics in 2010, developed formal models of decentralized search that typically lead to a market equilibrium with unemployed workers and unfilled job vacancies. To illustrate the main ideas, we focus primarily on the job search process of employees. However, a complete model would include employer search for workers, and how employee and employer searches interact to determine market equilibrium. Useful surveys of equilibrium search models of the labour market include Mortensen and Pissarides (1999); Rogerson, Shimer, and Wright (2005); and Rogerson and Shimer (2010).

Job search is an economic decision in that it involves both costs and benefits. There are two main aspects to the decision: (1) determining whether it is worthwhile *initiating* the job search process and, once begun, (2) determining when to *discontinue* the process. For employees, initiating a job search or continuing to search rather than accepting the first job offer that comes along may yield benefits in the form of a superior job offer involving higher wages or better working conditions. Similarly, by continuing to search rather than filling the job with the first "warm body" that becomes available, the employer may obtain benefits in the form of more-suitable or more-qualified applicants. In both cases, the magnitude of these benefits is uncertain; their size depends on the employee's expectations regarding the probability of receiving a superior job offer or on the employer's expectations regarding the quality of future applicants. Those engaged in search must make their decisions on the basis of expectations; that is, the information available *ex ante*. The realized or *ex post* benefits may turn out to be larger or smaller than the expected benefits.

The expected benefits have to be weighed against the costs of search. These include both the direct costs, such as the employer's costs of advertising positions and interviewing applicants, and the employee's costs of sending applications and travelling to interviews, and the indirect or opportunity costs. For employees, the opportunity costs are measured by the best alternative use of their time devoted to job search. For those who quit their previous job to search for a better one, their opportunity cost would be their previous wage. For others, the opportunity cost would be measured by the best job offer received so far or the wage that could be earned in some job that is known to be available. It could also be an individual's implicit home wage or the value of his or her time doing household work. For employers, the opportunity cost of continuing to search is the difference between the value of the output that would be produced by the best application received to date and the wages that would be paid to that applicant.

Not all job seekers are unemployed; some individuals will search for a better job while employed. Employed search has the advantage of being less costly. However, it may also be less effective because of the difficulties associated with contacting potential employers and following up promising opportunities while working, especially if employed on a full-time basis. In some circumstances, individuals may choose to quit their current job in order to search for a better one, while, in other circumstances, employed search will be the preferred method.

The central assumption in the economic analysis of job search is that individuals will search in an optimal fashion—that is, will choose their search activities in order to maximize their expected utility. Note, however, that the assumption of optimal search behaviour does not imply that all unemployed job seekers have *chosen* to be unemployed or that all search unemployment is voluntary in nature. Individuals who quit their previous job in order to search for a new job, the "job leavers" in Table 16.2, may have chosen unemployment. Rational employees would not do so unless the expected utility of searching for a new job exceeds the expected utility of remaining in the existing job. However, as Table 16.2 indicates, a substantial minority of the unemployed are "job losers"; many of these individuals may have preferred to remain in their previous job. Nonetheless, given that they have lost their previous job, rational individuals will carry out their job search in an optimal fashion. In the case of a person who is risk neutral, this assumption implies that the individual will choose the amount of search activity that maximizes the net expected benefit (expected benefits minus expected costs). Risk-averse employees will also take into account the costs and benefits of search, but will attach a greater weight to benefits and costs that are certain compared to those that are uncertain. The basic principles of optimal job search are most easily explained in the context of risk-neutral searchers. However, very similar principles and conclusions follow when individuals are risk averse.

In order to maximize the net expected benefits of job search, employees should continue searching until the marginal expected benefit of search equals the marginal expected cost. This condition is simply another example of the familiar rule: the net benefit of any activity is maximized by expanding the activity to the point at which its marginal benefit equals its marginal cost. Figure 17.1 shows the way in which the benefits and costs of search are likely to be related to the amount of time devoted to job search. The case in which search is worthwhile is illustrated (i.e., total expected benefits exceed total costs). For low levels of search, the marginal costs of search are fairly low because low-cost, usually informal, search processes can be used. For example, friends and relatives can be contacted, want ads examined, and perhaps a few telephone calls made. As the search continues, however, more-costly processes are often necessary to acquire additional labour market information. For example, it may be necessary to apply directly to a company or to sign up with an employment service. In some cases, it may even be necessary to change locations or to quit working if one already has a job. For these reasons, the marginal cost of search probably rises with the amount of job search undertaken, as depicted in Figure 17.1.

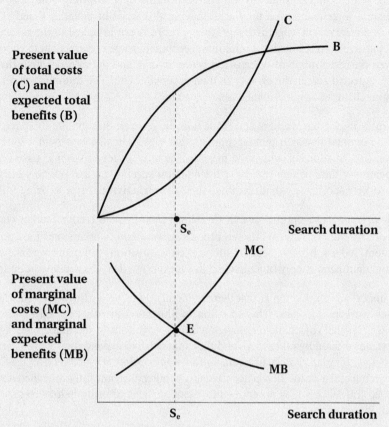

Figure 17.1 Optimal Job Search

The expected optimal time spent searching for a job will maximize the present value of the difference between the expected benefits and costs of search. The expected benefits, B, are increasing with time spent searching, and the expected costs of search, C, also increase with search duration. The optimal amount of search will maximize the difference between B and C. This difference is maximized when the expected marginal benefit of search equals the expected marginal cost, at expected search duration S_e. As shown in the bottom panel, shorter expected searches than S_e yield a situation where an extra "day" of search has a higher expected benefit than cost, and is, thus, worth conducting. Similarly, longer searches reduce net benefits.

The marginal benefits of search, on the other hand, probably are a declining function of the amount of search undertaken. One starts out the search process by pursuing the most-promising alternatives, and then continues examining further activities in the hope of finding an even better one. Obviously, a better alternative may occur; however, one may encounter diminishing returns with respect to the additional information. As search continues, it becomes less likely, but still possible, that a better offer will be received, simply because there are fewer options left to examine.

Given the costs and benefits of additional search, the rational individual will acquire labour market information and engage in search until the point E, where the marginal expected benefits equal the marginal cost. To the left of E, the benefits of additional search exceed the cost, and hence, additional search is worthwhile; to the right of E, the benefits of additional search are not worth the costs. In this sense, E will be an equilibrium, with S_e being the optimal amount of expected search activity. Note, however, that S_e is the *expected* amount of search required to maximize net benefits. The actual amount of search undertaken in any particular situation may turn out to differ from S_e. For example, a lucky individual who receives an extremely good job offer during the first week will experience a search duration less than S_e because the best course of action will be to accept the job and discontinue the search. Similarly, an unlucky individual may have to search longer than anticipated or accept a lower-paying job than expected.

The conditions for optimal search can, alternatively, be stated in terms of a **stopping rule**; that is, the individual should choose a minimum acceptable wage and search until a job paying this wage or better is found. The minimum acceptable wage is often referred to as a reservation wage, although this concept is not identical to the reservation wage discussed in Chapter 2 on labour force participation. Choosing a minimum acceptable wage is equivalent to choosing the expected search duration. On average, given the distribution of wage offers in the market and the rate at which firms can be contacted, the individual will require the expected search duration to find an acceptable job. The minimum acceptable wage is, therefore, chosen to equate the marginal benefits and marginal costs of search.

Note that these decision rules imply that workers and firms will, in general, discontinue their search activities before they are fully informed. That is, optimal decision making implies that it is typically worthwhile to acquire some information prior to making a decision (information for which the marginal benefits exceed marginal costs) but to not acquire all the available information. Because of diminishing returns to information acquisition, and possibly also rising marginal costs of information acquisition, workers and firms will discontinue their search activities prior to being fully informed.

Several implications follow from these optimal search decision rules. First, a labour market characterized by imperfect information will not "clear" instantaneously. While the process of *matching* workers and jobs proceeds, demand will not equal supply at each moment. Indeed, because search, information acquisition, and matching take time, unsatisfied demand (unfilled job vacancies) and unutilized supply (unemployed job seekers) will co-exist at any point in time.

A related implication of imperfect information is that there, generally, will be a distribution of wage rates even in a labour market with homogeneous workers and jobs. This situation is illustrated in panel (a) of Figure 17.2, in contrast to the full-information case shown in panel (b). Some employers will pay wages above the market average, both because they are not fully informed about wages offered by other firms and they may wish to expand their workforce at a rapid rate, an aspect that is discussed further below. Similarly, other firms may offer wages below the market average. In fact, this dispersion of wages is necessary for search to exist in the first place. Because workers are not fully informed about the wages offered by all firms, some unemployed job seekers may accept employment at firms offering below-average wages, an outcome that would not occur under full information.

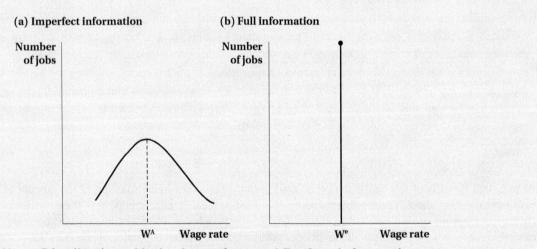

Figure 17.2 Wage Distributions Under Imperfect and Perfect Information

Panel (b) shows the case of perfect information, where employers and employees both know the entire distribution of wages, and the only equilibrium is the single wage, W^e. With imperfect information (in panel [a]), some employers will pay above the market average (W^A), not being aware that they could get away with paying less, and some employees will accept jobs paying less than W^A. If search is costly, the search process will not fully erode wage differences across individuals, and the wage dispersion around W^A will be self-sustaining in equilibrium.

Although conceptually simple, this model of imperfect information and search yields insights into several additional features of labour market behaviour. For example, it helps to understand why an unemployed job seeker might choose to turn down a job offer and remain unemployed. It also points out the potential role of randomness in labour market outcomes. In an environment with a distribution of wages for otherwise identical jobs, some workers will obtain high-wage jobs and other otherwise identical workers will be less lucky.

A further, and closely related, implication is that under imperfect information employers possess some short-run monopsony power, even though the market is otherwise perfectly competitive, and employers are wage takers in the long run. This situation, referred to as **dynamic monopsony**, is most readily understood by assuming that workers have some information about the distribution of wage rates available in the market—that is, the distribution illustrated in Figure 17.2(a)—but do not, in the absence of search, know the wage rates offered by individual employers. In these circumstances, when an unemployed job seeker receives a job offer, she must decide whether to accept the offer or continue searching. She will be more likely to accept an offer that appears to be above average (based on her beliefs about the distribution of wage rates available in the market) than one that appears to be below average. Thus, from the perspective of the employer with unfilled job vacancies, paying a high wage (relative to what other firms are believed to be paying) increases the probability that an offer will be accepted, and vice versa for offering a low wage. In other words, the employer faces an upward-sloping labour supply curve because the higher the offered wage the greater is the acceptance rate of job offers, or hiring rate.

WORKED EXAMPLE

Job Search and the Reservation Wage

Julia just graduated from college and is looking for a first job. Inexperienced workers in her line of work cannot get a permanent job right away and must first gain some experience in a fixed-term (12 months) job. After having gained experience on a first 12-month job, it is typically very easy to get another job. The way the job market works, people who apply for jobs get only a single offer at the end of each month. This means that Julia has to decide whether to accept the offer or wait until next month in the hope of getting a better offer. There are three types of jobs: the best jobs pay $2400 a month, "not as good" jobs pay $2200 a month, while the worst type of job pays $2000 a month. Each month, the offer is as likely to be from one of the three types; that is, the probability of each type of job offered is one-third.

Julia must now decide what to do once she gets an offer. Should she accept it or wait until next month? Obviously, if she gets a $2400 offer she should just take it since she won't find anything better next period. The difficult question is whether to accept a $2200 or, especially, a $2000 offer. This is a dynamic decision problem where the decision today depends on expectations about the future. In particular, since the probability of each job type is the same, the expected value of a future offer is $2200 a month (average of $2000, $2200, and $2400 a month).

We can now look at what happens when Julia gets offered $2200 a month. On the one hand, the cost of turning down the offer is the $2200 salary she won't receive this month. On the other hand, there is no benefit in waiting until next period since the expected offer she will get next month ($2200) is the same as what she already has on the table. So Julia should accept the $2200 offer.

Let's finally look at the $2000 offer. The cost of turning down the offer is now only $2000. The benefit, however, is that Julia will likely get a better offer next period. Since she can expect, on average, to get a $2200 offer next period, she will likely make $200 more in the 11 remaining months than if she was to take the $2000 offer right away. The expected benefit is, thus, $200 × 11 = $2200, which now exceeds the $2000 cost of turning down the offer. Julia should thus turn down the offer and wait until next period for a better offer.

Another way of characterizing Julia's decision is to say that her reservation wage is $2200; that is, that she won't accept a job offer unless it pays at least $2200 a month. We can also derive the distribution of the duration of unemployment implied by this reservation rule. Since 2/3 of offers are $2200 or $2400, the probability that Julia will leave unemployment (and accept a job) each month is 2/3. This is also known as the hazard rate (out of unemployment). So there is a 2/3 chance that unemployment will last for just a month. Further computations show that there is a 2/9 probability that unemployment will last exactly two months, a 2/27 probability that unemployment will last exactly three months, and so on.

Search theory simply generalizes this simple example to settings where we have a more realistic search process and distribution of wage offers. The basic principle nonetheless remains the same—people base their decisions on a reservation wage rule and, as a result, we observe a full distribution of unemployment durations.

This discussion also indicates that in markets characterized by imperfect information, the wage rate does not adjust instantaneously to equate labour demand and supply. Employers who find that their acceptance rate of job offers is low will, over time, adjust upward their offered wages, especially if it is very costly to leave jobs unfilled. Similarly, employers who discover that their offers are immediately accepted may lower their offered wages. These adjustments can be expected to occur gradually, because it takes time for employers to become aware of how their offered wages compare to those available elsewhere, as well as to observe the rate at which their offers are accepted.

Factors Determining Optimal Search

This framework is useful to illustrate how the optimal amount of search depends on the various factors underlying the cost and benefit schedules, and how search activity will respond to shifts in these schedules. For example, factors affecting the expected benefits of job search are the dispersion of wage offers (for otherwise comparable jobs) and the expected duration of the job. If there is little variation in the attractiveness of different jobs in terms of wages and working conditions, there is little point in continuing to search once an offer has been received. In contrast, if some jobs are much more desirable than others, the optimal strategy may be to continue searching even after receiving an average job offer. Similarly, if some potential jobs are more desirable than others, it will be rational to devote more time to search if it is anticipated that the duration of employment will be long, because of the longer period over which the benefits of a superior job can be enjoyed.

These two factors may help explain the observed differences in the average duration of unemployment across age and sex groups, as summarized in Table 16.3. Because of their limited work experience, youth typically face a less dispersed distribution of potential wages than older workers. In addition, many youth try out a variety of jobs before settling on a career; thus, on average, their expected duration of employment is much lower than is the case for adult workers. For both these reasons, there is less incentive for youth than for adult workers to continue searching in the expectation of obtaining a better job. These considerations are consistent with the observation that the average duration of unemployment of youth is significantly lower than that of adults.

Shifts in the schedules may affect the number of searchers, as well as the expected duration of search. For example, an increase in expected total benefits or a decrease in total costs will imply a larger number of people for whom search is worthwhile. As a consequence, the following may be observed: more entry and re-entry into the labour force, an increase in the number of quits as more employed workers seek a new job, and more search by the employed.

Given the central role played by imperfect information in the job search model, important factors determining the value of job search are the institutional mechanisms for disseminating labour market information. Since the introduction of the Internet, these mechanisms have been undergoing dramatic change. There are now literally hundreds of "jobs.com" sites in existence. These websites range from the very general to the very specialized (e.g., "Meat and Poultry Online"), significantly facilitating information exchange between employers and employees (see Kuhn and Skuterud 2004; Autor 2009; Nakamura et al. 2009; Kuhn 2014). Evidence on the effectiveness of online search and matching is discussed below.

Other factors affecting the benefits and costs of search include the number of employers with job vacancies, the rate at which employers make job offers, the value of "leisure" time (time spent not searching or working), the number of other searchers competing for the available jobs, and the occupational and regional segmentation of labour markets. Social and labour market policies can also alter the costs and benefits of search and, hence, its amount and duration. Unemployment insurance and portable pensions would reduce the total and marginal costs of search and, hence, increase the number of searchers and the optimal duration of search. Improving the arrangements for disseminating labour market information would increase the total benefits and, in most cases, the marginal benefits as well. Thus, the number of job seekers would increase but the expected duration would fall. The total amount of search unemployment may either increase or decrease, depending on which effect is larger.

The job search paradigm may also help explain why wages adjust slowly to excess supply or demand in the labour market. As noted above, the optimal search strategy involves choosing an acceptance wage and searching until a job offering this wage or better is found. Thus, wages are not adjusted downward even if an acceptable job is not found quickly. Over time, unemployed searchers will revise downward their acceptance wages if they discover that their initial beliefs regarding the distribution of wage offers and the rate at which job offers were made were too optimistic, as would be the case if there were more labour supply or less demand than originally anticipated. However, because this learning process takes time, the adjustment of wages to excess demand or supply will occur less quickly than in the presence of complete information.

EXHIBIT 17.1

Mandatory Notice and Unemployment

Employment protection laws take a variety of forms, including severance or redundancy pay, mandatory notice, and requirements to establish adjustment programs to assist displaced workers. In Canada, mandatory notice is the primary legal obligation on employers who wish to reduce their workforce for "economic" reasons. All jurisdictions (federal, provincial, and the territories) have some form of advance-notice requirement for individual layoffs or dismissals. Several provinces have additional requirements for mass layoffs. In addition, under Canadian common law, "reasonable" notice must be provided to employees dismissed for economic reasons. (See Kuhn 2000a for details.)

Does mandatory notice reduce unemployment? By giving employees time to search prior to the termination of their existing job, some may be able to move from one job to another without an intervening period of nonemployment, thus, reducing the incidence of unemployment. Others may be able to begin the search process during the notice period, and to thereby reduce the duration of unemployment.

The impact of mandatory notice on unemployment has been examined in Canadian studies by Jones and Kuhn (1995) and Friesen (1997). Both studies conclude that advance warning of mass layoffs can have positive benefits. For example, using a sample of workers laid off due to plant closures in Ontario, Jones and Kuhn find that even small amounts of notice are quite helpful in reducing the number of workers who experience some unemployment following displacement (the incidence of unemployment). For example, giving notice of less than one month reduces the proportion of workers in a shutdown who experience unemployment from 92 percent to 76 percent. However, Jones and Kuhn also find that there are few, if any, additional gains from providing notice of more than one month, and they even find some evidence that notice of more than six months can be harmful to workers.

Unfortunately, there appears to be little scope for using advance notice to reduce the long-term unemployment that results from many mass layoffs. In particular, Jones and Kuhn find that, no matter how much notice is given, about 30 percent of workers remain unemployed one year after shutdown. The reason appears to be that, except in small amounts, pre-displacement search is significantly less effective than post-displacement search in obtaining re-employment, a conclusion also reached in several U.S. studies of displaced workers (e.g., Swaim and Podgursky 1990; Ruhm 1992).

LO1, 2   Empirical Evidence on Job Search

A significant amount of job search takes place. Table 17.1 provides information on job search activity for 2015, based on the Labour Force Survey. Most of the unemployed are looking for full-time work. Among those individuals who are searching, Table 17.1 indicates that the most-common search activities are looking at job advertisements and directly contacting employers.

Use of the Internet by workers to scout for jobs and by employers to find and select applicants has increased at a rapid rate, and it can be expected to grow further as Internet use becomes more widespread and the websites more sophisticated. For instance, Statistics Canada's Canadian Internet Use Survey estimates that the percentage of Canadians who used the Internet to look for a job has increased rapidly in recent years and reached over 35 percent in 2012 (CANSIM Table 358-0153). Given that only about 5 percent of the adult population is unemployed at each point in time (see Figure 2.1), job search is clearly not confined to those classified as unemployed. Indeed, Skuterud (2005) finds that on-the-job search has been growing in the United States and Canada, and Stevenson (2009) finds that the vast majority of those who use the Internet for job search are employed. In addition to job boards, social media, such as Facebook, LinkedIn, and Twitter, are increasingly becoming an integral part of the job search process (Kuhn 2014).

TABLE 17.1	Search Activity of the Unemployed, 2015		
Group and Search Activity		**Number Using Activity (thousands)**	**Percent Using Activity[a] (%)**
Unemployed:	Did not search[b]	123	9.3
Unemployed:	Searched for full-time work	911	68.4
Unemployed:	Searched for part-time work	297	22.3
Search activity:	Looked at advertisements	678	50.9
	Contacted employers directly	583	43.8
	Placed or answered advertisements	416	31.2
	Checked with friends or relatives	229	17.2

NOTES:

[a]For search activities, the sum of the methods does not equal the total because many of the individuals use more than one method. Only the four most important activities are reported.

[b]Includes those on temporary layoff and future job starts.

SOURCE: Statistics Canada CANSIM database, Table 282-0050 (2016).

There is an extensive empirical literature estimating formal models of search behaviour, testing some of the propositions outlined in this chapter. Eckstein and van den Berg (2007) survey this literature. For example, in a series of papers exploiting administrative data, Belzil (1993, 1996) explores the relative efficiency of unemployed and employed job search. Belzil (1993) finds that if job quality is measured by the duration of the accepted job, then those who use employed job search, ultimately, obtain better jobs. In Belzil (1996), this finding is confirmed and refined. For younger workers, unemployed job search may actually be more effective. His findings may provide a partial explanation for the patterns reported in Table 16.3, where the incidence of unemployment is higher for young workers. Their higher unemployment incidence may reflect the rational choice to engage in unemployed job search in the pursuit of better job matches. Bloemen (2005) estimates a search model in which unemployed job seekers choose not only whether or not to accept a wage offer but also how intensively to search. Searching more intensively increases the job offer arrival rate but is also more costly. Thus, there is an optimal search intensity for each individual, given their characteristics and circumstances.

Bowlus (1998) and Ferrall (1997) also show the value of the search framework as a lens through which to view the unemployment experience of the young. Both authors use panel data from Canada and the United States from the late 1980s to follow young workers as they move into and out of jobs. By specifying an econometric model of the decisions that workers make in response to the jobs they find, both authors are able to identify key features of the "matching process" in Canada and the United States. Bowlus finds that the higher unemployment rate of young and low-skilled Canadian workers is consistent with greater search frictions in the Canadian labour market; the Canadian jobs are shorter, and harder to find. These greater frictions also map into a higher degree of monopsony power for Canadian employers, which helps sustain the frictions. Ferrall's study focuses on similar workers, but his emphasis is on the impact of UI on individuals as they leave school. In particular, he asks whether the Canadian UI system affects the search behaviour of these young workers. While his conclusions concerning the frictions in Canada's labour market are similar to Bowlus's, Ferrall finds that UI actually speeds up young Canadian's acceptance of their "first" job, as workers need to obtain employment in order to subsequently qualify for UI.

The dramatic growth in the use of online methods to advertise and search for jobs has also attracted research interest. Clearly, the Internet can substantially reduce the costs of acquiring information about jobs that are available and workers seeking employment. However, the extent to which it can improve the search and matching process remains unclear. One important challenge derives from the fact that the labour market is characterized not only by imperfect information but also by **asymmetric information**, which arises when either the buyer or seller has private information not available to the other party. In the search and matching process, job applicants have an incentive to provide information that favours their application, and to not reveal information that may be damaging. Recognizing this situation, employers may treat online applications with some skepticism. As stated by one recruiting executive (quoted in Autor 2001), online job boards are populated by "The unhappy (and, thus, probably not a desirable employee), the curious (and therefore likely to be a 'job-hopper'), the unpromotable (probably for a reason), and the unemployed (probably for a worse reason)."

A further problem is that, by making it almost costless to submit multiple applications, employers with posted openings are inundated with applications. When it was costly to submit a job application, only those who were seriously seeking employment would incur the necessary costs. However, when applying becomes almost costless, the applicant pool may contain many inappropriate and non-serious candidates. Employers are, thus, faced with an applicant pool that is both substantially larger and, on average, of lower quality.

In part in response to these problems and in part in response to potentially profitable opportunities, online job boards have evolved from their original "help wanted" form to more complex forms that essentially outsource the personnel recruiting functions of large employers. Nakamura et al. (2009) describe this evolution in the North American setting. One point they emphasize is that by lowering the costs of on-the-job search and making it easier for employers to identify potentially good hires among those currently working for other organizations, online job boards like Monster.com, CareerBuilder.com and Hotjobs.yahoo.com may advantage employed over unemployed job seekers. This may be one reason why on-the-job search has been growing rapidly at the same time that Internet penetration and use has been increasing dramatically. Thus, the Internet may facilitate employment-to-employment transitions, perhaps to the detriment of unemployment-to-employment transitions.

The presence of asymmetric information in the search and matching process leads to a demand for information intermediaries that attempt to verify claims made in job applications. These include Internet services that provide criminal record checks, verify claims about educational achievements, and so on. The collection of studies edited by Autor (2009) provides valuable insights into this rapidly evolving feature of the labour market.

Perhaps as a result of these challenges, research by Kuhn and Skuterud (2004) covering the period 1998–2000 found that shopping for jobs on the Internet did not reduce the time it took to find a new job, suggesting that the growing use of online methods was not improving the efficiency of the search and matching process. Similarly, Kroft and Pope (2014) took advantage of the "natural experiment" created by the website Craigslist, which expanded rapidly during the period 2000–2007, but at different times in different cities. Craigslist quickly became a leading job board in cities in which it was introduced, allowing Kroft and Pope to assess whether its entry into a city lowered the unemployment rate compared to cities in which Craigslist had not yet been introduced. The authors found no effect of the introduction of this widely used job board on the city unemployment rate.

However, a subsequent study by Kuhn and Mansour (2014) covering the period 2008–2009 and using very similar methods and data to those employed by Kuhn and Skuterud (2004) for the earlier 1998–2000 period did find evidence that Internet job search reduced the duration of unemployment, suggesting that workers and employers have been developing methods to use the Internet more effectively as a matching tool.

In summary, labour market search is an important activity among the unemployed, some of the employed, and many employers. Most fundamentally, the economic analysis of job search helps explain the co-existence of unemployed workers and unfilled vacancies and the process through which these are matched. More specifically, search theory offers insights into several phenomena, including the duration of unemployment, the cyclical behaviour of quits and labour force participation, the sluggish adjustment of wages to changes in economic conditions, and the consequences of public policies, such as unemployment insurance and the provision of labour market information. The costs associated with looking for work and recruiting workers online is low compared to traditional methods for job search and recruitment. The rapid growth in online search, as well as the use of social networking sites as a job search tool, constitute technological advances that appear likely to improve the search and matching process.

Sectoral Shifts and Unemployment

Matching unemployed workers to open job vacancies becomes a particularly challenging task in periods of major structural adjustment due to technological and economic change. While search theory typically looks at the case where a stable flow of jobs gets created and destroyed at each time period, a natural question to ask is whether unemployment would increase in periods of major structural adjustment. In particular, Lilien (1982) suggested that shifts in the sectoral composition of demand (by region, industry, or occupation) could raise the equilibrium level of unemployment, as time is required for labour and other resources to be reallocated to other sectors.

This **sectoral shift hypothesis** can be illustrated as follows. Consider two economies in which labour demand and labour supply are growing at equal average rates. If labour demand is growing at the same rate in each industry (or region or occupation) in economy A, but growing at above-average rates in some industries and below-average rates in other industries in economy B, the latter economy would have a higher unemployment rate due to the necessity for labour to be reallocated from those industries that are growing slowly (perhaps even declining) to those industries that are growing rapidly. For this reason, Lilien (1982) includes the variance of employment growth across U.S. industries as an additional variable explaining movements in the equilibrium level of unemployment in that country. Lilien's model was estimated for Canada by Sampson (1985) and Charette and Kaufman (1987). Both studies find a relationship between the variance of employment growth across industries and the unemployment rate.

Although periods of high dispersion of employment growth across industries are associated with periods of high unemployment, there is considerable disagreement as to whether this relationship confirms the structural shifts hypothesis. The problem arises because a standard macroeconomic model of the business cycle based on aggregate demand shocks is also likely to generate a positive relationship between the variance of employment growth across industries and unemployment (Abraham and Katz 1986). In particular, some industries are more cyclically sensitive than others, so that shocks to aggregate demand will have a differential effect across industries, producing a rise in the dispersion of employment growth across industries at the same time as unemployment increases. Thus, it is difficult to separate cause and effect; in particular, it is difficult to determine whether sectoral shifts exert an independent influence on unemployment, or whether aggregate shocks cause both a rise in unemployment and a cyclically induced increase in the dispersion of employment growth across industries. In a Canadian study that attempts to separate out the cyclical from noncyclical components of changes in sectoral composition of demand, Neelin (1987) finds that noncyclical shifts in the variance in employment growth across industries do not have an independent effect on unemployment. Rather, the causation runs in the reverse direction; economy-wide shocks that influence the aggregate unemployment rate also cause shifts in the industrial composition of employment. However, Neelin does find evidence supporting the sectoral-shifts hypothesis for changes in the regional composition of labour demand. Evidence reported in Gera (1991, Chap. 4) also suggests that increasing regional imbalances played an important role in the rise in unemployment in Canada during the 1970s and 1980s.

Adopting a different estimation framework to these studies, Altonji and Ham (1990) attempt to decompose the sources of employment fluctuations in Canada into those due to (1) U.S. aggregate shocks, (2) Canadian-specific aggregate shocks, (3) provincial shocks, (4) industry shocks, and (5) idiosyncratic shocks. They document the empirical difficulty of identifying the inherently "unobservable" shocks, and find that two-thirds of employment variation in Canada was due to U.S. shocks and one-quarter was due to aggregate Canadian shocks. Only one-tenth of employment variation could be explained by sectoral shocks, though they were more important in some individual industries and provinces.

Osberg (1991) analyzes microdata on the interindustry mobility of Canadian workers during the period 1980–1986. He finds that interindustry mobility falls sharply during economic downturns, in contrast to the implications of the sectoral-shifts hypothesis. Murphy and Topel (1987) report similar findings for the United States. The tendency for recessions to "chill" the process of intersectoral labour mobility may contribute to the slow recovery from economic downturns.

Structural unemployment will increase if there is a mismatch between industries and regions experiencing growth in labour demand and those experiencing growth in labour supply. However, there are incentives for employers to adjust their hiring to the available labour supply, as well as for workers to acquire characteristics in demand by employers. Beach and Kaliski (1986) examine changes in the demographic and industry characteristics of employment in detailed Canadian industries during the period 1966–1983, when most of the growth in labour supply involved entry by youth and women. They find that changes in industry employment structure generally accommodated the changes on the supply side; most industries increased their proportions of women and young workers employed, and industries that employed women intensively grew more rapidly than average. Thus, the interaction between changes in labour demand and those in the composition of labour supply facilitated employment growth and prevented the increase in structural unemployment that would occur in the absence of adjustments on both the demand and supply sides of the labour market.

Although the evidence supporting the sectoral-shifts hypothesis is limited, the message that some economic shocks may have more severe consequences for unemployment than others (holding constant the overall magnitude of the shock) is an important one. The recession of 1981–1982 had a much larger impact in the western provinces (especially Alberta and British Columbia) than in central Canada, whereas the 1990–1992 and 2008–2009 downturns adversely affected central Canada more than they did the western provinces. Because of the additional need for interregional reallocation of labour resources, adjustment to these shocks is more difficult than adjustment to shocks that have an even impact across regions.

Storer (1996) pursues this in analyzing the differential effects that oil price shocks have played in Ontario and Alberta. In this paper, the oil price is treated as a sectoral shock, though Storer notes the "hazy" distinction between a sectoral shock and an aggregate shock that has different effects across sectors. Nevertheless, he shows the important role played by this *observable* variable in explaining the differential unemployment experience in the two economies: oil price increases in the 1970s had detrimental effects on Ontario, but a positive effect on the labour market in Alberta, while the subsequent fall in oil prices in the 1980s reversed Alberta's advantage. While not looking at specifically sectoral issues, Carruth, Hooker, and Oswald (1995) also explore the remarkably high correlation between oil prices and Canada's aggregate unemployment rate, noting the similarity and robustness of the relationship in both Canada and the United Kingdom. These papers have the merit of isolating what the "shocks" may be that are the driving variables in microeconomic models of unemployment.

A distinctive feature of Canada's economy is its regional nature, which can result in large sectoral shifts across regions. The resource boom of the 2000s provides a good illustration. Beginning in the late 1990s, the world price of oil and other resources rose substantially, and, apart from temporary declines during the recessions of 2000–2001 and 2008–2009, remained elevated for about 15 years. Canadian exports of oil, natural gas, coal, potash and various metals increased markedly, resulting in an appreciation of the Canadian dollar and an economic boom in the resource-rich provinces. The higher Canadian dollar resulted in a loss of competitiveness of Canadian manufacturing goods, leading to layoffs and unemployment in central Canada, especially in Ontario and Quebec. At the same time, employment in the extractive resources sector in Alberta, Saskatchewan, and Newfoundland grew by about 50 percent over the period 1999–2013, resulting in a substantial movement of labour from central Canada and the Maritime provinces to the booming resource-rich provinces. This process continued until late 2014 when the world price of oil, as well as prices of many other resources, collapsed, leading to massive layoffs in the extractive resources sector. The regional sectoral shifts then reversed direction; that is, the value of the Canadian dollar fell, the moribund manufacturing sector began to increase output and employment, and unemployed workers moved from Alberta, Saskatchewan, and Newfoundland to parts of the country with better employment prospects.

The extent to which unemployment is associated with sectoral shifts and the process of labour reallocation is important for policy purposes. Policies that facilitate adjustment to change (training, mobility assistance) are more likely to be useful in periods characterized by substantial sectoral adjustment, whereas macroeconomic stabilization policies are more likely to be useful in response to aggregate shocks.

 # Displaced Workers and Unemployment

Other features of economic shocks may also contribute to the ease or difficulty of adjustment. During the past several decades, a considerable amount of economic dislocation involved losses in high-wage manufacturing jobs and growth in lower-wage service sector employment. In addition, there was substantial displacement among older workers with substantial job tenure. These features of displacement may contribute to a slow process of adjustment and high levels of unemployment. For example, adjustment may take longer if job losers need to change industry or occupation, or relocate to a region with more employment opportunities. Understanding the consequences of job loss and dealing with the necessary adjustments are important issues in a dynamic and ever-changing labour market.

In fact, **displaced workers**—those who have permanently separated from their previous employer; were not dismissed for cause; and had substantial prior attachment to their previous employer, occupation, or industry—have been the focus of considerable recent research. Much of this research stems from the particular challenge posed to policymakers by this subgroup of the unemployed. Because of their attachment to their previous employer, displaced workers may lose accumulated experience that is specific to their previous employer, industry, or occupation—the concept of specific human capital discussed in Chapter 9. Measuring the impact of displacement on these workers is difficult because we do not observe the path that their earnings would have followed if they had not been displaced. It is possible that their earnings would have declined anyway, for example, as their industry declined or monopoly rents were eroded.

An influential study by Jacobson, LaLonde, and Sullivan (1993) analyzed the consequences of displacement among workers in Pennsylvania. Their study has several key advantages: detailed administrative data linking workers and firms, several years of pre-displacement and post-displacement earnings, and of particular importance, a comparison group of non-displaced workers. They focus on workers with six or more years of tenure with the previous employer. Relative to the comparison group of non-displaced workers, earnings losses were very large—24 percent of expected earnings even six years after displacement.[2] The time pattern of earnings losses has some striking features. Not surprisingly, earnings drop precipitously, by about 50 percent, upon displacement, mainly because many job losers need time to become re-employed and, thus, have zero employment earnings. During the next two to three years, average earnings recover to an important extent, prior to levelling off. A salient feature is that average earnings plateau at a level substantially below their pre-displacement level and even further below the average earnings of the comparison group of non-displaced workers. There is little evidence in their data that earnings of displaced workers will ever return to their pre-displacement level or to the earnings levels experienced by their non-displaced counterparts. They also find that the earnings losses of displaced workers (relative to those who do not become displaced) began about three years prior to separation, suggesting that the events that lead to workers' separations cause their earnings to depart from their normal levels even prior to separation.

This study has subsequently been replicated using administrative data from other U.S. states and time periods (e.g. Couch and Placzek 2010) and survey data (e.g., Stevens 1997), with broadly similar findings. Earnings losses of displaced workers are substantial and persist for an extended period of time. Even six to 10 years after job loss, average earnings of permanent job losers are typically in the range of 11 to 15 percent of those of otherwise comparable non-displaced workers.

Farber (2005, 2015) analyzes U.S. data from over 30 years of Displaced Worker Surveys covering the period 1981–2013. These surveys have the important advantage of being based on a representative sample of the adult population. Even during periods of normal economic activity, job loss has substantial negative consequences for affected workers. For example, in the early 2000s (i.e. prior to the 2008–2009 financial crisis), 35 percent of displaced workers were not re-employed three years later, while about 13 percent of full-time job losers were re-employed part-time. Full-time job losers re-employed in full-time jobs earned 17 percent less than their earnings before displacement. The average earnings loss increased dramatically with prior job tenure. The consequences of losing one's job during the U.S. Great Recession from December 2007 to June 2009 were particularly severe. Only about 50 percent were re-employed in early 2010, and only about three-quarters of these were employed full time. This implies that only 35 to 40 percent of those who lost work during the Great Recession were employed full-time by early 2010. The adverse employment experience of job losers continued during the subsequent recovery. Those who lost jobs between 2011 and 2013 had very low re-employment rates and full-time employment rates.

Canadian evidence yields results similar to those reported for the United States. Morissette, Qui, and Chan (2013) use administrative data from Statistics Canada's Longitudinal Worker File to provide a comprehensive analysis of the incidence and consequences of permanent layoffs over the time period 1978 to 2008. This 30-year period includes the recessions of 1981–1982 and 1990–1992, the two most severe downturns experienced in Canada since the Great Depression. One noteworthy finding is that, apart from cyclical fluctuations, the risk of job displacement did not increase (or decrease) over this extended period of time, though there is evidence of a downward trend in permanent job loss since the mid-1990s. Permanent layoff rates for men range from 8–9 percent in strong economic conditions, like 2004–2007, to 13–14 percent in the 1981–1982 and 1990–1992 recessions. Comparable rates for women are much lower 4–5 percent in expansions, and 5–6 percent in recessions.

Short-term employment and earnings outcomes (one year after job loss) were also similar in the 2000s to those experienced by job losers in the late 1970s. For males, the probability of re-employment one year after layoff was about 85 percent at the beginning and end of this 30-year period, but this fell in recessions and rose in expansions. Females experienced a rise of 11 percentage points in re-employment rates, from 70 percent in the late 1970s to 81 percent in the mid-2000s. In assessing the earnings consequences of displacement, the authors consider two groups: a broad group that includes all permanent job losers and a narrower group consisting only of those who obtained a new job following displacement. For the broad group, earnings losses one year after job loss (relative to a comparison group of otherwise comparable non-displaced workers) averaged 23 percent for men and 31 percent for women. These earnings losses are highly sensitive to economic conditions. For example, men laid off in 1982 (the peak of the 1981–1982 recession) suffered one-year earnings losses of 30–40 percent, while those who permanently lost their job in 1988 (the peak year of the strong expansion of the 1980s) experienced earnings losses of 1–12 percent. Average earnings losses for the narrower group are much smaller: 12–14 percent for males and 14–17 percent for females.

Long-term earnings losses also display no upward or downward trend, but substantial cyclical fluctuations. Five years after job displacement the average earnings loss for the broad group was 17 percent for males and 23 percent for females. However, for the narrower group that had become re-employed five years later, earnings losses were much smaller: 3–4 percent for men and 2–6 percent for women. Morissette, Qui, and Chan (2013) also examine long-term earnings losses of two groups of particular policy interest—those with stable labour force attachment (defined as having earnings of at least $10,000 in six consecutive years prior to job loss) and high-seniority workers (those with the same employer for at least six years prior to layoff). As found in U.S. studies, these groups suffer large and long-lasting declines in earnings. Even restricting attention to the narrower group with positive labour market earnings following displacement, employees with stable prior labour force attachment experienced earnings losses of 10–17 percent after five years, while high-seniority workers suffered losses of 13–18 percent after five years.

Schirle (2009) uses data from the Survey of Labour and Income Dynamics to examine earning losses of displaced older workers—those who lose their job at between 50 and 69 years of age. In this study, displaced workers are defined as those who lost their job due to the company closing, the company moving, or being laid off due to business slowdown. An important challenge in examining earnings losses among older displaced workers is that many may not become re-employed but rather may retire from the workforce. For this group, re-employment earnings are not observed. The subset of those who do obtain re-employment may not be representative of the larger group of older displaced workers. Statistical techniques are required to take account of the self-selected nature of the sample of individuals who obtain a new job.

Schirle finds that, as with younger workers, older workers face large and persistent earnings losses after permanent job loss. Interestingly, once one statistically controls for job tenure, age plays only a modest role in the magnitudes of earnings losses. However, as also found in other studies, job tenure is a strong predictor of the magnitude of the loss in earnings. Schirle also finds that some earnings losses begin before displacement occurs, particularly among those workers who are laid off due to the company closing.

In their 1991 paper "Layoffs and Lemons," Gibbons and Katz point out another problem that laid-off workers may face. If worker ability is only imperfectly observed when workers are hired, but is observed better after the worker has been employed for some time, then it is a generally bad signal to be seen as having been fired. Despite protestations that they were laid off for economic reasons, workers may have a difficult time distinguishing themselves from the "lemons" who were fired because they were inferior employees. The one advantage that truly displaced workers have is that they can make a more credible case that they are not lemons, since the layoff was clearly beyond their control. Using the U.S. Displaced Worker Survey, they find evidence that workers who were the victims of mass layoffs indeed suffered lower post-layoff losses than comparable other laid-off workers. Doiron (1995b) has replicated this analysis in Canada with the Canadian Displaced Worker Survey. She also finds that, at least for white-collar workers, those who had lost their jobs due to a plant closing suffered 5 percent lower losses than the average job loser, but there was no advantage for similar blue-collar workers.

What explains the large earnings losses that persist for many years after permanent job loss? The leading explanation involves loss of human capital that is specific to the job, firm, industry, or occupation and thus not transferable to other settings, as discussed in Chapter 9. Evidence supporting this view includes studies by Jacobson, LaLonde, and Sullivan (1993); Neal (1995); and Parent (2000) that find that workers who change industries after job loss suffer much greater losses. Additional evidence supporting the specific human capital view is provided by Poletaev and Robinson (2008) using measures of the skill content of jobs. They find that the earnings losses experienced by displaced workers are closely associated with the magnitude of the change in the skill portfolio between the pre-displacement and post-displacement jobs. Job losers who obtain new employment with skill content similar to that in their previous job are less likely to suffer earnings losses, even when doing so involves changing industry or occupation, while those unable to become re-employed in a job with similar skill content are likely to experience large declines in earnings.

Another explanation is the presence of internal labour markets and wage profiles that depend on seniority. As discussed in Chapter 13, employers and employees may prefer wage structures such that workers earn less than their value to the firm early in their career and more than their value to the firm later in their career. This type of behaviour produces a wage profile that increases with tenure with the firm—indeed, one that increases with seniority more rapidly than does worker productivity. Employees with substantial tenure who permanently lose their jobs, thus, lose this "premium" (wages in excess of productivity) when they re-enter the job market and become re-employed at wages that more closely reflect their productivity. An additional factor is that some displaced workers may have been earning "economic rents"—wages in excess of productivity—and cannot be expected, on average, to be able to find new jobs that also pay wages in excess of worker productivity. For example, Kuhn and Sweetman (1998) find that earnings losses are larger for workers who lose jobs in the union sector and become re-employed in the non-union sector, compared with those who make a transition from the non-union to union sector or who remain in the union sector. The losses are similar in size to the union–non-union wage differential discussed in Chapter 15.

Permanent job loss has additional negative consequences, adding to the economic and social significance of labour market adjustment. A U.S. study by Sullivan and von Wachter (2009) concludes that displacement leads to a 15–20 percent increase in death rates, equivalent to a reduction in life expectancy of about 1.5 years for someone displaced at age 40. Eliason and Storrie (2009) examine the impact of job loss on overall and cause-specific mortality with Swedish data. They find a substantial rise in mortality among displaced Swedish men (an over 40 percent increase) during the first four years after job loss. For both men and women, displacement results in an approximate doubling of mortality due to suicides and alcohol-related deaths. Mental health problems arising from job loss are reported by Hamilton et al. (1997). Using high quality Norwegian administrative data, Black, Devereux, and Salvanes (2012) find that job displacements lead to a higher incidence of smoking and elevated indicators for heart disease.

There are also adverse consequences for the families of displaced workers. Charles and Stephens (2004) find that the incidence of divorce rises after a spouse's displacement, an effect that is not present for the onset of a disability. Lindo (2010) finds evidence that a husband's displacement reduces the wife's fertility. Parental job loss reduces the likelihood that teenaged children will pursue post-secondary education (Coelli 2009). Intergenerational impacts appear to be long lasting; children whose fathers were displaced have, as adults, lower annual earnings (about 9 percent) and have higher incidence of employment insurance (EI) and social assistance receipt (Oreopoulos, Page, and Huff Stevens 2008).

In summary, the research on the consequences of displacement yields a number of salient and consistent findings:

- For some individuals, earnings losses from permanent job loss are very large, especially for workers with prior stable labour force attachment and those with long tenure with their previous employer. Both groups represent a minority of job losers.

- A major part of the earnings loss arises not from post-displacement unemployment, but from re-employment at wages substantially below their pre-displacement levels.

- These substantial losses appear to be long lasting.

- In contrast, most unemployed workers become re-employed relatively quickly and do not suffer permanent earnings losses. Even among permanent job losers, most obtain new employment at wages close to those in their previous job.

- Older displaced workers are less likely to become re-employed than their younger counterparts. However, age appears to play only a minor role in the magnitudes of annual earnings losses, once one statistically controls for worker seniority.

These results create challenges for public policy. Adjusting to economic change benefits the economy and society as a whole, but it imposes large costs on a small number of affected individuals and families. No matter how generous UI may be in replacing temporary earnings loss during spells of unemployment, it appears that displaced workers suffer permanent damage to their earnings capacity. There is also growing evidence of significant negative consequences on the health and well being of displaced workers and their families. This recent research has resulted in growing interest in "wage insurance" or "job displacement insurance" that would provide insurance against the risk of permanently lower earnings following job loss and re-employment (LaLonde 2007; Parsons 2014). The United States has introduced wage insurance on a limited scale for some displaced workers. In Canada, the Expert Panel on Older Workers (2008) recommended enhanced benefits for displaced workers with long previous job tenure, and this recommendation was adopted by the federal government, initially on a temporary basis during the 2008–2009 recession, and subsequently on a continuing basis. Like many other examples in this book, this provides an illustration of the influence of labour market research on public policy.

LO5   High-Wage Unemployment

Traditional theories of unemployment merely assumed that unemployment was characterized by wages being set too high, above the market clearing level. While the minimum wage could account for this particular type of unemployment for a small subset of low-wage workers, it is harder to see why market forces don't simply push the wage back to its equilibrium level for the bulk of the workforce. Significant theoretical developments have shown, however, a number of reasons wages may remain too high in equilibrium once some key assumptions of the competitive model are reconsidered. Examples of such alternative approaches include implicit contracts, efficiency wages, and insider-outsider theories.

Implicit Contracts

While search theory is concerned with the process of matching job vacancies and unemployed workers, **implicit contract theory** deals with issues that may arise when firms and workers are already engaged in a continuing employment relationship. In particular, implicit contract theory seeks to explain phenomena such as rigid wages and the use of quantity adjustments (layoffs and rehires) rather than wage adjustments to respond to variations in product demand. Our emphasis in this section is on the way in which implicit contract theory can generate rigid wages and layoffs as the optimal arrangement between willing workers and firms.

Implicit contract theory is based on the view that wage and employment behaviour reflects **risk-sharing** between employers and employees. Risk-sharing arises because of differences in attitudes toward risk between workers and the owners of firms. Specifically, workers are believed to be more risk averse than the shareholders of firms. These differences in attitudes toward risk create potential gains from trade; that is, both parties can benefit from a risk-sharing arrangement. Because workers dislike fluctuations in their incomes, they prefer an arrangement whereby they receive a somewhat lower average or expected income, provided their income is sufficiently less variable (more certain). The owners of firms also prefer this arrangement because average or expected profits are higher (due to lower labour costs), albeit more variable because of the stabilization of workers' incomes. In effect, the employment relation involves two transactions: (1) provision of labour services by employees in exchange for payment by employers and (2) provision of insurance services by employers in exchange for payment of an insurance premium (acceptance of a lower wage) by employees. For reasons discussed below, workers are generally unable to purchase insurance against the risk of income fluctuations in regular insurance markets such as those that exist for accident, property, and life insurance. However, the continuing nature of the employment relationship makes feasible the implicit purchase of income insurance from the employer.

Seminal contributions to implicit contract theory were made by Azariadis (1975), Baily (1974), and Gordon (1974). A large literature, much of it highly technical in nature, has subsequently developed. Our purpose in this section is to present the basic elements of implicit contract theory in as nontechnical a fashion as possible. Further details are available in surveys by Azariadis (1979), Azariadis and Stiglitz (1983), Hart (1983), and Rosen (1985).

Differences in attitudes toward risk between employers and employees provide the basis for both parties to benefit from a risk-sharing arrangement. Two reasons workers may be more risk averse than the owners of firms have been advanced. Perhaps the most significant factor is that for many workers their wealth consists largely of the value of their human capital, which cannot be diversified. In contrast, individuals whose wealth consists largely of financial capital can reduce the risk of a reduction in their wealth by holding a diversified portfolio; that is, by acquiring shares in (or income claims on) a variety of companies. It is not possible to diversify wealth holdings in the form of human capital because markets analogous to the stock market do not exist for buying and selling claims on the incomes of different individuals or groups of individuals. Such markets would constitute a form of slavery and would, therefore, be illegal, even if there were sufficient demand to make markets for trading in such claims viable. Workers, therefore, are in the awkward position of having most of their wealth in one risky asset—their human capital. As a consequence, they seek alternative ways of reducing the risk of fluctuations in the return on that asset, their employment income.

A second reason for differences in risk attitudes involves sorting according to innate risk preferences. Those who are venturesome, perhaps risk neutral or perhaps even risk loving, may be more likely to become entrepreneurs and, thus, the owners of firms. Cautious or risk-averse individuals may be more likely to become employees and wage earners.

If workers dislike the risk of fluctuations in their employment income, why do they not purchase income insurance from private insurance companies? Private markets for income insurance do not exist because of two phenomena, moral hazard and adverse selection, that may result in the selling of such insurance being an unprofitable activity, despite the demand that exists for the product. **Moral hazard** exists when individuals can influence the risk against which they are insured. For example, suppose workers are insured against reductions in their income associated with becoming unemployed. The fact that they are insured could affect their behaviour such that they are then more likely to be unemployed and collecting insurance—perhaps because such workers who become unemployed search longer for a better job when they are insured or because they become more willing to accept a job with a high risk of layoff than they would if they were not insured. Thus, the profitability of selling such insurance is reduced, perhaps to the point at which selling such insurance is unprofitable.

Adverse selection occurs when the insurer cannot observe the risk that a particular insuree represents. The insurer, thus, charges each customer the same rate. However, the high-risk individuals are more likely and the low-risk individuals less likely to purchase insurance. Thus, the average risk among those who purchase insurance will be higher than the risk for the population as a whole. The insurer will, therefore, earn less than would be expected, perhaps even incurring a loss, on the basis of population risk statistics. Furthermore, raising its insurance rates may not increase profitability, because fewer individuals will purchase insurance at the higher rates, *and* those who decide not to purchase insurance because of the higher rates will be the customers facing the lowest risk. Thus, with each increase in its rates, the insurance company ends up selling to a smaller number of customers with a higher average risk. In these circumstances, there may be no price that would enable insurance to be sold at a profit.

The central hypothesis of implicit contract theory is that employees purchase income insurance indirectly from the employer. The continuing nature of the employment relationship enables the employer to deal with the moral hazard and adverse selection problems. The firm provides insurance only to its own employees, thus avoiding adverse selection. In addition, the firm controls the probability of income loss due to layoff or wage and/or hours reduction, thus avoiding the moral hazard problem.

Implicit contract theory applies to situations in which there is a long-term attachment between the firm and its workers. Many economists have suggested that in labour markets with these characteristics, wages do not adjust each period to equate demand and supply. In contrast, many product and asset markets behave like "Walrasian auction markets" in which the price adjusts each period to clear the market. According to implicit contract theory, this difference in behaviour reflects risk-sharing in the labour market. The continuing nature of the employment relationship enables the firm to stabilize its employees' incomes over several periods by paying a wage above that which would exist with continuous market clearing when product demand conditions are weaker than normal, and paying a wage below that which would exist with continuous market clearing when product demand conditions are stronger than normal.

Although employers and employees are assumed to be involved in a continuing employment relationship, the basic model of implicit contracts can be explained in a two-period setting. In the initial period, firms offer wage and employment contracts to workers, and workers decide which firm's contract to accept. The wages and employment stipulated in these contracts may be contingent on the state of product demand realized in the second period. The contracts agreed to in the first period are then carried out in the second. Thus, workers are mobile *ex ante* (in the initial period when they are choosing which firm's contract to accept) but immobile *ex post* (in the second period when the uncertainty about product demand conditions is resolved and the terms of the contract are carried out). The assumption of *ex post* immobility is intended to reflect the continuing nature of the employment relationship and the cost of severing that relationship.

These contractual arrangements are not formal written agreements—hence, the term "implicit contract"—but rather represent understandings that govern the behaviour of firms and workers. As stated by Okun (1981, p. 89), "Employers... rely heavily on the 'invisible handshake' as a substitute for the invisible hand that cannot operate effectively in the career labour market." The explicit contracts observed in the union sector may also reflect risk-sharing to some degree, but the purpose of the analysis is to explain behaviour in the unorganized sector.

To keep the analysis simple, we will assume that the workers are homogeneous, each with utility function u(y) where $y = w \times h$ is income, w is the wage rate, and h is hours worked. To focus on wages and employment, hours of work will be assumed to be constant at h. A worker is, thus, either employed, working h hours, or unemployed, working zero hours. With hours of work fixed, an employed worker's utility can be written in terms of the wage rate alone, u(w). An unemployed worker receives utility u(k), where k is the value of leisure time and any unemployment benefit received from the unemployment insurance program. (Workers on layoff receive no income from the employer.) Because workers are homogeneous, which workers are laid off (should layoffs be required) is randomly determined.

Let N_0 be the number of workers attached to the firm; this is the number of workers who agreed to join the firm's "labour pool" given the contract offered in the first period. The firm's labour supply curve in the second period is, thus, shown by S in Figure 17.3. At wage rates equal to or greater than the reservation wage k, the firm can employ up to N_0 workers. The firm cannot employ any workers at wage rates below k.

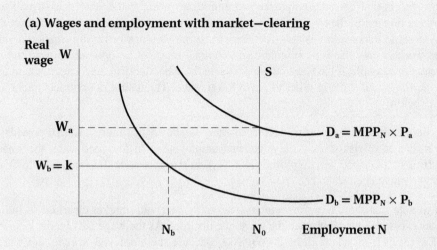

(a) Wages and employment with market–clearing

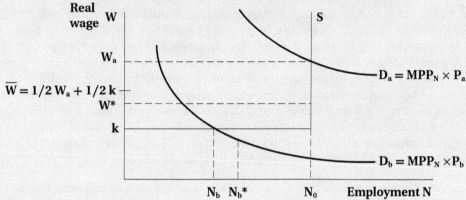

(b) Wages and employment with implicit contracts

Figure 17.3 Implicit Contracts

The base case without implicit contracts is shown in panel a. N_0 workers are attached to the firm, and the value of leisure is k. The supply curve to the firm is perfectly elastic at k for employment levels below N_0 and perfectly inelastic at N_0 for wages above k. The firm's labour demand can either be "high," D_a, or "low," D_b. Neither workers nor firms know which state will prevail before workers sign on with a firm. In the good state, N_0 workers are employed at W_a; in the bad state, N_b employed workers earn W_b, and unemployed workers "earn" k (not paid by the firm). Earnings variability can be reduced with implicit contracts. Panel b shows the case where workers and firms agree that, in the good state, employment will be at N_0 at a wage W^*. In the bad state, employment will be higher than before, at N_b^*, and wages will be W^*, higher than the market-clearing case. For workers, this represents a reduction in risk (fewer layoffs and constant wages). As long as W^* is not too low, risk-averse workers will find this attractive. For firms, the wage W^* is lower than the expected wage under market clearing, $\overline{W}$, so expected profits are higher. Firms and workers are, thus, better off with the risk-sharing.

We will discuss the case in which perfect competition prevails in the output market so that the price of output is not affected by the output produced and, hence, labour utilized. The analysis for other product market structures is similar. The firm's labour demand schedule is the locus of points for which wages are just equal to the value of the marginal product of labour, which, in turn, equals the marginal product of labour times the price at which the extra output is sold. That is, $D = VMP_N = MPP_N \times P$, where MPP_N is the marginal product of labour and P is the price of output.

There is uncertainty about the state of the product market. When product market conditions are strong, the product price and the demand for labour will be high. The opposite holds in weak product market conditions. For ease of exposition, we will assume that there are only two possible states of the product market—the "good state" in which the product price is high at P_a and the "poor state" in which the product price is low at P_b—and that these are equally likely to occur. The assumption of two equi-probable outcomes does not affect the analysis in any way except to make the results easier to present. An important assumption, however, is that both the employer and employees observe the state that is realized. When this **symmetric information** assumption holds, the two parties can make the implicit wage-employment contract contingent on the observed state. When asymmetric information exists—for example, if the firm has better information about the state of the product market than the workers do—this type of contingent contract may not be optimal because the firm will usually have an incentive to cheat. For example, if the wage rate depends on the state, the firm may want to claim that the poor state has been realized, whatever the actual state, in order to pay a lower wage. The nature of contracts under asymmetric information is discussed further below.

The behaviour of a continuously clearing labour market, as shown in Figure 17.3(a), provides a useful benchmark for examining the influence of risk-sharing on wages and employment. In the good state, the wage rises to W_a and all the workers in the firm's labour pool are employed ($N = N_0$). In the poor state the wage falls to W_b (equal to the reservation wage, k) and employment declines to N_b.

It is important to note that there is no involuntary unemployment with market clearing. In the poor state, the decline in demand produces excess labour supply and the wage rate declines. As the wage falls below k, some workers withdraw from employment. The result is an equilibrium at (W_b, N_b). Because the employed workers are paid the reservation wage, k, unemployed workers do not envy the employed workers. Workers are indifferent between being employed and unemployed, given the equilibrium wage rate and their value of leisure time.

As is well known, in the absence of externalities and other sources of market failure, the competitive market-clearing outcome produces an efficient allocation of resources. In the case analyzed here, the allocation of labour among firms was determined based on expected results. However, there remains the question of how to best utilize each firm's labour pool. The allocation of workers shown in Figure 17.3(a), including the fact that N_bN_0 workers are not employed in the poor state, is efficient in the sense that it maximizes the value of output produced and income generated in each state. However, with market clearing, workers face an uncertain income stream. Income may fluctuate because both the wage rate and employment depend on the state that is realized. Because of this income uncertainty, the market-clearing outcome is not, in general, a Pareto-optimal arrangement—that is, it is possible through risk-sharing to make at least one of the parties better off without making the other party worse off—even though it does produce an efficient allocation of labour resources. An optimal arrangement takes into account both efficiency and risk-sharing considerations.

A Pareto-optimal contract between a risk-neutral firm and risk-averse workers has the following features: (1) the real wage rate is independent of the state that is realized, so that employed workers receive the same real wage whatever the level of product demand, and (2) layoffs may occur in weak states of demand, though the number of workers laid off will be less than the number who would be voluntarily unemployed under market clearing. Figure 17.3(b) shows an example of an optimal wage-employment contract. Employed workers receive the wage W^* in each state. Employment equals N_0 in the good state and N_b^* in the poor state.

Several features of the optimal contract should be noted. First, the contract provides for a rigid real wage. Employed workers receive the same utility, whatever the state of product demand and the overall price level. The contract wage W^* is lower than the market-clearing wage in the good state and higher than with market clearing in the poor state. Second, there are layoffs in the poor state. However, the number of workers laid off ($N_b^* N_0$) is less than the number that would voluntarily withdraw from employment with market clearing ($N_b N_0$). Third, there is involuntary unemployment in the poor state, which is why layoffs are necessary. Employed workers receive utility u(W^*), whereas unemployed workers receive utility u(k); laid-off workers would prefer to be employed, given that the wage does not decline in the poor state.

The way in which both parties may benefit from a risk-sharing arrangement can be seen in Figure 17.3. Even though the firm is paying a higher wage and employing more workers in the poor state than with market clearing, the savings in labour costs in the good state are sufficiently large, given a contract wage W^* less than the expected wage W, that expected profits are higher under the implicit contract. The risk-neutral firm will therefore be better off with risk-sharing. Although their expected income is somewhat lower, risk-averse workers are also better off because their income is more certain. The reduction in the variability of workers' real income comes from two sources—real wage fluctuations are eliminated and more workers are employed in the poor state than with market clearing.

Workers' incomes are not fully stabilized, however. There remains some uncertainty due to the possibility of being laid off in weak demand conditions. In general, a contract that eliminates all income risk by stabilizing employment in addition to the wage is not optimal, because in order for it to be in the firm's interest to employ all N_0 workers in the poor state, the contract wage W* would have to be lower than the reservation wage k. In these circumstances, the workers would prefer not to be employed. Thus, the optimal contract reduces, but does not necessarily eliminate, the income uncertainty that workers face.

The optimal contract represents a trade-off between risk-sharing and production efficiency. On the basis of risk-sharing alone, the risk-neutral firm should absorb all the risk and the risk-averse workers should receive a fixed real income. For production efficiency alone, the real wage and employment should fluctuate, as shown in Figure 17.3(a). The optimal contract sacrifices some efficiency by employing more than N_b workers in the poor state. This inefficiency is reflected in the fact that the output produced by the additional N_b N_b* workers is less than the value of their leisure time. However, there is a benefit in terms of risk-sharing, because employing these additional N_b N_b* workers in the poor state reduces the probability of a worker being laid off and not receiving the contract wage W*. However, completely eliminating income uncertainty would be too costly in terms of production efficiency. The optimal contract strikes a balance between these two competing considerations.

Several conclusions emerge from this discussion of risk-sharing between the firm and its workers. Implicit contract theory can account for real wage rigidity, the use of layoffs to respond to reductions in demand, and the existence of involuntary unemployment. The optimal contract provides for a constant real wage and reduction in employment in the poor state. Because workers would prefer to be employed and earning the contract wage, the reduction in employment takes the form of layoffs. Those workers laid off are involuntarily unemployed based on actual results; given that the weak demand state occurs, that they are selected for layoff, and that the contract wage exceeds their reservation wage, they would prefer to be employed. However, the unemployment may be considered voluntary based on expected results, because the workers chose a wage-employment contract with some risk of layoff, and would make the same choice again in identical circumstances, given the Pareto-optimal nature of the contractual arrangement. Thus the unemployment is involuntary in a rather limited sense.

Although implicit contract theory does provide a rigorous microeconomic explanation for wage rigidity, layoffs, and involuntary unemployment (in a restricted sense), the theory has been criticized for its inability to explain unemployment in excess of the amount that would be observed if wages adjusted each period to equate labour supply and demand (Akerlof and Miyazaki 1980). Indeed, according to the basic implicit contract model discussed in this section, the number of workers involuntarily laid off in weak demand conditions is less than the number who would voluntarily withdraw from employment with market clearing. However, this implication of the model is closely related to the assumption that both parties observe the state of demand. When this symmetric information assumption is relaxed, optimal contracts may imply unemployment in excess of the amount that would occur with market clearing.

Because many of the key variables in implicit contract models are unobservable (that is one of the reasons they are called "implicit"), the empirical literature on this subject is not large. One approach adopted by researchers is to explore the features of "explicit" contracts, in order to gauge the degree to which it appears that firms are offering UI to their unionized workers. Ragan (1995) examines a sample of Canadian union contracts. He posits that risk-averse unions should prefer shorter contracts, since this allows more flexible renegotiation in response to changed market conditions. On the other hand, risk-neutral firms would prefer longer contracts. He then investigates whether union members are compensated for bearing the risk of longer contracts, and finds that, indeed, longer contracts are associated with higher wages. This provides favourable evidence for the underlying behavioural assumptions of implicit contract theory.

Beaudry and DiNardo (1991, 1995) use implicit contract theory to explain evidence of long-term attachment of workers to firms, which would otherwise be difficult to explain. For example, Beaudry and DiNardo (1991) show that the economic conditions that existed when a worker signed on with a firm have permanent effects on earnings. For example, if an employee started with a firm during a recession for a lower starting wage, this would have a significantly adverse effect on the entire profile of wages, as long as the employee remained at that firm. Allowing for the possibility of renegotiation, they also found that if economic conditions improved over the tenure of employment with the firm, the wage could be adjusted upward. The significant correlation of past economic conditions with current wages, thus, suggests that wages are not determined solely in a contemporaneously clearing spot market, and the attachment of workers to firms is, thus, consistent with a more general model where contracting is important. McDonald and Worswick (1999) replicate Beaudry and DiNardo's methodology with Canadian data, and reach similar conclusions. On the other hand, Kahn and Lang (1995) do not find that actual and desired hours line up with the predictions of implicit contract theory. Clearly, long-run firm-worker attachments are an important feature of the labour market, but the precise nature of this relationship, and its link to wages and unemployment, remain an important area for further research.

LO4   Efficiency Wages

Another explanation of wage rigidity and unemployment that has received considerable attention is the notion of efficiency wages. While implicit contract theory emphasized the role of wages and employment in risk-sharing, efficiency wage theory focuses on the effect of wages on incentives and worker productivity. The central hypothesis is that firms may choose to pay wages above the market-clearing level in order to enhance worker productivity.

Some of the basic features of efficiency wage theory were described in Chapter 10, where its implications for wage differentials were discussed. Here we focus on the theory's implications for unemployment.

The central assumption of efficiency wage theory is that firms may prefer to pay "above market" wages because doing so enhances worker productivity. There are several reasons firms may benefit from paying a wage above the level necessary to attract labour. In less-developed countries, higher wages may result in better-fed and, thus, healthier and more productive workers. In developed economies, wages may affect productivity in a variety of ways. Higher wages may improve worker morale, discourage shirking and absenteeism by raising the cost to workers of being fired, and reduce turnover. Firms may also prefer to pay high wages in order to reduce the threat of unionization or to obtain a larger and higher-quality pool of job applicants.

The incentive to pay high wages will generally differ across firms and industries. Efficiency wages are most likely to be observed when other methods of enhancing productivity, such as supervision and monitoring of employees or the use of piece-rate compensation systems, are costly or ineffective. The impact of employee work effort on the quality and quantity of output is also an important factor. Shirking by employees can have disastrous effects in some jobs (an example would be the operator in a nuclear power station or the driver of a bus), while in others the consequences are much less severe. Similarly, in some production processes the work is highly interdependent, so that poor work effort by one employee affects the output of the entire group, whereas in other situations only that employee's output is affected. Other determinants of efficiency wages may also differ from one firm or industry to another. For example, turnover is more costly to some employers than others because of differences in hiring and training costs. As discussed in Chapter 14 on unions, some firms are more likely to become unionized than others because of factors such as size and capital intensity. Thus, the incentive to pay high wages in order to discourage unionization will be stronger in some organizations than in others.

The primary objective of the model is to show why firms may be reluctant to hire an unemployed applicant, even if the applicant is willing to work for a lower wage than are the current employees. If we can show why this is rational for firms, then we can explain the logical possibility of the co-existence of unemployment and rigid wages. For concreteness, we present a model motivated by the nutritional efficiency wage model used in development economics (see Exhibit 17.2). To sketch the model, assume that labour, L, is supplied inelastically to the firm (a rice farm). Output depends only on the labour input, which is measured in "efficiency units," eL; L measures the quantity of labour (in hours), while e is the quality, or efficiency of the work. Output of rice is given by the production function,

$$Q = F(eL)$$

EXHIBIT 17.2

Nutritional Efficiency Wages

Some of the earliest papers on efficiency wages were motivated by their possible importance in the rural labour markets of low-income countries (Mirrlees 1975; Stiglitz 1976). There was significant concern that unemployment or underemployment was a defining feature of rural labour markets. In nutritional efficiency wage models, the labour market does not clear because wages cannot be cut without adversely affecting worker productivity and farm profits. If wages are the sole source of income for a worker, then, if wages are set too low, the worker will not be able to afford to eat enough food to be productive, especially in physically demanding farm labour. Thus, no matter how persistent workers may be in offering their services below the prevailing wage, employers will not be willing to hire them at the lower wage, and unemployment will result.

Because the basic ingredients of the model are more or less observable—worker wages, nutritional intake, and farm productivity—this type of efficiency wage model has received more empirical attention, at least in terms of direct evaluation of its assumptions, than those based on imperfect information. The first step in evaluating the model has been an estimation of the links between nutrition and labour productivity. Strauss (1986) estimates a relationship between individual caloric intake and farm productivity, and finds that better-fed farmers are also more productive. Of course, one obvious problem that Strauss must contend with is that the causality goes both ways: more-productive farmers (i.e., richer farmers) also tend to be better fed. Strauss goes to considerable lengths to build a convincing case that at least some of the correlation between caloric intake and productivity is the productivity-enhancing effect of better nutrition, a key ingredient of the efficiency wage model.

Foster and Rosenzweig (1994) examine the productivity of workers under alternative payment schemes—straight-time wages, piece rates, sharecropping, and own-farm self-employment. Controlling for nutritional health status—Body Mass Index (BMI), an index that measures weight for height—they find that workers who eat more (i.e., consume more calories) are more productive in those pursuits for which there is the greatest payoff: piece rate and own-farm work. Their research also addresses the moral hazard (shirking) explanation for efficiency wages. They find that workers who were paid by piece rates worked harder than those who were paid a flat-time wage. Work effort was measured by the decline in BMI after a day's work under different wage payment schemes. Evidently, those workers whose pay was not tied directly to their output did not "sweat" as much as those paid piece rates.

While these and other studies provide convincing evidence on the potential links between nutrition, health, and productivity, they still do not show that efficiency wages are an important feature of rural labour markets. As Subramanian and Deaton (1996) show, for example, in one part of rural India, daily nutrients for a farm worker can be purchased with about 5 percent of the daily agricultural wage. At this level, it is unlikely that wage rigidities could be generated by nutritional concerns. For a more-detailed discussion of these issues, see Strauss and Thomas (1995).

Clearly, the higher e is, the more efficiency units of labour are provided for each hour worked, and the higher is output. The key part of an efficiency wage model is that efficiency, e, depends on the wage paid:

$$e = e(W)$$

In the nutritional efficiency wage model, the efficiency of workers increases as they are paid more, thus they are able to eat better and work harder. The firm's profits are given by the difference between revenue and costs. If we normalize the price of output (e.g., rice) to one, profits are given by

$$\Pi \quad = \quad F\big(e(W) \times L\big) - WL$$

$$= \quad g(W;L) - WL$$

If there is full employment, the firm will have to pay the prevailing wage if it wants to hire any workers. In that case, the efficiency wage framework is less relevant—even if it would like to, the firm must at least pay the going wage rate. But consider the case where there are unemployed workers and the firm has some discretion in setting the wage. It faces a trade-off in making this decision. The firm reduces labour costs by paying a lower wage, but these labour savings may be offset by a drop in labour productivity, so that the lower wage actually reduces profits. The firm must balance the costs and benefits of higher wages. The solution is depicted in Figure 17.4.

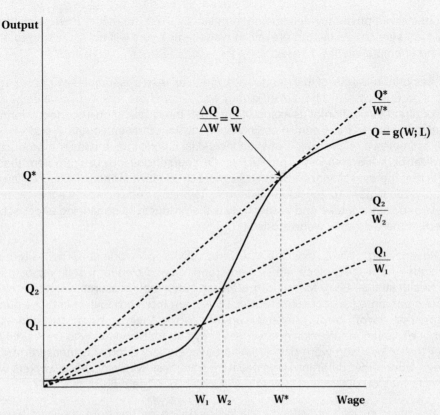

Figure 17.4 Determination of the Efficiency Wage

The efficiency wage, W*, is the wage that maximizes profits when worker productivity depends on how much he or she is paid. The efficiency relationship linking productivity (output) and wages is given by g(W; L). Maximizing profits can be shown to imply minimizing the cost per unit of output, W/Q, or equivalently, maximizing Q/W. Any ray through the origin has a slope (rise over run) equal to Q/W. Maximizing profits then requires choosing the wage on g(W; L) that lies on the steepest ray Q/W. The choice of a wage like W_1 yields output Q_1 and a slope of Q_1/W_1. The firm would do better by increasing the wage to W_2, but profits are maximized by raising the wage to W*, at the tangency between Q/W and g(W;L). This tangency implies that the slopes of the two functions are equal; that is $\frac{\Delta Q}{\Delta W} = \frac{Q}{W}$.

The relationship between productivity and the wage is summarized by the function g(W; L).[3] In our depiction, the function is S-shaped. The corresponding "story" is that productivity increases only slowly at first, as the wage is increased. Only after workers are able to obtain a minimum threshold diet do we see an increase in efficiency. Eventually, diminishing returns take over—paying workers higher wages beyond some point will have only small impacts on productivity (only so much of the extra wage goes to food, and increased eating has only limited effects on productivity beyond some point, as these authors are all too aware!). The average cost of producing any given output (with one worker) is W/Q. It can be shown that maximizing profits implies minimizing this cost, or maximizing output per dollar spent, Q/W. The firm's objective is to choose the wage to maximize profits, subject to the efficiency relationship. Diagrammatically, any ray through the origin represents a line with slope equal to Q/W. The firm's objective is to choose the wage on the g(W; L) function that has the steepest (highest) output per dollar spent (Q/W). Consider first the firm paying W_1. A worker with this wage produces Q_1, yielding output per dollar of Q_1/W_1. The firm would do better to increase the wage to W_2, yielding higher output per dollar, Q_2/W_2. This will continue to be true as long as the increase in the worker's productivity justifies the higher labour costs. The optimum occurs at W*, at the tangency between Q/W and g(W; L). This tangency is characterized by

$$\frac{\Delta Q}{\Delta W} = \frac{Q}{W} \text{ or } \frac{\Delta Q}{\Delta W} \times \frac{Q}{W} = 1$$

Notice that this expression implies that profits are maximized when the elasticity of output with respect to the wage is equal to one. The intuition is straightforward. An increase in the wage by 1 percent will increase labour costs by 1 percent, no matter what happens to output. So the firm should increase the wage until the increase in benefits is also 1 percent (i.e., output increases by 1 percent). In summary, as long as the efficiency wage, W^*, is higher than the going wage rate, the firm's optimal wage is independent of labour market conditions. No matter how much a worker offered to work for less, the firm would not want to hire him. Unemployment and rigid wages can co-exist.

A theoretically tighter link between efficiency wages, productivity, and unemployment is provided by Shapiro and Stiglitz (1984). Their model is more applicable to rich industrial economies, and is the basis of most current efficiency wage models. In their model, unemployment serves as a "worker discipline device." Monitoring employee effort is difficult, but if employees are caught shirking, they are fired. The cost to the employee of being fired depends on how long it will take him to find another job that pays as well. Employees are, thus, assumed to work hard when they fear losing their jobs. Their work effort will be greatest when their wage is high relative to the next-best alternative or when unemployment is high. The greater the unemployment rate, the longer the expected search period facing the fired worker, and therefore, the greater the cost of shirking on the present job. The co-existence of unemployment and rigid wages is, thus, maintained by the unwillingness of firms to cut wages because of the adverse work incentives on employees.

Testing whether efficiency wages are an important source of unemployment, let alone whether they exist, has been difficult. One problem is that the standard neoclassical theory also predicts a correlation between wages and productivity ($W = VMP$). It would be difficult to attribute such a correlation to a causal relationship between wages and productivity, at least as an alternative to the neoclassical model. One approach that researchers have taken is to look for evidence of cross-sector differences in wages that cannot be explained by productivity differentials, and that can reasonably be associated with efficiency wage considerations. Some of these results were outlined in Chapter 10, where it was noted that difficulties in controlling for unobserved productivity mean that a neoclassical explanation of the differentials cannot be precluded.

Insider-Outsider Theory

In the presence of excess supply, labour market equilibrium is restored by a decline in the real wage, and vice versa for excess labour demand. Persistent unemployment suggests that this natural equilibrating mechanism is not operating, or not operating sufficiently quickly. For this reason, explanations of persistent unemployment typically focus on the wage determination process, and in particular on reasons wages may not adjust to eliminate excess supply or demand. Both the implicit contract and efficiency wage theories provided explanations for real-wage rigidity and unemployment that are consistent with rational behaviour on the part of employers and employees. **Insider-outsider theory** is another explanation of wage inflexibility and unemployment, one that has received considerable attention, especially in the context of the persistence of high unemployment in several European countries. (References include Lindbeck and Snower 1986, 1987, 1988; Solow 1985.)

The central theme of insider-outsider theory is that wage setting is determined by bargaining between the employer and its existing workforce (the "insiders"), with unemployed workers (the "outsiders") exerting little, if any, influence on the outcome. This view is based on the proposition that it is costly for the firm to replace all or some of its existing workforce with new workers recruited from among the ranks of the unemployed. These costs give incumbent workers bargaining power that they can use to raise their wages, even in the presence of excess labour supply in the form of unemployed workers willing to work at lower wages.

Turnover costs are one potentially important source of insider power. As discussed in Chapter 6, there are often costs associated with recruiting and hiring new workers. There may also be significant costs associated with the dismissal of existing employees (severance pay, requirements for advance notice). Firm-specific training and work experience is another factor giving insiders power over outsiders. As discussed in Chapter 9, in the presence of firm-specific human capital, the employer is not indifferent between an experienced incumbent and an otherwise identical individual without the specific training.

In these circumstances, the fact that there exist unemployed job seekers willing to work at lower wages may not be enough of an incentive for employers to attempt to replace some or all of the existing workforce with new employees.

Another potential source of insider power stressed by Lindbeck and Snower (1988) is the ability of incumbent employees to not co-operate with or even to harass new hires, especially if new hires are replacing otherwise incumbent workers.

Analytically, the insider-outsider theory is similar to wage determination under collective bargaining, as discussed in Chapter 14. Through bargaining between the employer and incumbent insiders, the wage will be set above the market-clearing level, thus generating less employment than would occur in the absence of insider power. This reduced employment in sectors in which workers possess insider power will generate unemployment in the labour market as a whole, unless wages fall enough in other sectors (sectors in which workers do not have insider power, perhaps because turnover costs and firm-specific training are unimportant) to absorb the excess supply.

Insider-outsider theory has been used to explain the persistence of high unemployment combined with substantial real-wage growth among employed workers observed in many European countries since the 1970s. The persistence of unemployment, including the phenomenon of "hysteresis"—according to which the level of unemployment may drift upward or downward rather than tending to return to its natural or equilibrium level—is discussed later in this chapter.

There have been very few attempts to directly test the implications of insider-outsider theory. One exception is provided by Doiron (1995a). In that paper, she examines a set of union contract provisions from the International Woodworkers of America in British Columbia to estimate the implicit weight that insiders (current union members) place on outsiders (potential union members). She rejects the insider-outsider specification, whereby existing union members would prefer increased rents to existing members as opposed to the expansion of membership.

Blanchflower, Oswald, and Sanfey (1996) provide indirect evidence supporting a more general prediction of insider-outsider theory that workers earn rents at all. They examine cross-industry wage differentials in the United States. After controlling for worker demographic and education characteristics, they find that long-run profitability is correlated with wages. Thus, firm "ability to pay" is a significant determinant of wages. As long as individual productivity is fully accounted for, then this evidence is at odds with the purely competitive model and consistent with models emphasizing that some workers earn rents, as in insider-outsider models. However, their paper draws no links between rents and queues of workers to work in the high-paying industries, and provides no evidence linking rents and unemployment.

LO6, 7   Unemployment Insurance and Unemployment

The relationship between unemployment insurance (UI) and unemployment has been the subject of considerable theoretical and empirical research. UI is intended to provide workers with protection against the risk of income loss due to unemployment. However, the UI program may also affect the incidence and duration of unemployment by altering the incentives facing workers and firms. In this section, we examine the influence of UI on labour supply, job search, layoffs, seasonal unemployment, and interregional mobility. A brief description of the main features of Canada's UI system is also provided.

LO6   Economic Rationale for Unemployment Insurance

Because economic circumstances continually change, risk and uncertainty are often present. As discussed previously in the context of implicit contract theory, labour market risks are especially significant because workers are generally unable to diversify their human capital wealth. In addition, comprehensive private insurance markets, which would enable most workers to purchase insurance against the risk of unemployment (and possibly other sources of loss of labour market income), have generally failed to emerge despite the demand that evidently exists for such insurance. According to the economic theory of risk and insurance, this absence of private insurance markets is probably due to moral hazard and adverse selection. In the context of unemployment insurance, moral hazard implies that individuals with insurance are more likely to become or remain unemployed. Adverse selection in this context implies that the purchasers of insurance will be those who are most likely to become unemployed. Knowledge about the probability of becoming unemployed is private information known by the buyer of insurance but not by the seller. Relative to a situation without moral hazard and adverse selection, these two effects reduce the profitability of selling insurance, and may result in a situation in which the sale of insurance is not profitable at any price. For these reasons, the private sector may not provide the socially optimal amount of UI. In the absence of private-sector provision, governments in many countries have introduced unemployment insurance as part of social policy.

Unemployment insurance may also allow unemployed workers and their families to maintain consumption without depleting their assets or accepting jobs unsuited to their skills. Doing so can also yield macroeconomic benefits by acting as an "automatic stabilizer." In the absence of UI, consumption expenditure could decline substantially during economic downturns, reducing aggregate demand and exacerbating the recession. On the other hand, in periods of strong economic growth, the number of unemployed workers declines and contributions by employees and employers to UI will exceed benefits paid, thus acting as a drag on further expansion.

Studies of the impacts of UI on consumption, such as Gruber (1997) and Browning and Crossley (2001), provide strong support for the view that UI facilitates "consumption smoothing" among job losers. The positive effects on consumption are largest among families with no savings and without an employed spouse. As a consequence, UI programs can have important macroeconomic stabilization benefits in addition to those associated with their role of providing insurance against the risks inherent in a market economy.

However, despite these potential microeconomic and macroeconomic benefits, UI can have adverse side effects that lengthen unemployment spells, reduce labour market adjustment, and lower the standard of living. The policy challenge is to design the UI program to protect workers from labour market risks and act as an automatic stabilizer while minimizing undesirable side effects.

The following section briefly reviews the development of Canada's UI system, now called Employment Insurance (EI).

Canada's Unemployment Insurance System

The experience of the Great Depression, when unemployment soared to almost 20 percent (see Figure 16.1) and there was little in the way of a "safety net," led to the creation of publicly provided unemployment insurance in Canada and other countries. Canada's UI system was established in 1940, following the resolution, through a constitutional amendment, of the difficulties that had resulted in an earlier attempt to introduce UI being declared outside the legislative authority of the federal government. Although the federal government initially contributed, the UI fund is currently financed by premiums collected from employers and employees. Coverage is compulsory for those groups that come under the act, a feature that significantly reduces the effects of adverse selection. However, as the empirical evidence reviewed below indicates, moral hazard effects do occur. In most developed countries, moral hazard effects are also reduced by limiting UI eligibility to those who were involuntarily terminated from their job and who continue to be actively searching for work.

Canada's UI system has evolved significantly over time. Between 1940 and 1971 there were gradual enhancements in the eligibility, coverage, and benefit and financing provisions of the UI Act. Dramatic changes to these key features of the act were made in 1971–1972, including a substantial expansion in coverage (including to seasonal workers), an increase in the benefit rate (benefits as a proportion of previous earnings) to 66 percent, a reduction in the minimum period of employment required to qualify for benefits, an increase in the maximum benefit period, and the introduction of extended benefits in regions with high unemployment. With these changes, UI covered a much larger proportion of the labour force (about 90 percent) and became considerably more "generous." It also became regionally differentiated, so that the amount of insurance provided to unemployed workers varies across economic regions, depending on the local unemployment rate. The 1971–1972 changes were partially reversed by subsequent retrenchment and restructuring of the program. Nonetheless, the EI system of today contrasts sharply with that of pre-1971 in terms of coverage and its key features.

The period from 1980 to the mid-1990s saw continued modifications to UI, generally in the direction of reducing the generosity of the program changes that were made in 1971. The reforms of 1989 and 1994, for example, generally increased the qualification period, reduced the benefit rate, and reduced the maximum duration of benefits. One of the side effects of the 1989 change was the subsequent delay of passage of the enacting legislation by the Senate, which provided some limited "exogenous" variation in some of the UI program parameters. This variation was exploited in a number of papers (Green and Riddell 1997; Baker and Rea 1998) discussed in Chapter 3. (See Exhibit 3.1)

The mid-1990s witnessed dramatic changes, partly in response to concerns about the federal government's fiscal situation. In 1996, the Unemployment Insurance program was renamed Employment Insurance (EI), and several key parameters were changed. First, EI qualification became based on hours worked, not weeks. In the past, if an individual worked fewer than 15 hours per week, he or she would not be eligible to collect UI. Similarly, individuals working 15 or 50 hours per week accumulated the same credit toward UI eligibility, a feature that became increasingly questionable given the rise in the incidence of part-time work. The hours of work eligibility requirement continued to be greater in regions where the unemployment rate is lower. In addition, an "intensity rule" was introduced, whereby the replacement rate, while still 55 percent for most workers, was reduced slightly for repeat users. However, this contentious provision was later dropped in response to political opposition from regions (especially the Atlantic provinces) where repeat use of EI is more common.

The EI changes of 1996 were modified in the year 2000, primarily in the direction of relaxing some of the restrictions introduced in the 1996 reforms. Most importantly, the contentious intensity rule was dropped, so that the replacement rate became 55 percent for all beneficiaries, and not reduced for repeat users. The federal government also reduced the clawback of benefits for higher-income beneficiaries, especially those who had made no previous use of UI, or who were collecting maternity or parental benefits in the EI program. This change was part of a larger package of refinements to EI, designed to improve the provisions for maternity and parental benefits.

Compared to other developed countries, especially many in Europe, Canada's EI program is not particularly generous in terms of key parameters, such as the replacement rate and the maximum benefit duration. However, Canada is unusually generous in some respects, such as the treatment of seasonal workers, and relatively stingy in others, such as benefits provided to those with stable labour force attachment prior to job loss. As noted previously in this chapter in the section on displaced workers, much recent evidence indicates that the group who suffer the most from involuntary job loss consists of those who had been employed for a long time. Based on this evidence, the Expert Panel on Older Workers (2008) recommended enhanced EI benefits for job losers with lengthy work histories prior to displacement, a recommendation that was subsequently adopted by the federal government. As a consequence, the EI program currently distinguishes among three types of claimants: frequent claimants (those who had three or more claims in the past five years), long-tenured workers (those who paid into the EI system for at least seven of the past ten years and have received only limited EI benefits in the past five years), and occasional claimants (all others). Some EI regulations differ across these three groups; for example, long-tenured workers have enhanced benefit durations.

In Canada, as in most developed countries, those applying for unemployment benefits are required to register with the EI program and may be required to show evidence of active job search in order to maintain eligibility. They may also have their benefits cut off if they do not accept a "suitable" job offer. For most of the program's history, "suitable employment" was not explicitly defined in legislation and regulations, but it developed over time in the process of adjudicating EI appeals to be defined as a job that pays a comparable wage in the claimant's "usual occupation." In 2012, the federal government introduced new regulations that more explicitly define "suitable employment" both in terms of the range of wages and the commuting distance that are regarded as suitable. These changes appear to be principally directed at seasonal workers and repeat users that turn down employment opportunities in the "off season."

Despite many changes over time in Canada's unemployment compensation system, the program remains controversial and frequently criticized. For a recent assessment of the EI program, see the report of the Mowat Centre EI Task Force (2011) and the research studies carried out for that task force (Banting and Meadow 2012).

On the basis of economic theory, changes in the provisions of the UI system can be expected to affect labour force behaviour in several ways. Indeed, examining the impact of such changes provides a useful test of the theories of unemployment discussed previously in this chapter, and of the analysis of the incentive effects of alternative income maintenance schemes discussed in Chapter 3. UI potentially affects a large number of outcomes, such as the incidence and duration of search unemployment, temporary layoffs, employment instability, seasonal employment, labour force participation and labour supply, and interregional labour market mobility. Since this chapter focuses on the question of unemployment, we will focus the discussion on the effect of UI on search unemployment (incidence and duration) and labour supply. More-detailed surveys of the effects of unemployment insurance can be found in Gunderson and Riddell (2001), Krueger and Meyer (2004), Fredriksson and Holmlund (2006), Tatsiramos and van Ours (2014), and Moffitt (2014).

The Effect of Unemployment Insurance on the Incidence and Duration of Unemployment

Analysis of the relationship between unemployment and UI is complicated by the fact that the UI program has several key parameters, including the benefit rate, the minimum employment period to qualify for benefits, the maximum duration of benefits, the relation between weeks of previous employment and weeks of potential benefits, and the coverage of the labour force. Much of the empirical literature focuses on the consequences of changes in the benefit rate and the maximum duration of benefits, and our discussion reflects this emphasis. However, other program parameters are also important, and we discuss evidence regarding their impacts where this evidence is available.

UI can affect the incidence and duration of search unemployment by altering the costs and benefits of job search. Several cases need to be considered, depending on whether the individual is (1) employed, (2) unemployed and eligible for UI benefits, and (3) not eligible for benefits. For the employed, an increase in the benefit rate makes unemployed search more attractive relative to employed search. As a consequence, the incidence of unemployment is predicted to rise, and evidence appears to support this prediction. Kaliski (1985) notes that the ratio of employed to unemployed search rose sharply following the introduction in 1978–1979 of a reduced benefit rate and tighter qualification requirements.

For the unemployed who are eligible for benefits (because of a previous spell of employment), as shown in an important contribution by Chetty (2008), UI has both a moral hazard effect and a liquidity constraint effect. The former arises because UI benefits lower the marginal cost of search. According to the theory of optimal search, this is predicted to increase the average duration of job search. The liquidity constraint effect arises because, in the absence of UI, unemployed workers with limited assets or other sources of income will need to lower their consumption and possibly take a low-wage job or one unsuited to their skills. Borrowing against their expected future income is generally not feasible. The distinction between these two consequences of unemployment insurance benefits is important because the moral hazard effect is an undesirable side-effect of being insured, whereas the liquidity constraint effect is socially beneficial. Chetty (2008), for example, concludes that almost two-thirds of the additional time spent unemployed by UI recipients is the result of liquidity constraints and inability to borrow against future income.

The prediction that UI benefits lengthen unemployment spells has been extensively tested. In their survey of earlier studies, Krueger and Meyer (2004) conclude that more-generous UI benefits are associated with longer spells of unemployment, with an elasticity of about 1.0 (i.e., a 10 percent increase in benefit levels is associated with a 10 percent increase in unemployment duration). Canadian studies of this UI effect include Beach and Kaliski (1983) and Ham and Rea (1987). Beach and Kaliski use gross flows data and find that the 1978–1979 revisions, which lowered the benefit rate from 67 to 60 percent and tightened qualification requirements, resulted in an increase in the flow from unemployment to employment and a reduced duration of unemployment for all age-sex groups. Ham and Rea, using microdata on the employment and unemployment experience of individuals, find significant effects of UI entitlements on the duration of job search.

In many European countries, unemployment insurance benefits and durations depend on prior work experience (OECD 2007). In Austria, for example, those with less than three years of prior work experience are entitled to 20 weeks of benefits, whereas those with three or more years of previous work experience are entitled to 30 weeks of benefits. In addition, employers that permanently lay off workers with three or more years of job tenure are required to make severance payments. By exploiting these sharp discontinuities at three years of previous work experience and three years of tenure with the employer, Card, Chetty, and Weber (2007b) provide convincing evidence that these features have small to modest effects on the duration of unemployment following displacement. Entitlement to 30 weeks of benefits reduces the job finding rate by 5 percent to 9 percent, compared to workers displaced with less than three years of previous work experience. Similarly, the severance payment associated with reaching the three-year job tenure threshold reduces the job-finding rate by 8 percent to 12 percent. Interestingly, they also find that longer unemployment spells do not result in improved matches in the subsequent job, using both wages and the duration of the re-employment job as measures of job-match quality. Also with Austrian data, Lalive, van Ours, and Zweimuller (2006) exploit a policy change that resulted in some unemployed workers having a higher replacement rate, a second group having longer benefit durations, a third group with both, and a fourth group with neither. They find that a 5 percent increase in the benefit rate resulted in a one-half week increase in unemployment durations. Longer benefit durations also reduced the job-finding rate and lengthened unemployment spells. Consistent with job search theory, the effects of higher replacement rates take place, mainly, early in the unemployment spell, whereas the impacts of benefit duration occur closer to the benefit expiry date.

When UI benefits are exhausted, there is often a "spike" in the probability of leaving unemployment, as first noted in U.S. studies by Moffitt (1985) and Katz and Meyer (1990). This spike is also present in Canadian data (Belzil 1995), and is often interpreted as indicating that unemployed UI recipients search more intensively or become more likely to accept job offers as benefit exhaustion approaches. Some support for this view is provided by Krueger and Mueller (2008) who find, using time-use data, that UI recipients spend more time searching as they get closer to the end of their UI eligibility. However, as pointed out by Card, Chetty, and Weber (2007a), some care is required in interpreting the spike at benefit exhaustion. Some of those who exit unemployment at the end of their UI spell stop searching for work (i.e., withdraw from the labour force) rather than enter employment. The spike in the exit rate from unemployment is larger than the spike in the entry rate into employment.

Among the more convincing bodies of evidence that UI affects search behaviour are the results of Unemployment Insurance Bonus Experiments in the United States, surveyed in Meyer (1995, 1996). Woodbury and Spiegelman (1987) provide the earliest evidence on one specific experiment, conducted in Illinois. In that experiment, UI recipients were offered a $500 bonus if they found a job within 11 weeks and kept the job for at least four months. UI recipients were carefully assigned to treatment (bonus eligible) and control (conventional UI) groups, so that the effect of the bonus could be isolated. Woodbury and Spiegelman found that this bonus program significantly reduced the duration of unemployment, though not enough to offset the cost of paying the bonus. Their basic finding was confirmed in later versions of the experiment, and in those conducted in other states. Thus, while bonuses may not represent a useful policy tool in themselves, the results of the experiments point to the role that incentives play in affecting unemployment duration.

In the United States, the joint federal-state unemployment compensation system normally limits UI benefits to a maximum of 26 weeks. However, during economic downturns, UI maximum benefit durations are often extended because of the difficulty of finding employment during a period of economic weakness. An important part of the policy response to the Great Recession of 2007–2009 and the unusually weak labour market conditions that followed was an unprecedented extension of UI benefits to as much as 99 weeks, and that lasted until 2012. The timing of these extensions varied by state, depending on the level and change in state unemployment rates. Rothstein (2011) and Farber and Valetta (2013) exploit the numerous natural experiments created by the variation in benefit extensions across states and over time to examine the impacts of benefit duration on search activity and re-employment rates. Both studies find small but statistically significant negative impacts on the probability that UI recipients exit unemployment. For example, Rothstein's estimates imply that the UI extensions raised the unemployment rate in 2011 by 0.1 to 0.5 percentage points. Reductions in exit from unemployment can result from two different effects on labour market behaviour: (1) encouraging continued search rather than leaving the labour force, and (2) by reducing re-employment. Although both of these consequences play a role, the Rothstein study and Farber and Valetta study both conclude that most of the effect of extended benefits on unemployment results from reduced exits to nonparticipation; that is, "labelling" those not employed as being unemployed rather than being out of the labour force. Indeed, Farber and Valetta (2013), whose empirical analysis extends to late 2012, conclude that the effects of extended benefits on unemployment occur primarily through a reduction in labour force exits than through lower job-finding, which is more of a policy concern.

Changes in the benefit rate may also affect the search behaviour of those who are not eligible for UI. Such individuals may be entering the labour force for the first time, they may be re-entering after an extended absence from the labour force, they may not have sufficient recent work activity to qualify, they may have quit their previous job, or they may have exhausted their benefits. In these circumstances, it may be rational to accept employment quickly, even temporary work, in order to subsequently qualify for UI benefits—a phenomenon named the "entitlement effect" by Mortensen (1977). In effect, a job has two components: the income received directly, and a "ticket" entitling the worker to benefits in the event of unemployment. In addition to this entitlement effect, there may be spillovers from the unemployed who are UI eligible to the ineligible. Because unemployment benefits reduce search effort among the UI eligible, job seekers not receiving benefits are more likely to find employment. Evidence of this type of externality is found in studies by Levine (1993) for the United States and Lalive, Landais, and Zweimuller (2013) for Austria. Thus, the impact of UI benefits and maximum benefit duration on the overall unemployment rate is smaller than that on the UI eligible, both because not all unemployed workers receive UI and because shorter unemployment spells among the ineligible offset, at least to some extent, longer spells among UI recipients.

In summary, UI affects job search behaviour in several ways. For workers who qualify for UI, a more-generous benefit structure lowers the cost of job search, reduces the job-finding rate, and increases average search duration. It also makes unemployed search more attractive relative to employed search, thus increasing the incidence of unemployment. Empirical evidence generally supports these predictions of the theory of search behaviour. Offsetting these effects to some extent, more-generous benefits can reduce the duration of unemployment spells among those not eligible for UI.

 LO7   The Effect of Unemployment Insurance on Labour Supply

Unemployment insurance also affects employment and unemployment through its impact on labour force participation. This aspect was analyzed in Chapter 3 using the income-leisure choice model, and the reader may wish to review that discussion at this time. The analysis applies to situations in which employees can adjust their weeks of employment and nonemployment in response to the incentives inherent in the EI system. The many individuals for whom a job entails being employed throughout the year do not fit in this category. The relevant group consists of those who work less than a full year, either because the worker is laid off after a certain period of employment or because the job itself is short term in nature, as is the case in much seasonal work.

Our earlier analysis showed that more-generous EI will decrease weeks worked by those who, prior to the change, worked more than the minimum number of weeks required to qualify for benefits, whereas more-generous EI will increase weeks of employment for those who previously did not work enough to qualify. Most of the latter group would have been out of the labour force prior to the change. For these individuals, higher EI benefits make labour force participation sufficiently attractive to obtain at least enough employment to qualify for benefits. (In Chapter 3 we compared equilibriums with and without EI. The analysis of equilibriums with different EI benefit levels is very similar.)

These two responses have offsetting effects on employment, reducing weeks worked by those with relatively strong labour force attachment and increasing weeks worked by those with little or no labour force attachment. Total employment may, therefore, increase or decrease. However, the impact on labour force participation and unemployment is unambiguous. Labour force participation is predicted to rise because of the entry by those who wish to obtain enough work to qualify for EI. Those who previously qualified for benefits do not exit from the labour force, although they do work fewer weeks. Measured unemployment increases for both groups; those who previously qualified for EI because they now spend less time employed and more time unemployed, while those previously not eligible spend more time employed and unemployed and less outside the labour force.

These predictions of the income-leisure choice model refer to desired combinations of employment and nonemployment given the individual's preferences and constraints. Of course, not all workers can achieve their desired allocation of time to work and nonmarket activity, especially in the short run. However, as discussed in Chapter 8, firms have an incentive to offer jobs with more desirable and fewer undesirable characteristics, because doing so reduces the compensating wage that must be paid in equilibrium. Thus, if short-term employment is desirable for some workers, jobs with these features can be expected to emerge. In this way, changes in the EI system may affect not only employee behaviour but also employer behaviour and the structure of labour demand.

A variety of Canadian empirical evidence is available on these labour supply effects. Early studies by Cousineau and Green (1978), Rea (1977), and Sharir and Kuch (1978) found that the 1971–1972 changes to the EI program increased aggregate labour force participation, especially among groups with lower average rates of labour force attachment. Green and Riddell (1993) examine the labour supply effects of EI coverage of older workers, a group generally considered to have a low degree of labour force attachment. In particular, they study the impact of a 1976 change in EI regulations that disenfranchised workers between 65 and 70 years of age, who were covered by the EI program prior to this change. They find that a large proportion of these individuals withdrew from the labour force on the removal of EI eligibility.

Perhaps the most striking evidence of labour supply effects comes from the analysis by Kuhn and Riddell (2010) of the experience of Maine and New Brunswick over the period 1940–1991. The Canada–U.S. border separates Maine and New Brunswick in what is otherwise a relatively homogeneous region: largely rural, a similar resource base, a predominantly white Anglo-Saxon population, and average incomes below the respective national averages. Furthermore, in 1950, the unemployment compensation systems of these two regions were very similar. Subsequently, two major expansions of the Canadian program increased EI generosity substantially in New Brunswick, whereas little change took place in Maine's program. Kuhn and Riddell use a natural experiment methodology to analyze labour supply effects, using Maine as a comparison region to estimate what would have occurred in New Brunswick in the absence of the changes to Canada's EI program. They find large effects of EI on labour supply, measured by weeks worked during the year. For example, by 1990 about 13 percent of working-age men in Maine's northern counties (those near the border with NB) worked part year, versus 26 percent in New Brunswick. Their estimates attribute more than 75 percent of this large difference to the more generous Canadian EI program. The much higher incidence of part-year work in New Brunswick is partly due to an increase in labour supply by those who would otherwise (i.e., in the absence of a generous EI program) not participate in the labour force, and partly due to reduced labour supply by those who would otherwise work more weeks per year.

Repeat use of UI has also attracted the attention of researchers and policymakers. Corak (1993a, 1993b) uses EI administrative data covering the period 1971–1990 to examine patterns of employment and nonemployment among participants in the EI program. He finds a high degree of repeat use of EI. For example, during the latter part of the 1980s, about 80 percent of claimants in any year had previously received EI, with 40 to 50 percent having experienced five or more previous claims. The extent to which this degree of repeat use is due to the structure of labour demand (for example, the importance of seasonal work) or due to individuals adjusting their labour supply to the parameters of the EI program is an important question. Corak (1993b) shows that spell length of unemployment increases with repeat use of EI. Whether this reflects diminished human capital ("destroyed" by the experience of unemployment), repeated and compounding bad luck, or changed search behaviour remains unclear. For instance, Lemieux and MacLeod (2000) present evidence that because people learn how generous the EI system is after a first "exposure" to the system, they are more likely to change their behaviour and use EI repeatedly in the future. Further evidence of individual learning effects is provided by Gray and McDonald (2012) using longitudinal administrative data on individual worker EI claim histories over the period 1980 to 2003. They find that over the span of the first five claims filed by an unemployed worker there is an adjustment process which takes the form of recipients altering their work patterns to maximize benefits from the EI system.

One possible explanation for repeat use is the lack of experience rating, discussed in Chapter 3. Repeat users, and their employers, do not pay actuarially fair EI premiums. The primary objective of the 1996 intensity rule (since abandoned) was to partially rectify this by slightly reducing the benefits of repeat users. At the same time, the government planned a social experiment in order to evaluate the importance of incentives for repeat users to accept longer duration. It was called the Earnings Supplement Project, and was rigorously designed along lines similar to the Self-Sufficiency Project described in Chapter 3. The basic idea was to offer an earnings supplement to repeat EI users, topping up their wages and encouraging them to accept, possibly, lower-paying jobs. The experiment had to be scrapped, as it quickly became apparent that there would be no takers for the supplement. Instead, the budget was directed toward an intensive survey of repeat users: Survey of Repeat Use of Employment Insurance. Results based on this survey indicate that there is considerable heterogeneity within the group of repeat EI users, and so it is unlikely any single explanation or policy response will fit (Social Research and Demonstration Corporation 2001a, 2001b). The evidence from the survey, and the "failure" of the Earnings Supplement Project, is consistent with the view that employers and employees in high-turnover and seasonal industries adjust the terms of employment (job duration and pay) in response to the EI system and its lack of experience rating.

The regional extended benefit structure brought about by the changes made to the UI program in the late 1970s provided a relatively strong incentive for individuals in high-unemployment regions to work at least 10 weeks, and thereby qualify for up to 40 weeks of benefits (after the two-week waiting period). In their study of Canada–U.S. unemployment, Card and Riddell (1993) find evidence that, during the 1980s, Canadians increasingly adjusted their labour supply to the parameters of the UI program. In particular, for both males and females, the distributions of annual weeks of employment show "spikes" at 10 to 14 weeks (the minimum weeks required to qualify for UI), and the magnitudes of these spikes increased during the 1980s. As noted above, such behaviour could arise both because (1) some individuals who would otherwise (i.e., in the absence of UI eligibility) not participate in the labour force would now work for enough weeks to qualify for UI, and (2) some individuals who would otherwise work more weeks would now reduce their labour supply. By comparing the differences in these spikes over time and between Canada and the United States, Card and Riddell (1997) attribute as much as 80 percent of the increased unemployment differential to the increased likelihood that nonemployed individuals report being unemployed in Canada. In turn, the data suggest that the increased unemployment was associated with collection of UI benefits.

While they look at only aggregate measures of unemployment and UI generosity, Milbourne, Purvis, and Scoones (1991) show that by setting benefit levels as a function of the unemployment rate, UI benefits may increase the persistence of unemployment. Their results suggest that the increased generosity of UI and its link to benefits through the unemployment rate can account for most of the divergence of the unemployment rates between Canada and the United States that was observed during the 1980s.

The 1996 changes to Canada's UI program were the most sweeping since the dramatic expansion of the program in the 1970s. Gray (2004) provides a useful survey of the individual studies of these changes. Two key changes involved hours of work—the shift to a system based on hours rather than weeks of work, and the extension of coverage to individuals employed less than 15 hours of work per week. Studies by Green and Riddell (2000), Friesen (2002), and Sweetman (2000) explore the impact of these reforms on UI eligibility and hours of work. The principal conclusion of these studies is that the distribution of hours worked by Canadians changed substantially in response to the reforms. For example, there was a shift away from jobs limited to less than 15 hours per week and towards jobs lasting more than 15 hours per week. This shift suggests that the extension of coverage to all workers, no matter how many hours worked per week, removed a distortion in the labour market, as employers no longer had an incentive to restrict hours worked to less than 15 in order to avoid paying EI premiums. There was also a shift, especially in seasonal industries, toward longer work weeks among those who previously worked less than 40 hours per week. Again, this change suggests that the previous weeks-based system may have distorted hours-of-work decisions, leading workers and employers in seasonal industries to "spread out" the hours worked over sufficient weeks in order to qualify for EI. In terms of eligibility, in principle, using hours instead of weeks could allow more people to become eligible for EI, especially those working fewer than 15 hours per week who were previously ineligible. In fact, there is little evidence of a shift in EI eligibility patterns—the increased eligibility among some workers was offset by reduced eligibility among others. However, the move to an hours-based system had two important effects. First, it distributed EI benefits toward those who could accumulate more hours per week, predominantly men and seasonal workers, and away from part-time workers, predominantly women. Second, because EI entitlement could be accumulated more quickly in high weekly hours seasonal jobs, the average weekly duration of these jobs declined, providing further evidence that firms and workers adjust their terms of employment in response to parameters of the EI system.

In summary, the EI system has numerous effects on labour force behaviour. A substantial amount of empirical research has been devoted to estimating the size of these effects. Although there are some offsetting influences, the overall impact of a more generous EI benefit structure is to increase unemployment. This does not imply that improvements in EI generosity are undesirable or that changes that to some extent "tighten up" the EI program are desirable; rather, it highlights the fact that such changes affect our aggregate unemployment and labour force participation rates and that this should be considered in interpreting these statistics. More generally, the trade-offs inherent in the EI system need to be recognized in the design of EI financing and benefits. The more generous the benefit structure, the greater the insurance value of the program but also the larger the adverse incentive effects and the amount of induced unemployment. Optimal EI design must strike a balance between these social costs and benefits.

Summary

- The primary objective of this chapter is to provide an overview of the variety of theoretical explanations of unemployment, and to evaluate the extent to which UI plays a role in the Canadian unemployment experience. The most important lesson to take away is that unemployment is complex, and no simple explanation is sufficient. A corollary of this is that there is no single policy prescription that economists can provide that will yield "full employment."

- There are many theories of unemployment, but all have a common theoretical thread. In the conventional neoclassical (supply and demand) model, unemployment exists only when some factors prevent the wage from clearing the market. The various theories we review all attempt to provide foundations for unemployment by introducing realistic departures relative to the simple neoclassical model.

- Search theory provides a theory of frictional unemployment, and a model of individual behaviour in the presence of imperfect information. In this case, the imperfect information is incomplete knowledge about jobs that are available and the wages being paid for specific jobs. At the same time, employers with job vacancies face imperfect information about workers seeking employment and the characteristics of those workers.

- Structural unemployment occurs when there is a mismatch between labour demand and labour supply. The mismatch may exist along skill, occupation, or regional dimensions. A related type of unemployment arises when sectoral shifts require workers who lost their job in one sector to find a job in another sector or region of the economy.

- *High-wage unemployment.* Theoretical developments have proposed a number of reasons wages may remain too high in equilibrium once some key assumptions of the competitive model are reconsidered. The approaches we explore are implicit contracts, efficiency wages, and insider-outsider theories.

- *Deficient-demand unemployment and the business cycle.* In the standard Keynesian macroeconomic approach, unemployment is primarily due to cyclical fluctuations in the aggregate demand for labour. This source of unemployment is beyond the scope of this book and is covered in courses in macroeconomics.

- We review the motivation and development of unemployment insurance (UI or EI) in Canada, and evaluate the evidence linking UI to labour market behaviour. Whether one is looking at the impact of UI on the incidence and duration of unemployment, the layoff behaviour of firms, employment stability, labour supply behaviour, or interregional mobility, it is difficult to avoid the conclusion that UI "matters" in contributing to the observed patterns of labour supply and unemployment. However, this does not mean UI is a "bad" program, but merely that its many impacts must be taken into account in program design.

Keywords

adverse selection

asymmetric information

displaced workers

dynamic monopsony

frictional unemployment

implicit contract theory

insider-outsider theory

job search

matching

moral hazard

risk-sharing

sectoral shift hypothesis

stopping rule

structural unemployment

symmetric information

Review Questions

1. Discuss the costs and benefits of job search for younger workers and women. Relate these factors to their expected unemployment duration.

2. Discuss the implications of job search theory for the following phenomena:
    - Unemployment duration
    - The cyclical behaviour of quits
    - Wage rigidity over the business cycle

3. Explain why some job losers find new jobs relatively quickly at wages similar to those in their previous job, while others take longer to become re-employed and often earn much less in their new job. What policies might be implemented for those who experience large losses from job displacement?

4. Discuss the implications of implicit contract theory for the following phenomena:
    - Wage rigidity over the business cycle
    - Labour hoarding
    - Layoffs instead of wage reductions

5. Why don't we observe private insurance companies selling unemployment insurance? How could employers provide such insurance?

6. Discuss the various design features (policy parameters) of UI that can affect the benefits from such insurance, and therefore, the behaviour of recipients. What features of unemployment and other labour market behaviour might be explained, at least partially, by UI?

Problems

1. "Frictional unemployment is optimal." True or false? Discuss.

2. Assume that the productivity of farm labour depends on daily caloric intake, similarly to that depicted in Figure 17.4. Using this kind of diagram, compare the efficiency wages that would apply to the following two types of workers:

   • A landless labourer
   • A labourer with small plot of land on which he grows staple crops

   Describe the likely equilibrium unemployment rates and wage rates for landless labourers and small landholders. Judging partially on the basis of this example, what sorts of data and what empirical strategies might you use to see whether nutritional efficiency wages were an important element in the rural labour markets of poor, rural economies?

3. Assume that the following relationship describes individual productivity as a function of the wage paid:

$$Q = \begin{cases} = 0 & \text{for } W \le \$8 \\ = -20 + 3W - 0.05W^2 & \text{for } \$8 < W < \$30 \\ = 30 & \text{for } W \ge \$30 \end{cases}$$

   a. Plot this relationship, and interpret. *Hint:* You may use a spreadsheet if you wish.

   b. Note that the slope of the efficiency function is given by $\frac{\Delta Q}{\Delta W} = 3 - 0.10W$ in the range $\$8 < W < \$30$.

   Evaluate whether the following wages are profit-maximizing: $10, $20, and $30. Interpret and explain.

4. When examining the frequency distribution for various durations of unemployment, a common feature is a sharply noticeable concentration (or "spike") of individuals who find jobs at the maximum benefit period for UI. In other words, if the maximum number of weeks a person can collect UI is 26 weeks, there is a significant fraction of unemployed workers who find jobs after exactly 26 weeks of unemployment.

   a. Show how a labour supply explanation, similar to that developed in Chapter 3, could account for this pattern.

   b. Show how a search-based explanation could account for this phenomenon.

   c. What type of data and what empirical strategy would you employ to distinguish between the labour supply and search-based explanations?

5. a. Assume that the marginal benefit of a week's job search is given by

   $$MB = a - b \times \text{Weeks}; \ a, b > 0$$

   where "Weeks" is the cumulative number of weeks of searching. What factors will affect the returns to search; that is, what factors will cause a or b to be higher or lower?

   b. Assume, as well, that the marginal cost of a week's job search is given by

   $$MC = c + d \times \text{Weeks}; \ c, d > 0$$

   What factors will affect the marginal cost of search; that is, what factors will cause c or d to be higher or lower?

   c. Solve for the optimal number of weeks of job search for the parameters $a = 35$, $b = 1$, $c = 5$, $d = 1$.

   d. Find a general expression for the optimal number of weeks of search; that is, express the optimal number of weeks of search, W^*, as a function of a, b, c, and d. Use this expression to discuss what happens to W^* if there is an increase in b or an increase in d. Interpret.

6. A firm produces doughnuts in a competitive industry. Demand conditions are such that either it's a hot day and demand is low, or a cold day and demand is high. The firm does not know in advance what the weather will be, but there is a 50-50 chance it could be either (i.e., the probability of each type of day is one-half). If the weather is hot, the zero-profit equilibrium wage to pay its "baker" is $4 for a day; if the weather is cold, the zero-profit equilibrium wage to pay is $16 for the day. The doughnut firm cares only about profits and is risk neutral.

   The baker has a utility function defined over his wage for the day, $u = \sqrt{w}$. Assume that the baker cares only about the expected utility of his wage income.

   Show that the baker and the doughnut shop owner would both be better off (on average) if the firm paid the baker $9.50 irrespective of the weather. Interpret.

7. Illustrate how the adjustment process of Figure 17.6 could arise from a job search process whereby job seekers face a distribution of money wage offers and have an acceptance or reservation wage in money terms. That is, they will continue to remain unemployed and search (sample the distribution of money wage offers) until they receive their reservation wage. Indicate how an increase in aggregate demand and its accompanying increase in the aggregate price level may reduce search unemployment in the short run, but may not reduce it in the long run when the reservation wage adjusts to the inflation.

8. "Any microeconomic theory of behaviour that requires wage rigidities due to such things as unanticipated inflation, wage lags, or money illusion in the collective bargaining or job search process, could explain phenomena only in the short run, not in the long run." Discuss.

Endnotes

1. "UI" is used for convenience to refer to unemployment insurance in general, not a specific program.
2. "Expected earnings" refers to the earnings that would have been experienced without displacement. These are estimated using the outcomes experienced by the comparison group of nondisplaced workers.
3. Note we are conditioning on employment in this presentation. It is not difficult to derive the same conditions allowing the firm to choose both wages and employment.

References

CHAPTER 1

Angrist, J., and J.-S. Pischke. 2014. *Mastering 'Metrics: The Path from Cause to Effect.* Princeton University Press.

Wooldridge, J. M. 2016. *Introductory Econometrics: A Modern Approach,* Sixth Edition. Cincinnati: South-Western College.

CHAPTER 2

Ashenfelter, O., K. Doran, and B. Schaller. 2010. A shred of credible evidence on the long-run elasticity of labour supply. *Economica,* 77(308):637–650.

Biddle, J., and D. Hamermesh. 1990. Sleep and the allocation of time. *JPE* 98 (October):922–43.

Blundell, R., and T. MaCurdy. 1999. Labor supply: A review of alternative approaches. In *Handbook of Labor Economics,* eds. O. Ashenfelter and D. Card. New York and Oxford: Elsevier Science, North-Holland.

Camerer, C., L. Babcock, G. Loewenstein, and R. Thaler. 1997. Labour supply of New York City cabdrivers: One day at a time. *QJE* 112(2):407–41.

Del Boca, D., and A. Lusardi. 2003. Credit market constraints and labor market decisions. *LE* 10:681–703.

Farber, H. S. 2005. Is tomorrow another day? The labour supply of New York City cabdrivers. *JPE* 113(1):16–82.

Farber, H. S. 2015. Why you can't find a taxi in the rain and other labor supply lessons from cab drivers. *QJE* 130(4):1975–2026.

Fortin, N. M. 1995. Allocation inflexibilities, female labor supply, and housing assets accumulation: Are women working to pay the mortgage? *JOLE* 13 (July):524–57.

Hansson, I., and C. Stuart. 1985. Tax revenue, and the marginal cost of public funds in Sweden. *JPubEc* 27 (August):333–53.

Jones, S. R. G., and W. C. Riddell. 1999. The measurement of unemployment: An empirical approach. *Ecta* 67 (January):147–61.

Killingsworth, M. 1983. *Labor Supply.* Cambridge: Cambridge University Press.

Killingsworth, M., and J. Heckman. 1986. Female labor supply: A survey. In *Handbook of Labor Economics,* eds. O. Ashenfelter and R. Layard. New York: Elsevier.

Labour Canada. 1974. Trends in working time. Ottawa: Wages Research Division, Economics and Research Branch.

Oettinger, G. S. 1999. An empirical analysis of the daily labor supply of stadium vendors. *JPE* 107 (April):360–92.

Pencavel, J. 1986. Labor supply of men: A survey. In *Handbook of Labor Economics.* Vol. 1, eds. O. Ashenfelter and R. Layard. New York: Elsevier.

Pencavel, J. 1998. The market work behavior and wages of women: 1975–94. *JHR* 33(4):771–804.

Robbins, L. 1930. On the elasticity of demand for income in terms of effort. *Economica* (June):123–29.

Smith, A. 1776. *The Wealth of Nations.* London: Methuen and Company.

CHAPTER 3

Allen, D. W. 1993. Welfare and the family: The Canadian experience. *JOLE* 11 (Supplement, January):S201–23.

Atkinson, A. B. 1998. Social exclusion, poverty and unemployment. In *Exclusion, Employment and Opportunity,* eds. A. B. Atkinson and J. Hills, Centre for Analysis of Social Exclusion, London School of Economics.

Ashenfelter, O. 1983. Determining participation in income-tested social programs. *JASA* 78 (September):517–25.

Baker, M., J. Gruber, and K. Milligan. 2008. Child care, maternal labor supply, and family well-being. *JPE* 116(4) (August):709–745.

Baker, M., J. Gruber, and K. Milligan. 2015. Non-cognitive deficits and young adult outcomes: The long-run impacts of a universal child care program. NBER Working Paper No 21571.

Baker, M., and S. Rea. 1998. Employment spells and unemployment insurance eligibility requirements. *R.E.Stats* 80 (February):80–94.

Barrett, G. F., and M. I. Cragg. 1998. An untold story: The characteristics of welfare use in British Columbia. *CJE* 31 (February):165–88.

Berg, N., and T. Gabel. Did Canadian welfare reform work? The effects of new reform strategies on social assistance participation. *CJE* 48 (May):494–528.

Besley, T., and R. Kanbur. 1993. The principles of targeting. In *Including the Poor,* eds. M. Lipton and J. van der Gaag. Washington, D. C.: The World Bank.

Blank, R. 2002. Evaluating welfare reform in the United States. *JEL* 40 (December):1105–1166.

Blundell, R. Earned income tax credit policies: Impact and optimality. 2006. *LE* 13:423–443.

Brown, D. M. 1995. Welfare caseload trends in Canada. In *Helping the Poor: A Qualified Case for "Workfare."* Toronto: C. D. Howe Institute.

Charette, M., and R. Meng. 1994. The determinants of welfare participation of female heads of household in Canada. *CJE* 27 (May):290–306.

Christofides, L., T. Stengos, and R. Swidinsky. 1997. Welfare participation and labour market behaviour in Canada. *CJE* 30 (August):595–621.

Christofides, L. N., and C. J. McKenna. 1996. Unemployment insurance and job duration in Canada. *JOLE* 14 (April):286–312.

Dooley, M. 1999. The evolution of welfare participation among Canadian lone mothers, 1973–1991. *CJE* 32 (May):589–612.

Dooley, M., and J. Stewart. 1999. An analysis of changes in welfare participation rates in Ontario

from 1983–1994 using social assistance caseload data. Manuscript. McMaster University.

————. 1999. The duration of spells on welfare and off welfare among lone mothers in Ontario. *CPP* 25 (Supplement, November):S47–72.

Duclos, J.-Y., B. Fortin, G. Lacroix, and H. Roberge. 1998. The dynamics of welfare participation in Quebec. Laval University Working Paper No 9817.

Fortin B., G. Lacroix, and S. Drolet. 2004. Welfare benefits and the duration of welfare spells: Evidence from a natural experiment in Canada. *JPubEc* 88:1495–1520.

Fortin, P. 1995. The future of social assistance in Canada. Manuscript. University of Quebec at Montreal.

Fortin, P., and P.-Y. Cremieux. 1998. The determinants of social assistance rates: Evidence from a panel of Canadian provinces, 1987–1996. Manuscript. University of Quebec at Montreal.

Gottschalk, Peter. 2005. Can work alter welfare recipients' beliefs? *Journal of Policy Analysis and Management* 24(3):485–498.

Green, D. A., and W. C. Riddell. 1997. Qualifying for unemployment insurance: An empirical analysis. *EJ* 107 (January):67–84.

Hum, D., and W. Simpson. 1991. *Income Maintenance, Work Effort, and the Canadian M-income Experiment.* Ottawa: Economic Council of Canada.

Kottelenberg, M., and S. Lehrer. 2013. New evidence on the impacts of access to and attending universal child care in Canada. *CPP* 39(2):263–285.

Kuhn, Peter, and Chris Riddell. The long-term effects of unemployment insurance: Evidence from New Brunswick and Maine, 1940–1991. *ILLR* 63 (January 2010):183–204.

Lacroix, G. 2000. Reforming the welfare system: In search of the optimal policy mix. *In Adopting Public Policy to a Labour Market in Transition,* eds. W. C. Riddell and F. St-Hilaire. Montreal: Institute for Research on Public Policy.

Lemieux, T., and K. Milligan. 2008. Incentive effects of social assistance: A regression discontinuity approach. *Journal of Econometrics* 142(2):807–28.

MaCurdy, Thomas E. 1981. An empirical model of labor supply in a life-cycle setting. *JPE* 89(6):1059–85.

Milligan, K., and M. Stabile. 2007. The integration of child tax credits and welfare: Evidence from the Canadian National Child Benefit program. *JPubEc* 91(1-2) (February):305–326.

Moffitt, R. 2002. Welfare programs and labour supply. In *Handbook of Public Economics,* Vol. 4, eds. A. Auerbach and M. Feldstein.

Moffitt, R., and K. Kehrer. 1981. The effect of tax and transfer programs on labor supply: The evidence from the income maintenance experiments. In *Research in Labor Economics,* ed. R. Ehrenberg. Greenwich, Conn.: JAI Press.

Nichols, A., and J. Rothstein. The Earned Income Tax Credit (EITC). NBER Working Paper No 21211. Cambridge, Mass.: National Bureau of Economic Research.

Phipps, S. 1990. Quantity-constrained household responses to unemployed insurance reform. *EJ* 100 (March):124–40.

——— . 1991. Behavioural response to UI reform in constrained and unconstrained models of labour supply. *CJE* 24 (February):34–54.

Riddell, Chris, and W. Craig Riddell. 2014. The pitfalls of work requirements in welfare-to-work policies: Experimental evidence on human capital accumulation in the Self-Sufficiency Project. *JPubEc* 117:39–49.

Schirle, T. 2015. The effect of universal child benefits on labour supply. *CJE* 48 (May):437–463.

Social Research and Demonstration Corporation. 2000. The Self-Sufficiency Project at 36 months: Effects of a financial work incentive on employment and income.

Social Research and Demonstration Corporation. 2002. Making work pay: Final report on the Self-Sufficiency Project for long-term welfare recipients.

Stocker, G., and M. Ornstein. 2013. Quebec, daycare, and the household strategies of couples with young children. *CPP XXXIX* (2):241–262.

CHAPTER 4

Acemoglu, D., D. Autor, and D. Lyle. 2004. Women, war, and wages: The effect of female labor supply on the wage structure at mid-century. *JPE* 112(3):497–551.

Angrist, J., and W. N. Evans. 1998. Children and their parents' labor supply: Evidence from exogenous variation in family size. *AER* 88 (June):450–77.

Bailey, M. 2006. More power to the pill: The impact of contraceptive freedom on women's life cycle labor supply. *QJE* 121(1):289–320.

Baker, M., and D. Benjamin. 1999. How do retirement tests affect the labour supply of older men? *JPubEc* 71 (January):27–51.

——— . 2000. Public pension programs and attachment to the labour force. In *Adapting Public Policy to a Labour Market in Transition*, eds. F. St-Hilaire and C. Ridell, IRPP.

Beaudry, P., and T. Lemieux. 1999. Evolution of the female labour force participation rate in Canada, 1976–1994: A cohort analysis. *Canadian Business Economics* 7 (May):57–70.

Becker, G. 1960. An economic analysis of fertility. In *Demographic and Economic Change in Developed Countries*. Princeton: Princeton University Press.

——— . 1965. A theory of the allocation of time. *EJ* 75 (September):493–517.

——— . 1976. *The Economic Approach to Human Behavior*. Chicago: University of Chicago Press.

——— . 1989. Malthus was right after all: Poor relief and birth rates in southeastern England. *JPE* (February):93–114.

Card, D. 1994. Intertemporal labour supply: An assessment. In *Advances in Econometrics: The Sixth World Congress*, ed. C. A. Sims. New York: Cambridge University Press.

Dooley, M. D. 1994. The converging market work patterns of married mothers and lone mothers in Canada. *JHR* 29:600–20.

Fernandez, R., A. Fogli, and C. Olivetti. 2004. Mothers and sons: Preference formation and female labor force dynamics. *QJE* 119 (4):1249–99.

Goldin, C. 1990. *Understanding the Gender Gap: An Economic History of American Women*. New York: Oxford University Press.

Goldin, C., and L. Katz. 2002. The power of the pill: Oral contraceptives and women's career and marriage decisions. *JPE* 110(4):730–70.

Goldin, C. 1995. The U-shaped female labor force function in economic development and economic history. In *Investment in Women's Human Capital*, ed. T. P. Schultz. Chicago and London: University of Chicago Press.

Goldin, C., and C. Olivetti. 2013. Shocking labor supply: A reassessment of the role of World War II on women's labor supply. *AER* 103(3):257–262.

Gomez, R., and M. Gunderson. 2011. For whom the retirement bell tolls: Accounting for changes in the expected age of retirement and the incidence of mandatory retirement in Canada. *CPP* 37(4):513–539.

Greenwood, J., A. Seshadri, and M. Yorukoglu. 2005. Engines of liberation. *R. E. Studies* (January):109–33.

Gruber, J., and D. Wise, Eds. 1999. *Social Security and Retirement Around the World*. Chicago and London: NBER Conference Report Series. University of Chicago Press.

Hotz, V. J., J. A. Klerman, and R. J. Willis. 1997. The economics of fertility in developed countries. In *Handbook of Population and Family Economics*, eds. M. R. Rosenzweig and O. Stark. Amsterdam, New York, and Oxford: Elsevier Science, North-Holland.

Hyatt, D., and W. Milne. 1991a. Can public policy affect fertility? *CPP* 17:77–85.

——— . 1991b. Countercyclical fertility in Canada: Some empirical results. *Canadian Studies in Population* 18:1–16.

Lancaster, K. 1966. A new approach to consumer theory. *JPE* (January):132–57.

Lazear, E. 1986. Retirement from the labor force. In *Handbook of Labor Economics*, eds. O. Ashenfelter and R. Layard. New York: Elsevier Science.

Lumsdaine, R., and O. S. Mitchell. 1999. New developments in the economic analysis of retirement. In *Handbook of Labor Economics*, eds. O. Ashenfelter and D. Card. New York and Oxford: Elsevier Science, North Holland.

McElroy, M., and D. Yang. 2000. Carrots and sticks: Fertility effects of China's population policies. *AER* 90 (May):389–92.

Milligan, K. 2005. Subsidizing the stork: New evidence on tax incentives and fertility. *R.E.Stats* 87(3):539–55.

Mincer, J. 1963. Market prices, opportunity costs, and income effects. In *Measurement in Economics: Studies in Mathematical Economics and Econometrics in Memory of Yehuda Grunfeld*, eds. C. Chris et al. Stanford, Calif.: Stanford University Press.

Montgomery, M. R., and J. Trussell. 1986. Models of marital status and childbearing. In *Handbook of Labor Economics*, eds. O. Ashenfelter and R. Layard. New York: Elsevier Science.

Oral contraceptives: The liberator. 1999. *The Economist* (December 31).

Phipps, S. 1998. What is the income "cost of a child"? Exact equivalence scales for Canadian two-parent families. *R.E.Stats* 80 (February):157–64.

Schultz, T. P. 1997. Demand for children in low income countries. In *Handbook of Population and Family Economics*, eds. M. R. Rosenzweig and O. Stark. Amsterdam, New York, and Oxford: Elsevier Science, North-Holland.

Schultz, T. P., and Y. Zeng. 1995. Fertility of rural China: Effects of local family planning and health programs. *Journal of Population Economics* 8 (November):329–50.

——— . 1999. The impact of institutional reform from 1979 through 1987 on fertility in rural China. *China Economic Review* 10 (Fall):141–60.

Whyte, M., W. Feng, and Y. Cai. 2015. Challenging myths about China's one-child policy. *The China Journal* 74: 144–159.

CHAPTER 5

Autor, D. H., D. Dorn, and G. H. Hanson. 2013. The China Syndrome: Local labor market effects of import competition in the United States. *AER* 103 (October):2121–68.

Bank of Canada. 2011. Monetary Policy Report, January. Available at www.bankofcanada.ca/en/mpr/pdf/2011/mprjan11.pdf.

Beaulieu, E. 2000. The Canada–U.S. Free Trade Agreement and labour market adjustment in Canada. *CJE* 33 (May):540–63.

Betcherman, G., and M. Gunderson. 1990. Canada–U.S. free trade and labour relations. *Labour Law Journal* 41 (August):454–560.

Card, D. 1990. Unexpected inflation, real wages, and employment determination in union contracts. *AER* 80 (September):669–88.

Currie, J. 1991. Employment determination in a unionized public-sector labour market: The case of Ontario's school teachers. *JOLE* 9 (November):45–66.

Gaston, N., and D. Trefler. 1994. The role of international trade and trade policy in the labour markets of Canada and the United States. *World Economy* 17 (January):45–62.

——— . 1997. The labour market consequences of the Canada–U.S. free trade agreement. *CJE* 30 (February):18–41.

Gordon, S. 1996. Using mixtures of flexible forms to estimate factor demand elasticities. *CJE* 29 (August):717–36.

Hamermesh, D. 1986. The demand for labor in the long run. In *Handbook of Labor Economics*, eds. O. Ashenfelter and R. Layard. New York: Elsevier.

——— . 1993. *Labor Demand*. Princeton: Princeton University Press.

Hicks, J. R. 1963. *The Theory of Wages*. New York: Macmillan.

Johnson, G., and F. Stafford. 1999. The labor market implications of international trade. *In Handbook of Labor Economics,* eds. O. Ashenfelter and D. Card. New York and Oxford: Elsevier Science, North Holland.

Lemieux, T., W. B. MacLeod, and D. Parent. 2009. Performance pay and wage inequality. *QJE* 124 (February):1–49.

Lichter, A., A. Peichl, and S. Siegloch, S. 2015. The own-wage elasticity of labor demand: A meta-regression analysis. *European Economic Review* 80 (November):94–119.

Melitz, M. J., and D. Trefler. 2012. Gains from trade when firms matter. *JEP* 26 (Spring):91–118.

Nagatani, K. 1978. Substitution and scale effects in factor demands. *CJE* 11 (August):521–526.

Townsend, J. 2007. Do tariff reductions affect the wages of workers in protected industries? Evidence from the Canada–U.S. Free Trade Agreement. *CJE* 40(February):69–92.

Trefler, D. 2004. The long and short of the Canada–U.S. free trade agreement. *AER* 94 (September):870–895.

———. 2010. Canadian policy responses to offshore outsourcing. *In Offshore Outsourcing: Capitalizing on Lessons Learned,* ed. D. Trefler. Toronto and Ottawa: Rotman School of Management and Industry Canada.

CHAPTER 6

Aizcorbe, A. M. 1992. Procyclical labour productivity, increasing returns to labour and labour hoarding in car assembly plant employment. *EJ* 102 (July):860–73.

Buchmueller, T. C. 1999. Fringe benefits and the demand for part-time workers. *Applied Economics* 31 (May):551–63.

Cahuc, P., and S. Carcillo. 2010. Is short-time work a good method to keep unemployment down? *Nordic Economic Policy Review,* forthcoming.

Chemin, M., and E. Wasmer. 2009. Using Alsace-Moselle local laws to build a difference-in-differences estimation strategy of the employment effects of the 35-hour workweek regulation in France. *JOLE* 27 (October):487–524.

Crépon, B., and F. Kramarz. 2002. Employed 40 hours or not employed 39: Lessons from the 1982 mandatory reduction of the workweek. *JPE* 110 (December):1355–1389

Doiron, D. J., and G. F. Barrett. 2001. Working part time: By choice or by constraint? *CJE* 34 (November):1042–65.

Friesen, J. 2001. Overtime pay regulations and weekly hours of work in Canada. *Labour Economics* 8 (December):691–720.

Government of Canada. 2002. *Achieving Excellence: Investing in People, Knowledge and Opportunity.* Ottawa: Industry Canada. Available at www.innovationstrategy.gc.ca.

Gray, D. M. 1998. When might a distressed firm share work? Evidence from the short-time compensation programme in France. *British Journal of Industrial Relations* 36 (March):43–72.

———. 2000. The work sharing program in Canada: A feasible alternative to layoffs? C. D. Howe Institute Commentary, No 146.

Hamermesh, D. S. 1993. *Labor Demand.* Princeton: Princeton University Press.

———. 1989. Labour demand and the structure of adjustment costs. *AER* 79 (September):674–89.

———. 1995. Labour demand and the source of adjustment costs. *EJ* 105 (May):620–34.

Hamermesh, D. S., and G. A. Pfann. 1996. Adjustment costs in factor demand. *JEL* 34 (September):1264–92.

Hart, R. A. 1984. *The Economics of Non-wage Labor Costs.* London: Allen and Unwin.

———. 1987. *Working Time and Employment.* Boston: Allen & Unwin.

Hijzen, A., and D. Venn. 2011. The role of short-time work schemes during the 2008–09 recession. OECD Social, Employment and Migration Working Papers, No 115, OECD Publishing.

Houseman, S. N. 2001. Why employers use flexible staffing arrangements: Evidence from an establishment survey. *ILRR* 55 (October):149–70.

Huberman, M., and R. Lacroix. 1996. Le partage de l'emploi: Solution au chômage ou frein à l'emploi? Sainte-Foy: Les Presses de l'Université Laval.

Katz, L. F., and A. B. Krueger. 2016. The Rise and Nature of Alternative Work Arrangements in the United States, 1999–2015. Princeton and Harvard University, March.

Oi, W. 1962. Labour as a quasi-fixed factor. *JPE* 70 (December):538–55.

Rice, P. G. 1990. Relative labour costs and the growth of part-time employment in British manufacturing industries. *EJ* 100 (December):1138–46.

Rosen, S. 1968. Short-run employment variation in class I railroads in the U.S., 1937–1964. *Ecta* 36 (October):511–29.

Skuterud, M. 2007. Identifying the potential of work-sharing as a job-creation strategy. *JOLE* 25 (April):265–87.

CHAPTER 7

Alesina, A., E. Glaeser, and B. Sacerdote. 2005. Work and leisure in the U.S. and Europe: Why so different? *NBER Macroeconomics Annual,* eds. M. Gertler and K. Rogoff. Cambridge: MIT Press.

Allegretto, S., A Dube, and M. Reich. 2011. Do minimum wages really reduce teen employment? Accounting for heterogeneity and selectivity in state panel data. *IR* 50 (April):205–240.

Baker, M. 2005. Minimum wages and human capital investments of young workers: Work related training and school enrollment. Skills Research Initiative Paper 2005-B04. Ottawa: Human Resources Development Canada.

Baker, M., D. Benjamin, and S. Stanger. 1999. The highs and lows of the minimum wage effect: A time-series cross-section study of the Canadian law. *JOLE* 17 (April):318–50.

Beach, C., and M. G. Abbott. 1997. The impact of employer payroll taxes on employment and wages: Evidence for Canada, 1970–1993. In *Transition and Structural Change in the North*

American Labour Market, eds. M. G. Abbott, C. Beach, and R. P. Chaykowski. Kingston: IRC Press.

Beach, C., Z. Lin, and G. Picot. 1996. What has happened to payroll taxes in Canada over the last three decades? *Canadian Tax Journal* 44:1052–77.

Benjamin, D. 2001. Minimum wages in Canada. *In Labor Market Policies in Canada and Latin America: Challenges of the New Millenium,* ed. A. Berry. Norwell, Massachusetts: Kluwer Academic Publisher.

Blanchflower, D. G., A. J. Oswald, and P. Sanfey. 1996. Wages, profits, and rent-sharing. *QJE* 111 (February):227–51.

Boal, W. M., and M. R. Ransom. 1997. Monopsony in the labor market. *JEL* 35 (March):86–112.

Brochu, P., and D. A. Green. 2013. The impact of minimum wage on labour market transitions. *EJ* 123 (December):1203–35.

Brown, C. 1995. Myth and measurement: The new economics of the minimum wage: Review symposium: Comment. *ILRR* 48 (July):828–30.

———. 1999. Minimum wages, employment, and the distribution of income. *In Handbook of Labor Economics,* eds. O. Ashenfelter and D. Card. New York and Oxford: Elsevier Science, North Holland.

Brown, C., C. Gilroy, and A. Kohen. 1982. The effect of the minimum wage on employment and unemployment. *JEL* 20 (June):487–528.

Burkhauser, R. V., K. Couch, and A. Glenn. 1996. Public policies for the working poor: The earned income tax credit versus minimum wage legislation. In *Research in Labor Economics,* ed. S. Polachek. Greenwich, Conn: JAI Press.

Burkhauser, R. V., and T. A. Finegan. 1989. The minimum wage and the poor: The end of a relationship. *Journal of Policy Analysis and Management* 8 (Winter):53–71.

Campolieti, M., T. Fang, and M. Gunderson. 2005. Minimum wage impacts on youth employment transitions, 1993–1999. *CJE* 38 (February):81–104.

Campolieti, M., M. Gunderson, and B. Lee. 2012. The (non) impact of minimum wages on poverty: Regression and simulation evidence for Canada. *JLR* 33 (September):287–302.

Campolieti, M., M. Gunderson, and C. Riddell. 2006. Minimum wage impacts from a pre-specified research design: Canada, 1981–1997. *IR* 45 (April):195–216.

Card, D., and A. B. Krueger. 1994. Minimum wages and employment: A case study of the fast-food industry in New Jersey and Pennsylvania. *AER* 84 (September):772–93.

Card, D., and A. B. Krueger. 1995. *Myth and Measurement: The New Economics of the Minimum Wage.* Princeton: Princeton University Press.

———. 2000. Minimum wages and employment: A case study of the fast-food industry in New Jersey and Pennsylvania: Reply. *AER* 90 (December):1397–1420.

Currie, J. 1991. Employment determination in a unionized public-sector labour market: The case of Ontario's school teachers. *JOLE* 9 (November):45–66.

Dahlby, B. G. 1993. Payroll taxes. In *Business Taxation in Ontario,* ed. A. Maslove. Toronto: University of Toronto Press.

Davis, S. J., and M. Henrekson. 2005. Tax effects on work activity, industry mix and shadow economy size: Evidence from rich-country comparisons. In *Labour Supply and Incentives to Work in Europe,* eds. R. Gomez Salvador, A. Lamo, B. Petrongolo, M. Ward, and E. Wasmer. Cheltenhan, UK, and Northampton, MA: Edward Elgar Press.

Dube, A., T. W. Lester, and M. Reich. 2010. Minimum wage effects across state borders: Estimates using contiguous counties. *R.E.Stats* 92 (November):945–64.

Ehrenberg, R. G. 1995. Myth and measurement: The new economics of the minimum wage: Review symposium: Editor's introduction. *ILRR* 48 (July):827–28.

Fortin, N. M., and T. Lemieux. 2015. Changes in wage inequality in Canada: An interprovincial perspective. *CJE* 48 (May):682–713.

Freeman, R. B. 1995. Myth and measurement: The new economics of the minimum wage: Review symposium: Comment. *ILRR* 48 (July):830–34.

Goldberg, M., and D. Green. 1999. Raising the floor: The economic and social benefits of minimum wages in Canada. Canadian Centre for Policy Alternatives.

Green, D. 2015. The case for increasing the minimum wage: What does the academic literature tell us? Canadian Centre for Policy Alternatives.

Grenier, G., and M. Seguin. 1991. L'incidence du salaire minimum sur le marché du travail des adolescents au Canada: Une reconsidération des resultats empiriques. (The impact of the minimum wage on the labour market of teenagers in Canada: A reconsideration of the empirical results. With English summary.) *L'Actualité Économique* 67 (June):123–43.

Gruber, J. 1997. The incidence of payroll taxation: Evidence from Chile. *JOLE* 15 (Supplement, July):S72–101.

Hamermesh, D. S. 1993. *Labor Demand.* Princeton: Princeton University Press.

———. 1995. Myth and measurement: The new economics of the minimum wage: Review symposium: Comment. *ILRR* 48 (July):835–38.

Hill, J. R., and W. Spellman. 1983. Professional baseball: The reserve clause and salary structure. *IR* 22 (Winter):1–19.

Jones, J. C. H., and W. D. Walsh. 1988. Salary determination in the National Hockey League: The effects of skills, franchise characteristics, and discrimination. *ILRR* 41 (July):592–604.

Kesselman, J. 1996. Payroll taxes in the finance of Social Security. *CPP* 22 (June):162–79.

Lazear, E. P. 1995. *Personnel Economics.* Cambridge, Massachusetts: MIT Press.

Lin, Z. 2000. Payroll taxes in Canada revisited: Structure, statutory parameters, and recent trends. *Canadian Tax Journal* 48:577–625.

Manning, A. 2003. *Monopsony in Motion: Imperfect Competition in Labour Markets.* Princeton and Oxford: Princeton University Press.

Mascella, A., S. Teja, and B. S. Thompson. 2009. Minimum wages as an anti-poverty policy in Ontario. *CPP* 35 (September):373–79.

Matsudaira, J. 2014. Monopsony in the low-wage labor market? Evidence from minimum nurse staffing regulations. *R. E. Stats* 96 (March):92–102.

Merrifield, J. 1999. Monopsony power in the market for teachers: Why teachers should support market-based education reform. *JLR* 20 (Summer):377–91.

Neumark, D., and W. Wascher. 2000. Minimum wages and employment: A case study of the fast-food industry in New Jersey and Pennsylvania: Comment. *AER* 90 (December):1362–96.

Osterman, P. 1995. Myth and measurement: The new economics of the minimum wage: Review symposium: Comment. *ILRR* 48 (July):839–42.

Prescott, E. C. 2004. Why do Americans work so much more than Europeans? *Federal Reserve Bank of Minneapolis Quarterly Review* 28 (July):2–13.

Putnam, R. D. 2000. *Bowling Alone: The Collapse and Revival of American Community.* New York: Simon & Schuster.

Ransom, M. R. 1993. Seniority and monopsony in the academic labor market. *AER* 83 (March):221–33.

———, and D.P. Sims. 2010. Estimating the firm's labor supply curve in a "new monopsony" framework: Schoolteachers in Missouri. *JOLE* 28 (April):331–355.

Schaafsma, J., and W. Walsh. 1983. Employment and labour supply effects of the minimum wage: Some pooled time-series estimates from Canadian provincial data. *CJE* 16 (February):86–97.

Scully, G. 1995. *The Market Structure of Sports.* Chicago: The University of Chicago Press.

Sen, A., K. Rybczynski, and C. Van De Waal. 2011. Teen employment, poverty, and the minimum wage: Evidence from Canada. *LE* 18 (January):36–47.

Shannon, M., and C. M. Beach. 1995. Distributional employment effects of Ontario minimum-wage proposals: A microdata approach. *CPP* 21:284–303.

Staiger, D., J. Spetz, and C. Phibbs. 2010. Is there monopsony in the labour market? Evidence from a natural experiment. *JOLE* 28 (April):211–236.

Stigler, G. 1946. The economics of minimum wage legislation. *AER* 36 (June):358–65.

Sullivan, D. 1989. Monopsony power in the market for nurses. *Journal of Law and Economics* 32 (October):S135–78.

Swidinsky, R. 1980. Minimum wages and teenage unemployment. *CJE* 13 (February):158–70.

Thornton, R. J. 2004. Retrospectives: How Joan Robinson and B. L. Hallward named monopsony. *JEP* 18 (Spring):257–61.

Welch, F. 1995. Myth and measurement: The new economics of the minimum wage: Review symposium: Comment. *ILRR* 48 (July):842–49.

Wellington, A. 1991. Effects of the minimum wage on the employment status of youths. *JHR* 26 (Winter):27–46.

CHAPTER 8

Adams, J. 1985. Permanent differences in unemployment and permanent wage differentials. *QJE* 100 (February):29–56.

Adams, S. 2007. Health insurance and market reform. *JPubEc* 91(5–6):1119–1133.

Albouy, D., and C. Warman. 2013. Quality of life, firm, productivity, and the value of amenities across Canadian cities. *CJE* 46(2):379–411.

Aldy, J., and K. Viscusi. 2008. Adjusting the value of a statistical life for age and cohort effects. *R.E. Stats* 90(3):573–581.

Arunachalam, R., and M. Shah. 2012. Compensated for life: Sex work and disease risk. *JHR* 48(2):345–369.

Ashenfelter, O., and J. Abowd. 1981. Anticipated unemployment, temporary layoffs, and compensating wage differentials. In *Studies in Labour Markets,* ed. S. Rosen. Chicago: University of Chicago Press.

Ashenfelter, O., and M. Greenstone. 2004a. Using mandated speed limits to measure the value of a statistical life. *JPE* (February):S226–67.

Ashenfelter, O., and M. Greenstone. 2004b. Estimating the value of a statistical life: The importance of omitted variables and publication bias. *AER* 94 (May):454–60.

Averett, S., H. Bodenhorn, and J. Staigiunas. 2005. Unemployment risk and compensation in New Jersey manufacturing. *EI* 43 (October):734–739.

Baugman, R., D. DiNardi, and D. Holtz-Eakin. 2003. Productivity and wage effects of "family friendly" fringe benefits. *IJM* 24:247–259.

Bloom, N., J. Liang, J. Roberts, and J. Ying. 2015. Does working from home work? Evidence from a Chinese experiment. *QJE* 130(1):165–218.

Bonhomme, S., and G. Jolivet. 2008. The pervasive absence of compensating differentials. *Journal of Applied Econometrics* 24(5):763–95.

Brown, C. 1980. Equalizing differences in the labour market. *QJE* 94 (February):113–34.

Cousineau, J. M., R. Lacroix, and A. M. Girard. 1992. Occupational hazard and wage compensating differentials. *R.E.Stats* 74 (February):166–69.

Cropper, M., J. Hammitt, and L. Robinson. 2011. *Valuing Mortality Risk Reductions.* Washington, DC: Resources for the Future.

DeLeire, T., and H. Levy. 2004. Worker sorting and the risk of death on the job. *JOLE* 22(4):925–54.

Duncan, G., and B. Holmlund. 1983. Was Adam Smith right after all? Another test of the theory of compensating wage differentials. *JOLE* 1(4):366–379.

Ehrenberg, R. 1980. Retirement system characteristics and the compensating wage differentials in the public sector. *ILRR* 33 (July):470–84.

Ehrenberg, R., and P. Schumann. 1984. Compensating wage differentials for mandatory overtime. *EI* 22 (October):460–78.

Eriksson, T., and N. Kristensen. 2014. Wages of fringes? Some evidence on trade-offs and sorting. *JOLE* 32(4):899–928.

Farber, H. S., and H. Levy. 2000. Recent trends in employer-sponsored health insurance coverage:

Are bad jobs getting worse? *Journal of Health Economics* 19 (January):93–119.

Felfe, C. 2012. The motherhood wage gap—What about job amenities? *LE* 19(1):56–57.

Felfe, C. 2012. The willingness to pay for job amenities: Evidence from mothers' return to work. *ILRR* 65(2):427–454.

Fernandez, R., and C. Nordman. 2009. Are there pecuniary compensations for working conditions? *LE* 16:194–207.

Garen, J. 1998. Compensating wage differentials and the endogeneity of job riskiness. *R.E.Stats* 70 (February):9–16.

Gertler, P., M. Shah, and S. Bertozzi. 2005. Risky business: The market for unprotected commercial sex. *JPE* 113(3):518–50.

Goddeeris, J. H. 1988. Compensating differentials and self-selection: An application to lawyers. *JPE* 96 (April):411–28.

Goucher, J., and W. Horrace. 2012. The value of life: Real risks and safety-related productivity in the Himalaya. *LE* 19:27–32.

Gronberg, T., and W. R. Reed. 1994. Estimating workers' marginal willingness to pay for job attributes using duration data. *JHR* 29(3):911–31.

Gruber, J. 1994. The incidence of mandated maternity benefits. *AER* 84:622–641.

Gruber, J., and A. Krueger. 1991. The incidence of mandated employer-provided insurance: Lessons from workers' compensation insurance. In *Tax Policy and the Economy* 5:111–144. MA: MIT Press.

Gunderson, M., and D. Hyatt. 1996. Do injured workers pay for reasonable accommodation? *ILRR* 50 (October):92–104.

———. 2001. Workplace risks and wages: Canadian evidence from alternative models. *CJE* 34 (May):377–95.

Gunderson, M., D. Hyatt, and J. Pesando. 1992. Wage-pension trade-offs in collective arguments. *ILRR* 46 (October):146–60.

Guo, X., and J. Hammitt. 2009. Compensating wage differentials with unemployment: Evidence from China. *Environment Resource Economics* 42:187–209.

Hamermesh, D. S. 1999. Changing inequality in markets for workplace amenities. *QJE* 114 (November):1085–123.

Hatton, T., and J. Williamson. 1991. Unemployment, employment contracts, and compensating wage differentials: Michigan in the 1890s. *JEH* 51 (September):605–32.

Heywood, J., W. S. Siebert, and X. Wei. 2007. The implicit cost of family friendly work practices. *Oxford Economic Papers* 59:275–300.

Hintermann, B., A. Alberni, and A. Markandya. 2010. Estimating the value of safety with labour market data: Are the results trustworthy? *Applied Economics* 42(7–9):1085–1100.

Hwang, H.-S., W. R. Reed, and C. Hubbard. 1992. Compensating wage differentials and unobserved productivity. *JPE* 100 (August):835–58.

Johnston, C., C. Callón, K. Li, E. Wood, and T. Kerr. 2010. Offer of financial incentives for unprotected sex in the context of sex work. *Drug and Alcohol Review* 29(2):144–49.

Jones-Lee, M. 1989. *The Economics of Safety and Physical Risk*. Oxford: Basil Blackwell.

Kniesner, T., and J. Leeth. 2010. Hedonic wage equilibrium: Theory, evidence and policy. *Foundations and Trends in Microeconomics* 5(4):1–67.

Kniesner, T., K. Viscusi, and J. Ziliak. 2010. Policy relevant heterogeneity in the value of a statistical life: New evidence from panel data from quantile regressions. *Journal of Risk and Uncertainty* 40(1):15–31.

Kostiuk, P. F. 1990. Compensating differentials for shift work. *JPE* 98 (October):1054–75.

Leigh, J. P. 1986. Are compensating wages paid for time spent commuting. *AER* 18 (November):1203–13.

Leonardi, M., and G. Pica. 2013. Who pays for it? The heterogeneous wage effects of employment protection legislation. *EJ* 123 (December):1236–1278.

Li, E. H. 1986. Compensating differentials for cyclical and noncyclical unemployment: The interaction between investors' and employees' risk aversion. *JOLE* 4 (April):277–300.

Lluis, S., and J. Abraham. 2013. The wage-health insurance trade-off and worker selection: Evidence from the medical expenditure panel survey 1997 to 2006. *IR* 52(2):541–581.

Martinello, F., and R. Meng. 1992. Workplace risks and the value of hazard avoidance. *CJE* 25 (May):333–45.

Meng, R. 1989. Compensating differentials in the Canadian labour market. *CJE* 22 (May):413–24.

Meng, R., and D. Smith. 1990. The valuation of risk of death in public sector decision making. *CPP* 16 (June):137–44.

Miller, R. Jr. 2004. Estimating the compensating differential for employer-Provided health insurance. *International Journal of Health Care Finance and Economics* 4(1):27–41.

Montgomery, E., K. Shaw, and Benedict. 1992. Pensions and wages: an hedonic price theory approach. *IER* 33:111–128.

Moore, M., and W. K. Viscusi. 1990. *Compensation Mechanisms for Job Risks*. Princeton: Princeton University Press.

Morrisey, M. 2002. Why do employers do what they do compensating differentials. *International Journal of Health Care Finance and Economics* 1:195–201.

Moretti, E. 2000. Do wages compensate for the risk of unemployment? *Journal of Risk and Insurance* 20:45–66.

Mulalic, I., J. Van Ommeren, and N. Pilegaard. Wages and commuting: Quasi-natural experiments' evidence from firms that relocate. *EJ* 124:1086–1105.

Murphy, K., and R. Topel. 1987. Unemployment, risk and earnings. In *Unemployment and Its Structure of Labour Markets,* eds. K. Lang and J. Leonard. Oxford: Basil Blackwell.

Olson, C. 2002. Do workers accept lower wages in return for health benefits? *JOLE* 20(2):S91–S114.

Oyer, P. 2008. Salary or benefits? *Research in Labor Economics* 28:429–467.

Pierce, B. 2001. Compensation inequality. *QJE* 116 (November):1493–1525.

Powell, D. 2012. Compensating differentials and income taxes: Are the wages of Dangerous jobs more responsive to tax changes than the wages of safe jobs? *JHR* 47(4):1023–1054.

Rosen, S. 1986. The theory of equalizing differences. In *Handbook of Labor Economics,* Vol. 1. eds. O. Ashenfelter and R. Layard. Amsterdam: Elsevier.

Ruhm, C. 1998. The economic consequences of parental leave mandates: Lessons from Europe. *QJE* 113:285–317.

Sandy, R., and R. Elliott. 2005. Long-term illness and wages. *JHR* 40(3):744–768.

Schiller, B., and R. Weiss. 1980. Pensions and wages: A test for equalizing differences. *R.E.Stats.* 62 (November):529–38.

Shiller, R. 2005. Behavioral economics and institutional innovation. Yale University Cowles Foundation Discussion Paper No 1499.

Shogren, J., and T. Stamland. 2002. Skill and the value of life. *JPE* 110(5):1168–1173.

Smith, A. 1776. *The Wealth of Nations.* London: Methuen and Company.

Smith, R. S. 1981. Compensating differentials for pensions and underfunding in the public sector. *R.E.Stats* 63 (August):463–67.

Thaler, R., and S. Rosen. 1975. The value of saving a life: Evidence from the labor market. In *Household Production and Consumption,* ed. N. Terleckyj. New York: National Bureau of Economic Research.

Topel, R. H. 1984. Equilibrium earnings, turnover, and unemployment: New evidence. *JOLE* 2 (October):500–22.

Viscusi, W. K. 1993. The value of risks to life and health. *JEL* 31 (December):1912–46.

Viscusi, K., and J. Aldy. 2007. Labor market estimates of the senior discount for the value of statistical life. *Journal of Environmental Economics and Management* 53:377–392.

Viscusi, K., and J. Hersch. 2001. Cigarette smokers as job risk takers. *R.E.Stats* 83:269–280.

CHAPTER 9

Acemoglu, D., and J. Angrist. 2001. How large are human capital externalities? Evidence from compulsory schooling laws. *NBER Macroeconomics Annual* 2000.

Acemoglu, D., and D. H. Autor. 2010. Skills, tasks, and technologies: Implications for employment and earnings. In *Handbook of Labor Economics,* vol. 4B, eds. O. Ashenfelter and D. Card. San Diego and Amsterdam: Elsevier North-Holland.

Acemoglu, D., and J. S. Pischke. 1998. Why do firms train? Theory and evidence. *QJE* 113 (February):78–118.

———. 1999. The structure of wages and investment in general training. *JPE* 107(June):539–572.

Almond, D., and J. Currie. 2011. Human capital development before age five. In *Handbook of Labor Economics,* vol. 4B, eds. O. Ashenfelter and D. Card. San Diego and Amsterdam: Elsevier North-Holland.

Altonji, J. 1995. The effects of high school curriculum on education and labor market outcomes. *JHR* 30 (Summer):409–38.

Altonji, J., and C. R. Pierret. 2001. Employer learning and statistical discrimination. *QJE* 116 (February):313–350

Anderson, M. 2008. Multiple inference and gender differences in the effects of early intervention: A reevaluation of the Abercedarian, Perry Preschool, and Early Training projects. *JASA* 103 (December):1481–95.

Angrist, J. D., and A. B. Krueger. 1991. Does compulsory school attendance affect schooling and earnings? *QJE* 106 (November):979–1014.

Arcidiacono, P., P. Bayer, and A. Hizmo. 2010. Beyond signaling and human capital: Education and the revelation of ability. *AEJ Applied* 2 (October):76–104

Ashenfelter, O., and A. Krueger. 1994. Estimates of the economic return to schooling from a new sample of twins. *AER* 84 (December):1157–73.

Ashenfelter, O., and C. Rouse. 1998. Income, schooling, and ability: Evidence from a new sample of identical twins. *QJE* 113 (February):253–84.

Atkinson, A. B., T. Piketty, and E. Saez. 2011. Top incomes in the long run of history. *JEL* 49 (March):3–71

Autor, D. H. 2014. Skills, education, and the rise of earnings inequality among the "other 99 percent." *Science* 344 (May):843–51.

Autor, D. H., and D. Dorn. 2013. The growth of low-skill service jobs and the polarization of the U.S. labor market. *AER* 103 (August):1553–97.

Autor D. H., L. F. Katz, and M. S. Kearney. 2006. The polarization of the U.S. labor market. *AER* 96 (May):189–94.

Autor, D. H., F. Levy, and R. J. Murnane. 2003. The skill content of recent technological change: An empirical investigation. *QJE* 118 (November):1279–1333.

Baker, M., J. Gruber, and K. Milligan. 2005. Universal child care, maternal labour supply, and family well-being. *JPE* 116 (August):709–745.

———. 2015. Non-cognitive deficits and young adult outcomes: The long-run impacts of a Universal Child Care Program. National Bureau of Economics Research Working Paper No 21571, September.

Bar-Or, Y., J. Burbridge, L. Magee, and A. L. Robb. 1995. The wage premium to a university education in Canada, 1971–1991. *JOLE* 13 (October):762–94.

Beach, C., and G. Slotsve. 1996. *Are We Becoming Two Societies? Income Polarization and the Myth of the Declining Middle Class in Canada.* Toronto: C. D. Howe Institute.

Beaudry, P., and D. A. Green. 2000. Cohort patterns in Canadian earnings: Assessing the role of skill premia in inequality trends. *CJE* 33 (November):907–36.

Beaudry, P., and D. Green. 2005. Changes in U.S. wages, 1976–2000: Ongoing skill bias or major technological change? *JOLE* 23 (July):609–48.

Becker, G. 1964. *Human Capital.* New York: National Bureau of Economic Research.

Bedard, K. 2001. Human capital versus signaling models: University access and high school drop-outs. *JPE* 109 (August):749–75.

Behrman, J., Z. Hrubec, P. Taubman, and T. Wales. 1980. *Socioeconomic Success: A Study of the Effects of Genetic Endowments, Family Environment, and Schooling.* Amsterdam: North Holland.

Blackburn, M., and D. Bloom. 1993. The distribution of family income: measuring and explaining changes in the 1980s for Canada and the United States. In *Small Differences That Matter,* eds. D. Card and R. Freeman. Chicago: University of Chicago Press.

Boudarbat, B., T. Lemieux, and W. C. Riddell. 2010. The evolution of the returns to human capital in Canada, 1980–2005. *CPP* 36 (March):63–89.

Bound, J., and G. Johnson. 1992. Changes in the structure of wages in the 1980s: An evaluation of alternative explanations. *AER* 82 (June):371–92.

Burbidge, J. B., K. A. Collins, J. B. Davies, and L. Magee. 2012. Effective tax and subsidy rates on human capital in Canada. *CJE* 45 (February):189–219.

Canada Millenium Scholarship Foundation. 2004. Low-income Canadians' perceptions of costs and benefits—a serious barrier to higher education. Available at www.millenniumscholarships.ca/images/Publications/ipsos_en.pdf.

Card, D. 1995. Using geographic variation in college proximity to estimate the return to schooling. In *Aspects of Labour Market Behaviour: Essays in Honour of John Vanderkamp,* eds. L. Christofides, E. K. Grant, and R. Swidinsky. Toronto: University of Toronto Press.

———. 1999. The causal effect of education on earnings. In *Handbook of Labor Economics,* eds. O. Ashenfelter and D. Card. New York and Oxford: Elsevier Science, North-Holland.

Card, D., and John E. DiNardo. 2002. Skill-biased technological change and rising wage inequality: Some problems and puzzles. *JOLE* 20 (October):733–83.

Card, D., J. Kluve, and A, Weber. 2010. Active labour market policy evaluations: A meta-analysis. *EJ* 120 (November):F452–F477.

Card, D., J. Kluve, and A. Weber. 2015. What works? A meta analysis of recent active labor market program evaluations. National Bureau of Economic Research Working Paper No 21431, July.

Card, D., T. Lemieux, and W. C. Riddell. 2004. Unions and wage inequality. *JLR* 25 (Fall):519–62.

Ciccone, A., and G. Peri. 2006. Identifying human capital externalities: Theory with applications. *R.E.Studies* 73 (April):381–412.

Clark, D., and H. Royer. 2013. The effect of education on adult mortality and health: Evidence from Britain. *AER* 103 (October):2087–2120.

Coelli, M. 2009. Tuition fees and equality of university enrolment. *CJE* 42 (August):1072–1099

Currie, J., and D. Thomas. 1995. Does Head Start make a difference? *AER* 85 (June):34–64.

Deming, D. 2009. Early childhood intervention and life-cycle skill development: Evidence from Head Start. *AEJ App* (July):111–34.

Devereux, P. J., and R. Hart. 2010. Forced to be rich? Returns to compulsory schooling in Britain. *EJ* 120 (December):1345–64.

DiNardo, J., N. Fortin, and T. Lemieux. 1996. Labor market institutions and the distribution of wages, 1973–1992: A semi-parametric approach. *Ecta* 64 (September):1001–44.

DiNardo, J., and T. Lemieux. 1997. Diverging male wage inequality in the United States and Canada, 1981–88: Do institutions explain the difference? *ILRR* 50 (July):629–51.

DiNardo, J., and J.-S. Pischke. 1997. The returns to computer use revisited: Have pencils changed the wage structure too? *QJE* 112 (February):291–303.

Donald, S. G., D. A. Green, and H. Paarsch. 2000. Differences in wage distributions between Canada and the United States: An application of a flexible estimator of distribution functions in the presence of covariates. *R.E.Studies* 67 (October):609–33.

Dooley, M. 1986. The overeducated Canadian? Changes in the relationship among earnings, education, and age for Canadian men: 1971–1981. *CJE* 19 (February):142–59.

Dustmann, C., and U. Schoenberg. 2012. What makes firm-based vocational training schemes successful? The role of commitment. *AEJ App* 4 (April):36–61.

Ferrer, A., and W. C. Riddell. 2002. The role of Ccredentials in the Canadian labour market. *CJE* 35 (November):879–905.

Fields, E. 2009. Educational debt burden and career choice: Evidence from a financial aid experiment at NYU Law School. *AEJ App* 1 (January):1–21.

Foley, K., and D. A. Green. 2016. Why more education will not solve rising inequality (and may make it worse). In *Income Inequality: The Canadian Story,* eds. D. A. Green, W. C. Riddell, and F. St-Hilaire. Montreal: Institute for Research on Public Policy.

Fortin, N. M. 2005. Rising tuition and supply constraints: Explaining Canada–U.S. differences in university enrollment rates. In *Higher Education in Canada,* eds. C. Beach, R. W. Boadway, and R. M. McInnis. Kingston and Montreal: John Deutsch Institute and McGill-Queens University Press.

Fortin, N. M., D. A. Green, T. Lemieux, K. Milligan, and W. C. Riddell. 2012. Canadian inequality: Recent developments and policy options. *CPP* 38 (June):121–45.

Fortin, N. M., and T. Lemieux. 1997. Institutional changes and rising wage inequality: Is there a linkage? *JEP* 11 (Spring):75–96.

———. 2015. Changes in wage inequality in Canada: An interprovincial perspective. *CJE* 48 (May):682–713.

Freeman, R. B. 1976. *The Overeducated American.* New York: Academic Press.

Freeman, R. B., and K. Needels. 1993. Skill differentials in Canada in an era of rising labor market inequality. In *Small Differences That Matter,* eds. D. Card and R. Freeman. Chicago: University of Chicago Press.

Frenette, M. 2014. An investment of a lifetime? The long-term labour market premiums associated with a postsecondary education. Statistics

Canada, Analytical Studies Branch Research Paper Series, February.

Frenette, M., D. A. Green, and K. Milligan. 2009. Taxes, transfers, and Canadian income inequality. *CPP* 35 (December):389–411.

Frenette, M., and R. Morissette. 2014. Wages and full-time employment rates of young high school graduates and bachelor's degree holders, 1997 to 2012. Statistics Canada Analytical Studies Branch Research Paper Series, April.

Gathmann, C., and U. Schoenberg. 2010. How general is human capital? A task-based approach. *JLE* 28 (January):1–49.

Goldin, C., and L. F. Katz. 1996. Technology, skill, and the wage structure: Insights from the past. *AER* 86 (May):252–57.

———. 2008. *The Race between Education and Technology*. Cambridge: Harvard University Press.

Gottschalk, P. 1997. Inequality, income growth, and mobility: The basic facts. *JEP* 11 (Spring):21–40.

Green, D. A., and B. M. Sand. 2015. Has the Canadian labour market polarized? *CJE* 48 (May):612–46.

Hamilton, G. 1995. Enforcement in apprenticeship contracts: Were runaways a serious problem? Evidence from Montreal. *JEH* 55 (September):551–74.

———. 1996. The market for Montreal apprentices: Contract length and information. *Explorations in Economic History* 33 (October):496–523.

———. 2000. The decline of apprenticeship in North America: Evidence from Montreal. *JEH* 60 (September):627–64.

Heckman, J., R. LaLonde, and J. Smith. 1999. The economics and econometrics of active labor market programs. In *Handbook of Labor Economics,* eds. O. Ashenfelter and D. Card. New York and Oxford: Elsevier Science, North Holland.

Heckman, J., and J. Smith. 1995. Assessing the case for social experiments. *JEP* 9 (Spring):85–110.

Heisz, A., and B. Murphy. 2016. The role of taxes and transfers in reducing income inequality. In *Income Inequality: The Canadian Story,* eds. D. A. Green, W. C. Riddell, and F. St-Hilaire. Montreal: Institute for Research on Public Policy.

Iranzo, S., and G. Peri. 2009. Schooling externalities, technology, and productivity: Theory and evidence from U.S. states. *R.E.Stats* 91 (May):420–431.

Johnson, G. 1997. Changes in earnings inequality: The role of demand shifts. *JEP* 11 (Spring):41–54.

Juhn, C., K. M. Murphy, and B. Pierce. 1993. Wage inequality and the rise in returns to skill. *JPE* 101 (June):410–42.

Kambourov, G., and I. Manovskii. 2009. Occupational specificity of human capital. *IER* 50 (February):63–115.

Katz, L. F., and D. Autor. 1999. Changes in the wage structure and earnings inequality. In *Handbook of Labor Economics,* eds. O. Ashenfelter and D. Card. New York and Oxford: Elsevier Science, North-Holland.

Katz, L. F., and K. M. Murphy. 1992. Changes in relative wages, 1963–1987: Supply and demand factors. *QJE* 107 (February):35–78.

Krashinsky, H., and M. Gunderson. 2015. Returns to apprenticeship based on the 2006 Canadian Census. *ILRR* 68 (October):1078–1101.

Krueger, A. 1993. How computers have changed the wage structure: Evidence from microdata. *QJE* 108 (February):33–60.

LaLonde, R. 1986. Evaluating the econometric evaluations of training programs with experimental data. *AER* 76 (September):604–20.

———. 1995. The promise of public sector sponsored training programs. *JEP* 9 (Spring):149–68.

Lang, K., and D. Kropp. 1986. Human capital versus sorting: The effects of compulsory attendance laws. *QJE* 101 (August):609–24.

Lang, K., and E. Siniver. 2011. Why is an elite undergraduate education valuable? Evidence from Israel. *LE* 18 (December):767–77

Lemieux, T. 2006. Increasing residual wage inequality: Composition effects, noisy data, or rising demand for skill? *AER* 96 (June):461–98.

———. 2008. The changing nature of wage inequality. *Journal of Population Economics* 21 (January):21–48.

———. 2011. Wage inequality: A comparative perspective. *Australian Bulletin of Labour* 37 (Winter):2–32.

Lemieux, T., and D. Card. 2001. Education, earnings, and the "Canadian G. I. Bill." *CJE* 34 (May):313–44.

Lemieux, T., and W. C. Riddell. 2016. Top Incomes in Canada: Evidence from the Census. In *Income Inequality: The Canadian Story,* eds. D. A. Green, W. C. Riddell, and F. St-Hilaire. Montreal: Institute for Research on Public Policy.

Lleras-Muney, A. 2005. The relationship between education and adult mortality in the U.S. *R.E.Studies* 72 (January):189–221.

Lochner, L., and E. Moretti. 2004. The effect of education on criminal activity: Evidence from prison inmates, arrests and self-reports. *AER* 94 (March):155–89.

Manning, A., M. Goos, and A. Salomons. 2014. Explaining job polarization: Routine-biased technological change and offshoring. *AER* 104 (August):2509–26.

Milligan, K., E. Moretti, and P. Oreopoulos. 2004. Does education improve citizenship? Evidence from the U.S. and the UK. *JPubEc* 88 (August):1667–95.

Moretti, E. 2004a. Workers' education, spillovers and productivity: Evidence from plant-level production functions. *AER* 94 (September):656–90.

———. 2004b. Estimating the social return to higher education: Evidence from longitudinal and repeated cross-sectional data. *Journal of Econometrics* 121 (July–August):175–212.

———. 2004c. Human capital externalities in cities. In *Handbook of Regional and Urban Economics,* eds. V. Henderson and J. F. Thisse. New York and Oxford: Elsevier Science, North-Holland.

Moussaly-Sergieh, K., and F. Vaillancourt. 2009. Extra earning power: The financial returns to university education in Canada. C. D. Howe Institute.

Murphy, K. M., W. C. Riddell, and P. M. Romer. 1998. Wages, skills, and technology in the United States and Canada. In *General Purpose Technologies and Economic Growth,* ed. E. Helpman. Cambridge and London: MIT Press.

Murphy, K. M., and F. Welch. 1992. The structure of wages. *QJE* 107 (February):285–326.

Oreopoulos, P. 2006a. Average treatment effects of education when compulsory school laws really matter. *AER* 96 (March):152–75.

———. 2006b. The compelling effects of compulsory schooling: Evidence from Canada. *CJE* 39 (February):22–52.

Oreopoulos, P., and K. G. Salvanes. 2011. Priceless: The nonpecuniary benefits of schooling. *JEP* 25 (1):159–84.

Parent, D. 1999. Labour market outcomes and schooling in Canada: Has the value of a high school degree changed over time? Cirano, Scientific Series, Number 99s-42.

———. 1999. Wages and mobility: The impact of employer-provided training. *JOLE* 17 (April):298–317.

Picot, G. 1998. What is happening to earnings inequality and youth wages in the 1990s? Statistics Canada Analytic Studies Branch Research Paper Series, Number 116.

Picot, G., and A. Heisz. 2000. The performance of the 1990s Canadian labour market. *CPP* 26 (Supplement July):S7–25.

Poletaev, M., and C. Robinson. 2008. Human capital specificity: Evidence from the Dictionary of Occupational Titles and Displaced Worker Surveys, 1984–2000. *JLE* 26 (July):387–420.

Richardson, D. H. 1997. Changes in the distribution of wages in Canada, 1981–1992. *CJE* 30 (August):622–43.

Riddell, W. C. 2003. The role of government in post-secondary education in Ontario. Research Paper No 29, prepared for the Panel on the Role of Government in Ontario.

Riley, J. G. 1979. Testing the educational screening hypothesis. *JPE* 87:S227–52.

Rosen, S. 1977. Human capital: A survey of empirical research. In *Research in Labor Economics,* ed. R. Ehrenberg. Greenwich, Conn.: JAI Press.

Saez, E., and M. R. Veall. 2005. The Evolution of high incomes in North America: Lessons from Canadian evidence. *AER* 95 (June):831–849.

Sand, B. M. 2014. A re-examination of the social returns to education: Evidence from U.S. cities. *LE* 24 (October):96–106.

Smith, A. 1776. *The Wealth of Nations*. London: Methuen and Company.

Spence, A. M. 1974. *Market Signaling: Informational Transfer in Hiring and Related Screening Processes*. Cambridge, Mass.: Harvard University Press.

Topel, R. H. 1997. Factor proportions and relative wages: The supply-side determinants of wage inequality. *JEP* 11 (Spring):55–74.

Veall, M.R. 2012. Top income shares in Canada: Recent trends and policy implications. *CJE* 45 (November):1247–72.

Weiss, A. 1995. Human capital versus signalling explanations of wages. *JEP* 9 (Fall):133–54.

CHAPTER 10

Abowd, J. M., F. Kramarz, and D. N. Margolis. 1999. High wage workers and high wage firms. *Ecta* 67 (March):251–333.

Acemoglu, D., and D. H. Autor. 2011. Skills, tasks, and technologies: Implications for employment and earnings. In *Handbook of Labor Economics*, vol. 4B, eds. O. Ashenfelter and D. Card. San Diego and Amsterdam: Elsevier North-Holland.

Albouy, D. 2012. Evaluating the efficiency and equity of federal fiscal equalization. *JPubEc Economics* 96 (October):824–39.

Albouy, D., F. Leibovici, and C. Warman. 2013. Quality of life, firm productivity, and the value of amenities across Canadian cities. *CJE* 46 (May):379–411.

Barro, R., and X. Sala-i-Martin. 1999. *Economic Growth*, Cambridge, MA: MIT Press.

Beaudry, P., D. A. Green, and B. Sand. 2012. Does industrial composition matter for wages? A test of search and bargaining theory. *Ecta* 80 (May):1063–1104.

Bernard, A., R. Finnie, and B. St-Jean. 2008. Interprovincial mobility and earnings. *Perspective on Labour and Income* 9 (October):15–25.

Berry, C., and E. Glaeser. 2005. The divergence in human capital levels across cities. *Papers in Regional Science* 84 (August):407–44.

Bishop, J., J. Formby, and P. Thistle. 1992. Convergence of the South and Non-South income distributions, 1969–1979. *AER* 82 (March):262–72.

Borland, J., and R. G. Gregory. 1999. Recent developments in public sector labor markets. In *Handbook of Labor Economics*, eds. O. Ashenfelter and D. Card. New York and Oxford: Elsevier Science, North-Holland.

Brown, C., and J. L. Medoff. 1989. The employer size wage effect. *JPE* (October):1027–59.

Card, D. 1986. The impact of deregulation on the employment and wages of airline mechanics. *ILRR* 39 (July):527–38.

Card, D., A. R. Cardoso, and P. Kline. 2016. Bargaining, sorting, and the gender wage gap: Quantifying the impact of firms on the relative pay of women. *QJE* 131 (May):633–686.

Card, D., A. R. Cardoso, J. Heining and P. Kline. 2016. Firms and labor market inequality: Evidence and some theory. UC Berkeley mimeo.

Card, D., J. Heining, and P. Kline. 2013. Workplace heterogeneity and the rise of West German wage inequality. *QJE* 128 (August):967–1015.

Card, D., T. Lemieux, and W. C. Riddell. 2004. Unions and wage inequality. *JLR* 25 (Fall):519–62.

Chan, P. C. W., and R. Morissette. 2016, The impact of annual wages on interprovincial mobility, interprovincial employment, and job vacancies. Statistics Canada, Analytical Studies Branch Research Paper Series, April.

Cortes, M. 2016. Where have the middle-wage workers gone? A study of polarization using panel data. *JOLE* 34 (January):63–105.

Coulombe, S. 2006. Internal migration, asymmetric shocks, and interprovincial economic adjustments in Canada. *International Regional Science Review* 29 (April):199–223.

Coulombe, S., and K. Day. 1999. Economic growth and regional income disparities in Canada and the northern United States. *CPP* 25 (June):155–78.

Cousineau, J.-M., and F. Vaillancourt. 2000. Regional disparities, mobility and labour markets in Canada. In *Adopting Public Policy to a Labour Market in Transition*, eds. W. C. Riddell and F. St-Hilaire. Montreal: Institute for Research on Public Policy.

Day, K. 1992. Interprovincial migration and local public goods. *CJE* 25 (February):123–44.

Day, K., and S. Winer. 2012. *Interregional migration and public policy in Canada: An empirical study*. Vol. 223. Montreal and Kingston: McGill-Queen's Press.

Dickens, W., and L. Katz. 1987. Industry wage differences and industry characteristics. In *Unemployment and the Structure of Labor Markets*, eds. K. Lang and J. Leonard. Oxford: Basil Blackwell.

Dickens, W., and K. Lang. 1988. Why it matters what we trade: A case for active policy. In *The Dynamics of Trade and Employment*, eds. L. Tyson, W. Dickens, and J. Zysman. Cambridge: Ballinger.

Edin, P.-A., and J. Zetterberg. 1992. Interindustry wage differentials: Evidence from Sweden and a comparison with the United States. *AER* 82 (December):1341–49.

Farber, S., and R. Newman. 1987. Accounting for South/Non-South real wage differentials and for changes in those differentials over time. *R.E.Stats* 59 (May):215–23.

Ferrer, A., and S. Lluis. 2008. Should workers care about firm size? *ILRR* 62 (October):104–24.

Filer, R. 1986. The "starving artist"—myth or reality. *JPE* 94 (February):56–75.

Finnie, R. 2004. Who moves? A logit model analysis of inter-provincial migration in Canada. *Applied Economics* 36 (September):1759–79.

Fortin, N. M., and T. Lemieux. 2015. Changes in wage inequality in Canada: An interprovincial perspective. *CJE* 48 (May):682–713.

Freeman, R. B., and L. F. Katz. 1991. Industrial wage and employment determination in an open economy. In *Immigration, Trade, and the Labor Market*, eds. J. Abowd and R. Freeman. Chicago: University of Chicago Press.

Gaston, N., and D. Trefler. 1994. Protection, trade, and wages: Evidence from U.S. manufacturing. *ILRR* 47 (July):574–93.

———. 1995. Union wage sensitivity to trade and protection: Theory and evidence. *JIE* 39 (August):1–25.

Gera, S., and G. Grenier. 1994. Interindustry wage differentials and efficiency wages: Some Canadian evidence. *CJE* 27 (February):81–100.

Gibbons, R., L. Katz, T. Lemieux, and D. Parent. 2005. Comparative advantage, learning, and sectoral wage determination. *JOLE* 23 (October):681–724.

Goldschmidt, D., and J. F. Schmieder. 2015. The rise of domestic outsourcing and the evolution of the German wage structure. NBER Working Paper, July.

Gray, D., and H. Qiu. 2010. The responsiveness of industry wages to low-frequency shocks in Canada. *CJE* 43 (November):1221–1242.

Green, D.A. 2015. Chasing after good jobs. Do they exist and does it matter if they do? *CJE* 48 (November):1215–65.

Grey, A. 1993. Interindustry wage differentials in manufacturing: Rents and industrial structure. *CJE* 26 (August):525–35.

Grossman, G. 1986. Imports as a cause of injury: The case of the U.S. steel industry. *JIE* 20 (May):201–23.

———. 1987. The employment and wage effects of import competition. *Journal of International Economic Integration* 2 (Spring):1–23.

Gunderson, M. 1998. Government compensation: Issues and options, CPRN Discussion Paper, Number W03.

Gunderson, M., D. Hyatt, and W. C. Riddell. 2000. Pay differences between the government and private sectors: Labour force survey and census estimates, CPRN Discussion Paper, Number W10.

Gunderson, M., and C. Riddell. 1991. Provincial public sector payrolls. In *Provincial Public Finances*, ed. M. McMillan. Toronto: Canadian Tax Foundation.

———. 1995. Public and private sector wages: A comparison. Government and Competitiveness Series, School of Policy Studies, Queen's University.

Hendricks, W. 1994. Deregulation and labor earnings. *JLR* 15 (Summer):207–34.

Hou, F., and S. Coulombe. 2010. Earnings gaps for Canadian-born visible minorities in the public and private sectors. *CPP* 36 (March):29–43.

Katz, L. F., and L. H. Summers. 1989a. Can inter-industry wage differentials justify strategic trade policy? In *Trade Policies for International Competitiveness*, ed. R. C. Feenstra. Chicago: University of Chicago Press.

———. 1989b. Industry rents: Evidence and implications. *Brookings Papers: Microeconomics*:209–90.

Kleiner, M. 2006. *Licensing Occupations: Ensuring Quality or Restricting Competition?* Kalamazoo, MI: W.E. Upjohn Institute for Employment Research.

Kleiner, M., and A. Krueger. 2013. Analyzing the extent and influence of occupational licensing on the labor market. *JOLE* 31 (April):S173–S202.

Krueger, A. 1988a. Are public sector workers paid more than their alternative wage? Evidence from longitudinal data and job queues. In *When Public Sector Workers Unionize*, eds. R. Freeman and C. Ichniowski. Chicago: University of Chicago Press.

———. 1988b. The determinants of queues for federal jobs. *ILRR* 41 (July):567–81.

Krueger, A. 2005. The economics of real super-stars: The market for rock concerts in the material world. *JOLE* 23 (January):1–30.

Krueger, A., and L. H. Summers. 1987. Reflections on the inter-industry wage structure. In *Unemployment and the Structure of Labor Markets,* eds. K. Lang and J. Leonard. Oxford: Basil Blackwell.

Krueger, A. B., and L. H. Summers. 1988. Efficiency wages and the inter-industry wage structure. *Ecta* 56 (March):259–93.

Laporte, C., Y. Lu, and G. Schellenberg. 2013. Inter-provincial employees in Canada. Statistics Canada, Analytical Studies Branch Research Paper Series, September.

Lawrence, C., and R. Lawrence. 1985. Manufacturing wage dispersion: An end game interpretation. *BPEA* 1:47–106.

Lluis, S. 2009. The structure of wages by firm size: Evidence from Canada and the U.S. *Labour: Review of Labour Economics and Industrial Relations* 23 (June):283–317.

Marchand, J. 2015. The distributional impacts of an energy boom in Western Canada. *CJE* 48 (May):714–35.

Morissette, R. 1993. Canadian jobs and firm size: Do smaller firms pay less? *CJE* 26:159–74.

Morissette, R., and H. Qiu. 2015. Interprovincial employment in Canada, 2002 to 2011. Statistics Canada, Economic Insight, June.

Mueller, R. E. 1998. Public–private sector wage differentials in Canada: Evidence from quantile regressions. *Economics Letters* 60 (August):229–235.

Murphy, K., and R. Topel. 1987. Unemployment, risk and earnings. In *Unemployment and the Structure of Labour Markets,* eds. K. Lang and J. Leonard. Oxford: Basil Blackwell.

Oi, W., and T. Idson. 1999. Firm size and wages. In *Handbook of Labor Economics,* Vol. 3b, eds. O Ashenfelter and D. Card. Amsterdam: Elsevier Science.

Osberg, L., D. Gordon, and Z. Lin. 1994. Inter-regional migration and interindustry labour mobility in Canada: A simultaneous approach. *CJE* 27:58–80.

Ponak, A., and M. Thompson. 2005. Public-sector collective bargaining. In *Union-Management Relations in Canada,* 5th ed., eds. M. Gunderson, A. Ponak, and D. G. Taras. Toronto: Pearson Addison Wesley.

Postel-Vinay, F., and J.-M. Robin. 2002. Equilibrium wage dispersion with worker and employer heterogeneity. *Ecta* 70 (November):2295–2350.

Reder, M. 1955. The theory of occupational wage differentials. *AER* 45 (December):833–52.

Reilly, K. T. 1995. Human capital and information: The employer size-wage effect. *JHR* 30 (Winter):1–18.

Revenga, A. 1992. Exporting jobs: The impact of import competition on employment and wages in U.S. manufacturing. *QJE* 107 (February):255–84.

Rose, N. 1987. Labor rent sharing and regulation: Evidence from the trucking industry. *JPE* 6 (December):1146–78.

Roy, A. D. 1951. Some thoughts on the distribution of earnings. *Oxford Economic Papers* 3 (June):135–46.

Syverson, C. 2011. What determines productivity? *JEL* 49 (April):326–65.

CHAPTER 11

Abbott, M. and C. Beach. 2009. Immigrant earnings distributions and earnings mobility in Canada: Evidence for the 1982 landing cohort from IMDB micro data. CLSRN Working Paper No 13.

Akbari, A. 1995. The impact of immigrants on Canada's treasury, circa 1990. In *Diminishing Returns,* ed. D. DeVoretz. Toronto: C. D. Howe Institute and Laurier Institution.

Altonji, J., and D. Card. 1991. The effects of immigration on the labor market outcomes of less-skilled natives. In *Immigration, Trade, and the Labor Market,* eds. J. Abowd and R. Freeman. Chicago: University of Chicago Press.

Aydemir, A. 2011. Immigrant selection and short-term labor market outcomes by visa category. *Journal of Population Economics* 24:451–475.

Aydemir, A., and M. Skuterud. 2005. Explaining the deteriorating entry earnings of Canada's immigrant cohorts, 1966–2000. *CJE* 38(2):641–71.

Aydemir, A., and G. Borjas. 2011. Attenuation bias in measuring the wage impact of immigration. *JLE* 29 (January): 69–112.

Baker, M., and D. Benjamin. 1994. The performance of immigrants in the Canadian labour market. *JOLE* 12 (July):369–405.

———. 1995a. Labour market outcomes and the participation of immigrant women in Canadian transfer programs. In *Diminishing Returns,* ed. D. DeVoretz. Toronto: C. D. Howe Institute and Laurier Institution.

———. 1995b. The receipt of transfer payments by immigrants to Canada. *JHR* 30 (Fall):650–76.

———. 1997a. Asia-Pacific immigration and the Canadian economy. In *The Asia Pacific Region in the Global Economy: A Canadian Perspective,* ed. R. G. Harris. Calgary: University of Calgary Press.

Bloom, D. E., G. Grenier, and M. Gunderson. 1995. The changing labour market position of Canadian immigrants. *CJE* 28 (November):987–1005.

Borjas, G. 2003. The labor demand curve is downward sloping: Reexamining the impact of immigration on the labor market. *QJE* 118(4) (November):1335–74.

Borjas, G. J. 1985. Assimilation, changes in cohort quality, and the earnings of immigrants. *JOLE* 3 (October):463–89.

———. 1993. Immigration policy, national origin, and immigrant skills: A comparison of Canada and the United States. In *Small Differences That Matter,* eds. D. Card and R. Freeman. Chicago and London: University of Chicago Press.

———. 1994. The economics of immigration. *JEL* 32 (December):1667–1717.

———. 1995. The economic benefits from immigration. *JEP* 9 (Spring):3–22.

———. 1999. The economic analysis of immigration. In *Handbook of Labor Economics,* eds. O. Ashenfelter and D. Card. New York and Oxford: Elsevier Science, North-Holland.

———. 2014. *Immigration Economics.* Cambridge: Harvard University Press.

———. Forthcoming. The wage impact of the *Marielitos*: A reappraisal. *Industrial and Labor Relations Review.*

Borjas, G. J., R. Freeman, and L. Katz. 1992. On the labor market effects of immigration and trade. In *Immigration and the Work-force: Economic Consequences for the United States and Source Areas,* eds. G. Borjas and R. Freeman. Chicago: University of Chicago Press.

———. 1996. Searching or the effect of immigration on the labour market. *AER* 86 (May):246–51.

Borjas, G., J. Grogger, and G. H. Hanson. 2012. Comment: On estimating elasticities of substitution. *Journal of the European Economic Association* 10: 198–210.

Cadena, Brian, and Brian Kovak. 2016. Immigrants equilibrate local labor markets: Evidence from the Great Recession. *American Economic Journal: Applied Economics* 8(1):257–290.

Card, D. 1990. The impact of the *Mariel* boatlift on the Miami labor market. *ILRR* 43 (January):245–57.

———. 2001. Immigrant inflows, native outflows, and the local labor market impacts of higher immigration. *JOLE* 19 (January):22–64.

Card, D. 2003. Canadian emigration to the United States. In *Canadian Immigration Policy for the 21st Century,* eds. C. Beach, A. Green, and J. Reitz. Kingston and Montreal: McGill-Queens University Press.

Card, D. 2009. Immigration and inequality. *AER* 99 (May):1–21.

Carrington, W. J., and P. J. F. de Lima. 1996. The impact of 1970s repatriates from Africa on the Portuguese labor market. *ILRR* 49 (January):330–47.

Chiswick, B. 1978. The effect of Americanization on the earnings of foreign-born men. *JPE* 86 (October):897–921.

Citizenship and Immigration Canada. 1998. *The Economic Performance of Immigrants: Immigration Category Perspective.* Ottawa: IMDB Profile Series.

———. 1999. *The Economic Performance of Immigrants: Education Perspective.* Ottawa: IMDB Profile Series.

Clarke, A., and M. Skuterud. 2013. Why do immigrant workers in Australia perform better than those in Canada? Is it the immigrants or their labour markets? *CJE* 46(4):1431–1462.

Crossley, T. F., J. T. McDonald, and C. Worswick. 2001. Immigrant benefit receipt revisited: Sensitivity to the choice of survey years and model specification: Comment. *JHR* 36 (Spring):379–97.

DeVoretz, D. J., and C. Iturralde. 2001. Why do highly-skilled Canadians stay in Canada? *Policy Options* (March):59–63.

Dion, Patrice, and Mireille Vézina. 2010. Emigration from Canada to the United States from 2000 to 2006. *Canadian Social Trends,* Statistics Canada, no. 11-008-X:57–67.

Duleep, H. O., and M. C. Regets. 1992. Some evidence of the effects of admissions criteria on immigrant assimilation. In *Immigration, Language, and Ethnicity: Canada and the United States,* ed. B. R. Chiswick. Washington, D. C.: AEI Press; distributed by University Press of America.

Ferrer, A. D., A. Green, and W. C. Riddell. 2006. The effect of literacy on immigrant earnings. *JHR* 41 (Spring):380–410.

Ferrer, A., and W. C. Riddell. 2008. Education, credentials, and immigrant earnings. *CJE* 41 (February):186–216.

Finnie, R. 2001. The brain drain: Myth and reality—what it is and what should be done. School of Policy Studies, Queen's University, Number 13.

Foged, Mette, and Giovanni Peri. 2016. Immigrants' effect on native workers: New analysis on longitudinal data. *American Economic Journal: Applied Economics* 8(2):1–34.

Frank, J., and E. Belair. 1999. South of the border: Graduates from the class of 1995 who moved to the United States. Human Resources Development Canada and Statistics Canada.

Friedberg, R. 2001. The impact of mass migration on the Israeli labor market. *QJE* 116(4):1373–1408.

Friedberg, R., and J. Hunt. 1995. The impact of immigrants on host country wages, employment and growth. *JEP* 9 (Spring):23–44.

Globerman, S. 1995. Immigration and trade. In *Diminishing Returns,* ed. D. DeVoretz. Toronto: C. D. Howe Institute and Laurier Institution.

Grant, M. 1999. Evidence of new immigrant assimilation in Canada. *CJE* 32 (August):930–55.

Green, A. G. 1976. *Immigration and the Postwar Canadian Economy.* Toronto: Macmillan.

———. 1995. A comparison of Canadian and U.S. immigration policy in the twentieth century. In *Diminishing Returns,* ed. D. DeVoretz. Toronto: C. D. Howe Institute and Laurier Institution.

Green, A. G., and D. A. Green. 1995. Canadian immigration policy: The effectiveness of the point system and other instruments. *CJE* 28 (November):1006–41.

———. 1999. The economic goals of Canada's immigration policy: Past and present. *CPP* 25 (December):425–51.

Green, D. A. 1995. Intended and actual occupations of immigrants. In *Diminishing Returns,* ed. D. DeVoretz. Toronto: C. D. Howe Institute and Laurier Institution.

———. 1999. Immigrant occupational attainment: Assimilation and mobility over time. *JOLE* 17 (January):49–79.

Green, D., and C. Worswick. 2004. Entry earnings effects of immigrant men in Canada: The roles of labour market entry effects and returns to foreign experience.

———. 2012. Immigrant earnings profiles in the presence of human capital investment: Measuring cohort and macro effects. *Labour Economics* 19(2):241–59.

Head, K., and J. Ries. 1998. Immigration and trade creation: Econometric evidence from Canada. *CJE* 31 (February):47–62.

Helliwell, J. F. 1999. Checking the brain drain: Evidence and implications. *Policy Options* (September):6–17.

Hou, F., and G. Picot. 2014. Annual levels of immigration and immigrant entry earnings in Canada. *CPP* (June):66–81.

Hunt, J. 1992. The impact of the 1962 repatriates from Algeria on the French labor market. *ILRR* 45 (April):556–72.

Javdani, M., and K. Pendakur. 2014. Fiscal effects of immigrants in Canada. *Journal of International Migration and Integration* 15(4):777–797.

Kaushal, N., Y. Lu, N. Denier, J. S.-H. Wang, and S. Trejo. 2016. Immigrant employment and earnings growth in Canada and the USA: Evidence from longitudinal data. *Journal of Population Economics* 29(4):1249–1277.

Kesselman, J. 2001. Policies to stem the brain drain—without Americanizing Canada. *CPP* 27 (March):77–93.

Konig, E., and K. Banting. 2013. Inequality below the surface: Reviewing immigrants' access to and utilization of five Canadian welfare programs. *CPP* 39(4):581–601.

Kuhn, P. J., and I. Wooton. 1991. Immigration, international trade, and the wages of Native workers. In *Immigration, Trade, and the Labor Market,* eds. J.-M. Abowd and R.-B. E. Freeman. A National Bureau of Economic Research Project Report, Chicago and London: University of Chicago Press.

Lam, K.-C. 1994. Outmigration of foreign-born members in Canada. *CJE* 27 (May):352–70.

Lubotsky, D. 2007. Chutes or ladders? A longitudinal analysis of immigrant earnings. *JPE* 115:820–867.

McDonald, J. T., and C. Worswick. 1997. Unemployment incidence of immigrant men in Canada. *CPP* 23 (December):353–73.

———. 1998. The earnings of immigrant men in Canada: Job tenure, cohort, and macroeconomic conditions. *ILRR* 51 (April):465–82.

Oreopoulos, P. 2011. Why do skilled immigrants struggle in the labor market? A field experiment with thirteen-thousand resumes. *American Economic Journal: Economic Policy*:148–171.

Ostrovsky, Y. 2012. The dynamics of immigrant participation in entitlement programs: Evidence from Canada, 1993–2007. *CJE* 45(1):107–136.

Ottaviano, G., and G. Peri. 2012. Rethinking the effect of immigration on wages. *Journal of the European Economic Association* 10(1):152–97.

Picot, G., and A. Sweetman. 2005. The deteriorating economic welfare of immigrants and possible causes. Analytic Studies Branch Research Paper Series, No. 262, Catalogue No. 11F0019. Ottawa: Statistics Canada.

Schaafsma, J., and A. Sweetman. 2001. Immigrant earnings: Age at immigration matters. *CJE* 34:1066–99.

Sweetman, A., and C. Warman. 2013. Canada's immigration selection system and labour market outcomes. *CPP* 39 (Supplement):S141–S164.

Symposium on the Brain Drain. *Policy Options,* September 1999. Institute for Research on Public Policy.

Warman, C., and C. Worswick. 2015. Technological change, occupational tasks and declining immigrant outcomes: Implications for earnings and income inequality in Canada. *CJE* 48(2):736–772.

Wright, R. E., and P. S. Maxim. 1993. Immigration policy and immigrant quality: Empirical evidence from Canada. *Journal of Population Economics* 6 (November):337–52.

Zhao, J., D. Drew, and T. S. Murray. 2000. Brain drain and brain gain: The migration of knowledge workers from and to Canada. *Education Quarterly Review* 6 (May):8–35.

Zong, Jie, Hataipreuk Rkasnuam, and Jeanne Batalova. 2014. Canadian immigrants in the United States. http://www.migrationpolicy.org/article/canadian-immigrants-united-states, September. Accessed August 12, 2016.

CHAPTER 12

Akee, R., and M. Yuksel. 2012. The decreasing effect of skin tone on women's full-time employment. *ILLR* 65(2):398–426.

Akerlof, G. A., and R. E. Kranton. 2000. Economics and identity. *QJE* 115 (August):715–54.

Alensina, A., P. Giuliano, and N. Nunn. 2013. On the origins of gender roles: Women and the plough. *QJE* 128(2):469–530.

Altonji, J., and R. Blank. 1999. Race and gender in the labour market. In *Handbook of Labor Economics,* eds. D. Ashenfelter and D. Card. New York: Elsevier Science.

Andres, L., and M. Adamuti-Trache. 2007. You've come a long way, baby? Persistent gender inequality in university enrolment and completion in Canada, 1979–2004. *CPP* 33(1):93–116.

Arcidiacono P., P. Bayer, and A. Hizmo. 2010. Beyond signaling and human capital: Education and the revelation of ability. *AEJ App* 2 (October):76–104.

Arrow, K. 1973. The theory of discrimination. In *Discrimination in the Labour Market,* eds. O. Ashenfelter and A. Rees. Princeton, N. J.: Princeton University Press.

Arulampalam, W., A. L. Booth, and M. L. Bryan. 2007. Is there a glass ceiling over Europe? Exploring the gender pay gap across the wage distribution. *ILRR* 60 (January):163–86.

Ashenfelter, O., and T. Hannan. 1986. Sex discrimination and product market competition: The case of the banking industry. *QJE* 101 (February):149–74.

Azmat, G., and B. Petrongolo. 2014. Gender and the labour market: What have we learned from field experiments. *LE* 30:32–40.

Bacolod, M. P., and B. S. Blum. 2010. Two sides of the same coin: U.S. "residual" inequality and the gender gap. *JHR* 45 (Winter):197–242.

Badgett, M. V. L. 1995. The wage effects of sexual orientation discrimination. *ILRR* 48:726–39.

Baert, S., B. Cockx, N. Gheyle, and C. Vandamme. 2015. Is there less discrimination where recruitment is difficult? *ILLR* 68(3):467–500.

Bailey, M., B. Hershbein, and A. Miller. 2012. The opt-in revolution? Contraception and the gender gap in wages. *AEJ: Applied Economics* 4(3):225–234.

Baker, M., and D. Benjamin. 1994. The performance of immigrants in the Canadian labour market. *JOLE* 12 (July):369–405.

———. 1997. Ethnicity, foreign birth and earnings: A Canada/U.S. comparison. In *Transition and Structural Change in the North American Labour Market,* eds. M. Abbott, C. Beach, and R. Chaykowski. Kingston, Ont.: IRC and John Deutsch Institute.

Baker, M., D. Benjamin, A. Desaulniers, and M. Grant. 1995. The distribution of the male/female earnings differential:1970–1990. *CJE* 28 (August):479–501.

Baker, M., and K. Cornelson. 2016. Gender-based occupational segregation and sex differences in sensory, motor and spacial aptitudes. NBER Working Paper 22248.

Baker, M., and M. Drolet. 2010. A new view of the male/female pay gap. *CPP* 36 (December):429–64.

Baker, M., and N. Fortin. 1999. Women's wages in women's work: A U.S.–Canada comparison of the roles of unions and "public goods" sector jobs. *AEA Papers and Proceedings* 89(2):198–223.

———. 2001. Occupational gender composition and wages in Canada: 1987–1988. *CJE* 34 (May):345–76.

———. 2004. Comparable worth in a decentralised labour market: The case of Ontario. *CJE* 37 (November):850–78.

Baker, M., and K. Milligan. 2008. How does job-protected maternity leave affect mothers' employment? *JOLE* 26(4):655–691.

Baldwin, M., and C. Choe. 2014. Wage discrimination against persons with sensory disabilities. *IR* 53(1):101–124.

Baldwin, M., and W. Johnson. 2006. A critical review of studies of discrimination against workers with disabilities. In *Handbook on the Economics of Discrimination.* ed. William M. Rodgers III. Northampton, MA: Edward Elgar Publishing.

Barth, E., and H. Dale-Olsen. 2009. Monopsonistic discrimination, worker turnover, and the gender wage gap. *LE* 16:589–97.

Bartos, V., M. Bauer, J. Chythova, and F. Mateika. 2016. Attention discrimination: Theory and field experiments with monitoring information acquisition. *AER* 106(6):1437–1475.

Beaudry, Paul, and Ethan Lewis. 2014. Do male–female wage reflect differences in the returns to skill?: Cross-city evidence from 1980–2000. *AEJ: Applied Economics* 6(2):178–194.

Becker, E., and C. Lindsay. 1994. Sex differences in tenure profiles: Effects of shared firm specific investments. *JOLE* 12:98–118.

Becker, G. 1957. *The Economics of Discrimination.* Chicago: University of Chicago Press.

Belot, M., V. Bhaskar, and J. van de Ven. 2012. Beauty and the sources of discrimination. *JHR* 47(3):851–872.

Benson, A. 2015. A theory of job search and sex-based occupational clustering. *IR* 54(3):367–400.

Bertrand, Marianne. 2011. New perspectives on gender. In *Handbook of Labor Economics,* Vol. 4, edited by Orley C. Ashenfelter and David Card. Amsterdam: Elsevier.

Bertrand M., and S. Mullainathan. 2004. Are Emily and Greg more employable than Lakisha and Jamal?: A field experiment on labor market discrimination. *AER* 94 (September):991–1013.

Bertrand, M., and K. Hallock. 2001. The gender gap in top corporate jobs. *ILRR* 55:3–21.

Bharadwaj, P., and L. Lakdawala.2013. Discrimination begins in the womb. *JHR* 48(1):71–113.

Bjerk, D. 2008. Glass ceilings or sticky floors? Statistical discrimination in a dynamic model of hiring and promotion. *EJ* 118 (July):961–82.

Black, D. 1995. Discrimination in an equilibrium search model. *JOLE* 13:309–34.

Black, D., H. Makar, S. Sanders, and L. Taylor. 2003. The earnings effects of sexual orientation. *ILRR* 56(April):449–69.

Black, D. A., A. M. Haviland, S. G. Sanders, and L. J. Taylor. 2008. Gender wage disparities among the highly educated. *JHR* 43 (Summer):630–59.

Black, S., and E. Brainerd. 2004. Importing equality? The impact of globalization on gender discrimination. *ILRR* 57:540–59.

Black, S., and P. Strahan. 2001. The division of spoils: Rent-sharing and discrimination in a regulated industry. *AER* 91:814–31.

Black, S. E., and A. Spitz-Oener. 2010. Explaining women's success: Technological change and the skill content of women's work. *R.E.Stats* 92 (February):187–94.

Blackaby, D., A. Booth, and J. Frank. 2005. Outside offers and the gender pay gap: Empirical evidence from the UK academic labour market. *EJ* 115:F81–F107.

Blau, F. 1998. Trends in the well-being of American women (1970–1995). *JEL* 36:112–65.

Blau, F. D., and J. Devaro. 2007. New evidence on gender differences in promotion rates: An empirical analysis of a sample of new hires. *IR* 46(3):511–550.

Blau, F. D., and L. M. Kahn. 1981. Race and sex differences in quits by young workers. *ILRR* 34 (July):563–77.

———. 1997. Swimming upstream: Trends in the gender wage differential in the 1980s. *JOLE* 15(1, Part I):1–42.

———. 2000. Gender differences in pay. *JEP* 14:75–99.

———. 2006. The U.S. gender pay gap in the 1990s: Slowing convergence. *ILRR* 60 (October):45–60.

———. 2008. Women's work and wages. *The New Palgrave Dictionary of Economics* 8:762–72.

Blinder, A. 1973. Wage discrimination: Reduced form and structural estimates. *JHR* 8 (Fall):436–55.

Booth, A. 2009. Gender and competition. *LE* 18 (August):599–606.

Booth, A. 2013. Gender differences in risk behaviour: does nurture matter? *EJ* 122:F56–F78.

Boudarbat, B., and M. Connelly. 2013. The gender wage gap among recent post-secondary graduates in Canada: A distributional approach. *CJE* 46(3):1037–1065.

Bowlus, A. 1997. A search interpretation of male–female wage differentials. *JOLE* 15(4):625–657.

Brown, C., and M. Corcoran. 1997. Sex-based differences in school content and the male–female wage gap. *JOLE* 15(July):431–65.

Buser, T., M. Niederle, and H. Oosterbeek. 2014. Gender competitiveness and career choices. *QJE* 129(3):1409–1447.

Cannings, K. 1988. Managerial promotion: The effects of socialization, specialization and gender. *ILRR* 42 (October):77–88.

———. 1991. Family commitments and career success: Earnings of male and female managers. *RI/IR* 46(1):141–58.

Carpenter, C. S. 2008. Sexual orientation, work, and income in Canada. *CJE* 41 (November):1239–1261.

Carrell, S. E., M. E. Page, and J. E. West. 2010. Sex and science: How professor gender perpetuates the gender gap. *QJE* 125 (August):1101–44.

Charles, K. K., and J. Guryan. 2008. Prejudice and wages: An empirical assessment of Becker's *The Economics of Discrimination. JPE* 116 (October):773–809.

Christofides, L., A. Polycarpou, and K. Vrachimis. 2013. Gender wage gaps, sticky floors and glass ceilings in Europe. *LE* 21:86–102.

Christofides, L., and R. Swidinsky. 1994. Wage determination by gender and visible minority status: Evidence from the 1989 LMAS. *CPP* 20 (March):34–51.

Coate, S., and G. Loury. 1993a. Antidiscrimination enforcement and the problem of patronization. *AER* 83:92–98.

———. 1993b. Will affirmative-action policies eliminate negative stereotypes? *AER* 83:1220–40.

Daneshvary, N., C. J. Waddoups, and B. S. Wimmer. 2009. Previous marriage and lesbian wage premium. *IR* 48 (July):432–453.

Daymont, T., and P. Andrisani. 1984. Job preferences, college major and the gender gap in earnings. *JHR* 19 (Summer):408–28.

Dexter, E. 2015. Physical appearance and earnings, hair color matters. *LE* 32:15–26.

Dittrich, M., A. Knabe, and K. Leipold. 2014. Gender differences in experimental wage negotiations. *EI* 32(2):862–873.

Dohmen, T., and A. Falk. 2011. Performance pay and multidimensional sorting: Productivity, preferences, and gender. *AER* 101(April):556–590.

Doiron, D., and W. C. Riddell. 1994. The impact of unionization on male–female earnings differences in Canada. *JHR* 29:504–34.

Doucet, C., M. Smith, and C. Durand. Pay structure, female representation and the gender pay gap among university professors. *RI/IR* 67(1):51–75.

Drolet, M. 2001. The persistent gap: New evidence on the Canadian gender wage gap. Ottawa: Statistics Canada, Business and Labour Market Analysis Division.

———. 2002a. New evidence on gender pay differentials: Does measurement matter? *CPP* 28:1–16.

————. 2002b. Can the workplace explain gender pay differentials? *CPP* 28 Supplement:S41–S64.

————. 2011. Why has the gender wage gap narrowed? *PLI* 23(1):5–16.

Drolet, M., and K. Mumford. The gender pay gap for private sector employees in Canada and Britain. *BJIR* 50(3):529–553.

Edgeworth, F. 1922. Equal pay to men and women for equal work. *EJ* 32:431–457.

Eriksson, S., and J. Lagerstrom. 2012. The labour market consequences of gender differences in job search. *JLR* 33:303–327.

Escriche, L. 2007. Persistence of occupational segregation: The role of the intergenerational transmission of preferences. *EJ* 117 (April):837–57.

Escriche, L., G. Oleina, and R. Sanchez. 2004. Gender discrimination and the intergenerational transmission of preferences. *Oxford Economic Papers* 56:485–511.

Filer, R. 1983. Sexual differences in earnings: The role of individual personalities and tastes. *JHR* 18 (Winter):82–99.

————. 1986. The role of personality and tastes, in determining occupational structure. *ILRR* 39 (April):412–24.

Fisman, R., and M. O'Neill. 2009. Gender differences in beliefs on the returns to effort evidence from the world values survey. *JHR* 44 (Fall):858–70.

Flabbi, L. 2010. Gender discrimination estimation in a search model with matching and bargaining. *IER* 51 (August):745–83.

Flory, J., A. Leibbrandt, and J. List. 2015. Do competitive workplaces deter female workers: A large-scale natural field experiment on job entry decisions. *R.E.Studies* 82:122–155.

Fortin, N. 2005. Gender role attitudes and labour market outcomes of women across OECD countries. *Oxford Review of Economic Policy* 21(3):416–38.

————. 2008. The gender wage gap among young adults in the United States. *JHR* 43 (Fall):884–918.

Frederiksen, A. 2008. Gender differences in job separation rates and employment stability: New evidence from employer-employee data. *LE* 15:915–937.

Frick, B. 2011. Gender differences in competitiveness: Empirical evidence from professional distance running. *LE* 18 (April):389–398.

Fryer, R. G. 2011. Racial inequality in the 21st century: The declining significance of discrimination. *Handbook of Labor Economics* 4:855–971.

Fryer, R. G., and S. D. Levitt. 2010. An empirical analysis of the gender gap in mathematics. *AEJ App* 2(April):210–240.

Garratt, R., C. Weinberger, and N. Johnson. 2013. The state street mile: Age and gender differences in competition aversion in the field. *EI* 51(1):806–815.

Gayle, G., L. Golan, and R. Miller. 2012. Gender differences in executive compensation and job mobility. *JOLE* 30(4):829–872.

George, P., and P. Kuhn. 1994. The size and structure of native-white wage differentials in Canada. *CJE* 27:20–42.

Gerdes C., and P. Gransmark. 2010. Strategic behavior across gender: A comparison of female and male expert chess players. *LE* 17 (October):766–775.

Gielen, A., J. Holmes, and C. Myers.2016. Prenatal testosterone and the earnings of men and women. *JHR* 51(1):30–61.

Giuliano, L., D. Levine, and J. Leonard. 2011. Racial bias in the manager-employee relationship: An analysis of quits, dismissals, and promotions at a large retail firm. *JHR* 46(1):26–52.

Gneezy, U., K. L. Leonard, and J. A. List. 2009. Gender differences in competition: Evidence from a matrilineal and a patriarchal society. *Ecta* 77 (September):1637–1664.

Goldin, C. 2014. A grand convergence: Its last chapter. *AER* 104(4):1091–1119.

Goldin, C., and C. Rouse. 2000. Orchestrating impartiality: The impact of "blind" auditions on female musicians. *AER* 90 (September):715–41.

Gregory-Smith, I., B. Main, and C. O'Reilly III. 2014. Appointments, pay and performance in UK boardrooms by gender. *EJ* 124:F100–F128.

Gruber, J. 1994. The incidence of mandated maternity benefits. *AER* 84:622–24.

Gunderson, M. 1989. Male–female wage differentials and policy responses. *JEL* 27 (March):46–117.

————. 1994. *Comparable Worth and Gender Discrimination: An International Perspective.* Geneva, Switzerland: International Labour Office.

————. 1995. Gender discrimination and pay-equity legislation. In *Aspects of Labour Market Behaviour: Essays in Honour of John Vanderkamp*, eds. L. Christofides, E. K. Grant, and R. Swidinsky. Toronto: University of Toronto Press.

————. 2006. Male–female wage differentials: How can that be? *CJE* 39 (February):1–21.

————. 2010. Pay and employment equity legislation meet the market. In *Introducing Microeconomic Analysis: Issues, Questions and Competing Views*, eds. H. Bougrine, I. Parker, and M. Seccareccia. Edmond Montgomery Publications.

Gunderson, Morley, and Byron Lee. 2016. Pay discrimination against persons with disabilities: Canadian evidence from PALS. *International Journal of Human Resource Management* 27:1531–1549.

Gunderson, Morley, and Lin Xiu. 2014. Glass ceilings and sticky floors in Chinese pay distributions: Results from quantile regressions. *International Journal of Manpower* 35(2):306–326.

Gupta, N. D., A. Poulsen, and M. Villeval. 2013. Gender matching and competitiveness: Experimental evidence. *EI* 51(1):816–835.

Guryan, J., and K. Charles. 2013. Tast-based or statistical discrimination: The economics of discrimination returns to its roots. *EJ* 123:F417–F432.

Hamermesh, D., and J. Biddle. 1994. Beauty and the labor market. *AER* 84 (December):1174–94.

Hamermesh, Daniel. 2011. *Beauty Pays: Why Attractive People Are More Successful.* Princeton: Princeton University Press.

Hellerstein, J., and D. Neumark. 1999. Sex, wages, and productivity: An empirical analysis of Israeli firm-level data. *IER* 40:95–123.

Hellerstein, J., D. Neumark, and K. Troske. 1999. Wages, productivity, and worker characteristics: Evidence from plant-level production functions and wage equations. *JOLE* 17:409–46.

————. 2002. Market forces and sex discrimination. *JHR* 37:353–380.

Hersch, J., and L. Stratton. 1997. Housework, fixed effects and wages of married workers. *JHR* 32:285–307.

Heyman, F., H. Svaleryd, and J. Viachos. 2013. Competition, takeovers and gender discrimination. *ILLR* 66(2):409–432.

Hirsch, B., T. Schank, and C. Schnabel. 2010. Differences in labor supply to monopsonistic firms and the gender pay gap: An empirical analysis using linked employer-employee data from Germany. *JOLE* 28:291–330

Hoffmann, F., and P. Oreopoulos. 2009. A professor like me. *JHR* 44 (Spring):476–94.

Holzer, H., and D. Neumark. 2000. Assessing affirmative action. *JEL* 38:483–568.

Hou, F., and S. Coulombe. 2010. Earnings gaps for Canadian-born visible minorities in the public and private sectors. *CPP* 36 (March):29–43.

Hum, D., and W. Simpson. 1999. Wage opportunities for visible minorities in Canada. *CPP* 25 (September):379–94.

Janssen, S., and U. Backes-Gellner. 2016. Occupational stereotypes and gender specific job satisfaction. *IR* 55(1):71–91.

Janssen, S., S. Sartore, and U. Backes-Gellner. 2016. Discriminatory social attitudes and varying gender gaps within firms. *ILLR* 69(1):253–279.

Jarrell, S., and T. D. Stanley. 2004. Declining bias and gender wage discrimination? A meta-regression analysis. *JHR* 39:828–38.

Javdani, M. 2015. Glass ceilings or glass doors? The role of firms in male–female wage disparities. *CJE* 48(2):529–560.

Johnston, D., and W.-S. Lee. 2012. Climbing the job ladder: New evidence of gender inequality. *IR* 31(1):129–151.

Jones, J. C. H., and W. D. Walsh. 1991. Product market imperfections, job content differences and gender employment discrimination at the management level: Some evidence from the Canadian manufacturing sector in 1971 and 1981. *CJE* 24:844–858.

Kassenboehmer, S., and M. Sinning. 2014. Distributional changes in the gender wage gap. *ILLR* 67(2):335–361.

Kidd, M., and M. Shannon. 1994. An update and extension of the Canadian evidence on gender wage differentials. *CJE* 27:918–38.

————. 1996a. The gender wage gap: A comparison of Australia and Canada. *ILRR* 49 (July):729–44.

————. 1996b. Does the level of occupational aggregation affect estimates of the gender wage gap? *ILRR* 49 (January):317–29.

Kim, M. 2013. Pay secrecy and the gender wage gap in the United States. *IR* 54(4):648–667.

Klawitter, M. 2015. Meta-analysis of the effect of sexual orientation on earnings. *IR* 54(1):4–32.

Kolpin, V., and L. Singell, Jr. 1996. The gender composition and scholarly performance of economics departments. *ILLR* 49:408–23.

Kosteas, V. 2013. Gender role attitudes, labor supply and human capital formation. *IR* 52(4):915–940.

Kreisman, D., and M. Rangel. On the blurring of the color line: Wages and employment for black males of different skin tones. *R.E.Stats* 97(1):1–13.

Kuhn, Peter, and Kailing Shen. 2013. Gender discrimination in job ads: Evidence from China. *QJE* 128(1):287–336.

Kuhn, Peter, and Marie Villeval. 2014. Are women more attracted to co-operation than men? *EJ* 125:115–140.

Kurtulus, F. 2013. Affirmative action and the occupational advance of minorities and women during 1973–2003. *IR* 51(2):213–246.

Lamb, Danielle. 2013. Earnings inequality among Aboriginal groups in Canada. *JLR* 34:224–240.

Lavy, V. 2013.Gender differences in market competitiveness in a real workplace: Evidence from performance-pay tournaments among teachers. *EJ* 123:540–573.

Le, A., P. Miller, W. Slutske, and N. Martin, 2011. Attitudes towards economic risk and the gender pay gap. *LE* 18(4):555–561.

Leppel, K. 2014. Does job satisfaction vary with sexual orientation? *IR* 53(2):169–198.

Light, A., and M. Ureta. 1992. Panel estimates of male and female job turnover behaviour. *JOLE* 10 (April):156–81.

——— . 1995. Early career work experience and gender wage differentials. *JOLE* 13:121–54.

Longhi, S., C. Nicoletti, and L. Platt. 2012. Interpreting wage gaps of disabled men: The roles of productivity and of discrimination. *SEJ* 78(3):931–953.

Lowen, A., and P. Sicilian. 2009. Family-friendly fringe benefits and the gender wage gap. *JLR* 30:101–119.

Ludsteck, J. 2014. The impact of segregation and sorting on the gender wage gap: Evidence from German linked longitudinal employer-employee data. *ILLR* 67(2):362–394.

Lundberg, S. 1991. The enforcement of equal opportunity laws under imperfect information: Affirmative action and alternatives. *QJE* 106:309–26.

Lundberg, S., and R. Startz. 1983. Private discrimination and social intervention in competitive labor markets. *AER* 73 (June):340–47.

——— . 1998. On the persistence of racial inequality. *JOLE* 16:292–324.

Macpherson, D. A., and B. T. Hirsch. 1995. Wages and gender composition: Why do women's jobs pay less? *JOLE* 13(3):426–71.

Madden, J. 1972. *The Economics of Sex Discrimination.* Lexington, MA: Lexington Books.

Manchester, C., and D. Barbezat. 2013. The effect of time use in explaining male–female productivity differences among economists. *IR* 52(1):53–77.

Manning, A. 2003. *Monopsony in Motion.* Princeton, N.J.: Princeton University Press.

Manning, A., and J. Swaffield. 2008. The gender gap in early career wage growth. *EJ* 118 (July):983–1024.

Martel, M. 2013. Do ENDAs end discrimination for behaviorally gay men? *JLR* 34:147–169.

Matsa, D., and A. Miller. 2013. A female style in corporate leadership? *AEJ: Applied Economics* 5(3):136–169.

McDonald, J. A., and R. J. Thornton. 1998. Private sector experience with pay equity in Ontario. *CPP* 24(2):185–208.

McDonald, J. A., and R. J. Thornton. 2015. Coercive cooperation: Ontario's pay equity act of 1988 and the gender pay gap. *CEP* 33(4):606–618.

Meitzen, M. 1986. Differences in male and female job quitting behavior. *JOLE* 4 (April):151–67.

Meng, X. 2004. Gender earnings gap: The role of firm specific effects. *LE* 11:555–73.

Morgan, L. A. 2008. Major matters: A comparison of the within-major gender pay gap across college majors for early-career graduates. *IR* 47 (October):625–650.

Mueller, G., and E. Plug. 2006. Estimating the effect of personality on male and female earnings. *ILRR* 60 (October):3–22.

Mulligan, C. B., and Y. Rubinstein. 2008. Selection, investment, and women's relative wages over time. *QJE* 123 (August):1061–1110.

Munasinghe, L., T. Reif, and A. Henriques. 2008. Gender gap in wage returns to job tenure and experience. *LE* 15:1296–1316.

Nardinelli, C., and C. Simon. 1990. Customer racial discrimination in the market for memorabilia: The case of baseball. *QJE* 105 (August):575–95.

Neal, D., and W. Johnson. 1996. The role of premarket factors in black-white wage differences. *JPE* 104:869–95.

Neumark, D. 2012. Detecting discrimination in audit and correspondence studies. *JHR* 47(4):1128–1157.

Neumark D., R. Bank, and K. Van Nort. 1996. Sex discrimination in restaurant hiring: An audit study. *QJE* 111 (August):915–41.

Niederle, M., and L. Vesterlund. 2007. Do women shy away from competition? Do men compete too much? *QJE* 122 (August):1067–1101.

Oaxaca, R. 1973. Male-female wage differentials in urban labour markets. *IER* 14 (October):693–709.

Oettinger, G. S. 1996. Statistical discrimination and the early career evolution of the black-white wage gap. *JOLE* 14(1):52–78

O'Neil, J., and D. O'Neil. 2005. What do wage differentials tell us about wage discrimination? National Bureau of Economic Research Working Paper 11240.

Orazem, P., and J. Mattila. 1990. The implementation process of comparable worth: Winners and losers. *JPE* 98 (February):134–52.

——— . 1998. Male–female supply to state government jobs and comparable worth. *JOLE* 16(1):95–121.

Ors, E., F. Palomino, and E. Peyrache. 2013. Performance gender gap: Does competition matter? *JOLE* 33(3):443–499.

Paglin, M., and A. Rufolo. 1990. Heterogeneous human capital, occupational choice, and male–female earnings differentials. *JOLE* (January):123–44.

Pendakur, K., and R. Pendakur. 1998. The colour of money: Earnings differentials among ethnic groups in Canada. *CJE* 31(August):518–48

——— . 2002. Colour my world: Have earnings gaps for Canadian-born ethnic minorities changed over time? *CPP* 28:489–512.

——— . 2007. Minority earnings disparity across the distribution. *CPP* 33 (March):41–61.

——— . 2011. Aboriginal income disparity in Canada. *CPP* 37 (March):61–83.

Pesando, J., M. Gunderson, and J. McLaren. 1991. Pension benefits and male–female wage differentials. *CJE* 24:536–50.

Phipps, S., P. Burton, and L. Lethbridge. 2001. In and out of the labour market: Long term income consequences of child-related interruptions to women's paid work. *CJE* 34 (May):411–25.

Plug, E., D. Webbink, and N. Martin. 2014. Sexual orientation, prejudice and segregation. *JOLE* 32(1):123–159.

Ransom, M., and R. L. Oaxaca. 2005. Intrafirm mobility and sex differences in pay. *ILRR* 58 (January):219–37.

——— . 2010. New market power models and sex differences in pay. *JOLE* 28(2):267–90.

Reich, M. 1978. Who benefits from racism? *JHR* 13 (Fall):524–44.

Reilly, K., and T. Wirjanto. 1999. Does more mean less? The male–female wage gap and the proportion females at the establishment level. *CJE* 32:906–29.

Reitz, J., and R. Breton. 1994. *The Illusion of Difference: Realities of Ethnicity in Canada and the United States.* Toronto: C. D. Howe Institute.

Reitz, J. G., J. R. Frick, R. Calabrese, and G. C. Wagner. 1999. The institutional framework of ethnic employment disadvantage: A comparison of Germany and Canada. *Journal of Ethnic and Migration Studies* 25(3):397–443.

Rodgers III, W., and L. S. Stratton. 2010. Male marital wage differentials: Training, personal characteristics, and fixed effects. *EI* 48(3):722–742.

Roemer, J. 1979. Divide and conquer: Micro-foundations of a Marxian theory of wage discrimination. *Bell Journal of Economics* 10 (Autumn):695–706.

Ruhm, C. 1998. The economic consequences of parental leave mandates: Lessons from Europe. *QJE* 113:285–317.

Santos-Pinto, L. 2012. Labor market signaling and self-confidence: Wage compression and the gender pay gap. *JOLE* 30(4):873–914.

Schirle, T. 2015. The gender gap in the Canadian provinces. *CPP* 41(4):309–319.

Scholz, J. K., and K. Sicinski. 2015. Facial attractiveness and lifetime earnings: Evidence from a cohort study. *R.E.Stats* 97(1):14–28.

Sicherman, N. 1996. Gender differences in departures from a large firm. *ILRR* 49:484–505.

Simpson, W. 1990. Starting even? Job mobility and the wage gap between young single males and females. *Applied Economics* 22 (June):723–37.

Skuterud, M. 2010. The visible minority earnings gap across generations of Canadians. *CJE* 43 (February):347–72.

Smith, N., V. Smith, and M. Verner. 2013. Why are so few females promoted into CEO and vice president positions: Danish empirical evidence, 1997–2007. *ILLR* 66(2):380–408.

Sorensen, E. 1990. The crowding hypothesis and comparable worth. *JHR* 25 (Winter):55–89.

Smith, D. M. 2002. Pay and productivity differences between male and female veterinarians. *ILRR* 55 (April):493–511.

Solberg, E., and T. Laughlin. 1995. The gender pay gap, fringe benefits and occupational crowding. *ILRR* 48:692–708.

Stelcner, M., and N. Kyriazis. 1995. An empirical analysis of earnings among ethnic groups in Canada. *International Journal of Contemporary Sociology* 32 (April):41–79.

Sulzner, G. 2000. A pay equity saga: The Public Service Alliance of Canada vs. the Treasury Board of Canada Secretariat. *Journal of Collective Negotiations in the Public Sector* 29(2):89–122.

Ureta, M. 1992. The importance of lifetime jobs in the U.S. economy, revisited. *AER* 82 (March):322–35.

Vincente, Carole. 2013. Why do women earn less than men: A synthesis of findings from Canadian microdata. CRDCN Synthesis Series.

Waldfogel, J. 1998. Understanding the "family gap" in pay for women with children. *JEP* 12:3–12.

Warman, C., F. Woolley, and C. Worswick. 2010. The evolution of male–female earnings differentials in Canadian universities 1970–2001. *CJE* 43 (February):347–72.

Webber, D. 2015. Firm market power and the earnings distribution. *LE* 35:123–134.

———. 2016. Firm-level monopsony and the gender pay gap. *IR* 55(2):323–345.

Weichselbaumer, D., and R. Winter-Ebner. 2005. A meta-analysis on the international gender wage gap. *JES* 19 (March):479–511.

Weinberger, C. J., and P. J. Kuhn. 2010. Changing levels or changing slopes? The narrowing of the gender earnings gap, 1959–1999. *ILRR* 63 (April):384–406.

Wellington, A. J. 1993. Changes in the male/female wage gap: 1976–85. *JHR* 28 (2):383–411.

Yap, M., and A. M. Konrad. 2009. Gender and racial differentials in promotions: Is there a sticky floor, a mid-level bottleneck, or a glass ceiling? *RI* 64 (Fall):593-619.

Zabalza, A., and Z. Tzannatos. 1985a. The effect of Britain's anti-discrimination legislation on relative pay and employment. *EJ* 95 (September, comments and reply *EJ* 98:812–43):79–99.

———. 1985b. *Women and Equal Pay: The Effects of Legislation on Female Employment and Wages.* Cambridge: Cambridge University Press.

Zafar, B. College major choice and the gender gap. *JHR* 48(3):545–595

Zeytinoglu, I. U., and G. B. Cooke. 2008. Non-standard employment and promotions: A within-genders analysis. *IR* 50 (February):319–37.

Zhang, X. 2009. Earnings of women with and without children. *PLI* 21 (Summer):5–14.

CHAPTER 13

Abeler, J., S. Altmann, S. Kube, and M. Wibral. 2010. Gift exchange and workers' fairness concerns: When equality is unfair. *Journal of the European Economic Association* 88 (December):1299–1324.

Abowd, J., and M. Bognanno. 1995. International differences in executive and managerial compensation. In *Differences and Changes in Wage Structures,* eds. R. Freeman and L. Katz. Chicago: University of Chicago Press.

Abowd, J., and D. Kaplan. 1999. Executive compensation: Six questions that need answering. *JEP* 13:145–68.

Abramitzky, R., and V. Lavy. 2014. How responsive is investment in schooling to changes in redistributive policies and in returns. *Ecta* 82(4):1241–1272.

Aggarwal, R., and A. Samwick. 1999. The other side of the trade-off: The impact of risk on executive compensation. *JPE* 107 (February):65–105.

Altman, S., A. Falk, and M. Wibral. 2012. Promotions and incentives: The case of multistage elimination tournaments. *JOLE* 30(1):149–174.

Anderson, F., M. Freedman, J. Haltiwanger, J. Lane, and K. Shaw. 2009. Reaching for the stars: Who pays for talent in innovative industries? *EJ* 119 (June):F308–F332.

Asch, B. 1990. Do incentives matter? The case of navy recruiters. *ILRR* 43 (November):S89–106.

Asch, B., and J. T. Warner. 2001. A theory of compensation and personnel policy in hierarchical organizations with application to the United States military. *JOLE* 19 (July):523–62.

Ashenflelter, O., and D. Card. 2002. Did the elimination of mandatory retirement affect faculty retirement? *AER* 92:957–80.

Atkinson, A., S. Burgess, B. Croxson, P. Gregg, C. Propper, H. Slater, and D. Wilson. 2008. Evaluating the impact of performance-related pay for teachers in England. *LE* 16 (June):251–261

Baker, G. P., and B. J. Hall. 2004. CEO incentives and firm size. *JOLE* 22 (October):767–98.

Baker, G., and B. Holmstrom. 1995. Internal labor markets: Too many theories, too few facts. *AER* 85:255–59.

Baker, G., M. Gibbs, and B. Holmstrom. 1994a. The internal economics of a firm: Evidence from personnel data. *QJE* 109:881–919.

———. 1994b. The wage policy of a firm. *QJE* 109:921–55.

Bandiera, O., I. Barankay, and I. Rasul. 2007. Incentives for managers and inequality among workers: Evidence from a firm-level experiment. *QJE* 122 (May):729–773.

———. 2009. Social connections and incentives in the workplace: Evidence from personnel data. *Ecta* 77 (July):1047–94.

———. 2010. Social incentives in the workplace. *R.E.Studies* 77 (February):417–458.

Barmby, T., B. Eberth, and A. Ma. 2012. Incentives, learning, task difficulty, and the Peter Principle. *LE* 19:76–8.1

Barron, J., and K. Gjerde. 1997. Peer pressure in an agency relationship. *JOLE* 15:234–54.

Barth, E., B. Bratsberg, T. Hægeland, and O. Raaum. 2008. Who pays for performance? *International Journal of Manpower* 29(1):8–29.

Bebchuk, L., and J. Fried. 2003. Executive compensation as an agency problem. *JEP* 17 (Summer):71–92.

———. 2004. *Pay without Performance: The Unfulfilled Promise of Executive Compensation.* Cambridge: Harvard University Press.

Bell, B., and J. Van Reenen. 2013. Extreme wage inequality: Pay at the very top. *AER Papers and Proceedings* 103(3):153–157.

Benmelech, E., E. Kandel, and P. Veronesi. 2010. Stock-based compensation and CEO (dis)incentives. *QJE* 125 (November):1769–1820.

Bertrand, M., and K. F. Hallock. 2001. The gender gap in top corporate jobs. *ILRR* 55(1):3–21.

Bertrand, M., and S. Mullainathan. 2001. Are CEOs rewarded for luck? The ones without principals are. *QJE* 116 (August):901–32.

Bivens, J., and L. Mishal. 2013. The pay of corporate executives and financial professionals as evidence of rents in top 1 percent incomes. *JEP* 27(3):57–78.

Blakemore, A. (ed.). 1987. The new economics of personnel. *JOLE*: Supplement 5 (Part 2).

Bognanno, M. 2001. Corporate tournaments. *JOLE* 19:290–315.

Boning, B., C. Ichniowski, and K. Shaw. 2007. Opportunity counts: Teams and the effectiveness of production incentives. *JLE* 25:613–50.

Booth, A. L., and J. Frank. 1999. Earnings, productivity, and performance-related pay. *JLE* 17(3):447–463.

Borjas, G., and K. Doran. 2015. Prizes and productivity: How winning the fields medal affects scientific output. *JHR* 50(3):728–740.

Brenčič, V., and J. B. Norris. 2010. On-the-job tasks and performance pay: A vacancy-level analysis. *ILRR* 63 (April):511–44.

Brown, M., and J. S. Heywood. 2003. The determinants of incentive schemes: Australian panel data. *Australian Bulletin of Labour* 29(3):218–235.

Bryson, A., J. Forth, and M. Zhou. 2014. Same or different: The CEO labour market in China's public listed companies. *EJ* 124: F90–F108.

Bullon, F. M. 2010. Gender compensation differences among high-level executives in the United States. *IR* 49(3):346–370.

Burgess, S., C. Propper, M. Ratto, A. H. K. Scholder, and E. Tominery. 2009. Smarter task assignment or greater effort: The impact of incentives on team performance. *EJ* 120 (September):968–89.

Burkhauser, R., and J. Quinn. 1983. Is mandatory retirement overrated? Evidence from the 1970s. *JHR* 18:337–58.

Carmichael, L., 1988. Incentives in academics: Why is there tenure? *JPE* 96 (June):453–72.

———. 1989. Self-enforcing contracts, shirking and life-cycle incentives. *JEP* 365–83.

Chan, H., B. Frey, J. Gallus, and B.Torgler. 2014. Academic honors and performance. *LE* 31:188–204.

Chan, W. 1996. External recruitment versus internal promotion. *JOLE* 14:555–70.

Charness, G., and P. Kuhn. 2007. Does pay inequality affect worker effort? Experimental evidence. *JLE* 25: 693–723.

Chauvin K. W., and A. Ronald. 1994. Gender-earning differentials in total pay, base pay and contingent pay. *ILRR* 47(4):634–649.

Che, Y.-K., and S.-W. Yoo. 2001. Optimal incentives for teams. *AER* 91 (June):525–41.

Chen, K.-P. 2005. External recruitment as incentive device. *JOLE* 23 (April):259–77.

Chen, P., and P.-A. Edin. 2002. Efficiency wages and industry wage differentials: A comparison across methods of pay. *R.E.Stats* 84 (November):617–31.

Clark, R. L., and L. S. Ghent. 2008. Mandatory retirement and faculty retirement decisions. *IR* 47 (January):153–63.

Compensation strategy and design. 2002. Special issue of *JOLE* 20 (April).

Conyon, M. 2014. Executive compensation and board governance in U.S. firms. *EJ* 124:F60–F89.

Conyon, M., and K. Murphy. 2000. The prince and the pauper: CEO pay in the United States and the United Kingdom. *EJ* 110:640–671.

Copeland, A., and C. Monnet. 2009. The welfare effects of incentive schemes. *R.E.Studies* 76 (January):93–113.

Cowling, M. 2000. Performance related pay in Belgium and the Netherlands. *Applied Economics Letters* 7(10):653–657.

Crystal, G. 1991. *In Search of Excess: The Overcompensation of American Executives.* New York: W.W. Norton Co.

DeVaro, J., and A. Kauhanen. 2016. An "opposing response" test of classical versus market-based promotion tournaments. *JOLE* 34 (3).

DeVaro, J., and M. Waldman. 2012. The signaling role of promotions. *JOLE* 30(1):91–147.

Dohmen, T. J. 2004. Performance, seniority and wages: Formal salary systems and individual earnings profiles. *LE* 11 (December):741–63.

Dohmen T., and Falk A. 2006. Seemingly irrelevant events affect economic perceptions and expectations: The FIFA World Cup 2006 as a natural experiment. Working paper:1–16.

———. 2011. Performance pay and multi-dimensional sorting: Productivity, preferences and gender. *AER* 101(2):556–590.

Doucouliagos, H., J. Haman, and T. Stanley. 2012. Pay for performance and corporate governance reform. *IR* 51(3):670–703.

Drago, R., and G. Garvey. 1998. Incentives for helping on the job. *JOLE* 16:1–25.

Duflo, E., R. Hanna, and S. Ryan. 2012. Incentives work: Getting teachers to come to school. *AER* 102(4):1241–1278.

Duggan, M., and S. Levitt. Winning isn't everything: Corruption in Sumo wrestling. *AER* 92:1594–1605.

Ehrenberg, R., and M. Bognanno. 1990. Do tournaments have incentive effects? *JPE* 98 (December):1307–24.

Ellingsen, T., and M. Johannesson. 2007. Paying respect. *JEP* 21 (Fall):135–49.

Elvira, M. M., and M. E. Graham. 2002. Not just a formality: Pay system formalization and sex-related earnings effects. *Organization Science* 13(6):601–617.

Eriksson, T. 1999. Executive compensation and tournament theory: Empirical tests on Danish data. *JOLE* 17:262–80.

Fabling, R., and A. Grimes.2014. The suite smell of success: personnel practices and firm performance. *ILLR* 67(4):1095–1126.

Fairburn J. A., and J. M. Malcomson. 2001. Performance, promotion and the Peter Principle. *R.E.Studies* 68 (January):45–67.

Ferrall C., A. W. Gregory, and W. Tholl. 1998. Endogenous work hours and practice patterns of Canadian physicians. *CJE* 31(1):1–27.

Flabbi, L., and A. Ichino. 2001. Productivity, seniority and wages: New evidence from personnel data. *LE* 8 (June):359–87.

Frick, B., U. Goetzen, and R. Simmons. 2013. The hidden cost of high-performance work practices. *ILLR* 66(1):189–209.

Fuess, S. M., and M. Millea. 2002. Do employers pay efficiency wages? Evidence from Japan. *JLR* 23 (Spring):279–92.

Gabaix, X., and A. Landier. 2008. Why has CEO pay increased so much? *QJE* 123 (February):49–100.

Gabaix, X., A. Landier, and J. Sauvagnat. 2014. CEO pay and firm size: An update after the crises. *EJ* 124:F40–F59.

Gayle, G., L. Golan, and R. Miller. Promotion, turnover and compensation in the executive market. *Ecta* 83(6):2293–2369.

Gayle, G., and R. A. Miller. 2009. Has moral hazard become a more important factor in managerial compensation? *AER* 99 (December):1740–1769.

Geddes, L. A., and J. S. Heywood. 2003. Gender and piece rates, commissions, and bonuses. *IR* 42(3):419–444.

Georg, S. J., S. Kube, and R. Zultan. 2010. Treating equals unequally: Incentives in teams, workers' motivation, and production technology. *JLE* 28 (October):747–72.

Gersbach H., and A. Glazer. 2009. High compensation creates a ratchet effect. *EJ* (July):1208–1224.

Gibbons, R. 1987. Piece-rate incentive schemes. *JOLE* 5 (October):413–29.

———. 1998. Incentives in organizations. *JEP* 12:115–32.

Gibbons, R., and M. Waldman. 1998. Careers in organisations: Theory and evidence. In *Handbook of Labor Economics,* eds. O. Ashenfelter and D. Card, Vol. 3B. New York: North-Holland.

Gibbs, M. J., K. A. Merchant, W.A. V. D. Stede, and M. E. Vargus. 2009. Performance measure properties and incentive system design. *IR* 48 (April):237–63.

Gittleman, M., and B. Pierce. 2015. Pay for performance and compensation inequality: Evidence from the ECEC. *ILLR* 68(1):28–52.

Gneezy, U., and A. Rustichini. 2004. Gender and competition at a young age. *AER* 94(2):377–381.

Gneezy, U., M. Niederle, and A. Rustichini. 2003. Performance in competitive environments: Gender differences. *QJE* 118(3):1049–73.

Goldin, C. 1986. Monitoring costs and occupational segregation by sex: A historical analysis. *JOLE* 4(1):1–27.

Gomez-Mejia, L. R., and D. B. Balkin. 1992. Determinants of faculty pay: An agency theory perspective. *Academy of Management Journal* 35(5):921–955.

Goodman, S., and L. Turner. 2013. The design of teacher incentive pay and educational outcomes: Evidence from the New York City bonus program. *JOLE* 31:409–420.

Grant, H., and J. Townsend. 2013. Mandatory retirement and the employment rights of elderly Canadian immigrants. *CPP* 39(1):135–152.

Gregory-Smith, I., S. Thompson, and P. Wright. 2014. CEO pay and voting: Dissent before and after the crises. *EJ* 124:F22–F39.

Gunderson, M. 1983. Mandatory retirement and personnel policies. *Columbia Journal of World Business* (Summer):8–15.

———. 2001. Economics of personnel and human resource management. *Human Resource Management Review* 11(4):431–452.

Haley, M. R. 2003. The response of worker effort to piece rates: Evidence from the Midwest logging industry. *JHR* 38 (Fall):881–90.

Hallock, K. F. 2002. Managerial pay and governance in American nonprofits. *IR* 41(3):377–406.

———. 2009. Job loss and the fraying of the implicit employment contract. *JEP* 123 (Fall):69–93.

Hallock, K. F., and F. Klein. 2016. Executive compensation in American unions. *IR* 55(2):219–234.

Harbring, C., and B. Irlenbusch. 2003. An experimental study on tournament design. *LE* 10 (August):443–64.

Hamlen, W. 1991. Superstardom in popular music. *R.E.Stats* 73 (November):729–32.

Heisz, A. 1996. Changes in job tenure. *PLI* 8 (Winter):31–35.

Hermalin, B., and M. Weisbach. 1998. Endogenously chosen boards of directors and their monitoring of the CEO. *AER* 88(1):96–118.

Heywood, J. S., and U. Jirjahn. 2002. Payment schemes and gender in Germany. *ILRR* 56(1):44–64.

Heywood, J. S., and D. Parent. 2012. Performance pay and the black-white wage gap. *JOLE* 30(2):249–290.

Holmstrom, B., and P. Milgrom. 1994. The firm as an incentive system. *AER* 84:972–91.

Huck S., A. J. Seltzer, and B.Wallace. 2011. Deferred compensation in multiperiod labour contracts: An experimental test of Lazear's model. *AER* 101(2):819–843.

Hutchens, R. 1987. A test of Lazear's theory of delayed payment contracts. *JOLE* 5(2) (October):S153–70.

——— . 1989. Seniority, wages and productivity. *JEP* 3 (Fall):49–64.

Hvide, H. K. 2002. Tournament rewards and risk taking. *JOLE* 20 (October):877–98.

Ichniowski, C., K. Shaw, and G. Prennushi. 1997. The effects of human resource management practices on productivity: A study of steel finishing lines. *AER* 87:291–313.

Jensen, M., and K. Murphy. 1990. Performance pay and top management incentives. *JPE* 98 (April):225–64.

Jones, D. C., and T. Kato. 2011. The impact of teams on output, quality, and downtime: An empirical analysis using individual panel data. *ILRR* 64 (January):215–33.

Jones, D. C., P. Kalmi, and A. Kauhanen. 2010. Teams, incentive pay, and productive efficiency: Evidence from a food-processing plant. *ILRR* 63 (July):606–26.

Kahn, C., and G. Huberman. 1988. Two-sided uncertainty and "up-or-out" contracts. *JOLE* 6:423–44.

Kahn, L., and P. Sherer. 1990. Contingent pay and managerial performance. *ILRR* 43(3)(Special Issue):S107–S121.

Kandel, E., and E. Lazear. 1992. Peer pressure and partnerships. *JPE* 100 (August):801–17.

Kaplan, S., and J. Rauh. 2013. It's market: The broad-based rise in the teturn to top talent. *JEP* 27(3):35–55.

Kraft, K. 1991. The incentive effect of dismissals, efficiency wages, piece rates and profit sharing. *R.E.Stats* 73 (August):451–59.

Kosfeld, M., and S. Neckermann. 2011. Getting more work for nothing? Symbolic awards and worker performance. *Am. Econ. J. Microecon.* 3(3):86–99.

Kruger, A. 2005. The economics of real superstars: The market for rock concerts in the material world. *JOLE* 23 (January):1–30.

Larkin, I. 2014.The cost of high-powered incentives: Employee gaming in enterprise software sales. *JOLE* 32(2):199–227.

Lazear, E. 1979. Why is there mandatory retirement? *JPE* 87 (December):1261–84.

——— . 1981. Agency, earnings profiles, productivity and hours restrictions. *AER* 71:606–20.

——— . 1986. Raids and offer-matching. *Research in Labor Economics* 8:141–65.

——— . 1989. Pay equality and industrial politics. *JPE* 97:561–80.

——— . 1990. Pensions and deferred benefits as strategic compensation. *IR* 29:263–80.

——— . 1991. Labor economics and the psychology of organisations. *JEL* 5:89–110.

——— . 1995. *Personnel Economics.* Cambridge, Mass., and London: MIT Press.

——— . 1998. *Personnel Economics for Managers.* New York: Wiley.

——— . 1999. Personnel economics: Past lessons and future directions. *JOLE* 17:199–236.

——— . 2000. Performance pay and productivity. *AER* 90:1346–61.

——— . 2004. The Peter Principle: A theory of decline. *JPE* 112 (February):S141–63.

——— . 2007. *Personnel Economics: New Developments.* Oxford: Oxford University Press.

———. 2011. Leadership: A personnel economics approach. *LE* 19:92–101.

Lazear, E., and S. Rosen. 1981. Rank-order tournaments as optimum labor contracts. *JPE* 89 (October):841–64.

Lazear, E. P., and K. L. Shaw. 2007. Personnel economics: The economist's view of human resources. *JEP* 21 (Fall):91–114.

Lazear, E., and P. Oyer. 2004a. Wages and internal mobility. *AER* 94 (May):212–16.

——— . 2004b. Internal and external labor markets: A personnel economics approach. *LE* 11 (October):527–54.

——— . 2007. Personnel economics: The economist's view of human resources. *American Economic Association* 21(4):91–114.

Lemieux, T., W. B. MacLeod, and D. Parent. 2009. Performance pay and wage inequality. *QJE* 124 (February):1–49.

Leonard, J. 1990. Executive pay and firm performance. *ILLR* 43(Supplement):13–29.

Lindbeck, A. 1997. Incentives and social norms in household behavior. *AER* 87:369–77.

Loewenstein, G., and N. Sicherman. 1991. Do workers prefer increasing wage profiles? *JOLE* 9 (January):67–84.

Long, R., and T. Fang. 2012. Do employees profit from profit sharing: evidence from Canadian panel data. *ILLR* 65(4):899–927.

Lucifora, C., and F. Origo. 2015. Performance related pay and firm productivity: Evidence from a reform in the structure of collective bargaining. *ILLR* 68(3):606–632.

MacDonald, G., and M. S. Weisbach. 2004. The economics of has-beens. *JPE* 112 (February):S289–310.

Main, B., C. O'Reilly, and J. Wade. 1993. Top executive pay: Tournament or teamwork? *JOLE* 11:608–28.

Malcolsom, J. 1998. Individual employment contracts in labor markets. In *Handbook of Labor Economics,* eds. O. Ashenfelter and D. Card, Vol. 3B. New York: North-Holland.

Malmendier, U., and G. Tate. 2009. Superstar CEOs. *QJE* 124 (November):1593–1638.

Manning, A., and F. Saidi. 2010. Understanding the gender pay gap: What's competition got to do with it? *ILRR* 63 (July):681–697.

Mengistae, T., and L. C. Xu. 2004. Agency theory and executive compensation: The case of Chinese state-owned enterprises. *JOLE* 22 (July):615–37.

Mitchell, D., and M. Zaidi. (Eds.) 1990. The economics of human resource management. *IR* (Special Issue) 29(2).

Moldovanu, B., and A. Sela. 2001. The optimal allocation of prizes in contests. *AER* 91 (June):542–58.

Muñoz-Bullón, F. 2010. Gender-compensation differences among high-level executives in the United States. *IR* 49 (July):346–370.

Muralidharan, K., and V. Sundararaman. 2011. Teacher performance pay: Experimental evidence from India. *JPE* 119(1):39–76.

Murphy, K. 1985. Corporate performance and managerial remuneration. *Journal of Accounting and Economics* 7:11–42.

Murphy, K. J. 1999. Executive compensation. In *Handbook of Labor Economics,* eds. O. Ashenfelter and D. Card, Vol. 3B. Amsterdam: North-Holland.

Murphy, K. J., and J. Zabojnik. 2004. CEO pay and appointments: A market-based explanation for recent trends. *AER* 94 (May):192–202.

Neckermann, S., R. Cueni, and B. Frey. 2014. Awards at work. *LE* 31:205–217.

Neumark, D., and W. Stock. 1999. Age discrimination laws and labor market efficiency. *JPE* 107:1081–1125.

Oettinger, G. S. 2002. The effect of nonlinear incentives on performance: Evidence from "ECON 101." *R.E.Stats* 84 (August):509–17.

O'Flaherty, B., and A. Siow. 1992. On-the-job screening, up-or-out rules, and firm growth. *CJE* 25 (May):346–68.

——— . 1995. Up-or-out rules in the market for lawyers. *JOLE* 13 (October):709–35.

Ortin-Angel, P., and V. Salas-Fumas. 2002. Compensation and span of control in hierarchial organizations. *JOLE* 20 (October):848–76.

Oyer, P. 1998. Fiscal year ends and nonlinear incentive contracts: The effect on business seasonality. *QJE* 113 (February):149–85.

Oyer, P., and S. Schaefer. 2011. Personnel economics: Hiring and incentives. In *Handbook of Labor Economics,* O. Ashenfelter and D. Card, eds., Vol 4b. Great Britain: North-Holland.

Paarsch, H., and B. Shearer. 1999. The response of worker effort to piece rates: Evidence from the British Columbia tree planting industry. *JHR* 35:1–25.

Parent, D. 1999. Methods of pay and earnings: A longitudinal analysis. *ILLR* 53(1):71–86.

Parsons, D. 1986. The employment relationship: Job attachment, work effort, and the nature of contracts. In *Handbook of Labour Economics,* eds. O. Ashenfelter and R. Layard. New York: Elsevier.

Peach, E. K., and T. D. Stanley. 2009. Efficiency wages, productivity and simultaneity: A meta-regression analysis. *JLR* 30 (September):262–68.

Pekkarinen, T., and C. Riddell. 2008. Performance pay and earnings: Evidence from personnel records. *ILRR* 61 (April):297–318.

Pesando, J., and M. Gunderson. 1988. Retirement incentives contained in occupational pension plans and their implications for the mandatory retirement debate. *CJE* 21:244–64.

Pesando, J., M. Gunderson, and P. Shum. 1992. Incentive and redistributive effects of private sector union pension plans in Canada. *IR* 30:179–94.

Prendergast, C. 1999. The provision of incentives in firms. *JEL* 37:7–63.

Raff, D., and L. Summers. 1987. Did Henry Ford pay efficiency wages? *JOLE* 5 (October):57–86.

Reid, F. 1988. Economic aspects of mandatory retirement: The Canadian experience. *RI/IR* 43:101–13.

Reskin B. F. 2000. The proximate causes of employment discrimination. *Contemporary Sociology* 29(2):319–328.

Rosen, S. 1981. The economics of superstars. *AER* 71 (December):845–58.

———. 1982. Authority, control and the distribution of earnings. *Bell Journal of Economics* 13:311–23.

———. 1986. Prizes and incentives in elimination tournaments. *AER* 76:921–39.

Rosen, S., and A. Sanderson. 2001. Labour markets in professional sports. *EJ* 111 (February):F47–68.

Sen, A., H. Ariizumi, and N. Desousa. 2014. Evaluating the relationship between pay and research productivity: Panel data evidence from Ontario universities. *CPP* 40(1):1–14.

Sgobbi, F., and G. Cainarca. 2015. High performance work practices and core employee wages: Evidence from Italian manufacturing plants. *ILLR* 68(2):426–456.

Shannon, M., and D. Grierson. 2004. Mandatory retirement and older worker employment. *CJE* 37:528–51.

Shaw, K. 2009. Insider econometrics: A roadmap with stops along the way. *LE* 16 (December):607–17.

Shearer, B. 2004. Piece rates, fixed wages and incentives: Evidence from a field experiment. *R.E.Studies* 71:513–534.

Singh, P., and N. C. Agarwal. 2002. Union presence and executive compensation: An exploratory study. *JLR* 23 (Fall):631–46.

Sojourner, A., E. Mykerezi, and K. West. 2014. Teacher pay reform and productivity. *JHR* 49(4):945–981.

Stiroh, K. J. 2007. Playing for keeps: Pay and performance in the NBA. *EI* 45 (January):145–61.

Taylor, B. A., and J. G. Trogdon. 2002. Losing to win: Tournament incentives in the national basketball association. *JOLE* 20 (January):23–41.

Taylor, J. E. 2003. Did Henry Ford mean to pay efficiency wages? *JLR* 24 (Fall):683–94.

Terviö, Marko. 2008. The differences that CEOs make: An assignment model. *AER* 98:642–668.

Tranaes, T. 2001. Raiding opportunities and unemployment. *JOLE* 19 (October):773–98.

Wade, J. 1993. Top executive pay: Tournament or teamwork? *JOLE* 11:606–28.

Waldman, M. 1990. Up-or-out contracts: A signalling perspective. *JOLE* 8:230–50.

Warman, C., and C. Worswick. 2010. Mandatory retirement rules and the retirement decisions of university professors in Canada. *LE* 17 (May):1022–29.

Weisbach, M. S. 2007. Optimal executive compensation versus managerial power: A review of Lucian Bebchuk and Jesse Fried's *Pay*

without Performance: The Unfulfilled Promise of Executive Compensation. JEL 45 (June):419–28.

Zhou, X. 2000. CEO pay, firm size, and corporate performance: Evidence from Canada. *CJE* 33(1):213–51.

Zwick, T. 2012. Consequences of seniority wages on the employment structure. *ILLR* 65(1):108–125.

CHAPTER 14

Abbott, M. 1982. An econometric model of trade union membership growth in Canada, 1925–1966. Princeton University, Industrial Relations Section Working Paper, No. 154.

Abowd, J. M. 1989. The effect of wage bargains on the stock market value of the firm. *AER* 79 (September):774–809.

Ashenfelter, O., and J. Pencavel. 1969. American trade union growth: 1900–1960. *QJE* 83 (August):434–48.

Brown, J., and O. Ashenfelter. 1986. Testing the efficiency of employment contracts. *JPE* 94 (July):S40–87.

Bryson, A., R. Gomez, M. Gunderson, and N. Meltz. 2005. Youth-adult differences in the demand for unionization: Are American, British, and Canadian workers all that different? *JLR* 26 (Winter):155–167.

Campolieti, M., C. Riddell, and S. Slinn. 2007. Labor law reform and the role of delay in union organizing: Empirical evidence from Canada. *ILRR* 61 (October):32–58.

Card, D. 1986. Efficient contracts with costly adjustment: Short-run employment determination for airline mechanics. *AER* 76 (December):1045–71.

———. 1990. Unexpected inflation, real wages, and employment determination in union contracts. *AER* 80 (September):669–88.

Carruth, A., and A. Oswald. 1985. Miners' wages in post-war Britain: An application of a model of trade union behaviour. *EJ* 95(380):1003–1020.

Christofides, L. 1990. Non-nested tests of efficient bargain and labour demand models. *Economics Letters* 32 (January):91–6.

Christofides, L., and A. Oswald. 1991. Efficient and inefficient employment outcomes: A study based on Canadian contract data. In *Research in Labor Economics,* Vol. 12, ed. R. G. Ehrenberg. Greenwich, Conn.: JAI Press.

Conyon, M. 2014. Executive compensatioand board governance in U.S. firms. *EJ* 124:F60–F89.

Currie, J. 1991. Employment determination in a unionized public-sector labour market: The case of Ontario's school teachers. *JOLE* 9 (November):45–66.

Dertouzos, J., and J. Pencavel. 1981. Wage and employment determination under trade unionism: The international typographical union. *JPE* 89 (December):1162–81.

Doiron, D. 1992. Bargaining power and wage-employment contracts in a unionized industry. *IER* 33 (August):583–606.

Doiron, D., and W. C. Riddell. 1994. The impact of unionization on male–female earnings differences in Canada. *JHR* 29:504–34.

Dunlop, J. T. 1944. *Wage Determination under Trade Unions.* New York: Macmillan.

Farber, H. 1978. Individual preferences and union wage determination: The case of the United Mine Workers. *JPE* 86 (October):923–42.

———. 1983. The determinants of the union status of workers. *Ecta* 51 (September):1417–37.

Farber, H., and D. Saks. 1980. Why workers want unions: The role of relative wages and job characteristics. *JPE* 88 (April):349–69.

Farber, H., and B. Western. 2001. Accounting for the decline of unions in the private sector, 1973–1998. *JLR* 22 (Summer):459–85.

Fisher, T., and R. Waschik. 2000. Union bargaining power, relative wages, and efficiency in Canada. *CJE* 33 (August):742–65.

Flanagan, R. 2005. Has management strangled U.S. unions? *JLR* 26 (Winter):33–63.

Freeman, R. 1986. Unionism comes to the public sector. *JEL* 25 (March):41–86.

———. 1988. Contraction and expansion: the divergence of private sector and public sector unionism in the United States. *JEP* 2 (Spring):63–88.

Galarneau, Diane, and Thao Sohn. 2012. Long-term trends in unionization, in *Insights on Canadian Society.* Ottawa: Statistics Canada, November, pp. 1–6.

Godard, J. 2009. The exceptional decline of the American labor movement. *ILRR* 63 (October):82–108.

Hogan, C. 2001. Enforcement of implicit employment contracts through unionization. *JOLE* 19 (January):171–95.

Hosios, A. J., and A. Siow. 2004. Unions without rents: The curious economics of faculty unions. *CJE* 37 (February):28–52.

Johnson, S. 2002a. Canadian union density 1980 to 1998 and prospects for the future: An empirical investigation. *CPP* 38 (September):333–49.

———. 2002b. Card check or mandatory representation vote? How the type of union recognition procedure affects union certification success. *EJ* 112 (April):344–61.

Johnson, Susan. 2010. First contract arbitration: Effects on bargaining and work stoppages. *ILRR* 63(4):585–605.

Kaufman, B. E. 2002. Models of union wage determination: What have we learned since Dunlop and Ross? *IR* 41:111–58.

Kumar, P., and B. Dow. 1986. Econometric analysis of union membership growth in Canada, 1935–1981. *RI/IR* 41(2):236–53.

Legree, Scott, Tammy Schirle, and Mikal Skuterud. 2016. Can labour relations reform or reduce wage inequality? in *Income Inequality: The Canadian Story,* eds. David A. Green, W. Craig Riddell, and France St-Hilaire. Montreal: Institute for Research on Public Policy, pp. 399–434.

Lindbeck, A., and D. Snower. 1988. *The Insider-Outsider Theory of Employment and Unemployment.* Cambridge. MA: MIT Press.

Lipset, S., and N. Meltz. 2004. *The Paradox of American Unionism: Why Americans Like Unions More Than Canadians Do but Join Much Less.* Ithaca, New York: ILR Press.

Machin, S., and S. Wood. 2005. Human resource management as a substitute for trade unions in British workplaces. *ILLR* 58 (January):201–18.

MaCurdy, T., and J. Pencavel. 1986. Testing between competing models of wage and employment determination in unionized markets. *JPE* 94 (July):S3–39.

Magnani, E. 2003. Did globalization reduce unionization? Evidence from U.S. manufacturing. *Labour Economics* 10 (December):705–26.

Manning, A. 1994. How robust is the microeconomic theory of the trade union? *JOLE* 12 (July):430–59.

Martinello, F. 1989. Wage and employment determination in a unionized industry: The IWA and the B.C. wood products industry. *JOLE* 7 (July):303–30.

———. 2000. Mr. Harris, Mr. Rae, and union activity in Ontario. *CPP* 26 (March):17–34.

Martinello, F., and R. Meng. 1992. Effects of labor legislation and industry characteristics on union coverage in Canada. *ILRR* 46 (October):176–90.

Naylor, R. 2003. Economic models of union behaviour. In *International Handbook of Trade Unions,* eds. J. Addison and C. Schnabel. Cheltenham, UK: Edward Elgar.

Neumann, G., and E. R. Rissman. 1984. Where have all the union members gone? *JOLE* 2 (April):175–92.

Oswald, A. 1993. Efficient contracts are on the labour demand curve: Theory and facts. *LE* 1 (June):85–113.

Pencavel, J. 1971. The demand for union services: An exercise. *ILRR* 24 (January):180–90.

———. 1984. The tradeoff between wages and employment in trade union objectives. *QJE* 99 (May):215–32.

———. 2004. The surprising retreat of union Britain. In *Seeking a Premier Economy,* eds. D. Card, R. Blundell, and R. Freeman. Chicago: University of Chicago Press.

———. 2005. Unionism viewed internationally. *JLR* 26 (Winter):65–97.

Riddell, C. 2001. Union suppression and certification success. *CJE* 34 (May):396–410.

———. 2004. Union certification success under voting versus card-check procedures: Evidence from British Columbia, 1978–1998. *ILLR* 57 (July):493–517.

———. 2013. Labor law and reaching a first collective agreement: Evidence from a quasi-experimental set of reforms in Ontario. *Industrial Relations* 52(3):702–736.

Riddell, C., and W. C. Riddell. 2004. Changing patterns of unionization: The North American experience, 1984–1998. In *Unions in the 21st Century,* eds. A. Verma and T. Kochan. New York: Palgrave Macmillan.

Riddell, W. C. 1993. Unionization in Canada and the United States: A tale of two countries. In *Small Differences that Matter: Labor Markets and Income Maintenance in Canada and the United States,* eds. D. Card and R. Freeman. Chicago: University of Chicago Press.

Robinson, C. 1995. Union incidence in the public and private sectors. *CJE* 28 (November):1056–76.

Ross, A. 1948. *Trade Union Wage Policy.* Berkeley: University of California Press.

Schnabel, C. 2003. Determinants of trade union membership. In *International Handbook of Trade Unions,* eds. J. Addison and C. Schnabel. Cheltenham, U.K.: Edward Elgar.

Solow, R. 1985. Insiders and outsiders in wage determination. *Scandinavian Journal of Economics* 87 (April):411–28.

Swidinsky, R. 1974. Trade union growth in Canada: 1911–1970. *RI/IR* 29(3):435–50.

Svenjar, J. 1986. Bargaining power, fear of disagreement and wage settlements: Theory and empirical evidence from U.S. industry. *Ecta* 54 (September):1055–78.

Taras, D., and A. Ponak. 2001. Mandatory agency shop laws as an explanation of Canada–U.S. union density divergence. *JLR* 22 (Summer):541–68.

Visser, J. 2003. Unions and unionism around the world. In *International Handbook of Trade Unions,* eds. J. Addison and C. Schnabel. Cheltenham, U.K.: Edward Elgar.

Weiler, P. 1983. Promises to keep: Securing workers' rights to self-organization under the NLRA. *Harvard Law Review* 96 (June):1769–829.

Woojin, L., and J. Roemer. 2005. The rise and fall of unionised labour markets: A political economy approach. *EJ* 115 (January):28–67.

CHAPTER 15

Addison, J., and C. Belfield. 2001. Updating the determinants of firm performance: Estimation using the 1998 WERS. *BJIR* 39:341–66.

Addison, J., and C. Belfield. 2004. Unions and establishment performance: Evidence from the British Workplace Industrial/Employee Relations surveys. In *The Changing Role of Unions: New Forms of Representation,* ed. P. Wunnava. New York: M.E. Sharpe.

Addison, J., and J. Wagner. 1994. Unionism and innovative activity: Some cautionary remarks on the basis of a simple cross-country test. *BJIR* 32:85–98.

Allen, S. 1984. Trade unionized construction workers are more productive. *QJE* 99 (May):251–74.

———. 1988. Productivity levels and productivity change under unionism. *IR* 27:94–113.

Artz, B. 2012. Does the impact of union experience on job satisfaction differ by gender? *ILRR* 65(2):225–243.

Ashenfelter, O., and G. Johnson. 1972. Trade unions and the rate of change of money wages in United States manufacturing industry. *R.E.Studies* 39 (January):27–54.

Bahrami, B., J. D. Bitzan, and J. A. Leitch. 2009. Union worker wage effect in the public sector. *JLR* 30:35–51.

Banning, K., and T. Chiles. 2007. Tradeoffs in the labor union–CEO compensation relationship. *JLR* 28:347–57.

Barnichon, Regis, and Andrew Figura, 2015. Declining desire to work and downward trends in unemployment and participation. *NBER Macroeconomics Annual 2015,* eds. M. Eichenbaum and J. Parker.

Bastos, P., U. Kreickemeier, and P. W. Wright. 2010. Open-shop unions and product market competition. *CJE* 43(2):640–662.

Bebchuck, L., and J. Fried. 2004. *Pay without Performance: The Unfulfilled Promise of Executive Compensation.* Boston, MA: Harvard University Press.

Becker, B., and C. Olson. 1989. Unionization and shareholder interests. *ILRR* 42 (January):246–62.

Belman, D. 1992. Unions and firm profits. *IR* 31:395–415.

Belman, D., J. S. Haywood, and J. Lund. 1997. Public sector earnings and the extent of unionization. *ILLR* 50 (July):610–28.

Berg, P., E Kossek, K. Misra, and D. Belman. 2014. Work-life flexibility policies: Do unions affect employee access and use? *ILRR* 67:111–131.

Betts J., C. Odgers, and M. Wilson. 2001. The effects of unions on research and development: An empirical analysis using multi-year data. *CJE* 34:785–806.

Bilginsoy, C. 2013. Union wage gap in the U.S. construction sector: 1983–2007. *IR* 52(3):677–701.

Blackburn, M. L. 2008. Are union wage differentials in the United States falling? *IR* 47(3):390–418.

Blanchflower, D., and A. Bryson. 2004. What effect do unions have on wages now and would Freeman and Medoff be surprised? *JLR* 25 (Summer):383–414.

Blau, F., and L. Kahn. 1983. Unionism, seniority, and turnover. *IR* 22 (Fall):362–73.

Block, R., and P. Berg. 2009. Joint responsibility unionism: A multi-plant model of collective bargaining under employment security. *ILLR* 63:60–81.

Boal, W. 2009. The effect of unionism on accidents in the U.S. coal mining, 1897–1929. *IR* 48(1):97–120.

Bratsberg, B., and J. F. Ragan Jr. 2002. Changes in the union wage premium by industry. *ILRR* 56:65–82.

Bronars, S., and D. Deere. 1990. Union representation elections and firm profitability. *IR* 29:15–37.

Bronars, S., G. Deere, and J. Tracy. 1994. The effects of unions on firm behaviour. *IR* 33:426–51.

Brown, C., and J. Medoff. 1978. Trade unions in the production process. *JPE* 86:355–78.

Brown, S., and J. D. Sessions. 2004. Trade unions and international competition. In *The Changing Role of Unions: New Forms of Representation,* ed. P. Wunnava. New York: M.E. Sharpe.

Bryson, A., E. Barth, and H. Dale-Olsen. 2013. The effects of organizational change on worker well-being and the moderating role of trade unions. *ILRR* 66(4):989–1011.

Budd, J., and K. Mumford. 2004. Trade unions and "family-friendly" policies in Great Britain. *ILRR* 57:204–22.

Card, D. 1996. The effect of unions on the structure of wages: A longitudinal analysis. *Ecta* 64 (July):957–79.

———. 2001. The effect of unions on wage inequality in the U.S. labor market. *ILRR* 54:296–315.

Card, D., T. Lemieux, and W. Craig Riddell. 2004. Unions and wage inequality. *JLR* 25 (Fall):519–62.

Christensen, S., and D. Maki. 1981. The union wage effects in Canadian manufacturing. *JLR* 2:355–367.

Christofides, L., and R. Swidinsky. 1994. Wage determination by gender and visible minority status: Evidence from the 1989 LMAS. *CPP* 20:34–51.

Clark, K. 1984. Unionization and firm performance: The impact on profits, growth, and productivity. *AER* 74 (December):893–919.

Cleveland, G., M. Gunderson, and D. Hyatt. 2003. Union effects in low-wage services: Evidence from Canadian childcare. *ILRR* 56 (January):295–305.

Coles, M., and A. Hildreth. 2000. Wage bargaining, inventories, and union legislation. *R.E.Studies* 67 (April):273–93.

Corneo, G., and C. Lucifora. 1997. Wage formation under union threat effects. *LE* 4:265–92.

Cooke, W. 1989. Improving productivity and quality through collaboration. *IR* 28: 299–319.

———. 1990. Factors influencing the effect of joint union-management programs on employee-supervisor relations. *ILRR* 43:587–603.

———. 1992. Product quality improvement through employee participation: The effect of unionization and joint union-management administration. *ILRR* 46:119–34.

———. 1994. Employee participation programs, group-based incentives, and company performance: A union-nonunion comparison. *ILRR* 47:594–609.

———. 1997. The influence of industrial relations factors on U.S. foreign investment. *ILRR* 51:3–17.

Connolly, R., B. Hirsch, and M. Hirschey. 1986. Union rent seeking, intagible capital, and market value of the firm. *R.E.Stats* 68:567–77.

De Fina, R. 1983. Unions, relative wages, and economic efficiency. *JOLE* 1 (October):408–29.

Denny, K., and S. Nickell. 1991. Unions and investment in British manufacturing industry. *BJIR* 29:113–21.

DiNardo, J., N. Fortin, and T. Lemieux. 1996. Labor market institutions and the distribution of wages, 1973–1992: A semi-parametric approach. *Ecta* 64 (September):1001–44.

DiNardo J., and D. S. Lee. 2004. Economic impacts of unionization on private sector employees: 1984–2001. *QJE* 119(4):1383–1142.

DiNardo, J., and T. Lemieux. 1997. Diverging male wage inequality in the United States and Canada, 1981–88: Do institutions explain the difference? *ILRR* 50 (July):629–51.

DiNardo, J., K. Hallock, and J.-S. Pischke. 2000. Unions and the labor market for managers. London School of Economics Centre for Economic Performance Working Paper.

Doiron, D., H. Doucouliagos, and P. Laroche. 2013. Unions and innovation: New insights from the cross-country evidence. *IR* 52(2):467–491.

Doiron, D., and W. C. Riddell. 1994. The impact of unionization on male–female earnings differences in Canada. *JHR* 29:504–34.

Donado A., and K. Wälde. 2012. How trade unions increase welfare. *EJ* 122(September):990–1009.

Donado, A. 2015. Why do unionized workers have more nonfatal occupational injuries? *ILRR* 68(1):153–183.

Doucouliagos, H., and P. Laroche. 2003a. Unions and tangible investments. *IR* 42:314–37.

———. 2003b. What do unions do to productivity: A meta-analysis. *IR* 42:650–91.

———. 2009. Unions and profits: A meta-regression analysis. *IR* 48(1):146–184.

Drago, R. 1988. Quality circle survival. *IR* 27:336–51.

Duncan, G., and F. Stafford. 1980. Do union members receive compensating wage differentials? *AER* 70 (June):335–71.

Dustmann, C., and U. Schönberg. 2009. Training and union wages. *R.E.Stats* 91(2):363–376.

Ehrenberg R. G., and J. Schwartz. 1987. Public sector labour market. *Handbook of Labour Economics*, eds. O. Ashenfelter and R. Layard. North-Holland.

Ehrenberg, R., D. Sherman, and J. Schwarz. 1983. Unions and productivity in the public sector: A study of municipal libraries. *ILRR* 36 (January):199–213.

Elsby, Michael W. L., Bart Hobijn, and Aysegul Sahin. 2015. On the importance of the participation margin for labor market fluctuations. *Journal of Monetary Economics* 72:64–82.

Eren, O. 2007. Measuring the union-nonunion wage gap using propensity score matching. *IR* 46(4):766–780.

Even, W., and D. Macpherson. 2014. What do unions do to pension performance? *EI* 52(3):1173–1189.

Fallick, B., and K. Hassett. 1999. Investment and union certification. *JOLE* 17:570–82.

Fang, T., and A. Verma. 2002. Union wage premium. *Perspectives* 14 (Winter):17–23.

Feiveson, L. 2015. General revenue sharing and public sector unions. *JPubEc* 125:28–45.

Flanagan, R. 1999. Macroeconomic performance and collective bargaining: An international perspective. *JEL* 37:1150–75.

Forth, J., and N. Millward. 2002. Union effects on pay levels in Britain. *LE* 9:547–61.

Frandsen, B. 2014. The surprising impacts of unionization: Evidence from matched employer–employee data. Working paper.

Frandsen, B. 2016. The effects of collective bargaining rights on public employee compensation: Evidence from teachers, firefighters, and police. *ILRR* 69(1):84–112.

Freeman, R. 1980a. Unionism and the dispersion of wages. *ILRR* 34 (October):3–23.

———. 1980b. The exit-voice trade-off in the labour market: Unionism, job tenure, quits and separations. *QJE* 94 (June):643–73.

———. 1980c. The effect of unionism on worker attachment to firms. *JLR* 1 (Spring):29–62.

———. 1981. The effect of unionism on fringe benefits. *ILRR* 34 (July):489–509.

———. 1982. Union wage practices and wage dispersion within establishments. *ILRR* 36 (October):3–21.

———. 1984. Longitudinal analyses of the effects of trade unions. *JOLE* 2 (January):1–26.

———. 1986. Unionism comes to the public sector. *JEL* 25 (March):41–86.

———. 1993. How much has de-unionization contributed to the rise of male earnings inequality? In *Uneven Tides: Rising Inequality in America,* eds. S. Danziger and P. Gottschalk. New York: Russell Sage Foundation.

Freeman, R., and L. F. Katz. 1991. Industrial wage and employment determination in an open economy. In *Immigration, Trade and the Labour Market,* eds. by. M. Abowd and R. Freeman. Chicago: NBER, pp. 235–59.

Freeman, R., and M. Kleiner. 1990. The impact of new unionization on wages and working conditions. *JOLE* 8 (January):8–25.

———. 1999. Do unions make enterprises insolvent? *ILRR* 52:510–27.

Freeman, R., and J. Medoff. 1979. The two faces of unionism. *The Public Interest* (Fall):69–93.

———. 1984. *What Do Unions Do.* New York: Basic Books.

Gaston, N., and D. Trefler. 1995. Union wage sensitivity to trade and protection: Theory and evidence. *JIE* 39:1–25.

Grant, D. 2001. A comparison of the cyclical behavior of union and nonunion wages in the United States. *JHR* 36 (Winter):31–57.

Grant, E., R. Swidinsky, and J. Vanderkamp. 1987. Canadian union–non-union wage differentials. *ILRR* 41 (October):93–107.

Grant, E., and J. Vanderkamp. 1980. The effects of migration on income: A micro study with Canadian data 1965–1971. *CJE* 13 (August):381–406.

Green, D. 1991. A comparison of estimation approaches for the union-nonunion wage differential. UBC Department of Economics Working Paper, 91–13.

Green, F., S. Machin, and A. Manning. 1996. The employer size-wage effect: Can dynamic monopsony provide an explanation. *Oxford Economic Papers* 48:433–455.

Gunderson, M. 2005. Two faces of union voice in the public sector. *JLR* 26 (Summer):393–414.

Gunderson, M., D. Hyatt, and W. C. Riddell. 2000. Pay differences between the government and private sectors: Labour force survey and census estimates. Ottawa: Canadian Policy Research Networks. Available at www.cprn.org.

Hall, Robert E., and San Schulhofer-Wohl. 2015. Measuring job-finding rates and matching efficiency with heterogeneous jobseekers. NBER Working Paper 20939, February.

Hallock, K. 2002. Managerial pay and governance in American nonprofits. *IR* 41(3):377–406.

Hallock, K., and F. Klein. 2016. Executive compensation in American unions. *IR* 55(2):219–234.

Hammer, T. H., and A. Avgar. 2005. The impact of unions on job satisfaction, organizational commitment, and turnover. *JLR* 26 (Spring):242–66.

Hara, H., and D. Kawaguchi. 2008. The union wage effect in Japan. *IR* 47(4):569–590.

Hart, C., and A. Sojourner. 2015. Unionization and productivity: Evidence from charter schools. *IR* 54(3):422–448.

Hedrick, D., S. Henson, J. Krieg, and C. Wassell. 2011. Is there really a faculty union salary premium? *ILRR* 64:558–575.

Henson, S., J. Krieg, C. Wassell Jr, and D. Hedrick. 2012. Collective bargaining and community college faculty: What is the wage impact? *JLR* 33:104–117.

Hildreth, A. 1999. What has happened to the union wage differential in Britain in the 1990s? *Oxford Bulletin of Economics and Statistics* 61:5–31.

Hirsch, B. 1982. The interindustry structure of unions, earnings, and earnings dispersion. *ILLR* 36:22–39.

Hirsch, B. 1988. Trucking regulation, unionization, and labor earnings, 1973–85. *JHR* 23:295–317.

———. 1991a. Union coverage and profitability among U.S. firms. *R.E. Stats* 73 (February):69–77.

———. 1991b. Labour unions and the economic performance of firms. Kalamazoo, MI: Upjohn Institute of Employment Research.

———. 1992. Firm investment behavior and collective bargaining strategy. *IR* 31:95–121.

———. 1993. Trucking deregulation and labor earnings: Is the union premium a compensating differential? *JOLE* 11:279–301.

———. 2004a. Reconsidering union wage effects: Surveying new evidence on an old topic. *JLR* 25 (Spring):233–66.

———. 2004b. What do unions do for economic performance? *JLR* 25 (Summer):413–55.

Hirsch, B., and J. Addison. 1986. *The Economic Analysis of Unions: New Approaches and Evidence.* Boston: Allen and Unwin.

Hirsch, B., and D. A. MacPherson. 1998. Earnings and employment in trucking deregulating a naturally competitive industry. In *Regulatory Reform and Labor Markets,* eds. J. Peoples. Norwell, MA: Kluwer Academic, pp. 61–112.

———. 2000. Earnings, rents, and competition in the airline labor market. *JOLE* 18:125–55.

Hirsch, B., D. MacPherson, and E. Schumacher. 2004. Measuring union and nonunion wage growth: Puzzles in search of solutions. In *The Changing Role of Unions: New Forms of Representation,* ed. P. Wunnava. New York: M.E. Sharpe.

Hirsch, B., and E. J. Schumacher. 1998. Union, wages, and skills. *JHR* 33:201–19.

———. 2002. Private sector union density and the wage premium: Past, present, and future. *In The Future of Private Sector Unionism in the United States,* eds. J. T. Bennett and B. E. Kaufman, Armonk, NY: M. E. Sharpe, pp. 92–128.

Hirschman, A. 1970. *Exit, Voice and Loyalty.* Cambridge, Mass.: Harvard University Press.

Hoxby, C. 1996. How teachers' unions affect production. *QJE* 111:671–718.

Hyclak, T. 1979. The effect of unions on earnings inequality in local labour markets. *ILRR* 33 (October):77–84.

———. 1980. Unions and income inequality: Some cross-state evidence. *IR* 19 (Spring):212–15.

Ichniowski, C. 1986. The effects of grievance activity on productivity. *ILRR* 40 (October):75–89.

Ichniowski, C., R. Freeman, and H. Lauer. 1989. Collective bargaining laws, threat effects, and the determination of police compensation. *JOLE* 7:191–209.

Jakubson, G. 1991. Estimation and testing of the union wage effect using panel data. *R.E.Studies* 58 (October):971–91.

Jalette, P., and R. Hebdon. 2012. Unions and privatization: opening the "black box." *ILLR* 65:17–33.

Jarrell, S., and T. Stanley. 1990. A meta-analysis of the union-nonunion wage gap. *ILRR* 44:54–67.

Johnson, H., and P. Mieszkowski. 1970. The effects of unionization on the distribution of income: A general equilibrium approach. *QJE* 84:539–61.

Kahn, L. 1978. The effects of unions on the earnings of non-union workers. *ILRR* 31 (January):205–16.

———.1980. Union spillover effects on unorganized labour markets. *JHR* 15 (Winter):87–98.

———. 1998. Against the wind: Bargaining recentralisation and wage inequality in Norway 1987–91. *EJ* 108(448):603–45.

Karier, T. 1995. U.S. foreign production and unions. *IR* 34:107–18.

Katz, H., T. Kochan, and K. Gobeille. 1983. Industrial relations performance, economic performance, and QWL programs: An interplant analysis. *ILRR* 37 (October):3–17.

Kaufman, R. T. 1992. The effects of IMPROSHARE on productivity. *ILRR* 45:311–22.

Kim, D., and P. Voos. 1997. Unionization, union involvement, and the performance of gainsharing programs. *RI/IR* 52:304–29.

Klaff, D. B., and R. G. Ehrenberg. 2003. Collective bargaining and staff salaries in American colleges and universities. *ILRR* 57 (October):92–104.

Koevoets, W. 2007. Union wage premiums in Great Britain: Coverage or membership? *LE* 14:53–71.

Krieg, J., C. Wassell Jr., D. Hedrick, and S. Henson. 2013. Collective bargaining and faculty job satisfaction. *IR* 52(3):619–644.

Krol, R., and S. Svorny. 2007. Unions and employment growth: Evidence from state economic recoveries. *JLR* 28:525–535.

Krueger, Alan B., Judd Cramer, and David Cho. 2014. Are the long-term unemployed on the margins of the labor market? Brookings Papers on Economic Activity, Spring 2014 Conference.

Kudlyak, Marianna, and Fabian Lange. 2014. Measuring heterogeneity in job finding rates among the nonemployed using labor force status histories. IZA DP No. 8663, November.

Kuhn, P. 1998. Unions and the economy: What we know and what we should know. *CJE* 31:1033–56.

Kuhn, P., and A. Sweetman. 1998. Wage loss following displacement: The role of union coverage. *ILLR* 51:384–400.

Kumar, P. 1972. Differentials in wage rates of unskilled labour in Canadian manufacturing industries. *ILRR* 26 (October):631–45.

Kumar, P., and T. Stengos. 1985. Measuring the union relative wage impact: A methodological note. *CJE* 18 (February):182–9.

———. 1986. Interpreting the wage gap estimate from selectivity correction techniques using micro data. *Economic Letters* 20:191–95.

Laporta, P., and A. Jenkins. 1996. Unionization and profitability in the Canadian manufacturing sector. *IR/RI* 51:756–76.

Lee, D., and A. Mas. 2012. Long-run impacts of unions on firms: New evidence from financial markets, 1961–1999. *QJE* 127:333–378.

Leigh, J. 1982. Are unionized blue collar jobs more hazardous than non-unionized blue collar jobs? *JLR* 3 (Summer):349–57.

Lemieux, T. 1993. Unions and wage inequality in Canada and the United States. In *Small Differences that Matter,* eds. D. Card and R. Freeman. Chicago: University of Chicago Press.

———. 1998. Estimating the effects of unions on wage inequality in a panel data model with comparative advantage and nonrandom selection. *JOLE* 16:261–91.

Lewis, H. 1963. *Unionism and Relative Wages in the United States: An Empirical Inquiry.* Chicago: University of Chicago Press.

———. 1986. *Union Relative Wage Effects: A Survey.* Chicago: University of Chicago Press.

———. 1986. Union relative wage effects. In *Handbook of Labor Economics,* eds. O. Ashenfelter and R. Layard. New York: Elsevier Science.

———. 1990. Union/nonunion wage gaps in the public sector. *JOLE* 8:S260–328.

Long, R. 1993. The effect of unionization on employment growth of Canadian companies. *ILRR* 46:691–703.

Long, R. J., and J. L. Shields. 2009. Do unions affect pay methods of Canadian firms? A longitudinal study. *IR* 64(3):442–465.

Liu, W., J. P. Guthrie, P. C. Flood, and S. MacCurtain. 2009. Unions and high performance work systems: Does job security play a role? *ILRR* 63(1):108–126.

MacDonald, G. 1983. The size and structure of union-nonunion wage differentials in Canadian industry: Corroboration, refinement and extension. *CJE* 16 (August):480–85.

MacDonald, G., and J. Evans. 1981. The size and structure of union-nonunion wage differentials in Canadian industry. *CJE* 14 (May):216–31.

Machin, S. 1991. Unions and the capture of economic rents: An investigation using British firm level data. *International Journal of Industrial Organization* 9:261–74.

MacPherson, D. A., and J. B. Stewart. 1990. The effect of international competition on union and nonunion wages. *ILRR* 43:434–46.

Magnani, E., and D. Prentice. 2009. Outsourcing and unionization: A tale of misallocated (resistance) resources. *EI* 48(2):460–482.

———. 2010. Did lower unionization in the United States result in more flexible industries? *ILRR* 63(4):662–680.

Maki, D. 1983. Trade unions and productivity: Conventional estimates. *RI/IR* 38(2):211–25.

Maki, D., and S. Christensen. 1980. The union wage effect re-examined. *RI/IR* 35:210–30.

Maki, D., and L. Meredith. 1986. The effect of unions on profitability: Canadian evidence. *RI/IR* 41(1):54–68.

Mandelstamm, A. B. 1965. The effects of unions on efficiency in the residential construction industry: A case study. *ILLR* 18 (July):503–21.

Martinello, F. 2009. Faculty salaries in Ontario: Compression, inversion, and the effects of alternative forms of representation. *ILRR* 63(1):128–145.

Martinello, F., R. Hanrahan, J. Kushner, and I. Masse. 1995. Union certification in Ontario: Its effect on the value of the firm. *CJE* 28 (November):1077–95.

Mastekaasa, A. 2013. Unionization and certified sickness absence: Norwegian evidence. *ILRR* 66(1):117–141.

Medoff, J. 1979. Layoffs and alternatives under trade unions in U.S. manufacturing. *AER* 69 (June):380–95.

Mellow, W. 1981. Unionism and wages: A longitudinal analysis. *R.E.Stats* 63 (February):43–52.

Menezes-Filho, N. 1997. Unions and profitability over the 1980s: Some evidence on union-firm bargaining in the United Kingdom. *EJ* 107:651–70.

Menezes-Filho, N., D. Ulph, and J. Van Reenen. 1998. R & D and unionism: Comparative evidence from British companies and establishments. *ILRR* 52:45–63.

Meng, R. 1990. Union effects on wage dispersion in Canadian industry. *Economic Letters* 32 (April):399–403.

Mincer, J. 1983. Union effects: wages, turnover, and job training. In *New Approaches to Labor Unions,* ed. J. J. D. Reid. Greenwich, Conn.: JAI Press.

Mitchell, D. 1983. Unions and wages in the public sector: A review of recent evidence. *Journal of Collective Negotiations* 12(4):337–53.

Mitchell, M., and J. Stone. 1992. Union effects on productivity: Evidence from western U.S. sawmills. *ILRR* 46:135–45.

Moffat, J., and H. I. Yoo. 2015. Who are the unemployed? Evidence from the United Kingdom. *Economics Letters* 132:61–64.

Moore, W., and J. Raisian. 1983. The level and growth of union/non-union relative wage effects, 1967–1977. *JLR* 4 (Winter):65–80.

Morantz, A. 2013. Coal mine safety: Do unions make a difference? *ILRR* 66(1):88–116.

Murphy, K. 1999. Executive compensation. *Handbook of Labor Economics* 3:2485–2563.

Neumark, D., and M. Wachter. 1995. Union effects on nonunion wages: Evidence from panel data on industries and cities. *ILRR* 49:20–38.

Noam, E. 1983. The effect of unionization and civil service on the salaries and productivity of regulators. In *New Approaches to Labor Unions,* ed. J. J. D. Reid. Greenwich, Conn.: JAI Press.

Odgers, C., and J. Betts. 1997. Do unions reduce investment? Evidence from Canada. *ILRR* 51:518–36.

Pantuosco, L., D. Parker, and G. Stone. 2001. The effect of unions on labor markets and economic growth: An analysis of state data. *JLR* 22 (Winter):195–205.

Pearce, T., J. Groff, and J. Wingender. 1995. Union decertification's impact on shareholder wealth. *IR* 34:58–72.

Penceval, J. 2009. How successful have trade unions been? A utility-based indicator of union well-being. *ILRR* 62(2):147–156.

Podgursky, M. 1986. Unions, establishment size, and intra-industry threat effects. *ILLR* 39:277–284.

Porter, S. 2013. The causal effect of faculty unions on institutional decision-making. *ILRR* 66(5):1192–1211.

Quan, N. 1984. Unionism and the size distribution of earnings. *IR* 23 (Spring):270–7.

Rees, A. 1963. The effects of unions on resource allocation. *Journal of Law and Economics* 6 (October):69–78.

Rees, D. 1994. Does unionization increase faculty retention? *IR* 33:297–321.

Renaud, S. 1997. Unions and wages in Canada. Selected Papers from the 33rd Annual CIRA Conference. Quebec: Canadian Industrial Relations Association, pp. 211–26.

———. 1998. Unions, wages and total compensation in Canada. *IR/RI* 53:710–27.

Riddell, C. W. 1993. Unionization in Canada and the United States: A tale of two countries. In *Small Differences That Matter: Labor Markets and Income Maintenance in Canada and the United States,* eds. D. Card and R. Freeman. Chicago: University of Chicago Press and National Bureau of Economic Research.

Rios-Avila, F., and B. Hirsch. 2014. Unions, wage gaps, and wage dispersion: New evidence from the Americas. *IR* 53(1):1–27.

Rogers, S., A. Eaton, and P. Voos. 2013. Effects of unionization on graduate student employees: Faculty-student relations, academic freedom, and pay. *ILRR* 66(2):487–510.

Robinson, C. 1989. The joint determination of union status and union wage effects: Some tests of alternate models. *JPE* 97 (June):639–67.

Robinson, C., and N. Tomes. 1984. Union wage differentials in the public and private sectors: A simultaneous equations specification. *JOLE* 2 (January):106–27.

Ruback, R., and M. Zimmerman. 1984. Unionization and profitability: Evidence from the capital market. *JPE* 92 (December):1134–57.

Shippen, B. S. Jr., and A. K. Lynch. 2002. How international trade affects union wages: New evidence. *JLR* 23:131–44.

Simpson, W. 1985. The impact of unions on the structure of Canadian wages: An empirical analysis with micro data. *CJE* 18 (February):164–81.

Singh, P., and N. C. Agarwal, 2002. Union presence and executive compensation: An exploratory study. *JLR* 23:631–46.

Sloan, F., and K. Adamache. 1984. The role of unions in hospital cost inflation. *ILRR* 37 (January):252–62.

Sojourner, A., B. Frandsen, R. Town, D. Grabowski, and M. Chen. 2015. Impacts of unionization on quality and productivity: Regression discontinuity evidence from nursing homes. *ILRR* 68(4):771–806.

Walsworth, S. 2010. What do unions do to innovation? An empirical examination of the Canadian private sector. *IR* 65(4):543–561.

Starr, G. 1973. Union–non-union wage differentials: A cross-sectional analysis. Toronto: Research Branch, Ontario Ministry of Labour.

Stewart, M. 1995. Union wage differentials in an era of declining unionization. *Oxford Bulletin of Economics and Statistics* 57:143–66.

Warren, R., Jr. 1985. The effect of unionization on labor productivity: Some time series evidence. *JLR* 6 (Spring):199–207.

Swidinsky, R. 1992. Unionism and the job attachment of Canadian workers. *IR/RI* 47:729–751.

Swidinsky, R., and M. Kupferschmidt. 1991. Longitudinal estimates of the union effects on wages, wage dispersion, and pension fringe benefits. *RI/IR* 46:819–38.

Tzioumis, K., and R. Gomez. 2007. What do unions do to CEO compensation? London School of Economics Centre for Economic Performance Discussion Paper.

Vedder, R., and L. Galloway. 2002. The economic effects of labor unions revisited. *JLR* 23:105–30.

Wenchuan, L., J. P. Guthrie, P. C. Flood, and S. MacCurtain. 2009. Unions and the adoption of high performance work systems: Does employment security play a role? *ILRR* 63(1):109–127.

West, K. 2015. Teachers' unions, compensation, and tenure. *IR* 54(2):294–320.

Verma, A. 2005. What do unions do at the workplace? Union effects on management and HRM policies. *JLR* 26 (Summer):415–50.

Voos, P., and L. Mishel. 1986. The union impact on profits: Evidence from industry price-cost margin data. *JOLE* 4 (January):105–33.

White, F. 1994. The union/non-union earnings differential for professionals. Proceedings of the 30th Canadian Industrial Relations Association, pp. 269–280.

Waddoups, C. J. 2008. Unions and wages in Australia: Does employer size matter? *IR* 41(1):136–144.

Wagar, T. 1997. Is labor-management climate important: Some Canadian evidence? *JLR* 18:163–74.

Wilson, K. 1995. *The Impact of Unions on United States and Economy-wide Productivity.* New York: Garland.

———. 1998. The labour-management relationship and organizational outcomes. *RI/IR* 52:430–46.

Woodbury, S. 1985. The scope of bargaining outcomes in public schools. *ILRR* 38:195–210.

CHAPTER 16

Akerlof, G., and B. Main. 1980. Unemployment spells and unemployment experience. *AER* 70 (December):885–93.

Baker, M., M. Corak, and A. Heisz. 1998. The labour market dynamics of unemployment rates in Canada and the United States. *CPP* 24 (Supplement: February):S72–S89.

Beach, C., and S. Kaliski. 1983. Measuring the duration of unemployment from gross flow data. *CJE* 16 (May):258–63.

Blanchard, O., and P. Portugal. 2001. What hides behind an unemployment rate: Comparing Portuguese and U.S. labor markets. *AER* 91 (March):187–207.

Bowlby, G. 2005. Divergence in the Canadian and US labour markets. *CPP* 31 (March):83–92.

Brandolini, A., P. Cipollone, and E. Viviano. 2006. Does the ILO definition capture all unemployment? *Journal of the European Economic Association* 4 (March):153–79.

Card, D., and W. C. Riddell. 1993. A comparative analysis of unemployment in Canada and the United States. In *Small Differences That Matter: Labor Markets and Income Maintenance in Canada and the United States,* eds D. Card and R. B. Freeman. Chicago: University of Chicago Press.

———. 1997. Unemployment in Canada and the United States: A further analysis. In *Trade, Technology and Economics: Essays in Honour of Richard G. Lipsey,* eds. B. Eaton and R. Harris. Cheltanham: Edward Elgar.

Clark, K., and L. Summers. 1979. Labor market dynamics and unemployment: A reconsideration. *BPEA*:13–60.

Corak, M., and A. Heisz. 1995. The duration of unemployment: A user's guide. Statistics Canada Research Report 84.

Feldstein, M. 1973. The economics of the new unemployment. *Public Interest* 33 (Fall):3–42.

Hasan, A., and P. de Broucker. 1982. Duration and concentration of unemployment. *CJE* 15 (November):706–34.

Jones, S. 1993. The cyclical and seasonal properties of Canadian gross flows of labour. *CPP* 19:(March).

Jones, S., and W. C. Riddell. 1999. The measurement of unemployment: An empirical approach. *Ecta* 67 (January):147–61.

———. 2006. Unemployment and non-employment: Heterogeneities in labour market states. *R. E. Stats* 88 (August):314–23.

Kuhn, P., and M. Skuterud. 2004. Internet job search and unemployment durations. *AER* 94 (March):218–32.

Levesque, J. 1989. Unemployment and unemployment insurance: A tale of two sources. *PLI* 1 (Winter):49–53.

Macklem, T., and F. Barillas. 2005. Recent developments in the Canada–U.S. unemployment rate gap: Changing patterns in unemployment incidence and duration. *CPP* 31 (March):101–07.

Riddell, W. C. 1999. Canadian labour market performance in international perspective. *CJE* 32 (November):1097–1134.

———. 2000. Measuring unemployment and structural unemployment. *CPP* 26 (July):S101–08.

———. 2005. Why is Canada's unemployment rate persistently higher than in the United States? *CPP* 31 (March):93–100.

Statistics Canada. 1998. Labour Force Update: Canada–U.S. Labour Market Comparison. Ottawa: Statistics Canada.

———. 1999. Labour Force Update: Supplementary Measures of Unemployment. Ottawa: Statistics Canada.

CHAPTER 17

Abraham, K., and L. F. Katz. 1986. Cyclical unemployment: Sectoral shifts or aggregate disturbances. *JPE* 94:507–22.

Akerlof, G., and H. Miyazaki. 1980. The implicit contract theory of unemployment meets the wage bill argument. *R.E.Studies* 47 (January):321–338.

Altonji, J. G., and J. C. Ham. 1990. Variation in employment growth in Canada: The role of external, national, regional, and industrial factors. *JOLE* 8 (Part):S198–236.

Autor, D. 2001. Wiring the labor market. *JEP* 15:25–40.

Autor, D., ed. 2009. *Studies of Labor Market Intermediation.* Chicago: University of Chicago Press.

Azariadis, C. 1975. Implicit contracts and underemployment equilibria. *JPE* 83 (December):1183–1202.

———. 1979. Implicit contracts and related topics: A survey. In *The Economics of the Labour Market,* eds. Z. Hornstein et al. London: HMSO.

Azariadis, C., and J. E. Stiglitz. 1983. Implicit contracts and fixed price equilibria. *QJE* 98:1–22.

Baily, M. N. 1974. Wages and employment under uncertain demand. *R.E.Studies* 41 (January):37–50.

Banting, K., and J. Medow (eds.). 2012. *Making EI Work.* Montreal and Kingston: McGil-Queen's University Press.

Beach, C., and S. Kaliski. 1983. Measuring the duration of unemployment from gross flow data. *CJE* 16 (May):258–63.

———. 1986. Structural unemployment: Demographic change or industrial structure. *CPP* 12 (June):356–67.

Beaudry, P., and J. DiNardo. 1991. The effect of implicit contracts on the movement of wages over the business cycle: Evidence from micro data. *JPE* 99 (August):665–88.

———. 1995. Is the behavior of hours worked consistent with implicit contract theory? *QJE* 110 (August):743–68.

Belzil, C. 1993. An empirical model of job-to-job transition with self-selectivity. *CJE* 26:536–51.

Black, S., P. Devereux, K. Salvanes. 2012. Losing heart: The effect of job displacement on health. NBER Working Paper No. 18660. Cambridge, Mass.: NBER.

Blanchflower, D. G., A. J. Oswald, and P. Sanfey. 1996. Wages, profits, and rent-sharing. *QJE* 111 (February):227–51.

Bloemen, H. 2005. Job search, search intensity and labor market transitions. *JHR* 40:231–69.

Bowlus, A. J. 1998. U.S.–Canadian unemployment rate and wage differences among young, low-skilled males in the 1980s. *CJE* 31 (May):437–64.

Brencic, V. 2009. Employers' hiring practices, employment protection and costly search: A vacancy-level analysis. *LE* 16(5):461–79.

Browning, M., and T. Crossley. 2001. Unemployment insurance benefits levels and consumption changes. *JPubEc* 80(1):1–23.

Card, D., R. Chetty, and A. Weber. 2007a. The spike at benefit exhaustion: Leaving the unemployment system or starting a new job? *AER* 97(May):113–118.

———. 2007b. Cash-on-hand and competing models of intertemporal behavior: New evidence from the labor market. *QJE* 122(4):1511–560.

Card, D., and W. C. Riddell. 1993. A comparative analysis of unemployment in Canada and the United States. In *Small Differences That Matter: Labor Markets and Income Maintenance in Canada and the United States,* eds. D. Card and R. B. Freeman. Chicago: University of Chicago Press.

———. 1997. Unemployment in Canada and the United States: A further analysis. In *Trade, Technology and Economics: Essays in Honour of Richard G. Lipsey,* eds. B. C. Eaton and R. G. Harris. Cheltenham, U.K. and Lyme, N.H: Elgar.

Chetty, R. 2008. Moral hazard vs. liquidity and optimal unemployment insurance. *JPE* 116(2):173–234.

Charles, K. C., and M. Stephens, Jr. 2004. Job displacement, disability and divorce. *JOLE* 22(2):489–522.

Coelli, M. B. 2009. Parental job loss, income shock and the education enrolment of youth. Department of Economics, University of Melbourne, Working Paper 1060.

Corak, M. 1993a. Is unemployment insurance addictive? Evidence from the benefit durations of repeat users. *ILRR* 47 (October):62–72.

Couch, K. A., and D.W. Placzek. 2010. Earnings losses of displaced workers revisited. *AER* 100(1):572–589.

———. 1993b. Unemployment insurance once again: The incidence of repeat participation in the Canadian UI program. *CPP* 19:162–76.

Couch, K. A. and D. W. Placzek. 2010. Earnings losses of displaced workers revisited. *AER* 100(1):572–589.

Cousineau, J.-M., and C. Green. 1978. Structural unemployment in Canada: 1971–1974. Did it worsen? *RI/IR* 33(2):175–92.

Crossley, T. F., S. R. G. Jones, and P. Kuhn. 1994. Gender differences in displacement cost: Evidence and implications. *JHR* 29:461–80.

Della Vigna, S., and M. D. Paserman. 2005. Job search and impatience. *JOLE* 23 (July): 527–588.

Diamond, P. 1982. Wage determination and efficiency in search equilibrium. *R.E.Studies* 49:217–227.

Doiron, D. J. 1995a. Lay-offs as signals: The Canadian evidence. *CJE* 28 (November):822–35.

———. 1995b. A test of the insider-outsider hypothesis in union preferences. *Economica* 62 (August):281–90.

Eckstein, Z., and G. van den Berg. 2007. Empirical labor search: A survey. *Journal of Econometrics* 136:531–564.

Eliason, M., and D. Storrie. 2009. Does job loss shorten life? *JHR* 44 (Spring):277–302.

Expert Panel on Older Workers. 2008. Supporting and engaging older workers in the new economy. Ottawa: Expert Panel on Older Workers.

Farber, H. S. 2005. What do we know about job loss in the United States? Evidence from the Displaced Workers Survey, 1984–2004. *Economic Perspectives* 29(2):13–28.

———. 2015. Job loss in the Great Recession and its aftermath: U.S. evidence from the Displaced Workers Survey. NBER Working Paper 21216. Cambridge, Mass: NBER.

Farber, H., and R. Valletta. 2013. Do extended unemployment benefits lengthen unemployment spells? NBER Working Paper 19048. Cambridge, Mass: NBER.

Ferrall, C. 1997. Unemployment insurance eligibility and the school-to-work transition in Canada and the United States. *Journal of Business and Economic Statistics* 15 (April):115–29.

Fortin, P. 1996. The great Canadian slump. *CJE* 29 (November):761–87.

Foster, A. D., and M. R. Rosenzweig. 1994. A test for moral hazard in the labor market: Contractual arrangements, effort, and health. *R.E.Stats* 76 (May):213–27.

Fredriksson, P., and B. Holmlund. 2006. Improving incentives in unemployment insurance: A review of recent research. *Journal of Economic Surveys* 3.

Friesen, J. 1997. Mandatory notice and the jobless durations of displaced workers. *ILRR* 50(4):652–66.

———. 2002. The effect of unemployment insurance on weekly hours of work in Canada. *CJE* 35 (May):363–84.

Gera, S., ed. 1991. *Canadian Unemployment.* Ottawa: Economic Council of Canada.

Gibbons, R., and L. F. Katz. 1991. Layoffs and lemons. *JOLE* (October):351–80.

Gordon, D. 1974. A neoclassical theory of Keynesian unemployment. *EI* 12 (December):431–59.

Gray, D. 2004. Employment insurance: What reform delivered. Toronto: C. D. Howe Institute.

Gray, D., and T. McDonald. 2012. Does the sophistication of use of unemployment insurance evolve with experience? *CJE* 45 (August):1220–1245.

Green, D. A., and W. C. Riddell. 1993. The economic effects of unemployment insurance in Canada: An empirical analysis of UI disentitlement. *JOLE* 11 (January).

———. 1997. Qualifying for unemployment insurance: An empirical analysis. *EJ* 107 (January):67–84.

———. 2000. The effects of the shift to an hours-based entrance requirement. Report prepared for strategic evaluation and monitoring evaluation and data development, strategic policy. Human Resources Development Canada.

Grenon, L. 1998. Looking for work. *Perspectives on Labour and Income* 10 (Autumn):22–26.

———. 1999. Obtaining a job. *Perspectives on Labour and Income* 11 (Spring):23–27.

Gruber, J. 1997. The consumption smoothing benefits of unemployment insurance. *AER* 87(1):192–205.

Gunderson, M., and W. C. Riddell. 2001. Unemployment insurance: Lessons from Canada. In *Labor Market Policies in Canada and Latin America: Challenges of the New Millennium,* ed. A. Berry. Norwell, MA: Kluwer Academic Publisher.

Hall, R. E. 2011. The long slump. *AER* 101 (April):431–69.

Ham, J. C., and S. A. Rea. 1987. Unemployment insurance and male unemployment duration in Canada. *JOLE* 5 (July):325–53.

Hamilton, V. H., P. Merrigan, and E. Dufresne. 1997. Down and out: Estimating the relationship between mental health and unemployment. *Health Economics* 6(4):397–406.

Hart, O. D. 1983. Optimal labour contracts under asymmetric information: an introduction. *R.E.Studies* 50(January):3–35.

Holzer, H. J. 1988. Search methods used by unemployed youth. *JOLE* 6:1–20.

Jacobson, L. S., R. J. LaLonde, and D. G. Sullivan. 1993. Earnings losses of displaced workers. *AER* 83 (September):685–709.

Jones, S. 1995. *The Persistence of Unemployment.* Montreal: McGill–Queen's University Press.

Jones, S. R. G., and P. Kuhn. 1995. Mandatory notice and unemployment. *JOLE* 13 (October):599–622.

Kahn, S., and K. Lang. 1995. The causes of hours constraints: Evidence from Canada. *CJE* 28 (November):914–28.

Kaliski, S. F. 1985. Trends, changes and imbalances: A survey of the Canadian labour market. In *Work and Pay: The Canadian Labour Market,* ed. W. C. Riddell. Toronto: University of Toronto Press.

Katz, L., and B. Meyer. 1990. The impact of the potential duration of unemployment benefits on the duration of unemployment. *JPubEc* 41(1):45–72.

Kroft, K., and D. G. Pope. 2014. Does online search crowd out traditional search and improve matching efficiency? Evidence from Craigslist. *JOLE* 32 (April).

Krueger, A., and B. Meyer. 2004. Labor supply effects of social insurance. In *Handbook of Public Economics,* Vol. 4., eds. A. Auerbach and M. Feldstein. Amsterdam: North-Holland.

Krueger, A., and A. Mueller. 2008. Job search and unemployment insurance: New evidence from time use data. Princeton University, Industrial Relations Section, Working Paper No 532, August.

Krugman, P. 1994. Past and prospective causes of high unemployment. In *Reducing Unemployment: Current Issues and Policy Options.* Symposium sponsored by the Federal Reserve Bank of Kansas City, Jackson Hole, WY, August, pp. 25–27.

Kuhn, P. J. 2000a. Policies for an Internet labour market. *Policy Options* (October):42–47.

———. 2000b. Canada and the OECD hypothesis: Does labour market inflexibility explain Canada' high level of unemployment? In *Adopting Public Policy to a Labour Market in Transition,* eds. W. C. Riddell and F. St-Hilaire. Montreal: Institute for Research on Public Policy.

———. 2014. The internet as a labor market matchmaker. *IZA World of Labor*:18. Available at wol.iza.org.

Kuhn, P., and H. Mansour. 2014. Is Internet job search still ineffective? *Economic Journal* 124 (December):1213–33.

Kuhn, P., and C. Riddell. 2010. The long-term effects of unemployment insurance: Evidence from New Brunswick and Maine, 1940–1991. *ILRR* 63 (January):183–204.

Kuhn, P., and M. Skuterud. 2004. Internet job search and unemployment durations. *AER* 94 (March):218–32.

Kuhn, P., and A. Sweetman. 1998. Wage loss following displacement: The role of union coverage. *ILRR* 51(3):384–400.

Lalive, R., J. C. van Ours, and J. Zweimuller. 2006. How changes in financial incentives affect the duration of unemployment. *R.E.Studies* 73(4):1009–1038.

Lalive, R., C. Landais, and J. Zweimuller. 2013. Market Externalities of Large Unemployment Insurance Extension Programs. IZA Working Paper.

Lalonde, R. J. 2007. The case for wage insurance. Council on Foreign Relations. Available at http://www.cfr.org/publication/13661/caseforwageinsurance.html.

Levine, P. B. 1993. Spillover effects between the insured and uninsured unemployed. *ILRR* 47(1):73–86.

Layard, R., S. Nickell, and R. Jackman. 2005. *Unemployment: Macroeconomic Performance and the Labour Market.* Second edition. Oxford: Oxford University Press.

Lemieux, T., and B. MacLeod. 2000. Supply side hysteresis: The case of unemployment insurance in Canada. *JPubEc* 78 (October):139–70.

Lilien, D. 1982. Sectoral shifts and cyclical unemployment. *JPE* 90 (August):777–93.

Lindbeck, A., and D. J. Snower. 1986. Cooperation, harassment, and involuntary unemployment. *AER* 78:167–88.

———. 1987. Efficiency wages versus insiders and outsiders. *European Economic Review* 31 (February, March):407–16.

———. 1988. *The Insider-Outsider Theory of Employment and Unemployment.* Cambridge: The MIT Press.

Lindo, Jason M. 2010. Are children really inferior goods? Evidence from displacement-driven income shocks. *JHR* 45 (Spring):301–327.

McCall, J.J. 1970. Economics of information and job search. *QJE* 84:113–26.

McDonald, J. T., and C. Worswick. 1999. Wages, implicit contracts, and the business cycle: Evidence from Canadian micro data. *JPE* 107 (August):884–92.

Meyer, B. D. 1995. Lessons from the U.S. unemployment insurance experiments. *JEL* 33 (March):91–131.

———. 1996. What have we learned from the Illinois reemployment bonus experiment? *JOLE* 14 (January):26–51.

Milbourne, R. D., D. D. Purvis, and W. D. Scoones. 1991. Unemployment insurance and unemployment dynamics. *CJE* 24 (November):804–26.

Mirrlees, J. 1975. A pure theory of underdeveloped economies. In *Agriculture in Development Theory*, ed. L. Reynolds. New Haven: Yale University Press.

Moffitt, R. 1985. Unemployment insurance and the distribution of unemployment spells. *Journal of Econometrics* 28 (1):85–101.

Moffitt, R. 2014. Unemployment benefits and unemployment. IZA WOL – 13. Available at http://wol.iza.org/articles/unemployment-benefits-and-unemployment.

Morissette, R., H. Qui, and P. C. W. Chan. 2013. The risk and cost of job loss in Canada, 1978–2008. *CJE* 46 (November):1480–1509.

Morissette, R., X. Zhang, and M. Frenette. 2007. Earnings losses of displaced workers: Canadian evidence from a large administrative database on firm closures and mass layoffs. Statistics Canada Analytical Studies Branch Research Paper No. 291.

Mortensen, D. 1977. Unemployment insurance and job search decisions. *ILRR* 30 (4):505–517.

Mortensen, D. 1982. The matching process as a non-cooperative bargaining game. In *The Economics of Information and Uncertainty*, ed. J. J. McCall. Chicago: University of Chicago Press.

Mortensen, D. T., and C. A. Pissarides. 1999. New developments in models of search in the labor market. In *Handbook of Labor Economics*, eds. O. Ashenfelter and D. Card. New York and Oxford: Elsevier Science, North Holland.

Mowat Centre Employment Insurance Task Force. 2011. Making it Work: Final Recommendations of the Mowat Centre Employment Insurance Task Force. Toronto: Mowat Centre. Available at http://www.mowateitaskforce.ca/sites/default/files/MakingItWork-online.pdf.

Murphy, K., and R. Topel. 1987. Unemployment, risk and earnings. In *Unemployment and Its Structure of Labour Markets*, eds. K. Lang and J. Leonard. Oxford: Basil Blackwell.

Nakamura, A., K. Shaw, R. Freeman, E. Nakamura, and A. Pyman. 2009. Reducing search costs: Jobs online. In *Studies of Labor Market Intermediation*, ed. D. Autor. Chicago: University of Chicago Press.

Neal, D. 1995. Industry-specific human capital: Evidence from displaced workers. *JOLE* 13 (October):653–77.

Neelin, J. 1987. Sectoral shifts and Canadian unemployment. *R.E.Stats* 69:718–32.

Nickell, S., and R. Layard. 1999. Labor market institutions and economic performance. In *Handbook of Labor Economics*, eds. O.

Ashenfelter and D. Card. New York and Oxford: Elsevier Science, North-Holland.

Oreopoulos, P., M. Page, and A. Huff Stevens. 2008. The intergenerational effects of worker displacement. *JOLE* 26(3):455–83.

Osberg, L. 1991. Unemployment and inter-industry labour mobility in Canada in the 1980s. *Applied Economics* 23:1707–17.

Parent, D. 2000. Industry-specific capital and the wage profile. *JOLE* 18 (April):306–21.

Parsons, D. O. 2014. Job displacement insurance: An overview. IZA Working Paper No. 8223, May.

Phelps, E. S., et al. 1970. *Microeconomic Foundations of Employment and Inflation Theory*. New York: Norton.

Pissarides, C. 1985. Short run equilibrium dynamics of unemployment, vacancies and real wages. *AER* 75:676–90.

———. 1986. Unemployment and vacancies in Britain. *Economic Policy* 3:499–559.

Poletaev, M., and C. Robinson. 2008. Human capital specificity: Evidence from the Dictionary of Occupational Titles and Displaced Worker Surveys, 1984–2000. *JOLE* 26:387–420.

Ragan, C. 1995. A risk-sharing view of real wages and contract length. *CJE* 28 (November):1161–79.

Rea, S. A. 1977. Unemployment insurance and labour supply: A simulation of the 1971 Unemployment Insurance Act. *CJE* 10 (May):263–78.

Riddell, W. C. 1999. Canadian labour market performance in international perspective. *CJE* 32 (November):1097–134.

Rogerson, R., and R. Shimer. 2010. Search in macroeconomic models of the labor market. In *Handbook of Labor Economics*, eds. O. Ashenfelter and D. Card. Elsevier.

Rogerson, R., R. Shimer and R. Wright. 2005. Search-theoretic models of the labor market: A survey. *JEL* 43:959–988.

Rosen, S. 1985. Implicit contracts: A survey. *JEL* 23 (September):1144–75.

Rothstein, J. 2011. Unemployment Insurance and job search in the Great Recession. *BPEA* (Fall):143–213.

Ruhm, C. J. 1992. Advance notice and postdisplacement joblessness. *JOLE* 10 (January):1–32.

Sampson, L. 1985. A study of the impact of sectoral shifts on aggregate unemployment in Canada. *CJE* 18 (August):518–30.

Schirle, T. 2009. Earnings losses of displaced older workers: Accounting for the retirement option. CLSRN Working Paper No 22.

Shapiro, C., and J. E. Stiglitz. 1984. Equilibrium unemployment as a worker discipline device. *AER* 74 (June):433–44.

Sharir, S., and P. Kuch. 1978. Contribution to unemployment of insurance-induced labour force participation: Canada 1972. *Economics Letters* 1:271–4.

Skuterud, M. 2005. Explaining the increase in on-the-job search. Statistics Canada, Analytical Studies Branch, Research Paper 250.

Social Research and Demonstration Corporation. 2001a. Essays on the repeat use of unemployment insurance: The earnings supplement project.

———. 2001b. The frequent use of unemployment insurance in Canada: The earnings supplement project.

Strauss, J., and D. Thomas. 1995. Human resources: Empirical modeling of household and family decisions. In *Handbook of Development Economics*, Volume 3, eds. J. Behrman and T. N. Srinivasan. Amsterdam: North-Holland.

Solow, R. M. 1985. Insiders and outsiders in wage determination. *Scandinavian Journal of Economics* 87:411–28.

Stevenson, B. 2009. The Internet and job search. In *Studies of Labor Market Intermediation*, ed. D. Autor. Chicago: University of Chicago Press.

Subramanian, S., and A. Deaton. 1996. The demand for food and calories. *JPE* 104 (February):133–62.

Stigler, G. J. 1962. Information in the labour market. *JPE* 70 (October):94–105.

Stiglitz, J. E. 1976. The efficiency wage hypothesis, surplus labour, and the distribution of income in L.D.C.s. *Oxford Economic Papers* 28 (July):185–207.

Sullivan, D., and T. von Wachter. 2009. Job displacement and mortality: An analysis using administrative data. *QJE* 124 (August):1265–1306.

Stevens, A. H. 1997. Persistent effects of job displacement: The importance of multiple job losses. *JOLE* 15(1) (January):165–88.

Storer, P. 1996. Separating the effects of aggregate and sectoral shocks with estimates from a Markov-switching search model. *Journal of Economic Dynamics and Control* 20 (January/March):93–121.

Strauss, J. 1986. Does better nutrition raise farm productivity? *JPE* 94 (April):297–320.

Sweetman, A. 2000. The impact of EI on those working less than 15 hours per week. *Evaluation Report*. Ottawa: Human Resources Development Canada.

Swaim, P. L., and M. J. Podgursky. 1990. Advance notice and job search: The value of an early start. *JHR* 25 (Spring):147–78.

Tatsiramos, and J. C. van Ours. 2014. Labour market effects of unemployment insurance design. *Journal of Economic Surveys* 28(2):284–311.

Woodbury, S., and R. Spiegelman. 1987. Bonuses to workers to reduce unemployment: Randomized trials in Illinois. *AER* 77 (September):513–30.

Glossary

ability bias: a pitfall that is involved in the empirical estimation of human capital earnings functions; the estimate of the rate of return on education might be systematically higher than the true value due to the role of the unobserved variable of innate ability

Aboriginal earnings differentials: the discrepancy in the average earnings between Aboriginal Canadians and non-Aboriginal Canadians, often after adjusting for human capital levels (see also the definition for human capital)

added worker: a worker who normally does not participate in the labour force but searches for work in order to supplement the family income

administrative concept of value: a procedure for determining the value of a certain job that relies on explicit assessments of the average value of the job's characteristics; in contrast to the market, or economic, concept of value

adverse selection: a situation in which the insurer cannot observe the true risk involved in insuring the insuree, but the insuree knows it well; it imposes a difficulty on developing insurance contracts, such as implicit contracts (see also the definition for implicit contracts)

affirmative action: a particular form of equal employment opportunity legislation that seeks to implement a greater equality in results as opposed to focusing on more equal opportunities (see also the definition for equal employment opportunity legislation)

age-earnings profile: the relationship between age and/or labour market experience and the wage level of an individual as he or she ages; the shape of an earnings stream

alternative wage: the highest wage level that the worker could earn

working for another firm; it may or may not be a unionized position

assessed and non-assessed classes: assessed classes are those immigrants whose applications are subjected to an evaluation of their likely contribution and success in the Canadian labour market; immigrants in nonassessed classes do not undergo an evaluation based on those criteria

asymmetric information: a situation in which both parties to a contract do not have the same information as far as work effort, production costs, or firm profit is concerned; there is often a disincentive to reveal full information to the other party

bargaining power: the power the union possesses in collective bargaining to raise wages without facing a major cost in the form of reduced employment; alternatively, the power to achieve a wage-employment outcome that approaches its ideal outcome

bargaining range: the range of wage outcomes that could feasibly emerge from collective bargaining; the lower bound is the alternative wage and the higher bound generates zero profits for the firm (see also the definition for alternative wage)

bargaining unit: the group of workers whose wages and terms of employment are covered in the collective bargaining agreement (see also the definition for collective bargaining)

brain drain: an economic choice in which highly skilled and highly educated individuals emigrate from Canada; Canada is, thus, the source country rather than the host country

budget constraint: the locus of all combinations of income and leisure that the worker can potentially reach

given the wage and the level of nonmarket income

Canada/Quebec Pension Plan: these government programs, abbreviated CPP/QPP, are social insurance regimes providing payments to retired workers on the basis of their prior contributions to the regime; the payments are, thus, not in the form of demogrants and the program is not universal

certification: the legal process by which a group of unorganized workers attain representation by a labour union; the union then becomes the sole bargaining agent for that group

child care subsidies: a government program that allocates payments to working parents to either pay the full cost of or defray the cost of child care services

coefficient: a parameter of a regression model; a constant scalar value that, multiplied by the economic variable(s), gives the effect of the explanatory variable on the variable being explained (see also the definitions for regression analysis and parameter)

cohort effect: a labour supply choice or effect that refers to a group of individuals who all entered the labour force at the same time (contexts of life-cycle labour supply and effects on wage levels)

collective agreement coverage: the percentage of paid workers whose wages and working conditions are covered by a collective agreement; in North America, nearly all of them are actual union members

collective bargaining: a process under which the union negotiates wages, non-wage benefits, working conditions, and the terms of employment with the firm; the union negotiates on behalf of all workers, and the terms of the contract apply to all workers (see also the definition for unions)

comparable worth: a government policy designed to reduce the magnitude of the overall earnings gap between men and women; very similar to pay equity (see also the definition for pay equity)

comparative advantage: a wage advantage that a worker gets by choosing one employment sector versus another, relative to the advantage obtained by other workers

comparator jobs: a job class used to implement a pay equity scheme; the female-dominated job is paired with a male-dominated one thought to have very similar attributes and requirements

compensated elasticity: (of labour supply) the wage elasticity of labour supply adjusted for the income elasticity of labour supply; that is, the percentage change in the quantity supplied of labour divided by the percentage change in the wage after subtracting the income effect of the wage change

compensating risk premium: the rate at which the worker values a higher level of job safety in terms of the wage; the compensating differential that the worker offers to the labour market before the market wage differential is determined, and it is determined by his or her preferences for job safety versus income (see also the definition for compensating wage differentials)

compensating wage differentials: wage differentials designed to compensate a worker for amenities or disamenities associated with a job; positive for undesirable aspects and negative for desirable ones (see also the definition for wage differentials)

competitive: refers to the general situation where a market equilibrium is determined by the forces of supply and demand; in a competitive labour market, workers and firms are small

relative to the whole market and have no individual influence on the determination of wages, which are solely shaped by the overall supplies and demands in the market

competitive buyer of labour: a firm that obtains its labour in a competitive labour market; it faces a labour supply curve that is infinitely elastic at the going market wage, and is, thus, a wage "taker" (see also the definition for competitive market)

competitive market: an input market or an output market that meets the criteria of the model of perfect competition (a large number of buyers and/or sellers, a homogenous product/ service, perfect information regarding prices and quality, and free entry of new buyers and sellers)

complements: two production factors are complements when increasing the use of one factor in production makes the other one more productive; for instance, capital and labour are complements when capital investments increase the marginal product of labour

consumer's optimum: the worker's choice of market income received and number of hours worked within the labour supply model (context of the labour supply model)

consumption-leisure: the trade-off facing any worker in the labour supply model; also called the income-leisure trade-off

contract curve: the locus of all Pareto-efficient wage-employment combinations; drawn in wage-employment space (see also the definition for Pareto-efficient wage-employment outcome)

control group: in a research experiment, the group of subjects that is not subjected to a certain process and is compared to the treatment group (see also the definitions for program evaluation and treatment group)

conventional equal pay legislation: a government anti-discrimination policy that requires equal pay for equal work within the same job and within the same establishment

corner solution: a labour supply choice corresponding to either zero hours of leisure coupled with all hours allocated to work, or zero hours of work coupled with all hours allocated to leisure

cost minimization: the assumption applied to the behavioural motive of firms as they determine the demand for labour; it applies in cases in which the level of output desired is fixed (see also the definition for profit maximization)

counterfactual: a case involved in the research of labour market issues; an estimate of an alternative, hypothetical labour market equilibrium that would have occurred in the absence of an economic event (such as in the absence of immigration activity)

craft unions: a labour union that represents workers within a particular trade or occupation (see also the definition for unions)

cross-section microdata: data describing attributes of microeconomic units, such as firms and workers; there is a one-to-one correspondence between the unit of observation and a data value; the values vary over the dimension of economic actors at the same time period

crowding hypothesis: a supply theory of discrimination according to which women, facing barriers to entry in many occupations, tend to be forced into certain female-dominated occupations, thereby expanding the supply of labour (see also the definition for supply theories of discrimination)

deadweight loss: the loss in total output generated by an inefficient allocation of labour resources between two sectors (see also the definitions of inefficient allocation and two-sector model)

decertification: the reverse of the certification process (see also the definition for certification)

defined benefit plans: a special type of employer-sponsored pension plan in which the benefits are set at a certain percentage of wages and the length of time worked, and the contributions are determined by the financial requirements of the pension obligations

defined contribution plans: a special type of employer-sponsored pension plan in which the contributions are set at a certain percentage of wages, and the benefits are determined by the amount of money in the fund at the time of retirement

demand for union representation: an economic variable reflecting the preferences of workers for union representation; it depends on its expected costs and benefits

demand theories of discrimination: a source of labour market discrimination; demand for female labour is reduced relative to the demand for male labour, all other factors (especially productivity) held constant

demogrant: a lump-sum transfer allocated to the worker regardless of his or her work effort or how many or few hours that he or she works

derived demand: the demand for a productive resource or input that depends directly on the demand for the product or service it is employed to produce

diminishing marginal returns: a principle stating that as successive increments of a variable factor, such as labour, are applied to a fixed factor the marginal product of the variable factor declines; it applies only in the short run (see also the definition for marginal physical product)

discouraged worker: a jobless worker who has ceased searching for work

because he or she believes no work is available

disequilibrium: a state in which a market is not clearing so that quantity supplied is equal to quantity demanded; the transactions price is prevented from reaching the equilibrium price

displaced workers: workers who were formerly employed (and often attached to these jobs) but are permanently laid off and have lost their jobs; much research has been carried out on their subsequent job search

dualism: an analytical perspective that is an alternative to the neoclassical supply and demand approach; the labour market is segmented into two parts, the core and the periphery

dynamic labour supply: choices involving hours worked as a function of wages in the current period, as well as of wages in prior or subsequent periods; at the beginning of the time horizon, the worker plans his or her choices of how many hours to work in each subsequent time period over his or her career as a function of the wages and expected wages over his or her career

dynamic monopsony: a firm that is essentially a competitive buyer of labour, but may be facing an upward-sloping supply of labour in the short run; it thus has to raise the wage it pays in order to recruit workers at the margin (see also the definitions for competitive buyer of labour and monopsony)

Earned Income Tax Credits (EITC): income-tested wage subsidy

earnings function: a mathematical equation that models the wage earned by an individual; the wage is the dependent variable, and among the independent variables are level of education and level of experience

economic assimilation: the process by which a cohort of immigrants overcomes a negative entry effect and attains labour market outcomes (such

as wage levels) that are on a par with those of their native counterparts (see also the definition for entry effect)

economic rent: the difference between the going wage and the alternative wage (see also the definition for alternative wage)

efficiency wages: a wage that exceeds the competitive, market-clearing level and is designed to enhance the productivity of the worker; thought to elicit greater effort from the worker

efficient contract: an agreed-upon arrangement between the employer (the principal) and the employee (the agent) that minimizes the potential disincentives, such as employee shirking or employer cheating

efficient wage and employment contracts: collective bargaining agreements for which both the level of the wage and the level of employment are subjected to negotiation

elasticity of demand for labour: the percentage change in quantity of lsbour demanded that results from a 1 percent change in the wage rate

employed: the state of holding a paying job

employer-sponsored/occupational pension plans: a private tier of pension funds that allocate pensions to retired workers; the beneficiaries are former employees of these firms, and, typically, both the employer and the employee have contributed

employment: the market quantity of labour that is hired and inputted into the production process

employment equity: see the definition for affirmative action

employment insurance: income security program for non-elderly individuals

employment rate: the number of employed workers divided by the size of the working-age population

endogenous: determined within the model and system in which it appears; derived internally; opposite of exogenous, or predetermined outside the system

endogenous preferences: anti-discrimination policies that are designed to alter tastes, perceptions, preferences, and attitudes regarding traditional male and female occupations; the objective is to encourage more females to enter male occupations

endogenous variables: variables within an economic model whose fluctuations are explained or determined by the fluctuations of exogenous variables; also called the dependent variables of a model; the analyst has no control over the fluctuations (see also the definition for exogenous variables)

entry effect: the degree to which immigrants, upon arrival to Canada, earn lower wages than their native counterparts; also labelled the earnings penalty

equal employment opportunity legislation: a government policy designed to prevent discrimination in recruiting, hiring, promotion, and dismissals; influences personnel decisions rather than wage levels

equilibrium: the state of an economic model, such as the supply and demand framework, in which there are no forces acting to change the values of the economic variables

errors-in-variables problems: a difficulty involved in empirical analysis; an empirical proxy for an economic variable, such as job safety, does not measure the true variable very accurately

ethnic-white earnings differentials: differences between the average earnings levels of white Canadians and those of other ethnic groups, many of whom are visible minorities; these differences may stem from labour market discrimination

event study: a research methodology oriented around a particular occurrence; economic outcomes that occurred before this event are compared to those occurring after it in order to analyze the effect of the event

evolutionary wage change: a wage change reflected in a movement along an individual's age-earnings profile; these wage changes are associated with normal progress through one's career; there are, typically, increases during most of the career, but decreases are possible toward the end of the career

executive compensation: pay of executives, including salary and stock options

exit: a tactic for workers to exert pressure on their employers when and if they are dissatisfied with their terms of employment; that is, quitting the job; an alternative strategy to voice (see also the definition for voice)

exogenous variables: variables within an economic model whose fluctuations are controlled by the researcher; these variables serve to explain the fluctuations of endogenous variables (see also the definition for endogenous variables)

experience rating: an aspect of unemployment insurance programs in which premiums paid by the firm increase with the frequency with which its workers claim benefits

experimental evidence: a research technique that develops and carries out social experiments involving the parameters of the income maintenance scheme, and observes the labour market outcomes (context of supply and income maintenance schemes); for example, the negative income tax mechanism

explained and unexplained differentials: the two components of the Oaxaca decomposition of the observed wage gap; the first is attributable to differences in pre-market characteristics and the

second is due to differences in the rate at which they are valued on the labour market (see also the definitions for the Oaxaca decomposition and pre-market characteristics)

external production: a personnel practice whereby positions are filled from the pool of applicants outside the firm; the opposite of internal recruitment (see the definition for internal promotion)

external promotion: filling a position by bringing in a person from outside the firm, rather than promoting from within

facilitating policies: a particular form of equal employment opportunity policies that are designed to encourage greater employment opportunities and wages for the disfavoured group; there is less direct intervention in personnel decisions (see the definition for equal employment opportunity legislation)

factor of production: economic resources that function as inputs to the production process, such as land, labour, capital, and entrepreneurial ability

family class immigrants: one of the two non-assessed classes of immigrants; their applications are not evaluated according to the point system, but rather according to the immigrants' kinship with other immigrants who have been admitted

family-friendly work practices: workplace activities that are conducive to families balancing their time between work and family activities; examples include parental leave or flexible worktime arrangements

fertility: issues having to do with bearing children and raising a family; they have profound effects on labour supply patterns of both men and women

fixed costs: production costs expressed in levels that are invariant with respect to the level of output

fixed-effects model: a type of empirical wage-determination model in which the effect of many unobservable attributes on wage levels is removed from the estimation process; longitudinal data is required (see also the definition for panel data)

frictional unemployment: the type of aggregate unemployment associated with normal turnover in the labour force; individual workers often take time to find suitable jobs while they are jobless

full income: the amount of income that corresponds to the maximum number of hours worked

general equilibrium effects: the impact of an income maintenance scheme on labour market choices within a dynamic framework

general training: human capital development, often occurring on the job, that can be applied at other firms in addition to the firm that provides it

glass ceilings: a discriminatory barrier to upward job mobility thought to apply to higher-skilled women, preventing them from reaching the highest echelons of the pay scale

goods-intensive commodities: in the household production framework, utility-generating goods that require a relatively low amount of household time before they can be enjoyed by the household

gross flows: the total number of workers observed per month to be transitioning from one labour force state (i.e., employment, unemployment, or out of the labour force) to another; movements in the two directions are counted separately

Guaranteed Income Supplement (GIS): this program is very similar to the old age security regime (see the definition for Old Age Security (OAS))

hidden unemployment: the situation of jobless workers who are not officially classified as unemployed but

nonetheless may desire work or otherwise exhibit some attachment to the labour force

hold-up problem: a potential negative effect that unions can have on firm productivity; by threatening job action, they can appropriate some of the returns to investment in capital due to the immobility of capital

hours-of-work aspect: the element of the labour supply choice involving the number of hours that are worked per unit of time

household production model: a view of households as producers as well as consumers, and that the time of household members is an important ingredient in the production of household goods and services and, ultimately, in the economic well-being of the household

human capital: characteristics individuals can acquire to improve the productivity of their labour; the most common examples are education and other forms of training, but, more generally, can include health, nutrition, and other investments in human productivity

human capital earnings function: an empirical equation that relates the wage level of a worker to the level of education; it includes as explanatory variables the level of education and an estimate of the level of labour market experience

human capital investment decision: the choice an individual makes regarding the level of education or training to which he or she will devote time and resources

human capital theory: the theory of investment in human resources, in the form of training and education, with a view to raising the productivity of an individual

hysteresis: an extreme case of persistence in unemployment in which the actual rate of unemployment can drift upward or downward, without any tendency to return to an

equilibrium level (see also the definition for persistence)

ICTS: acronym for information and communication technologies; refers to the set of new technologies revolving around the Internet that have reshaped the way businesses and other organizations operate; examples include portable computing devices connected through wireless networks, web-based project management, and video-conferencing facilities

immobility: a state in which a factor of production, such as labour, is constrained as to which sectors, occupations, or regions it can enter

impact of immigrants: an important economic issue related to immigration; the degree to which immigration activity has an impact on the equilibriums in labour markets of the host country, and hence, on the welfare of native workers

imperfect information: a feature of labour markets in which the attributes of workers and the attributes of firms are unknown at the point of exchange, and are revealed only with the passage of time

implicit contracts: an agreement between the employer and the labour force that is not legally binding, but that tends to be self-enforcing because the firm's reputation and/or the worker group's reputation could be at risk if it did not respect the contract

implicit contract theory: theory of unemployment based on the idea that employers and employees implicitly agree (without a binding contract) to keep wages relatively constant in the presence of product demand shocks; as a result of this implicit contract, firms respond to a downturn by cutting employment instead of wages, which generates some additional unemployment (see also the definition for implicit contracts)

incidence of the tax: the distribution between the demanders and the suppliers of the true burden of a tax, net of any adjustment of the market price in response to the imposition of the tax

incidence of unemployment: the proportion of the individuals in the labour force who become unemployed in any time interval

income effect: the portion of the change in quantity demanded resulting from a price change that is attributed to the change in income, holding relative prices constant

income elasticity: (of labour supply) the percentage change in the quantity of labour supplied divided by the percentage change in the income

income-leisure: the trade-off workers face as they determine their labour supply behaviour; both income and leisure are considered to be goods, and the worker has to choose how many units of each he or she wants given the wage and other income

income maintenance schemes: a government program that compensates individuals with payments for income losses and/or income deficiencies

increased returns to education: the economic phenomenon of an apparent rise in the rate of return to education in the United States over the 1980s and 1990s (see also the definition for returns to schooling)

independent immigrants: see the definition for assessed and non-assessed classes

indifference curves: the locus of all combinations of income and leisure that yield equal utility to the worker (context of the labour supply model)

industrial unions: a labour union that represents all workers within a particular firm or industry as opposed to a certain trade or occupation (see also the definition for unions)

industry premiums: a difference in wages between two individuals attributable solely to the industries in which the workers are employed;

factors such as human capital requirements and the occupation have been accounted for; it sometimes reflects nonpecuniary differences

inefficient allocation: an allocation of labour between two sectors of the labour market that fails to maximize total production and income; typically accompanied by disequilibrium wages (see also the definition for two-sector model)

inferior good: a good whose quantity demanded decreases with the level of income

inflation targeting: a central bank policy of employing the standard tools of monetary policy with the aim of achieving a certain rate of inflation

insider-outsider theory: a theory that is designed to model aggregate unemployment; is based on rigid and unduly high real wages; and is sometimes applied to explain the persistently high unemployment in continental Europe during the 1990s

institutionalism: an analytical perspective that is an alternative to the neoclassical supply and demand approach; plays down the importance of the economic forces of supply and demand, and plays up the role of institutions, conventions, customs, social mores, and political forces

interindustry wage differentials: see the definition for industry premiums

interior solution: a labour supply choice corresponding to a positive number of hours of leisure and a positive number of hours of work

internal labour markets: labour markets in which the firm hires only its entry-level workers on the external market, and always fills its open positions by promoting workers from within the ranks of their present labour force

internal promotion: a common feature of internal labour markets whereby positions above entry level are filled from the ranks of the existing

labour force; there is no external recruitment for these positions (see also the definition for internal labour markets)

internal rate of return: an implicit, calculated rate of return of investment in human capital (context of human capital)

interoccupational wage differentials: see the definition for occupational premiums

intertemporal substitution: a labour supply response to an anticipated, evolutionary wage change over the course of the life cycle; the worker adjusts his or her working patterns and savings patterns over the entire life cycle in response to changes in wages at other periods

involuntary or voluntary unemployment: individuals are voluntarily unemployed if a suitable job is available but are unwilling to accept it at the going wage; they are involuntarily unemployed if they are willing to work at the going wage rate for their skills or occupation but are unable to find employment

isocost line: the locus of all combinations of inputs of labour and capital that generated the same level of total cost; represented graphically in capital-labour space

isoprofit curves: the locus of all combinations of the wage level and the employment level that yield equal profits to the employer; drawn in employment-wage space

isoprofit schedule: the locus of various combinations of the wage level and the job attribute (such as safety) that generate an equal level of profitability for the firm; drawn in wage-job attribute space

isoquant: the locus of all combinations of inputs of labour and capital that generate the same level of output; represented graphically in capital-labour space

job search: the process of workers seeking job offers and employment in the labour market; takes place in an environment of imperfect information

labour demand: the relationship between the amount of labour that firms are willing to hire over a given time interval and the wage level offered by workers

labour force: the number of people who are either employed or unemployed

labour force participation decision: the decision to either work or seek work in the labour market

labour force participation rate (LFPR): the ratio of the labour force to the size of the working-age population

Labour Force Survey: a monthly data set containing information on the labour market status of individuals

labour market discrimination: an instance in which seemingly equally productive workers, or workers having equal endowments of productivity-related attributes, of different races, genders, or ethnicities, are paid different wages

labour market outcomes: the phenomena generated from the labour market by the forces of labour supply and labour demand; primary examples are wages, employment levels, and unemployment levels

labour market turnover: the extent to which positions in the labour market are assumed by new workers; it includes quits, dismissals, layoffs, promotions, and rehires

labour shortages: influenced by the interaction of labour supply and demand in alternative market structures, including the degree of competition in the product market as well as the labour market

labour supply: the relationship between the amount of work that workers are willing to provide over a given time interval and the wage level offered by firms

labour supply model: the analytical framework employed for determining the number of hours of work

labour supply schedule: the functional relationship between the wage offered and the quantity supplied of labour

leisure: time per day that is not allocated to working for a wage

life-cycle labour supply: the configuration (or time path) of labour supply choices over an individual's adult life; analyzed as a function of wages, age, demographic factors such as fertility, and spousal income

line-to-line: a procedure for implementing a pay equity scheme; the female line is raised vertically to the male line; the average pay of the female-dominated occupations is raised to the average level of the male-dominated ones for each set of comparator jobs (see also the definitions for payline, comparator jobs, and pay equity)

logarithm: a mathematical function that is the inverse of the exponential function; frequently employed to transform economic data

long run: the time frame under which producers are able to adjust the quantities of all of the factors of production that they employ; a period in which all resources are variable and no resources are fixed

mandatory retirement: a personnel management practice in which a worker is compelled to retire upon reaching either a certain age or a certain length of service; tied to the termination date for a compensation contract

mandatory retirement provisions: provisions stipulating that the worker is compelled to withdraw from the labour force upon reaching a certain age

Maquiladora: Mexican corporations approved by the Mexican government that tend to assemble and export goods using duty-free imports; Maquiladora can be 100 percent foreign owned and managed, and are often located near the U.S. border

marginal cost: the increment to the firm's level of total cost that is obtained by producing one more unit of output

marginal labour force attachment: the state of being jobless but not necessarily actively searching for work; workers with marginal labour force attachment would not be considered officially unemployed, and they include discouraged workers (see also the definition for discouraged worker)

marginal physical product: the increment to the total product, or the level of production, that stems from a change in the level of a variable factor (such as labour) that is employed

marginal rate of substitution: the rate at which the worker is willing to trade an increment of leisure for an increment of income, and vice versa (context of the labour supply model)

marginal rate of technical substitution: the rate at which the firm can increase its employment of labour (capital) and reduce its employment of capital (labour) and still generate the same level of output; graphically, the slope of the isoquant curve

marginal revenue: the increment to the firm's total revenue obtained by producing and selling one more unit of output

marginal revenue product: the increment to the firm's total revenue obtained by hiring one more unit of a variable factor, such as labour on the input market

market-clearing model: the supply and demand model of equilibrium output and price determination; the market is said to clear when the equilibrium price is reached

market demand curve: the total demand for labour within a given labour market, representing the horizontal summation of the labour demand curves of the individual firms

market envelope curve: the outermost portions of the group of employers' isoprofit curves; sometimes called the outer shell, or the employers' offer curve; represents the maximum compensating wage any employer is willing to pay given a certain level of job safety (see also the definition for isoprofit schedule)

matching: the process by which workers searching for employment are paired with firms offering jobs; takes place in an environment of imperfect information

median voter model: a proposition holding that when economic choices over a single variable (such as the union wage level) are made in a democratic fashion, the choice made by the group will be identical to the choices made by the median voter (i.e., one whose preferences are halfway through the range of the preferences of all of the voters)

migration: geographical mobility on the part of workers

minimum wage laws: laws stipulating a floor on wages such that the employer is compelled to pay his or her employees a wage at least as high

monitoring costs: the costs incurred in ensuring that employees are not shirking and that employers are meeting their commitments in terms of remunerating their workers

monopolist: a firm that operates in a market in which there are no other firms producing and selling its product/service; there is a single seller of the good/service

monopsony: a structure for an input market for which there is only one buyer (single employer in the context

of a labour market); the labour supply curve facing the firm is upward sloping

moonlighting: the choice of accepting additional work at a wage rate lower than that of the first job

moral hazard: a situation in which individuals can influence their risk of suffering a loss for which they have obtained insurance coverage; it imposes a difficulty on developing insurance contracts such as implicit contracts (see also the definition for implicit contracts)

multiple regression: a regression model having more than one explanatory variable (see also the definition for regression analysis)

natural experiment: a research technique sometimes employed to isolate the impact of changes in one economic variable on the fluctuations of another economic variable; the possibility of unobserved and omitted economic variables affecting the estimation of that relationship is reduced

negative income tax: a special type of social assistance program containing an incentive structure that does not penalize the act of working; a level of income is guaranteed and the implicit tax rate on labour market earnings is not 100 percent, as is the case for conventional social assistance programs

neoclassical economics: the analytical approach used in mainstream economics; self-interested economic actors produce, consume, and exchange goods and services in markets

neoclassical supply and demand model: the analytical framework used for most of the field of labour markets; based on the self-interested choices of firms and workers who exchange services in labour market

net flows: the number of workers observed per month to be transitioning from one labour force state (i.e.,

employment, unemployment, or out of the labour force) to another; movements in the opposite direction are subtracted

noncompetitive market: an input or output market that does not meet the criteria of the model of perfect competition; for output markets, monopoly, oligopoly, or monopolistic competition; for input markets, monopsony, oligopsony, or monopsonistic competition

noncompetitive theories of discrimination: any theory regarding the nature of labour market discrimination such that the differentials are not eroded by the forces of competition in the labour market, but are permanent

nonexperimental evidence: a research technique that uses data and evidence relating measures of labour market supply to the parameters of the income maintenance scheme (context of labour supply and income maintenance schemes); it is the most commonly employed research technique, and it is based only on observed economic behaviour

nonmarket time: time per day not allocated to working for a wage; also called leisure time

nonpecuniary benefits: an amenity associated with a job that is not financial in nature; it thus has no bearing on wages or benefits

normal good: a good whose quantity demanded increases with the level of income (leisure in the context of the labour supply model)

Oaxaca decomposition: a mathematical equation that measures discrimination by decomposing the average wage differential between males and females into a portion attributable to differences in productive characteristics and a portion due to differences in the rates at which these productive characteristics determine wages; it is that latter element that is considered to be discriminatory

occupation: the function of a worker; the nature or content of the work performed

occupational premiums: a difference in wages between two individuals that is attributable solely to the functions of the workers (i.e., the trade) involved; factors such as human capital requirements and the industry of employment have been accounted for; it sometimes reflects nonpecuniary differences

offer-matching: the act of matching the salary offer that the raiding firm makes to one of the firms' top employees; a counteroffer from the current employer

offshoring: the delegation by firms of certain elements of internal production to an offshore foreign firm, usually for reasons of cost cutting and/or to specialize internal production on core competencies

Old Age Security (OAS): a government program that provides payments to retired workers in the form of a demogrant; it is a universal program, but the benefits are clawed back for higher-income recipients

omitted variable bias: a difficulty involved in empirical analysis; an economic variable thought to play an important role in determining the values of the endogenous variables (such as wages) is not included in the estimating equation at all

1/N problem: a pitfall involved in the remuneration practice of team-based compensation (all workers receive an equal share of the salary mass) whereby certain workers have an incentive to shirk

opportunity cost: the cost of the forgone alternative that has the highest value; the explicit costs of education and training plus the forgone earnings stemming from the training process (context of human capital investment)

optimal compensation system: a remuneration mechanism within a firm that generates a wage level such that the effort level and, hence, the workers' productivity is the highest possible given the level of labour costs

optimal degree of inequality: a characteristic of a remuneration system within an organization such that the degree of inequality of the salary scale achieves the proper trade-off between generating proper incentives for individual effort versus achieving cooperative teamwork when necessary

outsourcing: the delegation by firms of certain elements of internal production to an external entity (sometimes an offshore foreign firm) usually for reasons of cost cutting and/or to specialize internal production on core competencies

ordinary least squares: a statistical or econometric technique employed to estimate the values of parameters of regression models having a linear form; applicable under certain conditions (see also the definition for parameter)

overemployed: said of a worker who desires to work fewer hours at the going wage rate but is prevented from doing so due to labour market constraints

overtime premium: the wage premium that is awarded for hours worked beyond the standard work week, and that may be necessary to induce the overemployed worker to work longer hours (see also the definition for overemployed)

panel data: data consisting of the attributes of individuals (such as wages) that follow these individuals over time; time-series observations exist for the same individual

parameter: an element of a regression model that links the economic variables; typically, it takes the form of a slope coefficient or the intercept

term (see also the definition for regression analysis).

Pareto-efficient wage-employment outcome: a wage-employment outcome that makes the union as well off as possible given the level of profit for the firm, and makes the firm as well off as possible given the level of utility for the union; any other wage-employment outcome will necessarily make one party worse off

partial equilibrium effects: the impact of an income maintenance scheme on labour market choices within a static framework

pay equity: a government anti-discrimination policy that requires equal pay for work at different jobs that are assessed to have the same value; usually restricted to the public sector

payline: a mathematical tool in the form of a line that is used to implement pay equity schemes; the number of job evaluation points is related to the pay rates, and there is a line for both men and women

perfect capital markets: financial markets that allow an individual to borrow against his or her lifetime earnings and save for his or her lifetime earnings without constraint; in such markets an individual can base an investment decision on lifetime income rather than on current income

perfect monopsonistic wage differentiation: a particular type of monopsony equilibrium in which the employer is able to pay every single worker a different wage equal to the worker's reservation wage (see also the definition for monopsony)

persistence: the tendency for shocks that cause increases or decreases in the actual rate of unemployment to have very long-term effects that dissipate slowly; thus, the natural rate of unemployment is affected by changes in the actual rate of unemployment

phantom jobs: the situation in which an appropriate (usually male) comparator job does not exist (see also the definition for comparator jobs)

Phillips curve: a macroeconomic, negative mathematical relationship between the rate of unemployment and the rate of wage inflation

point system: the institutional procedure through which the applications of independent immigrants are evaluated; it consists of about a dozen criteria that can be evaluated in a relatively objective fashion

point-to-line: a procedure for implementing a pay equity scheme; all of the points of female-dominated occupations are raised vertically to the male line; the pay of the female-dominated occupations is raised to the average level of the male-dominated ones for each set of comparator jobs (see also the definitions for payline, comparator jobs, and pay equity)

point-to-point: a procedure for implementing a pay equity scheme; all of the points for female occupations are raised vertically to the nearest point among the male-dominated occupations; the pay of the female-dominated occupations is raised to the lowest level of the male-dominated one given a set of comparator jobs (see also the definitions for payline and pay equity)

polarization of wages: the economic phenomenon of an apparent rise in the earnings gap between the highly educated and the less-educated workers in the U.S. labour market; the distribution of wage levels among workers tends to diverge

policy capturing approach: a procedure for applying the administrative concept of value that simulates the market approach; the attributes of a job that have been estimated by the evaluators are then remunerated according to market rates prevailing for male-dominated jobs

positively selected: the degree to which immigrants, often having undergone an evaluation of their productive attributes according to the official point system, also possess unobservable characteristics (such as motivation) that strengthen economic assimilation (see also the definitions for economic assimilation and point system)

potential experience: the proxy variable for labour market experience that is frequently included in a human capital earnings function; typically, estimated as age minus years of schooling minus five (see also the definition for human capital earnings function)

potential income constraint: the highest level of income that can be reached corresponding to a given number of hours worked

preferences: the tastes the worker has for income versus leisure (context of labour supply model)

pre-market characteristics: the first component generated by the Oaxaca decomposition; also called the explained component of discrimination (see also the definition for the Oaxaca decomposition)

present value: the value of the right to receive a payment or a series of payments in the future, denominated in dollars of the current period

principal-agent theory: a conceptual framework employed to analyze certain remuneration practices; the principal is the firm, which hires the employee (the agent) to work on its behalf

private costs and benefits: the costs and the benefits that are incurred by and accrue solely to the parties that make an economic choice (such as an investment in human capital)

proactive system-wide: quality of a procedure for applying comparable worth policies whereby employers are required to have in place a bona fide job evaluative system achieving pay

equity; no complaint or grievance would have to be filed

production function: the technological relationship between the inputs to the production process and the level of output (see also the definition for factor of production)

production possibility frontier (PPF): a curve that shows the locus of combinations of the levels of outputs of two goods or services that can be produced in a full-employment, full-production economy where the levels of inputs and the state of technology are fixed; also called a transformation curve

productivity: the relationship between the level of output and the level of input employed to produce it; stated as a ratio of either the level of output divided by the level of input, or the change in output divided by the change in input (see also the definition for marginal physical product)

profitability: the level, or the margin, of profit, where profit is the total revenue of the firm minus the total costs

profit maximization: the assumed behavioural motive of firms as they determine the demand for labour: that they will choose to employ the level of labour which yields the greatest possible level of profit

program evaluation: a research procedure that seeks to assess the efficacy of labour market programs, such as job training, in obtaining a desired result

protectionist labour standards: employment regulations designed to improve working conditions in certain male-dominated occupations so that females may find them more attractive

public–private sector wage differentials: a difference in wages between two workers that is attributable solely to the fact that one works in the private sector and one works for the public sector; factors such as human capital requirements and the occupation have been accounted for; may reflect nonpecuniary differences (see also the definition for industry premiums)

quasi-panel: a research methodology employing data series that follow a group of individuals over several time periods; growth in economic variables, such as wages, can be observed

queuing theories: theories regarding the nature of labour market discrimination according to which the wage differentials stem from the payment of efficiency wages; the efficiency wages cause workers to queue up for well-paying jobs that tend to be held by the favoured group (see also the definition for efficiency wages)

raiding: a personnel management practice that involves very aggressive recruitment of workers of high skill level from competing organizations

real costs: concrete costs stemming from an economic choice that involves the use of productive resources; may or may not have a monetary value

reduced form: a form for an economic model in which only exogenous variables and parameters appear on the right side of the model's equations

refugee class: one of the two non-assessed classes of immigrants; their applications are not evaluated according to the point system, but rather on their personal histories in foreign countries

regional wage differential: a difference in wages between two individuals attributable solely to geographical location; factors such as human capital requirements have been accounted for

regression analysis: a tool for empirical analysis in which the fluctuations in the dependent (or explained) variable are assessed as a function of fluctuations in one or more independent (or explanatory) variables; the regression model is a mathematical equation describing the

relationship between a dependent variable and one or more independent variables; the primary elements are parameters and variables (see also the definition for parameter)

reservation wage: the lowest wage required to prevent the worker from withdrawing from the labour force or the wage threshold that will induce a nonparticipating worker to join the labour force

retirement decision: a labour supply decision that, typically, involves labour supply and savings decisions made over the entire life cycle; the worker chooses to no longer participate in the labour force

retirement test: a provision of a retirement pension program that penalizes the beneficiary to the extent that he or she continues to work for a wage

returns to schooling: empirical evidence on the private benefits, in the form of wage increases, from an investment to schooling; a quantitative estimate of the differences in earnings between groups of workers having various levels of education

risk sharing: a major element of the implicit contract approach to modelling wages and employment levels; workers accept lower wages in exchange for a greater degree of job security and a lower degree of wage variability

Roy model: a competitive model of wage determination in a labour market where different workers have different skills and productive abilities, and earn different wages in different sectors depending on their comparative advantage

R-squared: the proportion of the fluctuations in the dependent variable of a regression model that can be explained by fluctuations in the independent variable (see also the definition for regression analysis)

salaries as tournament prizes: a salary determination mechanism in

which much of the compensation reflects a prize for being selected as the most productive worker rather than reflecting the marginal revenue product (see also the definition for superstar)

sample selection bias: a difficulty involved in empirical analysis; the estimating sample is not representative of the underlying population whose economic behaviour the researcher wants to investigate; the sample is, typically, weighted toward workers with fairly extreme patterns of economic behaviour

sampling error: the error (inaccuracy) in the estimation process that stems from drawing data from a sample not totally representative of the population

scale effect: the change in quantity demanded of labour that results from a change in the wage rate, holding the relative prices of the inputs (usually labour versus capital) fixed; the portion of the change that is attributable solely to the level of output adjusting

sectoral shift hypothesis: a model for analyzing aggregate unemployment that stresses the role of adjustment of the allocation of labour in the face of frequent changes in technology and shocks to aggregate demand and supply; emphasizes the dispersion in employment growth across sectors of the labour market

selection bias: a complication involved in the empirical elimination of the union–non-union wage effect; the unobservable attributes of union workers are not the same as those of non-union workers

Self-Sufficiency Project (SSP): a pilot project involving social assistance recipients who were presented with strong financial incentives to accept paying jobs (see also the definition for experimental evidence)

shadow or implicit prices: the portion of the total market wage associated with a job amenity or disseminate; synonymous with a compensating wage differential

shock effect: a potential for the unionization of workers (with the accompanying increase in wages) to increase the level of production at the firm by inducing the firm to adopt more-efficient production techniques

shock effect: when management or employees are shocked into more-efficient practices from some external effect, such as a minimum wage increase

short run: the time frame under which producers are able to adjust the quantities of some but not all of the factors of production they employ; a period in which some resources are fixed but some are variable

signalling: an event whereby a worker on the supply side of the labour market reveals information relevant to his or her true innate productivity or quality; applies only in a climate of imperfect information (see also the definition for imperfect information)

simultaneity: a complication involved in the empirical elimination of the union–non-union wage effect; the union status can affect the wage, and vice versa, which can render a biased estimate

simultaneous equation bias: bias that occurs when two variables are endogenous and simultaneously influence each other.

social assistance: see the definition for welfare

social costs and benefits: the private costs and benefits faced by parties making an economic choice, plus the third-party effects or externalities that accrue to parties not directly involved (such as an investment in human capital)

specific training: human capital development, often occurring on the job, that can be applied only at the firm that provides it

standard errors: a statistical measure of the dispersion of an economic variable or an estimator for a parameter

statistical and signalling theories of discrimination: a practice in which female workers (or some other group treated unfavourably in the labour market) are assessed according to the average performance of all females, and have their wages set accordingly

statistical significance: an indication that the true value of the parameter of the regression model is different from zero (see also the definition for regression analysis)

stock options: a method of compensation that frequently applies to business executives; they have the option of buying the firm's stock in the future at a guaranteed price

stopping rule: the condition under which the process of job search comes to an end; the wage of the offered job is equal to or greater than the reservation wage (see also the definitions for job search and reservation wage)

structural unemployment: the aggregate unemployment associated with mismatches between the skills and/or the geographic location of the unemployed with the characteristics of job vacancies

substitution effect: the change in quantity demanded of labour that results from a change in the wage rate, holding the level of output fixed; the portion of the change attributable solely to the change in the relative factor prices

superstar: a worker whose compensation level far exceeds those of all of the other workers within the organization even though often his or her skill level is only slightly higher than the next most productive worker; the differential in salary is magnified relative to the differential in productivity

supply of union representation: an economic variable reflecting the costs of organizing and maintaining a union, and the costs of administering contract preferences of workers for union representation; depends on its expected costs and benefits; emanates from the staff of the union

supply theories of discrimination: a source of labour market discrimination; the supply of female labour is expanded relative to the supply of male labour, all other factors held constant

symmetric information: a situation in which the two parties in an employment relationship have the same amount of information regarding relevant variables, such as the firm's profits, labour market conditions, worker productivity, etc.

systemic discrimination: labour market discrimination that may be the unintended by-product or side effect of conventional employment or pay practices that perpetuate the existing gender composition of the workplace

teamwork: work effort by an individual that is cooperative in nature and is harmonized with the efforts of the co-workers; the cross-marginal products are positive and high in this case

tenure: the length of service an employee has with the firm

threat effect: a positive effect on the wages of the non-union sector that can stem from the possibility that those non-union workers could organize; the employers in the non-union sector grant a wage increase in order to discourage unionization (see also the definition for two-sector model)

time-intensive commodities: in the household production framework, these are utility-generating goods that require a relatively high amount of household time before they can be enjoyed by the household

time-series data: data describing macroeconomic variables, such as unemployment or inflation; there is a one-to-one correspondence between the time period and a data value, as the values vary over the dimension of time

total revenue product: the level of a firm's total revenue associated with an amount of a factor (such as labour) employed in the production process

transfer costs: costs stemming from an economic choice that do not involve the use of real, productive resources; they involve only a financial gain for one group and a financial loss for another

transitory wage: a wage that is not evolutionary, but rather temporary (see also the definition for unanticipated wage increase)

t-ratio: the ratio of the estimated parameter (i.e., the estimated slope coefficient or estimated constant) to the estimated standard of error of the estimated parameter

treatment group: a group of workers involved in a research experiment and subjected to a certain process; often they have participated in a program (see also the definition for program evaluation)

tripartite choice: in the household production framework, individuals allocate their time across three options: (1) leisure, (2) work in the market, and (3) work in home production; the distinction with the usual work-leisure framework is the division of nonmarket time into "leisure" and "household production"

two-sector model: an analytical framework based on supply and demand forces that can be used to analyze wage differentials between workers in unionized industries and those in non-unionized industries; also employed to analyze the male-female wage differential

unanticipated wage increase: a one-time, unexpected wage increase that occurs at a particular point in time over the age-earnings profile; not thought to influence labour supply

choices during other periods (see also the definition for dynamic labour supply)

uncompensated elasticity: (of labour supply) the total wage elasticity of labour supply; that is, the percentage change in the quantity supplied of labour divided by the percentage change in the wage

underemployed: a worker who is willing to work more hours at the going wage rate but is prevented from doing so due to labour market constraints

unemployed: the state of being jobless and actively searching for work, or being jobless on temporary layoff

unemployment: human resources that are not employed on the job market; workers actively searching for work and willing to work at the going market wage

unemployment insurance: an income maintenance program that allocates payments to workers who have suffered job loss; workers must have contributed while they were employed in order to be eligible for benefits

unemployment rate: the number of unemployed workers divided by the size of the labour force, which, in turn, is the sum of the number of unemployed workers plus the number of employed workers

union density: a quantitative measure of the extent of union organization; the number of organized union members divided by the number of potential union members

union membership: the state of belonging to a labour union; normally, involves the payment of dues

union–non-union wage differential: the percentage difference in wages between union workers and otherwise comparable non-union workers

union objectives: the goals of the labour union relating primarily to wages, employment levels, working

conditions, and the terms of employment

union status: the individual worker's attribute of belonging or not belonging to a labour union

unions: collective organizations of workers of a certain firm and/or occupations whose primary objective is to protect and improve the well-being of their members

unobserved heterogeneity: differences in attributes (often across individuals) of economic factors that are relevant for economic choices but are not observable to the researcher; for example, innate intelligence and entrepreneurial drive

up-or-out rules: a personnel management practice in which the firm's employees are evaluated at a certain stage of their career and either promoted or terminated at that stage

utility: the level of well-being or satisfaction the worker receives from consuming given levels of income and leisure (context of the labour supply model)

utility function: a function relating the level of consumer satisfaction or well-being to the level of consumption of one or more goods

utility maximizing: the assumption thought to guide the behaviour of the worker (context of the labour supply model)

value of a (statistical) life: estimates of the value of a worker's life that reflect only the compensating differential generated by the labour market for a risky job or occupation; represents the price that the market assesses in order to reduce the risk of death to zero

value of marginal product: the increment to the firm's total revenue obtained by hiring one more unit of a variable factor such as labour on the input market; applies only when the output market is perfectly competitive

(see also the definition for marginal revenue product)

variable costs: production costs expressed in levels that vary directly with the level of output

voice: a tactic for workers to exert pressure on their employers when and if they are dissatisfied with their terms of employment by resorting to collective expression through the union; an alternative strategy to exit (see also the definition for exit)

wage differentials: a difference in the wage levels that arises when workers and jobs are heterogeneous with respect to attributes such as vocation, risk of injury, or working conditions

wage dispersion: the degree of variation or variance within the distribution of wages within the labour market

wage rate: the market price for a unit of labour

wage-safety locus: the locus of tendencies between the various isoprofit curves and the indifference curves; generates the equilibrium combinations of the wage and the job attribute (usually job safety) that prevail in the labour market

wage structures: the hierarchy or grid of wage levels relative to each other; a set of wage premiums associated with worker or job attributes, such as education, training, and seniority

wage subsidy: a government program that allocates a wage supplement in addition to the wage paid by the employer; designed to encourage low-paid workers to increase their work hours

wages: the market price for a unit of labour

wait or queue unemployment: the phenomenon of unemployed workers who are unsuccessful in finding jobs in the union sector but waiting for those scarce jobs to open up; there is, thus, less pressure on the supply of labour to the non-union sector (see also the definition for two-sector model)

welfare: a social program (also called social assistance) that typically allocates demogrant payments to nonparticipants of the labour force; the amounts are based primarily on the survival needs of the family, and the implicit tax on labour market earnings is 100 percent

winner's curse: a possible result stemming from the personnel management practice of raiding other organizations (often competing organizations) for the most-talented workers; there is a risk that the pay offer will not be justified by the recruit's marginal productivity (see also the definition for raiding)

work incentives: the reward and/or penalty effect associated with an income maintenance scheme that applies to the work effort of recipients

workers' compensation: an income maintenance program allocating payments to workers who have suffered job-related illness or injury and are thus unable to work

worksharing: a special type of unemployment insurance regime in which workers are compensated for partial rather than total job loss; they receive indemnities for the working hours, which are reduced

years since migration: the number of years that have elapsed since the time in which the immigrant entered the host country; an important variable involved in assessing economic assimilation (see also the definition for economic assimilation)